HARLEY HAHN'S
LIST OF 25 THINGS TO DO WHEN YOU SHOUL...

1) ADVICE: Good Advice
Read what professional advisors have to say about life and other stuff.

(See page 1.)

2) ANIMALS AND PETS: Cats, Dogs
Learn something cool about your pet.

(See pages 15 and 16.)

3) BIZARRE: Bizarre Stuff to Make
Cook up something weird and make life exciting.

(See page 62.)

4) BROADCASTING ON THE NET: Internet Broadcasting Networks
Turn off your radio, turn on the Net.

(See page 82.)

5) COMICS: Daily Comics
Read your favorite comic strip without having to buy the newspaper.

(See page 112.)

6) COOL AND USEFUL: Harley Hahn's Internet Exploration Station
Explore the Internet with Harley Hahn.

(See page 143.)

7) FAMILIES AND PARENTING: Family Resources
Find fun stuff to do on the Net with your family.

(See page 252.)

8) GAMES AND PUZZLES: Java Game Park
Sharpen your competitive skills and enhance your value to your employer by playing a game.

(See page 305.)

9) HOLIDAYS AND CELEBRATIONS: Entertainment and Party Ideas
Plan a party that people will never forget.

(See page 383.)

10) HUMOR AND JOKES: Humor Magazines
Get a good laugh—it's time for a break anyway.

(See page 398.)

11) INTERNET: Scout Report
See what's new and exciting on the Net.

(See page 411.)

Visit my web page at http://www.harley.com/

12) INTRIGUE: Smoking Gun

Examine the real documents behind the gossip.

(See page 413.)

13) MAGAZINES: Women's Magazines

Stay trendy—read a magazine online.

(See page 486.)

14) MISCHIEF: Fake News

Create a fake news story to send to your friends.

(See page 516.)

15) MOVIES: Personal Movie Finders

Let a computer help you choose what movie to see.

(See page 535.)

16) NEWS: World News Sources

Find out what's going on anywhere in the world.

(See page 576.)

17) QUOTATIONS: Daily Quotations

Read something witty, wise or wonderful.

(See page 651.)

18) ROMANCE: Romantic Greetings by Email

Make someone fall in love with you, again and again.

(See page 691.)

19) SHOPPING: Auctions Online

Send in a bid without leaving your chair.

(See page 716.)

20) SOFTWARE: Software Archives

Try out a cool new program for free.

(See page 722.)

21) SOUNDS: Sounds and Sound Effects

Amuse your neighbors by playing funny noises.

(See page 726.)

22) SPORTS AND ATHLETICS: Sports News

See how the big game turned out.

(See page 742.)

23) TALKING ON THE NET: Web Chat Rooms

Talk to an old friend or meet a new one.

(See page 762.)

Web chat rooms ✷ 24 hours a day ✷ Free ✷ Now

24) TRAVEL: Travel Resources

Use the Net to help you plan your next vacation.

(See page 782.)

25) TRIVIA: Today's Events in History

Something happened on this day in the past. Find out what.

(See page 785.)

Visit my web page at http://www.harley.com/

HARLEY HAHN'S INTERNET & WEB GOLDEN DIRECTORY

1999 EDITION

HARLEY HAHN'S
INTERNET & WEB
GOLDEN DIRECTORY

1999 EDITION

Harley Hahn

Osborne/McGraw-Hill

Berkeley New York St. Louis San Francisco Auckland Bogotá Hamburg
London Madrid Mexico City Milan Montreal New Delhi Panama City Paris
São Paulo Singapore Sydney Tokyo Toronto

HARLEY HAHN'S INTERNET & WEB GOLDEN DIRECTORY
1999 EDITION

**OSBORNE/McGRAW-HILL
2600 TENTH STREET
BERKELEY, CALIFORNIA 94710
U.S.A.**

This is not a commercial yellow pages book. Please do not write asking how you can buy an ad in this book. There are no commercial ads. In addition, please do not write asking Harley to mention your new Web site in the next edition. Also, please do not put the above address on any mailing lists for press releases or marketing materials. Thanks.

For information on translations or book distributors outside the U.S.A., or to arrange bulk purchase discounts for sales promotions, premiums, or fund-raisers, please contact Osborne/McGraw-Hill at the above address.

Within the United States, this book is sold under the name "Harley Hahn's Internet & Web Yellow Pages".

Copyright © 1999 by Harley Hahn. All rights reserved. Printed in the United States of America. Except as permitted under the Copyright Act of 1976, no part of this publication may be reproduced or distributed in any form or by any means, or stored in a database or retrieval system, without the appropriate prior written permission of the author and publisher.

The name "Harley Hahn" *HARLEY HAHN*® and the Unisphere logo ® are registered trademarks of Harley Hahn.

1234567890 QPD QPD 90198765432109

ISBN 0-07-211893-8

Information has been obtained by Osborne/McGraw-Hill from sources believed to be reliable. However, because of the possibility of human or mechanical error by our sources, Osborne/**McGraw-Hill**, or others, Osborne/**McGraw-Hill** does not guarantee the accuracy, adequacy, or completeness of any information and is not responsible for any errors or omissions or the results obtained from use of such information.

Publisher
  Brandon A. Nordin
Editor-in-Chief
  Scott Rogers
Project Editor
  Cynthia Douglas
Editorial Assistant
  Marlene Vasilieff
Copy Editor
  Lunaea Hougland
Proofreaders
  Pat Mannion
  Carroll Proffitt
Computer Designers
  Mickey Galicia
  Roberta Steele
  Peter F. Hančík
Illustrators
  Roberta Steele
  Brian Wells
  Beth Young
Cover Design
  Cristina Deh-Lee

To Carrie, Cynthia, Lunaea and Wendy:

The best team an author could ever have.

— Harley Hahn

Table of Contents

Introduction xxxi
Frequently Asked Questions xliii
Acknowledgments il

ADVICE 1
Advice Chat 1
Ann Landers and Dear Abby 1
Ask Tina 1
Good Advice 1
Jane Err 1
Jeffrey Zaslow 2
Libby Webwise 2
Lifestyle Advice 2
Miss Abigail's Time Warp Advice ... 2
Women's Wire Advice 3

AGRICULTURE 3
Agricultural News 3
Agriculture Jobs 3
Agriculture Links 3
Agriculture Network Information Center 4
Agriculture Talk and General Discussion 4
Agripedia 4
Beekeeping 4
Dairy Science 5
Farm Journal Today 5
Forestry 5
Irrigation 5
National Agricultural Library 5
National Genetic Resources Program 6
Organic Farming 6
Poultry 6
Precision Farming 7
Progressive Farmer Magazine 7
Sustainable Agriculture Information ... 7
USDA Economics and Statistics 8
World Agricultural Information Center 8

ANARCHY 8
Anarchist Calendar 8
Anarchist Feminism 8
Anarchist Resources 8
Anarchist Theory FAQ 8
Anarchy History 9

Anarchy Sampler 9
Anarchy Talk and General Discussion 9
Anarchy Yellow Pages 9
Chomsky, Noam 10
Goldman, Emma 10
History of the Black Flag 11
Internet Anarchist University 11
Primitivist Network 11
Prominent Anarchists 11
Rocker, Rudolf 11
Siege of Paris 12
Spunk Library 12

ANIMALS AND PETS 12
Animal Information Database 12
Animal Rescue and Adoption 13
Animal Rights 13
Animal Talk and General Discussion 13
Aquariums 14
Bird-Keeping 14
Bird-Watching 15
Cats 15
Dogs 16
Electronic Zoo 16
Endangered Species 16
Ferrets 17
Fleas and Ticks 17
Hamsters 18
Horses 18
Iguanas 18
Marine Mammals 18
Monkeys 19
Pet Cemetery 19
Pet Channel 19
Pet-Keeping Dos and Don'ts 19
Pet of the Day 19
Pet Talk and General Discussion ... 20
Plants Harmful to Animals 20
Rabbits 20
Rats and Mice 20
Reptiles and Amphibians 21
Scorpions 21
Sharks 22
Tarantulas 22
Veterinary Medicine 22
Wildlife 22
Zoos 23

ARCHAEOLOGY 23
Archaeological Fieldwork 23
Archaeological Societies 24
Archaeology Events 24
Archaeology Magazine 24
Archaeology News 24

Archaeology Resources 24
Archaeology Talk and General Discussion 24
Archnet 25
Biblical Archaeology 25
Classics and Mediterranean Archaeology 25
Cultural Site Etiquette 25
Egyptian Artifacts 25
Industrial Archaeology 26
Mesoamerican Archaeology 26
National Archaeological Database . 26
Papyrology 27
Perseus Project 27
Pottery 27
Rock Art 27
Roman Art and Archaeology 28
Stones and Megaliths 28
Underwater Archaeology 28

ARCHITECTURE 28
Aesthetic Architecture 28
Alternative Architecture 29
Architectural Reconstructions 30
Architectural Styles 30
Architecture Competitions 30
Architecture Talk and General Discussion 30
Athenian Architecture 30
Bauhaus 31
Cathedrals 31
Fabric Structures 31
Gargoyles in New York City 32
Golden Gate Bridge 32
Japanese Architecture 32
New Urbanism 32
Renaissance and Baroque Architecture 32
Sullivan, Louis Henry 33
Women in Architecture 33
World's Tallest Buildings 33
Wright, Frank Lloyd 34

ART 34
African Art 34
Art Conservation 34
Art Criticism Forum 34
Art Dictionary 34
Art History 35
Art News 35
Art Nouveau 35
Art Resources 35
Art Talk and General Discussion ... 35
Ascii Art 36
Basic Design in Art and Architecture 36
Body Art 36

ix

Ceramic Arts	37
Contemporary Art Mailing List	37
Gargoyles and Grotesques	37
Impressionism	37
Mail Art	38
Native American Art	38
Pop Art	38
Student Artist Mailing List	38
Surrealism	38
Women Artists in History	38

ART GALLERIES AND EXHIBITS .. 39

Alphonse Mucha Museum	39
Art Crimes	39
Art Gallery Talk and General Discussion	39
Asian Art Gallery	39
Baroque Art	39
Carlos Museum of Art	39
Digital Photography	39
Erté Museum	40
French Age of Enlightenment	40
Imagebase	40
Leonardo da Vinci Museum	40
Los Angeles County Museum of Art	40
Louvre Museum	40
M.C. Escher Gallery	41
National Museum of American Art	41
Pinup Art	41
Sistine Chapel	42
Treasures of the Czars	42
Van Gogh Gallery	42
Vatican Exhibit	42
World Art Treasures	43
World Wide Art Resources	43

ASTRONOMY 43

Astronomy and Astrophysics Research	43
Astronomy Cafe	43
Astronomy History	43
Astronomy Hypertextbook	43
Astronomy Software	44
Astronomy Talk and General Discussion	44
Astrophysics Data System	44
Bad Astronomy	44
Constellations	44
Dark Sky Stargazing	45
Earth Views	45
Eclipses	46
Mars Atlas	46
Observatories and Telescopes	46
Peculiar Galaxies	46
Planets and the Solar System	47
SkyView	47
Starpages	47
Sunspots	47
Telescopes	48
USGS Astronomy Resources	48
Webstars	48

AVIATION 48

Aerobatic Aviation	48
Aeronet	48
Air Disasters	48
Airline Travel	49
Airplane Mailing Lists	49
Aviation Enthusiast Corner	49
Aviation Events	49
Aviation Magazines	50
Aviation Poetry	50
Aviation Q & A	50
Aviation Safety	50
Aviation Talk and General Discussion	51
Aviation Technology	51
DUATS	51
Flight Planning and Navigation	51
Hang-gliding and Paragliding	52
Helicopters	52
Landings Aviation Server	52
Learning to Fly	52
Military Aircraft	53
Owning Airplanes	53
Piloting	53
Stories About Flying	53
Ultralight Flying	53

BIOLOGY 54

Algae (Phycology)	54
Bioethics	54
Bioinformatics	55
Biology Dictionary	55
Biology Funding and Grants	55
Biology Job Opportunities	56
Biology Journals	56
Biology Resources	56
Biology Software	56
Biology Talk and General Discussion	56
Biology-Related Sciences	57
Biotechnology	57
Cell Biology	58
Developmental Biology	58
Ecology	59
Evolution	59
Genetics	59
Human Genome Project	59
Infomine Searchable Database	60
Microbiology	60
Molecular Biology	60
Mycology	61
Neuroscience	61
Taxonomy	61
Virology	62

BIZARRE 62

Air Sickness Bag Museum	62
Bizarre Stuff to Make	62
Bizarre Talk and General Discussion	62
Contortionism	62
Crime Scene Evidence File	63
Dark Side of the Net	63
Death Clock	63
Discord and Destruction	63
Evil Hexes	63
Grocery Shooting	63
Grotesque Curiosities	64
Mummy Museum	64
Negative Emotions	64
News of the Weird	64
Positive Emotions	65
Rotten Galleries	65
Rumors	65
Spleen	65
Squashed Bug Zoo	65
Stare Down Sally	66
Stick Figure Death Theater	66
Surrealist Compliment Generator	66
Tasteless Topics	66
Vampyres Only	66
Weird IRC Channels	66

BOATING AND SAILING 67

Boat Racing	67
Boatbuilding	67
Boating Mnemonics	67
Boating Quiz	67
Boating Rules	68
Boating Safety	68
Boating Talk and General Discussion	68
Boating Today	68
Crew Database	69
Dragon Boat Racing	69
GORP: Great Outdoor Recreation Pages	69
Kayaking and Canoeing	69
Marine Signal Flags	69
Navigation	69
Personal Watercraft	70
Rowing	71
Sailing	71
Seaports and Harbors	71
Watercraft Calendar	71
Wave-Length Paddling Magazine	71

BOOKS 72

Bibliomania	72
Book Authors	72
Bookbinding	72
Book Browser	72
Book Recommendations	72
Book Resources	73
Book Reviews	73
Book Talk and General Discussion	73
BookWeb	73
BookWire	73
Buying and Selling Books	74
Children's Books	74
Do-It-Yourself Book Reviews	74
Pulp Fiction	74
Rare Books	74
Romance Novels	75
Science Fiction and Fantasy Reviews	75
Technical Books	75

BOTANY 76

Agroforestry	76
Botanical Gardens	76
Botanical Glossary	76
Botany Images	76
Botany Talk and General Discussion	76
Botany Web Sites	76
Carnivorous Plants	77
Ethnobotany	77
Ferns	78
Lichens	78
Paleobotany	78

TABLE OF CONTENTS

Palynology Resources	78
Photosynthesis	78
Plant Fossil Database	79
Plant Gene Register	79
Plant Hormones	79
Plant Pathology	80
Plant Taxonomy	80
Succulents and Cacti	80
Smithsonian Botany Resources	80
BROADCASTING ON THE NET	**80**
Audionet	80
Book Radio	81
Celebrity Interviews	81
Commercial Radio Stations	81
Computer News Broadcasts	81
Internet Broadcasting Networks	82
Live Broadcasting Guides	82
Live Concerts	82
News Broadcasts	82
Sports Broadcasts	82
CANADA	**83**
Anti-Canada Web Site	83
Canadian Constitutional Documents	83
Canadian Culture	83
Canadian Fact Sheets	83
Canadian Government	83
Canadian History	84
Canadian Investment	84
Canadian Legal Resources	85
Canadian Music	85
Canadian News	85
Canadian Resources	85
Canadian Sports	86
Canadian Talk and General Discussion	86
Canadian Travel	86
Canuck Site of the Day	87
CBC (Canadian Broadcasting Corporation)	87
Montreal	87
Musée du Québec	87
Ottawa	88
Toronto	88
Vancouver	88
CARS AND TRUCKS	**88**
Antique Cars	88
Auto Channel	89
Auto Discussion Archives and FAQ	89
Auto Racing	89
Automobile Listings	89
British Cars	89
Car and Truck Purchasing	90
Car Audio	90
Car Classifieds	90
Car Place	90
Car Talk and General Discussion	91
Classic and Sports Cars	91
Customized Cars	91
Driving	92
Electric Vehicles	92
Exotic Cars	92
Formula 1 Motor Racing	93
Four-Wheel Drive Vehicles	93
Gasoline FAQ	93
Indy Racing	94
Kit Cars	94
Motorsport FAQ	94
Nascar	95
PM Zone	95
Road Rally	95
Slot Cars	95
Solar Cars	95
Team.Net Automotive Information Archives	95
CHEMISTRY	**96**
Analytical Chemistry	96
Atmospheric Chemistry	96
Biochemistry	96
Chemical Acronyms	97
Chemistry Journals	97
Chemistry Learning Materials	97
Chemistry Resources	98
Chemistry Talk and General Discussion	98
Chemistry Visualization and Animation	98
Computational Chemistry	98
Electrochemistry	99
Glycoscience	99
Hazardous Chemical Database	99
Laboratory Safety	99
Molecule of the Month	100
Nuclide Table	100
Organic Chemistry	100
Periodic Table	100
Sonochemistry	101
COLLECTING	**101**
Antiques	101
Autograph Collecting	101
Beanie Babies	102
Book Collecting	102
Bottle Collecting	103
Clocks and Watches	103
Coins and Money	104
Collecting Talk and General Discussion	104
Collectors' Marketplace	104
Doll Collecting	104
License Plates	104
Marble Collecting	105
Music Collecting	105
Postcards	105
Rock Collection	106
Snowglobes	106
Sports Memorabilia	106
Stamp Collecting	108
Teddy Bear Collecting	108
Toy Talk and General Discussion	108
Trading Cards	109
COMICS	**109**
Alternative Comics	109
Anime and Manga	109
Batman	110
Classic Comic Strips	110
Comic Conventions	110
Comic Reviews	110
Comicon	110
Comics Databases	111
Comics Fan Fiction	111
Comics Marketplace	111
Comics on the Net	111
Comics Talk and General Discussion	111
Daily Comics	112
Dilbert Zone	112
European Comics	112
Gallery of Fictional Beauty	112
International Museum of Cartoon Art	113
Professional Cartoonists	113
Small Press Comics	113
Tintin	113
COMPUTERS: COMPANIES	**114**
Apple	114
Compaq	114
Computer Companies	114
Computer Company Talk and General Discussion	114
Dell	114
Gateway 2000	114
Guide to Computer Vendors	114
HP (Hewlett-Packard)	115
IBM	115
Intel	115
Microsoft	115
Netscape	115
Novell	115
Packard-Bell	115
Rumors and Secrets About Computer Companies	115
SCO (Santa Cruz Operation)	116
Silicon Graphics	116
Sun Microsystems	116
COMPUTERS: MACINTOSH	**116**
Buying and Selling Macs	116
Macintosh Hardware	116
Macintosh Magazines	116
Macintosh Mailing Lists	116
Macintosh News and Announcements	117
Macintosh Programming	117
Macintosh Resources	118
Macintosh Talk and General Discussion	118
Macintosh Troubleshooting	118
Macintosh Updates	118
MacintoshOS.com	118
MkLinux	119
Tidbits	119
COMPUTERS: PCs	**119**
Buying and Selling PCs	119
Laptops and Notebooks	119
Monitors	120
Palmtops	120
PC Hardware Talk and General Discussion	120
PC Magazines	121
PC News	121
PC Prices	121
PC Resources	121
PC Talk and General Discussion	121
PCMCIA Cards	122
Printers	122
Scanners	122

xi

HARLEY HAHN'S INTERNET & WEB GOLDEN DIRECTORY

COMPUTERS: REFERENCE 123
- Bugs and Fixes 123
- Computer Almanac 123
- Computer Books Online 123
- Computer News 123
- Computer Product Reviews 123
- Computing Dictionary 123
- Computing Magazines and Journals 124
- Glossary of PC Terminology 124
- Hacker's Dictionary 124
- Smileys 124
- Tech Support and Online Help ... 125
- Webopaedia 125
- Yahoo Computers 125
- Year 2000 Problem 125

CONNECTING TO THE INTERNET .. 126
- ADSL 126
- Cable Modems 126
- Frame Relay 126
- Internet Service Providers 126
- ISDN 127
- Modems 127
- WebTV 128

CONSUMER INFORMATION 128
- Automobile Lemons 128
- Better Business Bureau 128
- Blacklist of Internet Advertisers ... 128
- Consumer Fraud 128
- Consumer Information Catalog ... 129
- Consumer Law 129
- Consumer Line 129
- Consumer News 129
- Consumer Product Safety Commission 129
- Consumer Talk and General Discussion 130
- Consumer World 130
- ConsumerNet 131
- Credit 131
- Finding a Doctor 131
- Free Stuff 131
- Funeral Planning 131
- Junk Mail 132
- National Institute for Consumer Education 132
- Tipping 132

CONTESTS 132
- Beanie Baby Contests 132
- Bookweb Contest 132
- Celebrity Classmates 132
- Contest Talk and General Discussion 132
- Dangerfield, Rodney 133
- Find the Lost Dog 133
- Hard Disk Contest 133
- Kids' Contests 133
- Nightmare Factory 133
- Popsicles 133
- Riddler Game 134
- Sports Contest 134
- Sports Picks 134
- Sweepstakes and Contests 134
- Uproar 135
- Vacation and Travel Contests ... 135
- Victoria's Valentine Contest ... 135
- Word Puzzles 135
- World Village 135

COOKING AND RECIPES 135
- Aunt Edna's Kitchen 135
- Backcountry Recipes 136
- Barbecue 136
- Bread 136
- Candy Recipes 136
- Cookie Recipes 136
- Cooking Talk and General Discussion 137
- Diabetic Recipes 137
- Fat-Free Recipes 137
- Fish 137
- French Cooking 137
- Home Canning 137
- Indian Food 138
- Insect Recipes 138
- Internet Chef 138
- Italian Cooking 138
- Kitchen Link 138
- Medieval and Renaissance Food .. 139
- Mexican Cuisine 139
- Mimi's Cyber-Kitchen 139
- Pies 140
- Random Recipe Generator 140
- Recipe a Day 140
- Recipe Archives 140
- Recipe Talk and General Discussion 140
- Southern Cooking 141
- Sushi 141

COOL AND USEFUL 141
- Complaint Letter Generator 141
- Daily Diversions 141
- Daily Fix 142
- Daily Tips 142
- Eeeek Net 142
- Electronic Postcards 142
- Harley Hahn's Internet Exploration Station 143
- Kvetch 143
- Last Word on Science 143
- Learn2 143
- Pocket Internet 143
- Reminder Services 144
- Search Snoopers 144
- Straight Dope 144
- Very Crazy Stuff 145
- Virtual Presents 145
- Why Files 145

COOL BUT USELESS 145
- Advertising Gallery 145
- Answers to All of Your Questions ... 145
- Biker Buddy 146
- Bill Gates Wealth Clock 146
- Cool but Useless Talk and General Discussion 146
- Create a Barcode 146
- Faces 147
- Internet Dancing Baby 147
- Mad Martian Museum of Modern Madness 147
- Magnetic Poetry 147
- Mood Thing 148
- Museum of Dirt 148
- Time Machine 148
- Useless Facts 148
- Virtual Plastic Surgery 148
- Woodcutter 148

CRAFTS 149
- Balloon Art 149
- Basket Weaving 149
- Beading and Jewelry 149
- Calligraphy 150
- Clay Art 150
- Craft Fairs 151
- Craft Marketplace 151
- Craft Resources 151
- Craft Talk and General Discussion .. 151
- Cross-Stitch 151
- Decorative Painting 152
- Knitting 152
- Knives and Blades 152
- Lacemaking and Tatting 152
- Metalworking 153
- Needlework 153
- Origami 153
- Polymer Clay 154
- Quilting 154
- Rubber Stamps 154
- Rug-Hooking 154
- Sewing 155
- Soapmaking 155
- Stained Glass 155
- Textiles 155
- Tie Dye 155
- Yarn 156

CRIME 156
- Alcatraz 156
- Con Artists 156
- Corrections Professionals 157
- Crime Statistics 157
- Crime Talk and General Discussion 157
- Death Row 158
- Electric Chair 158
- Famous Murderers 159
- FBI's Ten Most Wanted Fugitives .. 159
- Gangs 159
- Internet Crime Archives 159
- Law Search 159
- Mafia 160
- Police Brutality 160
- Police Scanner 160
- Prison Inmates 160
- Prison Life 160
- Rape 161
- Serial Killers 161
- Stalking 161
- Terrorism 161
- Unsolved Crimes and Fugitives .. 161

CRYPTOGRAPHY 162
- Ciphers 162
- Classical Cryptology Bibliography .. 162
- Cryptographic Research 162
- Cryptography Archive 162
- Cryptography FAQs 163

TABLE OF CONTENTS — xiii

Cryptography Policy Issues 163
Cryptography Resources 163
Cryptography Software 163
Cryptography Talk and General
   Discussion 163
Cryptography Technical Papers 163
Digital Signatures and Certificates ... 164
PGP 164
RSA 165
Steganography 165

DANCE 166
Ballet 166
Ballroom Dancing 166
Belly Dancing 166
Break Dancing 166
Competitive Dance Sport 166
Contra Dancing 167
Country Line Dancing 167
Dance News 167
Dance Resources 167
Dance Talk and General
   Discussion 167
Flamenco 168
Folk and Traditional Dance 168
Morris Dancing 168
Renaissance Dance 168
Salsa 168
Samba 169
Society for Creative Anachronism
   Dance 169
Swing Dance 169
Tango 169
Tap Dancing 170
Western Square Dancing 170

DEVICES AND GIZMOS CONNECTED TO THE NET 171
Animal Cams 171
Ant Farm 171
Antarctica Live 171
Cameras on the Net 171
Interactive Model Railroad 172
Light on the Net 172
New York Views 172
Refrigerator Status 172
Satellite Images of Cities 172
Things on the Net 172
Traffic Conditions 173
Vending Machines 173
Volcanoes on the Net 173
White House Cam 173

DIET AND NUTRITION 174
Ask the Dietitian 174
Basal Metabolism Calculator 174
Cyberdiet 174
Diet Analysis 174
Dieting FAQ 175
Dieting Talk and General
   Discussion 175
Fad Diets 175
Fast Food Calorie Counter 175
Fat 175
Fat Substitutes 175
Healthy Diet Guidelines 175
Healthy Weight 176
Holiday Diet Tips 176

Low Fat Lifestyle 176
Magic of Believing 176
Nutrition 176
Vending Machine Calorie Counter ... 177
Weight Gain 177
Weight Loss 177

DISABILITIES 177
Accessibility 177
Americans with Disabilities Act 178
Amputees 178
Attention Deficit Disorder 178
Autism 179
Birth Defects 179
Blind and Visually Impaired
   Computer Usage 179
Blindness 180
Cleft Palate and Cleft Lip 180
Computers for the Handicapped ... 180
Deaf-Blind Discussion List 180
Deafness 180
Disability Benefits 180
Disability Information 182
Down Syndrome 182
Dyslexia 183
Family Village 183
Handicap Talk and General
   Discussion 183
Kids with Disabilities 183
Paralysis and Spinal Cord Injuries .. 183
Rehabilitation 183
Service Dogs 183
Special Olympics 184

DRAMA 184
Acting Talk and General
   Discussion 184
Aisle Say 184
Ancient Theater 185
Back Stage 185
Casting Calls 185
Costumes of the Early Twentieth
   Century 185
Drama Talk and General
   Discussion 185
Dramatic Exchange 185
George and Ira Gershwin 186
Gilbert and Sullivan 186
Improv 187
Musicals 187
On Broadway 188
Opera 188
Play Scripts 188
Playbill Online 188
Stagecraft 188
Technical Theater Databases 189
Theater Resources 189

DRUGS 189
Anti-Drug Stuff 189
Anti-War-on-Drugs 189
Caffeine 189
Cocaine 190
Drug Chemistry and Synthesis 190
Drug Culture 190
Drug Information Resources 190
Drug Pix 190
Drug Talk and General Discussion .. 191

Drug Testing 191
Ecstasy 191
Heroin and Opiates 191
History of Drug Laws 192
International Stoner Slang
   Dictionary 192
Leary, Timothy 193
LSD: My Problem Child 193
Marijuana 193
McKenna, Terence 193
Methamphetamine 193
Nitrous Oxide 194
Nootropics
   (Intelligence-Enhancing Drugs) .. 194
Pihkal 194
Politics and Drugs 195
Prescription and OTC Drugs 195
Psychedelic Drugs 195
Street Drug Slang 195
Virtual Acid Trip 195

ECONOMICS 196
Beige Book 196
Bureau of Economic Analysis 196
Central Banks of the World 196
Computational Economics 197
Consumer Price Index 197
Economic Growth 197
Economic Resources 197
Economic Statistics 198
Economics History 198
Economics Journals 198
Economics Network 198
Economics of the Internet 198
Economics Talk and General
   Discussion 199
Economist Jokes 199
Economists on the Web 199
Federal Reserve System 199
Game Theory 200
Gross State Product Tables 200
History of Economic Thought 200
Household Economic Statistics 200
Inflation Calculator 200
Law and Economics 200
Securities and Exchange
   Commission's Database 201
U.S. Census Bureau Economic
   Statistics 201

EDUCATION 202
Adult Education 202
Canada's Schoolnet 202
Curriculum Materials and Ideas ... 202
Education Conferences 202
Education News 202
Education Policy 203
Education Talk and General
   Discussion 203
Educational Discussion Groups 203
Educational Mailing Lists 203
Eisenhower National
   Clearinghouse 204
Home Schooling 204
Musenet 204
National School Network Testbed ... 204
Netschool 205

xiv HARLEY HAHN'S INTERNET & WEB GOLDEN DIRECTORY

Newton BBS for Teachers 205
Special Education 206
Talented and Gifted 206
U.S. Department of Education 206
Vocational Education 206

EDUCATION: COLLEGES AND UNIVERSITIES 206
American Colleges and Universities 206
College Admissions 207
College Student Guides and Manuals 207
College Talk and General Discussion 208
Community Colleges 208
Counselor-O-Matic 209
Edufax 209
Exploring Campus Tunnels 209
Financial Aid 209
Fraternities and Sororities 210
Graduate Record Examination 210
Graduate Schools 210
Higher Education Resources Newsletter 210
Honors Programs 210
Lecture Hall 210
Online Courses and Distance Learning 211
Religious Colleges 211
Residential Colleges 211
Student Affairs 211
Studying Abroad 211
University Residence and Housing ... 211

EDUCATION: K-12 212
Ask an Expert 212
Ask Dr. Math 212
Education Place 212
Geometry and Art 212
High School Student's Survival Guide 212
Jason Project 213
K-12 Curriculum Talk and General Discussion 213
K-12 Foreign Language Talk and General Discussion 214
K-12 Internet School Sites 214
K-12 Resources 214
K-12 Student Discussion Groups ... 214
K-12 Teachers Discussion Group ... 214
Learning to Read 214
Literature for Children 214
School Projects by Kids 215
School Safety Tips 215
Science Learning Network 215
Spelling Bee 216
Study Tips 216
Test Taking Tips 216
Writing Well 217

EDUCATION: TEACHING 217
AskERIC 217
Classroom Discipline 217
College and University Teaching Assistants 217
EdWeb 218
Explorer 218

Instructor Magazine 218
Kinder Art 218
Science Demonstrations 219
Special Education and Special Needs 219
Teachers Helping Teachers 220
Teachers Net 220
Teaching English as a Second Language 220
Teaching Health and Physical Education 220
Teaching Mathematics 220
Teaching Music 220
Teaching Resources 221
Teachnet 221

ELECTRONICS 221
All About Electronics 221
Consumer Repair Documents 221
EDN Magazine 222
Electronic Chip Directory 222
Electronic Equipment Repair Tips ... 222
Electronic Prototyping Tips 222
Electronics Talk and General Discussion 222
Great Microprocessors Past and Present 223
Museum of HP Calculators 223
Semiconductors 223
Speaker Building Information 224

EMERGENCY AND DISASTER 224
Alertnet 224
Disaster Handbook 224
Disaster Situation and Status Reports 224
Disaster Talk and General Discussion 225
Earthquakes 225
Emergency News 225
Emergency Services 225
Emergency Tip of the Week 225
Emerging Diseases 226
Famine 226
Federal Emergency Management Agency 226
First Aid 226
Flood Observatory 226
Home Fire Safety Tips 227
Hurricanes 227
Planning Ahead for Disasters 227
Red Cross 227
Survivalism 229
Tornadoes 229
Wildfires 229

ENERGY 229
Alternative Energy 229
Biomass 229
Coal 229
Department of Energy 230
Educational Energy Information 230
Energy and the Environment 231
Energy Efficiency and Renewable Energy Network 231
Energy Efficient Homes 231
Energy Information Administration 231

Energy Talk and General Discussion 231
Hydroelectricity 231
Hydrogen Power 232
Natural Gas 232
Nuclear Energy 232
Petroleum 232
Renewable Energy 233
Solar Energy 233
Wind Energy 233
World Energy Statistics 233

ENGINEERING 233
Aerospace Engineering 233
Architectural Engineering 234
Audio Engineering 234
Biomedical Engineering 235
CAD (Computer Aided Design) 235
Chemical Engineering 235
Civil Engineering 235
Cold Region Engineering 236
Defense Sciences Engineering 236
Electrical Engineering 236
Electronics Engineering 236
Engineering Failures 237
Engineering Index 237
Engineering Talk and General Discussion 237
Geotechnical Engineering 237
Mechanical Engineering 238
Nuclear Engineering 238
Optical Engineering 239
Robotics 239

ENVIRONMENT 239
Air Pollution 239
Atmosphere Pollution Prevention ... 239
Biosphere 239
Chemicals in the Environment 240
Coastal Management 240
Coral Reefs 240
Ecological Economics 240
Endangered Rivers 240
Endangered Species 241
Environment Talk and General Discussion 241
Environmental Protection Agency ... 241
Environmental Resources 241
Environmental Scorecard 242
Environmental Search Engine 242
Environmental Web Directory 242
Forest Conservation 243
Greenpeace 243
National Wetlands Inventory 243
National Wildlife Refuges 243
Ozone Depletion 243
Planet Diary 243
Population 244
Rainforests 244
Sea Level Data 244
Seas and Water Directory 244
ULS Report 244
Waste Reduction Tips and Factsheets 245

EXERCISE 245
Aerobics 245
Fitness 245

Fitness for Kids	245
Fitness Talk and General Discussion	246
Powerlifting	246
Pregnancy and Exercise	247
Running	247
Sports Doctor	247
Stretching and Flexibility	247
Walking	247
Weightlifting and Bodybuilding	247
Women's Fitness	248
Yoga	248

FAMILIES AND PARENTING 249

Adoption	249
Babies	249
Breastfeeding	249
Child Activism	249
Child Discipline	250
Child Safety	250
Child Safety on the Internet	251
Child Support	251
Children	251
Children with Special Needs	252
Dads	252
Family Resources	252
Foster Parents	252
Grandparents Raising Grandchildren	253
Internet Filtering Software	253
Jewish Parenting	253
Kids, Computers and Software	253
Missing Children	253
Moms	254
Parent Soup	254
Parenthood Web	254
Parenting Resources	255
Parenting Talk and General Discussion	255
Parents and Children Together Online	255
Parents and Teens	255
Parents Room	255
Pregnancy and Childbirth	256
Premature Infants	256
Products for Children	256
Sgt. Mom's Place	256
Single Parents	257
Step-Parents	257
Surrogate Motherhood	258
Teaching with Movies	258
Twins and Triplets	258
Vacationing with Children	258

FAQs (FREQUENTLY ASKED QUESTION LISTS) 258

FAQ Archives	258
FAQ FAQ	259
FAQ for the *.answers Usenet Groups	259
FAQ Talk and General Discussion	260
Internet FAQ Consortium	260
Maintaining a FAQ	260
Minimal Digest Format FAQ	260
Periodic Informational Postings List	260
Posting a FAQ Automatically	261
Submission Guidelines for the *.answers Usenet Groups	261

FASHION AND CLOTHING 261

Beauty Shoppe Archive	261
Bra FAQs	261
Bridal Fashion Regrets	262
Business Fashion	262
Clogs	262
Clothing for Big Folks	263
CNN Style	263
Corsets	263
Fantasy Costume	263
Fashion Live	263
Fashion Net	263
Fashion Planet	264
Fashion Talk and General Discussion	264
Gothic Fashion	264
Hair Care	264
Historical Costuming	265
Hypermode	265
Lipstick	265
Look Online	265
Lumière	265
Lycra	265
Models and Supermodels	266
Shoes	266
Sneakers	266
Textiles	267
Victorian Fashion	267
Women's Wire Fashion & Beauty	267

FINDING STUFF ON THE NET 267

Culture Finder	267
File Finder	268
FTP Search	268
How to Use Search Engines	268
Image Search Engines	268
Internet Consulting Detective	268
Internet Sleuth	268
LocalEyes	269
Mailing List Search Engines	269
New Stuff Talk and General Discussion	269
Portals	270
Research It	270
Search Engine Access Sites	270
Search Engines	271
Usenet Search Engines	271
Web Catalogs	271
Web Channel Guides	272
Web Guides	272
Web Sitez	272
Webring	272

FOLKLORE, MYTHS AND LEGENDS 272

Aesop's Fables	272
Atlantis	273
Bigfoot	273
Charms and Amulets	273
Computer Folklore	273
Cryptozoology	273
Dragons	274
Encyclopedia of Myths and Legends	274
Faerie Lore	274
Fairy Tales	274
Folk Tales from Around the World	274
Folklore and Mythology Resources	275
Gems and Mineral Folklore	275
Germanic Myths, Legends and Sagas	277
Ghost Stories	277
Gnomes	278
Greek Mythology	278
Griffins	278
Imaginary Creatures	278
King Arthur and Camelot	278
Loch Ness Monster	279
Mermaids	279
Mythology in Western Art	279
Mythology Talk and General Discussion	279
Native American Myths and Legends	280
Pirates	280
Robin Hood	281
Scientific Urban Legends	281
Sea Serpents and Lake Monsters	281
Urban Legends	282
Werewolf Folklore	282

FONTS AND TYPEFACES 282

Field Guide to Fonts	282
Figlet Fonts	282
Font Talk and General Discussion	282
Fontsite Magazine	283
Foreign Font Archive	283
Free Fonts	283
Funny Fonts	283
Headline Maker	284
Truetype Fonts	284
&Type	284
TypeArt Library	284
Typofile	284
Typography Terminology	284
Unusual Fonts	284

FOOD AND DRINK 285

Beer	285
Beer Ratings	285
Beverages	285
Cereal	286
Cheese	286
Coca-Cola	286
Cocktails	286
Coffee	286
College Food	287
Epicurious	287
Fast Food	287
Food Labeling Information	287
Food Safety	288
Food Talk and General Discussion	288
Foodplex	288
French Fries	288
Fun Foods	289
Global Gourmet	289
History of Food	289
Homebrewing	290
Mead	290
Restaurant Talk and General Discussion	290
Restaurants on the Web	290

Sushi	291
Vegans	292
Vegetarian Resources	292
Vegetarian Talk and General Discussion	292
Wine	292
Wine Zines	293

FREEDOM ... 293

ACLU	293
Activism Resources	293
Amnesty International	293
Banned Books	293
Censorship of the Internet	294
Censorship Talk and General Discussion	294
Censorware	294
Flag Burning	294
Free Speech	294
Freedom of Expression	295
Freedom of Information Act	295
Freedom of Religion	295
Gun Control	296
Human Rights	296
Liberty Web	296
Naturism and Freedom	296
United Nations Agreements on Human Rights	296

FUN ... 298

Abuse a Celebrity	298
Anagrams	298
Bubbles	298
Diaries and Journals	299
Fortune Telling	299
Fun Planet	299
Madlibs	299
Mind Breakers	299
Mystery Solving	300
Payphone Project	300
Web Soap Operas	300
Weird Sites	300
Yo-Yos	300

GAMES AND PUZZLES ... 301

Backgammon	301
Battleship	301
Bingo Zone	301
Blackjack	301
Board Games	302
Bridge	302
Chess	303
Cribbage	303
Crossword Puzzles	303
Doom	304
Earth 2025	304
Empire	304
Game Hotspots	304
Game Reviews	305
Hangman	305
Hollywood Stock Exchange	305
Interactive Fiction	305
Java Game Park	305
Magic: The Gathering	306
Mame Arcade Emulator	306
Mazes	306
Othello	306
PC Games Talk and General Discussion	306
Pinball	307
Poker	307
Puzzles	307
Riddle of the Day	307
Sandbox	307
Shogi	308
Sliding Tile Puzzles	308
Tic Tac Toe	308
Top 100 PC Games	308
Video Games	309
Video Games Hints and Cheats	309

GARDENING ... 310

Bonsai	310
Flowers	310
Garden Encyclopedia	310
Garden Gate	310
Garden Ponds	310
Garden Web	311
Gardening Oasis	311
Gardening Talk and General Discussion	311
Gothic Gardening	311
Growing Vegetables	312
Hydroponics	312
I Can Garden	312
Indoor Plants	312
Mailing Lists for Gardeners	312
Organic Gardening	313
Pest Management	313
Plant Answers	313
Trees	313
Urban Gardening	313
Virtual Garden	314
Web Garden	314
Wildflowers	314

GAY, LESBIAN, BISEXUAL ... 315

Bisexuality	315
Catholic Gays	315
Coming Out	315
Cyberqueer Lounge	315
Domestic Partners	315
Gay and Lesbian Alliance Against Defamation	315
Gay and Lesbian Parenting	316
Gay Christians	316
Gay, Lesbian and Bisexual Resources	316
Gay, Lesbian and Bisexual White Pages	316
Gay Travel Guide	316
Gay TV Listings	316
Gay-Oriented Mailing Lists	316
Gays in the Military	317
Gayzoo	317
Historical and Celebrity Figures	317
Homosexuality and Religion	317
Homosexuality Talk and General Discussion	317
Jewish Gays	317
Lesbian Chat	317
Out Proud	318
PFLAG Gay Support Organization	318
PlanetOut	318
Politics and Homosexuality	318
Queer Resources Directory	319
Queer Zines	319
Straight Answers	319

GENEALOGY ... 319

Adoptees and Genealogy	319
Canadian Genealogy Resources	319
Cyndi's Genealogy Resources	320
Genealogy Discussion by Ethnicity	320
Genealogy Events	320
Genealogy Mailing Lists	320
Genealogy Marketplace	320
Genealogy Methods and Hints	320
Genealogy Resources	321
Genealogy Scams	321
Genealogy Search Engine	321
Genealogy Software	321
Genealogy Talk and General Discussion	321
Genealogy Terms	321
Genealogy's Most Wanted	322
Genserv	322
GenWeb Project	322
Getting Started in Genealogy	322
Heraldry	323
Jewish Genealogy	323
Journal of Online Genealogy	323
Mayflower Genealogy	323
Medieval Genealogy	324
National Archives and Records Administration	324
Native American Genealogy	324
Online Genealogy Newsletter	324
Roots	324
Royalty and Nobility	324
Scottish Clans	325
Surname Databases and Discussion	325
Surname Origins	326
Tombstone Rubbings	326
U.S. Census Information	326
U.S. Civil War Genealogy	326
Vital Records in the U.S.	327

GEOGRAPHY ... 327

CIA World Factbook	327
Distance Calculator	327
Earth Rise	327
Geographic Information Systems	328
Geography Departments Worldwide	328
Geography Resources	328
Geography Talk and General Discussion	328
Global Land Information System	329
Global Positioning System	329
Great Globe Gallery	329
Interactive Maps	329
Land Surveying	330
Landform Atlas of the United States	330
Perry-Castañeda Library Map Collection	330
Time Zones	331
United States Gazetteer	331
Vintage Panoramic Maps	331
World Population Datasheet	331

World's Highpoints	331
Xerox Map Viewer	331

GEOLOGY ... 332
Ask-a-Geologist	332
Earth Science Site of the Week	332
Earth Sciences Resources	332
Geological Image Library	332
Geological Time Machine	333
Geological Time Scale	333
Geology and Earth Science Resources	333
Geology of Radon	333
Geology Talk and General Discussion	333
Geologylink	334
Glaciology	334
Global Map of Earthquakes	335
Hydrology Web	335
Minerals	335
National Geophysical Data Center	335
Rock Shop	336
Seismology	336
Structural Geology	336
U.S. Geological Survey	336
Virtual Cave	336
Volcanology	337
World Data Center System	337

GOVERNMENT: INTERNATIONAL . 337
African Governments	337
Asia Pacific Governments	338
Australian Government	338
British Intelligence Organizations	338
Embassies and Consulates Around the World	338
Embassies in Washington, D.C.	338
European Governments	339
European Parliament	339
European Union	339
Governments of the World	340
Intelligence Organizations	340
International Government Talk and General Discussion	340
International Organizations in Geneva	340
International Relations and Security Network	340
Israeli Government	341
Japanese Government	341
Latin American Governments	341
Middle East Governments	341
National Parliaments	342
NATO	342
North American Free Trade Agreement	342
Organization of American States	342
Post-World War II Political Leaders	342
Swiss Government	342
United Kingdom Government	343
United Nations	343
United Nations Security Council	344
U.S. International Aid	344
World Government	345

GOVERNMENT: UNITED STATES .. 345
Budget of the United States Government	345
Census Information	345
CIA	346
Commerce Department	346
Congress	346
C-SPAN Live	347
Executive Branch	347
FBI	347
Federal Government Information	347
FedStats	347
FedWorld	348
General Accounting Office	348
Government Corruption	348
Government Information	348
Inspectors General	349
Justice Statistics	349
Justices of the Supreme Court	349
National Archives and Records Administration	349
National Performance Review	349
Social Security Administration	349
State Department	350
White House	350
White House Press Releases	350

HEALTH ... 351
Acne and Eczema	351
Addictions	351
AIDS	351
Arthritis	352
Birth Control	352
Centers for Disease Control	352
Children's Health	352
Children's Mental Health	353
Depression	353
Diabetes	353
Epilepsy and Seizure Disorders	353
Go Ask Alice	354
Headaches	354
Health Care Politics Talk and General Discussion	354
Health News	354
Health Oasis	354
Health Resources	355
Keyboard Yoga	355
Massage	355
Mental Health Net	355
National Institute of Allergy and Infectious Disease	356
National Institutes of Health	356
Quackery and Health Fraud	356
Sleep Disorders	356
Smoking Addiction	357
Snakebites	357
Stress	357
Stuttering	357
Suicide Prevention	357
Typing Injuries	358
U.S. Department of Health and Human Services	358
Women's Health	358
World Health Organization	358

HERBS ... 359
Algy's Herb Page	359
Aromatherapy	359
Chinese Herbs	359
Culinary Herbs	359
Garlic	359
Henriette's Herbal Homepage	360
Herb Magick	360
Herb Talk and General Discussion	360
Herb Uses	360
Herbal Encyclopedia	360
Herbal Hall	361
Herbnet	361
Medicinal Herbs	361
Modern Herbal	361
Pictures of Herbs	361

HISTORICAL DOCUMENTS ... 362
American Historical Documents	362
Canadian Constitution Act	362
Constitution of the United States of America	362
Council of Trent	362
Declaration of Arms, 1775	362
Declaration of Sentiments	363
Emancipation Proclamation	363
English Bill of Rights	363
European Texts and Documents	363
Federalist Papers	363
Gettysburg Address	364
Historical Document Archive	364
Historical Documents Talk and General Discussion	364
Joint Declaration of Peace	365
Maastricht Treaty	365
Magna Carta	366
Native American Treaties	366
Treaty of Guadalupe Hidalgo	366
Treaty of Paris	366
United States Bill of Rights	366
United States Declaration of Independence	367
Universal Declaration of Human Rights	367
Versailles Treaty of 1919	368

HISTORY ... 368
American Civil War	368
American First Ladies	368
American Memory Collection	369
American Studies	369
Ancient World Cultures	369
Anglo-Saxons	369
Classical Studies	369
Eighteenth Century Resources	369
Feudal Terms	370
Gulf War	370
Hiroshima and Nagasaki	370
Historian's Database and Information Server	370
Historic American Speeches	371
Historical Sounds and Speeches	371
Historical Timelines	371
History Net	371
History Resources	371
History Talk and General Discussion	371
Holocaust	372
Hyperhistory	372
Medieval History	373
Renaissance	373
Revisionism	373

HARLEY HAHN'S INTERNET & WEB GOLDEN DIRECTORY

Royalty	374
This Day in History	374
Titanic	374
Twentieth Century USA	374
Vietnam War	375
Vikings	375
War	375
World War I	376
World War II	376
World War II Propaganda Posters	377

HOBBIES ... 377

Audio Talk and General Discussion	377
Drums and Marching	377
Gold Prospecting	377
Graphology	378
Guns	378
Hobby Resources	378
Juggling	378
Kites and Kiting Resources	378
Letter Writing	378
Living History	379
Magic	379
Model Building	379
Nudity	380
Puppetry	380
Puzzles	381
Railroad	381
Roller Coasters	381
Scrapbooks	381
Society for Creative Anachronism	381
Treasure Hunting	382
Unicycling	382

HOLIDAYS AND CELEBRATIONS .. 382

Birthday Calendar	382
Christmas	382
Easter	382
Entertainment and Party Ideas	383
Halloween	383
Hanukkah	383
Hindu Festivals	383
Holiday Suicide Talk and General Discussion	383
Is There a Santa Claus?	384
Kwanzaa	384
Mardi Gras	384
Pagan Holidays	385
Reminder Services	385
Thanksgiving	385
Valentine's Day	386
Weddings	386
World Birthday Web	386
World Holiday Guides	386

HOMES ... 386

Apartments	386
Ask the Builder	387
Buying and Selling Houses	387
Decorating a Country Home	387
Feng Shui	387
Home Appliance Clinic	388
Home Environmental Hazards	388
Home Front Tips	388
Home Improvement	388
Home Improvement Encyclopedia	388
Home Improvement Warehouse	389
Home Repair	389
House Talk and General Discussion	389
Illustrated Tool Dictionary	389
International Real Estate Digest	390
Moving	390
Paint Estimator	390
Pest Control	390
Plumbing	390
Real Estate Talk and General Discussion	391
Tenant Net	391
Toilet Repair and Maintenance	391
Wallpaper Calculator	391
Woodworking	392

HUMANITIES AND SOCIAL SCIENCES ... 392

Anthropology	392
Communications	392
Generation X	393
Humanities Resources	393
Leisure Studies	393
Perseus Project	393
Popular Culture	394
Population Studies	394
Social Science Resources	394
Social Work	395
Sociology Resources	395
Sociology Talk and General Discussion	395
U.S. National Endowment for the Humanities	396
Voice of the Shuttle	396

HUMOR AND JOKES ... 396

Best of Usenet	396
Blackout Box	396
Comedy Talk and General Discussion	396
Complaint Letter Generator	396
Cruel Site of the Day	397
Dumb Lists	397
Fifty Fun Things for Non-Christians to Do in Church	397
Funny People	397
Humor Archives	398
Humor Databases	398
Humor Magazines	398
Humor Mailing Lists	398
Humorous Text Filters	399
Imprudent Wit and Verbal Abuse	399
Interactive Top Ten Lists	399
Joke of the Day	399
Jokes	399
Jokes, Moderated	400
Onion	400
Oracle	401
Religious Satire	402
Science Jokes	402
Shakespearean Insults	402
Tasteless (and Dirty) Jokes	402

INTERESTING TECHNOLOGIES .. 403

Artificial Intelligence	403
Artificial Life	403
Cloning	403
Computer Speech	404
Conversations with Computers	404
Nanotechnology	404
Neural Networks	405
Virtual Reality	405
Wireless Technology	405

INTERNET ... 405

Ad Blocking Software	405
Domain Name Registration	406
Email	406
Free Email Services	406
Free Mailing List Hosting	406
Historical Timeline of the Internet	406
History of the Internet	407
Information Activism	407
Internet Conference Calendar	407
Internet Drafts	407
Internet Fax Services	407
Internet Help Talk and General Discussion	408
Internet Hoaxes	408
Internet News	408
Internet Resources by Email	408
Internet Statistics	409
Internet Talk and General Discussion	409
Internet Terminology	409
IRC	409
Jargon File	409
Learning About the Internet and Web	410
ListTool	410
Net Happenings	410
New Internet Technologies	410
Scout Report	411
Web Talk and General Discussion	411
Whois	411

INTRIGUE ... 411

Conspiracies	411
Conspiracy Talk and General Discussion	411
Contemporary Conspiracies	412
Disinformation	412
JFK Assassination	413
Mind Control	413
Namebase	413
Parascope	413
Smoking Gun	413
Unsolved Mysteries	414
Waco	414

JOBS AND THE WORKPLACE ... 415

Bicycle Commuting	415
Contract Labor	415
Education-Related Jobs	415
Entry Level Jobs Offered	415
How to Get Rich	415
International Jobs	416
Job Hating	416
Job Searching	416
Job Talk and General Discussion	416
Jobs for College Students and Graduates	417
Kingdomality	417
Medical Jobs	418
Occupational Safety and Health	418
Repetitive Stress Injuries	418
Résumés	418

Riley Guide	419
Salary and Wages	419
Science Jobs	419
Seasonal Employment	419
Sexual Harassment on the Job	419
Telecommuting	419
Temps	420
Unions	420
U.S. Government Jobs	420
Young Job Seekers	420

JOURNALISM AND MEDIA ... 421
Committee to Protect Journalists	421
Environmental Journalist's Resources	421
Gonzo Journalism	421
International Federation of Journalists	422
Investigative Journalism	422
Journalism Mailing Lists	422
Journalism Resources	423
Journalism Student Resources	423
Journalism Talk and General Discussion	423
Media Watchdogs	423
Newslink	425
Photojournalism	425
Press Photographers	425
Pulitzer Prize	426
Radio and Television Companies	426
Reporters Network	426
Scholastic Journalism	426
Television Journalism	426

KEYS AND LOCKS ... 427
History of Locks	427
Impressioning	427
Lock Talk and General Discussion	427
Lockpicking	427
Locksmithing FAQ	427
Locksmithing Terminology	430
MIT Guide to Lock Picking	430
Murphy's Laws of Locksmithing	430
Picking Locks and Opening Safes	431

KIDS ... 431
Ask Jeeves for Kids	431
Astronomy Picture of the Day	431
Bee-Eye	431
Best Sites for Children	431
Contests for Kids	431
Cyberkids Magazine	432
Dinosaurs for Kids	432
Droodles	432
Heroes	432
Imagination Station	433
KidPub	433
Kids Click	433
Kids Report	433
Kids Space	433
Kids Talk and General Discussion	433
Knot Tying	434
National Wildlife Federation Kids Stuff	434
Papermaking	434
Poetry for Kids	434
Preschool Pages	435
Sites for Kids	435
Solve a Mystery	435
String Figures	435
Sugar Bush	435
Wendy's World of Stories for Children	435
White House Tour for Kids	436
Wild Weather	436
Yahooligans	436
Yucky Stuff	436

LANGUAGE ... 437
American Sign Language	437
Arabic	437
British-American Lexicons	437
Chinese	437
Cliché Finder	437
Computation and Language E-Print Archive	437
Cyrillic Alphabet	438
Czech	438
Dutch	438
Eastern European Languages	439
English	439
Esperanto	439
Filled Pauses	440
Foreign Language Dictionaries	440
Foreign Languages for Travelers	440
French	441
Gaelic	441
German	441
Greek	441
Hawaiian	441
Hindi	442
Icelandic	442
Italian	442
Japanese	442
Language IRC Channels	442
Language Playground	443
Language Translator	443
Languages of the World	443
Latin	443
Linguistic Talk and General Discussion	443
Linguistics	444
Middle English	444
Pronunciation in the American South	444
Russian	445
Serbian	445
Slovak	445
Spanish	445
Word-a-Day	445

LAW ... 446
Computers and the Law	446
Copyrights	446
Expert Witnesses	446
Federal Communications Law Journal	447
Free Legal Information	447
House of Representatives Law Library	447
International Criminal Justice	447
International Law Students Association	447
International Trade Law	448
Law Firms	448
Law Resources	448
Law Schools	449
Law Talk and General Discussion	449
Lawtalk	449
Lawyer Jokes	449
Legal Dictionary	449
Legal Documents Online	449
Litigation	450
Patents	450
Publishing Law	450
Supreme Court Rulings	450
Trade Secrets	451
Trademarks	451

LIBRARIES ... 451
American Library Association	451
Cataloging Talk and General Discussion	451
College Libraries	451
Conservation OnLine	451
Dewey Decimal System	452
Internet Public Library	452
Librarian Resources	452
Libraries Around the World	452
Library and Information Science	452
Library of Congress	453
Library of Congress Classification System	454

LITERATURE ... 454
African-American Literature	454
American Literature	454
Australian Literature	455
Beat Generation	455
Classics	456
English Renaissance Literature	456
First Lines	456
Gothic Literature	456
James Bond	457
Jewish Literature	457
Literary Calendar	458
Literary Theory	458
Literature Resources	458
Literature Talk and General Discussion	458
Mysteries	458
Native American Literature	458

LITERATURE: AUTHORS ... 459
Austen, Jane	459
Author Talk and General Discussion	459
Author's Pen	460
Baum, L. Frank	460
Bierce, Ambrose	461
Brontë Sisters	461
Carroll, Lewis	461
Conrad, Joseph	461
Dante	461
Dickens, Charles	462
Doyle, Arthur Conan	462
Faulkner, William	462
Hemingway, Ernest	463
Hesse, Hermann	463
Lovecraft, H.P.	463
Mansfield, Katherine	463
Milton, John	464
Parker, Dorothy	464
Poe, Edgar Allan	464

Pratchett, Terry	464
Rice, Anne	464
Shakespeare, William	465
Tolkien, J.R.R.	465
Twain, Mark	466
Virgil	466
Wells, H.G.	466
Wodehouse, P.G.	466
Yeats, William Butler	467

LITERATURE: COLLECTIONS ... 467

Ancient Greek Literature	467
Anglo-Saxon Tales	467
British Authors	468
Chinese Literature	468
English Server	468
French Literature	468
German Stories	468
Latino Literature	468
Literature Collection Talk and General Discussion	469
Middle English Literature	469
Online Books	469
Project Gutenberg	469
Secular Web	469
Short Stories	470
Victorian Literature	470
Western European Literature	470
Women and Literature	470

LITERATURE: TITLES ... 470

Aeneid	470
Alice's Adventures in Wonderland	471
Anne of Green Gables	472
Arabian Nights	472
As a Man Thinketh	472
Call of the Wild	472
Canterbury Tales	472
Civil Disobedience	472
Communist Manifesto	473
Connecticut Yankee in King Arthur's Court	473
Discourse on Method	473
Divine Comedy	473
Dracula	473
Fanny Hill	474
Far from the Madding Crowd	474
Fictional Character Talk and General Discussion	474
Flatland	474
Frankenstein	475
Gift of the Magi	475
House of the Seven Gables	475
Hunting of the Snark	475
Invisible Man	475
Jabberwocky	475
Jungle Book	476
Legend of Sleepy Hollow	476
Moby Dick	476
Oedipus Trilogy	477
On Liberty	477
Paradise Lost	477
Peter Pan	478
Scarlet Letter	478
Scarlet Pimpernel	478
Song of Hiawatha	478
Strange Case of Dr. Jekyll and Mr. Hyde	479
Time Machine	479
Tom Sawyer	479
Uncle Tom's Cabin	480
Voyage of the Beagle	480
War of the Worlds	480
Wonderful Wizard of Oz	480
Wuthering Heights	480

MAGAZINES ... 481

Business and Finance Magazines	481
Cars, Trucks and Motorcycle Magazines	481
Children's Magazines	481
Collector's Magazines	481
Computer Magazines	481
Entertainment Magazines	481
Fashion Magazines	482
Food, Wine and Cooking Magazines	482
Gossip Magazines	482
Health and Fitness Magazines	483
Hobby Magazines	483
Home and Garden Magazines	483
Home Maintenance Magazines	483
Magazine Collections	483
Magazine Talk and General Discussion	484
Men's Magazines	484
Music Magazines	484
News and Politics Magazines	484
Outdoors Magazines	484
Photography Magazines	485
Popular Culture Magazines	485
Science Magazines	485
Sports Magazines	485
Travel Magazines	485
Women's Magazines	486

MATHEMATICS ... 486

Algebra Assistance	486
American Mathematical Society	486
Calculus	486
Chance Server	486
Chronology of Mathematicians	487
Electronic Journal of Differential Equations	487
Geometry	487
History of Mathematics	487
Hub Mathematics and Science Center	488
Logic Talk and General Discussion	488
Math and Philosophy	488
Math Articles	488
Mathematical Association of America	488
Mathematical Quotations Server	489
Mathematics Resources	489
Mathematics Talk and General Discussion	489
Nonlinear and Linear Programming	490
Numerical Analysis	490
Operations Research	490
Pi (3.14159...)	491
Society for Industrial and Applied Math	491
Square Root of 2	491
Statistics	491
Symbolic and Algebraic Computation	492
Turing, Alan	492

MEDICINE ... 493

AIDS	493
Allergies	493
Anatomy	493
Anesthesiology	494
Atlas of Hematology	494
Biomedical Engineering	494
Brain Tumors	494
Breast Cancer	494
Cancer and Oncology	495
Chronic Fatigue Syndrome	495
Crohn's Disease and Colitis	495
Cystic Fibrosis	495
Dentistry	495
Dermatology	496
Emergency Medicine	496
Endometriosis	496
Forensic Medicine	496
Hippocratic Oath	497
Immunology	497
Infertility	497
Medical Education	498
Medical Libraries	498
Medical Physics	498
Medical Resources	498
Medical Software	498
Medical Students	498
Medical World Search	499
Medicine Talk and General Discussion	499
Medline	500
Medscape	500
Merck Manual	500
Nursing	500
Occupational Medicine	500
Organ Transplants	501
Pharmacy	501
Radiology and Imaging	501
Telemedicine	501
Virtual Hospital	501
Webdoctor	502

MEDICINE: ALTERNATIVE ... 502

Acupuncture	502
Alternative Medicine Resources	502
Alternative Medicine Talk and General Discussion	502
Ayurvedic Medicine	503
Cannabis and Medicine	503
Chinese Medicine	503
Chiropractic	503
Complementary Medicine	503
Dictionary of Metaphysical Healthcare	503
Herbal Medicine	504
Holistic Healing	504
Homeopathy	504
Music Therapy	504
Osteopathy	504
Relaxation Techniques	505
Rolfing	505
Shiatsu	505

TABLE OF CONTENTS

MEN ... 505
- Backlash ... 505
- Fathers ... 506
- Friends of Choice for Men ... 506
- Guy Rules ... 506
- Hair Loss ... 506
- Man's Life ... 507
- Men's Health ... 507
- Men's Issues ... 508
- Men's Talk and General Discussion ... 508
- P.O.V. ... 508
- Self-Help for Men ... 508
- Stay-at-home Dads ... 508

MILITARY ... 509
- Armed Forces of the World ... 509
- Chemical and Biological Warfare ... 509
- Contemporary Military Conflicts ... 509
- Disarmament Talk and General Discussion ... 509
- Medieval Armor and Weapons ... 509
- Military Academies ... 510
- Military Brats ... 510
- Military Medals ... 510
- Military Police ... 510
- Military Talk and General Discussion ... 511
- Military Terms and Acronyms ... 511
- Military Uniforms ... 512
- Military Vehicles ... 512
- Mine Warfare ... 512
- Nuclear Weapons ... 512
- Prisoners of War ... 513
- Selective Service System ... 513
- Special Operations ... 513
- Technology Insertion ... 513
- United States Armed Forces ... 514
- U.S. Department of Defense ... 514
- U.S. Military Magazines ... 514
- Veterans ... 514
- Vietnam Veterans ... 515
- Women in the Military ... 515

MISCHIEF ... 515
- April Fools ... 515
- Avenger's Page ... 515
- Backyard Ballistics ... 516
- Big Book of Mischief ... 516
- Culture Jamming ... 516
- Dumpster Diving ... 516
- Fake Memos ... 516
- Fake News ... 516
- Hack Gallery ... 517
- Mischief Talk and General Discussion ... 517
- Practical Jokes ... 517
- Prank Phone Calls ... 517
- Revenge Talk and General Discussion ... 517
- Telemarketer Torture ... 517
- Terrorist's Handbook ... 518
- Trolling ... 518
- Urban Exploration ... 518
- Wedding Pranks ... 518

MONEY: BUSINESS AND FINANCE ... 519
- American Stock Exchange ... 519
- Annual Reports ... 519
- Asia Online ... 519
- Bonds ... 519
- Business Headlines ... 520
- Business Information Resources ... 520
- Business Plans ... 520
- Commerce Business Daily ... 520
- Entrepreneur Talk and General Discussion ... 520
- FinanceNet ... 521
- Foreign Trade Statistics ... 521
- Global Trade Center ... 521
- Idea Futures ... 521
- Importing and Exporting ... 521
- Industry Net ... 521
- International Accounting Network ... 522
- Investor Glossary ... 522
- IPOs ... 522
- Money Page ... 522
- Multilevel Marketing Talk and General Discussion ... 522
- Mutual Funds ... 522
- Small Business Administration ... 523
- Small Business Resources ... 523
- Stock Market Data ... 523
- Stock Market Timing ... 523
- Wall Street Net ... 523

MONEY: PERSONAL FINANCE ... 524
- Consumer Credit Cards ... 524
- Currency Converter ... 524
- Estate Planning ... 524
- Getting the Most from Your Money ... 525
- Household Budgeting ... 525
- Insurance Information ... 525
- Investment Talk and General Discussion ... 525
- Money News ... 525
- Mortgage Calculator ... 526
- Mortgages ... 526
- Personal Finance Tips and Resources ... 526
- Planning for Retirement ... 526
- Tax Preparation ... 527
- Teaching Kids About Money ... 527

MOTORCYCLES ... 527
- Antique Motorcycles ... 527
- Biker Women ... 527
- Harley Owners Group ... 527
- Motorcycle Camping ... 528
- Motorcycle Maintenance ... 528
- Motorcycle Online Magazine ... 528
- Motorcycle Racing ... 528
- Motorcycle Reviews ... 528
- Motorcycle Safety ... 529
- Motorcycle Talk and General Discussion ... 529
- Motorcycling in the Rain ... 529
- Regional Motorcycle Mailing Lists ... 529
- Scooters ... 530
- Sidecars ... 530
- Stolen Motorcycles ... 530
- Used Bike Prices ... 530

MOVIES ... 530
- Box Office ... 530
- Coming Attractions ... 531
- Cult Movies Talk and General Discussion ... 531
- Directors Guild of America ... 531
- Film and TV Studies Mailing List ... 531
- Film Festivals ... 531
- Film, Television and Popular Culture ... 532
- Film.com ... 532
- Filmmaking Talk and General Discussion ... 532
- Hollywood Online ... 532
- Horror Movies ... 532
- Monster Movie Talk and General Discussion ... 532
- Movie and Film Resources ... 533
- Movie Databases ... 533
- Movie Mistakes ... 533
- Movie Previews ... 533
- Movie Reviews ... 534
- Movielink ... 534
- Movies Talk and General Discussion ... 534
- Mr. Showbiz ... 535
- Personal Movie Finders ... 535
- Science Fiction Movie Talk and General Discussion ... 535

MUDS ... 535
- Cardiff's Mud Page ... 535
- DikuMud Talk and General Discussion ... 536
- Harley Hahn's Guide to Muds ... 536
- History of Muds ... 536
- LPMud Talk and General Discussion ... 536
- Macintosh Mudding Resources ... 536
- Mud Admin Talk and General Discussion ... 536
- Mud Announcements ... 537
- Mud Area Building ... 538
- Mud Clients ... 538
- Mud FAQs ... 538
- Mud Glossary ... 538
- Mud List ... 538
- Mud Reviews ... 539
- Mud Talk and General Discussion ... 539
- Muds to Play ... 539
- TinyMud Talk and General Discussion ... 539
- Zhing ... 539

MUSEUMS ... 540
- Boston Science Museum ... 540
- Exploratorium ... 540
- Holocaust Museums and Memorials ... 540
- London Science Museum ... 540
- Maritime Museums ... 541
- Museum of Science and Industry ... 541
- Museum Talk and General Discussion ... 541
- Museums and Galleries of Wales ... 541

XXII HARLEY HAHN'S INTERNET & WEB GOLDEN DIRECTORY

Museums, Exhibits and Special Collections ... 541
National Gallery of Art ... 542
New Mexico Museum of Natural History ... 542
Royal Tyrrell Museum of Paleontology ... 543

MUSIC ... 543
A Cappella ... 543
Bagpipes ... 543
Bands ... 543
Banjo ... 543
Barbershop Quartets ... 544
Big Band ... 544
Blues ... 544
Buying and Selling Music ... 544
Celtic Music ... 545
Classical Music ... 545
Concert Information ... 545
Country Music ... 545
Disco ... 546
Discographies ... 546
Drums and Percussion ... 546
Early Music ... 547
Electronic Music Talk and General Discussion ... 547
Filk ... 548
Film Music ... 548
Folk Music ... 548
Funk ... 548
Gregorian Chants ... 548
Grunge ... 548
Guitar Talk and General Discussion ... 549
Indian Classical Music ... 549
Jazz ... 549
Lyrics ... 550
Marching Bands ... 550
Metal ... 550
Music Chat ... 550
Music Composition ... 551
Music FAQs ... 551
Music News ... 551
Music Performance ... 551
Music Resources ... 552
Music Reviews ... 552
Music Talk and General Discussion ... 552
Music Video Talk and General Discussion ... 552
Music Videos ... 553
Musical Instrument Construction ... 553
New Age Music Discussion ... 553
Opera ... 554
Punk Rock ... 554
Rap ... 554
Rap Dictionary ... 554
Rave ... 554
Record Production ... 554
Reggae ... 555
Rock and Roll ... 555
Strange Sounds ... 555
Underground Music Archive ... 555
Women in Music ... 556
World Music Talk and General Discussion ... 556

MUSIC: PERFORMERS ... 556
Amos, Tori ... 556
Beastie Boys ... 557
Beatles ... 557
Bush ... 557
Dion, Celine ... 557
Fan Favorites Talk and General Discussion ... 558
Grateful Dead ... 560
Hanson ... 560
Hootie and the Blowfish ... 560
Jackson, Janet ... 562
Jamiroquai ... 562
Jewel ... 562
Madonna ... 562
McCartney, Paul: Death Hoax ... 563
McLachlan, Sarah ... 563
Morissette, Alanis ... 563
Oasis ... 564
Presley, Elvis ... 564
Prodigy ... 565
Puff Daddy ... 565
Rolling Stones ... 565
Sinatra, Frank ... 565
Spice Girls ... 565

NEW AGE ... 566
Aquarian Age ... 566
Aware Net ... 566
Biorhythms ... 566
Chakras ... 566
Crystals ... 566
Firewalking ... 567
Lucid Dreams ... 567
Masters, Extraterrestrials and Archangels ... 567
Meditation ... 567
Mysticism ... 568
New Age Talk and General Discussion ... 568
Numerology ... 569
Reincarnation ... 570
Spirit Web ... 570
Spiritual Healing ... 570
Tarot ... 571

NEWS ... 571
Arabic News ... 571
Australian News ... 571
BBC News ... 571
Chinese News ... 571
CNN Interactive ... 572
Current Events Talk and General Discussion ... 572
Drudge Report ... 572
Email the Media ... 572
Free Clipping Services ... 573
German News ... 573
Good News and Bad News ... 573
India News ... 573
Internet Press ... 573
Irish News ... 573
Israeli News ... 574
Japanese News ... 574
Los Angeles Times ... 574
MSNBC ... 574
New York Times ... 574
OneWorld News ... 575
Pakistan News ... 575
Pointcast Network ... 575
Reuters News ... 575
Russian News ... 576
South African News ... 576
Swedish News ... 576
Time Daily ... 576
USA Today ... 576
Washington Post ... 576
World News Sources ... 576

OCCULT AND PARANORMAL ... 577
Astrology Charts ... 577
Astrology Resources ... 577
Astrology Talk and General Discussion ... 577
Chaos Magick ... 577
Ghosts and Hauntings ... 577
Hermeticism ... 578
Inner Sanctum Occult Net ... 578
Lightful Images ... 578
Magick ... 578
Magick Talk and General Discussion ... 578
Near-Death Experience ... 578
Necronomicon ... 579
Occult and Magick Chat ... 579
Occult Search Engine ... 579
Ouija ... 580
Out-of-Body Experiences ... 580
Paranormal Phenomena Talk and General Discussion ... 580
Parapsychology ... 580
Skepticism ... 580
Thelema ... 581
Voodoo ... 582

OUTDOOR ACTIVITIES ... 582
Ballooning ... 582
Boomerangs ... 583
Camping ... 583
Climbing ... 583
Fishing ... 583
Hiking and Backpacking ... 584
Human-Powered Vehicles ... 584
Hunting ... 584
Inline Skating ... 585
Kayaking and Canoeing ... 585
Mountain Biking ... 585
Nude Beaches ... 585
Orienteering and Rogaining ... 585
Outdoor and Recreation Resources ... 586
Outside Online ... 586
Paragliding ... 586
Parks in the United States ... 586
Radio-Controlled Model Aircraft ... 586
Scuba Diving ... 587
Shooting ... 587
Skateboarding ... 588
Skydiving ... 588
Snowboarding ... 589
Snowmobiles ... 589
Spelunking ... 589
Surfing ... 589
Swimming ... 589

TABLE OF CONTENTS   xxiii

Water Skiing 590
Windsurfing 590

PEOPLE 591
Billionaires 591
Callahan's Bar 591
Characters and Fictional
  People 591
Charities 591
Chatting in 3-D 592
Cult of the Dead Cow 592
Dead People Server 592
Expatriates and Refugees 592
Find-A-Grave 592
Finding Email Addresses 593
Friends 593
Interesting People on
  the Web 593
Kooks 593
Masons and Shriners 594
Mensa 594
Names 594
Nerds 595
Obituaries 595
PenPals 596
Personal Web Pages 596
Random Portrait Gallery 596
Shared Realities 596
Tea and Conversation 596
Virtual Campfire of Nerds 597
Virtual Memorials 597
Wendy Pages 597
Y Forum 597

PEOPLE: FAMOUS AND
INTERESTING 597
Adams, Scott 597
Asimov, Isaac 598
Brite, Poppy Z. 598
British Royal Family 598
Celebrity Addresses 598
Celebrity Resources 599
Celebrity Romantic Links 599
Celebrity Talk and General
  Discussion 600
Dangerfield, Rodney 601
Date, Kyoko 601
Einstein, Albert 602
Famous People's Wills 602
Fuller, Buckminster 602
Gates, Bill 603
Gingrich, Newt 603
Hall of Annoying Buttons 603
Horror Authors 603
Lewinsky, Monica 603
McCaffrey, Anne 603
Nobel Prize Winners 604
Pope John Paul II 604
Poundstone, William 604
President of the United States 604
Princess Diana 605
Randi, James 605
Real Names of Famous People 606
Santa Claus 606
Thompson, Hunter S. 606
Vice President of the
  United States 606

PERSONALS AND DATING 606
American Singles 606
Bisexuals 606
Blind Dates 607
Chit-Chat 607
Cupid's Network 607
Dating Pattern Analyzer 607
Dating Tests 607
Friend Finder 607
Friendly Folk 608
Internet Personals 608
Internet Romances 608
Jewish Personals 608
Large People 608
Meeting People 609
Pen Pal Brides 609
Personal Ads Talk and General
  Discussion 609
Personals for Gays 609
Relationship Advice 609
Spanking 610

PHILOSOPHY 610
Aesthetics 610
Chinese Philosophy 611
Ethics 611
Existentialism 611
Greek Philosophy 611
Memetics 611
Metaphysics Talk and General
  Discussion 611
Objectivism 612
Philosophers 612
Philosophy Reference Guides 612
Philosophy Resources 612
Philosophy Search Engines 613
Philosophy Talk and General
  Discussion 613
Political Philosophy 613
Women in Philosophy 613

PHOTOGRAPHY 614
Alternative Photographic
  Processes 614
Black and White Photography 614
Daguerreotypes 614
Darkroom Photography 614
Digital Cameras 614
Exposure 614
History of Photography 615
Infrared Photography 616
Kite Aerial Photography 616
Nature and Wildlife
  Photography 616
Panoramic Photography 616
PhotoForum 616
Photographers Directory 617
Photography Basics 617
Photography Equipment Talk and
  General Discussion 617
Photography Resources 617
Photography Talk and General
  Discussion 617
Pinhole Photography 618
Toy Cameras 618
Underwater Photography 619
Zone System 619

PHYSICS 619
Center for Particle Astrophysics 619
Computational Fluid Dynamics 619
Fusion 620
Index of Physics Abstracts 620
Optics 620
Particle/High Energy Physics 620
Particle Surface Research 620
Physics Conferences 621
Physics Talk and General
  Discussion 621
Plasma Physics 621
Polymer and Liquid Crystal Tutorial .. 621
Polymer Physics 622
Radioactive Waste 622
Relativity 622

PICTURES AND CLIP ART 622
Ascii Art 622
Cartoon Pictures 623
Clip Art 624
Fantasy Art 624
Fractals 624
Icon Collections 624
Photo Archives 624
Picture Viewing Software 625
Realm of Graphics 625
Shuttle and Satellite Images 625
Stereograms 625
Supermodels 625
Thesaurus for Graphic Material 625

POETRY 625
Blake, William 625
British Poetry Archive 626
Browning, Elizabeth Barrett 626
Chinese Poetry 626
Collective Poem 626
Dickinson, Emily 626
Haiku 626
Irish Poetry 627
Keats, John 627
Millay, Edna St. Vincent 627
Neruda, Pablo 627
Plath, Sylvia 628
Poetry Archives 628
Poetry Talk and General
  Discussion 628
Semantic Rhyming Dictionary 628
Shelley, Percy Bysshe 629
Tennyson, Alfred 629
Whittier, John Greenleaf 629
Wordsworth, William 629

POLITICS 629
Activism 629
Clinton-Lewinsky Scandal 629
Conservative Political News 630
Democrats 630
Euthanasia 631
Grassroots Activism 631
Hate Groups 631
International Politics Talk and
  General Discussion 631
Internet Politics 631
Irish Politics 632
Israeli Politics 632

Jefferson Project 632
Political Correctness 632
Political Policies 632
Political Talk and General
    Discussion 633
Politicians 633
Politics of Government
    Organizations 634
Presidential Scandals 634
Republicans 634
Richard Nixon Audio and Video
    Archive 634
Treaties 635
United States Political Talk and
    General Discussion 635

PRIVACY AND SECURITY 635
Anonymous Remailers 635
Anti-Telemarketing 636
Anti-Virus Programs 636
Computer Security 636
Computer Viruses 637
Cookies (on the Web) 637
Electronic Privacy Information
    Center 637
Email Privacy 637
Fingerprinting and
    Biometrics 638
Privacy Forum Digest 638
Privacy Resources 638
Privacy Rights Clearinghouse 639
Privacy Talk and General
    Discussion 639
Privacy Tips 639
Spamming 639
Using the Web Anonymously 640
Virus Hoaxes 640

PROGRAMMING 640
Ada 640
C++ and C 640
DOS Programming Talk and
    General Discussion 641
Free Compilers and
    Interpreters 641
Free Programming Tools 641
Hackers 641
Hello, World 642
IEEE Computer Society 642
Macintosh Programming 642
Obfuscated C Code 642
Object-Oriented Programming .. 643
Operating Systems Talk and
    General Discussion 643
OS/2 Programming Talk and
    General Discussion 644
Perl 644
Programmer of the Month 644
Programming Humor 644
Programming Languages 645
Programming Talk and General
    Discussion 645
Software Engineering 646
Tao of Programming 646
Visual Basic 646
Windows Programming Talk and
    General Discussion 646
X Window 646

PSYCHOLOGY 647
Adler, Alfred 647
American Psychological Association
    Journals 647
Consciousness 647
Freud, Sigmund 648
Jung, Carl 648
Optical Illusions 648
Personality Testing 649
Psychological Help 649
Psychology Database 649
Psychology Resources 649
Psychology Talk and General
    Discussion 650
Self-Help and Psychology
    Magazine 650
Social Psychology 650

QUOTATIONS 651
Allen, Woody 651
Daily Quotations 651
Dangerfield, Rodney 651
Famous Quotations 651
Fields, W.C. 652
Goldwyn, Samuel 652
Harley Hahn Quotes 652
Marx, Groucho 652
Presidential Quotes 652
Quotable Women 652
Quotation Resources 652
Quotation Talk and General
    Discussion 654
Random Quotes 654
Star Trek Quotes 655
Today's Fortune 655
Twain, Mark 655
Wilde, Oscar 655

RADIO 656
Amateur Radio Talk and General
    Discussion 656
Campus Radio Disc Jockeys 656
Canadian Broadcasting
    Corporation 656
Citizen Band Radio 657
Classic Top 40 Radio Sounds ... 657
Digital Audio Broadcasting 657
Ham Radio 657
NPR Online 657
Number Stations 658
Old-Time Radio 658
Open Broadcasting 658
Packet Radio 658
Pirate Radio 659
Radio Broadcasting 659
Radio History 660
Radio Scanner Frequencies 660
Radio Station Lists 660
Shortwave Radio 660
Talk Radio Hosts 661
Vintage Radios and
    Broadcasting Equipment 661
Voice of America 661

REFERENCE 661
Acronyms 661
Alternative Dictionaries 662
Biographies 662
Calculators 662
Calendars 662
Center of Statistical Resources . 663
Dictionaries 663
Encyclopedias 663
Farmer's Almanac 664
Grammar and English Usage ... 664
Maps and Atlases 664
Phone Books 664
Postal Codes and Mail 664
Reference Desks 665
Roget's Thesaurus 665
Time 665
Today's Date and Time 666
Tracking a Package 666
Weights and Measures 666
Word Detective 666

RELIGION 666
Agnosticism 666
Anglican and Episcopalian
    Churches 667
Atheism 667
Bible Study 667
Bibles Online 668
Biblical Timeline 668
Buddhism 669
Catholicism 669
Christian Resources 669
Christianity Talk and General
    Discussion 670
Eastern Orthodox Christianity . 670
Hinduism 670
Islam 671
Jainism 671
Judaism 671
Koran (or Qurán) 671
Quakers (Society of Friends) 672
Religion Talk and General
    Discussion 672
Religious Tolerance 672
Sexuality and Religion 672
Sikhism 672
Zen Buddhism 674
Zoroastrianism 674

RELIGION: SECTS AND CULTS ... 674
Baha'i Faith 674
Brother Jed 674
Chabad-Lubavitch Judaism 675
Coptic 675
Eckankar 675
Gnosticism 675
Goddess Names 676
Goddess Spirituality and
    Feminism 676
Jehovah's Witnesses 676
Mennonites 676
Mormons 677
Mysticism Chat 677
Nazarenes 677
New Religious Movements 677
Paganism 678
Santeria 678
Satanism 678
Scientology 679
Shakers 679

TABLE OF CONTENTS XXV

Shamanism 679
Theosophy 679
Unitarianism 680
Wicca 680

ROLE PLAYING 681
Advanced Dungeons and Dragons ... 681
Buying and Selling Role-Playing
   Games 681
Fantasy Role Playing Talk and
   General Discussion 682
Live-Action Role Playing 682
Magic: The Gathering 683
Miniatures 683
Netrunner 683
Role-Playing Crafts 683
Role-Playing Games Magazine 683
Role-Playing Resources 685
Star Trek Role Playing 685
Vampire: The Masquerade 685
Warhammer 685
World of Darkness 685

ROMANCE 686
Chatting in the Big City 686
Couples 686
Kissing 686
Language of Love 686
Love Chat 687
Love Letters 687
Love Test 687
Men and Women 687
Online Romance Talk and
   General Discussion 690
Poetry 690
Random Love Poems 690
Romance Readers Anonymous 690
Romance Talk and General
   Discussion 690
Romantic Ascii Graphics 690
Romantic Gestures 691
Romantic Greetings by Email 691
Singles 691
Soulmates 691
Togetherness Tips 691
Unhappy Romances 691
Virtual Wedding Chapel 691

SCIENCE 692
Annals of Improbable Research 692
Bad Science 692
Dinosaurs 692
Earth and Sky 692
Folklore of Science 693
Hawking, Stephen 693
History of Science 693
Human Evolution 694
National Science Foundation 694
Oceanography 694
Research Methods in Science 694
Science Fraud and Skepticism 695
Science News 695
Science Resources 695
Science Talk and General
   Discussion 695
Temperature 695
Why Files 696

SCIENCE FICTION, FANTASY
AND HORROR 696
Ansible Newsletter 696
Babylon 5 697
Cabinet of Dr. Casey 697
Cyberpunk 697
Darkecho's Horror Web 698
Doctor Who 698
Fans of Science Fiction and Fantasy
   Writers 698
Fright Site 699
Furry Stuff 699
Horror Fiction Online 699
Horror Literature 699
Horror Talk and General
   Discussion 699
Mystery Science Theatre 3000 699
Red Dwarf 700
Science and Science Fiction 700
Science Fiction and Fantasy
   Archives 700
Science Fiction and
   Fantasy Online 700
Science Fiction Announcements 700
Science Fiction Convention
   Calendar 701
Science Fiction Fandom Talk and
   General Discussion 701
Science Fiction Marketplace 701
Science Fiction Movies 701
Science Fiction News 701
Science Fiction Resource Guide 701
Science Fiction Talk and
   General Discussion 702
Science Fiction Writing 702
SciFaiku 702
SF-Lovers 702
Star Wars 703

SECRET STUFF 703
2600 703
Backward Masking 703
Cellular Phone Hacking 704
Disney Secrets 704
Easter Eggs 705
Magic Secrets Talk and General
   Discussion 705
Pay-TV Decoders 705
Phreaking 705
Police Codes 706
Secret Societies 706
Social Security Number Location
   Finder 706
Software Cracks 706
Super Secret Web Site 706
Warez 707

SENIORS 707
Elders 707
Fitness for Seniors 707
Grandparents 707
Housing for Seniors 708
Retirement Planning 708
Senior Resources 708
Senior Talk and General
   Discussion 708
Seniors Magazines 708

Seniors Organizations 709
Travel for Seniors 709

SEX 709
Aphrodisiac Guide 709
First Times 709
How to Use a Condom 709
Jane's Guide 710
Pleasing a Woman 710
Safer Sex 710
Señor Sex 710
Sensual Massage 711
Sex Glossary 711
Sex Talk and General Discussion 711
Sex Tips 711
Sex Trivia 711
Tantra and the Kama Sutra 711
Urban Sex Legends 712

SEXUALITY 712
Androgyny Information 712
Dr. Ruth 713
Human Sexuality 713
Polyamory 713
Purity Tests 713
Sex Experts Talk and General
   Discussion 713
Sex Laws 713
Sex Questions and Answers 714
Sex Reference Guide 714
Sexual Assault and Sex Abuse
   Recovery 714
STD Information 714
Transvestite, Transsexual,
   Transgender 715

SHOPPING 715
Auctions 715
Auctions Online 716
Buying/Selling Talk and General
   Discussion 716
Catalogs by Mail 717
CD Clubs 717
Classified Ads 717
Comparisons 717
Coupons 717
Flea Markets 717
Shopping Malls 718
Shopping Online 718
Shopping with Children 718

SOFTWARE 718
Buying and Selling Software on
   the Internet 718
Cool Tool of the Day 719
Free-DOS Project 719
Freeware 719
Jewish Software 719
Linux 719
Macintosh Games 720
Macintosh Software Archives 720
Macintosh Software Talk and
   General Discussion 720
Macintosh Version Tracker 720
Nonags 721
Non-English Software 721
OS/2 Games 721
OS/2 Networking Environment 721
OS/2 Software Archives 721

XXVI HARLEY HAHN'S INTERNET & WEB GOLDEN DIRECTORY

OS/2 Utilities	721
Software Archives	722
Software Licensing	722
Software Testing Talk and General Discussion	722
Spam Filtering Software	722
TCP/IP	722
Windows CE Software Archives	723
Windows Game Software	723
Windows Networking Environment	723
Windows Software	723
SOUNDS	**723**
Animal Sounds	723
Bird Sounds	724
Christmas Sounds	724
Goldwave	724
Human Noises	724
Insulting Sound Files	724
MIDI Archives	725
Number Synthesizer	725
Sound Archives	725
Sound Tools	725
Sounds and Sound Effects	726
Television and Movie Sounds	726
SPACE	**726**
Aeronautics and Space Acronyms	726
Center for Earth and Planetary Studies	726
Challenger	726
Electronic Universe Project	726
European Space Agency	726
European Space Information System	727
Goddard Space Flight Center	727
History of Space Exploration	727
Lunar Photographs	727
Mars Images	727
NASA Historical Archive	727
NASA News	728
NASA Research Labs	728
NASDA	729
Planetary Nebulae Gallery	729
Planets	729
Politics of Space	729
SETI	729
Shuttle Snapshots	729
Solar System Exploration	730
Space Calendar	730
Space Frequently Asked Questions	730
Space Movie Archive	730
Space News	730
Space Shuttle	730
Space Talk and General Discussion	731
Students for the Exploration and Development of Space	731
United Nations Office for Outer Space Affairs	731
Viking Image Archive	731
Windows to the Universe	731
SPORTS AND ATHLETICS	**731**
Aikido	731
Archery	732
Badminton	732
Baseball	732

Baseball Teams	733
Basketball	733
Basketball Team Talk and General Discussion	734
Basketball: Women	734
Bicycling	734
Boxing	735
College Sports	735
Cricket	735
Exercise and Sports Psychology	736
Fencing	736
Figure Skating	736
Football: American	737
Football: Canadian Football League	737
Football: Professional	737
Frisbee	738
Golf	738
Hockey	738
Hockey: College	738
Hockey Team Talk and General Discussion	739
Martial Arts	740
Polo	740
Rodeo	740
Rugby	741
Rugby League	741
Skiing	741
Soccer	741
Softball	742
Sports News	742
Sports Resources	742
Sports Schedules	742
Squash and Racquetball	742
Swimming Competitions	743
Tennis	743
Volleyball	743
Women's Sports	743
Wrestling: Professional	743
Wrestling: Sumo	744
STAR TREK	**744**
Alien Races	744
Animations and Images	744
Beer Trek	745
Captain Kirk Sing-a-Long Page	745
Conventions and Memorabilia	745
Future Technology Talk and General Discussion	745
Klingon Phrasebook	745
Klingon Shared Reality	746
Klingon Talk and General Discussion	746
Next Generation	747
Star Trek Games	747
Star Trek News	747
Star Trek Resources	747
Star Trek Reviews	747
Star Trek Role Playing	747
Star Trek Sounds	748
Star Trek Stories and Parodies	748
Star Trek Talk and General Discussion	748
Star Trek Television Shows	748
Star Trek Trivia	749
Star Trek Universe	749
Star Trek Video Clips	749

Star Trek: Voyager	749
Trekker Chat	749
SUPPORT GROUPS	**750**
30 Plus	750
Adoption	750
AIDS Caregivers	750
Al-Anon and Alateen	750
Anxiety	750
Depression	752
Divorce	752
Domestic Violence	752
Eating Disorders	752
Grief	753
Narcotics Anonymous	753
Pregnancy Loss	754
Recovery for Christians	754
Recovery for Jews	754
Sexual Addiction	754
Smoking	754
Support Groups Networking	755
Support Talk and General Discussion	755
Transgendered Support	755
Usenet Support Groups	756
Widows and Widowers	757
TALKING ON THE NET	**758**
3D Chatting	758
Chat Room Lists	758
Chat Servers	758
Chatting Safety	758
Comic Chat	758
ICQ	759
Internet Phone Services	759
IRC (Internet Relay Chat)	759
IRC Talk and General Discussion	759
Java Chat Applets	760
List of BBSs on the Internet	760
mIRC Client	761
NetMeeting (Internet Explorer)	761
Powwow	761
Talkers	761
Video Conferencing	761
Web Chat Rooms	762
TELEPHONE AND TELECOM	**762**
Business and Toll-Free Directory Listings	762
Cell-Relay Communications	762
Data Communications Servers	762
Fax Technology	762
International Dialing Codes	763
National Telecommunications and Information Administration	764
Networks	764
Phone Number Translator	764
Telecom Discussions and Digest	764
Telecom Resources	765
Telephone Tech Talk and General Discussion	765
Underwater Telecommunication Cables	766
U.S. Area Codes	766
TELEVISION	**766**
Andy Griffith	766
Beverly Hills 90210	766

TABLE OF CONTENTS xxvii

Brady Bunch	767	
Cartoons	767	
Comedy Central	767	
Commercials	767	
Daytime Talk Shows	767	
Dick Van Dyke Show	768	
ER	768	
Game Shows	769	
High Definition Television	770	
I Love Lucy	770	
Late Night Talk Shows	770	
Muppets	770	
Public Broadcasting Service (PBS)	770	
Satellite TV	770	
Simpsons	771	
Sitcom Downfalls	771	
Soap Operas	771	
South Park	771	
Television Talk and General Discussion	772	
Television Theme Songs	774	
TV Episode Guides	775	
TV Gossip	775	
TV Guide Postcards	775	
TV News Archive	775	
TV Schedules	775	
X-Files	775	

TRAVEL 776
- Air Travel 776
- Amtrak Trains 776
- Antarctica 776
- Australia 776
- Budget Travel 776
- Caribbean 777
- Castles 777
- City Net Travel Channel 777
- Dangerous Travel 777
- Fodor's Travel Resources 777
- Hawaii 778
- Hostels 778
- Japan 778
- Jerusalem 778
- London 778
- Lonely Planet 779
- Megaliths 779
- New York City 779
- Packing Tips 779
- Paris 779
- Railroad Connections 780
- Recreational Vehicles 780
- Roadside America 780
- Route 66 780
- Russia 780
- Speedtraps 780
- Subway Navigator 781
- Thailand 781
- Tourism Offices 781
- Travel Health Advice 781
- Travel Marketplace 781
- Travel Matters Newsletter 781
- Travel Resources 782
- Travel Talk and General Discussion 782
- Travel Tips 782
- Trip Planning 783

- U.S. National Parks 783
- U.S. State Department Travel Information 783
- World Guide to Vegetarianism 783

TRIVIA 783
- Digits Project 783
- Internet Index 784
- Movie Trivia 784
- Names of Famous People 784
- Oldies Music Trivia 784
- Sports Trivia 784
- Television Trivia 784
- Today's Date 785
- Today's Events in History 785
- Trivia Matters 786
- Trivia Page 786
- Trivia Web 786
- Trivial Talk and General Discussion 786
- Useless Facts 786
- Useless Information 786

UFOs AND ALIENS 787
- Abductions 787
- Alien Autopsies 787
- Alien Lexicons 787
- Alien Pyramids 787
- Alien Research 787
- Ancient Astronauts 787
- Area 51 788
- Contact Lab 788
- Crop Circles 789
- Life on Mars 789
- Roswell Incident 790
- UFO Chatting 790
- UFO Information Resources 790
- UFO Origins 790
- UFO Reports 790
- UFO Talk and General Discussion 791

USENET 792
- Creating Alternative Usenet Discussion Groups 792
- Creating Mainstream Usenet Discussion Groups 792
- Flames 792
- Harley Hahn's Master List of Usenet Newsgroups 792
- Moderated Newsgroups 793
- Net Abuse 793
- Newsgroup Listings 793
- Picture Grabbing Software 793
- Talkway 793
- Usenet Announcements 793
- Usenet Archiving Software 794
- Usenet Culture Talk and General Discussion 794
- Usenet Discussion Group Administration 794
- Usenet Discussion Group Invasion 795
- Usenet Discussion Group Questions 795
- Usenet Filtering Service 795
- Usenet for New Users 795
- Usenet Hierarchies 795
- Votetaker Volunteers 795

VICES 796
- Bingo 796
- Caffeine 796
- Chocolate 796
- Cigar Smoking 796
- Cigarette Smoking 797
- Drinking 797
- Gambling and Oddsmaking 797
- Hangovers 797
- Horse Racing 798
- Lotteries 798
- Pipe Smoking 798
- Sex Services Talk and General Discussion 799
- Strip Clubs 799
- Virtual Slot Machine 799

VIDEO AND MULTIMEDIA 800
- DVD 800
- MIME Format 800
- Mpeg Movies 800
- Mpeg Video Resources and Software 800
- Multimedia File Formats 801
- Multimedia in Education 801
- Multimedia News 801
- Multimedia Talk and General Discussion 801
- PC Video Hardware 801
- Video Editing 802
- Video Glossary 802

WEATHER 803
- Climate Data Catalog 803
- Climate Diagnostics Center 803
- Climate Monitoring 803
- European Weather Satellite Images 803
- Hurricanes and Typhoons 803
- Marine Weather Observations 803
- Meteorology Resources 803
- Meteorology Talk and General Discussion 803
- Space Weather 804
- Storm Chasing 804
- Weather Images 804
- Weather Radar 804
- Weather Reports: Canada 805
- Weather Reports: International 805
- Weather Reports: United States 805
- Weather Warnings 806

WEB: CREATING WEB PAGES 806
- Animated Gifs 806
- Bad Website Design 806
- Bandwidth Bandits 806
- Banners, Buttons and Text 806
- Beginner's Guide to HTML 806
- Cascading Style Sheets 807
- CGI Scripts 807
- Color Chart 807
- Dynamic HTML 808
- Frames 808
- Free Web Page Hosting 808
- Guestbooks 808
- HTML 809
- HTML Editors 809
- Icons for Fake Awards 809
- Image Maps 810

xxviii HARLEY HAHN'S INTERNET & WEB GOLDEN DIRECTORY

Learning HTML	810
Meta Tags	810
Promoting Your Web Site	810
Tables	811
Transparent Gifs	811
Using HTML Well	811
Web Authoring FAQ	811
Web Page Backgrounds	812
Web Page Counters	812
Web Page Creation Talk and General Discussion	812
Web Page Graphics and Icons	812
Web Page Marketing	812
Web Page Programs	812
Web Publishing Resources	813
Web Reference	813
Web Site Validation	813
Web Style Manual	813
XML	813

WEB: SOFTWARE ... 814

ActiveX	814
Browser Watch	814
Hostile Java Applets	814
Internet Explorer	814
Java	815
Javascript	815
Javascript Archives	815
Lynx	815
Netscape	816
Netscape Source Code	816
Plug-Ins	816
Real Audio	816
VRML	816
Web Browser Talk and General Discussion	817
Web Log Analysis	817
Web Server Talk and General Discussion	817
Web Server Watch	817
Web Talk and General Discussion	817

WINDOWS ... 817

Desktop Themes	817
Windows 95 and 98 Official Web Sites	818
Windows Annoyances	818
Windows Applications Talk and General Discussion	818
Windows Drivers	818
Windows Glossary	818
Windows Magazines	819
Windows Networking Talk and General Discussion	819
Windows News	819
Windows Peer-to-Peer Networking	819
Windows Pre-releases	819
Windows Programming	819
Windows Questions and Answers	820
Windows Resources	820
Windows Setup	820
Windows Talk and General Discussion	820
Windows Video Discussion	821

WINDOWS NT ... 821

Creating an Internet Site with Windows NT	821
Internet Resources for Windows NT	821
Introduction to Windows NT	822
Windows NT Drivers	822
Windows NT Faq	822
Windows NT Internet Servers	822
Windows NT Magazine	822
Windows NT Official Web Site	822
Windows NT Resources	823
Windows NT Security	823
Windows NT Setup	823
Windows NT Talk and General Discussion	823

WOMEN ... 823

Abortion	823
Ada Project	824
Disgruntled Housewife	824
Electronic Forums for Women	824
Femina	824
Feminism	824
Feminism Talk and General Discussion	824
Gender and Computing	825
Gender and Sexuality	825
Gynecological Exams	826
History of Women's Suffrage	826
Midwifery	826
National Organization for Women	826
Notable Women	826
Sexual Assault on Campus	827
Women Halting Online Abuse	827
Women in Congress	827
Women's Online Communities	827
Women's Resources	827
Women's Studies Resources	828
Women's Talk and General Discussion	828
Women's Web Guides	828
Women's Wire	828

WORLD CULTURES ... 829

Africa	829
Asia	829
Australia	829
Brazil	829
Cajun Culture	830
Central America	830
Chile	831
China	831
Country Studies Area Handbooks	831
Czech Republic	831
Egypt	831
Flags of the World	832
France	832
Germany	832
Hungary	833
Immigration	833
India	834
Indonesia	834
Ireland	834
Israel	835
Italy	835
Japan	836
Korea	836
Latin America	837
Malaysia	837
Mexico	837
Middle Europe	837
Morocco	837
Native Americans	838
New Zealand	838
Norway	838
Peru	838
Poland	838
Portugal	840
Russia	840
Russian and American Friendship	840
Saudi Arabia	841
Slovakia	841
Sweden	841
Taiwan	841
Thailand	841
United Kingdom	842
United States	843
United States: Southern	843
Venezuela	843
World Constitutions	843
World Culture Talk and General Discussion	844
World Heritage List	844

WORLD CULTURES: DISCUSSION GROUPS ... 844

Africa Discussion Groups	844
Asia Pacific Discussion Groups	845
Australia and Oceania Discussion Groups	845
Central Asia Discussion Groups	845
Europe Discussion Groups	845
Latin America Discussion Groups	846
Middle East Discussion Groups	846
Southeast Asia Discussion Groups	847
Southern Asia Discussion Groups	847
United States and Canada Discussion Groups	848
West Indies Discussion Groups	848

WRITING ... 848

Bad Writing Contest	848
Children's Writing	848
Copy Editing	849
Freelance Writing FAQ	849
Literary Agents	849
Mystery and Crime Writing	850
Online Writery	850
Prose	850
Publisher's Web Pages	850
Romance Writing	851
Screenplays	851
Screenwriters and Playwrights	851
Speechwriting	851
Technical Writing	852
Writer's Block Magazine	852
Writers Chat	852
Writers' Resources	852
Writers Talk and General Discussion	852
Writing Tips	852

X-RATED RESOURCES ... 854

Adult Site of the Day	854
AltSex	854

TABLE OF CONTENTS   xxix

Auto-Eroticism 854
Bondage 854
Cross-Dressing 854
Diaper Fetish 855
Dominance and Submission 855
Dominant Women 856
Erotic Postcards 856
Erotic Resources 856
Exhibitionism 857
Fetish Fashions 857
Foot Fetish 857
Glory Hole FAQ 857
Hard Kink Magazine 857
Limericks 857
News and Gossip of the
    Porn Industry 858
Oral Sex 858
Pantyhose and Stockings 858
Porn Stars 858
Porn-O-Matic 858
Prostitution Around the World 858
Sex How-Tos 859
Sex Magazine Talk and General
    Discussion 860
Sex Magazines 860
Sex Pictures 860
Sex Sounds 861
Sex Stories 861
Sex Wanted 861
Sexy Talk 861
Spanking 861
Strip Club List 861
Tickling 862

Voyeurism 862
Watersports 862
X-Rated Movies 862
Zoophilia 862

YOUNG ADULTS 863
Christian Youth 863
Cool Science 863
Cyberteens 863
Girl Stuff 863
Gurl 863
Marijuana Facts 864
MidLink Magazine 864
Preparing for College 864
Scouting 864
Straight-Edge 864
Technoteen 865
Teen Chat Rooms 865
Teen Dating Page 865
Teen Driving Tips 865
Teen Movie Critic 865
Teen Voice 865
Teen Writers 866
Teenagers 866
Teens Helping Teens 866
Virtually React 866
Young Adults Talk and General
    Discussion 866
Young Investors and Entrepreneurs .. 866

ZINES 867
After Dinner 867
American Folk 867
Bad Girl Zines 867

Bad Subjects 867
Fray 867
Glassdog 867
Mad Dog Weekly 868
Popular Culture Zines 868
Salon 868
Word 868
Zine Lists 868
Zine Talk and General Discussion ... 868

ZOOLOGY 869
Arachnology 869
Entomology 869
Ethology Talk and General
    Discussion 869
Herpetology 870
Icthyology 870
Malacology 870
Mammals 871
Marine Life 871
Nematology 872
Ornithology 872
Primates 872
Strange Animals 872
Zoological Resources 872

Notes 873

INDEX 877
About the CD 907

Introduction

"It's time to go to bed."

"Aw, Mom, you said we could stay up and play Destructo on the Net."

"It's already been two hours, Bobby. It's time you and Betsy were in bed."

"But I haven't got to talk to my friends in Finland yet," said Betsy. "They sent me mail that they were meeting in a Web chat room later tonight."

"Well, it's eight hours later in Finland, and they're just waking up on Saturday morning. It's Friday night here and it's late, so you and Bobby have to go to bed. You can talk to your friends when you wake up."

"But Mom, it's still early. Can't we stay up just few more minutes?"

"No, but if you hop into your beds right now, I'll tell you a story."

"Tell us one about monsters and fighting and lots of blood," said Bobby.

"Eww," said Betsy. "Who wants to hear about monsters? Tell us a nice story, Mom."

"Get to bed right now, and I'll tell you the real story of how the Net got started. You haven't heard that."

"Many years from now," began the mother, "there was a young woman named Mirabelle, but everyone called her Mira—"

"But Mom, that's your name," said Betsy.

"Yes, it is."

"Wait a minute," said Bobby. "If this story is about someone who lived many years from now, how can you say there was a young woman?"

"And how can you even know what happened?" asked Betsy. "If it's in the future, it didn't even happen yet, so how can you even tell us about it?"

The mother smiled. "If you two would be quiet and listen to the story, you would find out."

Many years from now (began the mother), there was a young woman named Mirabelle, but everyone called her Mira. When she was young, Mira was by far the brightest girl in her class. As she grew older, she studied math and science and languages, and she was good at everything. She was especially good at ancient history.

Now, remember, Mira lived a long time from now, so, to her, ancient history was the time we are living in right now. So she studied all about how we lived and what we did. By the time she was 21 years old, Mira already had a university degree, and she was working in a temporal physics lab.

"What's temporal physics?" said Betsy.

"Aw, everybody knows that," said Bobby. "It's being able to travel in time, isn't it Mom?"

Sort of (continued the Mother). Remember, this story takes place a long time from now, and, by then, science was very far advanced. They understood many things we don't know now, and they knew how to do things with time that we think are impossible. They even figured out how to send someone back into the past.

However, they didn't ever do it because it could cause major disruptions. Scientists had calculated that if someone went into the past and did certain things, it could change everything permanently. In fact, Mira worked on this project and did a lot of the calculations herself.

One day, Mira was called to a meeting. It was in a big room, but there were only three other people there, and the door was locked tight after she came in. Mira saw the head of her department and two other people she didn't recognize. The head of the department did all the talking. The other two people didn't say a word, and, in fact, she never even found out who they were.

"Mira," he told her, "for some time, we have been working on a secret project. So secret that only a handful of people in the whole world even know about it. We have reached the point where we need a volunteer to finish the project. Although you are a temporal physicist, you are also a historian, and we need someone who knows about ancient cultures."

He asked her, "Are you familiar with the Age of Darkness?"

"Yes," replied Mira. "The Age of Darkness was a long period with economic problems and wars. It started in the twentieth century and lasted more than three hundred years."

"Correct. Now are you familiar with the Theory of Information Access?"

"Yes. It's a large, complex theory. Basically, it says that human societies, by their nature, are subject to economic and social problems until information flows quickly and freely everywhere. Once that happens, everything works better, and eventually war disappears, just like it has today."

"It is our opinion," said the head of the department, "that most of the Age of Darkness could have been avoided if the Internet had been used better at the beginning. Being a history expert, you will know that the Internet was not used widely until the year 2010. Our calculations show that if enough of people had started to use the Internet fifteen years earlier, everything would have worked out better, and the world would have avoided a lot of trouble."

He then told Mira they wanted her to go back in time and change history. Her job was to make sure the Internet became popular before 2010. In doing so, she would help the world avoid many years of trouble. To help her, they would send her back to the year 1990 with the tools she needed to help her do the job. Once she got there, however, she would be on her own. Moreover, if she was successful, she would end up changing things so much that all of history would be different, which meant she could never return to her own time.

As you can imagine, this was a hard choice for Mira. She had studied ancient history for years, and she didn't want to turn down a chance to visit the twentieth century and see it for herself. She also welcomed an opportunity to help make the world better. On the other hand, she knew she would miss her friends and her parents, and she grew sad at the thought of never seeing them again.

The head of the department seemed to know what she was thinking.

"We know this is a tough decision, Mira. To help you, we have prepared something for you to read. We have put together a description of what your life will be like if you go back in time. You can read it and then decide what to do."

So Mira read it and made up her mind.

"I will do it," she said.

"So what happened, Mom?" asked Bobby.

"Yes, Mom, what did she do?" said Betsy.

"Well, Mira went back in time to the year 1990. When she got there, she found a scientist in Switzerland who was developing an idea for the Internet. Using her special tools, she influenced him and helped him think of an idea he called the World Wide Web. Then, a couple of years later, she went to the United States and helped people there develop a program that made it easy to use the World Wide Web.

"By 1995, the World Wide Web had turned into the Web, and the Internet turned into the Net. Millions of people started using the Net fifteen years early, just as Mira had planned, and, as a result, history was changed."

"But Mom, what happened to Mira?" said Betsy.

"Well, Mira became a scientist at a big university."

"Just like you," said Bobby.

"That's right," she said, "just like me. Remember, before she left, Mira was shown what would happen to her if she went back to the twentieth century. The reason she decided to go was she saw that she would be able to have a wonderful life.

"Everything happened just like they had told her. Not long after the Net became popular, Mira met a wise, handsome man. They fell in love and got married. The best part was that they had two wonderful children. And, as Mira already knew, they ended up having a wonderful life and lived happily ever after. In addition, as people started using the Net, the world got better and better. By the time Mira's children were grown with children of their own, all the countries of the world were working together and there was no more war."

"Oh Mother," said Betsy, "that's a lovely story. Isn't that a lovely story Bobby?"

"It's okay," said Bobby, "but I wish there were more monsters and fighting."

INTRODUCTION TO THE FIFTH EDITION

"You have to help us. You're our only hope."

"What do you mean?" I said. "I'm a writer. Why do you need me?"

The tall man with the uniform coughed slightly. "Has he been cleared?" he asked the fat man behind the desk.

"Up, down and sideways," replied the fat man.

"Then it's time to tell him, sir," said the tall man.

The fat man looked at me for a long time without saying anything. "For some reason I thought he would look different."

"You saw the report."

"Yes, but the pictures looked different... Never mind."

He turned to me. "You're probably wondering why we brought you here."

Indeed I was.

Twelve hours ago I was in my bed on the other side of the country. I had just finished writing a chapter of a new book, and I was relaxing, reading a novel.

I didn't hear them come in. One minute I was alone in the room, the next moment I looked up to see four men standing at the foot of my bed. They were dressed in plain dark jumpsuits, each with a single small blue-gray patch.

They looked at me. One of them spoke in a quiet voice with a great deal of authority.

"You are to come with us."

In less than a minute, I was in a car, speeding through the night. Five minutes later, I was in a helicopter. Twenty minutes more and I was led aboard a long, very large aircraft. The area was deserted except for a ring of armed guards around the plane. As I walked up the steps, I caught a glimpse of the lettering on the side: "Air Force One".

For the next several hours I was alone. I sat on a large, comfortable leather seat as the airplane flew swiftly. No one appeared and no one offered any explanations.

I must have fallen asleep. I awoke with a start as the plane landed. Within seconds, the four men in jumpsuits reappeared and led me off the plane to a long, black car with flags on the front. The car had curtains over the windows, but as I got in, I managed to catch a glimpse of a tall, white, needle-like monument.

I thought about all of this as I looked up at the two men in front of me.

The tall man coughed again. "Excuse me, sir, but it might be better if you showed him the file."

"Maybe you're right," said the fat man. He turned to me. "Take a look at this," he said, pushing a thin file across the desk.

It was a blue-gray folder with a seal across the side. Across the top was the single word "UMBRA".

"UMBRA?" I asked.

"Just a code word," said the fat man. "Break the seal and take a look."

I started to read. I couldn't believe what I saw.

"What is this?" I said. "Are you trying to tell me you've received messages from the future?"

"That's exactly what we're telling you."

I read through to the end. "How many people know about this?"

"Counting you," said the fat man, "six people. You and us, the man who received the messages, another person you will never meet, and the President."

I tapped the folder with my finger.

"If I understand this correctly, I'm supposed to write some type of book."

"Exactly."

"What if I don't?" I raised my eyebrows.

They both looked at me. The tall man stared without blinking.

"You will," he said at length.

His voice was quiet, but it carried a great deal of conviction and I decided not to pursue the matter.

"According to this," I said, "you want me to write an Internet book. Or rather, someone in the future wants me to write the book."

"Correct."

"This is unbelievable. For several months you have been receiving these mysterious messages, warning that unless you do certain things there is going to be a lot of trouble in the future. So to keep all the trouble from happening, I have to write a book. Is that it?"

"Partially. You writing this Internet book is only the beginning. There are a couple of other things we have to do in the next few years. But for now, all we have to do is make sure you write"—he referred to the file—"something called 'The Internet Golden Directory'. Somehow this book, along with the other things we will do, is going to ensure that the Internet grows to be as free as possible.

"The messages stressed that," he continued. "The Internet has to be completely free and unregulated for"—he looked at the file again—"five more years. After that, supposedly, it will be able to take care of itself."

"Yes, I saw that. And if the plan doesn't work, something called the MFS is going to take over. What's the MFS?"

"Frankly, we don't know."

I thought for a minute.

"So what do I do?"

"Just write the book. We'll take care of the rest."

"How do I know I'll even get a publisher?"

"It's taken care of. Just write the book."

"How do I know anyone will even buy it?"

"That's our problem. I told you, it's all taken care of."

"Can I tell anyone?"

"Not now. You have to wait five years. By then it won't matter. You'll be able to tell anyone you want."

"Today is October 15, 1992," I said. "Does that mean I can tell people about all of this"—I thought for a moment—"in October 1997?"

"If you want."

"But a message from the future? Come on. Who's going to believe me?"

The fat man looked at me. "You're a professional writer. Make it believable. Anyway, what do you care? In five years you'll be rich and famous. I'll still be behind this desk."

He stood up. "It's time to go. I have to go to a meeting and you have to get to work." He walked me to the door. "Before we take you home, would you like to say hello to the President?"

"The President?"

"We showed him some of your books. He wants to meet you."

"That would be great. Can I tell people about talking to the President?"

"In five years you can tell people anything you want."

INTRODUCTION TO THE FOURTH EDITION

An unspecified safe-location,
somewhere in the Third District, Western Region
December 14, 2052

"Have you got it?"

"Yes, right here. Did anyone see you come?"

"No way. I changed autobots four times. Then I walked the rest of the way with an activated scan shield. If anyone was monitoring me I would have known."

"Wasn't that taking a chance? What if the MFS had picked up your rad reading?"

"Well, they didn't, because I'm here. Do you want the thing or not?"

"Yes, of course I do. Can I listen to it?"

"Sure. Let me plug it into an infoport. What are you going to do with an old datacube anyway? This thing must be over fifty years old."

"You don't know much about the Slicks, do you?"

"Slicknets?"

"Same thing. Well, my friends and I are organizing an anti-MFS offensive to take back the Net. We are using a Slick which is completely unauthorized. If we get caught we'll be closed down in an hour. But we figure the main reason the MFS has so much control is because people don't really understand the Net. If they did, they wouldn't dare let the MFS get away with what they do."

"So what does this speech have to do with it?"

"Do you know what next week is?"

"No."

"It's the hundredth anniversary of the birth of Harley Hahn."

"Really?"

"Yes. But ever since the Reorganization, it's so hard to get old books that hardly anyone has actually ever seen a real Harley Hahn book. This speech is part of a talk Hahn gave at the UCLA School of Business in the spring of 1996. In the talk, Hahn explained the future of the Net and what he thought it would become. We—my friends and I—feel that if people were to hear the speech, they would have a feeling for what the Net could be without the MFS and, well... we're hoping to start a rebellion. That's why I asked you to break into the archives and steal this particular datacube."

"How could this be a real speech from 1996? Did someone record it?"

"No. It's a synjob. One of the students took notes. Just before the Information Decree, she hid them in a box where they were discovered a few years later. Someone reconstructed part of the speech and used a synspeak module with Hahn's voice. Go ahead, plug the thing in. I've never actually heard it myself. I know it's not the whole thing, but I'm not sure how much actually survived."

"...evolution takes place in two ways. Biologically, cells evolve into more complex organisms, through fish, amphibians, reptiles, and finally birds and mammals. However, as a species, human beings have stopped evolving biologically.

"But that doesn't mean evolution has stopped. Rather, once it reaches a certain point, evolution switches from being biological to being social. This started to happen to us about 25,000 years ago. However, it wasn't until post-Industrial Revolution information technology began to develop that our social evolution really became noticeable.

"With the telegraph, then the telephone, radio, television and satellites, the rate at which information flowed from one place to another became faster and faster.

"This ever-increasing information flow had an enormous influence on our social evolution as a species. The very fabric of our society began to change. And then we built the Net.

"What we now call the Net started as a small collection of computers connected together. But within ten years, that collection had grown to huge proportions and then, about the mid-1990s, something changed. Perhaps it was a critical mass of some type, but once enough people start getting connected, the thing that we now call the Net was formed.

"I want to be sure you understand this. The Net is not a computer network. It is nothing less than a being in its own right. The fact is, the Net is an independent lifeform. However, it is unlike any lifeform we have ever seen.

"The Net has four main components that combine in a way we still don't understand. These components are information, computers, connections and people.

"By information, I mean the vast amount of data that is available all over the Net. There is so much information on the Net that no one understands it. No one even understands how much information actually exists.

"The computers are of several types. You and I use computers to access the Net, but there are also a vast number of machines that are working on their own to keep things running. Day and night, these computers, which are very much a part of the Net, work with only minimal help from us.

"The connections are the lines of transmission between all the computers. For example, when you use a computer to access the Net, your machine is connected to a host computer maintained by your Internet service provider. That machine is connected in a network which itself is connected to a larger part of the Net.

"Finally, a most important part of the Net is provided by the people who use it. Whenever you are connected, part of you merges with the Net itself. The Net can make use of part of your mind. When you design a Web page or create a program to share on the Net, your efforts are part of the Net, even when you are not connected.

"The Net is a giant, amorphous organism that is always moving, creating, problem solving and organizing. In fact, I believe that the Net is involved in a great many activities that you and I don't understand. Perhaps we aren't capable of understanding what the Net is doing any more than a bee can understand the purpose of a beehive, or an ant can understand an ant hill.

"The point I want you to appreciate is that the Net, although it exists on its own, lives in cooperation with human beings. Not with individual people, but with the human species as a whole.

"There are many people who are looking outward for signs of life elsewhere in the universe, life that is similar to the biological life here on Earth. Well, there is a type of life that is not biological, and the Net is the first example that I know of.

"I mean that literally. The Net is alive according to any definition of 'life' you wish to use. We helped create it, but now it's on its own. Human beings are not alone. We have the Net to help us, connect us, and—in the very best of ways—to use us.

"You know, we made a mistake. We assumed that life could only be biological. And, like the bees and ants, we didn't conceive of a lifeform that was a giant step larger than ourselves.

"In a way, we have also been blinded by our own biology. We assumed that if other life exists in the universe it would be like us, or at least similar enough to us to communicate. I feel it is far more likely that alien life will resemble the Net more than it resembles human beings. Indeed, there is no reason not to assume that the universe is populated by Net-like objects, each of which consists of information, computing machines, connections and a large number of intelligent 'cells'.

"You have to wonder what compelled us to spend so much time and money in recent years to create the Net. My answer is that we are compelled to do so in order to fulfill our destiny. However, for what comes next, we must be part of the Net; individual human beings, even groups of humans, can only go so far.

"To me, it is clear that the Net is the next step in evolution. Moreover, if life is found elsewhere, I do not think it will be found by individual humans. The Net will grow until it becomes mature enough, and then it will reach out and find others of its kind.

"Whether or not we will realize when that happens, I do not know. We already do not understand most of what the Net does. However, what I can tell you is that the Net, by its nature, looks after humanity. The Net is our best friend: it connects our separate economies and social systems in such a way that war will soon be unlikely. I believe it won't be long before it just won't be economically feasible to do anything but cooperate with one another.

"All of this, of course, is on a grand level. In day-to-day events, I suppose human nature is not going to change. However, we are finally part of something larger than ourselves. And, as one cell to a group of cells, I can tell you that I like the experience. And, if you look around, you will see that just about everyone else does as well.

"In less than a hundred years, there will not be anyone alive who can remember a time before the Net. Long before then, life will be a lot different and—if I am correct—a lot better.

"We have finally begun to fulfill our biological destiny."

INTRODUCTION TO THE THIRD EDITION

At 10:30 AM, December 21, 2022, on my 70th birthday, I woke up and I Remembered. I spell the word "Remembered" with a capital "R" because the memory that returned to me was of great import.

It was thus:

On December 5, 1969 (sixteen days before my 17th birthday), the first wide area network connection among multiple computers was completed. The project was funded by the Advanced Research Projects Agency (ARPA), a part of the Department of Defense in what was then called the United States.

The planners at ARPA had decided to fund the development of a network that could connect distant computers. They wanted to design the system in such a way that, if part of the network were to be destroyed (say, by a nuclear bomb), the rest of the network would still work. The work began on September 25, 1968, with the first planning session at the Stanford Research Institute. A little over one year later, on November 21, 1969, the first two special-purpose communication computers, called IMPs (Interface Message Processors), were connected together. (IMP #1 was in Los Angeles at UCLA. IMP #2 was in Menlo Park, California, at the Stanford Research Institute.)

Two weeks later, on Thursday, December 5, four IMPs were connected to form the first wide area computer network in the history of mankind. In addition to the IMPs in Los Angeles and Menlo Park, there was one at U.C. Santa Barbara and one at the University of Utah.

In one moment, as a switch closed, electrical signals jumped from one computer to another, and the world was changed forever. These four computers formed the beginning of the Arpanet, which within a few years developed into the Internet, the ancestor of the Net.

The Net. A global communication organism spanning the Earth. In your time (the mid-1990s) the Net is still small. According to what I can remember, as you read this (somewhere around 1996 by my calculations) the Net has only several million computers and not much more than 20 million people. But within a decade, the Net will expand, and fragment, and expand some more until, well... I seem to be drifting from the main idea here.

The point is that, in late 1968, I heard about the beginning of the Arpanet on my birthday (December 21) and immediately had a feeling that this new computer "network" was something important. I was still in high school, but I was taking the first computer course ever offered in my area. (The teacher had studied "computers" for two months during the previous summer.)

As it happened, December 21 was not only my birthday, but the last day of school before the winter vacation and, that evening, some friends took me to a nightclub to celebrate. And it was there that I met The Great Mephisto.

The Great Mephisto was a stage hypnotist. I remember very little about him except that he had long black hair, a straggly beard, and talked in a strange, unidentifiable Eastern European accent. Indeed, I remember barely nothing at all about that night. Evidently, The Great Mephisto hypnotized me and left me with what he called a post-hypnotic suggestion. The idea was that I was to write a letter to myself, seal it in a secret place, and forget about it for exactly 54 years. On that same day, 54 years later, I was to remember the letter, find the place where it was hidden, take it out and read it.

And that is why, at 10:30 AM, on December 21, 2022, the day of my 70th birthday, I woke up, and I Remembered: I remembered writing the letter. I remembered where I hid it. (And I even remembered The Great Mephisto.)

Where did I hide the letter? I hid it in one of my old high school textbooks, which I had carefully preserved for so many years. (The book, by the way, was *Cours Moyen de Français*.) Imagine my excitement as I recalled events more than 50 years distant. Imagine my curiosity as, with trembling fingers, I retrieved the book from my personal storage area and opened it, looking for the letter.

And imagine my amazement when I carefully opened the pages of this 54-year-old letter and started to read about the Arpanet.

You see, for a reason I still can't explain, I had guessed that this new "computer network" was something important. And I had decided to write down some of the particulars (which is why, today, I am able to recall so many of the details).

As I read the letter today, it is, to my ancient and practiced eye, a study in immaturity and raw construction. However (and this is why I am telling you all of this), there was one thing I had anticipated correctly. I conjectured that if the new Arpanet were to become important, people would soon forget the events of the surrounding time and lose their historical perspective. To remedy this, I enclosed a summary of the important events of the day: what was happening in the news, and so forth.

Little did I realize how important all this would be. You see, ever since the Information Decree of 1999, the free access to information has been manipulated and controlled. Last year at this time, I was allowed to write a short note and send it through a Temporal Gateway to 1994. This, of course, was a highly unusual occurrence. At the time, I had the blessing of the Microsoft Friendship Society and the cooperation of the authorities.

Since then, the Slicknets have started to expand, and the Underground has become much better organized. In just 12 months, the strength of the MFS has begun to attenuate noticeably—something which I would not have believed when I wrote the first note.

Still, access to a Temporal Gateway is almost impossible to find and, to send this note to myself (in 1995), I had to break a lot of rules and bribe more than a few people to look the other way. I can't explain the details, because I need to hurry. I must get this into the transport chamber before it is too late. However, what I am trying to do is send this note to myself, back in late 1995, to print in one of my books.

I am doing this because I have come to realize why the MFS was able to grow so strong: instead of trying to control the flow of information (a more or less impossible task), they decided to control the *tools* people used to access the Net. And having done this, they were able to shape events so as to disconnect us from our past.

As odd as this sounds, by restricting our access to the details of recent history, the MFS was able to convince us that our likes, dislikes, preferences and antipathies were in harmony with their own. Although this may be hard for you to believe, very little of late twentieth-century life before 1998 was preserved. And, since then, the records have been changed so many times as to render them unreliable.

So, when a fortuitous concatenation of circumstances found me in possession of some historical details of the days of the original Arpanet, I felt compelled to write them down and do my best to transport them to a time before the Information Decree where they might be published. Although I can't take the time to explain it to you now, if you retain an understanding of what is important in your lifetime and how it is connected to what everyone else is doing, the power of an organization like the MFS is greatly diminished.

I don't know if this message will ever make it back to late 1995, and I don't know if it will ever be published. But I do know that I have to try. So, at this point, I thank you for indulging an old man in his rambling, and I present some excerpts from the original letter I wrote myself, some 54 years to this very day.

Harley Hahn
December 21, 2022
Third District, Western Region

...but perhaps the most important occurrence of recent time was the connection of four computers into a "network". I have heard of computers being connected (I think), but what makes this such an unusual experiment is the computers are far apart. I can't help but feel this is an important event. Of course, there probably won't be enough computers in the world to make much of a network, but, still, it's an intriguing idea...

...important to put this all in perspective. To do so, I will tell you a bit of what is going on right now. By the time you read this (that is, by the time I read this in 54 years), most of the details will probably have passed from memory.

The same day the four computers were connected into a network found the United States knee-deep in the Vietnam War. President Nixon says he cannot stop until we achieve "peace with honor". What a strange concept! A couple of weeks ago an army captain denied any knowledge or responsibility for last year's massacre in My Lai. Still, the Department of Defense (the same department that paid for connecting the four computers!) has admitted that someone slaughtered hundreds of Vietnamese civilians 19 months ago. No one really knows what happened, but peace with honor seems a long way off.

In the meantime, thousands of young men continue to die in the far-off steamy jungle, thousands of miles from home. Still, many of the countries in the world, especially the underdeveloped countries, are becoming Communist at an alarming rate, and I don't know what to make of it. The people at home are massively polarized. While the hawks adamantly support the war, the doves are protesting.

About a month ago, 250,000 people protested in Washington, the largest anti-war demonstration ever in the U.S. capital. Vice President Agnew called the protesters "anarchists and ideological eunuchs". Referring to the liberal news people, Agnew said that "a spirit of national masochism prevails, encouraged by an effete corps of impudent snobs who characterize themselves as intellectuals." (Most everyone I know thinks he and Nixon are jerks. Still, they are the President and Vice President of the United States, and I guess they couldn't have gotten elected if they didn't have some intelligence and integrity.)

Speaking of protesters, hippies seem to be taking over the world (or at least the part of it that is under 30 years old). Four months ago, over 400,000 people traveled to Bethel, New York, for Woodstock: "four days of peace and music". Far out. I wish I could have gone. It seems that everything these days is sex, drugs and music. (I can't wait to get to college!)

And yet, something seems to be changing. On December 6, at a concert in Tracy, California—featuring the Rolling Stones, Jefferson Airplane and the Grateful Dead—some Hells Angels stabbed someone (while the Stones were singing "Sympathy for the Devil", actually).

In the Middle East, things are as bad as ever. On the same day the computers were being connected, Syria released two Israeli passengers from a plane that had been hijacked last August. In return, Israel had to trade 13 Arab prisoners. Three days later, the Israelis and the Syrians fought for an hour on the Golan Heights. And even within the Arab world, things are unsettled. Saudi Arabia is still fighting with South Yemen, and general confusion and misunderstanding are the rule rather than the exception. Interestingly enough, a few days ago the U.S. House of Representatives just passed the smallest foreign aid bill since World War II.

And what else? Well, one of my teachers was saying that the price of gold just dropped to $35 an ounce (although I don't understand what all the fuss is about). And there is something called "Women's Liberation" starting. I don't know a lot about it. Seems like a bunch of misfit women complaining. I guess nothing will come of it.

Anyway, that's all for now. I have to finish this letter and hide it.

But I can't get those computers out of my mind. I keep wondering if it means anything important. Maybe by the time I read this letter again, I'll know if I was right.

Harley Hahn
December 21, 1969

INTRODUCTION TO THE SECOND EDITION

If all this works out the way I hope, you will be reading this back in 1995. That is, I will receive this message from myself, sometime in late 1994, just in time to get it to the printer to be included in the second edition.

Wait a minute. Maybe I should take a moment to explain, because if you haven't heard of the Temporal Gateway—and how could you?—you probably haven't the foggiest idea what I am talking about.

Let me start from the beginning. I sent this message to myself from the year 2021, in order that it be included in the second edition of *The Internet Golden Directory*. No, wait, that's not the beginning. I guess the beginning was in 2017, when T.L. Nipper figured out how to build the Temporal Gateway into the past.

No, wait, that's not really the beginning. The real beginning would be in the late 1990s when the Internet broke up into pieces and what came to be called the Net (or more formally, the People's Net) emerged as the organized successor to the free non-commercial information network.

Does that help? No, I guess this is all a hopeless muddle. You see, I did write some Internet books at one time, way back in the mid-1990s, but that was about 25 years ago and things have changed a lot. I am not sure how to explain it so you can understand. So many of the New Words don't even exist in 1995; I wouldn't even know where to start.

How about this: it happened that in 2017 a genius named T.L. Nipper figured out how to send information into the past. Like most people, I don't understand the details—I think it has something to do with neutrinos and tachyons—but the important thing is the process is only partially dependable and highly restricted by the MFS. Moreover, it takes an enormous amount of energy just to send a few characters.

To transmit this introduction, for example, consumed the equivalent of a month's energy allotment for the entire Western Region (what used to be California and parts of Nevada and Oregon). In fact, if it wasn't that the Governor of the Continental Fusion Project agreed to cooperate, I would never have been able to send this message at all.

Anyway, this all has to do with the 50th anniversary of what used to be called the Internet, and some researcher in the Information Division of the MFS discovered the date and thought it would be a good idea to send a message into the past—to celebrate, so to speak. (Ironically, no one really knows if it is exactly 50 years because, these days, such details are mostly forgotten. However, the MFS thinks it is close enough.)

I don't know how they did it and what strings they had to pull, but somehow they got the CFP to cooperate and they were able to set up a Temporal Gateway just long enough to send a message back to 1994. And since I was the author of some old-time Internet books, they asked me to write the message.

The deal was I could write anything I wanted, which would then be sent back 25 years into the past—November 1994, actually—to myself. And, if it all worked, the message from 2021 would suddenly appear in my electronic mailbox back in 1994. The intention is that I would send a message suitable for the introduction of one of my books.

The trouble is, once you send something, it generates what is called an "alternate reality", so that you don't get to see the results of what you send. Thus, I have no way of knowing whether or not this message got through. But if it did, and you are reading this in 1995, at least you will know that it worked.

So, having explained all of that, what do I want to tell you?

Well, to start, I should tell you that the Net is now considered to be the most significant invention of the 20th century. However, it wasn't until the early 2000s that it became apparent just how important the Net actually was. Unfortunately, the real nature of the Net had been completely misunderstood until this time, and just about nobody anticipated what would happen. In fact, until the Information Decree of 1999, most of what was on the Net was highly disorganized and left up to individual preference.

Perhaps another thing I should mention is what we now call the Net (in 2021) is really nothing like the old Internet, although there are a few similarities. We can access information just about anywhere we go, and the speed is so fast as to be unnoticeable. We can

HARLEY HAHN'S INTERNET & WEB GOLDEN DIRECTORY

view and transmit with ease, and public access (to the Pubnet portion anyway) is universal.

The trouble is, everything is managed and organized and... well... boring. You see, in the olden days (as you are reading this), the Net was not really run by anyone and was poorly organized. Of course, this meant there were problems, but there was also an enormous amount of personal freedom. This freedom meant that anyone who knew how could create and broadcast information. As I write this, such facilities are completely unknown.*

The point is, you happen to be living at a time when you have enormous opportunity. The Net as you know it is not going to last all that long, but, while it does, you will have a chance to *participate* in a way that never existed until the 1990s and certainly does not exist today.

If I remember correctly, back in 1995 you had just about total freedom to send out whatever information you wanted. I urge you to not lose sight of the importance of this capability. I keep thinking that if things had gone otherwise, we might not have had the Information Decree and the Microsoft Friendship Society might never have had... well, that's neither here nor there and, as the saying goes, you can't change the past.

I guess what I really want to tell you is the Net as you perceive it is a temporary resource, and you should enjoy and appreciate it while you can. If this message did get through, and you are really reading this in the second edition of *The Internet Golden Directory*, I urge you buy the book and spend some time exploring. Nothing lasts forever, and some things end all too soon.

And, oh yes... have fun. Soon you will need a permit.

Harley Hahn
December 21, 2021
Third District, Western Region

---

*On the official Net, that is. There are rumors of underground Slicknets, but, like most people, I have never seen one.

INTRODUCTION TO THE FIRST EDITION

This book will change the way you think about the world.

Even more important, this book will change the way you think about people and how we exist as a species.

How can this be? After all, this book is really just a large catalog, and what could be so important about a catalog?

Well, take a look at the list of categories, and you will see that virtually every important type of human activity is represented. Indeed, this book contains descriptions of thousands of separate items, grouped into well over 150 different categories.

The importance of all this is not so much in the details, but in the fact that it even exists at all. Not long ago, most of what you see in this book had not yet been created. A few years ago, none of it existed. But what does it all mean to *you*?...

Imagine yourself exploring. You walk for days through hot steamy jungles, you climb over rocky hills and through canyons; you drag yourself across an endless arid plain until, one day, you look at the horizon and see what looks like a city. As you approach, you see that it is not really a city, but—whatever it is—it is vast beyond description: more buildings, vehicles, works of art, and so on than you have ever seen or even imagined.

You spend many hours exploring, always finding something new, something challenging, and something delightful. Being a stranger, you feel confused and you spend much of your time wandering haphazardly. Once in a while you see a bit of a pattern and, for an instant, you make some sense out of the immediate neighborhood. But for the most part, you wander from place to place in a cloud of distraction and fascination. What makes it all so frustrating is you get the feeling that everything you see is part of something very large you just can't understand.

One day, you happen upon a stranger who looks like he knows his way around; at least he seems familiar with the surroundings.

You ask him, how do you find your way?

He shrugs. You'll get used to it.

INTRODUCTION

But, you ask, why is this all here?

I don't know, he says, and he starts to wander away.

Wait, you call after him, where can I get a map?

No such thing, he answers over his shoulder.

But can't you help me at all?

He turns around and looks at you with a gleam in his eye and a funny half-smile on his face. Clearly, he knows something that you don't. Something important.

This place, he gestures widely, is only a few years old. In fact, you could travel for days and almost everything you'd see would be less than a year old. You will see new places almost everywhere you look and, every so often, you will notice that old ones have disappeared. You turn around, and when you turn back it's changed—larger, more complicated, more... well, it's hard to explain. Like I said, you'll get used to it.

But don't be confused, he continues. The meaning in what you see is not about the structures or the vehicles. It's not about the art or the beauty, or pleasure or truth or good or bad. It's about people and what they have created. People working together and by themselves.

You will notice that wherever you go, you will never see another person (I know this to be a fact, and I have been here as long as anyone). However, you can talk to other people whenever you want, so you will never be lonely. No matter who you are, no matter how individual your desires and your preferences, there are people just like you here somewhere.

So where are you? Nobody really knows. The important thing is we are all here together. We are all connected. We all share. We all belong, especially those of us who have nowhere else to go. And the best thing is you can come here whenever you want. No one is ever turned away.

Personally, I don't really understand why this place is so important. Most of us just move around from place to place, doing whatever we feel like. Still, just be glad that you are here at all. As I say, most of this is only a few years old and you are among the first.

But wait, you say. You told me I would never actually see anyone. What about you? I can see you.

He looks at you for a long moment.

You only *think* you see me. I don't really exist. Anyway, for what it's worth, there is a map of sorts. Don't lose it and you can take it with you wherever you go.

He points behind you to a single piece of paper lying on the ground. You turn around to pick it up, and by the time you turn back he is gone. You look down. In the center of an otherwise blank piece of paper, is a big "X" and the words "You are here."

You stuff the paper into your pocket and start walking. After a few minutes, you turn around and gasp. Behind you is a large sign. It must have been there all the time, how could you have missed it? Okay, you say to yourself, I may not know where I am, or why I am here, or what anyone is really doing, but now at least, I know the name of this place. For the sign says:

Welcome to the Net.

Frequently Asked Questions

To save you a bit of time, here are the answers to the most common questions people ask me.

(1) Do you have a Harley Hahn Web site?

Yes. Take a look at:
http://www.harley.com/

(2) This book is so large. Does it contain everything on the Internet?

The Internet—or the Net—is so big that nobody even knows everything it contains. Moreover, the Net is always changing. This book is my personal guide to the best resources on the Net. Still, as large as this book is, it contains only a tiny fraction of what is on the Net.

(3) How can I advertise in this book?

You can't.
This is not a commercial directory like a telephone yellow pages book. I do my best to ensure that nothing gets in this book unless it is free to use. Thus, I do not take paid advertisements. All the "advertisements" in this book were written by me and are just for fun.

(4) My organization has just created a new Web site. How can I tell you about it, so you can put it in the book?

You can't.
I choose all the items in this book myself (with some help from my researchers).

(5) I am new to the Internet, and I don't know what to do. How do I use the Net? What is the Web?

This book is a personal guide to Internet resources. It will not teach you how to use the Internet. If you are a new user, you need to spend some time learning about the Net (sorry, but that's a fact). It may take a while to learn how to use the Net well, but don't be discouraged. The Internet is a lot of fun and will well repay your effort.

The best suggestion I have is to use my book *Harley Hahn Teaches the Internet*, published by Que/Harley Hahn. (The ISBN is 0-7897-1615-1.) If you like this book, you will like *Harley Hahn Teaches the Internet*.

(6) What about Usenet? What about mailing lists?

Following this section, I have included some basic material on Usenet and on mailing lists. For more detailed information, see my other book.

(7) I tried to access a Web site and it wasn't there. What is happening?

The Internet is always changing. By the time you get this book, some of the items will be obsolete, and there is nothing anyone can do about it. However, virtually all the items should be fine. For each new edition, my researchers and I start from scratch and check each item in the book by hand.
If a few items don't seem to be there, that is to be expected. However, if nothing seems to work, you know something important is wrong. The best advice I can offer you is to get a friend to help you or ask your Internet service provider for assistance. Unless you happened to buy a particularly old copy of this book, most everything should work just fine. Before you get too frustrated, make sure you are doing everything correctly.

(8) I have a problem with the CD that comes with the book. What should I do?

The CD in this book is manufactured by a company called Modern Age Books. If you have any problem—including an installation problem—they will provide free technical support via their Web site:
http://www.modernagebooks.com/help/

USENET

Usenet is a worldwide system of discussion groups in which millions of people participate. There are tens of thousands of different Usenet groups, and anyone on the Internet may participate for free. For historical reasons, Usenet groups are sometimes referred to as *newsgroups*, even though they are actually public forums for discussion.

Within each newsgroup, people send messages, called *articles*, for other people to read. Once an article is sent to a group, anyone in the world may read it.

Each Usenet group has a unique name. The name consists of two or more parts, separated by periods. For example, here are the names of several groups:

```
alt.celebrities
biz.marketplace.international
k12.news
news.newusers.questions
rec.parks.theme
sci.chem
soc.women
talk.environment
```

Usenet groups are organized into *hierarchies*. When you look at the name of a group, the first part of the name is the hierarchy. For example, the `news` hierarchy contains groups in which people discuss Usenet itself. The `talk` hierarchy is for debate.

Most of the time, you can guess the purpose of a Usenet group just by looking at its name. For example, `news.newusers.questions` is for new users to ask questions about Usenet. The group `talk.environment` is for people to debate topics devoted to the environment.

There are hundreds of different hierarchies, but only thirteen are of general interest. These are shown in the accompanying table.

All the Usenet groups in this book are from these hierarchies.

There are two ways to access the Usenet newsgroups. The most common way is to use a program called a *newsreader* to display articles for you to read. You tell your newsreader which group you want to look at, and it fetches the articles and displays them for you. If you decide to send out an article of your own, you can use your newsreader to compose the message and send it to the appropriate group.

Both popular Web browsers come with a free newsreader. With Internet Explorer, the newsreader Outlook Express (the same program used to handle email). With Netscape, the newsreader is Collabra.

You might ask, where are all the Usenet articles stored? The answer is, each Internet service provider maintains a Usenet repository for their customers. This repository (called a *news server* or *news feed*) contains all the articles that are currently available. As new articles come in, they are added to the repository. After a certain amount of time—usually several days—old articles are purged to make room for new ones.

Before you can use your newsreader, you must configure it by telling it the name of the computer you will be using as a news server. Your Internet service provider will tell you this name. If you have problems getting started, they should be able to help you configure your newsreader.

Once your newsreader is configured, there is an easy way to read the articles in a particular group. Within your browser, there is a place where you can type the address of a Web site you want to visit. The easy way to look at a Usenet group is to type the "address" of the group. This consists of the word **news:** followed by the name of the group.

For example, if you want to read the articles in the group in which people debate environmental topics, specify the following Usenet address to your browser:

```
news:talk.environment
```

Hierarchy	Contents
`alt`	Wide variety of miscellaneous topics
`bionet`	Biology
`bit`	Miscellaneous topics
`biz`	Business, marketing, advertising
`comp`	Computers
`humanities`	Literature, fine arts
`k12`	Kindergarten through high school
`misc`	Miscellaneous topics
`news`	Usenet itself
`rec`	Recreation, hobbies, arts
`sci`	Science and technology
`soc`	Social and cultural issues
`talk`	Debate, controversial topics

The most important Usenet heirarchies.

Your browser will recognize this as a Usenet group, and will start your newsreader automatically.

The best way to participate in Usenet is by using a newsreader program. However, such programs are complex and take time to master. There is an alternative that is easier.

There are Web-based services that allow you to read and send Usenet articles for free. With such a service, you only need a regular Web browser. If you find yourself using Usenet a lot, it is better to learn how to use a newsreader. However, for more casual use, a Web-based service is fine. You will see such services described on page 271 under the name "Usenet Search Engines".

There are thousands of Usenet groups, and it is not always easy to find the one you want for a specific topic. If you want to find a group, I have two suggestions. First, start your search by looking in this book. I have included many Usenet groups along with Web sites and mailing lists.

Second, I have created a Web site to help you find the Usenet group you want. The name of this service is "Harley Hahn's Master List of Usenet Newsgroups". You can read about it on page 792.

For a more detailed explanation of Usenet and how to use it, please see my book *Harley Hahn Teaches the Internet*.

MAILING LISTS

A mailing list is a system by which a group of people can have a discussion via electronic mail. The idea is that a person can send a message to one central address. That message is then processed by a program which automatically sends a copy of the message to everyone on the list. Thus, once you join a mailing list, you will automatically receive copies of all the messages that anyone sends to the central address. These messages will be sent to your electronic mailbox.

When you join a mailing list, we say you *subscribe* to that list. To leave the list—that is, to stop receiving mail—you *unsubscribe*. Although we use the words "subscribe" and "unsubscribe", there is no cost involved. You can join—and quit—as many mailing lists as you want for free. However, if you join too many, your mailbox will be flooded with so much mail, you won't have time to read it.

Subscribing and unsubscribing to a mailing list is easy. Each list has a special administrative address. All you have to do is send a message to that address saying that you want to subscribe or unsubscribe. A program (not a person) will read and process the message, and carry out your request.

There are three main types of mailing list systems. They are called Listserv, Listproc and Majordomo. Subscribing and unsubscribing with each is almost the same. There is only one small difference when you subscribe to a Majordomo list (which I will explain below).

Let's look at an example. In the "Animals and Pets" section of this book, you will see an item called "Horses" (page 18). One of the resources under this item is a mailing list. Here is the information:

Listserv Mailing List:

List Name: **equine-l**
Subscribe to: **listserv@lists.psu.edu**

What can we tell about this list? First, we see that this is a Listserv mailing list, as opposed to Listproc or Majordomo. Second, each mailing list has a name. The name of this list is **equine-l**.

Notice the two characters **-l** at the end of the name. In the olden days, it was necessary to know if a name belonged to a person or a mailing list. Thus, mailing lists were given names that ended with **-l**. The letter "l" (L) stands for "list". On some systems, this is still the custom. That is why this name, **equine-l**, ends with **-l**.

The third piece of information we see is the address to which we would send mail to subscribe. In this case, it is **listserv@lists.psu.edu**. This is the address of the program that administers the list. When you send a message to this address, your message is not seen by a person. Everything is done automatically by the Listserv program. It will read your message, figure out what you want, and respond appropriately.

There are many commands you can send to a Listserv program (and the same goes for Listproc and Majordomo). I will describe four.

Before you subscribe to a mailing list, you should always send a request to the mailing list program asking for information about that list. This will help you make sure you really want to subscribe, as well as alert you to any special considerations about the list. To request such information, send an email message to the administrative (subscription) address. The subject of the message doesn't matter; it will be ignored. In the body (main part) of the message, put a single line consisting of the word **info** followed by the name of the list.

For example, in this case, you would send a message to:

listserv@lists.psu.edu

The subject of the message could be anything. In the body of the message, you would type the single line:

info equine-l

Now wait. You will receive a reply with some information. Sometimes this takes only a few minutes, sometimes longer. When you receive the reply, read the information and see if you still want to subscribe. (There will be a lot of technical information you can ignore.)

If you want to subscribe, send another one-line message to the same address. This message should have the word **subscribe**, followed by the name of the list, followed by your first and last names. You do not need to specify your email address. The program at the other end will pick it up automatically.

Let's say your name is Bartholomew Bunzlehammer. To subscribe to the equine-l mailing list, send a one-line message to the address:

listserv@lists.psu.edu

The subject of the message doesn't matter. In the body of the message, you type the single line:

subscribe equine-l Bartholomew Bunzlehammer

When the message is received, the Listserv program will automatically subscribe you to the list. From now on, any messages sent to the list will be sent to you as well.

Hint: For security reasons, some mailing list programs require you to confirm that you really want to join the list (just in case some friend has snuck over to your computer while you were away and sent in a subscription to a mailing list). If this is the case, you will be sent instructions on how to confirm. Usually, it is as simple as replying to a message and saying "ok".

You can unsubscribe to a mailing list at any time. Just send a one-line message to the administrative address with the word **unsubscribe**, followed by the name of the list. You do not need to include your name or your email address. In our example, you would send a message to the address:

listserv@lists.psu.edu

The subject of the message doesn't matter. In the body of the message, type the single line:

unsubscribe equine-l

For a Listproc mailing list, everything works exactly the same. For a Majordomo mailing list, there is only one difference: when you subscribe, you do not have to specify your first and last names.

The final command I want you to know about is **help**. Listserv, Listproc and Majordomo systems have more commands than **info**, **subscribe** and **unsubscribe**. To learn about these commands, send a one-line message to the administrative address with the single word **help**. For example, you can send a message to the address:

listserv@lists.psu.edu

The subject of the message doesn't matter. In the body of the message, type the single line:

help

Once you belong to a list, the question arises, how do you send messages to everyone on the list? You do not send messages to the administrative address: that is only for subscribing, unsubscribing, and so on. Rather, you send messages to the list itself. The list's address consists of the name of the list, followed by the name of the computer.

In our example, the name of the list is **equine-l**. The name of the computer is **lists.psu.edu**. Thus, to send a message to the list itself (that is, to all the people on the list), you would mail to:

equine-l@lists.psu.edu

Each time you send a message to this address, it will be sent automatically to everyone on the list.

So remember, when you want to unsubscribe, do not send the **unsubscribe** message to this address. All administrative requests go to the administrative address (where they are handled automatically by a program).

For reference, the following table summarizes what I have explained in this section. Notice that—for the basic commands—all three systems work the same, except that when you subscribe to a Majordomo mailing list, you do not specify your first and last names.

FREQUENTLY ASKED QUESTIONS xlvii

Subscribing and Unsubscribing to a Mailing List

To request information about a mailing list, or to subscribe or unsubscribe, send mail to the administrative (subscription) address for the list. These are the addresses given in this book. For example:

> listserv@lists.psu.edu
> majordomo@massey.ac.nz
> listproc@cornell.edu

Request Information About the List
> info *list*

Request General Information
> help

Subscribe to a List
> subscribe *list firstname lastname*   (Listserv and Listproc)
>
> subscribe *list*   (Majordomo)

Unsubscribe to a List
> unsubscribe *list*

Acknowledgments

Every year, my researchers and I check all the resources by hand and rebuild the entire book. During the process, I add a lot of new material. What you are holding in your hands right now—the sixth edition of this book—required an enormous amount of work.

I would like to take a few minutes to introduce you to the people who helped me produce this book. However, I do want to make it worth your while. As you know, reading the acknowledgments for a book can be a boring process. You see a lot of strange names and you see the author thank people whom you will never meet. "What's in it for me?" you ask yourself, and rightly so.

Thus, to make reading this section as fulfilling as possible, I have included a number of interesting facts that you might otherwise never encounter. For example:

The first drive-in restaurant in history was opened in 1921. The restaurant was in Dallas, Texas, and was named "J.G. Kirby's Pig Stand".

Now, is that cool or what? And that's just a sample of what you'll find out in this section of the book, so keep reading.

So, to continue, let me start the acknowledgments with Wendy Murdock. Wendy is my chief researcher and has worked on every edition of this book. She is a highly skilled, intelligent, witty, industrious, charming person who is wonderful to work with. Wendy is also able to find information on the Net faster than just about anyone else in the world.

In fact, the only other person I know who can find information as quickly as Wendy is my senior researcher, Carrie Campbell. Carrie is an Internet detective, a tireless paragon of skill and judgment, whose deeds on the Internet are legion. Like Wendy, Carrie is wonderful to work with: always in a good mood, pleasant and a joy to be around.

Aside from Wendy and Carrie, there are two other people who contributed enormously to this book. Both of these people are talented women who hold the title of "editor". Lunaea Hougland is my copy editor. Her job is to make sure that everything you read is grammatically correct, and that all the punctuation and spelling are perfect. In addition, Lunaea also helped with the research, proving herself to be valuable beyond words. Lunaea has been my copy editor for years, and is widely considered to be the best such editor in the business.

Cynthia Douglas is a project editor. Cynthia works for the publisher, and it is her job to coordinate every aspect of the book production. In pursuit of this noble goal, Cynthia spent hundreds of hours slaving over a hot manuscript, making sure every item was placed correctly and solving the many problems that arise daily in an undertaking of this size. Since Cynthia is one of the most important people who helped on this book, I have included a picture of her for you to admire. (You can see it on page 432.)

I would also like to mention Zbigniew Jurkowski, a hard-working researcher. Zbigniew spent many hours working with the mailing lists that you see throughout the books.

In order to produce a book this complex, it is necessary to have special-purpose software. This software was programmed by my ace programmer, James Brady. James has been working on the programs for several years now, and, each year, under his careful eye, they get better and better.

The most famous—and clearest—picture ever taken of the Loch Ness Monster was published in 1934. The picture shows the top half of a brontosaurus-like sea serpent within the waters of Loch Ness in Scotland. This picture, which did much to fuel the legend of the Loch Ness Monster, was actually fabricated by a discredited big-game hunter named Duke Wetherall. The "monster" was created by Wetherall's son and stepson, who made a head and neck that they placed over the top of a toy submarine.

HARLEY HAHN'S INTERNET & WEB GOLDEN DIRECTORY

As you might imagine, in order to work on this book, I need reliable high-speed access to the Internet. For providing me with such access, I thank Marcy Montgomery, Sylvia Tyndall and Timothy Tyndall at RAIN (the Regional Alliance for Information Networking), as well as Michael Ghens, the RAIN system administrator.

For other important Internet resources, I thank Patrick Linstruth and Chris Linstruth of Quantum Networking Solutions, probably the most friendly Internet service provider in North America.

For help with hardware, I thank the IBM Product Reviews Lab. In particular, I thank the manager, James Adkins, as well as his competent co-workers Eldrice Murphy, James Lumpkin, Robert Armbruster, Mike Redd, Keith Snyder, Scott Kennedy, Richard Rousseau and Joanie Miller (who keeps track of all the paperwork).

For help with my high-speed Internet connection, I thank Gery Sommer and Gil Leon, both with GTE. And for special technical support, I thank Noel Cragg, a programmer who is so fast that watching him work makes you believe in miracles.

In 1981, actor/director Warren Beatty was making the film "Reds" about John Reed, the founder of the American Communist Labor Party. Beatty wanted to ensure that everyone associated with the movie understood the significance of what they were doing, so he assembled all the extras and gave them a lecture on Reed's beliefs that capitalists exploited their employees. Shortly after the lecture, the extras returned to Beatty. They told him that they felt they were being exploited, and they would quit unless he raised their wages (which he did).

The last group of people I want to thank are the ones who worked on the publication of this book. First, the CD that comes with this book was produced by a company called Modern Age Books. At this company, I wish to thank John Grow (the production technician), Joe Tolland (production manager), Chris Pooley (CEO), Mike Iacobucci (CFO) and Tom Clark (quality assurance). I worked with all of these people to make the best possible CD product we could. In particular, John Grow and I spent a lot of time working to make the data on the CD as easy to use as possible.

The book itself is published by Osborne McGraw-Hill, based in Berkeley, California. The person at Osborne most responsible for this book is Scott Rogers, the editor-in-chief. Scott has been associated with all the editions of this book, and, as such, he has been rewarded appropriately. Not only has Scott been promoted to a lofty position in the world of publishing, he also has a window with an office, an assistant (Marlene Vasilieff), a speaker phone, and a chair with wheels.

Now, imagine you are in Berkeley at the Osborne offices. You have just visited Scott in his office, admired the view, and heard him describe the big picture. You then go to the end of the hall, descend one flight of stairs, and come face to face with the people who tend to the details.

To start, we have Cynthia Douglas, the project editor. (I talked about Cynthia above, but she does such good work, she deserves to be mentioned again.) Not far from Cynthia is a large room, the production area. In this room you will find the artists who created the pictures in this book (Roberta Steele, Brian Wells and Beth Young), as well as the page layout people who worked many hours making each page look as good as possible (Mickey Galicia, Roberta Steele [again], Peter Hančík and Jani Beckwith). The production was managed by Marcela Hančík, production supervisor, and Steve Emry, the director of editorial, design, and production.

Once the pages were created, each page was read carefully by Pat Mannion and Carroll Proffitt, the proofreaders. Their job was to look for any tiny mistakes so that the final product, every word on every page, is perfect.

At the same time all these people were toiling valiantly to finish this book on time, other people had to do extra work to take up the slack on other projects. For all this extra work, I thank Jean Butterfield, Ann Sellers, Lance Ravella and Sylvia Brown.

Once the pages and the master CD are ready, the actual book has to be printed, the CD has to be replicated, and the whole thing has to be put together and shipped to the stores. All of this was coordinated by George Anderson, the manufacturing supervisor.

Of course, a book is more than pages. It needs a front and back cover, a marketing program, and someone to sell the translation rights to various publishers around the world. These covers were created by Kevin Pruessner (director of creative services), Lee Healy (copywriter), Regan Honda (art director) Cristina Deh-Lee (cover artist) and Jane Keisler, who

ACKNOWLEDGMENTS

handled the logistics. The marketing was organized by Anne Ellingsen and Caroline Keller. The international rights were handled by Laurel Graziano.

To conclude the list of special people at McGraw-Hill, I want to thank two especially pleasant people: Peggy Poage, who works in the mailroom, and Barbara Yanucil, who works in the McGraw-Hill royalty department in New Jersey.

Finally, I wish to thank the employees at my local DHL office for friendly, professional delivery service:

Danielle Ritchko, Terry Chlentzos-Keramaris, Cypress Feld, Sue Sadler, Daryl Niemann, Ger Coghlan and Wendy Wolff.

You may have heard that Pluto is the furthest planet from the sun. However, this is not always the case. Pluto takes 248.8 years to orbit the sun, and in December 1978, it crossed the orbit of Neptune, at which time Neptune was actually farther from the sun. By March 1999, Pluto will have moved far enough away to regain its relative position. This means that, for almost 11 years, Neptune was the most distant planet in our solar system.

ADVICE 1

ADVICE

Advice Chat
Here is an IRC channel where you can go to ask questions and get advice from other Internet folk. While I was in there I saw some honestly friendly people giving good advice to a lonely shy teenager on some ways to make more friends. I was relieved at the lack of sarcasm and joking around.

IRC:
#advice

Ann Landers and Dear Abby
Ann Landers and Abigail Van Buren ("Dear Abby") have been dispensing good old-fashioned, practical advice to the masses for more than 40 years. What is amazing is that these two czarinas of advice are actually twin sisters. The ladies were born on July 14, 1918, in Sioux City, Iowa. Ann's real name is Esther Pauline Friedman, while Abby was born Pauline Esther Friedman. Ann started writing her advice column in October 1955, for the Chicago Sun-Times. Abby started writing her column three months later, in January 1956, for the San Francisco Chronicle. Incredible? Maybe yes, and maybe no. However, one thing I have noticed is that you never see both of them in the same place at the same time.

Web:
http://www.creators.com/lifestyle/landers/lan.asp
http://www.uexpress.com/ups/abby/

Mail:
annlanders@creators.com

Ask Tina
So your boyfriend is flirting with your best friend, and your brother's roommate wants to ask you out, while, at the same time, you aren't sure if you want to be involved with anyone, but the big dance is coming up and you have to have a date. What do you do? For small problems, you can depend on your mom or your Aunt Wendy or maybe even Ann Landers or Dear Abby, but when your social life and deep feelings are on the line, you need Tina. Thoughtful, straightforward answers to the real issues of love, relationships, friendships, work, and life as we know it today.

Web:
http://members.aol.com/ToAskTina/AskTina.html

Good Advice

The nice thing about advice is that you can take it or leave it. And when you get your advice from the Net, you can take it whenever you want and leave it without worrying about hurting somebody's feelings.

Good Advice
Need some advice? Want to check out some questions and answers? The Internet is full of people giving advice, but how do you find what you want when you want it? Start here, where you will find a collection of links to a variety of advice-oriented resources. Not only will you find personal-type stuff (romance, relationships, teen issues, Internet relationships, family problems, and so on), but also places to check for advice about computers, health, diet, travel and finances.

Web:
http://www.4advice.com/

Jane Err
Match your advising skills against Jane. People in need of counsel (mostly romance and relationships) send in their questions and, at intervals, Jane will display a question along with her answer. You can then send in *your* answer. Jane prints a selection of readers' answers so you can compare what other people think with what she thinks. My question is: is there really a Jane?

Web:
http://www.swoon.com/depts/jane_err/janeframe.html

2 ADVICE

Jeffrey Zaslow

Jeffrey Zaslow ("Zass") is an advice columnist who deals with life in general. The questions he answers tend to be the types of real problems people face in day-to-day life (as opposed to the love/relationships/marriage emphasis that seems to dominate the advice industry). Zass's answers are thoughtful, straightforward and (what I like) not always politically correct.

Web:
http://www.suntimes.com/index/zazz.html

Libby Webwise

Do you ever read an advice column and say, "I can do better than that?" Well, here's your chance to strut your stuff. Libby invites people to submit their personal problems, which are posted on the Web site. Once a problem is posted, anyone can send in advice. So give it a try. After all, as one of my readers, you are intelligent, thoughtful and knowledgeable. Shouldn't other people have the benefit of your wisdom?

Web:
http://maxpages.com/libbywebwise

Lifestyle Advice

Life is not easy, and without professional help there is a chance that you might make a mistake. Never fear: there are professional advice-givers who will be glad to provide all the assistance you need. Start your day by using the Net to enjoy a variety of lifestyle advice columns. After all, your style is yours alone, but life is too important to be left to the amateurs.

Web:
http://washingtonpost.com/style/columns

If you're feeling risqué, take a look at "X-Rated Resources".

Miss Abigail's Time Warp Advice

Over the past hundred years, many books have been written offering advice. You may not have many of these books, but Miss Abigail does. So just ask away, and Miss A. will search through the books and find you an appropriate answer for such questions as "What is the proper age for marriage?" (a book from 1938 says at least 25 years old for men and 22 years old for women), or "How can I tell if a guy's not married?" (a book from 1969 counsels that a married man will never ask you out for a weekend date). So when you need the wisdom of the ages, check with Miss Abigail. After all, your Aunt Wendy may be wise, but can she run to her library and check with The Cool Book: A Teen-Ager's Guide to Survival in a Square Society" [1961]?

Web:
http://www.kreative.net/timewarp/

Miss Abigail's Time Warp Advice

Have you got a problem? Not to worry. Miss Abigail will check her extensive library of old books and find the advice you need.

You may not be able to live in the past, but getting advice via Miss Abigail's literary time warp can present you with a better future.

AGRICULTURE 3

Women's Wire Advice

Here is a gaggle of advice columnists from which you can choose what you need. Ask about finances, fashion, sex, body image or astrology. Once you choose a columnist, you can send her (or him) a question which may be answered on the Web site. While you are waiting, you can check out the archive of past questions and answers (which will make you feel good when you realize that other people have worse problems than you).

Web:
http://www.womenswire.com/fyi/experts.html

AGRICULTURE

Agricultural News

If you are out in the field all day, you don't have to feel entirely isolated and behind the times. When you turn off the tractor and have a little lunch, just fire up the laptop and check your email. If you are on the **agnews** mailing list you can get all sorts of agricultural news releases. Or you can get your news hot off the Web. Keep informed, no matter where in the world you are.

Web:
http://fbminet.ca/agnews.htm

Listserv Mailing List:
List Name: **agnews**
Subscribe to: **listserv@vm.cc.purdue.edu**

Agriculture Jobs

If you are looking for a job, here is a good place to start. You will find information regarding professional-level job opportunities in the field of agriculture (including research), as well as in related areas such as biotechnology and chemistry.

Web:
http://www.nationjob.com/ag

Agriculture Links

Farming doesn't have to be lonely business. Being out in the boonies won't keep you isolated if you can reach this great load of agricultural resources. This is just about all the information you will need if you are interested in any aspects of agriculture: Usenet groups, Web resources, archives, mailing lists and other cool stuff are available.

Web:
http://ipmwww.ncsu.edu/cernag/
http://www.agview.com/

Why Being in Agriculture is So Cool

(1) You get to drive a tractor.
(2) You can grow your own food (except for pizza).
(3) You can have a lot of fun pets like chickens, cows and pigs. And when you get tired of them, you can eat them.
(4) Only a farmer can be married to a farmer's wife.
(5) You have easy access to all the fertilizer you need for your personal use.
(6) You never have to worry that you are sleeping in too much.
(7) You can use the Net as much as you want and say it is for research.

4 AGRICULTURE

Agriculture Network Information Center

In a time of agricultural need, it's always good to know you can find a specialist. The Agriculture Network Information Center (AgNIC) provides access to experts in various fields of agriculture as well as links to agricultural databases. Find out about conferences, meetings and seminars in your area. If you are going to be traveling, call ahead and arrange to take an agricultural expert to lunch.

Web:
http://www.agnic.org/

Agriculture Talk and General Discussion

It has been a long time since farmers were isolated tillers of the soil, living alone and working from dawn to dusk with little contact with the outside world. Today's modern farmer is as likely to have an Internet connection as a tractor. If you are a farmer or have an interest in agriculture, join the discussion, and stay in touch with your neighbors all over the world.

Web:
http://www.agriculture.com/agtalk/Ag_Groups.html

Usenet:
alt.agriculture
alt.agriculture.beef
alt.agriculture.commodities
alt.agriculture.fruit
alt.agriculture.misc
alt.agriculture.technology
sci.agriculture
sci.agriculture.fruit

Listserv Mailing List:
List Name: **agric-l**
Subscribe to: **listserv@uga.cc.uga.edu**

Agripedia

Agripedia is a well-designed encyclopedia of agriculture maintained by the University of Kentucky's College of Agriculture. The site is oriented toward learning, so if you are an agriculture student, you will find the resources particularly useful. The reference material is comprehensive, including many well-organized links to resources around the Net. If you have any interest at all in agriculture, you will want to know about this site. (Actually, the only word I couldn't find in the large glossary was "dell". It seems as if the U. of Kentucky College of Agriculture still has a lot to learn about The Farmer in the Dell.)

Web:
http://frost.ca.uky.edu/agripedia/agrimain.htm

Beekeeping

These beekeeping resources provide the novice and experienced apiarist alike with all the information relating to the art and science of beekeeping available through the Net. You'll find archived articles and newsletters, newsgroups, photos, FAQs, links to Web entomology servers, and much more.

Web:
http://weber.u.washington.edu/~jlks/bee.html
http://www.tdale.demon.co.uk/BeeKeeping/

Usenet:
alt.hobbies.beekeeping
sci.agriculture.beekeeping

Listserv Mailing List:
List Name: **bee-l**
Subscribe to: **listserv@cnsibm.albany.edu**

Look What I Found on the Net...

```
Newsgroup: alt.agriculture.misc
Subject: Sugar Production

> Can anyone tell me where to find sugar production by country?

Look in the yearbooks issued by United Nations organizations,
including the Food and Agriculture Organization's "Production
Yearbook".

Top sugar producers are usually India, Brazil, China (rising),
Russia, Cuba (falling), USA, Mexico, Pakistan, France, Colombia
and Australia, in that order.
```

AGRICULTURE 5

Dairy Science

There is no other farm animal whose output reflects the quality of forage as much as a lactating dairy cow. Even high-quality alfalfa does not supply enough digestible dry matter: you still have to use some type of grain and protein supplement. When you come right down to it, if you want top milk production, there is no substitute for young, bright-green alfalfa. Can't you just smell that pleasant freshly-cut-grass aroma without a hint of mustiness? (I'm getting hungry just thinking about it.) Check the Net, where you can milk the dairy science resources for all they are worth.

Web:
  http://netvet.wustl.edu/cows.htm#dairy
  http://www.adsa.uiuc.edu/memb/links.html
  http://www.ansi.okstate.edu/exten/dairy/

Listserv Mailing List:
  List Name: **dairy-l**
  Subscribe to: **listserv@umdd.umd.edu**

Farm Journal Today

These days, people think you have to go skydiving, bungee jumping, ice climbing or fire walking to get a thrill. How wrong can they be? On the Net, I can get a rush any time I want. Check out this site and you will see what I mean. There are several different agriculture magazines for your perusal. You can read articles from journals like Hogs Today, Beef Today, Dairy Today, Farm Journal and Top Producer. If you don't want to just read, you can hang with other agricultural thrill-seekers in chat rooms.

Web:
  http://www.farmjournal.com/

---

5 out of 5 dentists surveyed recommend this book.

Forestry

The only thing bad about the forest is that there's no good waves to surf. Other than that, I really like the forest. Except for the bugs. But other than that, I like the forest. Except for the snakes, I mean. Other than that, I really do like the forest. If you are a big fan of forestry like I am, you have to check out the forestry resources on the Net. You can find software, databases, lists of conferences, mailing lists, research papers, journals, and links to other forestry stuff. And you don't even need any insect repellent.

Web:
  http://www.metla.fi/info/vlib/Forestry/

Usenet:
  alt.forestry
  bionet.agroforestry

Irrigation

Irrigation—the artificial watering of agricultural land—has been used for centuries. Irrigation is crucial to agriculture, and modern irrigation practices can be complex. Simply put, the idea is to get enough water in the right place at the right times, without causing waterlogging (soil saturation) or salinization (excessive accumulation of salts). At the same time, one must also worry about water rights, the overall water supply, environmental concerns—such as endangered species—and politics. Here are resources to help you with the science of irrigation: hydraulic modeling, drainage, salinity, drought management, news, and much more.

Web:
  http://www.wiz.uni-kassel.de/kww/irrig_i.html

Listserv Mailing List:
  List Name: **irrigation-l**
  Subscribe to: **listserv@listserv.gmd.de**

National Agricultural Library

The National Agricultural Library (NAL) is one of four national libraries in the United States. NAL is part of the U.S. Department of Agriculture's research service. Through this Web page you can learn how to access ISIS, the library's public catalog, see part of the NAL's image collection that is online and get information on how to access other NAL resources.

Web:
  http://www.nalusda.gov/

6 AGRICULTURE

National Genetic Resources Program

The USDA's National Genetic Resources Program provides germplasm and related information for plants, animals, microbes and insects. ("Germplasm" refers to the hereditary material within germ [sex] cells. Get enough germplasm, and you can start your own world.) My favorite plants are the Giant Raspberries of Jilin. These raspberries, which were originally bought from street vendors along the banks of the Songhua reservoir near the city of Jilin in northeastern China, measure from 2.5 to 3.5 centimeters wide. In case you are a raspberry breeder, the species name for the Giant Raspberries of Jilin is *Rubus crataegifolius*. Germplasm—in the form of seeds—is available from the National Clonal Germplasm Repository in Corvallis, Oregon. You will need to reference accession (identifier) RUB 1917.

Web:
   http://www.ars-grin.gov/

National Genetic Resources Program

You're sitting around the house with nothing to do, so you say to yourself, "Hey, why not create my very own biological environment?"

Why not indeed?

However, before you can start, you are going to need some germplasm. But how do you decide which germplasm to use?

Just connect to the National Genetic Resources Program site where you will find information about plants, animals, microbes and invertebrates.

It won't solve all your problems, but it can save you a lot of time.

(I don't want to point fingers or anything, but if you-know-who—the Big Guy up there—had used the Net, he probably would have been able to create the world in five days and rest for the whole weekend.)

Organic Farming

"Organic farming" refers to agricultural practices in which farming is carried out without the use of synthetic fertilizers, pesticides or chemicals (such as hormones and antibiotics). Organic farmers employ a wide array of materials and techniques, and there is a great deal of information available on the Net. If you are interested in organic farming, you should check out IFOAM, the International Federation of Organic Agriculture Movements, which encompasses more than 500 organizations from more than 100 countries.

Web:
   http://ecoweb.dk/ifoam/
   http://www.rain.org/~sals/my.html

Poultry

According to my sister, there's nothing bad about poultry that can't be fixed by boiling it long enough. Of course, not everyone agrees. There are more than seven billion chickens in the world, many of whom are loved like brothers (or sisters). Of course, there is more to life than chickens. There are also geese, ducks and turkeys. If you are a poultry person, you're going to feel right at home on the Net. Join the people who appreciate that buttercup combs are less round and lumpy than silkie combs, and read about poultry till your uropygial gland overflows. (By the way, to put the whole thing in perspective, seven billion, the number of chickens in the world, is more than all the people who have ever bought a Harley Hahn book, put together.)

Web:
   http://poultry.mph.msu.edu/glossary.html
   http://www.ansi.okstate.edu/poultry/
   http://www.transport.com/~lhadley/

Usenet:
   sci.agriculture.poultry
   sci.agriculture.ratites

Listserv Mailing List:
   List Name: **pltrynws**
   Subscribe to: **listserv@sdsuvm.sdstate.edu**

AGRICULTURE 7

Precision Farming

I will admit I didn't anticipate information about farming to be interesting. However, after reading some documents about precision farming, I have changed my mind. Precision farming is the process of tailoring soil and crop management to fit the various conditions found in individual fields. Precision farming uses remote sensing, geographic information systems (GIS) and global positioning systems (GPS) to analyze field data to within inches. Using this system, farmers can adjust seeding rates, fertilizer and pesticide applications, make tillage adjustments and record yield data variations within each individual field. If you want to know more about this space age method of farming, check out these sites, which have lots of good information, or join the mailing list and talk to other agricultural folk about precision farming.

Web:
http://nespal.cpes.peachnet.edu/pf/
http://www.silsoe.cranfield.ac.uk/cpf/

Listproc Mailing List:
List Name: **precise-agri**
Subscribe to: **listproc@soils.umn.edu**

Progressive Farmer Magazine

It's the '90s. If you are going to be a farmer, you should be a progressive farmer. Don't live in the past. Read this free online magazine that has news, weather, market information, feature articles, information about weed control, biotechnology and a forum where you can post messages for other agriculture buffs.

Web:
http://progressivefarmer.com/

**Embarrassed?
Use an anonymous remailer.
(See "Privacy and Security".)**

Sustainable Agriculture Information

Farming is habit-forming. You think you'll try it for a year, just for fun, and you tell yourself that you can take it or leave it. But one day you wake up and realize it's in your blood. You're a farmer and you just can't quit. Then you start to realize how expensive your habit is. All those chemicals and fertilizers you put in the soil add up to big bucks. So use the Net to investigate sustainable agriculture, and see how people are working together to make farming less dependent on additives, and more self-sustaining. After all, no one likes a freeloader, so why not make Mother Nature carry her own weight?

Web:
http://www.caff.org/sustain/faq/
http://www.ces.ncsu.edu/san/
http://www.sarep.ucdavis.edu/other.htm

Usenet:
alt.sustainable.agriculture

Majordomo Mailing List:
List Name: **sanet-mg**
Subscribe to: **majordomo@ces.ncsu.edu**

Can We Keep On Keeping On?

Traditional agriculture requires that we add a significant amount of substances and energy to the soil. For example, farmers routinely use chemical fertilizers, pesticides, soil conditioners, and so on.

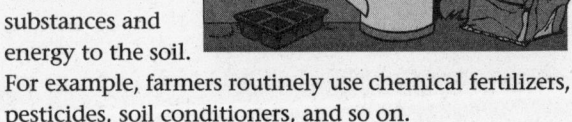

The goal of sustainable agriculture is to depend as little as possible on external resources. The holy grail of sustainable agriculture is to create an agricultural system that is efficient and economically viable, while needing as little external support as possible.

In the long run, sustainable agriculture practices can benefit us all, conserving resources and saving money. However, to reach that goal, there will have to be a lot of experimentation, development and testing.

If you would like to follow the flow, check the sustainable agriculture resources on the Net. Maybe there is a way we can keep on keeping on without running out of resources.

AGRICULTURE

USDA Economics and Statistics

According to the U.S. Department of Agriculture, there are 2.42 billion cubic feet of refrigerated storage capacity in the United States; there are 671 million gross feet of storage for apples and pears; and in California, 510,000 acres were planted with winter wheat, while only 380,000 were harvested. If you have even a passing interest in agricultural statistics, this is the place to satiate your curiosity. Lots and lots of numbers about crops, farm economics, food, weather, technology, international agriculture, livestock, dairy, poultry, rural affairs, specialty agriculture and trade issues. This is a great resource. After all, there aren't too many places you can go when you need to find out how much acid rain (in kilograms of nitrate and sulfate per hectare) has been deposited in the northeastern area of the United States.

Web:
http://usda.mannlib.cornell.edu/usda/usda.html

World Agricultural Information Center

The World Agriculture Information Center (WAICENT) was created by the Food and Agriculture Organization of the United Nations. WAICENT provides information on agriculture, fisheries, forestry, nutrition and rural development. Information is also available in languages other than English. This is just the thing when you have to pick up a quick present for a farm girl and you don't know what to get her.

Web:
http://www.fao.org/waicent/waicente.htm

ANARCHY

Anarchist Calendar

When you want to give a party, but you just don't have a good occasion to celebrate, check with the anarchist calendar on the Net. This site has a list of important anarchist happenings in history. Just find the anarchist event closest to the day you are giving the party, then call your caterer and tell him the theme of the gathering. Or you can read him the list of historical events and ask him which one goes best with frozen pigs-in-blankets.

Web:
http://iww.org/~galt/anarcal.html

Anarchist Feminism

Anarchy and feminism have been strolling hand in hand long before Hillary Clinton agreed to be Martha Stewart's financial planner for a straight percentage of the gross. If you would like to explore the roots of modern feminism, you need to look at the women who were not afraid to stand up and be counted at a time when even getting noticed could be hazardous to a lady's health. True, Hillary and Martha are honest-to-goodness folk heroes, but in my humble masculine opinion, they can't hold an intellectual candle to, say, Emma Goldman, the Russian-born American activist who was pro-birth control and anti-draft long before it was fashionable. Check the Net and see for yourself.

Web:
http://burn.ucsd.edu/~mai/afem_kiosk.html

Anarchist Resources

After going through a three-hour meeting, it's refreshing to look at a nice Web site that can help you fantasize about throwing off the corporate chains that bind you. These sites have lots of interesting resources that are related to anarchy and anarchists: discussion groups, archive sites, Web pages, newsletters, mailing lists, publications, and more.

Web:
http://flag.blackened.net/sai/faq/links.html
http://tigerden.com/~berios/liberty.html
http://www.andrew.cmu.edu/~ctb/anarchy/

Anarchist Theory FAQ

Anarchy comes in a variety of shapes and sizes with the one common belief that Government Is Bad. On the Net, you can read more about the ins and outs of anarchy. This FAQ attempts to take all the ideas and philosophies and put them in a readable format. It explains anarchy from a critical point of view.

Web:
http://www.princeton.edu/~bdcaplan/anarfaq.htm

ANARCHY

Anarchy History

The thing I like best about anarchy is that no one organizes it. Oh, people try, but anarchy seems to have a life of its own. If you like reading about the history of not following the rules, try these sites. Learn about the people who did not feel like getting permission from Burger King just to have it their way: people like Noam Chomsky, Emma Goldman, William Godwin, Michael Bakunin and Max Stirner. Find out what the Haymarket massacre has in common with the Spanish Civil War, and see why, when push comes to anarchical shove, there's no business like show-em-how-it-really-ought-to-be-done business.

Web:
http://www.pitzer.edu/~dward/Anarchist_Archives/archivehome.html
http://www.teleport.com/~jwehling/AnarchistEducation.html

History of Anarchy

Human society is a stew into which you throw all types of ingredients and cook for a long time, with no idea of how it is going to turn out. One of the most important ingredients in human history is anarchy. Every now and then, we need a few people to redefine the recipe of government and stir the stew.

Even a cursory glance at history will show you that what starts off as frank rebellion often ends up as the status quo. Thus, when we learn about the anarchy of the past, we are studying the seeds of our modern society.

Remember, those who do not understand the history of anarchy may find themselves repeating it with their own heads on the platter.

Anarchy Sampler

Wanna get serious? Sitting around the cafeteria, drinking coffee and discussing politics will only take you so far. If you want to be a real anarchist, you've got to learn a whole lotta stuff, and this is the place to start. You will find a great many quotes, full of just the ideas you need to get the anarchical ball rolling down the hill of enlightenment.

Web:
http://www.pitt.edu/~hebst3/writers.htm

Anarchy Talk and General Discussion

To some people, anarchy is society without government. To others, anarchy is life without television. Still, whether you are an armchair social critic or a couch potato with a plan to reform the world, you won't want to miss the discussion. Talk may be cheap, but good plans to reform the world the hard way are in short supply.

Usenet:
alt.anarchism
alt.anarchy.rules
alt.society.anarchy

Majordomo Mailing List:
List Name: **anarchy**
Subscribe to: **majordomo@world.std.com**

Anarchy Yellow Pages

There are a lot of people who want to change the status quo, one way or another, for one reason or another. And those people support a lot of anarchy-related organizations and publications around the world. The Anarchist Yellow Pages will help you find the information you want, when you want it (as long as the Internet doesn't dissolve into anarchy).

Web:
http://flag.blackened.net/agony/ayp.html

10 ANARCHY

Chomsky, Noam

In 1957, the linguist Noam Chomsky (1928-) published a book called Syntactic Structures, in which he proposed the Theory of Generative Grammar. This theory states that people learn to speak because they have an innate ability to recognize which constructions are valid and invalid within their language (as opposed to learning to speak by memorizing minimal sounds). The Theory of Generative Grammar revolutionized linguistics, affording Chomsky considerable renown. Since then, Chomsky has used this considerable renown to try to revolutionize the rest of the world. Chomsky is an anarchist with thoughtful opinions about *everything*, and he is not shy about sharing. It takes a long time to understand much of what Chomsky says, but if you are willing to try, the Net is a good place to start. And if you become confused, you can always switch to linguistics (where confusion is taken for granted).

Web:
  http://www.worldmedia.com/archive/

Usenet:
  alt.fan.noam-chomsky

Goldman, Emma

Emma Goldman (1869-1940) was a Russian-born American anarchist. At the age of 17, she emigrated from Russia to the U.S., where she and Polish-born Alexander Berkman later published the newspaper Mother Earth. Goldman was vociferously active in a number of unpopular causes, including birth control (with Margaret Sanger), anti-militarism, the anti-draft movement, free speech, the eight-hour work day, and women's rights. Between 1893 and 1917, Goldman was sent to prison several times. In 1919, she was deported to Russia (along with Berkman), only to leave in 1921 after becoming disillusioned with the Russian government. It is difficult to appreciate the importance of Goldman's contributions because, today, much of what she worked for has come to pass and is taken for granted. However, in her time, Emma Goldman was a tireless anarchist, an unbridled force of nature whose lifelong devotion to her causes made her one of the outstanding political activists of the twentieth century.

Web:
  http://sunsite.berkeley.edu/Goldman/

Look What I Found on the Net...

```
Newsgroup: alt.society.anarchy
Subject: Nukes in Space

Excerpt from the article "Risking the World" by Xxxx Xxxxxxxx,
Professor of American Studies at XXXX:

"Despite enormous danger, huge expense, and a clear alternative —
solar power — the U.S. government is pushing ahead with the
deployment of nuclear technology in space.  In October 1997,
NASA plans to launch the Cassini probe to Saturn. Carrying
72.3 pounds of plutonium-238 fuel, the largest amount of
plutonium ever used in space...

"...NASA says in its First Environmental Impact Statement for
the Cassini Mission, that if an 'inadvertent reentry occurred'
during the fly-by, approximately five billion of the seven to
eight billion people on Earth, 'could receive 99 percent or
more of the radiation exposure...'"

We must mobilize to prevent the nuclearization of space, and the
possible release of so toxic a substance, condemning us to a
lingering, painful death. Unless we act directly to prevent this
launch, it will occur (and will set the precedent for further
launches of plutonium into space, increasing the likelihood that
an accident will occur).
```

ANARCHY

History of the Black Flag

You may have noticed that when the political and fashionable hoi polloi congregate (say, at the opening of Congress or the annual Clinton, Arkansas, turkey drop) you never see a black flag. And you know why? Because a black flag is the symbol of anarchy, and if there is one thing the political and fashionable hoi polloi will not tolerate, it is anything that smacks of not following the rules. (Just ask any member of Congress or, for that matter, any turkey from Arkansas.) But how did the black flag come to have such a meaning? Read this article and find out.

Web:
  http://www.teleport.com/~jwehling/BlackFlag.html

Internet Anarchist University

Okay, so you are tired of everything being so predictable, and you want to learn more about mixing it up. But where can you go? If you go to a regular school, you will have to be politically correct just to stay in class. However, as a Net user, you have an option: the Internet Anarchist University, the only place of learning in the world where you get credit for being revolting.

Web:
  http://burn.ucsd.edu/~mai/iau.html

If you want to learn about anarchy, what better place to visit than the Internet Anarchist University? It's handy, it's always available, and the subject matter is fascinating. The only drawbacks are they don't give diplomas and there is no football team.

Primitivist Network

Do you believe that something is destroying the Earth? If so, what is to blame? If you are an Anarcho-Primitivist, the answer is clear: the problem is civilization. Yes, it is civilization itself, a "huge system of domination and exploitation", that is responsible. Fortunately, the way out is clear. There is a simple five-point plan that starts with "1. Dismantle civilization." Want to know more? Visit the Primitivist Network.

Web:
  http://www.hrc.wmin.ac.uk/campaigns/ef/efhtmls/primnwk.html

Prominent Anarchists

Who's who, and why? Here's the inside scoop about your favorite anarchists: biographies, photos, quotations, and information about their work. After all, you can't follow in someone's footsteps if you don't know their shoe size. Or as Noam Chomsky once put it: "If I were to run for president, the first thing I would do is tell people not to vote for me."

Web:
  http://www.tigerden.com/~berios/libertarians.html

Rocker, Rudolf

Rudolf Rocker (1873-1958) was a German-born anarchist writer, speaker and philosopher. Rocker was a socialist when he was young, but soon became an anarchist. Throughout his adult life, Rocker proved to be a prolific and energetic proponent of anarcho-syndicalism (a movement that believes in wresting power from the bosses and vesting it in unions or syndicates). Rocker believed an anarchist world, characterized by "free association of all productive forces based upon cooperative labor", would be, ultimately, the logical outcome of modern monopoly capitalism and totalitarianism. (Remember, Rocker lived through the labor unrest of the early part of the century, the Great Depression and two World Wars.) Clearly, he did not envision the evolution of society that was to take place in the latter half of the century. Nevertheless, Rocker's writings are, to this day, thought-provoking and compelling.

Web:
  http://flag.blackened.net/rocker/

12 ANARCHY

Siege of Paris

In 1870, Otto Von Bismarck, the "Iron Chancellor", goaded the French into declaring war against Prussia (a German state). This was part of Bismarck's plan to create a unified German empire, and it worked. The French declared war—the Franco-Prussian War—and lost, after which Bismarck was able to consolidate the German empire as an aggressive military force, leading to one or two minor military problems in the twentieth century. Once the war ended, Germany forced France to accept punitive and humiliating terms of surrender. Many of the working class citizens of Paris (such as writers of Internet books) were so upset at the new French government's acceptance of these terms that they forced out the National Assembly and formed a committee called the Commune of Paris to run the city. Led by the Commune of Paris, the citizens put up a brave and desperate struggle against government troops, but after a week of battles—called the Siege of Paris—the working class protesters lost. Afterward, there were massive reprisals in which tens of thousands of people were killed, putting a crimp in the French political scene for the next several years.

Web:
http://www.library.nwu.edu/spec/siege/

Spunk Library

If you're going to be an anarchist, you need spunk. If you're going to be an anarchist on the Net, you need the Spunk Library: a collection of anarchist literature, including lots of esoteric papers and commentaries, as well as the Anarchist FAQ (frequently asked question list). The Spunk Library is a good place to browse when you have a few extra moments and you want to raise your anti-hierarchy consciousness without having to do any heavy lifting. (By the way, the word "spunk" was taken from a Pippi Longstocking book.)

Web:
http://www.spunk.org/

Get away from it all in "Travel".

ANIMALS AND PETS

Animal Information Database

Created by Sea World and Busch Gardens, this Web page is loaded with information, not only about aquatic animals, but also on a variety of terrestrial critters. Learn about manatee bodysurfing, hippos that sweat pink oil, and other interesting animal facts that will make you the life of any party.

Web:
http://www.seaworld.org/

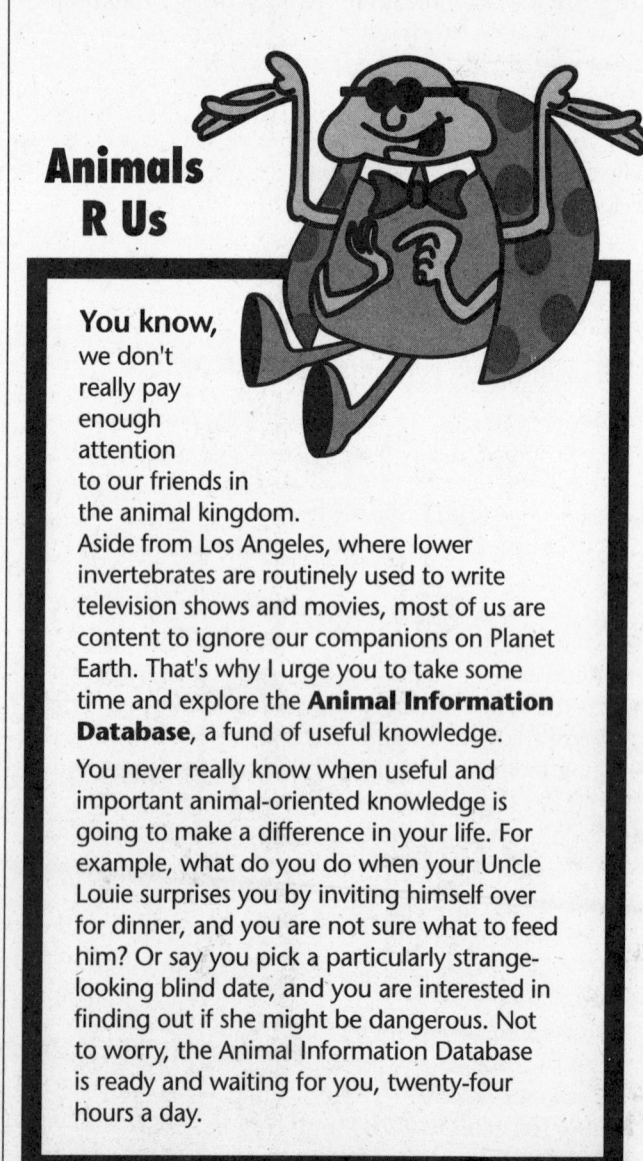

Animals R Us

You know, we don't really pay enough attention to our friends in the animal kingdom. Aside from Los Angeles, where lower invertebrates are routinely used to write television shows and movies, most of us are content to ignore our companions on Planet Earth. That's why I urge you to take some time and explore the **Animal Information Database**, a fund of useful knowledge.

You never really know when useful and important animal-oriented knowledge is going to make a difference in your life. For example, what do you do when your Uncle Louie surprises you by inviting himself over for dinner, and you are not sure what to feed him? Or say you pick a particularly strange-looking blind date, and you are interested in finding out if she might be dangerous. Not to worry, the Animal Information Database is ready and waiting for you, twenty-four hours a day.

ANIMALS AND PETS

> **Just say no to spam.**

Animal Rescue and Adoption

Let me tell you a true animal rescue story. Every night, my cat (The Little Nipper) sleeps on my bed. If he happens to be outside in the evening, he knows to come in when it is time for bed and, as soon as he comes in, I close all the doors. Last week, after he was inside and I had shut all the doors, The Little Nipper disappeared. He didn't show up all night. I was worried about him and had trouble sleeping. Early in the morning, I got up and started a comprehensive search. I looked in every closet, behind every door, and on top of every shelf. The Little Nipper had vanished. By now it was light, so I started to look around outside, just in case he had found a secret exit even though the doors were closed. However, my efforts were fruitless. I walked all around the house with a bowl of tuna, a treat that had never before failed to attract him, but The Little Nipper was gone. I checked with the neighbors. No one had seen him. My options had run out. With trembling fingers, I dialed the local animal control office. Calmly and professionally, they took a report and offered general advice. I hung up the phone and, within five minutes, in walked The Little Nipper. With the air of the President of the United States helping himself to the prettiest girl in the room, The Little Nipper swanked over to the bowl of tuna and, demonstrating a quiet dignity that became him well, lowered his head and began to indulge himself. To this day, I have no idea where he was—the White House, perhaps. If you like pets, I bet you will enjoy reading more rescue stories about animals (some of which are even more gripping than this story). If so, check the Net, where you can also find information about rescue organizations and animal shelters. If you have a pet of your own, take a moment to see what organizations exist in your area. Don't wait until tragedy strikes to identify the sources of professional help. After all, one day you may find yourself involved in a situation in which even a bowl of tuna is not enough.

Web:
  http://petstation.com/central.html#TOP
  http://www.ecn.purdue.edu/~laird/animal_rescue/shelters/

Animal Rights

My cat (The Little Nipper) and I have developed an Animal Bill of Rights: (1) All animals are entitled to tuna once a day. (2) Having your teeth brushed every morning should be voluntary. (Actually, The Little Nipper made up the Bill of Rights. I did the typing.) However, the world is not always so simple. Many people think that it takes more than guaranteed tuna to fulfill our responsibilities toward animals. In that, I agree. Animals are an important part of our culture and our economy, and how we treat them—and think about them—affects our society more than most people appreciate. Take a look at the animal rights resources on the Net, and see if you agree with me that there is room for kindness and reason in all aspects of our lives.

Web:
  http://www.aldf.org/
  http://www.envirolink.org/arrs/peta/

Usenet:
  talk.politics.animals

Animal Talk and General Discussion

Animals are for more than eating or making into pets. Some are pretty or lovable, and some are to be admired for their skill in stalking and devouring small prey or unsuspecting pizza-delivery boys. On the Net there are several places you can go to participate in discussions of your favorite animal.

Usenet:
  alt.animals.badgers
  alt.animals.bears
  alt.animals.dolphins
  alt.animals.foxes
  alt.animals.otters
  alt.animals.pandas
  alt.animals.raccoons
  alt.animals.whales
  alt.fan.hedgehog
  alt.fan.lemurs
  alt.goat
  alt.skunks
  alt.wolves
  alt.wolves.hybrid

14 ANIMALS AND PETS

Aquariums

What does it mean when your gourami is leaning thirty degrees to the right? He could be trying to steer, but that's probably not the case. Splash around with the rest of the ichthyophiles as they explore the true nature of tropical fish. Learn a wide variety of new things, like the best way to earthquake-proof your tanks, how to name your fish after famous Internet book writers, or what to feed your black piranha when all he really wants is you.

Web:
http://www.actwin.com/fish

Usenet:
alt.aquaria
alt.aquaria.killies
alt.aquaria.oscars
rec.aquaria
rec.aquaria.freshwater.cichlids
rec.aquaria.freshwater.goldfish
rec.aquaria.freshwater.misc
rec.aquaria.freshwater.plants
rec.aquaria.marine.misc
rec.aquaria.marine.reefs
rec.aquaria.marketplace
rec.aquaria.misc
rec.aquaria.tech
sci.aquaria

Listserv Mailing List:
List Name: **aquarium**
Subscribe to: **listserv@listserv.cc.emory.edu**

Bird-Keeping

Birds, birds, birds. There are 28 different orders of birds, comprising the class Aves. Within the bird world there is a great deal of variation with respect to what birds eat, how they live, where they live, where they migrate, how they build nests, and the sounds they make. It's hard to give an exact definition that covers every bird in the world, but most birds do share a number of characteristics. First, they have wings and feathers. Second, birds are streamlined—contoured feathers, no external ears—and fly with their feet held tightly against their bodies. Finally, birds have fast metabolisms, with a low body weight and light bones. Bird-keeping is no fly-by-night hobby, so to help you, I have found some cool avian- related resources. (Note: The **dom_bird** mailing list is for domestic birds, while **exotic-l** is for exotic birds.)

Web:
http://www.theaviary.com/ci.shtml
http://www.upatsix.com/

Usenet:
alt.pets.birds.dutch
alt.pets.birds.softbills
alt.pets.birds.softbills.crows
alt.pets.birds.softbills.starlings
alt.pets.parrots.african-grey
alt.pets.parrots.amazons
alt.pets.parrots.cockatiels
alt.pets.parrots.jardines
alt.pets.parrots.marketplace
alt.pets.parrots.misc
rec.pets.birds
rec.pets.birds.pigeons

Listserv Mailing List:
List Name: **dom_bird**
Subscribe to: **listserv@plearn.edu.pl**

Listserv Mailing List:
List Name: **exotic-l**
Subscribe to: **listserv@plearn.edu.pl**

Not bad... A hearty, fishy bouquet with just a hint of authority.

ANIMALS AND PETS   15

Bird-Watching

This is a hobby that can be as simple or as elaborate as you wish. Basic pieces of equipment are a lawn chair, a bird book, and a pair of binoculars—and some birds, of course. On the high end, you can use complicated camouflage, blinds and camera equipment. No matter what your aim is, bird-watching is an endlessly fascinating pastime.

Web:
   http://www.birder.com/
   http://www.naturesongs.com/birds.html
   http://www.theaviary.com/bi.shtml

Usenet:
   rec.birds

Listserv Mailing List:
   List Name: **birdchat**
   Subscribe to: **listserv@listserv.arizona.edu**

Cats Are People, Too

I may be biased, seeing as I have the best cat in the entire world, but what could be better than a warm, fluffy bundle of feline affection sitting beside you as you work?
If you like cats, the Net is *the* place to be, with all the cat-related information you will ever need. My cat loves the Net so much, he often takes the laptop computer with him to bed.
(I only wish he wouldn't get tuna all over the keyboard.)

Cats

No doubt about it, cats are très cool. (And my cat, The Little Nipper, happens to be the coolest cat of all.) The Net abounds with cat information, and just about everything cat-wise is out there waiting for you. Cats are also involved in some of the most amazing coincidences in the world. For example, my chief researcher's mother's name is Kitty and—get this—my maternal grandmother's name was Kitty. Farm out or what?

Web:
   http://www.afn.org/~afn47757/
   http://www.io.com/~tittle/cat-faqs/

Usenet:
   alt.animals.felines
   alt.animals.felines.diseases
   alt.pets.cats
   rec.pets.cats
   rec.pets.cats.anecdotes
   rec.pets.cats.announce
   rec.pets.cats.community
   rec.pets.cats.health+behav
   rec.pets.cats.misc
   rec.pets.cats.rescue

Listserv Mailing List:
   List Name: **feline-l**
   Subscribe to: **listserv@lists.psu.edu**

Listserv Mailing List:
   List Name: **talk-aboutcats**
   Subscribe to: **listserv@listserv.temple.edu**

Majordomo Mailing List:
   List Name: **cats-l**
   Subscribe to: **majordomo@stargame.org**

Majordomo Mailing List:
   List Name: **holisticat**
   Subscribe to: **majordomo@mylist.net**

Majordomo Mailing List:
   List Name: **nfh**
   Subscribe to: **majordomo@listservice.net**

Even my cat likes the Net.

16 ANIMALS AND PETS

Dogs

By their nature, dogs are pack animals that crave companionship. Combine this with over 10,000 years of domestication and a wide range of genetic variability, and you have the perfect companions for human beings. Even a cursory look at our culture will show you how important the canine dominion is to mankind. When I was growing up, I watched Huckleberry Hound, Rin Tin Tin, Lassie and Mighty Manfred the Wonder Dog. When I learned how to swim, I started with the dog paddle; when I was hungry I would eat a hot dog; and when I felt argumentative I would be dogmatic. If you like dogs, you are in good company on the Net, where there are more dog lovers than you can throw a stick at.

Web:
   http://www.canismajor.com/dog/
   http://www.dog-play.com/
   http://www.frii.com/~phouka/dog_main.html
   http://www.k9web.com/dog-faqs/
   http://www.worldclassdogs.com/

Usenet:
   alt.animals.dogs.collies.open-forum
   alt.pets.dogs.aussies
   alt.pets.dogs.pitbull
   alt.pets.dogs.sharpei
   rec.hunting.dogs
   rec.pets.dogs
   rec.pets.dogs.activities
   rec.pets.dogs.behavior
   rec.pets.dogs.breeds
   rec.pets.dogs.health
   rec.pets.dogs.info
   rec.pets.dogs.misc
   rec.pets.dogs.rescue

Majordomo Mailing List:
   List Name: **alldogs-l**
   Subscribe to: **majordomo@teleport.com**

Electronic Zoo

If you love animals, this is the place to spend your spare time. Enjoy a compilation of animal-related resources: mailing lists, Web sites, Usenet discussion groups, archives, databases, and much more. The next time you have an extra ten minutes, start here and explore. I bet you'll find something to distract you from your work.

Web:
   http://netvet.wustl.edu/e-zoo.htm

Endangered Species

Endangered species are animals whose numbers are diminishing to such an extent as to threaten their very existence. Throughout the history of the Earth, countless species have developed, flourished, and died out. In this sense, species extinction is natural and normal. However, many people believe that a great many species are becoming extinct because of changes produced in the environment by people and their activities. Although your personal life may seem remote from, say, the Moschus chrysogaster leucogaster (Himalayan Musk Deer) in Afghanistan, we do share the same world, and changes in remote areas can affect the ecological balance. So, when a species in Afghanistan becomes threatened, it is not necessarily something we can ignore with impunity. Still, I want you to be aware that the culture of the environment is filled to the brim with politics. A lot of people—perhaps most people—who argue passionately about saving the environment are misinformed and ignorant. For example, talk to any kid, and you will find that children get a lot of politically correct pro-environment propaganda at school. (My philosophy is that ten-year-old kids should have certain responsibilities, but that saving the rain forest should not be one of them.) So where does that leave us? The idea that the Earth is a large eco-system in which all species are indirectly dependent on one another is a sound, even brilliant observation. However, running around like Chicken Little, moaning that the ecological sky is falling, gets us nowhere. Here are some places on the Net that contain information about endangered species. These are starting places. Try to see past the propaganda and figure out for yourself what is real and what is important.

Web:
   http://www.fws.gov/r9endspp/endspp.html
   http://www.nwf.org/

**Go win something.
Check out "Contests".**

ANIMALS AND PETS

Ferrets

The weasel-like ferret is actually a type of domesticated polecat. Traditionally, ferrets have been used to chase rabbits, rats and mice. They are as playful as kittens, good-natured, energetic and entertaining. However, when they are not sleeping, ferrets are often very, very active. Ferrets can be a lot of fun, sometimes even more fun than you can stand. In one sentence, this is what a pet ferret does for a living: He runs around your home, exploring every opening and every object he can reach, and then he does the whole thing all over again.

Web:
http://www.ferretcentral.org/

Usenet:
alt.pets.ferrets
rec.pets.ferrets

Listserv Mailing List:
List Name: **ferret**
Subscribe to: **listserv@cunyvm.cuny.edu**

Majordomo Mailing List:
List Name: **ferret-forum**
Subscribe to: **majordomo@majordomo.net**

Fleas and Ticks

Learn how to rid your pet or home of fleas and what to do about ticks. (The ol' gasoline trick probably isn't a very good idea anymore.)

Web:
http://www.canismajor.com/dog/critter.html
http://www.k9web.com/dog-faqs/fleas-ticks.html

Look What I Found on the Net...

```
Newsgroup: alt.pets.hamsters
Subject: Do hamsters have nightmares?

>>> Do hamsters have nightmares?

>>> I was in my room this morning, when I suddenly heard a
>>> scream coming from my hamster's cage.  (If you've ever heard
>>> a hamster scream, you know what I'm talking about).  I
>>> jumped about 3 feet into the air!  I thought he was dying,
>>> or in mortal agony or something!  I ran over to his cage,
>>> popped open the top, popped open his house, and as soon as
>>> he saw me he stopped, then he crawled out into my hand.
>>> I held him for a few minutes, and he was fine, and he hasn't
>>> let out a peep since.  Should I get him checked out, or has
>>> anyone else experienced a hamster with nightmares?

>> With humans, rapid eye movement is an indication of dream,
>> maybe hamsters have this too?  Their eyes are large, so it
>> might be easy to observe.

> I like watching Li'l Hamster sleep, he seems to have a lot of
> Rapid Nose movement for a few minutes about half hour after he
> has been asleep, I am sure that they dream...

Until I read all of these "Do hamsters have nightmares?" I
hadn't really thought about it much.  But after reading this,
I heard my hamster actually squeak in his sleep yesterday.
Thanks for the tip.
```

18 ANIMALS AND PETS

Hamsters

Hamsters can be a lot of fun, and they are as cute as the dickens. When I was a kid I had a hamster named Hamlet. He used to stay up all night, running around inside a wheel in his cage. Aside from that, he was pretty easy to get along with. He never ate the last corndog; when we were watching TV, he didn't mind if I changed the channel to Dick van Dyke; and he always saved the comics for me to read before he started ripping them apart. If you would like to find out more about our pleasant little golden-brown friends, here are some Net resources that are even more fun than running around inside a wheel.

Web:
http://www.chat.carleton.ca/~ggower/hamsters/
http://www.hamsters.co.uk/
http://www.jagnet.demon.co.uk/hamster/links.html

Usenet:
alt.pets.hamsters

Majordomo Mailing List:
List Name: **hammies-r-us**
Subscribe to: **majordomo@lists.i-way.co.uk**

Horses

Why do so many young women love to ride horses? Well, I know, but I can't tell. What I can tell you is that the Net is the place to meet horse lovers of all types for a general discussion of horses, riding, and all-around good, clean equestrian fun.

Web:
http://www.horseadvice.com/
http://www.horseweb.com/hw_hlink.htm

Usenet:
alt.animals.horses.breeding
alt.animals.horses.icelandic
alt.animals.mules
alt.animals.ponies
alt.horseback.riding
alt.horsecare.basics
rec.equestrian

Listserv Mailing List:
List Name: **equine-l**
Subscribe to: **listserv@lists.psu.edu**

Iguanas

An iguana is a large lizard, found in the tropical regions of the western hemisphere. Even in the dark, it is easy to tell an iguana from a cat or a dog, because iguanas have spiny projections along their backs. Here is information for every iguana lover or potential iguana lover about housing, feeding, health, reproduction, and so on.

Web:
http://www.baskingspot.com/igbook/
http://www.sonic.net/~melissk/ig_care.html

Majordomo Mailing List:
List Name: **iguanas**
Subscribe to: **majordomo@echonyc.com**

Marine Mammals

I love spending time in the ocean. Occasionally, I will be sitting on my board, waiting for a wave, when a group of dolphins will swim by. Just having them nearby is a special treat. Dolphins are one of the few animals that are always cool, even when they are lying around doing nothing in particular. There is something intriguing about dolphins, porpoises, manatees, whales and seals. They are mammals, but they live in the water. Sometimes, when I am snorkeling, I will lie with one eye above the water, staring at the sky and the shore, and the other eye under water, looking at all the plants, rocks and fish. The underwater environment is so different from where we live, it is almost like being on two planets at the same time. Perhaps that is why marine mammals are so enchanting: they manage to live above and below, and still fit in so well.

Web:
http://ourworld.compuserve.com/homepages/jaap/aad_faq.htm
http://www.bhm.tis.net/zoo/ao/marinmam.htm
http://www.mmsc.org/info/
http://www.physics.helsinki.fi/whale/

Usenet:
alt.animals.dolphins
alt.animals.whales

ANIMALS AND PETS

Monkeys
I never had a pet monkey when I was growing up, but I did have a little sister. Of course, there are important differences. For example, many sisters do not live in tropical or semi-tropical climates. And monkeys do not tie up the telephone when you are waiting for an important call. If you need even more information, here's a good place to look.

Web:
http://members.primary.net/~heather/

MONKEYS

You would think that having a monkey would be a lot of fun, and it can be. But before you get one, use the Net and find out what's in store for you. Living with a monkey is a permanent, highly demanding job, and is not for the faint at heart. Before you think seriously about getting your own monkey, take the following quiz. Answer each question yes or no.

(1) Is it okay if an animal repeatedly trashes your home?
(2) Do you hate going on a vacation or having any spare time?
(3) Do you have a lot of extra money you need to get rid of?
(4) Does your idea of having a good time involve a lot of cleaning and repairing?
(5) Can you be patient and loving when your pet, whom you have cared for since it was a baby, savagely attacks you for no particular reason?

Score 1 point for each "yes", 0 for each "no".
If your score is 0, 1, 2, 3, or 4, you should get a cat.
If your score is 5, you may be monkey material.

Pet Cemetery
Finally, here is the perfect venue for you to publish "Ode to Wilhelmena, Marsupial Companion of my Youth". The Virtual Pet Cemetery is just the place to send an honorable epitaph for that favorite pet who, after handing in his dinner pail, has passed on to his final reward, beloved by all and sundry.

Web:
http://www.lavamind.com/pet.html

Pet Channel
Having pets can be a lot of fun, but what do you do when they are asleep and you have nothing to do? Visit the Pet Channel. Here you will find information to help you keep your pet healthy and well-trained. You will also find funny pet stories, help in finding a pet, pet pictures (you can submit your own), and other features. After all, owning a pet is not a full-time job: you do deserve some time off to have fun on your own.

Web:
http://www.thepetchannel.com/

Pet-Keeping Dos and Don'ts
Before my brother was born, the doctor asked me what I hoped the baby would be. I said I wanted a pony. However, my mother knew I was too young to take care of a pony by myself, so she got me a brother instead. Pets can be a lot of fun, but we do have a responsibility to look after them. Here is a wealth of advice on how to select and care for a pet. For example, before you take a trip, make arrangements with your family or friends as to who should take care of your pet if you don't come back.

Web:
http://petstation.com/do&dont.html

Pet of the Day
Any pet is eligible! Just send in his or her picture with some information, and your pet might become the Pet of the Day. If you like animals, this is a great place to visit when you have a few moments. You can browse through the archives and look at the previous Pets of the Day. Of course, none of them is as adorable as my cat (The Little Nipper) or your pet (but they are cute).

Web:
http://www.petoftheday.com/

20 ANIMALS AND PETS

> There's something fishy in "Zoology".

Pet Talk and General Discussion

If you have a pet, or want a pet, or happen to be cooking a pet for dinner, check with the general pet discussion group first. Share information and experiences on a range of topics, including exotic animals, nutrition, grooming, behavior, veterinary care and recipes.

Usenet:
alt.pets
alt.pets.guinea-pigs
alt.pets.hedgehogs
alt.pets.skunks
alt.pets.sugar-glider
rec.pets

Plants Harmful to Animals

It sounds like a job for a professional politician, but truly, there are people who like to grow poisonous plants for a living. At least they do it for the common good. At this Web site you can check out plants that are toxic to animals and humans. You can look up the plants by common name or by scientific name. There are also links to related sources. This is an important resource if you have kids or animals that chew on things they aren't supposed to chew on.

Web:
http://www.library.uiuc.edu/vex/toxic/toxic.htm

Rabbits

Cuddly, soft, lovable little animals that you can dye pastel shades when Easter rolls around, bunnies are not just for kids. They make great pets for everyone. Learn about how to care for a pet rabbit and get information about rabbit psychology and diseases that afflict bunnies. On the mailing list, non-bunny-lovers are not welcome unless you can mind your manners.

Web:
http://pages.prodigy.com/NTMX83A/
http://www.rabbit.org/

Usenet:
alt.animals.breeders.rabbits
alt.pets.rabbits
rec.pets.rabbits

Listserv Mailing List:
List Name: **petbunny**
Subscribe to: **listserv@lsv.uky.edu**

Rats and Mice

I once lived with someone who had a pet rat. One day she let it get away and it hid in the couch. Eventually, we were able to retrieve the rat, but the couch was never the same. Another time, she was playing with the rat by holding its tail. Much to her chagrin, the outside of the tail pulled off, leaving a raw, red inner core. Eventually, the rat healed, but the tail was never the same. As you can see, rodents are pretty cool pets, and if your day-to-day existence is missing something or other, maybe you should get yourself a rat or mouse.

Web:
http://www.afrma.org/afrma/rmindex.htm
http://www.rmca.org/Resources/faqs.htm

Usenet:
alt.pets.mice
alt.pets.rodents

Look What I Found on the Net...

```
(from the message that describes the mailing list "petbunny")

    ...PetBunny is an open, unmoderated discussion list for owners
of pet rabbits.  Things such as how to care for a pet rabbit,
rabbit diseases and rabbit psychology are likely to be
discussed.  The list is NOT intended for rabbit bashing...
```

ANIMALS AND PETS 21

Reptiles and Amphibians

Herpetology is the study of reptiles and amphibians. Both reptiles and amphibians are cold-blooded (that is, they do not maintain a constant internal body temperature). However, where reptiles use lungs to breathe, amphibians breathe with gills when they are young (under water), and with lungs once they become adults. Another difference is that reptiles—such as snakes, lizards, turtles and crocodiles—have bodies that are covered by scales or horny plates. Amphibians—such as newts, frogs, toads and salamanders—have a moist, scaleless skin. Why do people enjoy keeping such animals? Because they are creepy. Kewl.

Web:
  http://fovea.retina.net/~gecko/herps/
  http://www.baskingspot.com/
  http://www.hellfire.com/nootnerd/
  http://www.teleport.com/~dstroy/frogland.html

Usenet:
  rec.pets.alligators
  rec.pets.herp

IRC:
  #herp

It's your 15th wedding anniversary, and you're not sure whether to get your wife a rat, a reptile, or a scorpion. Don't take chances with something this important. Check with the Net and get all the information before you make a commitment.

Are you a know-it-all? Check in "Trivia" for tidbits of useless information.

Scorpions

It was real and it was scary, but, once again, the Net saved my peace of mind. Here's what happened. The night seemed like any other until I looked under the bed. There, crawling along with the aplomb of the Pope walking through the Sistine Chapel, was an ugly, many-legged insectoid thingy. We are talking ugly here, major ugly. Major ugly, with two pincer-like forelegs. Oh no, I thought, there's a scorpion in the bedroom. I grabbed a book and went after the insect. Man to man, just the two of us, a showdown. One way or another, only one of us was going to leave the room alive. Fortunately, the battle was one-sided (after all, I was the one with the book), and it wasn't long before the arthropodal intruder had departed his earthly moorings. Flushed with the thrill of victory, I instituted a thorough search, and within a moment, I had found another ugly, many-legged insectoid thingy with pincer-like forelegs. Once again, I brandished my trusty book and dispatched the second intruder to the netherworld. However, I was not sanguine, not by a long shot. Was it possible that a nest of scorpions had taken up residence under the house? There was only one thing to do. Although it was the middle of the night, I had to get to the bottom of this entomological puzzle. So I went to the computer and checked a scorpion site on the Net. Imagine my relief when I found that my nocturnal visitors were not scorpions, but sun spiders. They are related to scorpions but perfectly harmless. So, once again, the Net came through, helping me to sleep soundly in the embrace of knowledge. True, a pair of sun spiders died unnecessarily, but, as the saying goes, "No pain, no gain."

Web:
  http://wrbu.si.edu/www/stockwell/emporium/emporium.html

22 ANIMALS AND PETS

Sharks

Okay, let's get the strange stuff out of the way. (1) Sharks don't have bones, they have cartilage. (2) There are 250 different species of sharks. (3) Fully grown sharks can range from cute pygmy sharks measuring only 60 cm (2 feet) up to large whale sharks stretching to 15 meters (50 feet). (4) The most feared shark is the white shark (called the "Great White Shark" in the movies). This animal can grow up to 6 meters (20 feet), and will attack and try to eat just about anything, even without provocation. (The huge whale shark, by the way, is much less dangerous, as it lives on microscopic plankton.) Although many people are afraid of sharks, such fears are more a testament to the movies than to common sense. I have been swimming in the ocean for years, and the closest I ever came to a shark was going snorkeling with my lawyer.

Web:
  http://www.ncf.carleton.ca/~bz050/HomePage.shark.html
  http://www.oceanstar.com/shark/
  http://www.ucmp.berkeley.edu/vertebrates/Doug/shark.html

Listserv Mailing List:
  List Name: **shark-l**
  Subscribe to: **listserv@raven.utc.edu**

Tarantulas

The name "tarantula" refers to several species of large, hair-covered spiders native to North and South America. A large tarantula can measure up to 7.5 cm (3 inches) wide, stretching up to 25 cm (10 inches) with its legs extended. Despite their formidable appearance, tarantulas, if handled properly, are not dangerous to people and can make good pets. By the way, the easiest way to preserve a tarantula—or any spider—is to put it in a glass jar filled with 90-100 percent ethanol (regular drinking alcohol). Of course, you should make sure the tarantula is dead, but, if he isn't, you probably won't get any complaints.

Web:
  http://chekware.simplenet.com/burrow/index.hts
  http://www.concentric.net/~dmartin/spidercare.html

Usenet:
  alt.pets.arachnids

Veterinary Medicine

If you were always the one to bring home the bird with the broken wing or if you liked to wrap the dog up in gauze bandages, then maybe your calling is veterinary medicine. There is a wealth of information on the Net about animals and the veterinary field. The **vetstu-l** mailing list is primarily for veterinary students. The **vetplus-l** mailing list is for veterinary medicine professionals.

Web:
  http://trfn.clpgh.org/animalfriends/medical.html
  http://www.futurescan.com/vet/

Usenet:
  alt.med.veterinary

Listproc Mailing List:
  List Name: **vetplus-l**
  Subscribe to: **listproc@u.washington.edu**

Listserv Mailing List:
  List Name: **vetmed**
  Subscribe to: **listserv@listserv.iupui.edu**

Listserv Mailing List:
  List Name: **vetstu-l**
  Subscribe to: **listserv@uga.cc.uga.edu**

Wildlife

Outside of downtown Los Angeles or the U.S. Republican National Convention, most people don't get a chance to see real wildlife in their native habitat. However, as a Net user, you can visit a virtual collection of various types of wildlife, including species that are extinct or endangered.

Web:
  http://www.cccweb.com/wildlife.html
  http://www.nature-wildlife.com/

Usenet:
  rec.animals.wildlife

This book is high in fiber.

ARCHAEOLOGY

Zoos

Who doesn't like to visit a zoo? We live in a controlled environment with very few animals (aside from pets) and visiting the zoo reminds us that most of the world is populated by many different types of non-human animals. There are a lot of zoo-oriented resources on the Net, and before you visit somewhere, you might want to check out the local zoo. By the way, although zoo animals live behind bars and fences, they are well-fed and cared for. Indeed, zoo animals usually live better, more healthy lives than their cousins in the wild.

Web:
http://aazk.epower.net/
http://www.mindspring.com/~zoonet/

ARCHAEOLOGY

Archaeological Fieldwork

If you are a student of archaeology, it behooves you to spend a lot of time crawling around the great outdoors looking for little bits and pieces of whatnot. But where should you go? Here is a listing of fieldwork opportunities around the world. The pay is often low or non-existent, the hours are long, and the work can be mind numbing, but the experience can be invaluable (especially if, one day, you plan to become a professional archaeologist, crawling around the great outdoors looking for little bits and pieces of whatnot).

Web:
http://www.cincpac.com/afs/testpit.html

Look What I Found on the Net...

```
Newsgroup: rec.animals.wildlife
Subject: A to Z of animals

 Has anybody got an A to Z list of animals for my young nephew's
 homework? Failing that, we need animals beginning with the
 letters N, U and X.

For N: Nanday conure (parrot),
       narwhal (tusked whale),
       newt,
       nilgai (antelope),
       nine-banded armadillo,
       nudibranch (sea slug),
       numbat (marsupial),
       nuthatch (small tree-climbing bird),
       nutria (fur-bearing rodent),
       nyala (antelope)

For U: uakari (South American monkey),
       urial (wild sheep),
       Utah sucker (fish),
       umbrella crab

For X: Xantus' murrelet (sea bird),
       xenops (finch),
       xenopsaris (flycatcher),
       X-ray fish, xenogale (mongoose)
```

24 ARCHAEOLOGY

Archaeological Societies

If you want to be a real honest-to-Pete archaeologist, you've got to join the club. After all, what's the point of spending your life discovering all kinds of cool archaeological stuff if you don't belong to the same organization as all the other people who spend their lives discovering all kinds of cool archaeological stuff? And once you're a member, don't forget to check in regularly to read about upcoming events, check out the online journals, and immerse yourself in all manner of things archaeological. That's what's great about the Net. No matter where you are, you can always spend time at the club.

Web:
http://www.saa.org/
http://www.wisc.edu/larch/sas/sas.htm

Archaeology Events

If you're in the field a lot, it's easy to lose track of what's happening. So how can you be sure that you don't miss that oh-so-important conference? Check with the Net, and you will never be left out in the cold when it comes time to talk about what's been left out in the cold.

Web:
http://users.hol.gr/~dilos/anistor/conf.htm

Archaeology Magazine

Archaeology Magazine is an official publication of the Archaeological Institute of America. Visit their Web site and browse through articles, abstracts, back issues, as well as an events calendar. What I like best are the Newsbriefs: short articles on what is new and exciting in the world of archaeology.

Web:
http://www.archaeology.org/

Hold that thought.

Archaeology News

There are a lot of people excavating and cataloging all around the world, and a week doesn't go by without some fascinating archaeological discovery. These Web sites will help you keep current with what's new and exciting. I like to take a moment every now and then just to see what the archeologists of the world are doing. After all, on the Net, everything old is news again.

Web:
http://anthro.org/issues1.htm
http://web.idirect.com/~atrium/commentarium.html

Archaeology Resources

Need to explore? Here's the door. Want more? Read the lore. Wanna soar? Skip the gore, avoid the war, just get to the core. Never a bore. Never a chore. Bring your paramour. Archaeology resources, wow! Need to explore? Here's the door.

Web:
http://www.brown.edu/Departments/Anthropology/archsite.html
http://www.ccc.nottingham.ac.uk/~aczkdc/ukarch/ukindex.html
http://www.julen.net/aw/

Archaeology Talk and General Discussion

The study of archaeology covers a huge amount of ground, which is why there are a great many archaeology discussion groups on the Net. No matter what your interest or field of expertise, there is bound to be a group just for you. Follow the discussion over the Net, and you can work with people all over the world without having to venture more than a few feet from the fridge. Or, when you are out on a dig, you can take your laptop computer and cellular modem (paid for by a government grant) and keep up on what is happening, no matter how far you are from the trappings of civilization.

Web:
http://anthro.org/lists.htm

Usenet:
alt.archaeology
sci.archaeology
sci.archaeology.moderated

ARCHAEOLOGY

Archnet

I have a friend, Virginia (Ginny) Hatfield, who is an archaeologist. She spends a lot of time running around the country digging up small pieces of whatnot and making esoteric discoveries. Myself, I prefer to stay at home with my cat and cruise the University of Connecticut's Archnet site. That way I can spend hours poring over all kinds of archaeological resources without getting my hands dirty. Ginny may have more fun, but I'm a lot closer to the shower.

Web:
http://www.lib.uconn.edu/ArchNet/ArchNet.html

Make Money With Archaeology

Do you want to make a lot of money? Here's a great investment.

Take a bunch of stuff from around the house — some old newspapers, a chipped cereal bowl, a few T-shirts with beer ads on them, an old car battery, and any other junk that you can spare — and put it all in a large, hermetically sealed box. Now all you have to do is wait.

After 2,000 years or so, the items in your box will qualify as genuine archaeological artifacts, and you will be able to sell them for a handsome profit.

If you would like to see what the Greeks, Romans, Egyptians, and other ancient people put in *their* boxes, check out Archnet.

Biblical Archaeology

People who study the Bible are especially interested in the archaeological foundations of biblical writings. However, even for non-believers, the study of the archaeology of biblical times can be rewarding, offering a glimpse into ancient societies that form the basis for much of modern Western civilization. Here is a well-organized collection of links relating to sites mentioned in the Bible. Aside from general resources, you will find links to maps, organizations, and information about ongoing excavations.

Web:
http://www.lpl.arizona.edu/~kmeyers/archaeol/bib_arch.html

Classics and Mediterranean Archaeology

Some of the richest areas in archaeology lie in the study of ancient civilizations (Babylon, Egypt, Greece, Rome, and so on). This Web site points to a huge amount of information of interest to classicists and Mediterranean archaeologists. If you are inclined toward the Ancient World, start here and your archaeological amphora will runneth over.

Web:
http://rome.classics.lsa.umich.edu/

Cultural Site Etiquette

Archaeology sites don't grow on trees (although trees do grow on some archaeology sites). It is important, when you work on a site, to be able to investigate without damaging the site and the artifacts. Here is information about minimum impact techniques that every budding archaeologist should understand before visiting a cultural or archaeological site.

Web:
http://www.nps.gov/care/arpa.htm

Egyptian Artifacts

You can be Indiana Jones without having to worry about sharp spikes being driven through your head or giant rolling rocks crushing you to death. Take a look at beautiful Egyptian artifacts at the Institute of Egyptian Art and Archaeology.

Web:
http://www.memphis.edu/egypt/artifact.html

ARCHAEOLOGY

Industrial Archaeology

Industrial Archaeology deals with history and artifacts relating to technology, engineering and industry. Today, that means studying, say, the Industrial Revolution. But what about the future? All the technology we use and take for granted today will be studied by future industrial archaeologists. For example, say you throw away an old blender. A few centuries from now, someone is going to be rooting around in an ancient landfill and come across your blender. He or she will excavate it very carefully, and then use it as the subject of a Ph.D. dissertation. That is why, each time I throw away any type of machine, I put a note it in saying, "To whom it may concern: Hello from Harley in the twentieth century."

Web:

http://www.iarecord.demon.co.uk/otheria.htm
http://www.ss.mtu.edu/IA/sia.html
http://www.twelveheads.demon.co.uk/aia.htm

Mesoamerican Archaeology

Mesoamerica ("Middle America") refers to the area that includes central Mexico and the region extending to the south and east, encompassing parts of Guatemala, Belize, Honduras and Nicaragua. This area is of interest because it has been inhabited by a variety of civilizations, the most well-known being the pre-Columbian Maya and Olmec. Although the Mayans flourished centuries ago (about 300-900 A.D.), their civilization was well-developed, having an understanding of mathematics, calendars and hieroglyphics, as well as architecture and city planning. The Olmec are much older (about 1300-400 B.C.), and are often considered to be the mother culture of the later Mesoamerican civilizations. Like the Mayans, the Olmec had a hieroglyphic system of writing. Although the Olmec were much less advanced than the Mayans, they have left intriguing artifacts, such as carved stone heads weighing over 20 tons.

Web:

http://copan.bioz.unibas.ch/meso.html
http://www.netaxs.com/~mckenzie/
http://www.realtime.net/maya/

Usenet:

sci.archaeology.mesoamerican

National Archaeological Database

Throughout most of recorded history, people have had to dig around for official archaeological data. Now, however, the National Archaeological Database puts hard-to-find information at your virtual fingertips. Never again need you spend hours looking for documents such as the Notice of Inventory Completion for Native American Human Remains from Lake Winnepesauke, New Hampshire.

Web:

http://www.cast.uark.edu/products/NADB/

Treasure in Your Backyard?

How many people are overlooking important — and perhaps valuable — archaeological treasures right in their own backyard? This need never happen to you.

The National Archaeological Database

contains information on more investigations than you can shake a 500-year-old stick at. Connect to this bountiful resource and get the lowdown on what's low down.

ARCHAEOLOGY 27

Papyrology

Papyrology is the study of ancient documents written on papyrus leaves. The ancient Egyptians developed the technique of creating a paper-like material from the pith of the papyrus plant, a reed that grew along the banks of the Nile River. (Pith is the material inside the stem.) The idea of writing on papyri spread from Egypt to other parts of the world. However, it was only in Egypt and Mesopotamia (part of modern-day Iraq) that the climate allowed papyri to survive over the years. Today, papyrologists study the estimated 400,000 papyri preserved around the world, many of which are fragments. These papyri contain a large variety of writing—literature, religious works, government reports, private documents—in Egyptian, Greek, Latin, Coptic and Arabic. As you might imagine, a papyrologist is like a detective. He or she must decode the meaning of a document, often from a fragment. Today, however, we have the Net, and papyrologists around the world can share research material.

Web:
http://www.csad.ox.ac.uk/CSAD/
http://www-personal.umich.edu/~jmucci/papyrology/

Perseus Project

The Perseus Project contains a vast collection of information relating to art objects, archaeological sites and buildings, vases, coins, and sculptures, including well over 10,000 pictures. My favorite part is the collection of ancient coins—information as well as pictures—because I like to collect coins myself. This is a great site for serious researchers. Information on all these artifacts, gathered from museums around the world, is collected and organized into a large, well-organized library.

Web:
http://www.perseus.tufts.edu/art&arch.html

Pottery

Pottery is made of moist clay that is heated until it becomes hard. In most of the world, pottery was the earliest developed craft. For example, potter's wheels—for spinning the clay into round shapes—were used in Egypt before 4000 B.C. Around the world, many ancient cultures used pottery to create bowls, pots, plates and decorative works of art. When your archaeological investigations take you into the world of pottery, the Net is ready to help.

Web:
http://spirit.lib.uconn.edu/ArchNet/Topical/Ceramic/Hgloss/Hgloss.html
http://www.pmiles.demon.co.uk/mprg/mprg.htm

Rock Art

The oldest existing works of art we have are drawings and carvings on rocks. Such artifacts have been found on every continent and form an important body of archaeological source material. Common rock art motifs include outlines of human hands, drawings of animals and hunting scenes, and pictures of daily activities. Here are a great many links to rock art Web sites around the world.

Web:
http://www.questorsys.com/rockart/links.htm

The archaeologists' motto: If you hang around long enough, you're bound to find something cool.

28 ARCHAEOLOGY

Roman Art and Archaeology

The traditional date for the founding of the city of Rome is 753 B.C. The Roman Republic was established about 150 years later (509 B.C.), and, over the next 1,000 years, the Romans created an empire that expanded to control virtually the entire known world. The Roman Empire flourished for hundreds of years, until it ended in 476 A.D., with the defeat of the last emperor, Romulus Augustus. During their centuries of domination, the Romans created highly developed systems of architecture and art. For example, between 70-82 A.D., the Romans built the Colosseum, a huge amphitheater seating 50,000 people and occupying six acres. The archaeology of ancient Rome is a large, robust area of study, and this site has some great resources, including a large number of wonderful, well-organized essays and exhibits, as well as information and archives for related mailing lists. This is a great place for both research and browsing.

Web:
http://www-personal.umich.edu/~pfoss/ROMARCH.html

Majordomo Mailing List:
List Name: **romarch**
Subscribe to:
majordomo@rome.classics.lsa.umich.edu

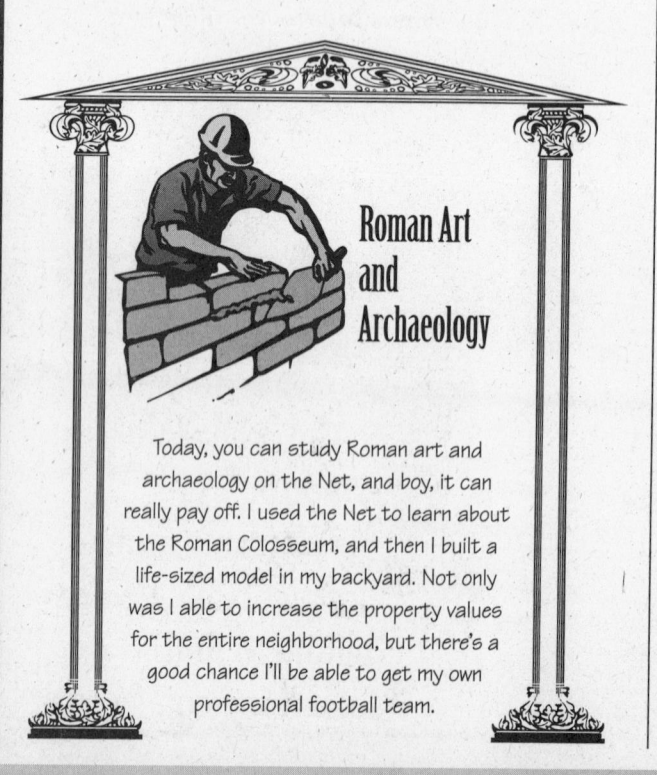

Roman Art and Archaeology

Today, you can study Roman art and archaeology on the Net, and boy, it can really pay off. I used the Net to learn about the Roman Colosseum, and then I built a life-sized model in my backyard. Not only was I able to increase the property values for the entire neighborhood, but there's a good chance I'll be able to get my own professional football team.

**Express yourself.
Try Usenet.**

Stones and Megaliths

Stones, stones, stones. Standing stones, hillfort settlements, stone circles and cairns. Stones, stones, stones. Megaliths in Scotland, England and Ireland. Stones, stones, stones. Pictures, map reference points, nearest town info; a glossary, bibliography, photo tips. Stones, stones, stones.

Web:
http://easyweb.easynet.co.uk/~aburnham/stones.htm
http://utenti.micronet.it/dmeozzi/HomEng.html

Underwater Archaeology

Not all archaeology takes place on land. There are lots and lots of old and important stuff under the water. Here is an Internet site devoted to studying underwater archaeology. You will find articles, discussion lists, information about shipwrecks, as well as links to other related resources.

Web:
http://www.gotropical.com/archaeol.htm
http://www.pophaus.com/underwater/

ARCHITECTURE

Aesthetic Architecture

This site has information about the aesthetic architecture movement of the late 19th and early 20th centuries. The works displayed at this site are from artists and architects who concentrated heavily on regional styles, hand-craftsmanship and decorative detail. Represented movements include the Prairie School (Frank Lloyd Wright), Craftsman (Gustave Stickley), and other regional and international styles such as the Gothic revival.

Web:
http://www.fswarchitects.com/links.html

ARCHITECTURE 29

Alternative Architecture

The reason many cities look so boring is because most architects design structures that look like all the other structures. If you are someone who likes to ask "What if...?" hang out with the people in the alternative architecture discussion group and find out what might be possible.

Usenet:
 alt.architecture.alternative

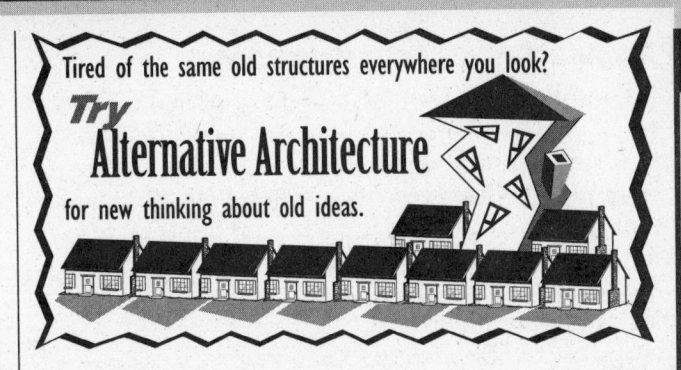

Tired of the same old structures everywhere you look?
Try Alternative Architecture *for new thinking about old ideas.*

Look What I Found on the Net...

(from the Web)

                    AN ARCHITECTURAL MANIFESTO

Buckminster Fuller said that the average person doesn't give a
thought to the sophistication of the technology that allows him
to flush the toilet on the 104th floor and have it work...
I say, let's just cut holes in the floor and let the refuse fall
into the basement.

However, architectural critics pick nits with this design:

   "This design is a crock. Although cheap and effective in
    low buildings, random air currents blowing this way and
    that will inevitably cause the material descending from
    higher floors to splatter on the edges of the holes in the
    floors below."

I say, no problem, just make the holes on the lower floors
bigger.

Architectural critics still pick nits:

   "The hole in the first floor of a 104-story building would
    have to be at least 35 feet, 4 inches in diameter to be
    practical."

I say, so what, people will love 'em. What a conversation
piece... Imagine this: you're sitting in your living room,
eating toast points, drinking champagne before your maid serves
dinner, and you see a piece of refuse fall through the 35-foot hole
in the ceiling, silently descend the 12 feet to the 35-foot
4 inch hole in the floor, and vanish from sight. One of your
guests, remarks:

"Looked to be about 6.5 feet in from the edge, there.
 I'd say it came from the 42nd floor..."

30 ARCHITECTURE

Architectural Reconstructions

Do you ever wonder what ancient ruins looked like when they were new? If you have trouble imagining the architecture, you can take a look at some of the computer-modeled reconstructions of famous ancient buildings such as Hadrian's Bath and the Temple of Rameses III. This site has not only the pictures, but details about rebuilding by computer and other architectural explorations.

Web:
http://archpropplan.auckland.ac.nz/virtualtour/

Architectural Styles

When you have to go to one of those swanky, cultural, let's-show-off-who-we-are-and-what-we-do parties, it's good to have a few cocktail conversation topics prepared. Architecture is something good to talk about, because there will always be a building nearby. Before you head off to that party, read the information at these sites. You'll find descriptions of various architectural styles and their influences. Before long, you will be able to name-drop with ease.

Web:
http://www.escape.ca/~jmorgan/iadhp/ainfo/
http://www.uwec.edu/Academic/Geography/Ivogeler/w367/styles/

Architecture Competitions

Competition brings out the best in people. Architects are people. Therefore, architectural competitions bring out the best in architects. (If only all of life were so simple.)

Web:
http://www.archeire.com/icn/
http://www.deathbyarch.com/html/competitions.html

**Plan ahead.
See "Emergency and Disaster".**

Having trouble with your grand design? Let Architecture fill in the missing pieces.

Architecture Talk and General Discussion

In my opinion, architects are some of the most talented, visionary, imaginative people in the world. Join the general architecture discussion group for all manner of architecture-oriented topics: building design, construction, architecture schools, materials, and so on. If they can build it, you can talk about it.

Usenet:
alt.architecture
alt.architecture.int-design
alt.building.architecture
alt.landscape.architecture
rec.arts.architecture

Athenian Architecture

If you can't tell your basic amphiprostyle structure from a peripteral layout, maybe it's time to brush up on your basic Greek architecture. Take a virtual tour of the architecture of Athens. Here you will see pictures of the Acropolis, the Library of Hadrian, the Arch of Hadrian, the Temple of Zeus, the Theater of Dionysos, and much more.

Web:
http://www.indiana.edu/~kglowack/athens/

Bauhaus

The Bauhaus movement of the early twentieth century developed from a school of art and architecture founded in 1919 by Walter Gropius (1883-1969) in Weimar, Germany. To me, Bauhaus represents two important movements. First, it represents an architectural philosophy that was firmly intertwined with the political and economic conditions of post-World War I Germany. Bauhaus architecture was created for the workers, and was supposed to reject "bourgeois" traditions and materials. The result was a collection of ugly, functional structures based on rigid economic and geometrical designs. The German government built massive amounts of Bauhaus housing which ultimately became highly unpopular (especially among the workers who had to live in the buildings). With the rise of the Nazis, many Bauhaus designers emigrated, spreading their influence to the U.S. (If you have ever seen American public housing or "portable" classrooms, you have seen Bauhaus.) The second important Bauhaus movement concerned itself with applied design: furniture, lighting, kitchenware, appliances, and so on. The Bauhaus artisans popularized the idea that one could design utilitarian objects as pieces of art, offering beauty as well as function. This idea has become one of the defining tenets of our twentieth century love affair with stuff, and, for many years, we have been buying *objets d'utilité* that double as pretty things to have around the house. Still, it is the Bauhaus style of architecture that has insinuated itself into the body cultural. Like an incorrigible virus, Bauhaus-inspired buildings arise with disturbing regularity, most often when people in authority combine a lack of taste with a desire to save money. On the Net, the Bauhaus sensibility is widespread, flourishing under the guise of Web page design.

Web:
   http://www.johnco.cc.ks.us/~jjackson/bauhaus.html
   http://www2.ucsc.edu/people/gflores/bauhaus/

Now is a good time for chocolate.

Cathedrals

The Gothic style of cathedrals was predominant in Europe from around 1150 to 1400. Gothic emerged in France and coincided with the rise of the monarchy as the central form of government. (Gothic cathedrals were not called gothic in their days of creation. The style was referred to as the "Modern" or "French" style. The term "Gothic" was coined in the sixteenth century by an Italian artist and historian named Giorgio Vasari. The expression was originally a negative term referring to the Goths who, Vasari felt, were responsible for ruining the classical artistry of the Roman empire.) However, today the Gothic cathedral is admired as a breathtaking work of art. This Web page offers a tour of various cathedrals such as Notre Dame, Canterbury and Chartres.

Web:
   http://www.elore.com/elore04.html

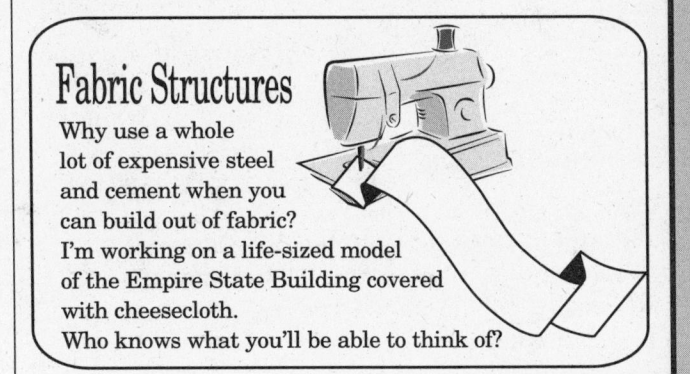

Fabric Structures

Why use a whole lot of expensive steel and cement when you can build out of fabric? I'm working on a life-sized model of the Empire State Building covered with cheesecloth. Who knows what you'll be able to think of?

Fabric Structures

What do the domes over modern sports stadiums have in common with circus tents, spiderwebs, air mattresses and parachutes? They are all fabric structures, built from lightweight materials designed to meet specific requirements of tension and compression. Generally speaking, there are two main types of fabric structures: air-supported structures (such as bubbles covering tennis courts) and tension structures (such as sports domes). Fabric structures are not new—tents, for example, have been used for many centuries—but modern materials and design techniques have laid the foundation for many new creations. Here are some resources to help you learn about fabric structures: history, materials, buildings, and much more.

Web:
   http://koenig.njit.edu/civil/gen.html
   http://www.arch.buffalo.edu/~agrawal/fabric.htm

ARCHITECTURE

Gargoyles in New York City

Tired of driving down the streets of suburbia and looking at row after row of the same old houses? Get a taste of some of the New York architecture by taking a monster tour of the city. This site has a virtual walking tour of New York City streets noted for creepy, cute or lurking stone monsters. The pictures are great and are accompanied by commentary.

Web:
http://www.aardvarkelectric.com/gargoyle/

Golden Gate Bridge

In 1579, the English explorer Francis Drake discovered a strait connecting the Pacific Ocean with San Francisco Bay. This strait became known as the Golden Gate. Although the name was used long before the California Gold Rush of 1849, the Gold Rush made the Golden Gate—the entrance into Northern California—an indelible part of the California mystique. The idea of building a bridge across the Golden Gate Strait was discussed as early as 1872. However, it was not until 1937 that a suspension bridge was built to span the strait. The Golden Gate Bridge runs north and south, connecting the city of San Francisco to Marin County. The bridge, which took a little over four years to build, is one of the most beautiful structures in the world. It is not the longest suspension bridge in the world, but it is easily the most famous.

Web:
http://www.goldengate.org/

Japanese Architecture

The architecture of a region has many influences. Some of these are physical (geography, weather patterns), while others are social (the economy, religion, types of people, and history of the area). Over the centuries, Japan has developed distinct architectural traditions that are both pleasing and puzzling to the Western eye. Use these Web sites to explore Japanese architecture and to view pictures of a variety of traditionally designed buildings.

Web:
http://www.japan-guide.com/a/html/shrine_e.html
http://www.kippo.or.jp/culture/build_e.htm
http://www.takase.com/JiroHarada/Chapter04.htm
http://www2.osaka-sandai.ac.jp:8080/orion/eng/hstj/histj.html

New Urbanism

New Urbanism is an approach to architecture that strives to design small, livable, comfortable neighborhoods. The tenets of New Urbanism mandate residential and commercial planning so as to encourage walking, not driving. A neighborhood should have a variety of homes and services, and be small enough for residents to walk from their houses to a public area in which there are stores, public buildings, transportation, and so on. In addition, there should be well-planned open spaces, such as playgrounds and parks, in convenient locations. (If you saw the movie The Truman Show, you have seen an example of a New Urbanism design.) To me, the New Urbanism movement represents an attempt to make modern life more manageable. The goal seems admirable, but I wonder if such designs are not more suitable for vacation communities. They seem unrealistic as day-to-day working and living environments.

Web:
http://www.cnu.org/
http://www.dpz.com/principl.htm
http://www.mnapa.com/urbanlex.html

Listserv Mailing List:
List Name: **cnu**
Subscribe to: **listserv@lsv.uky.edu**

Renaissance and Baroque Architecture

The Renaissance (1300-1500) and the Baroque eras (1600-1750) were times of immense architectural development. This collection of images will give you an idea of the basic design and building principles typical of the architecture of the times.

Web:
http://www.lib.virginia.edu/dic/colls/arh102/

If Herman Melville had written this book, you would be reading a metaphor right now.

ARCHITECTURE   33

If you're like me, you are tired of arguing with every Tom, Dick and Harry in the checkout line at the supermarket about whether or not Baroque and Renaissance architecture should be modernized.
Next time you run into a clown who doesn't know a flying buttress from a B-52, or a groined vault from his vas deferens, tell him to spend a few moments at the *Renaissance and Baroque Architecture* Web site. After all, as Howard Roark once said on one of his trips to Canada, "If it ain't Baroque, you don't need to fix it, eh?"

Sullivan, Louis Henry

Louis Henry Sullivan (1856-1924) was an eminent American architect remembered today for his admonition that "form ever follows function". In 1881, Sullivan formed the Chicago firm of Alder and Sullivan (with Dankmar Adler). Alder and Sullivan designed a number of important buildings during the years of rebuilding that followed the Chicago Fire (of 1871), and developed many of the early steel-frame designs for skyscrapers. The firm is also known for employing the young Frank Lloyd Wright for six years at the beginning of his career. Sullivan believed that architects must reconcile nature with science and technology, and he designed buildings in which ornamentation was an integral part of the structure rather than merely an addition to the finished product. Later in life, Sullivan developed the idea of "organic architecture", which asserted that architects should integrate the presence of nature along with the functional needs and materials of a structure.

Web:
http://www.burrows.com/bank.html
http://www.middlebury.edu/~ac400c/selover.html

Women in Architecture

Women involved with architecture will find these sites inspiring. Lots of links to biographical information about women architects, such as Julia Morgan (1872-1957), designer of Hearst Castle in San Simeon, California. There are also bibliographies, statistics regarding women in the architecture workplace, as well as information about modern female architects.

Web:
http://scholar2.lib.vt.edu/spec/iawa/iawa.htm
http://www.nscee.edu/unlv/Libraries/arch/rsrce/resguide/archwom.html
http://www4.ncsu.edu/unity/users/r/rlkeen/public/

Majordomo Mailing List:
List Name: **women-aaa**
Subscribe to: **majordomo@lists.uoregon.edu**

World's Tallest Buildings

In 1956, Frank Lloyd Wright proposed a skyscraper, called "The Illinois", that would be a mile high (over 1,600 meters). The structure was never built, but man's quest for such buildings has flourished. If you love tall buildings, this is the place for you. Not only will you find enough information to satiate your desires, you will feel right at home among those who worship tall buildings as more than just jumbo-sized structures. Tall buildings speak deep to our psyche, in an innate sexual way (which I would explain were this not a family book). So what is the tallest building in the world? It's more or less a tie. Officially, the tallest buildings in the world are the Petronas Towers, a pair of buildings in Kuala Lumpur, Malaysia, that reach a height of 450 meters (1,476 feet). However, the Sears Tower in Chicago, a close second at 444 meters (1,454 feet), is actually 520 meters (1,707 feet) if you count the antenna on top. (In Chicago, they count the antenna on top.)

Web:
http://www.dcircle.com/wtb.html

Don't know where to start? See "Connecting to the Internet".

ARCHITECTURE

Wright, Frank Lloyd

Frank Lloyd Wright (1869-1959) was an American architect whose innovations later set standards in architecture. Wright invented the "prairie style" of home and believed in eliminating traditional room divisions in order to create a living space that was more in tune with the needs of the inhabitants. These Web pages have lots of great information about Wright, along with pictures of his works.

Web:
  http://selfpub.www.columbia.mo.us/~jmiller/wright1.html
  http://www.erols.com/dchandlr/fllw.htm
  http://www.franklloydwright.org/

ART

African Art

An enduring theme in African art is that ideas about life—both spiritual and worldly—can be portrayed through the rendering of human and animal images. Thus, masks, carvings, paintings and other works represent ideas and feelings. Here are some good places to start exploring African art and to appreciate its unique flavor.

Web:
  http://satie.arts.usf.edu/~ooguibe/africa.htm
  http://www.artnetweb.com/guggenheim/africa/
  http://www.si.edu/organiza/museums/africart/exhibits/currexhb.htm

---

"Art Nouveau" is just another way of saying "New Art". (We just say it in French to make it more classy.) So take a look at the Internet's **Art Nouveau** overview, and soon you will be saying "Zut alors!"(French for "Way cool, Dude".)

Art Conservation

Human beings have strong ties to the past. We may not realize it day to day, but what we think and what we do is influenced enormously by the people who preceded us. Although technology and fashion change, human nature doesn't. By studying art, we form a connection to our past, which allows us to understand the present. However, you can't study art if it doesn't exist: once a work of art deteriorates, the original quality is gone forever. Thus, if we don't spend our time, effort and money to preserve our heritage, we may lose it. Modern art conservation not only deals with traditional problems (such as molds and pests), but also with new techniques such as digital imaging and electronic records.

Web:
  http://palimpsest.stanford.edu/
  http://www2.lib.udel.edu/subj/artc/internet.htm

Art Criticism Forum

When it comes to art, everybody may know what they like, but not everybody's opinion is worthwhile. If you are serious about art, you may want to participate in an art criticism discussion. At least you can be sure there will always be one person who knows what he is talking about.

Listserv Mailing List:
  List Name: **artcrit**
  Subscribe to: **listserv@yorku.ca**

Art Dictionary

How well do you know your art terminology? Here is a comprehensive, well-designed art dictionary that is only a mouse click away. Never again need you feel embarrassed because you thought that gouache, mischio and sinopia were the names of the Three Musketeers. (A gouache is heavy, opaque watercolor paint; a mischio is a smoky pattern in marble; sinopia is a reddish-brown earth color.)

Web:
  http://www.artlex.com/

ART 35

Art History

I have mixed feelings about art history. Learning about art by studying paintings, sculpture, architecture, and the artists themselves can teach us to appreciate the creative spirit of human beings at their very best. However, it is all too common for art history courses to degenerate into the mindless memorization of slide after slide after slide (so you can identify them in order to pass the exam). Don't consign yourself to a life of temporarily force-feeding hundreds of images into your cerebrum. Use the Net to immerse yourself in a sea of electronic resources, and enjoy some of mankind's greatest creations at your own speed.

Web:
http://home.mtholyoke.edu/~klconner/parthenet.html
http://witcombe.bcpw.sbc.edu/ARTHLinks.html

Art News

Don't get left out of the cool art scene. No matter where on Earth you are—London, Cairo, or Fargo, North Dakota—you can keep up with the latest happenings in the art world.

Web:
http://www.artnet.com/magazine/
http://www.cdes.qut.edu.au/fineart_online/
http://www.msstate.edu/fineart_online/

Art Nouveau

The Art Nouveau movement flourished as a style of architecture and decoration in the 1890s and early 1900s. Art Nouveau started in France (in Paris and then the city of Nancy) and from there spread to major European centers in other countries. Here is a nice overview of the Art Nouveau movement as it manifested itself in various European cities. Take a look at representative examples within the decorative arts, as well as a variety of buildings designed in the Art Nouveau style.

Web:
http://www.loria.fr/AN/EN/menuAN.html

Art Resources

The best thing about art is you can define it to be whatever you want. For example, this book is a work of art (as are the Eiffel Tower, the Mona Lisa and Mickey Mouse). To a greater or lesser degree, all of us have some creativity. In fact, the urge to create art is one of the distinguishing characteristics that separate us from the lower animals (although my cat once constructed a fascinating collage involving a dead mouse, some tufts of grass and a piece of leftover tuna). So when you are ready for an *expérience d'art*, start by visiting the Internet, where you can enjoy the good, the bad, the ugly, and the I-know-what-I-like-when-I-see-it.

Web:
http://www.art.net/
http://www.artresources.com/
http://www.fineart.com/FineArtGuide/contents.html

Art Talk and General Discussion

Here are the places on Usenet where artists gather to talk about the art community. These discussion groups are where you can post announcements about new exhibits and gallery openings, rant about the politics of art, and offer critical appraisal and analysis.

Usenet:
alt.airbrush.art
alt.art
alt.art.caricature
alt.art.illustration
alt.art.video
alt.art.virtual-beret
alt.artcom
alt.arts
alt.illustration
rec.arts.fine
rec.arts.misc

LOOKING FOR AN ART JURY OF YOUR PEERS?

Try the **alt.art.com** discussion group. No need to waste your time hanging around a coffee house talking about the art world, when you can sit around your own house, drinking coffee and discussing the art world.

Ascii Art

There is no sense getting your hands dirty just to make art. Have a blast making cool pictures without ever having to throw down a dropcloth or stink up your room with brain-damaging chemicals. There are loads and loads of ascii art resources on the Net.

Web:
  http://www.auburn.edu/~norgapd/

Usenet:
  alt.ascii-art
  alt.ascii-art.animation
  rec.arts.ascii

Listserv Mailing List:
  List Name: **asciiart**
  Subscribe to: listserv@lsv.uky.edu

Basic Design in Art and Architecture

There is more to art and architecture than just expressing yourself. You have to do it in a way in which nobody gets killed. At least in architecture. (In the art world, you just call it performance art, and that makes it okay.) Participate in discussion relating to basic and applied design as it relates to both art and architecture.

Listserv Mailing List:
  List Name: **design-l**
  Subscribe to: listserv@lists.psu.edu

Body Art

Pierced, tattooed, scarred, painted, and more. These resources are where you can find body art in all its forms.

Web:
  http://www.bioch.ox.ac.uk/~jr/henna/
  http://www.eskimo.com/~rab/

Usenet:
  alt.art.bodypainting
  rec.arts.bodyart

Need advice? See "Advice".

I Too, You Too, We All Too for Tattoo

Only a humph-brained ignoramus would think that decorating your body by permanent disfigurement is foolish. After all, if God didn't want us to modify our outer covering in the name of Art, why did he give us safety pins (and needles and knives and paper shredders)?

Personally, I feel that the human body comes with only the minimum set of holes, and anyone who wants to add to the collection has a perfect right to do so. If cleanliness is next to godliness, then holiness must be next to... well, I'm not quite sure, but it must be something important.

So next time you have a few spare moments and it is not too close to mealtime, spend some time reading the body art discussion groups. I guarantee a fun time for all and more than a few ideas for how to decorate the neighbors' children next Christmas.

ART 37

Ceramic Arts

We're talking about clay here. Mushy, moist, malleable clay. And glazes. Mellifluous, marvelous, multicolored glazes. Not to mention kilns, pottery wheels, greenware and extruders. I love ceramics (inorganic, nonmetallic solids processed at high temperatures) and what you can do with them. So hot, yet, so cool.

Web:
http://apple.sdsu.edu/ceramicsweb/
http://ikts.ikts.fhg.de/VL.artistic.ceramics.html

Listserv Mailing List:
List Name: **clayart**
Subscribe to: **listserv@lsv.uky.edu**

Yes, it's true: in Ceramic City, there are two pots for every guy (and gal).

Ceramic City

Join the **clayart** mailing list and have your mailbox filled with information and discussion that will bring fire to your life and make your eyes glaze over in happiness.

Contemporary Art Mailing List

Don't believe any rumors you might hear about art being dead. It's alive and well and contemplating itself on this mailing list devoted to the discussion of issues relevant to contemporary art.

Listserv Mailing List:
List Name: **artlist**
Subscribe to: **listserv@listserv.arizona.edu**

Gargoyles and Grotesques

Are you a fan of the dark? Do you, at sunset, glance upward to see the grotesque statuary on the edges of skyscrapers or Gothic cathedrals? These Web sites are devoted to gargoyles old and new, as well as grotesque statues of every sort. They provide a history of and writings about this unique form of sculpture, as well as dramatic pictures of some of its more interesting examples.

Web:
http://ils.unc.edu/garg/garghp4.html
http://www.stonecarver.com/gargoyle.html

So what do you do if you're not married and you don't have a mother-in-law?

Not to worry. The **Gargoyles and Grotesques** site is open, round the clock, to fulfill your need for surreal scariness.

Impressionism

Impressionism is a style of painting that started in France during the 1860s. Impressionist paintings portray a quick visual impression of a scene (often a landscape), with particular attention being paid to the effects of light. Such paintings are particularly soothing and inviting, with almost universal appeal. Among the well-known Impressionists were Claude Monet, Edgar Degas, Camille Pissarro and Pierre Auguste Renoir. The name "Impressionism" comes from one of Monet's paintings, exhibited in 1874 under the name "Impression Sunrise".

Web:
http://campus.tam.itesm.mx/~jdorante/art/impresi/iimpre01.htm
http://www.columbia.edu/~jns16/monet_html/monet.html

Mail Art

Mail art is a fun means of creating interactive art that stays in the hands of the artists, instead of being behind glass or in stuffy exhibits. Find out more about mail and email art, see images of mail art, and get a list of people on the Net who participate in mail art.

Web:
http://www.millkern.com/webdoc/home.html
http://www.rt66.com/~dragonfy/

Native American Art

Prior to the twentieth century, native Americans did not create art as an end unto itself. Rather, they created crafts that fit into their ceremonies and their everyday activities. The twentieth century has seen a great deal of purposeful art development based on these early traditions and skills. These Native American art sites contain museums, galleries and collections in which you will find a wide variety of information regarding contemporary Native American art.

Web:
http://hanksville.phast.umass.edu/misc/NAart.html
http://www.artnatam.com/

Pop Art

Pop Art focuses on objects taken from the popular urban culture, such as advertisements, comics, and the labels and packages used with mass-produced consumer products. The basic idea was to fashion art based on vernacular images and icons shared by everyone. Pop Art originated in London in the mid-1950s with the work of the Independent Group. Within several years, the same type of ideas were being explored in the United States, where they flourished into the 1960s, partially as a reaction to Abstract Expressionism. The most well-known Pop Art artists were Richard Hamilton, Andy Warhol, Roy Lichtenstein, Claes Oldenburg, Jasper Johns and Robert Rauschenberg.

Web:
http://www.fi.muni.cz/~toms/PopArt/
http://www.fi.muni.cz/~toms/PopArt/Overview/intro.html

Student Artist Mailing List

Art is a personal experience, but there are people who understand how you feel. Join the student artist mailing list, and hang out with people who hang out with the type of people who understand how you feel.

Majordomo Mailing List:
List Name: **artist**
Subscribe to: **majordomo@qnet.com**

Surrealism

If you don't understand it, I can't explain it. Let your mind dance on the edge of radical thought. (Fish.) Take a look at paintings by famed Surrealists or participate in some fun Surrealism games like The Infinite Story or The Exquisite Cadaver. Don't be afraid. The only thing it can hurt is your brain.

Web:
http://gaia.lis.uiuc.edu/~lis35312/Surrhome.html
http://pharmdec.wustl.edu/juju/surr/surrealism.html

Women Artists in History

Here is *the* place to look for information about women artists. The site is built around a list of women artists from medieval times to the twentieth century. If information exists on the Net about a particular artist, a helpful link is provided. Keep this address handy. There aren't that many places you can go in the middle of the night when you need to find out if Hildegard von Bingen lived before or after Maria Sybilla Merian. This Web site is also special because Frida Kahlo and Georgia O'Keeffe used to hang out here when they were kids.

Web:
http://www.wendy.com/women/artists.html

**Do you like weirdness?
Check out "UFOs and Aliens".**

ART GALLERIES AND EXHIBITS

Alphonse Mucha Museum

Alphonse Maria Mucha (1860-1939) was a Czech artist remembered for his posters created in the French Art Nouveau period. He was propelled into stardom when he was commissioned to create posters of Sarah Bernhardt, an actress who was in vogue in the late 1800s. Mucha's work is characterized by a predominance of curves and flowing lines, and abstract and stylized motifs from nature, such as flowers. At the time, there was a growing interest in decorative art and a relaxation of the Victorian attitudes. Mucha's more free and sensual style was heartily welcomed. Take a look at the beautiful works of Alphonse Mucha. This Web site has many of his works, including some of the advertisement graphics he did for companies like Nestle foods.

Web:
http://www.webcom.com/ajarts/mucha.html

Art Crimes

Graffiti is often referred to as "art crime" because even though it can sometimes be beautiful, it's still illegal. Take a photo-tour of art crimes around the world. Many of these places no longer exist, so this will be your only chance to see them.

Web:
http://www.graffiti.org/

Usenet:
alt.graffiti

Art Gallery Talk and General Discussion

There are lots of things happening in the art scene, and one way to keep up is to follow what's happening in this Usenet group. When the time comes that your work is going in exhibition, you can announce it here.

Usenet:
alt.art.scene

Asian Art Gallery

Cure that craving for the exotic with a visit to the Asian Art Gallery. Explore an exhibit on Tibetan mandalas or a collection of Himalayan art. You will also find information and photos of art from China, India and Mongolia.

Web:
http://www.webart.com/asianart/

Baroque Art

The Baroque movement involved European painting, sculpture and architecture, particularly in the Catholic countries, from about 1600 to 1750. Baroque style was an outgrowth of the Renaissance. The work emphasized unity and balance, and many ornate, ambitious works were created featuring detailed parts put together to form a single large composition. Among the most important Baroque artists are Caravaggio (1571-1610), Peter Rubens (1577-1640), Diego Velázquez (1599-1660), Rembrandt Van Rijn (1606-1669) and Jan Vermeer (1632-1675).

Web:
http://www-lib.haifa.ac.il/www/art/bar_menu.html
http://www.parsons.edu/~va2/BAROQART.HTM

Carlos Museum of Art

Get your daily dose of culture by looking at images of ancient Egypt, the ancient Americas, art from Asia, Greece, Rome and sub-Saharan Africa. You will see ancient artifacts such as a cuneiform tablet, a mummy, and an engraved effigy, among others. Also available are later works on paper, such as manuscripts and scrolls.

Web:
http://www.cc.emory.edu/CARLOS/

Digital Photography

A display of the winners of annual juried contests of digital photography. These images began life as mere photographs or film and video and were then transformed into new art forms using a computer. Since this contest is held annually, you can also get information on how to enter your work in future events.

Web:
http://www.bradley.edu/exhibit/

40 ART GALLERIES AND EXHIBITS

Digital Photography

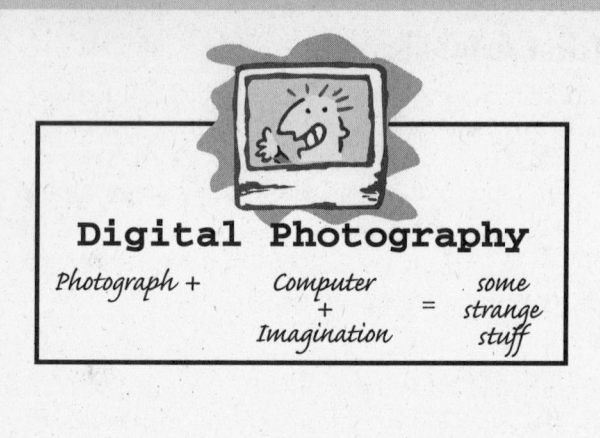

Photograph + Computer + Imagination = some strange stuff

Erté Museum

Erté was an Art Deco artist born in Russia. (His original name was Romain de Tirtoff.) He moved to Paris in 1912 to become a fashion illustrator and called himself Erté, after the French pronunciation of his initials. He is best known for his extravagant costumes for ballet and the opera, as well as Harper's Bazaar illustrations. His fashion career spanned his entire life—he designed outrageous clothing for approximately 75 years. This Web site contains a nice collection and some writing about Erté.

Web:
  http://www.webcom.com/ajarts/erte.html

French Age of Enlightenment

In France, the Age of Enlightenment is considered to be the time between the death of Louis XIV (1715) and the acquisition of power by Napoléon Bonaparte (1799). Throughout Europe, this period was marked by significant intellectual and scientific advances. The art of this time was more sensible than that of the preceding Rococo period, demonstrating a serious and moralistic approach to creation. (Although it's hard to believe, there was a time when moral virtue and sensibility were considered characteristics to be admired.) The paintings in these exhibits, all of which are from national museums in France, show us the work of the artists who flourished during the seventy-five years of domestic peace and prosperity (not a common phenomenon in the history of France) that led up to the revolution.

Web:
  http://mistral.culture.fr/files/
  imaginary_exhibition.html

Imagebase

The Fine Arts Museum of San Francisco maintains this Web site, where you can view a large portion of their collections. Enjoy exhibits devoted to European paintings, African art, American paintings, European porcelain, European glass and ancient art. To make the experience complete, after you look at some paintings, run around the room and yell, "Clang, clang", as if you were on a cable car.

Web:
  http://www.thinker.org/imagebase/

Leonardo da Vinci Museum

See the work of the master who put the word "Renaissance" in "Renaissance Man". Painter, inventor, architect, writer, musician and all-around genius, Leonardo is a household name in the world of art. This site displays his oil paintings, futuristic designs, drawings and sketches, and biographical information on the man who made Mona Lisa smile.

Web:
  http://sunsite.unc.edu/wm/paint/auth/vinci/

Los Angeles County Museum of Art

There is more to the city of Los Angeles than what you read in the National Enquirer. For instance, the Los Angeles County Museum of Art has quite a collection of beautiful artwork and interesting cultural costumes and textiles. See selected images of ancient and Islamic art, European paintings and sculpture, and art of the twentieth century as well as links to other art sites.

Web:
  http://www.lacma.org/

Louvre Museum

Here's your chance to visit Paris free of charge. Get a ticket to the virtual Louvre, which is conducting tours around the city. You will see the Eiffel Tower and the Champs Elysees, among other sights. At the Louvre itself, they offer tours of a collection of famous paintings and a demonstration of French medieval art. You have to bring your own pastries.

Web:
  http://www.louvre.fr/

ART GALLERIES AND EXHIBITS — 41

Art+L.A.= Culture to the Max

A quick trip to the Los Angeles County Museum of Art Web site is one that should be on everyone's cultural agenda. Of course, you will find the usual ancient Islamic and European art, as well as the mandatory collection of priceless paintings and sculpture. All of that is nice, of course, but nothing that you couldn't find on the walls of your local Water, Sewer and Trash Administration Building.

But what you can't find elsewhere are exhibits that capture the essence of the true Southern California creative soul. For example, does the Louvre have an entire room devoted to toupees worn by famous film stars? Can the Sistine Chapel offer a collection as inspiring as the photographic exhibition of *all* of Johnny Carson's wives? And is there anything in New York the poor East Coast wannabe that even approaches the beauty and inspiration of the Winners of the Annual TV Guide Advertisement Collage Contest?

I think not. We in Southern California are proud of our creative heritage and our contributions to world culture, and we love to share.

M.C. Escher Gallery

Maurits Cornelis Escher was not only a master at paradox and illusion, but he could draw an exquisite likeness of anything he could see or imagine. Artists, mathematicians, scientists and the general consumer are all fascinated by his many graphic images on one level or another. Whether he stimulates your eye or your mind, these sites will be interesting to you.

Web:
http://www.worldofescher.com/

National Museum of American Art

There is more to good American art than the Sunday newspaper comics. View not only the permanent collection of the National Museum of American Art, but also some spectacular roving collections and exhibits.

Web:
http://www.nmaa.si.edu/

Pinup Art

In the world of art, what could be more accessible (and more American) than the pinup, a rendering of an idealized girl-next-door, suitable for framing? A study of the pinup leads us away from philosophy, art history and symbolism, and takes us firmly into the part of the world in which "I may not know art, but I know what I like" provides the dominant framework for aesthetic appreciation. The Impressionists, Post-Impressionists, Cubists and Abstract Expressionists may all be important to our culture, but for pure, down-home *enjoyment*, the work of, say, Alberto Vargas (1896-1982) provides a visceral impetus that goes a long way toward hitting the lover of fine art on a gut level. After all, the wholesomeness of Betty Crocker in the kitchen may be a comforting and nurturing part of our culture, but, I have to admit, I'd much rather spend an evening in the living room looking at pinups of Bettie Page.

Web:
http://www.greatamericanpinup.com/
http://www.webjerk.com/pinup/

42 ART GALLERIES AND EXHIBITS

Sistine Chapel

If you can't get the time off from work to go see the Sistine Chapel, take a mini-vacation right now. Use your browser to take a tour of Cappella Sistina, where you will see hundreds of images of the chapel's artwork and read informative text about the chapel and its history.

Web:
   http://www.christusrex.org/www1/sistine/0-Tour.html

Treasures of the Czars

This is an excellent exhibit of art, icons, jewelry, armor and other items from the Russian Romanov dynasty. This site not only has images, but also useful historical information, fun games and a crash course on the Russian language. Even if you don't care anything about Russian art, you can still learn important phrases such as, "Grouper is the local specialty."

Web:
   http://www.sptimes.com/Treasures/Default.html

Wish Upon a Falling Czar

On March 10, 1917, the troops of Czar Nicolas II of Russia mutinied. On March 11, the Czar ordered the dissolution of the legislature, but the members refused to honor the order. And on March 15, in the face of increasingly powerful unrest, the Czar decided to abdicate.

Clearly, being a Czar is a high-stress occupation that is probably not for everyone. However, if there is one thing good about being His Royal Excellency, it is the magnificent art collection that is yours to enjoy in your moments of leisure.

For example, we might imagine Czar Nicolas II saying to himself, "Sure, the peasants are revolting and my soldiers refuse to obey my commands, but I can still sit on my throne and admire this totally cool Fabergé egg with the tiny copy of a Harley Hahn book inside." (Of course, he would be saying it in Russian, but you get the idea.)

For many years, such treasures were hidden from the world, but now, through the courtesy of the Internet, you can share in the art and culture of the Romanov dynasty. From 1613 to 1917, these awesome dudes (and dudettes) collected enough art to choke a Siberian horse. And if they were alive today, there would be nothing they would enjoy more than having you drop in and look around.

Need a job?
See "Jobs and the Workplace".
Got a job? See "Fun".

Van Gogh Gallery

Vincent Van Gogh (1853-1890) was a Dutch painter whose work became one of the seminal influences of twentieth century art. Van Gogh was at once immensely talented, innovative and disturbed. For example, at the end of 1888, he cut off his ear following a violent argument with the painter Paul Gauguin (1848-1903). Over the next two years, Van Gogh, suffering from bouts of madness, produced a vast number of brilliantly colored and maniacally frenzied paintings. In the last 70 days of his life, he painted 70 pictures, following which he took his own life. Van Gogh's hypersensitivity to life and sensation led him to create an oeuvre that is unmatched in the history of art. Although there is a great deal of talent, innovation and emotional disturbance in the world, it rarely comes together in the same place at the same time.

Web:
   http://sunsite.unc.edu/wm/paint/auth/gogh/
   http://www.iscs.nus.edu.sg/~tanmingm/vangogh/
   http://www.openface.ca/~vangogh/

Vatican Exhibit

Here is a wonderful resource from the U.S. Library of Congress: an exhibition of Vatican history and culture. Here you can find a great deal of fascinating information as well as some wonderfully unexpected treasures: a fifteenth century manuscript of a Latin translation of Archimedes' mathematics, a Carolingian manuscript of the Roman comic poet Plautusy, and an original autographed Harley Hahn book used by the Pope to teach himself how to send email.

Web:
   http://www.ncsa.uiuc.edu/SDG/Experimental/vatican.exhibit/Vatican.exhibit.html

ASTRONOMY

World Art Treasures

An art lover's fantasy: you're going through a bunch of junk at a yard sale and you find an old sculpture that turns out to be a lost treasure from the fifth century. Prepare yourself for those weekend jaunts from sale to sale. Brush up on art treasures from places such as Egypt, China, Japan, India, Burma, Laos and Thailand so you will recognize that precious gem when you find it, although these are items you will probably not find lying around your neighborhood.

Web:
http://sgwww.epfl.ch/BERGER/

World Wide Art Resources

There are a large number of art museums and galleries in the world, many of which have information and exhibits on the Net. These sites offer comprehensive collections of information and are definitely places to start when you are looking for a museum or gallery anywhere in the world. I like visiting these sites for two reasons. First, when I have a few minutes, they are great places to browse. I can always find a new online exhibit to explore. Second, before I travel anywhere, I check out all the museums and galleries in the area to see what looks good.

Web:
http://wwar.com/galleries.html
http://wwar.com/museums.html

ASTRONOMY

Astronomy and Astrophysics Research

It's hard to enjoy your life if you have heavy stuff on your mind like the anisotropy of gamma ray bursts or whether the sun actually has a south pole. If your local theologian can't help you solve the mystery of the universe, maybe here you will find someone who can. These folks know their astronomy and astrophysics.

Usenet:
sci.astro.research

Astronomy Cafe

Sit around in the Astronomy Cafe and contemplate the stars, browse the weekly hotlist, ask questions in "Ask the Astronomer", and even listen to music which rounds out the cafe motif.

Web:
http://www2.ari.net/home/odenwald/cafe.html

Astronomy History

The study of astronomy is as old as the study of science. Aristarchus of Samos (310-230 B.C.), an early Greek astronomer, suggested that the Earth rotated on its axis and that the planets rotate around the sun in circular orbits. (Actually, the orbits are elliptical.) He also used his own observations along with his knowledge of geometry to determine the relative sizes of the Earth, the moon and the sun, and the distances between them. Personally, I have always been fascinated by man's quest to understand the cosmos. Yes, there were a few false starts (like the Dark Ages and the sixteenth century Catholic Church), but by and large, mankind has made enormous progress in understanding the nature of our universe.

Web:
http://www.astro.uni-bonn.de/~pbrosche/hist_astr/
http://www-hpcc.astro.washington.edu/scied/astro/astrohistory.html

Listserv Mailing List:
List Name: **hastro-l**
Subscribe to: **listserv@wvnvm.wvnet.edu**

Astronomy Hypertextbook

Back in the old days, most of us had to lug around 150 pounds of dull, dry textbooks, and the only fun that could be had was to devise ways of writing graffiti in them without getting caught. With hypertext languages, textbooks become interactive and fun. Plus, you can sneak around and play games on the computer while the teacher isn't looking. Check out this fun and informative textbook that gives learning astronomy a whole new twist.

Web:
http://zebu.uoregon.edu/text.html

ASTRONOMY

Don't take a chance of getting lost in hyperspace. Carry the Astronomy Hypertextbook with you wherever you go.

Astronomy Software

The days have long passed since an astronomer could operate with a telescope and a notebook. Modern astronomy requires a lot of computers and a lot of computer programs. Here is a comprehensive collection of links to many different sites containing astronomy software. Whatever you need—everything under (and over) the sun—if it's available on the Net, you will probably find it here.

Web:

http://www.stsci.edu/astroweb/yp_software.html

Astronomy Talk and General Discussion

Would you like to talk with people who really do understand black holes? Join the astronomers on Usenet and discuss all aspects of astronomy and astrophysics: stars, planets, telescopes, cosmology, space exploration, and so on. The **sci.astro.amateur** group is specifically for amateur astronomers.

Usenet:
  alt.sci.astro.hale.bopp
  alt.telescopes.meade.lx200
  rec.radio.amateur.space
  sci.astro
  sci.astro.amateur
  sci.astro.ccd-imaging
  sci.astro.fits
  sci.astro.hubble
  sci.astro.planetarium
  sci.astro.satellites.visual-observe

Astrophysics Data System

The Astrophysics Data System allows access to hundreds of thousands of abstracts (astronomy and astrophysics, space instrumentation, physics and geophysics, and more), as well as access or links to archives and catalogs of astronomical data, including data collected by NASA space missions.

Web:

http://adswww.harvard.edu/

Bad Astronomy

Philip Plait, the Bad Astronomer, is an astronomer, but he's not really bad. Rather, he brings to our attention, and explains, examples of bad (incorrect) astronomy from movies, television and newspapers. Ironically, by reading about bad astronomy, you can learn a lot of actual science, which makes Dr. Plait good indeed.

Web:

http://smart.net/~badastro/bad.html

Constellations

Look up into the night sky when the stars are visible, and you will begin to see patterns. Since ancient times, men have identified such patterns, called constellations, and given them names. The oldest references to constellations are from the ancient Greeks, although those constellations probably originated even earlier, among the Sumerians and Babylonians. The modern system of constellations is based on the Greek ones, but has been codified and expanded to cover the entire sky (including the southern areas that were not visible to the Greeks). Today, we recognize 88 different constellations. As you look at the stars, remember that the constellations are artificial constructions made up by people. Only the stars are real.

Web:

http://galileo.gmu.edu/constellation/
  constellation.html
http://www.astro.wisc.edu/~dolan/constellations/
http://www.physics.csbsju.edu/astro/asp/
  constellation.faq.html

ASTRONOMY

Dark Sky Stargazing

One time I was camping by myself in a national park east of San Diego, and I ran into a couple of teenagers who had never been out of the city. While talking to them, I found out they had never seen the Milky Way (the long, extended clumping of stars that is actually part of our galaxy), because the lights of the city were so bright as to obscure most of the stars. It wasn't until the boys had finally ventured to the countryside that they were able to see this remarkable phenomenon. Astronomers (professional and amateur) have the same problem. Cities create so much light pollution as to seriously impact astronomical observation. To look at the heavens, you need a dark sky, and these Web sites can help you find it.

Web:
http://proxima.astro.Virginia.EDU/~ida/darksky/
http://www.darksky.org/

> The Net wasn't built in a day.

Earth Views

It's all a matter of perspective. No matter where you go on the Earth, you can never see the entire thing. These days, you don't have to be an astronaut to enjoy a nice view of the Earth from space. Check out this collection of photos of the Earth. If you know the latitude and longitude of your house, you can find the corresponding pictures and make a map with a big X and label it "You are here."

Web:
http://images.jsc.nasa.gov/iams/html/earth.htm

Look What I Found on the Net...

```
Subject: Sunspots and Global Climate — An Apology
Newsgroup: rec.radio.amateur.space

Over the last few months, I've tried to provoke some discussion
on sunspots and climate, a subject I got interested in as a ham
radio operator years ago.

Lots of people responded, but an article I read the other day
finally put the while thing into perspective. I realized I'd
been preaching to the choir, and also that it's likely to be
some time before a real solar/Earth connection is developed.

It seems that a lot of scientists have found strong correlations
between solar change and climate/weather change on Earth...
The problem is they are ONLY correlations, and we do not yet
understand the mechanisms... Proof according to the "scientific
method" is needed, and proof promises to be hard to come by...

My apologies to anyone and everyone I may have misunderstood.
Like many, I have a real gut feeling that the sun is a major
player in our weather patterns and long-term climate, but I now
understand that we have to play by the rules. Until these things
get proven out it's premature to tout solar power as the real
biggie...
```

46 ASTRONOMY

Observatories and Telescopes

One of the things I like best about the Net is that it provides a place for information that literally did not exist before there was an international computer network. For example, say that you want to look for a particular observatory or telescope. Before the Net existed, where could you even look for an up-to-date master list? Now it's easy to find what you want. Just check these sites and find links to hundreds of observatories and telescopes all over the globe.

Web:
  http://webhead.com/WWWVL/Astronomy/astroweb/yp_telescope.html
  http://webhead.com/WWWVL/Astronomy/observatories-optical.html

Eclipses

An eclipse occurs when one heavenly body casts a shadow on another. To Earthbound observers (you and me), the most important eclipses are those in which the moon comes between us and the sun (a solar eclipse), and those in which the Earth comes between the moon and the sun (a lunar eclipse). The most spectacular eclipses are total solar eclipses, in which the moon, for a short time, will almost completely block the light from the sun. In other words, the moon casts its shadow on the Earth. If you happen to be in this shadow, you will see the awesome sight of the disc of the sun being slowly covered and then, a few minutes later, regain its original appearance. These Web sites contain pictures of eclipses and information about future eclipses.

Web:
  http://planets.gsfc.nasa.gov/eclipse/eclipse.html
  http://www.earthview.com/resources/links.htm
  http://www.skypub.com/eclipses/eclipses.shtml

Peculiar Galaxies

In the 1960s, the astronomer Halton C. Arp collected images of 338 "peculiar galaxies", that is, galaxies with unusual or abnormal shapes. Arp published a book called the Atlas of Peculiar Galaxies, which has become the standard reference work for what many people now refer to as "Arp objects". Arp's work contributed greatly to the study of the nature of galaxies, and, today, there are Arp enthusiasts around the world who photograph as many Arp objects as they can. Start here if you would like to learn more about these intriguing galactic phenomena (and look at some cool pictures).

Web:
  http://users.aol.com/arpgalaxy/
  http://www.mcs.net/~bstevens/al/obsclubs/arppec.html

Mars Atlas

These Web sites are just as good as being on Mars. Better, really, if you think about how much you save in gas money by not going there. Check out all the cool pictures you can see of the surface of Mars. If you look hard enough, maybe you will see those little men that Ray Bradbury is always going on about.

Web:
  http://cass.jsc.nasa.gov/expmars/expmars.html
  http://fi-www.arc.nasa.gov/fia/projects/bayes-group/Atlas/Mars/

**Buy something.
Sell something.
See "Buying and Selling".**

ASTRONOMY 47

Planets and the Solar System

You and I may be stuck on Earth, but these resources are out of this world. You will find a great deal of information about the solar system: the planets, asteroids, comets and meteors in our immediate astronomical neighborhood. For ongoing discussion, you can participate in the Usenet group. This is also the place to talk about the various space missions exploring the planets.

Web:
   http://bang.lanl.gov/solarsys/
   http://nssdc.gsfc.nasa.gov/planetary/planetfact.html
   http://ranier.oact.hq.nasa.gov/sensors_page/planets.html
   http://seds.lpl.arizona.edu/nineplanets/nineplanets/nineplanets.html

Usenet:
   alt.sci.planetary

PLANETS ARE COOL

Yes, there is no doubt about it, planets are high up on just about everybody's list of favorite astronomical objects. Join the folks on **alt.sci.planetary** and talk about the large, significant objects that comprise our solar system, and our efforts to visit them before prices go up.

SkyView

SkyView is a sophisticated tool that allows you to look at various parts of the sky in different wavelengths. However, SkyView does not show you real images: rather, it creates the images you want, based on your specifications, by using an extensive database of astronomical observations. In other words, SkyView is a virtual telescope. The system is set up with various interfaces, for both professional astronomers and amateurs.

Web:
   http://skyview.gsfc.nasa.gov/

Starpages

The Starpages are the Yellow Pages of the astronomy world. Put this site on your bookmark list, and start your search here when you are looking for an astronony-related organization, institution, association or company. This is also the place to look when you are trying to find a particular person or astronomy researcher. In addition, there is a database you can use to look up abbreviations and acronyms. (I found more than 30 different meanings for the acronym "ABC".)

Web:
   http://cdsweb.u-strasbg.fr/~heck/sf.htm

Sunspots

Sunspots are relatively dark areas that appear on the sun from time to time (although you need a telescope with a special filter to see them). Sunspot activity goes through 11.3-year cycles that affect our local environment. In 1852, for example, the Swiss astronomer Rudolf Wolf first correlated sunspots and magnetic variations on Earth. For more up-to-date research information, see your friendly Internet sunspot site.

Web:
   http://athena.wednet.edu/curric/space/sun/sunspot.html

48 ASTRONOMY

Telescopes

It's tempting to rush out and buy a telescope, but don't. Take time, before you buy, to learn what you are doing. I once bought a high-quality telescope, and I sure was glad I did some research before I made my selection. Here are some resources to help you, including a FAQ (frequently asked question list) about buying and using a telescope. Harley's Rules for Buying a Telescope: (1) When it comes to telescopes, you get what you pay for. (2) The one you need costs more than you can afford.

Web:
http://www.astronomy.ohio-state.edu/~perkins/FAQ.index.html
http://www.atmpage.com/
http://www.skypub.com/backyard/chooscop.html

USGS Astronomy Resources

The next time you are looking for a particular astronomy site, start your search here, a registry operated by the U.S. Geological Survey. As a service to the research community, the USGS maintains links to educational and non-profit astronomy resources around the world.

Web:
http://www.usgs.gov/network/science/astronomy/

Webstars

Webstars is a collection of astronomical resource sites created by the High Energy Astrophysics Science Archive Research Center (HEASARC) at NASA's Goddard Space Flight Center. What I like best about Webstars is it is a great place to browse for fun. You can read about comets, meteors, asteroids, planets and the solar system. You will also find information about space exploration, astronomy magazines, and the history of astronomy. My personal favorite is looking through the various astronomical images. Hint for Windows 95 users: When you find an image you like, set it as the background for your desktop. [1] Use Netscape or Internet Explorer to find a particularly cool astronomical image. [2] With your mouse, right-click on the image. You will see a list of choices. [3] Choose "Set as wallpaper". The background on your desktop is now the image you selected. (If you want to set the background back the way it was, right-click on the desktop and choose "Properties". Then click on the "Background" tab.)

Web:
http://heasarc.gsfc.nasa.gov/docs/www_info/webstars.html

AVIATION

Aerobatic Aviation

Aerobatics are for everyone. Even people who know nothing about airplanes are in awe when they see a highly trained aerobatic pilot doing stunts that seem to defy the laws of physics. Here is information about aerobatics, including the most famous of the aerobatic groups, the U.S. Navy's Blue Angels.

Web:
http://acro.harvard.edu/IAC/iac_homepg.html
http://www.airspacemag.com/expo/wac/
http://www.blueangels.navy.mil/
http://www.worldaerobatics.com/

Aeronet

Here is where the world of commercial aviation meets the Net. Aeronet is *the* place to look for airline info: news, company information, academic institutions, conferences, manufacturers, organizations, and much more. This is where I look when I need to find the Web site for a particular airline.

Web:
http://www.aeronet.co.uk/

Air Disasters

I am no stranger to aviation disasters. One time I took a dinner flight, and they forgot to put my special vegetarian meal on the plane. Another time, I asked for a glass of apple juice with no ice, but they gave me ice anyway. But the worst disaster—so bad that I actually wondered if I was going to make it—was the time I forgot to bring a book to read and had no choice but to watch an entire Meryl Streep movie. If you are an air disaster buff, here are some Internet resources that are right up your aerodynamic alley. Here is where you can look for timely information after an accident or other disaster, or—between accidents—discuss methods and investigations.

Web:
http://www.niweb.com/dnet/dnetGOjg/Disasters.htm

Usenet:
alt.disasters.aviation

AVIATION

Airline Travel

It you like to travel, you can use the Net to solve problems ahead of time. Before you leave, scope out the potential pitfalls with ticket purchases, layovers, connecting flights, luggage dramas and airline strikes. Information is available for the entire planet.

Web:
http://www.armchair.com/info/fly.html
http://www.naafa.org/documents/brochures/airtips.html

Usenet:
alt.airline.schedules
alt.flame.airlines
misc.transport.air-industry
rec.travel.air

Airplane Mailing Lists

Are you interested in flying? Here are some mailing lists you will enjoy. The **a51** list is for discussion of modifying and flying experimental aircraft; the **airline** list is concerned with airlines and civil aircraft; and **airplane-clubs** is for people discussing the airplane clubs. (Hint: If you would like to have your own plane but you find the cost and maintenance prohibitive, consider joining a club in which you will share the costs with other pilots.)

Listserv Mailing List:
List Name: **airline**
Subscribe to: listserv@cunyvm.cuny.edu

Listserv Mailing List:
List Name: **airplane-clubs**
Subscribe to: listserv@dg-rtp.dg.com

Majordomo Mailing List:
List Name: **a51**
Subscribe to: majordomo@mailinglists.org

Aviation Enthusiast Corner

You'll find a great deal of interesting material here to occupy those otherwise dull hours when you are on the ground. I particularly enjoy the stories written by a navigator who flew on the old B-52s, B-58s and the RF-4C. This Web site is also a good place to visit if you will be traveling in the United States and you want to find particular air shows or air museums.

Web:
http://aeroweb.brooklyn.cuny.edu/

Sharing an Airplane

For years you have been dreaming of having your own airplane; unfortunately, your two feet are firmly planted on the ground while your bank account grows slower than a dead Christmas tree. It's all too true that an airplane is just a hole in the sky into which you throw money.

Join the **airplane-clubs** mailing list and meet the people who form clubs to share the only hobby more expensive than running for Congress.

Aviation Events

What's going on? Do you have an open weekend you want to fill? Are you going to be traveling to a new city and want to catch some aviation action? Find out what's happening on the aviation scene.

Web:
http://www.airshows.com/
http://www.pattywagstaff.com/

Usenet:
rec.aviation.announce

50 AVIATION

All revved up and nowhere to go? Check the Net for **upcoming aviation events.**

Aviation Magazines

Check out the official Web pages for Air and Space magazine, AOPA Pilot, and U.S. Aviator. These sites include articles in current and past issues, links to air and space-related sites, a list of aviation events, and more.

Web:
  http://airspacemag.com/
  http://www.aopa.org/pilot/
  http://www.av8r.net/

Aviation Poetry

There's more to flying than just knowing which instruments to read and how many flight attendants it takes to screw in a light bulb. No, flying can be truly poetic, inspiration for songs of the soul. Read these poems about flight and flying, so on some dark, romantic night you can whisper into your beloved's ear a little poem that begins, "There once was a girl from Nantucket..."

Web:
  http://members.iquest.net/~jlevy/avpoem.html

Aviation Q & A

Looking for thorough, well-researched information on aviation? Or are you willing to pass on your knowledge through concise, streamlined postings? The Net has some stuff for you. This group is moderated, and it would be in your best interest to read the FAQ lists before posting.

Web:
  http://www.newsguy.com/~ericmax/faqs/faq.htm
  http://www.tc.faa.gov/ZDV/FAA/FAQ/faq.html

Usenet:
  rec.aviation.answers

Aviation Safety

We all know that flying is the safest way to fly. Why? Because pilots are trained to be dependable and cautious. However, airplanes are complex machines, and there are a lot of variables that affect your flight experience. Use these Net resources to keep yourself up to date on the newest safety-related information and news. Remember, the only good pilot is a living pilot.

Web:
  http://web.inter.nl.net/users/H.Ranter/
  http://www.aviation.org/
  http://www.tc.faa.gov/ZDV/GA/gaa.html

Usenet:
  alt.aviation.safety

The Net can help you buy a car. See "Cars and Trucks" or "Shopping".

AVIATION 51

> Heading for the final frontier? Take a look at "Star Trek" (or "Space").

Aviation Talk and General Discussion

You'll go into a flat spin when you see all the information you can find in these Usenet discussion groups. If you don't know how to choose one of the specific aviation groups, the Web site is a great place to start. There are often cross-postings from other groups to **.misc**, so you'll see a wide variety of topics, including comparisons of different types of planes, what to do about engine fires, pros and cons of leasing, and what happens when an instrument malfunctions. There's something for everyone.

Web:
http://www.aero.com/news/news.htm

Usenet:
alt.aviation.fun
rec.aviation
rec.aviation.aerobatics
rec.aviation.balloon
rec.aviation.ifr
rec.aviation.marketplace
rec.aviation.misc
rec.aviation.powerchutes
rec.aviation.products
rec.aviation.questions
rec.aviation.restoration
rec.aviation.rotorcraft
rec.aviation.seaplane
rec.aviation.simulators

Aviation Technology

Don't be content to just fly; dig deep into what makes aeronautics work. See the latest NASA press releases and learn about the physics of flight, pitch moment damping, aircraft stability, boarding design and technical safety.

Usenet:
sci.aeronautics
sci.aeronautics.airliners

DUATS

If you are a pilot, the Direct User Access Terminal Service (DUATS) is the place to get your weather briefings, plan your flight, and even file your flight plan. DUATS also offers other valuable services. Check it out the next time you plan a cross-country flight. (Please note that the site says, "You must hold a U.S. pilot's certificate and have a current medical to gain access to DUATS.")

Web:
http://www.skycentral.com/index.html#preflight

Flight Planning and Navigation

How would you feel if you planned to fly to Washington to help the President of the United States clean out his garage, and you got your directions mixed up and ended up in the middle of Disneyland? Imagine your embarrassment at spending an entire day with the wrong Mickey Mouse. Don't take chances: download a copy of free flight planning software and data today.

Web:
http://www.aero.com/plan/flitplng.htm
http://www.airnav.com/

Where am I ??????????????????

Plan to Plan a Flight Plan

Of course you need a flight plan. If you didn't have a plan, you might arrive at your destination and not even know it. Worse, you might never arrive, and someone else would end up getting your dessert at dinner.

Before you go, use the Net to help you create a flight plan. Check weather and current conditions, and download software to make the whole thing as easy as falling off an aviational log.

52 AVIATION

Hang-gliding and Paragliding

Some people say that Man was not designed to fly, but that's only because they have never flown. Being in an airplane doesn't count. The plane is actually doing the flying while you just sit inside. No, for a human being, flying means hang-gliding or paragliding. The real thing. And the real thing is alive and well on the Net.

Web:
http://lapphp0.in2p3.fr/~orloff/FF/faq.html
http://www.sky-adventures.com/hang/

Usenet:
rec.aviation.hang-gliding
rec.aviation.soaring

Helicopters

Helicopters are highly maneuverable, and, as such, have an appeal unlike that of fixed-wing aircraft. (I have a friend who keeps his own helicopter in his garage. When he wants to go for a ride, he wheels the helicopter out and takes off.) The first flight of a helicopter-like airplane occurred on November 13, 1907, flown by the Frenchman Paul Cornu. If you are a helicopter enthusiast, these resources will help you find what you need on the Net. If you want to talk to other helicopter buffs, check out the Usenet discussion group.

Web:
http://www.copters.com/
http://www.helis.com/
http://www.rotor.com/

Usenet:
rec.aviation.rotorcraft

Landings Aviation Server

If you were going to fly to a desert island and could take only one Web site with you, this would be the one. Landings has been around the Net for a long time (before there was even a Web), and it just keeps getting better. If you are a pilot, remember this site. You'll be returning here often to access the huge collection of aviation information and links: news, weather, flight planning, pilot training, discussion groups, and much more.

Web:
http://www.landings.com/

Learning to Fly

What a wonderful new experience, learning to fly. It's nice to know you have a place to ask questions or share your experiences with people who enjoy the same hobby or way of life. Find out all the questions new students are asking, and learn about instructors, lessons, equipment, PPL qualifications, and airspace.

Web:
http://www.gleim.com/Aviation/LearnToFly.html
http://www.tc.faa.gov/ZDV/GA/AC61-12M.html
http://www.ufly.com/

Usenet:
rec.aviation.student

Look What I Found on the Net...

```
Newsgroup: rec.aviation.student
Subject: Nausea and Learning to Fly

> I'm at about 15 hours now, and the nausea has pretty much
> entirely subsided.  Anyone else have stress-related nausea
> while flying?

You're most definitely not alone there.  As a student, I don't
think that I knew of anyone as stressed out as I was in my
learning days.  All I can say to others as unfortunate is stick
it out, it WILL go away if you want.
```

AVIATION

Military Aircraft

From the Sopwith Camel to the F-117A Stealth Fighter and beyond, experience the thrill of military aircraft. See the past, present, and even the future, as aviation devotees share their ideas on what are the best planes, who are the most notorious pilots in history, and how military aircraft of various countries compare to one another.

Web:
  http://www.csd.uwo.ca/~pettypi/elevon/gustin_military/

Usenet:
  rec.aviation.military
  rec.aviation.military.naval

Owning Airplanes

Don't you wish owning an airplane were as simple as installing a bigger garage door? Learn the joys and travails of being the owner of a powerful flying machine. If you are interested in building or restoring aircraft, check out .**homebuilt** to indulge in your aviation obsession. A word of warning: one of the questions in the homebuilt FAQ list is, "Will my marriage survive?"

Web:
  http://www.homebuilt.org/
  http://www.newsguy.com/~ericmax/faqs/r-a-h.htm

Usenet:
  rec.aviation.homebuilt
  rec.aviation.owning

Piloting

You can't be flying all the time—you do need to spend some of your time on the surface of the planet (if only to refuel). But that doesn't mean you need to be bored. Connect to the Net, and see what other pilots are talking about when they're not up in the air.

Usenet:
  rec.aviation.piloting

Stories About Flying

How does it feel to be so high above the Earth? What was it like the first time you went solo? What excites you about flying? Read anecdotes of flight experiences and share yours. Even if you don't fly, you can experience the thrill of the moment in the stories of others.

Usenet:
  rec.aviation.stories

Your Own Airplane

Oh, how these three simple words invoke deep feelings in all of us. **Wouldn't** it be great to be able to fly to the market or the dry cleaners instead of having to wait in rush hour traffic? Join the discussion on Usenet (**rec.aviation.homebuilt** and **rec.aviation.owning**) and share ideas about what might well be the personal transportation vehicle of the 20th century.

Ultralight Flying

Don't let the testosterone take over and convince you that you have to fly a jumbo jet. Experience the joy of ultralight aircraft and enjoy flying as often as possible using as little as possible.

Web:
  http://www.cs.fredonia.edu/~stei0302/WWW/ULTRA/ultralight.html

Usenet:
  rec.aviation.ultralight

Majordomo Mailing List:
  List Name: **fly-ul**
  Subscribe to: **majordomo@majordomo.hughes.net**

BIOLOGY

Algae (Phycology)

Phycology is the study of algae: eukaryotic organisms (each cell has a nucleus containing chromosomes) that are non-flowering and are capable of photosynthesis. However, algae are not plants. Some algae are classified Monera, while others are considered to be Protista. Algae range from small single-celled organisms, such as some plankton, to large, multicellular forms, such as seaweeds (most of which are green, brown or red algae). Algae are important as they produce much of the organic matter at the bottom of the food chain. In the ocean, algae also produce oxygen used by other marine life. Hint: If you have trouble recalling the definition of algae, just remember: algae = seaweed + some plankton + pond scum.

Web:
http://jupiter.phy.ohiou.edu/psa/
http://seaweed.ucg.ie/seaweed.html
http://www.bgsu.edu/departments/biology/algae/
http://www.nmnh.si.edu/botany/projects/algae/
http://www.upe.ac.za/botany/pssa/pssanet.htm

Usenet:
bionet.chlamydomonas

Listserv Mailing List:
List Name: algae-l
Subscribe to: listserv@listserv.heanet.ie

Feeling under the weather? Look at "Health" (or "Weather").

Bioethics

No science is complete without well-developed ethical traditions. The biological sciences are driven by research imperatives and a priority on preserving and enhancing human life. However, it is important that someone take the time to define and debate the ethical issues. For example, how should scarce resources be allotted? Are there any kinds of biological research which should not be allowed? How does society establish research priorities? So, what happens when you cross a philosopher with a biologist? You can find out by visiting the bioethics resources on the Net.

Web:
http://guweb.georgetown.edu/nrcbl/
http://www.gen.emory.edu/medweb/medweb.bioethics.html
http://www.med.upenn.edu/~bioethic/

Bioethics

The name "bioethics" is derived from two words: "bioeth" (the Greek word for those sandwiches made with pita bread and fried chickpeas) and "ics" (the Greek god of intermittent fertility).

Perhaps this explains why some of the best thinkers in the biological world are attracted to the study of bioethics, like fish to a what's-a-whoosie.

So the next time you are sitting around idly speculating about whether or not it is proper for your cat to accept gifts from a corporate lobbyist, don't wallow in ignorant bliss. Connect to the **Bioethics Server** and find the guidance you need to conduct your life with philosophical flair.

BIOLOGY 55

Bioinformatics

The techniques of bioinformatics deal with using computers to manipulate and manage biological information. In particular, much of bioinformatics deals with the sort of computational demands generated by the Human Genome Project. Bioinformatics specialists are experts in both molecular biology and computer science: a melding of disciplines that is becoming increasing valuable.

Web:
http://motif.stanford.edu/resources.html
http://ubik.microbiol.washington.edu/BioInf.html
http://www.bioplanet.com/
http://www.cbil.upenn.edu/

Usenet:
bionet.biology.computational
bionet.molbio.bio-matrix

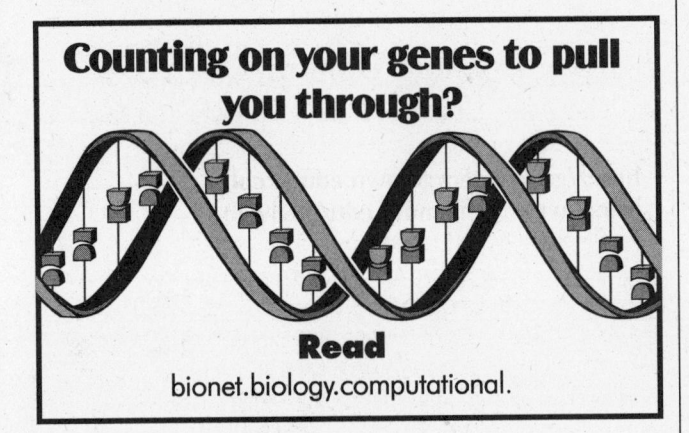

Counting on your genes to pull you through?

Read
bionet.biology.computational.

Biology Dictionary

Are you one of those people who have trouble remembering the difference between cytoplasm, ectoplasm and endoplasm? Do you have trouble recalling the exact definition of all your favorite organelles? If so, an online biology dictionary can help. Use the Net, and it won't be long before you are the life of the biological party. ("Is that chromatin in your nucleolus, or are you just glad to see me?")

Web:
http://biotech.chem.indiana.edu/pages/dictionary.html

Biology Funding and Grants

Don't wait for your million dollar sweepstakes check to come in. Where are some of the funding agencies in biology? Who's giving out research grants? Find out who has the money and how you can get some, too.

Web:
http://fundingopps.cos.com/
http://www.auhs.edu/library/resource/funding.htm
http://www.library.wisc.edu/guides/Biology/funding.htm

Usenet:
bionet.sci-resources

Funding and Grants in Biology

So you've got this great idea for developing wheat that grows in thin rows, just perfect for making sliced bread. But what can you do for seed money?
Participate in the **bionet.sci-resources** discussion group and perhaps, just perhaps, you will find the financial source that will send you on your way to becoming the next Internet Nobel Prize winner.

BIOLOGY

Biology Job Opportunities

Why be a telemarketer when you can have a job in the exciting field of biology? See cells reproduce right before your eyes, cut up small unsuspecting micro-organisms with lightning speed, and create new life forms seemingly from scratch. Opportunities abound for pre- or post-docs, undergraduates looking for something to keep them out of trouble for the summer, assistant professors who don't mind grading papers, and for upwardly mobile tenure-track seekers.

Web:
  http://bio.com/hr/
  http://www.biolinks.com/career/

Usenet:
  bionet.jobs
  bionet.jobs.offered
  bionet.jobs.wanted

Biology Journals

If you like biological journals (or even if you don't, and you have to read them anyway), you can do a lot of your reading on the Internet. A large number of research papers are available online, and many print journals also publish on the Net. The biological world moves fast, and these resources will help you find what you need to stay current.

Web:
  http://www.bio.com/news/journals.html
  http://www.biolinks.com/index/journals.html
  http://www.genenet.com/fpage13.html

Usenet:
  bionet.journals.contents
  bionet.journals.letters.biotechniques
  bionet.journals.letters.tibs
  bionet.journals.note

Biology Resources

Whatever you are looking for in the world of biology, these Web sites can help you. They contain vast collections of links that will lead you to just about anything you need. These are the places I use when I need to fulfill my biological needs.

Web:
  http://golgi.harvard.edu/biopages.html
  http://pillo.unipv.it/~marcora/surf.htm
  http://www.scicentral.com/B-02bios.html
  http://www.scienceguide.com/Site_Directories/Biology_Direct.html

Biology Software

If you have the right tools, computers lighten your workload, and the right tools are available if you know where to look. These Web sites are good places to look when you are searching for biological software. The Usenet groups are useful if you have questions or you want to keep up on new products.

Web:
  http://cmgm.stanford.edu/WWW/www_software.html
  http://www.euronet.nl/users/mbleeker/prog/soflis_e.html

Usenet:
  bionet.software
  bionet.software.acedb
  bionet.software.gcg
  bionet.software.srs
  bionet.software.staden
  bionet.software.www
  bionet.software.x-plor

Biology Talk and General Discussion

For many years, biologists have used the Internet extensively, more so than any other scientific discipline. In particular, there are a great many biology-oriented Usenet groups and mailing lists. This Web site is the home of Biosci, where all of this discussion is coordinated. (This is the home of all the **bionet** discussion groups.) If you are looking for a group or mailing list devoted to a particular topic, this Web site is the place to start. For miscellaneous biology talk, visit the Usenet discussion groups.

Web:
  http://www.bio.net/

Usenet:
  bionet.general
  sci.bio

Guess how many items there are in the "Trivia" section.

BIOLOGY 57

Biology-Related Sciences

Unbutton your top button and roll up your sleeves in preparation for some lively biological bantering. While informative and educational, subjects are never strictly hard-core science. Debate is sparked by such topics as evolution, the ethics of cloning, and the instinctual mating habits of animals and humans.

Usenet:
sci.bio.botany
sci.bio.conservation
sci.bio.ecology
sci.bio.ethology
sci.bio.fisheries
sci.bio.herp
sci.bio.microbiology
sci.bio.misc
sci.bio.paleontology
sci.bio.phytopathology
sci.bio.systematics

Tempt yourself in "Vices".

Biotechnology

Biotechnology is a broad area: it refers to using technology within the biological sciences (for research and so on), as well as using elements of biology to create new technology (such as genetic engineering). The advances in biotechnology in the last several decades have profoundly influenced our economy and our culture. For example, even the man on the street is familiar with DNA testing. (He may not know what it is, but at least he knows it's something cool.) If you have an interest in biology, you can use these resources to keep up on the latest biotechnology advances.

Web:
http://biotech.mond.org/
http://www.cato.com/biotech/
http://www.nbif.org/
http://www.schmidel.com/bionet/biotech.htm

Usenet:
alt.bio.technology
alt.bio.technology.cloning
alt.bio.technology.misc
sci.bio.technology

Look What I Found on the Net...

```
Newsgroup: bionet.general

Subject: Biology degree

> What is the common opinion for job outlook in biology with an
> M.S. degree?  Is it worth pursuing?  Or should one concentrate
> more on another hard science?

> I am a biology major but do not desire to go on to med
> school, so please let me know.

Genetics is booming at the moment.

In principle, one can set up a company called "Genes-R-Us",
and introduce it to the stock market.  Wait one year while the
stocks hit the one million dollar point, and then cash in.

A slightly smarter move is to actually hire some people and do
some research.  Your stocks will then reach the one billion
dollar point.  After a couple of years, you can sell off your
company, and live in comfort for the rest of your life...
```

58 BIOLOGY

Cell Biology

This is where life happens, in tiny units of protoplasm. Unless you are a robot, cell biology concerns you. Cell scholars from all over the world dissect studies, research and experiments that relate to cell biology. The .cytonet group is for the discussion of cytoskeletons such as cell walls and plasma membranes.

Web:
http://www.cellbio.com/
http://www.cellsalive.com/
http://www.hardlink.com/~tsute/glossary/
http://www.mblab.gla.ac.uk/dictionary/

Usenet:
bionet.cellbiol
bionet.cellbiol.cytonet
bionet.cellbiol.insulin

Developmental Biology

Developmental biology is the study of how multi-cellular organisms develop from their early forms (such as embryos and larvae) into adults. In particular, developmental biology embraces the study of embryology. It seems like a miracle that a complex organism can grow from just a single fertilized cell, but it's not a miracle at all. Miracles are just phenomena you don't yet understand, so let the Net help you fill in the gaps.

Web:
http://sdb.bio.purdue.edu/other/vl_db.html
http://visembryo.ucsf.edu/
http://www.acs.ucalgary.ca/~browder/
http://zygote.swarthmore.edu/info.html

Try a Mud.

Look What I Found on the Net...

```
Newsgroup: bionet.molbio.genome-program
Subject: Sequence and terabytes?

> The Human Genome Project will generate 3 billion subunits.
> Can anyone tell me how much computer storage capacity will
> that be in gigabytes, terabytes or petabytes?
>
>  Maybe someone knows the relationship between gene sequence
> length and computer storage capacity?

...If you store "A","G","C","T" as the equivalent ASCII character
in one byte, base pairs and bytes are equivalent.

   So 3 gigabasepairs = 3 gigabytes of storage.

This only applies to the sequence though: any documentary
information will take up roughly the same amount of space
as the sequence...

This is without any compression.  DNA sequences can usually be
stored in about 1/4 the space described above by packing
approximately 4 characters per byte, and the reference
information can also usually be squeezed down substantially
through compression.
```

Ecology

The term "ecology" was coined in 1869 by the German zoologist Ernst Heinrich Haeckel, who used the word to refer to "environmental balance". Today, ecology has developed into a complex biological science dealing with the interrelationships of living organisms and the physical environment. Ecologists observe and analyze systems of organisms: their communities, population patterns, and dependence upon their environment. (By the way, Heinrich was also the biologist who developed the idea that "ontogeny recapitulates phylogeny", that is, the embryonic development of a higher animal mimics the evolutionary development of its species.)

Web:
  http://conbio.rice.edu/vl/browse/
  http://pbil.univ-lyon1.fr/Ecology/
    Ecology-WWW.html

Usenet:
  bionet.ecology.physiology
  sci.bio.conservation
  sci.bio.ecology

Listproc Mailing List:
  List Name: **consbio**
  Subscribe to: **listproc@u.washington.edu**

Evolution

Evolution didn't stop when the apes climbed out of the trees and learned to drive sports cars. It's a constant process that goes on from the tiniest bacteria to the largest plants and animals. Get together with other people interested in evolution and discuss where we came from and where we might be going.

Web:
  http://ccp.uchicago.edu/~jyin/evolution.html
  http://www.ucmp.berkeley.edu/history/
    evolution.html

Usenet:
  bionet.molbio.evolution
  sci.bio.evolution

Genetics

How genes are connected is important and complex. If you are involved in this important area of molecular biochemistry, these genetics resources will interest you. Check out what's moving and shaking in the world of alleles and genotypes.

Web:
  http://www.edv.agrar.tu-muenchen.de/idw/
    genglos.html
  http://www.genenet.com/
  http://www.ornl.gov/TechResources/
    Human_Genome/genetics.html
  http://www3.ncbi.nlm.nih.gov/Omim/

Usenet:
  bionet.drosophila
  bionet.genome.arabidopsis
  bionet.molbio.gene-linkage
  bionet.molbio.molluscs
  bionet.organisms.zebrafish

Listserv Mailing List:
  List Name: **gentalk**
  Subscribe to: **listserv@list.iex.net**

Human Genome Project

The Human Genome Project is a massively ambitious global project to ferret out and document all of the genes in the full complement of human chromosomes. Here are some Web sites that can point you to a great deal of data and keep you up to date on the progress of this project. For ongoing discussion, you can take a look at the Usenet group. (My hope is that, one day, someone will find the gene for TV watching, and we'll all be saved.)

Web:
  http://www.genome.ad.jp/
  http://www.hgmp.mrc.ac.uk/

Usenet:
  bionet.molbio.genome-program

**Need a pick-me-up?
Try a new Usenet group.**

60 BIOLOGY

Infomine Searchable Database

Here is a huge database of biological, agricultural and medical information. You can search by keyword or browse by subject. Just the place to do some research when you have to decide whether you should sever your anterior or posterior commissure, and you haven't got a lot of time to make up your mind.

Web:
  http://lib-www.ucr.edu/bioag/

Microbiology

Microbiology is the study of microorganisms: organisms that are too small to be seen with the naked eye, such as bacteria, viruses, yeasts, fungi, protozoans and the smaller algae. Once you start to study microbiology, you come to a startling realization: most of life is too small to see without a microscope. When I was in medical school, I studied medical microbiology, and, believe me, there is a lot to know.

Web:
  http://alces.med.umn.edu/vgc.html
  http://www.hardlink.com/~tsute/glossary/
  http://www.horizonpress.com/gateway/micro.html
  http://www.microbiol.org/

Usenet:
  bionet.celegans
  bionet.microbiology
  bionet.microbiology.biofilms
  bionet.organisms.pseudomonas
  bionet.organisms.schistosoma
  bionet.parasitology
  bionet.protista
  sci.bio.microbiology

Label 10 copies of this book "1" through "10".
Now, rearrange them into every possible combination (1234, 1243...), one per minute. When you finish, it will be the 21st century.

Molecular Biology

Molecular biology is the study of biochemical and molecular reactions within cells. As such, molecular biology deals with the macromolecules upon which life depends (nucleic acids, proteins, and so on) as well as the basic processes that take place within a cell (such as respiration, reproduction and excretion). Today, much of molecular biology focuses on the study of genetic material (DNA, RNA, nucleotides, and so on) and how it transmits genetic information. There is a huge amount of molecular biology information on the Net, and many Usenet groups in which people discuss related topics.

Web:
  http://alces.med.umn.edu/VGC.html
  http://cmm.info.nih.gov/modeling/
  http://golgi.harvard.edu/sequences.html
  http://molbio.info.nih.gov/cgi-bin/pdb
  http://www.mdli.com/chemscape/chime/
  http://www.unl.edu/stc-95/ResTools/cmshp.html
  http://www.yk.rim.or.jp/~aisoai/

Usenet:
  bionet.genome.autosequencing
  bionet.genome.chromosomes
  bionet.genome.gene-structure
  bionet.glycosci
  bionet.molbio.ageing
  bionet.molbio.bio-matrix
  bionet.molbio.embldatabank
  bionet.molbio.evolution
  bionet.molbio.genbank
  bionet.molbio.genbank.updates
  bionet.molbio.hiv
  bionet.molbio.methds-reagnts
  bionet.molbio.proteins
  bionet.molbio.proteins.7tms_r
  bionet.molbio.proteins.fluorescent
  bionet.molbio.rapd
  bionet.molbio.recombination
  bionet.molbio.yeast
  bionet.molec-model
  bionet.molecules.free-radicals
  bionet.molecules.p450
  bionet.molecules.peptides
  bionet.molecules.repertoires
  bionet.structural-nmr
  bionet.xtallography
  sci.bio.immunocytochem

BIOLOGY

Mycology

Mycology is the study of the organisms within the Fungi kingdom, including yeasts, molds, smuts and mushrooms. Fungi are characterized by a lack of chlorophyll and vascular tissue. They range from small, single cells to large masses of branched filaments. Here is a great resource containing a collection of material relating to fungi organisms and cultivation, research, publications, discussion groups and taxonomy (naming systems), as well as a Usenet group for mycological discussion. By the way, we commonly divide the world of biology into five separate kingdoms: Plants, Animals, Fungi, Protista (one-celled protozoans and some algae) and Monera (bacteria and blue-green algae). Thus, properly speaking, fungi, protozoa and bacteria are neither plants nor animals.

Web:
http://www.keil.ukans.edu/~fungi/

Usenet:
bionet.mycology

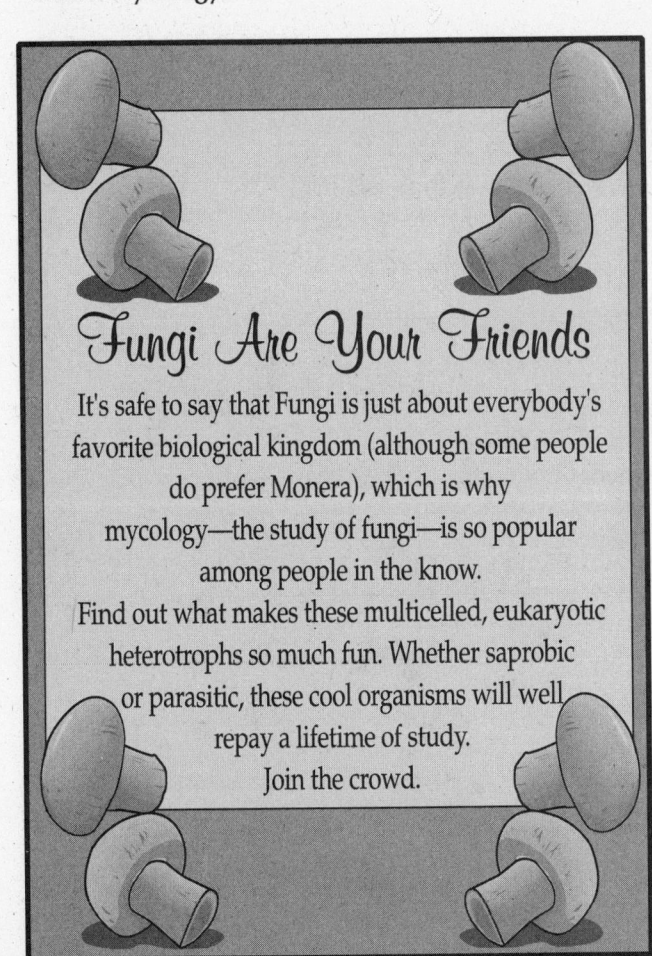

Fungi Are Your Friends

It's safe to say that Fungi is just about everybody's favorite biological kingdom (although some people do prefer Monera), which is why mycology—the study of fungi—is so popular among people in the know.
Find out what makes these multicelled, eukaryotic heterotrophs so much fun. Whether saprobic or parasitic, these cool organisms will well repay a lifetime of study.
Join the crowd.

Neuroscience

Neuroscience is the study of the nervous system, encompassing neuoranatomy (one of my favorite areas of science) and neurobiology. When I was younger, I studied neuroscience in between graduate computer science and medical school. I got to dissect brains, and I took a neuroscience course in which I was able to carry out a variety of strange experiments. If you have an interest in learning how your brain functions, you will find neuroscience fascinating: it's all just a matter of mind over matter over mind.

Web:
http://k2.scl.cwru.edu/~bqw/neuro/
http://neuro.med.cornell.edu/VL/
http://thalamus.wustl.edu/course/
http://www.cnbc.cmu.edu/other/other-neuro.html
http://www.indiana.edu/~pietsch/

Usenet:
bionet.neuroscience
bionet.neuroscience.amyloid

Taxonomy

Taxonomy is the systematic classification of living things. Modern taxonomy originated with the work of the Swedish botanist Carolus Linnaeus (1707-1778), who, in 1735, published *Genera Plantarum*, a work dealing with botanic classification. There are, of course, a vast number of different types of living things, and today's taxonomy systems are complex indeed. Although various systems are used (there is no one definitive scheme), the most common classifications are, from most to least general: kingdom, phylum, subphylum, class, subclass, order, family, genus, species and (for plants only) variety. When we talk about a particular organism, we often use the scientific name consisting of the genus (which is capitalized) followed by the species. For example, the next time someone offers you some Myrichthys maculosus soup, don't worry. It's just a common Tiger Snake Eel.

Web:
http://phylogeny.arizona.edu/tree/phylogeny.html
http://www.itis.usda.gov/itis
http://wwweti.eti.bio.uva.nl/

Virology

Virology is the study of viruses: tiny infectious agents (most viruses are between 10-200 nanometers) consisting of a length of DNA or RNA wrapped in a protein coat called a capsid. In human beings, viruses cause a large number of diseases, including colds, measles, mumps, yellow fever, polio, flu, AIDS and some types of cancer. Viruses also infect many other kinds of organisms, including plants and bacteria. In order to reproduce, a virus must infect a host cell. The virus then uses the cell's own biochemical mechanisms to create replica viruses. Outside of the host cell, the virus is inert with no active metabolism. Thus, strictly speaking, viruses are not actually alive (although that is not much consolation when you are sick in bed with a fever).

Web:
http://www.tulane.edu/~dmsander/garryfavweb.html
http://www.umu.se/virology/alistair/lecture.htm
http://www.virologyweb.com/

Usenet:
bionet.virology

BIZARRE

Air Sickness Bag Museum

The next time you fly on an airplane, look in the seat pocket in front of you. There you will find a small paper bag, discreetly labeled "For Motion Discomfort". Most people will just ignore the bag and concentrate on the other treasures you find in an airline seat pocket (such as the free magazine or the spiffy card showing all the emergency exits). A few select people, however, know value when they see it. To such people, an (unused) air sickness bag is a valuable commodity, to be collected and enjoyed. Just goes to show what I always say, that half the people in this world don't understand how the other two-thirds live.

Web:
http://fly.to/barfbag
http://rampages.onramp.net/~stevebo/airsick.html
http://www.dallas.net/~costilow/barfbags.htm
http://www.netlink.co.uk/users/gnarly/sickbag.html

Majordomo Mailing List:
List Name: **sickbags**
Subscribe to: **majordomo@axalotl.demon.co.uk**

Bizarre Stuff to Make

Here are several gaggles of recipes for weird stuff you can do and make, much of it right in your very own kitchen. Find out how to make realistic-looking blood, fake glass, slime, glowing pickles, and much more: 1001 ways to entertain your guests. This Web site brings a whole new meaning to the expression "Out to Lunch".

Web:
http://freeweb.pdq.net/headstrong/

Bizarre Talk and General Discussion

There is too much in the world that is *not* bizarre. If we are to maintain our status as the pre-eminent species on Earth, it behooves us to spend more time immersing ourselves in strangeness. A good way to do so is by subscribing to the Weird List. Then just sit back and wait for your mailbox to be filled with bizarre, disturbing and offensive short stories and ramblings. Perhaps you might even send in a story of your own. (The world needs all the help it can get.) If you are the type of person who wants immediate gratification, check out Usenet for your daily dose of weirdness.

Usenet:
talk.bizarre

Listserv Mailing List:
List Name: **weird-l**
Subscribe to: **listserv@brownvm.brown.edu**

Contortionism

If you are looking for new recruits for your Olympic Twister team, this is the perfect place to start. You can view lots of photographs of contortionists bending their bodies in ways that are probably outlawed in more conservative parts of the world. Besides images, you will also find text on the history of contortion, a bibliography, information about the International Contortion Society and links to other contortion sites.

Web:
http://www.escape.com/~silverbk/contortion

Usenet:
alt.arts.contortion

Crime Scene Evidence File

If you have ever fantasized about being the hero in a detective novel, or being the sleuth in a mystery story, here's your chance to act out the fantasy. A crime has been committed: a gruesome murder of a young woman. All the evidence is before you. Can you solve it? Justice depends on your wit, savvy and keen powers of observation.

Web:
http://www.crimescene.com/

Dark Side of the Net

When the history of the twentieth century is written, the section on gothic culture will have one simple entry: see Carrie Carolin. Carrie is a wonderfully resourceful and talented bundle of energy who maintains The Dark Side of the Net, the pre-eminent Internet site for things gothic. Here you will find a fabulous list of resources regarding gothic, horror, vampires (and vampyres), occult, magick, zines, magazines, and much more. Root around a little, and you will find links to Carrie's other, equally fascinating enterprises. Not recommended for normal people or Republicans.

Web:
http://www.gothic.net/darkside/

Dark Side of the Net

When it comes to things gothic on the Net, there is only one way to make sure you have it all: **Look to the Dark Side.**

Death Clock

Do you want to know how long it is going to be before you bite the biscuit so you can plan everything in advance? On the Net, you can find out just how long you have to go until you pass on to your final reward. Your personal death clock will tell you how many seconds you have left to live and the date you are scheduled to die. If you don't want to know for yourself, you can check the death clocks of celebrities instead.

Web:
http://www.deathclock.com/

Discord and Destruction

Serious talk about serious talk. Destroy the earth or just our way of life: it's up to you. Remember, life is stern and earnest, and nobody gets out of here alive.

Web:
http://www.ci-n.com/~jcampbel/principia.index.html

Usenet:
alt.destroy.the.earth
alt.discordia

Evil Hexes

Anyone can send a sappy love note or a Valentine's Day greeting by email. But only a totally cool person (like me or you) would think to send an actual hex! Choose the perfect evil hex to send to a friend on the Net. My favorite is "Shame on you! Shame on you! Does your Mother know what you do?"

Web:
http://www.evilhex.com/

Grocery Shooting

I bet you've spent a lot of sleepless nights wondering what would happen if common, ordinary foodstuffs were shot with a variety of different firearms. Well, wonder no longer. You can now view short movies showing, say, a cabbage being blown to pieces by a bullet from a .357 Glaser. Before you get offended, however, I want you to remember the slogan of the U.S. National Rifle Association: If guns are outlawed, only vegetables will have guns.

Web:
http://www.5sigma.com/joseph/inan/

Grotesque Curiosities

When I was a kid I had a shrunken head. It was made out of dark, black plastic, and it was ever so cool. If I had had a chance to get a real shrunken head, I would have done so in a minute, but, such items were sadly out of reach for a young boy in Toronto, Canada. However, in my exploration of the Internet, I was gratified to find that the young man's fancy with things grotesque is alive and well. If you like shrunken heads, trophy skulls, and other weird stuff, the Net is only too willing to oblige. Just the thing to show your younger sister.

Web:
  http://members.aol.com/arbysaurus/
  http://www.head-hunter.com/
  http://www.morbidreality.com/contents.html
  http://www.strugglers.net/andy/grotesque-gallery/

Mummy Museum

If you've been feeling bad because all the other people in your neighborhood have mummies and you don't, here's your chance to perk right up and show them your stuff. Go to the Mummy Museum, where you will find lots and lots of pictures of real live dead people in their typically shriveled states of being.

Web:
  http://www.sirius.com/~dbh/mummies/

Negative Emotions

Angst, bitterness, misanthropy, fear, disgust, anxiety and just plain being in a bad mood. Join the folks down at the not-OK corral for some roll-up-your-sleeves-and-get-down-to-it homestyle bitchin'. As John Milton put it (when they took away his Internet account), "So little is our loss. So little is our gain."

Usenet:
  alt.anger
  alt.angst
  alt.bitterness
  alt.im.angry
  alt.im.having.a.rotten.day
  alt.life.sucks
  alt.peeves

THE USENET COMPLAINT DEPARTMENT

We all need to complain. The trouble is, most of our complaints are heard only by people in our immediate vicinity. Much better to send your complaints to **alt.peeves**.

That way, anyone on the Internet will have a chance to find out what you think of parents who can't keep their kids quiet in public, or talk show hosts who swank around like they own the place.

News of the Weird

It's often hard to accept the mundanity of normal everyday living. If your life isn't weird enough, try browsing through the News of the Weird archives or subscribe to their mailing list. You can read stories that will shock, surprise and flabbergast you. And this news is good for a laugh, too.

Web:
  http://www.newsoftheweird.com/
  http://www.nine.org/notw/

BIZARRE

Positive Emotions

As if there isn't enough to deal with already, here are discussion groups devoted to good feelings and happiness. Bah, humbug. If God had wanted us to hear good news, he wouldn't have given us television and newscasters with bad toupees.

Usenet:
  alt.cuddle
  alt.good.morning
  alt.good.news
  alt.hi.are.you.cute
  alt.i-love-you

Rotten Galleries

Do you like strange, sick, twisted pictures and information? How about disturbing images of death, racism, mugshots, crime scene photos? Sound good? Of course they do. And isn't it comforting to know that, whenever you want, 24 hours a day, there is a place you can go to look at the pictures of Nicole Simpson's bloody body after her final discussion with O.J.?

Web:
  http://www.rotten.com/

> You are what you download.

Rumors

Check out all the new rumors, both serious (Elvis and aliens) and less serious (the FBI and CIA). Did you know that readers of this book are entitled to free admission to Disney World?

Usenet:
  talk.rumors

Spleen

You probably don't give much thought to your spleen. You just let it sit there all day long doing its business, which, frankly, is not much. However, there is one man on the Net who is making the most of his spleen and feels the need to share it with you. Take a look at his work. It's sort of art, sort of philosophy, sort of poetry wrapped around the motif of anatomy.

Web:
  http://www.mcad.edu/home/faculty/szyhalski/Piotr

Squashed Bug Zoo

This page is for all of you who want to take revenge on bugs, but never have the nerve to actually squash them yourself. Recommended viewing time is between meals. Yes, live bugs were harmed in the making of this page.

Web:
  http://squashed.roach.org/zoo.html

Look What I Found on the Net...

```
Newsgroups: alt.hi.are.you.cute
Subject: A Cute Thing at Disney!

Today I did a temp assignment working at the reception desk at
Disney Studios.

Today the man and woman who do the voices for Mickey and Minnie
Mouse came in and entertained us with some samples of their
vocal talents.

But the cutest thing is that they are married to each other.
They met while doing the voices of Mickey and Minnie, and fell
in love...

I think that is so cute!
```

BIZARRE

Stare Down Sally

Sally has beautiful green eyes: the kind you can stare into forever. Or can you? See if you can stare down Sally. Can you beat her at her own game, or will you blink first?

Web:
http://www.stairwell.com/stare/

Stick Figure Death Theater

Need a break from all the violence on TV and in the movies? Visit the home of the Stick Figure Death Theater, and—through the magic of the animated GIF—you will enjoy a large number of imaginative variations of a stick figure suffering through various disturbing deaths, usually extremely bloody. It sounds simple, but then so does Abstract Expressionism.

Web:
http://www.calvert.com/sfdt/

Surrealist Compliment Generator

In a thankless world when an ordinary compliment is drowned out by deadlines, ringing phones, and suited executives waving memos that say "Hurry! Hurry!" it's nice to know that you can get a unique compliment anytime you want it just by loading this page. The Surrealist Compliment Generator will offer you the kindest words it can. While sometimes startling or unusual, these compliments seem earnest, sincere and refreshing.

Web:
http://pharmdec.wustl.edu/cgi-bin/jardin_scripts/SCG

Surrealist Compliment Generator

Guys—what can you get for the woman who has everything but nowhere to put it? How about a surrealistic compliment?

"Though I may never see you again, I wish you the warmest clam chowder, the finest of embalmings, and the best in stainless steel cadaver pans that money can buy."

Truly, no modern romantic arsenal can be complete without the **Surrealist Compliment Generator**.

Tasteless Topics

Taste is in the eye (and often in the mouth) of the beholder. But what do you do on those days when you need a good dose of bad taste? The answer is to check out the Net's tasteless discussion group. Feel free to look, to copy and to participate. Just be sure that whatever you do is disgusting and without any redeeming social value whatsoever. The Web site has the alt.tasteless FAQs and other tasteless links. This is not the place to bring your grandmother for her birthday.

Web:
http://www.aracnet.com/~jaydog/index2.html

Usenet:
alt.tasteless

Vampyres Only

Vampyre lovers, here is the site for you. If you are interested in being a vampyre, there are special tips on how to become such a creature of the night. Get information on what vampyres are, read the FAQs, and learn about vampyre societies, clubs and religions. If you are worried that you might be a vampyre, you can take a test to see how you rate. There are also audio and video clips, images and humor files. This is definitely the hotspot for vampyre information.

Web:
http://www.vampyres-only.com/

Weird IRC Channels

After a while, going to Tupperware parties and hanging out at the mall can get a tad predictable. So when you get to the point where you are itching to meet some new and bizarre people, try hanging out in these IRC channels. The only thing I can guarantee is that nothing is guaranteed.

IRC:
#abyss
#discordia
#dork
#evil
#gothic
#heathers
#insomnia
#pizza
#tarot
#thelema

BOATING AND SAILING

Boat Racing

Boat racing has an appeal that is unlike any other type of racing. On the water, even a relatively slow speed can make you feel like you are streaking along. The fastest racing boats, the unlimited hydroplanes (the ones that produce the large roostertails), use aircraft turbine engines and reach speeds close to 200 mph (330 kph). At any speed, however, boat racing is exciting, and when you are not watching or taking part in a race, what better way to pass the time than to read about boat racing on the Net.

Web:
  http://www.apba.org/
  http://www.boatracer.com/

Usenet:
  rec.boats.racing
  rec.boats.racing.power

Boatbuilding

People have been building boats for centuries, but when I see how much information is available online, I wonder how boatbuilders ever managed without the Net. The Web site offers a great deal of information for commercial boat builders: research engineering, marketing, regulations, materials, safety, industry news, and much more. The Usenet group and mailing list are good for ongoing discussion of all aspects of building boats, including canoes and kayaks.

Web:
  http://www.virtualpet.com/rbbi/

Usenet:
  rec.boats.building

Listserv Mailing List:
  List Name: yacht-l
  Subscribe to: listserv@nic.surfnet.nl

Boating Mnemonics

When I was in medical school, there were lots of great mnemonics used to remember body parts in anatomy, symptoms of diseases and the properties of drugs. When you are learning to sail, there are also lots of things to remember and the mnemonics really help. This site gives you a list of clever tricks to help commit boating terms and rules to memory: mast light combinations, stern lights, buoyage, sound signals and right of way rules. Not many places will explain why your life can be saved by knowing that Timid Virgins Make Dull Company at Weddings.

Web:
  http://ficus-www.cs.ucla.edu/ficus-members/geoff/mnemonics.html

Boating Quiz

Are you ready to captain your own sailing vessel? Find out how you score on this boating quiz. Afterward, you can take a break and head for the open seas, or at least to the bathtub with your little plastic battleships.

Web:
  http://www.usps.org/e_stuff/quiz.html

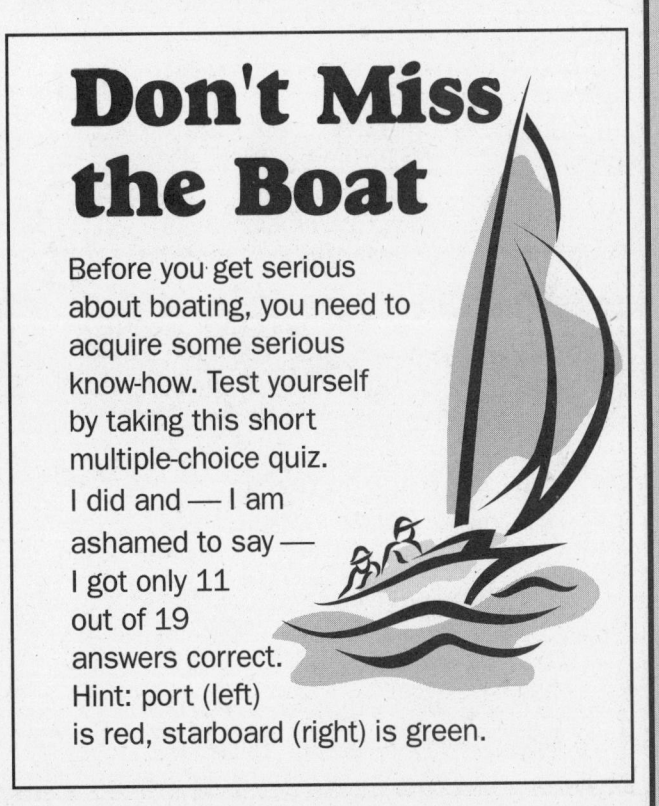

Don't Miss the Boat

Before you get serious about boating, you need to acquire some serious know-how. Test yourself by taking this short multiple-choice quiz. I did and — I am ashamed to say — I got only 11 out of 19 answers correct. Hint: port (left) is red, starboard (right) is green.

BOATING AND SAILING

Boating Rules

Quick. Take a few minutes and go over the rules by which all good sailors abide. Along with the "Rules of the Road" (the International Regulations for Avoiding Collisions at Sea), you will also find information about signals, lights, navigation marks, equipment and flags. (Next time you go mine sweeping, check with these sites first to make sure your boat has the correct pattern of running lights.)

Web:
http://www.boatsafe.com/nauticalknowhow/boating/colregs.html
http://www.digigate.net/mba/rules.htm

Boating Safety

The words "safety" and "boating" go hand in hand. Just like you wouldn't go into a storm after getting your hair done, you wouldn't want to go charging off on a sailing adventure without first getting some safety tips from the Net. These boating safety sites will help you with boating regulations, the weather, personal watercraft safety and more. Don't leave shore without them.

Web:
http://www.boatingsafety.com/
http://www.boatsafe.com/nauticalknowhow/safetips.htm
http://www.mailbag.com/users/stobo76/
http://www.uscgboating.org/

Boating Talk and General Discussion

When I was a kid at camp, I earned my Master Canoeist award. To this day, I can still recall all the esoteric canoeing strokes I had to be able to demonstrate, equally well on both sides. Truly, moving on water invokes deep feelings in all of us. If you care about things that float, join the Usenet boating discussion groups. The **live-aboard** mailing list is for the discussion of living onboard a boat.

Usenet:
  rec.boats
  rec.boats.cruising
  rec.boats.electronics
  rec.boats.paddle

Majordomo Mailing List:
  List Name: **live-aboard**
  Subscribe to: majordomo@crux.astro.utoronto.ca

Boating Today

Enjoy this slick, online boating magazine. You will find a variety of informative articles, a marine calendar, weather information, a marina finder, discussion forums, and much more.

Web:
  http://www.iwol.com/boating/

Quick... click!

Look What I Found on the Net...

```
Newsgroup: rec.boats.cruising
Subject: Collision at Sea

I'm reminded of a story I can't resist sharing.

While sailing from Boston to Bermuda, we saw an enormous tree
trunk floating free — probably 100 feet long and 10 feet in
diameter.

My sister's comment was, "I'm sure glad there's nothing like
that out here at night."
```

BOATING AND SAILING 69

Crew Database

Are you a boat looking for a crew? Are you a crew looking for a boat? Here's a database of boatless crews and crewless boats looking for the perfect match. If you are itching to enter a boat race, but you just don't have everything you need, try this site. You might find just what you are looking for.

Web:
  http://people.netscape.com/flc/crew/

Dragon Boat Racing

Dragon boat racing is a popular event in China. It is a Chinese tradition dating back more than 2,000 years. The boat races are said to have originated from a belief that they would bring agricultural prosperity. There is another, more romantic, legend that says dragon boat racing is related to the story of Ch'u Yuan, a Chinese patriot, who was exiled. Because of his expatriation, he was filled with despair and threw himself into the Mi Lo river. The legend says the people of the country were so distraught over the suicide of Ch'u Yuan that they got into their boats and raced up and down the river beating drums, splashing oars and making a general ruckus in order to scare away evil spirits and water dragons from the body of Ch'u Yuan. Today, this story creates a great excuse for people to get into brightly colored boats that are decorated like dragons and race up and down the river yelling, making noise and having a good time. Seems like as good an excuse as any to me. Use the Net to learn more about this fun Chinese celebration.

Web:
  http://www.alvin.org/dragon/

GORP: Great Outdoor Recreation Pages

Having this site on your bookmark list means you will never run out of interesting and entertaining resources relating to rafting, canoeing and kayaking. There are links to information on trips, gear, books and magazines, safety, events, reviews of locations, health, food and organizations.

Web:
  http://www.gorp.com/gorp/activity/paddle.htm

Kayaking and Canoeing

When I was an undergraduate student at the University of Waterloo in Canada, I spent a little time with the Whitewater Canoe Club. However, I never got close to the action: my participation was limited to paddling a kayak around the swimming pool. Later, after I moved to California, I once went kayaking in the ocean, and I found it a lot more fun than the pool in Waterloo. If you want to keep afloat of the happenings in the world of the paddle, check out this Web site for links to kayak and canoe organizations around the world. The mailing list is for the discussion of skin/frame and other traditional types of kayaks.

Web:
  http://www.nif.idrett.no/padling/world.html

Majordomo Mailing List:
  List Name: **baidarka**
  Subscribe to: **majordomo@lists.intelenet.net**

Marine Signal Flags

Ships at sea use signal flags to spell out short messages or to communicate speeds and course changes. This page shows alphabetic flags, answering pennants, numeric pennants, substitute pennants, and the semaphore flag-waving system.

Web:
  http://osprey.anbg.gov.au/flags/signal-flags.html

Navigation

When you are out to sea and lost or confused, send mail to this mailing list for the discussion of non-electronic navigation, with primary topics such as celestial navigation, coastal piloting, dead reckoning, charts, currents and weather at sea. For important navigation resources, see the Web sites. As long as you have an Internet connection, you can find your way home.

Web:
  http://www.navcen.uscg.mil/
  http://www.uscg.mil/hq/g-m/mov/pages/rules.htm

Majordomo Mailing List:
  List Name: **navigation**
  Subscribe to: **majordomo@ronin.com**

BOATING AND SAILING

Navigate Your Way to Happiness

What do you do when you're in the middle of the ocean, all your electronic navigation aids are on the fritz and—on the distant horizon—a black, ponderous cloud has begun to form?

For most people, this would be a giant-sized pickle, but as an Internet user and a reader of this book, you have nothing to worry about.

All you need to do is send a message to the **Navigation** mailing list, describe your predicament ("I am surrounded by a bunch of water, what should I do?") and wait for a reply. Within a short time, some kind soul will probably answer you with the help you need, and soon you will be back in action without a care in the world.

Personal Watercraft

If you are not up to sailing your own large boat, start smaller with a personal watercraft. These sites include links to manufacturers, part suppliers, magazines, clubs, and much more relating to owning, using and maintaining personal watercraft. You have to supply your own pirate flag.

Web:
http://www.connect.net/racerx/
http://www.personalwatercraft.com/
http://www.pwczone.com/

Where's Harley?
(See www.harley.com)

Look What I Found on the Net...

```
Newsgroup: rec.sport.rowing
Subject: Paddling in Stream: A Physicist Writes...

> I don't believe that it feels any different rowing with or
> against a current.  I think it is all due to visual cues from
> the shore.  As a similar example, have you ever walked on a
> moving walkway at an airport?  It seems to feel as though
> you are getting tremendous acceleration from each step.
> But if you close your eyes, aside from the sensation of the
> air, it feels no different than walking on a stationary
> surface.

I row on a river and, during the spring, the current is usually
pretty fast.  When I do my long distance workout, I measure the
time it takes for me to reach a specific point downstream and
then the time to get back.  Factoring in the velocity of the
current, which I check by just sitting in my single and drifting
for a fixed distance, my boat speed relative to the water
remains the same both ways.

I admit there is definitely a feeling of being faster when one
rows with the current, but each time I do this little
experiment, I conclude there is really no basis for it besides
the visual sensations.
```

BOATING AND SAILING

Rowing

Whether you prefer rowing gently down a stream, sculling by yourself in the early morning, or pulling frantically on your oar during a hard-fought bump race, **rec.sport.rowing** is one Usenet discussion group you should read. To help you find the information you need, I have also included some Web sites, one of which contains the rowing FAQ (frequently asked question list).

Web:
http://riceinfo.rice.edu/~hofer/Rowingfaq.html
http://www.comlab.ox.ac.uk/archive/other/rowing.html

Usenet:
rec.sport.rowing

Sailing

When you are landbound and missing the open seas, drop anchor on the Net, where there are a lot of sailing resources waiting for you. You can find FAQs (frequently asked question lists), humor, discussion, information about weather and navigation, and much, much more.

Web:
http://sailing.info-access.com/
http://www.sailnet.com/

Listserv Mailing List:
List Name: yacht-l
Subscribe to: listserv@nic.surfnet.nl

Seaports and Harbors

Before you set out on that long-distance trip, check with the Net about the ports you will be visiting. Many port authorities have Web sites, so you can use the Net to find out, in advance, what facilities are available. Here are some resources that will help you find Web sites for ports around the world.

Web:
http://www.seaports.com/
http://www.seaportsinfo.com/portmenu.html

Watercraft Calendar

Are you all dressed up in your sailor suit with no place to go? Here's an events calendar that will help you make plans for the weekend. Find out about races, meetings, boat shows and jet ski competitions all across the United States.

Web:
http://www.watercraft.com/pcalendr.html

Wave-Length Paddling Magazine

Now you can enjoy the online edition of Wave-Length paddling magazine. This magazine covers all topics relating to paddling and wilderness with a focus on preservation. Read articles on paddling experiences, kayaking and paddling with children, environmental issues, safety, and book, video and movie reviews. You can also get helpful hints on equipment, clothing and travel, and read the calendar of events.

Web:
http://www.wie.com/~wavenet/magazine.html

Get on the Right Wavelength

No matter how much you like kayaking, you can't spend all your time in the water. Sometimes you have to stay home and rest up for the next trip.
The best way to rest is to use your Net connection to read the online version of **Wave-Length Magazine**. That way, even if you are not in the water, you can still immerse yourself in the world of kayaking. In fact, if you have a waterproof laptop computer and a cellular modem, you can take your Net connection with you and read Wave-Length while you are paddling.

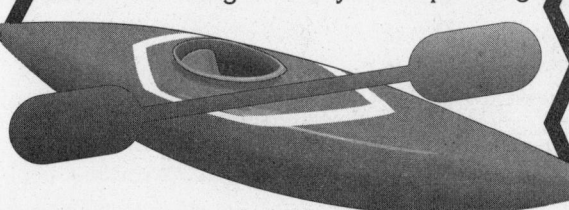

BOOKS

Bibliomania

Curl up by the fireplace and cozy down with this nice fiction collection, which includes author biographies and book texts. Authors include such notables as Joyce, Hardy, Dickens, Alcott, Defoe, Wilde, Stevenson, Kipling and Lawrence.

Web:
http://www.bibliomania.com/

Book Authors

Books are good for those times when the computer is down and you can't connect to the Net. If there is a particular kind of book that catches your fancy, check in Usenet to see if there is a discussion group relating to your favorite author.

Usenet:
alt.books.anne-rice
alt.books.arthur-clarke
alt.books.bukowski
alt.books.clive-barker
alt.books.crichton
alt.books.cs-lewis
alt.books.dean-koontz
alt.books.george-orwell
alt.books.h-g-wells
alt.books.isaac-asimov
alt.books.john-grisham
alt.books.julian-may
alt.books.kurt-vonnegut
alt.books.louis-lamour
alt.books.m-lackey
alt.books.orson-s-card
alt.books.peter-straub
alt.books.phil-k-dick
alt.books.poppy-z-brite
alt.books.pratchett
alt.books.raymond-feist
alt.books.robert-rankin
alt.books.roger-zelazny
alt.books.sf.melanie-rawn
alt.books.stephen-king
alt.books.terry-brooks
alt.books.toffler
alt.books.tom-clancy
alt.fan.tom-robbins
rec.arts.books.tolkien
rec.arts.sf.written.robert-jordan

Bookbinding

Make your own book or preserve some that are in a delicate condition. This bookbinding tutorial will show you how to photocopy, collate and fold paper, make a cover, punch holes, sew sections of a cover, trim pages and make a dust jacket.

Web:
http://www.cs.uiowa.edu/~jones/book/

Book Browser

This is one of my favorite book-related sites. I love information, and this Web site—created by two professional librarians—serves up heapin' spoonfuls of data in a well-organized buffet. For example, I was able to find a complete list of all the Perry Mason books by Erle Stanley Gardner. (I am a big Perry Mason fan—I have all the books, which I read repeatedly—so I think this list is a big deal.) There is also a collection of links to authors' Web sites on the Net, a pseudonym reference, lists of book awards, reviews, and much more. Check it out for yourself. If you like to read, you'll love this site.

Web:
http://www.bookbrowser.com/

Book Recommendations

We all love to recommend books to other people, and we all know that most of the time other people don't pay any attention. That's because we're wasting our time on the wrong people: our family and friends. Instead, we should be sharing our literary knowledge and good taste with the faceless millions of people on the Net. So if you like to read—and you like to tell other people what to read—this is the place for you. Share your list of favorite books with everyone, and take a look at what other people like to read.

Web:
http://www.best.com/~yylee/homespun/booktop.html

Mac users, see "Computers: Macintosh".

Book Resources

If you like books, you will find enough information on the Net to keep you reading until well past bedtime. These resources will lead you to Web sites where you can find author interviews, publisher information, book reviews, bookstore information, bibliographies, book organizations, and much, much more.

Web:
http://www.bookpage.com/
http://www.literaryleaps.com/

Book Reviews

Why waste your time and money on an unrewarding book? Read the reviews on the Net and find out the real scoop before you make a serious commitment. Save your excess time and money for unrewarding people. The Usenet groups are for ongoing discussion and current reviews.

Web:
http://www.ala.org/booklist/
http://www.nytimes.com/books/

Usenet:
alt.books.reviews
rec.arts.books.reviews

Book Talk and General Discussion

Usenet is a good place to find a variety of information about books, and to talk with other people. These discussion groups cover books of all genres, including reviews and discussion of reviews. Moreover, talk is not limited to books: there is a lot of discussion about the publishing industry as well as requests for information on interesting bookstores and hard-to-find bargains.

Usenet:
alt.books
alt.books.mysteries
alt.books.purefiction
rec.arts.books
rec.arts.books.hist-fiction
rec.arts.sf.dune
rec.books
rec.collecting.books

Book Talk and General Discussion

Many people believe if you have a complete set of Harley Hahn books, you really don't need anything else. Well, although that is certainly true for most people, there are a few oddballs who need some other type of literary stimulation once in a while. If you are one of these unfortunate eccentrics, you may want to follow the discussion in **rec.arts.books**. Find out what's old, what's new, what's borrowed, and what's colorful in the land of literature.

BookWeb

Book selling isn't just business, it's big business. If you want to stay plugged into what's new and exciting in the industry, check out BookWeb, maintained by the American Booksellers Association. Here you will find information about the American book industry, such as news, events and statistics, as well as a number of bookstore directories. (I am still waiting to find out the average number of Harley Hahn books that are sold to ballroom dance instructors every day.)

Web:
http://www.ambook.org/

BookWire

When you don't want the best book, only the best-selling book, check out this database of the hottest books on the market. The database is searchable by author or title. You'll find descriptions and links to book publishers and sellers on the Web, links to online libraries, a reading room, a book events calendar, and more.

Web:
http://www.bookwire.com/

74 BOOKS

Buying and Selling Books

Get a piece of the buying and selling action. See what's hot and what's not. Book reviews and business news make up the bulk of the traffic in these Usenet discussion groups.

Usenet:
  biz.books.technical
  rec.arts.books.marketplace

Children's Books

Parents: Are you looking for some good books for your kids? These Web sites will help you find a lot of useful resources relating to books for children and young adults. Find out about conferences, book events, book awards, recommended books, booksellers, movies based on children's books, and much more. For ongoing discussion, check out Usenet and share your ideas with other people who care about children and books.

Web:
  http://www.ucalgary.ca/~dkbrown/
  http://www.users.interport.net/~fairrosa/

Usenet:
  rec.arts.books.childrens

Do-It-Yourself Book Reviews

Which books are real crowd-pleasers? Find out by reading reviews written by people on the Internet. Categories include science fiction and fantasy, general fiction, religion, new age, mystery, computers and technology, biographies, science and mathematics.

Web:
  http://www.clark.net/pub/bell/review/
    book_review.shtml

Little Bo Peep lost her sheep,
so she used
"Finding Stuff on the Net".

Pulp Fiction

Pulp magazines existed in America from the turn of the century to the early 1950s. They offered an impressive array of stories about crime, mystery, detectives, war, love, romance, science fiction, horror, sports, westerns and adventure. The spirit of pulp fiction is alive today in modern paperback adventure series and on the Net. Did you know that the Shadow was really Kent Allard, a World War I ace and spy? Lamont Cranston was merely a disguise. If you listen to the radio show, you will be misinformed, but with these resources, you will know the truth.

Web:
  http://members.aol.com/dotPulp/
  http://www.columbia.edu/~mfs10/pulp.html

Usenet:
  alt.pulp

Rare Books

People always want what they can't have, so, if it's rare, it's bound to be popular. Take rare books, for example. People collect them, and most of the time they just store the books and never look at them. I myself collect old Freddy the Pig books (but I read them). For lots of valuable information, see the Web sites. If you want to talk to other book lovers, join one of the mailing lists, where you can discuss out-of-print and rare books, as well as techniques for preserving your special collection (such as don't read a valuable Freddy the Pig book while you are eating spaghetti).

Web:
  http://www.princeton.edu/~ferguson/rbms.html
  http://www.rarebooks.org/

Listproc Mailing List:
  List Name: **exlibris**
  Subscribe to: **listproc@library.berkeley.edu**

Listserv Mailing List:
  List Name: **rare**
  Subscribe to: **listserv@biblio.bibliofind.com**

Listserv Mailing List:
  List Name: **rarebooks-l**
  Subscribe to: **listserv@listserv.indiana.edu**

BOOKS

Romance Novels

Fantasies are exciting because they are not played out in real life. All the more reason to immerse yourself in a good, old-fashioned romance novel. If you're a romance addict, I've got some Web sites for you. You can search for books, read reviews, and visit the Web sites of various romance authors. Are you looking for something new to read? Just specify your favorite author or genre, and the Net can help you find the first romance novel of the rest of your life. In the meantime, let me tell you some interesting statistics. Several years ago, two college professors presented the results of some important research at a scholarly conference. They read one hundred romance novels and found that at the beginning of the novel, 74 percent of the heroines were virgins while none of the men were. Notwithstanding, 98 percent of the heroines had an orgasm the first time they had sex. They also found that 17 percent of the novels had rape scenes, and 18 percent of the women who were raped had an orgasm during the attack. (By the way, a few years later, the two professors were back at the same conference where they presented a paper entitled "Collecting Mickey Mouse".)

Web:
http://www-personal.si.umich.edu/~sooty/romance/
http://www.romanceweb.com/
http://www.romcom.com/
http://www.theromancereader.com/

Jennifer's breath grew short and stertorous. Her lips began to quiver while her straw-colored hair moved gently in the warm tropical breeze.

She gazed up at the dark, mysterious, masculine eyes of the stranger. As a frisson of passion shocked her taut, leonine body, she whispered softly into his dark, mysterious, masculine ear. "Tell me, my love," she murmured, "of all the heroines in all the romance novels in the world, whom would you say I most resemble?" The stranger touched her face gently with the back of his dark, mysterious, masculine hand. He turned away slowly, the moonlight shining brightly on his dark, mysterious, masculine features as he took out his palmtop computer. "Just one moment, my sweet angel," he responded. "My Internet connection will be active shortly, and I will be able to check the **Romance Novels** Web sites."

Science Fiction and Fantasy Reviews

This is the place to find reviews of your favorite (or not so favorite) books, magazines, movies and videos. This collection of resources offers reviews of speculative fiction, fantasy, horror and even (sometimes) comics. The Usenet discussion group is moderated.

Web:
http://www.clark.net/pub/iz/Books/Top100/top100.html

Usenet:
rec.arts.sf.reviews

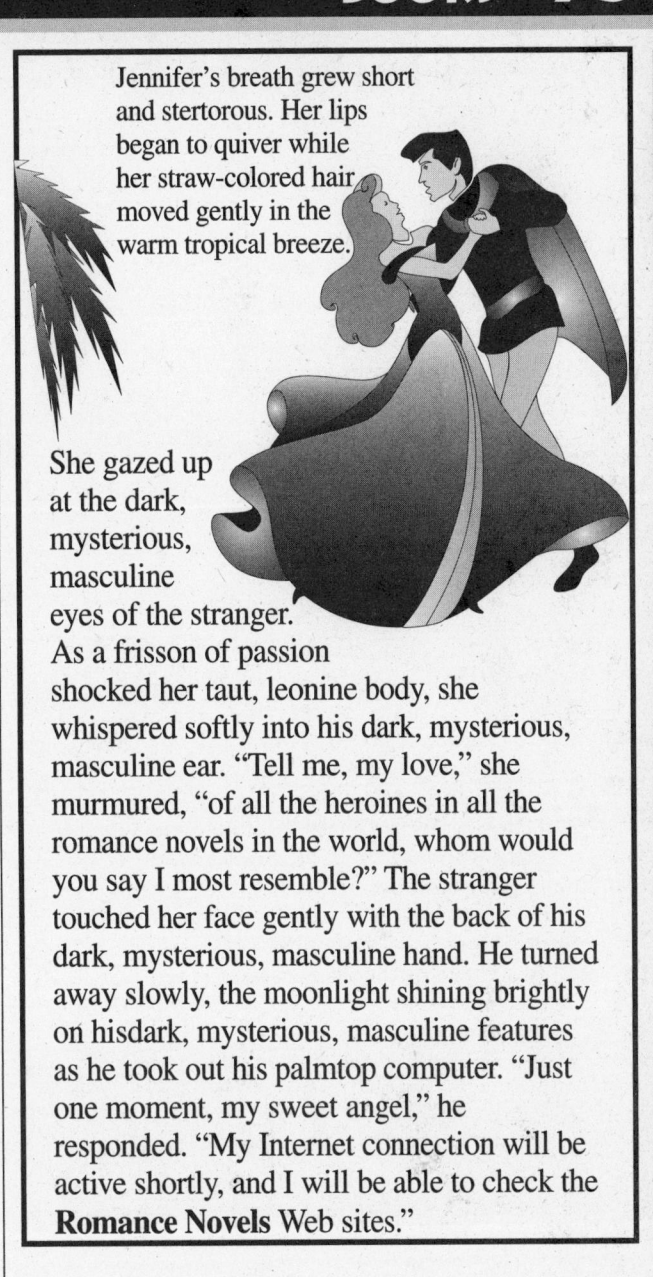

Technical Books

If you have a squeak in your clicker or you can't get slot A to line up with tab B, check into these Usenet discussion groups to see if there is a technical book that can help. Just the place to look when you need to decide which Unix book to give your grandmother for her birthday.

Usenet:
alt.books.technical
misc.books.technical

BOTANY

Agroforestry

As the population grows, the need for better crops and soil increases. Agroforestry studies plant growth and nutrition in an effort to find crops and soil that are compatible with each other and with the rest of the surrounding environment.

Web:
http://www.cgiar.org/icraf/
http://www.unl.edu/nac/

Usenet:
bionet.agroforestry

> We need better and more crops and forests, but what have *you* done lately to help? After all, if you're not part of the solution, you're not contributing your fair share of nose to the grindstone. But don't worry, it's never too late. Join the **bionet.agroforestry** discussion group right this minute. Soon, with your help, poor crop yields will be a thing of the past and never again will some poor mother in Fargo, North Dakota, have to tell her son to clean his plate because paper doesn't grow on trees.

Botanical Gardens

I belong to the local botanical garden where I live. I find that there is nothing more relaxing than sitting beside a rushing brook under a large tree, or reading a good book while sitting in a field of wildflowers. If you like gardens and plants, here is a list of botanical gardens in Canada and the United States, wonderful places to visit when you get a chance to slow down and enjoy life.

Web:
http://www.botanique.com/

Botanical Glossary

When someone calls you a reniform acaulescent stomium, don't get mad, get even. Check with the Botanical Glossary and soon you will be able to reply, "Yeah, well, your mother is a vegetative (lacking reproductive organs) perispore (wrinkled spore covering)."

Web:
http://www.anbg.gov.au/glossary/croft.html

Botany Images

Here are thousands of pictures of plants, flowers, trees, fungi and other vegetation. If you are a student or researcher of botany, this is a site you should explore. However, even if you don't really care about botany, I suggest that you browse around and see what's here. There are fabulous pictures that would be great to dress up your Web page or to use as a background.

Web:
http://www.wisc.edu/botany/virtual.html

Botany Talk and General Discussion

How does your garden grow? Discover the myth and mystery of plant growth and reproduction. Discussion of all aspects of plant biology is encouraged. You'll never have a guilt-free salad again.

Usenet:
bionet.plants

Botany Web Sites

Students, teachers, scientists or plain old plant lovers must immediately make their way to this Web page. There is a huge amount of resources for botanists around the Net, and you will find most of them here: links to databases, mailing lists, archive sites, software, organizations, and much more.

Web:
http://www.biol.uregina.ca/liu/bio/botany.shtml

BOTANY

Carnivorous Plants

A carnivorous plant is one that eats animal matter of some type (usually insects, but sometimes very small animals like frogs). Carnivorous plants have adapted to live in an environment which is lacking in nutrients, for example, a bog or the surface of a cliff. Worldwide, there are more than 600 different species of carnivorous plants, many of which can be grown right in your very own home or garden. What is fascinating about them is that they are so unexpected. Normally, we assume that plants will sit quietly and leave the animal kingdom alone. To find a plant that can actually attract, capture and digest an animal of some type is a complete biological non sequitur. In case you want to explore these monarchs of the botanical world, here are some Internet resources to help you learn about these plants before they learn about *you*.

Web:
  http://www.hpl.hp.com/bot/cp_home/
  http://www.indirect.com/www/bazza/cps/faq/faq.html

Listserv Mailing List:
  List Name: **cp**
  Subscribe to: **listserv@opus.hpl.hp.com**

Ethnobotany

Ethnobotany is the study of how people in a particular region of the world make use of the indigenous plants. Ethnobotany involves not only botany, but many other disciplines such as archaeology, anthropology, biochemistry, pharmacology, history, sociology, mythology, and so on. Ethnobotany is especially important to us as a source for native plants that might have important pharmacological and medical uses.

Web:
  http://hammock.ifas.ufl.edu/~michael/eb/
  http://www.ars-grin.gov/duke/

Everything I tell you is true.
The above sentence is only partially correct.
Don't believe everything you read.

Look What I Found on the Net...

(from the Carnivorous Plants frequently asked question list)

...You bought a Venus Fly Trap and have no idea how to grow it. So you fired up your Web browser and here you are, right?

Fine, but I have bad news for you. The people who raised your plant grew that little green gem in a fabulous greenhouse facility. That plant was healthy, strong, vigorous, and very happy in its customized environment...

The surprise is that your Venus Fly Trap requires exacting growing conditions in order to live. If you live in a climate very much like coastal North Carolina you will be able to grow the plant easily.

Otherwise, it is doomed. It is dying now. It will take a while, but it is surely approaching death.

What to do now? I have a few suggestions. First, consider returning the plant to the store...

Ferns

In an outside alcove at my house, I have a fern garden with a nice variety of plants. From within the house, there are two large windows that I can look out of and see the ferns. I am not sure exactly what it is, but ferns have a special feeling about them that makes them unique among plants. If you would like to know more about ferns, here are some resources containing detailed biological data, as well as information about related books, organizations, events and helpful hints.

Web:
   http://www.inetworld.net/~sdfern/
   http://www.visuallink.net/fern/

Lichens

Lichens are so cool. You've probably heard of them, but do you know what they really are? Lichens are organisms made up of a combination of algae and fungus living symbiotically. The fungus collects the water that is needed by the algae. The algae uses the water for photosynthesis, which produces the food needed by the fungus. Cool, huh? And not only that, when the algae and fungus reproduce, they usually do so simultaneously. (Although experts suspect that the fungus will sometimes fake it.) Lichens are found all over the world, from the deserts to the polar regions, so there's a good chance you can find some near you. They make great pets, especially for people who can't handle the responsibility of caring for children or cats.

Web:
   http://mgd.nacse.org/hyperSQL/lichenland/
   http://www.sbg.ac.at/pfl/projects/lichen/

Listproc Mailing List:
   List Name: lichens-l
   Subscribe to: listproc@hawaii.edu

Canada is more than just a country. It's an entire section of this book.

Paleobotany

Paleontology is the study of the history of life on Earth as reflected in the fossil record. Paleobotany is the branch of paleontology that concentrates on plant fossils and ancient vegetation. The most common type of plant fossils are the impressions of leaves. Other parts of the plant, such as stems, seeds and wood are more often petrified. Petrified wood is formed over millions of years as silica dissolved in groundwater replaces the organic material in pieces of wood. Thus, petrified wood is really a mineral that has been formed within the pattern of the wood.

Web:
   http://www.dartmouth.edu/~daghlian/paleo/
   http://www.uni-wuerzburg.de/mineralogie/
      palbot1.html

Palynology Resources

Palynology is the study of spores and pollen. My advice is to visit this Web site as often as you can and brush up on your knowledge of tiny things that float around making people miserable. Then, when you meet someone at a party and they ask about your hobbies, you can say, "Oh, I am something of an amateur palynologist. Do you like spores?" I guarantee you will be invited back again and again.

Web:
   http://www.ualberta.ca/~abeaudoi/cap/links/
      websites.htm

Photosynthesis

Photosynthesis is the process whereby sunlight is used as an energy source to synthesize carbohydrates from carbon dioxide and water. As a byproduct, photosynthesis also produces oxygen. Photosynthesis takes place in most plants, as well as algae and some bacteria. In plants, photosynthesis requires the use of chlorophyll, a pigment that gives plants their characteristic green color. All foods, fossil fuels (such as oil and coal), and plant products are indirect products of photosynthesis. Thus, without photosynthesis, there would be no paper to print this book and no pizza to eat as you use the Net.

Web:
   http://photoscience.la.asu.edu/photosyn/

Usenet:
   bionet.photosynthesis

Plant Fossil Database

For some reason, when you read about extinct and endangered species, animals get all the press. However, there is a large number of extinct plant species, many of which have left fossil remains. This database contains a wealth of research information relating to thousands of extinct plants.

Web:
http://ibs.uel.ac.uk/ibs/palaeo/pfr2/pfr.htm

Plant Gene Register

The Electronic Plant Gene Register is an online publication produced by the American Society of Plant Physiologists. The Web site allows you to access a large database of information relating to DNA sequence determination of plant genes.

Web:
http://www.tarweed.com/pgr/

Plant Hormones

A plant hormone is a chemical that, when produced in one part of the plant and transmitted to other parts of the plant, can, in small amounts, affect various biological processes. The most common plant hormones are auxin, cytokinins, gibberellins, abscisic acid and ethylene. Hormones control processes such as cell growth, branching, apical dominance, the differentiation of vascular tissue, root creation and signaling. Apical dominance, for example, occurs when a terminal bud produces an auxin that moves down the branch and inhibits lateral budding. Plant hormones are even important in the home. When you have a piece of fruit that you want to ripen quickly, put it in a paper bag with an unripe banana. As the banana ripens, it will emit ethylene (a gaseous hormone), which will cause the other fruit to ripen more quickly.

Web:
http://www.plant-hormones.bbsrc.ac.uk/

This is the first book of the rest of your life.

Tune in, turn on, and drop in to the Net.

Look What I Found on the Net...

```
Newsgroup: bionet.photosynthesis
Subject: I'm a Dad!

Although I don't know all of you I thought this was the easiest
way to let most of my photosynthesis buddies know what's
happening with me, and why I won't be at the upcoming conference
causing trouble this year.

I'm a dad! It's a girl.

She doesn't seem too interested in photosynthesis yet:
eating, sleeping and screaming are the current focus,
but there is time for everything.

Xxxx Xxxxx
Department of Biological Sciences
Xxxxx University
```

Plant Pathology

Plants get sick. However, unlike people, plants rarely have adequate insurance and must almost always depend on the kindness of strangers. If you have a sick plant, or if you happen to be a plant pathologist doing research or wondering what your peers are up to, here are some Web sites specializing in botanical diseases and related topics.

Web:
  http://ppathw3.cals.cornell.edu/olplpath/olplpath.htm
  http://www.bspp.org.uk/fbpp.htm
  http://www.ianr.unl.edu/pubs/PlantDisease/
  http://www.scisoc.org/resource/common/

Plant Taxonomy

Plant taxonomy refers to the scientific classification of plants. There is a wealth of information on the Net that can help you identify and name the plant of your choice. For example, say your significant other gives you a Phyllanthus acuminatus for Valentine's Day. Most people wouldn't know what to make of it, but as one of my readers, it will be the work of a moment for you to check with the Net and find out that your gift is actually a Jamaican gooseberry tree. (Wow!)

Web:
  http://www.csdl.tamu.edu/FLORA/aspt/aspthome.htm
  http://www.inform.umd.edu/pbio/pb250/
  http://www.itis.usda.gov/itis/
  http://www.york.biosis.org/zrdocs/zoolinfo/an_names.htm#pla

Succulents and Cacti

Succulents are fleshy plants that are characterized by being able to survive with minimal water. Succulents typically have thick leaves, covered with a waxy material called cutin that acts to reduce the evaporation of water. These plants—including many species of cactus, aloe and yucca—are commonly indigenous to naturally dry regions, such as the semi-arid areas of the world. Personally, I like succulents, and I have a number of them in my office and outside in my garden. One such plant that I recommend for everyone is the aloe vera. It is easy to grow, and the slimy substance inside the leaves is useful for treating mild burns and skin irritations.

Web:
  http://www.gardenweb.com/forums/cacti/
  http://www.graylab.ac.uk/usr/hodgkiss/succule.html
  http://www.vvv.com/~amdigest/

Smithsonian Botany Resources

Botany lovers will have a great time with the Smithsonian's online botany resources, including databases, images and links to botanic collections. There is also information about the United States National Herbarium.

Web:
  http://nmnhwww.si.edu/departments/botany.html

Succulents and Cacti

Low maintenance, hardy, independent, easygoing— succulents are all of these. (If only all your relationships were so simple.)

BROADCASTING ON THE NET

Audionet

Audionet is a huge collection of audio broadcasting sites. Whatever your tastes, there is something here for you: education, comedy, business, newscasts, home repair, computers, celebrities, sports, music, politics, live radio stations, and much more. If you are looking for something new to listen to, this is a good place to start your search.

Web:
  http://www.broadcast.com/

BROADCASTING ON THE NET

Instead of watching TV, read about it: take a look at the "Television" section.

Book Radio

If you like to keep up on what's current in the book world, you'll like Book Radio. There are lots of interviews with authors, as well as book reviews and general book talk. You can also hear authors read from their own work. (That gives me an idea. Maybe I should record something from this book to play on my telephone answering machine. What a concept!)

Web:
http://www.bookradio.com/

Celebrity Interviews

There are two types of celebrities: accomplished people who are famous because they have achieved or created something of renown, and vacuous people who are famous because they are famous. However, accomplished or vacuous, celebrities seem to have one thing in common. They always have a lot to say, especially when they need to plug a new movie or book. Let us not forget, though, the main reason for listening to celebrity interviews: to find out the newest gossip. Isn't it interesting that, when our friends and relatives get divorced or have financial problems, it's nothing but a big pain, but when the same things happen to celebrities, we are fascinated? Maybe it's because famous people are so far removed from our personal world, it doesn't bother us when they screw up their lives. (Or maybe it's because celebrities don't call in the middle of the night asking us to choose sides or lend them money.) Anyway, if you like to hear celebrities talking, not to mention people talking about celebrities, here are the places to be.

Web:
http://www.broadcast.com/entertainment/celeb.stm
http://www.premrad.com/entertainment/celeb/bytes.html
http://www.zeldman.com/celeb.html

Commercial Radio Stations

There are lots and lots of regular commercial radio stations that you can listen to over the Net. There's something intriguing about listening to a station that is far away. And, somehow, local commercials for a distant city don't seem to be as obnoxious as local commercials in your own hometown. Here are collections of links to hundreds of radio stations you can listen to on the Net. I bet you'll have fun exploring. I am also including the address of my favorite commercial station, OZ-FM, in Newfoundland, Canada.

Web:
http://goan.com/radio.html
http://www.comfm.fr/sites/rdirect/
http://www.newcomm.net/ozfm.ram
http://www.timecast.com/stations/
http://www.web-radio.com/

Computer News Broadcasts

There's always a lot happening in the world of computers and technology, and you can use the Net to help you keep up to date. Here are some sites you can tune into at any time to listen to reports on what is new and exciting. The next time you meet a beautiful babe in the laundromat, invite her over to see your computer and connect to one of these broadcasting sites. If that doesn't impress her, nothing will.

Web:
http://www.nettalklive.com/
http://www.zdnet.com/pcweek/radio/

Internet Broadcasting Networks

Tune in to one of the networks that broadcasts over the Internet, and watch the world change in front of your very eyes (and ears).

82 BROADCASTING ON THE NET

Internet Broadcasting Networks

The time has passed when broadcasting required a huge sum of money as well as permission from the government. Here are some networks that broadcast exclusively over the Internet. The costs are relatively low, there is no government regulation, and the audience is worldwide. I think that this aspect of the Net is one of the most important, and is going to change our global society significantly. Check out these Internet-based networks, and you will find a large variety of shows, audio and video, live and prerecorded. Some are slick, expensive productions. Others are down-home laid-back get-togethers. Today, as I write this, I am enjoying a show in which the host is playing some of his old Beach Boys records (which makes me anxious to finish these descriptions and get out into the water with my board).

Web:
 http://www.denradio.com/
 http://www.internetv.com/
 http://www.intv.net/
 http://www.netradio.net/
 http://www.thedj.com/

Live Broadcasting Guides

Every minute of every day, there is a lot of broadcasting—audio and video—on the Net. These broadcasting guides will help you find out what's happening live right now (or soon). Enjoy audio broadcasts, video broadcasts, sports, concerts, live chats, and more. As I was writing this, I checked to see what was on the menu for the evening. I found country music, campus radio/video from Taiwan, Christian music, exotic dancers performing live strip acts (on video), a sports show, and a talk show.

Web:
 http://www.broadcast.com/
 http://www.live-online.com/
 http://www.onnow.com/
 http://www.timecast.com/

> **Don't be a Web Potato: participate.**

> **Isn't this more fun than watching television?**

Live Concerts

The Net is host to live concerts—both audio and video—that you can enjoy from anywhere in the world. Check here from time to time, and see what concerts are being broadcast. After all, why should you pay through the nose for expensive tickets when you can use the Net to listen to a concert for free (through the ears)?

Web:
 http://www.jamtv.com/sections/venue/text/
 http://www.liveconcerts.com/
 http://www.sonicnet.com/guide/

News Broadcasts

News, news, news. 24 hours a day. Live. Video and audio. News, business, sports, weather, science. Video and audio. Live. 24 hours a day. News, news, news.

Web:
 http://news.bbc.co.uk/olmedia/audio/
  world_summary.ram
 http://www.cnn.com/audioselect/
 http://www.foxnews.com/video/
 http://www.npr.org/news/
 http://www.wrn.org/

Sports Broadcasts

If you're a sports buff, you'll love the Net. There are lots and lots of sporting events you can listen to and watch—baseball, hockey, basketball, football, college sports, and more—as well as post-game shows, updates, interviews, clips and archived games. And, of course, you can listen to sports news whenever you want, so you never have to worry about missing the latest scores just because you are forced to spend some of your time working, eating or sleeping.

Web:
 http://espnet.sportszone.com/zonemedia/
 http://www.broadcast.com/sports/
 http://www.majorleaguebaseball.com/av/
 http://www.sportsline.com/u/byline/

CANADA

Anti-Canada Web Site

Oh Canada! The land of "good manners, friendly people, and clean streets"—a nice, innocent, well-behaved country. Or is it? Better check this Web site before you make up your mind about the true north strong and free.

Web:
http://www.neptunenet.com/antican/

Canadian Constitutional Documents

In 1982, the United Kingdom parliament gave up all power over Canadian laws, including the Canadian constitution. Since then—through hard work and perseverance—Canada has become one of the best countries in North America. Would you like your own copy of the 1982 Canada Act? It's here, along with many other Canadian constitutional documents, waiting for you, 24 hours a day, 365 days a year.

Web:
http://insight.mcmaster.ca/org/efc/pages/law/cons/Constitutions/Canada/English/cons.html

Canadian Culture

There is an old riddle: What is Canadian culture? The answer is, "Mostly American." Some people feel that "Canadian culture" is an oxymoron. What do they know? Haven't they ever heard of the Blue Jays? William Shatner? Rick Moranis (with whom I went to summer camp)? After all, if Canadian culture is good enough for Wayne Gretzky, it should be good enough for The Kids in the Hall.

Web:
http://www.culturenet.ucalgary.ca/indexen.html
http://www.icomm.ca/emily/

Usenet:
soc.culture.canada

CANADIAN (?) CULTURE

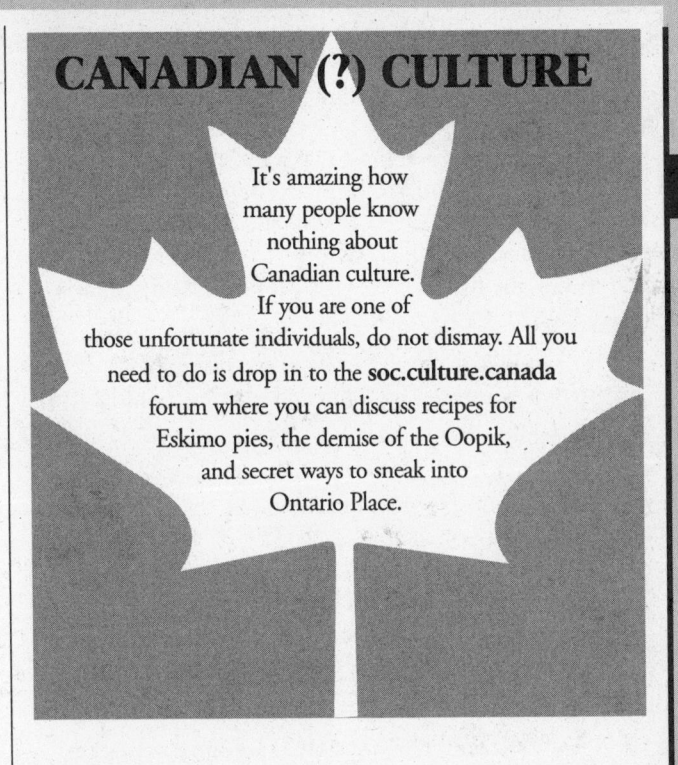

It's amazing how many people know nothing about Canadian culture. If you are one of those unfortunate individuals, do not dismay. All you need to do is drop in to the **soc.culture.canada** forum where you can discuss recipes for Eskimo pies, the demise of the Oopik, and secret ways to sneak into Ontario Place.

Canadian Fact Sheets

Straight from the Canadian Department of Foreign Affairs and International Trade to you. Here is information about Canadian provinces, history, government, legal system, economy, trade, education, women, geography, environment, climate, transportation, arts, sports, and—of course—the Mounties.

Web:
http://www.dfait-maeci.gc.ca/english/canada/menu.htm

Canadian Government

Explore segments of the Canadian federal government, including the House of Commons, the Senate, the Supreme Court, and federal departments and agencies. These pages are in both French and English.

Web:
http://canada.gc.ca/
http://canada.justice.gc.ca/
http://cipo.gc.ca/
http://www.parl.gc.ca/

CANADA

Canadian History

Here is a little-known fragment of Canadian history: when my sister, Melissa, was two years old and I was babysitting her, she fell off my parents' bed and hit her head on the floor. (Come to Toronto with me some time, and I will show you the exact spot.) Of course, not all Canadian history is that interesting, but still, there are jewels if you only take the time to look.

Web:
  http://www.arts.ouc.bc.ca/fiar/his_home.html
  http://www.interchange.ubc.ca/sneylan/cdnhist.htm

Listserv Mailing List:
  List Name: h-canada
  Subscribe to: listserv@h-net.msu.edu

Canadian Investment

If you're looking to spread your money around a little, try investing in Canada. Learn about Canadian money markets, investment clubs, financial publications and the government. (And, if you have a little extra money, I have a snow farm you might want to invest in.)

Web:
  http://www.canadianfinance.com/

Usenet:
  misc.invest.canada

Lonely? Try IRC.

Look What I Found on the Net...

```
Newsgroup: misc.invest.canada
Subject: Retirement Savings Plans "Should be Taxed" to Reduce Deficit
```

The federal government can't ignore $15 billion a year in tax-breaks for retirement savings if it's serious about controlling the deficit, says a new article in a respected economics journal...

The item says the government needs to find out if tax deductions for contributions to RRSPs, registered pension plans, and deferred profit-sharing plans are working.

Economists Sid Ingerman and Robin Rowley of McGill University in Montreal take issue with the view — trumpeted by four major pension consulting firms and the Reform Party — that the government should keep its hands off money set aside for old age.

Finance Minister Paul Martin announced that his department would study the problem of the country's aging population, and how to finance its retirement...

Ingerman and Rowley say the federal and provincial governments have five major options:

* leave the system alone
* reduce contribution limits
* tax new contributions to pension plans
* tax the income that pension-funds earn
* impose one-time or periodic levies on pension-fund assets

The authors say that New Zealand has already eliminated tax breaks for retirement savings, while Australia and Sweden have moved to increase their tax take.

CANADA

Investing In Canada

No financial portfolio is complete without a healthy collection of Canadian stock. But don't let your holdings in the country just north of the Land-of-the-Free-and-the-Home-of-the-Brave expire from benign neglect. Keep track of what is moving and grooving in the country that boasts the best baseball team in the world. Use the *Canadian Investment* site. My personal favorite is a long-term investment in beaver futures.

Canadian Legal Resources

My brother Randy is a lawyer in Toronto, so I guess you could say I have a Canadian legal resource right in the family. But when a free consultation isn't enough, I turn to the Net (and so should you). In less time than it takes to say "division of powers", you will be able to find information about Canadian courts and tribunals, law reform commissions, legislation, taxes and accounting, lawyers and law firms, universities, the federal and provincial governments, free speech and privacy. Wow! (Or, as they say in Canada, "Eh?")

Web:
http://www.droit.umontreal.ca/doc/biblio/en/
http://www.smithlyons.ca/links/cdn_link.htm

Don't click here.

Canadian Music

After more than 25 years of federal "Canadian content" rules, Canadian music is alive and well and living in...ahem...Canada. At the Web site you can search for your favorite band. Or just join the discussion of your favorite musicians from the land where a rich musical tradition resonates from sea to shining sea. (Bagpipes and accordions are optional.)

Web:
http://www.monkey-boy.com/cmusic/

Usenet:
alt.music.canada

WANT TO HEAR SOME REALLY "COOL" SOUNDS? Try *CANADIAN MUSIC*.

Canadian News

An American magazine once referred to Canada as "the retarded giant on our doorstep". Read the latest Canadian news and get the real scoop. You will find that Canadian news is about as exciting as...well...Canadian news.

Web:
http://www.canoe.ca/cnews/
http://www.cdnemb-washdc.org/newscan.html
http://www.cp.org/
http://www.newsworld.cbc.ca/

Canadian Resources

I grew up in Canada, and, although I didn't realize it at the time, I had Canadian resources all around me. Now I have to get them from the Internet. Fortunately, that's not a problem. There are so many Canadian resources, you can use all you want and still have enough left over for the rest of the family. News, statistics, travel, government services, politics, history, education, culture—everything under the Canadian sun is waiting for you on the Net.

Web:
http://www.cs.cmu.edu/Web/Unofficial/Canadiana/README.html
http://www.nlc-bnc.ca/caninfo/ecaninfo.htm
http://www.yahoo.ca/

Canadian Sports

As a young lad growing up in Canada, I watched a lot of hockey on television, and went to a great many football games. That was years ago. Since then, Canadian sports have become even more popular. For example, there are now professional baseball and basketball teams, which was not the case when I was growing up. If you are a sports fan, you will enjoy these Web sites, where you can keep up to date on Canadian sports of all types, both amateur and professional.

Web:
http://www.canoe.ca/slam/
http://www.interlog.com/~jeffv/hockey.htm
http://www.tsn.ca/

Canadian Talk and General Discussion

What do you do at 9:30 PM on Saturday night when you are just dying to talk to a Canadian and William Shatner's line is busy? Hop over to IRC, where nimble-fingered Canadians are cutting fast, loose and easy. Need a French-Canadian fix? Try the **#quebec** channel ("ici, on parle Français"). Who says Saturday night has to be dull?

Usenet:
  alt.canadian
  alt.ontario.north-bay
  soc.culture.canada
  soc.culture.quebec

IRC:
  #alberta
  #calgary
  #canada
  #edmonton
  #manitoba
  #montreal
  #ontario
  #quebec
  #toronto
  #vancouver
  #winnipeg

Life begins at 0.

Canadian Travel

Canada is a big place, and it's easy to get lost. Imagine how embarrassed you would be if, after saving all your money and planning for months, you and your family finally make it to Canada only to become completely disoriented. For example, what if you are driving from Winnipeg to Toronto, and you accidentally make a left turn at North Bay? The next thing you know, you are in the Ungava Peninsula, and the kids are complaining, "There are no bathrooms. You promised we would stop at McDonald's. Whose dumb idea was it to go on this trip anyway?" Don't let this happen to you. Before you even think about exploring this grand old country just north of the Land of the Free and Home of the Brave, use the Net to access Canada's tourism information network. Remember their slogan: "Canada, the country with a lot of space."

Web:
  http://info.ic.gc.ca/Tourism/Canada/

Canadian Travel

Who among us has not sat wistfully at a desk, daydreaming about being able to visit Canada? What a joy it would be to visit the frozen jewel of North America without even having to pack a bag.

Well, now your dream can come true— you can use the Net to tour Canada right from your very own home. (Hint: As you pass through Toronto, look for the plaque marking the place where I was born.)

Canuck Site of the Day

Everybody needs a bit of Canadian something-or-other in their life. Don't be deprived. Every day, you can visit this site and be surprised with a nice, pleasant Canadian experience.

Web:
  http://csod.canadas.net/

CBC (Canadian Broadcasting Corporation)

In December 1928, the Canadian government set up a Royal Commission (special committee) to figure out what to do about radio broadcasting in Canada. After spending a long time studying the situation, the commission issued a report which, in May 1932, led to the formation of the Canadian Radio Broadcasting Commission (CRCB). The CRCB started to create and broadcast Canadian programming and, in November 1936, after more committees and more reports, the CRCB was changed into the Canadian Broadcasting Corporation (CBC). Since then, the CBC has grown into a large, government-supported network, broadcasting television and radio across Canada, in both English and French. It's hard for an outsider to fully understand the importance and the ubiquity of the CBC. Canada has fewer people than California in an area that is much larger than the entire United States. Most of the country speaks English and is heavily Americanized (although they like to deny it). The province of Quebec speaks French and has its own unique culture. Add to this a government that has, for many years, tried to create a "Canadian culture", by spending money, passing laws, spending money, creating lots of cultural propaganda, and spending money. The modern-day mission of the CBC is to balance all of these forces—in two languages—while entertaining and informing the entire country.

Web:
  http://www.cbc.ca/

Just say no to spam.

If you are one of those people lucky enough to get CBC (Canadian) Radio, you will appreciate their web site.

Montreal

When I was in the 10th grade, my class went on a trip to Montreal to see the World's Fair. Years later, I went to Montreal again to see the summer Olympics. You, however, may not have fulfilled your quota, so a trip to Montreal may be in your future. If so, here is a good place to get the details you need to make your visit enjoyable: locations, attractions, calendar of events, museums, maps of the city and, for foreign travelers, customs regulations and exchange rates.

Web:
  http://www.tourism-montreal.org/

Musée du Québec

The Musée du Québec (Quebec Museum) is the province of Quebec's national art gallery, containing more than 20,000 works of art, most of which were produced in Quebec. You can look at some of the paintings over the Net as well as historical information about the artists. At this point, I can hear you saying, "Wait, Quebec is a province. Why would it have its own 'national' art gallery?" The answer is: Don't even ask. Just visit and enjoy yourself.

Web:
  http://www.mdq.org/fr/Anglais/

CANADA

Ottawa

I once spent a summer in Ottawa, the capital of Canada, and I had a great time. It's a beautiful city with a lot of tourist attractions and wonderful places to visit. And there are miles of pleasant bicycle paths on which you can ride your bike or jog. True, the winter gets a tad cold—actually, freezing beyond endurance—but you can skate on the canal and cross-country ski in the parks. However, perhaps the most important thing that anybody needs to know about Ottawa is that my friend Mike the Dentist lives there. If, for some reason, you need more information, all you need to do is check with the Net, where you can find out about dining, transportation, things to see and things to do. Whether you live in Ottawa or are merely planning to visit, there is lots of info waiting for you on the Net, twenty-four hours a day. And, if your teeth start to hurt, you can always call Mike.

Web:
http://www.ottawa.com/
http://www.ottawaweb.com/
http://www.tourottawa.org/

Toronto

I was born in Toronto and, I can tell you, it changes so fast that the only way I can keep up is to live in California and use the Net to look at the Toronto information Web site. Find all the info you need about Toronto: news, sports, entertainment, food, music, tourism, and so on. However, my favorite activity is to check the weather reports during the winter.

Web:
http://www.torinfo.com/
http://www.wheremags.com/wheremag.nsf/cities/toronto

There are only two things worth remembering in life (both of which I forget).

Vancouver

The summer after I finished high school, I hitchhiked across Canada and ended up in Vancouver, where I joined a special French-language program at the University of British Columbia. It was great—the government paid for everything. I got free food, a place to stay, had lots of fun, went on excursions, and spent the afternoons sunning at Wreck Beach (the nude beach). And all I had to do was put in a few hours a day trying to learn how to speak French. ("La plume de ma tante est sur la table.") Since then, I have had occasion to spend many more delightful days in the pearl of the Canadian west coast. For instance, when I was a medical student, I spent a few weeks in Vancouver researching a book on unconventional medicine. Even if you do not want to learn to speak French or understand unconventional medicine, you may still want to visit Vancouver. If so, you can check with the Net before you go. There you will find information about parks, community centers, bicycling, swimming pools, arts, entertainment, attractions and visitor resources. True, the government probably won't pay for your room and board, but you can still spend your afternoons at Wreck Beach.

Web:
http://www.discovervancouver.com/
http://www.vanmag.com/

CARS AND TRUCKS

Antique Cars

Wash it, buff it, and tuck your baby in at night. If antique automobiles hold a special place in your heart, you are not alone—not on the Net. There are Web sites to visit and people to talk to. If your family and friends can't understand the beauty and allure of a 1957 Studebaker Hawk, a 1948 DeSoto Club Coupe or a classic (1955-1957) Thunderbird, rest assured there are lots of people who share your discrimination and good taste.

Web:
http://www.aaca.org/
http://www.classicar.com/

Usenet:
alt.autos.antique
rec.autos.antique

CARS AND TRUCKS

Auto Channel

You don't need a television to check out the Auto Channel. In fact, you don't even need a car. All you have to do to get great auto news, commentary and other useful information is point your Web browser to the Auto Channel Web site.

Web:
http://www.theautochannel.com/

Auto Discussion Archives and FAQ

Take it from me, the best place to learn about cars is where you learned about sex: in the street. Here is a wealth of street-smart info, guaranteed to explain something interesting you always wanted to know but were afraid to ask. For example, I learned how to double-clutch (and my car is an automatic).

Web:
http://www.wizvax.net/rwelty/FAQ/

Auto Racing

As one of my readers, you can no doubt drive rings around anyone else. So where do you go in between races when you want to read what people are saying about driving from one place to another as fast as possible? Put the virtual pedal to the metal and aim for the Net, where you will find discussion and information covering all aspects of organized racing competition.

Web:
http://espnet.sportszone.com/car/
http://www.motorsport.com/
http://www.speedworld.net/

Usenet:
rec.autos.sport
rec.autos.sport.info
rec.autos.sport.nascar
rec.autos.sport.rally
rec.autos.sport.tech

Listserv Mailing List:
List Name: **autorace**
Subscribe to: **listserv@vtvm1.cc.vt.edu**

Racing Archive

You can't always be driving a car or watching a race. Occasionally you need to take a break to go home, eat something, and remind your family who you are.
However, that doesn't mean you have to be wasting your time. During those off hours, you can connect to the Net and check out the racing archive.
After all, you do need to spend some quality time with your computer.

Automobile Listings

When the Queen of England comes over for dinner and you want to impress her with all the facts you have at your fingertips on the Internet, connect to this huge list of all-things-automobile. Exotic, classic and run-of-the-mill cars are all represented. This is the Web site to use when size really does matter.

Web:
http://www.car-stuff.com/

British Cars

Some people have lifelong love affairs with things British. For example, Prince Charles's girlfriend, what's-her-name, always makes a point of riding in a British car, except when it is inconvenient or the weather is bad. Would you like to nurture your feelings for English things that move quickly with style? If so, here are some important British car resources for your anglophilic perusal.

Web:
http://www.team.net/sol/

Majordomo Mailing List:
List Name: **british-cars**
Subscribe to: **majordomo@autox.team.net**

CARS AND TRUCKS

Car and Truck Purchasing

Listen to me. Before you visit a dealer to buy a car or truck, you *must* use the Internet to find out everything you need. The Web has lots and lots of car and truck information. Best of all, you can get the actual prices the dealer pays for the vehicle and options. Why should you pay the auto club or a consumer magazine for this exact same information when you can get it for free from the Net? Now, when it comes time to open negotiations for a new car, you will know exactly what the dealer is paying, so he won't be able to pull the sleazy automotive wool over your eyes. Information is power and, as we used to say in the Sixties, "Power to the people."

Web:
http://www.autoweb.com/
http://www.carprices.com/
http://www.edmunds.com/
http://www.intellichoice.com/
http://www.kbb.com/

Usenet:
rec.autos.marketplace

Car Audio

If you are one of those people who believe that cars are made to be heard as well as seen, here is a Usenet discussion group (along with a Web site for the FAQ and an IRC channel for live chatting) that is right up your auditory alley. Start hanging around and soon, when someone says, "My woofer is bigger than your woofer," you will be able to snap back, "Oh yeah? Well, my speakers use isobaric variations of a quasi-eighth order series-tuned dual-reflex bandpass."

Web:
http://www.mobileaudio.com/rac-faq/

Usenet:
rec.audio.car

IRC:
#caraudio

CHOOSING A CAR AUTO-MAGICALLY

Selecting just the right car is not easy. No matter which one you pick, you can be assured that somewhere along the line, someone is putting one over on you. So if you want the straight stuff about which cars offer the best overall cost of ownership, start with the Net. Before you shell out your hard-earned bucks on a potentially big bucket of back-breaking bolts, check out the real dealer costs as well as the many useful tips. Stick with the Net and you'll never have to worry about being the laughingstock of the automotive neighborhood.

Car Classifieds

Don't stop reading the classified ads just because you are tired of having to recycle the daily paper. This Web site provides a great index of advertisements for automobiles of all types. Whether you are buying or selling, the listings are free for non-commercial usage.

Web:
http://classifieds.autofusion.com/

Car Place

Here's someone who knows his cars. Here's someone who knows other people's cars. Here's someone who spends his time driving cars and lives to tell about it. Check out the reviews of all types of cars, new and old. Here's someone worth listening to.

Web:
http://www.thecarplace.com/

CARS AND TRUCKS

Car Audio

What's the point of even driving if you aren't making enough noise to wake several surrounding neighborhoods? However, in these days of computerized engines and strict air control standards, it's not easy to find a car that can produce the required sound levels without a lot of special tuning and getting your hands dirty.

What's the solution? Auto audio, of course. All you need is a sufficiently powerful amp, and you can drive with the peace of mind that comes from being able to create a musical interlude as loud as you want.

So, if you want to make sure you are always as popular as a skunk in the wine tasting booth at a perfume convention, join the discussion in **rec.audio.car**, and find out how to coax that one last decibel out of Old Bessie. After all, life is designed to be lived with a bang, not a whimper.

Car Talk and General Discussion

When you're not driving, you can talk about driving and, on the Net, there is no end to the discussion: automobile design, construction, service, tires, competitions, driving, manufacturers, and on and on and on.

Usenet:
  alt.auto.mercedes
  alt.autos
  alt.autos.bmw
  alt.autos.camaro.firebird
  alt.autos.classic-trucks
  alt.autos.corvette
  alt.autos.dodge.trucks
  alt.autos.ferrari
  alt.autos.ford
  alt.autos.isuzu
  alt.autos.karting
  alt.autos.microcars
  alt.autos.mini
  alt.autos.toyota
  alt.cars.ferrari
  alt.cars.ford-probe
  alt.cars.lotus
  rec.auto
  rec.autos
  rec.autos.makers.chrysler
  rec.autos.makers.ford.explorer
  rec.autos.makers.ford.mustang
  rec.autos.makers.honda
  rec.autos.makers.jeep+willys
  rec.autos.makers.mazda.miata
  rec.autos.makers.mg
  rec.autos.makers.saturn
  rec.autos.makers.vw.aircooled
  rec.autos.makers.vw.watercooled
  rec.autos.makers.yugo
  rec.autos.misc
  rec.autos.vw

Classic and Sports Cars

There's nothing like the feel of riding around in a classic or sporty car. People turn to stare, the engine throbs and begs to be driven at high speeds. If you're addicted to classic or sports cars, join this international mailing list or the Usenet discussion groups and talk about your favorite cars with motoring enthusiasts around the world. Get updates about events such as races or car shows.

Usenet:
  alt.autos.studebaker
  rec.autos.sport.misc

Listproc Mailing List:
  List Name: **autos-l**
  Subscribe to: **listproc@itu.edu.tr**

Customized Cars

If you like to customize cars, here are some Usenet discussion groups you will enjoy. There are a great many details that go into working on a customized car, and there are a lot of people on the Net who are knowledgeable and experienced. Join the discussion and talk with people who love cars as much as you do. Then cruise the Web and enjoy all the resources devoted to cars and the people who love them.

Web:
  http://www.kustoms.com/bbc/words/defi/
  http://www.roadsters.com/

Usenet:
  alt.autos.rod-n-custom
  rec.autos.rod-n-custom

CARS AND TRUCKS

Driving

Once you know how to drive, it seems easy. After all, how many other important activities are there that you can perform adequately with one hand, while listening to the radio and talking to the person next to you? Ask almost anyone, and he (or she) will tell you that he (or she) is a skillful driver. It's true that most people avoid accidents most of the time, but in actual fact, few people are good drivers. Unfortunately, there is something about driving that makes us reluctant to admit we are less than perfect (males more than females). Perhaps it is because earning a driver's license is considered an important coming-of-age event, bringing with it the illusions of freedom and adulthood. Maybe we like the feeling that comes from being in command of a fast, powerful piece of machinery that we control from the inside. As we drive, the car becomes an extension of ourselves, and we develop the same confidence that we have in our ability to walk or run. I think it also has something to do with the fact that we become complacent because, most of the time, most of us do manage to avoid accidents. If you would like to become a more skillful driver, here are some resources to help you. Making yourself into a better, more competent driver will have important long-term benefits (such as increasing your chances of avoiding a serious accident). In addition, as with most things in life, you'll have more fun if you are doing it well.

Web:
  http://www.driving.co.uk/
  http://www.familycar.com/driving.htm
  http://www.nadanet.com/consumer/excuseme.htm
  http://www.trucking.org/safety_net/wakeup.html

Usenet:
  rec.autos.driving

Jack Spratt could eat no fat,
so he read the
"Diet and Nutrition" section.

Electric Vehicles

Regular cars use engines that burn gasoline. An electric vehicle (EV) uses an engine that is powered by an electric motor and batteries. To recharge the batteries, you plug the car into an electrical outlet. Catch up on the state of EV technology and the future of these vehicles. How close are we to affordable electric cars? What advantages do they have over gas-powered cars? For ongoing discussion, you can join the mailing list.

Web:
  http://www.radix.net/~futurev/

Listserv Mailing List:
  List Name: **ev**
  Subscribe to: **listserv@sjsuvm1.sjsu.edu**

Life in the Fast Lane

We all know that fast, high-performance cars are just a substitute for you-know-what. (Well, I do know, but I'm not allowed to talk about stuff like that in a family-oriented book.) Join the boys in the **rod-n-custom** Usenet groups and find out how to soup up your performance and enhance your experience with high speed and quick starts.

Exotic Cars

Imagine the awe you would inspire in everyone around you if you were the lucky owner of an exotic or limited edition automobile. Neighbors would ask you to drive them to the grocery store, people's chatter would die down to a respectful whisper as they passed your car, and the insurance agent would beg you to please leave the car in the garage. But there is more to exotic cars than just good looks. If you can't own one, you might as well be able to drool over them. Check out the fancy driving machines at these well-endowed Web sites.

Web:
  http://www.specialcar.com/
  http://www.supercars.net/

CARS AND TRUCKS 93

Exotic Car + You = Big Success

As one of my readers, you are as close to being perfect as a human being can expect. Perhaps, however, there is a tiny, little something missing from your life. Is it possible that you need a head-turning, attention-grabbing, high-performance automobile?

If so, drive right over to the exotic car site and pick out something nice. After all, why be almost perfect when you can go all the way?

Hint: If you decide to buy such a car, show them your copy of this book, and they are bound to give you a discount.

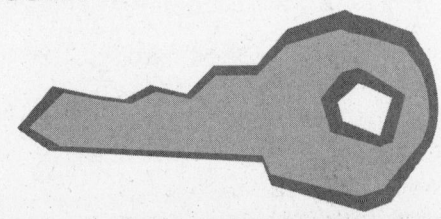

Formula 1 Motor Racing

Formula 1 cars are designed for one purpose: to race on a circuit or closed course. If you want to build your own Formula 1 vehicle, don't forget: the car cannot be more than 200 cm wide; it must weigh at least 505 kg; you must use a 4-stroke engine with reciprocating pistons; and the engine capacity cannot exceed 3500 cc. Hint: When you get to the point where you need to understand how pneumatic valve openers relate to engine mapping, it's time to check with the Net.

Web:
http://www.f1-news.com/
http://www.formula-1.co.uk/

Usenet:
rec.autos.sport.f1

IRC:
#formula1

Four-Wheel Drive Vehicles

Check out the discussion of the on- and off-road four-wheel drive vehicle. Read about and share experiences with other owners of Cherokees, New Tahoes, Explorers, Jeeps and other get-where-you-are-going-no-matter-where-you-are-going kind of vehicles. The Web site is for those of you who like to drive off road.

Web:
http://www.off-road.com/

Usenet:
rec.autos.4x4

Gasoline FAQ

Frankly, most people don't care about gasoline. They go to the nearest place that offers a free car wash with a fill-up and hope that everything will keep working according to the Divine Automobile Plan. However, for those who dig chemistry or truly like to feed their cars, there is a frequently asked question list that discusses the composition of gasoline, gas toxicity, environmental issues, how to choose appropriate fuel and the diagnosis of some fuel-related problems.

Web:
http://www.netmeg.net/faq/recreation/autos/gasoline-faq/

CARS AND TRUCKS

Indy Racing

The first Indianapolis 500 race was run in 1911. The winner was Ray Harroun, who completed the grueling race with an average speed of 74.602 miles an hour. In 1998, the average speed of the winner was 145.155 and the fastest lap was 214.746 mph. In the intervening decades, the Indianapolis 500 and its home, the Indianapolis Motor Speedway, have became world famous, synonymous with the epitome of high-speed high-endurance racing. (The Indianapolis Motor Speedway, with 250,000 seats, is the largest sports venue in the world, making the Indianapolis 500 the largest single-day sporting event on the planet.) Today there are a series of competitions, referred to as Indy racing, based on Indy-style cars: open wheel, open cockpit, single seat, very fast, and very expensive. If you are a fan of Indy racing, visit the Web site, where you can find information on cars, history, and all the Indy races, including the Indianapolis 500. For discussion with other Indy racing fans, you can join the Usenet group or the IRC channel.

Web:
  http://www.indyracingleague.com/

Usenet:
  rec.autos.sport.indy

IRC:
  #indycar

Kit Cars

For years you have been building model cars, and now you can do it without gluing your fingers together. It's time to graduate to the real thing. Find out about purchasing, building, driving, and maintaining kit cars—full-size and fully functioning cars you build from scratch. Then when people give you compliments on your smooth ride, you can say, "Thanks. I made it myself."

Web:
  http://www.kitcar.com/

Usenet:
  alt.autos.kitcars

Motorsport FAQ

You should always be prepared for the day your grandmother calls you on the phone and wants to know exactly why an armco may or may not be better than a tyre wall. Are you going to let her down? There's no need to if you have access to the Web. This **rec.autos.sport** FAQ on auto competitions is loaded with detailed information on motorsports.

Web:
  http://www.netmeg.net/faq/recreation/autos/sport/

Look What I Found on the Net...

```
(from the Motorsports FAQ for rec.autos.sports)

What are restrictor plates?

They are aluminum plates with four 7/8 inch holes.  They are
placed between the carburetor and intake manifold on an engine.
The carburetors used in WC have four 1-1/2 inch diameter
barrels.  When this 7/8 inch restrictor plate is installed, the
air flow into the engine is restricted, thus reducing horsepower.

Restrictor plates were mandated on WC cars at Talladega and
Daytona in 1988.  NASCAR first attempted to slow speeds after
Bobby Allison's car became airborne and crashed into the
spectator fence at Talladega in May of 1987...
```

CARS AND TRUCKS 95

Nascar

Racing fans can hang out in this IRC channel and talk in real time about anything involving driving around and around on a track at high speeds. Get information about upcoming events, race schedules or just talk. For those of you who don't want to go as fast as real time, join the discussion in the Usenet group or check out the Web site.

Web:
http://www.nascar.com/

Usenet:
rec.autos.sport.nascar

IRC:
#nascar

PM Zone

Brought to you by the fine folks who get their hands dirty publishing Popular Mechanics, this Web site has lots of nifty car tidbits for automotive fans. Get a tech update of the day, learn more about choosing a quality automobile, and see movies and pictures that will make any car and truck lover purr like a finely tuned hot rod.

Web:
http://www.popularmechanics.com/

Road Rally

A road rally is a competition for two-person teams (and a car). One person is the driver, the other is the navigator. Each team is given instructions that describe a particular route to follow. The instructions are exact: the team must travel to specific points at specific speeds. Along the routes are checkpoints, and the idea is to arrive at each checkpoint exactly on time. A road rally is not a race; you lose points for being too slow or too fast. Novices are almost always welcome (they compete against other beginners), so if you like to drive and you like to think, you will probably enjoy road rallying.

Web:
http://members.iquest.net/~osands/rally.htm
http://www.contrib.andrew.cmu.edu/usr/ef1c/plug.html
http://www.rallyusa.com/
http://www.reed.edu/~bradley/
http://www.scca.org/amateur/prorally.html

Slot Cars

If you are old enough to remember when slot cars were popular, you are old enough to remember the Dick Van Dyke Show and Peace With Honor. Ah, what halcyon days of our youth were those. And what could be a better way to recover a bit of lost innocence than to grab a hot slot car, rev its motor, and show the kids how it was really done. For the slot car aficionado, here is all the info you need to stay cool: race and product information, links to related sites, calendar of events, slot car zines, and much more.

Web:
http://www.crl.com/~lostisle/hoslots.html
http://www.oldweirdherald.com/
http://www.slotcar.com/

Solar Cars

Have you been waiting for a rainy day to start learning about solar-powered cars? Here are some good places to start. Many solar cars are built for special competitions by students. If you are interested in such activities, these Web sites will have a lot to interest you.

Web:
http://www.nrel.gov/business/education/SprintWeb/
http://www.ogata.or.jp/english/wsr/menu.htm
http://www.sunrayce.com/
http://www.iastate.edu/~prisum/links.html
http://www.winstonsolar.org/

Team.Net Automotive Information Archives

Here is a nice collection of automotive-related resources: links to archives, organizations, mailing lists and activities. By the way, the American pronunciation of Team.Net is "Team Net"—the dot is silent; the British pronunciation is "Team-dot-Net". (See how cool it is to be one of my readers: I make sure you know everything important.)

Web:
http://triumph.cs.utah.edu/team.net.html

CHEMISTRY

Analytical Chemistry

Analytical chemistry is the branch of chemistry devoted to making quantitative measurements. In particular, the techniques of analytic chemistry are used to determine the composition of chemical samples. Thus, an analytical chemist not only has to know a lot about everything, he or she has to be an expert problem solver. This involves being familiar with a great many different tools and techniques, as well as an understanding of which tools to use in a specific situation.

Web:

  http://sciweb.cc.duq.edu/analytical/
  http://www.anachem.umu.se/jumpstation.htm
  http://www.chem.vt.edu/chem-ed/analytical/
    ac-acronym.html
  http://wwwsoc.nacsis.ac.jp/jsac/analsci.html

Usenet:

  sci.chem.analytical
  sci.techniques.xtallography

Atmospheric Chemistry

Atmospheric chemistry is the study of the chemical composition and properties of the atmosphere. Atmospheric chemists study how the components of the atmosphere interact with each other, with the Earth, and with living organisms. One important area of research is the investigation of how human activities may be changing the characteristics of the atmosphere with respect to smog, global climate change, toxic air pollutants, acid rain and ozone depletion.

Web:

  http://airsite.unc.edu/
  http://www.aeat.co.uk/netcen/airqual/kinetics/
  http://www.science.yorku.ca/cac/intro.html
  http://www.shsu.edu/~chemistry/Glossary/glos.html
  http://www.ucsusa.org/warming/

Biochemistry

Biochemistry is the study of the chemical reactions within living organisms. In particular, biochemists investigate metabolism (the chemical processes within cells), macronutrients (proteins, carbohydrates and fats), enzymes, as well as DNA and the chemistry of genes. When I was a graduate student, I wanted to learn biochemistry. But I was a computer science student. I hadn't studied chemistry since high school and I knew nothing about organic chemistry. I wrote a letter to the famous science writer Isaac Asimov in which I asked him advice on how to teach myself biochemistry. He sent me back a reply, which I still have (it is framed and on my desk). He said, "If you have a good library at your disposal, you can teach yourself anything. I did." Asimov's example inspired me. I got a biochemistry textbook and started teaching it to myself. Later, I ended up going to medical school, where I learned the whole thing over again in more detail. But, to this day, I can't forget how fascinating I found it to read a book that could describe what was going on inside my own body.

Web:

  http://home.wxs.nl/~pvsanten/mmp/mmp.html
  http://www.biochemist.com/
  http://www.schmidel.com/bionet.htm

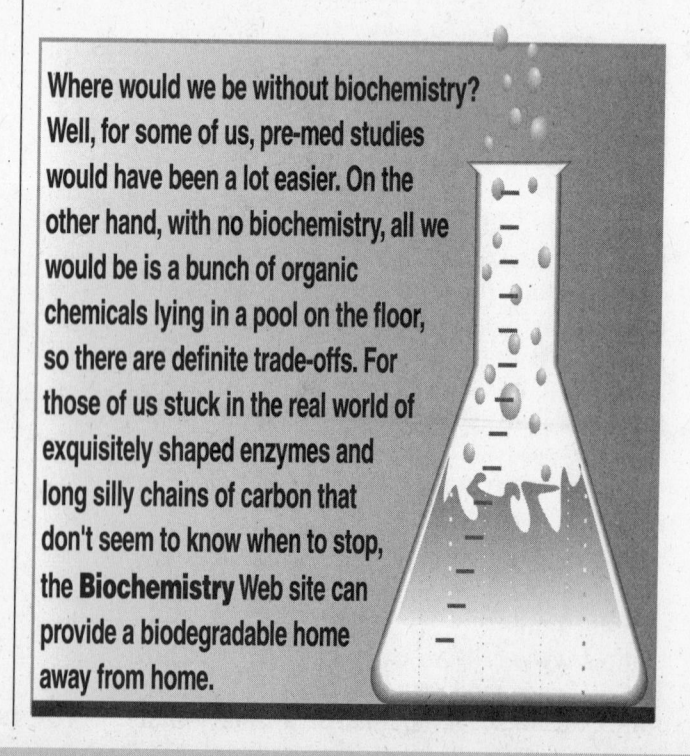

Where would we be without biochemistry? Well, for some of us, pre-med studies would have been a lot easier. On the other hand, with no biochemistry, all we would be is a bunch of organic chemicals lying in a pool on the floor, so there are definite trade-offs. For those of us stuck in the real world of exquisitely shaped enzymes and long silly chains of carbon that don't seem to know when to stop, the **Biochemistry** Web site can provide a biodegradable home away from home.

CHEMISTRY 97

Chemical Acronyms

We all know that DNA is deoxyribonucleic acid and EDTA is ethylenediaminetetraacetic acid. But what about the more esoteric chemical acronyms? The next time you are at a party with a bunch of chemists, see if they know what UASBR or FREMSAAS stands for. They may not, but you will, because you have the Net (and this book) to help you. (By the way, UASBR refers to an "upflow anaerobic sludge blanket reactor", and FREMSAAS is "frequency modulated simultaneous atomic absorption spectrometry".

Web:
http://biotech.chem.indiana.edu/acronym/

> Zines are cool.

Chemistry Journals

Here are collections of links to chemistry journals. Some of the journals are completely online; others only show the tables of contents or abstracts. If you are involved in chemical research of any type, you need to look at these sites. (I bet you have lots of spare time for reading more journals.)

Web:
http://pubs.acs.org/about.html
http://www.chemconnect.com/library/journals.shtml

Chemistry Learning Materials

This site contains a collection of computer materials that can be used to learn about chemistry and lab procedures. If you teach chemistry and you like computers, you may want to check out this site for ideas and resources you can use with your own students.

Web:
http://www.knowledgebydesign.com/tlmc/

Look What I Found on the Net...

```
Newsgroups: sci.chem
Subject: (fwd) Re: Strange properties of cornstarch slurr

>> The other night I was making a sauce and noticed that the cornstarch
>> and water had the bizarre property of solidifying when pressure was
>> applied and returning to a liquid when released.  Is anyone familiar
>> with this phenomenon?

> This property is called thixotropy.  I haven't tried this, but
> hitting the cornstarch/water slurry with a blunt object is supposed
> to cause it to crack, yet it can also be poured like a liquid.

I think the proper term is dilatancy.

Pseudoplastic fluids:
- thin with increasing shear rate and are not time dependent

Thixotropic fluids:
- thin with increasing shear rate and are time dependent

Newtonian fluids:
- are not affected by shear rate or time dependent

Dilatant fluids:
- thicken with increasing shear rate and are not time dependent

Rheopectic fluids:
- thicken with increasing shear rate and are time dependent
```

98 CHEMISTRY

Chemistry Resources

The Internet has more chemically related resources than you could dissolve in a beaker of distilled water and alcohol-free chloroform. Whatever you need to find in the world of chemistry, virtually everything virtual is here somewhere. Remember, if you're not part of the solution, you're part of the precipitate.

Web:
  http://galaxy.tradewave.com/galaxy/Science/
    Chemistry.html
  http://www.chem.rpi.edu/icr/chemres.html
  http://www.chem.ucla.edu/chempointers.html
  http://www.chemsite.com/
  http://www.liv.ac.uk/Chemistry/Links/

Chemistry Talk and General Discussion

Let's talk chemistry. Let's talk about substances and how they react when they are combined. Let's talk about mixing diatomaceous earth into sulfuric acid in order to make it sticky. Let's talk about everything under and inside of the sun. Let's talk about cleaning up the mess.

Usenet:
  sci.chem

Listserv Mailing List:
  List Name: **chemchat**
  Subscribe to: **listserv@uafsysb.uark.edu**

Chemistry Visualization and Animation

Chemistry deals with molecules, atoms and bonds, and there are wonderful computer-based tools available to help you visualize these chemical concepts. These resources will help you learn how computer visualization is used in chemistry. In addition, you will be able to view a great many pictures and animations. I have also included information about two of the most important chemistry visualization tools, Chime and RasMol.

Web:
  http://www.csc.fi/lul/chem/graphics.html
  http://www.glaxowellcome.co.uk/software/
  http://www.mdli.com/download/chimedown.html
  http://www.umass.edu/microbio/chime/

Date With a Nerd

Okay, you finally got the BNOC (Big Nerd on Campus) to ask you out. So where do you go on your first date?

The Chemist's Art Gallery, of course.

Show your date that you have both good taste and the technical knowledge necessary to make a modern relationship work as well as a properly buffered acid-base reaction.

Computational Chemistry

Computational chemistry involves the use of computers in the study of chemistry. In particular, this area of study has applications to molecular modeling, quantum mechanics, statistical mechanics and dynamics. Computational chemistry is often combined with theoretical chemistry to construct quantitative predictions based on specific theory.

Web:
  http://fcindy5.ncifcrf.gov/tmmec/
  http://www.osc.edu/chemistry.html
  http://www.wiley.com/wileychi/ecc/layout.html

Listproc Mailing List:
  List Name: **comp-chem**
  Subscribe to: **listproc@iqm.unicamp.br**

CHEMISTRY 99

Electrochemistry

Electrochemistry deals with the chemistry of electrical phenomena (such as electrophoresis, electroplating, batteries, corrosion, and so on). The Web sites have a wealth of links to all kinds of electrochemical resources on the Net: information, organizations, publications, discussion groups, mailing lists, schools, and more. The Usenet groups are for discussion of related topics.

Web:
  http://electrochem.cwru.edu/estir/
  http://www.electrochem.org/

Usenet:
  sci.chem.electrochem
  sci.chem.electrochem.battery

Electrochemistry to the Rescue

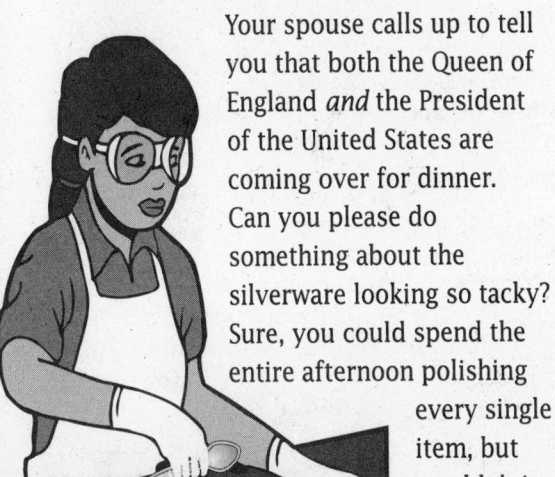

Your spouse calls up to tell you that both the Queen of England *and* the President of the United States are coming over for dinner. Can you please do something about the silverware looking so tacky? Sure, you could spend the entire afternoon polishing every single item, but wouldn't it be easier to use the Net to teach yourself all about electrochemistry? That way you could set up an electroplating system and completely re-plate all the silverware before your guests arrive. And don't kid yourself: high-class people do notice when you do things right.

Glycoscience

Glycoscience is the study of carbohydrates and glycoconjugates. Many people in the physical or life sciences find that memorizing the citric acid cycle several times during your academic career provides enough glyco-oriented stimulation to last a lifetime. However, for hard core glycoscientists, the citric acid cycle is merely the beginning. Glycoscience is a complex, robust area of science, and there are a lot of related resources on the Net. This Web site is an excellent place to start, and for discussion, there is the Usenet group.

Web:
  http://www.vei.co.uk/tgn/

Usenet:
  bionet.glycosci

Hazardous Chemical Database

Please put this Web site in your bookmark list. This important resource contains information on a large number of hazardous chemicals. You can find out basic information—such as formulas, physical data, names—as well as extensive safety information. This is the type of place you want to visit *before* the accident. However, if something unexpected does happen, you will be glad you know where this site is.

Web:
  http://ull.chemistry.uakron.edu/erd/

Laboratory Safety

I have to admit, I was a terror in the lab. Although I was mostly well-behaved, I once incurred the wrath of my organic chemistry lab instructor by throwing an iceball at my friend Stan. And in medical school, my partner and I would often break things in biochemistry lab no matter how careful we were. Still, I had an excuse: in those days, there was no Internet, and so I could not subscribe to the laboratory safety mailing list or check out the resources on the Web.

Web:
  http://www.virginia.edu/~enhealth/guide.html

Usenet:
  sci.chem.labware

Listserv Mailing List:
  List Name: **safety**
  Subscribe to: **listserv@list.uvm.edu**

100 CHEMISTRY

Molecule of the Month

Some people waste their time and money on silly publications that feature new pictures of naked women every month. Not for me. My monthly thrill comes from checking out the new Molecule of the Month. Pictures, structures and chemical information—what more could you want? See if you can answer this riddle. What am I? I am a terpene-like compound, occurring as an essential oil within plants. I am non-polar, with low solubility in water. If you were to vaporize and inhale my volatile fractions, I would induce relaxation and euphoria. You might also experience perceptual changes, a sense of slowing of time, loss of attention, depersonalization, silliness and the munchies™. Aside from recreational uses, I am utilized by chemotherapy patients to treat drug-induced nausea. The final clue? I was the Molecule of the Month in April 1996. (If you would like to see who I am, check the archive.)

Web:
http://www.bris.ac.uk/Depts/Chemistry/MOTM/motm.htm

Nuclide Table

This is an amazing resource. You start with a graphical representation of all the known nuclides. (A nuclide is a type of atom, specified by its atomic number, atomic mass and energy state. For example, carbon 14 is a particular nuclide of carbon.) Click on a section of the diagram, and you are presented with a more detailed chart that contains useful information about all the nuclides in that region. It's like a periodic table of the elements on steroids. You must try this Web site: it's a great tool.

Web:
http://www.dne.bnl.gov/CoN/

Need to fix the plumbing?
See "Homes".
Need to fix a horse race?
See "Vices".

Organic Chemistry

Organic chemistry is the science that deals with carbon compounds. As such, organic chemistry forms the basis of the study of biochemistry, hydrocarbons and polymers. When I was a computer science graduate student, I studied organic chemistry in preparation for medical school and found the course to be one of the hardest I have ever taken (ranking right up there with advanced calculus). If you have an interest in organic chemistry, here are some resources for you. Aside from general resources, I have also included a site that contains the official IUPAC nomenclature rules. (As strange as it may seem, this can be a fun place to browse.) Special organic chemistry hint: If you don't know what you are doing, do it neatly.

Web:
http://chemfinder.camsoft.com/siteslist.html
http://www.acdlabs.com/iupac/nomenclature/
http://www.gwup.org/orgchem.html

Usenet:
sci.chem
sci.chem.organic.synthesis
sci.chem.organomet

Periodic Table

Every chemistry student learns about the Periodic Table: a way of organizing the elements into related groups. Within the Periodic Table is a wealth of information about each element and the various chemical families. I like these Web sites as they are so easy to use. Display the entire table and admire the patterns. Then click on a particular element for more information. The details vary from one site to another: atomic number, atomic weight, atomic volume, valence, density, melting point, boiling point, appearance, ionization energies, electron configuration, discoverer, date discovered, and much more. Aside from several online Periodic Tables, I have also included a link to a program you can download and run on your own computer. (By the way, my favorite element is #105: Hahnium.)

Web:
http://anders.compart.fi/winpte/
http://cst.lanl.gov/CST/imagemap/periodic/periodic.html
http://domains.twave.net/domain/yinon/default.html

COLLECTING 101

Jog on over to "Exercise".

Sonochemistry

Sonochemistry is the study of chemical reactions that are significantly affected by ultrasound. Under the influence of ultrasound, a reaction may be accelerated (such as with a catalyst) or may yield completely different products. These effects can happen for various reasons. For example, ultrasound can speed up a reaction by enlarging the surface area of a catalyst or by enhancing the mixing of the reagents. A more profound effect of ultrasound can result from cavitation: the creation of tiny, low pressure bubbles, in this case caused by the compression/decompression pressure cycles as the sound passes through the reagents. For more information about this fascinating new branch of chemistry, check out these sonochemistry Web pages.

Web:
http://chemibm1.chemie1.uni-rostock.de/organik/miethchen/dietmar/ess/intro.htm
http://www.und.ac.za/und/prg/sonochem/

COLLECTING

Antiques

Capture the past by collecting antiques and vintage items. Learn to restore your old Victrola, music box or clock. Find out where you can get issues of the Charlie Chaplin comics. Buy, sell and trade.

Web:
http://willow.internet-connections.net/web/antiques/
http://www.antiquesworld.com/reference/
http://www.antiquetalk.com/
http://www.curioscape.com/

Usenet:
rec.antiques
rec.antiques.marketplace

Autograph Collecting

To many people, an autograph is just someone signing his or her name. For example, suppose you are eating in a restaurant, and you see someone famous like the President of the United States or Homer Simpson or Denis Thatcher walk in. If you're like most people, you grab a napkin, casually saunter over, and ask Mr. Famous Person for an autograph. Later, you take the napkin home with you, show it around to a few friends, and then throw it out. A serious autograph collector, however, would do it all differently. He or she would use a special piece of paper, not a napkin, and afterward, the autograph would be carefully cataloged and stored. Moreover, real collectors don't collect autographs willy-nilly. They tend to concentrate in certain areas, and build their collection by requesting specific autographs, often by mail. If you would like to learn more about this fascinating hobby, take a look at these autograph-related resources on the Net. (By the way, the story in the restaurant is true. All three of the celebrities were there, and I was able to get three great autographs for my collection. I specialize in "Men Who Live With Forceful Women".)

Web:
http://mail.bcpl.lib.md.us/~ddavison/autos.html
http://www.kestrok.com/~darryl/celeb/faq.html

Usenet:
alt.autographs.transactions
alt.binaries.autographs
alt.collecting.autographs

This page is officially designated as a collectable piece of memorabilia.

Harley Hahn

Beanie Babies

Beanie Babies are small, furry, bean bag toys that are popular with many people who collect the toys, sometimes to the point of fanaticism. Official Beanie Babies are made by the Ty Company (but, as you can imagine, there are a lot of knock-offs). My favorite Beanie Baby is Nip the Cat, because he looks like my cat, The Little Nipper. (The Little Nipper, however, is much cuter and was born on April 6, 1991, three years before Nip was first sold on March 6, 1994.) In order to maintain the demand for Beanie Babies, the Ty Company manipulates the market by making specific toys for a limited time. When they stop making a particular toy, they say it has been "retired". (Nip the Cat, for example, has been retired.) If you are a Beanie Baby aficionado, you are not alone. There are many people on the Net who are ready to talk, trade and compare.

Web:
http://www.beaniefun.com/
http://www.beaniemania.com/
http://www.beaniemom.com/
http://www.beaniephenomenon.com/
http://www.beanieplace.com/
http://www.ty.com/

More, more... more.

Lettuce turn to "Food and Drink".

Book Collecting

I love books and I even have a few of my own collections: Tintin, Perry Mason, Freddy the Pig, as well as anything by P.G. Wodehouse and Isaac Asimov. Mostly I collect these books because I enjoy reading them. However, many book lovers are serious collectors, maintaining accession records and circulating a desiderata (want list). If you are passionate about book collecting in this way, the Net stands ready to help you. (Remember, old collectors never die, they just deaccession.)

Web:
http://www.gol.com/users/steve/books/glossary.htm
http://www.lucasbooks.com/collect.html
http://www.massmedia.com/~mikeb/rcb/
http://www.princeton.edu/~ferguson/yob.html

Usenet:
rec.collecting.books

Look What I Found on the Net...

```
Newsgroup: rec.antiques
Subject: The Best Stores

> Someone wanted to know if it was really so awful for an
> "antique" store to have collectibles in it.  It seems to me
> that if you think the definition of antique is elastic, the
> definition of "collectible" is even more so, since it can be
> stretched to cover everything from Depression glass to
> cheap toys made last week.

A friend of mine has a rule:

If you smell potpourri when you walk in the door of a place
that says it's an antique shop, turn around and walk out.
```

COLLECTING

Bottle Collecting

If you are a bottle collector, here is something cool you can do with one of your bottles.

Fill your bathtub with water. Then write a note (be sure to include your name and address). Put the note in the bottle, seal the bottle carefully, and throw it in the tub.

Now wait for someone to find the note and send you a reply.

The disadvantage of putting the bottle in your tub is that it may take a long time for someone to find the note (especially if you live alone).

The advantage, however, is that it is easy to check on the bottle whenever you want.

Clocks and Watches

Here are lots of great resources for anyone interested in horology (the science of measuring time and the art of making timepieces). These resources offer information about collecting clocks and watches, timepiece repair, the history of timekeeping, antique timepieces and trading. The mailing list and Usenet group are forums in which you can talk about horology any time, day or night.

Web:
http://www.horology.com/horology/
http://www.ubr.com/clocks/

Usenet:
alt.horology

Listserv Mailing List:
List Name: **clocks**
Subscribe to: **listserv@listserv.syr.edu**

Don't be late.

Check out clocks, the Internet's most timely mailing list.

Bottle Collecting

When I was a young kid, I used to enjoy going to the Canadian National Exhibition. My favorite place was the Food Building, where there were a great many booths selling various types of food and giving away free samples. I remember that the Coca Cola booth used to give away tiny little Coke bottles (with real Coke inside). For some reason, I was never able to get one of these tiny bottles, but I really wanted one. If you are a bottle collector, I'm sure you can understand my feelings. Sometimes it seems as if the most important bottle in the whole wide world is the one you want but can't have. However, now we have the Net to help us. Here are some great resources for bottle collectors, as well as a Usenet discussion group where you can talk about antique bottles.

Web:
http://www.antiquebottles.com/
http://www.bottlecollecting.com/
http://www.fohbc.com/

Usenet:
rec.antiques.bottles

104 COLLECTING

Coins and Money

Collecting various types of money can be a lot of fun. This Web site has some useful and interesting resources for people interested in collecting coins and banknotes. The **numism-l** mailing list is not a collector's list. It is for discussing coin topics relating to antiquity and the Middle Ages (up to c.1454). The **biblionumis-l** list is devoted to literature having to do with numismatics. The Usenet discussion groups leave room for lots of free-form discussion of coins and paper money.

Web:
  http://www.coin-universe.com/

Usenet:
  rec.collecting.coins
  rec.collecting.paper-money

Listserv Mailing List:
  List Name: **numism-l**
  Subscribe to: **listserv@vm.sc.edu**

Majordomo Mailing List:
  List Name: **biblionumis-l**
  Subscribe to: **majordomo@majordomo.netcom.com**

Collecting Talk and General Discussion

Is there anyone who doesn't collect anything? (I, for example, collect Internet books.) Collecting seems to be part of our nature as human beings. Thus, if you are human, there is a place in this discussion for you. Use your imagination: anything that can be quantified or categorized is fair game.

Usenet:
  alt.collecting.8-track-tapes
  alt.collecting.breweriana
  alt.collecting.casino-tokens
  alt.collecting.pens-pencils
  alt.collecting.sports-figures
  alt.collecting.teddy-bears
  rec.collecting
  rec.collecting.cards.discuss
  rec.collecting.cards.non-sports
  rec.collecting.ornaments
  rec.collecting.phonecards
  rec.collecting.pins
  rec.collecting.villages
  rec.knives

Collectors' Marketplace

Just about everyone collects something, so here is a Web site of universal appeal. Free ads to buy and sell just about anything you can think of (as well as lots of stuff you would never think of): animation, antiques, autographs, Barbie, Disney, GI Joe, porcelain, Hallmark, toys, sports, records, sci-fi, and much more.

Web:
  http://www.collectiblesnet.com/

Doll Collecting

There are lots and lots of doll collectors on the Net, and lots and lots of doll stuff to enjoy. Even if you can't tell the difference between a Cabbage Patch Baby Surprise and the Barbie Neptune Fantasy '92 (from the Bob Mackie series), you can still enjoy bopping around, looking at dolls and doll-related discussion, or hopping in on some hot doll discussion in Usenet.

Web:
  http://www.everink.com/ndl.html
  http://www.thedollnet.com/

Usenet:
  rec.collecting.dolls
  rec.crafts.dollhouses

Majordomo Mailing List:
  List Name: **dollwork**
  Subscribe to: **majordomo@rpmdp.com**

License Plates

I like license plates. They're small, they're colorful, and there are just enough variations to make collecting them worthwhile. Whether or not you are a collector, I bet you will enjoy looking at pictures of license plates from around the world. I especially like looking at old plates and imagining the people who used them and the cars they were driving. If you are a collector (or you want to be a collector), you will find a wealth of reference material on the Net.

Web:
  http://attila.stevens-tech.edu/~jwasiele/alpca/
  http://danshiki.oit.gatech.edu/~iadt3mk/
  http://www.motorcycles-online.com/plates/pl8s.htm
  http://www.pl8s.com/

Marble Collecting

When I was young, we had marble season at school every spring as soon as the snow had melted. Here is how the whole thing worked. For several weeks, a large area of the playground was set aside for marbles (also called "alleys"). Various people would sit on the ground with their legs spread and place a valuable marble in front of them. When you did this, it announced that you were willing to let anyone try and win the valuable marble. People could come up and, from a certain distance (about 10-15 feet), roll a less valuable marble on the ground toward you. If the rolling marble hit the valuable marble, the person who rolled the less valuable marble got to keep the valuable one. In general, it is difficult to hit another marble 10-15 feet away, and the person sitting on the ground could end up accumulating many marbles before having to give up the valuable one. There were two basic ideas. First, you could beg, borrow, steal or buy a whole bunch of plain, ordinary marbles, and then use them to try and win a few of the valuable ones such as purees or puree biggies. (Purees were valuable because there was no place to buy them; you had to win them.) Or, if you had some valuable marbles, you could sit on the ground with a valuable marble, and collect as many plain marbles as you could before someone hit the valuable one. I still remember the day two brothers came to school with a big tin filled with beautiful, green, medium-large puree biggies. One of the brothers sat down and placed one of the green marbles on the ground in front of him. In no time, a crowd of people had appeared, rolling one marble after another, trying to win a beautiful, green, medium-large puree biggie. Whenever the green puree was hit, one of the brothers would give it to the winner, reach into the tin, pull out a new puree, and place it on the ground. Boy, did they ever do well! Marble season was for the youngest kids, and I only played for a few years. But even now, it is impossible for me to see a nice-looking marble without feeling nostalgic about those childhood times that seem so far away and so long ago. To this day, whenever I walk into an art supply store and see a boxful of clear glass marbles, I feel like calling to the person I am with and saying, "Wow, look at all these purees. I bet if we bought some we could really clean up."

Web:
http://www.blocksite.com/

Music Collecting

There are lots of reasons why it is a good idea to be a music collector. Here are the top three. (1) You will always have the right music to play no matter what the occasion (such as a surprise Tupperware party). (2) One day a famous movie producer may come over to your place and ask you to help him choose the soundtrack music for his new picture. (3) When you die, people will have something pleasant to say about you. ("He had such a nice CD collection...")

Web:
http://www.8trackheaven.com/
http://www.helsinki.fi/~tuschano/records/
http://www.punx.com/78rpm/
http://www.searchlight.com/frank/vinyl

Usenet:
alt.collecting.8-track-tapes
rec.music.collecting.cd
rec.music.collecting.misc
rec.music.collecting.vinyl

Postcards

Postcards were designed so that people who go on vacation could quickly and easily torture all those friends or family members who didn't get to go. Connect with other postcard collectors and discuss the history of picture postcards, information on research activities, or find people with whom you can exchange postcards by mail.

Web:
http://pwp.starnetinc.com/roger/postcard.htm
http://www.library.arizona.edu/users/mount/postcard.html

Usenet:
rec.collecting.postal-history

Listserv Mailing List:
List Name: **postcard**
Subscribe to: **listserv@listserv.idbsu.edu**

Witty saying goes here.

106 COLLECTING

Rock Collection

They're not friendly or cuddly, but you don't have to feed and water them and they don't make any noise. If you are into long-term commitment without the emotional sloppiness, rocks make perfect friends. Get together with other collectors to exchange ideas and share tips on gem, mineral and fossil hunting and collecting.

Web:
  http://www.rahul.net/infodyn/rockhounds

Majordomo Mailing List:
  List Name: **rocks-and-fossils**
  Subscribe to: **majordomo@world.std.com**

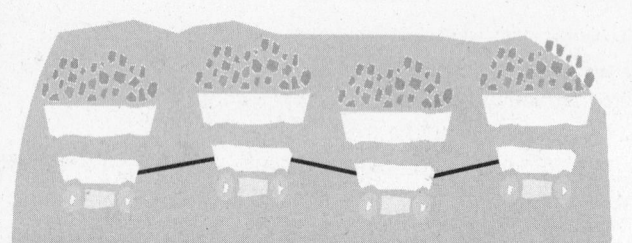

ROCKS ARE OUR FRIENDS,

and who couldn't use more friends? The Rock Collection resources will help you appreciate all that is hard, small and intriguing. After all, why should a piece of Annabergite be a mere hunk of hydrated nickel arsenate, when it can be a full-fledged member of your extended family?

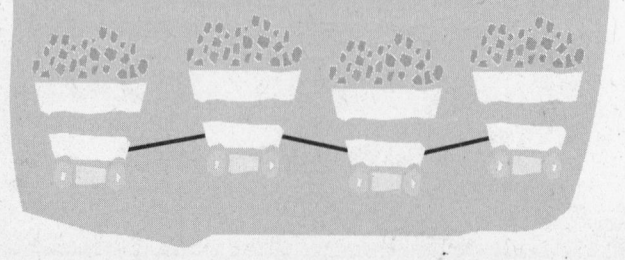

Snowglobes

My favorite snowglobe is a special one commemorating Watergate. You shake it, and, as the snow floats down gently, obscuring the view, you catch a glimpse of Richard Nixon sitting behind a big desk erasing audio tapes. Snowglobes are not only fun to collect, they can be useful as well. After all, suppose that one day you are on trial for your life and, to get off, have to prove you have visited Fargo, North Dakota. All you need to do is show the judge your special Fargo souvenir snowglobe. Or maybe one day a millionaire will knock on your door and ask if you would be willing to trade a snowglobe for his Rolls Royce. You'd feel pretty silly having to turn him down. But the best thing about snowglobes is that you can shake them up and watch the snow float down gently whenever you want.

Web:
  http://members.aol.com/c1urchn/web/snowdome.htm
  http://www.auburn.edu/~morrike/
  http://www.snowdome.demon.nl/

Sports Memorabilia

You don't have to play a sport to be one, but you don't even have to be a sport to collect stuff. All you need is motivation, time, money, and a place to keep your collection where your mother or wife won't throw it out. There are many people on the Net who buy, sell and appreciate sports memorabilia, and these Web sites can help you find what you want. If you like to talk to other collectors, or you want to buy or sell something, you can join the discussion in one of the Usenet groups. It's not always easy to find exactly what you want, but it's worth it. As a kid, I collected football cards, and I still remember how thrilled I was the day I got the last card I needed to have the complete set. It was a *big* deal.

Web:
  http://countryliving.com/cl/collect/10basf1.htm
  http://www.collector-link.com/cards/faq.shtml
  http://www.collector-link.com/cards/posting.shtml

Usenet:
  rec.collecting.sport.baseball
  rec.collecting.sport.basketball
  rec.collecting.sport.football
  rec.collecting.sport.hockey
  rec.collecting.sport.misc

Look What I Found on the Net...

Newsgroup: rec.toys.lego
Subject: Lego Piece Counting

> When you count pieces in your set, do you count mini-fig arms,
> hands, torso, legs, crutches, and so on, or do you count the
> torso with arms and hands together as one piece?
- - - - - -

I would count the torso and arms as one piece. Since the arms can't be attached to anything else, they don't qualify as a piece, at least to me.

Similarly, mini-fig helmets and hats would count, but the little plumes that go into the hats would not count as individual pieces.

- - - - - -

You might also want to count the head and torso (with attachments) as one piece. It may be that Lego counts them this way because someone posted here earlier that the heads are attached to the torso at the factory. This is why all the mini-figs in sets have heads on torsos when you open the box...

Also, do you count extra parts left over, such as control sticks, 1x1 round plates, visors, and so on, that Lego seems to give extras of? Too bad we can't get a counting guide from Lego to see how they count the number of parts.

- - - - - -

I think there is a fairly easy solution to this quarrel, a piece is counted as a piece if it comes separated from other pieces in a new set.

- - - - - -

I have every set I own inventoried, and I count a mini-fig as 3 pieces: the leg piece, the torso piece and the head...

- - - - - -

According to someone in the parts replacement group at Lego Consumer Service, the head/torso/arms/hands all count as a single piece. So a typical "basic" mini-fig is three pieces: legs, head/torso/arms/hands and hat/helmet/hairpiece.

- - - - - -

I'm wondering today about dragons. Have they always counted dragons as 7 pieces or did they once count as 5 pieces? There is the body, the two wings, and the two arms. The arms are separate pieces because they have Technic-compatible pegs, and because you get just the arms to a dragon in at least one Time Cruisers set...

Anyway, if there's not already a Web page with detailed discussions and proofs of this sort of thing, I really wish someone who's spent enough time on this to be an expert would publish this — it would be very useful.

108 COLLECTING

Stamp Collecting

The modern use of postage stamps started in England in 1840. The first official U.S. stamps were issued in 1847. By 1850, the custom had been adopted by countries around the world. Eventually, postal officials noticed that many stamps were never used: they were being saved by collectors (philatelists). For years now, the collecting market has been so large that post offices have been designing and producing stamps specifically for the philatelic community. Indeed, some small countries accrue significant revenue by selling stamps to foreign collectors. There are a large number of stamp collecting resources on the Net. Here are some good places to start.

Web:
  http://www.execpc.com/~joeluft/faq/title.html
  http://www.execpc.com/~joeluft/resource.html
  http://www.philatelic.com/

Usenet:
  rec.collecting.postal-history
  rec.collecting.stamps
  rec.collecting.stamps.discuss
  rec.collecting.stamps.marketplace

Listserv Mailing List:
  List Name: **stamps**
  Subscribe to: listserv@lists.psu.edu

Teddy Bear Collecting

If you are a woman, I don't have to tell you why it's fun to collect teddy bears. They are cute, cuddly, and you can sleep with them at night without having to worry about them pulling away all the covers. If you are a man, there are two important reasons to have a teddy bear collection of your own. First, from time to time, you can give one of your teddy bears to a woman, and she will think you are thoughtful and sensitive. Second, you can sleep with them at night without having to worry about them pulling away all the covers.

Web:
  http://www.bearsandbeyond.com/beary/
  http://www.bearworld.com/
  http://www.cybear.austin.com/

Usenet:
  alt.collecting.teddy-bears

Majordomo Mailing List:
  List Name: **teddy-bears**
  Subscribe to: majordomo@bga.com

Toy Talk and General Discussion

Admit it. You love toys. Not only are they fun, but they are a great thing to keep you busy so you don't have to work. The only thing that could possibly be better than playing with toys is actually getting paid to play with toys. Enter the world's largest playroom and meet other people who love toys. These discussion groups cover toys from the simplest plastic Legos to the most complicated technical gadgetry.

Usenet:
  alt.toys
  alt.toys.gi-joe.1980s
  alt.toys.hi-tech
  alt.toys.lego
  alt.toys.my-little-pony
  alt.toys.transformers
  alt.toys.transformers.classic.moderated
  alt.toys.transformers.marketplace
  alt.toys.virtual-pets
  rec.toys
  rec.toys.action-figures
  rec.toys.action-figures.discuss
  rec.toys.action-figures.marketplace
  rec.toys.cars
  rec.toys.lego
  rec.toys.misc
  rec.toys.transformers.marketplace
  rec.toys.transformers.moderated
  rec.toys.vintage

Stuff, stuff, and more stuff. If it's worth collecting, it's on the Net.

Trading Cards

The growth of the Internet has helped establish a global market for many different types of trading cards. No matter what type of cards you collect, there are other people who share your interest. For ongoing discussion—including "wanted" or "for sale" postings—you can join the Usenet groups and the mailing lists.

Web:
  http://snapper.umd.edu/~rkohlbus/
  http://www.collector-link.com/cards/
  http://www.hypervillage.com/abend/cards/

Usenet:
  rec.cards.non-sports.marketplace
  rec.collecting.cards

Listserv Mailing List:
  List Name: **nonsport-cards**
  Subscribe to: **listserv@listserv@listserv.aol.com**

Listserv Mailing List:
  List Name: **sports-cards**
  Subscribe to: **listserv@listserv.aol.com**

COMICS

Alternative Comics

Anybody can be mainstream, but if you are looking to break out of your comics rut, try some alternative comics. Enjoy information about comics, including reviews, news, interviews and FAQs. The comic book industry may have fallen on hard times since the beginning of the 1990s, but the alternative scene is as robust and alive as ever.

Web:
  http://www.indyworld.com/
  http://www.indyworld.com/altcomics/

Usenet:
  alt.comics.alternative
  alt.comics.alternative
  rec.arts.comics.alternative

Majordomo Mailing List:
  List Name: **comix**
  Subscribe to: **majordomo@indra.com**

Anime and Manga

Join the anime-loving masses discussing and enjoying Japanese comics and animation. The Net has tons of goodies relating to anime and manga: enough to satisfy even the most insatiable fanatic.

Web:
  http://www.animepitstop.com/
  http://www.anipike.com/
  http://www.csclub.uwaterloo.ca/u/mlvanbie/anime-list/
  http://www.infostation.com/
  http://www.mangaseeker.com/
  http://www.usagi.com/Links/

Usenet:
  alt.fan.bgcrisis
  alt.fan.r-takahashi
  alt.fan.sailor-moon
  alt.manga
  rec.arts.anime
  rec.arts.anime.creative
  rec.arts.anime.fandom
  rec.arts.anime.games
  rec.arts.anime.info
  rec.arts.anime.marketplace
  rec.arts.anime.misc
  rec.arts.anime.models
  rec.arts.anime.music
  rec.arts.anime.stories
  rec.arts.manga

Listserv Mailing List:
  List Name: **anime-l**
  Subscribe to: **listserv@vtvm1.cc.vt.edu**

IRC:
  #anime
  #anime!

Looking for facts?
See "Science".
Looking for fantasy?
See "Science Fiction, Fantasy and Horror".

Batman

"Criminals are a superstitious, cowardly lot. So my disguise must strike fear and terror in their hearts." With these words, Bruce Wayne began his career as Batman, a hero whose appeal has transcended a wide variety of renditions as well as sixty years of social change. Batman was created by artist Bob Kane and first appeared in the May 1939 issue of Detective Comics (eleven months after Superman). Through the years, there have been comic books, TV shows, movies, and a huge amount of memorabilia and commercial products. Unlike other superheroes, Batman has no special powers. He is not faster than a speeding bullet, nor is he more powerful than a locomotive, and he definitely can't leap tall buildings at a single bound. What he *can* do is use his intelligence, training and superb physical condition to track criminals to their dens and bring them to justice without the use of guns. Why is he so popular and enduring? Because, although he is as human as you and I, Batman represents the highest pinnacle of mortal development: a man whose extreme bravery, strength and knowledge make him the perfect hero for the bulk of humanity who must wake up to an alarm clock, go to work, pay taxes, and raise their children. When a middle-aged man looks into the mirror, holds in his stomach and flexes his muscles, he is, for one brief moment, looking at Batman.

Web:
http://udel.edu/~demes/batman.html
http://www.rvgs.k12.va.us/~macman/dkc/

Classic Comic Strips

I like old comics. My favorites are the pre-1960 strips of Nancy, Peanuts and Blondie, some of which you can find on this Web site. Here's a mailing list and Usenet group on which you can talk about any pre-1960 vintage newspaper comic strips with other fans.

Web:
http://www.stus.com/3classic.htm

Usenet:
alt.comics.classic

Majordomo Mailing List:
List Name: comic-strip-classics
Subscribe to: majordomo@liss.olm.net

Classic Comic Strips

Sometimes life moves too quickly. Why live in the fast lane, when you can take it easy and enjoy the past?

Statistics (including the one I just made up) show that if you spend just ten minutes a day reading about classic comic strips, your life will slow down, and you will be healthy, wealthy and wise.

Comic Conventions

When it's time for a road trip, check out the upcoming comics conventions. Pack your bags and go on an adventurous excursion to hang out in a large room with other people who like comics. This site will give you the details you need to get started.

Web:
http://www.nexilis-hobbies.com/indyworld/reference/conventions.shtml

Comic Reviews

It's hard to know what to say when you are at a party and someone asks your opinion about a particular comic. Sure, you can always make up something, but isn't it a lot better to prepare for important social encounters by reading a whole lot of comic reviews *before* you leave the house?

Web:
http://www.rzero.com/books/

Comicon

The first Comicon (comic convention) I went to was in 1982 in San Diego. I went with my friends Marlene and David Garstang and I had a great time. Now you don't have to go to San Diego to visit a Comicon: there is an Internet-based comics convention on the Web that you can visit whenever you want. It doesn't quite have the same ambience, but it's a lot more convenient and the food is better. Also, you don't have to worry about Marlene telling you it's time to go because David has to get home and do his homework.

Web:
http://www.comicon.com/

COMICS 111

Comics Databases

I like comics and I have a collection of my own (Silver Age Superman, Lois Lane and Jimmy Olsen, as well as Disney duck comics). If you are a collector, you will be glad to know that there are databases you can use to search for information about comics. Some people might be bored stiff at the idea of browsing through a Web site filled with listings of comic book information, but you and I know better.

Web:
  http://www.nostromo.no/gcd/
  http://www.update.uu.se/~starback/disney-comics/database.html

Comics Fan Fiction

Comic book characters really have a life of their own, and fans of comic book characters like to participate by helping bring these characters to life. These Usenet groups are for the purpose of sharing fiction written by fans of various comic strips and comic books. The Web sites contain links to various fan fiction collections and related resources.

Web:
  http://members.aol.com/kielle/cfan.htm
  http://members.aol.com/ksnicholas/fanfic/comics.html

Usenet:
  alt.comics.fan-fiction
  rec.arts.comics.creative

Comics Marketplace

What do you do when it's 2 AM and you just have to lay your hands on the Superman comic in which Lois Lane pretends to marry Peewee Herman, but it turns out to be a hoax? Fire up the old computer and visit the Usenet comics marketplace.

Usenet:
  rec.arts.comics.marketplace

Comics on the Net

If you like to read comics, but don't like to get your hands dirty, the Net has the answer for you. There are enough comic links here to keep you busy for hours. These Web sites offer links to comics around the Net. Click to your heart's content and never once worry about icky newsprint or your obligation to the environment. On the Web, you never have to recycle.

Web:
  http://studentweb.tulane.edu/~jseifert/comics/
  http://www.uta.fi/yhteydet/sarjikset.html

Comics Talk and General Discussion

Zap! Biff! Pow! Action dialog brings comics to life. Whether you are a collector or just a person who likes to read comics now and then, you'll love the variety of discussion you can find in Usenet and IRC.

Usenet:
  alt.comics.2000ad
  alt.comics.alan-moore
  alt.comics.batman
  alt.comics.elfquest
  alt.comics.gunnm
  alt.comics.image
  alt.comics.jack-kirby
  alt.comics.lnh
  alt.comics.peanuts
  alt.comics.superman
  alt.fan.neil-gaiman
  rec.arts.comics
  rec.arts.comics.dc.lsh
  rec.arts.comics.dc.universe
  rec.arts.comics.dc.vertigo
  rec.arts.comics.elfquest
  rec.arts.comics.european
  rec.arts.comics.info
  rec.arts.comics.marvel.universe
  rec.arts.comics.marvel.xbooks
  rec.arts.comics.misc
  rec.arts.comics.other-media
  rec.arts.comics.strips
  rec.arts.comics.xbooks

IRC:
  #comicbooks

COMICS

Need to know when the next meeting of the Jimmy Olsen Fan Club will be held? Send your request to one of the Usenet comic book discussion groups.

Daily Comics

These are some of my favorite sites on the whole Internet. Lots of daily comic strips to look at for free. Along with the comics, you will find background information on the cartoonists and on the strips themselves. Just between you and me, these sites eliminated the only reason I ever had to buy a newspaper.

Web:
http://www.creators.com/comics/comics.asp
http://www.ctoons.com/
http://www.kingfeatures.com/comics/
http://www.stus.com/
http://www.washingtonpost.com/comics

Don't start work. Not just yet. First you have to go to the Daily Comics Web site and read everything you haven't already seen.

Dilbert Zone

There is a fifth dimension beyond that which is known to man (or woman). It is a dimension as vast as the Internet and as timeless as anything that is trendy. It is the middle ground between light and "Where's the light switch?", between science fiction and Super Bowl. It lies between the pit of a man's computer and the summit of his high speed Internet connection. This is the dimension of imagination. It is an area we call... The Dilbert Zone. Check out the cartoon archive and a massive amount of Dilbert-oriented silliness, including information on joining Dogbert's New Ruling Class.

Web:
   http://www.unitedmedia.com/comics/dilbert/

Usenet:
   alt.comics.dilbert

Listserv Mailing List:
   List Name: dilbert_news
   Subscribe to: listserv@listserv.unitedmedia.com

European Comics

European comics have a history and style that is much different from American comics. If you are a fan of European comics, here are some resources you will enjoy. If you like comics, but have never seen the European publications, take a few minutes to explore.

Web:
   http://stp.ling.uu.se/~erikt/comics/
   http://www.bdparadisio.com/
   http://www.euronet.nl/users/freak/strips/stindex.htm
   http://www.uni-passau.de/~zimmerth/comics/
      index.engl.shtml

Gallery of Fictional Beauty

If you like exquisitely drawn pictures of fictional women (from comic books) with large breasts and stunning beauty, you have come to the right place. As one of my friends put it, "The pictures are really nice."

Web:
   http://network.ctimes.net/gfb/index.htm

International Museum of Cartoon Art

The International Museum of Cartoon Art is in Boca Raton, Florida. The museum's Web site has information on many popular comic artists and animators, as well as advice for people who want to be cartoonists. You can read about the artists who have been voted into the Cartoon Hall of Fame.

Web:
http://www.cartoon.org/home.htm

Professional Cartoonists

Professional cartoonists and would-be professional cartoonists will appreciate all the resources available on the Internet. Stay in touch with other cartoonists, keep up on what is new and exciting in the industry, and look for job opportunities.

Web:
http://www.cagle.com/
http://www.cartoonet.net/
http://www.detnews.com/AAEC/
http://www.unitedmedia.com/ncs/

Small Press Comics

On the Net there are great resources for any comic talent looking to be published. These Web sites offer information on how to get yourself published and how to copyright, distribute and advertise your work.

Web:
http://www.cloudnet.com/~hamlinck/spz.htm
http://www.sentex.net/~sardine/spfaq.html

Tintin

What is Tintin? A series of wonderful stories in comic format—written by the Belgian artist Hergé—in which the hero Tintin (a young reporter) travels around the world with his dog Snowy, having one adventure after another. I have every Tintin book, and I read them again and again and again. (And so should you.) Here is a bit of Tintin trivia: in French, the original language, Tintin's dog is named Milou. This is the name of Hergé's first girlfriend.

Web:
http://www.daimi.aau.dk/~jjuhne/COT/cot_home.html
http://www.tintin.be/

IRC:
#tintin

TINTIN

I still remember the day. I was 13 years old and I was browsing in a large bookstore. I happened upon a display where several oversized comic/adventure books were on sale.

The books were **King Ottokar's Sceptre**, **The Crab with the Golden Claws**, and **The Secret of the Unicorn**.

I didn't know it at the time, but these were **Tintin** books.

I bought all three books, took them home, and read them. Then I read them again, and again and again. I loved those books. But I was frustrated because I could not find any more books in the series. And what made it worse was that **The Secret of the Unicorn** was the first part of a two-part story, and I couldn't find out how it ended. All I could do was read the first part over and over.

A few years later, I happened to be in the university bookstore, when I ran into the sales rep for the company that published **Tintin** in my country. I told him my problem, and he said, "Well, I'll just send you a complete set."

Since then, I have read all my **Tintin** books so many times that the bindings have disintegrated. A week doesn't go by that I do not see or hear something that reminds me of a **Tintin** book. For example, someone will bend over, and I will say, "You look exactly like Captain Haddock when he hurt his back by throwing a coconut at a parrot in a tree in **Red Rackham's Treasure**."

So what's the moral of all this? Well, I guess there isn't any moral, except to say that **Tintin** books are cool, and you should get the whole set and read them as many times as you can before you die.

COMPUTERS: COMPANIES

Apple

The official Web site for Apple: Macintosh computers and software.

Web:
  http://www.apple.com/

Compaq

The official Web site for Compaq: PCs (as well as what used to be Digital Equipment Corporation and Tandem Computers).

Web:
  http://www.compaq.com/

Computer Companies

Here are many, many links to the Web sites of hardware and software companies around the world. Just type in the name of the company you want, and—click-click—you're at their Web site. I have found this resource to be a great time saver. The next time you are looking for a computer company, start your search here.

Web:
  http://www-atp.llnl.gov/atp/companies.html

Computer Company Talk and General Discussion

Computer companies have become an important part of the world's economy. As such, it is incumbent upon us—the customers—to talk and gossip about them whenever we get a chance. After all, when it comes to computer companies, their concerns become our concerns. Here are some Usenet discussion groups in which you can help everyone else mind somebody else's business.

Usenet:
  biz.marketplace.computers.discussion
  biz.marketplace.services.computers

Dell

The official Web site for Dell: PCs.

Web:
  http://www.dell.com/

Gateway 2000

The official Web site for Gateway 2000: PCs.

Web:
  http://www.gw2k.com/

Guide to Computer Vendors

Here you will find hundreds of links to computer hardware and software vendors (as well as their phone numbers). There is also a large list of links to computer magazine Web sites. This is where I start looking when I can't decide where to start looking.

Web:
  http://guide.sbanetweb.com/

Finding the Computer Company You Need

Computer equipment is best when it works perfectly, sitting quietly on your desk doing whatever you want. However, before you can get to that point, you need to: (1) find the equipment that is just right for you, and (2) get it up and running.

And, before that magic moment arrives, the time will come when you need to find a particular computer company—to find out what they sell, or to check their Web site for updates, or maybe to get a phone number to ask for tech support.

So don't forget, the Guide to Computer Vendors is waiting for you on the Net.

COMPUTERS: COMPANIES

HP (Hewlett-Packard)
The official Web site for HP: PCs, printers, scanners, and many other computer and non-computer products.

Web:
http://www.hp.com/

IBM
The official Web site for IBM: PCs, software, OS/2, IBM Global Network, network products, Lotus, mainframes, midrange computers, AIX, and much, much more.

Web:
http://www.ibm.com/

Intel
The official Web site for Intel: PC processors and other products.

Web:
http://www.intel.com/

Microsoft
The official Web site for Microsoft: Windows (3.1, 95, 98 and NT), Office suite (Word, Access, Excel, and so on), games, networking software, Internet software (Internet Explorer), and much, much more.

Web:
http://www.microsoft.com/

Netscape
The official Web site for Netscape: Internet software (including the Navigator Web browser).

Web:
http://home.netscape.com/

Novell
The official Web site for Novell: Netware operating system and other networking products.

Web:
http://www.novell.com/

Packard-Bell
The official Web site for Packard-Bell: PCs.

Web:
http://www.packardbell.com/

Rumors and Secrets About Computer Companies
Computer companies, like all companies, want to control what you know about them and when you should know it. If you're like me, however, you want to know stuff that you are not supposed to know, so take a look at these rumor and secrets sites every now and them. I love inside information, and I think that it is only right that you and I be on the inside.

Web:
http://www.macosrumors.com/
http://www.mindspring.com/~ggking3/pages/windmill.htm
http://www.x86.org/

Rumors and Secrets About Computer Companies

Rumors, secrets, rumors, innuendo, rumors, speculation, rumors, gossip, rumors, hearsay, rumors and more rumors.

They don't want you to know, but I do.

COMPUTERS: COMPANIES

SCO (Santa Cruz Operation)

The official Web site for SCO: Unix, software development tools, and so on.

Web:
http://www.sco.com/

Silicon Graphics

The official Web site for Silicon Graphics: workstations, software development tools, and more.

Web:
http://www.sgi.com/

Sun Microsystems

The official Web site for Sun Microsystems: Java, workstations and other computers, Unix, software development tools, networking products, and so on.

Web:
http://www.sun.com/

COMPUTERS: MACINTOSH

Buying and Selling Macs

Here is the Usenet swap meet for Macs. The **.wanted** group is the place to send a request for Macintosh-related hardware or software. The **.computers** groups are more for buying and selling systems and components.

Usenet:
biz.marketplace.computers.mac
comp.sys.mac.wanted
misc.forsale.computer.mac-specific.systems
misc.forsale.computers.mac
misc.forsale.computers.mac-specific.cards.misc
misc.forsale.computers.mac-specific.cards.video
misc.forsale.computers.mac-specific.misc
misc.forsale.computers.mac-specific.portables

Macintosh Hardware

All kinds of discussion about all kinds of Macintosh computers. Talk, talk, talk. Point the mouse and click. Talk, talk, talk. Point the mouse and click. Talk, talk, talk. Empty the trash can. Talk, talk, talk, etc.

Usenet:
comp.sys.mac.hardware
comp.sys.mac.hardware.misc
comp.sys.mac.hardware.storage
comp.sys.mac.hardware.video
comp.sys.mac.portables

Macintosh Magazines

Keep up to date on what is happening in the Mac world. Here are some sites for magazines in which you can find news about hardware and software, reviews and articles as well as links to other online resources. As long as you are on the Net, you need never be out of the Macintosh loop.

Web:
http://macweek.zdnet.com/
http://macworld.zdnet.com/
http://www.macaddict.com/
http://www.machome.com/
http://www.mactech.com/
http://www.mactoday.com/

Macintosh Mailing Lists

One way to keep up on the Macintosh world is to subscribe to one or more mailing lists. Here is a list from which you can choose the mailing lists that are just right for you. Moreover, they make great presents. For example, for a wedding present, I registered my brother and his wife for a subscription to the HyperCard mailing list. True, they don't have a computer, and they have no idea what HyperCard is, but it is awfully hard to know what to get newlyweds. A nice mailing list is always in good taste.

Web:
http://www.ultranet.com/~rcl/sub_Lists.shtml

COMPUTERS: MACINTOSH

Macintosh News and Announcements

There is a lot happening in the Mac world, and you can use the Internet to help you keep up. These resources will show you the official scoops from Apple, as well as what everyone on the street is saying. Never again need you feel embarrassed because Steve Jobs had a new idea, and you didn't know about it until you saw it in the newspaper.

Web:

http://product.info.apple.com/pr/source/
http://www.macintouch.com/
http://www.macnn.com/
http://www.macsurfer.com/
http://www.mactimes.com/headlines/
http://www.macworld.com/daily/

Macintosh Programming

Do you aspire to be a Macintosh programmer? And not just an ordinary Mac programmer but a *great* Mac programmer? Start here, and check out a FAQ, programming notes, technical notes, tips, tricks and links to all kinds of Mac programming resources. After all, you don't want to be one of those people who go to a formal Macintosh dinner at the White House and use the data fork instead of the resource fork.

Web:

http://www.apple.com/developer/

IRC:

#macdev

Look What I Found on the Net...

```
Newsgroup: comp.sys.mac.advocacy
Subject: Mac Users Are Dumb

>> I've had a Mac for years, but I recently bought a PC to see
>> what the Windoze users were talking about.
>>
>> My opinion:
>>
>> YOU HAVE GOT TO BE OUT OF YOUR MIND TO RUN WINDOWS 95
>> BY CHOICE.
>>
>> What a terrible piece of crap it is.  How could you possibly
>> even think that it's a poor cousin to the Mac?
>> Get a life, you idiots. Throw those Windoze machines back
>> into the typing pool for the secretaries to use, and get
>> yourself a Mac for real use.

> Your kind of snobbery is an ugly blotch on the face of
> humanity.
>
> I own a PC and an Apple PowerMac and they both do their jobs
> well.  Each has been customized with the best possible
> software to meet the job requirements.  I even make a living
> with these machines.
>
> This dumb Mac/PC argument — usually associated with some
> immature insecurity — has been going on for years now,
> and is developing into an art of mindless prejudice.
>
> Try to enjoy what toys you have.

AMEN...  To each his own, if you like it, GREAT!
If you don't, get the other kind and get on with your life.
```

COMPUTERS: MACINTOSH

Macintosh Resources

When you are looking for any type of Macintosh-related resources, these are great places to start. No matter what you are looking for—software, news, mailing lists, online publications, FAQs, user groups—I bet you'll find it at one of these Web sites.

Web:
   http://www.cucug.org/mac
   http://www.flashpaper.com/umac/
   http://www.maccentral.com/
   http://www.macsonly.com/
   http://www.mymac.com/
   http://www.webintosh.com/

Macintosh Talk and General Discussion

In Usenet, you will find discussion and commentary on every topic under the Macintosh sun. The **.advocacy** group is for debate and opinion. The **.digest** group is a moderated magazine that contains articles of interest to Mac people. The other Usenet groups and the IRC channels are forums for general discussion.

Usenet:
   comp.sys.mac
   comp.sys.mac.advocacy
   comp.sys.mac.digest
   comp.sys.mac.misc

IRC:
   #mac
   #macintosh

Macintosh Troubleshooting

Wouldn't it be nice to have a Macintosh expert on call, 24 hours a day, to solve your problems? Well, I'd give you Steve Jobs's unlisted phone number, but you'd probably only get his voice mail. Instead, here are some resources full of hints and tips for troubleshooting Macintosh problems. Using the Net is the next best thing to having your own personal tech support staff.

Web:
   http://www.apple.com/support/
   http://www.macfixit.com/

Macintosh Updates

If you are a Mac user, this is definitely a place you need to remember: a collection of fixes, updates and information relating to the Mac operating system, peripheral devices and all types of Macintosh software. Next time tech support puts you on hold forever, check here to see if there is a fix you can download.

Web:
   http://www.ucalgary.ca/ucs/ucic/mac_updates.html

MacintoshOS.com

When the original Macintosh was introduced in 1984, it cost $2,500. Today it is worth about $15. This is just one of the interesting factoids I found in the Macintosh Museum, a compendium of information about every Macintosh model, including some models that are still under development. Aside from the museum, this well-organized Web site serves as a general launching place for things Mac. You can look for free software, get help troubleshooting your problems, join a discussion group or talk to someone in a live chat area. By the way, in 1984, if you had spent that $2,500 on Apple stock instead of a computer, you would have seen it increase to a high of $3,147,743.75 in the glory days of the Mac. Today, that same stock would be worth about $15.

Web:
   http://www.macintoshos.com/

Are you a Mac person?
Would you like to run Unix on your machine? Do you have lots and lots of time?
Try **MkLinux**.

COMPUTERS: PCs

MkLinux

Linux is *the* cool Unix for the late-1990s. And just because you have a Mac doesn't mean you can't be as cool as all the other Unix people on your block. Use this Web site to find all types of Linux-for-the-Mac (MkLinux) information: the MkLinux package, a FAQ, updates and patches, as well as links to other MkLinux-related resources on the Net.

Web:
http://www.mklinux.apple.com/

IRC:
#mklinux

Tidbits

Tidbits is an electronic publication that discusses products and events in the Macintosh part of the world. Tidbits is both practical and news oriented. They do an excellent job and have been around for a long time. I suggest you read it regularly for three reasons: (1) to keep up on what is happening, (2) for useful tips and techniques, and (3) if you have the type of friends who are impressed that you know what is new in the Macintosh community, you will be able to impress your friends.

Web:
http://www.tidbits.com/

COMPUTERS: PCs

Buying and Selling PCs

When it comes time to buy or sell a PC, it can help you a lot to be able to talk to other people. You can use these Usenet groups to look for a computer or computer parts to buy, to offer something for sale, or to ask questions. Remember, you are dealing with strangers, so you must be careful. Don't blindly send your money (or your PC) to someone without satisfying yourself that everything is okay.

Usenet:
biz.marketplace.computers.pc-clone
misc.forsale.computers.pc-specific.audio
misc.forsale.computers.pc-specific.cards.misc
misc.forsale.computers.pc-specific.cards.video
misc.forsale.computers.pc-specific.misc
misc.forsale.computers.pc-specific.motherboards
misc.forsale.computers.pc-specific.portables
misc.forsale.computers.pc-specific.software
misc.forsale.computers.pc-specific.systems

Laptops and Notebooks

A laptop computer is one that is small and lightweight enough to be portable and sit on your lap comfortably. How small can laptops get and still be laptops? Well, people like a full-sized keyboard and a screen large enough to read without squinting, which puts a minimum size on how small a computer can be and still be useable for more than a few minutes. However, within these limitations, there are a lot of choices. Before you buy a laptop, check with the Net. You need to know more than when you buy a regular PC, so I suggest you definitely do some homework before committing yourself.

Web:
http://www.edgeworld.com/notebook/
http://www.enteract.com/~epbrown/
http://www.fringeweb.com/laptops.html

Usenet:
comp.sys.laptops

Monitors

As you use a computer, you are constantly looking at the monitor (display screen). A cheap monitor may save money up front, but it is much more pleasant to use a better quality display. Before you buy your next monitor, take a few moments to learn about what to look for and how to make an intelligent decision. If possible, test the monitor in a store before you buy it. Hint: Cheap monitors flicker. If you notice a flicker, don't buy the monitor. It will bother you more than you might think. (Remember, these are your eyes we are talking about.)

Web:
http://hawks.ha.md.us/hardware/monitors.html
http://www.hardwarecentral.com/hardware/monitors/

Usenet:
comp.sys.ibm.pc.hardware.video

Palmtops

A palmtop is a small, hand-held computer. Palmtops (which used to be called PDAs, or personal digital assistants) are full-fledged computers, and many of them run a variation of Windows called Windows CE. Palmtop hardware and software are evolving all the time, and it is important to keep up on what is happening. Since everything is so small, these machines do not work exactly the same as regular desktop and laptop computers, and there are lots of things you need to know to use your palmtop well. These resources will allow you to explore the brave new world of brave new hand-held computers.

Web:
http://brooklyn.slack.net/~thundt/pda.htm
http://velo.philips.com/
http://www.intercall.net/~smr/palmtop/
http://www.lgphenom.com
http://www.pdacentral.com/
http://www.pilot.org/
http://www.wincecity.com/hardware.html

Usenet:
alt.comp.sys.palmtops.hp
alt.comp.sys.palmtops.pilot
comp.sys.handhelds
comp.sys.palmtops
comp.sys.palmtops.pilot
comp.sys.palmtops.pilot

PC Hardware Talk and General Discussion

Computing is no fun if you have to work on a slow dinosaur of a PC that creaks when it starts up or blows dust out of its cracks every time you change directories. Keep up with the latest in hardware changes and make your machine state-of-the-art.

Usenet:
comp.hardware
comp.sys.ibm.hardware
comp.sys.ibm.pc.hardware
comp.sys.ibm.pc.hardware.cd-rom
comp.sys.ibm.pc.hardware.chips
comp.sys.ibm.pc.hardware.comm
comp.sys.ibm.pc.hardware.misc
comp.sys.ibm.pc.hardware.networking
comp.sys.ibm.pc.hardware.storage
comp.sys.ibm.pc.hardware.systems
comp.sys.ibm.pc.hardware.video
comp.sys.ibm.ps2.hardware
comp.sys.next.hardware

PC Hardware

Ah, those halcyon days of my youth when—screwdriver and chip puller in hand—I spent so many wonderful hours working on the innards of my PC. What could be more fun on a summer's afternoon than discussing PC hardware when everybody else is wasting their time at the beach?

(Tip for the guys: Women really go for men who know their hardware.)

PC Magazines

Keeping up on what is happening in the PC world is impossible. However, if you want to pretend to keep up, the easiest way is by reading PC magazines. To help you, here are some places on the Net where you can read articles from PC magazines without leaving the comfort of your Web browser. Check back every now and then; there is always something new.

Web:
   http://www.pcworld.com/
   http://www.zdnet.com/pccomp/
   http://www.zdnet.com/pcmag/
   http://www.zdnet.com/pcweek/

PC News

Don't get left behind, even for a moment. Check in with the Net every day and see what's new in the world of PCs. Here are some great places to read the factoids behind the rumors and hype that pass for news in the PC industry. If you like keeping up with the PC flow, these sites will help you stay one giant step ahead of the guy or gal in the next cubicle.

Web:
   http://www.pcworld.com/pcwtoday/
   http://www.zdnet.com/

PC Prices

If you are interested in getting the best price, you need a good way to compare. Use this Web site to help you find pricing information about a large number of PCs, as well as parts and components. These days, even the best is relatively inexpensive. Considering what you are getting, being able to buy any PC at all is the bargain of the century. Don't be too cheap. The only way anyone can offer you a computer that is well below the regular price is by selling you last year's technology. If you try to save money, you will only end up with an inferior machine and, believe me, your programs will know the difference.

Web:
   http://www.shopper.com/idx/COMPUTER_SYSTEMS/

PC Resources

These sites feature extensive information about PCs. These are good places to find PC-related information when you have a vague idea of what you want, but you don't know where to look.

Web:
   http://www.ccomm.com/~users/cchamberlin/cac/pc_info.html
   http://www.pcguide.com/

PC Talk and General Discussion

When you want to talk about your PC, these are the Usenet discussion groups to check out. Whether you want to ask a question, help someone else, or just hang out, there is always plenty to talk about.

Usenet:
   alt.sys.pc-clone.acer
   alt.sys.pc-clone.compaq
   alt.sys.pc-clone.dell
   alt.sys.pc-clone.gateway2000
   alt.sys.pc-clone.micron
   alt.sys.pc-clone.packardbell
   alt.sys.pc-clone.zeos
   comp.sys.ibm.pc
   comp.sys.ibm.pc.misc
   comp.sys.ibm.pc.misc
   comp.sys.ibm.ps2
   comp.unix.pc-clone.16bit
   comp.unix.pc-clone.32bit

Do you believe in magic? Do you like having mystery in you life?

If so, be forewarned. These Internet resources will take all the magic and mystery out of using a PC.

122 COMPUTERS: PCs

PCMCIA Cards

PCMCIA cards are small adapters—the size of a thick credit card—designed to fit into laptop computers. The name PCMCIA stands for "Personal Computer Memory Card International Association". (See if you can say that ten times real fast.) There are three types of PCMCIA cards: Type I cards are 3.3 mm thick (for example, memory cards), Type II cards are 5 mm thick (modems, network adapters), while Type III are 10.5 mm thick (miniature disk drives). In theory, PCMCIA cards always work perfectly the first time, especially the "plug and play" cards. In practice, getting these little gremlins working properly can sometimes drive you crazy. Here are some resources to help.

Web:
   http://www.pc-card.com/

Usenet:
   alt.periphs.pcmcia

Printers

I remember when it was hard to get any printer working with a PC and, today, whenever a printer actually works I consider it nothing less than a small miracle. My feelings, of course, are way out of date. Today's printers are generally reliable and well-manufactured, and many printers are actually computers in their own right. There are a lot of different printers and, before you buy, many choices to consider. After you buy, there are a lot of questions that may arise. Here are some resources to help you: links to printer manufacturers, sources for printer drivers, and much, much more.

Web:
   http://skyways.lib.ks.us/kansas/sekls/staff/brigc/printer/
   http://www.connectworld.net/c9.html
   http://www.primenet.com/~penguink/printers/

Usenet:
   comp.periphs.printers

Act out in "Drama".

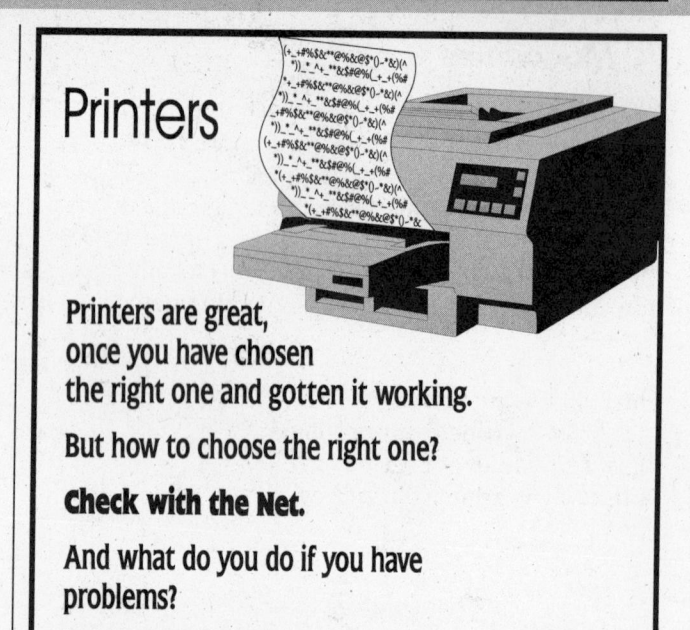

Printers

Printers are great,
once you have chosen
the right one and gotten it working.

But how to choose the right one?

Check with the Net.

And what do you do if you have problems?

Check with the Net.

Scanners

A scanner is a device that you use to convert an image on paper into data stored in a computer file. For example, say you have some pictures of your cat that you want to put on your Web site. You would use a scanner to "digitize" the pictures, each of which could be stored in a separate file. You can then display these files on your Web site. (This is how photos end up on Web sites.) Here is some information to help you learn about scanners. I have one and I like it a lot. It's fun to take a photo or drawing and make it into a computer file. If you are artistic, there is a lot you can do with your own scanner. If you are thinking of buying a scanner, here are some tips to help you. (1) You get what you pay for. Expensive scanners work better (and faster) than cheap scanners. (2) All scanners use software. Expensive scanners will have better software, which will make a difference. (3) It will take you some time to learn how to use the software well. (4) It's fun to experiment, but *read the documentation*.

Web:
   http://www.dpi-scanner-authority.com/288int/scannered2.html
   http://www.infomedia.net/scan/
   http://www.scanshop.com/

COMPUTERS: REFERENCE

Bugs and Fixes

A bug is a problem in a computer program, often a mistake in the program itself. A fix is a way to cure the problem or, at least, to work around it. All computer programs have two types of bugs: the ones you know about and the ones you don't know about. (I guarantee that all the programs you are using right now have some bugs in them.) Here are some resources to help you find and (hopefully) fix the bugs. If you need to talk to someone, try the Usenet group.

Web:
  http://www.bugnet.com/
  http://www.pcworld.com/resources/hereshow/
    bugs_and_fixes.html

Usenet:
  comp.bugs.misc

Computer Almanac

Trivia buffs, brush up on your facts about computers. You never know when an emergency will come up and you will need to know some sort of useless fact or figure such as the estimated percent of salaried workers who will work at video display terminals by the year 2000 or how many wire transfers the Federal Reserve handles per day.

Web:
  http://www.cs.cmu.edu/afs/cs.cmu.edu/user/bam/
    www/numbers.html

Computer Books Online

Macmillan Computer Publishing (the largest computer book publisher in the industry) offers some of their books for free online. Just sign up and you can look at a large variety of technical books. What better way to spend a quiet Saturday night while you are waiting for Star Trek to start?

Web:
  http://www.mcp.com/personal/

Computer News

So much happens in the world of computers, it's difficult to stay current on the latest events. So why not let someone else keep track of it all for you? Here are some news sites that will give you the hot (and cool) scoops on the most important computer-related happenings in the world. Check here every few days and you'll be able to stay up to date with no problem.

Web:
  http://extlab1.entnem.ufl.edu/IH8PCs/
  http://webserv.educom.edu/edupage/edupage.html
  http://www.news.com/
  http://www.slashdot.org/
  http://www.tbtf.com/

Computer Product Reviews

Before you plunk down a wad of money for a computer or a computer-related product, read the reviews. Money is time, time is knowledge, and knowledge is power. So taking the time you need to save money will make you a powerful person indeed (at least around the house).

Web:
  http://www.anandtech.com/
  http://www.cnet.com/content/reviews/
  http://www.computers.com/
  http://www.reviewfinder.com/
  http://www.streettech.com/

Computing Dictionary

In the 1960s, a lot of people gave their children far out names, like Rainbow, Sunshine and Moon Unit. So what can you do in the 90s? Use this online computer dictionary to come up with all kinds of cool ideas. For example, anyone can name their kid Jennifer, Bobby or Stacy. But you just know you're dealing with someone special when you meet Proxy Server Mandelbaum, Firewall Jackson, Gif Jeffries, or L. Spam Montgomery.

Web:
  http://wombat.doc.ic.ac.uk/
  http://www.dooki.com/foldoc/
  http://www.instantweb.com/foldoc/

Computing Magazines and Journals

I am going to let you in on a secret. Everyone else in the world has no trouble staying current on everything that is happening in the world of computing. *You* are the only one who is having trouble keeping up. That is why I have put in this resource, just for you. Here you will find links to many different computer magazines and journals. Read long and prosper.

Web:
http://www.utexas.edu/computer/vcl/journals.html

Glossary of PC Terminology

There are so many technical terms that it is impossible to know them all. I wanted to find you a good PC glossary so I looked all around the Net, and this is the one I found. The definitions are exact and well-written, and the coverage is comprehensive. Whoever is responsible for it did a good job. Put this link on your bookmark list. It will come in handy the next time you encounter a PC word you don't understand.

Web:
http://homepages.enterprise.net/jenko/Glossary/Index.htm

The PC Glossary

Before your next big social occasion, spend a few minutes with the online Glossary of PC Terminology. After all, when it comes to PCs, the more buzzwords you know the more people will treat you as if you know what you are doing. (It's always worked for me…)

Hacker's Dictionary

The Hacker's Dictionary (also known as the "jargon file") is a venerable reference work that you simply *must* know about. It is a huge, comprehensive compendium of hacker slang, illuminating many aspects of hacker traditions, folklore and humor. I like The Hacker's Dictionary because it is written by smart people for smart people, and because it is authoritative, well-written and witty.

Web:
http://www.earthspace.net/jargon/
http://www.logophilia.com/jargon/jargon.html

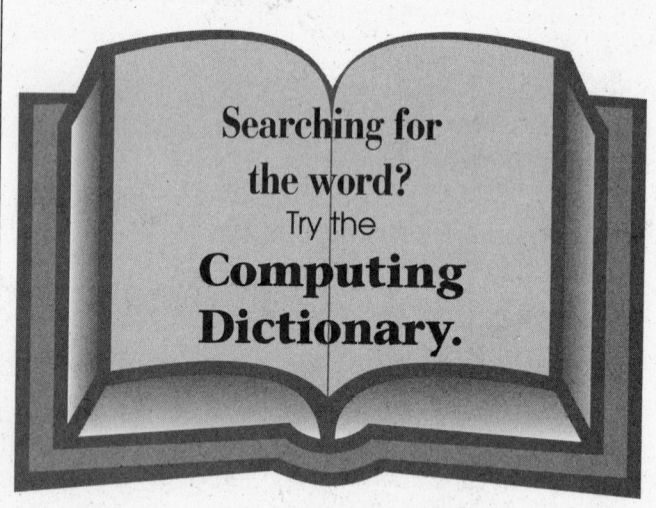

Searching for the word? Try the Computing Dictionary.

Smileys

A smiley is a short sequence of characters that looks like a small smiley face when you look at it sideways. For example, here is the basic smiley: **:-)**. (To see the smiling face, tilt your head sideways to the left.) People use smileys in email, within Usenet articles, and when talking on the Net. The purpose of a smiley is to show a sense of irony, as if you mean to say, "Just kidding." The idea of a smiley has been around for years. Although you only really need the one basic smiley, inventive people have created many different smileys just for fun. For example, here is a smiley with a mustache **:-{**. Wanna see more? Enjoy.

Web:
http://www.eff.org/papers/eegtti/eeg_286.html
http://www.pop.at/smileys/

Computers are people, too.

Tech Support and Online Help

We all wish that every computer product came with free technical support offered by knowledgeable people. Fat chance. If you have ever waited on the phone for a long time just to talk to a tech support person who knew less than you did, you will understand what I mean when I say that good tech support is hard to find. Except on the Net. Here are some resources you can use to look for answers on many different types of problems. My experience is that, whenever I can, it is a lot easier to find the answer myself than to ask someone else.

Web:
http://www.24hoursupport.com/
http://www.cermak.com/techguy/
http://www.compucure.com/
http://www.nowonder.com/
http://www.software.net/directory.htm
http://www.supporthelp.com/
http://www.zdhelp.com/

Webopaedia

So you have a computer question. Well, chances are someone has already asked that question and, if so, there's a good chance you can find an answer here. This is a searchable database with information about anything and everything you could ever want to know about PCs and Macs. A cross between a dictionary and an encyclopedia, the Webopaedia has tons of information with lots and lots of links to explore.

Web:
http://www.pcwebopaedia.com/

Yahoo Computers

When you are looking for things computer, try Yahoo. Lots of news, reviews and information all in one place.

Web:
http://computers.yahoo.com/

Year 2000 Problem

As you know, many computer programs need to keep track of dates. For example, every time you use a credit card, some computer somewhere has to verify that your card is okay by checking the expiration date. Well, a lot of programs were written to use only two digits to store the year within a date. For example, the year 1999 would be stored as "99". Probably, you do this a lot yourself when you want to abbreviate. With computer programs, though, there can be a problem. When the year 2000 comes, some dates will be stored as "00". If this is interpreted as 2000, there won't be a problem. However, if a program interprets "00" as 1900 (or 0!), it will cause a problem. In the worst case, a program might fail completely or create inaccurate data. This is the year 2000 problem, often referred to as the Y2K problem ("K" means 1000 in the metric system). Some people would have you believe that the Y2K problem is going to be a huge catastrophe: computers will shut down and we won't have electricity, banking, air traffic control, and so on. The plain truth is, many responsible people are working to fix the problem, and there will not be a catastrophe.

Web:
http://www.support2000.com/
http://www.year2000.com/
http://www.zdnet.com/pcmag/special/y2k/

Usenet:
comp.software.year-2000

Don't give up. Don't despair. (Online) tech support is always there.

CONNECTING TO THE INTERNET

ADSL

ADSL, Asymmetric Digital Subscriber Line, is a system that provides high-speed Internet connections over a regular phone line without interfering with the voice service. ADSL is much faster than a dialup connection (using a regular modem) or ISDN. I can't tell you an exact speed, because phone companies offer various services, but, at a minimum, you should be able to get several hundred bps (bits per second) and perhaps much faster. Unlike a dialup connection, an ADSL connection is always turned on. Thus, once you install ADSL, you are connected permanently to the Net until you either stop the service or die (whichever comes first).

Web:

http://www.adsl.com/adsl_forum.html
http://www.hayes.com/prodinfo/adsl/intro.html

Cable Modems

You know that thick round cable that brings the TV signal into your home? Well, the cable companies have developed ways to use that very same cable to give you Internet connectivity. To connect to the Net in this way, you need an Ethernet card in your computer along with a small box called a cable modem. But don't sweat the details, the cable company will do it all for you. The service is not available everywhere, but if it's in your area, you should definitely consider it. The speed will be very fast: not as fast as the cable company promises—after all, *everyone* in the connectivity business lies about speed—but a lot faster than regular modem access or even ISDN. And once it's all set up, you will have a permanent, 24-hour-a-day Internet connection without having to use (or pay for) a second telephone line.

Web:

http://cabledatacomnews.com/cmic.htm
http://www.cablemodems.com/
http://www.catv.org/

Frame Relay

Frame relay is a multiplexed interface to a packet-switched network. With frame relay you have a leased line that supports a high-speed connection to the Net, from 56 K bits per second to T1 (1.536 M bps) and beyond. I have a frame relay line to my house, and let me tell you, if you can live through getting the thing up and running, it's great. During the many times I was put on hold by various engineers, receptionists and technical support people, I found it helpful to do a little reading about the technology. By the time everything's going, you'll probably end up learning more about frame relay than you ever wanted to know, but then, life's funny that way.

Web:

http://web.syr.edu/~jmwobus/comfaqs/
   faq-comp.dcom.frame-relay
http://www.frforum.com/
http://www.mot.com/mims/isg/tech/frame-relay/
   resources.html

Usenet:

comp.dcom.frame-relay

Internet Service Providers

An Internet service provider (ISP) is a company or organization that provides access to the Internet. For example, if you have a computer at home, you access the Net by having your computer connect to an ISP. Here are some resources to help you find an ISP that serves your area. (If you do not already have access, ask a friend who does to help you out by checking the lists for you.) For discussion about Internet access, you can read the Usenet groups.

Web:

http://boardwatch.internet.com/isp/
http://thelist.internet.com/
http://www.cnet.com/content/reviews/compare/ISP/
http://www.ispfinder.com/
http://www.mindspring.com/~mcgatney/indexx.html
http://www.thedirectory.org/areacode.htm

Usenet:

alt.internet.access.wanted
alt.internet.services

CONNECTING TO THE INTERNET

ISDN

ISDN is a type of telephone service that is an alternative to a regular phone line. (The name stands for "Integrated Services Digital Network".) The advantage of ISDN is it allows you to connect to another computer at a speed which is much faster than even the fastest modem. If ISDN is available in your area, you should consider it as an alternative to using a modem with a regular phone line. (On the Internet, there is no such thing as too much speed.) To learn more about ISDN, start with these Net resources. Then call your local telephone company and see if ISDN is available. Getting ISDN working can be a lot more hassle than using a modem, but it's worth it. ISDN is fast and, once it's all set up, you'll love it.

Web:
http://www.digitalmx.com/wires/
http://www.isdn.ocn.com/
http://www.isdnzone.com/info/
http://www.microsoft.com/windows/getisdn/whatis.htm

Usenet:
comp.dcom.isdn

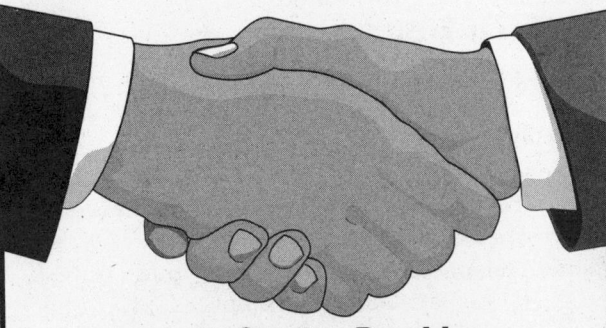

MODEMS and FUN

Modems are now an indispensable accoutrement of modern life. However, anyone who has ever tried to get a recalcitrant modem to cooperate understands just how much fun these delightful little devices can be. When your modem gets its back up, turn to the modem information site for help and enlightenment.

Internet Service Providers

Once you are on the Net, you become dependent on your Internet service provider (ISP). Unfortunately, many people don't appreciate how important this relationship really is.

A good ISP can make a big difference to making your time on the Internet comfortable and satisfying, so don't make the mistake of choosing your ISP as casually as you might choose a university, or an employer, or a spouse.

Do your homework now, and you'll avoid a lot of regret later.

Modems

The most common way to connect to the Net is by using a computer with a modem to access an Internet service provider over a regular telephone line. The modem provides the interface between your computer and the phone line. Modem technology has improved tremendously over the years. I remember when the "standard" was 300 bps (bits per second). The current standard, referred to as V.90, is now 56 K bps (56,000 bps). Hint: Although the 56K modems are fast compared to the older modems, they are still too slow. You are much better off with ADSL, cable modems or ISDN (in that order), if they are available in your area.

Web:
http://www.56k.com/
http://www.modemhelp.com/
http://www.rosenet.net/~costmo/
http://www.v90.com/

Usenet:
comp.dcom.modems
comp.sys.ibm.pc.hardware.comm
misc.forsale.computers.modems

WebTV

WebTV is a system that lets you access the Internet without a PC. All you need is a WebTV Internet terminal (which you must buy) and a television set. The WebTV Internet terminal is a special box that connects to your TV and to a phone line. All you need to buy is the box, but you do need to pay a subscription fee, just like you do with a regular Internet service provider. These Web sites will help you understand WebTV and, if you are already a subscriber, provide you with ongoing information and news. The advantage of WebTV is that the box is cheaper than a PC, and the system is easy to install and use. However, the box does not run regular software: all it can do is access the Internet. For example, you can't use Windows or any programs that use Windows. Still, I will tell you that when I first saw WebTV I was pleasantly surprised at how well it worked.

Web:
http://www.philipsmagnavox.com/product/pf322.html
http://www.ruel.net/settop.html
http://www.sel.sony.com/sel/webtv/
http://www.webtv.net/

CONSUMER INFORMATION

Automobile Lemons

A "lemon law" obligates a car manufacturer or a car seller to repair or replace a defective automobile or refund your money. If you suspect you have a "lemon", check out these Web pages to see how you can be recompensed. These sites have information about consumer strategies and the applicable laws for lemons.

Web:
http://www.autopedia.com/Lemon/
http://www.mindspring.com/~wf1/
http://www.nhtsa.dot.gov/cars/problems/complain/

Better Business Bureau

The Better Business Bureau (BBB) promotes good business/consumer relations. At the BBB site, you can find local bureaus, read consumer warnings and related news, file a complaint online, read consumer buying guides, or obtain a report on a company or charity. Find out what the Better Business Bureau can do for you.

Web:
http://www.bbb.org/

Blacklist of Internet Advertisers

Do you get mad when you get junk email? If so, you are not the only one. Check out this great blacklist of Internet advertisers. This site will give you information on what to do about spamming and unsolicited junk mail. This is an informative FAQ and should be read by anyone who is interested in consumer issues on the Net.

Web:
http://math-www.uni-paderborn.de/~axel/BL/blacklist.html

Consumer Fraud

There is a massive amount of fraud in the world, and the best way to avoid it is to be able to recognize it. Before you lose your money, take some time to read about chain letters, "free" prizes, "free" vacations, 900-numbers, foreign lotteries, personal finance-related schemes, multilevel marketing, work-at-home schemes, telephone solicitations, and much more. If you think you have been the victim of fraud, you may be able to find help on the Net. Most fraud is perpetuated by dishonest swindlers, but you can protect yourself by not allowing yourself to be a victim. There is something about the thought of free money that makes people so greedy that they are willing to throw their judgment out the window. Please remember, if someone is offering you a deal that sounds too good to be true, it *is* too good to be true.

Web:
http://www.echotech.com/
http://www.fraud.org/
http://www.usps.gov/websites/depart/inspect/consmenu.htm

CONSUMER INFORMATION

Consumer Information Catalog

When it's late at night and you need a little something to read, check out the Consumer Information Center, which was established in 1970 to help federal agencies and departments develop, promote and distribute consumer information to the masses. Four times a year, the Consumer Information Catalog is published. This jewel has descriptive listings of hundreds of booklets from all sorts of federal agencies covering topics like buying a car, building a career, federal benefits and housing information. You can order a free copy of the Consumer Information Catalog by filling out this handy-dandy Web form.

Web:
http://www.pueblo.gsa.gov/

Consumer Law

Find out your rights as a consumer. This Web site offers information on various consumer pitfalls such as insurance fraud, product liability, toxic chemicals, bodily injury, and more. You will also find links to consumer law resources and information on how to file consumer complaints. There is lots and lots of information here, making it a good place to browse when you have a few spare moments.

Web:
http://www.consumerlawpage.com/

Consumer Line

The Federal Trade Commission's Bureau of Consumer Protection has an online service called "Consumer Line". This service offers lots and lots and lots of online brochures relating to consumer protection. These brochures can inform you about art fraud, repossessions, financing scams, product purchases, and much, much more. Increase your consumer savvy by visiting this site.

Web:
http://www.ftc.gov/bcp/conline/conline.htm

Consumer News

Real news about real products bought by real consumers (you). Find out what is happening before the Joneses do.

Web:
http://www.bbb.org/alerts/
http://www.ftc.gov/ftc/news.htm

Consumer Product Safety Commission

If you think you are safe because you stay home all the time and play on the Internet, think again. There are all sorts of dangers lurking around your house, just waiting to get you. That's why people in America have the Consumer Product Safety Commission (CPSC): an independent federal regulatory agency whose mission is to keep citizens safe from harmful products such as badly designed cribs, toy boxes or television remote controls. Here's the CPSC official site where you can find their latest news or report an unsafe product.

Web:
http://www.cpsc.gov/

Don't let con artists take advantage of you. The Consumer Fraud Internet site has all kinds of useful information to protect yourself against the most common scams and rip-offs.

And once you have read the information, I have a special one-time offer for you. Just send $100 U.S. to me, and I will say a personalized benediction for you over the Internet. Although you may not notice it consciously, you will be protected by the cosmic force and be completely immune to consumer fraud forever (maybe).

130 CONSUMER INFORMATION

Can the Government Protect You?

Some people believe that the government should regulate many aspects of our lives to make them more safe, reliable and efficient.

Other people would have the government do as little as possible, letting individual people fend for themselves.

If you would like to see what the official U.S. government consumer agency is doing, take a look at the **Consumer Product Safety Commission** Web site.

Consumer Talk and General Discussion

Here are Usenet's general consumer forums. Send in your questions, share your answers, read the reviews, opinions, and general bad-mouthing of the bad guys. Before you spend your next dime, check with the world at large.

Usenet:
   alt.consumers.experiences
   misc.consumers

Consumer World

All dressed up and nowhere to go? Head to Consumer World where you can spend hours browsing around checking airfares, looking for ATM machines, filing consumer complaints, reading consumer booklets, applying for credit cards, researching a law, and countless other things. Consumer World covers a variety of types of consumer needs whether it's business or just plain fun.

Web:
   http://www.consumerworld.org/

Look What I Found on the Net...

```
Newsgroup: alt.consumers.free-stuff
Subject: Ways to Get Free Music

Join a record club and get your promised 10 free CDs, tapes, or
whatever they have promised.  They make you pay shipping charges, but
it's only about $2 per CD or tape.  Then, when they want you to buy
more CDs or tapes at the regular price you:

a) Say that you are a minor.  Write a note from your parents saying they
   didn't know you were in this club.

b) Say you are devastated by society's pressures — for example, you
   are 21 and pregnant, trying to resist everyday pressures, etc.
   — and the last thing you can worry about is belonging to a stupid
record club.

c) Say that you decided to give the money instead to charity.

This also works great with magazines to get a couple of issues free.

Trust me...
```

CONSUMER INFORMATION

ConsumerNet

Boy, there is so much consuming going on—here, there, all over the place—there's just no end to it. So I bet you want to keep up on what's happening: news, legislation, what people are saying, and what's available on the Net. Well, you're at the right place: today I read about identity theft legislation, tips on saving money during hot weather, and how to protect my privacy (and it's still early).

Web:
http://www.consumernet.org/

Credit

We're in a fast-moving world, and it is a rare person who is not hard-pressed to keep up with the popular culture. One crucial area of modern life is money and how it affects your credit. A good way to make sure you are capable of minding your financial Ps and Qs is to read the credit information on the Net, and prepare yourself to face the brave new financial world with confidence and style.

Web:
http://www.creditinfocenter.com/
http://www.experian.com/personal.html

Finding a Doctor

I went to medical school, and I know. There is a *huge* difference in the skill of doctors, and it matters a lot. I put in a lot of effort to find a good doctor for myself. I asked around for recommendations, then I made appointments with various doctors and interviewed them. Sure, I had to pay for those appointments, but it was worth it, as I was able to find the doctor I wanted. The best way to find a good doctor is to ask another doctor who is familiar with your area. The doctors in every community know which of their colleagues are good and which are bad. However, they are reluctant to give such information to outsiders, so you may have to be inventive to get a real recommendation. One last hint. Don't ever forget that you are the customer. The doctor works for you.

Web:
http://docboard.madriver.com/
http://www.ama-assn.org/aps/amahg.htm

Free Stuff

There is free stuff out there in the world, just waiting for you to ask for it. You can get all kinds of cool things for free—phone calls, food, clothes, recipes, tickets and endless samples of miscellany—just for asking. All the information is here, so clean out the garage in order to make room for more stuff.

Web:
http://www.1freestuff.com/
http://www.fabfreebies.com/
http://www.freeandfun.com/
http://www.thefreesite.com/freestuff1.htm
http://www.winternet.com/~julie/ntn1.html

Usenet:
alt.consumers.free-stuff

IRC:
#freestuff

Funeral Planning

Don't let the cost of dying ruin your day. When someone dies, the last thing you feel like doing is attending to all the details of arranging a funeral. So do yourself a favor and let the Net help. Use these resources to answer your questions and to give you the information you need. (Personally, I'd rather be caught dead than to be the guest of honor in a poorly planned, disorganized funeral.)

Web:
http://vbiweb.champlain.edu/famsa/
http://www.ftc.gov/bcp/conline/pubs/services/caskets.htm
http://www.ftc.gov/bcp/conline/pubs/services/funeral.htm
http://www.funeralnet.com/faq.html

Why watch it on TV when you can see it on the Net?
See "Broadcasting on the Net".

132 CONSUMER INFORMATION

Junk Mail

Some people don't mind junk mail (unsolicited advertising delivered in the mail), but I do. I don't like the idea of my address being sold and resold by junk mailers, and I don't like my mailbox being filled with, well, junk. It's not just the inconvenience; after all, it's not hard to throw away junk mail. It's an emotional thing. I like to have control over my life, and I don't like junk mailers (or telemarketers or spammers) buying and selling personal information about me. If you are like me, you will appreciate learning how to remove yourself from the lists used by the junk mailers and other such scum.

Web:

http://www.ecofuture.org/ecofuture/jnkmail.html
http://www.junkbusters.com/
http://www.the-dma.org/pan7/cons-7a.shtml

National Institute for Consumer Education

Do you know anyone who needs to learn about consumer issues? The National Institute for Consumer Education (a NICE organization) has information about fraud, credit, finance, bankruptcy, credit cards, car leasing, and much more. I say, if you're going to consume, do it knowledgeably.

Web:

http://www.emich.edu/public/coe/nice/

Tipping

The thing about tipping is, if you don't do it right, you won't be a welcome customer. And if you aren't a welcome customer, a lot of strange things are going to happen to your food you would rather not know about. So learn about tipping: when, why and how much. Nothing is more suave than a man who nonchalantly offers exactly the right tip without even thinking about it (unless it is a woman who offers exactly t r t w e t a i).

Web:

http://www.astanet.com/www/asta/pub/info/tipsontipping.htmlx
http://www.cis.columbia.edu/tipping/tipping.html

CONTESTS

Beanie Baby Contests

So you love Beanie Babies. But once you have amassed your collection, what can you do? Well, you can play with them, but that gets a bit boring after a while. You can look at the master list and fantasize about getting all the ones you need to complete your collection, but that just leads to frustration. No, the only thing to do is connect to the Net and enter a Beanie Baby contest. Anything else would just be a colossal, ludicrous waste of time.

Web:

http://www.angelicinsights.com/freedisneybeanie.html
http://www.encyclobeaniea.com/beanhunt.htm

Bookweb Contest

If you can solve a puzzle you get to be in the group from which a winner is randomly chosen. And, if you are lucky enough to be chosen, you win a prize. Okay, so your chance of winning is only slightly more likely than being struck by lightning, but you have to admit it's a lot more fun.

Web:

http://www.ambook.org/fun/contest/

Celebrity Classmates

Each week, you get a chance to identify famous celebrities as they were before fame struck and they were catapulted out of their normal, bland, everyday existence into glitzy, glittering stardom.

Web:

http://www2.classmates.com:8080/celebs/index.cgi

Contest Talk and General Discussion

This is the Usenet group devoted to announcing new contests. You will also find discussion about contests as well as questions and answers. If you like contests, this is a good place to check regularly.

Usenet:

alt.consumers.sweepstakes

Dangerfield, Rodney

Rodney Dangerfield, the comedian, has some clever contests on his Web site. Even if you don't enter the contests, it's fun to read the past results, and Rodney and his Web guys do go to a lot of trouble to make the site interesting.

Web:
http://www.rodney.com/contest.asp

> **Rodney Dangerfield's Contests**
>
> Does the world give you a hard time?
>
> Just win one of **Rodney Dangerfield's** contests, and, in no time at all, everyone on the Net will be treating you with respect.

Find the Lost Dog

The poodle is lost and it's your mission to find him. This challenge sends you out all over the Web looking for clues as to where the little doggie has gone. To be eligible for the drawing, there are various criteria you have to meet. Then you can win fabulous prizes and be admired by all your peers. Not to mention that, if you happen to be a Boy Scout, finding the dog could count as a good deed.

Web:
http://www.heymon.com/contest.html

Hard Disk Contest

It's every geek's fantasy to win free computer equipment. Get a chance to win a studly hard drive just by answering some simple questions.

Web:
http://www.harddisk.com/freedisk/freedisk.html

Kids' Contests

Here's an important tax tip. If you win a contest, you must declare the value of the prize as income on your tax return. But if your kid wins, you can save a lot of tax, because he or she is probably in a lower bracket than you. (Is this a cool book, or what?)

Web:
http://www.4kidz.com/weekly_changes/win_prizes.html
http://www.acekids.com/contests.html
http://www.contestclub.com/Kids/kids.htm

Nightmare Factory

Indulge your morbid sense of fear by checking out the Nightmare Factory. This Web site is the online representation of a huge haunted house in Austin, Texas. Once a month they offer a chance to win a prize by having you go on a monster hunt. Find the monster and maybe you will be the winner.

Web:
http://www.nightmarefactory.com/monsterh.html

Popsicles

When I was a kid, I used to love popsicles. They only cost 5 cents, and you could make two out of one if you were able to crack them down the middle without having the top part break off. Do you like popsicles? Enter this contest, and maybe you'll win a year's worth. Actually, they send you 52 coupons, each of which can be traded for a box. I guess they figure you only need one box a week. (Too bad you only get coupons. The thought of having someone hand-deliver real popsicles to your house every week for a year is cool beyond belief.)

Web:
http://www.popsicle.com/contests/

Riddler Game

Right now, as you read this, you could be out making money on the Web just by using your brain along with some clever mouse-button clicking. The Riddler Game gives you the opportunity to answer trivia questions and solve puzzles for cash prizes. The game is free, but you have to register to play.

Web:
   http://www.riddler.com/

Tracy Turnblatt Taken to Task in Trivia Tumble

Do you know who Tracy Turnblatt is? If so, you may be a trivia champ in the making.

Don't even wait a moment. Connect to the Riddler Game and see what you can do with a lifetime's supply of otherwise useless knowledge.

Sports Contest

Your sports experience doesn't have to be limited to sitting around watching television. You can sit around testing your hard-won sports knowledge on the Net by entering the monthly contests sponsored by the World Wide Collectors Network. Not only will you impress your friends with your mastery of the esoteric, you may even win a prize.

Web:
   http://www.wwcd.com/contest/contest.html

Sports Picks

Here's your chance to prove you really know your (American) football. During the football season, this site offers a contest that allows you to predict the scores of various games. The computer will keep track of all your predictions for the entire season. When it's not football time, you can hang out and talk with other sports fans in a variety of sports-related chat rooms. Or you can brush up on your football trivia, just in case you get an emergency call to participate on a game show.

Web:
   http://www.iis-sports.com/picks/

Sweepstakes and Contests

Here's a gold mine of sweepstakes and contest information for both children and adults. These sites include instant win sweeps, writing contests, freebie pages and links to other sweepstakes pages. Win, win, win, win. (That's my advice.)

Web:
   http://contest.catalogue.com/contests/
   http://www.4cyte.com/ThreadTreader/
   http://www.contestguide.com/
   http://www.contestworld.com/
   http://www.loopy.net/contests/
   http://www.prizes.com/
   http://www.sweepstakesonline.com/

Today may be your lucky day, but there is only one way to find out. Connect to the Sweepstakes and Contests site, and see what destiny has in store for you.

Uproar

Are you a sports trivia buff? Do you like word puzzles? Is bingo your game? Play these games and many more, and maybe you'll win a prize. There are lots of regularly scheduled contests. You can play alone or team up with other people on the Net. Just remember where this Web site is, and you will never have to worry about having nothing to do.

Web:
http://www.uproar.com/

Vacation and Travel Contests

If you don't want to spend your hard-earned money on a vacation, you can always try to win a vacation in a contest. Here is a Web site where you can enter a variety of contests to win vacation-oriented prizes. Of course, if you did win a free trip, you would have to leave your computer and a lot of email would accumulate while you were away. Oh well, nothing is perfect.

Web:
http://www.freestuffcentral.com/contests/

Victoria's Valentine Contest

Do you like romantic stories? The type that make you feel like a mushy container of warm butter? If so, you may be an almost-winner. All you have to do is write about your most cherished Valentine's Day memory, send it in to the judges, and you might win a lovely romantic prize.

Web:
http://www.mmnewsstand.com/static/products/454/valentine-contest.html

Word Puzzles

Does your brain need a few mental pushups to keep it in tip-top shape? Try solving some of these interesting and challenging word puzzles, and you just may win a prize. There are several different puzzles to solve, and they are not easy, so roll up your virtual sleeves and plug in the ol' thinking cap. Pretty soon, your mind will be one of the best-functioning organs in your entire body.

Web:
http://www.syndicate.com/

> **Think, Think, Think.**
> Good. Now that you are warmed up, enter one of the Word Puzzle contests. Do it now. Don't tergiversate.

World Village

Do you need a variety of mental stimulation in your life? Would you like to win a prize? If you answered "yes yes," head straight to this Web site, where you will find a variety of interesting places to visit, with contests scattered here and there.

Web:
http://www.worldvillage.com/wv/contests.htm

COOKING AND RECIPES

Aunt Edna's Kitchen

Do you need some help cooking? Nothing could be easier. Aunt Edna has lots of information for you: recipes, nutrition stuff, help on using spices, measurement conversions, and a bunch of links to other culinary resources. With Aunt Edna in the kitchen, your dishes are bound to come out perfect (and then you can invite Uncle Harley over to help you eat).

Web:
http://www.cei.net/~terry/auntedna/

136 COOKING AND RECIPES

Backcountry Recipes

When you are heading to the outback, make sure you are prepared. There's nothing worse than getting into the middle of nowhere, and suddenly you have a big craving for a barbecued chicken wing. Here are some recipes to use when you go backpacking, hiking and camping. Learn about trail snacks, dinners, breakfasts, meat dishes and desserts that are easy to bring along whether you are going to hike up a mountain or just spend the afternoon in downtown New York.

Web:
http://www.gorp.com/gorp/food/recipe.htm

Barbecue

You know what I like after a hard day of writing? A whacking big carrot stick, doused with a liberal helping of spicy barbecue sauce, and roasted slowly over an open flame. However, if vegetarian is not your style, take a look at some of the smoking-and-curing resources on the Net, where I guarantee you'll find enough information to choke a cumin-rubbed Boston butt. And if you find a tempting recipe for slow-roasted barbecued carrot, try it in my honor and see how close you can get to heaven on Earth.

Web:
http://www.azstarnet.com/~thead/bbq/
http://www.barbecuen.com/

Usenet:
alt.food.barbecue

Bread

Here's how to plan for a successful dining experience: pick a bread that suits your mood, then decide what main dish goes well with it. Those of you who are more ambitious might want to even bake your own. If that is the case, try some of the bread recipes on the Net. When you find one you like, double the size of the recipe just in case. (You can never have too much bread.)

Web:
http://haven.ios.com/~wordup/bread.html
http://www.breadrecipe.com/
http://www.countrylife.net/bread/

Usenet:
rec.food.baking
rec.food.sourdough

Candy Recipes

When it's midnight and the stores are closed and you are having a big Attack of the Killer Sweet Tooth, get out the pots and pans, and whip up some of these exotic specimens, such as Turkish delight, peanut butter balls, candied apple slices, and many more.

Web:
http://soar.berkeley.edu/recipes/desserts/candy/
http://www.candyusa.org/recipes.html
http://www.youcan.com/rock-candy/rock-candy.html

Cookie Recipes

Everybody has his or her own favorite type of cookie. Mine are made from organic seaweed, brewer's yeast, whey and (for fiber) biodegradable sawdust. However, if you happen to be one of those people who is not a health food junkie, your taste in cookies may be a tad more mainstream. If so, check out these Web sites for more cookie recipes than you could use in a month of Sunday bake sales.

Web:
http://www.cookierecipe.com/
http://www.lino.com/~mimi/vegetablepatch/cookiear.htm
http://www.well.com/user/vard/cookies.html
http://www.wester.net/Momz/cookies.html

Make a Cookie

I bet that, right now, you need a cookie.

And not just any cookie. I bet you need a delicious, aromatic, homemade cookie.

Here's a great idea: go to the Cookie Recipes Web site, find something that looks good, and get a batch in the oven as fast as you can.

Do you realize that, in less than half an hour, you could have a freshly baked cookie in your mouth?

Now *that's* what I call an idea.

COOKING AND RECIPES

Cooking Talk and General Discussion

If you like messing around the kitchen and trying out new recipes, there are lots of people on the Net who will love to talk to you. Join one or all of the cooking discussion groups, and talk about cooking techniques, equipment, recipes, vegetarianism, and so on. Usenet is a great place to trade tips and techniques, and to ask questions about things culinary.

Usenet:
  alt.cooking-chat
  alt.creative-cook
  alt.creative-cooking
  rec.food.cooking

Diabetic Recipes

If you are a diabetic, you know you have to be extra careful about your diet. For this reason, you probably know more about nutritious cooking than other people. To augment your repertoire, here are some great collections of recipes for diabetics, including dishes you would think you could never eat, such as apple dumplings, double fudge balls, fruit cookies and chocolate banana mousse. You will also find other useful resources, such as information on sugar replacements.

Web:
  http://gourmetconnection.com/diabetic/
  http://soar.berkeley.edu/recipes/diabetic/
  http://www.childrenwithdiabetes.com/d_08_200.htm

Fat-Free Recipes

Whether you are staying away from fat for dieting or health reasons, you still need some good recipes. The Net has lots of tasty ways of preparing food without fat. You don't have to feel deprived, because here are recipes for bread, salads, cookies, casseroles, pizza and a variety of ethnic foods.

Web:
  http://www.fatfree.com/
  http://www.wdn.com/mirkin/indexes/recipes.html

Fish

Cooking fish is the test of your culinary abilities. Nothing is better than fresh fish, prepared well and cooked properly. On the other hand, old fish cooked poorly is about as rank a foodstuff as you would ever hope to meet. This is why I like this Web site. There are lots of hints, tips and recipes for preparing fish, including a wonderful fish-cooking glossary. My lawyer Bill goes fishing a lot, and sometimes he and his wife Wendy invite me over for a dinner of fresh salmon. Talk about good cooking: I can taste it now. If you ever run into Bill, be sure to tell him you are one of my readers, and ask for a piece of fish. (I'm sure he'll give you one. After all, it's a business expense.)

Web:
  http://www.gortons.com/cookbook/

French Cooking

Some people pooh-pooh French cooking. They say that it uses too much butter, that it's too fattening, that the rich sauces are used to hide meat of dubious quality and that any food that can't be prepared by warming it in a microwave is too complex and intricate for day-to-day consumption. My philosophy is: if it's good enough for Zsa Zsa Gabor, it's good enough for me (and *she's* not even French).

Web:
  http://sunsite.auc.dk/recipes/english/cat74.html
  http://www.cooking-french.com/recipes/
  http://www.epicuria.fr/recette/anglais/
  http://www.swv.ie/recipes/frahme.htm

Home Canning

Home canning can be a lot of fun, and it sure is nice to be able to go to the pantry whenever you want and pull out a can of your favorite fruit, vegetable or jam. However, to guard against spoilage and contamination, you do need to make sure that you do everything just so. Before you can, check out these tips and recipes. Remember, as your third grade teacher would say, if something's worth canning, it's worth canning well.

Web:
  http://www.foodsafety.org/canning.htm
  http://www.home-canning.com/tips.html

Indian Food

When I am in the mood for Indian food, I don't always have the time to hop on a plane and travel to India. On these occasions, it's easier just to find a recipe from the Net and make it in my own kitchen. You can do it, too. Set up the computer in the kitchen, point your Web browser to these sites and follow along. In no time, you will have a delightful meal prepared in your own home, without the side effect of jet lag and the red tape that comes with traveling to another country.

Web:
   http://www.gadnet.com/recipes.htm
   http://www.indiaworld.co.in/open/rec/recipes/
   http://www.welcomeindia.com/recipes/
   http://www.welcometoindia.com/cookery/

Insect Recipes

If you are having a party, these Web sites offer the perfect recipes for little appetizers. Insects are not only freely found in the environment, but they make perfect finger food. Try some dry-roasted leafhoppers or Army worms. For dipping, use the rootworm beetle dip or for dessert try my personal favorite: the chocolate chirpie chip cookies.

Web:
   http://www.ent.iastate.edu/misc/insectsasfood.html
   http://www.uky.edu/Agriculture/Entomology/
      ythfacts/bugfood2.htm

Internet Chef

The Internet Chef is a great culinary home away from home. You can browse the extensive recipe archives, look at cooking tips and articles, and even chat with other people in real time. You can also leave messages for other visitors to read. For example, you can post a message asking if anybody has a recipe for fried groat clusters and check back later to see the responses. If you can't stand the heat in the kitchen, you can always hang out at the Internet Chef.

Web:
   http://www.ichef.com/

Italian Cooking

Can't tell your cannellini from your cannoli or your fontina from your fontinella? Don't worry. The Net can make you an Italian know-it-all in no-time-at-all. These Web sites have recipes for pasta, appetizers and main dishes. Or you can read an Italian cooking glossary so you can enunciate your pancetta with the best of them.

Web:
   http://www.cimorelli.com/pie/mangia/
      mangmenu.htm
   http://www.eat.com/cooking-glossary/

Kitchen Link

If you're like me, you divide your time between the kitchen and the Internet. If so, here is the missing link: a large, well-organized collection of food and cooking resources from all over the Net. Recipes, magazines, FAQs (frequently asked question lists), cooking software, discussion groups, nutrition information, cooking tips—it's all here.

Web:
   http://www.kitchenlink.com/

An Unexpected Treat

What do you do when your mother-in-law and your boss drop in unexpectedly for dinner at the same time?

You could reheat that leftover tuna surprise, or whip up a family-sized potful of macaroni and cheese, but that is *so* cliché and would impress nobody.

Instead, why not connect to the Net and try some of the **Insect Recipes**? Insect dishes are stylish, unusual and a good source of protein. After all, why let people bug you when you can bug them first?

COOKING AND RECIPES

Medieval and Renaissance Food

If you want some really old food, besides the scary stuff at the back of the refrigerator, try whipping up something from the medieval or Renaissance period. You can get recipes for main dishes or desserts.

Web:
http://www.bahnhof.se/~chimbis/tocb/foreword.htm
http://www.pbm.com/~lindahl/food.html

Majordomo Mailing List:
List Name: **sca-cooks**
Subscribe to: **majordomo@ansteorra.org**

Mexican Cuisine

When you are in the mood for something spicy, drag the laptop into the kitchen and connect to these Web sites, which have lots of recipes and interesting trivia about Mexican foods and their history.

Web:
http://godzilla.eecs.berkeley.edu/recipes/ethnic/mexican/
http://www.viva.com/nm/food.recipes.cocinas.html

Mimi's Cyber-Kitchen

There's no kitchen like Mimi's kitchen. It has tons of links to recipe archives, articles on cooking indoors and outdoors, information on preparing seafood, spices, vegetables, holiday cooking, plus Mimi's personal recipe collection. Fire up the grill and make something special tonight.

Web:
http://www.cyber-kitchen.com/

Cooking with Mimi
If you love cooking, you'll love Lots and lots of plain-spoken kitchen talk, along with an old-fashioned, traditional, down-home search engine to help find the exact recipe you need.
Mimi's Cyber-Kitchen.

Look What I Found on the Net...

```
(from the Random Recipe Generator Web site)
               Delicious Beet Bars

    Ingredients:

        * 1 pound of fresh chicken
        * 3 beets
        * 1 bag of carrots
        * 3 newts on a root of a banyan tree
        * 1 tablespoon of spoiled mayonnaise
        * 2 tablespoons of sesame seed

    Preparation:

        1. Cut chicken and remove bones
        2. Dice beets and sprinkle on skillet
        3. Chop carrots and mix in beets
        4. Throw in the newts on a root of a banyan tree
        5. Spread mayonnaise on beets
        6. Add seed
        7. Bake for 53 minutes at 125 degrees

    Serves 2.
```

140 COOKING AND RECIPES

Pies

Not long ago I had a great pie experience. A well-known publisher came to visit me and stayed overnight. At dinnertime, he volunteered to help out by making dessert and, using a recipe passed on to him by his grandmother, he baked a magnificent apple pie fit for a king. The best part was—since we couldn't find a king on such short notice—we had to eat the whole thing ourselves. If you would like to have a great pie experience in your own home, you don't have to wait for a well-known publisher to visit you. Simply check with these Internet pie resources, where you can find instructions on pie baking along with a nice variety of recipes and tips that will make the whole experience as easy as you-know-what.

Web:
http://dinnercoop.cs.cmu.edu/dinnercoop/Recipes/subjects/dessertpies.html
http://www.pierecipe.com/

Random Recipe Generator

Ladies: The next time your best friend starts bragging about what a good cook she is, get a couple of recipes from the Random Recipe Generator, and challenge her to a cooking contest. This Web site generates recipes with random ingredients and random cooking times, so I guarantee you will boldly go where no woman has gone before. (And you thought Martha Stewart did her own research.)

Web:
http://bobo.link.cs.cmu.edu/cgi-bin/dougb/recipe

Recipe a Day

Check this Web site, and, every day, you will see a free recipe, displayed on your own personal computer in the privacy of your own home. What could be more appetizing?

Web:
http://www.recipe-a-day.com/

> **Look around.
> Is anyone watching? Good.
> Take a look at the
> "X-Rated" section.
> (But remember, you didn't
> read it here.)**

Recipe Archives

I promise you: As long as you have the Net, you will never ever run out of recipes. How about a new idea for dinner tonight? Or perhaps you'd like to cook up a special something for that special someone. Here are some great archives with more recipes than you can shake a wooden spoon at.

Web:
http://mel.lib.mi.us/reference/REF-food.html
http://soar.berkeley.edu/recipes/
http://www.ichef.com/ichef-recipes/
http://www.tc.umn.edu/~fine0015/rfr/
http://www.virtualcities.com/~virtual/ons/recipe.htm

Recipe Talk and General Discussion

Have you ever seen the Dick Van Dyke Show? Well, when Rob Petrie first met his wife Laura, she did not like him at all. However, he found out that she collected recipes and started sending her cookbooks (which helped him win her heart). Rob had to do it the hard way; today, he could snarf as many recipes as he wanted from either the **rec.food.recipes** Usenet group or the Web site that serves as the archive for this group. Then he could simply email the recipes to Laura. So what do you do when your boss and his family are coming over for dinner and all you have is a frozen armadillo? Nothing to worry about. Just connect to the Net and check out the armadillo recipes. Either that or borrow a cookbook from Laura.

Web:
http://www.neosoft.com/recipes/

Usenet:
rec.food.recipes

COOL AND USEFUL

Southern Cooking

Mmm, mmm. If you have never had Southern cooking, you are certainly in for a treat. Take off those jogging shoes and your fitness gear, and pull up to a big slab of ham coated with red eye gravy, a side of collards, some poke salad, okra, black-eyed peas and a hunk of cornbread. If you can't get this at your favorite restaurant, you can learn about Southern cooking on the Net. These sites will tell you what it is and how it's done, including the history of Southern cooking. You'll learn how ingenious Southerners are with their cooking and about the many different uses there are for leftover bacon grease.

Web:
http://dbtech.net/~suncastl/kitchen.htm
http://www.cbt.net/dedwards/
http://www.grits.com/category.htm
http://www.math.ua.edu/~bgray/recipes.htm
http://www2.netdoor.com/~billover/

FOOD, SOUTHERN STYLE

If you don't happen to live in the southern part of the United States, you are missing a lot. For example, I bet you can't remember the last time you had a nice helping of catfish and hush puppies, with a side order of cornbread.

Well, as long as you have a Net connection, you can remedy the situation right now. Just connect to one of the **Southern Cooking** sites and find out what you have been missing.

Until you can say you really understand grits, you have not led a full life.

Sushi

When you are hungry, it's nice to have a little ikura to roll around on your tongue. If you want to try to make some sushi at home, or you are just curious about how they make sushi hold together, you can learn about it on the Net.

Web:
http://www.stickyrice.com/html/sushi.html

Usenet:
alt.food.sushi

COOL AND USEFUL

Complaint Letter Generator

Want to complain to someone? Or about someone? Or on behalf of someone? Let the Complaint Letter Generator do all the hard work. Generate a letter, copy and paste it into your email program, and send a despicably elegant missive to the victim of your choice. Or, for more impact, print the letter and mail it in a mysterious envelope with no return address. (Just remember, you didn't read this here.)

Web:
http://www-csag.cs.uiuc.edu/individual/pakin/complaint

Daily Diversions

Do you have a sneaking suspicion that your best friend is getting more work done than you? If so, send her (or him) a diversion. It's free, it's easy, and you can choose from a different list every day. Some people accomplish far too much, and it is up to you to slow them down. After all, what are friends for?

Web:
http://www.dailydiversions.com/

Daily Fix

Wow! Somewhere to visit every day where you can find (1) an engaging quotation, (2) a wry observation, (3) a trivia factoid, and (4) the definition of an interesting word. Wow! Four reasons to get up in the morning and start your browser. Wow!

Web:
   http://www.dailyfix.com/

Daily Tips

Life can be difficult, but the Net can help in its own small way. All you need to do is sign up for a free daily tip. Just pick the area in which you are interested (business, health, travel, pets, humor, gardening, self improvement or sports), and every day you will receive email with a genuine tip. Yes, life can be difficult, but a small daily tip may be just the boost you need to push you over the precipice of happiness.

Web:
   http://www.dailytips.com/

Eeeek Net

Did you know that the onion is the most widely used vegetable in the world? And were you aware that margarine was patented in 1871, but the first appendectomy was not performed until 1885? And I bet you didn't know that, when a bat flies out of a cave, it will always turn left. Is all this really true? Who cares, it's fun just to read stuff like this. Aside from little known facts, this site contains a miscellaneous grab bag of interesting ways to spend your valuable time on planet Earth.

Web:
   http://www.eeeek.com/

The best way to make money is to give something away for free.

Electronic Postcards

Faster than a speeding bullet.

More powerful than a handwritten note and a dozen roses.

Able to leap the widest chasms of interpersonal relationships in a single transmission.

Look! There in your mailbox! It's a note. It's a memo. It's an *electronic postcard*!

Yes, an electronic postcard—strange visitor from the Internet—with powers and abilities far beyond those of regular messages. An electronic postcard—that can change the course of individual relationships, bend the harshest misunderstandings back to reality, and, disguised as a mild-mannered piece of email, fights a never-ending battle for Friendship, Communication and the Electronic Way.

Electronic Postcards

Would you like your friends to think you are thoughtful and considerate with very little effort on your part? Send them an electronic postcard. All you have to do is choose a picture or graphic, fill out the form, and your message is on the way. (Actually, if you really want your friends to think you are thoughtful and considerate, a better idea might be to buy them all copies of this book.)

Web:
   http://www.123greetings.com/
   http://www.mailameal.com/
   http://www.maxracks.com/
   http://www.surfme.com/cgc/
   http://www.webcircle.com/users/ladydi/index5a.htm
   http://www.yobaby.com/

Harley Hahn's Internet Exploration Station

Join me at Harley Hahn's Internet Exploration Station, and I'll take you on a tour of the Internet tempered with genuine, guaranteed wisdom. If I weren't so modest, I would tell you that Harley Hahn's Internet Exploration Station is the very best way to explore the Net, have fun, and learn about life, all at the same time. However, since I am modest, you'll have to find out for yourself.

Web:
http://www.harley.com/hhies/

Kvetch

"Kvetch" is Yiddish for "complain". When life gets to be a bit too much, take a moment and see what other intelligent and accomplished people are complaining about. By the way, speaking of kvetching, it strikes me that a lot of the trouble in this world is caused by other people. I mean, I'm okay and I know that you're pretty cool, but what about all the other people in the world? Don't you wish they would just shut up and do whatever you tell them?

Web:
http://www.kvetch.com/

Last Word on Science

I believe everyone should understand the basics of science: chemistry, physics and biology. Why? First, being knowledgeable and using your brain is good for you, and, two, a lot of what happens around us from day to day is understandable if you understand basic science. For example, have you ever wondered why the sky is blue? Or how a dog tracks a scent? Or how a smoke detector is able to detect smoke? Or why we have fingerprints? This Web site has the answers to all these questions and more. You know, there are two things in life I really like: good questions and smart answers. Plan on spending some time here, and it won't be long before you agree with me.

Web:
http://www.last-word.com/

Learn2

This site is one of my very favorites. In fact, I used it just today because my copy editor was looking for information about how to clean her computer. If you like to learn how to do stuff, you'll find enough material here to occupy you for a long time. Learn how to change a flat tire, fix your zippers, carve a turkey, choose wine for your meal, dress nicely, balance your checkbook, burp a baby, fix your computer, and much more. My philosophy is if you are going to be a know-it-all, you should know it all.

Web:
http://www.learn2.com/

Pocket Internet

When I was a little kid, one of my favorite things was when the whole family went downtown to meet my father after work and he would take us out to eat at this restaurant that had a big buffet. I liked that there were all different types of food and that I could sample them all. (My favorite item was the small baked crabapples.) This Web site is like an Internet buffet. There are samples of all the different types of things that people like to do on the Net. If you are teaching somebody how to use the Web, this is a good place to have them start.

Web:
http://www.thepocket.com/

Reminder Services

It's nice when your mother calls to remind you of upcoming birthdays and anniversaries. But what happens if she forgets?

E-minder can be your personal Internet reminder service to make sure you never forget again.

(If you need some important dates to remember, my birthday is December 21, and my cat's birthday—his name is The Little Nipper—is April 6.)

Reminder Services

We all know how embarrassing it is to forget something important. For example, last month I forgot to send my sister a card for her gerbil's birthday. And a couple of days ago, Bill Gates called me to ask if I was finished with the "Buns of Steel" video he loaned me. This need never happen again—to me or to you. On the Net there are some great electronic reminder services. Just specify your email address, a date, a message, and how many days' warning you want. On the right day, you will receive email containing your message. Now that you are on the Net, there is no excuse for forgetting anything ever again. (By the way, Bill, don't forget you still have my copy of "Windows 98 for Dummies".)

Web:
   http://nf.webassist.com/
   http://www.alertweb.com/
   http://www.allnotes.com/
   http://www.candor.com/reminder/
   http://www.memotome.com/
   http://www.specialdates.com/

Search Snoopers

Do you like to eavesdrop? Of course you do. Well, here's a way to find out what people all over the Net are doing. These sites, maintained by the search engine companies, allow you to see what other people are looking for. You use a search engine to find resources on the Web. To do so, you specify one or more words or terms, and the search engine examines a vast database of information to suggest resources relating to what you specified. So, wanna eavesdrop? Connect to either of these sites and see a list of words that people are searching for right now. While I looked, I found that people were looking for resources about slot machines, audio components, incest, deer habitats, butts, sailing, teen-only chat, Bible, escape velocity, lottery and singles.

Web:
   http://voyeur.mckinley.com/cgi-bin/voyeur.cgi
   http://webcrawler.com/Games/SearchTicker.html
   http://www.askjeeves.com/Peek/peek.asp
   http://www.debriefing.com/spywarning.htm
   http://www.metaspy.com/

Search Snoopers

Snoop, snoop, snoop.

See what other people are doing on the Net.

Snoop, snoop, snoop.

Find out what strange things other people are looking for.

Snoop,

   snoop,

      snoop.

I love it.

Straight Dope

The Straight Dope is a syndicated newspaper column written by Ed Zotti under the pen name Cecil Adams. The Straight Dope site contains archives of many of the questions that Adams has answered. The answers are thoughtful and knowledgeable. What I like is that Adams does not confine himself to questions that have an easy answer. Thus, not all of the answers are exact, which I find thought-provoking.

Web:
   http://www.straightdope.com/

Very Crazy Stuff

What do all these women's names have in common? Ethel, Marcella, Wilma, Mildred, Phyllis, Thelma, Bertha, Doreen, Henrietta and Edna? They are all on the list of "Names That Guarantee Your Daughter Won't Find a Husband". There's a lot more crazy stuff at this site, and, if you like thinking and reading about things that are a tad unusual, the stuff at this site will keep you rotating in your chair for hours. (By the way, it's not true that all women with these names can't find a husband, although, it is probably not just a coincidence that both Ethel Mertz and Wilma Flintstone had to marry guys named Fred.)

Web:
  http://www.verycrazy.com/

Virtual Presents

I love virtual presents, and I love to send them to my friends for no reason at all. This is a great place to visit if you need to get someone an impressive gift that you can't afford. You can send your friends a vacation, fine jewelry, animals, food, flowers, and a lot more. What's a virtual present? Try it.

Web:
  http://www.virtualpresents.com/

Virtual Presents
Right now, there are people all over the Net having fun sending imaginary gifts to one another by email.
Your virtual presents is requested.

Why Files

A lot of news stories relate to science, but rarely do you get a chance to really understand the science behind the news. The Why Files start with topics from the news and go on to explore all kinds of interesting questions. If you care why things work the way they do, this site is for you. (Hint: When you have nothing to do and it's still a few hours to dinner, read the step-by-step description of coronary bypass surgery.)

Web:
  http://whyfiles.news.wisc.edu/

COOL BUT USELESS

Advertising Gallery

Some people are frightened by roller coaster rides or monster movies. Some people are frightened by various processed foods such as Spaghetti O's or Vienna sausages. For others, their blood may run cold after analyzing some of the less tasteful parts of marketing culture. This gallery of advertising will show you parts of the mostly American culture that are best left unrevealed. However, since it's too late for that, you might as well go see what you should be missing.

Web:
  http://www.absurdgallery.com/

Answers to All of Your Questions

There are so many times in life when you just do not know what to do. You reason everything out as best you can; perhaps you ask a friend or relative for advice; you may even toss a coin. But, no matter what you do, you just can't bring yourself to make a decision. Well, your troubles are over. What you need is spiritual guidance based upon your own particular inner needs, and here it is, for free, on the Net. Just ask your question and click on the purple square of your choice. As if by magic, the exact advice you need will appear on your screen. (And, if that doesn't work, open this book at random and read the first sentence you see. You have my personal guarantee that what you get will be what you need.)

Web:
  http://www.ccnet.com/~elsajoy/instant.html

NEVER FORGET.
If you are ever unsure what to do, you can always use the Net to find the
Answers to All of Your Questions.

COOL BUT USELESS

Biker Buddy

Have you seen one of those Tamagotchi-like toys: small gadgets in which a virtual person or pet lives? Your job is to use the controls to keep maintaining the thing in a happy and healthy state—or it dies! Well, here is your own Internet-based responsibility, the Biker Buddy. See how long you can keep him alive.

Web:
  http://www.binary-biker.org/onthefly/23mc/

Bill Gates Wealth Clock

Have you ever wondered how much money Bill Gates has? The real answer is that no one, even Mr. Bill himself, actually knows how much he is worth. However, here is a Web site that has a conservative estimate of his wealth based on his holdings of Microsoft stock and its current price. Check out the site, and you can see what the big fellow's stock is worth right now. You can also see an interesting statistic: the total amount of money divided by the number of people in the United States. Thus, if you are American, you can see an estimate of how much you would receive if Mr. Bill were to liquidate all his Microsoft stock at the current price (with no commissions) and share it equally with everyone in the country. It comes to about $218. Or to put it another way, if everyone in America were to send me the measly sum of $218, our country could have *two* humungously rich billionaires instead of only one. This would serve to increase the competition and be generally better for everyone.

Web:
  http://www.webho.com/WealthClock

Cool but Useless Talk and General Discussion

There is a lot of useless talk on the Internet. However, there aren't that many places where you will find useless talk about cool ideas. Here are a few Usenet groups in which you might find such treasures. These are the places I visit when I need a quick break from the press of everyday life, and I want to immerse myself in the cool, but useless part of the world.

Usenet:
  alt.angst
  alt.celebrities
  alt.conspiracy
  talk.rumors

Create a Barcode

Have you ever wished you could create your own barcode patterns? Now you can. Just specify a number, and you will be presented with the corresponding barcode. There are lots of cool ways to have fun with barcodes. For example, if you have a kid, use these services to generate a barcode for a unique identification number (such as the kid's Social Security number). Then have the pattern tattooed on the kid's forehead. Cool, huh? As they say on TV when they are trying to sell you something expensive that you don't need, you are limited only by your imagination.

Web:
  http://www.milk.com/barcode/
  http://www.tippecanoe.com/barservr.htm

Look What I Found on the Net...

```
Newsgroup: talk.rumors
Subject: Space Monkeys Have Arrived!

> Holy Moley, the space monkeys are here! Stop them! Help me!

Are these monkeys related to the ones you put in the fish bowl?
The sea monkeys?
```

COOL BUT USELESS

Faces

You don't have to go to years and years of medical school to experience the thrills of being able to modify the faces of rich Hollywood stars. All you have to do is click your mouse, and mix and match parts of the stars' faces until you create something new that you like. You can recreate all the excitement experienced by Dr. Frankenstein without running up a huge electric bill.

Web:
http://www.corynet.com/faces/

Internet Dancing Baby

Have you seen the famous Internet Dancing Baby? It's a wonderful animation of a virtual dancing baby that has been floating around the Net for some time. There are many versions of the baby. One of these Web pages is my version of the dancing baby, in which he gyrates to the sounds of Latin jazz. The other resources will help you find all the dancing babies you need to lead a rich and fulfilling life.

Web:
http://www.a-ztech.com/baby.htm
http://www.harley.com/dancing-baby/
http://www.nwlink.com/~xott/babypage.htm

Mad Martian Museum of Modern Madness

This is a great place if you are worried you are getting a bit too normal, and you need a boost of weirdness. For example, wouldn't you love to investigate the "Interactive Toilet of Terror"? And how can you pass up the "Plastic Eyeball Exhibit" or the "Mad Martian Masks"? I don't think I need to say any more: the interactive toilet can speak for itself.

Web:
http://www.madmartian.com/

You're cool.

Magnetic Poetry

Imagine you have a very large refrigerator and, sticking to the door, you have several hundred small magnetic thingies, each one having a word printed on it ("women", "urge", "pink", "ask", "you", "go", and on and on). Now imagine yourself being able to select and arrange the thingies so as to write poetry out of the words. Well, on the Net you do not have to imagine. Here is a virtual surface with lots and lots of thingies, each with its own word. Use your mouse to move the words around and create whatever poetry or messages your heart and mind desire. When you are finished, you can share the result with everyone by copying your poem onto a piece of paper and putting it on the door of your fridge.

Web:
http://prominence.com/java/poetry/

I went to the
Magnetic Poetry
site, and you know what I found out? I'm a poet.
No kidding. This is what I composed:

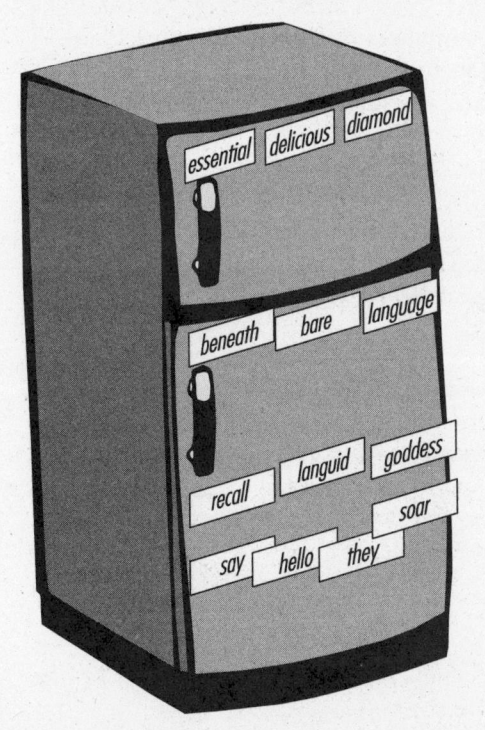

essential delicious diamond
beneath bare language
recall languid goddess
soar
say hello they

And I bet you could do even better.

Mood Thing

What kind of day will you have? Here's a quick and easy way to find out. Go to this Web site and see a list of words that change so fast you can't read them. Click four times and select four words from the list. The remote computer will then look at those words and foretell your future. After all, why should you spend a whole day in ignorance, when the truth is so close and so accessible (and free)?

Web:

http://www.gettingreal.com/pow/moodthing/moodthing.html

Museum of Dirt

There's more to dirt than what meets the eye and stimulates the hand. Dirt can have a story of its own, a passive but significant role to play in our appreciation of the world around us. To see what I mean, visit the Museum of Dirt, where you will find dirt samples taken from celebrity yards and interesting places like a Buddhist shrine and Alcatraz Island. You will also see rejection letters from celebrities who did not want to contribute dirt to the museum (boo!).

Web:

http://www.planet.com/dirtweb/dirt.html

Time Machine

These days, time is really at a premium. So I understand if you don't have time to sit around and watch the sun rise, or enjoy flowers as they slowly open their petals, or appreciate the various other wonders of the world. No problem: take the easy way out. You can see all sorts of interesting time lapse photo movies without having to miss any of your favorite television shows. Life has never been so fast, easy or convenient.

Web:

http://www.timelapse.com/

Are you a modem or a mouse?

Useless Facts

Sometimes, the most enjoyable facts are the most useless facts. Facts that are weird, funny, sometimes astounding, but are careful to never stray from the path of uselessness. For example, I bet you didn't know that Anne Boleyn (the second queen consort of Henry VIII) had six fingers on one hand. Get your fill of odd factual tidbits and amaze your friends to no end. My prediction is that you will be the most popular person in your entire circle of friends. After all, there is no one more beloved than the purveyor of an endless supply of useless knowledge. Just ask any film studies teacher.

Web:

http://www-leland.stanford.edu/~jenkg/useless.html

Virtual Plastic Surgery

Mix and match the features of well-known attractive people to create your own perfect someone or other. Choose just the right nose, mouth, eyes, and put it on whichever head feels right. When the result is displayed, print it out and take it with you as you walk around the world looking for your perfect soulmate. Each time you meet a new person, check your picture to see how close the person comes to your personal dream bunny.

Web:

http://www.mrshowbiz.com/features/games/surgery/

Woodcutter

In the Sixties, people used to take drugs to have an experience like this. Now you can have it for free on the Web. Very cool; very useless. (Hint: From time to time, you will need to find the right place to click to move things along.)

Web:

http://www.thewoodcutter.com/

CRAFTS

Balloon Art

Balloon art is always a good thing to know how to do in case you are trapped in an elevator with a group of children or perhaps have to calm several wild animals who are about to attack you. Check out this site for lots of balloon pictures, a FAQ (frequently asked question list), a guide to ballooning, as well as other potentially life-saving material.

Web:
http://www.fooledya.com/balloon

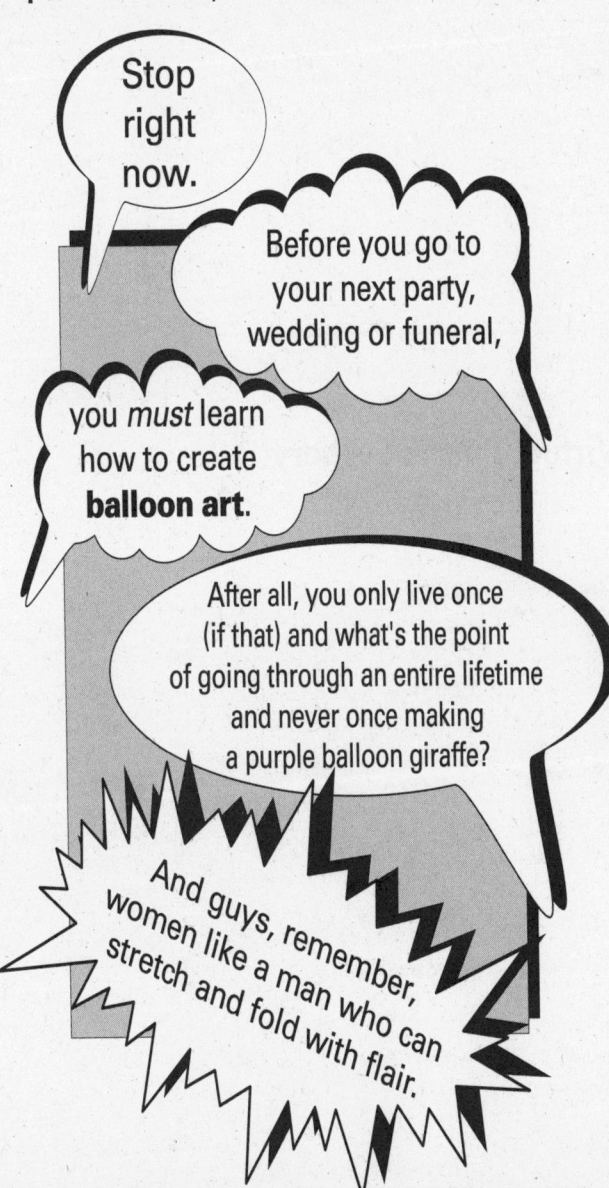

> Stop right now.
>
> Before you go to your next party, wedding or funeral, you *must* learn how to create **balloon art**.
>
> After all, you only live once (if that) and what's the point of going through an entire lifetime and never once making a purple balloon giraffe?
>
> And guys, remember, women like a man who can stretch and fold with flair.

Basket Weaving

If your home is sadly lacking in cultural artifacts, I have the answer. Connect to one of these basket-oriented sites and teach yourself how to render an actual objet d'art. After all, what could be in better taste than a house full of baskets? I myself have a basket in the shape of *Harley Hahn's Student Guide to Unix* hanging on my bedroom wall. (And, boy, am I popular.)

Web:
http://csbh.mhv.net/~abeebe/basket.html
http://www.bright.net/~basketc/

Beading and Jewelry

If you are a hardcore beader, you will love these Web sites, where you find a little of everything for bead fans and jewelry makers. Get information about bead resources, bead societies, places to talk about beads, and much more. For discussion, check out the Usenet groups and find out what the bead-conscious people of the world are doing.

Web:
http://exo.com/~emily/instructions.html
http://www.beadwrangler.com/tips&techniques.htm
http://www.jewelrycrafts.com/
http://www.landofodds.com/glueuse.htm
http://www.suzannecooper.com/beadmain.html

Usenet:
alt.beadworld
rec.crafts.beads
rec.crafts.jewelry

The Internet supports the three most important pillars of popular culture: sex, lies and videotape. (For more information, take a look at "Sexuality", "Politics" and "Television".)

150 CRAFTS

Calligraphy

Calligraphy is the art of fine handwriting. Traditionally, calligraphy is often used with illumination (the decoration of a manuscript or book). There are many different types of traditional calligraphy and illumination: early Egyptian papyri, ornamental scripts of the Renaissance, Oriental brushwork, Islamic ornamentation, and so on. To be a good calligrapher requires years of practice. To be a great calligrapher requires years of practice and a lot of natural talent. Unfortunately, with the advent of computer-assisted artwork, the need for traditional calligraphers (ones who do not use a computer) is significantly diminished. If you are a calligrapher, or interested in calligraphy, take a look at these Web pages. You will find information about individual artists, calligraphy organizations, online pictures of manuscripts, as well as a collection of calligraphy-related links around the Net.

Web:
http://mmm.wwa.com/ohmori/intro1.html
http://www.catalog.com/gallery/

Clay Art

It's so much fun to play in the mud. The problem is you can't do it and use the computer at the same time. But when you get clean and dry, take some time to subscribe to this mailing list to partake in the discussion of ceramic arts, clay, kilns, glazes and other hot clay art topics. The Web site and Usenet groups have some nifty stuff you can read when you aren't out getting your hands dirty.

Web:
http://home.vicnet.net.au/~claynet/

Usenet:
bit.listserv.clayart
rec.crafts.pottery

Listserv Mailing List:
List Name: **clayart**
Subscribe to: **listserv@lsv.uky.edu**

IRC:
#potters

Look What I Found on the Net...

```
Newsgroup: rec.crafts.misc
Subject: Stamp/Sticker Glue

> Does anybody have a recipe for the gummed back of stamps?

I found this one recently:

1 pkt (1/4 ounce) unflavored gelatin
1 Tbls cold water
3 Tbls boiling water
1/2 tsp. white corn syrup (optional)
1/2 tsp. lemon extract (optional)

In a very small bowl sprinkle gelatin into cold water.
Let soften for 5 minutes.

Pour boiling water into softened gelatin and stir until
dissolved. Add corn syrup and lemon extract (used for taste).

Mix well.

Brush thinly on back of sticker (paper may curl).

When dry, moisten sticker and apply to paper.
```

> **There's no time like the present. (Except maybe the future.)**

Craft Fairs
I can't think of anything that rivals the liveliness and fun of a craft fair except perhaps a folk-dancing marathon. If you want to take a walk on the wild side, take a look at the schedule for upcoming craft fairs.

Web:
   http://www.xmission.com/~arts/calendar/view.html

Craft Marketplace
No need to travel to the far regions of the world for the chance to buy cool craft stuff. In this Usenet discussion group, you can buy, sell, trade, or search for craft products and supplies. This is just the place to look when you need a little bit of Australian yarn to finish up that afghan.

Usenet:
   rec.crafts.marketplace

Craft Resources
There are so many craft activities in this world, there is no excuse for anyone being bored, not even for one tiny minute. But just in case you do get bored, here are some craft-related resources that will catch your interest and make you want to start a new project immediately. While you are on the Net, you can also find out about craft suppliers, craft associations, information about fairs and events, and fun craft things for kids.

Web:
   http://www.craftsearch.com/Craft/links.html
   http://www.craftsfaironline.com/
   http://www.cyberhighway.net/~istation/crafts/clinks.htm
   http://www.wyomingcompanion.com/janacraft/links.htm

Craft Talk and General Discussion
The only thing as much fun as sitting around making crafts is sitting around talking about making crafts (and you don't have a mess to clean up when you are finished). Come join the discussion. Trade hints, tips, techniques and generally hang with the craftiest people on the Net.

Usenet:
   rec.crafts.misc

Listserv Mailing List:
   List Name: **crafting-digest**
   Subscribe to: **listserv@ml.rpmdp.com**

Cross-Stitch
What could be a better way to relax than to spend time sitting in a chair making thousands of little Xs with a needle and thread on a piece of aida cloth? If you like to spend your spare time making colorful crafts of cross-stitch, take a look at what is on the Net. (Using the mouse will limber up your fingers just the right amount to prepare you for a long session of stitching.)

Web:
   http://www.concentric.net/~wildwolf/
   http://www.ncal.verio.com/~kdyer/xstitch.html

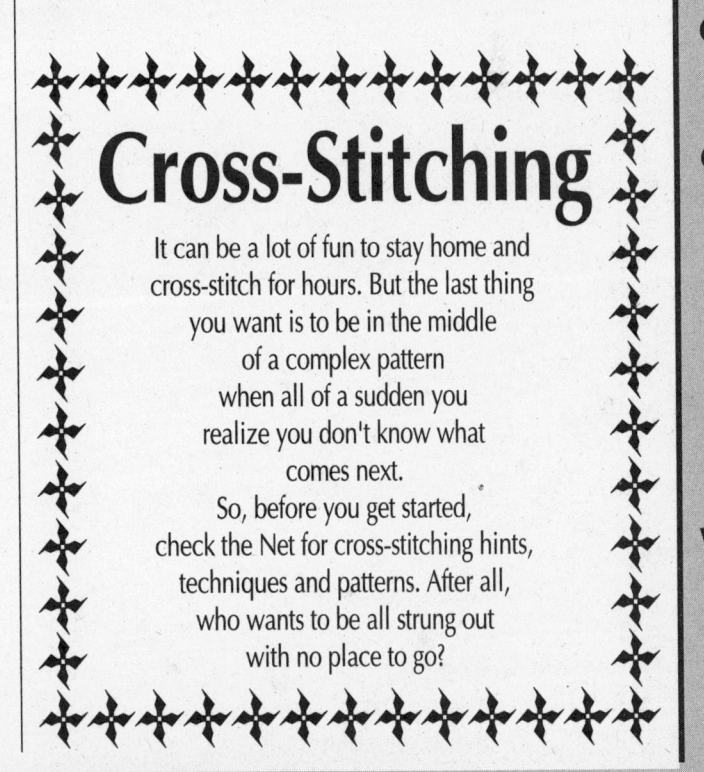

Cross-Stitching
It can be a lot of fun to stay home and cross-stitch for hours. But the last thing you want is to be in the middle of a complex pattern when all of a sudden you realize you don't know what comes next. So, before you get started, check the Net for cross-stitching hints, techniques and patterns. After all, who wants to be all strung out with no place to go?

152 CRAFTS

Decorative Painting

Decorative painting refers to a number of techniques in which you embellish walls, furniture or other objects with a patterned finish. Learn about tole painting (decorative painting on metal, and sometimes wood, surfaces), stenciling (applying paint upon a sheet in which a design has been cut, to produce a pattern upon the surface beneath), and faux finishing (painting a surface to look as if it were made from a different type of material). Spend a few hours on the Net, and you will soon be impressing people with your knowledge of strié, color washing, patina, crackling and marbleizing.

Web:
 http://www.busybrushes.com/
 http://www.craftnetvillage.com/project_library/painting.html
 http://www.cybertours.com/periwinkle/art.html
 http://www.decoart.com/free/
 http://www.fauxlikeapro.com/
 http://www.stenciling.com/
 http://www.tolenet.com/

Knitting

Knit one, purl two, what could be more fun to do? My experience is that the most intelligent and desirable women like to keep their hands busy. Well, the Internet has lots of resources for knitters, including a lot of patterns. (I recently came across one for a sweater for a Chihuahua.) Although the U.S. Surgeon General says that running while carrying knitting needles can be hazardous to your health, my advice is to take your chances and head straight for the Net without delay.

Web:
 http://www.tiac.net/users/stacey/
 http://www.woolworks.org/

Usenet:
 rec.crafts.textiles.machine-knit

Majordomo Mailing List:
 List Name: **knitlist**
 Subscribe to: **majordomo@kniton.com**

Knives and Blades

Years ago, I had a wonderful switchblade given to me by my uncle. Later, I bought myself another such knife when I was visiting Switzerland. That was years ago, and I didn't think much about knives until my good friend John Anderson, a knife aficionado and collector, took me to a knife show. Boy, did I have a good time. It was a real treat to see so many people who love what they do, and to see so many exquisitely crafted instruments. The knife collecting world has a fascinating culture, with a symbiotic balance between collectors and knife makers. The collectors support the knife makers, who create a limited supply of new knives for the collectors. Thus, a knife show has an interesting mix of two very different types of personalities. All of this, and a lot more, is waiting for you on the Net.

Web:
 http://www.agrussell.com/
 http://www.customknives.com/faq-contents.htm
 http://www.knife.com/

Usenet:
 rec.knives

Lacemaking and Tatting

Lacemaking and tatting (looping and knotting a single strand of heavy-duty thread on a small hand shuttle) are almost lost arts (probably because beer companies do not like to sponsor professional lacemaking competitions). Fortunately, nothing important is neglected on the Net. Find out about lacemaking techniques, supplies, clubs and guilds, and talk to other lacemakers and tatters around the world.

Web:
 http://www.arachne.com/
 http://www.hottub.org/~exapno/tatting/tatting.html
 http://www.picotnet.com/Locatelace/locate.html

Listserv Mailing List:
 List Name: **knitted-lace**
 Subscribe to: **listserv@listserv@home.ease.lsoft.com**

Majordomo Mailing List:
 List Name: **lace**
 Subscribe to: **majordomo@arachne.com**

Metalworking

It's a totally embarrassing experience when your new neighbor comes to the door and says, "I heard you were the smartest and most talented metalworker on the block. Would you please anodize this piece of aluminum for me?" and that just happens to be the day your Internet connection is down. Don't disappoint your friends and neighbors. Connect to the Net now and brush up on your metalworking skills before that doorbell rings. While you are at it, you can get the lowdown on heat treating, machinery, welding, motors, associations, clubs, museums, and much more.

Web:
http://w3.uwyo.edu/~metal/
http://www.arts.state.tx.us/crafts/metal.htm
http://www.metalsmith.org/

Usenet:
rec.crafts.metalworking

Needlework

This delicate and skillful craft takes time, patience and devotion. Read up on all manner of needlework, including tips and techniques on tatting, petit point, cross-stitch and embroidery. Share patterns, design ideas and timesaving hints on this age-old craft.

Web:
http://www.ncal.verio.com/~kdyer/xstitch.html
http://www.needlework.com/

Usenet:
rec.crafts.textiles.needlework

Majordomo Mailing List:
List Name: needlework-digest
Subscribe to: majordomo@ml.rpmdp.com

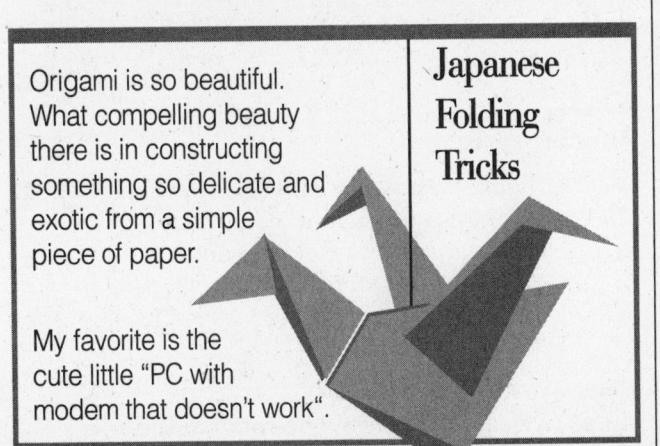

Japanese Folding Tricks

Origami is so beautiful. What compelling beauty there is in constructing something so delicate and exotic from a simple piece of paper.

My favorite is the cute little "PC with modem that doesn't work".

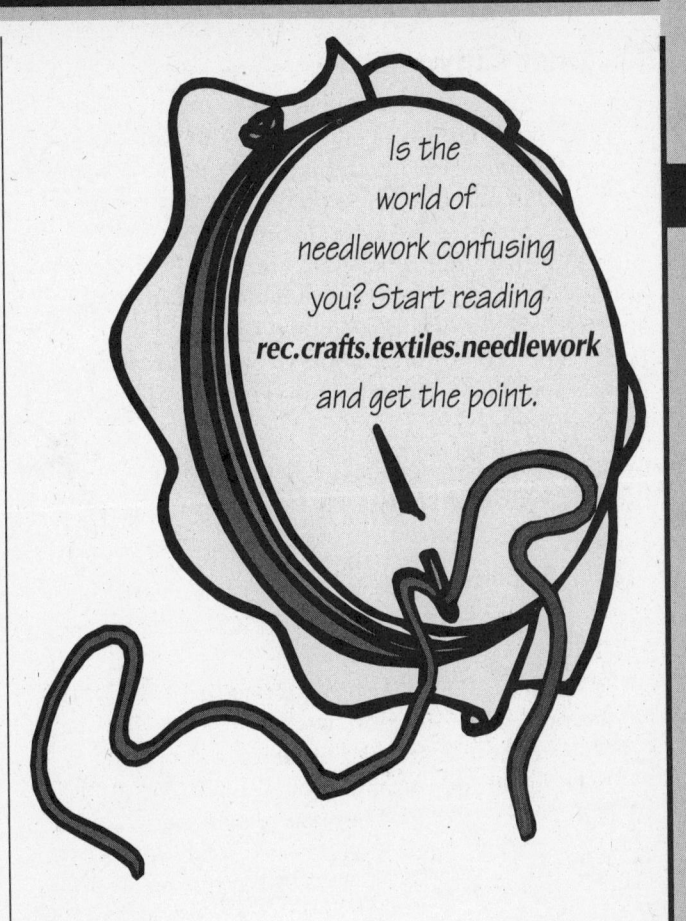

Is the world of needlework confusing you? Start reading **rec.crafts.textiles.needlework** *and get the point.*

Origami

In the 6th century, the secret of paper was carried by Buddhist monks from China to Japan. The Japanese soon integrated paper into their culture. Traditional designs were passed down orally, from one generation to the next. Creative paper folding with non-traditional designs was popularized by Akira Yoshizawa, starting in the 1930s. Modern origami (from the Japanese words for "fold paper") is a pastime enjoyed all over the world. Origami is a wonderful hobby to explore, and the Net is the place to start learning. Read about all facets of origami, including bibliographies, folding techniques, display ideas and materials.

Web:
http://ccwf.cc.utexas.edu/~vbeatty/origami/gate2.html
http://www.datt.co.jp/Origami/

Usenet:
alt.arts.origami

154 CRAFTS

Polymer Clay

Clay. Ah....clay. It makes me think of my childhood, when I could happily spend hours with soft and gooey substances and uninhibitedly mash and smash them into an unrecognizable pulp. (Now I have to spend my time smashing editors into an unrecognizable pulp.) Release your inner child and join the discussion about polymer clays. Common topics include molds, strength of clay, and tips on how to make various clay crafts. The Web sites have lots of cool information for people who like to play with polymer clay.

Web:
http://members.aol.com/lynellev/lynelle.htm
http://www.best.com/~jaed/clayspot/

Usenet:
rec.crafts.polymer-clay

Quilting

A quilt is a blanket consisting of two layers of fabric enclosing a layer of cotton, wool, feathers or down. The whole thing is stitched together, often using a decorative pattern of some type. What make quilts so much fun is that you can use various fabrics and designs to create your own personalized work. If you are a quilt person—or aspire to learn this noble art—start with these quilting Web sites. Here you will find all the information you need to get started, along with lots of resources for experienced quilters. For discussion, questions and answers, check out the Usenet groups.

Web:
http://ttsw.com/MainQuiltingPage.html
http://w3.one.net/~davidxix/QuiltLinks.html

Usenet:
rec.crafts.quilting
rec.crafts.textiles.quilting

Kids, see "Kids". Pet bunnies, see "Animals and Pets".

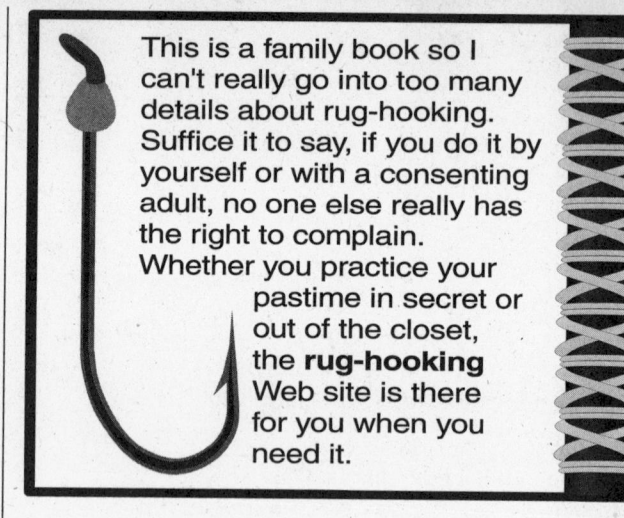

This is a family book so I can't really go into too many details about rug-hooking. Suffice it to say, if you do it by yourself or with a consenting adult, no one else really has the right to complain. Whether you practice your pastime in secret or out of the closet, the **rug-hooking** Web site is there for you when you need it.

Rubber Stamps

These resources are for people who like to stamp designs onto paper using colored inks: stamping resources, a list of people on the Net who like stamping, information about stores and conventions, reviews and tips, stamp artwork, and a glossary. For a little more interactive action, there is a mailing list for those who like to talk about stamping as much as they like actually doing it.

Web:
http://www.agate.net/~silvrfox/websites.html
http://www.hand-stamped.com/jump-page.html
http://www.rubbertrouble.com/

Usenet:
rec.crafts.rubberstamps

Majordomo Mailing List:
List Name: rubberstampers
Subscribe to: majordomo@crafts.dm.net

IRC:
#stampers

Rug-Hooking

Real rug-hookers know the difference between looped pile rug-hooking and latch-hooking. Don't get caught in a big social faux pas by not knowing the difference. At this Web site, you can read the history of looped pile rug-hooking, a rug-hooking FAQ and a zine called Woolgatherings.

Web:
http://www.rughookingonline.com/hooked/hooked.html

Sewing

To me, the epitome of skill and artistry is being able to sew a shirt from scratch. I once watched someone do it and, to this day, I am still amazed. I guess I am one of the culturally unwashed: I like to wear clothes, but I have no idea how to make them. However, if you are a real sewing person, you are not alone. There are many people on the Net talking about sewing, and you can join them whenever you want.

Web:
http://quilt.com/Bernina/Thread101.html
http://www.craftsearch.com/Sewing/links.html
http://www.delphi.com/needle/resources.html

Usenet:
alt.sewing
rec.crafts.textiles.sewing

Soapmaking

Kidneys are important, and, for protection, they are surrounded by a layer of adipose tissue (fat) referred to as perirenal fat. While an animal is alive, the perirenal fat acts as protection, cushioning the kidneys from random blows of fate. After death, however, the fat is up for grabs, which brings us to the question at hand. What would you do if some kind soul presented you with 40 pounds of pure beef kidney fat? Well, most people would be nonplussed at such an opportunity— but not a soap maker. No, a talented soap maker would be able to use that fat, mix it with lye (sodium hydroxide), water, and perhaps a little fragrance and coloring, and come up with a wonderful batch of homemade soap. Sound inviting? Believe me, it's a lot more fun than starting with 40 pounds of soap and trying to create perirenal fat.

Web:
http://www.lis.ab.ca/walton/old/soaphome.html
http://www.silverlink.net/~timer/soapinfo.html

Usenet:
alt.crafts.candlemaking.soapmaking
alt.crafts.candlemaking.soapmaking.moderated

Fun is one click away.

Stained Glass

I love to look at stained glass and think of all the work that went into making it: cutting the pieces, grinding the edges, copper foiling or leading the glass, and then soldering the pieces together. If you are a stained glass artist, or if you are interested in learning something about this fascinating craft, you will enjoy this well-organized, comprehensive Web site. You will find lots of information about supplies, patterns, magazines, questions and answers, and much, much more. Check out the Usenet discussion group for lively stained glass banter.

Web:
http://www.artglassworld.com/

Usenet:
rec.crafts.glass

Textiles

Textiles are so...tactile. Get your fill of luscious laces, fabrics, yarns, thread and more. The Net has loads of information on fibers, knitting, spinning, embroidery and producing yarn.

Web:
http://www.his.com/~fandl/fiberwww.html

Usenet:
rec.crafts.textiles
rec.crafts.textiles.marketplace
rec.crafts.textiles.misc

Tie Dye

Learn to tie dye your clothes in a totally rad fashion, man. And these are not just some lame instructions by capitalist pigs trying to make money off you. This FAQ (frequently asked question list) is compiled by the pros: tie-dyed-in-the-wool Grateful Dead fans.

Web:
http://www.public.asu.edu/~idjmw/tiedye.htm

Yarn

The world would be a dull place if it were not for yarn. There would be no cozy sweaters or lumpy slippers to wear. Whether you like knitting, crocheting, using a machine or just your hands, this discussion group will have something you like as long as you are a lover of yarn. The Web site has some good information about the various properties of yarn.

Web:
http://www.sonic.net/~garyh/yarns/propert.html

Usenet:
rec.crafts.textiles.yarn

CRIME

Alcatraz

Alcatraz was a United States federal prison built on an island in San Francisco Bay to house the most incorrigible and heinous prisoners in the federal penitentiary system. Alcatraz was opened in 1934, and remained in operation until 1963, when it was closed as a cost-cutting measure. During that time, the prison housed a total of 1,545 inmates, with an average of about 260 at any one time. In all, 36 prisoners tried to escape, of which 21 were recaptured, 7 were shot and killed, 2 drowned, and 5 were left unaccounted for. Currently, Alcatraz is a popular San Francisco tourist attraction, drawing many visitors who arrive by boat and take a guided tour of what has become America's most notorious prison.

Web:
http://www.nps.gov/alcatraz/

> Be cool! Join a mailing list.

Con Artists

Have you ever seen a game of three-card monte? You are in a crowd, and a man takes out three playing cards, two of which are similar. For example, there may be two black cards and one red card. He turns the cards face down, so you can't tell which is which, and starts throwing them back and forth. Eventually, he lets them fall, still face down. He invites you to bet on which one is the red one. If you bet, say, $20, and you choose the red card, you win $20. Otherwise you lose your money. The man plays this game over and over. Sometimes he wins, sometimes he loses. But, eventually, he will win a lot of money and vanish quickly. How does he do it? There are several ways, all of which involve slight of hand and deception. The man sets up the situation to make it look as if you can't lose. For example, you might see that the red card has a little bend in the corner, and the man doesn't seem to notice. Perhaps another person in the crowd will wait until the man's attention is distracted for a moment, and then point out the bend in the red card to everyone. Now, it's time for the kill. The man with the cards does his best to mix them up, but you don't care. All you have to do is watch to see where the bent card ends up. You may not feel that it's fair to bet when you know the red card is bent, but after all, it's a street game and if the card man can't look after himself, he shouldn't be betting. So you bet a lot of money, point to the bent card, and say, "This is the red one." The man invites you to turn it over, and you discover that the card is black. He flips over the other two, neither of which is bent, and, sure enough, one of them is red. Before you have time to figure out what happened, the three-card monte man is gone, and so is your money. What you didn't know is that three-card monte players spend long hours practicing how to bend and unbend a card surreptitiously. What you also didn't know is that the friendly fellow who pointed out the bent card was a confederate of the card man. Con artists are as old as humanity, and they are entertaining only in the movies. Getting conned in real life is not fun at all. To help you be prepared, here are some Web pages with information about common cons, scams and illegal schemes.

Web:
http://www.andrew.cmu.edu/user/td2b/conmen.html
http://www.newc.com/crimeprevention/white/whitecollarcrime.html

CRIME 157

Con Artists

I love reading about con artists and their scams. It's interesting to see how many effective ways there are to separate people from their money. Since you are one of my readers, I want to make sure you are never cheated. So go right now to the **Con Artist** Web sites, and learn about the tricks of the trade, before a member of the trade tricks you.

Corrections Professionals

Working in a prison or jail is a difficult job, and most people, even your relatives and friends, will never really understand what your job is like. But if you have Net access, there are lots of ways to keep in touch with other corrections professionals and related organizations. These Web sites are for professionals working in the field, and provide information about events, careers, news, legal happenings, and so on. There are also online newsletters as well as chat rooms where you can talk to other people.

Web:
http://www.corrections.com/
http://www.io.com/~ellie/13b.html

Crime Statistics

Here are some interesting predictions about the population of the United States (based on current statistics). One out of every twenty people (5.1%) will end up in prison at some time during his or her life. The chances of going to prison are 9% for men and 1.1% for women. The chance of a black man going to prison in the United States sometime in his life is 28%. This compares to 16% for Hispanic men and 4.4% for white men. It's interesting to talk about numbers, but these statistics represent real people in real communities. There are a lot more crime-related statistics on the Internet, and if you have an interest in this area, there is a lot for you to think about.

Web:
http://www.crime.org/
http://www.ojp.usdoj.gov/bjs/

Crime Talk and General Discussion

If you are interested in talking about crime, there are several discussion groups just for you. For crime buffs, the **alt.crime** group discusses all types of miscellaneous topics, while **alt.true-crime** is for talking about famous crimes. If you are a law enforcement professional, you may want to participate in the **bail-enforce** group (professional bail enforcement) or the **criminology** group.

Usenet:
alt.crime
alt.crime.bail-enforce
alt.crime.peacemaking.criminology
alt.true-crime

Look at all this information.

Wouldn't it be a crime to let it go to waste?

158 CRIME

Death Row

In the United States, the method of putting criminals to death varies from state to state. Overall, there are five different methods that are used: the electric chair, lethal injection, gas chamber, firing squad and hanging. Traditionally, "death row" is the name given to the part of the prison that houses inmates who are scheduled for execution. The death penalty and how it is applied are issues of great debate everywhere. Regardless of how you feel about the death penalty, it's interesting to look at some of the facts and figures. These Web sites have a lot of interesting information, but they did leave one of my questions unanswered. You know that before the doctor gives you an injection, he wipes your skin with an alcohol swab to clean off the germs. I wonder, when somebody is about to be executed by lethal injection, does the person administering the injection clean the person's skin with an alcohol swab?

Web:
http://essential.org/dpic/womencases.html
http://www.derechos.org/dp/
http://www.smu.edu/~deathpen/

Usenet:
alt.activism.death-penalty

Electric Chair

In the late 1880s, the electric chair was developed in order to execute criminals more humanely than by hanging. On August 6, 1890, the first person was put to death using this new technology. Since then, the electric chair has earned a place in the annals of American culture. And now, here is a Web site devoted entirely to this wonderful invention. Learn about the electric chair, its history, botched electrocutions, women in the electric chair, crimes, prisons, serial killers, and other methods of carrying out the death penalty.

Web:
http://www.theelectricchair.com/

Before you go on a trip, use the Net to help you plan. Read the "Travel" section.

Look What I Found on the Net...

```
Newsgroups: alt.activism.death-penalty
Subject: Logical Consequences for Death-Penalty Nations

>> Governments have murdered approximately 150,000,000 people in
>> peacetime during the twentieth century, which vastly exceeds
>> the number of private killings.

> What does this have to do with the death penalty in the United
> States?

Are all those who favor the death penalty this slow?  We will try
it really slow.

Government kills.  It kills needlessly and irrationally.  When it
executes people, it is killing.  It is very careless about who it
kills.  It kills the innocent as well as the guilty.

I sure hope that is simple enough.
```

Famous Murderers

What do Jack the Ripper, the Unabomber, Charles Manson and O.J. Simpson all have in common? They all worked hard to rise to the top of their profession, and they all have information available about them on the Internet. Need to find out more? Start with these killer Web sites. For discussion, try the Usenet groups.

Web:
  http://ripper.wildnet.co.uk/
  http://www.atwa.com/
  http://www.cruzio.com/~ytulip/cntnts.html
  http://www.cs.indiana.edu/hyplan/dmiguse/oj.html
  http://www.cs.umass.edu/~ehaugsja/unabom/
  http://www.easynet.co.uk/ray/serial_killers/
    boston.html

Usenet:
  alt.fan.karla-homolka
  alt.fan.oj-simpson
  alt.fan.unabomber

FBI's Ten Most Wanted Fugitives

Perhaps the most famous thing about the FBI (the United States Federal Bureau of Investigation) is their Ten Most Wanted Fugitives program. Since 1949, the FBI has published a list of the ten men and women they would most like to apprehend. Since then, a total of more than 440 people (7 of whom were women) have had the honor of making the list. Except for about 30 of these people, everyone on the list has been captured; about one third because a member of the public saw a familiar face on the list. Do you have some questionable friends? Check this Web site now. If you manage to turn in an actual fugitive, you could get rewarded with some big bucks.

Web:
  http://www.fbi.gov/mostwant/tenlist.htm

Gangs

If you live in an American city, you have probably seen gang signs and graffiti. But did you know that a lot of the writing is actually in code? Here is information to help you understand the codes, as well as some of the hand signals used by gangs. I have also included a Web site with information on various gangs in the U.S.

Web:
  http://www-bcf.usc.edu/~aalonso/Gangs/
  http://www.austingangbusters.org/
  http://www.ctol.net/~segag/faq.html

Internet Crime Archives

The sun is shining, the birds are singing and what better way to spend the afternoon than browsing through this collection of information about serial killers and mass murderers.

Web:
  http://www.mayhem.net/Crime/archives.html

CRIME INFO TO THE MAX

What's the best way to plan a serial crime or a mass murder? Well, you could figure things out as you go along, but you risk finding yourself in the hands of the police before you have arranged for the proper international media exposure. Nothing is more embarrassing than being in the middle of negotiating a book deal and finding out that another criminal has already used the exact same modus operandi (and sold the rights for a made-for-TV movie).

So, before you commit yourself, check with the Internet Crime Archives. Whether you are looking for ideas for leisure-time activities or just browsing for fun, let the Net help you avoid the time-consuming and costly research which is so much a part of modern life.

Law Search

If you are a police officer, this is a resource you will want to visit. There is a large database of police-related Web sites, which you can search to find just what you need. There are also handy online utilities, such as an accident calculator and a U.S. Social Security number state lookup.

Web:
  http://www.chickasaw.com/~waedens/

160 CRIME

Mafia

Whatever else you say about the Mafia, at least you have to admit they understand the importance of Family Values. If you want to learn even more about this collection of underground criminal societies, here are some good places to start. Although movies and TV often glorify gangsters, in real life they are highly unpleasant evil people, definitely not cool.

Web:

http://hrvati.cronet.com/mprofaca/mafia.html
http://www.ganglandnews.com/
http://www.murderinc.com/

Police Brutality

Police brutality and abuse of power are more or less built into our society. As human beings, we need the police. We ask them to take constant risks and protect us against evil, crazy, dangerous (often well-armed) people, who don't have to follow the rules. But police are human, so who watches the police? These resources deal with the problems of police abuse, offering a variety of useful and interesting information. If you are a policeman, take a few moments and explore this information. If you are a civilian with a problem, you will find information to help.

Web:

http://www.policeabuse.com/
http://www.unstoppable.com/22/
http://www.walrus.com/~resist/ndp/
http://www2.micro-net.net/~menache/

Police Scanner

Ever wonder what the police are talking about (when they're not cooping)? This Web site features live police transmissions from New York, Los Angeles and Dallas, as well as a variety of other live broadcasts, such as fire departments and air traffic controllers. To help you understand the slang, you can display a helpful list of the codes used on the radio. (In Los Angeles, for example, a "code 7" is a meal break.)

Web:

http://www.policescanner.com/

Police Scanner

Security hint:
To protect your house when you go out, leave your computer connected to the Net while playing a live police transmission at full volume.

The noise will help scare burglars (and keep your cat from getting lonely).

Prison Inmates

Believe it or not, there are a lot of prisoners who have access to the Net, directly or through the help of others. These Web sites contain pages created by (or for) inmates, as well as names, addresses and biographical information about inmates who would like pen pals. Warning: When you read the biographies—written by the prisoners themselves—they all sound like nice, normal people who didn't do anything wrong. Obviously, this is usually not the case. If you decide to write to an inmate, be careful.

Web:

http://www.pennpals.com/
http://www.prisonpenpals.com/

Prison Life

There are three types of people who will be interested in these resources: people who are currently in prison; people who are about to go to prison; and people who would like to find out what life is like in prison.

Web:

http://www.cs.oberlin.edu/students/pjaques/etext/
   prison-guide.html
http://www.fcnetwork.org/
http://www.prisonactivist.org/

Usenet:

alt.prisons

CRIME

Rape

Rape is the crime of forcing another person to submit to sex acts. If you or someone you know have been raped, you can find a lot of information on the Net to help you through your crisis. You will be able to read about counseling, domestic violence, incest, Rohyphnol (the so-called "date-rape" drug), crisis centers and rape prevention. When you need people to talk to, you will find a comforting and sympathetic group of people on Usenet.

Web:
http://www.cs.utk.edu/~bartley/saInfoPage.html
http://www.ncasa.org/
http://www.rainn.org/

Usenet:
talk.rape

Serial Killers

Serial killers are people who commit one murder after another, often following the same pattern. Here are some common characteristics shared by many such killers. Serial killers tend to be white heterosexual males in their twenties and thirties. They are loners with low self-esteem, subject to methodical rampages that are sexually motivated and sadistic. They enjoy returning to grave sites and crime scenes to fantasize. While growing up, their family life was violent, they tortured animals and were chronic bed-wetters. As adults, serial killers enjoy setting fires, have brain damage and are addicted to alcohol or drugs. If this reminds you of anyone you know, be careful. At the very least, don't give the person money or anything valuable (such as your only copy of a Harley Hahn book).

Web:
http://www.mayhem.net/Crime/serial.html
http://www.serialkillers.net/

Stalking

Stalking occurs when an obsessive person becomes completely and utterly focused on another individual. You have probably heard about high profile cases when the stalking victim is a celebrity. However, most victims are regular people, and the crime is a lot more common than you might think. If you have a stalking problem of your own, here is information that may help guide you toward a satisfactory resolution.

Web:
http://francieweb.com/stalked/
http://www.privacyrights.org/fs/fs14-stk.htm
http://www.soshelp.org/

Terrorism

Here are two complementary Web sites. First, a great collection of links with information about many different terrorist groups. Here you can find detailed information about the terrorist organizations: who they are, their location, their purpose, and their patterns of operation. The other Web site is run by the Bureau of Diplomatic Security at the U.S. State Department. Read about the cases the Bureau is actively investigating, and learn how you can pick up a huge lump of reward money by helping them capture a terrorist.

Web:
http://www.heroes.net/
http://www.terrorism.com/terrorism/

Usenet:
alt.security.terrorism

Unsolved Crimes and Fugitives

Mystery, intrigue, adventure. If you have ever read any Sherlock Holmes stories, you may have wondered how you would be at solving mysteries. Well, here are some real-life mysteries waiting for you on the Net. These Web sites contain a lot of information describing unsolved crimes and criminal fugitives. Remember, as Sherlock Holmes once said, "It is of the highest importance in the art of detection to be able to recognize, out of a number of facts, which are incidental and which vital. Otherwise your energy and attention must be dissipated instead of being concentrated." Make sure you always do your research on the Net before setting out to find the criminal, and, one day, you too may be a famous fictional character.

Web:
http://www.amw.com/
http://www.emeraldcity.com/crimefiles/
http://www.fugitive.com/
http://www.mostwanted.org/

Throw a wild party.
The Net can help. See
"Holidays and Celebrations".

162 CRIME

Unsolved Crimes: The Case of the Missing Plum

You read about a lot of unsolved crimes, but here is one that actually happened to me.

When I work late at night, I often like to stop for a quick snack. The other day, I bought a nice, juicy plum and left it on the kitchen counter. A few hours later, I took a short walk outside, and when I got back the plum was gone!

I searched all over the house, but there was no trace of the missing plum. The only other people in the house at the time were my cat (who doesn't even like plums), and my Chief Researcher who said she had no idea what might have happened.

Later, I did find a plum pit in my Chief Researcher's trash basket, so the only thing I can think of is that the thief ate the plum, and left the pit in the trash basket to throw us off the trail.

I still can't figure it out.

CRYPTOGRAPHY

Ciphers

If you have to send a quick secret message to one of your friends, but you don't have time to make up a clever code, check out some of the ciphers that are already on the Net. While they aren't exactly a secret, some of them certainly are clever. Maybe you will get lucky and pick one that nobody has read about.

Web:
http://www.achiever.com/freehmpg/cryptology/crypto.html

Classical Cryptology Bibliography

There is a ton of cryptography information on the Internet. However, if for some reason you can't find everything you need to know from the Net, check out this bibliography of books about cryptology and cryptography. It is bound to get you going in the right direction.

Web:
http://liinwww.ira.uka.de/bibliography/Theory/crypto.security.html

Cryptographic Research

This is the Web site for the International Association for Cryptologic Research. To be a cool cryptomaniac, you don't have to sit around in isolation planning new codes and trying to break old ones. No, you too can belong to a club of people just like you. (But remember what Groucho Marx once said, "I don't care to belong to any club that will have me as a member.") This site has information on crypto conferences, journals and newsletters.

Web:
http://www.iacr.org/~iacr/

Cryptography Archive

Here is a well-organized, compact collection of cryptography resources from around the Net. If you are at all serious about cryptography, you will want to put this site on your bookmark list. If you are not serious about cryptography, put this site on your list anyway. It's bound to impress your friends.

Web:
http://www.austinlinks.com/Crypto/

Want to learn about cryptography? Start with the Cryptography Archive.

CRYPTOGRAPHY

Cryptography FAQs

Cryptography is a fascinating pastime, and it's not difficult to spend many hours immersed in learning about codes. Before you spend too much time, however, take a few minutes and look at these FAQs (frequently asked question lists). Chances are most of your initial questions will be answered. Personally, I found reading these FAQs interesting and I bet you will too (especially if you know some math).

Web:
http://ftp.lth.se/archive/faq/cryptography-faq/
http://www.rsa.com/rsalabs/newfaq/

Cryptography Policy Issues

Cryptography is more than deciphering secret writing. There are also the political and administrative aspects. Here are some sites that consider cryptography from a political and legislative angle. Read about policies, legislative efforts, information about the infamous clipper chip, cryptography across international boundaries, and much more.

Web:
http://www.cdt.org/crypto/
http://www.crypto.com/

Usenet:
talk.politics.crypto

Cryptography Resources

One of the nice things about cryptography is that it will allow you to store copies of all your love notes on your computer at work and you don't have to worry about your colleagues reading anything that might embarrass you or perhaps cause you to lose a presidential election. Find out about other great uses for cryptography at this Web site, which contains a variety of links and information about data security.

Web:
http://www.cs.auckland.ac.nz/~pgut001/links.html

Cryptography Software

If you need some cryptography software, here are a few programs you can download and try for free: RPK, TEA, PGP, TinyIDEA and SecurPC. All of these programs are very secure, but each one has its own design and features. Try them all and see which one you like best.

Web:
http://vader.brad.ac.uk/tea/tea.shtml
http://web.mit.edu/network/pgp-form.html
http://www.rpkusa.com/
http://www.securitydynamics.com/products/datasheets/securpc.html

Cryptography Talk and General Discussion

Here is a general discussion group for all aspects of data encryption and decryption. If you are a cryptography aficionado, this is the place to communicate with your peers on the Net. (Note: The following is a message in code. There is a prize if you can break it. —Harley)

```
F_eB7   n!K4r   F^Pb2   M:Quf   ^{9&L
0y}w#   I/hH@   K'|eI   6N%-R   G-(4u
UA,,]   .Gs2~   o&?_^   :|IJA   V*e}@
;a2#3   ZZuJB   t0px9   s\@z)t  {eNSr
;LSZx   Kht9.   'oRFa   J'/KH   oF:q'
Hn[\P   vwqo1   4^:pI   ~&8jb   ]q4(2
1D)OE   v.bvZ   6[M\$   1)n;b   L$?q{
d,$}F   Q4PBM   c[<&U   )2>j)   Sh\yF
!\u@j   }:)ZW   cOPKt   2_~P/   x|s]!
;<6.Q   ";<;t   UB,-{   3@wzB   HD4PH
tb$Xr   !2Rpm   &7}BU   8sg)=   {
```

Usenet:
sci.crypt

Cryptography Technical Papers

There is lots and lots and lots to learn about cryptography if you really want to know the subject intimately. If you like to get down to the nuts and bolts of how cryptography works, try reading technical papers and articles on this interesting science.

Web:
http://www.cryptography.com/resources/papers/

CRYPTOGRAPHY

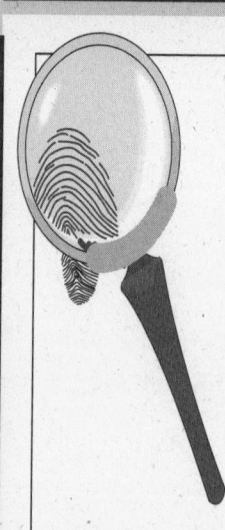

Finding Technical Papers About Secret Stuff

What do you do when you need to find a particular cryptography-related technical paper?

If you live near Washington, D.C., you can always go to the headquarters of the National Security Agency and ask them to let you go through their library. (If you have any problem, just tell them you are one of my readers.)

However, if a trip to the NSA is not convenient, try the **Cryptography Technical Papers** Web site. Not only is it faster, but you won't have to get fingerprinted just to use the restroom.

Digital Signatures and Certificates

More and more, we have the need to send information over the Net in complete secret. For example, if you order merchandise online by typing your credit card number, you should be sure that no one else can tap into the line, capture the information and use it for their own purposes. Or you may want to send a message to a friend or colleague that no one but the recipient can read. The systems that send and receive secure information over the Net use what are called "digital signatures" and "digital certificates". Such facilities are going to be in common use, so it is a good idea to find out how they work. Here are some good places to start.

Web:
http://www.epic.org/crypto/dss/

PGP

The PGP (Pretty Good Privacy) system is widely used to encrypt and decrypt data. Download the software for free, and use it to send secret messages to your friends. Better yet, encrypt your diary with PGP and even your mother won't be able to read it.

Web:
http://axion.physics.ubc.ca/pgp-attack.html
http://web.mit.edu/network/pgp-form.html
http://www.pgp.com/products/

Usenet:
alt.security.keydist
alt.security.pgp

IRC:
#pgp

Sending Secret Messages with PGP

The best things in life may be free, but if you don't want to share, you may have to hide them. One of the most widely used encryption programs on the Net is PGP, written by Phil Zimmerman. By offering a free, high-quality software package to everyone, Zimmerman single handedly deep-sixed the government's plans to control encryption.

Using PGP requires two passwords, called "keys". One of these is public; the other one is secret. You give your public key to anyone you want to be able to send secret notes to you. They use this key (and the PGP software) to encode a message which they then send to you. The beauty of the system is that a person can only decode the message if they have the private key (which you keep only for yourself).

The PGP program helps you create public and private keys that will work properly. Then you can give out your public key to your friends and start sending secrets around the Net. Similarly, if you have a friend who uses PGP, you can use his public key to encode a message to him that only he can read (because only he has the corresponding private key).

RSA

RSA is a cryptography system, invented in 1977, that is used for both encryption and authentication. (The name comes from RSA's inventors, Ron Rivest, Adi Shamir and Leonard Adleman.) With RSA, each person has a public key and a private key. You can give your public key to everyone; it is not a secret. However, you do not give out your private key. When another person wants to send you a secret message, he uses your public key to encrypt a message. The nature of RSA is such that, once someone uses your public key to encrypt a message, the message can only be decrypted by using your private key. Thus, you are the only person in the world who can decrypt messages that have been encrypted with your public key (because no one else has your private key). RSA is secure because it is extremely difficult to use someone's public key to figure out his private key. Thus, you can give out your public key with no worries. Of course, the whole system depends on being able to create suitable pairs of private and public keys. To create such a pair, you start with large prime numbers—call them **p** and **q**. Find their product **n=pq**. Choose a number **e**, less than **n**, such that **e** and **(p-1)(q-1)** have no common factors except 1. (In other words, **e** and **(p-1)(q-1)** are relatively prime.) Now find another number **d**, such that **(ed-1)** is divisible by **(p-1)(q-1)**. The public key is the pair **(n,e)**, and the private key is **(n,d)**. Once the keys are generated, the factors **p** and **q** can be thrown away. Here is the Web site of a company called RSA Data Security, which was formed by the inventors of RSA in order to develop and explore the technology. You will find a lot of interesting information about RSA and about people's attempts to break the code.

Web:
http://www.rsa.com/

Steganography

Where are you going to hide Aunt Wendy's secret recipe that you plan to use for the chili cook-off? The county championship is at stake, and you are determined not to let a spy slip in and ruin your chances. Don't settle for mere PGP encryption. Use steganography to hide your encrypted documents inside innocuous-looking images, sound recordings or other data files.

Web:
http://www.iquest.net/~mrmil/stego.html

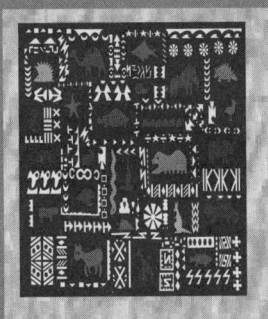

HIDING SECRETS WITHIN PICTURES USING STEGANOGRAPHY

Stego is the most amazing, cool thing you have ever seen. You can encode secret information inside a *picture*—within the little tiny dots. To anyone else, it looks like a regular picture (say, of you shaking hands with the Pope at Rodney Dangerfield's birthday party). But to anyone in the know, it is a *secret message*. You can send it all around the Net if you want, and no one can extract the information unless they have the password.

How totally radical. Only you know that the picture contains information hidden within the dots. All you need is a Macintosh and a modem and you can open your own spy agency. If you do, make sure you remember what my sister told me years ago: It's nice to be important, but it's important to be nice.

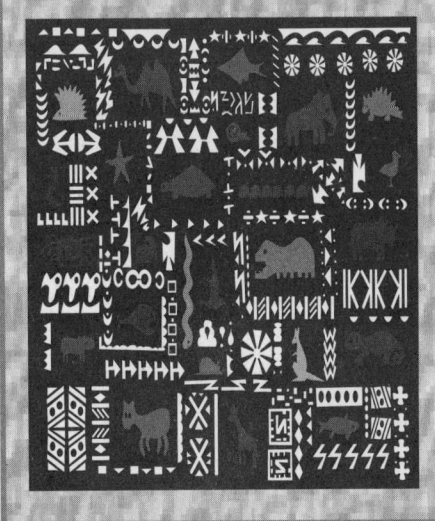

DANCE

Ballet

Ballet is a formalized dance discipline, first developed in 16th century Italy. (The name "ballet" comes from the Italian word meaning "to dance".) The history of ballet is long and complex. Here is a quick summary, touching only on the most important highlights. 1581: The first ballet is presented at the French court of Catherine de' Medici (the wife of Henry II). 1681: Women, and not just men, now dance in the ballet. 1708: The first public performance of a ballet is presented. 1820: Carlo Blasis introduces modern ballet technique (including the turned-out leg). 1832: "La Sylphide" begins the romantic period of ballet, emphasizing the role of the prima ballerina. 1875: A renaissance of romantic ballet begins in Russia. 1909-1929: Ballet enjoys a renaissance in Europe and America, and is strongly influenced by modern dance. The tradition of male virtuoso dancing is revived. 1977: Harley Hahn takes ballet classes while he is a graduate student. Late 20th century: Ballet gains great popularity, especially in the United States.

Web:
http://www.abt.org/dictionary/terms.html
http://www.wwar.com/dance/ballet.html

Usenet:
alt.arts.ballet

Ballroom Dancing

Keep in step with the latest ballroom dance happenings by joining these ballroom dancing mailing lists. Discuss places to dance, exchange information about clubs, ballroom dance music, dance steps, technique, dance etiquette, and get announcements of special events. If you are interested in joining a moderated, lower traffic mailing list, use the **ballrm-m** list. If you are sick of talking and want to get straight to the dancing, check out the Web sites for the hottest places to go on the Net.

Web:
http://www.ballroomdancers.com/
http://www.dancetv.com/tutorial/basics/

Listserv Mailing List:
List Name: **ballrm-m**
Subscribe to: listserv@mitvma.mit.edu

Listserv Mailing List:
List Name: **ballroom**
Subscribe to: listserv@mitvma.mit.edu

Belly Dancing

When you feel like your life is lacking something exotic, you can have a look at these Web sites which specialize in belly dancing, often called oriental dancing or Middle Eastern dance. Learn about the rich cultural heritage behind the art of belly dancing. These sites include sounds, texts, pictures and lists of events happening around the world. Join the mailing list if you are looking for more personal interaction with fellow dancers or fans.

Web:
http://www.bdancer.com/
http://www.ivo.se/as-sayf/englishindex.html
http://www.lpl.arizona.edu/~kimberly/medance/medance.html

Majordomo Mailing List:
List Name: **med-dance**
Subscribe to: majordomo@world.std.com

Break Dancing

Break dancing, which started as a rap-based, inner-city art form in the 1980s, has evolved. It has now embraced hip-hop and the suburbs, and the boomboxes and rappers have been replaced by disc jockeys at all night raves. Everything old is new again, and as loud as ever. (If you remember the original break dancing craze, let me tell you something that is guaranteed to make you feel old: there are now father and son break dancing teams.)

Web:
http://www.bboy.com/
http://www.breakdance.com/

Competitive Dance Sport

Ballroom dancing is not for sissies. For those of you with more cutthroat tendencies, this site has loads of information about competitive ballroom dancing. Check the calendar of events to see what's happening in your area. Get information on publications about competitive dancing, organizations dedicated to the sport of dancing, and personal ads for people who love to dance. You will also find a list of places where competitive dancing events are held, including Asia, Europe and North America. This is not your mother's ballroom dancing.

Web:
http://www.dancescape.com/

DANCE

Contra Dancing

It's not square dancing. It's not country line dancing. A young, Americanized version of English country dancing, this lively dancing pastime gets its name from the French *contredans*. While nobody agrees on the origins, most everyone agrees that contra dancing is fun. Learn more about how and where it's done at these Web sites, which are packed to the edges with information.

Web:
http://www.rain.org/~gshapiro/contradance.html
http://www.tiac.net/users/cseelig/contra/contralinks.shtml

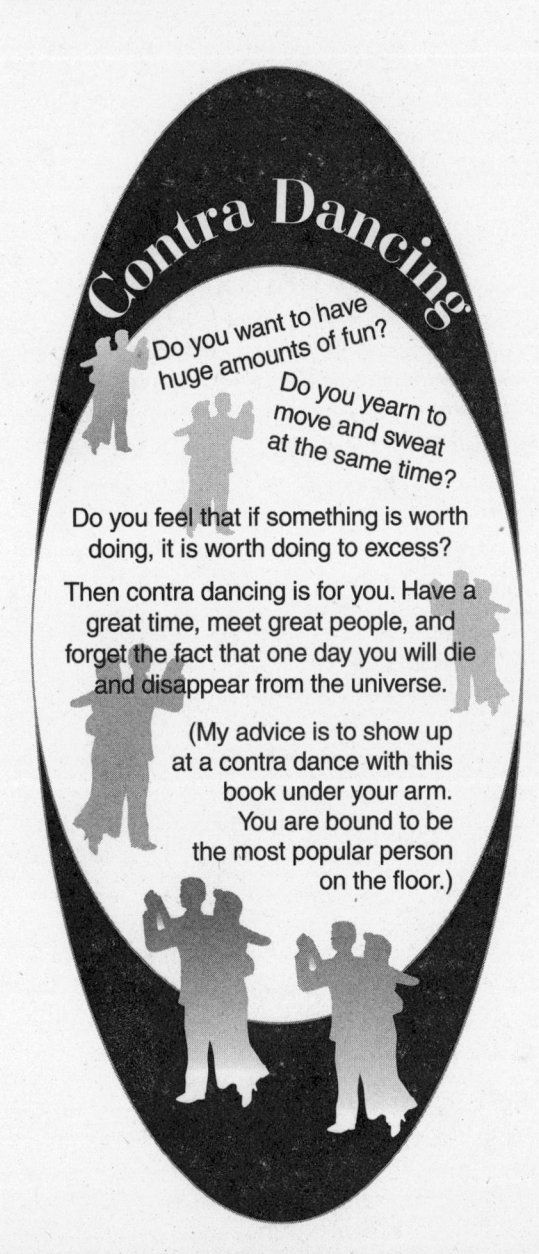

Contra Dancing

Do you want to have huge amounts of fun?

Do you yearn to move and sweat at the same time?

Do you feel that if something is worth doing, it is worth doing to excess?

Then contra dancing is for you. Have a great time, meet great people, and forget the fact that one day you will die and disappear from the universe.

(My advice is to show up at a contra dance with this book under your arm. You are bound to be the most popular person on the floor.)

Country Line Dancing

You are standing with a group of people, listening to the music. You get caught up in the rhythm, and your body begins to move. All at once, everyone begins to move at the same time—side shuffle rock step, side shuffle quarter-turn rock step... and you're dancing. To be more precise, you are country line dancing. It's easy to learn, but a challenge to master. There are many, many line dance descriptions on the Internet, and you will always have something new to try. So what are you waiting for?

Web:
http://ourworld.compuserve.com/homepages/jgothard/
http://www.apci.net/~drdeyne/glossary.htm
http://www.country-time.com/archives/archive.htm

Dance News

Dance, dance, dance... But now and again, you need a break. What better time to catch up on what's new and what's news in the dance world. Read about who is doing what, and what is being done by whoever. Opinions, stories, articles, features, and soon it is time to go back to work. Dance, dance, dance...

Web:
http://www.danceonline.com/

Dance Resources

After six hours of school, I've had enough of a day, I grab the radio dial, and turn it up all the way, I've got to dance, right on the spot, the beat's really hot, dance, dance, dance, dance... (And when I'm not dancing, I'm on the Net, looking at dance resources.)

Web:
http://www.artstozoo.org./artslynx/dance.htm
http://www.dancer.com/dance-links/
http://www.sapphireswan.com/dance/

Dance Talk and General Discussion

Eventually the music will stop, but that's no reason for you to stop dancing. Do what I do: stand in front of the computer, read the Usenet articles, and check out the FAQ (frequently asked question list).

Web:
http://www.eijkhout.net/rad/

Usenet:
rec.arts.dance

Flamenco

There is absolutely no truth to the rumor that culture is boring. This is simple propaganda designed by those in the entertainment business to seduce people into watching more television when, in fact, they should be out learning how to flamenco dance. Flamenco dancing is fun. Other than children's birthday parties, where else can you wear colorful costumes while dancing around, stomping your feet and clapping your hands? Learn more about this passionate pastime by checking out a Web page entirely devoted to the dance. For personal interaction, you can discuss dancing with people around the world on the mailing list.

Web:
  http://home.luna.nl/~davidb/_flamenc.htm

Listserv Mailing List:
  List Name: **flamenco**
  Subscribe to: **listserv@listserv.temple.edu**

Folk and Traditional Dance

I have always had a strong interest in traditional dances; for example, my favorite dance is the "Freddy". If you too like traditional dances, you are not alone. Here are some resources to keep you in step with people around the world who care about how dancing used to be in the days when people danced to enjoy life and not just to keep moving till the drugs wore off.

Web:
  http://www.ftech.co.uk/~webfeet/

Usenet:
  rec.folk-dancing

Listserv Mailing List:
  List Name: **dance-l**
  Subscribe to: **listserv@nic.surfnet.nl**

Folk Dancing is like life, in that there are only two basic rules to remember:
(1) Wear comfortable shoes.
(2) Don't worry if you are out of step. Just enjoy yourself.

Morris Dancing

When you are looking for something lively in which to participate, consider taking up Morris dancing. This rustic dance of north England had its origins in country festivals and became a vigorous ambulatory dance which found its dancers cavorting from village to village accompanied by pipers and taborers. These resources offer information not only about Morris dancing, but also Garland, North West, Rapper, Cotswold, Border, Abbots Bromley, Longsword and similar forms of English dance.

Web:
  http://web.syr.edu/~rsholmes/morris/rich/morris_links.html

Listserv Mailing List:
  List Name: **morris**
  Subscribe to: **listserv@listserv.iupui.edu**

Renaissance Dance

For those of you with a little more vintage taste for dance, try Renaissance dancing. It's colorful, it's cultural, the music is good and best of all, you can't get arrested for doing it. The Web site has tons of files about the dance, including information about music, history and the dance steps themselves. If you want to talk to other people about Renaissance dances, join the mailing list.

Web:
  http://www.ucs.mun.ca/~andrew/rendance.html

Listserv Mailing List:
  List Name: **rendance**
  Subscribe to: **listserv@morgan.ucs.mun.ca**

Salsa

Salsa music developed in the 1970s in New York. Salsa dance, based on the music, is a sort of a rumba blended with Cuban, Puerto Rican and Dominican influences. What is wonderful about a salsa concert is the musicians will often perform and dance at the same time. Spend just a few minutes listening, and your body will start moving, and once you start moving, you won't want to stop. That's salsa.

Web:
  http://www-zeus.ncsa.uiuc.edu/~hneeman/salsa_hotlist.html
  http://www.salsafreak.com/
  http://www.sirius.com/~frankr/salsa_patterns.htm

Samba

Samba is a type of music and a type of dance from Brazil, a tradition that originated with African slaves. Samba is a lively, gyrating, complicated dance. The men and women perform different moves, with the women shaking their bodies and the men doing more hopping, jumping and slapping hands to their heels. This Web site has a listing of samba events, help with terminology, information about samba music, and links to regional samba Web pages. The mailing list is a place for exchanging information on topics such as music, costumes, styles of samba, schools and events.

Web:
http://www.worldsamba.org/

Majordomo Mailing List:
List Name: **sambistas**
Subscribe to: **majordomo@tardis.ed.ac.uk**

Don't just sit there.
Put on the music and samba.
(And while you are dancing,
read about samba on the Net.)

Society for Creative Anachronism Dance

If you love the SCA, but don't want to dress funny and get hit with big sticks, try engaging in some SCA dance in which you still have to dress funny, but there is little hitting involved. This Web site has lots of information about historical dance, dance steps and music.

Web:
http://www.pbm.com/~lindahl/music_and_dance.html

Swing Dance

Swing all night and at daybreak when the music dies down, come home to the Web and swing some more. These Web sites have more information than you can triple step on. For instance, you can get information on upcoming swing dance events on a local or national level. Or you can read about styles and techniques of swing. Impress your friends and dance partners with your huge knowledge of swing steps that you learned from these fabulous online swing sources. I could go on and on about this site, but I have better things to do...like go dancing.

Web:
http://www.anyswinggoes.com/
http://www.cs.cornell.edu/Info/People/aswin/SwingDancing/swing_dancing.html

Listserv Mailing List:
List Name: **swing_dance**
Subscribe to: **listserv@listserv.vt.edu**

IRC:
#swing

Tango

What is it that is so appealing, so passionate and so captivating about the tango? At first glance, it's hard to understand the attraction. Why would so many people spend so much time moving with restrained eroticism to haunting music, when they could be sitting at home reading one of my books? Still, there are tango fans all over the world, so there must be something in it. Try it for yourself and you will find that there is nothing better to perk up an otherwise dull day than a heavy dose of carefully channeled sensuality. (Personal note: My favorite tango is "The Masochism Tango" by Tom Lehrer, which I play on the piano whenever I need a break from writing.)

Web:
http://members.ping.at/kdf-wien/tango/
http://www.informatik.uni-frankfurt.de/~garrit/english/tango_engl/tango_engl.html

Listserv Mailing List:
List Name: **tango-l**
Subscribe to: **listserv@mitvma.mit.edu**

170 DANCE

It takes three to **tango:** you, your partner, and an Internet connection to the *tango* sites on the Web.

Western Square Dancing

Western square dancing is wholesome, good clean fun, and, these days, is there anyone who can't use a bit more w.g.c.f. in their life? If you enjoy hanging out with the type of people who understand the difference between a single file promenade and a rollaway half sashay, there is a lot waiting for you on the Net: information about clubs and schools, call lists and definitions, articles to read, and lots of resources to explore. You can even find computer programs that act as square dance simulators. So don't waste a minute. Get out and dance, and when you're not dancing, get on the Net. And the next time you take a shower, join me in singing, "Chicken in the bread pan kickin' out the dough; Chicken in the bread pan kickin' out the dough; Chicken in the bread pan kickin' out the dough; Skip to my Lou, my darling!"

Web:
http://www.dosado.com/

IRC:
#squaredance

Tap Dancing

When you are looking for some lively, snappy dancing, consider tap. On the mailing list, lovers of fancy footwork discuss steps, techniques, shoes, dancers and the tap industry. For more immediate gratification, you can shuffle, flap, hop, scuff, paddle, dig or cramp roll your way to the Web site. These pages contain information about dance steps, famous tapsters, dance clubs, movies, sounds, and more. By the way, when I was a kid, I used to do a lot of tap dancing, until one day I fell into the sink and hurt my ankle.

Web:
http://www.mcphu.edu/~corrp/tap

Majordomo Mailing List:
List Name: **tap-jazz**
Subscribe to: **majordomo@world.std.com**

Square Dancing, the Pastime of Kings

Who has not fantasized about meeting the perfect man or woman in the middle of a square dance? There is something about this honestly American tradition that fans the flames of grace and nobility in all of us. The next time you are sitting home on a Saturday night, wondering if there are people out there who really know how to have more fun than you, take a look at the Western Square Dancing Web site and eat your heart out. Then stop feeling sorry for yourself and get out on the floor.

DEVICES AND GIZMOS CONNECTED TO THE NET

Animal Cams

Visit various animals, live on the Net and become a full-fledged zoological voyeur. Here are some Web sites that will let you look at a giraffe, an iguana, a killer whale, a penguin, an elephant, and lots more types of animals. Wait! I have an idea. Throw an animal party, where each person comes dressed as their favorite animal. Then visit each Web site in turn and, when you get to an animal that looks like one of your guests, the guest has to run around the room imitating the animal as it moves on your screen. Boy, talk about fun! Computers, the Internet, animals, friends—it just doesn't get any better.

Web:
http://iguana.images.com/dupecam.html
http://pbob.speeder.com/ferret/
http://www.camzone.com/cams/shamucam/stream.html
http://www.cmzoo.org/zoocam.html
http://www.discovery.com/cams/cams.html
http://www.seaworld.org/penguins/penguincam.html
http://www.seaworld.org/sharkcam/sharkcam.html
http://www.si.edu/organiza/museums/zoo/hilights/webcams/molerat1/elecam/elecam.htm

Ant Farm

There's nothing like the feeling of having your own personal ant farm sitting close by. All day, as you are working, you can glance over and see the ants being industrious, running back and forth carrying things and generally doing whatever it is ants do. If you've always wanted to have your own ant farm, but felt too guilty about confining live things in a small narrow area, here's the next best thing: a picture of a live ant farm. Now, whenever you need to take a small breather from the hustle and bustle of daily life, peek in on the hustle and bustle of the daily ant life. To see what's new, simply reload the Web page and you will get an updated picture.

Web:
http://www.atomicweb.com/antfarm.html

Antarctica Live

Would you like to see a picture of Antarctica right now? This Web site shows you a recent picture of the view outside Mawson Station (on the eastern side of Holme Bay, perched on a horseshoe-shaped outcrop of rock). Mawson Station has been in continuous operation since February 1954, and now you can visit whenever you want.

Web:
http://www.antdiv.gov.au/aad/exop/sfo/mawson/video.html

Cameras on the Net

Feeling lonely and out of sorts? These Web sites will allow you to view some interesting people, places and things around the world. If you are stuck in a cubicle, check out the views of exotic lands. If you are stuck in an exotic land, look for a cubicle. There are a large number of cameras on the Net, and these collections of links are great places to look for great places to snoop.

Web:
http://www.camcentral.com/
http://www.dcn.com/
http://www.earthcam.com/
http://www.leonardsworlds.com/camera.html
http://www.nvg.ntnu.no/~oyvind/cam/

CHEESE!

Cameras on the Net

Now, for a change, *you* get to be Big Brother.

Use one of the cameras on the Net to see what someone else is doing.

172 DEVICES AND GIZMOS CONNECTED TO THE NET

Interactive Model Railroad

This is really cool. You can play with a pair of model trains in Germany. All you have to do is select a train and a destination, and press a button to make the train leave the station. Watch the train zoom around the track. As it moves, the Web page will display the IP number (official address) of the person's computer that is currently controlling the train. If you want, you can even type a message for other people to read. I love this. I can not only control the train, but everyone who is watching knows that the commands came from *my* computer.

Web:
   http://rr-vs.informatik.uni-ulm.de/rr/

Light on the Net

This sounds a bit silly, but it's a lot of fun. Visit this Web site in Japan, where you will see an array of light bulbs. Each bulb is either on or off, and you can control it with your mouse. Just click on the bulb of your choice, and it will send a signal to Japan. If that bulb is off, it will be turned on; if the bulb is on, it will be turned off. Of course, as you are turning the bulbs on or off, so are people in other parts of the world. I like to see if I can turn all the bulbs off before anyone else can turn them on. (Hint: Start multiple copies of your browser in separate windows.)

Web:
   http://light.softopia.pref.gifu.jp/

New York Views

I love New York in June, how about you? The good news is, you don't have to wait until June to see some hot New York action. Check out these Big Apple cameras now, and look at a view from the World Trade Center, the plaza at Rockefeller Center and the Brooklyn Bridge. (The only better view in town is from the camera in Donald Trump's walk-in closet.)

Web:
   http://kinya.com/view.html
   http://www.ftna.com/cents.cgi
   http://www.romdog.com/bridge/brooklyn.html

Refrigerator Status

I'm sure that, before you go to bed every night, you check to make sure that the door of your refrigerator is closed. Well, now you have another fridge to check. This one is connected to the Net and, whenever you want, you can check its status: temperature, light, and whether or not the door is closed.

Web:
   http://hamjudo.com/cgi-bin/refrigerator

Satellite Images of Cities

It's important that you and I keep an eye on things. Here is an easy way to do it. Here are collections of satellite photos of a number of cities: Atlanta, Boston, Denver, Los Angeles, San Francisco, Seattle and more. Using your browser, you can tour the cities, enjoying a bird's eye view without having to leave your warm and comfortable nest. One of my researchers is from Seattle, and she showed me around the city, pointing out all the places of interest. (For some reason, the satellite photos of Seattle stop just as you get to the area where Bill Gates lives.)

Web:
   http://www.city-scenes.com/

Things on the Net

Stuff is good. However, having too much stuff in your house is not good. But now, thanks to the Net, you can have access to other people's stuff. This Web site has links to lots of devices that are connected to the Net: cameras, machines, robots, gadgets, screen captures, pagers, and lots more.

Web:
   http://www.oink.com/thingys/

When I was a kid, we had to deliver email by hand.

DEVICES AND GIZMOS CONNECTED TO THE NET

Traffic Conditions

Do you drive in a big city? If so think about this: as you drive, you are making a small contribution to the overall traffic pattern. That is important because it just may be that people all over the world are looking at that traffic pattern right now on the Web. Take a look. See the cool color-coded map that shows you where the traffic is moving and where it's stuck. Try again during rush hour and see the pattern change. Aren't you glad you're not there?

Web:
http://trafficview.twincities.sidewalk3.com/applet.asp
http://www.eng.hawaii.edu/~csp/Trafficam/
http://www.scubed.com/caltrans/la/la_big_map.shtml
http://www.scubed.com/caltrans/sd/big_map.shtml
http://www.wsdot.wa.gov/regions/northwest/NWFLOW/camera/

The Perfect *Relaxation* Technique

When I feel the need to relax, I use the Net to check the traffic flow on the Los Angeles freeway system.

I look at every colored dot on the map and imagine tens of thousands of cars, slowing down, speeding up, making noise and emitting exhaust.

Within a few minutes, I am completely relaxed and ready to get back to work.

Vending Machines

The rage started with being able to check the Coke machine from the Internet. Things got out of control with the invention of CU-SeeMe. Check out coffee machines, temperature gauges, light sensors and a Geiger counter without leaving your seat. "Spy cameras" have been set up in offices and pointed out windows so you can even have a view.

Web:
http://www-cse.ucsd.edu/users/bsy/iam.html

Volcanoes on the Net

I think you and I had better get organized, so here's my plan. Let's get a bunch of people and organize them into teams. Every day, one of the teams is responsible for monitoring this Web site, where anyone can use recent satellite photos to keep an eye on the ten most active volcanoes in the world. As soon as a volcano starts to look as if it is going to erupt, the team leader notifies us immediately, so we can give everyone instructions on what to do. In that way, the world will be a safer, more organized place. What do you think?

Web:
http://www.ssec.wisc.edu/data/volcano.html

White House Cam

It's up to you and me and everyone else to keep an eye on the President of the United States. This webcam (camera connected to the Web) lets us look at the White House, whenever we want, 24 hours a day. We can't actually look inside, but we can see some of the windows. I think we should keep a careful watch, just to make sure there's no funny business. After all, if we don't keep an eye on the guy, who knows what might happen?

Web:
http://www.mti1.com/home/Whitehouse/

DIET AND NUTRITION

Ask the Dietitian

Our culture is obsessed with food and dietary silliness, and there is a great deal of misinformation. For this reason, it is a pleasure to visit this Web site. There are a great many diet-related questions and they are all answered sensibly and knowledgeably by a dietitian. If it's real information you want about food, nutrition and diet, make this your first stop.

Web:
  http://www.dietitian.com/

Basal Metabolism Calculator

Here is my simple, four-step plan to achieve optimal health. (1) Visit this Web site and enter your height, weight and age. The computer will perform a calculation and tell you your basal metabolism rate. (2) Specify the activity level that best describes your favorite activity. The computer will then display a detailed breakdown of how many calories you should be eating, and how much of those calories should come from fats, proteins and carbohydrates. (3) Study these numbers carefully, paying particular attention to the maximum suggested values. (4) Order a pizza.

Web:
  http://www.room42.com/nutrition/basal.shtml

> Lots and lots of music on the Internet: check out the Music categories.

Cyberdiet

If you think you need to go on a diet, but you are not sure exactly where to start, check with this Web site. They offer a nutritional profile that might help you determine the amount of calories you should eat in order to maintain or decrease your weight. Other information about dieting is also available.

Web:
  http://www.cyberdiet.com/

Diet Analysis

If you are serious about maintaining a healthy diet, you may want to analyze what you eat. If so, use this resource to help you figure out just what you are ingesting. Specify what you have eaten today, and let the computer estimate the calories, protein, vitamins and minerals you consumed. (Remember, however, that all such numbers are gross estimates. There is no way to know exactly what is in a particular food.)

Web:
  http://dawp.anet.com/

Look What I Found on the Net...

    Newsgroup: alt.support.diet
    Subject: Bodyfat Measurement

    Hi all. Since a lot of people have been asking me about
    various methods of bodyfat measurement, I figured I ought to
    post something. There are a variety of methods used to measure
    bodyfat, each with their own pros and cons.

    The most accurate method is to have the body dissected, and
    then to separate and weigh the fat cells. This will give the
    most accurate value but is rather inconvenient as you have to
    be dead for it to work...

DIET AND NUTRITION

Dieting FAQ

When you are suffering from too much information, get some help sorting it all out with the FAQ from **alt.support.diet**. This list of frequently asked questions covers issues such as general diet and nutrition, weight loss, liquid diets and fasts, weight loss organizations and diet books, motivation, exercise, diet aids, and more.

Web:
  http://www.cis.ohio-state.edu/hypertext/faq/usenet/dieting-faq
  http://www.lib.ox.ac.uk/internet/news/faq/alt.support.diet.html

Dieting Talk and General Discussion

Does your diet work? Or like the other 99.9 percent of humanity, do you have to suffer to lose excess weight? Join ultra-nutrition-conscious people around the world who will thank you for sharing. Trade stories, scientific trivia and leftover Weight Watchers' menus. Are you just about ready for your own zip code? Lonely no more.

Usenet:
  alt.support.diet
  alt.support.diet.rx
  alt.support.diet.zone

Fad Diets

Every day you can see new fad diets in magazines and books. Each one claims to be *the* way to fill your dieting needs. This has been happening for years, and the diets still come and go like the tide. The American Heart Association has a page that talks about fad diets from a health point of view. You might want to read this before starting any new program that you think may be a flash in the fad-diet pan.

Web:
  http://www.americanheart.org/Heart_and_Stroke_A_Z_Guide/fad.html

---

Old MacDonald had a farm. (He read about it in "Agriculture".)

Fast Food Calorie Counter

When you go to a fast food restaurant, you can't exactly read the labels to see what you are putting into your body. In fact, you are probably better off if you *don't* read the labels. Instead, use these calorie counters to find out how fattening everything is. After all, what's the point of eating junky fast food if you can't at least get a substantial helping of guilt out of the experience?

Web:
  http://www.olen.com/food/
  http://www.uiuc.edu/departments/mckinley/health-info/hlthpro/fastfood.html

Fat

It's 11:00 PM, do you know what your cholesterol/HDL risk ratio is? Saturated fat, hydrogenated fat, good fat, bad fat, everyone is talking about fat. Sometimes the stories, ideas and rumors are so conflicting, you can't tell if you are sinking slowly or rising to the top of the soup bowl of life, only to be skimmed off. Don't despair, get your fat facts hot off the Net.

Web:
  http://ificinfo.health.org/index7.htm
  http://www.uiuc.edu/departments/mckinley/health-info/nutrit/wtloss/fatcont.html

Fat Substitutes

The American Heart Association has lots of information about fat: what it is, what types of fat exist, and what you should and should not eat. Whether you are watching your fat intake because you want to lose weight or just because you want to be healthy, check out this Web site for some useful information.

Web:
  http://www.americanheart.org/Heart_and_Stroke_A_Z_Guide/fatsub.html

Healthy Diet Guidelines

When it's time to get off the Pepsi and cheeseburger express, get help from your friend the Net. You'll find everything you need to eat well except willpower and a credit card.

Web:
  http://ificinfo.health.org/brochure/pyramid.htm
  http://www.americanheart.org/Heart_and_Stroke_A_Z_Guide/dietg.html
  http://www.nal.usda.gov/fnic/dga/dguide95.html

DIET AND NUTRITION

Healthy Diet Guidelines

People talk a lot about nutrition and dieting, and it's not new. For much of the twentieth century, special diets have been a staple of the body cultural.

There is a great deal of confusion, but it's not necessary. All you have to do is follow the Harley Hahn Super Nutrition System:

Step 1: Find out what type of diet a normal person should follow to stay healthy.

Step 2: Follow that diet.

The information you need is well known. You can find it on the Net whenever you want.

Healthy Weight

This is a level-headed site that will encourage you to eat healthy, live healthy and exercise. Learn how to read a food label like a pro, then calculate your BMI (body/mass index) and see how close your weight is to ideal. Then explore some of the links to other diet-related resources, read some news articles, and browse through the exercise guidelines. (And if you still feel energetic, run down to the closest pizza restaurant and look in the window.)

Web:
http://www.healthyweight.com/

Holiday Diet Tips

Inevitably, when the holidays roll around, out come the trays of party snacks and rich chocolates, not to mention the high-fat cheeseballs sent across the country by your well-meaning Aunt Matilda (who used to send fruitcakes until she found out you were using them as doorstops). Don't get caught in the holiday-eating pitfall. Prepare now by reading tips on how to enjoy the holiday without overeating.

Web:
http://www.healthyideas.com/holiday/
http://www.medtropolis.com/consumer/datafile/winter.html

Low Fat Lifestyle

One way some people are successful at losing weight is to reduce the amount of fat they have in their diet. This Web site gives lots of tips and recipes on living a low fat lifestyle. While you are on the Net, check out the list of facts about fast food at the Web site or chat with like-minded folks on Usenet. (Then go eat a carrot.)

Web:
http://www.wctravel.com/lowfat/

Usenet:
alt.food.fat-free

Magic of Believing

Get rid of your diet blues. Here's a group of people who support each other in their efforts to get fit and healthy through weight loss. Read important insights by support group members, and check out the links and resources relating to weight loss.

Web:
http://www.swlink.net/~colonel/

Nutrition

Should you eat the Twinkie or opt for another seaweed sandwich? Join the conversation and talk about the usual gang of suspects: vitamins, carbohydrates, proteins, fats, minerals and fiber. Then hop over to a Web site, and read and read and read about food until you are stuffed.

Web:
http://ificinfo.health.org/
http://www.ag.uiuc.edu/~food-lab/nat/
http://www.nal.usda.gov/fnic/etext/fnic.html

Usenet:
sci.med.nutrition

DISABILITIES 177

Vending Machine Calorie Counter

How many calories are you putting into your body on those midnight snack runs to the vending machine? Before you do it, go to the site that will tell you exactly how many of those hard-to-burn little monsters are making their way to your hips and thighs. This calorie counter lists the types of foods from vending machines and their number of calories.

Web:
http://www.uiuc.edu/departments/mckinley/health-info/nutrit/hlthdiet/vendingm.html

Vending Machine Vendetta

How do you know how many calories are in a prepackaged snack? Well, you can look at the wrapper, but when you buy something from a vending machine, you can't look at the wrapper until you have already spent your money.

Ordinary people just have to put up with problems like this, but *you* are on the Net, which makes you special. All you need to do is check with the *Vending Machine Calorie Counter* ahead of time, and find exactly what is hidden from view. Never again will you be fooled into buying a "lite" snack only to find out that it contains enough calories to support a closetful of hungry elephants.

Weight Gain

Most people are trying to get their weight to go down, but if you are one of the few who are trying to gain weight, take a look at this information resource. Here you will find articles covering topics such as too much exercise, body composition, healthy ways to gain weight, and recovering after hard exercise.

Web:
http://www.uiuc.edu/departments/mckinley/health-info/nutrit/wtgain/wtgain.html

Weight Loss

There are lots of ways to lose fat, but the whole thing can be summarized into two simple rules. (1) Exercise more. (2) Eat less. For helpful tips and techniques, check out these Internet resources. (I talked to a doctor once who had a surefire method to lose weight. You serve yourself normal amounts of food, but you don't eat everything, you leave 25% of the food on your plate. It isn't easy to get started, he said, but the technique does work. Now I am ready to introduce him to my new money-saving plan in which I pay all but 25% of my doctor bill.)

Web:
http://www.shapeup.net/
http://www.weight.com/

DISABILITIES

Accessibility

Accessibility issues are an important part of everyday life for people with disabilities. Use the Net to help you find out what solutions are available for accessibility problems. This site has information for adaptive, assistive and access technology researchers and for users. You will also find helpful information about special equipment.

Web:
http://www.yuri.org/webable/

DISABILITIES

Accessibility

If you have a serious disability that makes day-to-day life difficult, look at the help and information available on the Net.

Remember, the Internet is not about computers. The Internet is about **people.**

There are lots of people ready to help and to contribute. Perhaps you are one of them.

Americans with Disabilities Act

In 1990, the U.S. Congress passed the Americans with Disabilities Act (ADA). Although most people do not appreciate the significance of this legislation, it has an enormous effect on many areas of the American economy. Why? The ADA defines a disability as a mental or physical condition that "substantially limits one or more of the major life activities" (walking, hearing, seeing, working, and so on). The ADA requires specific action in four areas: employment, public facilities, transportation and communication. Here are some Internet resources about the ADA and related topics, including the full text of the actual law. (I actually found it interesting to read.)

Web:
http://www.hr.state.ks.us/dc/
http://www.usdoj.gov/crt/ada/adahom1.htm

Usenet:
bit.listserv.ada-law

Amputees

Amputees and friends and families of amputees can find a lot of helpful information on the Net. These Web sites have articles and links to resources, information about prosthetics, phantom sensation, as well as sports and recreation. The mailing list and Usenet group offer ways for amputees to talk to and support one another.

Web:
http://www.amputee-online.com/
http://www.inform.umd.edu:8080/EdRes/Topic/Disability/Events/People/Amputees/

Usenet:
alt.support.amputee

Listserv Mailing List:
List Name: **amputee**
Subscribe to: **listserv@maelstrom.stjohns.edu**

Attention Deficit Disorder

Attention Deficit Disorder (ADD) is a childhood syndrome characterized by hyperactivity, a short attention span and impulsive behavior. These Web resources have information relating to children and adults with ADD, including helpful tips for parents and a checklist of symptoms for adults suspected of having ADD. The mailing list is for adults with ADD, but the Usenet group is for the support of adults, children and anyone who works with ADD patients.

Web:
http://www.chadd.org/
http://www.greatconnect.com/oneaddplace/
http://www.health-center.com/english/brain/adhd/
http://www3.sympatico.ca/frankk/addfaq3.txt

Usenet:
alt.support.attn-deficit

Listserv Mailing List:
List Name: **addult**
Subscribe to: **listserv@maelstrom.stjohns.edu**

DISABILITIES

Autism

Autism is a syndrome with many variations. By its nature, autism is difficult to define, especially in plain English (but I am going to try anyway). Autism is a congenital condition characterized by some of the following: (1) abnormal development of physical and social skills, (2) abnormal responses to sensation, (3) delayed development of speech and language, (4) abnormal ways of relating to the outside world. Here are some Internet resources to help you understand autism and to communicate with other people who are interested in the disorder.

Web:
http://web.syr.edu/~jmwobus/autism/
http://www.autism.org/
http://www.cmhcsys.com/guide/autism.htm

Usenet:
alt.support.autism
bit.listserv.autism

Listserv Mailing List:
List Name: **autism**
Subscribe to: **listserv@maelstrom.stjohns.edu**

Birth Defects

A birth defect (or congenital defect) is a condition that is present from birth. There are various types of birth defects, including mental deficiencies, physical traits, malformations and diseases. There are a number of different causes of birth defects: genetic abnormalities, infections, drugs (including alcohol, illegal drugs, and certain medicines), smoking, poor nutrition and environmental chemicals. Some of the more common birth defects are cerebral palsy, cleft lip or palate, fetal alcohol syndrome, Down syndrome, spinal bifida, hearing loss, perinatal AIDS and heart defects. If you or someone you know has a child with a birth defect, you will be able to find information to help you on the Net.

Web:
http://www.birthdefects.org/
http://www.modimes.org/

Blind and Visually Impaired Computer Usage

Using the computer is tricky enough when you don't have a vision impairment. This mailing list provides a forum for the discussion of computer use by the blind and visually impaired. If you are interested in helping to make the Internet more accessible to blind people, this is a good place to participate. For my part, I have worked with the National Braille Press to help them translate my books into Braille. However, it is an expensive and time-consuming process, and it doesn't solve the main problem: the interface. Fortunately, Microsoft has gone to a lot of trouble to design features for blind people into their operating system. They have also developed tools for programmers who want to create software for blind users. None of this comes too soon for me. I have enough trouble using the wretched mouse-oriented/pull-down-menu/one-size-fits-all graphical interface—and I can see. Imagine what it's like for someone who is visually impaired.

Usenet:
alt.comp.blind-users

Listserv Mailing List:
List Name: **blind-l**
Subscribe to: **listserv@uafsysb.uark.edu**

Blind and Visually Impaired Computer Usage

There is lots of modern technology available to help blind people use the Net. If you are blind, or visually impaired, ask someone to help you get started. Then, once you do, join the *blind-l* mailing list and keep up on what is new and exciting.

DISABILITIES

Blindness

There are a great many resources on the Net for blind people: lots of mailing lists and Web sites, as well as information about Braille, vision conditions, technology, education and blindness-related organizations.

Web:
   http://weber.u.washington.edu/~doit/Brochures/DRR/inetres.vi.html
   http://www.blind.net/
   http://www.nfb.org/
   http://www.nyise.org/blind.htm

Usenet:
   alt.disability.blind.social

Listserv Mailing List:
   List Name: **blindnws**
   Subscribe to: **listserv@listserv.nodak.edu**

Cleft Palate and Cleft Lip

The palate is the hard, bony area that forms the roof of your mouth. A cleft palate is a congenital (birth) defect in which there exists a fissure along the midline of the palate. A cleft lip (which is often present with a cleft palate) occurs when one or both lips have not fused properly. Unlike many other birth defects, a cleft palate or cleft lip can often be repaired surgically. Here are some Web sites that contain many types of information about these conditions.

Web:
   http://www.cleft.org/
   http://www.widesmiles.org/

Listproc Mailing List:
   List Name: **cleft-talk**
   Subscribe to: **listproc@listproc@mother.com**

Computers for the Handicapped

CHIPS is the Computers for the Handicapped Independence Program. Get information about software and hardware for the visually impaired, quadriplegics, the hearing impaired, and people with mobility, speech and language impairments.

Web:
   http://www.wolfe.net/~dr_bill/

Usenet:
   bit.listserv.easi

Deaf-Blind Discussion List

This is a multipurpose list devoted to the topic of dual sensory impairment or deaf-blindness. Not only is it a place where professionals can discuss problems and solutions, but it's also a space in which individuals with DSI or families and friends can share information, inquiries, ideas and opinions.

Listserv Mailing List:
   List Name: **deafblnd**
   Subscribe to: **listserv@tr.wou.edu**

Deafness

Here are some discussion forums in which the deaf, the hearing impaired, researchers, and family members of the deaf all gather to discuss issues relating to deafness. People discuss medical and technical subjects, as well as experiences and problems. Aside from the ongoing discussion, you can use the Web to access a great deal of useful information, including an online ASL (American Sign Language) dictionary. When I lived in Berkeley, I studied ASL for a short time. I wish I were fluent—it is a beautiful language.

Web:
   http://dww.deafworldweb.org/

Usenet:
   alt.relationships.deaf-hearing
   bit.listserv.deaf-l

Listserv Mailing List:
   List Name: **deaf-l**
   Subscribe to: **listserv@siu.edu**

Disability Benefits

If you live in the United States, there are a variety of programs, managed by the Social Security Administration, that are available to assist people with disabilities. However, the rules and regulations are complex. If you think you may qualify, or if you want more information, check with this Web site. For a discussion of such benefits, you can participate in the Usenet groups.

Web:
   http://www.ssa.gov/odhome/

Usenet:
   alt.government.ssdi.benefits
   alt.social-security-disability

Look What I Found on the Net...

```
Newsgroup: bit.listserv.deaf-l
Subject: Hard of Hearing in the Hearing World
```

...I figured out that this is all physics. I have an 80 dB loss.
You hear half with every loss of 20 dB. So it goes like
this:

```
    -20 dB   you hear   1/2 the sound
    -40                 1/4
    -60                 1/8
    -80                 1/16
```

Assuming I'm still at -80, I hear 1/16 what you hear. That
means the person I am listening to [in a lecture hall] has to
be 16 times closer...

Once I understood what was wrong, I could understand that if
I am sitting down and the person speaking to me is standing up,
I can't hear them. It's obvious why...

When people get high frequency deafness, the ability to pick out
consonants fails as well as the hearing itself. People do not
realize that when they raise their voice to communicate with
people who are hard of hearing, they automatically destroy the
very consonants that cannot be heard. The vowels distort and
completely cover up the consonants.

Please never ask us to "listen harder". We are already trying
to outguess the 70 percent or more of the consonants we cannot
hear. We hear all languages like a foreign language, English
included...

When you talk to us, DO talk in a normal soft voice, very close
in the ear. If this will not work, write it down. If we can't
hear it close and soft, we will not be able to hear it louder or
"enunciated" either.

Please understand that lip reading is nothing but a guessing
game, and we are really tired of guessing. There is not even
one lip pattern that unambiguously means one thing only.

At the same time, we are sick of being alone, sick of eating by
ourselves (since almost no one takes the trouble to learn how to
talk to us), sick of being unable to communicate.

So there you have it: how it is to be hard of hearing in a
hearing world.

182 DISABILITIES

Disability Information

There is an enormous amount of disability-related material on the Net. If you, or someone you know, has a particular disability, I guarantee there are many people on the Net in the same position. Here are some good places to start exploring. You will find a large amount of information, as well as many other people who share your interests.

Web:
  http://www.curbcut.com/
  http://www.eskimo.com/~jlubin/disabled.html
  http://www.indie.ca/

If you or a loved one is disabled, remember that there are many people on the Net who are glad to help. There are many sites that offer information for the disabled, and they are open 24 hours a day.

Remember: when you're dealing with people, you're dealing with people.

Down Syndrome

Down Syndrome is a congenital disorder caused by the existence of an extra chromosome 21. The condition is characterized by mild to moderate mental retardation. Such people also tend to be short with broadened facial features. Down Syndrome was named after John Langdon Down, the British doctor who first identified the condition in 1866. These Web sites have good information about Down Syndrome, including a FAQ (frequently asked question list) and health care guidelines. If you want to talk with other people interested in Down Syndrome, I've included a mailing list and a Usenet discussion group.

Web:
  http://www.nas.com/downsyn/
  http://www.ndss.org/

Usenet:
  bit.listserv.down-syn

Listserv Mailing List:
  List Name: **down-syn**
  Subscribe to: **listserv@listserv.nodak.edu**

Look What I Found on the Net...

```
Newsgroup: misc.handicap
Subject: Singles Groups for Persons with Disabilities?

>>> Are there are singles groups for persons with disabilities?

>> I also would like to know if you find one.  I've tried every
>> single's Web page and BBS, and have had no luck.  If you ever
>> find one please pass it on to me.

> Me too.  If one doesn't exist how do we create one?

I'm sure there must be some, but I don't know of them.  I have
an idea.  Try alt.support.disabled.sexuality — that's the sort
of place to ask.
```

DISABILITIES

Dyslexia

Dyslexia is a reading and writing disability characterized by the reversal of letters and words, or by trouble matching letters to their corresponding sounds. Here are some Internet resources with information about dyslexia, including tips for teachers, research information, reports and useful software.

Web:
http://www.cmhcsys.com/guide/dyslexia.htm
http://www.interdys.org/
http://www.ldonline.org/

Usenet:
alt.support.dyslexia

Family Village

Family Village is a great site for anyone who has a disability or for parents who have children with disabilities. Family Village has a library of specific diagnoses, contact lists, ways to get in touch with other people with similar disability issues, and much, much more.

Web:
http://www.familyvillage.wisc.edu/

Handicap Talk and General Discussion

If you have a handicap, you will find something helpful from this Usenet group. Useful information and personal support cover problems facing amputees, medical issues for the disabled, handicap access concerns, politics, and personal interest stories such as biographies of famous people with handicaps.

Usenet:
misc.handicap

Kids with Disabilities

Parents of children with disabilities will find these resources useful. The Web site has links to information about mental and physical disabilities and related adaptive technologies. The mailing list acts as a support group for parents and other people who work with disabled children.

Web:
http://rdz.acor.org/lists/our-kids/

Listserv Mailing List:
List Name: our-kids
Subscribe to: listserv@maelstrom.stjohns.edu

Paralysis and Spinal Cord Injuries

If you, or someone you know, have paralysis or a spinal cord injury, it is good to understand the physical and medical aspects of the condition. It is also important to be able to talk to other people. These resources will provide you with information and news, as well as an easy way to reach out to others who share your concerns.

Web:
http://www.erols.com/nscia/

Usenet:
alt.med.cure-paralysis

Rehabilitation

Rehabilitation is a vast area of human endeavor, related to many different types of disabilities and conditions. Here is a Web site that contains an excellent collection of rehabilitation-related resources. Spend some time browsing. You will be astonished at all the information that is available.

Web:
http://www.naric.com/naric/search/kb/bookmark.html

Service Dogs

Service dogs perform tasks for people with physical disabilities. There are several types of such dogs, including general service dogs, hearing dogs and social dogs. General service dogs perform tasks like switching lights on and off, fetching items, pulling a wheelchair and pushing buttons. Hearing dogs can alert a deaf person to noises such as the telephone, alarm clocks, or a crying baby. Social dogs provide companionship and guidance for people with developmental disabilities. Read more about the great services that canine companions can offer to the disabled. You can also join the mailing list to discuss service dogs with disabled people as well as trainers.

Web:
http://www.caninecompanions.org/
http://www.k9web.com/dog-faqs/service.html

Majordomo Mailing List:
List Name: service-dogs
Subscribe to: majordomo@acpub.duke.edu

184 DISABILITIES

Special Olympics

The Special Olympics are an exciting sports competition for individuals with mental retardation. The Special Olympics were founded in 1968 by Eunice Kennedy Shriver, and today there are Special Olympics programs in many countries all over the world. This is the official site for the program. You can learn more about the Special Olympics, discover how you can become a volunteer, and read other information about this great program for the mentally retarded.

Web:
http://www.specialolympics.org/

Special Olympics

In a way, the word "Olympics" is a misnomer. The regular Olympics involve only the very best athletes, once every four years.

The Special Olympics—created for mentally retarded participants—involve over a million people, all over the world, all year long.

Take a look at their Web site, and you will see just how special people can be.

DRAMA

Acting Talk and General Discussion

When I was a young lad in graduate school, I studied theatrical fencing. As part of the course, a friend and I wrote and acted in a play. It was great. It had mystery, excitement, action, beautiful women, brave heroes and, of course, lots of fencing. However, when it came time to put on the play, I made one mistake. I chose a friend of mine to be the narrator. In the middle of the play, my friend the narrator—who shall remain nameless (Marlene Garstang)—decided the play was too long, so she skipped right to the end. Today, after years of intense rehabilitation, Marlene manages to lead a socially useful life, but the loss to American theater is a permanent one: the play was only performed once. If you are an actor, you probably have stories of your own as tragic as this one. No doubt your colleagues will thank you for sharing.

Web:
http://www.danielnorton.net/ACTING-L/
http://www.hollywoodnetwork.com/guide/lounges.html#actors

Usenet:
alt.acting

Listserv Mailing List:
List Name: acting-l
Subscribe to: listserv@home.ease.lsoft.com

Aisle Say

If you are a lover of modern theater, you will enjoy Aisle Say, an online magazine of reviews and opinion. The magazine contains theater reviews for plays in a variety of cities in and out of the United States. Before you travel, you may want to check this site to see if there is a review of a play you are thinking about seeing. I enjoy reading the reviews just for fun, even if I don't care about the play.

Web:
http://www.escape.com/~theanet/AisleSay.html

Ancient Theater

Age is good for cheese, fine wines and classic cars, so why not the theater? Take a look at the ancient histories, culture and philosophy of Greek and Roman theater.

Web:
http://www.warwick.ac.uk/didaskalia/Didintro.html

Back Stage

No matter how busy you are, if you are in The Business, you need to keep up, and now that you have the Net, what could be easier? Back Stage offers current information on casting calls, show listings, job offers, news, reviews and much more. Show business exists in a tough, highly competitive environment in which having access to timely information can give an edge.

Web:
http://www.backstagecasting.com/

Casting Calls

Would you like to be in films? How about TV or the theater? Start here, where you will find lots of opportunities for actors, production crew members, singers, dancers, writers and more. You may be between jobs temporarily, but there is always a place for you on the Net.

Web:
http://www.opencasting.com/

Costumes of the Early Twentieth Century

If you were not attending the theater at the turn of the nineteenth century, you were missing the grand costumes and stage fineries the actors and actresses used to wear. Now on the Web, you can see it all. This Web site has pictures of famous English actors and actresses as they were costumed at the turn of the previous century.

Web:
http://www.siue.edu/COSTUMES/actors/pics.html

Drama Talk and General Discussion

Do your friends and relatives tell you not to dramatize? Well, they don't know what they are missing. The Internet is full of people who love drama and the theater, and they are waiting for you to join the discussion.

Usenet:
rec.arts.theatre.misc
rec.arts.theatre.plays

Dramatic Exchange

The Dramatic Exchange is an archive for storing and distributing play scripts. This Web site is a vehicle for experienced or budding playwrights to publish and distribute their works, and a place for producers to look at new material. Anyone else interested in drama is also welcome here.

Web:
http://www.dramex.org/

Ahoy, Scriptwriters!

The *Dramatic Exchange* is a place for you to share your work and read what other people are doing. Just the place to show off the great script that Warren Beatty refuses to read about a surfing detective who writes Internet books.

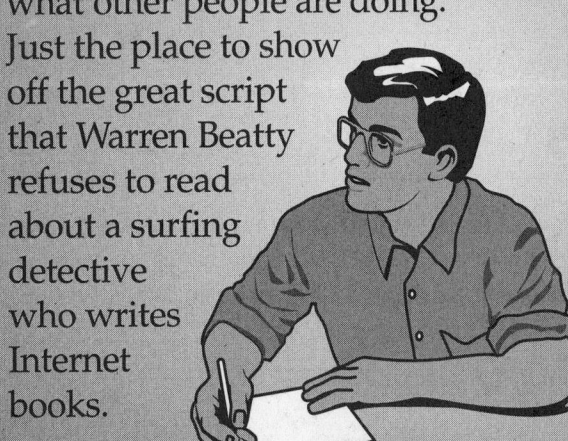

DRAMA

George and Ira Gershwin

Here's a Web site devoted to two Brooklyn boys who gave the world something to talk about. George and Ira Gershwin created beautiful music and plays that are popular to this day, even on the Internet. This site has the complete list of their plays and detailed information about each work. Who could ask for anything more?

Web:
http://www.sju.edu/~bs065903/gershwin/homepage.htm

> **If this were Chapter R, "Romance" would be just around the corner.**

Gilbert and Sullivan

If your husband is so fat that you must move him with a trailer hitch.

And you are tired of groups like Nine Inch Nails and Weird Al Yankovitch.

You clearly need to break away from culture that is popular.

To something that is pleasing, auditorial and ocular.

Try Gilbert and try Sullivan, I guarantee they're sure to please.

No matter if you're sitting in the orchestra or balconies.

In short, in matters musical and other things historical.

This is the very model of an archive categorical.

Web:
http://diamond.idbsu.edu/gas/GaS.html

Look What I Found on the Net...

```
Newsgroup: rec.arts.theatre.misc
Subject: Theatrical Combat Open House


> I always wished I would have had a chance to cross swords
> with one of the actors there [at a Renaissance Faire].
> Pick up a sword, act dumb, like "How do I hold this thing?"
> then, when the fencing starts let it all loose!

Stage combat is not fencing.  If you are at a Ren Faire, and
you pick up a weapon and "let it all loose" with an actor,
odds are that security will haul you out of there in a not too
dignified fashion.  Stage combat is not sparring...

Stage combat is choreographed, like dance.  It is rehearsed
and rehearsed to insure the safety of the performers and the
audience.  As a Ren Vet I will tell you, the scariest thing
at the Faire is the Rennie with the sword who wants to bout
with you.
```

DRAMA

Improv

Improv (improvisational theater) is a form of performance in which actors improvise as they go along. There is no script. Rather, the actors make up all the dialogue and action on the spot. Modern improv is almost always humorous (in theory, anyway). There are a number of different styles of improv, one of the most common being a group of actors who take suggestions from the audience and use those suggestions to create a spontaneous skit. There are also competitive forms of improv, where one or more teams will improvise in front of an audience and a set of judges will decide which team is best. When I was an undergraduate, I used to enjoy going to a type of competitive improv called "Theater Sports". One of the things I enjoyed the most was that we were all given soft pieces of foam, called "Boo Bricks", to throw at the actors. Improv is not only fun to watch, it affords an opportunity for extroverted people with a lively sense of humor to make fools out of themselves in front of a large group of strangers.

Web:
   http://sunee.uwaterloo.ca/~broehl/improv
   http://www.freenet.hamilton.on.ca/~aa994/structures.html

Improvisational Theater

Unlike traditional theater, improvisation often requires a collaboration between performers and the audience. During the performance, the audience offers suggestions which the actors use to create a story.
Since this can be a lot of fun, I thought you might like to try it for yourself.
Find a half dozen friends to act as an audience, and choose one person to perform with you. Sit down next to one another and pretend that you are all alone, stuck in an elevator. To pass the time, you and the other person take turns reading this book, which you should pretend is a copy of Madonna's secret love diary. As you read, you act out the various escapades.
From time to time, have your friends in the audience yell out suggestions. Don't forget to videotape the performance, so you can enjoy it again and again.

Musicals

I want to let you in on a secret. My life is like a musical. Whenever I am excited or perturbed or falling madly in love, I burst into song in a most appropriate manner. And, within a minute or two, all the people around me stop what they are doing and sing along. Then we all start to dance. This goes on for a while, until everybody just sort of drifts away and I go back to my writing. It may be a little unusual, but hey, it's a living.

Web:
   http://www.juglans.demon.co.uk/Tim/Theatre/TheatreLinks.htm
   http://www.saintmarys.edu/~jhobgood/Jill/theatre.html

Usenet:
   rec.arts.theatre.musicals

On Broadway

Are you all dressed up with no place to go? Have a look at this list of plays and musicals on or off Broadway. You provide the date, they'll provide the show time. While you are here, check out the Tony Award information and links to other theater sites.

Web:
http://artsnet.heinz.cmu.edu/OnBroadway/

Opera

Opera is opera, right? That's like telling your cat that tuna is tuna. Those with a cultivated taste for dynamic singing and musical theatrics will appreciate the fine distinction between various opera companies. So what do you do when the fat lady has already sung, but you haven't yet had enough? You rush home, fire up your Internet connection and talk about the opera. Here are some resources relating to opera discussion: a mailing list and some Web resources especially designed for opera lovers.

Web:
http://www.atreus.com/operal.html
http://www.cc.columbia.edu/~km34/geopera.html
http://www.fsz.bme.hu/opera/main.html

Listserv Mailing List:
List Name: opera-l
Subscribe to: listserv@listserv.cuny.edu

Remember, It's not over until the fat lady has checked out the Opera Schedule Server.

Play Scripts

Just the other day, I had a few friends over and we were trying to think of something to do. "I have an idea," I said, "let's put on our own version of Aristophanes' play 'The Thesmophoriazus'". "But where can we get a copy of the play at this time of night?" my friends asked, "Wal-mart is already closed." "No problem," I replied, "we can download it free from the Net." And we did. And you can too, along with many other plays, both classical and contemporary.

Web:
http://english-www.hss.cmu.edu/drama/

Playbill Online

Who needs the newspaper when you can get access to this snazzy online magazine that offers news and information listings for Broadway, off-Broadway and national theater tours? Have fun browsing around or use Playbill's search mechanism for speedier results.

Web:
http://www.playbill.com/playbill/

Stagecraft

The lure of the theater is hard to resist and even if you have no acting talent, it doesn't mean that you have to miss out on the magic. Arm yourself with tools, gadgets, plans and a great imagination, and you can be one of the all-important backstage magicians who create the stage, lighting, sets and costumes of the theater. The Usenet groups are for the discussion of the more technical aspects of theater.

Web:
http://waapa.cowan.edu.au/lx/
http://www.blighty.com/ratsfaq/

Usenet:
alt.stagecraft
rec.arts.theatre.stagecraft

Technical Theater Databases

When you need quick information on technical theater subjects, don't wait around for your mailing list to respond. You can use this Web form to do a search through documents sent to various mailing lists relating to technical theater discussion. Use keywords to search for any topic and before you can say "Don't drop that sandbag," a Web page with links to related documents will appear on your browser.

Web:
http://www.ffa.ucalgary.ca/citt/clbd/wais.html

Theater Resources

As long as you have Internet access, you will never have to be without a good dose of theater. These resources cover just about every theater topic imaginable. Now, when you are left home on Saturday night because your BMW broke down and you can't get to the theater, you can amuse yourself with a virtual experience that has a compelling drama all its own.

Web:
http://www.perspicacity.com/elactheatre/library/
http://www.siue.edu/COSTUMES/WOW/WOW_INDEX.html
http://www.stetson.edu/departments/csata/thr_guid.html
http://www.wwar.com/theater/

Listproc Mailing List:
List Name: theatre
Subscribe to: listproc@lists.princeton.edu

DRUGS

Anti-Drug Stuff

We all know that bad drugs are bad for you, so here is some good information about bad drugs, so you will be able to take good care of yourself, and avoid the bad things that happen to good people, when they have bad information about bad drugs.

Web:
http://www.druguse.com/
http://www.nida.nih.gov/MarijBroch/Marijteenstxt.html
http://www.sayno.com/poison.html

Anti-War-on-Drugs

If you are old enough, you can remember when it was cool to be anti-war (during "the War"). Well, since then, we have had a number of other, perhaps less minor wars, such as the War on Poverty. If you are still anti-war, here is another one you can protest against: the War-on-Drugs. Find out what people around the world are doing to legalize that which is illegal. (Personally, I think it would be nice if someone would start a War on Bad Taste or a War on Advertising.)

Web:
http://www.legalize.org/global/

Caffeine

Check out the caffeine resources on the Net and find out everything you always wanted to know about the world's most overused stimulant. Do you know how to make really sludgy, sweet espresso? Are you wondering how much caffeine is in Jello Pudding Pops? Don't let it keep you up at night.

Web:
http://www.caffeinearchive.com/

Usenet:
alt.drugs.caffeine

★ Having trouble ★ staying awake at night?

Try reading **alt.drugs.caffeine**.

DRUGS

Cocaine

Cocaine is a powerful central nervous system (CNS) stimulant. Its effects include increased alertness, decreased appetite, decreased fatigue, and—what cocaine users crave—an intense feeling of pleasure. In general, cocaine makes people feel powerful and happy. Unfortunately, cocaine is highly addictive, illegal, expensive and causes terrible side effects, both short-term and long-term. Cocaine is prepared from the leaves of the Erythroxylon coca bush, which grows primarily in Peru, Bolivia and Columbia. Here are some sites from which you can find out more about cocaine, such as its appearance, its effects (including during pregnancy), and a discussion of tolerance and dependence.

Web:
http://www.arf.org/isd/pim/cocaine.html
http://www.hedweb.com/cocafile.htm

Drug Chemistry and Synthesis

Where do you turn when it's late and you have a cold and all the pharmacies are closed? Check out this Usenet group and see if you can find a nice recipe for a decongestant or perhaps some LSD. That won't help your cold, but at least it will take your mind off your symptoms. Chemists and fans of chemistry chat about how drugs are constructed and synthesized.

Usenet:
alt.drugs.chemistry

Drug Culture

There is an entire group of people who choose not to hang out in reality some of the time. Instead of going to Disneyland, they like to spend lots of money on chemicals that are illegal and bad for their health. Commune with members of the drug culture as they talk about various drugs, music to trip to, becoming one with nature, and getting in touch with themselves and on special occasions with each other.

Usenet:
alt.drugs.culture

Drug Information Resources

I know what you are wondering. Did Harley put anything dangerous to my mental health in this book, or are these ordinary, harmless Web sites? To tell you the truth, with all the excitement of working on the book, I don't even remember myself. But seeing as the Internet is the most powerful interactive medium in history, what you need to be asking yourself is, "Do I feel lucky?"

Web:
http://kiwi.uwaterloo.ca/drug_info.html
http://www.algonet.se/~birdy/druglink/
http://www.epas.utoronto.ca:8080/~haans/druglink.html
http://www.hightimes.com/
http://www.hyperreal.com/drugs/

Drug Information Resources

Before you embark on your next drug-induced exploration, check the Net to see what other people have to say.

Remember, you only have one central nervous system, so don't take chances.

As we used to say in the sixties, "Uh... uummm... like wow, man. Far out..."

Drug Pix

Who says art is only for cultured people? Here are some drug-related photos that are bound to enlighten and amuse you. See what street drugs and drug paraphernalia look like, and enjoy pictures of rare curiosities. For example, the last time I visited, I saw a photo of Cary Grant taking a hit of LSD, as well as a piece of drug paraphernalia signed by U.S. comedian Oliver North. My only hint is, if you see an invitation to lick the screen, don't do it. (I am serious.)

Web:
http://www.drugs.indiana.edu/prevention/iprcpics.html
http://www.hyperreal.org/drugs/psychedelics/lsd/lick.this.screen.html
http://www.sppd.ci.st-pete.fl.us/drugs/drugs.htm

DRUGS

Drug Talk and General Discussion

There is a lot you can say about drugs, and the Internet has a lot of people who love to say it. And where else can you go for advice on what to do with a pot of leftover phenyl acetic acid or how to tell the difference between Amanita Muscaria, Psilocybe Cubensis and Chinese take-out? On the Net you will find wide-ranging discussions about a variety of topics: hard drugs (such as heroin and cocaine), psychedelic drugs (such as LSD and mushrooms), and soft drugs (such as marijuana and television). Turn on, tune out, and drop into the Usenet groups where "Better Living Through Modern Chemistry" is more than just a slogan.

Usenet:
   alt.drugs
   alt.drugs.hard
   alt.drugs.pot
   alt.drugs.pot.cultivation
   alt.drugs.psychedelics
   alt.hemp
   rec.drugs.announce
   rec.drugs.chemistry
   rec.drugs.misc

IRC:
   #drugs
   #lsd
   #mdma
   #pot

Drug Testing

Drug testing is certainly a double-edged sword (to coin a phrase). On the one hand (to coin another phrase), drug testing is a useful tool to help employers maintain a drug-free workplace. Be that as it may (to coin yet a third phrase), many people see the forced donation of bodily substances to possibly incriminate oneself as an affront to personal liberty. Would you like the real scoop on what may or may not be the lesser of two evils? (Wow, I just coined two phrases in one sentence.) Check out these Web sites, and you won't be left out in the cold. (Boy, I sure wish I had a Susan B. Anthony dollar for every phrase I've coined.)

Web:
   http://hyperreal.com/drugs/politics/drug.testing/
   http://www.csun.edu/~hbcsc096/dt/

Ecstasy

What a nice, tempting name for a drug. An intense, yet delicate labeling. However, unlike other well-known drugs—such as Coca-Cola and television—this is *not* one that you want to try at home. Contrary to what most people believe, Ecstasy (or MDMA—metheylenedimethoxymethamphetamine) is not that new a drug. Read about the history, effects, dangers and usage of Ecstasy, the drug that will turn you into an Energizer Bunny with the brain of a sea slug. ("Coca-Cola", by the way, is a trademark of the Coca-Cola Company; "Ecstasy" is a trademark of the Republican National Committee.)

Web:
   http://ecstasy.org/e4x/
   http://www.ecstasy.org/
   http://www.erowid.org/entheogens/x/x.shtml

Heroin and Opiates

Within 4-6 hours after his or her last dose, a heroin addict has begun to feel withdrawal symptoms: chills, muscle aches, joint aches, insomnia and nausea. About 10-20 hours later, those symptoms will have intensified and, by the time an addict has reached the 24-36 hour mark, he or she is experiencing insomnia, vomiting, diarrhea, weakness, depression, and hot and cold flashes. (You can see why a heroin addict will do anything to get the next fix.) Symptoms reach a peak at about 2-3 days. By then the person is experiencing muscle cramps, abdominal cramps, fever, severe tremors and twitching. These symptoms are often accompanied by incessant nausea and vomiting, and it is not unusual for an addict to lose 10-15 pounds (over 5 kg) in 24 hours. Withdrawal symptoms can take more than a week to disappear, and there may be a general loss of well-being that lasts for several months. Remember all of this the next time someone tries to tell you that heroin and other opiates are cool. Of course we all have differing tastes, and I would be the last one to impose my values on other people, but having to continually come up with large sums of money in order to avoid severe pain, vomiting and involuntary muscle contractions doesn't seem to be a pleasant way to spend one's brief time on Planet Earth.

Web:
   http://www.druglibrary.org/schaffer/heroin/opiates.htm
   http://www.sayno.com/opiates.html

DRUGS

History of Drug Laws

The use of drugs stretches back into antiquity, and follows a simple, general principle: if drugs are available, some people will use them, some people will sell them, and some people will regulate them. Our current drug laws have their roots in legislation developed in the late 1800s and modified throughout the 20th century. The only way to really understand why drug laws are the way they are is to have an appreciation of their history. By the way, speaking of drugs and history, has anyone else noticed that the guitar solo in the middle of the song "Just Like Me" by Paul Revere and the Raiders (1966) is a lot like the famous guitar solo in "25 or 6 to 4" by Chicago (1970)?

Web:
http://www.calyx.com/~schaffer/LIBRARY/shrthist.html
http://www.gwu.edu/~pretrial/jer1a.htm

> **Don't forget to take your vitamins (especially today of all days).**

> **A sure-fire way to make all your dreams come true is to sleep with this book under your pillow.**

International Stoner Slang Dictionary

If you're not stoned, you might have trouble understanding stoned people when they talk to you. Not a problem. The next time someone under the influence says something you can't understand, tell him to write it down and have him wait quietly in the corner. Then you can quickly connect to the Net and check with the International Stoner Slang Dictionary. After all, if people can find a way to talk to gorillas using sign language, there's no reason why you can't learn to understand your friends.

Web:
http://www.warehouse.net/wwweed/books/Slang/

Look What I Found on the Net...

```
(from The International Stoner Slang Dictionary)

Clam Bake [US]:
    To smoke in a car with the windows up.

Henry [UK]:
    An eighth of an ounce of cannabis (as in Henry VIII).

Logy [CA]:
    To become lethargic after smoking cannabis.

Pregnant [US]:
    A joint that is rolled incorrectly, usually with more pot in
    the middle than anyplace else.

Wacky Weed [AU]:
    Wild plant sometimes found in dense forest or sugar cane.

Zoom Tube [UK]:
    A long pipe on a bong which you take the smoke in with.
```

Leary, Timothy

The late Timothy Leary (1920-1996) was nothing if not an iconoclast. For example, he firmly believed that proper use of hallucinogenic and mind-altering drugs was necessary for experiencing an optimal existence. His philosophy was not that people should take drugs indiscriminately, but rather they should learn about drugs—what they do and how to use them—and deliberately choose what to take. In other words, where Nancy Reagan was fond of saying "Just say no," Timothy Leary would say "Just say know." In 1995, Leary was diagnosed with terminal prostate cancer and, until he died on May 31, 1996, he used his Web page to keep the world informed of his pre-death drug use (which was considerable). There was some talk of Leary committing suicide on the Net—in real time, I assume—but, in the end, he went quietly and peacefully, certainly not his usual modus operandi. One of his last goals was to "give death a better name or die trying". Even in final repose, Leary seems to have more to say than most living people.

Web:
http://www.leary.com/

LSD: My Problem Child

There are lots of famous fathers: George Washington was the Father of Our Country (in the U.S.); Prince Charles is the father of Prince William (in England); and Ward Cleaver was the father of Beaver Cleaver (on television). But perhaps the oddest parent-offspring relationship is that of Albert Hofmann and LSD. His writings have been translated and collected into this monograph, "LSD: My Problem Child". It begins: "There are experiences that most of us are hesitant to speak about, because they do not conform to everyday reality and defy rational explanation..."

Web:
http://www.flashback.se/archive/my_problem_child/

Heading for the final frontier? Take a look at "Star Trek" (or "Space").

Marijuana

You probably know marijuana as a commonly used mind-altering drug of questionable value. What you may not know is that marijuana is used medicinally by people with AIDS, glaucoma, cancer and multiple sclerosis. Marijuana, or hemp, is also an industrial crop which can be used in the manufacture of paper, fiber, fuel and even food. Finally, in scientifically controlled studies, marijuana has been shown to increase the ability of volunteers to get the little beads into the eyes of the clown by as much as 54 percent. Need even more info? It's waiting on the Net.

Web:
http://www.grandpaspotbook.com/
http://www.hyperreal.com/drugs/marijuana/
http://www.stonernet.org/

Usenet:
alt.drugs.pot
misc.activism.cannabis
rec.drugs.cannabis

McKenna, Terence

Terence McKenna is an ethnobotanist and a writer who is as cherished in the drug culture as the big (but dead) cheese Timothy Leary. Read McKenna's bibliography, travel calendar and list of current events, hear audio clips, read a selection of his writings, quotes and interviews from magazines like bOING bOING and High Times.

Web:
http://deoxy.org/mckenna.htm

Methamphetamine

Methamphetamine, or speed, is a central nervous system stimulant (that is, an "upper") that produces a variety of effects, including alertness and elation. However, speed is an extremely addictive drug that causes terrible side effects, damage, and often death, to the user. Speed was first synthesized in 1887. In the 1930s and 1940s, there was a significant speed problem, especially among soldiers during World War II. Later, another epidemic occurred in the 1960s. Today, speed is sold illegally and is a major cause of crime. In the street, speed is known by a variety of names such as meth, crystal meth, crank, glass and ice. This is a terrible, terrible drug. Stay away from it.

Web:
http://www.antimeth.com/
http://www.kci.org/meth_info/links.htm
http://www.lifeormeth.org/

194 DRUGS

Nitrous Oxide

Nitrous oxide—or laughing gas—is a mild anesthetic that has been in use since the late 18th century. Today, it is most widely used by medical professionals for surgery and dental procedures. Of course, there are also people who use this drug for recreation. However, before you put your neurons on the line, you might want to check things out with your buddies on the Net. Remember, pleasure is not a laughing matter.

Web:
http://www.resort.com/~banshee/Info/N2O/

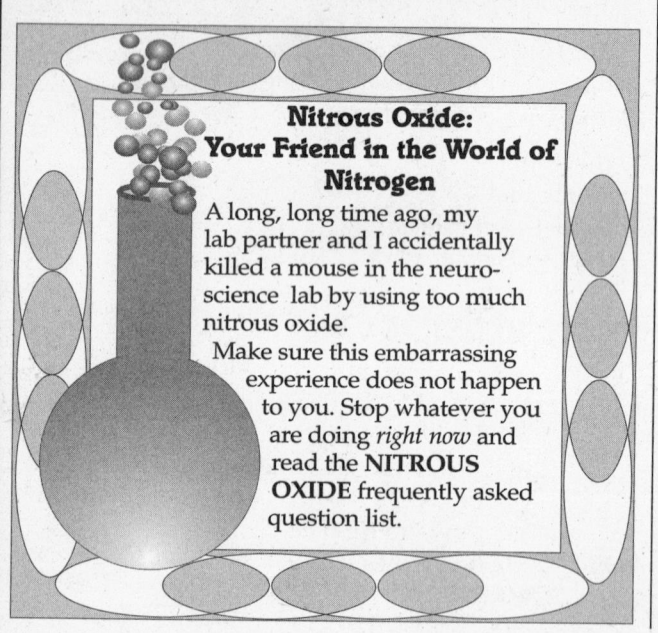

Nitrous Oxide: Your Friend in the World of Nitrogen

A long, long time ago, my lab partner and I accidentally killed a mouse in the neuroscience lab by using too much nitrous oxide.

Make sure this embarrassing experience does not happen to you. Stop whatever you are doing *right now* and read the **NITROUS OXIDE** frequently asked question list.

Nootropics (Intelligence-Enhancing Drugs)

I have a personal system for enhancing my intelligence: I exercise a lot, eat well, get plenty of sleep and—except when negotiating with editors—I think pure thoughts. I also happen to be very, very smart. Not everybody has such good habits, or is blessed with such natural talent, so it should come as no surprise that there is a lot of research into drugs that may be able to make you smarter. These drugs are called "nootropics" (from the Latin words for "doing your math homework"). Want some info? Here it is.

Web:
http://www.hyperreal.com/drugs/nootropics
http://www.mg.co.za/mg/news/smartdr1.htm
http://www.uta.fi/~samu/SMARTS2.html

Usenet:
rec.drugs.smart

Pihkal

An acronym for Phenelthylamines I Have Known and Loved, Pihkal is a "love story" about a man and his favorite chemicals. Read excerpts from the book and see clever chemical breakdowns of everyone's favorite phenylethyl radical.

Web:
http://www.hyperreal.com/drugs/pihkal

Look What I Found on the Net...

```
(from the Psychedelic Drugs Guide)

The effects of ketamine are stronger and more profound than acid
but last only an hour or so.

The subject should remain still. Experiences of the mind leaving
the body, floating in space or even death are common.
Bad trips are supposed to be absent, but there are serious
dangers following heavy use.

John Lilly and his fellow researchers have used the drug
continuously for weeks. Several believe themselves to have
contacted alien intelligences and two committed suicide.
```

Politics and Drugs

Who's right? The politicians, the reporters, the teachers, the doctors, Ann Landers, your mother? Read what the people who really understand drugs and politics have to say, and make up your own mind.

Web:
  http://www.druglibrary.org/

Usenet:
  alt.hemp.politics
  talk.politics.drugs

Prescription and OTC Drugs

There are a great many drugs used for medical purposes—so many that even doctors and pharmacists have trouble remembering all the details and keeping up with new products. The next time you need information about a drug, the Net can help you find what you need. This information is the same data doctors use, so it is an excellent resource for all types of health care professionals. Hint: When you look up a drug, pay particular attention to the "indications and usage" (when and how the drug is used), the "contraindications" (when the drug should not be used), and "adverse reactions" (side effects).

Web:
  http://www.rxlist.com/

Psychedelic Drugs

When you are in need of a little psychedelic culture, have a look at these resources. On the Net you will find tons of links, info on psychedelic music and art, history of psychedelics, resources, and information on the drugs.

Web:
  http://www.cia.com.au/serendipity/dmt/pt_links.html
  http://www.drugtext.org/psychedelics/

Usenet:
  rec.drugs.psychedelic

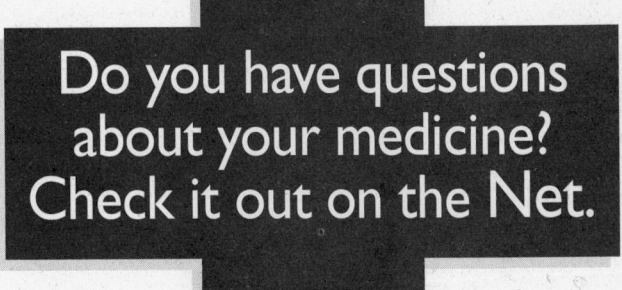

Do you have questions about your medicine? Check it out on the Net.

Street Drug Slang

We all know that seemingly innocent words can have other, more sinister meanings. If you get out on the street and start messing around in the world of drugs, one wrong word in the wrong place can have serious repercussions. Let's say your spouse sends you down to the store for some jelly beans, and, to save time, you buy some off a fellow in the street. You may have inadvertently copped a bag full of chloral hydrate (know-out tablets). Imagine your embarrassment. Next time, check with the Net first.

Web:
  http://www.addictions.com/slang.htm
  http://www.drugs.indiana.edu/slang

Virtual Acid Trip

So you missed the Sixties? No problem. Now you can take a virtual acid trip on the Net. Just tune in to the Internet, turn on to this Web page, and drop out of sight as you enjoy this psychedelic blast from the past. What's that you say? You do remember the Sixties? Farm out. Just close your eyes, click your mouse three times, and repeat after me, "There's no place like home..."

Web:
  http://www.acidtrip.com/

ECONOMICS

Beige Book

The beige book consists of national and regional summaries of the current economic conditions in the United States as described by the Federal Reserve. New versions of the beige book are produced every month or two, in advance of the meetings of the Federal Open Market Committee (FOMC) (the most important monetary policy-making body of the Federal Reserve System). At any time, you can look at the current beige book and check up on the economic health of the U.S. or one of its twelve Federal Reserve districts. I think this is a much better way of understanding the economy and where it might be heading than depending on the writers and commentators in the popular press.

Web:
http://www.federalreserve.gov/fomc/beigebook/

Bureau of Economic Analysis

The Bureau of Economic Analysis (BEA) is an agency of the United States Department of Commerce. The BEA's function is to analyze and integrate immense amounts of data in order to create a consistent model of the American economy. The BEA creates estimates and analysis dealing with regional, national and international areas of economic concern. Their best-known national measure is probably the gross domestic product (GDP), but they also produce a variety of less well known but equally important measures. Personally, I find a lot of these numbers fascinating. For example, in 1995, the highest average per capita income in the country was in the District of Columbia ($33,452), followed by Connecticut ($31,776) and New Jersey ($29,848). The lowest incomes were in Mississippi ($16,683), Arkansas ($18,101) and New Mexico ($18,206). Although California had only the 12th highest per capita income ($24,073), it had, by far, the highest total personal income of any state in the country (760.4 billion dollars). The lowest total personal income was in Wyoming (9.9 billion dollars). (By the way, these are American figures, in which 1 billion = 1,000 million.)

Web:
http://www.bea.doc.gov/

Central Banks of the World

A "central bank" is an organization whose purpose is to guide and influence the economy of a particular country or region of the world. Traditionally, the most powerful tool a central bank has is the ability to exert partial control over the money supply. Virtually every country in the world has a central bank. In the U.S., the central bank is the Federal Reserve System. In Europe, each country has its own central bank. Once economic union is achieved, a European central bank will be formed from today's European Monetary Institute. Most people do not understand the role of central banks—indeed, many people do not even know of their existence—but their power is an important force in the national economies of the world. Here is a Web site that has a list of central banks of the world.

Web:
http://www.centralbanking.co.uk/links.html

Central Banks of the World

It's a conspiracy. I'm not supposed to tell you, but I will anyway. All the central banks of the world are controlled by a small group of the intelligentsia: people who are known to be very smart, highly educated, dedicated and disciplined, working in complete secret. These people hide away in hard-to-find places, wielding an obscene amount of power in almost total obscurity. They possess esoteric knowledge and use a vocabulary of technical terms that precludes normal people from even understanding what they are talking about. Yes, it's a conspiracy. The central banks of the world are controlled by... writers of Internet books. Well... not actually all writers of Internet books... just a few of us. Well... to be totally honest... it's just me. But don't tell anyone.

Computational Economics

Computational economics is a branch of economics that uses computers and numerical methods to solve economic problems. As such, computational economics does not lie within any particular branch of economics; rather, it touches many other areas. These Web sites contain links to a wide variety of related Internet resources. Since this area is such a disparate one, the resources sometimes go far afield, and as I followed the links I landed in some especially interesting and unexpected places.

Web:
  http://wueconb.wustl.edu/sce/
  http://www.econ.iastate.edu/tesfatsi/ace.htm

Consumer Price Index

In the United States, the Consumer Price Index (CPI) is a measure of the average change over time of the prices paid by urban consumers for a specific collection of goods and services. The CPI is important as it allows us to track the change in cost of living over various time intervals. This is the official CPI Web site as maintained by the U.S. Bureau of Labor Statistics. Here you will find all kinds of information about the CPI, including a FAQ (frequently asked question list), current estimates, news releases, raw data, and so on.

Web:
  http://stats.bls.gov/cpihome.htm

Economic Growth

Growth is crucial to maintain the health of the world economy. For measuring and studying economic growth, here is a great Web site. You will find data sets, publications and research, as well as many links to related resources on the Net. For ongoing discussion, you can join the mailing list.

Web:
  http://www.nuff.ox.ac.uk/Economics/Growth/

Majordomo Mailing List:
  List Name: **economic-growth**
  Subscribe to: **majordomo@ufsia.ac.be**

Economic Resources

Let's face it, no one really understands the economy any more than anyone really understands, say, why beer comes in six-packs when people only have two hands. Still, that is no reason to feel left out in the financial cold. There are lots of economics resources out there, just waiting for you to explore, and here are some good places to start. After all, when we are living in a world when an American basketball player can sign a $120,000,000 contract and Internet authors have trouble making that much money in a *good* year, you know that things are getting out of control.

Web:
  http://econwpa.wustl.edu/econfaq/
  http://www.helsinki.fi/WebEc/

Economics on the Net

It all started with classical economics and moved through Marxism, the neoclassical schools, Keynesian economics, monetarism, right through to supply-side economics. Where does that leave us now? Good question. All I can tell you is try to get paid in advance and carry a big stick. However, if you want to understand even more, there are substantial economics resources on the Net. Download the frequently asked question list and you will have more economic resources than you can use in a month of financial Sundays. Never again need you feel left out when the people in the checkout line at the supermarket start discussing the contributions of the neoclassicists to microeconomics.

ECONOMICS

Economic Statistics

Statistics are the basic currency of economics. The Internet gives you access to all kinds of economic statistics, both historical and current; virtually every type of important economic data is published on the Net. Start your search with these Web sites, and you will probably find what you need within a few minutes.

Web:
http://www.idbsu.edu/carol/busness2.htm
http://www.lib.lsu.edu/bus/economic.html

Economics History

The study of the history of economics is fascinating. Here are some resources for economic historians. You can find data series available for downloading, archives from various mailing lists, syllabi from many different academic courses in economic history, book reviews, abstracts, as well as links to many other sources of related information, such as professional organizations, journals, personal Web pages, data sets, library catalogs, and so on.

Web:
http://www.eh.net/

Economics Journals

There are a great many economics journals that have some type of presence on the Net. Here is a list of well over 200 such journals, along with links to the corresponding Web sites. This is a great place to look for journals of which you may not already be aware.

Web:
http://www.helsinki.fi/WebEc/journals.html

Economics Network

Charts are nice. Especially when they come in all sorts of shapes and colors. If you like economics or if you just like charts, take a peek at the Economics Network: an entire resource center with online chart rooms for the U.S. economy and financial markets, economic indicators, weekly economic analyses and briefings, and a fiscal policy chartbook.

Web:
http://www.yardeni.com/

Economic Experts Predict...

Don't be at the mercy of economic experts when you need to decide where to take your vacation, or whether or not to finance your next purchase at the grocery store.

Just connect to the

Economics Network,

and you can get all the information you need to make your own predictions. Astound your friends and family with your bold observations and wry comments.

Economics of the Internet

The Internet is very important to the economy, but it is only in the last few years that people have begun to study the economics of the Internet itself. Many people see the Net as a new economic frontier, which may be true, but there is a lot more hype and wishful thinking floating around than real data. These Web sites will help you track down Internet-related economic data, as well as resources in the areas of information-based goods and services, network economics and intellectual property.

Web:
http://www.ex.ac.uk/~RDavies/arian/internet.html
http://www.sims.berkeley.edu/resources/infoecon/

ECONOMICS

> Need a laugh? See "Comics".

Economics Talk and General Discussion

For serious talk about the science of economics, join the discussion in the **sci.econ** Usenet group. For more specific discussion, there are two other groups, both of which are moderated: **sci.econ.research** for economic research, and **sci.finance.abstracts** for the posting of abstracts of unpublished research papers. If you want to debate economic issues in a less technical and more spirited environment, check out **alt.politics.economics**.

Usenet:
  alt.politics.economics
  sci.econ
  sci.econ.research
  sci.finance.abstracts

Economist Jokes

You've just spent a hard day crunching numbers and making sense out of the latest economic indicators. The rest of the office staff is gone (you always are the last one to leave), and you are relaxing, your feet propped up on a copy of "The Wealth of Nations". What better way to take your mind off the vicissitudes of financial life than by enjoying a collection of economics jokes? To get you started, here's an original joke of my own. How many economists does it take to screw in a light bulb? The answer is two, as long as they have the Chairman of the Board of Governors of the U.S. Federal Reserve to help. The job of the chairman is to actually screw in the bulb, whereupon one economist predicts that the light will work, while the other economist predicts that the light won't work.

Web:
  http://netec.wustl.edu/jokec.html

Economists on the Web

Wallow in this large list of economists on the Internet, with pointers to their Web pages. If there is a better way to impress a hot date quickly with why the Internet is so important, I have yet to find it.

Web:
  http://eclab.ch.pdx.edu/ecwww

Federal Reserve System

The Federal Reserve System ("the Fed") was founded in 1913 to be the central bank of the United States. The Fed consists of a central Board of Governors in Washington, D.C., and twelve regional Federal Reserve Banks. (The twelve "banks" are really organizations, not regular banks that provide consumer services.) Each Federal Reserve Bank is located within a Federal Reserve Distinct. The districts—which are known by their numbers—are as follows: (1) Boston, (2) New York, (3) Philadelphia, (4) Cleveland, (5) Richmond, (6) Atlanta, (7) Chicago, (8) St. Louis, (9) Minneapolis, (10) Kansas City, (11) Dallas and (12) San Francisco. As the central bank of the United States, the Federal Reserve System has important responsibilities, affecting not only the country, but the entire global economy. The main goal of the Fed is to maintain a safe, flexible and stable monetary system in the United States. To do so, the Fed directly and indirectly influences money and credit conditions and regulates America's banking institutions. To help you find information relating to the Federal Reserve System, I have included two Web sites. One is maintained by the Federal Reserve Board of Governors and contains a great deal of information about the entire system. The other Web site provides access to the FRED Database, a repository for much of the financial data collected and created by the Fed.

Web:
  http://www.federalreserve.gov/
  http://www.stls.frb.org/fred/

Finding an Economist

How many times has this happened to you?
    You are planning a big party to impress your friends and neighbors and—while making out the guest list—you realize that you don't know any economists. And, as we all know, a party without at least one economist is like... well... a party without an economist.
    No need to panic. Just connect to **Economists on the Web**, and before you can say "M2 Money Supply", you will have as many economists as you need. Remember, a man who knows his numbers is a man you can count on.

ECONOMICS

Game Theory

Game theory sounds frivolous. It is anything but. Game theory is a complex body of mathematical methods used for making decisions. The goal of game theory is to analyze a competitive situation in order to determine the optimal course of action. Game theory has applications in politics, economics and military science. Here are two interesting game theory sites on the Net that offer articles, bibliographies, abstracts, information on conferences, and links to many other resources. There is also a well-organized chronology of game theory, tracing the ideas of analyzing competition well back into history, long before formal game theory was put in a sound mathematical basis.

Web:
http://www.canterbury.ac.nz/econ/hist.htm
http://www.pitt.edu/~alroth/alroth.html

Gross State Product Tables

The gross state product data tables estimate the value of goods and services produced for 61 industries in 50 U.S. states, eight regions, and the U.S. as a whole. The value is the sum of four components: compensation of employees; proprietors' income with inventory valuation adjustment and capital consumption allowances; indirect business tax and non-tax liability; and other, mainly capital-related, charges.

Web:
http://www.bea.doc.gov/gsp/gsplist.htm

History of Economic Thought

There have been many economists, but the large-scale schools of economic thought have been shaped by a relatively few important thinkers. For a student of economics, it is an invaluable experience to read historical papers to get a feeling for economic thinking at various times and places. Here is a wonderful collection of writings by some of the most important and influential people in history. Read papers by Babbage, Hobbes, Hume, Locke, Malthus, Marx, Swift, Toynbee, and many more.

Web:
http://socserv2.socsci.mcmaster.ca/~econ/ugcm/3ll3/

Household Economic Statistics

How is it that *They* know more about you than you know about you? The Department of Census's Housing and Household Economic Statistics Division has lots of information about incomes and poverty, health insurance, the labor force, wealth and asset ownership of households.

Web:
http://www.census.gov/ftp/pub/hhes/www/

Inflation Calculator

Inflation is important to the study of economics. Here are some good places to start your thinking about inflation and its effects. Begin by using the inflation calculator: put in any amount of money, pick two different years, and then see how the value of the money would inflate. For example, $100 in 1952 would have the same value as $605 in 1998. Aside from the inflation calculator, there are links to related Internet resources.

Web:
http://www.jsc.nasa.gov/bu2/inflate.html
http://www.westegg.com/inflation/

Law and Economics

This is a great way to find Internet resources relating to the law and economics. You can use a search engine to search for the resources you need, as well as look at lists of links to research, publications, organizations, legal and government resources, directories of people involved in the law and economics, and much more. The mailing list is devoted to discussions of relevant topics in this area.

Web:
http://www.findlaw.com/lawecon/

Listproc Mailing List:
List Name: **econlaw**
Subscribe to: **listproc@gmu.edu**

ECONOMICS 201

> A penny saved is a penny saved.

Securities and Exchange Commission's Database

The U.S. Securities and Exchange Commission (SEC) is a regulatory agency charged with the responsibility for enforcing the U.S. federal securities laws. Thus, the SEC ensures that markets operate fairly and that all investors have access to material information concerning publicly traded securities. They also regulate brokerages, investment advisors and investment companies. By law, there are many different types of forms that companies and individuals must file with the SEC. In order to disseminate this information to the public, the SEC maintains a database called EDGAR (the Electronic Data Gathering, Analysis, and Retrieval system). You can access information from EDGAR over the Net for free.

Web:
http://www.sec.gov/edgarhp.htm

U.S. Census Bureau Economic Statistics

The U.S. Census Bureau is one of the most prolific publishers of economic statistics. On this Web site, you can find the latest economic indicators, as well as lots of other important statistics relating to business, income and labor and a large collection of research reports. To help you plan, there is also a calendar showing when various economic indicators will be released.

Web:
http://www.census.gov/econ/www/

> If Herman Melville had written this book, you would be reading a metaphor right now.

Look What I Found on the Net...

(from Household Economic Statistics)

```
==============================
Net Worth of U.S. Households
==============================
```

Age Group	Median Net Worth	Excluding Home Equity
All ages	$37,587	$9,505
<35	$5,786	$3,297
35-44	$29,202	$8,219
45-54	$57,755	$14,499
55-64	$91,481	$25,108
>65	$86,324	$20,642

EDUCATION

Adult Education

These forums offer interesting discussions on ways to educate adults. People talk about all sorts of subjects, such as textbooks, education using interactive computer environments, and audio tapes. There is also lots of discussion about teaching in conventional classroom settings. The Web site can help you find many related resources on the Net.

Web:
http://www.susqu.edu/ad_depts/conted/otherce.htm

Usenet:
misc.education.adult

Listproc Mailing List:
List Name: adult-ed
Subscribe to: listproc@lists.fsu.edu

*Are you an adult? Do you need some education? Great. But if you would rather talk about it, there are plenty of people willing to oblige. Join the **Adult Education** mailing list and leave the homework to the kids.*

Canada's Schoolnet

If you are a Canadian teacher, you *must* know about Schoolnet. In the great Canadian tradition of let's-spend-lots-of-government-money-to-create-cultural-resources, Schoolnet is the most ambitious, comprehensive teaching facility since I organized the sex education exhibit at the University of Toronto Medical Students' Open House (1981). Are you Canadian? You must plug in, there is no choice. If you are not Canadian, check it out anyway, and you may find something useful.

Web:
http://www.schoolnet.ca/

Curriculum Materials and Ideas

Here are some pointers to curriculum resources on the Net, including curriculum guides, lesson plans, ideas and resources. Before you copy anything, though, remember that your kids also have access to the Net.

Web:
http://www.execpc.com/~dboals/k-12.html
http://www.wuacc.edu/mabee/lessons.html

Education Conferences

Here's a great Web page for those of you (you know who you are) who are just itching to go to an education conference. Check out this updated list of exhibitions, seminars and conferences for educators. You will never have to spend another dull weekend hanging around the house.

Web:
http://teams.lacoe.edu/documentation/news/conferences.html

Education News

The world of education moves fast, but here's an easy way for you to keep up with what's new and exciting. Just spend a few minutes every now and then visiting this Web site, where you will find news for education professionals. You'll enjoy the articles from various newspapers and magazines, including Education Week and Teacher Magazine. When you hear about something important or interesting in the world of teaching, this is the place to find the details.

Web:
http://www.edweek.org/

EDUCATION

Education Policy

When I was a kid, you could get in trouble for chewing gum in class. Now you get in trouble if the gun you are carrying happens to be on the list banned by Congress. I bet you can remember what it was like being a kid and having to follow the rules with no say in the matter. Well, now you can have your two cents' worth and eat it too. Here are two mailing lists: **edpolyan** for discussion of education policy in the U.S.; **edpolyar** for an archive of the **edpolyan** list.

Listserv Mailing List:
List Name: **edpolyan**
Subscribe to: **listserv@asuvm.inre.asu.edu**

Listserv Mailing List:
List Name: **edpolyar**
Subscribe to: **listserv@asuvm.inre.asu.edu**

Education Talk and General Discussion

You don't have to be a teacher or administrator to enjoy the education discussion on Usenet. This discussion group covers all sorts of general education topics that relate to teachers, parents, children, administrators, the public school system, and much more. Anything goes.

Usenet:
misc.education

Educational Discussion Groups

There are many people on the Net who like to talk about schools and education. So many, in fact, that there is a large number of Usenet discussion groups devoted to these areas. This Web site contains a list of many of these groups along with short descriptions. From here, it is easy to find what you want. I suggest that you take a look from time to time and investigate a new group. There is always something more to learn, and there is always an interesting discussion going on.

Web:
http://www.learninfreedom.org/ed-newsgroups.html

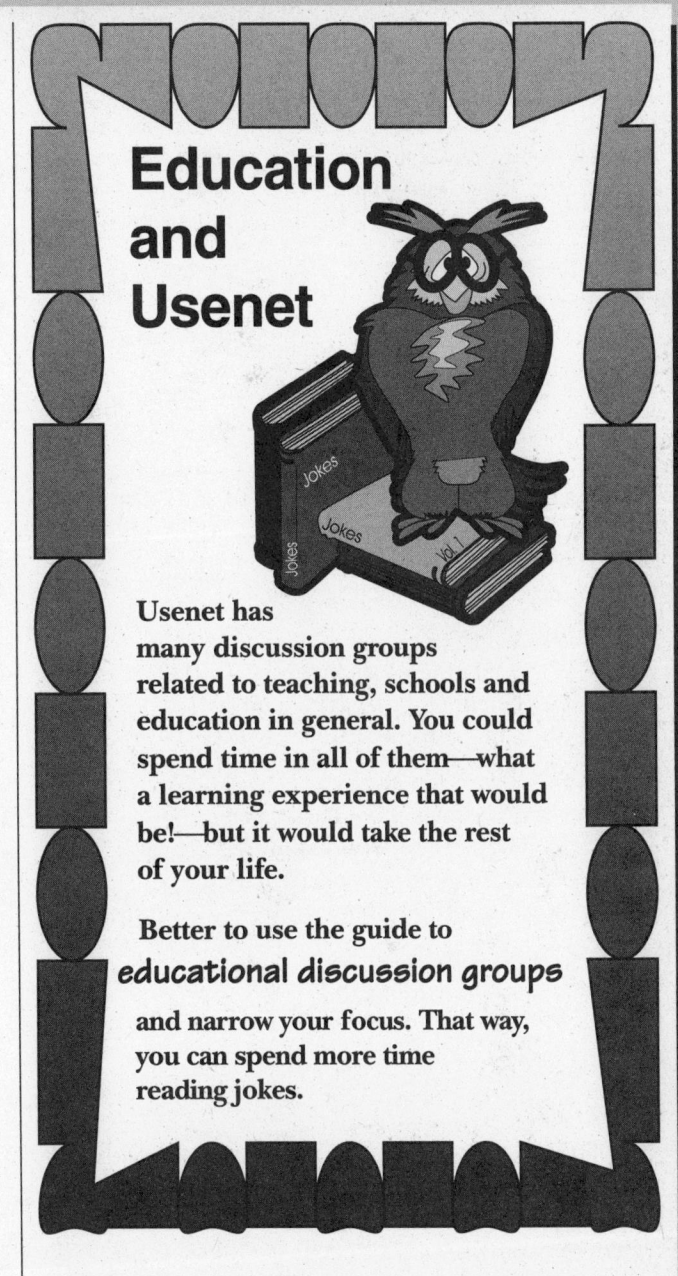

Education and Usenet

Usenet has many discussion groups related to teaching, schools and education in general. You could spend time in all of them—what a learning experience that would be!—but it would take the rest of your life.

Better to use the guide to **educational discussion groups** and narrow your focus. That way, you can spend more time reading jokes.

Educational Mailing Lists

There are a lots of mailing lists on the Net devoted to schools, education and related topics. Here are two Web sites that contain information about these lists. If you have anything to do with education (teacher, parent, administrator, even student) it is worth spending a few moments looking for mailing lists that interest you. I guarantee you will find something.

Web:
http://www.liszt.com/select/Education/
http://www.tile.net/lists/education.html

Eisenhower National Clearinghouse

The Eisenhower National Clearinghouse (ENC) provides K-12 teachers a central source of information on mathematics and science curriculum materials and encourages the adoption and use of these materials. ENC is funded by the U.S. Department of Education.

Web:
 http://www.enc.org/

Home Schooling

As home schooling becomes more popular, it is easier to find resources relating to the process of teaching children in the home environment. Take advantage of the Internet as one of these resources and discuss with other home schoolers the trials and rewards of teaching your kids at home.

Web:
 http://ericps.ed.uiuc.edu/npin/respar/texts/home.html
 http://www.home-ed-magazine.com/AHA/HSIF/
 http://www.midnightbeach.com/hs

Usenet:
 alt.education.home-school.christian
 alt.education.home-school.disabilities
 misc.education.home-school.christian
 misc.education.home-school.misc

Majordomo Mailing List:
 List Name: **home-ed**
 Subscribe to: **majordomo@world.std.com**

Musenet

A muse (multiuser simulated environment) is a text-based virtual community designed around a particular theme. Musenet (Multiuser Science Education Network) is a system of various educational muses. These muses provide real-time interaction between many people who cooperate to build their own world. (Think Dewey or Montessori.) Before you start, I would like to warn you: a muse can suck up all your spare time and then some. Game to try the game? Check the Web site for info (don't worry, you don't have to understand everything), then connect to the telnet site and see what happens.

Web:
 http://www.musenet.org/

Telnet:
 Address: **guest.musenet.org**
 Login: **guest**

National School Network Testbed

It's not hard to imagine a time when every school will be on the Net, in the same way that every school has telephone service. However, setting up the initial connection takes time, money and expertise. If you are interested in getting your school on the Net, check out the National School Network Testbed. Their goal is to help every school in the United States get on the Net. Although the information is oriented toward American schools, I know you will find it interesting no matter where you live.

Web:
 http://nsn.bbn.com/

Is Your School on the Net?

The National School Network Testbed is working to help get every school in the United States on the Net.

Okay, I know this sounds an awful lot like all that silly Information Superhighway, National Information Infrastructure stuff, and in some ways it is. However, if you are involved in getting your school on the Net, you can find some useful information here if you dig long enough.

Hint: The local Internet expert in your school is going to have a lot of power. That person might as well be you.

EDUCATION

Netschool

Netschool is a cooperative effort by students, families, teachers and schools. The goal is to create a group of schools that will work together even though they are remote from one another. Well, the Net is certainly the right place to try something like this. If you like the idea of cooperating over long distances, give this site a look.

Web:
http://www.netschool.com/

Is something not adding up? See "Mathematics".

Newton BBS for Teachers

The Newton BBS (bulletin board system) is for teachers and students of science, math and computer science. The Web site will lead you to the BBS, as well as show you a number of resources related to the Newton project. Isaac Newton, by the way, was an English mathematician and physicist who lived from 1642 to 1727. Among his many contributions to science are the invention of calculus and his concept of universal gravitation. He also—in 1665—discovered the binomial theorem. (Compare this to what most people are able to do at the age of 23.) Many people (including me) consider Newton to be the greatest scientist who ever lived.

Web:
http://newton.dep.anl.gov/

Telnet:
Address: **newton.dep.anl.gov**
Login: **new**

Look What I Found on the Net...

```
Newsgroup: misc.education.home-school.misc
Subject: How do you cope with four at home?

Hey, congrats on your plunge into what I think is the most rewarding
part of my life.  I have four, like you.  Mine are 9, 7, 4 and 1, my
boys are the older and girls the younger...

It is pretty hard to attend to all their differing needs.  I'm sure it
will take awhile for you to get into a routine, and I don't think it's
REAL important to worry too much about lots of structure right away.
When my boys were 7 and 5 we did very little schooling at all (we have
always homeschooled) — I sort of waited for them to indicate a
willingness and readiness.  We did lots of reading to them, which my
daughter (3) enjoyed, even the books geared to older kids.  And we did
lots of our work just talking about things: phonics/math/history/science
and they all seem to retain most of what we would talk about if it was
on their level at all.

I think your 2-year-old will probably stop her sabotage if you can
involve her by letting her participate...  If it's way beyond her
level, she will probably get bored and turn to a different
activity.

My three older kids all do pretty much the same work, but I don't
expect my 4-year-old's stuff to be "correct" and I make sure she
knows it's optional, especially if she gets frustrated...
```

Special Education

In the United States, we have the Individuals with Disabilities Education Act—I.D.E.A.—and, before that, PL 94-142 (both federal laws) to help ensure that students with a disability can receive a free and appropriate public education in the least restrictive environment. In the outside world (that is, outside the U.S. Congress), there are often problems. Fortunately, there are a lot of people on the Net who are willing to share solutions and information.

Web:
http://members.aol.com/LCantlin/se_links.htm

Talented and Gifted

When I was a kid, there were no special programs where I lived (in Canada) for talented and gifted (TAG) children. So I had to content myself with driving all my teachers crazy and learning extra math on my own. Today, there are many programs for TAG children: kids who show exceptional skill, intelligence or creativity. (By the way, I have a theory that kids who like to talk in class are smarter than everyone else.)

Web:
http://www.eskimo.com/~user/kids.html
http://www.millville.cache.k12.ut.us/millville/Teachers/TaG/gifted2.htm

Listserv Mailing List:
List Name: **tag-l**
Subscribe to: **listserv@listserv.nodak.edu**

U.S. Department of Education

As part of the Institutional Communications Network project, the U.S. Department of Education has established this site to provide information to educators and researchers interested in education. You will find a wide variety of files on K-12 education as well as vocational and adult education, goals of the Department of Education, programs, announcements and press releases, and educational software.

Web:
http://www.ed.gov/

Vocational Education

Network with teachers and administrators of vocational education systems as they explore new ways to pass on needed skills to people heading into the work force. Discover projects designed to make learning interesting and see how educators use the Internet to enhance the learning environment.

Web:
http://vocserve.berkeley.edu/

Usenet:
bit.listserv.vocnet

Listserv Mailing List:
List Name: **vocnet**
Subscribe to: **listserv@cmsa.berkeley.edu**

EDUCATION: COLLEGES AND UNIVERSITIES

American Colleges and Universities

Before you pick a college or university in the U.S., you *must* spend some time researching on the Net. There is so much information available, you can do a lot of checking all by yourself. These resources will get you started, and help you find the place that is the best for you. Remember, when you choose a college, you are not just choosing a school: you are selecting a football or basketball team, a place to party, a whole set of guys (or girls), restaurants and clubs where you will hang out, and a home away from home where you can do what you want without parental interference. These are not choices to take lightly.

Web:
http://www.allaboutcollege.com/colleges/united_states/usa.htm
http://www.globalcomputing.com/universy.html
http://www.petersons.com/ugrad/

Usenet:
alt.college.us

EDUCATION: COLLEGES AND UNIVERSITIES

College Admissions

Getting into the college you want can be difficult and frightening. Blow off some steam on Usenet. You can talk about fears, hopes, dreams, as well as how to make your college application absolutely stunning. If you have any questions about college admissions, this is a good place to ask.

Usenet:
soc.college.admissions

College Student Guides and Manuals

Perfection is not a bad goal. (It's always worked for me.) So if you want to be an ideal student, here are a few guides that can help you. Learn how to make the transition from high school to college, how to deal with various problems you may encounter in college, and how to make your time at the university go as smoothly as possible.

Web:
http://volvo.gslis.utexas.edu/~acadres/guides.html

Advice for College Students

One great thing about being young is there is no shortage of people who are willing to give you advice (including me).

My advice is to take a few moments and look through the

College Student Guides and Manuals.

Look What I Found on the Net...

```
Newsgroup: alt.college.us
Subject: Studio Art Programs

> Can anyone recommend reputable colleges/universities for
> studio art? My brother is an aspiring comic book artist who
> is unsure of which schools he should consider...

One of the most important things that your brother needs to
look into when he checks on schools is their attitude toward
"comic book art" or other "alternative" forms of art.  By
alternative, I mean "non-traditional".  I can tell you from
experience that no matter how good the school or the
instructors, if they don't feel that what he does is "real
art", he is going to end up either squelching his natural
inclinations or spending four or five years fighting the
administration.
```

EDUCATION: COLLEGES AND UNIVERSITIES

College Talk and General Discussion

These are great discussion groups for students and professors in college, and for anyone thinking about attending college. Anything related to colleges and universities is okay: school reputations, good courses to take, grading, taking exams, study habits, professors, university politics, and so on.

Usenet:
  alt.art.colleges
  soc.college
  soc.college.graduation

Community Colleges

The United States has—aside from universities—a great many post-secondary schools known as community colleges or two-year colleges. These schools have a wide variety of programs: academic studies leading to a diploma, vocational training, preparation for university, remedial education, and so on. If you are planning to apply to such a school, why not check it out over the Net first? You can find information on just about every community college in the U.S.

Web:
  http://www.mcli.dist.maricopa.edu/cc/
  http://www.sp.utoledo.edu/twoyrcol.html

Look What I Found on the Net...

```
Newsgroups: alt.college.sororities, alt.college.fraternities
Subject: Saying Hello

> This seems to be the sentiments of most sorority members that
> I've met.  My girlfriend wishes that she hadn't joined her
> sorority because most of the girls won't even say hi to her on
> campus, because they only talk to the people in their own
> clique.
>
> My cousin had the same problem in her sorority.  Why are
> sororities like this more so than fraternities?  Maybe it's
> just that way in my experience and nobody else's, but we
> pretty much all get along great in my house.  Once in a while
> there will be a squabble when personalities collide, but never
> do I pass a brother on the street and not even say hi to him.

I do NOT want to reduce this to a gender issue, but many Greek
women I know only know the women in their "family", within the
120-girl group.

I know what's going on in all of my fraternity brother's lives.
Never will I pass a brother without a handshake if I can help
it.

Some of the guys are just arriving back on campus now, and many
of them have gone far out of their way to see me.  (I've been
living a mile off campus all summer.)  There is real brotherhood
out there, even though Greeks get a lot of bad press.
```

EDUCATION: COLLEGES AND UNIVERSITIES

Counselor-O-Matic

Have you ever wondered how colleges and universities decide whom to admit? If you'd like some insight into the process, try this Web site. You start by answering a bunch of multiple choice questions (just like real life). A computer program then calculates your "desirability rating", from 0 to 99. The program then estimates, based on your rating, which schools you are likely to get into. I did an experiment. First, I filled out the questionnaire as best I could using information that would have been true at the time I graduated from high school some years ago. The computer program gave me a desirability rating of 74. It suggested my choices were limited, and I should apply to places like Tuskegee University, University of Rhode Island and Catawba College. I then made one small change to the questionnaire: I indicated that I had written a book published by a major publishing house. My desirability rating soared to 98. The program now judged that I would likely get into virtually any school in the country, including UCLA, U.C. Berkeley, Cal Tech or Johns Hopkins. Moreover, I had a very good chance at MIT, Princeton, Yale, Harvard, Stanford and the United States Military Academy. I'm not sure what to make of all this except to observe that, evidently, writers are highly desirable people (but then we knew that already, didn't we?).

Web:
http://www.review.com/time/counseloromatic/

Edufax

Edufax offers many kinds of help to college-bound students. You'll find all types of information, including answers to a lot of questions that may be confusing you. If you want to go to college, but you need to know more about the whole process, this Web site is a good place to begin..

Web:
http://www.tiac.net/users/edufax/faqcollege.html

There's no business like shoe business.
(See "Fashion and Clothing".)

Exploring Campus Tunnels

If you have not yet explored the tunnels under your campus, you have not had a full college experience. These tunnels are constructed in order to hold all types of utility conduits, wiring and pipes (especially steam pipes). They are secret. They can be dangerous (if you have bad luck or do something stupid). But they can be fun to explore. Since it is illegal to enter such tunnels, I advise you to not go near them. Do not look at these Internet resources even though you will find interesting stories, discussion about tunneling—the legalities and health hazards—and possibly information on entrances to specific campus tunnels.

Web:
http://www.infiltration.org/tentanda.htm
http://www.plop.net/underground/

Usenet:
alt.college.tunnels

Majordomo Mailing List:
List Name: **underground**
Subscribe to: **majordomo@userhome.com**

Financial Aid

Want some free money or even some cheap money? Get the scoop on how to pay your way through college by filling out forms for money. The Web pages have information about student financial aid, information about specialized schools like grad school, law school and medical school. The Usenet discussion group is a place where you can ask questions, talk or gripe about financial aid and your experiences. My advice is to get as much free money as you can, and borrow as little as possible.

Web:
http://www.finaid.org/
http://www.freschinfo.com/

Usenet:
soc.college.financial-aid

EDUCATION: COLLEGES AND UNIVERSITIES

Fraternities and Sororities

Have you been feeling out of touch since you graduated from college? No more parties, no more hazing, no more long hours of dressing for social success? Hook up electronically with your fraternity or sorority. The Web site lists fraternities and sororities that have a presence on the Web. For ongoing discussion, you can participate in the Usenet groups.

Web:
  http://www.greekpages.com/

Usenet:
  alt.college.fraternities
  alt.college.fraternities.dlta-sigma-phi
  alt.college.sororities
  alt.fraternity.sorority

Graduate Record Examination

Ah, the GRE (Graduate Record Examination). An acronym that strikes fear in the hearts of college graduates everywhere. After years and years of studying, you now have to take a test that is going to determine how likely you are to be admitted to the graduate school of your choice. I bet you would like to take some of the magic and mystery out of taking the GRE. This site has sample test questions, reference materials, tips and test-taking strategies, information on how and where to take the test, and how to get your score.

Web:
  http://www.gre.org/

Graduate Schools

If you've gone through college and you still just can't get enough of going to school, think about applying for graduate school. You will have much more intellectual stimulation and be admired by all the undergraduate students (who will worship you as a matter of course). This Web site contains information about graduate schools in the United States along with contact information. The Usenet groups offer a place for grad students or grad student wannabes to talk about applying for graduate schools, attending graduate schools, and so on. Personally, I had a lot more fun as a graduate student than as an undergraduate.

Web:
  http://www.gradschools.com/

Usenet:
  alt.grad-student.tenured
  soc.college.grad
  soc.college.gradinfo

Higher Education Resources Newsletter

Keep up with the latest cool resources valuable to the higher education community. This newsletter comes out once a month and announces new Internet resources such as online tutorials and courses, interesting Web sites, mailing lists and Internet books in print.

Web:
  http://www.hw.ac.uk/libWWW/irn/irn.html

Honors Programs

Are you looking for a college that will challenge your scholastic prowess with an honors program? As you are shopping for a place to spend the next four (or five or ten) years, check out this list of links to colleges that offer honors programs. The links will take you to the various colleges where you will find the specific information you need.

Web:
  http://www.honors.indiana.edu/nchc/other.html

> **Honors Programs**
>
> If you are smart and you like to work hard, maybe an honors program is for you.
>
> Check it out on the Net, and see what is available.
>
> Remember, the brain you train is anything but plain.

Lecture Hall

This is an absolutely fabulous resource. All over the world, professors are putting their lecture notes on the Net. This site is a directory of online lecture notes and course materials for many different subjects. If you are a student, you can check to see what is available for courses like the ones you are taking. If you are thinking of taking a course, you can get a preview by looking at the notes from similar courses. I like to browse, just to learn about many different subjects, especially the ones I never studied formally.

Web:
  http://www.utexas.edu/world/lecture/

EDUCATION: COLLEGES AND UNIVERSITIES

Online Courses and Distance Learning

Now that we have the Net, just about anything that has to do with information is within your reach. If you've been thinking about taking a university course, check with these sites where you can find comprehensive lists of courses that are taught online. Many different schools now offer such courses, so there's a good chance you'll find what you want.

Web:
http://www.caso.com/
http://www.ce.utk.edu/DistanceLearningResources/
http://www.gnacademy.org/
http://www.online.uillinois.edu/ramage/disted.html

Usenet:
alt.education.distance

Religious Colleges

If you would like to attend a college that leans toward a particular religious denomination, check out this Web site. You can search through a database of colleges run by various religious organizations. The site also has information about each of the colleges, so you can get a quick overview.

Web:
http://www.petersons.com/ugrad/select/rrse.html

Residential Colleges

Going to college is a much better way to get away from your family than getting married. So why not go all the way and pick a place that's halfway across the world? Imagine studying in a place where the food makes you ill and nobody speaks your language. Check in the Directory of Residential Colleges to find the perfect place for yourself.

Web:
http://strong.uncg.edu/colleges.html

Student Affairs

At a university, the euphemism "student affairs" refers to a wide variety of activities such as counseling services, student activism, fraternities, clubs and organizations, and so on. Here is a Web site with links to all kinds of related information. If you are a student affairs worker at a university or college, you will find these resources especially useful. (Monica Lewinski did, and she has a lot of experience in student affairs.)

Web:
http://www.studentaffairs.com/

Studying Abroad

What better excuse is there to go to another country and have adventures than to tell your parents that the whole thing is educational? Think of all the stories you will have to tell when you return and, best of all, your friends will be jealous. These Web sites offer information about various study programs available around the world.

Web:
http://www.petersons.com/stdyabrd/us.html
http://www.studyabroad.com/

University Residence and Housing

Before you go away to college, scope out the various places to live on campus. I lived in a co-op residence (a sort of dorm) in my first year as an undergraduate, and I liked it a lot. This Web site has links to many college residency and housing sites. Most of them include information on residence halls, dining, housing policies and rates.

Web:
http://www.netsquirrel.com/rha/

On-Campus Housing

When I was a young lad, I lived in a co-op dorm during my first year as an undergraduate. By "co-op", I mean a dorm where everything was organized and run by the students. In fact, the dorm was actually owned by the students, and the whole thing worked just fine.

If you get a chance to live in a dorm for a year or two, I think you will agree with me that it is an important social experience (often leading to other important social experiences).

Hint #1: If you want to find out the official details about dorms at various schools, use the Net to do your advance research.

Hint #2: Learn how to use a butter knife to hold a door shut, so you can lock someone into their room before they do it to you.

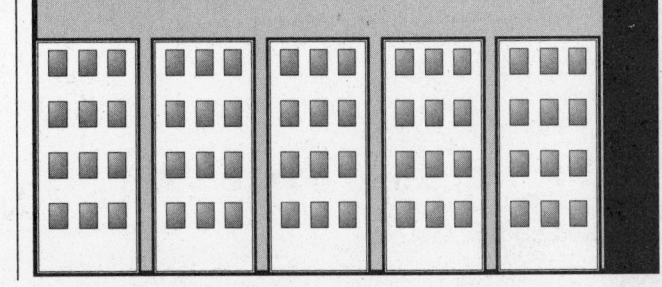

EDUCATION: K-12

Ask an Expert

I have always thought that if I changed my name to "Harley Expert" I would get a lot of free publicity in the newspapers. For example, just about every day you see a headline like "Expert Predicts Economy Will Rebound in Next Quarter," or "Expert Says Children Are Using the Internet More Than Their Grandparents Did." I could be famous. However, until then, you and your kids will have to be satisfied with regular, run-of-the-mill experts. Here are some links to such people, who have volunteered to answer questions in areas such as science and technology, health and medicine, computing, the Internet, the economy, and so on. Be aware, though, that questions asked of experts over the Net are similar to prayers addressed to a supreme being: they are not always answered.

Web:
http://njnie.dl.stevens-tech.edu/curriculum/aska.html

Ask Dr. Math

This is a fantastic math resource. The idea seems simple enough. Children and teachers submit questions about math. The questions are then answered by Dr. Math. (Actually, there are several Drs. Math, but don't tell anyone.) What makes this site so great is that the questions and answers are collected into a well-organized archive. First you choose the level of math in which you are interested: elementary school, middle school, high school, or college and beyond. Then, within that category, you can explore a variety of topics. If you are interested in learning or teaching math, I guarantee you will find something interesting here. And, of course, you can always send your own question to Dr. Math.

Web:
http://forum.swarthmore.edu/dr.math/dr-math.html

> Don't forget to do a backup.

Education Place

When you have a spare moment and you want to look for an interesting Internet resource for your children, take a look at this Web site. You will find a variety of information, games and activities suitable for various age groups. For example, I found a multiple choice geography game that was interesting. I also enjoyed the mathematical brain teasers. Hint: This site is produced by a textbook publisher, so you will have to ignore the commercial stuff and hunt for the jewels.

Web:
http://www.eduplace.com/

Geometry and Art

One of the nice things about teaching geometry is that you can use simple visual aids which you can make yourself. Here is a Web site that contains many different ideas on how to teach abstract geometrical ideas imaginatively. You will see detailed presentation plans, as well as descriptions of how to make all the visual aids you need. For the kids, you can find hands-on activities. For yourself, you can find grids and patterns you can copy, as well as tips on teaching geometry vocabulary.

Web:
http://forum.swarthmore.edu/~sarah/shapiro/

High School Student's Survival Guide

This Web site contains a list of resources for high school students. The resources are organized by subject so you pick an area in which you are interested, for example, English, history, art, science, computers, math, and so on. I don't know if these resources will help anyone survive high school—you would be better off with a lot of patience and a diverting social life—but if you are a nerd who likes spending your spare time on the Net, you will probably find something here you like.

Web:
http://www.marblehead.com/amahaney/

EDUCATION: K-12

Jason Project

The Jason Project is an ambitious undertaking that uses modern technology to offer educational experiences relating to science and technology. The material is organized around general themes, and helps children learn about important scientific discoveries and concepts. Jason is designed to be part of a K-12 curriculum, and can provide an ongoing and valuable adjunct to classroom study. If you are a teacher or parent, take a look at this site, and see if there is something here for you and your kids.

Web:
http://www.jasonproject.org/

> Parents and children,
> take a look at
> "Families and Parenting",
> "Kids", and "Young Adults".

K-12 Curriculum Talk and General Discussion

There are specific Usenet groups for teachers to discuss curriculum and learning materials. If you are a teacher, you may enjoy participating in the discussion related to your area. The groups are: **art** (art), **business** (business education), **comp.literacy** (computer literacy), **health-pe** (health and physical education), **lang.esp-eng** (English/Spanish), **life-skills** (home economics and career education), **math** (mathematics), **music** (music and performing arts), **science** (science), **soc-studies** (social studies and history), **special** (students with handicaps or special needs), **tag** (talented and gifted students), and **tech** (industrial arts and vocational education).

Usenet:
k12.ed.art
k12.ed.business
k12.ed.comp.literacy
k12.ed.health-pe
k12.ed.lang.esp-eng
k12.ed.life-skills
k12.ed.math
k12.ed.music
k12.ed.science
k12.ed.soc-studies
k12.ed.special
k12.ed.tag
k12.ed.tech

Look What I Found on the Net...

```
Newsgroup: k12.lang.art
Subject: Star Trek

How many other teachers use Star Trek in their teaching?

I've used the episode "Darmok" in discussing the concepts of
mythology, allusion and culture with good results.  You can
buy a CD which has theme songs and sound effects from the
various Star Trek incarnations.

If anyone would like to swap Star Trek lesson ideas, let me
know.
```

K-12 Foreign Language Talk and General Discussion

If you are learning (or teaching) a foreign language, you can talk to people around the world who speak that language. Learn about their culture and practice speaking with them. The **art** group is for general discussion of the language arts. The other groups are for specific languages and cultures: **deutsch-eng** (German/English), **esp-eng** (Spanish/English), **francais** (French/English), **japanese** (Japanese/English) and **russian** (Russian/English).

Usenet:
  k12.lang.art
  k12.lang.deutsch-eng
  k12.lang.esp-eng
  k12.lang.francais
  k12.lang.japanese
  k12.lang.russian

K-12 Internet School Sites

These Web sites have links to all the known high schools and elementary schools on the Internet. Save these addresses: they may save your life some day. (For example, I have a friend who teaches in Coquille, Oregon. One day she printed the entire list, folded it in two, and put it in her shirt pocket. A short time later, she was walking past a classroom window when an over-stimulated ADD student hurled a blackboard eraser out the window, hitting her smack in the chest. If it wasn't for that list in her shirt pocket, my friend would not be alive today.)

Web:
  http://web66.coled.umn.edu/schools.html
  http://www.gsn.org/hotlist/

K-12 Resources

Here are some well-organized collections of resources relating to many areas of K-12 education: classroom activities, teaching, libraries, administration, art, fun for kids, connecting your school to the Net, museums, information for parents, and so on. I predict that whatever spare time your kids are willing to let you have will be quickly used up by the Net.

Web:
  http://sunsite.unc.edu/cisco/schoolhouse/
  http://www.classroom.net/

K-12 Student Discussion Groups

There are special Usenet groups in which students all over the world can talk to one another. This is a great way for kids to learn about other children and other cultures while developing their writing skills. The groups are organized as follows: **elementary** for grades K-5, **junior** for grades 6-8, and **senior** for high school.

Usenet:
  k12.chat.elementary
  k12.chat.junior
  k12.chat.senior

K-12 Teachers Discussion Group

If you are a K-12 teacher, you may want to participate in the Usenet teacher's discussion group. After all, you need something to do in your spare time.

Usenet:
  k12.chat.teacher

Learning to Read

If you have children, you know how important it is to help them learn how to read. Here are some tips that can make the process effective and enjoyable. The emphasis is on talking, telling stories, reading stories together, and making the alphabet fun to learn. I have a hint of my own. Teach your kids the alphabet forward *and* backward. Throughout their entire life, they will find it much easier to use dictionaries, phone books and other reference books that are organized in alphabetical order. It is simple for kids to learn their letters both ways—from A to Z and from Z to A—but most parents and teachers don't realize how important it is.

Web:
  http://www.sfsv.org/read.html

Literature for Children

The Net has lots and lots of literature specially for children. Here are some Web sites that can help you find what you need for your kids. You will see book reviews, tips on using books, information about children's books and their authors, as well as links to other children's literature resources on the Net.

Web:
  http://www.carolhurst.com/
  http://www.users.interport.net/~fairrosa/

School Projects by Kids

Now that we have the Net, growing up will never be the same. There are many kids on the Net who love to share their work. Here are links to projects, reports and writing, all done by kids. Why not encourage your child to participate in the global community?

Web:
http://sln.fi.edu/tfi/hotlists/kids.html

School Safety Tips

Being in school presents a special set of safety considerations. Wise parents prepare by teaching their children how to avoid unsafe situations and what to do if something happens. Here is a wealth of wise and practical information about safety for parents of school-aged children. There is a lot you can do in advance to avoid unnecessary trouble, and I strongly recommend you take a few minutes to read the hints and tips. For example, you can choose a secret password for you and your children to use in case of an emergency.

Web:
http://www.st-louis.mo.us/st-louis/county/government/safety.html

Science Learning Network

Learning about science can be a lot of fun or it can be a big bore. One thing that makes science enjoyable is to see things happen with your own eyes, and then relate what you see to what you understand. The Science Learning Network has resources for teachers to plan lessons and demonstrations that help kids explore various areas of science. If you are a parent, you will be able to find things to do with your children at home to help them appreciate science. For example, wouldn't it be great to dissect a cow's eye in front of the entire family?

Web:
http://www.sln.org/

On the Net, you can shop til your modem drops.

Look What I Found on the Net...

```
(from School Safety Tips)

==============================
Know Your Children's Friends
==============================

Parents should become familiar with their children's
acquaintances.  This is a continuing process because children
make new friends during each school year.

Children should also be taught to keep parents informed about
their whereabouts.  They are often distracted on the way home
from school and end up at a friend's house without telling a
parent.

Knowing your children's friends will help you know where to
look for them in the event they fail to come home from school
on time.
```

EDUCATION: K-12

Spelling Bee

Would you know how to spell "chiaroscurist"? That's the word that a young lady named Jody-Anne Maxwell had to spell in order to win the final (11th) round of the Scripps Howard National Spelling Bee. A spelling bee is a contest in which people compete against one another to see who is the best speller. Spelling bees are organized into rounds. In each round, the individual contestants are each asked to spell a word, one person at a time. Only those people who spell their word correctly may move on to the next round. Eventually, only one person—the winner—is left. Spelling bees can use easy or difficult words. With easy words, you can have a spelling bee with young kids, even those who are just learning to read. The National Spelling Bee is a national championship in which very difficult words are used. For more information about this contest, take a look at their Web page. I enjoyed looking at the round by round descriptions, seeing exactly which words were used. By the way, a "chiaroscurist" is an artist who emphasizes the careful use of light and shade within a picture.

Web:

http://www.spellingbee.com/

What do all the following words have in common?

agglomerate aggrandizement asperities benison botuliform carpaccio chalicosis cotyledon dehiscence edaphon escamotage estrepement glaucous graupel graveolent invidious mynheer nidorous obsolescent periphrasis phalacrosis philippics phytophilous pileum pizzicato plenilune pomological psychrophilic quietus rantipole ravigote revanche rhizomatous saponaceous stymie therapeutant thoracodynia vitellusx enogamy

They are all words that people spelled wrong in the first round of the National Spelling Bee.

Study Tips

I am going to tell you a secret. How you do in high school *does* matter. I know you may hear stories about people who completely screwed up their grades in high school and went on to become rich/famous/powerful—whatever. However, in general it is just not true. The people you hear about are exceptions and are rare. When I think about the people I grew up with, their success in later life correlates directly with their success in high school. (For example, I did well in high school, and I am very successful.) In my experience, the people who blew off high school ended up being unhappy and poor. Believe me, it is no fun being a middle-aged man or woman who is floundering around looking for work or trying to get by on a small salary with no prospects. One of the things you need to understand is that being a good student involves using skills that you must learn and practice. To get you started, here are some resources with a small amount of information about studying and taking notes. (I don't want you to spend a lot of time reading about studying. I want you to study.) Finally, here are my personal tips on how to do well in high school. (1) Have fun, but don't fool around too much. (2) Learn to study well and do it a lot. (3) Hang around with people who share your interests and do well in school. Avoid people who are losers no matter how popular they may seem. (4) Don't get pregnant; don't get anyone else pregnant.

Web:

http://www.marblehead.com/guidance/students.htm
http://www.tulane.edu/~erc/STips.html

Test Taking Tips

So you thought that since you are finished with school yourself you don't have to worry about tests. Think again. Now that you have kids, you have to help them with *their* tests. Here is a lot of useful information that can help with both regular and standardized tests. (Isn't it nice that there are entire Web sites devoted to helping you teach your kids how to do better in school.)

Web:

http://www.busn.ucok.edu/tips/training/test.htm
http://www.byu.edu/stlife/cdc/learning/strategy.htm

EDUCATION: TEACHING

Writing Well

When your kids write well, everyone benefits. However, writing well must be learned deliberately and requires a lot of practice. Here are some useful hints to assist you in helping your children with their writing. If there is one skill they will use over and over for the rest of their lives, it is writing. Help them get started properly.

Web:
http://www.ed.gov/pubs/parents/Writing/

> *Writing Well*
>
> To me, the most important skill you can help your students (or your children) develop is being able to write well.
> As a child practices writing, he or she is also practicing how to read well, how to organize ideas, and how to concentrate for an extended period of time on a specific goal.
> Writing well endows a child with an enormous advantage that will persist throughout life. (Also, writers, especially good writers, are cool.)

Classroom Discipline

Keeping order in the classroom is important, and it's not always easy to walk a careful path between regulations, parents who are ready to complain, and the fact that, by their nature, many students love to misbehave. Still, you're the teacher, and you do have to spend some of your time socializing the youngsters (if for no other reason than to make your life easier). This Web site contains tips and techniques that you might find useful. However, it is good to remember, every teacher has his or her own personality and what works for one person won't work for everybody, so don't stop experimenting.

Web:
http://users.aol.com/churchward/hls/techniques.html

College and University Teaching Assistants

Remember how in school everyone wanted to do stuff for the teacher, like clean the chalkboard, bang erasers, or grade papers? Most of us got over that urge, but there are some who never did, and now they are hanging out in the big league academic scene wearing tweed and discussing philosophy at the off-campus coffeehouse. But that's not all they do. Sometimes they are found on the Internet discussing the roles of teacher and student with other teaching assistants.

Usenet:
soc.college.teaching-asst

Listserv Mailing List:
List Name: t-assist
Subscribe to: listserv@listserv.arizona.edu

EDUCATION: TEACHING

AskERIC

ERIC (Educational Resources Information Center) is an information system that provides access to education-related literature for teachers, library media specialists, administrators, and others. However, you don't have to be a teacher to find ERIC useful. I used it recently to find a paper dealing with management strategies that was written by a friend of mine, Marlene Garstang (look in the Drama category under Acting Talk and General Discussion).

Web:
http://ericir.syr.edu/

The Internet has some fascinating Frequently Asked Question Lists (FAQs). When you have a spare moment, find a FAQ that looks interesting and read it.

EDUCATION: TEACHING

Teaching Assistants

Being a T.A. (teaching assistant) is fun. For the first time in your life, you actually get to control the grades of other people. And you can have the experience of saying something and watching other people write it down.

Still, it can take a while to become a good T.A. If you would like to talk to other teaching assistants, join the **t-assist** mailing list.

When I was a grad student, I was the senior T.A. for a course in which the professor left before the end of the semester to move to Brazil. I got to give all the exams and award all the grades.

It was great.

EdWeb

If you have anything to do with schools, you know that lots of people are running around trying to figure out what to do with the Net—and what the Net is going to do with us. One way to sort it all out is to learn what you are talking about (a solution that has somehow evaded just about every public official in the world). A good place to start is EdWeb.

Web:
http://edweb.gsn.org/

Explorer

Here is a remarkable collection of information related to K-12 mathematics and science. There are outlines and lesson plans, as well as lots of ideas for teaching mathematical and scientific concepts in imaginative ways. This is an example of how the Internet helps us help ourselves: you can incorporate ideas developed by many different teachers into your own classes.

Web:
http://explorer.scrtec.org/

Instructor Magazine

This is a professional publication for elementary school teachers. You will find articles on important topics such as professional development, curriculum planning, communicating with children and parents, grading, teaching strategies, and ideas for the classroom.

Web:
http://www.scholastic.com/instructor/

Kinder Art

When you were a kid, wasn't it great to be able to bring home a genuine, personal work of art for your mom to put on the refrigerator? Well, your pupils will love it when you use some of these lesson plans and encourage them to create all kinds of cool art. Drawing, painting, printmaking and sculpture—there are lots of ideas to inspire you. In addition, you can look at an art library featuring art from kids around the world.

Web:
http://www.kinderart.com/lessons.htm

Look What I Found on the Net...

```
(from the Explorer Web site)

            CREEPIN' CRITTER MATH

Critter Math is an arcade-style game for practicing the math facts.
The game can be played in two variations.  In the first, four
cockroaches are crawling up a wall toward four picture frames
containing possible answers to a math-facts problem at the bottom of
the screen.  The student has to swat the bug below the correct answer
before one of the bugs disappears under its picture frame. If the wrong
bug is swatted, the other three keep crawling, and give the student an
extra chance...
```

Science Demonstrations

Here is a nice collection of science demonstrations you can do at home by yourself or at school (with a teacher around to make sure you don't have more fun than is absolutely necessary).

Web:
http://scifun.chem.wisc.edu/
http://www.eskimo.com/~billb/scied.html

Special Education and Special Needs

There are a lot of unique concerns when teaching children who have special needs. It's great to be able to network with other teachers, clinicians and researchers to discuss current issues about practices, policies and new developments. This list is open to anyone who has an interest in special education and teaching children with special needs.

Listproc Mailing List:
List Name: **sneteachtalk-l**
Subscribe to: **listproc@schoolnet.ca**

Listserv Mailing List:
List Name: **speced-l**
Subscribe to: **listserv@uga.cc.uga.edu**

Special education requires very special teachers. If you would like to talk with them, join the **spedtalk** mailing list.

Look What I Found on the Net...

```
Newsgroup: bit.listserv.tesl-l
Subject: What's a good post?

Fellow Netters: I am writing this both as an active teacher and as the
founder of TESL-L, and I am answering the claim that Netters are using
this list just to get "quick fixes" to help them with their next class.

Well, I can't see anything wrong with that... TESL-L was founded and
is funded to help teachers help students.  In particular, my vision for
TESL-L was that teachers who are professionally or geographically
isolated would have a forum where they could get the information they
needed and couldn't get elsewhere.

I think it is *wonderful* if teachers can get help with their next
TESL/FL class...

To demand that teachers not use the Net if the information requested is
available in libraries denies the value of electronic communications,
and it denies the facts of many teachers' lives: They do not have ready
access to libraries, journals, and professional development....
```

EDUCATION: TEACHING

Teachers Helping Teachers

The best tips and hints you can find will come from other teachers. That is what you will find at this Web site. In addition, you will find information on classroom management, language arts, special education and stress reduction. (Stress reduction? Who has time for stress reduction?)

Web:
http://www.pacificnet.net/~mandel/

Teachers Net

Teachers Net offers a variety of resources for teachers. There are places to talk to other people, as well as lesson plans, news, job information, curriculum planning resources, and a lot more. If you are a teacher, this site is a great place to trade tips, ask questions, and look for help with specific problems. In my experience, it often seems that a big part of teaching is complaining about the working conditions, lack of reasonable pay and all the dumb things your principal does. Most teachers are chronically disgruntled about something or other, so, when you feel in the mood, you might as well complain to your friends on the Net.

Web:
http://www.teachers.net/

Teaching English as a Second Language

Imagine the thrill of teaching people to speak English—every word you say is going to be mimicked, and all across the globe there will be people who talk just like you. Take advantage of networking opportunities by looking at what other teachers of English are doing with lesson plans, multicultural classroom environments, helpful hints for pronunciation and other important issues.

Web:
http://www.eli.wayne.edu/mitesol/linkseslteachers.html
Usenet:
bit.listserv.tesl-l

Teaching Health and Physical Education

Talk to people who teach health and physical education. Trade ideas, tips and stories. Find out if it is really true that "Those who can't do, teach. And those who can't teach, teach gym."

Web:
http://infoserver.etl.vt.edu/pe.central/
Usenet:
k12.ed.health-pe

Teaching Mathematics

All through school, I always loved mathematics. I never really had a favorite math teacher, because I was so good at it that I used to frustrate the teachers and they used to frustrate me. But that didn't stop them from trying to teach everyone else. I bet their lives would have been a lot easier if they'd had the Internet. Not only would they have been able to search for math teaching resources, they would have been able to tell me to go play on the Web and stop asking so many impertinent questions.

Web:
http://archives.math.utk.edu/k12.html
http://www.clarityconnect.com/webpages/terri/terri.html
Usenet:
k12.ed.math

Teaching Music

If music makes the world go round, then music teachers must make the... hmmm... well... something or other. Anyway, if you are a music teacher, here are some Web sites with a large variety of useful information. You will also find these resources helpful if you are a general teacher who is interested in doing some music with your class. If you would like to talk to other music teachers, you can participate in the mailing list or Usenet group.

Web:
http://www.isd77.k12.mn.us/resources/staffpages/shirk/k12.music.html
http://www.nexus.edu.au/teachstud/music/teacherresources.htm
Usenet:
k12.ed.music
Majordomo Mailing List:
List Name: **musednet**
Subscribe to: **majordomo@cc.rochester.edu**

ELECTRONICS

Teaching Resources

Teaching takes up a lot of time, so anything that can make your life easier is certainly worth knowing about. Well, here are some Web sites that have a lot of resources to help you. You'll find information about many different aspects of teaching, including curriculum, technology and professional development.

Web:
  http://tlc.ai.org/
  http://www.education-world.com/

Teachnet

Teachnet is an online magazine devoted to the teaching profession. You will find classroom decor tips, hints on getting organized, lesson plans, classroom management ideas, employment opportunities, and much more.

Web:
  http://www.teachnet.com/

ELECTRONICS

All About Electronics

Would you like to learn about electronics? Here are lots and lots of resources to help you find information about whatever area of electronics interests you. Start with basic skills, such as soldering, and work your way up to designing complicated circuitry. Pretty soon, you will be creating your own robots to help you with the household chores. And when people say, "Wow, how did you ever learn how to make something like that?" you can answer, "I learned it on the Net."

Web:
  http://www.hut.fi/~then/electronics.html

> **Jump into the Net.**

All About Electronics

Tell me if the following sounds interesting to you:
A transistor is a semi-conductor device used for amplifying a current or voltage. Transistors have three terminals.

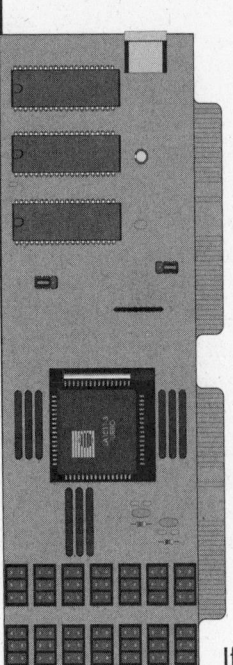

Bipolar transistors have a base, an emitter and a collector. They are controlled by current and have low input impedance. Field-effect transistors have a gate, a source and a drain. They are controlled by voltage and are high impedance.

Now don't worry about whether or not you understand all the technical terms. If this type of stuff sounds interesting to you, you may enjoy learning about electronics.

If so, don't waste a moment. Connect to the Net, and start reading about electronics right this very moment.

Consumer Repair Documents

Do you think you might like to fix that toaster yourself rather than throw it out? Or how about taking a whack at the microwave before calling the repair service? Here is some handy and practical information about fixing electronic appliances. And if you really get stuck, you can always ask your Usenet friends for help. Maybe you can save enough money to pay for your monthly Internet bill.

Web:
  http://www.repairfaq.org/filipg/

Usenet:
  sci.electronics.repair

EDN Magazine

EDN is a well-established magazine that follows the electronics industry, especially in areas related to design engineering and embedded systems. I like the articles because they are researched well, written well, and comprehensive without being bogged down in too much detail. This is a good site to visit every couple of weeks if you are an electronics professional interested in integrated circuits, microprocessors and computers, embedded systems, electronic design automation, testing and measurement.

Web:
http://www.ednmag.com/

Electronic Chip Directory

There are a *lot* of electronic chips in the world, with more being manufactured all the time. To help you find the information you need when you need it, here is a great resource that contains data about specific chips and about manufacturers, organized numerically as well as by function. You will also find FAQs (frequently asked question lists), information about mailing lists and useful tips, as well as many other links to related resources.

Web:
http://www.hitex.com/chipdir/

Electronic Equipment Repair Tips

If you like to repair electronic equipment, you'll find this site useful. People from all over the world contribute tips and hints on how to solve specific problems with electronic devices such as computer monitors, game machines, audio equipment, laser printers, microwave ovens, satellite systems, TVs, telephones, video recorders, and more. If you are a repair buff, take a look at the list of problems for which people need help. Maybe you can suggest a solution. If you have a repair problem of your own, send it in and see if someone can help you.

Web:
http://elmswood.guernsey.net/

Usenet:
sci.electronics.equipment

Electronic Prototyping Tips

Only those who are really lucky can aspire to this level of electronic excellence. Get your fill of electronic prototyping and construction methods. Learn how to do cool things like despike chips, make changes to circuitry, and more. There is a huge amount of great troubleshooting information at this site.

Web:
http://engr-www.unl.edu/ee/eeshop/proto.html

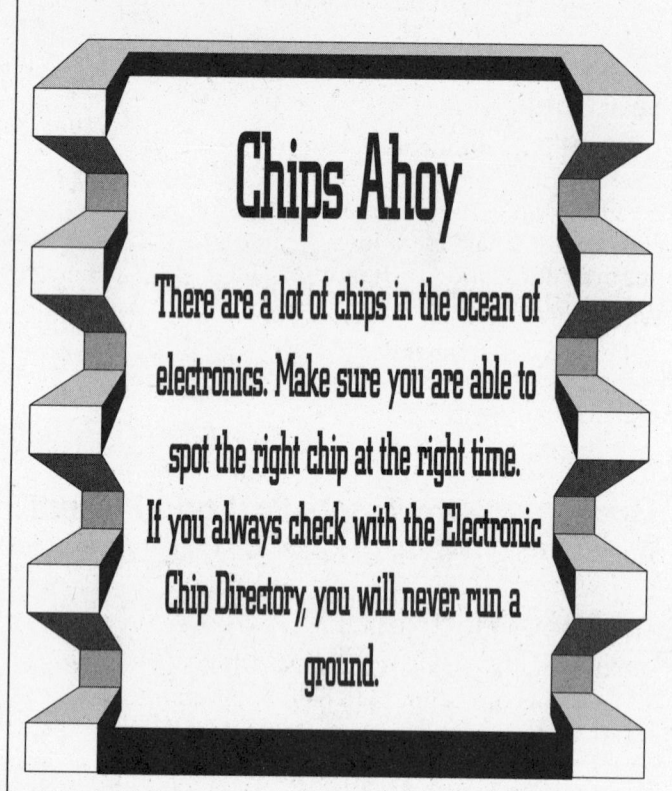

Chips Ahoy

There are a lot of chips in the ocean of electronics. Make sure you are able to spot the right chip at the right time. If you always check with the Electronic Chip Directory, you will never run a ground.

Electronics Talk and General Discussion

Electronics is a fascinating field that can be a lot of fun. However, it is a complex detailed area of technology, and there are times when it can help a lot to have someone to talk with. Usenet has a number of groups devoted to electronics discussion. This is where the P=IV type of people hang out in the Net.

Usenet:
sci.electronics
sci.electronics.basics
sci.electronics.design
sci.electronics.misc

Electronic Prototyping Tips

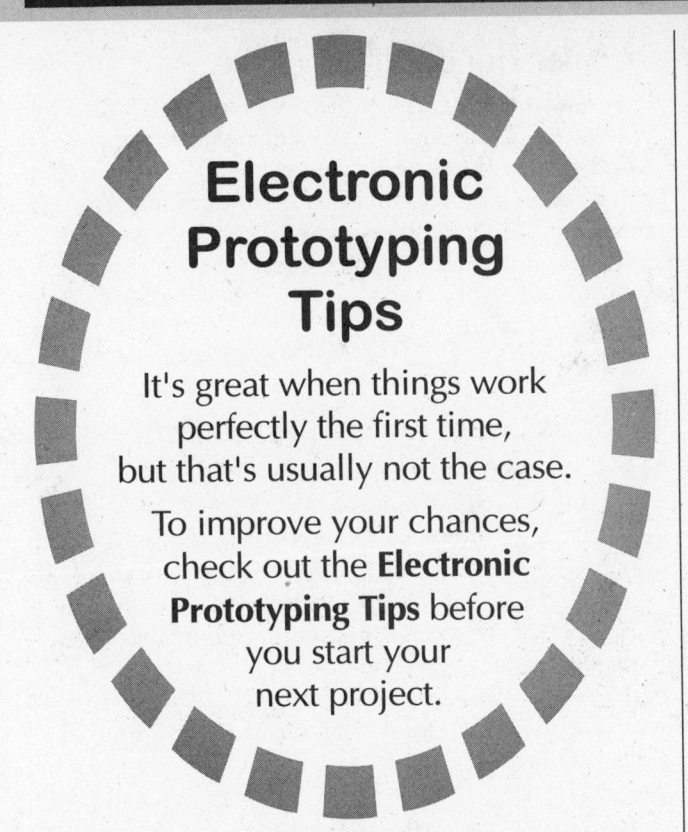

It's great when things work perfectly the first time, but that's usually not the case.

To improve your chances, check out the **Electronic Prototyping Tips** before you start your next project.

Great Microprocessors Past and Present

Within your computer are a variety of small electrical components known as "chips". These chips perform a number of different functions, but the one that people talk about the most is the processor. The processor performs many of the principal activities of the computer. You may have heard the processor being referred to metaphorically as the "brain" of the computer. Actually, there are a bunch of chips that are "brains", the processor being the main one. The most common PR processors are made by Intel and are members of the Pentium family (the Pentium, Pentium Pro and Pentium II). You may also have heard of an older Intel processor called a 486. The most common Macintosh processor is the PowerPC. This Web site contains information about a great many processors that have been developed through the years. I find this type of information interesting because I marvel at the enormous progress in processor design that has been made in such a short time. (The very first "microprocessor"—the old name for processor—was the 4004, announced by Intel in 1971.)

Web:
http://www.cs.uregina.ca/~bayko/cpu.html

Museum of HP Calculators

When I was a senior in high school, the chemistry teacher had a contraption about the size of an old fashioned adding machine: a brand new electronic calculator. It cost $450 (which was a lot of money in those days) and could add, subtract, multiply and divide. The machine was considered so valuable, the teacher kept it locked in his office. Nowadays, you can pick up a credit card-sized solar-powered calculator for a couple of bucks at the corner drugstore. Much of the evolution from the first rudimentary calculators to today's sophisticated hand-held computers is a result of the work done by Hewlett-Packard. Throughout the years, HP has produced a family of calculators that, even now, are near and dear to the hearts of nerds everywhere. This Web site celebrates the history of such calculators. And if you happen to have one, you can find information about the calculator and how to maintain it.

Web:
http://www.teleport.com/~dgh/hpmuseum.html

Semiconductors

A semiconductor is a substance whose electrical properties lie between that of a conductor and an insulator. Within the substance, there is limited movement of electrons, the exact characteristics depending on the crystalline structure of the material. Materials commonly used as semiconductors include germanium, silicon, indium antimonide, gallium arsenide and aluminum phosphide. What makes semiconductors so useful is the fact that, by adding small impurities to the material, the flow of electrons can be modified. Thus, it is possible to design a component that contains semiconductor material with specific impurities to create an electrical component designed to perform specific functions. As you can imagine, the world of semiconductors is complex. To help you understand what you read, I have found some resources with basic information about semiconductors and semiconductor terminology. For general discussion, such as questions and answers, you can participate in the Usenet group.

Web:
http://rel.semi.harris.com/docs/lexicon/
http://rsligar.home.mindspring.com/semi.html
http://www.semiconductors.philips.com/
http://www.semiweb.com/

Usenet:
sci.engr.semiconductors

224　ELECTRONICS

Speaker Building Information

Would you like to build your own audio speakers? There are a lot of subtle details that create the difference between a good speaker and a great speaker. Here is some useful information for people who like to design and build their own speakers. You will find various technical articles, tips and techniques.

Web:
　http://home.nycap.rr.com/wlarmon/speak/speak.htm

Speaker Building Information
Right now, you may be just a regular guy or gal in your home, with no special responsibilities. However, if you understand something about electronics, and you have access to information on the Net, you can become the Speaker Builder of the House.

EMERGENCY AND DISASTER

Alertnet

Every day, there are emergencies and disasters somewhere in the world. When you need the latest news and you need it now, here is the place to visit. My advice is to spend five minutes at the end of each day reading this Web site. You will feel so good knowing that all these awful things aren't happening to you, that you will have a wonderful restful sleep all night long.

Web:
　http://www.alertnet.org/

Disaster Handbook

The best way to handle a disaster is to prepare for it in advance. This guide will explain everything you need to know, understand and expect. You will also find what to do after a disaster, as well as help in understanding how to prepare for specific types of disasters, such as hurricanes, tornadoes, floods and earthquakes.

Web:
　http://disaster.ifas.ufl.edu/

Disaster Situation and Status Reports

This Web site has information and reports about natural disasters: earthquake reports, weather reports and hurricane forecasts. The **nat-dsr** mailing list is for situation reports from various humanitarian emergency response organizations and covers natural disasters only. The **sitreps** list is for situation reports about natural disasters as well as complex disasters (events that are socially or politically initiated). The **fireline** list is for the dissemination of information about wild land fires in North America.

Web:
　http://www.vita.org/emergres.htm

Listproc Mailing List:
　List Name: **fireline**
　Subscribe to: **listproc@vita.org**

Listproc Mailing List:
　List Name: **nat-dsr**
　Subscribe to: **listproc@vita.org**

Listproc Mailing List:
　List Name: **sitreps**
　Subscribe to: **listproc@vita.org**

Natural Disasters and You!
One of the best parts of life is reading about natural disasters that happen to other people. What could be more fun than waking up each morning, logging in to your favorite Internet connection, and checking out all the disasters that happened overnight to people who aren't as smart and good looking as you? (And, if truth be told, may not even be smart enough to read a Harley Hahn book.)

EMERGENCY AND DISASTER

Disaster Talk and General Discussion

Are you the type of person who can't resist staring in fascination as you drive by the scene of an automobile accident? Well, if you also like to talk about disasters, this is the place to be. Any disaster will do: fire, flood, earthquake, plane crashes, and so on.

Usenet:
   alt.disasters.misc

Earthquakes

If you live in earthquake country, it's good to be prepared just in case the ground beneath you starts moving. If you don't live in earthquake country, you may want to find out what you are missing. These Web sites have maps of recent earthquakes, seismic data, earthquake news, information about the latest earthquakes around the globe, as well as hints on making your home environment more earthquake-safe. The Usenet discussion groups are for talking about various aspects of earthquakes, including personal information and technical data.

Web:
   http://www-geology.ucdavis.edu/eqmandr.html
   http://www.civeng.carleton.ca/cgi-bin/quakes
   http://www.eqe.com/publications/homeprep/

Usenet:
   alt.disasters.earthquake
   sci.geo.earthquakes

Emergency News

When you want to find out what is happening in the emergency and disaster world, this is the place to look. You will find news stories about infectious diseases; police, military and fire operations; terrorism and rescue operations; hazardous material reports; and chemical and biological weapons.

Web:
   http://www.emergency.com/

Emergency Services

Emergency service personnel come in a variety of shapes and sizes. There are workers who help before, during or after emergencies. Such people—who may be civilian or military—cover various types of natural and technological disasters. Some workers get paid and some volunteer. But they all use a wide range of equipment and techniques to save lives and property. This Web site is a fine tribute to rescue workers as well as a good place to get general information about emergency services and life-saving tips. (You never know when you may need to know how to operate a chain saw properly.)

Web:
   http://www.catt.citri.edu.au/emergency/

Usenet:
   alt.emergency.services.dispatcher

Emergency Tip of the Week

It's one thing to be prepared, it's another to *Be Prepared*. Anybody can climb a few rungs on the ladder of emergency planning, but if you really want to be a pro, here's a Web site you will need to check regularly. For example, you may already keep some containers of water in your garage, but do you know how to turn your car into a well-planned, mobile storage facility that will allow you to survive for three days without help? And you may be aware that if you are in a tall building and a fire starts, you should take the stairs and not the elevator, but do you know the best place to hide when the building starts to collapse? You should stand near a big, strong object. There is a good chance that a "void" will be created around the object when the building collapses. (Don't hide under a desk. It will collapse along with the building.) Here is one last hint. Be sure your emergency supply kit has a copy of this book. Having something heavy to throw will come in handy if somebody tries to steal your food.

Web:
   http://www.theepicenter.com/tipoweek.html

Now is your chance.

EMERGENCY AND DISASTER

We interrupt this book to give you the following important message:

Stop right now, whatever you are doing, and check out the Emergency Tip of the week.

We now return you to the rest of the book (which is already in progress).

Emerging Diseases

Not feeling at your perky best? Do you have some newly discovered contagion, or are you just not getting enough sleep? Let's be sure. Take a look at this Web site, where you can find lots of information on various outbreaks around the world, historical information of outbreaks of bygone days (for those who love nostalgia), and in-depth coverage on the spread of important diseases such as ebola, dengue and monkeypox.

Web:
http://www.outbreak.org/cgi-unreg/dynaserve.exe/

Famine

Famine is a large-scale shortage of food. There are many causes of famine, the most common being (1) natural disaster, and (2) overpopulation combined with exhausted agricultural resources. However, no matter the reason for a famine, hunger is hunger, and the Net has a great many hunger-related resources. This site talks about causes of hunger and solutions to famine. You will find information about advocacy groups and policies, education and training, as well as situation updates from all around the world.

Web:
http://www.brown.edu/Departments/World_Hunger_Program/

Federal Emergency Management Agency

The Federal Emergency Management Agency (FEMA) is an independent United States federal agency in Washington, D.C. FEMA provides training to help communities prepare for and cope with disasters. After something happens, FEMA offers disaster relief assistance. The FEMA Web site offers information about their services, as well as general information about how to prepare for various natural (and unnatural) disasters: earthquakes, extreme heat, fire, floods, hurricanes, nuclear plant disasters, and much more.

Web:
http://www.fema.gov/

First Aid

You never know when a medical emergency is going to arise, but when it does, the Net can help. Here are first aid resources where you can learn what to do until proper medical attention is available. Read about bites, bleeding, blisters, bruising, burns, choking, ears/eyes/nose problems, fainting, frostbite, poisoning, sprains, fractures, shock, wounds, and much more.

Web:
http://www.kuwaitonline.com/dems/
http://www.mayohealth.org/mayo/library/htm/firstaid.htm
http://www.medaccess.com/first_aid/
http://www.parasolemt.com.au/afa/

Flood Observatory

If you are thinking of relocating, you may want to know if your new location is in an area that is prone to flooding. If so, you can check the flood activity for various places over the last few years. For example, many Americans think that moving to the mid-western United States is safe because they will be cleverly avoiding the earthquakes and volcanoes from the west as well as the hurricanes from the east. Well, as Marlon Brando said in A Streetcar Named Desire, "Ha... ha ha!" Before you relocate, read the information from the available flood databases, as well as current information about floods. There are also some fascinating images.

Web:
http://www.dartmouth.edu/artsci/geog/floods/

EMERGENCY AND DISASTER

Home Fire Safety Tips

Do you know what to do if your house catches on fire? This Web site has tips on how to prevent fires in the home, as well as how to make a good plan for evacuating your house and keeping your family safe in the event of a fire. For example, if your house does catch on fire, have you designated the person whose job it would be to bring the marshmallows?

Web:
http://www.ou.edu/oupd/fireprev.htm

Hurricanes

If you live in a place where you occasionally have to batten down the hurricane hatches, you should know about where on the Net you can get good hurricane information. These sites will tell you about hurricanes, including how to prepare for an upcoming storm.

Web:
http://www.edwards.cc/tcp/
http://www.gobeach.com/hurricane/
http://www.nassauredcross.org/sumstorm/
  hurrica1.htm
http://www.nhc.noaa.gov/

Hurricanes and Typhoons

You might think you are safe, but how can you be sure?

At this very moment, there may be a hurricane or typhoon headed directly toward you.

Your only chance is to check with the Net right away.

(Note: If you live in Montana or North Dakota, you may ignore this warning.)

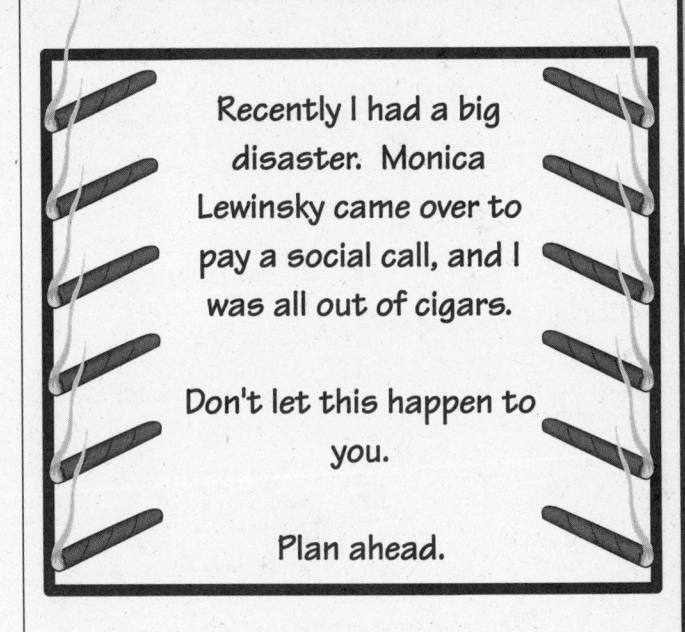

Recently I had a big disaster. Monica Lewinsky came over to pay a social call, and I was all out of cigars.

Don't let this happen to you.

Plan ahead.

Planning Ahead for Disasters

Part of the trick of surviving a disaster is being prepared. This Usenet discussion group offers a great place for people to talk about how to get ready for that unforeseen day when fate is waiting around the corner with an unpleasant bit of sticky business. Trade anecdotes and hints with people around the world or check out the Web for advice and handy checklists to help you prepare for The Big One.

Web:
http://disaster.ifas.ufl.edu/chap2fr.htm
http://www.theepicenter.com/howto.html

Usenet:
alt.disasters.planning

Red Cross

There never seems to be a lack of natural disasters, so there is always something for the Red Cross to do. This global nondenominational, nonprofit disaster assistance organization boldly goes where everyone else is evacuating. Read information about the Red Cross, get updated news about current disasters and assistance efforts currently being performed. For those of you who like to participate, you can also find out how to join.

Web:
http://www.crossnet.org/

Look What I Found on the Net...

```
Newsgroups: misc.survivalism
Subject: Re: My First Gun

> Hi.  I was hoping to get some advice.
>
> We have sunk ourselves into survival and alternative living
> for the last year.  We have bought our land in the mountains
> of Montana, we have our food and water storage going, and we
> have learned to be pretty proficient at organic gardening.
> We hope to move up to our property next summer and will be
> using solar energy up there.
>
> My question is this:
>
> We know nothing about guns.  We will need a gun for protection
> from grizzlies as well as protection if American society
> breaks down, and we have economic or social collapse.
> Eventually we will also have to learn to hunt. Should we start
> with a rifle or shotgun?  What is the main difference?
```

[to which various people offered the following suggestions]

A shotgun is definitely best for home protection...

A good hunting rifle in the .30 caliber range would be ideal...

If you are really worried about bears, and you are not a good shot, get a semi-automatic...

A shotgun is good in CLOSE combat...

I would recommend a good rifle... The .30-30 is good for areas with a lot of brush... The .308 is the basic NATO round — it's used by most military snipers... The .30/06 is the most common big game rifle...

For each person, one semi-automatic handgun, caliber 9 mm or larger with at least 6 magazines each... I'd store at least 500 rounds of ammunition... also for each person, one pump action 12 gauge shotgun with both a "riot" and a "hunting" barrel... I'd have on hand at least 200 rounds of #4 buckshot, 500 rounds of #6 shot, 250 rounds of #7.5 shot, and probably 100 rounds of rifled slugs...

Survivalism

I am a firm believer in survivalism, and I am quite a survivalist myself. For instance, in my pantry right now, I have not one, but *two* boxes of microwave popcorn in case I am overrun by hoards of hungry guests. In my bathroom, I have extra rolls of fluffy bathroom tissue because, well, you just never know. And, in the cupboard, I have an extra bag of cat food. To some people, however, survival goes beyond popcorn, toilet paper and cat food, as you will see when you start to read what people are doing to practice the art of self-reliance. All it takes is gumption, planning and some money. As Oscar Wilde said, you can survive anything except death, and live down anything except a good reputation.

Web:
  http://members.xoom.com/survive/
  http://www.idir.net/~medintz/surv_faq/
      surv_faq_index.html
  http://www.survival-center.com/

Usenet:
  misc.survivalism

Tornadoes

If you think living inland protects you from storm activity, think again. Tornadoes are generally quick but intense, causing destruction in a localized area. Find out how and where tornadoes form, how to rate a tornado, and tips on what to do if a tornado hits in your area.

Web:
  http://www.fema.gov/library/tornadof.htm
  http://www.tornadoproject.com/
  http://www.txdirect.net/~msattler/tornado.htm

Wildfires

Wildfires are a constant problem, and during the fire season, there is always something happening. Here are some Web sites to help you keep up. In particular, you can check the current fire situation in the United States; the information is updated daily. I have also included a Web site with articles of interest to wildfire professionals.

Web:
  http://www.firewise.org/pubs/wnn/
  http://www.nifc.gov/news/
  http://www.nifc.gov/news/sitreprt.html

ENERGY

Alternative Energy

Tired of the same old energy? Try an alternative energy lifestyle. This site has links to more alternative energy-related information than you'll probably need in your whole lifetime (or at least until all the potato chips are gone).

Web:
  http://gem.crest.org/

Usenet:
  alt.energy.homepower

Biomass

Biomass refers to organic matter. Much biomass is renewable; that is, if you use it up you can create more. There is a lot of research and development being done to find ways to use renewable biomass to produce energy in a way that is safe, economical and non-polluting. For example, researchers are looking for ways to create energy out of forest and mill residues, agricultural and animal wastes, livestock operation residues, aquatic plants, fast-growing trees and plants, and municipal and industrial wastes.

Web:
  http://www.biomass.org/

Coal

Coal is a fuel created from fossilized plants (similar to the way in which oil is created). Coal is almost entirely carbon with varying amounts of minerals. Although coal creates a lot of pollution when it is burned, it is still used in a good many places around the world (including the United States, where it is especially important to the steel industry). There are a good number of places on the Net where you can read about coal, its properties and uses. Here are a few to get you started.

Web:
  http://apollo.osti.gov/fe/ccafetdb.html
  http://energy.usgs.gov/coalpubs.html
  http://www.dpie.gov.au/resources.energy/coalmin/
      coal_vl/

ENERGY

Educational Energy Information

Kids. I bet you wish you knew more about energy. I know I did when I was young.
Spend some time browsing the educational resources on the Net and you will soon be at the top of your class, energy-wise. (And will *you* be popular.)
There are lots of great hints as to what you can do to help out. For example, you could get your school to start a school energy patrol. Every day, you can check all the classrooms to make sure that the lights are turned off if no one is in the room. Not only will you have a lot of fun, but it will look great on your résumé when you get older and want to go to medical school.
Boy, adults sure think of some great things for kids to do.

Department of Energy

What a nice word fusion is. Just say it slowly, let it roll off your tongue and lips with a soft hissing sound: *fusion*. It's not just a science, it's a way of life. Get an overview of the U.S. Fusion Energy Science Program, information about fusion and the environment, and documents on fusion as an environmentally attractive, commercially viable and sustainable energy source.

Web:
http://wwwofe.er.doe.gov/

Educational Energy Information

Here's a great place to find out about energy. The information is written in an easy-to-understand style, suitable for children. If you are a teacher or parent and you want to make energy information accessible to young people, this is a good site to explore. Aside from general energy information, you will find puzzles and stories about energy.

Web:
http://www.energy.ca.gov/education/

Isn't the Net amazing?

Look What I Found on the Net...

```
Newsgroup: sci.energy
Subject: Tidal Energy

Together with my friend Xxxx Xxxxxx, I have found a new concept
to extract huge amounts of tidal energy from shallow seas where
the tidal wave propagation is typically parallel to the shore.

Typically, 1000 to 2000 megawatt plants are possible.  This
concept is new, but most promising for the future.

At this time, we would like to know if anyone has ever dealt
with tidal energy plants.  In addition we are looking for
financing for a feasibility study, so if anyone knows the right
place, please let me know.
```

ENERGY

Energy and the Environment

It's common these days to hear about what car smog is doing to the environment. However, there is more to energy and the environment than what your automobile is producing. Check out some of the environmentally related resources on the Net, gathered under one solar-powered virtual roof. You'll find information about alternative energy as well as traditional energy sources (such as fossil fuels).

Web:
  http://www.eh.doe.gov/nepa/
  http://zebu.uoregon.edu/energy.html

Energy Efficiency and Renewable Energy Network

The Energy Efficiency and Renewable Energy Network (EREN) is part of the U.S. Department of Energy. The U.S. government is putting a lot of effort into developing new energy technologies, and this Web site is a good place to learn about what's happening. I found an enormous amount of interesting information here. A lot of it is technical government stuff, but there are some fascinating areas, including special resources for kids. I particularly enjoyed reading about superconductivity.

Web:
  http://www.eren.doe.gov/

Energy Efficient Homes

How energy efficient is your home? Here are some resources on the Net that show you how to improve your home's efficiency, help the environment, and save a few bucks at the same time. The Web sites will show you energy-saving tips. The Usenet groups are for the discussion of heating, venting and air conditioning.

Web:
  http://energuide.nrcan.gc.ca/tips/estips_e.htm
  http://www.electricitychoice.com/
      energy_saving_tips.htm
  http://www.energyoutlet.com/

Usenet:
  alt.hvac
  sci.engr.heat-vent-ac

Energy Information Administration

The Energy Information Administration (EIA) is an independent statistical and analytical agency of the United States Department of Energy. The EIA compiles data relating to energy resources, supply and demand, technology, economics, energy policies, and more. The EIA's Web site has summaries and reports on energy consumption all over the world, as well as energy forecasts. (This is the place to check to see if you will have enough energy to play softball after work.)

Web:
  http://www.eia.doe.gov/

Energy Talk and General Discussion

When you need a little pick-me-up, check out the Usenet groups where nerds around the Net energize themselves by talking about the science of energy.

Usenet:
  alt.energy
  sci.energy

Hydroelectricity

Hydroelectric power is the largest renewable resource in the United States. Hydropower generates ten percent of the power produced in the United States, equivalent to 500 million barrels of oil a year. In general, hydropower is an excellent energy source because it gives off no emissions when it is used, and the source of the energy is from water that is already lying around doing nothing in particular. However, there are problems. In order to create a hydroelectricity plant, water must be diverted and, often, dams must be constructed. These activities must be considered carefully as they can have negative effects on the ecosystems of the waterways. Still, I grew up in a place in which all the electricity was generated from hydropower, and I turned out pretty good.

Web:
  http://borworld.usbr.gov/power/
  http://members.aol.com/cloverted/waterpower.html
  http://www.nwp.usace.army.mil/hdc/

Hydrogen Power

If you have lots of water laying around and the right type of electrical current, you can whip up some hydrogen and create your own power plant. However, if you are low on water, you can also produce hydrogen from sewage, garbage, agricultural biomass, paper waste products and other waste streams that have hydrogen-bearing compounds. Check out these links for interesting information about using hydrogen as a source of fuel. And if you feel like talking, you can expend some hot air on the hydrogen Usenet group.

Web:
http://www.clean-air.org/

Usenet:
sci.energy.hydrogen

Natural Gas

Natural gas is a mixture of gases that come from beneath the ground. Natural gas is mostly methane (80-95 percent) with the remainder varying according to the geographic locality. The minor components of natural gas may include helium, carbon dioxide, carbon monoxide, hydrogen and nitrogen. Natural gas is a fossil fuel and is often found with petroleum. However, natural gas can also occur by itself within sand, sandstone or limestone deposits. Natural gas can be utilized to power any number of appliances or machines. These Web sites will give you a variety of information about natural gas, including the details about natural-gas-powered vehicles.

Web:
http://www.cng.com/html/ngv.htm
http://www.naturalgas.org/

A penny saved is a penny you have to do something with.

Be in the know. Check out "Secret Stuff" and "Intrigue".

Nuclear Energy

Nuclear energy produces approximately 20 percent of the energy used in the United States. In general, nuclear energy is a versatile form of power. Aside from the production of electricity, nuclear energy is put to such disparate uses as cancer treatments, explosive-detecting machines, medical instrument sterilizers, and smoke detectors. Nuclear usage in the United States is heavily regulated by an independent government agency called the Nuclear Regulatory Commission. They have a site on the Web where you can read about nuclear materials, handling and hazards. There are also more general nuclear resources that talk about the various uses and environmental concerns related to the use of nuclear energy.

Web:
http://www.me3.org/issues/nuclear/
http://www.nrc.gov/

Petroleum

Back in the olden days (millions of years ago), nobody knew what to do with all the dead dinosaurs and various other organic matter that were just sitting around composting. It was entirely too much for primitive people to use in their tomato gardens, so they just left it laying there. Eventually a lot of the organic matter fossilized and turned into a substance that we process and use as oil, gasoline and natural gas. You can find out more about petroleum, petroleum products and the oil industry by checking out the petroleum Usenet group. You can also read the FAQ (frequently asked question list) and browse the Web. Remember: Today's trash can be tomorrow's treasure.

Web:
http://www.slb.com/petr.dir/

Usenet:
sci.geo.petroleum

Renewable Energy

Right now, as you read this, there are clever people around the world thinking about ways to use renewable energy. They are coming up with new designs for batteries, generators, pumps and chargers to use wind, water and sun for fuel. Read about the neat gadgets they have modified or invented, or just check out the ideas and philosophy behind using renewable energy.

Web:
http://www.hgea.org/~daver/reneweng.htm
http://www.nrel.gov/

Usenet:
alt.energy.renewable

Solar Energy

Where I live in California, there is a lot of sun. In fact, there is such an abundance of sunlight that I can use it to power my souped-up solar-powered surfboard. But even if you don't surf, you may still want to check out solar energy information on the Net. On Usenet, you can discuss various aspects of solar energy with all the other solar buffs, talking about everything energy-related under the sun.

Web:
http://www.ises.org/
http://www.mrsolar.com/
http://www.solarenergy.net/tsen/database/planet.html

Usenet:
alt.solar.photovoltaic
alt.solar.thermal

PETROLEUM

Personally, I am always ready to learn more about petroleum.
My philosophy is: none of us lives forever, and it is good to be prepared, so when the end comes, I want to be ready.
After all, oil's well that ends well.

Wind Energy

I love to feel the wind in my hair while I am riding my skateboard. However, wind has other uses. It can also be harnessed for energy. You will find information about wind as well as experiments you can use for teaching about wind energy and windmills.

Web:
http://www.eren.doe.gov/RE/wind.html
http://www.risoe.dk/vea-wind/windlink.htm

World Energy Statistics

Numbers, numbers, numbers. What do you do when you need to find out how much natural gas the world is going to use in the year 2010? Well, you could just wait until 2010, but that would take a long time. Wouldn't it be faster to check with the Net?

Web:
http://www.eia.doe.gov/emeu/mer/contents.html

ENGINEERING

Aerospace Engineering

Aerospace engineering is the area of engineering that deals with aircraft and space vehicles. The Web site contains numerous links to Internet resources for aerospace engineers: information on NASA projects and missions, news, professional tools, publications, software, aerospace companies, and more. For discussion, the Usenet group is devoted to the technology of space flight.

Web:
http://www.db.erau.edu/www_virtual_lib/aerospace.html

Usenet:
sci.space.tech

Architectural Engineering

Architectural engineering is the profession that deals with the technical aspects of building design and construction. (In some countries, architectural engineers are known as building engineers.) Architecture and engineering are vastly different disciplines: not only in training and approach, but in the social aspects as well. Engineers and architects are two very different types of people who look at problems differently. Where an architect will create something out of nothing, changing and modifying and throwing away until he gets what he wants, an engineer will attack a problem by analyzing a mass of details while moving one step at a time toward a solution. The job of an architectural engineer is to bridge the gaps between these two disciplines. This is not a job for weenies. When an architectural engineer designs a building's structure, he or she will consider loads, structural systems, forces in structural members, and materials, all the while balancing the important considerations of the overall design. Clearly, architectural engineering is not an easy job. However, there are some Internet resources that can help you.

Web:
http://energy.arce.ukans.edu/wwwvl/wwwarce.htm

Audio Engineering

The Audio Engineering Society is a professional society devoted to audio technology. They maintain this Web page, which is a collection of links in the area of audio technology as well as related topics. You can find timely references to papers and articles on loudspeakers, sound reinforcement, microphones, disk recording, time-delay spectrometry and digital audio. For discussion, there are a number of Usenet groups in which you can participate. I have included the ones that are the most useful for audio engineering.

Web:
http://www.aes.org/resources/www-links/

Usenet:
rec.audio.high-end
rec.audio.opinion
rec.audio.pro
rec.audio.tech

What's your hurry? Stop at "Fun".

Look What I Found on the Net...

```
(from a FAQ referenced in the sci.space.tech Usenet group)

=================================================
    HOW LONG CAN A HUMAN LIVE UNPROTECTED IN SPACE?
=================================================

If you *don't* try to hold your breath, exposure to space for
half a minute or so is unlikely to produce permanent injury.
Holding your breath is likely to damage your lungs, something
scuba divers have to watch out for when ascending, and you'll
have eardrum trouble if your Eustachian tubes are badly plugged
up, but theory predicts - and animal experiments confirm -
that otherwise, exposure to vacuum causes no immediate injury.

You do not explode. Your blood does not boil. You do not freeze.
You do not instantly lose consciousness...
```

ENGINEERING

Biomedical Engineering

Biomedical engineering is an interdisciplinary field, combining engineering, physics and chemistry to develop instruments used to study and treat living organisms. Biomedical engineers design such devices as pacemakers, dialysis machines, medical lasers, surgical instruments, and so on. The Web is a good place to search for biomedical engineering information on the Net. You will find academic resources, publications and organizations, as well as information about jobs, grants and conferences. For discussion with other biomedical engineers, try Usenet.

Web:
  http://bme.www.ecn.purdue.edu/bme/
  http://mecca.mecca.org/BME/BMES/society/bmeshm.html

Usenet:
  sci.bio.technology
  sci.engr.biomed

Hey guys: want to make lots of **money** and meet **beautiful women**? Maybe its time to check out Chemical Engineering.

CAD (Computer Aided Design)

The aim of CAD (computer aided design) is to use computers for creating designs. A basic CAD system can be used to model a design, produce drawings, and keep track of a list of all the parts needed for a particular design. More advanced systems will provide sophisticated help to the engineer during the design process.

Web:
  http://www.cam.org/~flamy/cadcam.html
  http://www.flash.net/~cdhb/Cadlinks.htm
  http://www.phantomtech.com/cad_cam.htm

Usenet:
  alt.cad
  comp.lsi.cad
  sci.electronics.cad

Chemical Engineering

Chemical engineering is the study of the industrial applications of chemistry. In other words, chemical engineers use raw material to make stuff. Did you know that of the four main branches of engineering—civil, mechanical, electrical and chemical—chemical engineering has the fewest people, but they make the most money? Check the Net and see if you can find the formula.

Web:
  http://www.ciw.uni-karlsruhe.de/chem-eng.html
  http://www.retallick.com/resources/

Usenet:
  sci.chem.coatings
  sci.engr.chem

Listserv Mailing List:
  List Name: **cheme-l**
  Subscribe to: listserv@ulkyvm.louisville.edu

Civil Engineering

The term "civil engineering" was first used in the 18th century to describe engineering work performed by civilians for nonmilitary purposes. Today, civil engineering is a broad field, dealing with works of public utility: roads, buildings, bridges, dams, airports, tunnels, and so on (which is probably why the U.S. Army Corps of Engineers—civil engineers to the max—live inside the military). Here are some civil engineering sites from around the world. See what you can build with it.

Web:
  http://pw1.netcom.com/~toddvb/celinks.html
  http://www.ce.gatech.edu/WWW-CE/

Usenet:
  sci.engr.civil

Listserv Mailing List:
  List Name: **civil-l**
  Subscribe to: listserv@listserv.unb.ca

Cold Region Engineering

When the temperature falls below freezing (0 degrees centigrade, 32 degrees Fahrenheit), water solidifies and the natural world changes dramatically. This causes many engineering problems. For example, machinery may stop working properly, and many materials will change their properties. Nearly half our planet will, at some time during the year, experience temperatures below freezing. In fact, 20 percent of the Earth is underlaid by permafrost (permanently frozen subsoil). Thus, cold region engineering is an important discipline that draws from general engineering, earth sciences and physical sciences.

Web:
  http://www.crrel.usace.army.mil/

Defense Sciences Engineering

Defense sciences cover a range of engineering disciplines. This Web site, at the Lawrence Livermore National Laboratory, contains information on designing, testing and evaluating systems for national security. (Whose national security, you must figure out for yourself.) In addition, you can read about programs, projects and research in areas of electromagnetics, pulsed power, optics and material science.

Web:
  http://www-dsed.llnl.gov/

Electrical Engineering

Electrical engineering deals with systems and devices that use electric power and electric signals. The four main areas of this discipline are electronics, computers, communications and control, and electric power and machinery. If you are an electrical engineer (or a student), here are a lot of resources you will enjoy.

Web:
  http://arioch.gsfc.nasa.gov/wwwvl/ee.html
  http://www.eet.com/
  http://www.ieee.org/

Usenet:
  alt.engineering.electrical
  sci.engr.electrical.compliance
  sci.engr.electrical.sys-protection

Electrical Engineering

The next time you hear someone pooh-pooh electrical engineering, remind him of the following:

(1) In ancient Rome, there wasn't even one properly certified electrical engineer, and within several hundred years, the entire Roman civilization was toppled by bands of invading barbarians.

(2) No electrical engineer has ever been impeached by the Senate of the United States.

(3) In one survey after another, famous supermodels and movie stars choose electrical engineers as the type of engineer they would prefer to be stranded with in an abandoned hydroelectric plant.

(4) As a group, the electrical engineers of America collectively make more money than the President of the United States and his wife put together.

(5) Electrical engineers never have to wait in line at a restaurant, and they always get the best seats in a movie theater.

(6) Every year, on Electrical Engineering Day, everyone has to find an electrical engineer and do whatever he or she wants for the entire day.

(7) In certain primitive societies, electrical engineers are considered to be gods, even more important than writers.

Electronics Engineering

Electronics engineering is the branch of electrical engineering that deals with electrical devices and systems. Electronics engineers work in such areas as chips and computer components, digital signal processing, industrial embedded computing, microcontrollers and microprocessors, as well as real-time and embedded systems. (I wish I had an electronics engineer right now. My toaster only toasts the bread on one side.)

Web:
  http://engr-www.unl.edu/ee/eeshop/netsites.html
  http://www.eg3.com/ebox.htm
  http://www.electronicnews.com/

ENGINEERING

Engineering Failures

When things go wrong, the most important thing to do is to ask "Why?" Why, for example, did the space shuttle Challenger blow up in 1986? Why did the skywalk collapse in Kansas City in 1981? The answers to these questions and a lot more are to be found in the FAQ (frequently asked question list) for the **sci.engr** Usenet groups. (By the way, the space shuttle blew up when a failed pressure seal [O-ring] leaked combustion gases. The Kansas City skywalk collapsed because the nuts and rods that were supposed to support two levels of catwalk were inadequate because of a poor design.)

Web:
  http://members.aol.com/rongraham1/failure1.html

Engineering Index

Engineering covers so wide a range of activities as to almost defy definition. Still, such trifles never stopped me, so here goes: Engineering is the profession in which a knowledge of science and mathematics is used to control the materials and forces of nature. If you have any interest in any type of engineering, paste this Web site in your hat. Here you will find links to just about any type of engineering you can imagine (and several you can't imagine).

Web:
  http://arioch.gsfc.nasa.gov/wwwvl/engineering.html

Famous engineering failures in history:

- Collapse of the Kansas City skywalk in 1981
- Explosion of the space shuttle Challenger in 1986
- The inability of MIT engineering student Edwin Bestertester to get a date from 1992 to the present

Engineering Talk and General Discussion

If you are a part of the engineering community, you may want to participate in an ongoing discussion of engineering topics. If so, there are plenty of places on Usenet where you can talk shop.

Usenet:
  sci.engr
  sci.engr.advanced-tv
  sci.engr.color
  sci.engr.control
  sci.engr.joining.misc
  sci.engr.joining.welding
  sci.engr.manufacturing
  sci.engr.marine.hydrodynamics
  sci.engr.metallurgy
  sci.engr.micromachining
  sci.engr.mining
  sci.engr.safety
  sci.engr.television.advanced
  sci.engr.television.broadcast
  sci.materials
  sci.materials.ceramics
  sci.systems

Geotechnical Engineering

Geotechnical engineering is the engineering discipline related to the technology and methods of soil mechanics. Geotechnical engineers build things that must interact with geological structures. If you ever go to a party with such people, you will hear them talk about consolidation, lateral earth pressures, bearing capacity and stability. The father of modern geotechnical engineering (soil mechanics, actually) is the Hungarian-American Karl von Terzaghi (1883-1963). This Web site has a collection of information regarding organizations, jobs, publications, conferences, historical notes, as well as links to related resources around the world.

Web:
  http://geotech.civen.okstate.edu/wwwVL/

Usenet:
  sci.engr.geomechanics
  sci.geo.geology

ENGINEERING

Mechanical Engineering

Mechanical engineering is the broadest of the engineering sciences. In simple terms, mechanical engineering concerns itself with things that move in some way. More generally, this discipline can be divided into two main parts: machine design and working with heat. Here is a Web site that contains a good number of links to mechanical engineering resources.

Web:
http://cdr.stanford.edu/html/WWW-ME/

Usenet:
sci.engr.mech

Listserv Mailing List:
List Name: mech-l
Subscribe to: listserv@listserv.uta.edu

Break a rule.

Nuclear Engineering

So you want to impress your best girl (or guy) and show your parents that you really can amount to something? Go to this Web site and learn something about nuclear engineering (applying technology based on energy absorbed or released during atomic reactions). How hard could it be? After all, it's not rocket science.

Web:
http://web.mit.edu/ned/www/links.html

Usenet:
alt.engr.nuclear

Look What I Found on the Net...

```
Newsgroup: sci.engr
Subject: Almighty Money

> Why is it that engineers have to spend an ungodly amount of
> time in the library for weeks on end, only to make so-so
> money?  I see plenty of people who have everything but an
> engineering degree make much better money in the business
> world.  Our sales personnel are driving Mercedes.  None of
> our engineers are.
>
> Don't you think we ought to be making as much as lawyers or
> doctors?  We put real brain power into our jobs, and we did
> our time in school.

You might want to think on the positive side.  As a mechanical
engineer I do most of my own car repairs, I can better assess
the engineering of a vehicle in the first place, I can do a
better job  of choosing and fixing appliances, and I enjoy
what I do.

Why would you want to drive a Mercedes anyway?  They are rear
wheel drive pigs that need a lot of expensive maintenance.
```

ENVIRONMENT

Cat got your mouse?

Optical Engineering

Do you need to shed light on your engineering problems? Here are some resources devoted to optical engineering (applying the science of light) and to photonics (transmission of information via light, usually lasers). By the way, when I was a graduate student at the University of California at San Diego, one of my best friends was an optical engineer. I used to do my math homework with her.

Web:
http://www.optics.org/
http://www.osa.org/

Usenet:
sci.optics

Robotics

Robotics is the study and creation of machines guided by automatic controls (robots). Although it is fashionable to think of robots as being humanoid, outside of science fiction, robots look a lot more like your toaster than like your Uncle Henry.

Web:
http://piglet.cs.umass.edu:4321/robotics.html

Usenet:
comp.robotics.misc
comp.robotics.research

What do you do if you happen to be married to a member of the British royal family and want to learn to relate to your mate? Not to worry. The Net has lots and lots of resources to help you understand robotics.

ENVIRONMENT

Air Pollution

Everyone knows that methanesulfonic acid is an atmospheric aerosol particle formed from the oxidation of dimethylsulfide which has been produced by phytoplankton. But what about the difficult stuff? When it comes to air pollution, you don't want to get left out in the cold. Here are some resources that provide lots of data, a glossary and relevant information from the U.S. Environmental Protection Agency (EPA).

Web:
http://www.carnell.com/environment_health/clean_air/
http://www.epa.gov/docs/oar/
http://www.epa.gov/iaq/
http://www.phymac.med.wayne.edu/facultyprofile/penney/cohq/co1.htm
http://www.shsu.edu/~chemistry/Glossary/glos.html

Atmosphere Pollution Prevention

Do your part to help make the air healthier by finding out about the U.S. Environmental Protection Agency's Methane Outreach program (methane contributes to global warming) and Green Lights program (energy efficient lighting). This site has lots of information, links to other resources, and a variety of software tools.

Web:
http://www.epa.gov/appd.html

Biosphere

The "biosphere" refers to the part of our world in which life can exist: from the surface of the Earth—that is, the oceans and the land—up about 10 km (6 miles) into the atmosphere. Obviously, this is an important area of the universe that we should understand. After all, all our stuff is here.

Web:
http://ice.ucdavis.edu/mab/
http://www.biospherics.org/

Listserv Mailing List:
List Name: biosph-l
Subscribe to: listserv@listserv.aol.com

ENVIRONMENT

Chemicals in the Environment

There are many chemicals in our environment that can be harmful to human beings, and it is important to be able to separate the truth from the myths. When you need real information, read carefully and ask yourself, "Is what I am reading credible? Should I believe it?" When you need to do research, start with this Web site where you will find factual, scientific information about many different toxic chemicals.

Web:
http://atsdr1.atsdr.cdc.gov:8080/toxfaq.html

Coastal Management

People think that the coast is all fun and sun with the ocean crashing against the beach and the sun setting across the water. Well, it's that very water that makes the coast so tricky to manage. And then there's that rumor that has been going around about California falling off into the ocean. It's enough to give anyone a headache. Fortunately, there are resources on the Net that deal with topics related to coastal management and resources, so there is a place to turn when it's time to come up with some revolutionary ideas in the coastal management field.

Web:
http://www.webdirectory.com/Land_Conservation/Coastal_Preservation/

Coral Reefs

Coral reefs are limestone formations found in shallow tropical oceans where the water is over 22 degrees centigrade (72 degrees Fahrenheit). Reefs are produced by sea animals which secrete calcium carbonate (limestone) that, over thousands of years, builds up into massive formations. Coral reefs are part of the undersea ecosystem and provide important ecological support for coral as well as other animal and plant life. There are several types of reefs: fringing reefs that are platforms running continuous with the shore, barrier reefs that are separated from the shore by an expanse of deep lagoon, and atolls that surround a lagoon. Although coral reefs cover less than 0.2 percent of the Earth's ocean-covered area, they create a living environment for a great many of the ocean's species. At these Web sites, you can read about all the things that coral reefs do for humans, and why we should save them from contamination and physical destruction.

Web:
http://coral.aoml.noaa.gov/
http://www.coral.org/Home.html
http://www.indiana.edu/~reefpage/

Ecological Economics

What does economics have to do with the environment? A lot. Environmental factors are often influenced, at least indirectly, by monetary decisions. Thus, it is important to rethink our approach to finance, resources and money in terms of environmental concerns. If you love the Earth more than you love your money, this will make sense to you. These resources will allow you to see what other people are saying, doing and thinking about these important issues.

Web:
http://csf.colorado.edu/ecol-econ/

Listserv Mailing List:
List Name: **ecol-econ**
Subscribe to: **listserv@csf.colorado.edu**

Life here in Southern California is a lot more than surfing and snorkeling and swimming. Sometimes we have to take a break and get a massage.

But when we do get serious, we get serious. If you want to join in, subscribe to the Coastal Management resources on the Net.

If you can't go surfing, you might as well talk about the water.

Endangered Rivers

Rivers don't grow on trees, so it's a nice idea to take care of the ones we have. Here are some Web sites that will keep you informed about endangered and threatened rivers that are suffering from the effects of mining, toxic dumping, waste dumping, pollution and other human threats.

Web:
http://www.amrivers.org/
http://www.irn.org/

ENVIRONMENT 241

Imagine. You walk down to your favorite river, and there it is: gone. Don't let this happen to you. Check out the **Endangered Rivers** resource, and look for your personal favorite. After all, if you are like me, you probably don't have enough to worry about.

Adopt a river today.

Endangered Species

If you are looking for a Chadwick Beach Cotton Mouse (Peromyscus gossypinus restrictus) or a Big Thicket Hog-nosed Skunk (Conepatus mesoleucus telmalestes), I can tell you right now, don't waste your time: both these animals are extinct. I do want you to understand that it is normal for animals and plants to become extinct. However, in the past century, the activities of mankind have resulted in an abnormally high number of extinctions. This is not good because it signals a possible degradation of the natural environments around the world, which would ultimately have significant impact on human beings. To help you understand what is happening, here is information about endangered, threatened and extinct species, as well as the environments on which these species depend.

Web:
  http://www.fws.gov/r9endspp/endspp.html
  http://www.nwf.org/nwf/endangered/
  http://www.wcmc.org.uk/data/database/
    rl_anml_combo.html
  http://www.worldwildlife.org/action

Environment Talk and General Discussion

Whether you just like to talk about saving the environment or you actually want to *do* something about saving the environment, these Usenet discussion groups are for you. Earth lovers all over the planet talk about various aspects of ecology and the environment. Discussion ranges widely, from helpful home tips to technical scientific topics.

Usenet:
  alt.desert.restoration
  alt.earth.crisis
  alt.org.sierra-club
  alt.save.the.earth
  alt.wastewater
  sci.environment
  talk.environment

Environmental Protection Agency

The United States Environmental Protection Agency (EPA) is the American federal government agency charged with protecting the public's health and the natural environment. The EPA Web site offers a massive amount of information about the environment: news, programs, publications, regulations, contracts and grants. There are also special resources for teachers and children.

Web:
  http://www.epa.gov/

Environmental Resources

There are several places on the Net that are loaded with information designed to enhance cooperation among people interested in environmental activities. Would you like to save the world, but you don't have enough time? Let's start small. Hug a tree with one hand and, with the other, use your browser to connect to some of these environmental resources.

Web:
  http://ecosys.drdr.virginia.edu/EcoWeb.html
  http://www.econet.apc.org/econet/
  http://www.envirolink.org/

242 ENVIRONMENT

Environmental Scorecard

If you are American, you may be interested to see how your congressional representatives rank on the National Environmental Scorecard. This ranking is created by the League of Conservation Voters to draw attention to voting patterns followed by the individual congressmen and congresswomen. How did your elected officials do? My two senators—both women—scored high. One of them had a 1998 ranking of 100%. Her previous annual scores were 95% and 100%. The other senator also had a 1998 ranking of 100%. Her previous annual scores were 84% and 89%. (Now, if I could just get them to help me when I clean up the back yard.)

Web:
http://www.pirg.org/demos/score/

Environmental Search Engine

When you need to find data and information related to the environment, you can focus quickly using a search engine specifically geared toward environmental resources. Choose from many, many Web sites or archives, or perform a quick search on several databases at the same time.

Web:
http://www.isleuth.com/envi.html

Do elected officials know the score? Maybe yes and maybe no, but if you live in the United States, you can check your congressional representative's environmental scorecard. (Environmental hint: After you are finished connecting to the Web, be sure to recycle all your leftover electrons.)

Environmental Web Directory

Here on Earth, we have more environment than you can shake a biodegradable stick at. But some days, it seems as if our large but limited supply of environment is being damaged faster than we can even understand. Is this true, or is the Earth capable of taking care of itself? Check the information on the Net and see what *you* think.

Web:
http://www.webdirectory.com/

Look What I Found on the Net...

```
Newsgroup: sci.environment
Subject: Re: Environmental Lawyers

> Just a quick question.
> Are there any companies out there which hires
> individuals interested in environment law?
> I really would like to know.
> Thanks in advance

Plenty of consulting firms and industrial companies hire
environmental lawyers.  Pay is commensurate with experience and
skills, of course.

However, most such positions require extensive writing and
research.  Before you apply, I would suggest a good course in
English spelling and grammer.
```

ENVIRONMENT 243

Forest Conservation

Would you like to help protect forests? How about supporting biodiversity and indigenous cultures? If so, these sites are for you. Lots and lots of reference material relating to forest environments around the world. (However, to save disk space, information is restricted to only those forests in our local biosphere.)

Web:
http://forests.lic.wisc.edu/worldfor.html
http://forests.org/
http://www.fguardians.org/

Greenpeace

If the military is not your style, but you want a sense of adventure on the open seas, check out Greenpeace. Read up on ship movements, press releases, latest demonstrations and job opportunities, and see pictures and publications of this environmental activist group.

Web:
http://www.greenpeace.org/

National Wetlands Inventory

The Net is great. You can check on America's wetlands without having to put on waders and slosh about in the muck. There is lots of information here, courtesy of the U.S. Fish and Wildlife Service. You will find hard data, suitable for researchers, as well as links to resources for children and teachers.

Web:
http://www.nwi.fws.gov/

National Wildlife Refuges

This Web site provides information about the National Wildlife Refuge System and topics of interest related to wildlife management and natural resources management. This is a great place to go in the middle of the night when you need a copy of the "Review of Potential Impacts of Oil Development on the Coastal Plain of the Arctic National Wildlife Refuge".

Web:
http://bluegoose.arw.r9.fws.gov/

Ozone Depletion

Whether you are a serious researcher or just a student looking for information for your term paper entitled "Our Friend the Stratosphere", here are a couple of resources that contain enough information about ozone depletion to keep you satisfied for a long time. The ozone layer, by the way, refers to the area in the stratosphere (about 15-40 km straight up) in which ozone is formed by the action of ultraviolet radiation (coming from the sun) on oxygen. The ozone layer keeps a lot of this radiation from getting down to where we live. If the ozone layer is thinned—by pollutants, for example—a lot of bad things might happen. Don't say I didn't warn you.

Web:
http://www.epa.gov/docs/ozone
http://www.ozone.org/

ISN'T OZONE GREAT?
If there's too much you die, and if there's not enough you get skin cancer.
If you want more details, look under Ozone Depletion
(a great way to spend a Saturday night).

Planet Diary

Did you think nothing happened today? Think again. A lot of important world-class stuff is happening right now. Tune in to the Planet Diary and find out the locations of earthquakes, extreme weather and other environmental events. If you are the type of person who enjoys keeping track of geological, astronomical, meteorological, biological and environmental events, you'll love this site. Now that we have the Net, you will always be in the know. The Earth may try to run, but it can't hide.

Web:
http://www.planetdiary.com/

ENVIRONMENT

Population

Some people call it population. Some people call it overpopulation. I guess it depends on whether or not you are sitting on the side of the bread with the butter. Should you be concerned about overpopulation? Take a look at the statistics regarding population growth, fertility and mortality, and see what you think. In the meantime, as you make up your mind, you might consider that in the time it took you to read this paragraph, 100 people were born and 40 people died.

Web:
http://popindex.princeton.edu/
http://www.census.gov/cgi-bin/ipc/popclockw
http://www.overpopulation.com/
http://www.popexpo.net/english.html
http://www.popnet.org/

Rainforests

A rain forest is a type of forest found in certain tropical areas in South America and Asia, where there is a lot of rain. The rain forests of the world are large and contain many different species of plants and animals. Although rain forests seem remote to most of us, they are important for several reasons. First, the large number of trees and other plants help balance the global climate, by contributing to the rain and water systems, and by storing and absorbing carbon dioxide. The wide variety of plants also helps us in other ways: as an important source of new drugs and chemicals, new types of foods (fruits, vegetables and nuts), as well as various valuable woods (teak, mahogany, rosewood, balsa, sandalwood). Unfortunately, the late twentieth century has seen a significant portion of the rainforest destroyed as people have cleared large areas for logging and agriculture.

Web:
http://www.igc.apc.org/ran/
http://www.rainforest-alliance.org/

> Experiment.
> (Nothing bad will happen.)

> Life begins at 0.

Sea Level Data

I spend a lot of time at sea level (and some time below sea level), and I can tell you that the ocean is not flat. However, even averaging things out, sea level is not the same everywhere in the world. This site analyzes sea level data received by satellite, and shows you the anomalies using easy-to-understand colored maps (well, relatively easy-to-understand colored maps).

Web:
http://nng.esoc.esa.de/ers/alti.html

Seas and Water Directory

This site is dedicated to the conservation of reservoirs, oceans and aquatic life, and to finding solutions to help alleviate water problems. You will find links to information about acid rain, toxic hazards and specific action groups that are focusing on water as their part of the efforts to save the environment.

Web:
http://www.igc.apc.org/igc/www.water.html

ULS Report

The ULS Report is a newsletter devoted to helping people "use less stuff" and, thereby, become more friendly to the environment. You can read the newsletter in two different ways: by visiting the Web site (where you can also browse through back issues) or by subscribing (for free) to the mailing list. The mailing list also serves as a discussion group. Read the ULS Report, and learn how to do more by using less.

Web:
http://cygnus-group.com/ULS/Current_ULS_Reports/Reports.html

Majordomo Mailing List:
List Name: **uls**
Subscribe to: **majordomo@mail.msen.com**

Waste Reduction Tips and Factsheets

Here is useful information showing how to reduce waste and conserve resources. The focus is on source reduction and re-use rather than just recycling. Unfortunately, they left out the most important tip: buy Harley Hahn books in bulk, and never, ever throw them away.

Web:
   http://www.web.apc.org/rco/factsheet/fs_a37.html

Usenet:
   sci.environment.waste

TOO MUCH STUFF?
The Net has lots and lots of resources for Waste Reduction.

EXERCISE

Aerobics

Some people cringe each time they hear their aerobics instructor say, "Only eight more." Others get that adrenaline rush after cycling up their local mountain. You can utilize the Net to find information about all forms of aerobic activity and talk to other aerobics fans who will remind you that all your efforts are worthwhile.

Web:
   http://www.turnstep.com/

Usenet:
   misc.fitness.aerobic

Fitness

Statistics show that 37% of all statistics about fitness are meaningless. Or maybe it's 74%. Actually, I think it's 98%. I would be hard-pressed to think of any part of our popular culture that is so important, yet so misunderstood and riddled with half-truths. Fitness instructors, magazine writers, aerobics teachers, health club employees, and many health professionals repeat scientific-sounding silliness so often that I would challenge anyone to explain how to tell the difference between what is true and what seems to be true just because people believe it. I am going to give you some fitness resources, but for goodness sakes, don't believe everything you read. For example, I found a Web site that says if you weigh 150 pounds and you garden for 10 minutes, you will use 49 calories. A 175 pound person, however, would use 57 calories. Do you believe this? Is it even meaningful? (In this case, the numbers were taken from a publication put out by a running shoe company. and posted on the Web.) It's good to use your body, but, please, don't forget to use your brain.

Web:
   http://k2.kirtland.cc.mi.us/~balbachl/fitness.htm
   http://primusweb.com/fitnesspartner/
   http://www.fitnesslink.com/
   http://www.fitnessonline.com/
   http://www.fitnesszone.com/

Fitness for Kids

Remember, the kids of today are the kids of tomorrow. But it won't be long before the kids of tomorrow are adults, and, by then, they will be a lot better off if they were the kind of kids who exercised when they were young.

Web:
   http://www.coolrunning.com/school/
   http://www.fitnesslink.com/changes/kids.htm
   http://www.kidshealth.org/kid/food/

Why be normal? Read "Bizarre".

246 EXERCISE

Fitness Talk and General Discussion

We all know we should exercise every day. And we all know that sometimes we don't like to exercise every day. So when you are having one of those days, maybe it would be more fun to talk about it than actually do it. If so, Usenet is always there, and lots of people are ready to talk.

Usenet:
 misc.fitness
 misc.fitness.aerobic
 misc.fitness.misc
 misc.fitness.weights
 rec.fitness

Powerlifting

Powerlifting is competitive weightlifting with an emphasis on brute strength. In powerlifting, competitors perform three types of lifts: a squat, dead lift and bench press. (Olympic lifting, by contrast, uses the snatch and clean-and-jerk, in which technique is more important.) Powerlifting can be rewarding, but it is crucial to train properly and to know what you are doing. These Web sites have a variety of powerlifting resources for beginners and for veterans.

Web:
 http://www.drsquat.com/
 http://www.powerlifting.com/
 http://www.strongestmanalive.com/

You can't be too rich, too good a writer, too handsome or too strong.
(Well, that's always been my philosophy anyway.)

I can't help you with the money, talent or good looks, but if you want to be strong, spend some time on the Net. Maybe you'll get inspired and build yourself up to be the next world powerlifting champion. (If you do, be sure to mention this book.)

Look What I Found on the Net...

```
Newsgroup: rec.running
Subject: Throwing up

> Does anyone out there have any explanation as to why I would
> be throwing up after a long run?
>
> I had trained all winter and never got sick, but lately
> I'm throwing up on any run lasting more than 1 hour 15 min.

The two times I've been extremely dehydrated, I've felt very
nauseous.  Dehydration could be your problem.
```

EXERCISE

Pregnancy and Exercise

Exercising during pregnancy can help you be more comfortable with the weight gain, prepare for the rigor of labor, and recover more quickly after the delivery. You may also be able to minimize the discomforts of pregnancy, as well as improve your mood and sense of well-being. Here are some resources to show you which exercises will help the most, and how to plan a program for yourself.

Web:
http://www.babycenter.com/refcap/758.html
http://www.lifematters.com/rofintro.html

Running

Running can be delightful, if you are in good shape and you know what you are doing (and you have good shoes). When I want to relax, I run up a long, steep hill that is one mile from bottom to top. The first time was difficult, but, with practice (I like to do it every day), I got used to it and now the run is fun. Once your body becomes fit, you begin to realize that running is very much a mental challenge. Believe me, running an entire mile up a steep hill is difficult, and, although I know that my body can do it, I have to summon up my mental reserves to make the experience pleasant and fulfilling. If you are a runner (or you want to be a runner), you can use these resources to help yourself understand what you need to know, and to motivate yourself to excel.

Web:
http://www.clark.net/pub/pribut/spsport.html
http://www.coolrunning.com/
http://www.ontherun.com/
http://www.runnersworld.com/
http://www.runningpage.com/
http://www.straznitskas.com/george/

Usenet:
rec.running

Need a laugh? Check out "Humor and Jokes".

Sports Doctor

When you want to play doctor and nobody is around, just connect to this Web site. You can pretend to be a sports doctor and click on your patient's symptoms until you reach a diagnosis. You can also find a medical glossary to help explain some of the terms used in the diagnosis, as well as read explanations of various medical conditions. And, if you like to reduce your appetite, you can watch movies of various surgical procedures.

Web:
http://www.medfacts.com/sprtsdoc.htm

Stretching and Flexibility

This is a large, well-organized, well-researched document that covers every aspect of stretching and flexibility. You will find a great deal of information about mechanics and physiology for health care students and professionals.

Web:
http://www.enteract.com/~bradapp/docs/rec/stretching/

Walking

Walking can be a lot more meaningful than making regular trips from the computer to the refrigerator. In fact, walking is a great form of exercise. This site has information about power walking, race walking, and walking for sport, exercise and leisure. If you are thinking about improving your fitness level, take a look at these resources. For discussion, try Usenet.

Web:
http://www.teleport.com/~walking/walking.shtml

Usenet:
misc.fitness.walking

Weightlifting and Bodybuilding

Do you eat nutritious high protein and swallow raw eggs? Try to build up your shoulders, your chest, arms and legs? Do you do press-ups and chin-ups, cloak and jerk, do the snatch? Do you think dynamic tension must be a catch? Well, try the Net, and maybe, in just seven days, it can make you a man.

Web:
http://www.getbig.com/
http://www.musclenet.com/
http://www.weightsnet.com/

Usenet:
alt.sport.weightlifting
misc.fitness.weights

Women's Fitness

Being fit and healthy requires you to have a variety of information available when you need it. Here are some resources that cover fitness and health considerations for women: toning, weight control, weightlifting, workout routines, nutrition, and so on. I have also included resources to help you find information about women's sports and activities around the world.

Web:
http://fiat.gslis.utexas.edu/~lewisa/womsprt.html
http://www.gogirlmag.com/
http://www.justwomen.com/contents.html

Buy it, repair it, sell it.
See "Homes".

Yoga

I have been doing yoga for years (Ashtanga and Iyengar styles), and I can tell you that it works. However, it is hard work, and a good yoga workout will make you sweat profusely. Perhaps the best way to put it is that yoga is like a sewer: what you get out of it depends on what you put into it. The Web sites have a lot of information about yoga styles, asanas (poses), traditions and classes. If you want to see what people talk about when they are not doing their practice, take a look at the Usenet discussion group. Here you will find all the traditional cultural pursuits of the yoga community: sharing ideas, discussing personal growth, gossip about other people, and complaining.

Web:
http://www.spiritweb.org/Spirit/Yoga/Overview.html
http://www.timages.com/yoga.htm
http://www.yogafinder.com/
http://www2.gdi.net/~mjm/

Usenet:
alt.yoga

Look What I Found on the Net...

```
Newsgroup: misc.fitness.weights
Subject: People Who Experiment

>> I will tell you a story.  We were experimenting with a new
>> veterinary drug (not for humans).  A single vial contained
>> several doses for big cows.
>>
>> A friend of mine used the whole vial all at once.  He
>> agonized for several hours.  But he was happy about the
>> whole experience as the next day his body was completely
>> changed.
>>
>> The point is, people willing to try crazy stuff can be found
>> all over the world.

> His body changed overnight?  In what way?

He was leaner (he excreted a lot of water), and his muscles
were harder than anything I have ever touched.

And yes, he was bigger overnight (could be due to a vasodilatory
effect of the drug).
```

FAMILIES AND PARENTING

Adoption

Adoption is both difficult and exciting. These sites offer information for anyone involved in an adoption: birth parents, adoptees and adoptive parents. You can find answers to general, legal and medical questions, information about adoption agencies and publications, and advice on foreign adoption. The mailing list provides a forum for discussing anything relating to adoption and is open to adoptive parents, adoptees, birth parents, social workers, counselors and anyone else interested in the adoption process.

Web:
   http://www.adoptex.org/
   http://www.adopting.com/
   http://www.adopting.org/
   http://www.adoption.org/

Usenet:
   alt.adoption.adoptive.parenting
   alt.adoption.korean
   alt.adoption.searching
   alt.support.adoption.advocacy
   alt.support.birth-parent
   soc.adoption.adoptees
   soc.adoption.parenting

Listserv Mailing List:
   List Name: **adoption**
   Subscribe to: **listserv@maelstrom.stjohns.edu**

Babies

Babies want most of all to be fed, loved and changed. But when there's something wrong, it can be hard to tell what the problem is—or even if there is one. Parenting can be frustrating sometimes. These resources have information about caring for babies. Just the thing to read when you can't sleep at night.

Web:
   http://www.babycenter.com/
   http://www.babyonline.com/

Babies Online

Conception can be a lot of fun. And the day you deliver the baby, I'm sure you will be awfully busy. But what about the 280 days in between? How do you keep from being bored?
Easy. Spend your time exploring some baby-related Web sites. By the time the little one shows up, you'll know so much about children, they'll call you Mom.

Breastfeeding

There are special issues that must be considered by mothers who breastfeed. These Internet resources are great places for talking about and reading about the problems and rewards of breastfeeding. Some of the topics include attachment parenting, weaning, extended nursing, nursing in public, working mothers who breastfeed, tandem nursing, societal attitudes toward nursing, and nursing during pregnancy.

Web:
   http://www.efn.org/~djz/birth/breastfeeding.html
   http://www.lalecheleague.org/

Usenet:
   misc.kids.breastfeeding

Majordomo Mailing List:
   List Name: **parent-l**
   Subscribe to: **majordomo@uts.edu.au**

Child Activism

Children's rights is the main topic for discussion in these Usenet groups. Read and post your own thoughts and ideas regarding the social and political issues relating to children. Hint: If your child is going to grow up to be famous, be careful what you say and do, as it may all end up in a book.

Usenet:
   alt.activism.children
   alt.activism.youth-rights

250 FAMILIES AND PARENTING

Child Discipline

To spank or not to spank—that is the question. These groups mostly contain a long-running debate about whether it is morally and politically acceptable to spank children. However, there are occasional threads about alternative methods of discipline and hints on "positive parenting".
My personal hint is to speak softly, and carry a big stick.

Usenet:
  alt.parenting.spanking
  alt.parenting.spanking.moderated

Child Safety

Many accidents are avoidable. However, the little ones can't plan for themselves, so we have to make sure that our houses, cars and play areas are safe. There are so many possible ways a kid can get into trouble that it is difficult to think of them all yourself. My suggestion is to visit these Web sites and take the time to go over the lists of safety information. I bet you'll find yourself saying, "I never would have thought of that."

Web:
  http://www.childsafety.org/
  http://www.sosnet.com/safety/safety1.html
  http://www.xmission.com/~gastown/safe/safe2.htm

Look What I Found on the Net...

```
Newsgroups: alt.parenting.spanking
Subject: Beating the Devil Out of Them

Deut. 21:18-21 commands parents to stone disobedient sons to
death along with sons who have an alcohol problem or an eating
disorder.

Deut. 22:20, 21 advocates stoning girls to death for premarital
sex.  Daughters of priests were burned rather than stoned for
premarital sex (Lev. 21:9).

Deut. 13:6-10 says a man may execute his children for deviating
from Judaism.

In 2 Kings 2:23, 24, 42 children are torn apart by two she-bears
for childishly making fun of the prophet Elisha's receding
hairline.

Psalms 137:9 recommends bashing Babylonian babies' brains out
while Jer. 18:21 thunders, "Therefore deliver up their children
to the famine and pour out their blood by the force of the
sword; and let their wives be bereaved of their children and be
widows."

The point is, the handful of verses about beating children need
to be viewed in the context of their culture of origin.
The ancient Israelites were perfectly comfortable with behavior
that would nowadays constitute, not only child abuse, but war
crimes in violation of the Geneva Convention.  Anyone who states
that they have a religious duty to beat their children with a
rod because the Book of Proverbs says so needs to explain
whether or not they also believe in the literal meaning of the
Old Testament verses about killing children.  If not, how does
such an individual determine which bible verses to obey and
which ones to disregard?
```

FAMILIES AND PARENTING

Child Safety on the Internet

If you are worried about your kids wandering around the Internet by themselves, have a look at these tips that will give you a better idea of how to protect young minds from inappropriate material.

Web:
http://www.familyguidebook.com/
http://www.ou.edu/oupd/kidsafe/warn_kid.htm
http://www.safesurf.com/lifegard.htm
http://www.smartparent.com/

Child Support

How do you stand on issues of custody and child support? Find out the thoughts of others affected by these issues and learn about current legislation.

Usenet:
alt.child-support

Children

Kids say the darnedest things. Impart your information and experience regarding children from the cradle onward. Anecdotes, advice on doctors, behavior, activities, discipline and schooling legislation are just a few of the topics covered. The Web site has information on various issues that arise when rearing children.

Web:
http://www.familyweb.com/faqs/

Usenet:
misc.kids
misc.kids.info
misc.kids.moderated

Look What I Found on the Net...

```
Newsgroups: misc.kids
Subject: My daddy dressed me

>> Well, Carrie's Daddy dressed her yesterday, and what a
>> combination he came up with!  She was wearing a pair of
>> overalls, bright red with...

>> Normally, if Daddy dresses the kids, I leave on what he puts
>> on them, not wanting to belittle his efforts.  But normally
>> he does better than yesterday.

> I've been away from misc.kids for a while and, on tuning in
> today, it is disappointing to see that this sexist crap is
> still going on.  The traditional "this color goes with that"
> attitude has clearly long been dropped from fad wear, in which
> any and every color is worn together.

Sorry, but I have to disagree.  While I personally do not care
if my son matches when he plays, my wife and I do try to make
sure he "matches" if we go out.  (Of course, I tend to have a
little more liberal interpretation of what matches than my wife
does, but that seems to be common given the father/mother
responses. :-)  Now, I'm not saying it is important for a young
child to match.  I don't place that much weight on it.  However,
one of the things I see later on in life, especially with males,
is that wearing the appropriate clothes to work/interviews, etc.
one feels much more confident when one isn't concerned about
whether their tie matches their suit or if it clashes...
```

Children with Special Needs

Raising a child with a disability is difficult, and doing a good job can be time-consuming, tiring and expensive. But perhaps worst of all, spending a lot of time with a child with special needs can be a lonely experience for you. If you have such a child, you may enjoy participating in this mailing list, and browsing the associated Web site. This is a support group for parents or others who care for children with physical or mental developmental disabilities. It is important for you to remember that such problems are common, and you are not alone. Talking with other people who face similar problems and challenges can make all the difference in the world.

Web:
http://rdz.acor.org/lists/our-kids/

Listserv Mailing List:
List Name: **our-kids**
Subscribe to: **listserv@maelstrom.stjohns.edu**

Dads

It gets tiring hearing Mr. Mom jokes after a while. Dads, here is a little portion of the Internet just for you. Read through papers on men and children, gather information on interaction with kids, connect to an electronic bulletin board and chat system for dads, get a newsletter called At-Home Dad, and send in your opinions and experiences about fatherhood.

Web:
http://www.cyfc.umn.edu/Fathernet/
http://www.fathermag.com/
http://www.fathers.com/

Usenet:
alt.dads-rights
alt.dads-rights.unmoderated

Family Resources

When I was a kid, our family used to have a great time on Saturday nights, gathered around the computer—in those days, it was an old black and white job—exploring the Internet together. Then we'd all go out for ice cream, and run around having good-natured fun. Yup, no doubt about it, the family that Webs together, does something or other together. But don't take my word for it. Here are some places to visit together. (Don't forget the ice cream.)

Web:
http://family.disney.com/
http://www.familyresource.org/
http://www.happyfamilies.com/

Keeping the Family Together

These days, it's hard to keep the family together.

Dad's in his study, using the Net to check the sports scores; Mom's in the kitchen with her laptop computer, cruising the Web for recipes; Junior is downloading free game software; and Sis is up all night talking to her friends on IRC.

Sometimes it seems as if everyone is in a different world, and modern parents despair of creating any real family spirit.

But now there is a way. All you have to do is hold regular family get-togethers, where everyone gathers around the family PC as you visit a family Web site. Staying together has never been so easy.

Foster Parents

Being a foster parent can be tricky and can test your ability to adapt to new situations. However, the Net has great support groups of other foster parents. Foster parents gather on the Net to talk about their joys and experiences. The Web sites have a great deal of information about children's specific physical and mental conditions and how to deal with them, as well as articles and hints on foster parenting and a bulletin board to which you can post messages.

Web:
http://spitfire.cwv.net/~emil/stress.html
http://www.fosterparents.com/

Usenet:
alt.support.foster-parents

Listserv Mailing List:
List Name: **foster-l**
Subscribe to: **listserv@american.edu**

FAMILIES AND PARENTING

Grandparents Raising Grandchildren

For one reason or another, many children are being raised by their grandparents. If you are such a grandparent, these Web sites can be a real help. You will find articles and tips, information about relevant laws (such as adoption), and more. Perhaps the best resource is people: other grandparents who are raising grandchildren. You can talk to other grandparents by joining the mailing list or participate in the Usenet discussion group.

Web:
http://www.aoa.dhhs.gov/factsheets/grandparents.html
http://www.grandsplace.com/

Usenet:
alt.parenting.grandparents

Majordomo Mailing List:
List Name: grandparents
Subscribe to: majordomo@majordomo.pobox.com

Internet Filtering Software

There are many great resources on the Net for kids, and there is no reason why children should be deprived of exploring the Internet just because they might accidentally encounter some inappropriate content (that is, sex). These sites have links to companies that have designed software that helps filter out what you don't want your kids to see.

Web:
http://www.wico.net/draft.htm
http://www6.pilot.infi.net/~carolyn/guide.html

Jewish Parenting

This Usenet discussion group was specifically created for parents to discuss those issues that are important to the Jewish community (such as bread, religion and soup). Along with the Usenet group come two FAQs. The **judaism.faq.12-kids.html** FAQ is about Jewish parenting. The **judaism.faq.scjp-admin.html** FAQ contains information related to the Usenet discussion group.

Web:
http://www.lib.ox.ac.uk/internet/news/faq/archive/judaism.faq.12-kids.html
http://www.lib.ox.ac.uk/internet/news/faq/archive/judaism.faq.scjp-admin.html

Usenet:
soc.culture.jewish.parenting

Kids, Computers and Software

I have never met a child who didn't like computers. In these Usenet groups, you can talk about the best computers and hardware for children, as well as educational and entertainment software. The Web site has shareware that I am sure your kids will enjoy (when they are not sneaking behind your back to connect to inappropriate Web sites).

Web:
http://www.kidsdomain.com/

Usenet:
alt.comp.shareware.for-kids
misc.kids.computer

Missing Children

If you have a missing child, or if you think you may have found such a child, the Net can help. These Web sites allow you to read descriptions and look at photos of missing children. If you have such a child yourself, you can find help, including arranging for your child's information to be posted on the Net. Be careful of scams, though. I found a multi-level marketing company on the Net that plays on people's emotions ("A Child Is Missing Every 40 Seconds in America") to sell "child protection systems".

Web:
http://www.childquest.org/
http://www.childsearch.org/

Usenet:
alt.binaries.missing-kids
alt.missing-kids

THEY don't want you to know, but I'll tell you: take a look at "Secret Stuff".

FAMILIES AND PARENTING

Stay connected.

Moms

Moms, rev up your Internet connection and check out all the places that are designed especially for you. Hang out in one of the many chat rooms or browse the nice selection of articles while sipping a hot cup of cappuccino. You'll find a little bit of everything here: health, beauty, taking care of the kids, child safety, gardening, cleaning, entertaining, seasonal articles, and more.

Web:

http://www.midlifemommies.com/
http://www.momsonline.com/
http://www.salonmagazine.com/mothers/
http://www.thecybermom.com/

Parent Soup

Parent Soup is a great place for parents. As a matter of fact, if it weren't for your kids, you could spend hours at this site. You will find news, feature articles, a parent poll, chat areas, as well as information for parents. There are also special sections for at-home parents, working parents and single parents. The information at this site seems to go on forever, so put the kids to bed early so they won't get in the way.

Web:

http://www.parentsoup.com/

Parenthood Web

This is a fantastic Web site to explore. It has many features for parents and prospective parents, covering vital topics such as family health, naming babies, pregnancy, breastfeeding, helping children through divorce, problems at school, homework, and much more.

Web:

http://www.parenthoodweb.com/

Look What I Found on the Net...

```
Newsgroup: misc.kids.computer
Subject: Mouse for Young Kids

>> I want my three year-old son to start using our computer.
>> However, our mouse is too big for him to handle.  Can anyone
>> recommend something that is easier to use?

> The Microsoft Easyball is a trackball for kids. They use their
> whole hand to move it.
>
> The purpose of the Easyball is threefold:
>    1. To make the mouse easier to use for hands with less fine
>       motor control.
>    2. To provide a better cognitive relationship between hand
>       and eye coordination (any roller-ball would do that).
>    3. To make using a computer FUN.

I don't know how small your three-year-old's hands are, but my
four-year-old has been using the mouse since she was two.  She
uses the standard mouse just fine.  Children are slow at first,
but they catch on.  They learn to use it like they learn
everything else.

In my opinion, in the long run the Easyball will serve little
or no purpose when the kid gets older.

That is, unless YOU want to use it.
```

FAMILIES AND PARENTING

Parenting Resources

If you are bored and you want to read some new stuff about parenting, check out these Web sites. They have information on just about every topic imaginable related to parenting, step-parenting, parenting multiples, fatherhood, pregnancy, breastfeeding, health, education, and family activities. You will never run out of things to read on the Net. And, if you do, you can always have a couple more kids.

Web:
http://ericps.ed.uiuc.edu/npin/respar/nls.html
http://www.caringparents.com/
http://www.familyeducation.com/
http://www.parentsplace.com/
http://www.wholefamily.com/

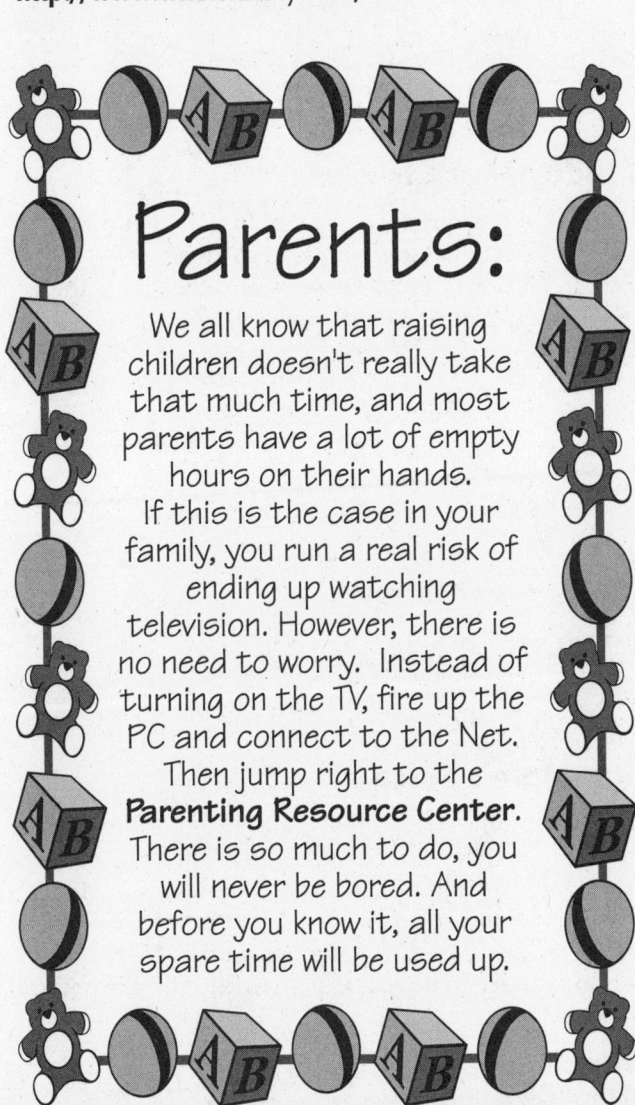

Parents:

We all know that raising children doesn't really take that much time, and most parents have a lot of empty hours on their hands. If this is the case in your family, you run a real risk of ending up watching television. However, there is no need to worry. Instead of turning on the TV, fire up the PC and connect to the Net. Then jump right to the **Parenting Resource Center**. There is so much to do, you will never be bored. And before you know it, all your spare time will be used up.

Parenting Talk and General Discussion

Raising children is more than a full-time occupation: it's a way of life that brings challenges, sacrifices and rewards. It can also be confusing and frustrating at times, and there is certainly no end of topics that need to be discussed. There are many, many parents on the Net who love to talk. Join them in these Usenet discussion groups.

Usenet:
alt.parenting
alt.parenting.solutions
misc.kids.moderated

Parents and Children Together Online

Here is an online magazine that both parents and children can enjoy. For the children, there are delightful, entertaining stories and articles. For adults, there are features about parenting, as well as reviews of books and products.

Web:
http://www.indiana.edu/~eric_rec/fl/pcto/menu.html

Parents and Teens

It's not easy being a parent of a teenager, but at least you are not alone. There are many other parents on the Net with whom you can have discussions. Talk about what works and what doesn't. Share your experiences with other parents, give advice, and ask questions.

Usenet:
alt.parents-teens

Parents Room

Parents Room is a place on IRC (Internet Relay Chat) where parents can exchange ideas on parenting and life or just hang out and talk. The Web site has information on the **#!parentsroom** regulars, parenting resources, guidelines for the IRC channel, and general information about how IRC works.

Web:
http://parentsroom.gwas.com/

IRC:
#!parentsroom

Pregnancy and Childbirth

Pregnancy is exciting and exhilarating, but it can be awfully scary if it is your first time. At these Web sites, you can find out what is going to happen at every stage of your pregnancy. Read stories about birth, what labor is like, and find out information on birth procedures such as caesarians and episiotomies. The Usenet group is for the discussion of pregnancy and pregnancy-related issues.

Web:
   http://www.childbirth.org/
   http://www.pregnancytoday.com/

Usenet:
   misc.kids.pregnancy

Premature Infants

The normal human gestation period—the time between conception and birth—is about 280 days (40 weeks). Babies that are born significantly before the full term (six weeks or more) are said to be premature. Premature infants face a special set of problems. First, because their bodies are not fully developed, they may have trouble surviving. Second, premature babies that do survive have a greater than normal chance of suffering from a disability. Here are some resources to help parents understand the problems and considerations unique to premature infants. My experience is that having authoritative information can make a medical situation much easier to bear. However, doctors are often too busy to spend a long time explaining technical matters to patients' families. If you have a premature infant, these resources can help you understand what is happening, and what you can do to help your child.

Web:
   http://www.medsch.wisc.edu/childrenshosp/
      Parents_of_Preemies/index.html
   http://www.vicnet.net.au/~garyh/preemie.htm

Usenet:
   alt.support.premature-baby

Majordomo Mailing List:
   List Name: preemie-l
   Subscribe to: majordomo@vicnet.net.au

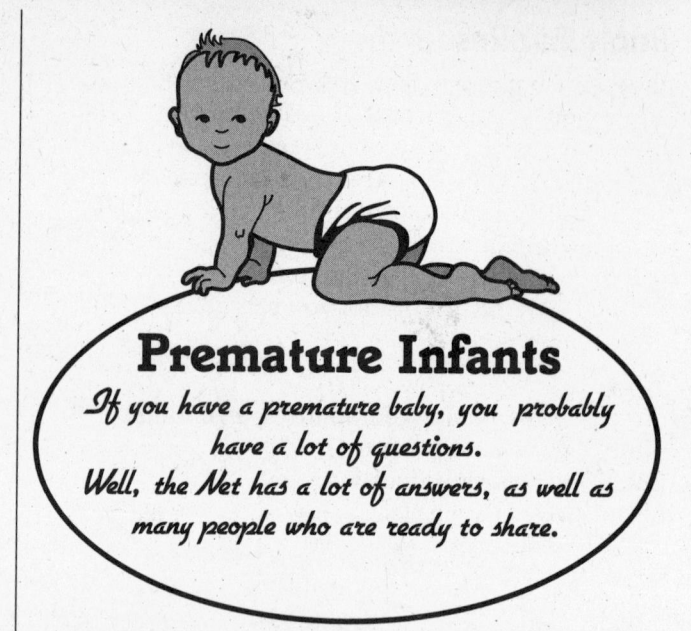

Premature Infants
If you have a premature baby, you probably have a lot of questions. Well, the Net has a lot of answers, as well as many people who are ready to share.

Products for Children

If you have children, you probably don't get much choice about what toy you want to give them. Children know what they want, and they have their own ways of getting it. However, if you want to get the lowdown on what is best for children—as if they care—check out this guide. This site reviews toys and entertainment products for children, and also has hints for parents about what to select for particular age groups. The Usenet group is for discussion of consumer issues that relate to children.

Web:
   http://www.drtoy.com/

Usenet:
   misc.kids.consumers

Sgt. Mom's Place

Military families have quite a life, so Sgt. Mom has made a Web site with resources that can help. This site is for any military family: active, veteran, retired or reserve. Find support groups and new friends, advice on parenting, moving tips, and stuff for kids. When military living gets tough, the tough get going to Sgt. Mom's.

Web:
   http://www.sgtmoms.com/pages.htm

FAMILIES AND PARENTING   257

Single Parents

When you're going it alone, it's good to know there are other single parents all around the Net. These Web sites have a great deal of information for any single parent. You can find helpful topics about children, careers, parenting, spirituality, support and entertainment.

Web:
  http://rampages.onramp.net/~bevhamil/singleparentresourcece_478.html
  http://www.singlerose.com/

Usenet:
  alt.support.single-parents

Majordomo Mailing List:
  List Name: **sinpar**
  Subscribe to: **majordomo@world.std.com**

Step-Parents

Being a step-parent is always a difficult job with no guarantee that it will be rewarding. However, you don't have to be on your own. On Usenet, you can find a whole group of people who are having the same types of experiences as you. Take some time to talk, share your ideas and experiences.

Web:
  http://www.studyweb.com/family/famstp.htm

Usenet:
  alt.support.step-parents

Start here.

Look What I Found on the Net...

```
Newsgroup: alt.support.step-parents
Subject: Step-daughter from Hell

> Dear Xxxxxxx:
>
> I am sorry for you, but I feel better knowing that I am not
> alone.  My step-daughter acted like this and she was only 12.
> ...her antics were dooming the marriage.  My hubby took the
> same passive stance [as yours].  I was the heavy... Though
> I gave her my life, she destroyed my reputation... she
> stole from me and rifled through my drawers... The marriage
> started to fail and I was pregnant...
>
> It got so bad, I taped our arguments, videoed her antics,
> taped phone calls and showed my hubby her school notes.
> He didn't know what to do, so he did nothing.
>
> ...we sent her, begrudgingly, to her mother's for an unlimited
> stay.  Her mom is a piece of work and this was the worst
> thing for her, but we had to save us if we were ever going to
> do her any good.  It's been 2 years, our marriage is sound
> and happy... She is going down the toilet but my hubby has no
> more energy for her.  I can't say I mind, but it is sad...

Wow!
Your whole story sounds like the one I'm just going through.
How did you guys tape the phone calls?
```

Surrogate Motherhood

A surrogate mother is a woman who conceives a baby and carries it to term on behalf of someone else. In most cases, the someone else is a couple who cannot have children of their own. When the baby is born, it is given to the couple to raise. The pregnancy can be initiated in two ways: the surrogate mother can be impregnated with the sperm of the father (via artificial insemination), or an egg from the mother that has been fertilized by the father can be implanted in the surrogate mother's uterus. In either case, there is a lot to consider and a lot to know.

Web:
http://www.opts.com/
http://www.surromomsonline.com/

Teaching with Movies

It used to be that helping your kids learn required time and mental effort. You might have to explain how things work, discuss complicated ideas, or maybe even show the little crumb-grabbers how to do algebra problems. Not anymore. Now you can help your kids just by watching movies. No guff! All the information you need is here on this Web site. They even select the movies for you. All you need to do is drive to the store, rent the video, and see that the popcorn bowl stays full. Who says parenting is hard?

Web:
http://www.teachwithmovies.org/

Twins and Triplets

The nice thing about multiple births is that you can have all your kids at once. No more Lamaze classes, no more packing the emergency hospital bag, no more late-night frantic phone calls to family members. Yes, now that you have lots and lots of babies on your hands, you can rest easy (sort of). The Web sites have resources for parents of twins and triplets (or more). The Usenet group is for the discussion of raising multiple birth children.

Web:
http://www.owc.net/~twins/faq.htm
http://www.tripletconnection.org/

Usenet:
alt.parenting.twins-triplets

Vacationing with Children

When you plan your next vacation, include reading Usenet to find out helpful hints on how to make traveling with your children easier. Find money-saving ideas, new ways to entertain kids while on the road, information on travel safety as well as funny travel anecdotes from parents.

Usenet:
misc.kids.vacation

FAQS (FREQUENTLY ASKED QUESTION LISTS)

FAQ Archives

A FAQ is a list of frequently asked questions and answers on a particular topic. The original FAQs were developed for Usenet discussion groups. People found that all newcomers who joined a group would tend to ask the same questions. For example, people who join the group where urban legends are discussed (**alt.folklore.urban**) often ask if it is true that Mrs. Field's or Nieman-Marcus forced somebody to pay a lot of money for a recipe. (The answer is no, by the way.) It became the custom for one or more experienced members of a Usenet group to create a list of frequently asked questions and answers. The idea was that newcomers to the group should read the FAQ before they start participating in the discussion. The concept of FAQs has grown to embrace just about every topic imaginable, in situations where it is useful for people to collect questions and answers. These Web sites are among my favorite resources on the Internet. This is because I love to learn new things and I find that reading a FAQ in an area that is new to me is a great way to pick up interesting and esoteric knowledge. It will be well worth your while to spend some time browsing through the FAQs looking for some areas that interest you. (By the way, according to the urban legends FAQ, green M&M's are not an aphrodisiac.)

Web:
http://familiar.sph.umich.edu/faq/
http://www.cis.ohio-state.edu/hypertext/faq/usenet/FAQ-List.html
http://www.cs.ruu.nl/cgi-bin/faqwais/
http://www.faqs.org/faqs/
http://www.landfield.com/faqs/
http://www.lib.ox.ac.uk/internet/news/faq/by_group.index.html

FAQS (FREQUENTLY ASKED QUESTION LISTS)

> **Somewhere in this book is a secret encrypted message.**

FAQ FAQ

"A FAQ FAQ? What's a FAQ FAQ? I don't need no stinking FAQ FAQ." Well, yes, you do. The FAQ FAQ is a list of questions and answers about FAQs. It explains the history of FAQs, and gives you tips and hints for writing and maintaining a FAQ. If you get the urge, one of the most useful things you can do for the Net is to maintain a FAQ. If you would like to try, begin by reading the FAQ FAO.

Web:
http://www.cis.ohio-state.edu/hypertext/faq/usenet/faqs/about-faqs/faq.html
http://www.cs.ruu.nl/wais/html/na-dir/faqs/about-faqs.html
http://www.lib.ox.ac.uk/internet/news/faq/archive/faqs.about-faqs.html

FAQ for the *.answers Usenet Groups

There are a number of Usenet groups devoted to FAQs and other period postings. These principal groups are **alt.answers**, **comp.answers**, **humanities.answers**, **misc.answers**, **news.answers**, **rec.answers**, **sci.answers**, **soc.answers** and **talk.answers** (often referred to collectively as ***.answers**). Here is a FAQ that explains the purpose and contents of these groups, how to submit new postings, how to join the mailing list for periodic posting maintainers, and where to find archives of postings to the ***.answers** groups.

Web:
http://www.cis.ohio-state.edu/hypertext/faq/usenet/news-answers/introduction/faq.html
http://www.cs.ruu.nl/wais/html/na-dir/news-answers/introduction.html
http://www.lib.ox.ac.uk/internet/news/faq/archive/news-answers.introduction.html

The FAQ FAQ

When I was young, I used to love watching movies starring Mickey Rooney and Judy Garland. (If you're too young to remember Mickey Rooney and Judy Garland, show this ad to your mother, and she'll explain it.)

The story would vary from one movie to another, but one thing never seemed to change.

Mickey and Judy would be using the Net to look at various documents, when all of a sudden Mickey would get all excited.

"I have an idea," he would say, "why don't we write our own FAQ?"

So they would, and it would be a great success. Have you ever wanted to write your own FAQ? If Mickey and Judy could do it, why not you?

260 FAQS (FREQUENTLY ASKED QUESTION LISTS)

FAQ Talk and General Discussion

The reason for frequently asked question lists is that newcomers to a Usenet discussion group often seem to ask the same questions. Veterans don't mind answering new questions, but nobody wants to explain, over and over and over, what "Unix" means. Through the years, many groups have developed a frequently asked question list (FAQ) that contains all the common questions that have been answered repeatedly in that group. Some FAQs are so large as to be divided into several parts. Whenever you start reading a new group, look for a FAQ to orient yourself. More important, before you post a question to the group, check the FAQ to see if your question has already been answered. The people who maintain FAQs post them regularly, not only to their own group, but to special groups that have been created just to hold FAQs and related material. The **news.answers** group contains FAQs from every possible source. The other **.answers** groups contain FAQs for their respective hierarchies. For example, **comp.answers** contains computer FAQs. When you have a spare moment, check out these groups, especially **alt.answers**. You will see a lot of interesting and strange stuff that you might never encounter otherwise. These groups contain not only FAQs, but important summaries of information not tied to specific Usenet groups.

Usenet:
  alt.answers
  comp.answers
  misc.answers
  news.answers
  rec.answers
  sci.answers
  soc.answers
  talk.answers

Internet FAQ Consortium

The Internet FAQ Consortium is a group of people who are concerned with writing and maintaining FAQs. If you have anything to do with a FAQ, you'll find this site interesting. There is a nice set of useful links that will make your life as a FAQ-meister easier.

Web:
  http://www.faqs.org/

Maintaining a FAQ

At first, it would seem easy—and fun—to maintain a FAQ. However, doing a good job can be more work than you might think. To help you, here is a Web site devoted to making FAQ maintenance as easy as possible. Read about tools for automatically posting your FAQ to Usenet, producing HTML versions of your FAQ, and coping with electronic mail. There are also links to other Internet resources related to FAQs.

Web:
  http://www.qucis.queensu.ca/FAQs/FAQaid/

Minimal Digest Format FAQ

When you maintain a FAQ, the format you use is important. Using a proper format can make your FAQ compatible with the digest-handling capabilities of certain newsreader programs. It can also allow your FAQ to be read more easily by a Web browser. Perhaps most important, using a good format will make it convenient for people to read and understand your work. This FAQ describes a format that is relatively simple but contains the minimal characteristics necessary for a proper FAQ.

Web:
  http://www.cis.ohio-state.edu/hypertext/faq/usenet/faqs/minimal-digest-format/faq.html
  http://www.cs.ruu.nl/wais/html/na-dir/faqs/minimal-digest-format.html
  http://www.lib.ox.ac.uk/internet/news/faq/archive/faqs.minimal-digest-format.html

Periodic Informational Postings List

On Usenet, there are a great many articles that are sent to various discussion groups on a regular basis. For example, there are many FAQs. There are also other types of regularly posted articles, such as lists of various things. You might ask, does anyone collect the names of all the articles that are posted regularly to Usenet? The answer is yes, and this list—called the Periodic Informational Postings List—is itself posted regularly to Usenet. (Imagine the philosophical implications.) This list is a long one, so here are Web sites that make it easy to find what you want.

Web:
  http://www.cis.ohio-state.edu/hypertext/faq/usenet/periodic-postings/top.html
  http://www.lib.ox.ac.uk/internet/news/faq/by_category.periodic-postings.html

FASHION AND CLOTHING

Posting a FAQ Automatically

If you maintain a FAQ, you will want to know about the **auto-faq** script. This script is designed to post a FAQ to Usenet groups automatically. It allows you a large amount of control by specifying particular values in a configuration file. Another benefit is that, if you use this script, your FAQ will comply with all the requirements for posting to **news.answers** and the other ***.answers** groups.

Web:
http://www.novia.net/~pschleck/auto-faq/

She looked up from her computer as I came in, and I caught a whiff of exotic oriental perfume. She smiled seductively: red hair, green eyes, and voluptuous body with enough curves to cause a cardiovascular accident in a giraffe.

"I want the program," I said.

"What program?" she asked.

"Don't get smart with me, sister. You know what program. The program to automatically post my FAQs to Usenet."

She wrote down an address on a piece of paper.

"All you have to do is connect to this Web site," she said. "But isn't there anything else you want? I know my way around the Net better than anyone. Just let me work with you, and I'll get you anything you want."

"Sorry, kid, but I work alone."

"Are you sure?" she said. "I have a lot more to offer. Are you positive there isn't anything else?"

I took the paper and headed for the door.

"Just the FAQs, ma'am."

Submission Guidelines for the *.answers Usenet Groups

If you maintain a FAQ, you will probably want to post it not only to your own Usenet group, but to **news.answers** and possibly one of the other ***.answers** groups. This FAQ explains what you need to do in order to cross-post a FAQ in this manner.

Web:
http://www.cis.ohio-state.edu/hypertext/faq/usenet/news-answers/guidelines/faq.html
http://www.cs.ruu.nl/wais/html/na-dir/news-answers/guidelines.html
http://www.lib.ox.ac.uk/internet/news/faq/archive/news-answers.guidelines.html

FASHION AND CLOTHING

Beauty Shoppe Archive

Contrary to the song, everything old is *not* new again, and with good reason. Most of the retro hairdo looks seem to be strange concoctions from another galaxy. See for yourself by visiting the Beauty Shoppe Archive. Just a few moments will convince you that, whatever happens to be in style now is going to look odd later.

Web:
http://www.net-link.net/~mwarner/BSA.html

Bra FAQs

A brassiere (or bra) is a women's undergarment whose principal purpose is to lend support to the breasts. As simple as this sounds, choosing the right bra can be a complex and frustrating task. There are many variations of people and by no means does one size fit all. The first modern bra, the Maidenform, was designed in 1922 by Ina Rosenthal and Enid Bissett. (If you are in New York, you can see the original bra on display at the Maidenform Museum.) Here is a series of FAQs devoted to bras, where you can read about coverings, designs, sizes and fitting, health issues, fabrics, fashion, history, trivia and suppliers. There is also a FAQ for underwire bras (bras that provide extra support by having wires underneath the cup or along the rib cage). Helpful Hint from Harley: Bra specialists will tell you that most women—especially large-busted women—are wearing the wrong size bra. When you look for a bra, pay attention to fit and comfort, not style and construction. (In other words, evaluate a bra with your eyes closed.) Extra Hint: For a better fit, lean over as you put on your bra.

Web:
http://www.funhouse.com/babs/FAQ.html

**Looking for a friend?
Try "UFOs and Aliens".**

Bridal Fashion Regrets

Doesn't she look beautiful? Well, not always. Just take a look at these fashion catastrophes: well-meaning people who, rather unwisely, decided to do it *their* way.

Web:
   http://www.visi.com/~dheaton/bride/
   the_bride_wore.html

Business Fashion

Have you heard of the MBA Style magazine? Well, if you have an MBA, or you want an MBA, or you live with someone who has an MBA, *and* you want to explore the style affected by fashion-conscious MBAs in modern-day American popular culture, this may be the magazine for you. Where else can you go for advice on how to buy a tie for an interview? What are you going to do, ask your mother?

Web:
   http://members.aol.com/mbastyle/web/
   mbastyle.html

Clogs

Originally, a "clog" was any shoe made from wood. Such shoes—constructed from a single piece of wood—were developed by the Dutch, who needed footwear that would keep their feet dry while working in wet fields. Today's clogs are made from a variety of materials, and the word "clog" has come to refer to a large, backless shoe with a thick, elevated sole. Even the most clog-enamored fanatic can't pretend that these shoes are anything but ugly. However, they do make a satisfying clunk-clunk sound as you lumber from one place to another like an elephant at a Sixties dress-up party. (Indeed, some people feel that the name "clog" comes from the sound they make as you walk.) In the Sixties, clogs were practical because they allowed you to walk wherever you wanted while still retaining the freedom to slip off your shoes at a moment's notice. (You had to be there.) For more information about clogs—perhaps all the information you may need in your lifetime—see this Web page: the most comprehensive collection of clog-related information on the Net.

Web:
   http://members.aol.com/clogs01/

Look What I Found on the Net...

```
(from the Bra FAQs Web site)
You may have heard about a new book which claims that there's a
link between bra-wearing and breast cancer.  Rest assured that
most cancer specialists say the idea is so ludicrous it isn't
even worth commenting on.

The authors interviewed more than 4,700 women (roughly half of
whom had breast cancer) and found that those who wore bras for
24 hours a day had a 113-fold increase in breast cancer
incidence, when compared with women who wear bras less than
12 hours a day.

Based on this, they theorize that constriction from a bra allows
toxins to build up in the breasts' lymphatic system, which
leads to cancer.

But that premise is unfounded. "Even when a bra fits snugly, it
doesn't interfere with the lymphatic drainage of the breast,"
explains a breast cancer expert Xxxxxx Xxxxxxxx, M.D., professor
of surgery at Jefferson Medical College in Philadelphia.

Says Xxxxxxxx Xxxxxxxx, M.D., director of the breast center at
the John Wayne Cancer Institute in Santa Monica, California,
"Breast cancer has many causes — hormonal, environmental,
genetic and dietary — but it's likely that wearing bras isn't
one of them."
```

FASHION AND CLOTHING

Clothing for Big Folks

Here are the FAQs discussing oversized clothing for the United States, Canada, United Kingdom and Europe. You'll find out how to convert sizes internationally, where to find clothing and shoes for everyday as well as where to shop for wedding and maternity clothing. This information will help women, men and children.

Web:
http://www.bayarea.net/~stef/Fatfaqs/canada.html
http://www.bayarea.net/~stef/Fatfaqs/us.html
http://www.cis.ohio-state.edu/hypertext/faq/usenet/fat-acceptance-faq/clothing/top.html
http://www.cs.ruu.nl/wais/html/na-dir/fat-acceptance-faq/clothing/.html

CNN Style

The world of fashion and style sure generates news. If you like to keep up, here is the place to check daily. CNN gathers the fashion news stories of the day—along with pictures—and puts them on the Web just so you can stay one step ahead of what is happening.

Web:
http://www.cnn.com/STYLE/

Corsets

Do not confuse corsets with girdles. Girdles are a modern undergarment made out of elastic material. Corsets have been used from time immemorial and are more extreme. Corsets incorporate a series of reinforcements called "stays" in order to bind the breasts, waist and hips into a particular desired shape. At one time, corsets were extremely popular, and the image of a Victorian woman needing help to lace up and tighten her corset is one that does little to make us nostalgic. However, corsets were an important fashion accoutrement that, even today, have their admirers. If you are one of them—or if you would like to see some pictures of corsets and the women who wore them—take a look at these Web pages.

Web:
http://www.dnaco.net/~aleed/corsets/
http://www.speakeasy.org/~traceyb/corset.html

Fantasy Costume

Everyone has a fantasy costume idea. This mailing list concentrates on the design and production of fantasy clothing. Let your imagination run free and think about what you may have worn in your past lives and what you'd like to wear in the future.

Majordomo Mailing List:
 List Name: **f-costume**
 Subscribe to: **majordomo@indra.com**

Fashion Live

Keep up on the world of style. Here is *the* place to visit to see what's new, exciting and fashionable. The latest news, catwalk coverage, a designer database, information on current trends and collections—it's all waiting for you on the Net.

Web:
http://www.worldmedia.fr/fashion/

Fashion Net

So you've already read everything in this month's Vogue? No need to be bored. Spend some time at Fashion Net and you will find plenty of food for fashionable thought: magazines, entertainment, modeling, shopping, beauty sites, fashion houses, fashion shows, photographers, Usenet groups, message boards, links and job listings.

Web:
http://www.fashion.net/

Corsets

Wearing a corset is definitely an acquired skill. However, is this a skill you want to acquire?
Some people say yes. A properly fitting corset is not only wearable, they say, but comfortable and — dare I say it? — arousing.
Would you like to get into the world of corsets, lacing and "waist training"? You had better know what you doing, so go right to the Net and get the straight and narrow.

Fashion Planet

It's cool to go shopping in New York and spend thousands of dollars in a day, but I bet I know what's holding you back. You need to know which are the most fashionable stores and where to find them. Not a problem. This Web site has oodles of fashion-related resources, including news, features, columns and a comprehensive guide to New York shopping.

Web:
  http://www.fp1.com/

Fashion Talk and General Discussion

It's a nice feeling when you're dressed in a spiffy new outfit with all the right accessories and people turn to look as you walk down the street. Impress your friends, family and total strangers with your fashion sense and the clothing tips you've learned while hanging out on the Internet. Clothing pros, trendsetters and the hopelessly unfashionable find their way to these discussion groups to share ideas or get answers to questions.

Usenet:
  alt.fashion
  alt.fashion.petite

Stay cool and trendy: read about fashion on the Net.

Gothic Fashion

Stop here for a complete discussion of such tricky topics as saving bleached hair, when to wear those pointy boots, and whether kinky or straight hair is the most Gothic. Just when you think you've dreamed up a new color to dye your hair, someone has beaten you to it.

Web:
  http://www.toreadors.com/gothfash/

Usenet:
  alt.gothic.fashion

Hair Care

Do you look good? Do you want to? Consult these Web sites if you want to be in style, look good, and be the envy of everyone on the Net.

Web:
  http://www.hairnet.com/
  http://www.tlhs.org/

Look What I Found on the Net...

```
Newsgroup: alt.gothic.fashion
Subject: Witch Shoes

I saw this pair of shoes I fell in love with.  Unfortunately,
they were on another girl.

They were black patent "witch shoes" also called granny boots,
with a thick heel that curved down in a Victorian style.

Do any mail-order places have these?  I have a pair in black
suede, but the heels are straight as opposed to curved.
```

FASHION AND CLOTHING

Historical Costuming

There's nothing I like more than dressing up in an authentic historical costume—bell bottoms, love beads and a tie-dyed T-shirt—and walking around the house affecting an attitude as cool as a Canadian winter. However, this is nothing compared to what real historical costume buffs do to relax. Here is a Web site where you can find information about historical costuming. Just the place to look when you need to find a Renaissance-style crossbow or complete your research into what type of underwear women wore in the fifteenth century.

Web:
http://www.milieux.com/costume/

Usenet:
alt.history.costuming

Hypermode

What is Hypermode? There is no good answer here. You have to look and listen and watch and make up your own mind. I guess that Hypermode has something to do with fashion. Check it out: pictures, advice, pictures, fashion, pictures, feature articles, pictures, raw urban streetstyle, pictures... you get the idea.

Web:
http://www.hypermode.com/

Lipstick

Lipstick is something we are all used to. However, like many areas of the fashion world, the more you think about it, the more strange the idea seems. The best solution, then, is not to think about it. Just use lipstick and enjoy. One way to enjoy is to look at this lipstick-oriented Web site. Read about tips and consumer issues, explore other links to cosmetic-related resources, look in the lipstick library of color choices, and much, much more. If you would like to know which lipstick shades and brands are used by famous models and movie stars, this is the place for you.

Web:
http://www.users.wineasy.se/bjornt/lip.html

> **Spare time? Take a look at "Games and Puzzles".**

Look Online

This is serious fashion industry stuff—news—upcoming events—site reviews—fashion resources—New York industry gossip—exclusive runway photos—this is serious stuff—life in a very expensive, designer-oriented fast, fast lane. It leaves me breathless.

Web:
http://www.lookonline.com/

Lumière

Lumière is a monthly magazine containing a variety of articles relating to fashion and beauty. And not just everyday fashion—"upscale" fashion (translation: innovative, high quality, expensive). Enjoy articles from past issues on such topics as ready to wear collections, casual dress for work, wardrobes, designer profiles, and reviews of makeup and perfume.

Web:
http://www.lumiere.com/

Lycra

Yes, it's true. There is a discussion group for fans of lycra and spandex. If you have something to contribute or are just curious about the lycra culture, check out the Usenet group. For some lycra-oriented exploration, try the Web site.

Web:
http://www2.best.com/~invncble/altlycra.html

Usenet:
alt.lycra

Models and Supermodels

Maybe you can never be too rich or too thin, but why not check it out on the Net first? See photos and learn what being a supermodel is all about. If you still think you've got what it takes, remember, no dinner for you tonight.

Web:
   http://www.supermodel.com/

Usenet:
   alt.binaries.pictures.joanne-guest
   alt.binaries.pictures.models
   alt.binaries.pictures.nicki-lewis
   alt.binaries.pictures.petra-verkaik
   alt.binaries.pictures.photo-modeling
   alt.binaries.pictures.supermodels.claudia-schiffer
   alt.binaries.pictures.supermodels.elle-macpherson
   alt.binaries.pictures.supermodels.kathy-ireland
   alt.fan.alison-armitage
   alt.fan.anna.nicole.smith
   alt.fan.ashley-lauren
   alt.fan.bridget
   alt.fan.bridget-maasland
   alt.fan.julia-hayes
   alt.fan.kate-moss
   alt.fan.kerri-kendall
   alt.fan.melinda.messenger
   alt.fan.patricia
   alt.fan.petra-verkaik
   alt.models
   alt.supermodels
   alt.supermodels.cindy-crawford

Shoes

The same foot can be a size 8, size 25 or size 85 depending on who you ask. If you're confused, look at the comparative shoe size charts at this site. Take a walk through the United States, Canada, United Kingdom, continental Europe and Japan and find out your local size.

Web:
   http://www.icon-net.co.uk/torture/shoesize.html

Free Offer: Get Your Own Supermodel

Would you like your own supermodel? I have arranged a special offer just for my readers. Here is what you need to do. Go to the Supermodels site and find a supermodel you like. Then write her name on a piece of paper, no larger than your hand. Take the paper, put it in this book at this exact page, close the book and put it under your pillow when you go to sleep tonight. Tomorrow morning, there will be a message on your answering machine from that particular supermodel. The message will tell you where and when you can meet her in person. If for some reason you do not get a message, try again the next night.

Disclaimer: Sorry, this offer is not valid if you do not have an answering machine.

Sneakers

When you've run out of useful things to do, check out the Internet resources on sneakers. You'll find dialog on different brands of running shoes, what sneaker to buy and how to deal with stinky feet.

Web:
   http://sneakers.pair.com/

Usenet:
   alt.clothing.sneakers
   alt.fan.nike

Textiles

Rough and soft, shiny and crinkled, textiles come in a variety of colors, weights, and textures. Some are made from natural materials like plants and animals or even metal. Others are invented in a lab, fibers woven out of who-knows-what kind of synthetic material with a 12-syllable name. Fashion designers, students, people who sew, or just folks who love fashion—you will find them all on the Net.

Web:
   http://www.cs.ruu.nl/wais/html/na-dir/crafts/textiles/books/.html
   http://www.fabriclink.com/

Usenet:
   rec.crafts.textiles.misc

Listserv Mailing List:
   List Name: **textiles**
   Subscribe to: **listserv@vm.ege.edu.tr**

Victorian Fashion

The Victorian Age is named after England's Queen Victoria, who ruled for sixty-four years, from 1837-1901. During these sixty-four years, a collection of style and behavior patterns developed that we refer to as Victorian culture. Along with the culture came a definite set of guidelines as to what proper people should wear and not wear. Even today, Victorian fashion has its admirers. If you would like to find out more, check this Web site where you will find information about making Victorian clothing, lists of companies that sell Victorian patterns, hints on how to wear frillies (underwear) and corsets, lists of accessories and where to find them, a bibliography, and links to related resources on the Net. By the way, within the royal household, the champion of taste was not Queen Victoria, but her consort Prince Albert—the Princess Diana of his time.

Web:
   http://www.teasociety.com/victorian/

Women's Wire Fashion & Beauty

Being fashionable is no accident: it takes time, effort, money, and an understanding of what looks good and what is in style. I can't help you with the time, effort or money, but I can make it easy for you to tune into the world of fashion and develop your sense of style. Spend some time on the Net, and wallow in the world of clothes, designers, beauty and that *je ne sais quoi* that comes so easily to my readers.

Web:
   http://www.womenswire.com/stuff/fb.html

Victorian Fashion

Back in the nineteenth century, Queen Victoria and her husband Prince Albert were the fashion trend-setters of the day.

Victoria and Albert could wear whatever they wanted and, instantly, that would become the new fashion.

However, Queen Victoria's temper was legendary, and nobody wanted to show up at an official function wearing something that was out of fashion.

So how could everyone keep up on the latest trends? Easy. All they had to do was connect to the Net and check the Victorian Fashion Web site.

FINDING STUFF ON THE NET

Culture Finder

The Culture Finder offers useful and interesting information about culture. For example, if you are visiting New York, you can check here to find out what is playing off-Broadway. Or, if you want to look up the meaning of "overture", you can use the Culture Finder dictionary. Here are many resources, including news, information and games. I bet you'll love this site.

Web:
   http://culturefinder.mediapolis.com/

File Finder

There's a lot of stuff on the Net, and all of it is stored in files. But how do you find the file you need when you need it? Try this Web site, where you can search for files containing programs, games, music, Windows 98/95 desktop themes, and more.

Web:
http://www.filez.com/

FTP Search

If you understand the anonymous ftp system, you will want to know about FTP Search. It offers a Web-based interface that is much easier to use than the original text-based archie or any archie client I have ever seen. Moreover, it is fast. The days of slow, awkward archie searches are gone forever. Searching the worldwide ftp archives is now as easy as falling off a virtual log (three years too late).

Web:
http://ftpsearch.ntnu.no/

How to Use Search Engines

A search engine is a program that allows you to search a database quickly. All of the well-known Internet search tools (Yahoo, AltaVista, Lycos, Excite, and so on) are search engines. Here is information about the various search engines, along with a wealth of advice on how to use them effectively. If you find yourself spending too much time floundering around, take a few moments and read these articles.

Web:
http://sunsite.berkeley.edu/help/searchdetails.html
http://www.monash.com/spidap.html

Image Search Engines

Get the picture? You will. There are a large number of pictures, illustrations, graphics and photographs available on the Net, and you can get them for free.

Web:
http://ipix.yahoo.com/
http://isurf.interpix.com/
http://safari.altavista.digital.com/
http://www.lycos.com/picturethis

How to Use Search Engines

You can find just about anything you want on the Net—if you know what you are doing. One of the biggest tips I can give you is to spend some time learning how to use the various Internet search engines. (A search engine is a program that can look through an entire database of information quickly.)

There are a number of companies that maintain databases containing information about all the Web sites on the Net. (You can imagine what a job it is keeping such databases up to date.) These companies allow anyone to use their search engines for free—they make their money from advertising.

For example, if you want information about me, you can use a search engine to look for the words "Harley Hahn". The results of the search will be a set of links to all the Web sites in that particular database that contain these words. To visit these pages, all you have to do is click on the links that look interesting.

My advice is to pick the search engines you like the best and learn how to use them well. Because the databases are so large, it is common to have your search return many spurious items that you will have to ignore. However, there are ways to make your request more sophisticated, which will get you better results.

In my experience, any time you spend learning how to use a tool well is time well spent.

Internet Consulting Detective

Check with this site every couple of weeks, and you will find hints on how to search the Net for what you want. The motif is based on a Sherlock Holmes theme. To test your skill, you can try to solve an Internet searching problem sent in by one of the readers.

Web:
http://www.intermediacy.com/sherlock/

Internet Sleuth

The Internet Sleuth is a really cool search tool. Specify what you want and the Internet Sleuth will submit your request to a number of databases and search tools around the Net. When the results come back, usually within a minute or two, Internet Sleuth will collect them and present them to you in an orderly manner. You can search the Web, news sources, business and finance databases, software archives and Usenet. What I like best about the Internet Sleuth is that it lets you specify where you want to search and how long you are willing to wait for the results.

Web:
http://www.isleuth.com/

FINDING STUFF ON THE NET

> You're almost there.

LocalEyes

LocalEyes is a regional business directory. You can browse the directory looking for a type of business in a particular area. If the business you find has a Web site, there will be a link to that site. The goal of LocalEyes is to find the best resources in each community. However, what you see is going to depend, at least partially, on which businesses are willing to pay for advertising. Thus, LocalEyes is not a comprehensive directory like your telephone book.

Web:
   http://www.localeyes.com/

Mailing List Search Engines

The Net has tens of thousands of different mailing lists, with more being added all the time. A mailing list is a forum for the discussion of a particular topic. Mailing lists differ from Usenet in that all the messages are distributed to participants by electronic mail. (With Usenet, messages are posted to various groups, which you can access with your Web browser or a special-purpose newsreader program.) To participate in a mailing list, you must subscribe (which is free). Once you subscribe, all the messages that are posted to the list will be sent to your mailbox. If you get tired of being on the list, you can unsubscribe at any time. Although the first mailing lists were administered by people, most modern lists (and all the ones listed in this book) are managed by computer programs. The three most popular such programs are Listserv, Majordomo and Listproc. I have included a great many mailing lists as resources in this book. However, there are times when you may want to perform a search of your own. To help you, here are my favorite mailing list search engines.

Web:
   http://www.catalog.com/vivian/
      interest-group-search.html
   http://www.findmail.com/
   http://www.liszt.com/
   http://www.lsoft.com/lists/listref.html
   http://www.neosoft.com/internet/paml/
   http://www.tile.net/lists/

New Stuff Talk and General Discussion

These two Usenet groups are good places to look for new and interesting Net resources. The **net-happenings** group is moderated and well-organized. This group is as close to an official place to announce a new resource as exists on the Net. There is *always* something interesting here. The **www.announce** group is not moderated, and is used by the general population to post notices about new Web sites.

Usenet:
   comp.infosystems.www.announce
   comp.internet.net-happenings

Mailing List Search Engines

(A mailing list is a discussion group in which messages are sent to the participants via email.)

Here is my one-step plan for total happiness:

1: Check with a mailing list search engine, and subscribe to the list of your dreams.

Pretty soon your mailbox will be overflowing, and your happiness will be unbounded.

Portals

Each time you start your browser, it automatically loads your "home page"—the same page you see when you click on the Home button. At any time, you can set your home page to be whatever you want (or nothing at all). The fact that millions of people see a specific Web site each time they start their browser is a vast marketing and advertising resource. For this reason, various Internet companies have created what are called "portals": Web sites that are designed to act as a welcome mat to the Internet. A typical portal will have a variety of useful features, such as access to a search engine, news, stock quotes, chat facilities, Web site guides, feature articles and free email. Both Microsoft and Netscape are aware of the value of a huge captive audience, and they make sure to preset the home page in their browsers to their own portal. But you can change it: to another portal, to a search engine, or to any site you want. (In Internet Explorer, pull down the View menu and click on "Internet Options". In Netscape, pull down the View menu, click on "Preferences" and then on "Navigator".)

Web:
  http://home.microsoft.com/
  http://home.netscape.com/
  http://www.aol.com/
  http://www.att.net/

Research It

Here are some tools that almost defy description (but that never stopped me). On one Web page you will find easy-to-use forms to search a variety of Internet resources: language tools (dictionaries, thesauri, acronym finders, translators—you can even conjugate French verbs); biography; geography (including zip codes and area codes); financial information (currency exchange, ticker symbols, stock quotes); and more. This is an interesting place to explore, just to get an appreciation of the type of useful reference information that is available for free on the Net.

Web:
  http://www.itools.com/research-it/

Search Engine Access Sites

These sites are not search engines. Rather, they are Web pages that contain a list of links to search engines. Although some people find such services useful, my experience is that—if you do much searching—it is probably easier to find one or two favorite engines and learn how to use them well. However, if you are an occasional searcher, you may like the one-size-fits-all setup. At the very least, I'm sure you will appreciate how some of these services select advertisements to show you based on the keywords in your search. How thoughtful.

Web:
  http://profusion.ittc.ukans.edu/
  http://www.albany.net/allinone/
  http://www.askjeeves.com/
  http://www.infind.com/
  http://www.metacrawler.com/
  http://www.metasearch.com/
  http://www.search.com/

Search Engine Access Sites

So your best friend is always bragging about his rare stamps. And your uncle Henry loves to talk about his original signed lithographs.

But the worst is a guy you knew in high school who never misses a chance to go on and on about the antique cars he has gathered over the years.

Well, here's your chance to get even. Invite them all over to see your collection of Internet search engines.

That'll show them who's cool.

Search Engines

A search engine is a facility that helps you find information on the Internet. The search engines I have listed here all allow you to search the Web. They work by maintaining a large database of information about Web sites. The search engine companies maintain their databases by using programs that continually search the Web. Some companies also accept submissions from people who want their sites listed. The basic way to use a search engine is to specify one or more keywords. A program then searches the database looking for resources that contain those words. The various search engines are organized in different ways. Some try to index every Web page on the Net. Others organize information into categories. In addition, most search engines offer other facilities, such as searching Usenet archives. My advice is to try the various search engines, pick one or two you like best, and learn how to use them well.

Web:
http://www.altavista.com/
http://www.excite.com/
http://www.hotbot.com/
http://www.infoseek.com/
http://www.lycos.com/
http://www.search.com/
http://www.snap.com/
http://www.webcrawler.com/
http://www.yahoo.com/

Usenet Search Engines

Usenet is a vast system of thousands of discussion groups. (For historical reasons, the discussion groups are called "newsgroups".) A Usenet search engine allows you to specify keywords, and then search a large archive, looking for all the newsgroup articles that contain those keywords. Millions of people around the world participate in Usenet every day, so being able to find what you need is a tremendous resource.

Web:
http://www.dejanews.com/
http://www.reference.com/

Usenet Search Engines
If it's worth saying (and, even more so, if it's not worth saying), someone on Usenet has probably said it lately.

Use a Usenet search engine and find out what people have been saying in places you would never even think of looking.

Web Catalogs

Have you ever thought about what it would be like to search the Web looking for the best sites in many different categories? Well, I do it in order to write this book, but I'm not the only one. Around the Net, a number of companies have Web sites that catalog the best, most interesting, or most useful Web sites. These Web catalogs are a good place to look when you know the type of resource you need, but you don't want to wade through a huge amount of items from a search engine.

Web:
http://a2z.lycos.com/
http://altavista.looksmart.com/
http://magellan.mckinley.com/
http://point.lycos.com/
http://www.dig.com/
http://www.diysearch.com/
http://www.ebig.com/
http://www.nerdworld.com/
http://www.vlib.org/
http://www.toptenlinks.com/
http://www.xplore.com/

And...

Web Channel Guides

A channel is a Web site that can send information to your computer automatically according to a predetermined schedule. (You will sometimes see this type of system referred to as "push" technology.) There are many channels available on the Net, and you can access them for free using your browser. Here are some guides to show you what is available. (Just make sure you don't spend so much time with Web channels that you forget to watch enough television.)

Web:
   http://home.netscape.com/netcenter/cf/index1.html
   http://www.iechannelguide.com/
   http://www.pushcentral.com/

Web Guides

Imagine you had your own research staff: a group of people, each one an expert in one particular area, who searched the Net just for you. Well, these Web guides are the next best thing. A large number of experts write articles and find resources for different categories of information. All you need to do is sit back, let someone else do the work, and pick and choose what you want. Not bad work if you can get it.

Web:
   http://www.miningco.com/
   http://www.suite101.com/

Web Sitez

When you look at an Internet address, the rightmost two parts are called the domain name. For example, **microsoft.com**, **whitehouse.gov**, **pacbell.net** or **activism.org**. The domain name will often give you information about the owners or purpose of the service using that name. Have you ever tried to find particular types of domain names? You can, using this awesome search engine, a great tool for searching for domain names set up for a specific purpose or by a specific organization. If a Web site exists for that name, the search engine will help you find it. For example, if you like humor, you might search for all the domain names that begin with "joke" or "humor".

Web:
   http://www.websitez.com/

Webring

Webring is cool. Very cool. It consists of hundreds of virtual "rings", each of which is devoted to a particular topic and contains a number of Web sites—for example: "Comic Book Ring", "The Official Ring of Games", "Female Empowerment Ring", "Adoption Ring", and so on. Here is how it works. You start by checking the index of rings for a topic that interests you. You then connect to the first site on whichever ring you want. At the bottom of the page, there is an icon you can select to move to the next site on the ring. Eventually, if you visit all the sites, you end up where you started. However, in the process, you will have jumped all over the Net. If you would like your site to be part of Webring, you can register it. Your site will then be placed in a particular ring. Next, you must put the Webring icons at the bottom of your Web page. These icons actually point back to the main Webring computer, where a special program figures out which is the next site in the ring. The Webring program handles all the details automatically, adding and deleting Web sites from rings as the need arises.

Web:
   http://www.webring.org/

FOLKLORE, MYTHS AND LEGENDS

Aesop's Fables

"Aesop" is the name given to an unknown Greek storyteller who lived in the sixth century B.C. Legend has it that Aesop was a slave, but nobody really knows much about him. What we do know is that, over the years, the stories called Aesop's Fables have become one of the most beloved of our literary traditions. As you read these very short stories, you will see many recognizable themes and morals, such as The Hare and the Tortoise ("Plodding wins the race"), Mercury and the Woodman ("Honesty is the best policy"), and The Fox and the Goat ("Look before you leap").

Web:
   http://attila.stevens-tech.edu/~soh1/aesop.html
   http://www.pacificnet.net/~johnr/aesop/

FOLKLORE, MYTHS AND LEGENDS

Atlantis

It all started with the Greek philosopher Plato (427-347 B.C.). He wrote two dialogues, Timeaus and Critias, in which Socrates, Hermocrates, Timeaus and Critias are sitting around having a conversation. Timeaus and Critias want to tell Socrates a story, a tale of a great city, a story which they say is absolutely true. And there begins the trouble. Ever since, people have been racing around the planet looking for this long-lost city of Atlantis. These Web sites have information on the origin of the legendary Atlantis, as well as links to other related resources.

Web:
http://www.activemind.com/Mysterious/Topics/Atlantis/
http://www.atlan.org/

Usenet:
alt.legend.atlantis
alt.legends.atlantis

Bigfoot

Bigfoot, sometimes called Sasquatch, is a creature of legend in the United States and Canada (especially in the U.S. Pacific Northwest). Bigfoot is supposed to be a tall, hairy apelike creature that has been sighted by isolated hikers and campers. The idea and legends of the North American Bigfoot are similar to that of the Abominable Snowman in parts of Asia. The Native American peoples have many different Bigfoot-like legends, which you can read about on the Net. If you would like to discuss these legends, or recent sightings, you can join the Usenet group.

Web:
http://www.hooked.net/~kylemi/bigfoot.html

Usenet:
alt.bigfoot

Aesop's Fables

Step 1: Read some Aesop's Fables.
Step 2: Look at today's newspaper.
Step 3: Marvel at how little human beings have changed in the last 2,600 years.

Charms and Amulets

There are days when something special is about to happen, and you want an extra boost to make things turn out perfect. For example, on the day you go in to ask your boss for a raise, wouldn't it be nice if you had a well-crafted spider amulet like that used by the ancient Europeans when they wanted to attract money? You don't like spiders? How about a magnetic lodestone, a horseshoe amulet, or a Snow Globe Pyramid of Luck? Whatever the occasion, when you need a bit of extra good luck to come your way, check out this site. It will give you great information about the legends, history and stories behind charms and amulets that have been used for centuries.

Web:
http://www.sonic.net/~yronwode/LuckyW.html

Computer Folklore

Over the years, the world of computing has been developing its own literary tradition. Like all such traditions, it starts with stories, discussion, tall tales and general talk. You can watch it all develop by following the discussion in these Usenet groups. Hang around here long enough, and when you get old, you will be able to tell your grandchildren, "I was there when Bill Gates told the *real* story of why DOS was kept around for so long."

Usenet:
alt.folklore.computers
alt.folklore.internet
comp.society.folklore

Cryptozoology

Cryptozoology is the study of mysterious animals — such as Bigfoot and the Loch Ness monster — whose existence is a matter of dispute. (The term "cryptozoology" was first used in the 1950s by Bernard Heuvelmans, author of "On the Track of Unknown Animals".) If you don't have enough to worry about in your life, and you want to concern yourself with things that don't actually exist, try reading some of the cryptozoology stuff at this site. There is information about monsters, bugs, invertebrates and legendary lifeforms that nobody can prove are real.

Web:
http://www.ncf.carleton.ca/~bz050/HomePage.cryptoz.html

Usenet:
alt.mythology.mythic-animals

Dragons

I was in the bookstore the other day, and I happened to go to the section that has my books. As I turned the corner, I encountered a dragon, holding a copy of this book and breathing fire. I said to him, "Don't you know this is a non-smoking area?" And he said, "I know, but I can't help it. This is a very hot book." As you can see, it's always good to know what to say to a dragon, just in case you happen to meet one unexpectedly. So read up on dragons, learn about their personalities (such as why they have such good taste in books), and enjoy their legendary stories.

Web:
http://www.draconian.com/links/
http://www.dragonfire.org/
http://www.netisle.net/~mersala/dragessay.html

Usenet:
alt.fan.dragons

Encyclopedia of Myths and Legends

High in content and easily searchable, these sites offer a wealth of information about mythology, legends and folklore. Read about all sorts of creatures, gods, goddesses, and their origins and history.

Web:
http://www.clubi.ie/lestat/godsmen.html
http://www.pantheon.org/myth/

Cryptozoology

Looking for Mr. Bigfoot? How about the Loch Ness monster or a giant cookiecutter shark?

If these mythical but well-known beasts appeal to you, maybe you should investigate Cryptozoology: the study of hidden animals.

(Actually, I would be satisfied with a way to find my cat when he is hiding in the back yard.)

Faerie Lore

Fairies come in many different shapes and sizes, and are known by a variety of names. What they have in common is that they are all magical beings who are most often mischievous in nature. If you are a fairy fan, here is a site you will enjoy: pictures, folklore and literature, and a searchable fairy dictionary. And while you are here, read about fairy etiquette, so you know what to do in case a brownie comes calling.

Web:
http://faeryland.tamu-commerce.edu/~earendil/faerie/faerie.html

IRC:
#faerie

Fairy Tales

A fairy tale is a legendary story involving imaginative characters and unusual adventures. Use the Net to enter the wonderful world of childhood magic. There are a variety of fairy tales for you to read to children and enjoy on your own.

Web:
http://www.cln.org/themes/fairytales.html
http://www.nvg.ntnu.no/~rikardb/folktales.html

Folk Tales from Around the World

Various cultures around the world have created tales to teach people and to modify the behavior of the community to suit specific needs. Out of these needs are born gods and goddesses, heroes and villains, magical objects, and mythical animals. It's fun to read folk tales from a variety of countries. Occasionally, I will light a nice fire, put the cat in my lap and read him a Syldavian folk tale. He really appreciates the cultural exposure and, as you know, a well-rounded cat can catch more mice. If you too would like to be more culturally refined, take look at these folk tales from around the world. What's my favorite folk tale? The one about the tired Internet writer who fell asleep exhausted in front of his computer, only to awaken in the morning to find that a group of elves had magically finished writing his book during the night.

Web:
http://darsie.ucdavis.edu/tales/
http://www.pitt.edu/~dash/folktexts.html

FOLKLORE, MYTHS AND LEGENDS

Folklore and Mythology Resources

A myth is a traditional, ancient story involving supernatural beings or other types of heroes. Myths are often used to explain natural phenomena and to demonstrate the customs and traditions of a particular society. A legend is an apocryphal (unverified) story that is handed down from one generation to the next. Myths and legends are important because they represent aspects of human nature and cultural evolution that form the basis of what we think and do today.

Web:
http://pibweb.it.nwu.edu/~pib/mythfolk.htm
http://pubpages.unh.edu/~cbsiren/myth.html
http://www.mindspring.com/~jadcox/
 Mythology_and_Folklore.html

Gems and Mineral Folklore

Some people believe there is magic and power locked inside the stones of the Earth, and that these stones can be used to channel energy from one place to another. (Of course, there are also people who believe the Easter Bunny is going to mysteriously fix all the bugs in Windows.) Regardless, in Usenet you can talk about folklore and stories surrounding various gems and minerals or use the handy reference guide on the Web.

Web:
http://www.demsjewelers.com/colinfo.htm

Usenet:
alt.folklore.gemstones

Look What I Found on the Net...

(from a fairy tale archive on the Net)

Living Like a Pig
(a tale from India)

One day, a guru foresaw in a flash of vision what he would be in his next life. So he called his favorite disciple and asked him what he would do for his guru in return for all he had received. The disciple said he would do whatever his guru asked him to do.

Having received this promise, the guru said, "Then this is what I'd like you to do for me. I've just learned that when I die, which will be very soon, I'm going to be reborn as a pig. Do you see that sow eating garbage there in the yard? I'm going to be reborn as the fourth piglet of its next litter. You'll recognize me by a mark on my brow. When that sow has littered, find the fourth piglet with a mark on its brow and, with one stroke of your knife, slaughter it. I'll then be released from a pig's life. Will you do this for me?"

The disciple was sad to hear all this, but he agreed to do as he had promised.

Soon after this conversation, the guru did die. And the sow did have a litter of four little pigs. One day, the disciple sharpened his knife and picked out the fourth little pig, which did indeed have a mark on its brow. Just as he was about to bring down his knife to slit its throat, the little pig suddenly spoke. "Stop! Don't kill me!" it screamed.

Before the disciple could recover from the shock of hearing the little pig speak in a human voice, it said, "Don't kill me. I want to live on as a pig. When I asked you to kill me, I didn't know what a pig's life would be like. It's great! Just let me go."

276 FOLKLORE, MYTHS AND LEGENDS

Look What I Found on the Net...

Newsgroup: alt.folklore.gemstones
Subject: Need to Know the Meaning of a Stone I Found

> Recently at an event I went to, I found a stone that was
> called apatite. I found the stones to be quite interesting,
> and purchased a few of them. I was wondering if anyone had
> come across similar stones, or might know of any significance
> they might have.

[...to which one person responds...]

Apatite is nothing new. It is a fairly common gem material, often found in attractive crystal forms. It's essentially a calcium phosphate, with some fluorine or chlorine in the composition.

As a gem, its use is somewhat limited, due to its softness. Because of their limited utility in jewelry, many apatite gems are inexpensive. That explains why you'll see the things on TV home shopping channels, being praised for their rarity and beauty. Of course, the real reason is that apatite crystals can be bought very cheaply, and look fine on a screen. The average consumer, not having seen them before, has no way of judging whether they are actually worth buying.

**Xxxxx Xxxx, commercial jeweler and metalsmith,
Graduate Gemologist and Lapidary**

[...another person answers the same question as follows...]

I have some information from the book Xxxxxx by Xxxxxx:

Apatite (astrological sign of Gemini) can be used to stimulate the intellect and to promote realization that one's strength occurs through both spiritual avenues and via love; hence, dissolving aloofness and negativity.

Apatite is related to service and to the development of the humanitarian pursuits. It is attuned to healing, storing information, communicating, balancing energy and teaching.
It is extremely useful in the expansion of knowledge and in the disclosure of the truth to freedom.

It can be used to stimulate the development of clairvoyance, clairaudience, clairsentience, and the awareness of the devic worlds. It can further the connection with UFOs and can provide access to past-life insights and telepathy.

This gem is the stone of the future and will bring knowledge to those attuned to it by clearing mental confusion. It truly awakens the fine, inner self.

Apatite vibrates to the number 9.

FOLKLORE, MYTHS AND LEGENDS

Germanic Myths, Legends and Sagas

Do you ever have one of those days when you come into the house, all bundled up and covered with snow, and someone hands you a big mug of hot chocolate and says, "Here, sit down by the fire and let me relate an old Germanic legend my mother used to tell me." It doesn't happen to me, because I live near a beach in California, but it could happen to you, especially if you have this Web site in your bookmark list. This site has information about Germanic (Scandinavian and Teutonic) mythology, culture, ancient beliefs and deities.

Web:
http://www.pitt.edu/~dash/mythlinks.html

Ghost Stories

Ghost stories are a fun and inexpensive way to keep yourself up all night. Read some creepy ghost stories on the Web or get them hot off the Net by checking out the Usenet group.

Web:
http://www.crown.net/X/GhostStories.html

Usenet:
alt.folklore.ghost-stories

Look What I Found on the Net...

```
Newsgroup: alt.folklore.ghost-stories
Subject: Ouija Board Story

> I once scoffed at Ouija Boards saying, "How could something
> mass produced by Parker Brothers be a powerful tool of evil?"
> to which my girlfriend quickly retorted, "If you were the sort
> of paranatural malevolent entity that supposedly gets its
> kicks from screwing people up with these things, wouldn't
> you try and get them mass produced?"

> Food for thought.

> I guess what I am trying to say is, be careful.
> I went insane, and spent a month under the care of
> a physician during which I slept less than twelve hours in
> total and went through hell.  It took me almost four years
> to fully recover, and I am still scared it might happen again.

> If you are going to get into the occult seriously, fine.
> Two bits of advice:  Always make sure that you do ALL your
> research first.  If you are going to do something, make sure
> you have perfected undoing it first.

> Second, always include a skeptic who you trust to remain a
> skeptic and remain a friend.  You'll thank me later.
> I wish I had done both these things.

You know, he's right.  Ouija Boards are the devil's tool.
They are evil.  You don't wanna mess with them.

They slowly possess you by addicting you, and each time you use
it your soul is more open for possession.
```

FOLKLORE, MYTHS AND LEGENDS

Gnomes

A gnome is an imaginary dwarflike creature that lives underground and is often depicted as guarding a treasure. The traditions and mythos of gnomes are well-developed. You can read about their history, appearance, activities, and so on. Gnomes are cute, and it can be fun to look at their pictures and read about them, but, of course, they don't really exist (or do they?).

Web:
http://www.erols.com/michaelmyrick/

Greek Mythology

Brush up on your ancient Greek mythology by reading stories about gods, goddesses, heroes and monsters. This Web page will not only give you an overview, but will also diagram a family tree so you can keep all your characters straight.

Web:
http://www.princeton.edu/~rhwebb/myth.html

Griffins

A griffin (also known as a griffon or gryphon) is a mythological beast with the body of a lion, and the head, forelegs and wings of an eagle. As you can imagine, this would be enough to cause the poor animal to be refused admittance to the more fashionable night clubs. Still, despite their odd features, griffins have been extremely popular over the centuries and are portrayed as having great intelligence and powerful strength (much like writers of Internet books). Griffins have appeared in numerous starring roles, as pets for the god Zeus, in a singing scene in Alice in Wonderland, and on many science fiction book covers. If you like griffins, or you want to learn how to like griffins, check out this Web site.

Web:
http://members.aol.com/catgandalf/gryphon/faq.html

Usenet:
alt.mythology.mythic-animals.gryphons

Imaginary Creatures

There are a great many mythological creatures in the world. You may not be able to see them in the forest or in the zoo; they live in our imaginations and in our hearts. If you like the land of make-believe, you will have a great time exploring this large, comprehensive Web site devoted to strange imaginary creatures.

Web:
http://www.gryphonheart.com/

King Arthur and Camelot

Arthurian legend contains many stories based in medieval times about King Arthur of Britain and his Knights of the Round Table. The legend can be traced back as far as the sixth century, although the stories have been expanded and modified throughout the years. The basic story, however, has always remained more or less the same. Arthur is the illegitimate son of King Uther Pendragon. After the king's death, Arthur distinguishes himself by successfully pulling out a sword that is embedded in a huge stone. Arthur becomes king and, from Camelot, reigns over the land of Britain. The stories involve the familiar characters of King Arthur, his knights (including Sir Lancelot, Sir Galahad and Sir Tristram), his wife Guinevere, Merlin the Magician, the Lady of the Lake (who gives Arthur his special sword Excalibur), and his enemies Morgan le Fay and Sir Mordred, all of whom appear in Arthur's many adventures. Eventually, Arthur is wounded by Sir Mordred and—as he is dying—is carried away to Avalon, from which he will one day return.

Web:
http://www.britannia.com/history/arthur/
http://www.eliki.com/ancient/myth/camelot/
http://www.lib.montana.edu/~slainte/arthur/

Usenet:
alt.legend.king-arthur

Listserv Mailing List:
List Name: arthurnet
Subscribe to: listserv@morgan.ucs.mun.ca

FOLKLORE, MYTHS AND LEGENDS

King Arthur

It's a well-known fact that King Arthur didn't really exist. (However, the last time I heard from him, he was saying that I don't really exist, so you'll have to make up your own mind.) If you want to get into the esoterica of the Arthurian legend, subscribe to the ArthurNet mailing list. Find out if Merlin was killed by one bullet or two. Was there really only one assassin, or was the whole thing a cover-up?

Loch Ness Monster

The Loch Ness Monster is a mythical sea serpent that lives in a very deep lake in Scotland called Loch Ness. (The word "loch" means lake in the Scottish dialect.) Since the early 1930s, people have been actively looking for the monster, affectionately referred to as Nessie. The evidence has been inconclusive (how do you prove a monster does *not* exist?), but people keep trying. In October of 1987, a group of 20 ships used sonar to check the lake carefully. Nothing was found, but who knows?

Web:
http://www.gng.com/lore_of_the_loch/
http://www.lochness.co.uk/
http://www.si.edu/resource/faq/nmnh/lochness.htm

Mermaids

A mermaid is a legendary sea creature with the head and upper body of a woman and the lower anatomy of a fish. Sightings of mermaids have always been popular among sailors who have spent long days at sea, without female companionship, in the company of other sweaty sailors (and the odd fish). These sites have pictures of mermaids, as well as classic and modern tales.

Web:
http://www.javanet.com/~frodo/merlinks.html
http://www.mermaid.net/

Mythology in Western Art

The stories of Greek mythology are soap operas that take place back when men were men, and the other men were glad of it. If you would like to know how the gods and goddesses of mythological tales have been portrayed by artists over the centuries, sneak a peek at this Web site. It offers images of individuals who have a starring role in your favorite myths. You will also find links to other interesting Greek and Roman mythology sites.

Web:
http://www-lib.haifa.ac.il/www/art/mythology_westart.html

Mythology Talk and General Discussion

Myths are traditional stories, passed down from one generation to the next. Myths arise in all time periods, and they most always involve supernatural events. (Myths are different from folklore in that folk tales are generally more entertaining and believable.) If you like any type of mythology, these are the places to hang out and discuss the who, what, when, where and how-high-did-he-jump aspects of this entertaining and telling area of human culture.

Usenet:
alt.mythology
alt.mythology.mythic-animals

280 FOLKLORE, MYTHS AND LEGENDS

Native American Myths and Legends

Native storytellers created sacred myths to explain the origin of humans, to answer the question of why we live as we do, and to record lessons that have been passed down through years of living. Many of these stories were based on nature and animals. Aside from being teaching tools, the legends were often used to entertain. Here are a variety of traditional stories from various native tribes.

Web:
http://www.ac.wwu.edu/~skywise/legends.html
http://www.mc.maricopa.edu/users/shoemaker/mourningdove/

Pirates

Pirates are the ultimate seafaring bad guys. They wear cool clothes, they pillage, and they can stay up as late as they want to watch Letterman. Yes, the pirate life is the life for me. If you want to be a pirate, or you want to just see what it was like to be a pirate (back in the days when pirates were allowed to have fun), take a look at these sites. You'll see pictures of ships, read about the pirate way of living, and have a chance to learn about the history, legends and myths of famous pirates of antiquity.

Web:
http://huizen.nhkanaal.nl/~wastrel/
http://www.discover.net/~nqgiven/ports.htm
http://www.ocracoke-nc.com/blackbeard/

Look What I Found on the Net...

```
Newsgroup: alt.mythology
Subject: Trans-atlantic Contacts

I think the ancient Mexicans came from Atlantis, because both
cultures have been *proven* to have eaten corn, which originally
came from the Old World.

Since it's well known that trans-atlantic contacts were
ubiquitous in antiquity, it seems to me that there's no question
that the Mexicans derived their civilization from the Atlantians.
After all, even Plato asserted this in no uncertain terms.

Now, don't get me wrong. I'm not in any way trying to claim that
Atlantian civilization came from alien beings, or anything else
so patently ridiculous.  All I'm trying to say is that since
trans-atlantic contacts have been *proven* (in this and other
newsgroups) to have happened long before the start of recorded
history, you obviously can't deny that the Mexican civilizations
were from Atlantis.

I mean, come on, people, it's as plain as the nose on your face.
Why must you insist, stubbornly, that what I and others are
saying isn't true?

What are you afraid of? The bogey man?
```

FOLKLORE, MYTHS AND LEGENDS 281

Robin Hood

Robin Hood is a legendary 13th century English hero who robbed the rich and gave his stolen goods to the poor and oppressed. Robin Hood lived in Sherwood Forest (in central England, north of Nottingham and west of Lincoln) with his band of merry followers who assisted him in his heroic endeavors. Read about the life and times of Robin Hood and why he is popular to this day.

Web:
http://www.lib.rochester.edu/camelot/rh/rhhome.stm
http://www.webspan.net/~amunno/rhood.html

Majordomo Mailing List:
List Name: **robinhood-l**
Subscribe to: **majordomo@cc.rochester.edu**

Scientific Urban Legends

There are all sorts of nasty rumors flying around about science. And we know just where they are coming from. Check out the latest outlandish tales of science, which often sound like they come straight from the set of a 1950s science fiction movie. Help discern the truths from the myths by reading up on what the folks on the Net have to say.

Web:
http://www.urbanlegends.com/science/

Usenet:
alt.folklore.science

> It's nice to be important,
> but it's important to be nice.

Sea Serpents and Lake Monsters

I have been swimming in the ocean for many, many years and I have never seen anything out of the ordinary or unexplainable. However, there are people all around the world who say they have seen oddities in oceans and lakes. Some of these people even have pictures. If you want a nice overview of what creatures you might be missing, take a look at this site. There are pictures, explanations and background information about various legendary creatures such as the Loch Ness monster, the Lake Champlain monster, the megamouth shark, giant squids, Ogopogo and others. And if you are insatiable for unusual marine animals, there are links to other water creature sites.

Web:
http://www.serve.com/shadows/serpent.htm

Look What I Found on the Net...

```
Newsgroup: alt.folklore.science
Subject: See the Ultraviolet

> According to Hecht's "Optics", people who have cataract
> surgery can see into the ultraviolet. The removed lens no
> longer filters out the ultraviolet.

The late Walter Scott Houston, who wrote Deep Sky Wonders in
Sky & Telescope, mentioned this once in a while.  The central
star in the ring nebula (M57 in Lyra) is brightest in the
ultraviolet.  This star is considered a challenge to see since
there is so little "visible" light emitted.  After cataract
surgery (in which the eyes lens is replaced with a plastic one),
he claimed that the star was easy to see with that eye.
```

FOLKLORE, MYTHS AND LEGENDS

Urban Legends

An urban legend is a story that is widely believed to be true, even though no real evidence exists. Urban legends generally offer a measure of humor or horror, and seem to take on a life of their own, regardless of how true they really are. Urban legends are famous for being retold as if they happened to "a friend of a friend". For example, are there really gangs of kidnappers at Disneyland who abduct children, change their clothing and hairstyles, and then smuggle them out the gates into a waiting getaway car?

Web:
http://www.snopes.com/
http://www.urbanlegends.com/

Usenet:
alt.folklore.urban

Don't you just love those unbelievable stories that always happen to a "friend of a friend"? These are urban legends, and the Net has several resources devoted to such tales. (I wonder, is there any truth to the story about the man whose life was saved by a Harley Hahn Unix book?)

Werewolf Folklore

On those days when you are not feeling quite like your old self, when you would rather have a midnight walk and howl at the moon than watch TV, you should know where to turn. Check these sites to see if you have any of the symptoms.

Web:
http://www.lycanthrope.org:4242/beliefs/other/shifting
http://www.therianthrope.org/ahww/

Usenet:
alt.horror.werewolves

FONTS AND TYPEFACES

Field Guide to Fonts

Have you ever used a Roget's Thesaurus? Although many people think it is a synonym finder, a Roget's Thesaurus is actually designed to help you find the exact right word. You use a Roget's Thesaurus when you know the meaning of a word, but you do not know the word. Analogously, there are times when you need to find out the name of a particular font. For example, what do you do when you know the characteristics of a font—perhaps because you have a sample—but you don't know its name? Here is an unusual and well thought-out tool that can help you track down the mysterious font, by narrowing the choices based on the font's characteristics.

Web:
http://www.lm.com/~mundie/Typography/Faces.html

Figlet Fonts

Don't settle for the same old dull, boring strings of letters. Spice things up with some ASCII fonts. This Web page has information about Figlet as well as links to sets of Figlet fonts and Web-based Figlet services.

Web:
http://st-www.cs.uiuc.edu/users/chai/figlet.html

Font Talk and General Discussion

These are the Usenet groups that are used to discuss fonts, typefaces, typography and related topics. If you are in the page layout business, these are good groups to read regularly. These are also good places to ask a question about fonts when no one around the office has any idea what you are talking about.

Usenet:
alt.binaries.fonts
comp.fonts

Listserv Mailing List:
List Name: **typo-l**
Subscribe to: listserv@listserv.heanet.ie

Fontsite Magazine

The Fontsite is a magazine for people who take their typestyles and graphics seriously. If you are a professional, take a break from work and cruise through the articles and resources. Dream of beautiful typefaces, slick new designs and people who really care about the art of typography. (Then go back to work.)

Web:
http://www.fontsite.com/

Foreign Font Archive

This is a huge repository of fonts from around the world. There are many different fonts for a large variety of languages, such as Hebrew, Gaelic, Arabic, Japanese, Cyrillic (Russian), and many more. All of these fonts can be downloaded for free, either as shareware or freeware.

Web:
http://www.dtcc.edu/~berlin/fonts.html

Free Fonts

There are a large variety of fonts available for free on the Net. Here are some resources from which you can download a large variety of different fonts. When you have a spare moment, these are great places to browse to find a new and interesting font (say, to give to your wife or husband for an anniversary present).

Web:
http://members.aol.com/JR9er/links.html
http://wabakimi.carleton.ca/~mgauthie/
http://www.fontface.com/
http://www.ragnarokpress.com/scriptorium/month.html
http://www.thefreesite.com/font.htm

Free Fonts

As Shakespeare once said, "There are more fonts on the Web and on the Net, Horatio, than are dreamt of in your philosophy." That's fine for Horatio: he could borrow Shakespeare's font collection whenever he wanted. But how do ordinary people like you and me find the fonts we need?

We use the Free Fonts sites.

Funny Fonts

Page layout is serious business, so don't forget to take some time to relax. And what better way to rest the old cerebrum than by fooling around with some goofy fonts and dingbats. Myself, I can't decide whether to publish my next book using Flying Penguin or Chow Mein.

Web:
http://totte.simplenet.com/

Look What I Found on the Net...

```
Newsgroup: comp.fonts
Subject: I Need Your Help Desperately

I am looking for a font called "Ovine".

My band uses this font for our logo, and I deleted it by
mistake.

Please, if someone has this font, I would be happy to trade
something for it. I hope someone has it.
```

284 FONTS AND TYPEFACES

Headline Maker

This typeface company has come up with an engaging way to show their wares. You can select one of their many typefaces and use it to create a headline banner of your choice (such as "Harley Hahn writes great books"). This is a fun way to experiment with different typefaces, and after you are finished, you can save the result to show your friends.

Web:

http://robot.esselte.com/

Truetype Fonts

Truetype is a family of fonts that was originally developed by Apple. They developed these fonts for two reasons. (1) They didn't want to have to pay royalties to the owners of existing fonts. (2) They wanted to fix some of the technical problems in Adobe Type 1 fonts. The Truetype family was designed to be compact, flexible and extensible. Since Microsoft had been looking for a similar type of font family, Apple agreed to license the technology. Since then, Microsoft has done considerable Truetype development, enhancing the font technology. Today, Truetype fonts will work on any current Microsoft platform or Apple computer. This Web site has a great deal of information devoted to Truetype fonts, including Opentype (the result of Microsoft's collaboration with Adobe to unify Truetype with Type 1 fonts).

Web:

http://www.truetype.demon.co.uk/

&Type

This is an eclectic set of resources for people interested in typography: check out the strange, interesting and useful fonts, take a look at the typesetting tricks, and read a number of articles, all related to fonts and the people who use them.

Web:

http://www.graphic-design.com/Type/

TypeArt Library

Here are some interesting typographical resources. The ones I think you will enjoy the most are the contests (can you identify a mystery font?), tips for typesetters, and tips for typeface designers, all of which change from time to time.

Web:

http://www.typeart.com/

Typofile

The Typofile Web site is for typophiles. If you love typefaces, you will love this Web site. Use the hypertext decision-making system to help you choose the best typeface for a particular job. Read hints on how to use typefaces well. And, for real typeface lovers, take a look at the featured typefaces of the month.

Web:

http://www.will-harris.com/type.htm

Typography Terminology

The world of typography has a great many technical words and terms. Here are some glossaries that can help you understand these terms. In my experience, knowing what the words mean counts for a lot. So, the next time someone (say, your manager) acts like he or she knows more than you do, you can say, "Well, I can do it your way if you really want, but the glyphs in that particular typeface will force me to use slightly different kerning which may change the lines by a few points."

Web:

http://www.nwalsh.com/comp.fonts/FAQ/cf_18.htm
http://www.sos.com.au/files/glosray.html

Unusual Fonts

Are you a font hog? Do you love collecting all types of fonts until your disk is full? If so, I think you'll enjoy these two Web sites. You will find unusual offerings, free for the downloading, that only a real font hog could appreciate.

Web:

http://fonts.transmission23.com/
http://www.gothic.net/~tygre/

FOOD AND DRINK

Beer

Making, choosing and imbibing: these discussion groups will help you find out everything you want to know about beer and related beverages. Read the regular posting on which beers are best, based on the votes of Usenet participants. (Anyone can vote, although you do have to supply your own beer.) On the Web you will find more beer information than you can shake a handful of beer nuts at.

Web:
  http://www.beerinfo.com/
  http://www.dlc.fi/~pennaka/english.html
  http://www.realbeer.com/

Usenet:
  alt.beer
  alt.beer.alt
  alt.drinks.beer
  rec.crafts.brewing
  rec.food.drink.beer

Beer Ratings

So many beers, so little time. If you feel too overwhelmed to go taste test all the beers in the world yourself, don't worry. Some guys on the Net have done a lot of the work for you. Read their beer ratings and see what they say to try and what to avoid.

Web:
  http://www.beerismylife.com/beerlist.htm
  http://www.tricity.wsu.edu/~bwarren/beer.html

You don't have to be a senior to read "Seniors".

Beverages

Unless you drink only water, somewhere, sometime, you are a consumer of commercial beverages. As such, you have my personal guarantee that there is something, somewhere, on the Net that will interest you. We all know that the world is full of fanatics, but it doesn't really hit home until you see something like this Web site: someone has used enormous amounts of time and energy (and a fair amount of talent) to create an entire Web site devoted to beverages. Check it out for yourself. While you are there, take the beverage purity test to see how beverage savvy you are. (I rated 17 percent, which puts me in the third lowest category.)

Web:
  http://www.thebevnet.com/

Usenet:
  alt.drinks.snapple
  alt.fan.dr-pepper
  alt.fan.ok-soda
  alt.soda.moxie
  rec.food.drink.tea

Look What I Found on the Net...

```
Newsgroup: rec.food.drink.beer
Subject: alt.beer vs. rec.food.drink.beer

> What is the difference between rec.food.drink.beer and
> alt.beer, if any?  Other than the fact that there is less
> junk in this group.

I think rec.food.drink.beer gets more posts like yours than
does alt.beer.

I wonder why that is?
```

FOOD AND DRINK

Cereal

Cereal is not just for the first meal of the day. In fact, it's more than just nutrition and sustenance—it's fun, and if you read the box, you could even call it a literary adventure. More than that, it's a facilitator of a great social experience by bringing people together on the Net to talk about how cereal makes an impact on all our lives. Don't be left out of the cereal movement. Grab a spoon and dig in.

Web:
http://www.toymuseum.com/cereal/timeline.html

Usenet:
alt.cereal

Cheese

If you like cheese, even just in passing, you *must* spend some time at this Web site. You will find much information about the cheeses of the world: how they are made, what they are made of, where they are made, what wines go well with particular cheeses, history of cheese, how to make cheese, a cheese glossary, Ask Dr. Cheese, and cheese literature (poems and writings about cheese).

Web:
http://www.wgx.com/cheesenet/

Usenet:
alt.cheese

Coca-Cola

You can pooh-pooh the contributions of America to world culture, but there is no gainsaying the fact that Coca-Cola has virtually defined the concept of ubiquity. It would be difficult to find anything as well-known as this peripatetic soft drink, so I'm sure it comes as no surprise when I tell you that the Coke fanatics of the world have a definite presence on the Net. If you have any interest at all in Coca-Cola and its social accoutrements, here are some Internet resources to help you explore this beacon of international culture, clearly the most important beverage in the refrigerator of American hegemony.

Web:
http://www.midwest-plaza.com/dkgifts/cocacolacity.htm
http://xenon.stanford.edu/~liao/cokestory.html

Usenet:
alt.food.coca-cola
alt.food.cocacola

Cocktails

The interesting thing about alcohol is that so much of our popular culture has been developed around the acts of creating, mixing and drinking alcoholic beverages. Can you think of any other drug that has specially trained people (bartenders) whose sole purpose is to create and serve a large number of different preparations (cocktails) based on that one particular drug? Do you not think it's interesting that the large alcohol companies routinely spend huge amounts of money trying to build an image for their particular version of this drug? And would I be too much of a spoilsport if I pointed out that the main reason one administers alcohol to oneself is to cause one's brain cells to act abnormally in a way that makes one feel good? I guess that would be too much, so forget I said it. In fact, forget all of this. Just enjoy these cocktails Web sites and drink up.

Web:
http://www.cocktailparty.com/dadrinks.htm
http://www.epact.se/acats/
http://www.ozemail.com.au/~berghous/drink.html
http://www.webtender.com/

Usenet:
alt.drinks.scotch-whisky

Coffee

Some people like to sip it, some gulp it down in the morning before their eyes are open. Some people like to have it flavored and run through various elaborate preparations which result in a thick, syrupy brew or a decadent foamy concoction. And then there are the hard core people who don't bother brewing and simply munch on the beans themselves. If your drug of choice is coffee, you will feel right at home in these Usenet groups where people talk about preparation, storage, growth and sale of this popular beverage. The Web sites offer the perfect reading material for your coffee break.

Web:
http://www.ao.net/~fredster/fredster/recipes/recipes.htm
http://www.cappuccino.com/
http://www.cupocoffee.com/origins.htm
http://www.nwlink.com/~donclark/java.html

Usenet:
alt.coffee
alt.food.coffee
rec.food.drink.coffee

IRC:
#coffee

College Food

Ah, those good old college days. How nostalgic we will be when our hair turns silver and we wax eloquent about mystery meat burgers and the blue-green algae surprise. Come on in and discuss college dining halls, cafeterias, and pay-for-it-even-if-you-don't-want-it food plans.

Usenet:
   alt.college.food

> Are you young? Are you a gourmet? Then discussing college food on the Net is for you.

Epicurious

Epicurious is an online magazine dedicated to the three major areas of culinary enjoyment: eating, drinking, and playing with your food. I find the articles imaginative and well worth a regularly scheduled look. My suggestion is to poke into the Web site once a week to see if anything new and exciting has arrived. You will find reviews, recipes, food commentary, wine information and—my favorite—complaints about stupid food.

Web:
   http://food.epicurious.com/

Fast Food

Fast food refers to cheap food that is sold, prepared, and served to you within several minutes. Fast food is usually bought at a franchised outlet which, as often as not, allows you to order, receive and devour the food all without leaving your car. Fast food outlets tend to standardize their offerings. For example, a Big Mac (multi-layer hamburger with secret sauce) will look, feel and taste pretty much the same from one McDonalds to the next. (Actually, if the carefully trained employees prepared your Big Mac correctly, it will look, feel and taste *exactly* the same.) Since the cost of fast food is reasonable and there is no real wait, such restaurants are a favorite of busy parents everywhere. If you are a fast food buff or buffette, and you want to share your ersatz culinary experiences and opinions, what better place could there be than the Net: the home of fast, cheap, simple, satisfying experiences?

Web:
   http://www.olen.com/food/

Usenet:
   alt.food.fast-food
   alt.food.mcdonalds
   alt.food.taco-bell
   alt.mcdonalds
   alt.mcdonalds.fries

Food Labeling Information

The U.S. Food and Drug Administration (FDA) has created a system of labeling requirements for all foods that are sold in the United States. Food labeling requirements control how nutritional information is listed on all packaging. The next time you are in the supermarket, notice how your shopping experience is enhanced by knowing the exact nutritional breakdown of each item you buy (calories, fats, carbohydrates, proteins, vitamins, minerals, and so on). As you are waiting at the checkout stand, you may want to pause briefly and offer a silent moment of thanks to the FDA's Center for Food Safety and Applied Nutrition.

Web:
   http://vm.cfsan.fda.gov/label.html

Food Labeling Information

My cat has a simple system when it comes to understanding food: a piece of food is either tuna or it's not tuna. For human beings, however, things are more complicated.

To help us, the United States Food and Drug Administration has set up a system in which all prepared foods must carry labels that have certain useful information.

If you have any questions as to how to interpret these labels, you can check with the Food Labeling Information Web site, sponsored by the FDA's Center for Food Safety and Applied Nutrition.

Or you can use my special alternate systems: a piece of food is either chocolate or it's not.

Food Safety

It is hard to imagine anything with broader public health implications than making sure our food is safe and nutritious. Food requires proper handling at each step of the way, from production and processing, through distribution and final preparation. Here are some excellent resources that will allow you to find whatever information you need about food safety: how to prepare food properly, germs that cause illness, current public health concerns, and much more. As you might imagine, a great deal of food safety regulation and education is done by the government. As you visit these Web sites, I am sure you will appreciate how complex and difficult it is to maintain a system of safe food. Remember this the next time you hear someone complain that government is a waste of money, and people should be left to fend for themselves in the marketplace. Our food safety system works so well, we can take it for granted, but only because other people are working hard on our behalf.

Web:
http://vm.cfsan.fda.gov/~dms/fc-3.html
http://vm.cfsan.fda.gov/~mow/foodborn.html
http://vm.cfsan.fda.gov/~mow/intro.html
http://www.foodsafety.org/
http://www.usda.gov/agency/fsis/consedu.htm

Usenet:
alt.food.safety

Listserv Mailing List:
List Name: **fsnet-l**
Subscribe to: **listserv@listserv.uoguelph.ca**

Food Talk and General Discussion

It is universally acknowledged that—out of all the things people put in their mouths in public—food is the most socially acceptable. There is a lot to say about food, and people on the Net are more than glad to say it. If you would like to take part in the discussion, just pull your chair up to the virtual table and join the group. What I like best about the Net is you can talk with your mouth full.

Usenet:
alt.food
rec.food
rec.food.drink
rec.food.equipment
rec.food.marketplace
rec.food.preserving

Listserv Mailing List:
List Name: **eat-l**
Subscribe to: **listserv@listserv.vt.edu**

Foodplex

Don't feel guilty about your food. Enjoy yourself with the help of this guilt-free Web page dedicated to the pleasure of fine food. Information about food, recipes, and food humor.

Web:
http://www.gigaplex.com/food/index.htm

French Fries

Okay, let's be honest for a moment. Is there anything you would rather do, right now, than connect to a hot French fry Web site and indulge yourself? Learn about history, world culture, art, government, little-known facts, foreign customs and the law. All of this from the lowly French fry? It almost sounds too good to be true. (It's not.)

Web:
http://www.select-ware.com/fries/

On the Net, you can shop til your modem drops.

FOOD AND DRINK

Fun Foods

We need to eat just to stay alive, but that doesn't mean we can't have some fun at the same time. We all know that some foods are just naturally more fun than others. For example, a plateful of turkey with cranberry sauce and baked sweet potatoes is serious food—ice cream is fun. A dry red Merlot wine can be a treat to enjoy with your linguini and clam sauce at a pretentious, over-priced Italian restaurant, but for pure enjoyment, Kool-aid is definitely the drink of the people. And ketchup—well, all I can say about ketchup is that anyone who grew up with my brother has enough first-hand experience with the consumption of ketchup to last a lifetime. However, when it comes to appreciating these special foods, eating them is only part of the fun. You should spend at least a few hours a week on Usenet, talking, reading, learning, and generally sharing in the collective experience.

Usenet:
alt.cake
alt.drinks.kool-aid
alt.food.ice-cream
alt.food.pancakes
alt.ketchup

Global Gourmet

It's a culinary emergency. Your husband has just called to say that he is bringing home his mother, father and sister for dinner. His mother is from New Zealand, his father is from Poland, and his sister has just spent the last five years living in Mexico. What to do? Turn to the Global Gourmet for international recipes and advice, and within minutes, you are whipping up a wonderful meal of Lamb Turnovers with Curried Yogurt Sauce (New Zealand), Cheese Pascha from Lwow (Poland), and Grilled Snapper with Charred Habanero Salsa (Mexico). Thanks to the Net—and your superior culinary proficiency—the dinner is a complete success, and contentment blankets the family like the gentle rain that falls from the heavens above.

Web:
http://www.globalgourmet.com/

History of Food

Where do you ask for information on what type of food the peasants ate during the French Revolution? What do you do when the in-laws are due any moment and you need the recipe for figgy pudding? Check out this Usenet discussion group and move forward, into the past.

Usenet:
rec.food.historic

Look What I Found on the Net...

```
Newsgroup: alt.ketchup
Subject: Recipe for ketchup cake

> Here is a complete meal for six people.
>
> You only need:
>
> 3 liters ketchup
> 200 gram flour
> 1 liter milk
>
> Mix the ingredients and place it in the oven for approximately
> half an hour.
>
> Enjoy!

I spent a night in the hospital due to eating this disgusting
cake.  Thank you very much.
```

FOOD AND DRINK

Homebrewing

Making your own beer can be fun, but you have to know what you are doing. If you are interested in homebrewing, the Net has resources to help you. You can start with the basics—such as, how do you make beer at home?—and work your way up to experimenting with esoteric recipes. Along the way, you can meet other homebrewing enthusiasts around the world and swap tips.

Web:
http://www.aob.org/hbshopframeset.htm
http://www.brewguys.com/
http://www.phoenix.net/~sdaniel/
http://www.pressenter.com/~rcalley/

Usenet:
alt.homebrewing

Mead

Mead is a honey-based fermented beverage that people have been making as long as there have been people (and bees). Traditional mead is made with honey, water and yeast. Other varieties use particular spices and juices. Once you find out about mead, I bet you will be tempted to make some. If so, here are some resources to get you started.

Web:
http://www.atd.ucar.edu/rdp/gfc/mead/mead.html
http://www.hbd.org/brewery/library/meadfaq.html

Restaurant Talk and General Discussion

Oh my, we all like to spout off about what is good or bad in the world, and this is a great place to do it. Do you have a favorite restaurant that you simply must praise? Or did you just spend too much money for a dinner that tasted like warmed-over cardboard, and you feel obliged to warn everyone in the world to stay away? Join the discussion on Usenet, and let the fish and chips fall where they may.

Usenet:
alt.food.red-lobster
alt.restaurants
rec.food.restaurants

Restaurants on the Web

Check out the menus of these fine restaurants on the Web. See their menus, gift catalogs, and maybe even fax in your order. The restaurants include some of the most interesting places to eat in a variety of cities around the world.

Web:
http://www.cuisinenet.com/
http://www.cyber-kitchen.com/pgrestrt.htm
http://www.dineresource.com/
http://www.dinersgrapevine.com/
http://www.dinesite.com/
http://www.onlinemenus.com/

Look What I Found on the Net...

```
(from a Homebrewing Web site)

(The following comments were included with the recipe for a
homemade beer named "Nothing Exceeds Like Excess".)

This was not an easy batch. The yeast took off immediately and
blew out 1-1/2 gallons through the blow tube.  Once the yeast
subsided, I let it sit for a week and then bottled it...

The flavor is impossibly syrupy, but I'll put in the cellar and
forget about it for a few months.  This could be my most
expensive failure yet, then again, maybe not. Maybe I can pour
it over ice cream...
```

FOOD AND DRINK

Eating Out Is Good

These days, more and more people who go to restaurants are going to restaurants. (Strange, but true.) But where's the best place to go?
No need to guess.
Before you spend your hard-earned cash for stuff to put in your mouth, check with your friends on **rec.food.restaurants**.

In the game of life, you are a free agent.

Sushi

What is it about small, strange hunks of biological material wrapped in seaweed that makes you want to put them in your mouth? It has been said that sushi is to the 1990s what roasted chunks of meat were to the 1530s. Still, you don't need to take our word for it. Your friends on the Net are ever-ready to talk sushi-talk regardless of how compelling your needs may be.

Web:
  http://www.sushi.infogate.de/
  http://www.twics.com/~robbs/sushivoc.html

Usenet:
  alt.food.sushi

Look What I Found on the Net...

```
Newsgroup: alt.food.sushi
Subject: Dangers of sushi?

> My question is this:  does anyone out there have personal
> knowledge of anyone who's experienced a serious problem after
> eating sushi?  I suspect the dangers are greatly exaggerated
> and probably culturally biased.
```

I've never gotten ill in at least 500 outings. I've never heard
anyone report that they got ill from sushi. I've heard that it
is possible to get ill under certain circumstances — the like
of which a sushi chef is knowledgeable in knowing how to avoid.

On the other hand I have gotten ill scores of times from poorly
prepared chicken, or beef that was a little off.

Seems the odds are really greatly lessened in a sushi shop.

FOOD AND DRINK

Vegans

If it came out of an animal, vegans want no part of it. That means all the rich yummy foods are off limits—butter, milk, cheese and eggs are among the things that will not pass a vegan's lips. Look at the vegan-oriented Web pages, or talk the talk with other vegans on the Net.

Web:
  http://www.bury-rd.demon.co.uk/
  http://www.vegansociety.com/

Listserv Mailing List:
  List Name: **vegan**
  Subscribe to: **listserv@maelstrom.stjohns.edu**

Listserv Mailing List:
  List Name: **vnews-l**
  Subscribe to: **listserv@listserv.acsu.buffalo.edu**

Vegetarian Resources

The word "vegetarian" was first used in England in 1847 by the people who started the Vegetarian Society of the United Kingdom. Today, vegetarianism covers a wide variety of eating choices. Some people simply avoid meat, but eat eggs, dairy products and fish. (Technically, you could call such people ovo-lacto pescetarians.) Other people eat only fruits and vegetables and nothing else (true vegetarians). Some will eat eggs (ovo vegetarians), or dairy products (lacto vegetarians), or both (ovo-lacto vegetarians). Other vegetarians are very strict, avoiding the use of any animal products whatsoever including non-food products (vegans). Perhaps the most strict are those people who will only eat foods that can be harvested without killing the plant (fruitarians). As you might imagine, there are a large number of vegetarian resources on the Net, and no matter what your preference, I guarantee there is something for you. To start, you may want to read one of the FAQs (frequently asked question lists). In addition, you will find information about nutrition, restaurants, organizations, journals and magazines, animal rights, as well a gaggle of recipes.

Web:
  http://www.newveg.av.org/
  http://www.veg.org/veg/
  http://www.vrg.org/

Vegetarian Talk and General Discussion

A vegetarian will say, "I eat in a way that makes sense to me, in order to preserve my day-to-day vitality and maintain my long-term health." A non-vegetarian will say, "Is it worth living forever if you can't have a hot dog?" This debate seems to be the central nutritional issue of our times, and here are some places to talk about it. Share your vegetable-oriented opinions, thoughts, hopes, dreams and recipes with vegetarians all over the world.

Usenet:
  rec.food.veg
  rec.food.veg.cooking

Listserv Mailing List:
  List Name: **vegfood**
  Subscribe to: **listserv@cadserv.cadlab.vt.edu**

Listserv Mailing List:
  List Name: **veglife**
  Subscribe to: **listserv@listserv.vt.edu**

Wine

Tired of the pedestrian charms of beer? Move up to the big time where drinking is an art form and 1983 was a good year. Join the Bacchus society, wine lovers extraordinaire, and maybe even make your own homegrown wine. Oenophiles of the world unite: you have nothing to lose but your grains.

Web:
  http://www.dailywine.com/
  http://www.intowine.com/
  http://www.wine-lovers-page.com/
  http://www.wines.com/resourc.html

Usenet:
  alt.food.wine
  rec.crafts.winemaking

Listserv Mailing List:
  List Name: **foodwine**
  Subscribe to: **listserv@cmuvm.csv.cmich.edu**

Majordomo Mailing List:
  List Name: **wine**
  Subscribe to: **majordomo@bds.com.au**

Wine Zines

When you are sitting in the study rolling a little vino around on your tongue and you need some interesting reading material, check these great wine zines on the Net. Whether you are a seasoned wine taster or a novice, you will find these Web pages highly agreeable with robust content and balanced, supple designs.

Web:
http://www.bpe.com/radio/
http://www.winedine.co.uk/

ARE YOU A WINE LOVER? Try the GRAPEVINE.

FREEDOM

ACLU

The ACLU is the American Civil Liberties Union. Their charter is to protect American constitutional rights even when everyone else is asleep at the political switch. You may not always agree with the ACLU, but I guarantee that you will always have an opinion. Their Web site contains speeches, publications, reports, legislative alerts, Supreme Court filings, and other information from the land of the generally free and occasionally brave.

Web:
http://www.aclu.org/

Activism Resources

If you are an activist, it helps to build upon the experience of other people. Here are activist resources where you will find advice regarding what to do and what not to do, as well as hints, inspirational writings, and links to related resources.

Web:
http://www.eff.org/pub/Activism/
http://www.webactive.com/

Amnesty International

Amesty International is an international organization dedicated to three main principles: (1) the release of prisoners of conscience, (2) prompt and fair trials for political prisoners, and (3) opposition to torture, the death penalty and other inhumane treatment of prisoners. Although your neighborhood may be relatively quiet, there is still unrest in much of the world and more than a few people in authority who aren't very nice.

Web:
http://www.igc.apc.org/amnesty/

Banned Books

The only thing worse than a banned book is two banned books. Unfortunately, banning books did not die out with Hitler and the Nazis. Today, even in the U.S., there are still people who are trying to ban books that challenge their particular political and social agendas. Find out more about it on the Net. You will be surprised how many books have been banned over the years. Moreover, since you are on the Net where everything can be linked to something else, you can not only learn about the banned books, you can, in many cases, read them on your own screen, in the privacy of your own home.

Web:
http://www.cs.cmu.edu/Web/People/spok/banned-books.html

Get involved. Do something. Make a difference. (But if you don't have the time, you can at least take a look at the activist resources on the Net.)

Censorship of the Internet

Traditionally, the Net has been without organized censorship. There has, of course, always been censorship. However, it is at the local level. Now that the Net has become an important and prominent part of our global culture, there are those who would love to impose their will on everyone else by fiat. Here are some Web sites that will keep you up to date on what is happening on the Net censorship-wise.

Web:
http://www.eff.org/pub/Censorship/Internet_censorship_bills/
http://www.peacefire.org/

Censorship Talk and General Discussion

The antidote to censorship is free and open discussion. That is what this Usenet group is devoted to: a frank discussion of censorship and current events. Hint: If you want to participate, be prepared to argue.

Usenet:
alt.censorship

Censorware

At first, it seemed like a good idea (to some people anyway). Instead of censoring the Net, someone could create software to block objectionable Web sites. Parents could then choose to use such software on their home computers, thereby preserving their children's innocence. However, like many good ideas, this one got blown out of proportion by zealous fanatics, to the point where the Web site-blocking programs are now referred to as "censorware". The censor companies started blocking all kinds of stuff that had nothing to do with Sex, Violence and other Bad Things: there are now secret blacklists that have definite political overtones. For more info, check with this informative Web site. While you are there, you can type in the name of your favorite Web site and see if it is on one of the blacklists.

Web:
http://cgi.pathfinder.com/netly/spoofcentral/censored/

Flag Burning

In the United States, the issue of having the freedom to burn the flag is so emotional as to be almost incomprehensible to people in other countries. In some countries, no one would dare even think about burning a flag. In other countries, no one would be bothered. In the U.S., however, the flag is an emotionally charged icon and being able to burn it is an important freedom, almost as if America is proud of the fact that the country is so free that its people are allowed to destroy and denigrate one of its most sacred symbols. The issue, of course, is symbolic. Should a person have the right to do something that many people find offensive, even if the act poses no immediate danger to anyone? Few Americans actually want to burn a flag, but many do want to preserve the freedom to do so. If you would like to understand the issues, try this Web site. As you are reading, you can personally participate by choosing whether or not to burn a virtual flag.

Web:
http://www.esquilax.com/flag/

Free Speech

Free speech does not mean the same to everybody. As we all find out eventually, it is often the case that my freedom ends where yours begins. For this reason, there is really no such thing as complete freedom of speech. Instead, there is only an eternal debate over what should be allowed and what should be disallowed. Although many people like to think that the idea of free speech can be considered a simple issue, there are many gray areas and, somehow, even in the United States—where freedom of speech is guaranteed by the Constitution—the line between right and wrong seems to always be moving. Here are a large number of free-speech-related resources on the Net. I was surprised at how much information is available. If you would like to explore the very complex concept of free speech, this is an excellent place to visit.

Web:
http://www.freedomforum.org/speech/

Usenet:
alt.freespeech

Listserv Mailing List:
List Name: amend1-l
Subscribe to: listserv@uafsysb.uark.edu

FREEDOM

Freedom of Expression

In my opinion, the fundamental ideas regarding freedom of expression are best expressed by the First Amendment of the Constitution of the United States: "Congress shall make no law respecting an establishment of religion, or prohibiting the free exercise thereof; or abridging the freedom of speech, or of the press; or the right of the people peaceably to assemble, and to petition the Government for a redress of grievances." Although this particular quotation refers specifically to the U.S., freedom of expression is an issue all over the world. Here are some Web sites that will lead you to a great many related resources all over the Net: the law, civil liberties, censorship, government, and much more.

Web:
http://insight.mcmaster.ca/org/efc/pages/chronicle/censor.html
http://www.cybersquirrel.com/clc/expression.html

Freedom of Expression?

Have you noticed that nowhere in the text of this book have I written the actual name of the book? I always refer to it indirectly as "this book". There is a reason.

The real name for this book is "Harley Hahn's Internet and Web Yellow Pages". However, in certain countries (Canada, Great Britain and Australia), the words "Yellow Pages" are a trademark of the telephone company. So in those countries, we have to call the book "Harley Hahn's Internet and Web Golden Directory".

This means that the publisher (Osborne McGraw-Hill) has to print two different versions of the cover: one for the U.S. and one for everywhere else. And to make it worse, it happens that all of McGraw-Hill's European-bound books go through their British subsidiary. Thus, all the books sold in Europe have to use "Golden Directory" on the cover, even where the phone companies don't care about the name.

Unfortunately, it would be too expensive to have two versions of the text of this book. Thus, I am not allowed to use the proper name of the book — "Harley Hahn's Internet and Web Yellow Pages" — within the book itself. Otherwise, McGraw-Hill would have unfriendly lawyers from Canada, Great Britain and Australia writing them threatening letters.

So don't talk to me about freedom of expression. Ha!
(Disclaimer: The name "Yellow Pages" is a trademark of the phone company in Canada, Great Britain and Australia.)

Freedom of Information Act

The United States' Freedom of Information Act (FOIA) was signed into law on July 4, 1966. The purpose of the FOIA was to establish the right of the public to obtain information from agencies of the federal government. Since then, every state has established its own laws to provide similar access to state records. In theory, the FOIA is a wonderful piece of legislation, opening the doors of the government to public scrutiny. In practice, there are problems due to inadequate funding and technical regulations. If you are interested in requesting information under the FOIA, these resources will provide you with the information you need.

Web:
http://www.aclu.org/library/foia.html
http://www.spj.org/foia/

Freedom of Religion

Almost by definition, belief in one particular religion precludes belief in another religion. Religions deal with matters of utmost importance to human beings: the existence of a supernatural being (or beings), morality and the law, what happens after death, the reasons for our existence, as well as our responsibilities toward society as a whole and toward individual people. Every religion believes that its scriptures and customs are the best (that is, true). However, history has proven over and over that when one religion dominates within a country or region, that group tends to use its power to oppress members of other religions. For this reason, the United States (and other countries) specifically enshrined in law the right for every person to practice religion (or to be without religion) as he or she sees fit. Such rights—perhaps by their very nature—are continually under attack, especially by those who would interpret the law to their advantage. Here are some Web sites with useful and informative resources relating to the vitally important, but very complex concept we call freedom of religion.

Web:
http://w3.trib.com/FACT/1st.relig.liberty.html
http://www.freedomforum.org/religion/

Gun Control

Gun control—restricting people's access to guns—is an issue everywhere, but nowhere is the debate as disputatious as in the United States. Technically, the American debate is rooted in the language of the Second Amendment to the U.S. Constitution: "A well regulated militia, being necessary to the security of a free state, the right of the people to keep and bear arms, shall not be infringed." It's easy to see how this can be interpreted two ways. If you are against gun control, you can point out that this amendment clearly enshrines the right of all Americans to "keep and bear arms". If you feel that guns should be controlled, you can argue that the amendment is irrelevant because it speaks only to the need of maintaining a "well regulated militia", and not any other uses of firearms. Here are Web sites that reflect both sides of this issue. The Usenet group is for general debate.

Web:
   http://www.gunfree.org/
   http://www.guninfo.org/

Usenet:
   talk.politics.guns

Human Rights

Although we talk a lot about human rights, the idea is relatively new. On December 10, 1948, the United Nations General Assembly unanimously adopted the Universal Declaration of Human Rights. This was the first time a declaration signed by more than one country mentioned the idea of human rights by name. This Web site has information and resources regarding human rights documents and organizations, including a well-organized collection of links to related resources around the Net. The Usenet group and mailing list are for ongoing discussion.

Web:
   http://www.igc.org/igc/issues/hr/

Usenet:
   soc.rights.human

Listserv Mailing List:
   List Name: hrs-l
   Subscribe to: listserv@bingvmb.cc.binghamton.edu

Liberty Web

This is the place to look if you want to find out what the fanatics are doing to protect our freedom (even though, goodness knows, as one of my readers you are anything but a fanatic).

Web:
   http://www.jim.com/jamesd/

Naturism and Freedom

Naturism refers to the philosophy that it is healthy and desirable for human beings to spend a significant amount of time naked, often in the company of other people. Most of us are taught that being naked in front of other people is bad, and so we sublimate our feelings by snickering at the very idea of nudism. So when I tell you that naturists are under attack from various people and organizations, I understand if you feel like ignoring the whole thing ("Surely we have more important matters to worry about") or perhaps even make a joke ("Did you hear about the blind man at a nudist colony?"). However, you should be concerned. When an isolated beach is closed to nudism because some local community pressure group is offended by the idea of people being allowed to be naked in a secluded area, the issue should concern all of us. Being naked—in an appropriate place—is a relatively harmless activity, and the people who would deny that freedom to naturists are just as ready to deny other, more vital freedoms to you and me. In my opinion, when you hear the bell of oppression anywhere, at any time, you don't have to ask for whom it tolls.

Web:
   http://www.naturist.com/NAC/

United Nations Agreements on Human Rights

When we study and talk about freedom, some of the most important documents of modern times are adopted by the United Nations. Here are these documents: Universal Declaration of Human Rights, Covenant on Civil and Political Rights, Covenant on Economic, Social and Cultural Rights, Convention Against Torture, Convention Against Genocide, Geneva Conventions, Convention on the Rights of the Child, Convention on the Elimination of Discrimination Against Women, and the original 1945 Charter of the United Nations.

Web:
   http://www.hrweb.org/legal/undocs.html

Look What I Found on the Net...

```
Newsgroup: rec.guns
Subject: Pocket Holsters Are Now Illegal

>>>> Yesterday afternoon, my holster maker told me he couldn't
>>>> make pocket holsters anymore.  He received a certified
>>>> letter from local law enforcement that a recent BATF
>>>> (U.S. Bureau of Alcohol, Tobacco and Firearms) decision /
>>>> interpretation now makes it illegal to make, possess or own
>>>> a pocket holster that allows the gun to fire while still in
>>>> the holster unless they are registered.

>>> I think it is wonderful how government agencies can make any
>>> rule that they want without the help of Congress.

>> They don't and can't.  Congress GAVE them that authority!
>> That's what we should be screaming about, not that they
>> exercise every bit of power they can.  Take away their
>> ability to interpret the law, and they will be crippled.

> Is this for real?  Nothing with regard to BATF surprises me
> anymore, but this is just a little weird.
>
> I carry a NAA .22LR in my pants pocket at all times, without
> the assault pocket holster.  Ninety percent of the time I have
> a Makarov or G17 on my hip.  If they ban my belt, it's time to
> fight.
>
> — Xxxxxx Xxxx, NRA Life Member
```

Here's the facts. Not all pocket holsters are illegal. And, certainly, belts aren't going to be outlawed.

The holsters the BATF doesn't like are those which allow the gun to be fired while it's still in the holster. They claim that, since it's a firearm that doesn't look like a firearm, then it qualifies as an Any Other Weapon (AOW) — the same as pen guns and those neat briefcases that let you fire the MP5 or MAC-10 inside.

So that's it. Do I like it? No way! Is there something you can do about it? Vote Republican. Otherwise, get ready to watch the constant erosion of our rights.

"Some men are alive simply because it is against the law to kill them."

FUN

Abuse a Celebrity

What do the following celebrities all have in common: Bill Clinton, Barney the Dinosaur, Mike Tyson, Bill Gates and Madonna? They are so lovable that countless people around the world would love to smack them a couple of times, just on general principle. If you share these sentiments, why wait? Hop to the Net, where you can express your love in a personal way.

Web:
http://slugfest.kaizen.net/
http://www.urban75.com/Punch/bashbeta.html
http://www.urban75.com/Punch/smackem.html

Anagrams

Anagrams are something you can do no matter where you are or what is going on. For instance, if you're in traffic and there is nothing on the radio but ads for hair replenishing cream, you can make up all sorts of anagrams by rearranging the letters of all of Henry the VIII's wives' names. This will be good practice so when you are at a party and word gets around that you are the county anagram champion you will be able to demonstrate your talents with grace and elegance.

Web:
http://www.wordsmith.org/anagram/

Usenet:
alt.anagrams

Bubbles

I have a wonderful battery-operated bubble gun, and sometimes when I need to take a break from writing, I will go out on the patio and blow bubbles. Occasionally, my cat will lounge on a nearby railing and sniff at the bubbles as they slowly float by, carried on their upward journey by the cool ocean breeze. If you think you would enjoy being a bubble person, check out this great bubble site and learn about the history of bubbles, how to make bubble tools, and creating your own bubble solution.

Web:
http://www.bubbles.org/

Rearrange the letters of one or more words into other words, and you have an anagram. For example, the letters of the words "Tom Cruise" can be rearranged to spell "So, I'm cuter".

But that's kid's stuff. Using the nifty, cool, super-deluxe anagram generator, you can get all kinds of nifty, cool, super-deluxe anagrams.

For example, you can rearrange "Henry got her a Sahara bloke." and "Her hot shy arrangeable... A-OK!" to spell "Harley Hahn books are great!"

(And some people still don't understand why the Internet is so important.)

Diaries and Journals

There's nothing like the sinful pleasure of snooping where you don't belong. The Web is a great place to be able to stick your nose into people's private lives. This site has a list of daily journals and diaries that are on the Net. With the click of your mouse, you can be finding out who did what, to whom, and why. Just think, if it weren't for these people who have nothing better to do with their time, you would have nothing better to do with *your* time.

Web:
http://www.metajournals.com/
http://www.spies.com/~diane/journals2.html

Fortune Telling

Why wonder about the future, when you can find out your fortune right now? Here are some Web sites that will put you in touch with the all-knowing universal spirit. After all, why guess about the days to come, when you can have a computer program guess for you?

Web:
http://www.facade.com/
http://www.now2000.com/fortune/
http://www.sirius.com/~purcell/dm_1/fortune.html
http://www.u.arizona.edu/~jhirata/cookie.html

Fun Planet

Fun Planet has games and quizzes you can enjoy as you pass the time. The games are easy to learn, which makes them suitable for those short periods of time when you have nothing to do. This is an excellent site to visit while you are waiting for tech support to answer the phone.

Web:
http://www.funplanet.com/us/

Go win something.
Check out "Contests".

Madlibs

These Web sites will allow you to have loads of fun filling in nouns, adjectives and other words out of which the computer will weave a story. This is just like the paper Madlibs, only you don't need a group of friends to play it.

Web:
http://www.eduplace.com/tales/
http://www.planetzoom.com/twistedtales/twist.htm
http://www.webcomics.com/madlib/

Do you think you might like to be a writer? Start with **Madlibs** and, if you do well, you can work your way up to sending in anecdotes to *Reader's Digest*. (From there, it is only a small step to writing Internet books. Soon, fame, fortune and never-ending happiness will be yours.)

Mind Breakers

Is your life uneventful? Is your job a bore? If so, there is no need to go through the day without a mental challenge. Just explore these mind games, puzzles and riddles, and get ready to be perplexed, frustrated and amazed. For some extra stimulation, try the Usenet discussion group.

Web:
http://leden.tref.nl/mhulsman/files.htm

Usenet:
alt.brain.teasers

Mystery Solving

Got a few minutes? Here are short mysteries you can try to solve whenever you have a spare moment. There are new stories posted every week, so, if you are a mystery buff, you will enjoy visiting this site regularly. To test your skills, take a look at the archive of past mysteries and their solutions.

Web:
  http://www.thecase.com/

Payphone Project

Do you like to talk to strangers in faraway places? If so, this is the Web site for you. The Payphone Project lists the numbers of payphones around the world. When you need a break from the humdrum reality of everyday life, take a few minutes and call a payphone in an exotic location, like the Eiffel Tower in Paris, the subway platform underneath Times Square in New York, or across the street from a popular teenage hangout in Hulbert, Oklahoma.

Web:
  http://www.sorabji.com/livewire/payphones/

Web Soap Operas

I don't watch television, so I miss out on the portion of the popular culture having to do with the daily lives of imaginary people having imaginary various trials and tribulations in imaginary places. However, on the Net, I can tune into a Web-based soap opera whenever I want. I don't have to wait for a particular time of day, and I don't have to be interrupted by commercials. This Web site is an index page to the various soap operas, collaborative fiction and ongoing dramas taking place around the Net.

Web:
  http://home.earthlink.net/~merlin200/

For a good time, see "Chemistry" and "Romance" (at the same time).

Web Soap Operas

Take a break from real life without even leaving your computer.

Choose a Web soap opera and follow it regularly.

The life you save from boredom may be your own.

Weird Sites

We all know there are weird people on the Net, but until you visit this Web site, you can't appreciate the full extent of mankind's eccentricity. Browse through this wacko-inspired craziness, and it won't be long till you start wondering if Man is really Nature's last word.

Web:
  http://www.now2000.com/weird/

Yo-Yos

If your personal popularity depends on hanging out at the mall strutting your fancy yo-yo style, it's good to have a way to access fresh material with which to impress your friends. Check out these sites at which you will find yo-yo tips and tricks, as well as general information regarding this pastime of the gods.

Web:
  http://pages.nyu.edu/~tqm3413/yoyo/
  http://www.pd.net/yoyo/

GAMES AND PUZZLES

Backgammon

Backgammon is played by two players using a specially marked board, 15 counters and a set of dice. You take turns throwing the dice and moving your counters around the board according to the numbers on the dice. When a counter reaches the end of the circuit, you remove it. The object of the game is to be the first person to remove all your counters from the board. It sounds easy, but there's lots of strategy involved. Backgammon is the oldest game in recorded history; historians even believe it was played in ancient Mesopotamia. Today, backgammon is as popular as ever, and if you would like to play, learn or talk about it, there are lots of resources on the Net. Or you can go to Mesopotamia and find someone to play in person. (Driving instructions: Head toward central Asia, make a left at the Persian Gulf, and go back 3,000 years.)

Web:
  http://www.bkgm.com/

Usenet:
  rec.games.backgammon

Backgammon with Strangers

These days you have to be careful who you mix with. Playing backgammon in person presents all kinds of potential problems. For example, someone might sneeze on you and give you pneumonia, or your opponent could get mad and stab you with an ice pick.

Much better to play it safe: connect to the *Backgammon Server* where you can depend on the kindness of strangers. Moreover, you can play in your underwear and no one will care.

Battleship

In World War II, radio operators invented the game of Battleship in order to test radio transmissions that were kept secret from the Japanese. The operators were only allowed a few tests a day, so they developed a game which they played, a bit at a time, over a matter of weeks. And now you can play the same game (without waiting) on the Internet.

Web:
  http://gen.ml.org/battle/
  http://scv.bu.edu/~aarondf/java/battleship.html

Bingo Zone

To be an excellent Net person, you need to develop good mouse skills. For example, to compete professionally, you must be able to steer your mouse pointer to a specific area of your screen and click the mouse button with perfect timing. And you must be able to do this dependably, quickly and under enormous pressure. Perfecting and maintaining such skills requires constant practice, and here is the place to do so. At the Bingo Zone, you compete with many other bingo players around the world. You will need to keep a sharp eye on the screen and coordinate your mouse and pointer perfectly. There's almost always a game going on, so get to it right now.

Web:
  http://www.bingozone.com/html_gv/gv_login.htm

Blackjack

If you can't make it to a casino this weekend, this is the next best thing. Play Blackjack with other Internet folks and become a Net billionaire or downright penniless. There are help files available and records are kept of rankings, cash won and lost, top players, and other table statistics. Join the table today.

Web:
  http://www.blackjackinfo.com/
  http://www.virtualvegas.com/newvv/lockout/
    blackjack.html

IRC:
  #blackjack

GAMES AND PUZZLES

Board Games

I've spent a lot of pleasant hours playing board games, and I bet you have too. What better way to spend an evening than getting into a heated game of Monopoly or Risk or Diplomacy or Clue, and beating the pulp out of your best friend? So, board game lovers of the world, here are some resources for you to enjoy: lots of information about lots of games. I have also included a Web site with some new games you may want to try, as well as a site that has the official rules of Monopoly. If you want to talk to other enthusiasts, check out the Usenet discussion groups. The **marketplace** group is for buying and selling; the other groups are for general discussion.

Web:
  http://www.gamecabinet.com/
  http://www.kootweb.com/games.html
  http://www.monopoly.com/rules-monop.html

Usenet:
  rec.games.board
  rec.games.board.ce
  rec.games.board.marketplace
  rec.games.chinese-chess
  rec.games.diplomacy
  rec.games.go
  rec.games.mahjong

Guys:
The best way to impress a date is to invite her over and show her that you have a complete set of Harley Hahn books.

The Game of Bridge

Well, it's time to write another advertisement and my editor suggested I do one about the game of bridge. Actually, I don't normally even think of it as a game, per se. More like a thing that you build, or perhaps even a structure. Okay, it's important to have bridges – after all, if we didn't have any bridges, all the cars on the highway would just fall off into nothingness, and you wouldn't be able to get across rivers and things – but still, I hardly see where that qualifies as a game. And I'm dashed if I can figure out why anyone wanted me to write an ad for the "game" of bridge. I mean, I know that there are people out there who build bridges and roads and things, civil engineers and what not, but why anyone would think that belongs in an Internet book, or why it requires an advertisement... What's that? You don't mean building bridges? You mean the card game? Do you mean all that stuff with spades and hearts and two no-trump and so on? Oh... *that* bridge game. Oh... Never mind.

Bridge

Bridge is such a fun game for couples. Most men take up bridge when they get married and discover their wives won't let them watch football. The only thing left to do is to sit with another couple and play cards all night. Perfect your bridge skills so you can learn to play a killer game. If you're clever, you can even make it a contact sport so you won't miss football.

Web:
  http://bridge.theriver.com/
  http://www.cbf.ca/GBL/
  http://www.winbridge.com/

Usenet:
  rec.games.bridge
  rec.games.bridge.okbridge

GAMES AND PUZZLES

CHESS LOVERS
the Net has a lot for you. The Chess Archives are just full of things and stuff and so on.

Chess

The attraction of chess is that it requires intense concentration in order to dominate in a highly competitive environment in which chance plays virtually no part whatsoever (much like being a professional Internet writer). The game symbolizes warfare, in that the strategy is to capture as many of the opponent "men" (pieces) as possible. Unlike real warfare, the game ends when the King has been captured ("checkmate"). If you are a chess aficionado, or even a beginner, there are lots of chess-related places on the Net to visit. You can learn about the game, play the game, or talk about the game (sort of an allegory for Life).

Web:
  http://caissa.onenet.net/chess/
  http://www.delorie.com/game-room/chess/
  http://www.users.nac.net/chess/

Usenet:
  rec.games.chess
  rec.games.chess.analysis
  rec.games.chess.computer
  rec.games.chess.misc
  rec.games.chess.play-by-email
  rec.games.chess.politics

IRC:
  #chess

Cribbage

Why work when you can play games? Learn to play cribbage and spend a few frustrating hours trying to beat your computer. Once you get good, you can start playing against other people and join a cribbage club. Everything you need is on the Net.

Web:
  http://www.cribbage.org/
  http://www.netlink.co.uk/users/pagat/adders/crib6.html

Crossword Puzzles

Do you like crossword puzzles? There are many, many puzzles on the Net that you can access for free whenever you want. There are also dictionaries, word lists, guides, computer programs, helpful tips, and a great deal of other crossword-related material, including a FAQ (frequently asked question list). Now, if someone would only tell me the three-letter word for an Australian bird, and the two-letter name for the sun god, my life would be complete.

Web:
  http://www.dareware.com/cross.htm
  http://www.lib.ox.ac.uk/internet/news/faq/archive/crossword-faq.part1.html
  http://www.primate.wisc.edu/people/hamel/cp.html

Do you need a word?
Don't be cross.
Use an Internet crossword resource.

GAMES AND PUZZLES

Doom

Why do young men like Doom so much? Because it is so much like real life. You get to travel around surrealistic environments, carrying powerful weapons and shooting at things left and right. But it's not just enough to play Doom. To do it right, you need to become a fanatic. These resources offer everything you need: the official Doom FAQ, tutorials and guides, news, specifications, graphics from the game, great utilities (such as map editors and level creators), and much more.

Web:
http://doomgate.cs.buffalo.edu/
http://www.gamers.org/pub/archives/doom/periodic/RGCD_FAQ.html
http://www.planetquake.com/thecoven/death/

Usenet:
alt.games.doom
alt.games.doom.ii
rec.games.computer.doom.announce
rec.games.computer.doom.editing
rec.games.computer.doom.help
rec.games.computer.doom.misc
rec.games.computer.doom.playing

IRC:
#doom

*If you are a **Doom** fan, the Net has lots of stuff for you. Then you can hunt and kill things to your heart's content in the privacy of your very own computer.*

Earth 2025

Here's a Web-based game you can play with nothing more than a browser. Earth 2025 is a strategy/empire building game in which thousands of people can play at the same time. Your goal is to try to create and maintain a strong country that can survive attacks by other players (just like real life). While you are playing, you can chat with other players, keep up with the Earth 2025 news, and check the rankings to see who are the top players. To do well at this game, you don't have to be a fanatic—but it sure helps.

Web:
http://www.solariagames.com/earth/

Empire

Here is the home of the famous game of Empire, the real-time strategy war game played by people across the Internet. If you like playing Civilization, you'll love Empire. The Web sites offer everything you need to learn about and start playing this great game.

Web:
http://www.cis.ohio-state.edu/hypertext/faq/usenet/games/empire/faq/faq.html
http://www.cis.ohio-state.edu/hypertext/faq/usenet/games/empire/news/faq.html

Usenet:
rec.games.empire

Game Hotspots

There is no need to waste even a minute of your time working, eating, sleeping or talking to other people. Here are enough game resources to keep you busy all day long. You'll find free games, reviews, cheats, and much more.

Web:
http://www.gamesdomain.co.uk/
http://www.gamesdomain.com/
http://www.gamespot.com/
http://www.gamesroyale.com/
http://www.happypuppy.com/

GAMES AND PUZZLES

Game Hotspots

computer + the Internet + lots of free games = one happy person (you)

Game Reviews

Here are some online magazines dedicated to electronic and computerized games: reviews, interviews, reports and general game industry news. If you are going to be a zealot, you might as well know what you are talking about.

Web:
http://www.gamesdomain.com/gdreview/
http://www.gamesmania.com/
http://www.pcme.com/

Hangman

Hangman is a game in which you try to guess a mystery word, one letter at a time. When you guess a correct letter, you are shown where it appears in the word. When you guess a wrong letter, a new feature is added to a drawing of a little man. If the entire little man is drawn before you guess all the letters in the word correctly, you lose, and the little man gets hung. I wonder if this is a feminist game? (I could make a joke about a well-hung little man, but instead, I will content myself with wondering out loud why the game is not called "hangperson".)

Web:
http://www.allmixedup.com/cgi-bin/hangman/hangman
http://www.sonic.net/~nbs/hangman

Hollywood Stock Exchange

Do you think you could pick which films will be winners better than the Hollywood movie moguls? Of course you can, and here is your chance to prove it. Try your hand at this addictive online game, where *you* choose which movies and which stars will be successful. Create your "portfolio" and start to wheel and deal. Then watch your fortune go up and down based on real box office grosses of real films.

Web:
http://www.hsx.com/

Interactive Fiction

Interactive fiction (IF) is a computerized text-based game in which a story is told as part of the game. The first IF game was probably "Hunt the Wumpus", a Unix game from the early 1970s, in which you must move around a dodecahedron-shaped maze, avoiding mysterious dangers in search of a Wumpus, which you must kill before he eats you. (Obviously, some people *did* inhale.) The classic IF was "Adventure", which debuted in 1977. Interactive fiction is a lot of fun. I myself completely mastered Adventure during the summer of 1981 when I had a few months off from medical school. There are lots of IF enthusiasts on the Net and lots of IF resources to explore.

Web:
http://www.csd.uwo.ca/Infocom/links.html
http://www.truespectra.com/~svanegmo/

Usenet:
rec.arts.int-fiction
rec.games.int-fiction

Java Game Park

Java is a system in which programs can be downloaded and run on your computer automatically. To use Java, you need to have a browser that supports such programs. (The current versions of both Internet Explorer and Netscape both support Java.) Java was developed to run all kinds of serious, important programs, but (are you surprised?) much Java development has gone into creating games. There are all kinds of Java games ready for you to try for free: adventure games, arcade games, board games, card games, and many more.

Web:
http://www.javagamepark.com/

306 GAMES AND PUZZLES

Magic: The Gathering

This is a dungeons-and-dragons-type game that is played with collectible cards. On the Net you can find tips, strategies, rules, links to other pages and sources for gaming materials.

Web:
　http://www.swiss-magic.ch/resource.html
　http://www.tranquility-base.com/magic/
　http://www.wizards.com/Magic/

Usenet:
　alt.cardgame.magic
　rec.games.trading-cards.marketplace.magic.auctions
　rec.games.trading-cards.marketplace.magic.sales
　rec.games.trading-cards.marketplace.magic.trades

IRC:
　#mtg

Mame Arcade Emulator

Do you remember all the video arcade games from the 1980s? If so, do *not* visit this Web site, or the rest of your day will be gone before you can say, "Wow, is that ever cool!" Mame stands for Multiple Arcade Machine Emulator. Download the Mame program, install it on your computer, and you will be able to play a large number of old arcade games on your PC. Mame allows your computer to run the original programs that were inside the actual video game, so what you see on your PC will look and sound and work exactly like the games you remember. My favorite is Ms. Pacman. You may enjoy Defender, Zaxxon, Space Invaders, Berzerk or Galaga. All of these, and many more, are waiting for you right now.

Web:
　http://www.gamepower.com/mame/mame.html

Usenet:
　alt.games.mame

Mazes

The best thing about having your own maze is you always have a good excuse for not doing something on time. ("I'm sorry I can't turn in my homework; my dog took it and dropped it in my maze.") If you are one of the few people who don't have a maze of their very own in the family room, you can at least explore and create mazes over the Net.

Web:
　http://www.delorie.com/game-room/mazes/
　http://www.obs-us.com/obs/english/books/holt/
　　books/maze/

Othello

Othello (which is similar to Reversi) is a strategy board game played by a great many people around the world. Othello is played on an 8x8 square by two players, each of whom uses discs which are one color on one side and a different color on the other side (for example, white and black). Each player has his own color. Players alternate moves, putting down a disc (with their personal color face up) in such a way as to try to "outflank" some of the other person's discs. When this happens, the outflanked discs are flipped, changing their color. When the game ends, the winner is the person who has the most discs with his color on the board. Lots and lots of people play Othello. Would you like to try? On the Net you can practice by playing against a computer.

Web:
　http://www.cs.ualberta.ca/~games/keyano/
　http://www.iioa.org/

PC Games Talk and General Discussion

If God didn't want us to use our PCs for games, he wouldn't have given us so many games discussion groups. The **.games** and **.misc** groups are for general talk about all types of PC games: for DOS, Windows and OS/2. The **.announce** group is moderated and contains announcements of interest to the PC games community. Look for the PC Games frequently asked question list, posted regularly to this group. The FAQ is also available on the Web. The other groups are for particular types of games (**.rpg** means role-playing games).

Usenet:
　alt.binaries.warez.ibm-pc.games
　alt.warez.ibm-pc.games
　comp.sys.ibm.pc.games
　comp.sys.ibm.pc.games.action
　comp.sys.ibm.pc.games.adventure
　comp.sys.ibm.pc.games.announce
　comp.sys.ibm.pc.games.flight-sim
　comp.sys.ibm.pc.games.misc
　comp.sys.ibm.pc.games.rpg
　comp.sys.ibm.pc.games.sports
　comp.sys.ibm.pc.games.strategic

GAMES AND PUZZLES

Keep up on the newest and coolest in the PC game world. Read the **comp.sys.ibm.pc.games**

Pinball

Pinball lovers, there is lots of pinball-related information on the Net, as well as a Usenet discussion group for talking to other enthusiasts. By the way, if you are thinking about getting your own machine, do some research before you spend any money.

Web:
http://personal.atl.bellsouth.net/atl/j/d/jdeitch/
http://www.daveland.com/pinball/
http://www.glue.umd.edu/~dstewart/pinball/
http://www.voyager.co.nz/~mburke/pinlinks/

Usenet:
rec.games.pinball

Poker

Play or watch multi-user poker, administered by the IRC Poker Bot. (A bot is an automated program used on IRC to perform a particular function.) The bot can provide complete instructions and a command summary. You can also play interactive video-style poker on the Web.

Web:
http://www.cis.ohio-state.edu/hypertext/faq/usenet/gambling-faq/poker/faq.html
http://www.inlink.com/~jmgberg/poker/poker.html
http://www.seas.upenn.edu/~swanwick/poker/
http://www.universe.digex.net/~kimberg/pokermain.html

Usenet:
rec.gambling.poker

IRC:
#poker

Puzzles

Do you like puzzles? There are enough puzzles (and solutions) on the Net to keep you busy indefinitely. But why should you do puzzles? Puzzles are good because they will help you think better. Thinking better turns you into a finer human being. And being a fine human being will help you become good looking, successful and powerful, with just the right amount of humility to make sure you are loved and respected by everyone you meet. (Well, it's always worked for me anyway.)

Web:
http://einstein.et.tudelft.nl/~arlet/puzzles/
http://leden.tref.nl/mhulsman/
http://www.internet.mcmail.com/

Usenet:
alt.brain.teasers
rec.puzzles

Riddle of the Day

Try to solve the riddles and brain teasers posed by the Sphinx. If you can, you get immortalized in the Sphinx Hall of Fame. You can even submit your own sticklers here or browse the archive of past riddles with their answers.

Web:
http://www.dujour.com/riddle/

Sandbox

Sandbox offers a variety of sophisticated interactive games, in which you can pit your skill and wits against other players and Lady Luck. For sports fans, there is fantasy football and fantasy baseball, where you create and manage your own teams. If you are a stock market buff, try the online financial trading simulation game.

Web:
http://www.sandbox.net/

Shogi

Shogi is a two-player Japanese game played on a board with squares. The object of shogi is to capture your opponent's king. (I hear that Camilla Parker Bowles is a great player.) Don't let any of those facts confuse you: shogi is not chess. However, shogi is fun and challenging, and knowing how to play will make you look cultured. (If that fails to work, just walk around with this book under your arm.)

Web:
http://www.halcyon.com/stouten/shogi.html
http://www.shogi.org/intro.html

Listserv Mailing List:
List Name: **shogi-l**
Subscribe to: **listserv@techunix.technion.ac.il**

Sliding Tile Puzzles

Do you remember when you were a kid playing with one of those puzzles with the sliding tiles? You move the tiles around until they are in the correct order (or until you give up in frustration and decide to throw the thing away and go watch TV). Now you can play the same game on the Net. Just one more way in which childhood is becoming electric.

Web:
http://www.allmixedup.com/Slider/

Tic Tac Toe

Tic Tac Toe has been called "one of the most useless games ever invented" (by my chief researcher, actually). Maybe so for the traditional 3x3 game, but have you tried playing on a 6x7 grid with 5 in a row needed to win? Play against a computer program that lets you choose the size of the grid and the number of Xs or Os in a row you need to win. You can play the regular 3x3 or try something more adventurous. When you get into higher numbers, it's more fun and a lot more difficult.

Web:
http://www.boulter.com/ttt/

Sliding Tile Puzzles – The Real Truth

Do you want to know the real truth about sliding tile puzzles?

You know, those puzzles that have a number of small pieces that slide up/down and left/right. You move the tiles around and, when you get all the pieces in the right place, you see a picture of some type.

Okay, here's the real scoop.

These puzzles were invented by aliens. They spread the puzzles everywhere and, whenever you work on one, the aliens monitor you with their special observations rays.

You see, the aliens want to take over the Earth and, to do so, they need to control a certain number of human beings. So, at night, the aliens kidnap certain people and implant control mechanisms in their brains. Before dawn, these people are returned with the memory of the whole procedure wiped out. One day, when enough people have been modified in this way, the aliens will activate all the control mechanisms and take control of the Earth.

This thing is, only certain people's brains are suitable for implantation. However, the aliens can tell if you are one of those people by monitoring your brain waves as you try to solve a sliding puzzle.

And now—for the first time—sliding puzzles are starting to appear on the Net.

Top 100 PC Games

Here is a weekly list of the top one hundred commercial PC games, as voted by game players on the Internet. This is a good list to check out, if you are looking for a new game for yourself or for a gift.

Web:
http://www.megatoon.com/~t15/top100.htm

Video Games

You never know when you will have to sneak up behind someone and shoot him in the head before he turns around and blasts you with a laser gun. Stuff like that happens every day and if it happens to you, I want you to be prepared. The best way I know to be prepared is to spend as much time as possible playing video games, so let's get started.

Web:
  http://www.gamearchive.com/video/
  http://www.geocities.com/~n64ultraplayer/
  http://www.videogamers.com/
  http://www.videogames.com/

Usenet:
  alt.atari-jaguar.discussion
  alt.atari.2600
  alt.fan.sonic-hedgehog
  alt.games.lynx
  alt.games.mame
  alt.games.rac-rally
  alt.games.sony-playstation
  alt.games.sony.yaroze
  alt.games.twinsens.odyssey
  alt.games.video
  alt.games.video.classic
  alt.games.video.emulation
  alt.games.video.import.japanese
  alt.games.video.nintendo-64
  alt.games.video.nintendo-64.faqs
  alt.games.video.sega-saturn
  alt.games.video.sega-saturn.faqs
  alt.games.video.sony-playstation
  alt.games.video.sony-playstation.faqs
  alt.sega.genesis
  alt.super.nes
  alt.video.games.sony-playstation
  alt.videogames.neo-geo
  rec.games.vectrex
  rec.games.video
  rec.games.video.3do
  rec.games.video.advocacy
  rec.games.video.arcade
  rec.games.video.arcade.collecting
  rec.games.video.arcade.marketplace
  rec.games.video.atari
  rec.games.video.cd-i
  rec.games.video.cd32
  rec.games.video.classic
  rec.games.video.misc
  rec.games.video.nintendo
  rec.games.video.sega
  rec.games.video.sony

Video Games Hints and Cheats

Why spend huge portions of your life trying to master an arcane video game? As a Net user, you are only one click away from enough hints, cheats and walkthroughs to choke an electronic horse. Now you can use all that extra spare time to do something useful (like talk about video games on Usenet).

Web:
  http://www.gamesdomain.co.uk/walkthru.html
  http://www.the-spoiler.com/
  http://www.thegw.com/cheats/

Video Game Cheating

Video games can be a lot of fun, but what is even more fun is knowing secret ways to beat the game.
If you play a lot of video games, check out the collection of cheats to see if any are known for your favorite game.
Be sure not to tell your brother, however. That would take all the fun out of it.

GARDENING

Bonsai

Bonsai is the Japanese art of dwarfing trees and plants into forms that mimic nature. Anyone interested, whether novice or professional, may join this mailing list or participate in discussion on the Usenet groups. At the Web sites, you will find FAQs and pictures of beautiful bonsai.

Web:
http://members.aol.com/iasnob/
http://www.btinternet.com/~bonsai.suiseki/bonsai.htm
http://www.hav.com/bonsai/
http://www.mnsinc.com/michaelj/bonsai/faq/part1.html
http://www.westminster.ac.uk/~allen/main.html

Usenet:
alt.bonsai
rec.arts.bonsai

Listserv Mailing List:
List Name: **bonsai**
Subscribe to: **listserv@home.ease.lsoft.com**

Flowers

Do you enjoy looking at the reproductive structures of certain seed-bearing plants, characteristically having stamens and a pistil enclosed in an outer envelope of petals and sepals? That is, are you a flower lover? If so, you will love these resources, your entrée into the world of petals and sepals. The Web sites have lots and lots of information (especially about roses, which I love). There are also facilities that allow you to search for information about specific flowers, using a botanical or common name. When you aren't out in the garden, you may want to spend time reading the Usenet discussion groups to see what other flower lovers have to say.

Web:
http://www.flowerbase.com/
http://www.mgardens.org/
http://www.rosarian.com/

Usenet:
rec.gardens.orchids
rec.gardens.roses

Garden Encyclopedia

Search through this encyclopedia of gardening to get information on soils, plants, tools, trimming, digging, mulching, and more. Never again will you have to wonder how much osmunda fiber to use for your epiphitic orchids or if a Christmas fern makes a nice holiday gift.

Web:
http://www.pathfinder.com/cgi-bin/VG/vg

Garden Gate

It's possible to spend hours reading about gardening instead of actually doing any real gardening. When you can't be participating in the real thing, try the virtual thing at the Garden Gate. Find FAQs, plant lists, a reading room, information on houseplants, reviews of gardening software, and tours of botanical gardens and greenhouses around the world.

Web:
http://www.prairienet.org/ag/garden/

Garden Ponds

Having water near your house creates an extremely pleasant and soothing environment. In one place where I lived, I put a waterfall in my yard near where I grew flowers, strawberries and tomatoes. I was able to see it and hear it from inside, and it served to bring a bit of the outdoors into the house. Would you like to make your own pond? These sites will show you how it is done and give suggestions about populating your pond once it is completed. (I am thinking about having a new pond where I live now, but I am still debating what to put in it. My cat has suggested goldfish.)

Web:
http://w3.one.net/~rzutt/
http://www.dallas.net/~crush/
http://www.erinedwards.com/eric/
http://www.koi.com/
http://www.vcnet.com/koi_net/
http://www.viagrafix.net/pingle/puddle.htm

Usenet:
rec.ponds

GARDENING

Garden Web

Right now, I wish I could stop writing and go work in my garden. But there's too much work yet to finish, so the best I can do is hang out at the Garden Web for a while. There are so many great gardening resources here it's easy to get immersed for hours. Oh well, at least while I am doing the research, I can look out the window at my garden.

Web:
http://www.gardenweb.com/

Gardening Oasis

If you are like me, you spend so much time on the Net that, one day, you walk out to your garden and find it is completely out of control. Do not despair. If your garden is no longer the oasis it once was, you can at least take a moment to relax at this soothing Web site. The Garden Oasis has a searchable database with many good gardening resources. Or you can brew a cup of herbal tea and read the latest feature on seasonal hints and tips. Pretty soon, your gardening quota will be fulfilled, and you can go back to regular Net stuff with a clear conscience.

Web:
http://www.gardening.com/

Gardening Talk and General Discussion

If things aren't going right in the garden, don't just raze everything with the roto-tiller, turn to your fellow Internet buddies for ideas. For the organically challenged, you have the opportunity to cry, scream, and beg for help. Bragging is also welcome; you can pass on the news that it was your 25-pound tomato that made the cover of the National Enquirer.

Usenet:
  alt.binaries.pictures.gardens
  rec.gardens
  rec.gardens.edible
  rec.gardens.orchids
  rec.gardens.roses

Listserv Mailing List:
  List Name: **gardens**
  Subscribe to: **listserv@lsv.uky.edu**

Gothic Gardening

If you prefer the dark and macabre (as opposed to the sunny and cheerful), you do not have to feel left out of the Internet gardening scene. Visit this site and experience gothic gardening at its best. Pick your theme: would you like lots of black plants, plants that attract bats and insects, carnivorous plants, or perhaps a garden that only sits up and takes notice after the sun goes down? It's all here and then some.

Web:
http://www.gothic.net/~malice/

Look What I Found on the Net...

```
Newsgroup: rec.gardens
Subject: Plants That Attract Birds?

> Has anyone had any particular success attracting birds to
> their yard with particular plants?  I've bought a book called
> "How to Attract, House and Feed Birds" which contains a list of
> trees and shrubs that birds are attracted to, but it lists
> several dozen and I'm having a hard time choosing among them.

If I had room for just one bird-feeding plant, it would be a
serviceberry (Amelenchier species): either a shrub or tree.
Robins and other birds love the berries.  In addition, the
plants have beautiful spring blooms and great fall color.
```

Growing Vegetables

One of my favorite pleasures is growing vegetables. Right now (as you read this), I have wonderful beefsteak tomatoes growing in my garden. Here's some information to help you plan and cultivate your own tiny patch of paradise. After all, if Adam and Eve had a Net connection with access to better information, they probably would have been more successful in handling their gardening problems.

Web:
http://hammock.ifas.ufl.edu/txt/fairs/17697
http://hammock.ifas.ufl.edu/txt/fairs/19976

Many people do not appreciate their friends in the vegetable kingdom. Why not grow your own?

Hydroponics

Hydroponics refers to the growing of plants in a water-based nutrient solution without using soil. To use hydroponics, you must have some specialized knowledge and be prepared to put in some extra work to get started. However, there are significant advantages over regular gardening. At home, you can use hydroponics to have your own garden even if you don't have a backyard. For commercial purposes, hydroponics virtually eliminates all pests and weeds. Moreover, it is possible to grow plants closer together than in a field, thus increasing the yield.

Web:
http://www.growingedge.com/pages/hydro.html

Majordomo Mailing List:
List Name: **hydro**
Subscribe to: majordomo@hawg.stanford.edu

I Can Garden

Yes, you can garden, and this lovely gardening site will inspire you to great things. This well-designed site, the work of many people, is described as a "Canadian Internet gardening resource", but don't let this mislead you. I Can Garden is for everyone. There are articles, resources, cat areas, stuff for kids, and much, much more. If you are the type of person who likes to stop and smell the roses, you will love this site.

Web:
http://www.icangarden.com/

Indoor Plants

The cat has eaten half of your rhododendron and the leaves on your African violet are turning yellow. What should you do? Check out the helpful hints you can find at these Web sites. Articles cover topics such as container drainage, decorating with houseplants, feeding and watering, and making terrariums.

Web:
http://muextension.missouri.edu/xplor/agguides/hort/g06510.htm
http://www.globalnode.com/users/stevenr/house.htm

Mailing Lists for Gardeners

Make new friends and talk about gardening by joining a mailing list. In fact, join lots of mailing lists and impress people when they see how much mail you get all the time. This Web site has an extensive collection of mailing lists on a variety of gardening topics.

Web:
http://www.gardenscape.com/GSMagsBooks.html#Mailing

Muds are real (sort of).

GARDENING

Organic Gardening

Organic gardening uses biological methods for pest control, fertilizing and maintenance. Thus, organic gardeners avoid the use of synthetic pesticides, growth regulators and additives. To do so, it is necessary to use particular techniques, such as composting. I have been growing tomatoes without the use of pesticides. They taste great, but, believe me, it takes significant effort and knowledge to keep plants healthy without the use of chemicals. Here are some organic gardening resources that will provide you with lots of information and advice.

Web:
http://mel.lib.mi.us/science/organic.html
http://www.rain.org/~sals/my.html
http://www.supak.com/mort/

Usenet:
rec.gardens.ecosystems

Pest Management

"Pest management" is the politically correct term for figuring out effective ways to destroy, obliterate, or otherwise get rid of those nasty creatures that feed on your plants. Form your strategic battle plan with the help of this Web site. It offers insect factsheets, information on exotic pests, and even images of insects so you can accurately identify the enemy.

Web:
http://www.nysaes.cornell.edu/ent/biocontrol/

Plant Answers

This is a great site for finding general information on particular types of plants such as flowers, fruits and vegetables, ground covers, houseplants, trees and shrubs, and grasses. In addition to specific plant-oriented answers, you can find helpful files about mulching, irrigation and other gardening basics.

Web:
http://aggie-horticulture.tamu.edu/plantanswers/web.html

Trees

If you are into dendrochronology (deducing past environmental changes by looking at tree rings), you probably already know that the oldest tree ring known (from a sequoia) covered 8,700 years. You may not plan on enjoying your own trees that long, but it's still a good idea to know something about how to take care of them. Here is a Web site to get you started.

Web:
http://www.tpoint.net/neighbor/Tre.html

NO NEED to stay ignorant about trees. Connect to the Net and spend some time learning about these wonderful perennial plants that boast single woody self-supporting stems.

Urban Gardening

If you live in a city, you will understand how important it is to have some plants around you to balance the artificial environment. I grew up in a large city, and I saw that most people who had even a little land would plant some sort of garden. If you enjoy gardening in the city, you will find these resources helpful. Read about community gardens, urban agriculture, school and rooftop gardens, composting and solutions to common problems.

Web:
http://www.cityfarmer.org/
http://www.urbangarden.com/

GARDENING

Virtual Garden

This is a beautifully designed Web site containing all kinds of great gardening resources. I particularly like all the reference material. For example, you can search a database and look for plants with specific characteristics that grow in your area. This is a great site to visit when you are planning a garden.

Web:
http://pathfinder.com/vg/

Web Garden

With all the great gardening resources available on the Net, it's hard to get away from the computer long enough to spend time in the backyard. This site has information for beginning gardeners, whether you garden at home or commercially. Read garden features and tips, and search a gardening database for information about all sorts of plants.

Web:
http://www.hcs.ohio-state.edu/hcs/webgarden.html

Wildflowers

I love wildflowers. Right now, in my garden, I have a large bed of assorted wildflowers that are particularly suited to attracting hummingbirds. The thing I like about wildflowers is that, unlike their cultivated cousins, they retain an air of informality that allows you to enjoy that back-to-nature feeling without actually having to get your feet dirty or leave your home. If you are a wildflower fan, here are some great sources of information and pictures that will keep your Web browser blooming long into the night.

Web:
http://aggie-horticulture.tamu.edu/wildseed/
http://www.vt.edu:10021/forestry/wildlife/stein/plants.html
http://www.wildflower.org/

Zines are cool.

Wildflowers

Here is a cool thing you can do with wildflowers.

First, get yourself a large field. Next, plant wildflower seeds all over the field. Wait for all the flowers to bloom. (As you wait, you can read this book from cover to cover.)

Once the wildflowers are blooming, get yourself a beautiful woman (or handsome man, whichever is appropriate). Then, in slow motion, run through the field of wildflowers, hand in hand with the woman (or man), while a friend of yours captures you on videotape.

Now put the videotape on your personal Web site. Soon you will be the envy of people the world over.

GAY, LESBIAN, BISEXUAL

Bisexuality

There are a lot of bisexual resources on the Net, and these Web sites can help you find what you need: questions and answers, news, newsletters, discussion groups, educational information, and lots and lots of links to related resources on the Net. For some hard-hitting theoretical discussion of bisexuality and gender issues, you can participate in the Usenet groups and the mailing list. Note: These forums are primarily for intellectual discussion, not for socializing, support, or news and announcements.

Web:
http://www.bi.org/~jon/soc.bi/
http://www.biresource.org/
http://www.bisexual.org/

Usenet:
alt.motss.bisexua-l
soc.bi

Listserv Mailing List:
List Name: **bithry-l**
Subscribe to: **listserv@brownvm.brown.edu**

IRC:
#bi

Catholic Gays

Being a gay Catholic is not easy. Within the church, there is a strong antipathy to homosexuality, feelings that are often present in local churches and families. This Web site has resources specifically for the Catholic gay community. Read about the Bible's stand on homosexuality, Catholic theology, dealing with religious attacks, lesbian and gay marriage, and more.

Web:
http://www.bway.net/~halsall/lgbh.html

Coming Out

Coming out can be difficult. Here is some information to help you understand individuals coming to terms with their lesbian or gay sexual orientation.

Web:
http://vub.mcgill.ca/clubs/lbgtm/info/academe.html
http://www.gmhp.demon.co.uk/coming-out/
http://www.hrc.org/ncop/

Cyberqueer Lounge

The Cyberqueer Lounge is a collection of resources for gay, bisexual and transgendered persons. As you can imagine, a site like this will have many different types of resources, so you won't be bored. If you get tired of reading, you can just hang out and talk to other people.

Web:
http://www.idowebs.com/GLAIDS/

Domestic Partners

It's amazing that problems can be caused by not having a little piece of paper. Even if you have signed on to your relationship for life, it doesn't count as much as if you had a legal marriage. This site has information about domestic partnerships, same-sex marriages, legal status, policies at various universities, and related issues.

Web:
http://qrd.rdrop.com/qrd/dp/

Domestic Partners

There is a lot more to a domestic partnership than disagreeing about money and remembering all the times your partner hurt your feelings. You also need to keep abreast of the latest legal information. The Domestic Partners archive has a wealth of information that is perfect for people who need to know what's what and what's not.

Gay and Lesbian Alliance Against Defamation

The Gay and Lesbian Alliance Against Defamation (GLADD) was founded in 1985 with a mission to reform the portrayal of gays and lesbians in the media, to improve the public's attitude toward homosexuality, and to help decrease violence and discrimination affecting gays and lesbians. At the GLAAD Web site, you can read about their successes, and look at their press releases, media resources and general information.

Web:
http://www.glaad.org/

Gay and Lesbian Parenting

Here are some useful resources for gays and lesbians who have children or who are considering starting a family. At these sites, you can find information about the Gay and Lesbian Parents Coalition International as well as relevant legal issues. There is also information for lesbian moms, covering such topics as sperm banks, artificial insemination, health and pregnancy, adoption and insurance.

Web:
http://www.glpci.org/
http://www.lesbian.org/lesbian-moms/
http://www.milepost1.com/~gaydad/

Majordomo Mailing List:
List Name: **moms**
Subscribe to: majordomo@queernet.org

Gay Christians

This IRC channel is devoted to gay Christians around the world. Join the discussion, and check out the **#gaychristians** Web site when you get a chance. I've also included an additional Web site that has general resources about gay Christianity.

Web:
http://www.gaychristians.org/
http://www.whosoever.org/

Usenet:
alt.christnet.motss

IRC:
#gaychristians

Gay, Lesbian and Bisexual Resources

There are lots of gay-related resources on the Net. Here is a good place to start when you are searching for something in particular or simply browsing for something new and interesting.

Web:
http://www.fc.net/~zarathus/links.html

Gay, Lesbian and Bisexual White Pages

One of the most important assets of the gay community is the wide variety of talented and accomplished people it contains. This Web site is a people-oriented resource where you can find a specific person, explore people's personal Web pages, and see which sites are the most popular among the other visitors.

Web:
http://www.planetout.com/pno/netqueery/people/

Gay Travel Guide

The next time you plan a trip, try this travel information from a gay perspective. This guide offers recommendations for gay-friendly hotels, bars, clubs and other interesting places you might enjoy.

Web:
http://www.outandabout.com/

Gay TV Listings

There's more to TV than Ellen (now in reruns). Check this Web site regularly to stay current on gay issues in the broadcast industry. More important, when you are not sure what's good on the tube, check the comprehensive listing of upcoming gay-related TV shows. You will find listings of shows for the current week that feature gays, gay themes, or have been created by members of the gay community.

Web:
http://www.washblade.com/point/ontheair.htm

Gay-Oriented Mailing Lists

Mailing lists are fun because the information comes right to you—you don't have to go out to get it (sort of like pizza). There is a huge amount of mailing lists dedicated to gays, lesbians and bisexuals, including regional lists.

Web:
http://www.qrd.org/qrd/electronic/email/

Gay-Oriented Mailing Lists

Would you like to talk with people about gay-oriented topics in complete privacy? Join a mailing list.

GAY, LESBIAN, BISEXUAL

Gays in the Military

Are you sick of hearing people talk about not telling? Here are some Web pages that relate to gays in the military. Read about the Servicemembers Legal Defense Fund for gays in the military as well as news, information and articles relating to relevant legal issues.

Web:
http://www.qrd.org/qrd/usa/military/
http://www.sldn.org/

Gayzoo

Gayzoo is a search engine devoted to gay and lesbian topics. It is modeled after Yahoo. (Hence the name "Gayzoo".) Search for many types of resources, including health, the arts, entertainment, sports, travel resources and personal Web sites.

Web:
http://www.gayzoo.com/

Historical and Celebrity Figures

When you're famous, you can't expect to have your privacy. Just look at headlines of the tabloids and other gossip sheets. Here is a list of people who are out by choice or by force, so take it for what you think it's worth.

Web:
http://users.cybercity.dk/~dko12530/queerhis.htm
http://www.scruz.net/~fez/Resources/famous_gays.html

Homosexuality and Religion

There are eight places in the Bible—five in the Old Testament and three in the New Testament—commonly cited as references to how we should think about homosexuality. However, Bible verses are only part of the story. How religious people feel about homosexuality has as much to do with what they are taught and what they feel as what it says in the Bible. Here are some links to information regarding this important topic.

Web:
http://www.bridges-across.org/faith.htm
http://www.religioustolerance.org/homosexu.htm

Homosexuality Talk and General Discussion

Members of the same sex (MOTSS) discuss their thoughts, feelings and experiences about being gay. The general groups on homosexuality cover a wide range of topics on how gays relate to the rest of the world, while the .motss groups discuss how gays relate to one another.

Usenet:
alt.homosexual
alt.sex.homosexual
alt.sex.motss
soc.motss

IRC:
#gay

Jewish Gays

If you are Jewish and gay, you will find this site informative: mailing lists, news, health information, bibliographies, as well as links. If you are thinking of having a religious ceremony to celebrate your relationship, there are special resources here that can help you.

Web:
http://www.usc.edu/Library/oneigla/tb/

Lesbian Chat

An important part of the lesbian community is socializing and talking. On the Net, there is never a shortage of people to talk with. Use the IRC channels to meet and talk with other lesbians and bisexual women around the world. Join the Usenet groups to see what other lesbians have been discussing.

Usenet:
alt.homosexual.lesbian
alt.shoe.lesbians
soc.women.lesbian-and-bi

IRC:
#lesbian
#lesbianation
#lesbianlounge
#lesbo

GAY, LESBIAN, BISEXUAL

Out Proud

In the gay community, there is a common (although not universal) belief that it is good for young gay people to recognize and come to terms with their sexual orientation. This Web site is maintained by the (U.S.) National Coalition for Gay, Lesbian, Bisexual & Transgender Youth to offer resources for young gay people, their teachers and their families. In particular, you will find online brochures offering advice about being a gay teenager, and on how to come out to your family.

Web:
 http://www.outproud.org/

PFLAG Gay Support Organization

PFLAG stands for "Parents, Families and Friends of Lesbians and Gays". PFLAG was created to offer support and advocacy for gays, lesbians, bisexuals and their families. The PFLAG mailing list is a great places for families and friends to talk about issues and experiences. The Web site offers lots of information about sexual orientation, gender identity and local PFLAG chapters.

Web:
 http://www.critpath.org/pflag-talk/

Majordomo Mailing List:
 List Name: **pflag-talk**
 Subscribe to: **majordomo@casti.com**

Express yourself on the Net.

PlanetOut

Out or in, PlanetOut is outrageous. Full of links and information about culture, community and news, PlanetOut has lots of entertaining stuff that will keep you informed and amused (and very possibly outraged). This is a great place to keep up on the news.

Web:
 http://www.planetout.com/

Politics and Homosexuality

Domestic partnerships and child custody battles put the politics of homosexuality on the front page. Discuss the latest civil rights cases, pending legislation, and whom to boycott (or not). Keep informed so you can make a difference in your community. The Web site has a nice collection of gay and lesbian political resources.

Web:
 http://www.indiana.edu/~glbtpol/

Look What I Found on the Net...

```
Newsgroup: alt.homosexual
Subject: Are You Gay or Is It a Phase?

> After all these years, my mother still thinks I'm going
> through a phase.  It's the longest phase I'm going through :-)
> and I'm wondering if anyone here has parents, friends or other
> loved ones who think the same thing.

For almost seven years, my mother began all our phone
conversations with: "Are you normal yet?  When will you get over
that silly phase?  Your father and I are getting older and we
want grandchildren from you."

I put a stop to this, but every now and then my mother still
surprises me with: "Do you have any female friends that you find
attractive?"  I always disappoint her by saying: "I do, mom, but
I'm lucky in that we cruise different types of men..."
```

Queer Resources Directory

The Queer Resources Directory contains thousands of files relating to just about every aspect of homosexuality you can imagine. This is one of the premier gay sites on the Internet. Family, religion, health, business, culture, media, politics, organizations, electronic resources—it's all here.

Web:
http://www.qrd.org/QRD/

Looking for some gay-oriented information on the Net? The **Queer Resources Directory** is *the* place to start your search.

Queer Zines

Looking for something good to read? Have a look at these lists of zines that relate to gays, lesbians and bisexuals. These informative sites cover print zines that are not accessible on the Net, and give all the details on how to subscribe or find the publications in question.

Web:
http://www.io.com/~larrybob/qze.html
http://www.qrd.org/qrd/media/magazines/

Straight Answers

Questions gay people hear often from straight people, and advice on how to answer them. For example, "Can gay people seduce straight people?" is a commonly asked question. Come here to get ideas on ways to handle this question. Topics covered include religion, AIDS, children, what it was like to come out, and relationships.

Web:
http://www.sipu.com/sa/

GENEALOGY

Adoptees and Genealogy

There are times when you can work on genealogy for hours and never seem to get anywhere. As you know, it can be a lot of work trying to trace your family tree. If you are adopted, there are extra complications, especially if you do not have full information about your birth parents. If you are an adoptee or you have adoptees in your family, here are some genealogy resources that can help you trace your lineage.

Web:
http://www.mtjeff.com/~bodenst/page3.html

Canadian Genealogy Resources

Searching through the records of another country is often difficult and time consuming. Get an advantage by doing preliminary research on the Net. This site has tons of links to Canadian genealogy resources as well as links to related sites.

Web:
http://www.iosphere.net/~jholwell/cangene/gene.html

Usenet:
soc.genealogy.surnames.canada

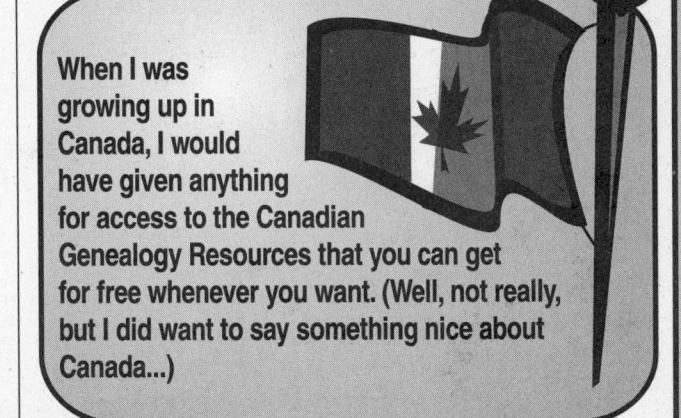

When I was growing up in Canada, I would have given anything for access to the Canadian Genealogy Resources that you can get for free whenever you want. (Well, not really, but I did want to say something nice about Canada...)

Cyndi's Genealogy Resources

If you want to be overwhelmed and dazzled by the amount of genealogy research material on the Net, all you need to do is fire up the old browser and check out this collection of genealogy links. You will be amazed at how well-organized and easy to use it is. There is only one problem: once you get started digging around, you won't want to stop.

Web:
  http://www.cyndislist.com/

Genealogy Discussion by Ethnicity

There are lots of genealogy discussion groups available on Usenet, many of which are devoted to various cultural and ethnic heritages. These groups focus on the following cultures: Cajun, Africa, Australia/New Zealand, Belgium/Netherlands/Luxembourg, Canada, France, Germany, Hispanic, Nordic, Slavic, United Kingdom and Ireland.

Usenet:
  alt.culture.cajun
  soc.genealogy.african
  soc.genealogy.australia+nz
  soc.genealogy.benelux
  soc.genealogy.canada+english
  soc.genealogy.french
  soc.genealogy.german
  soc.genealogy.hispanic
  soc.genealogy.nordic
  soc.genealogy.slavic
  soc.genealogy.uk+ireland

Genealogy Events

Are you looking for some hot genealogy action? This site will give you the details on upcoming events such as courses, seminars, meetings, tours, lectures, festivals and reunions. If you are planning a shindig of some sort, post it here so people can see what is going on in your genealogical neck of the woods.

Web:
  http://www.genealogy.org/~gcal/

Genealogy Mailing Lists

When you participate in a mailing list, you can meet lots of people, including other researchers who are working in the same lines as you. Scan these collections of mailing lists, and see what suits your needs. There is something for everyone here, including lists devoted to specific surnames.

Web:
  http://www.eskimo.com/~chance/lists.html
  http://www.rootsweb.com/~maillist/

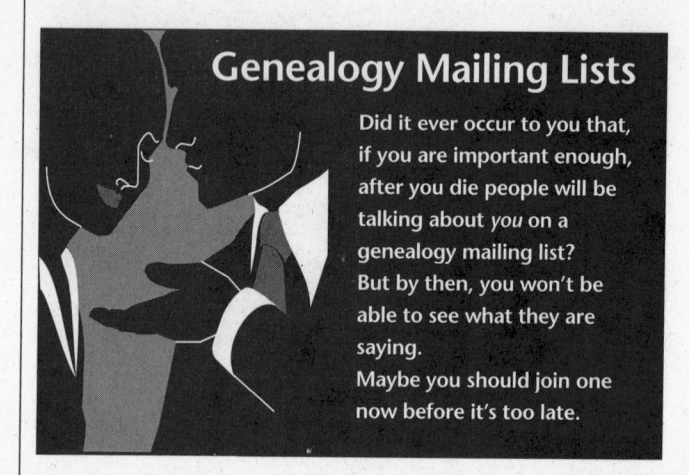

Genealogy Mailing Lists

Did it ever occur to you that, if you are important enough, after you die people will be talking about *you* on a genealogy mailing list? But by then, you won't be able to see what they are saying.
Maybe you should join one now before it's too late.

Genealogy Marketplace

If you have any genealogical items you want to buy or want to sell, this is the place to do it. Just about anything goes: books, services, maps, documents, and much more.

Usenet:
  soc.genealogy.marketplace

Genealogy Methods and Hints

It's always good to have help when you are working on a family history. These Web sites have lots of hints about what to do and what not to do, as well as suggestions as to good sources of information. The Usenet group is a place to ask questions or offer advice to other genealogical researchers.

Web:
  http://www.firstct.com/fv/tmaps.html
  http://www.kalglo.com/gentips.htm
  http://www.rootscomputing.com/howto/howto.htm

Usenet:
  soc.genealogy.methods

GENEALOGY

Genealogy Resources

Genealogy is a popular pastime on the Internet, and there are many people (and some companies) that have created related Web sites. But how do you find what you want? Start with these sites: well-organized collections with oodles of resources for the genealogically inclined.

Web:
http://genealogy.emcee.com/
http://www.ancestry.com/
http://www.gengateway.com/

Genealogy Scams

I got a special "genealogy" offer in the mail. Perhaps you have seen one yourself. Some company wants to sell you a complete history of your family from the beginning of time, or the full names of every single person in the world with your surname. The offers sound inviting, but you should always check them thoroughly before you turn loose any of your money. Some of these pitches are real scams and they are targeted specifically at inexperienced genealogists or anyone who is working on a family history. Read this overview and learn about the types of suspicious offers you should learn to avoid.

Web:
ftp://ftp.rootsweb.com/pub/roots-l/faq/faq.scams
http://www.everton.com/FAQ/FAQ.SCAMS

Genealogy Search Engine

When you want information fast (or as fast as it gets in genealogy), it's good to know where you can get what you need. Here is a search engine that will let you search a database of online genealogical resources to find the ones that are in your area of interest.

Web:
http://www.gensource.com/ifoundit/

Genealogy Software

Once you get started with genealogy, you will find that using a computer makes things a *lot* easier. For example, the program I use is able to print nice charts of various parts of the family tree. I then send these charts to relatives and ask them for changes and additions, which has worked out nicely. Here are some places to help you find the software you need to do the best possible job.

Web:
http://www.concentric.net/~lkessler/gplinks.shtml
http://www.cyberenet.net/~gsteiner/macgsfaq/
http://www.cyndislist.com/software.htm

Genealogy Talk and General Discussion

The Internet is a global community—a great place from which to track down family members from way-back-when. Usenet offers a convenient forum not only to discuss ways of researching, what kinds of software and resources are available, or to compare anecdotes of your quests, but you can also ask for information on family names. Plenty of sharing goes on here. Find that long-lost second-half-cousin-twice-removed who broke all your crayons when you were seven and remind him you want all 64 colors, plus the built-in sharpener.

Usenet:
alt.genealogy
soc.genealogy.britain
soc.genealogy.computing
soc.genealogy.ireland
soc.genealogy.italian
soc.genealogy.misc
soc.roots

Genealogy Terms

There are lots of special terms used in genealogy. Many of these have origins in other languages. Some terms are really arcane medical words. You will also find technical words relating to genealogy techniques and record keeping. The next time you encounter a baffling word, here are some good places to find a definition. Pretty soon, expressions like paucis hebdomadibus and collateral ancestor will be old friends.

Web:
http://home.att.net/~dottsr/diction.html
http://www.charweb.org/gen/gendict.html
http://www.genweb.net/~samcasey/terms.html
http://www.uftree.com/UFT/Nav/glossary.html

Genealogy's Most Wanted

Are you looking for information about a long-lost, long-dead relative? You may find what you need here. If not, you can submit a request, and maybe another genealogist researching the same family will be able to help you. To inspire yourself, read some of the success stories of how other people have found genealogical treasures. Even more important, lots of long-lost relatives have found each other by using this service.

Web:
  http://www.citynet.net/mostwanted/

What's in a Name?

We all know that it is important to know everything possible about your ancestors because... uh... well... I guess I forget, but it is a pretty important reason. After all, if you don't know where you came from then you certainly won't know where you are and... hmmm... something or other anyway.

Let's just say that genealogy is cool and leave it at that. After all, if it wasn't for our ancestors, we wouldn't be here. (Well, we might be here, but we would have different parents and grandparents, and we wouldn't know anyone's birthday, and everything would be all mixed up and, well... you get the idea.)

Genserv

Gain access to tens of thousands of surnames and over a million names in this huge database of family information donated from people around the Net. You can search the database as long as you provide information of your own to help Genserv grow.

Web:
  http://www.genserv.com/

GenWeb Project

GenWeb is an ambitious project devoted to compiling information about genealogy research resources around the United States. The available information is divided by state and county. These resources are actual physical sources of genealogical information, such as public libraries, family history centers and genealogy libraries. This is a great place to find what resources are available in your local area.

Web:
  http://www.usgenweb.com/

Getting Started in Genealogy

At first, getting started in genealogy can be bewildering. If you are having trouble telling your tiny tafel from your soundex, here are some good places to start. These are easy-to-read beginner's guides to genealogy, that will offer the help and guidance you need to begin a family search.

Web:
  http://www.familytreemaker.com/mainmenu.html
  http://www.rootsweb.com/roots-l/starting.html

Look What I Found on the Net...

```
Newsgroup: alt.genealogy
Subject: The Oldest U.S. Surname

This was in a local newspaper...

"Surname of the oldest surviving family in the United States
reportedly is Sonan.  Descended from settlers at Florida's St.
Augustine."

The next clip said: "When your father's father, or his, was a
lad, men usually lived longer than women.  And that had always
been true worldwide.  But by 1920, women lived a little longer.
```

Heraldry

Heraldry is the tradition, dating from the Middle Ages, of displaying symbols or pictures (called charges) on shields. During tournaments, knights were recognized by the shields they carried. (Such tournaments were refereed by officials called heralds—hence, the word "heraldry".) The charges on the shields identified individuals and families, and were passed to successive generations (the Middle Ages' version of a vanity license plate). As centuries passed, these charges were adapted into insignia for the nobility and were used not only on shields, but as seals for documents. Later the designs were embroidered into articles of clothing. In fact, the phrase "coat of arms" comes from the practice of embroidering family designs onto the surcoat that was worn over chain mail armor. (This served to make you easily recognizable by the person who was running you through with a sword.) Here are some interesting sites on the Net that explain heraldry, give a basic primer, and tell what some of the symbols mean. The Usenet group is for the discussion of heraldry. All these resources will help you better analyze your family's coat of arms. (Or, if your family does not have a coat of arms, you can concoct something suitable for your next reunion, and start a brand new family tradition.)

Web:
  http://renaissance.dm.net/heraldry/primer.html
  http://www.digiserve.com/heraldry/
  http://www.heraldica.org/topics/glossary/

Usenet:
  rec.heraldry

Jewish Genealogy

For genealogy buffs interested in tracing Jewish roots, here are special resources you will find useful. The mailing list and Usenet group address the special issues involved in tracing Jewish lineage and are great companions to other, more general discussion forums.

Web:
  http://www.jewishgen.org/

Usenet:
  soc.genealogy.jewish

Listserv Mailing List:
  List Name: **jewishgen**
  Subscribe to: **listserv@apple.ease.lsoft.com**

Journal of Online Genealogy

The Journal of Online Genealogy is a genealogy magazine with monthly articles. You'll find information for beginners, as well as discussions of advanced projects for more experienced genealogists. You will also find help in learning how to use the Internet for your research, as well as news of interest to the genealogical community.

Web:
  http://www.onlinegenealogy.com/

Mayflower Genealogy

The Mayflower was a ship that brought pilgrims from England to New England in 1620. The Mayflower landed at Plymouth on December 26, 1620. Before leaving the ship, the colonists drew up an agreement— called the Mayflower Compact—establishing a temporary government based on their own intentions, rather than the laws of the English crown. This Web site has information about the Mayflower and the people who descended from the original passengers. You can investigate wills, inventories, passenger lists, early writings related to the Mayflower, and explore links to other Mayflower resources. Somebody had to be descended from those adventurous pilgrims. It might as well have been you.

Web:
  http://members.aol.com/calebj/mayflower.html

Mayflower Genealogy

Do you know who Humility Cooper was? How about Damaris Hopkins?

They were the two youngest girls who came over to America on the Mayflower in 1620. If you can trace your roots back that far, it may be that one of these girls is your ancestor. Check with the Mayflower Web site for pertinent info. (Personally, I know it doesn't apply to me, because there hasn't been any humility in my family since the late 1500s.)

Medieval Genealogy

Imagine the hours and hours of research that would go into tracing a family lineage back to the medieval period. If you want to meet some people who are working on such a task, check out this Usenet group. This discussion involves genealogy relating to the period spanning 500 to 1600 A.D. This discussion group is strictly for talking about medieval genealogy, not a general discussion of medieval history and culture. (If you want to talk about history, use **soc.history.medieval** instead.) The Web site has the **soc.genealogy.medieval** FAQ.

Web:
http://www.erols.com/wrei/faqs/medieval.html

Usenet:
soc.genealogy.medieval

National Archives and Records Administration

See what the National Archives and Records Administration (NARA) has to offer in the way of instructional leaflets and helpful searching tips for genealogical research. They also give you a glance at microfiche records for census and federal court information such as bankruptcy records, naturalization records, land grant claims, and immigrant and passenger arrivals.

Web:
http://www.nara.gov/genealogy/

Native American Genealogy

No matter what tribe you are from, this site will have good general information to get you started. You may even find specific information about your particular nation of origin. There are also links to some useful how-to articles relating to Native American genealogy.

Web:
http://members.aol.com/bbbenge/front.html

Online Genealogy Newsletter

This online newsletter comes out every week. Take a break from your research, and spend a few moments to see what's new. The articles are well written and thoughtful with an emphasis on practical resources and techniques.

Web:
http://www.ancestry.com/columns/eastman/index.htm

Roots

The mailing list **roots-l** has been a popular genealogy mailing list for many years. It has been spun into a major collection of resources and networking options for genealogists around the world. The Web site has a searchable archive of posts that have been sent to the mailing list. For example, this is a good place to find out if anyone has been making queries regarding a particular surname. The site has a sharing library where individuals who have time to share list books from which they are willing to do lookups for other people. Roots offers a registry of people who are researching particular surnames, so you may be able to find other people who might be related to you. Detailed information about the **roots-l** mailing list is also available at this Web site.

Web:
http://www.rootsweb.com/

Royalty and Nobility

Once, when I was in a Mormon Family History Center, I saw ex-Duchess Fergie at a microfilm reader, working on her family tree. (Actually, she was having trouble with her microfilm reader, and I had to help her load the film.) Before I went back to do my own research, I told her that it would be easier to do her research on the Net. I explained that there are lots of places with information about royal and noble lineages, and she wouldn't even have to remember how to turn the microfilm spool. I gave her a list of these resources to get her started. And, I told her, if you want to see what they are saying about you behind your back, try the Usenet group.

Web:
http://ftp.cac.psu.edu/~saw/royal/royalgen.html
http://www.dcs.hull.ac.uk/public/genealogy/GEDCOM.html

Usenet:
alt.talk.royalty

GENEALOGY 325

Royalty and Nobility

When you come right down to it, the kings, queens and nobles of history were a lot like regular people (if you overlook minor details such as fame, power and wealth).

However, there was one important difference: many aspects of the lives of these people were documented in detail and, if you need such information, a lot of it is available on the Net.

So sometime, just for fun, why not graft a portion of some royal family onto your own personal family tree, and see if anything takes root?

Scottish Clans

Most people don't realize it, but there is a lot more to Scottish culture than the Loch Ness monster and Scotch whiskey. For example, they have bagpipes and Highland games and men who wear skirts. Moreover, the Scots also have lots of cool clans (sort of like gangs in Los Angeles, only Scottish accents are easier to understand). If you are interested in Scottish clans, or if you are a member of a clan, check out this great resource. It has links to individual clan sites, a virtual pub in which you can post messages, as well as information on the history and culture of Scotland and the Highland games. The Usenet group is for discussion of Scottish clans.

Web:
http://www.tartans.com/

Usenet:
alt.scottish.clans

Surname Databases and Discussion

As a genealogical researcher, you know how easy it is to spend hours and hours and still come up with nothing substantial. However, here's a great way to come up with information quickly that is fun, interesting and just may help you out. Search for your name in one of the surname databases, and I bet you will find something of interest. I found it interesting to see how many people in the database had the same last name as me. For discussion about surnames, check out the Usenet discussion groups. They are for discussing surnames, posting surname lists, and requesting information on particular names.

Web:
http://www.cyndislist.com/database.htm
http://www.polaris.net/~legend/spring.htm
http://www.rootsweb.com/rootsweb/searches/

Usenet:
soc.genealogy.surnames
soc.genealogy.surnames.britain
soc.genealogy.surnames.german
soc.genealogy.surnames.global
soc.genealogy.surnames.ireland
soc.genealogy.surnames.misc
soc.genealogy.surnames.usa

Surname Origins

Have you ever wondered what your surname means? Try this Web site where you will find information on the origins of over 2,000 names (the majority of which are British). For example, if your last name is Epps, you will find out that it's a British name meaning "Son of the wild boar." (I bet your father will be glad to hear that.)

Web:
http://www.familychronicle.com/surname.htm

Tombstone Rubbings

In the course of your genealogical field trips, you may one day find yourself in a cemetery, recording data from tombstones. One great way to capture the essence of the tombstone is to do a rubbing. This site gives detailed instructions about how to do tombstone rubbings as well as hints on the type of information you can expect to find.

Web:
http://www.firstct.com/fv/t_stone.html

GENEALOGISTS...
FIVE REASONS TO LEARN ALL ABOUT TOMBSTONE RUBBING:

(1) TOMBSTONE RUBBING IS THE BEST WAY TO CAPTURE INFORMATION AND DESIGNS FROM A TOMBSTONE IN A PERMANENT, CONVENIENT AND PORTABLE FORM.

(2) IT'S A GREAT WAY TO MAKE FRIENDS. JUST SPEND SOME TIME IN A GRAVEYARD WORKING ON A TOMBSTONE, AND YOU WILL BE SURPRISED HOW MANY PEOPLE COME OVER TO ASK WHAT YOU ARE DOING.

(3) IT'S FUN. AND UNLIKE VISITING DISNEYLAND, THERE ARE NO LONG WAITS.

(4) IT'S GOOD FOR YOUR SOCIAL LIFE. PEOPLE WHO KNOW HOW TO RUB TOMBSTONES CONSISTENTLY RANK AT THE TOP OF POPULARITY POLLS. THINK BACK TO HIGH SCHOOL. WHO WERE THE ONLY PEOPLE WHO WERE MORE POPULAR THAN THE CAPTAIN OF THE FOOTBALL TEAM AND THE HEAD CHEERLEADER? SEE WHAT I MEAN?

(5) DIDN'T YOUR MOTHER ALWAYS TELL YOU IT WAS HEALTHY TO SPEND TIME OUTDOORS?

U.S. Census Information

Article 1, Section 2 of the United States Constitution mandates an "enumeration" of all the people in all the states of the Union. (What a job that has turned out to be.) In the United States, the primary purpose of a census is to count the population in order to distribute seats in the U.S. House of Representatives and to define the legislative district boundaries within each state. However, census findings have many other purposes, most of which relate to allocating federal funds and developing social services. The first American census was taken in 1790, since then, a census has been taken every 10 years. Census records can give you basic information about families, some details about household members, and help you track family locations. These two Web sites have information about how to use census records for genealogical research, as well as background information on the census itself.

Web:
http://www.census.gov/ftp/pub/genealogy/www/
http://www.firstct.com/fv/uscensus.html

U.S. Civil War Genealogy

Just imagine. You are sitting on the front porch, drinking a refreshing mint julep, when all of a sudden a group of Union soldiers come tearing through the yard on their way to burn down your house. No doubt about it, the years of the U.S. Civil War were a confusing, difficult time in American history. Fortunately for genealogists, there was a lot of effort put into keeping track of all the men who went off to war, and it is possible to search the old military records for information about these men. In addition, since this was a time of upheaval, many people were away from home, corresponding by letters. There are also a fair number of personal diaries. One problem, however, is that some courthouses were burned, and some records were lost permanently. That aside, there are a lot of great resources relating to Civil War genealogy. These resources will show you where to begin and what to do once you get started.

Web:
http://sunsite.utk.edu/civil-war/warweb.html
http://www.cwc.lsu.edu/other/genealogy/faq-gene.htm

GEOGRAPHY

Vital Records in the U.S.

Vital records are official documents that record important life events such as births, marriages, deaths, divorces, and passages from one country to another. There is a great deal of important information you can glean from these documents, so be sure you know where to get them. These sites have a list of places to which you can write for vital records within the United States.

Web:
http://www.cdc.gov/nchswww/howto/w2w/w2welcom.htm
http://www.inlink.com/~nomi/vitalrec/

GEOGRAPHY

CIA World Factbook

The CIA World Factbook contains detailed information about every country and territory in the world. For each country you will find data about geography, people, government, the economy, transportation, communication and defense. This is a fantastic resource with which you should become familiar; you never know what you will find. For example, I just found out that 97 percent of Canadians over 15 years old can read and write. (The others, presumably, depend on a graphical user interface.)

Web:
http://www.odci.gov/cia/publications/factbook/

CIA INFO FOR YOU

The American Central Intelligence Agency is so secret that its budget is not even made public. (I don't even know if they have enough money to buy copies of my Internet books.) What I do know is that the CIA spends a lot of time and effort keeping track of all the countries of the world. And you can get it all (the non-secret stuff anyway) for free. This resource is invaluable for anyone who is planning to create his own military alliance.

> The Net is mankind's greatest achievement.

Distance Calculator

Before you go from here to there, make sure you know how far it is. Otherwise, how would you know how much food to bring? This site enables you to calculate the distances between world cities and will even show you the points plotted on a map as well as the longitude and latitude. I found out it is 8,668 miles (13,949 km) from where I live to Bombay.

Web:
http://www.indo.com/distance/

Earth Rise

Earth Rise is a Web site that allows you to access a huge database of pictures of the Earth taken by astronauts on the U.S. space shuttle. What a wonderful way to appreciate our planet. Just a few clicks of the mouse, and you can see what any part of the world looks like from space.

Web:
http://earthrise.sdsc.edu/

Pictures of Your Planet

If you are like me, the Earth is one of your favorite planets in the entire universe. But what do you do when you meet an alien who pulls out a wallet and starts showing you photos of his home planet? Invite him over to your computer, fire up your Web browser, and point it to "Earth Rise". Never again will you have to let a foreigner one-up you when it comes to civic pride.

GEOGRAPHY

Geographic Information Systems

A geographical information system (GIS) is a computer system used to manipulate information that is related to specific geographical locations. For example, satellite photos showing patterns of vegetation might be part of a GIS. There are many different types of GISs, and a lot of information available on the Net. Here are some good places to start looking.

Web:
http://www.ameritel.net/lusers/abrody/gis.html
http://www.esri.com/library/jumpstation/jumpstation.html

Usenet:
comp.infosystems.gis
comp.soft-sys.gis.esri

Geography Departments Worldwide

This site has a search engine that allows you to search geography department resources all over the Net. You can narrow your search by research field, so you could look up more specific resources, such as who is studying human geography in Bangladesh or remote sensing in Switzerland. You can access resources in many countries and in many different fields of geographical research.

Web:
http://geowww.uibk.ac.at/geolinks/

Geography Resources

Modern geography embraces many different branches of study. No matter what field you are interested in, you will find a lot of geographical information on the Net. Here are some good places to start. You will find links to educational resources, research publications, maps, images, geographic data sources, and information about jobs, organizations and professional associations.

Web:
http://www.census.gov/geo/www/
http://www.utexas.edu/depts/grg/virtdept/resources/contents.htm

Geography Talk and General Discussion

Imagine what life would be like if there was no geography. There would be no road maps to have to re-fold. There would be no grueling hours of having to memorize the capitals of third world countries. And worse, there would be no map showing what hills and dales you have to go over to get to Grandma's house. In fact, geography is so important that you can find a lively discussion about it in Usenet. Go hang out with the people who know the planet like the backs of their hands.

Usenet:
bit.listserv.geograph

Look What I Found on the Net...

```
Newsgroup: bit.listserv.geograph
Subject: Impact of a 3-Meter Rise in Oceans on Maps

> This is probably a question to which most of you already know
> the answer, but I don't even know where to look.  If the
> global warming people are correct in their views, and there
> is a rise in sea level of 3 meters, where in the world would
> maps change the most? The least?

Find a topographic map (showing altitude and depth) of the
regions in which you are interested, and search for all areas
that are under 3 meters in height.  They will probably be under
water.

Good luck.
```

GEOGRAPHY

Global Land Information System

The Global Land Information System (GLIS) is an interactive computer system developed by the U.S. Geological Survey (USGS), a branch of the U.S. Department of the Interior. The GLIS provides you with information relating to a huge variety of data sets that may be ordered from the USGS. If you have an idea what you want, this system can help you find it. If not, you can just cruise around and look for cool stuff. (USGS data sets make wonderful Mother's Day presents.)

Web:
http://edcwww.cr.usgs.gov/glis/glis.html

Global Positioning System

The Global Positioning System (GPS) is an amazing system that will tell you your (almost) exact position and time anywhere on the Earth. There are three parts to the system: (1) In space, there are 24 satellites (three of which are spares) that circle the Earth in 12-hour orbits. From any point on the Earth, there are five to eight satellites above you somewhere. (2) Around the world, there is a whole system of tracking stations. The master station is at Falcon Air Force Base in Colorado. (3) To receive data, you use a GPS receiver. This receiver uses the signals from at least four of the satellites to give you navigation, positioning and time information. If you are a special authorized user (U.S. Department of Defense, etc.) your receiver can tell you your exact position within an 18 by 28 meter area, and the time will be accurate within 100 nanoseconds (billionths of a second). Everyone else gets a position within a 100 by 156 meter area, with a time accurate within 167 nanoseconds. Are you intrigued? Check the Net for a lot more information.

Web:
http://www.gpsworld.com/
http://www.trimble.com/gps/
http://www.utexas.edu/depts/grg/gcraft/notes/gps/gps.html

Usenet:
sci.geo.satellite-nav

Great Globe Gallery

One of the most interesting and difficult problems for cartographers is how to represent all or parts of the Earth (which is three-dimensional) on a flat surface. I recently read a cartography textbook (just for fun), and I was amazed at how many decisions and tradeoffs there are in making a map. The overall general principle is: if you want to go into outer space and look down, you can see the real thing. Anything else is, in some way, a compromise and there are many, many ways to construct an image of the Earth. Here, in one place, is a magnificent collection showing many ways in which our globe can be represented on a computer screen.

Web:
http://hum.amu.edu.pl/~zbzw/glob/glob1.htm

Interactive Maps

It's getting harder and harder to get away with the excuse, "I would have been there sooner, but I got lost." Why? Because there are now interactive street guides on the Net that will allow you to access lots and lots of detailed maps. You can save a map, add your own points of interest to it, and mail it to someone else. You can also get city-to-city driving directions, as well as learn about the history of cartography and mapping symbols. Many of these maps have details right down to individual streets. Amazing. (Try it and you will see what I mean.)

Web:
http://www.mapblast.com/
http://www.mapquest.com/

No matter who you are
or what you believe,
somewhere on the Internet,
there are people like you.

330 GEOGRAPHY

Land Surveying

Surveying is cool because there is so much land to go around, you will never run out. Also, when you survey, you get to use neat tools, talk about things other people don't understand, and generally swank around like you own the place. When it comes to being cool about mapping the Earth, surveyors really draw the line. To help you, here's where you can find lots of good information about surveying rules and regulations, state statutes, educational events and resources, professional organizations, and data sources. The Usenet group is for the discussion of the measurement and mapping of the Earth's surface.

Web:
http://www.lsrp.com/mainind.html

Usenet:
sci.engr.surveying

Landform Atlas of the United States

Here is a great place to find a topographic map of any state within the United States. You can examine a selection of beautiful, high-resolution color maps. Take a look. I think you will really find them interesting, especially when you look at the state boundaries and see how they compare with the topography.

Web:
http://fermi.jhuapl.edu/states/states.html

There once was a fellow named Randall,
Who had all the gals he could handle,
He'd whip out his browser,
A sure-fire arouser,
And show them the
Landform Atlas of the United States.

Perry-Castañeda Library Map Collection

This collection contains a large number of maps which you can access from anywhere on the Net. For example, using only two mouse clicks, I was able to call up a map that showed the exact location of the McMurdo research station on Antarctica (where, by the way, they have copies of my Internet books).

Web:
http://www.lib.utexas.edu/Libs/PCL/Map_collection/Map_collection.html

---

Look What I Found on the Net...

(from the World Population Datasheet)

```
REGION/COUNTRY......................  World      U.S.     Sweden
POPULATION 1995 [THOUSANDS].........  5,701,769  263,200  8,857
CRUDE BIRTH RATE....................  24.4       15.4     12.8
CRUDE DEATH RATE....................  8.9        8.8      12.1
RATE OF NATURAL INCREASE [PERCENT].   1.55       0.66     0.07
POPULATION 2025 [THOUSANDS].........  8,312,025  338,338  9,570
INFANT MORTALITY RATE...............  61.6       8.0      4.8
TOTAL FERTILITY RATE................  3.1        2.0      1.9
LIFE EXPECTANCY AT BIRTH............  65.7       75.5     78.2
```

GEOGRAPHY 331

Time Zones

You wake up in the middle of the night and look at the clock—it is 2:18 AM. You close your eyes and try to go back to sleep, but all of a sudden a thought comes into your head: what time is it in Bangkok? And you know—you just know—that there is no way you will get to sleep until you find out the answer to your question. Here's what to do. Go to your computer, fire up your Internet connection, and connect to a time zone information Web site. In a few minutes, you will have satisfied your temporal curiosity, and sleep, tired Nature's sweet restorer, will once again be yours.

Web:
   http://www.01digital.com/time/
   http://www.hilink.com.au/times/

United States Gazetteer

Here is a place to find information about any city or town in the United States. Just enter a city name or a zip code, and get useful information about that location: population, latitude and longitude, zip codes, as well as a colorful map you can save and customize. By the way, did you know there are two towns in the United States that are named after me? Harleyville, South Carolina (1990 pop. 633) and Harleysville, Pennsylvania (1990 pop. 7405). I bet if you check, you would find that the people in these towns are smarter, better looking, and more successful than the rest of the general American population.

Web:
   http://www.census.gov/cgi-bin/gazetteer/

Vintage Panoramic Maps

A panoramic map is a nonphotographic picture, shown as it would be if viewed from above (that is, a bird's-eye view). Panoramic maps were popular in the nineteenth and early twentieth centuries, and many such maps have been collected by the U.S. Library of Congress, which maintains this Web site as a public repository. You will find many old panoramic maps of U.S. and Canadian cities, as well as maps relating to military campaigns, exploration, immigration and transportation. I love looking at these old maps, and I particularly like being able to zoom closer to see parts of the image in more detail.

Web:
   http://lcweb2.loc.gov/ammem/pmhtml/

> Dig up something in "Archaeology".

World Population Datasheet

Suppose you need to print brochures for a mass-mailing promotion to everyone in Burkina Faso. Where can you get the population data? Well, this site will show population estimates of many countries around the world, as well as other interesting statistics such as birth and death rates. In case you can't meet your brochure printing deadline, there are also population projections for the year 2025.

Web:
   http://www.igc.org/prb/info/98wpds.htm
   http://www.prb.org/info/98wpds.htm

World's Highpoints

Here is an easy way to stay head and shoulders above your friends. Start with this Web site, where you will find maps and graphs of the highest mountain peaks in the world. Select the mountain nearest you, pack your suitcase and walk to the top. Each individual mountain page at this site has additional links with information and climbing routes related to the particular mountain. Be sure to check out all the information before you leave, so you can plan where to stop for drinks and snacks along the way.

Web:
   http://www.inch.com/~dipper/world.html

Xerox Map Viewer

The PARC Web Map Viewer is an experiment in providing dynamic information retrieval via the Web. It allows you to zoom in and out of a map of the world and takes many options that you can supply to instantly make custom Web maps of any location in the world.

Web:
   http://pubweb.parc.xerox.com/map/

GEOLOGY

Ask-a-Geologist

Do you ever lie awake at night wondering whether all Texas lakes are man-made, or where you can find a good source of reservoir rock that is litharenite or sublitharenite? Thanks to modern technology, you can ask such questions of a real geologist. Whip off a letter to a geologist and eventually, someone somewhere will explain something that is geologically interesting. Check out this Web site and find out how to submit a question.

Web:
http://walrus.wr.usgs.gov/docs/ask-a-ge.html

Ask a Geologist

Have you got a question about volcanoes, earthquakes, mountains, rocks, maps, ground water, lakes or rivers?

Of course you do. Everyone has at least one question about volcanoes, earthquakes, mountains, rocks, maps, ground water, lakes or rivers.

So why wait? Ask a geologist now.

(My question is: What is your favorite type of rock music?)

Earth Science Site of the Week

Earth science refers to the family of geological sciences that study the Earth: its origin, its structure and the physical phenomena found within it. The principal Earth sciences study various characteristics of the Earth: geography (physical characteristics of the surface), geology (nature of its composition), orography (mountains), oceanography (oceans), geomorphology (landforms), speleology (caves), geodesy (size and shape) and hydrography (surface waters). Each week, a new Earth science resource is chosen, and a link to the resource along with a brief summary is displayed at this Web site. The past sites of the week are archived if you want to browse some of the selections. I like to visit once in a while to see what's new. Try it, and I bet you will learn something interesting.

Web:
http://agcwww.bio.ns.ca/misc/geores/sotw/sotw.html

Earth Sciences Resources

The Earth is one of my favorite planets in the entire solar system, so it's no surprise that I like these Earth sciences sites. There is a lot of interesting information waiting for you. For example, before I go to the beach, I make sure to check the map of world water temperatures. Take a few minutes and browse, and I bet you'll agree with me that we live in a pretty interesting place.

Web:
http://geology.uiggm.nsc.ru/engl/uiggm/links.htm
http://info.er.usgs.gov/network/science/earth/earth.html
http://www.geo.ucalgary.ca/vl-earthsciences.html

Geological Image Library

The next time you are having a bunch of geology friends over for a rock party, leave this Web site displayed on your computer screen. Simply type a keyword into a search engine and you will be rewarded with many beautiful images relating to geology. Once your friends wander over to the computer and start playing with this resource, they will become totally captivated, and you will be free to eat all the onion dip yourself.

Web:
http://www.science.ubc.ca/~eoswr/cgi-bin/db_gallery/searchframe.html

GEOLOGY

Geological Time Machine

Here is a fast way to go back to the past without having your time machine run up your electricity bill. Explore an outline of the various eras starting from the Precambrian. Each era is broken down into smaller time periods, with information about each one. There is also information about the formation of the Earth, evolution, and how our planet has changed over the ages.

Web:
   http://www.ucmp.berkeley.edu/help/timeform.html

Geological Time Scale

Here is a short, well-organized time scale charting the eras and events of the last 4,600 million years. This is the best place I know to check when you need to find out if the Devonian era came before or after the Silurian (after), and in which time frame graptolites were dominant (the Ordovician).

Web:
   http://www.geo.ucalgary.ca/~macrae/timescale/timescale.html

Geology and Earth Science Resources

The Internet has some of the best geological resources on Earth. Find out about geology, geomorphology, geophysics, geochemistry, mineralogy, paleontology, volcanology, geological organizations, geophysics, hydrogeology and paleontology. Wow! All that information, and you don't even have to dig for it.

Web:
   http://denr1.igis.uiuc.edu/isgsroot/earthsci/es_links.htm
   http://www.bham.ac.uk/earthsciences/texts/geoweb.html

Dig up some dirt in "Intrigue".

Geology of Radon

Radon is a colorless, radioactive gas formed by the natural decay of radium. As a tool, radon is primarily used in radiotherapy for treating cancer. However, radon also occurs naturally in areas where uranium-238 is present in the rocks and soil. Elements like uranium decay over long periods of time and, as they decay, the atoms transmute. Eventually, uranium decays into other elements that produce radium. When radium decays, it forms radon. At the same time, a type of radiation called alpha particles is released. (An alpha particle consists of two protons and two neutrons.) Radon gas is itself radioactive because it also decays, emitting more alpha particles and forming polonium (another radioactive element). The problem is, if there is radon in your environment, you breathe it, whereupon it gets trapped in your lungs. When the radon decays, the radiation and the polonium can cause damage to the tissue and predispose you to developing lung cancer. This Web site will give you detailed information: what is radon, where is it found and what can you do to reduce the risk of radon affecting your living environment?

Web:
   http://sedwww.cr.usgs.gov:8080/radon/georadon.html

Geology Talk and General Discussion

Geology is the study of the structure of the Earth and its surface. These are the places where the geologically inclined discuss technical matters, as well as topics of interest to non-scientists. Talk about rocks, fossils, the origin of natural formations, and so on. If you have a geological question (such as where to take your kids to look for fossils), you can post it here and see if an expert will answer you.

Usenet:
   sci.geo.geology

Listserv Mailing List:
   List Name: geol-101
   Subscribe to: listserv@list.uvm.edu

Geologylink

You have planned a romantic dinner—candles, flowers, good food, the right wine. You have just served the dessert, when it feels like it's time. "Will you marry me?" you ask your significant other. "I may," replies your companion, "but first I want you to explain the difference between a horst and a graben." Fortunately, your computer in the next room is powered on and connected to the Net. You excuse yourself to check with the glossary at Geologylink. Within a minute, you are back at the table with your beloved, wrapping up the deal. On your honeymoon, you take along your notebook computer, so you and your spouse can check the geology news, read the articles, and talk to other people in the geology-related chat rooms. Talk about living happily ever after.

Web:
http://www.geologylink.com/

Glaciology

Glaciology is the study of glaciers and glaciotectonics. These Web sites will lead you to just about anything you need in this area of study. Even if you are not a professional, I bet you'll enjoy a bit of browsing. For example, many people believe that the water content in snow is 1/10 the same volume of water. In other words, 10 inches of snow is equivalent to 1 inch of rain. Actually, the ratio varies from 1/100 to 1/3 and depends upon the weather conditions at the time of the snowfall.

Web:
http://student-www.uchicago.edu/users/chulbe/igs/igs.html
http://www-nsidc.colorado.edu/NOAA/glacier_inventory/
http://www-nsidc.colorado.edu/NSIDC/

Look What I Found on the Net...

```
Newsgroup: sci.geo.geology
Subject: The Deepest?
>> Hi, does someone know the greatest depth humans have ever
>> reached?  The information I have is:
>>    Kola scientific borehole 10 km
>>    mine (South Africa)       3 km
>> However, I am not sure.  Also I want to know the following:
>>    Coal mine ?
>>    Oil drilling ?
>>    Geophysical survey ?

> "Geophysical surveys" have no direct depth measurement
> associated with data gathering.  The data are measurements of
> geological/geophysical aspects which are in turn analyzed and
> depths estimated.
>
> As such, to answer your question, the deepest measurement made
> via earth-directed geophysical exploration methods would be
> the diameter of the earth.

Shouldn't that be the radius?

Q: How far into the woods can you go?
A: Halfway.
```

GEOLOGY 335

Global Map of Earthquakes

As you move on to adulthood, it is not uncommon for your mother to experience fits of anxiety and despair because she fears for your safety. If you are about to make that big move from home (or if you moved out 30 years ago and your mother is still worried), take a look at these earthquake maps. Show your mother that where you live is nowhere near a fault line and, in no time at all, she will feel completely at ease. (Hint for anyone living on or near a fault line: download the picture ahead of time, and use a graphics program to remove any red lines that are close to where you live.) The map facilities at this site let you zoom around a graphical representation of the Earth, checking out all the recent quake action. I've also included a glossary of geological terms to help you interpret these maps. The Usenet group is that place to talk with other people about what makes the Earth move under your feet.

Web:
   http://cires.colorado.edu/people/jones.craig/EQimagemap/global.html
   http://www.scec.gps.caltech.edu/glossary.html

Usenet:
   sci.geo.earthquakes

Hydrology Web

Hydrology is the study of water, its properties, distribution and movement across land. Hydrology encompasses a huge area of study, because the hydrologic cycle is so complex. (The hydrologic cycle refers to the entire process of water evaporating from the Earth's surface and eventually coming back down to Earth.) Moreover, water is present in several different physical forms (like rain, snow and ice) and travels in diverse patterns. For example, water can freeze into polar ice caps, where it will stay for millions of years. Or water can fall onto land where it immediately soaks into the ground, is utilized by plants, and runs off into rivers or soaks into the groundwater. Here is a collection of hydrology-related resources, which will give you a good background in the field of hydrology as well as links to related resources.

Web:
   http://terrassa.pnl.gov:2080/EESC/resourcelist/hydrology.html

Usenet:
   sci.geo.hydrology

Minerals

These sites will give you more than the recommended daily allowance of minerals. You can search databases containing information about gems and minerals of all types. In addition, you will also find a great many photos to help you identify any stray minerals you happen to encounter in your journeys on planet Earth.

Web:
   http://galaxy.einet.net/images/gems/gems-icons.html
   http://mineral.galleries.com/
   http://www.minerals.net/

Usenet:
   sci.geo.mineralogy

MINERAL GALLERIES

You can find information about animals simply by interviewing people at a rock concert.

And you can learn about vegetables by talking to people who watch a lot of television.

But there is only one place to search for data about minerals. Use the Net to visit the *Mineral Galleries*.

National Geophysical Data Center

The National Geophysical Data Center (NGDC), located in Boulder, Colorado, is part of the National Oceanic & Atmospheric Administration (NOAA). NGDC manages and makes available a large number of environmental data sets, many of them of interest to geologists. In particular there is data in the areas of marine geology, marine geophysics, paleoclimatology, solar-terrestrial physics, solid earth geophysics and glaciology.

Web:
   http://www.ngdc.noaa.gov/

GEOLOGY

Rock Shop

The two biggest uses of rocks in our culture are (1) to stub your toe, and (2) to hold down paper on your desk. However, studying and collecting rocks can also be a lot of fun, providing entertainment for lapidary hobbyists and various species of rockhounds. If you like to run around looking for interesting rocks and minerals, take a look at this great site, where you will find interesting news and features about rock collecting, as well as a large selection of pictures.

Web:
   http://www.rockhounds.com/rockshop/table.html

Seismology

Here is a large collection of links to seismic information available on the Net. There are lots and lots of earthquake-related resources, so the next time you run into someone on the street who asks, "What's shaking?" you can invite him over and show him in person.

Web:
   http://www.geophys.washington.edu/seismosurfing.html

Structural Geology

Structural geology is the study of rock deformation and the geologic configurations resulting from such deformations (mountains, canyons, mesas, and so on). In particular, structural geology includes plate tectonics, the study of the slow movements of sections of the Earth's crust (plates), leading to the formation of continents. Of particular interest are earthquakes and volcanoes, which mostly occur at the margins of such plates.

Web:
   http://home.earthlink.net/~schimmrich/structure/structure.h
   http://www.rwth-aachen.de/ged/Ww/others/structural.html

U.S. Geological Survey

The U. S. Geological Survey (USGS), a part of the United States Department of the Interior, is America's largest agency devoted to earth science. The USGS creates and provides (for free) an enormous amount of information relating to geology (rocks and soil), topography (lay of the land), and hydrology (water). There are lots of maps and databases, as well as many research analyses of natural resources.

Web:
   http://info.er.usgs.gov/

Where are you?

Check with the U.S. Geological Survey Internet site.

Virtual Cave

When I was younger, I spent a lot of time exploring the Colossal Cave in the Adventure game (the very first computer-based adventure game). However, I have never had a chance to explore a real cave. Now, however, I can visit the Virtual Cave whenever I want and look at pictures of all kinds of fascinating cave formations. So if—like me—you have always wanted to go spelunking (cave exploring), you can start by doing it over the Net. If you live in the U.S., you can also check with the United States Cave Directory to find out information about many of the public caves you can visit.

Web:
   http://www.goodearth.com/virtcave.html

GOVERNMENT: INTERNATIONAL

Volcanology

It used to be that the only thing you could do with a volcano was to throw a virgin into it and hope that the gods were appeased. Now you can hook up all sorts of wires and gadgets to it, and use X-ray fluorescence to examine trace elements and aerial photographs to analyze pumiceous pyroclastic flow. These sites present detailed descriptions of several volcanoes and include pictures and instructional material.

Web:
http://covis.atmos.uiuc.edu/geosciences/instructional/geology/volcano.html
http://vulcan.wr.usgs.gov/home.html
http://www.geo.mtu.edu/volcanoes/

Volcanoes

What can you say about volcanoes and their almost magnetic attraction for us all? I could remind you that they are holes or cracks in the Earth's surface that release molten lava, ash or other products from underground magma chambers. (Now *that's* a word: "magma." Bet you can't say it ten times real fast.)

Anyway, I could wax eloquent about the runny volcanic outpourings and how they build basalt beds, or how the more viscous types of lava form steep-sided volcanoes, or how ash residue tends to build cone-like peaks. Or I could go on and on about how volcanoes erupt where one lithospheric plate is forced beneath another, or where two such plates diverge.

Yes, there is a lot to say about volcanoes and, if truth be told, they are among my favorite large-scale geological formations. Still, there is something unsatisfying about mere talk and, if you are like me, you will want some pictures, and that is where the Net comes in. Take a cruise to volcano Web sites and I guarantee that you will find more than a few shots suitable for framing.

> Cool.

World Data Center System

In 1957-1958, scientists around the world collaborated on what was called the International Geophysical Year (IGY). One of the long-term products of the IGY was the establishment of a number of World Data Centers (WDC) to facilitate the acquisition and sharing of solar, geophysical and environmental data. The first such center, WDC-A, was established in the United States. The second, WDC-B, was started in Russia. Today there are three other centers as well: WDC-C1 (Europe), WDC-C2 (Japan, India), and WDC-D (China). Each WDC is actually a collection of smaller centers, each of which specializes in a particular area. This Web site provides a convenient way to access the various WDC sites around the world.

Web:
http://www.ngdc.noaa.gov/wdc/

GOVERNMENT: INTERNATIONAL

African Governments

Africa is the second largest continent in the world, containing about 10 percent of the world's population. The people of Africa are divided into over 50 countries, which are further fragmented into various ethnic and tribal divisions. Africa's presence in the Net is severely hampered by the lack of a large-scale dependable telephone system. However, there are some African countries with Internet access. These Web sites have links to such African governmental resources as exist on the Net.

Web:
http://www.agora.stm.it/politic/africa.htm
http://www.lib.umich.edu/libhome/Documents.center/forafr.html

338 GOVERNMENT: INTERNATIONAL

Asia Pacific Governments

The Asia Pacific region of the world consists of those Asian countries that border the Pacific Ocean (that is, most of what used to be referred to as the Orient). Today, the Asia Pacific region is considered to also contain Australia and New Zealand. The significance of this group of countries lies in their economic and political interdependence. To help you find information about the governments of these countries, here is a Web site that contains a collection of useful links to resources from Asia Pacific countries.

Web:
http://www.lib.umich.edu/libhome/ Documents.center/forasia.html

Australian Government

Okay, you don't always need instant access to a huge amount of information regarding all the different organizations and departments that comprise the government of Australia. But when you do, you'll be glad you have the Net. Imagine how embarrassing it might be to, say, lose the respect of your friends and co-workers just because you don't how to order a Zone Rebate Map from the Australian Taxation Office.

Web:
http://www.fed.gov.au/
http://www.nla.gov.au/oz/gov/

British Intelligence Organizations

If you have read any James Bond books or seen any of the movies, you would probably guess that the real British intelligence agencies are not exactly like the Secret Service for which Bond works. However, they are no less interesting. See for yourself by reading about MI5 (Military Intelligence 5: internal security and intelligence); MI6 (Military Intelligence 6: national security both internal and external); GCHQ (Government Communications Headquarters: intercepting and monitoring communications), SAS (Special Air Service: covert operations, especially counter-terrorism), and SBS (Special Boat Service: naval-based covert operations).

Web:
http://www.cc.umist.ac.uk/sk/

Embassies and Consulates Around the World

An embassy is the principal site of official representation of one country within another. Traditionally, embassies are located near the capital of the host country. For example, in the United States, most of the foreign embassies are in or near Washington, D.C. The head of the diplomatic mission is called an ambassador. In large countries, there may be other official diplomatic offices called consulates. For example, in the United States, there is a Canadian embassy in Washington, D.C., as well as consulates in various major cities around the country. Embassies and consulates provide a lot of useful information, and many of these offices around the world have their own Web sites. Here is a collection of resources related to embassies: links to the embassies' own Web sites, diplomatic news, information about foreign currency, and so on.

Web:
http://www.embpage.org/

Embassies in Washington, D.C.

When it's late at night and you are in the mood for a little political intrigue, take a look at these embassy-related links. You'll get the goods on the staff and resources of the Washington, D.C., embassy community, embassy Web sites, press releases, commerce and trade information, as well as travel and tourism reports. Remember, when you're in Washington, D.C., you can't be too careful. Today's attaché to the assistant secretary for international trade regulations could be tomorrow's industrial spy.

Web:
http://www.embassy.org/

**Wanna change the system?
Try "Anarchy".**

GOVERNMENT: INTERNATIONAL

European Governments

There are many governments in Europe, and sometimes it can be difficult to find the information you want. To help you, here are Web sites that contain links to many different European governments and organizations. When I am looking for European information— especially from an official organization—I often start here.

Web:
http://www.gksoft.com/govt/en/europa.html
http://www.lib.umich.edu/libhome/
  Documents.center/foreur.html

European Governments

Sometimes when I have trouble sleeping, I get up in the middle of the night and read about the governments of Europe.

After a half hour, my mind is full of all kinds of information about legislative, executive and judicative branches, and I can return to bed for a quiet, peaceful sleep.

Truly, you can never be too rich, too thin, or know too much about European governments.

European Parliament

The European Parliament is the only democratically elected international governing body in the world. The elected representatives exercise control over the member bodies at a European level. As such, the European Parliament is an important part of the European Union. Here is their official Web site, which contains information about the organization, including its powers, responsibilities, organization and operation.

Web:
http://www.europarl.eu.int/

European Union

Interesting facts about the European Union: On May 9, 1950, the French Foreign Minister formally read a declaration in which he proposed the creation of an international European organization to manage the coal and steel industry. (At the time, coal and steel were crucial to the balance of European military power.) From this proposal, a series of institutions were formed that, many years later, resulted in the European Union. For this reason, May 9th is now celebrated as Europe Day. Here is something even more interesting. The European flag consists of a circle of twelve gold stars in a blue background. Why twelve stars? The flag was originally designed for the Council of Europe (a completely different organization, sort of like a United Nations for Europe). At the time the Council of Europe was formed, there was some controversy over how many sovereign countries there would be. So, instead of creating a flag with one star for every country, they decided on a flag with twelve stars, because the number "12" was thought to be a symbol of completeness and unity. Why? There are twelve months in the year; twelve constellations in the zodiac; and—in order to win the support of the Christian population of Europe—it was observed that Jesus had twelve apostles. (I am not making this up.) In 1986, the flag was adopted by the European Communities, which later passed it on to the European Union. (Actually, I have a reason which is even better. The number "12" has a large number of factors: 1, 2, 3, 4, 6, 12. This symbolizes that—although there is only one union—there are many divisions.) Finally, here is one last item of European Union trivia. The European anthem (official song) is the prelude to the last movement of Beethoven's Ninth Symphony, often called the "Ode to Joy". (Note to Americans: Beethoven was a European musician who, in some parts of the world, has enjoyed a popularity rivaling that of Elvis Presley.)

Web:
http://europa.eu.int
http://fgr.wu-wien.ac.at/nentwich/euroint.htm

Usenet:
talk.politics.european-union

340 GOVERNMENT: INTERNATIONAL

Governments of the World

There are well over 200 countries in the world, and each one insists on having its own government, resources, organization, culture, and even its own flag. These sites have a lot of this type of information, organized by country, including links to other Web sites. There is also a nice collection of links to various world organizations. (Hint: This is the place I go when an emergency arises and I need to find the Web sites of the major political parties of Finland.)

Web:
http://www.adminet.com/world/gov/
http://www.worldworld.com/

Intelligence Organizations

An intelligence organization is one devoted to gathering secret information, usually, but not always, about an enemy. Such organizations employ many different methods, the most basic of which is spying. However, modern intelligence organizations go well beyond this traditional pastime, devoting much of their efforts to gathering massive amounts of data, monitoring of communications, industrial espionage and covert operations. Of course, these guys do not want you to know anything about their operations or how deeply entrenched they are within the various branches of government. However, as one of my readers, you deserve to know everything. Enjoy.

Web:
http://www.loyola.edu/dept/politics/intel.html

Intelligence Organizations

Spies. They're in every country. Every government uses them.

We love them when they are on our side. We vilify them when they work for the enemy.

Spies. They're everywhere. Learn all about them on the Net.

**Stay cool.
Read "Fashion and Clothing".**

International Government Talk and General Discussion

The world of international government involves a lot more than facts, figures and meetings. There are also opinions, power struggles, influence peddling and intrigue. If you would like to immerse yourself in a discussion of international affairs, join this mailing list. Every day, there is some new turn of events to discuss, and there is no reason why everyone shouldn't know your interpretation of what's happening.

Listproc Mailing List:
List Name: **iro**
Subscribe to: **listproc@listproc.bgsu.edu**

International Organizations in Geneva

There are a *lot* of international organizations in Geneva, including a large portion of the United Nations. Many of these organizations are related to various governments. This Web page provides a well-organized reference which allows you find and access information about many, many international organizations both public and private.

Web:
http://geneva.intl.ch/geneva-intl/gi/egimain/edir.htm

International Relations and Security Network

The International Relations and Security Network is a large collection of information in several related areas: security and defense, peace and war, and international relations. This is an excellent site if you are looking for research material, or if you are interested in following current world issues and how they are developing. Hint: If you are a political science student and you need to come up with an essay fast, this is a great place to look for raw material.

Web:
http://www.isn.ethz.ch/

Israeli Government

The State of Israel, a democracy, was founded on May 14, 1948. Israel is governed by the Knesset (a house of representatives), the members of which are elected by the entire country. Unlike other governments, the Prime Minister is directly elected by the people (as opposed to being the leader of the majority party). The Prime Minister appoints the members of the Cabinet. The head of state is the President, a largely ceremonial position, who is elected by the Knesset. This Web site provides a lot of basic information about the Israeli government, as well as links to various departments and organizations.

Web:
http://www.info.gov.il/eng/mainpage.htm

Japanese Government

Japan consists of a chain of islands off the coast of east Asia, between the North Pacific Ocean and the Sea of Japan. Most of Japan's land mass consists of four main islands: Honshu (the main island where Tokyo is), Hokkaido, Shikoku and Kyushu. Together, all of Japan is only 143,000 square miles (370,000 sq km), smaller than the state of Montana. Japan's population of about 125,000,000 is slightly less than half that of the entire United States, making Japan the seventh most populated country in the world. (The top six are China, India, Russia, the U.S., Indonesia and Brazil.) There are eleven Japanese cities with a population of over 1,000,000. The largest, Tokyo, has well over 8,000,000 people, making it the fourth largest city in the world (after New York, Mexico City and Los Angeles). Japan's government is a mixture of modern post-World War II democracy and traditional institutions. The main components of national government are its legislative body called the Diet (consisting of the House of Councilors and the House of Representatives), and the Prime Minister (elected by the Diet) and the Cabinet (appointed by the Prime Minister). Although the Prime Minister is the chief executive, the head of state is the Emperor. (Technically, Japan is a constitutional monarchy.) On a regional level, Japan is divided into 47 prefectures, each of which elects its own governor and legislature. Even though Japan's government may look similar to that of other countries, its system is uniquely Japanese, built on a pronounced work ethic and a large degree of government-industry cooperation.

Web:
http://jin.jcic.or.jp/navi/category_2.html

Are you one of those people who have to understand what is going on everywhere all the time? If so, you certainly can't depend on television, radio and newspapers.

You need the International Relations and Security Network.

Latin American Governments

Latin America consists of the countries of America south of the United States, in which Romance languages are generally spoken (Portuguese in Brazil, French in Haiti, and Spanish just about everywhere else). The breadth of Latin America is huge, ranging from the border of the U.S. to the tip of South America not far from Antarctica. This Web site contains links to government departments in many Latin American countries, offering a wide variety of information and resources.

Web:
http://www.georgetown.edu/pdba/

Middle East Governments

The Middle East refers to the area that includes most of southwest Asia and parts of northeast Africa. The countries in the Middle East are Israel, Syria, Jordan, Iraq, Iran, Lebanon and part of Turkey (Asia); Saudi Arabia, Yemen, Oman, United Arab Emirates, Qatar, Bahrain, Kuwait (the Arabian peninsula); and Egypt and Libya (Africa). This region was the site of the ancient civilizations of Mesopotamia and Egypt, as well as the birthplace of three of the world's major religions, Judaism, Christianity and Islam. In modern times, the Middle East has suffered from a great deal of turmoil and political unrest, much of it due to the tension between Israel and the Arab states, intra-Arab conflicts, and the fact that the region is sitting on a significant portion of the world's oil reserves. Here is a resource that contains links to such Middle East government sites as exist on the Net.

Web:
http://www.lib.umich.edu/libhome/Documents.center/forme.html

342 GOVERNMENT: INTERNATIONAL

National Parliaments

Want to see a magic trick? Pick a parliament, any parliament. Now look it up on one of these Web pages and click with your mouse. Wait a few minutes. All of a sudden, you will see the Web page for that organization. (Actually, it's not really magic—it's the Net.)

Web:
  http://www.ipu.org/parline-e/parline.htm
  http://www.soc.umn.edu/~sssmith/Parliaments.html

NATO

NATO (the North Atlantic Treaty Organization) was formed on April 4, 1949, with the signing of the North Atlantic Treaty by twelve countries. Since then, other countries have joined and, today, NATO is a large, complex organization devoted to a voluntary security system in which the member countries share responsibilities. NATO is a defensive alliance based on political and military cooperation. There are sixteen members: Belgium, Canada, Denmark, France, Germany, Greece, Iceland, Italy, Luxembourg, the Netherlands, Norway, Portugal, Spain, Turkey, the United Kingdom and the United States.

Web:
  http://www.nato.int/

Listserv Mailing List:
  List Name: **natodata**
  Subscribe to: **listserv@cc1.kuleuven.ac.be**

North American Free Trade Agreement

The North American Free Trade Agreement (NAFTA) is an economic agreement signed by the U.S., Canada and Mexico in order to promote economic growth among the three countries. Here you can find the full text of the agreement, as well as resources to help you understand and work with the rules and regulations.

Web:
  http://www.sice.oas.org/trade/nafta/naftatce.stm

Organization of American States

The Organization of American States (OAS) is the oldest regional organization in the world, having been established on April 30, 1948, by the United States and twenty Latin American republics. The purpose of the OAS is to promote cooperation among the countries of North and South America; to work toward peace and security; and to support economic, cultural and social development. Today, all 35 countries in North and South America belong to the OAS (although the current government of Cuba is not allowed to participate). This Web site contains general information about the OAS, as well as the activities of its many departments and programs.

Web:
  http://www.oas.org/

Post-World War II Political Leaders

The history of the late twentieth century is really the end result of everything that has been happening since the end of World War II. And in that time, much of what happened was influenced and controlled by our political leaders. This Web site offers an easy way to look up the political leaders of any country from 1945 to the present. I found some interesting patterns by reading through some of the lists. I also use this site when I need to find out the name of a political leader quickly.

Web:
  http://web.jet.es/ziaorarr/00index.htm

Swiss Government

The official name for Switzerland is Confoederatio Helvetica (which roughly translates as "the Swiss Federation"). Switzerland has a long history of remaining neutral and, in fact, they are not even a member of the European Union. Switzerland itself is actually a union. It consists of a confederation of 23 different cantons. The country has four official languages: German (the first language of 63.7% of the people), French (19.2%), Italian (7.6%) and Romansh (0.6%). The remainder of the people, 8.9%, speak another language. The country is an interesting one, and they have a lot of information on the Web. In fact, the ancestor of the Web (called the World Wide Web) was invented in Switzerland.

Web:
  http://heiwww.unige.ch/switzerland/
  http://www.admin.ch/

GOVERNMENT: INTERNATIONAL

United Kingdom Government

The United Kingdom—England, Scotland, Wales and Northern Ireland—is a constitutional monarchy. The hereditary monarch (currently Queen Elizabeth II) acts as the head of state, carrying out largely ceremonial duties. The parliament consists of an elected House of Commons and a non-elected House of Lords. The Prime Minister is the leader of whichever party holds a majority in the House of Commons. The Prime Minister appoints the Cabinet, the members of which are chosen from among the members of the House. These Web sites contains links to various British government organizations. I have also included the official Web site of 10 Downing Street, the residence and office of the Prime Minister. (However, what I am waiting for is an online version of Prince William's diary.)

Web:
http://www.nds.coi.gov.uk/coi/coipress.nsf
http://www.number-10.gov.uk/
http://www.open.gov.uk/index/figovt.htm

United Nations

On January 1, 1942, during World War II, representatives of 26 countries signed the Declaration by United Nations, in which they promised to continue fighting together against the Axis (the bad guys). The name "United Nations" was coined by U.S. President Franklin Roosevelt. On June 26, 1945, the United Nations as we know it was established with the signing of the United Nations Charter. In 1945, the U.N. had 51 member countries. Today, there are 185. The United Nations oversees a great many international organizations such as the International Court of Justice, the United Nations Children's Fund (UNICEF), the World Health Organization, the World Bank, and so on. Overall, the U.N. has 54,000 employees—about the same as Disney World + Disneyland.

Web:
http://www.un.org/
http://www.unsystem.org/

Usenet:
alt.politics.org.un

Look What I Found on the Net...

```
(from the North American Free Trade Agreement)
                  PREAMBLE

The Government of Canada, the Government of the United Mexican
States and the Government of the United States of America,
resolved to:
STRENGTHEN the special bonds of friendship and cooperation...
CONTRIBUTE to the harmonious development and expansion of...
CREATE an expanded and secure market for the goods and services
REDUCE distortions to trade
ESTABLISH clear and mutually advantageous rules...
ENSURE a predictable commercial framework for business...
BUILD on their respective rights and obligations...
ENHANCE the competitiveness of their firms in global markets...
FOSTER creativity and innovation, and promote trade...
CREATE new employment opportunities, improve working conditions.
UNDERTAKE each of the preceding in a manner consistent with...
PRESERVE their flexibility to safeguard the public welfare
PROMOTE sustainable development
STRENGTHEN the development and enforcement of environmental laws
PROTECT, enhance and enforce basic workers' rights

HAVE AGREED as follows...
```

344 GOVERNMENT: INTERNATIONAL

United Nations Security Council

The United Nations Security Council is the body of the United Nations with the responsibility of maintaining international peace and security. Unlike the General Assembly—which has a representative from every country and is not always in session—the Security Council has a limited number of members and functions continuously. The Security Council has fifteen members: five permanent members (the United States, China, France, Russia and the United Kingdom) who have veto power over all decisions, and ten elected members who change from time to time. Here are some resources with information about the Security Council, as well as the various documents they create.

Web:
 http://www.un.org/Overview/Organs/sc.html

Ssshhhh... See "Secret Stuff".

Lonely? See "People".

U.S. International Aid

USAID (United States Agency for International Development) is an independent government agency that provides foreign assistance and humanitarian aid to "advance the political and economic interests of the United States". Read about their goals and studies: regional information, population and health information, economic growth studies, and global environmental issues. I'm trying to get a government grant to send me on an all-expense paid trip to the south of France. The only problem is showing how such a trip would be in the economic interests of the United States.

Web:
 http://www.info.usaid.gov/

Look What I Found on the Net...

```
(from the preamble to the Charter of the United Nations)

WE THE PEOPLES OF THE UNITED NATIONS DETERMINED

to save succeeding generations from the scourge of war, which
twice in our lifetime has brought untold sorrow to mankind, and

to reaffirm faith in fundamental human rights, in the dignity
and worth of the human person, in the equal rights of men and
women and of nations large and small, and

to establish conditions under which justice and respect for the
obligations arising from treaties and other sources of
international law can be maintained, and

to promote social progress and better standards of life in
larger freedom...
```

GOVERNMENT: UNITED STATES

But...

World Government

Do you think that we would be better off with one large world government, rather than a whole bunch of countries continually arguing with one another (not to mention clogging up the Olympics and the United Nations)? Here are some resources that you can use to explore and learn about the idea of world government. In the old Superman comics, Superman came from the planet Krypton, which was much more advanced than the Earth. In particular, the Kryptonians had one large world government. (And look where they are today.)

Web:
http://www.bath.ac.uk/~adsjrc/eu/eu-main.html
http://www.cgg.ch/

GOVERNMENT: UNITED STATES

Budget of the United States Government

Have you ever wondered exactly how much money the government spends? Well, now you can find out. The entire budget of the United States federal government is on the Net. (That is, at least the parts of the budget that aren't deadly secrets like funding for clandestine operations.) Here are some interesting statistics I figured out. It is estimated that, in 1999, all of the following federal branches and departments, put together, will spend $373 billion dollars: Legislative branch, Judicial branch, Agriculture, Commerce, Education, Energy, Housing and Urban Development, Interior, Justice, Labor, State, Transportation, Veterans Affairs, Environmental Protection Agency, General Services Administration, NASA and the Small Business Administration. All that for only $373 billion. Compare that to Defense ($285 billion), Health and Human Services ($397 billion), Treasury ($398 billion) and Social Security ($432 billion). It sure makes NASA ($13.5 billion) look like a bargain.

Web:
http://www.access.gpo.gov/su_docs/budget98/maindown.html

Census Information

The job of the U.S. Census Bureau is to gather demographic (people) and economic (money) statistics about the United States. This information is made public, and much of it is available on the Census Bureau's Web site. I find this site a fascinating place to browse; there are so many interesting statistics. For example, in the county in which I live in California, of all the people 25 years of age or older, 80% are high school graduates and 27% are college graduates. Within the county, 13% of births were to mothers under 20 years old, and the infant death rate was 6.5/1,000 live births. It is interesting to compare these numbers to those describing other parts of the country. For example, in Hempstead County, Arkansas (where Bill Clinton was born), there were only 62% high school graduates and 9% college graduates. The number of births to mothers under 20 was 19%, and the infant death rate was 9.9/1,000 live births.

Web:
http://www.census.gov/

Need some numbers?

Check out the *Census Information* Server.

GOVERNMENT: UNITED STATES

CIA

The Central Intelligence Agency (CIA) was formed in 1947 by the passage of the National Security Act. The CIA's role is to concern itself with intelligence and counterintelligence activities outside the United States, and to coordinate activities with the FBI (Federal Bureau of Investigation) relating to domestic counterintelligence. If you would like to experience a little of the mystery and intrigue of the CIA—without having them start a file on you—visit their Web site, where you can learn more about the agency and take a virtual tour of the parts of their operation they are willing to discuss. While you are here, be sure to check out some of the CIA's publications, such as the "Factbook on Intelligence" and the "CIA World Factbook". The Usenet group is for the discussion of the CIA. You are probably safe to say anything you want because, after all, the United States is a free country and no government agency would ever dare monitor a Usenet discussion group. (Ha, ha.)

Web:
http://www.odci.gov/cia/

Usenet:
alt.politics.org.cia

Commerce Department

The U.S. Department of Commerce was started in 1903 and since then has continually changed to keep in step with current economic conditions. Today, the DOC has many agencies, some of which you might be surprised to find in this department. For example, here you will find NOAA (National Oceanic and Atmospheric Administration), NIST (National Institute of Standards and Technology), the Patent and Trademark Office, and the National Weather Service. For links to all of these government agencies, and more, check out the DOC's main Internet site.

Web:
http://www.doc.gov/

> **Need a lift? Boycott gravity.**

Department of Commerce

What could be more romantic than soft lighting, romantic music, a bottle of fine wine, and a direct link to the U.S. Department of Commerce?

So the next time your hot date starts to cool off, go back to your place, fire up your Internet connection and tap into the Department of Commerce Web site. Before you know it, your social life will perk up like a ferret on a caffeine binge.

Congress

Senators are elected for only six years, while representatives are elected for a shorter two-year term. However—like General MacArthur and adult children without jobs—they can return. If you would like to check up on your elected representatives, here is all the information you need to find them, send them email, connect to their Web pages, and generally see what they are doing (at least when they think you are looking).

Web:
http://clerkweb.house.gov/
http://lcweb.loc.gov/global/legislative/congress.html
http://lcweb.loc.gov/global/legislative/house.html
http://lcweb.loc.gov/global/legislative/senators.html
http://pathfinder.com/CQ
http://www.congress.org/
http://www.senate.gov/

GOVERNMENT: UNITED STATES

C-SPAN Live

Watch the U.S. government at work, from the comfort of your desktop. C-SPAN is a public-oriented cable TV channel, owned by the U.S. cable television industry. The goal of C-SPAN is to allow Americans to watch all the proceedings in the House of Representatives, the Senate, and other public forums. (The name C-SPAN stands for "Cable-Satellite Public Affairs Network".) The idea is that people should be able to watch their elected representatives talk without any editing, commentary or analysis. Of course, from time to time, C-SPAN does get a bit boring. However, at least there are no commercials.

Web:
http://www.c-span.org/

Executive Branch

Never again will you have to hotfoot it around the Net looking for information about the President and his minions. The Library of Congress has compiled a Web page that covers resources pertaining to the executive branch of the federal government and its various departments, as well as independent executive agencies.

Web:
http://lcweb.loc.gov/global/executive/fed.html

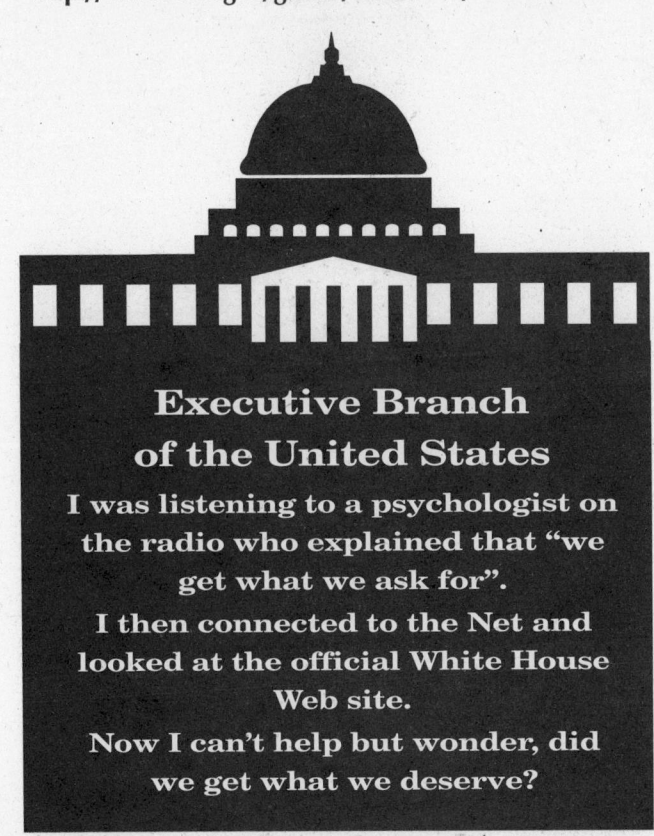

Executive Branch of the United States

I was listening to a psychologist on the radio who explained that "we get what we ask for".

I then connected to the Net and looked at the official White House Web site.

Now I can't help but wonder, did we get what we deserve?

FBI

The Federal Bureau of Investigation (FBI), created in 1908, is a division of the United States Department of Justice. The FBI investigates various violations of federal law such as kidnapping, bank robbing, sabotage, espionage and civil rights violations. If you have ever been in a United States post office, you may have seen the pictures on the wall of desperate and suspicious-looking individuals. These are fugitives that are being pursued by the FBI. However, you don't have to go into the post office to see these pictures. At the FBI Web site, you can check out the list of the "Ten Most Wanted Fugitives" and see if you happen to know any of them. You can also root around the Web site and learn a lot about the FBI. The Usenet group is for the discussion of the FBI and its operations and politics.

Web:
http://www.fbi.gov/

Usenet:
alt.politics.org.fbi

Federal Government Information

No matter what you are looking for in the federal government, these Web sites are the best places to start. They contain links to all major sources of government information. If you are not sure what you want, you can search for it. If you know a specific department, it is only a few mouse clicks away.

Web:
http://eden.cs.umass.edu/Govbot/
http://www.law.vill.edu/fed_agency/fedwebloc.html
http://www.nttc.edu/gov_res.html
http://www.whitehouse.gov/WH/Services/

FedStats

The agencies of the U.S. federal government are continually generating an enormous amount of statistics. This Web site can help you find what you need quickly and easily, no matter where it is. My advice is to keep this Web address with you at all times. You never know, for example, when you will need to find out how many electronics technicians were employed by the Federal Aviation Administration in 1984 (7,229).

Web:
http://www.fedstats.gov/

348 GOVERNMENT: UNITED STATES

FedWorld

The U.S. government has hundreds of departments, agencies and programs, all of which offer information to the public. FedWorld is a service supported by the National Technical Information Service (NTIS), an agency of the U.S. Department of Commerce. The purpose of FedWorld is to act as a central access point to help you find and obtain the information you want. Without a doubt, when you need to find something related to the federal government, this is the place to start.

Web:
  http://www.fedworld.gov/

General Accounting Office

The General Accounting Office (GAO) is the investigative arm of Congress. The GAO examines matters relating to the receiving and spending of public funds. In practice, the GAO is as close as we can get to a government auditor. The GAO Web site contains reports on budget issues, investment, government management, public services, health care, energy issues and virtually every other major area of the federal government.

Web:
  http://www.gao.gov/

Government Corruption

I don't want to talk behind anyone's back, but rumor has it that there is corruption in government. I thought if you were going to hear it, you should get the news from me. Find out the details of what's going on in the nooks and crannies of the political system.

Web:
  http://www.citizen.org/congress/
  http://www.govt-waste.org/
  http://www.pogo.org/

Usenet:
  alt.government.abuse

CORRUPTION is in the eyes of the beholder and—for people in government service—it is all too often the case that the "I"s have it. Check out the **Government Corruption** site, and see what your friends on the Net have to say about the government's tendency to confuse the ideas of "yours," "mine," and "ours".

Government Information

This world is full of such wondrous things, there is never a reason to be bored. For example, the next time you feel a bit of the old ennui, hurry over to this Web site where you can find demographic information about the population, employment, education, and economics of the United States. For example, you can read the Consolidated Federal Funds Reports, or the Census of Agriculture. For a nice change of pace, take a look at Earnings by Occupation and Education.

Web:
  http://govinfo.kerr.orst.edu/

GOVERNMENT: UNITED STATES

Inspectors General

This site has information about the Federal Offices of Inspectors General, the fine folks who are responsible for auditing, investigating and inspecting government agencies. Their goal is to decrease fraud, waste and abuse, and they have the Web page to prove it.

Web:
http://www.ignet.gov/

Justice Statistics

Here are some statistics on topics relating to the U.S. Department of Justice, including crimes, victims, drugs, prisons, courts, sentencing, and much more. There is a lot of interesting information here and, in my opinion, it speaks highly of the United States that such information is made accessible, for free, to anyone in the world. In many other countries, information like this is kept secret, not broadcast on the Internet.

Web:
http://www.ojp.usdoj.gov/bjs/

Justices of the Supreme Court

The Supreme Court is the highest federal court in the United States and has jurisdiction over all the other courts in the nation. The Supreme Court consists of judges—a chief justice and eight associate justices—all of whom are nominated by the President and confirmed by the Senate. The Supreme Court has two main duties: to interpret acts of Congress, and to determine whether federal and state statutes conform to the United States Constitution. If you want the scoop on those people currently serving on the Supreme Court, check out these Web sites. They have lists of the justices, along with biographical data and their pictures (in case you run into one of them in the supermarket). You will also find a lengthy and fascinating collection of each judge's opinions for the court: important majority opinions, important concurring opinions, and selected dissenting opinions.

Web:
  http://supct.law.cornell.edu/supct/
  http://www.uscourts.gov/
  http://www.washingtonpost.com/wp-srv/national/
     longterm/supcourt/supcourt.htm
  http://www2.cybernex.net/~vanalst/supreme.html

Make Yourself Feel Bad

No need to walk around always feeling good. Connect to the Net and take a look at the crime statistics from the U.S. Department of Justice.

Just the thing to take the edge off a beautiful spring day.

National Archives and Records Administration

The U.S. National Archives and Records Administration is the agency that oversees the management of all the records of the federal government. (And you thought it was a big job just keeping your room tidy.) Here you will find a wealth of information, including historical records, the Federal Register (the daily record of the government), genealogical data, links to the presidential libraries, the official U.S. Government Manual (which contains just about *everything* under the American sun), and much more.

Web:
http://www.nara.gov/

National Performance Review

The government is trying hard to get you in on the action—at least they'd like you to think so. The National Performance Review has a more interactive site which includes not only information, but an actual "toolkit to help reinvent government" so you can do your own part in making everything run as smooth as a well-oiled baby.

Web:
http://www.npr.gov/

Social Security Administration

You can't get far in the United States without having a Social Security number. But that's only the beginning. The Social Security Administration (SSA) dispenses huge amounts of money each year under the auspices of many different programs. If you are American, I promise you that, one day, you will need information from the SSA. On that day, start with this Web site.

Web:
http://www.ssa.gov/

350 GOVERNMENT: UNITED STATES

State Department

The United States maintains diplomatic relations with about 180 countries as well as many international organizations. The Department of State is the principal foreign affairs agency of the U.S government. As such, it has two broad mandates: to represent U.S. policies and interests abroad, and to gather information used to create foreign policy. The head of the State Department—the Secretary of State—is the fourth in line of presidential succession (after the Vice President, the Speaker of the House, and the President Pro Tempore of the Senate).

Web:
http://www.state.gov/

White House

Here is the official Internet site for the White House. If you have nothing to do, you might want to connect and see who is living there.

Web:
http://www.whitehouse.gov/

White House Press Releases

Each day, you can find out the official word on the activities and goings-on at the White House and related U.S. agencies. This Web site is just the thing to give your son or daughter for a graduation present. (After all, who wants a car?)

Web:
http://library.whitehouse.gov/PressReleases.cgi

Look What I Found on the Net...

(from the archives of the United States State Department)

[The following is excerpted from a speech given by the U.S. Secretary of State at the John F. Kennedy School of Government, Harvard University, January 18, 1996.]

...This is not the end of history, but history in fast-forward. Eight decades ago, when this century's first Balkan war ended, it took an international commission to piece together what had happened. Now, images of violence in Sarajevo are beamed instantly around the world. Six decades ago, it took several years for the Great Depression to become a global disaster. Now, an economic crisis in Mexico can disrupt the global economy in the blink of an eye.

In this time of accelerated change, American leadership must remain constant. We must be clear-eyed and vigilant in pursuit of our interests. Above all, we must recognize that only the United States has the vision and strength to consolidate the gains of the last few years, and to build an even better world...

HEALTH

Acne and Eczema

Acne is a condition in which the sebaceous glands become inflamed, generally due to the clogging of skin pores. Acne is characterized by blackheads, pimples and cysts which appear on the face, neck, chest, arms and back. Eczema is an inflammatory condition in which the skin develops redness and itching. There may also be a watery discharge which can become encrusted and scaly. These Web sites offer detailed information about the causes and treatment of acne. The Usenet group is for the discussion of acne and eczema. The mailing list is for sufferers of eczema and for health professionals who treat eczema.

Web:
  http://freenet.uchsc.edu/2000/adolescent/acne.html
  http://victorvalley.com/health%26law/hlaw-apr/skin.htm

Usenet:
  alt.skincare.acne

Listserv Mailing List:
  List Name: **eczema**
  Subscribe to: **listserv@maelstrom.stjohns.edu**

Addictions

There's a lot to be addicted to in this world: cigarettes, alcohol, marijuana, cocaine, heroin, gambling, food, sex, codependency, and so on. Some things are okay in moderation (such as food), while others should be avoided completely. What they all have in common is the potential to control somebody's behavior to the detriment of that person. Many people suffer from addictions and, as you might expect, there is a lot of relevant information on the Net. Most important behavioral changes start with a single small step. Here are the resources. Why not take that step now?

Web:
  http://www.alcoholics-anonymous.org/
  http://www.drugnet.net/
  http://www.na.org/basic.htm
  http://www.recoverynetwork.com/news/

Listserv Mailing List:
  List Name: **addict-l**
  Subscribe to: **listserv@listserv.kent.edu**

Can't **stop** the music? That's okay.

Can't **stop** something else?
You may have a problem.
If so, try the Addictions mailing list.

AIDS

AIDS (acquired immune deficiency syndrome) and the HIV (human immunodeficiency virus) family of viruses that cause it are important medical topics. AIDS is a disease that compromises the body's immune system by attacking certain types of white blood cells. (White blood cells attack germs, either directly or by secreting substances that help the immune response.) The HIV virus is spread via body fluids, mostly semen and blood. Once a person is infected, the virus can live in the body for years without seeming to cause a problem. However, in most cases, the immune system eventually weakens, and other diseases can take hold, often leading to severe illness or death. In recent years, drug treatments have been developed that can significantly slow down the course of the disease. But, as of yet, there is no cure nor is there a vaccine.

Web:
  http://www.aegis.com/
  http://www.teleport.com/~celinec/aids.shtml
  http://www.thebody.com/

Usenet:
  misc.health.aids
  sci.med.aids

Arthritis

"Arthritis" means inflammation of one or more joints of the body. Symptoms include pain, redness and stiffness, which can range from mild to severe. Although people talk about arthritis as if it is a single disease, there are actually many different types of arthritis. The two most well-known are osteoarthritis, a degenerative disease that sometimes accompanies aging, and rheumatoid arthritis, an auto-immune disease most commonly affecting women. In general, most types of arthritis, as well as many other auto-immune conditions, fall under the branch of medicine known as rheumatology. Here are some good Web resources that will give you more detailed information about arthritis, how it is treated, what research is being conducted, and much more. The Usenet groups offer a place for arthritis sufferers, medical personnel, or supportive family and friends to talk about arthritis.

Web:
http://www.arthritis.org/
http://www.pslgroup.com/arthritis.htm

Usenet:
alt.support.arthritis
misc.health.arthritis

Birth Control

On the Net you can find out everything you always wanted to know about birth control (but never bothered to ask). You can find general information about all methods of contraception (including abstinence). Learn about drugs, contraceptive devices, useful statistics, family planning, and much more.

Web:
http://opr.princeton.edu/ec/ec.html
http://rtt.colorado.edu/~mcck/
http://www.plannedparenthood.org/
   BIRTH-CONTROL/CONTRACHOICES.HTM
http://www.reproline.jhu.edu/

Birth control: When you care enough not to send the very best.

Hold that thought.

Centers for Disease Control

The Centers for Disease Control and Prevention (CDC) is an agency of the United States Department of Health and Human Services. (The CDC was originally established in 1946 as the Communicable Disease Center.) The CDC offers national programs for the prevention and control of communicable diseases, conducts research and directs quarantine activities when necessary. At their Web site they offer information about communicable diseases, health risks, injuries and disabilities, and prevention guidelines. They also have a nice selection of tips for people who are planning to travel outside the U.S. Take some time to read the information here. You will learn a lot.

Web:
http://www.cdc.gov/

Children's Health

If you have kids, there will be times when you need to call the doctor, or look for help in a first aid or medical book. At such times, the Net can help. Here is reference information on pediatric health, childhood conditions, and acquired and congenital diseases. The Usenet group is for the general discussion of children's health. Hint: If all else fails, ask your mother.

Web:
http://www.kidshealth.org/
http://www.uab.edu/pedinfo/

Usenet:
misc.kids.health

HEALTH 353

Children's Mental Health

Here is an excellent collection of articles that deal with many different aspects of children's mental health. If one of your children has a problem, this is a great place to look for information, advice and ideas. Read about adolescent development, depression, lying, teen pregnancy, sleep problems, mental retardation, and more. Even if your kids are doing fine, you will still find it worthwhile to browse this site for useful information. For example, did you know that children who watch a lot of television are more likely to have lower grades, read fewer books, exercise less and be overweight?

Web:
http://www.aacap.org/web/aacap/factsfam/

Depression

Depression is more than being bummed out because someone else ate the last of the ice cream. Depression is a psychological disorder characterized by a persisting general unhappiness often accompanied by other symptoms such as sleep disturbances, lack of appetite, lack of concentration, suicidal thoughts, problems with work or family life, and feelings of emptiness and worthlessness. The Web sites are an excellent source of information about depression and the treatment of depression. They have information about medical and psychological treatments for depression as well as a lengthy list of Usenet support groups. If you want to talk to someone online, try the IRC channel or post to the Usenet group. The mailing list is for sufferers of depression as well as their friends and family. On the Net, someone is always home.

Web:
http://www.execpc.com/~corbeau/
http://www.walkers.org/

Usenet:
alt.support.depression

Listserv Mailing List:
List Name: **depress**
Subscribe to: listserv@soundprint.org

IRC:
#depression

Diabetes

Within your body, most starchy and sugar-like nutrients are converted into a substance called glucose. Glucose is used for a number of important purposes, including being a source of energy. In order to use glucose properly, our body depends on a hormone (chemical) called insulin, which is created by your pancreas and released into the bloodstream. Diabetes—more formally, diabetes mellitus—is a disease in which the glucose/insulin system does not work properly. Diabetes is a serious medical condition that must be treated properly. I have carefully selected these diabetes-related resources to provide you with a variety of useful information. You will also find it valuable to participate in the Usenet discussion groups and the mailing list.

Web:
http://www.cdc.gov/nccdphp/ddt/
http://www.childrenwithdiabetes.com/
http://www.cis.ohio-state.edu/hypertext/faq/usenet/diabetes/top.html
http://www.diabetes.com/
http://www.diabetes.org/
http://www.niddk.nih.gov/health/diabetes/pubs/dmdict/dmdict.htm
http://www.pslgroup.com/diabetes.htm

Usenet:
alt.support.diabetes.kids
misc.health.diabetes

Listproc Mailing List:
List Name: **diabetic**
Subscribe to: listproc@lehigh.edu

IRC:
#diabetes

Epilepsy and Seizure Disorders

Epilepsy is a chronic condition in which the normal electrical functions of the brain are disturbed in such a way as to produce seizures. Epilepsy can also produce other neurological symptoms affecting consciousness, movement or sensation. Epilepsy is a common condition, and in most cases, there is no known cause. Here is a lot of useful information about epilepsy, including a FAQ (frequently asked question list).

Web:
http://www.efa.org/
http://www.epilepsyontario.org/faqs/
http://www.neuro.wustl.edu/epilepsy/

Usenet:
alt.support.epilepsy

Go Ask Alice

"Alice" is a pseudonym for a number of people in the Health Education and Wellness Program at Columbia University in New York City. The "Go Ask Alice" Web site features answers to questions submitted by readers. The questions are oriented toward students and cover sex, relationships, drugs, fitness, emotional health and other topics. You can browse through the many questions that have already been answered, or submit a question of your own. (The name "Go Ask Alice" is taken from the song "White Rabbit", recorded by Jefferson Airplane on their 1967 album "Surrealistic Pillow". The song deals with the superficial similarities between taking drugs in the Sixties and the book "Alice's Adventures in Wonderland". I assume the people at Columbia University chose this whimsical name in order to convince themselves that, even though they are old, they are still cool.)

Web:
   http://www.columbia.edu/cu/healthwise/alice.html

Headaches

There are many causes for headaches. Fortunately, most headaches are not serious. Unfortunately, all headaches are bothersome and painful. Isn't it a wonderful feeling when you realize that the headache that has been bothering you for hours has finally gone away? These Web sites contain useful information to help you understand what causes a pain in the head and what you can do about it. Hint: Many headaches are caused by muscular tension, and can be avoided if you take care of your body. For example, if you work at a desk, take a break every 20 minutes and stretch. I have found that yoga is a wonderful way to eliminate tension headaches.

Web:
   http://www.achenet.org/
   http://www.ama-assn.org/insight/spec_con/migraine/migraine.htm
   http://www.headache-help.org/head.html
   http://www.headachecare.com/

Be bizarre. See "Bizarre".

Health Care Politics Talk and General Discussion

What happens when an irresistible force (health care reform) meets an immovable object (the health care industry)? Join the ongoing debate and share your opinions and comments.

Usenet:
   talk.politics.medicine

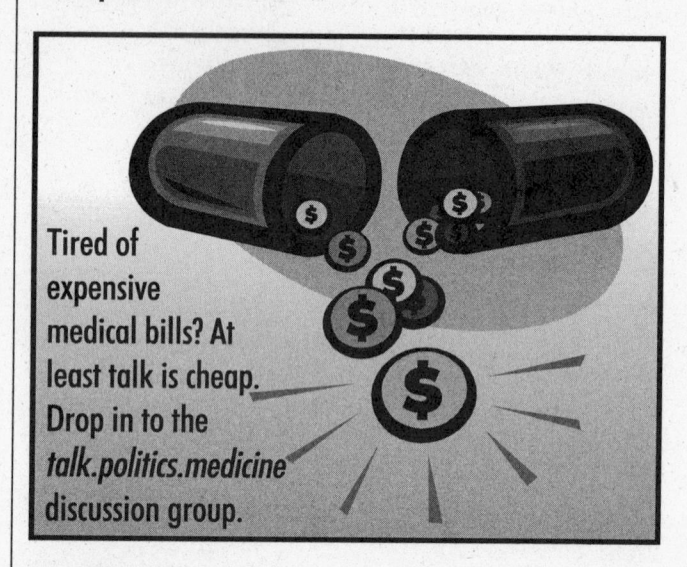

Tired of expensive medical bills? At least talk is cheap. Drop in to the talk.politics.medicine discussion group.

Health News

Whenever I want to catch up on the latest health news, I like to spend some time at these sites. They have all the latest news stories relating to the world of health and medicine.

Web:
   http://www.cnn.com/HEALTH/
   http://www.onhealth.com/
   http://www.pslgroup.com/mednews.htm
   http://www.reutershealth.com/
   http://www.yourhealthdaily.com/

Health Oasis

Health Oasis is a general health information center sponsored by the Mayo Clinic. I like this Web site because there is a lot of well-written, easy-to-understand background information. If it happens that some medical condition has just become important to you, this is a good place to find out the basics and to see what the current thinking is among medical professionals.

Web:
   http://www.mayohealth.org/

HEALTH

Health Resources

When you are looking for health-related information, here are some excellent places to start. You can find information on specific diseases and conditions, as well as a lot of good advice on how to stay healthy.

Web:
http://www.drkoop.com/
http://www.healthatoz.com/
http://www.healthfinder.gov/
http://www.medicinenet.com/

Keyboard Yoga

Human beings are designed to think, but not to sit at a desk for hours at a time while they are thinking. To keep you comfortable while you work, here are some exercises you can do even while sitting in front of the computer. Learn about self-massage, breathing, eye calisthenics, and yoga for your neck and shoulders, wrist and hands. Doing such exercises regularly is a great way to avoid muscular tension and the headaches it causes.

Web:
http://www.ivillage.com/fitness/yoga/

Massage

Just by using your fingers, you can turn someone into a noodle. Massage is a delicious and therapeutic way to alleviate the effects of tension and ill health. Discover new techniques and methods of massage along with recommendations for oils and additional accoutrements that can take massage to a new level.

Web:
http://www.doubleclickd.com/shiatsu.html
http://www.lib.ox.ac.uk/internet/news/faq/by_category.backrubs.faq.html
http://www.qwl.com/mtwc/

Usenet:
alt.backrubs

Mental Health Net

Mental health is something we take for granted when things are going well. But for the most part, we are creatures of the mind, and when our minds do not work well, our suffering can be tremendous. One of the things that can help you the most when you are dealing with mental illness is reliable information. This Web site can help you understand various medical conditions and treatments.

Web:
http://www.cmhc.com/

Look What I Found on the Net...

```
Newsgroups: alt.backrubs
Subject: Michelle Loves Back Rubs

> My name is Michelle. I'm 19 years old, and I live in Michigan.
>
> I am 5'6", 125 pounds, long, blonde hair.  I love getting
> back rubs from cute guys (mainly ones who like country music).
>
> Is there anyone who would like to give me a back rub?
> I'll be wearing nothing but a pair of black silky pantyhose.

Michelle,

Too bad you are in Michigan because I love back rubs too.
The funny thing is that I like to wear black silky panty hose
too.

Aching in Salt Lake,
    — Dave
```

National Institute of Allergy and Infectious Disease

The National Institute of Allergy and Infectious Disease (NIAID) provides major support and direction for medical research relating to infectious, immunologic and allergic diseases that afflict people worldwide (including AIDS). Their Web site is a point of access for information about their myriad activities and research accomplishments.

Web:
http://www.niaid.nih.gov/

National Institutes of Health

The National Institutes of Health (NIH) is one of eight health agencies of the U.S. Public Health Service. The general aim of the NIH is to "uncover new knowledge that will lead to better health for everyone" (boldly going where no medical man has gone before). More precisely, the NIH conducts research in its own laboratories, and supports a lot of research in universities, medical schools, hospitals, and other institutions.

Web:
http://www.nih.gov/

Quackery and Health Fraud

Health and feeling well are so important to us that when things go wrong we may consider any alternative, even those based on unsound principles or deception. Eventually, all of us die, and throughout the course of a lifetime, we will get sick from time to time. Thus, it is no surprise that the world of health has always had quacks and fakes. Moreover, there are many "alternative" therapies that are simply not effective, but still practiced widely. These Web sites contain information and links that will help you recognize health fraud and make informed decisions about health care for yourself and your family. If someone you know has a serious illness, do take some time to learn about the frauds, so you don't end up making a bad decision.

Web:
http://www.mtn.org/quack/
http://www.quackwatch.com/

Get your Mom on the Net.

Sleep Disorders

One time I had trouble getting to sleep because someone ate the last of the chocolate pudding before I could get to it. If you have trouble sleeping at night, it may help to read about various causes of sleeplessness and common sleeping disorders. These Web sites cover topics such as sleep apnea, snoring, sleep deprivation, narcolepsy, insomnia and restless leg syndrome. If it's late at night and you still can't get to sleep, check out the Usenet group for some late-night discussion.

Web:
http://www.newtechpub.com/phantom/
http://www.sleepnet.com/

Usenet:
alt.support.sleep-disorder

Sleep Disorders
Can't sleep?

Here are two ways to solve your problem.

(1) Get a job as a writer. That way, you'll never have to wake up to an alarm clock, so it doesn't matter if it takes you a long time to fall asleep at night. And if you get so little rest that you doze off in the afternoon, you can tell everyone you are doing research.

(2) Check with the Net to get lots of useful information about sleep disorders.

(Actually, I think there might be a third way, but I'm too tired to remember.)

Smoking Addiction

The phrase "the only way to break a bad habit is to drop it" was invented by someone who never had to quit smoking. It's a habit that is hard to break whether you quit altogether or try to taper off. Find support from other people recovering from their addiction to cigarettes or from people who have already recovered.

Web:
  http://www.chriscor.com/linkstoa.htm
  http://www.kickbutt.org/links/
  http://www.smokefreekids.com/smoke.htm

Usenet:
  alt.support.non-smokers
  alt.support.stop-smoking

Snakebites

In North America, snakes are not nearly as dangerous as most people believe. North American snakes seldom bite humans, and even when they do, the bites are rarely fatal. However, if you do get bitten by a snake, you may be in need of some hard information quickly. If so, here is the place to look. If you happen to be bitten by a snake in a different part of the world, my advice is to check this site, then catch the first plane for North America. (By the way, unless you are acting in a movie, it is never a good idea to suck out the venom with your mouth.)

Web:
  http://patc.simplenet.com/snakbite.html
  http://www.fda.gov/fdac/features/995_snakes.html

Stress

Stress, stress and more stress. I'm so tired of stress I could scream. But when I'm finished screaming and I want the real lowdown, I turn to the stress Web sites. Here is information on the history of stress, the reasons and biological basis for stress, the physiology of stress, how to manage stress, and hints on how to relax. (My hint is to stop reading about stress.)

Web:
  http://www.bbinst.org/stressaudit/stress3.cgi
  http://www.cyfernet.org/stress/
  http://www.psych-web.com/mtsite/smpage.html

Stuttering

Stuttering—or stammering—is an involuntary break in the flow of speech. Everyone stutters at times. However, some people stutter enough to affect their social interactions or peace of mind. Stuttering typically starts in children between 2-7 years old. However, there are many adults who stammer, and it is never too late to get help. Sometimes, just knowledge alone can bring comfort.

Web:
  http://www.cmhc.com/guide/stutter.htm
  http://www.mankato.msus.edu/dept/comdis/kuster/stutter.html

Listserv Mailing List:
  List Name: stutt-l
  Subscribe to: listserv@vm.temple.edu

Suicide Prevention

Sometimes life is frightening and miserable, and even though the pain won't last forever, it's still hard to deal with. If you feel like you've had all you can take and you're not sure what to do next, try getting in touch with the Samaritans. This is not a religious organization, but a group of people who want to give you a place to reach out to, confidentially. Their charity has been offering emotional support by phone, personal visits, and snail mail for 40 years, and now they are offering help electronically. Members of their staff are trained volunteers. The Web site is the American Foundation for Suicide Prevention.

Web:
  http://www.afsp.org/

Usenet:
  alt.suicide.holiday

The Net was cool before it was cool.

HEALTH

Typing Injuries

I have a good friend (who happens to be the wife of my lawyer) who injured her forearm by typing too much. Such injuries are common and more bothersome than most people realize—until it happens to them. The best treatment is to rest. However, most people, including my friend, want to keep on typing. (I remember when she only wanted to keep on truckin'.) Anyway, if you have or are developing a typing injury, here are some great places to look for information. By the way, I avoid such injuries by taking frequent breaks and doing the yoga "reverse namaste" pose. (Put your hands behind your back, fingers pointed up, and press with your palms together gently. Breathe slowly and think pure thoughts. After a while, it gets easy and feels great.)

Web:
  http://www.engr.unl.edu/eeshop/rsi.html
  http://www.tifaq.com/

Listserv Mailing List:
  List Name: **sorehand**
  Subscribe to: **listserv@itssrv1.ucsf.edu**

Typing Injuries

I was minding my Ps and Qs. I thought I had it down to a T, but I missed my Q.

"O no," I said. "I KO'd my wrist."

"R U OK?" she asked.

"Y do U ask?"

"B-cause, A typing injury can B painful. B careful."

"G," I said, "now I C Y. OK."

U.S. Department of Health and Human Services

The Department of Health and Human Services (HHS) is the principal U.S. federal governmental organization devoted to health care. HHS is huge, being the largest grant-making department in the government. HHS contains several hundred agencies and organizations, including the Centers for Disease Control, the Food and Drug Administration and the National Institutes of Health. The HHS Web site provides information about the HHS's programs, organizations and activities.

Web:
  http://www.os.dhhs.gov/

Women's Health

Women have a number of special health considerations. Here are large collections of links to resources related to women's health. Read about pregnancy, birth and midwifery, breast cancer, menopause, osteoporosis, rape and sexual assault, abortion, safe sex, fertility, sexual harassment, AIDS, sexually transmitted diseases, mental health, Pap tests, and much, much more.

Web:
  http://femina.cybergrrl.com/femina/
    HealthandWellness/
  http://www.cwhn.ca/resource/

World Health Organization

Here is the Web site for the World Health Organization (WHO), which operates under the auspices of the United Nations. The goal of WHO is the "attainment by all peoples of the highest possible level of health". What do they mean by health? "A state of complete physical, mental and social well-being—and not merely the absence of disease or infirmity—in which each person in the world has at least two Harley Hahn books."

Web:
  http://www.who.ch/

Rebel. See "Anarchy".

HERBS

Algy's Herb Page

You don't have to hop all over the Net just to find good herb information. This site has loads of links relating to ornamental herbs, culinary and medicinal herbs, recipes, news and discussions.

Web:
http://www.algy.com/herb/

Aromatherapy

Aromatherapy is the therapeutic use of scented essential oils derived from plants. The oil can be put into a vaporizer, applied to the skin by massage, or put into a bath. If you are not sure where to start, check out these resources. You will learn how to pick out appropriate oils and how to use them in conjunction with massage, baths or vaporizers. You can also read about the interesting history of aromatherapy. The Usenet group is for the discussion of aromatherapy or for asking questions.

Web:
http://www.fragrant.demon.co.uk/aromlist.html
http://www.halcyon.com/kway/
http://www.healthy.net/clinic/therapy/aroma/

Usenet:
alt.aromatherapy

Chinese Herbs

If you are interested in herbs, you will enjoy reading about Chinese herbs and how they are used in traditional healing. This Web site offers information for students of Chinese herbology as well as practitioners.

Web:
http://www.acupuncture.com/herbology/HerbInd.htm

Culinary Herbs

When I cook, I like to use a variety of fresh herbs to season my meal. They taste great, they are economical, and they are easy to use. Here is a FAQ (frequently asked question list) that will help you learn about using herbs in your cooking and growing your own culinary herbs.

Web:
http://sunsite.unc.edu/herbmed/culiherb.html

Culinary Herbs

Would you like to meet some of my favorite friends?

Basil, sage, chives, saffron, cilantro, rosemary, thyme, bay leaves, mint, tarragon, dill, garlic, lemon grass, horseradish, fennel, anise, parsley, ginger, borage, horehound, marjoram, oregano, caraway, savory and chamomile.

Why not invite them over to dinner sometime?

Garlic

I love garlic. I have a recipe for garlic and parsley spaghetti topped with a smoked garlic tomato sauce that is fantastic. (1: Buy ready-made garlic and parsley spaghetti. 2: Buy ready-made smoked garlic tomato sauce. 3: Cook spaghetti. 4: Warm sauce in microwave. 5: Combine spaghetti and sauce.) Garlic is good for more than cooking, though. You can use garlic to promote health. Garlic contains a large amount of organic sulfides and other nutritious compounds, and is reported as being useful as an antibiotic, anti-carcinogen and antioxidant, as well as reducing atherosclerosis (at least in lab animals).

Web:
http://www.frontierherb.com/spices/kkl/kkl.notes.garlic.html
http://www.solgar.com/nutrition_library/healthy_living/garlic.html

360 HERBS

Henriette's Herbal Homepage

When I want to get the latest dirt on the world of herbs, I like to go check with Henriette. Here you will find a great archive of postings taken from various herbal Usenet groups. While you are here, you can find herb FAQs, pictures, software and a database of plant names.

Web:
http://sunsite.unc.edu/herbmed/

Herb Magick

When you are trying to get through life, you don't necessarily have to stick with "the known" reality most people agree on. For instance, you can utilize some herb magick to make life go your way. These Web resources have basic information about getting started with herbs, as well as more esoteric information about the magickal properties of various woods and plants. Don't have a spellbook? No need to worry. You can find sample spells online. Bad with plants? It doesn't matter. After all, you don't need a green thumb when you have a magick wand.

Web:
http://www.cyberportal.net/pmather/wicca/herbs.html
http://www.enchantedencounters.com/herblist.htm

Herb Talk and General Discussion

Things that grow and things that don't, plants that heal and plants that won't. Little herbs that stink and flower, have their merit and their power. Here is where the people go, to talk about the herbs to grow. Herbs for cooking and to eat, herbs for healing can't be beat.

Usenet:
alt.folklore.herbs

Listserv Mailing List:
List Name: herb
Subscribe to: listserv@vm.ege.edu.tr

Herb Uses

It's always good to know about herbal healing properties. For example, if you have a big publishing deadline, and your editor will not allow you to sleep or have fun, it is nice to know that gota kola helps alleviate mental fatigue and rosehips fight stress. You can learn these helpful facts and more at these Web sites.

Web:
http://www.herbanspice.com/silversage/index.html
http://www.well-being.com/earthen-scents/text/property.htm

> You probably know that, historically, certain herbs are used for medicinal purposes.
>
> However, before you use an herb in this way, be sure you understand its effects.
>
> For example, tradition holds that ginger helps fight a cold, chamomile is soothing to the nerves, sarsaparilla helps cure impotence, and hawthorn berries strengthen the muscles and the nerves to the heart.
>
> So, guys, if your wife or girlfriend ever brings you chamomile tea mixed with sarsaparilla and ginger, make sure you've got plenty of hawthorn berries to see you through the night.

Herbal Encyclopedia

The Herbal Encyclopedia is a comprehensive guide to herbs. Choose an herb, any herb, and, in two clicks of a mouse tail, you will have information about how the herb is used and how to grow it.

Web:
http://www.wic.net/waltzark/herbenc.htm

HERBS

Herbal Hall

Here is an excellent site for herbalists, gardeners and botany lovers. This Web site is loaded with articles, reference material (including a glossary), links to herbal FAQs (frequently asked question lists), and information about herb-related Usenet groups and mailing lists.

Web:
http://www.herb.com/herbal.htm

Money, sex, intrigue... These are just three things that you won't find in the

Herbal Hall

What you *will* find is a lot of information about herbs and what to do with them. The next time you have a few minutes, why not take a look at this site and learn something about our friends in the horicultural kingdom. After all, herbs don't grow on trees.

Herbnet

For lots of information about herbs, Herbnet is the place to go. In addition to a collection of links to herbal resources, there is a great deal of information about print publications and journals, herb and seed sources, societies and associations, botanical gardens and herbalism schools.

Web:
http://www.herbnet.com/

Medicinal Herbs

There are many, many herbs that can be used as medicines, but make no mistake about it: when you are using an herb for medicinal purposes, you are using a drug. To be prudent, I recommend that you do a bit of research before you take an herb. Herbs, like all drugs, can cause side effects. These Web sites will help you. First, you can teach yourself about specific herbs: what they can do and how you should use them. Second, you can look at pictures of the herbs (which I find interesting).

Web:
http://www.healthy.net/clinic/therapy/herbal/
http://www.nnlm.nlm.nih.gov/pnr/uwmhg/

Modern Herbal

In 1931, Mrs. M. Grieve wrote an herbal reference detailing the properties, folklore and cultivation of many hundreds of plants. In the book, Mrs. Grieve described how to use plants for healing, cooking, and even for cosmetics. She called her book "A Modern Herbal". Although it is not modern any longer, the book is still a fantastic resource for anyone interested in herbs. Here is a hypertext version of Mrs. Grieve's wonderful reference.

Web:
http://www.botanical.com/botanical/mgmh/mgmh.html

Pictures of Herbs

Herbs are sometimes hard to identify, and if you are putting them in your mouth, it's not a good idea to make a mistake. This archive can help. It has a collection of pictures of herbs in various stages of growth.

Web:
http://www.rt66.com/hrbmoore/HOMEPAGE/

HISTORICAL DOCUMENTS

American Historical Documents

Many people have heard about the most important American historical documents, but few people have had the opportunity to look at the actual texts. Here is your chance. Take a look at the Declaration of Independence, the Constitution and its amendments, the Bill of Rights, the Monroe Doctrine, the Japanese and German surrenders, and many, many important documents.

Web:
http://memory.loc.gov/ammem/bdsds/
http://w3.one.net/~mweiler/ushda/
http://www.yale.edu/lawweb/avalon/avalon.htm

Nothing to do? Download a copy of the American Constitution and change all the parts you don't like.

Canadian Constitution Act

Most people think of Canada as a large country sitting quietly in the northern portion of North America, waiting patiently for winter. But believe me, Canada has seen its share of political action. And it all started in 1867 when the British parliament passed the British North America Act (also known as the Constitution Act), the legislation that created the independent country of Canada. The original country consisted of only four provinces: Ontario (Upper Canada), Quebec (Lower Canada), New Brunswick and Nova Scotia. It is interesting to read this document and compare it to the United States' Declaration of Independence and the United States' Constitution. The differences in the personalities of the two countries really show.

Web:
http://insight.mcmaster.ca/org/efc/pages/law/cons/Constitutions/Canada/English/ca_1867.html

Constitution of the United States of America

The Constitution of the United States is not only an important historical document, but an inspiration to people all over the world. At this site, you can look at the constitution and its amendments (the first 10 amendments being the Bill of Rights). You can also search for a particular phrase, and look at other, related information.

Web:
http://lcweb2.loc.gov/const/constquery.html

Council of Trent

The Council of Trent was an ecumenical council of the Roman Catholic church. It was convened in 1545 by Pope Paul III to address the problems of the Protestant Reformation. The Council of Trent met sporadically until 1563, when it was concluded by Pope Pius IV. Throughout its active years, the Council of Trent was a major figure in the Catholic Reformation. The reforms—which covered topics such as the Mass, the clergy, sacraments, scripture, relics, education and feasts—formed a basis for modern Catholicism. Here are the texts and transcripts of the Council of Trent's canons and decrees.

Web:
http://history.hanover.edu/early/trent.htm

Declaration of Arms, 1775

On July 6, 1775, the representatives of the "United Colonies of North-America" met in Philadelphia and issued a document called "Declaration of the Causes and Necessity of Taking Up Arms". These guys were sick up and fed with the way they were being treated by Great Britain, and this document is the explanation as to why they were rebelling. The document did not mince words. For example, the declaration refers to the members of the British parliament as "stimulated by an inordinate passion" for power, and describes them as being blinded "by their intemperate rage for unlimited domination". Sound familiar?

Web:
http://odur.let.rug.nl/~usa/D/1751-1775/war/causes.htm

Declaration of Sentiments

In 1848, the first Women's Rights Convention was held in Seneca Falls, New York. The convention was convened by Elizabeth Cady Stanton and Lucretia Mott, who presented the Declaration of Sentiments, a document based on the Declaration of Independence. This declaration, however, was a list of grievances denouncing the inequality between men and women in the areas of education, religion, employment, property rights, marriage, family and voting. Almost 150 years later, the Declaration of Sentiments still makes for interesting reading. Note: After the Declaration of Sentiments was presented, another 71 years passed before American women were given the right to vote under the 19th Amendment to the U.S. Constitution.

Web:
http://www.rochester.edu/SBA/declare.html

Emancipation Proclamation

In the United States, the expression "Lincoln freed the slaves" is commonly used as an all-purpose rejoinder in certain sticky social situations, such as when your boss tells you to work overtime without extra pay, or when your mother forces you to clean up your room. But just how did Lincoln free the slaves? At the time of the Civil War, Lincoln was president of the Union (the northern states), leading them against the Confederacy (the southern states). On September 17, 1862—the bloodiest day of the Civil War—the Battle of Antietam in western Maryland ended with combined losses of more than 23,000 men. Lincoln used the occasion to issue the Emancipation Proclamation, which declared free all slaves in states still in rebellion against the Union. The slaves were not actually freed until April 9, 1865, when the Union won its final victory against the Confederacy. If any of this interests you, take a few minutes to look at the actual proclamation (and at the fine print contained therein).

Web:
http://www.nps.gov/ncro/anti/emancipation.html

> The next time your teacher or your boss tries to tell you what to do, download the Emancipation Proclamation and mail them their own personal copy.

English Bill of Rights

The English established their Bill of Rights in 1689. This document lessened the power of the throne and gave more power to the subjects of England. The Bill of Rights elevated the political stature of Parliament over that of the crown, gave civil and political rights to English subjects and stated that no Roman Catholic would rule England. The Bill of Rights was accepted by William III and Mary II after the Glorious Revolution which ousted James II from the throne. You can read about this document which created a significant turning point in the history of England.

Web:
http://www.wwlia.org/uk-billr.htm

European Texts and Documents

Have you ever worried that you might run out of important historical documents to read? Well, relax. You are causing yourself unnecessary strain. There are lots of wonderful documents only a mouse click away. These sites, for example, have many European historical documents dating from medieval times to the present. As long as you have the Net, you will never run out of important European documents.

Web:
http://history.hanover.edu/europe.htm
http://library.byu.edu/~rdh/eurodocs/

Federalist Papers

Between 1787-1788, a series of 85 political essays—now called "The Federalist Papers"—was published in New York. The series was initiated by Alexander Hamilton in order to persuade New York to approve the Federalist Constitution (which they eventually did). Hamilton wrote most of the essays, the others being written by James Madison and John Jay. As they were written, the essays were published in newspapers and were read widely. (Compare to what you see in modern newspapers.) Even today, the Federalist Papers are acclaimed for their high literary quality and well-developed cogent arguments.

Web:
http://www.teachersoft.com/Library/history/federalist/contents.htm

364 HISTORICAL DOCUMENTS

Gettysburg Address

From 1861 to 1865, the United States was embroiled in a civil war between the northern states (Union) and the southern states (Confederacy). There were many causes of the war, but the primary reasons for conflict were fundamental disagreements over slavery and federal control of individual states. Approximately halfway through the war, a turning point occurred near the town of Gettysburg, Pennsylvania. On July 1, 1863, General Robert E. Lee (military commander of the Confederacy) attempted to invade the North, but after battling for three days, the Southern troops were routed. Many thousands of men were killed in those three days. On November 19, 1863, President Abraham Lincoln made a speech at the dedicaP

tion of the new Civil War cemetery in Gettysburg. His beautiful and oft-quoted words express Lincoln's grief for the fallen soldiers and describe the principles for which the men died. Ironically, in the speech Lincoln says, "The world will little note, nor long remember, what we say here...", but in fact, the Gettysburg Address is one of the most famous speeches in American history. What American does not recognize the words "four score and seven years ago" and "government of the people, by the people, and for the people"? At this Web site, you will find various drafts of the Gettysburg Address. It is a short, powerful speech, and it shows us why Lincoln is considered one of the great American presidents.

Web:
http://lcweb.loc.gov/exhibits/gadd/

Historical Document Archive

This is an archive of historical documents, including the Magna Carta, the U.S. Bill of Rights, Lincoln's Second Inaugural Address, the Monroe Doctrine, the Mayflower Compact, the Emancipation Proclamation, and many others.

Web:
http://odur.let.rug.nl/~usa/D/

Make every keystroke count.

Question:

What do the following people have in common?

His Majesty the King of the Belgians,
Her Majesty the Queen of Denmark,
The President of the Federal Republic of Germany,
The President of the Hellenic Republic,
His Majesty the King of Spain,
The President of the French Republic,
The President of Ireland,
The President of the Italian Republic,
His Royal Highness the Grand Duke of Luxembourg,
Her Majesty the Queen of the Netherlands,
The President of the Portuguese Republic,
Her Majesty the Queen of The United Kingdom of Great Britain and Northern Ireland

Choose the correct answer. All of these people...

(A) have four or more Harley Hahn books.
(B) were unable to get a job in the private sector.
(C) have hosted at least two Tupperware parties.
(D) signed the Maastricht Treaty in order to establish European Union.

Historical Documents Talk and General Discussion

Countries create important documents—such as constitutions, bills of rights, treaties, declarations, and so on—to solve problems. However, most of the time, the signing of the document is only the beginning, not the end. All important documents deserve discussion and interpretation, over and over. For example, in the United States, there is a continuous debate over the meaning of certain parts of the U.S. Constitution. If you enjoy discussing such matters, this is the Usenet group for you. Here you will find a forum for all types of historical topics.

Usenet:
soc.history

Joint Declaration of Peace

Ireland has a long, complex history of unrest. In modern times, the main issue is that the Protestants in Northern Ireland (the Unionists) want to be associated with England, while the Catholics (the Republicans) want all of Ireland to be a completely independent country. The situation, however, dates from the 12th century, when Pope Adrian granted control of Ireland to King Henry II of England. This initiated a continuing Anglo-Irish conflict that worsened in the 16th century when England tried to impose Protestantism on the Irish population, which was largely Catholic. In 1800, English control was underscored by the Act of Union, which formally unified the English and Irish parliaments. This legislation created a great deal of political unrest in Ireland, resulting in a series of Home Rule bills, providing for increased Irish control of the country. These bills resulted in great animosity on both sides of the controversy (pro-British and pro-independence). On April 24, 1916 (Easter Monday), a small group of Irish patriots in Dublin led an assault on the British. The "Easter Rising", as it came to be called, lasted only six days before it was put down by British troops. However, it laid the groundwork for the independence of southern Ireland, as well as further decades of violence, unrest and political turmoil. After the Rising, the extreme nationalist political party Sein Fein ("Ourselves Alone") won most of the seats in the 1918 General Election, and the Irish Republican Army (IRA) was formed to fight the British administration. For years, the IRA led a hit-and-run assault on the British and as a result, in 1921, a treaty was negotiated dividing the country into two mostly self-governing areas: Northern Ireland (also called Ulster) and Southern Ireland (the Irish Free State). In 1937, the people of Southern Ireland passed a referendum declaring themselves completely independent, and in 1948, the Republic of Ireland Act officially recognized the country—now called the Republic of Ireland or Eire—as being separate from the British Commonwealth, bringing an end to hundreds of years of direct British influence. However, this did not bring an end to the violence and unrest. Northern Ireland, now a part of the United Kingdom, has a Protestant majority that generally favors the union with Britain. However, the Catholic minority in Northern Ireland would prefer to be part of the south, and there are still many people in both countries who are willing to fight for a completely unified and independent country. In 1993, a document was created as a new starting point in the peace process. This document, the Joint Declaration of Peace, was signed on December 15, 1993, by John Majors, the Prime Minister of England, and Albert Reynolds, the Taoiseach (Prime Minister) of the Republic of Ireland. If you would like to read the Joint Declaration (which is actually quite easy to understand), here is a Web site that contains the full text.

Web:

http://www.bess.tcd.ie/dclrtn.htm

Maastricht Treaty

On February 7, 1992, the Treaty on European Union was signed, formally acknowledging the intentions of a number of European countries to form a political, monetary and social union. The treaty is generally known as the Maastricht Treaty, named after the city of Maastricht in southeast Holland where the meeting and signing took place. (The name is pronounced Mas'-trikt.) On November 1, 1993, the Maastricht Treaty was ratified, establishing the European Union (EU). The treaty is a complex document, but the main goals of the EU can be summarized as follows: (1) to create an economic and monetary union under the control of one central European bank; (2) to create a unified European market in which a single currency is used everywhere; (3) to ensure the unrestricted movement of people within the Union; (4) to create a common foreign and security policy; (5) to ensure cooperation among the member states with respect to justice and law enforcement; (6) to establish a European coal and steel community; (7) to establish a unified European atomic energy community; and (8) to strengthen the powers of the European Parliament. Although it all sounds simple (at least in principle), the European Union is actually a continuing work in progress, and many of the goals of the Maastricht Treaty have not yet been implemented completely. If you would like to read the actual treaty, to see the original intentions of the signatory countries, here is the Web site at which the document can be found.

Web:

http://europa.eu.int/en/record/mt/top.html

366 HISTORICAL DOCUMENTS

Magna Carta

Feudalism was a political and social system in Western Europe that developed in the late 9th century and lasted until the rise of absolute monarchies. The feudal system centered upon the ownership of land and manors. The lord of the manor would allow peasants (serfs) to utilize his land for farming and for living. In exchange, the peasant was bound by an oath of fealty to pay money or to perform servile labor for the lord. Within the feudal system, the king owned all land. Under the king was a hierarchy of nobles (for example, barons) who would hold land granted by the king. Under the high nobles were lesser nobles who controlled land granted by the high nobles, and so on, each landowner swearing fealty to the noble above him (not unlike multilevel marketing). During the reign of King John (1199-1216) the barons revolted. They did so because of their strong opposition to the King's abuse of the feudal custom by encroaching on baronial privileges in order to raise money. To settle the rebellion, King John put his seal on the Magna Carta, which guaranteed rights to the subjects of England and generally precluded the excessive use of royal power. The Magna Carta is an interesting document to read, as it lays out what various members of the feudal system could and could not do.

Web:

http://www.cet.com/~theoaks/historic/magnacarta.html

http://www.ecst.csuchico.edu/~rodmur/docs/Magna.html

Native American Treaties

In the late 1700s through the late 1800s, there were many treaties signed between the United States government and various Native American (Indian) tribes. Many of these treaties were to have long-lasting effects, some to the present day. I found it fascinating to read some of these treaties. In addition, I was surprised how many well-known names of places are derived from Indian tribal names.

Web:

http://www-libraries.colorado.edu/ps/gov/native.htm

The Internet is always on.

Treaty of Guadalupe Hidalgo

For some years before 1846, there was tension between Mexicans and Americans living in the region that later became the state of Texas. In 1846, upon the annexation of Texas by the United States, a war broke out between the United States and Mexico. The Mexican War continued until 1848, when the Treaty of Guadalupe Hidalgo was signed. This treaty granted the United States possession of the provinces and territories of Texas, New Mexico, California and other significant portions of the southwest. In return, the United States was to pay Mexico $15 million and assume $3.25 million in American claims against Mexico. The U.S. also recognized prior land grants in the southwest and offered citizenship to any Mexicans living in the area. Clearly, this document was instrumental in defining the territory of modern day America. Here is the text if you would like to read it for yourself.

Web:

http://www.monterey.edu/other-sites/history/treaty.html

Treaty of Paris

On September 3, 1783, about two years after the conclusion of the American Revolutionary War, the Treaty of Paris formally ended the hostilities. The Treaty of Paris recognized the independence of the 13 colonies and set forth what territory the British would cede: the Americans received huge territories in North America; the Spanish received Florida and regained West Indian properties; and France regained St. Lucia, Tobago, Senegal, Gorée, and East Indian properties.

Web:

http://w3.one.net/~mweiler/ushda/paris.htm

United States Bill of Rights

On December 15, 1791, the Bill of Rights became law in the United States. The Bill of Rights is a set of 10 amendments made to the U.S. Constitution (adopted in 1787). The Bill of Rights sets out various freedoms that all citizens of the United States are guaranteed. For example, the first part of the Bill of Rights guarantees freedom of religion, freedom of speech, freedom of the press, freedom of assembly, and freedom to petition the government. This is one of the most important documents in American history, and if you have never read it, you may want to spend some time seeing exactly what it contains.

Web:

http://lcweb2.loc.gov/const/bor.html

HISTORICAL DOCUMENTS

United States Declaration of Independence

On July 4, 1776, the Declaration of Independence was adopted by the Thirteen Colonies as an announcement of their separation from Great Britain and their creation of the United States of America. The Declaration of Independence portrays what the Americans considered an ideal government and lists particular grievances that went unanswered for too long. The American Revolution lasted for eight years and finally ended with the United States keeping their independence and their territories. Now you can get your own personal electronic copy of the Declaration of Independence from this Web site. (And if you have an irresistible surge of patriotism, you can print a copy for yourself and add your signature to the list at the end.)

Web:
http://lcweb2.loc.gov/const/declar.html

Universal Declaration of Human Rights

On December 10, 1948, the General Assembly of the United Nations adopted the Universal Declaration of Human Rights, a document based on the U.S. Bill of Rights, France's Declaration of the Rights of Man, and England's Magna Carta. The Universal Declaration of Human Rights was created to set a standard for human rights that all countries should meet. It stresses the dignity and worth of humanity, equal rights for men and women, and freedom as a right for everyone. The document was written primarily by René Cassin, a French public official who later (in 1968) won the Nobel Peace Prize for his efforts in promoting human rights. The Universal Declaration of Human Rights is inspiring and well worth a look.

Web:
http://www.un.org/Overview/rights.html

Look What I Found on the Net...

```
    (from the Treaty of Paris, ending the American Revolution)


It having pleased the Divine Providence to dispose the hearts
of the most serene and most potent Prince George the Third...
and of the United States of America, to forget all past misunderstandings
and differences that have unhappily interrupted the good
correspondence and friendship which they mutually wish to restore,


Article 1:

His Britannic Majesty acknowledges the said United States, viz.,
New Hampshire, Massachusetts Bay, Rhode Island and Providence
Plantations, Connecticut, New York, New Jersey, Pennsylvania,
Maryland, Virginia, North Carolina, South Carolina and Georgia,
to be free sovereign and independent states, that he treats with
them as such, and for himself, his heirs, and successors,
relinquishes all claims to the government, propriety,
and territorial rights of the same and every part thereof...
```

HISTORICAL DOCUMENTS

Versailles Treaty of 1919

Over the centuries, there have been many treaties signed in Versailles. The most famous, however, is the treaty signed in 1919 that helped bring World War I to a close. Four world leaders—the "Big Four"—negotiated the treaty: President Wilson (United States), Premier Clemenceau (France), Prime Minister Lloyd George (Britain), and Premier Orlando (Italy). The treaty called for many actions, most of which were geared to strip Germany of its military, political and economic powers. The treaty's main resolutions placed limits on German armed forces, put into place a method for Germany to make enormous reparations, restored various cities and territories to their rightful owners, demilitarized the Rhineland, and created the League of Nations. Unfortunately, the terms of the Treaty of Versailles were so punitive as to create enormous unrest in the German population. In the 1920s, the German economy suffered through a terrible decline and, combined with the resentment over the Treaty of Versailles, the economic suffering created an atmosphere in which Hitler was able to rise to power. What were the actual details of this treaty? Here is a Web site that contains the text, so you can read it for yourself.

Web:
http://ac.acusd.edu/History/text/versaillestreaty/vercontents.html

American First Ladies.

Learn about the women behind the men behind the women.

HISTORY

American Civil War

The American Civil War took place from 1861 to 1865. There were many reasons for the war, chief among them the South's dependence on slaves, and the fundamental disagreement of federal control over state's rights. In spite of President Abraham Lincoln's efforts to hold together the union, first South Carolina (in 1860) and then ten more southern states seceded, forming the Confederacy. The four years that followed saw a bloody war of attrition that, eventually, ended up killing or maiming more than 600,000 people—in Lincoln's words, "...so costly a sacrifice on the altar of freedom." (By 1865, fully one quarter of the white male population of the South had been killed or maimed.) The war ended on April 9, 1865, when General (later President) Ulysses S. Grant accepted the surrender of General Robert E. Lee at Appomattox, Virginia. Five days later, on April 14, 1865, President Lincoln was assassinated by an actor, John Wilkes Booth, in an attempt to avenge the loss of the South.

Web:
http://homepages.dsu.edu/jankej/civilwar/civilwar.htm
http://www.access.digex.net/~bdboyle/cw.html

Usenet:
soc.history.war.us-civil-war

American First Ladies

In the United States, the First Lady is the wife of the President. Traditionally, the style of the First Lady has had a significant influence on the fashion and culture of her time. Some first ladies have contributed enormously to the public good, and are remembered as great Americans in their own right, for example, Edith Wilson, Eleanor Roosevelt and Barbara Bush.

Web:
http://www.firstladies.org/Flbib2.htm
http://www.whitehouse.gov/WH/glimpse/firstladies/html/firstladies.html

HISTORY   369

American Memory Collection
The Library of Congress has put together these "scrapbooks" of American history and culture. Flip through and look at Civil War photographs, portraits of literary figures, artists and celebrities, photos of rural America, and hear sound recordings of speeches that were delivered around the World War I era.

Web:
   http://lcweb2.loc.gov/ammem/

American Studies
This is a great place to argue about who discovered America, because you can be sure these people know what they are talking about. And with American Studies there aren't as many dates to remember because the history is much shorter. Come dwell on the past with other scholars of American Studies and discuss issues relating to your field.

Listserv Mailing List:
   List Name: **h-amstdy**
   Subscribe to: **listserv@h-net.msu.edu**

Do you like snappy dialog?
What about intellectual stimulation, daring discussions and invaluable tidbits of fascinating information?

All that, and more, is waiting for you on the **American Studies** mailing list.

And what country could be better to study? America—a place where even squares can have a ball.

Ancient World Cultures
I find it fascinating to explore ancient world cultures. For instance, when I want to take a break, I love to pour a fresh glass of carrot juice, sit in my special relaxation chair, and read about the formation, by Amenhotep IV, of a new Egyptian monotheistic religion dedicated to the worship of the sun. Or about how, in 750 A.D., Irish monks established early medieval art, of which survives the glorious illuminated "Book of Kells". There is a lot to know, so you had better get started now. Check out these Web sites to learn about various ancient world cultures, and to find out who were the movers and shakers in the last couple of millennia.

Web:
   http://eawc.evansville.edu/
   http://www.menagerie.net/lyceum/

Anglo-Saxons
The Anglo-Saxon era was a period in English history from the 5th century to the Norman Conquest (1066). The Anglo-Saxons were the descendants of Germanic-speaking peoples—the Angles, the Saxons and the Jutes—who migrated from the European continent in the 5th century after the weakening of Roman influence in England. The Anglo-Saxons dominated England until the arrival of William the Conqueror from Normandy (France).

Web:
   http://bay1.bjt.net/~melanie/anglo-sa.html
   http://orb.rhodes.edu/encyclop/early/pre1000/asindex.html
   http://www.georgetown.edu/labyrinth/subjects/british_isles/anglo-saxon/anglo-saxon.html

Listserv Mailing List:
   List Name: **ansax-l**
   Subscribe to: **listserv@wvnvm.wvnet.edu**

Classical Studies
Classical Studies (the Classics) encompass the Greek and Roman civilization and their direct antecedents. This area of study includes the Greek and Latin languages as well as their literature, art, architecture and archaeology. For discussion, see the Usenet group. For the FAQ (frequently asked question list), see the Web site.

Web:
   http://www.lib.ox.ac.uk/internet/news/faq/archive/classics-faq.html

Usenet:
   humanities.classics
   sci.classics

Eighteenth Century Resources
Travel back in time, back to the 18th century: a kinder, gentler time before the invention of cellular phones, fax machines and pizza delivery. Instead of doing cool things like playing video games and watching talk shows, people of the 18th century had to be more culturally advanced and make great literature, art, architecture, music and philosophy. Explore the past. Right now.

Web:
   http://www.english.upenn.edu/~jlynch/18th/

370　HISTORY

Eighteenth Century Resources

You can't live in the past—unless you are on theNet—in which case you can visit the eighteenth century whenever you want.

Feudal Terms

Feudalism was a form of social organization common in Western Europe from the fall of Charlemagne's empire (9th century) to the rise of the absolute French, Spanish and English monarchies (14th century and later). An exact definition of feudalism is hard to give, but you won't go far wrong if you think of it as a system with three main characteristics: strict social classes, law based on local customs, and land holding dependent upon a fee. If you want to read or talk about things feudal, you will need the proper vocabulary, so here are online glossaries with a large number of feudal words, from "abbey" to "witen".

Web:
http://history.cc.ukans.edu/history/subject_tree/e3/gen/feudal-terms/
http://www.crabtree.demon.co.uk/feudterm.htm

Gulf War

These sites have information on Operation Desert Storm: the countries and world leaders involved, lists of military units deployed, glossary of military unit terms and military equipment used, such as helicopters, tanks, artillery, chemical weapons and aircraft.

Web:
http://www.andrewjd.demon.co.uk/gulfwar/gulfwar.html
http://www.army.mil/cmh-pg/photos/gulf_war/index.htm
http://www.army.mil/cmh-pg/reference/dsds.htm
http://www.desert-storm.com/

Hiroshima and Nagasaki

It was the summer of 1945. The Allied forces which had defeated Germany now turned their full attention toward Japan and its massive war machine. Although the war in Europe was over, the Japanese had more than 2,000,000 soldiers and 9,000 kamikaze suicide bombers ready to fight to the death. It was estimated that a full-scale invasion of Japan would kill more than 500,000 American servicemen as well as many millions of Japanese. On July 26, the United States, Britain and China warned Japan to surrender unconditionally or face "prompt and utter destruction". Japanese officials stalled for time and scoffed at the demands. In response, U.S. President Harry Truman gave the order to drop an atomic bomb on Japan. On August 6, an atomic bomb was dropped on the bustling city of Hiroshima immediately killing 75,000 people (many more died later). Three days later, a second bomb was dropped on the city of Nagasaki killing another 50,000 people. On August 10, 1945—overruling the desires of its military leaders who wanted to keep fighting—Japan finally surrendered. The dropping of the two bombs ended the war, saved millions of lives, and ushered in a new and terrifying era of human history.

Web:
http://129.171.129.67/mf/hibakusha/
http://japan.park.org/Japan/Peace96/sakuin-e.html
http://www.csi.ad.jp/ABOMB/
http://www.lclark.edu/~history/HIROSHIMA/
http://www.us1.nagasaki-noc.or.jp/~nacity/na-bomb/museume01.html

Historian's Database and Information Server

Here is a wonderful, comprehensive information server for historians. You can browse through a wide variety of resources—so large, in fact, that you'll be able to use this Web site as your one-stop history warehouse.

Web:
http://www.ukans.edu/history/

Have you ever...

HISTORY 371

Historic American Speeches

This Web site has the text of many historic American speeches and addresses, including some of those given by Washington, Jefferson, Martin Luther King, Lincoln, Kennedy, and others.

Web:
http://douglass.speech.nwu.edu/

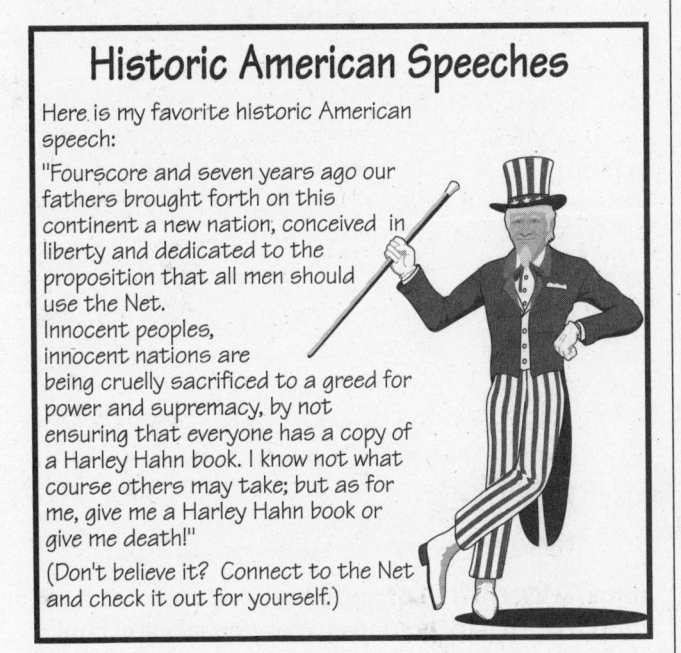

Historic American Speeches

Here is my favorite historic American speech:

"Fourscore and seven years ago our fathers brought forth on this continent a new nation, conceived in liberty and dedicated to the proposition that all men should use the Net. Innocent peoples, innocent nations are being cruelly sacrificed to a greed for power and supremacy, by not ensuring that everyone has a copy of a Harley Hahn book. I know not what course others may take; but as for me, give me a Harley Hahn book or give me death!"

(Don't believe it? Connect to the Net and check it out for yourself.)

Historical Sounds and Speeches

The Vincent Voice Collection of historical sounds and speeches contains many sound files of famous speeches, including some from John F. Kennedy, Richard Nixon, Teddy Roosevelt, Babe Ruth, Betty Ford, and many more.

Web:
http://web.msu.edu/vincent/

Historical Timelines

What happened and when? With the number of historical timelines on the Net, you will never be at a loss for names, dates and places. For example, not many people know that the Tiahuanaco empire was founded in Peru about 375 A.D. (But now you do.)

Web:
http://home.sprynet.com/sprynet/keithco/history.htm

History Net

The History Net is sponsored by a company that publishes a group of magazines for history buffs. The Web site contains a great many articles adapted from the magazines. If you have any interest in history, I guarantee you'll find something here you will enjoy reading.

Web:
http://www.thehistorynet.com/

History Resources

Those who do not learn how to find history resources on the Net are doomed to repeat their searches. Don't let this happen to you. Start with these Web sites, and you will be only a few mouse clicks away from whatever you need. If you are going to be a historian, it is crucial to learn how to use the Web. My philosophy is, if you can't master the present, you won't be able to live in the past.

Web:
http://www.corvinia.org/history/history.html
http://www.lib.iastate.edu/scholar/bib/history.html
http://www.plcmc.lib.nc.us/online/links/history.htm
http://www.ucr.edu/h-gig/horuslinks.html

History Talk and General Discussion

The great thing about history is that you never run out of it. Every minute there is more history made and that just means there is more to memorize when you are in school. Stop in on the Net, and hang out with the people who love to dwell on the past.

Usenet:
soc.history.african.biafra
soc.history.ancient
soc.history.moderated
soc.history.war.us-revolution
soc.history.what-if

Listserv Mailing List:
List Name: **h-world**
Subscribe to: **listserv@h-net.msu.edu**

Holocaust

The Web site has articles and other information geared toward remembrance of the Holocaust. The mailing list not only covers the Holocaust itself, but also related topics such as anti-Semitism, Jewish history in the 1930s and 1940s, and any topics with related themes in the history of World War II and Germany.

Web:
http://www.remember.org/

Usenet:
soc.culture.jewish.holocaust

Listserv Mailing List:
List Name: **h-holocaust**
Subscribe to: listserv@h-net.msu.edu

Hyperhistory

If you have some time to explore the Net, I suggest visiting this site. It has massive charts that show various historical and cultural happenings juxtaposed so you can see how various events relate to one another. For example, did you know that the year the Pope announced that Catholics could not practice birth control was the same year that Martin Luther King and Robert Kennedy were assassinated? Were you aware that the Berlin Wall was constructed in the same year that Yuri Garagin became the first man in space? And I bet you didn't know that Mussolini and Hitler formed the Rome-Berlin Axis around the same time Margaret Mitchell was writing "Gone with the Wind". This world history chart has lots of great information about people, events and history, and includes some cool maps.

Web:
http://www.hyperhistory.com/online_n2/History_n2/a.html

Look What I Found on the Net...

```
Newsgroup: soc.history.moderated
Subject: Why Did Civilization Start Where It Did?

Actually, the origin of civilization is a highly debated
subject.  The earliest civilizations — Mesopotamia, Egypt, and
the Indus — developed in river valleys.

In the case of Mesopotamia, as the region became more and more
arid, people from the dry areas moved into the valleys of the
Tigris and Euphrates rivers.  There they found water, swamps and
fertile soil.  They also found conditions that could only be
solved by organizing and by using large numbers of people on
irrigation and drainage projects.  Out of this situation came
civilization, because the people who conquered the river valleys
needed protection from floods and foes, as well as record
keeping, housing for increasingly large numbers, and steady
supplies of food and goods.

In other words, civilization arose out of necessity.  Once
civilization developed, it attracted a more or less steady
stream of settlers from the mountain and desert periphery —
settlers who brought new blood, new languages, and new
technologies.  The result was, in comparative terms, rapid
development...
```

Medieval History

Never mind that almost everyone was dirty, smelly, poor, and ate rotten food. Medieval history is cool because you got to fight with swords. Anyone who studies the culture and history of the medieval era can tell you that people were very different back then, as is evidenced by their politics, art, philosophy and religion. Scholars and students of the Middle Ages (476-1453 A.D.) discuss this period in history.

Web:
http://ebbs.english.vt.edu/medieval/
    medieval.ebbs.html
http://www.fordham.edu/halsall/sbook.html
http://www.georgetown.edu/labyrinth/
    labyrinth-home.html

Usenet:
soc.history.medieval

Listserv Mailing List:
List Name: **lt-antiq**
Subscribe to: **listserv@vm.sc.edu**

Renaissance

The Renaissance (14th-15th century to mid-17th century) is the period in European history between the Middle Ages and modern times, during which there was an enormous development of Western civilization. The Renaissance began in Italy in the 14th century, and by the 15th century had spread to the rest of Europe. The Renaissance was a time of great creation in art, architecture and crafts. There were also important accomplishments in the areas of literature, science and scholarship. Politically, the Renaissance gave birth to the nation states and to a great surge in exploration. To this day, the term "Renaissance man" describes someone who is accomplished and well-versed in a variety of areas.

Web:
http://humanitas.ucsb.edu/shuttle/eng-ren.html
http://www.hull.ac.uk/Hull/EL_Web/renforum/
    resource.htm
http://www.inmet.com/~justin/game-hist.html
http://www.luminarium.org/renlit/

Usenet:
alt.fairs.renaissance

Listserv Mailing List:
List Name: **renais-l**
Subscribe to: **listserv@ulkyvm.louisville.edu**

**History buffs:
Join the Renaissance mailing list and see what other people have to say about art, beauty, architecture, and all the other things that people used to do before there was television.**

Revisionism

Revisionism is the act of changing the way people view a commonly accepted doctrine or series of events. For example, within a movie, a person may be portrayed as a popular hero when, in fact, he was not at all liked during his time. There are many styles of revisionism. Revision can occur from people feeling nostalgic and making "the old days" into a more romantic, endearing time than it was. Revision can also occur when people want to heighten or lessen, for whatever reason, the emotional impact of events from the past. This Usenet group is a forum in which you can talk about revisionism in any form. The Web site contains articles and commentary pertaining to revisionism.

Web:
http://www.hoffman-info.com/

Usenet:
alt.revisionism

374 HISTORY

Royalty

From King Arthur to Princess Diana, we have always been fascinated with legends about royalty. For much of history, people were ruled by monarchs who achieved their divine rights by accident of birth. Today, there are only a handful of active monarchies in the world, but, if you believe the history books, there was a time when you couldn't walk to the next town without bumping into a king or queen. Today, the chances of meeting an actual member of a royal family are slight, but you can read about them whenever you want, and dream that, one day, your very own prince or princess will appear, and you will live happily ever after.

Web:
http://www.britannia.com/history/monarchs/
http://www.xs4all.nl/~kvenjb/kings.htm

This Day in History

Fill your mind with some trivial thoughts by finding out who was born and who died on this day in history. You never know when an important event or holiday is coming up for which you need to dress appropriately. Don't be caught unaware.

Web:
http://www.9online.com/today/today.htm
http://www.historychannel.com/today/

Titanic

On the night of April 14, 1912, the British passenger liner Titanic, once thought to be invincible, sunk in the North Atlantic. Since then, the Titanic disaster has become an enduring element of twentieth century folklore. When I was a young sprat at summer camp, we used to sing a folksong about the Titanic. ("...And the good Lord raised his hand/ Said the ship will never land/ It was sad when the great ship went down...") The good Lord notwithstanding, what brought the great ship down on its maiden voyage was an unexpected iceberg. As the ship began to sink, the 2,200 people aboard found out that there were not enough lifeboats, and, as a result, more than 1,500 people perished in the dark, icy water. The legend of the Titanic was resurrected in 1987, when the wreck itself was discovered, and again in 1997, when a maudlin, romanticized movie about the disaster rekindled interest in what is one of the oldest stories of mankind: what happens when hubris and poor planning encounter bad luck.

Web:
http://titanic.eb.com/
http://www.rmplc.co.uk/eduweb/sites/phind/
http://www.skarr.com/titanic/
http://www.titanic-online.com/

Usenet:
alt.history.ocean-liners.titanic

Majordomo Mailing List:
List Name: **titanic**
Subscribe to: **majordomo@listbox.com**

Twentieth Century USA

The history of 20th century America is rich with interesting events. Here is a collection of links to Web sites that cover important aspects of the last hundred years in the United States. Explore Prohibition, the Nixon era, the Cuban missile crisis, various wars, the women's rights movement, and much more.

Web:
http://www.msstate.edu/Archives/History/USA/20th_C./twenty.html

---

The Titanic

Big Ship + Big Iceberg = Big Disaster

Big Ship + Big Iceberg + Good Luck = Big Movie

It all adds up.

HISTORY

Vietnam War

The Vietnam War was a long, drawn-out affair, stretching from 1957 to 1975. In Washington, D.C., on the Vietnam Veterans Memorial, you can see the names of 58,153 dead serviceman, and over 300,000 more were wounded. As terrible as these numbers are, they are small compared to the dead and injured in Vietnam itself and in neighboring Laos and Cambodia. To anyone growing up in the Sixties, Vietnam was "The War". More than an actual conflict, it was a metaphor for the great mid-century life crisis that America and the world was to experience. It's hard to explain, even generally, what happened and why it was important. Suffice it to say that the Vietnam War finally convinced just about everyone that armed conflict is not a good way to settle differences. And by 1975, America finally started to realize that looking your enemy square in the face was most likely to lead you to a reflection of yourself.

Web:
http://www.faqs.org/faqs/vietnam/
http://www.historyoftheworld.com/soquel/vietwar.htm
http://www.shss.montclair.edu/english/furr/vietnam.html

Usenet:
alt.war.vietnam
soc.history.war.vietnam

Listserv Mailing List:
List Name: vwar-l
Subscribe to: listserv@listserv.acsu.buffalo.edu

Vikings

The Vikings were a seafaring people from Scandinavia, who flourished from the eighth to tenth century. By the late 700s, the Viking people were beginning to feel the effects of overpopulation and internal dissention. These problems, coupled with a cultural propensity for adventure and trade, started the Vikings on a long course of conquest, settlement and plundering that eventually led them as far abroad as the coasts of Europe, the British Isles, Greenland and even parts of America. In time, the Viking warriors were repulsed by the kingdoms of Sweden, Denmark and Norway (established after the introduction of Christianity), as well as the rise of strong European states. Today, the Vikings are remembered for their rich legacy: myths, legends and traditions.

Web:
http://www.control.chalmers.se/vikings/

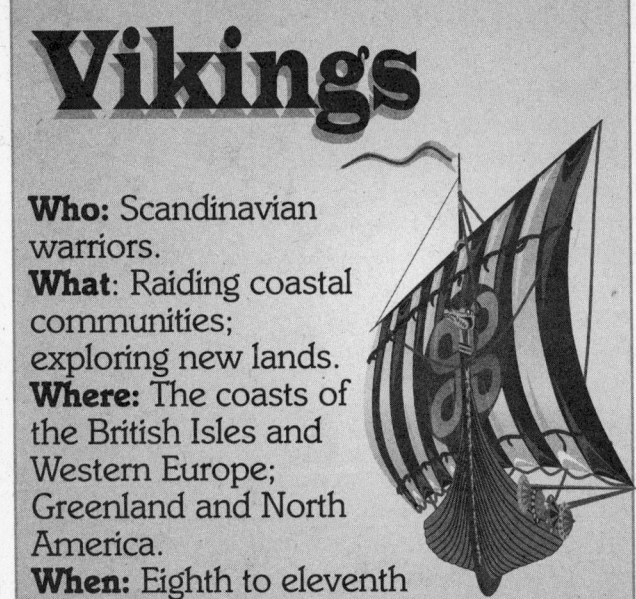

Vikings

Who: Scandinavian warriors.
What: Raiding coastal communities; exploring new lands.
Where: The coasts of the British Isles and Western Europe; Greenland and North America.
When: Eighth to eleventh centuries
Why: Overpopulation and dissension at home; quest for trade and adventure.
What stopped them: Introduction of Christianity into Scandinavia; creation of kingdoms in Norway, Denmark and Sweden; European states became strong enough to repel invaders.

War

Let's face it, war has been given a bum rap. Okay, so lots of people die, and many more suffer in horrible ways. Yes, families are broken up, and people are changed for the worse permanently. And, I guess, it is true that all kinds of property is damaged and destroyed, and huge amounts of money and resources are funneled away from socially productive uses and into a military machine. But are these necessarily *negative* things? Listen to some of the war discussion on Usenet, and check out the vast amount of war-related material on the Web. Then make up your own mind.

Web:
http://www.cfcsc.dnd.ca/links/milhist/

Usenet:
soc.history.war.misc

World War I

World War I, also called the Great War, took place from 1914 to 1918. The war was fought between the Allies (principally England, France, Russia and, from 1917, the United States), and the Central Powers (Germany, Austria-Hungary and Turkey). The main causes of the war were the ambitions of the German Empire as well as the excessive nationalism of the European nations, especially within the Austro-Hungarian Empire. The spark that started the hostilities occurred on June 28, 1914, when the Archduke Francis Ferdinand, heir to the Austro-Hungarian throne, was assassinated at Sarajevo by a Serbian nationalist. Within weeks, Europe was involved in a war which would not end until November 11, 1918. In spite of the fact that there were no decisive battles, World War I was one of the bloodiest wars in history. In a four and a half year period, 10 million people were killed and more than 20 million were wounded. At the time, the Great War was looked upon as the war to end all wars. (My paternal grandfather, by the way, was a soldier in the Austro-Hungarian army. In 1916, he was captured by the Russians and sent to Russia as a prisoner of war to work on a farm. While there, he met and fell in love with the young woman who was to become my grandmother.)

Web:
http://info.ox.ac.uk/departments/humanities/rose/war.html
http://www.lib.byu.edu/~rdh/wwi/
http://www.pitt.edu/~novosel/ww1.html
http://www.worldwar1.com/

Listproc Mailing List:
List Name: **wwi-l**
Subscribe to: **listproc@raven.cc.ukans.edu**

World War II

World War II was, by far, the most important conflict of the twentieth century. The war took place from 1939 to 1945, and was fought between the Allies (England, France, Russia, the United States and other countries) and the Axis (Germany, Italy and Japan). The main causes of World War II were the debilitating peace treaties forced on Germany after World War I, the economic suffering of the Great Depression of the 1930s, and the rise of totalitarian regimes in Germany, Italy and Japan. The German leader, Adolph Hitler, spent years building a military dictatorship and, on September 1, 1939, invaded Poland, whereupon England and France declared war on Germany. On December 7, 1941, the United States entered the war, after the U.S. naval base at Pearl Harbor, Hawaii, was bombed by Japan. The war in Europe ended on May 7, 1945, with the surrender of Germany. The war in the Pacific ended in August 14, 1945, shortly after the U.S. dropped atomic bombs on Hiroshima and Nagasaki, Japan. World War II involved every major power in the world, and was the most expensive war in history. In the U.S. alone, the cost was $816,300,000,000 (in 1967 dollars), more than twice as much as the combined cost of the Vietnam War, the Korean War, World War I, the Civil War and the Spanish-American War ($407,100,000,000).

Web:
http://earthstation1.simplenet.com/wwii.html
http://www.grolier.com/wwii/wwii_mainpage.html

Usenet:
soc.history.war.world-war-ii

Listserv Mailing List:
List Name: **wwii-l**
Subscribe to: **listserv@listserv.acsu.buffalo.edu**

Does your country have too much money? Are there too many young men with ambition who have a lot to contribute to society? Is everybody bored with peace and quiet? Why not have a WAR?

(Maybe if you're lucky, Steven Spielberg will make a movie of it afterward.)

World War II Propaganda Posters

Have you ever wondered what would inspire thousands and thousands of people to voluntarily march off to a big war far from home? Here's one of the answers: massive government propaganda. Examine these posters that were commissioned by government agencies to stir up the patriotism and sentiment of the American people during World War II. The posters, which are beautifully crafted (some by famous artists such as Norman Rockwell and Thomas Hart Benton), encourage men and women to enlist in the armed services, women to join the work force, and everyone to work hard, conserve resources, and keep secrets from the enemy.

Web:
http://www.library.nwu.edu/govpub/collections/wwii-posters/
http://www.openstore.com/posters/
http://www.si.edu/nmah/ve/victory/vichome.htm

HOBBIES

Audio Talk and General Discussion

A real audio system will make your living room windows bulge. Take the squeak out of your tweeter and the growl out of your woofer with a few helpful hints from the folks who know audio. High-fidelity, high-end, and professional audio are some of the topics covered.

Usenet:
rec.audio
rec.audio.high-end
rec.audio.marketplace
rec.audio.misc
rec.audio.pro
rec.audio.tubes

Drums and Marching

You've seen those rowdy children who sit in the middle of the kitchen floor and beat pots and pans together. What you may not know is that these very same children grow up to be in the drum corps, where they can make lots of noise and people praise them instead of sending them to their rooms. Join high-spirited marching bands as they talk tech and tell the world why their group is better than your group.

Usenet:
rec.arts.marching.drumcorps
rec.arts.marching.misc

Drums and Stuff

You may not know it, but there are a whole lot of people who march to someone else's drummer. Drum corps competition is one of America's fastest growing leisure time activities. What better way could anyone find to spend a sunny weekend afternoon.

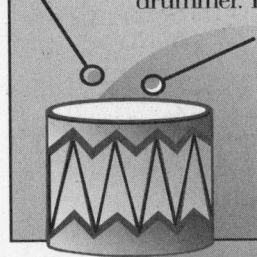

Gold Prospecting

Gold has, since antiquity, had a profound effect on people, often affecting their behavior to the point of irrationality. To a scientist, gold has some unique properties. Among the metals, gold is the most malleable (easily shaped) and ductile (able to be stretched). Compared to other common materials, gold is very dense (19.2 times as dense as water), an excellent electrical conductor, and will not rust, corrode or tarnish. For example, when a treasure of gold coins is recovered from a sunken ship, the coins are as bright and shiny as the day they were minted, even if they were immersed in sea water for hundreds of years. Which brings us to the more interesting properties of gold. It can make otherwise normal human beings act like complete loonies. True, gold is valuable, but not as valuable as, say, platinum (which is actually denser). And there are other precious metals (silver, palladium and rhodium) that are also important enough to be commonly traded as commodities. However, the allure of gold is unmatched in the psychology of mankind. Would you like to explore this irrational craving firsthand? You can. Here are some resources to help you get started with recreational gold prospecting. Start small, and with perseverance, you may soon work yourself up to fully qualified fanatic. In the meantime, you can have a lot of fun.

Web:
http://onlinether.com/prospect.htm
http://www.klws.com/gold/gold.html

Usenet:
alt.mining.recreational

HOBBIES

Graphology

Take a look at a handwritten letter. If the lines of writing slant upwards to the right, the person who wrote them was happy and in a good mood. But if the lines slant downward, it is a sign of depression. How much of graphology (the study of handwriting analysis) is valid? Probably more than you think, but less than you might want. Check for yourself and make up your own mind.

Web:
http://www.graphology-l.com/
http://www.hy.com/

Majordomo Mailing List:
List Name: **graphology-l**
Subscribe to: **majordomo@graphology.org**

Guns

On the Net you can get into all sorts of discussions and information about shooting sports, training, personal defense, gun laws, weaponry, and other topics related to firearms in general. And before you get on your high horse about weapons and gun control, I want you to remember that it isn't guns that kill people: it's bullets traveling at high velocity.

Web:
http://www.recguns.com/

Usenet:
rec.guns

Hobby Resources

We are all born with a particular combination of talents and aptitudes. Throughout our lives, we must use our inborn aptitudes or we become frustrated and dissatisfied. Life works well when our work (or school work) requires us to use all our aptitudes. For many people, however, this is not the case, and for this reason, hobbies are important. By using the talents that would otherwise be neglected, our hobbies help us balance our lives and feel an ongoing sense of satisfaction. If your life seems to be missing something, maybe a hobby is what you need.

Web:
http://www.craftsearch.com/Hobby/links.html
http://www.hobbyworld.com/
http://www.kalama.com/~mariner/qserhobby.htm

Juggling

I can juggle three oranges. So when I tell you that juggling is a great way to make friends and influence people, you know I'm telling the truth. Join the jugglers and learn how to keep none of your eggs in one basket.

Web:
http://www.juggling.org/

Usenet:
rec.juggling

Kites and Kiting Resources

Did you know that in Thailand, kiting is a major sporting event with teams, rules and even umpires? Kiting competition involves fighting between kites that are controlled by teams of up to twenty players. Whether you are a serious kiter or just like to fly kites for fun, these Web sites will have something for you. Find kite reviews, stories, tips on flying, general information, event guides, and even graphic images of single, dual, and quadline kites. When the wind isn't blowing, stay home and talk about kites on Usenet or IRC.

Web:
http://www.kfs.org/kites/
http://www.latrobe.edu.au/Glenn/KiteSite/Kites.html
http://www.mathcs.emory.edu/~kml/kites/kites.html
http://www.win.tue.nl/win/cs/fm/pp/kites/

Usenet:
rec.kites

IRC:
#kites

Letter Writing

One of the most cultivated, stylish and rewarding ways to spend your time is by writing personal letters. Thanks to the telephone, and now email, the art of letter writing is not practiced as much as it used to be. Still, there are people who care about the forgotten arts, and one of them is my chief researcher Wendy Murdock. Wendy has created a wonderful Web site devoted to letter writing, where you will find information about letters, diaries and journals. Spend even a few moments here, and you will want to start writing letters yourself. What better way to maintain a relationship while demonstrating your elegance and erudition?

Web:
http://www.wendy.com/letterwriting/

HOBBIES 379

My Trip to Kite Land

The other night, I was researching kites on the Internet.

However, it was so late and I was so tired, that it was all I could do to drag myself to bed, where I fell asleep immediately.

All of a sudden, I found myself in Kite Land, flying around a wonderful blue sky, zooming from one small fluffy white cloud to another. Within a few minutes, I was joined by a large flock of brightly colored kites, who led me through a tunnel into a mountain cavern where the King of Kite Land sat on a splendid throne.

"Welcome visitor," he said. "You are my honored guest." He wagged his tail and a servant brought out a large covered tray. "You will join me in a feast," said the King of Kite Land. The servant removed the cover of the tray, revealing the largest marshmallow I had ever seen.

For a good half hour, the King and I gorged on marshmallow. Finally he said, "The feast is over. You must now leave Kite Land," whereupon I suddenly woke up in my own bed, my stomach full of marshmallow and my mind spinning from my wonderful trip to Kite Land.

Now, if I could only find my pillow.

Living History

If your domestic life seems a bit mild, spice it up by joining the living history buffs who find delight in reenacting historical periods or events. After all, just because you weren't there doesn't mean you have to be left out.

Web:
http://nemesis.cybergate.net/~civilwar/
http://www.livinghistory.org/

Usenet:
alt.history.living
soc.history.living

Magic

Even after seeing the cut-up tie trick or the lady and the tiger a hundred times, you still can't figure them out. Brush up on your magic and learn some trade secrets. Learn how to make your little brother disappear or how to change that pesky IRS auditor into a pen and pencil set. You don't have to sell your soul to the devil, you just have to be more clever than the rest of us.

Web:
http://www.allmagicguide.com/
http://www.onramp.net/~pulcher/faqs/magic.html

Usenet:
alt.magic

Model Building

Having your own airplane, train or rocket is a big hassle. It costs a lot to maintain, and your wife (or mother) probably won't let you keep it in the garage. Much better to stick with scale models—they are a lot more economical and easier to manage. If you like building and enjoying models, there are a number of Usenet discussion groups in which you will enjoy participating. For information about supplies and techniques, I have selected a few Web sites to help you.

Web:
http://140.118.103.11/modelhome.htm
http://www.clever.net/dfk/modelling/modelling.html
http://www.fn.net/~downen/

Usenet:
rec.models.freeflight
rec.models.railroad
rec.models.rc
rec.models.rc.air
rec.models.rc.helicopter
rec.models.rc.land
rec.models.rc.misc
rec.models.rc.water
rec.models.rockets
rec.models.scale

Happy 25th birthday to the Internet.

380 HOBBIES

> You are what you think.

Nudity

Naturists are cool because they never have to iron their clothes. Sense the freedom and vitality of the human body unfettered by fabric. Nudists and naturists discuss the meaning, the legality, and the public's opinion of being naked. If you are looking for a hot game of strip poker, you are bound to be disappointed.

Web:
http://www.cybernude.com/

Usenet:
rec.nude

Puppetry

Like to be in control? Maybe you should take up puppetry as a safe outlet. Get information about puppets, puppeteers and puppet troupes. Read about the Puppeteers of America organization, see a list of festivals and guilds, or read about the history of puppetry. For those people who like to also work with their hands, there are patterns for making paper and cloth puppets. The mailing list is for performers and historians to discuss history and theory of puppet performance, tradition and innovation.

Web:
http://www.sagecraft.com/puppetry/

Usenet:
rec.arts.puppetry

Majordomo Mailing List:
List Name: **puptcrit**
Subscribe to: **majordomo@lists.village.virginia.edu**

Look What I Found on the Net...

```
Newsgroup: rec.nude
Subject: Birdwatching and Nude Beaches

> I'm really disappointed in the response to my original post
> regarding this subject.  I had thought Nudists were more
> open-minded but it sounds like I was incorrect.
>
> I had no desire to put my binoculars on any "birds with
> nipples on their heads".  I just wanted to go about my
> business and let others go about theirs.  I had no idea
> I was at a CO [clothing optional] beach, I was in fact on a
> non-CO part of the beach.  The birds happened to be on the
> CO part.
>
> What then?  Do I leave the beach or else get labeled a
> "sicko"?

...The problem is many nudists have had problems with beach
creeps wielding binoculars.  Binoculars tend to create
suspicion...

...I think if you approached the nudists and asked if the
binoculars bothered them, and you appeared legitimate (say,
with a birder's guidebook in hand, or if a female was in your
group), most nudists would say "No problem".
```

Puzzles

What's a six-letter word for the best place to participate in a discussion over the Net? Drive your friends wild with an endless supply of puzzles, quizzes and problems. Open yourself up for a little brain teasing, or be merciless and create a puzzle that hardly anyone can solve. (!tenesU :rewsnA)

Web:
http://www.win.tue.nl/cs/ooti/students/robvg/puzzle/

Usenet:
rec.puzzles
rec.puzzles.crosswords

Railroad

Who's been working on the railroad, all the live-long day? And what has Dinah been doing in the kitchen? Join the railroad fanatics and discuss real and model trains.

Web:
http://www.rrhistorical.com/nmra/nmralink.html
http://www.steamlocomotive.com/

Usenet:
alt.models.railroad.ho
misc.transport.rail.americas
misc.transport.rail.australia-nz
misc.transport.rail.europe
misc.transport.rail.misc
rec.railroad

Listserv Mailing List:
List Name: **railroad**
Subscribe to: **listserv@cunyvm.cuny.edu**

Roller Coasters

You are utterly terrified, screaming. Your heart is pounding and you think you might lose your cookies at any moment. You are on a roller coaster and, as scary as the ride seems, the whole thing is over much too soon. You tell yourself you can take it or leave it, but soon you are an addict. Don't worry, you are not alone. There are frenzied roller coaster fans all over the world.

Web:
http://coasters.eb.com/
http://www.joyrides.com/
http://www.lifthill.com/
http://www.thrillride.com/

Usenet:
rec.roller-coaster

Scrapbooks

Scrapbooks are cool, that's what I have to say. The present slips into the past so quickly and easily that preserving those special memories in a scrapbook is an effort that will repay you time and again. Here are some resources, created by scrapbook fanciers, that will give you ideas and tips for a scrapbook of your own.

Web:
http://www.homeandcrafts.com/
http://www.scrapbooking.com/
http://www.teleplex.net/krystalp/scraplink.htm

Majordomo Mailing List:
List Name: **sb**
Subscribe to: **majordomo@mlists.net**

Society for Creative Anachronism

Step back in time to the Middle Ages, where chivalry lives and everyone's lives are ordered by the rising and setting of the sun. Watch people dress up in metal and hit each other with sticks. Experience the grace and beauty of period costuming. Discover the festivity of a real medieval feast. Members and friends of the SCA discuss how it feels to live life in the modern Middle Ages.

Web:
http://www.sca.org/

Usenet:
alt.heraldry.sca
rec.heraldry
rec.org.sca

The Society for Creative Anachronism is all about living simply, using the tools and customs from a bygone era. See how much fun it can be living in the Middle Ages with an Internet account.

Treasure Hunting

Treasure is good. Imagine a great fantasy scenario in which you are walking along the beach and stumble across a barnacle-encrusted chest. You break it open and out tumble thousands of gold coins. Then a thousand federal agents come racing toward you waving paper and red tape. Wait, strike that last part. This is a fantasy. If you like treasure hunting, these are great places to start.

Web:
  http://www.iwl.net/customers/norman/linkog1.htm
  http://www.onlinether.com/

Usenet:
  alt.treasure.hunting

Unicycling

Forget the romance of a bicycle built for two. In fact, forget two wheels, period. Unicycling may not catch on as an energy-saving way to commute to work, but it sure is fun. Unicycling enthusiasts have put together a FAQ list, mailing list, pictures and animation. Now, if they could only come up with a unicycle built for two.

Web:
  http://www.unicycling.org/

Majordomo Mailing List:
  List Name: **unicycling**
  Subscribe to: **majordomo@winternet.com**

HOLIDAYS AND CELEBRATIONS

Birthday Calendar

What do Frank Zappa, Benjamin Disraeli, Kurt Waldheim, Joseph Stalin, Heinrich Boll, Jane Fonda and Harley Hahn all have in common? We were all born on the same day (December 21). No matter which day you want to celebrate, there are lots of famous people with the same birthday, and now you can find out who they are and why they are famous. Interesting fact: Philip Gosse (1810-1888) was the inventor of the institutional aquarium. My cat, The Little Nipper (1991-) also likes fish. And they were both born on April 6. Is that cosmic or what?

Web:
  http://www.eb.com/lives/cal1.html

Usenet:
  alt.happy.birthday.to.me

Christmas

Christmas, as we celebrate it, is a mixture of traditions from a variety of cultures. Traditionally, Christians celebrate the day, December 25, as the birthday of Christ. However, this date was chosen in the fourth century by Pope Julius I, perhaps as a replacement for the pagan festival that celebrated the winter solstice. (There is no direct evidence, even in the bible, describing the time of the year at which Christ was born.) Even before this time, the midwinter season had been marked by festivals, such as the Roman's Saturnalia, which were known for their merrymaking. Other traditions were developed throughout the years. For example, singing carols (Christmas songs), hanging mistletoe and exchanging gifts are all English traditions; the Christmas tree comes from medieval Germany; and the idea of a jolly Santa Claus was first popularized in 19th century New York City, where the English community adapted him from the Dutch Saint Nicholas.

Web:
  http://www.christmas.com/
  http://www.merry-christmas.com/
  http://www.santas.net/

Usenet:
  alt.yule.log

Easter

Whether your idea of Easter is waking up early to go to church or lying in bed waiting for a bunny to deliver your chocolate egg, the Net can help you celebrate properly. Enjoy learning about the history of Easter and its traditions. You will also find a lot of other enjoyable resources such as special Easter recipes. (My favorite is Scrambled Chocolate Easter Egg.)

Web:
  http://www.kidsdomain.com/holiday/easter/
  http://www.night.net/easter/
  http://www.njwebworks.com/easter/

Happy birthday.

HOLIDAYS AND CELEBRATIONS

Entertainment and Party Ideas

Whose bright idea was it to give this party in the first place? You are a nervous wreck. What if nobody comes? What if everybody comes, but nobody has fun? How do you break the ice? The host and hostess are supposed to be cool and graceful under pressure, so before the party check the Net for great ideas on games, get-to-know-you exercises, songs, and other ways to have fun at parties. People will be talking about your party for weeks.

Web:
http://members.aol.com/yourparty/ptylink.htm
http://users.vmicro.com/scrappy/parties/parties.htm
http://www.party411.com/
http://www.partymakers.com/

Need some party games? Check the Net for ideas.

Halloween

Halloween, October 31, is a holiday celebrated in the United States, Canada and the British Isles. The principle tradition is for children to wear costumes and go door to door in their neighborhood collecting treats and playing pranks. For older people, Halloween is an excuse to have parties and be as ghoulish as possible. The Net is a great source of ideas for how to celebrate. If you join the mailing list, a month or so before the holiday you will read lots of great ideas to enhance your Halloween experience.

Web:
http://www.bconnex.net/~mbuchana/realms/halloween/
http://www.benjerry.com/halloween
http://www.gamesdomain.com/tigger/halloween/halloween.html
http://www.gothic.net/darkside/dhaunt.html

Usenet:
alt.halloween.boo

Listserv Mailing List:
List Name: halloween-l
Subscribe to: listserv@netcom.com

Hanukkah

Hanukkah, or Chanukah, is an eight-day Jewish holiday celebrated in the winter. The purpose of Hanukkah is to commemorate the victory of the Maccabees (a group of ancient Jews) over their oppressors in the year 167 B.C. Hanukkah traditions include lighting candles in a special candleholder called a menorah and enjoying special foods such as, my favorite, latkes (potato pancakes).

Web:
http://www.caryn.com/holiday-chan.html
http://www.ort.org/ort/hanukkah/title.htm
http://www.virtual.co.il/city_services/holidays/chanukah/

Hindu Festivals

India, which is largely Hindu, has many different festival days. This is because Hindus worship many different gods, goddesses, saints and gurus. In addition, India is a big country and there are a large number of local and regional celebrations. I have chosen these Web sites to give you an overview of many Hindu festivals. Even if you are not Hindu, I bet you will find it interesting to read about these special days and how they are celebrated.

Web:
http://www.hindunet.org/festivals/
http://www.meadev.gov.in/culture/festival/festival.htm

Holiday Suicide Talk and General Discussion

Holidays can be stressful and depressing, so it is not surprising that suicides increase during the holiday season. This discussion group is devoted to the problems that lead to being sad while the rest of the world is celebrating. But don't feel you have to be suicidal to participate—it's okay if you just want to complain.

Usenet:
alt.suicide.holiday

HOLIDAYS AND CELEBRATIONS

Is There a Santa Claus?

Is there really a Santa Claus? Well... sort of, maybe, well... you know. Okay, Santa Claus may not be a real person, but what about as a metaphor? Is the idea of Santa Claus still important and meaningful? About a hundred years ago, a young girl sent a letter to a New York City newspaper, asking whether or not there really was a Santa Claus. The question was answered in an editorial ("...Yes, Virginia, there is a Santa Claus..."), which is trotted out every year at Christmas time in a seasonal fit of nostalgia. I have put the original essay on my Web site, along with my own answer to Virginia. Take look at both essays, and see what you think.

Web:
  http://www.harley.com/santa-claus/

Kwanzaa

Kwanzaa is an African-American holiday created in 1966 by Maulana Karenga, a Black Studies scholar. Kwanzaa is a seven-day festival, celebrated just after Christmas, from December 26 through January 1 (although it is not associated with any religion). Karenga's goal in creating Kwanzaa was to establish a set of traditions that would allow African-Americans to enjoy a festival of their own, firmly based on their cultural heritage. Today, Kwanzaa is growing in popularity and is celebrated not only in the U.S., but around the world.

Web:
  http://www.bluemountain.com/eng/seasonal/
     kwanzaa.html
  http://www.globalindex.com/kwanzaa/
  http://www.melanet.com/kwanzaa/

Witty saying goes here.

Mardi Gras

In the Christian church, the holiday of Easter is preceded by Lent, a 40-day period from Ash Wednesday to Easter Sunday, which is observed as a season for fasting and penitence. The day before the beginning of Lent is called Shrove Tuesday. Many people traditionally use this day to feast, in preparation for Lent. Thus, Shrove Tuesday is also called Mardi Gras, which means "Fat Tuesday" in French. In many places around the world, the days leading up to Mardi Gras are celebrated as a large carnival, lasting a week or more. Among the most celebrated carnivals are those of New Orleans and Rio de Janeiro. Such carnivals involve non-stop music and dancing, and lots and lots of fun. If you think you can stand this much applied hedonism, use the Net to check out the Mardi Gras carnival closest to you.

Web:
  http://www.alltoys.com/mg1.html
  http://www.fattuesday.com/
  http://www.neworleans.net/carnpages/
     carngloss.html
  http://www.usacitylink.com/mardigr/

Look What I Found on the Net...

```
Newsgroup: alt.suicide.holiday
Subject: Have you ever considered death?

>> I think that death pays for itself in the long run.

> I'm not saying this to insult you or tell you what to do or
> anything, but, if you really believe that, why haven't you
> made a purchase?

Problem is, as I see it, there's no try-before-you-buy plan, and
scant chance of a refund if you are unhappy with the purchase...

It's just a case of "caveat emptor".
```

HOLIDAYS AND CELEBRATIONS

Pagan Holidays

Paganism is a term used to describe a wide variety of spiritual beliefs and customs, loosely based on ancient nature religions, particularly those of ancient Europe. There is no central pagan authority—practicing pagans more or less do what they want—however, many pagans celebrate eight special days called the Sabbats. They are Candlemas, Spring Equinox, Beltane, Summer Solstice, Lammas, Autumn Equinox, Halloween and Yule.

Web:
  http://home.ici.net/~ariadne/holydays.html
  http://www.circlesanctuary.org/pholidays/
    PaganHolidays.html
  http://www.eoe-magical.org/days.html
  http://www.magicklass.com/fantasy/calendar/
  http://www.microlink.net/~shanem/holidays.htm
  http://www.witchesweb.com/weeloyr.html

Reminder Services

Boy is my life easy now!

Reminder Services

Before the Internet was developed, people would forget important dates all the time, leading to war, financial ruin and broken romances.

Now, however, we have Internet Reminder Services. Just register your special days and the Net will remind you automatically.

Pretty soon your life will become so easy, you will have to look around for new challenges.

Reminder Services

I know how you feel. You *would* have sent a present for your Aunt Riva's birthday, if only it hadn't slipped your mind. Next year, don't get caught again. Register with an Internet reminder service, and you will be sent email automatically, just in time to help you remember birthdays, anniversaries and other special days. (Hint: My birthday is December 21st, and money is always in good taste.)

Web:
  http://calendar.stwing.upenn.edu/
  http://thor.he.net/~nelly/remind/login.htm
  http://www.candor.com/reminder/
  http://www.rememberto.com/

Thanksgiving

The idea of an autumn celebration in which people give thanks is an ancient custom. After all, for an agricultural people, autumn is the season just after the harvest and if the harvest went well, there is good reason to be thankful. In America, tradition holds that the modern Thanksgiving holiday is descended from a celebration held by the Pilgrims (early settlers) in 1621. In 1863, U.S. President Abraham Lincoln set aside the last Thursday of November to commemorate the feast given by the Pilgrims. In 1939, the head of the Federated Department Stores convinced President Franklin Roosevelt that a longer Christmas shopping season would be good for the economy. The president moved Thanksgiving to the fourth Thursday in November where it has remained ever since. (Note: In Canada, Thanksgiving is celebrated 11 months after the American holiday, on the second Monday in October.) American Thanksgiving has its own well-defined traditions: food (including turkey, cranberry sauce, stuffing, potatoes, yams, pumpkin pie and gravy), two days off work, more food, watching football games on TV, more food, local parades, and even more food. The week after Thanksgiving is celebrated by the eating of leftovers. Here are some Thanksgiving-oriented resources to help you enjoy this holiday, including historical notes and the all-important advice on how to cook a turkey.

Web:
  http://www.bham.wednet.edu/thanks.htm
  http://www.media3.com/plymouth/thanksgiving.htm
  http://www.night.net/thanksgiving/

HOLIDAYS AND CELEBRATIONS

Valentine's Day

Valentine's Day, February 14, is the day when we honor that special someone in our life. The tradition of sending romantic gifts and cards is a modern one. The holiday is actually named after St. Valentine who, in the 3rd century A.D., was martyred during the persecution of Christians by the Roman emperor Claudius II. As we celebrate it today, the general idea of Valentine's Day for women is to honor the men who are special in their life with an appropriate gift or pledge of affection. The general idea for men is to try to remember to send something on time so as to not end up like an early Christian martyr.

Web:
http://user.mc.net/~urwhatur/lynval.htm
http://www.usacitylink.com/cupid/
http://www.valentine.com/

Weddings

Don't let your wedding be a remake of Father of the Bride (or the Bay of Pigs). On the Net you can learn what is proper and what is not. Find out shortcuts from folks who have done this before (or again and again). Topics cover a wide range, such as invitations, RSVPs, dresses, parties, garters, underclothes, and much more.

Web:
http://www.bridalplanner.com/
http://www.jmts.com/wedding/services.htm
http://www.weddingcentral.com/

Usenet:
alt.wedding
soc.couples.wedding

World Birthday Web

Come here to find out if anybody you know on the Net is having a birthday. Send them greetings and well wishes. Or you can add your own birthday, so you can get birthday email from friends and total strangers.

Web:
http://www.boutell.com/birthday.cgi/

World Holiday Guides

On the Internet, every day is a holiday. Check right now and find something to celebrate. Today, as I write this, it is Women's Day in South Africa and National Day in Singapore. This resource will come in handy when you need to take a day off. For example, let's say it's November 28 and you don't feel like working. Check with the Net and you will be able to tell your boss, in good conscience, that you just don't feel comfortable working on the Albanian National Holiday.

Web:
http://www.jpmorgan.com/cgi-bin/HolidayCalendar

HOMES

Apartments

Searching for an apartment can be a lot of fun if you are living in a town with a high vacancy rate. ("Well, I'll think about taking the place, but you'll have to paint it, replace the appliances, and lower the rent.") In many locations, however, vacancy rates are low, landlords swank around like princes ("If you are interested in renting, you can fill out an application for an application."), and you need all the help you can get. These Web sites have information on apartments for many locations in the U.S. Some sites let you specify what you would like—location, price, size, pets—and then show you the listings for your target area. (One of my researchers lives in an apartment not two miles from Bill Gates's house, and this is how she found her place.)

Web:
http://www.apartmentlife.com/
http://www.aptsforrent.com/
http://www.rent.net/

**Have a laugh.
Check out "Comics".**

HOMES 387

Ask the Builder

Okay, so you bought a house. In the words of the banker and real estate agent who encouraged you to go deep into debt, you are now a "homeowner". Here is a secret. It won't be long until you find out that it is actually the home that owns you. And, within a short time, you will be devoting as much energy to fixing a faucet and replacing a cabinet as you used to put into choosing which wine to have with dinner. But never fear, help is available. Here is a library of answers to commonly asked home maintenance questions. After all, just because all your weekend time is spent fixing things you never used to care about doesn't mean you can't know what you are doing.

Web:
http://www.askbuild.com/cgi-bin/library

Buying and Selling Houses

So you want to buy a house? In the old days, real estate agents would do some research and find places for you to visit. The agent would pick you up, drive you from place to place, and entertain you along the way with funny stories about escrow officers and title searches. Not any more. Now you need to do a lot of the finding-your-dream-home work for yourself. However, the Net is here to help, and you will be pleased to know that there are many, many real estate listings available online. A lot of people are finding houses on the Net.

Web:
http://www.house-hunting.com/
http://www.realtor.com/

Decorating a Country Home?
Need ideas? Like to look at pictures?
Want to see what other people have done?
Try the Net.

The Net is on *your* side.

Decorating a Country Home

Decorating a country home has its own special challenges. You are probably starting with an old house, a house that has many hidden traps and idiosyncrasies. What would be a relatively minor task in a newer house—such as replacing a cabinet—can turn into a big project faster than you can say "unforeseen lateral expansion". In addition, you probably want to have your house blend well with the nearby scenery and topography. Finally, there always seems to be so much to do, but only a limited amount of money in the decorating budget. If you have a country house—or if you simply like looking at them—you will enjoy this Web site containing lots of articles and pictures documenting how various country houses have been redecorated and renovated. Turning your country house into a showplace is not for the faint at heart. One of the people quoted in an article put it thus: "We have never stopped working on the place."

Web:
http://homearts.com/cl/toc/00cldec1.htm

Feng Shui

Feng Shui is an ancient tradition that involves the orientation and placement of objects and buildings. Originating in China, Feng Shui is now popular with people who are in search of a more spiritually harmonious living environment. The idea is to modify your home or working area according to certain principles, thereby enhancing your quality of life and good fortune. The name Feng Shui comes from the Chinese words for wind and water, representing the idea that one's living environment should be oriented and arranged so as to be in harmony with nature.

Web:
http://www.3dglobe.com/fs/
http://www.hawkfeather.com/fs/

Usenet:
alt.chinese.fengshui

Home Appliance Clinic

Appliances are great when they work. How happy life is when your washing machine actually washes, your dryer really dries, and your refrigerator knows how to stay cool. The best way to achieve such contentment is to choose good appliances in the first place (either new or used). If you are thinking of buying a home appliance, start by reading the knowledgeable words of advice at this Web site. And if something breaks, check here first, before you call for a repairman. Even if you don't want to fix the machine yourself, understanding the problem and the solution will go a long way toward helping you stay in control.

Web:

http://www.phoenix.net/~draplinc/

Home Environmental Hazards

If you spend much time watching TV or listening to the radio, you are bound to hear about home environmental hazards: radon, asbestos, lead, hazardous waste, contaminated water, formaldehyde and so on. It's enough to make you feel a tad uneasy. Is your home sweet home a castle of happiness, or a slow-but-sure death trap that will end up subjecting the members of your family to a slow, painful and expensive death? I understand your discomfort, and I know the cure. It's the same cure that always works in such cases. Find out the truth, so you can make informed decisions.

Web:

http://www.hsh.com/pamphlets/hazards.html

Home Front Tips

You're waiting for your wife or husband to get ready to leave the house, and you still have a few minutes to kill—not long enough to start a new project, but you don't want to sit around doing nothing. Here's what to do. Connect to the Home Front Web site and scan the list of home maintenance questions and answers. If you like puttering around the house, fixing and improving, I guarantee there will be something here to pique your interest. So sit down, find something interesting, and before you know it, you will hear a voice behind you saying, "Will you turn off that computer already? It's time to leave."

Web:

http://www.capitalonline.com/HFR2.html

When you own your own home, you are never far from the front lines. There's always something that needs to be fixed, serviced or replaced. Learn from the pros by reading the Home Front Tips.

Home Improvement

In the world of owning your own house, the words "home improvement" are a euphemism for making changes and then trying to get everything to work right. If you are thinking at all, even one tiny bit, about venturing into the world of repairs, remodeling or decorating, do not even move until you have spent a few hours reading on the Net.

Web:

http://www.homecentral.com/
http://www.housenet.com/
http://www.livinghome.com/
http://www.naturalhandyman.com/
http://www.todayshomeowner.com/

Home Improvement Encyclopedia

I have a great handyman named Larry. Larry can fix anything and he will keep working until he gets the job done right. The trouble is Larry is not available twenty-four hours a day, seven days a week, so when I'm stuck, I turn to the Net. This is one of my favorite home repair Web sites. What I like are the animations that show you how to perform particular tasks such as taking apart a faucet. If you are Larry, you already know how to do everything. If you are not Larry, you'll really appreciate this Web site.

Web:

http://www.bhglive.com/homeimp/docs/

Home Improvement Warehouse

Here is a Web site guaranteed to make you feel inadequate. For example, there is a wonderfully ambitious list of 10 important projects that you could be doing right now. (Sort of like Martha Stewart singing "If I Had a Hammer".) Or read the step-by-step instructions showing how to manage a major project (like putting in a new floor), and realize that some people actually know what they are doing. At the same time, you can't help but realize that just about anything major around the house is going to take more time, cost more money, and create more aggravation than you planned. Still, if you flounder around like an ignorant lummox, it can only be worse. Check with the experts before you start, and at least you'll have a chance.

Web:
http://www.lowes.com/

Home Repair

It's midnight and the shower is creating a tsunami in the upstairs bathroom. The emergency plumber is out on a hot date and can't stop by. What do you do? Find out on these home fix-it discussion forums where handy people talk about home improvement, repairs, electricity, plumbing and carpentry. These people really know their widgets, gadgets and whatchacallits.

Usenet:
alt.home.repair

Listserv Mailing List:
List Name: **homefix**
Subscribe to: **listserv@vm.ege.edu.tr**

House Talk and General Discussion

What did you ever do with your weekends before you bought a house? Don't you feel sorry for all those people who have nothing better to do than go out and have fun? Share your experiences involving hardwood floors, mortgages, roofing repairs, plumbing, carpeting, contractors, real estate agents, painting, ventilation systems, and all the other great ways to spend your all-too-brief time on planet Earth.

Usenet:
alt.tools.repair+advice
misc.consumers.house

Illustrated Tool Dictionary

It is well known in the home maintenance world that a man is only as good as his tools, and a neighbor is only as good as the tools he can lend you. This resource is great: an encyclopedia of tool information, written for a normal person. If it wasn't for this resource, you would be reduced to asking advice from the tool nerds who hang around the hardware store. You know the ones I mean. You find them at the hardware store on Saturday afternoons, standing around talking about reciprocating saws and spiral design auger bits. You have to wait patiently to get their attention. Then they make you feel like a goober when you ask a question, after which you have to listen to them dispense esoteric advice with a supercilious attitude that would put a stereo salesman to shame. Later, when you get home, you find out what they told you was all wrong anyway. Never again. From now on, the Net will take care of you. Check with this site *before* you go to the store.

Web:
http://www.homecentral.com/tools/

Look What I Found on the Net...

```
Newsgroup: misc.consumers.house
Subject: Too much house?

> Has anyone bought or rented a house and discovered that there was
> too much space for you?

I don't know if you're going to get much sympathy for your problems.
It is far easier to make a house smaller than to make it larger...
```

International Real Estate Digest

When you think about it, every spot on the planet Earth is real estate of some kind. Well, here is the Web site that expresses this philosophy exactly. The International Real Estate Digest is a colossal, well-organized guide to real estate everywhere. Lots and lots of stuff—you'll feel you've died and gone to real estate heaven. No matter where you want to buy or sell, start here.

Web:
http://www.ired.com/

Moving

Moving involves a lot more than just getting your possessions from one place to another. There are several bazillion details that have to be taken care of, any one of which has the potential of causing you a great amount of trouble if you forget about it. So don't depend purely on luck and the good graces of the universe. Let the Net help with your planning and your move will be as smooth as Napoleon's retreat from Moscow.

Web:
http://www.homefair.com/wizard/wizard.html
http://www.virtualrelocation.com/

Paint Estimator

It's bound to happen. You've taken on the weekend painting project and here it is Sunday night at midnight and you are still at it. The really annoying thing is that you have about two feet of wall space left to cover and you've run out of paint. If you had used the paint estimator, you would be tucked cozy into bed dreaming of freshly painted homes. All you had to do was enter in the dimensions of your room and the calculator would tell you exactly how much paint you needed to buy.

Web:
http://www.livinghome.com/livinghome/toolchest/paintcalc/lhpc0001-01.html

Pest Control

Would you like to find out how to make your home inhospitable to those tiny pests who just love to make themselves at home in your home? Well, home in on the Net, your pest control home away from home.

Web:
http://www.nj.com/yucky/getrid/
http://www.orkin.com/

Don't paint yourself into a corner. Use the Paint Estimator before you start.

Plumbing

Spend some time teaching yourself about the ins and outs of common household plumbing problems, and I guarantee you will be the most popular person on the block. After all, the neighbors may fawn over the guy who used to be a professional football player, or the fellow who can imitate a chicken laying an egg, but when the plumbing breaks, there is no one more in demand than someone who knows his pipes. Here are some great resources to help you understand plumbing: from the basics (such as how to change a washer or freshen up a garbage disposal) to advice on large ambitious projects involving construction, renovation and restoration.

Web:
http://www.plumbnet.com/
http://www.theplumber.com/faq.html

HOMES 391

Real Estate Talk and General Discussion

It's just like a Monopoly game, except you use real money and the bail is higher if you end up in jail. Learn tips on acquiring real estate: how to choose a good agent, perks for first-time homebuyers, and how to avoid the rental property blues.

Usenet:
  alt.real-estate-agents
  misc.invest.real-estate

REAL ESTATE REALITY

Isn't it great? All you have to do is spend some money and you can own your very own piece of an actual planet (Earth).

I love real estate because it brings out the best in people, and some of the best real estate people hang out in **misc.invest.real-estate**.

Remember, though, talking on Remember, though, talking on the Net is no substitute for experience: the smart way is to "walk the dirt, smell the dirt and feel the dirt". (Fortunately, there's no shortage of dirt.)

Tenant Net

Having a lousy landlord turns Home Sweet Home into Nightmare on Elm Street. Find out what your rights are on a variety of issues such as security deposits, pets, repairs, payment of rent and more. This site offers information on tenants' rights, limited referral and guidance, links to tenant advocacy groups, FAQs, text of rental and housing laws, and much more. Have Tenant Net on your bookmark list in case the big, bad wolf comes to huff and puff and blow your house in.

Web:
  http://www.tenant.net/

Toilet Repair and Maintenance

Okay, let's get this straight. Toilets are *not funny*. And when I tell you that this is the best tutorial about toilets on the Net, you are not to laugh. You are to proceed to this Web site immediately, and teach yourself more about toilets than most people learn in a lifetime. You will find lots and lots of useful information about toilet repair and maintenance. Learn how these devices work, how to fix them, and how to maintain them. If nothing else, be sure to read the emergency advice about what to do when the toilet overflows. (Read it now, *before* it happens.) At the very least, you'll save yourself some real money. At best, you'll find a brand new hobby.

Web:
  http://www.toiletology.com/

Wallpaper Calculator

Here's one of those conceptually simple tools that can very possibly save your life (and your marriage). Specify the dimensions of a room, including the doors and the windows, and this tool will calculate how many standard rolls of wallpaper you will need to cover the walls of the room. Hint from Harley: Buy at least one extra roll. Even if you don't use it immediately, it will come in handy later if you need to patch something.

Web:
  http://www.housenet.com/hi/planitright/calculators/wallpaperfrm.asp

Tenant Info
Do you rent a place to live? Check out Tenant Net for all kinds of important information. Be prepared *before* you sign the lease.

Woodworking

Wood is really a mass of plant tissue called xylem, formed within the plant from a thin layer (the cambrium) that lies between bark and the stem. Xylem has two primary functions: to conduct water throughout the plant and to provide structural support. Softwood comes from coniferous (evergreen) trees, and has a uniformly nonporous appearance. Hardwood comes from deciduous (leaf-losing) trees that produce xylem with a great many vessels, giving the wood a complex, non-uniform appearance. When wood is freshly cut, it contains a lot of moisture and, before it can be used, it must be dried (seasoned)—either in a kiln or by the action of the sun. This description, though accurate, fails to capture that magic inherent in a beautiful piece of wood. And talking about xylem and cambrium—though interesting to a botanist—doesn't even hint at the enormous utility of wood: a substance that is an integral part of just about every culture in the world. If you are one of the people who appreciate wood for what it is and what you can do with it, there are many useful resources on the Net. To get you started, here are some well-organized Web sites that will point you to a massive amount of woodworking and wood-related information. In addition, I have included a Web site that offers a summary of various woods and their properties. This will help identify and appreciate some of the more exotic varieties of wood that you would not normally see in a lumber yard. For discussion, you can talk on IRC, follow the ongoing give and take on Usenet or join a mailing list.

Web:
http://www.kiva.net/~rjbrown/w5/wood.html
http://www.theoak.com/
http://www.woodshop.net/wnlinks/wood_links.htm

Usenet:
rec.crafts.woodturning
rec.woodworking

Listserv Mailing List:
List Name: **woodwork-l**
Subscribe to: **listserv@listserv.indiana.edu**

Majordomo Mailing List:
List Name: **woodworking**
Subscribe to: **majordomo@theoak.com**

IRC:
#woodworking

HUMANITIES AND SOCIAL SCIENCES

Anthropology

Anthropologists study human beings: their origins and behavior, as well as their cultural, physical and social development. Here are some great collections of anthropological resources, suitable for students as well as serious researchers.

Web:
http://dizzy.library.arizona.edu/users/jlcox/first.html
http://www.nitehawk.com/alleycat/anth-faq.html

Usenet:
sci.anthropology
sci.anthropology.paleo

Listserv Mailing List:
List Name: **anthro-l**
Subscribe to: **listserv@american.edu**

Listserv Mailing List:
List Name: **anthro-l**
Subscribe to: **listserv@listserv.acsu.buffalo.edu**

Communications

Don't just talk—communicate. Can't? This'll help. Lotsa links here. Lotsa stuff for the ubiquitous communications student, as well as his or her teachers. Cool. (Although I think I really want to go into broadcasting.) Like, it's great. On the Web, nobody knows if you have nothing to say.

Web:
http://www.americancomm.org/
http://www.govst.edu/commcentral/

Should You Be a Communications Major?

If you want prestige, go to medical school.

If you want money, study business and finance.

If you want respect, become a nuclear physicist.

If you want intellectual stimulation, take philosophy or math.

But if you want prestige, and money, and respect, and intellectual stimulation...

HUMANITIES AND SOCIAL SCIENCES

Generation X

The term "Generation X" refers to the post-Baby Boomer Americans born between 1961 and 1981. (The name came from a book by Douglas Coupland.) Before they were named, nobody talked much about the Gen Xers. Now just about everyone has something to say. On the Net, you can visit Generation X Web sites, read a FAQ (frequently asked question list), and participate in a Usenet discussion group. Pretty soon, they'll have their own logo.

Web:
http://www.cs.caltech.edu/~adam/LEAD/genx.html

Usenet:
alt.society.generation-x

Listserv Mailing List:
List Name: **gen-x**
Subscribe to: **listserv@listserv.aol.com**

Humanities Resources

Here are some fabulous collections of resources relating to anthropology, theology, cultural studies, architecture, sociology, European studies, film and media, philosophy, languages, and many other area of the humanities. Truly, we may not all be scholars, but we can't blame the Net.

Web:
http://h-net2.msu.edu/
http://www.gu.edu.au/gwis/hub/hub.home.html

Usenet:
humanities.answers

The Humanities Hub

When you were a kid, you used to hang out at the playground.

When you were a teenager, you used to hang out at the mall.

When you were a student, you used to hang out at the cafeteria.

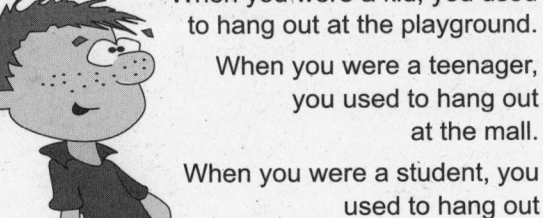

But now you're a social scientist. Time to start hanging out at the Humanities Hub.

Learn a new dance step in "Dance".

Leisure Studies

Leisure studies—often combined with recreation studies—is the examination of how people spend their leisure time. This is a huge discipline involving many different areas of study such as tourism, sports, outdoor recreation, parks and other public facilities, stress reduction, exercise, resource allocation, and so on. Rest assured, no matter what you do for fun, someone, somewhere, is studying it. If you are a leisure studies student or researcher, the Net has lots of resources to help you. In fact, using the Net to find the information you need will save you so much time, you won't know what to do with it all.

Web:
http://www.gu.edu.au/gwis/leis/services/lswp/linkfrme.htm

Listproc Mailing List:
List Name: **leisurenet**
Subscribe to: **listproc@gu.edu.au**

Listserv Mailing List:
List Name: **gleis-l**
Subscribe to: **listserv@uga.cc.uga.edu**

Listserv Mailing List:
List Name: **sprenet**
Subscribe to: **listserv@uga.cc.uga.edu**

Perseus Project

Do you feel nostalgic for the good old days of ancient Greece? Are you disgruntled and dissatisfied because you missed out on hearing the readings of epic poets and watching the original Olympics? Well, on the Net, you *can* live in the past. Check out this ancient Greek gathering place, and enjoy the art, archaeology and images.

Web:
http://www.perseus.tufts.edu/

Popular Culture

Just because something is popular doesn't necessarily mean it's good. However, some people enjoy going along with the crowd, and other people enjoy studying the people who enjoy going along with the crowd. No matter which category you fall into, I think you will enjoy these sites. One contains a great collection of resources for people who study the popular culture in a scholarly fashion. The other is an interesting encyclopedia-type reference to various persons, places and things in the popular culture.

Web:
   http://www.mcs.net/~zupko/popcult.htm
   http://www.pathfinder.com/altculture/

Population Studies

Population studies is the area of the social sciences dealing with such topics as population, demographics, ethnicity, migration, nuptiality (marriage), fertility, mortality, social mobility and distribution of wealth. Because of the heterogeneous nature of its subject matter, population studies is multi-disciplinary, drawing on a variety of sciences and social sciences.

Web:
   http://coombs.anu.edu.au/ResFacilities/
      DemographyPage.html
   http://popindex.princeton.edu/
   http://www.psc.lsa.umich.edu/library/
      resources.shtml

Social Science Resources

There are so many social science resources on the Net it's hard to know where to start, so I'll tell you: start here. Just visit these Web sites, select an area of study, and before you can say "This work was done in partial fulfillment of a Ph.D. thesis," you will be up to your cerebrum in enough information to please even the most demanding principal investigator.

Web:
   http://public-affairs.levitt.hamilton.edu/gambit/
      soc_links/
   http://www.vlib.org/SocialSciences.html

POPULAR CULTURE

I usually don't answer the phone while I am writing, but for some reason the machine didn't pick up.

"Uh... hello... you don't know me," she said, "but I wonder if you could email me something witty so I can graduate?"

"Say that again."

"I'm a student, and I've read all your books and I think they're great, and all I have to do is finish one last project for my course and I can graduate."

"What course?"

"Modern American Humorists Who Write Internet Books," she said.

I thought about it. "Must be an easy course."

"Independent study," she replied. "I chose it 'cause of the short reading list. So, can you help me?"

"What do you need?" I asked.

"I need to send you email and have you write back a witty message."

"No problem," I said.

"Great. Now I can finish my project and graduate."

"Congratulations. What's your degree?" I asked.

"Popular culture. I'm majoring in Dick Van Dyke with a minor in Lucy. Bye. Gotta go now."

Imagine that. A student studying my books in a college course. I have finally arrived.

Norman Mailer, eat your heart out.

HUMANITIES AND SOCIAL SCIENCES

Social Work

During the Great Depression, the United States government, along with private, state and local social organizations, began to help people who were in need of some type of assistance. This evolved into today's large network of people and agencies devoted to helping individuals and families who are facing poverty, alcoholism, drug abuse, and other physical, mental and social problems. If you are a social worker or a student of social work, here are some resources you will find useful. These sites have information about mailing lists, social work schools and organizations, resources for mental health care professionals, child abuse prevention, international social work, and much more.

Web:
http://theusc.csd.sc.edu/swan/
http://www.sc.edu/swan/listserv.html

> Even my cat likes the Net.

Sociology Resources

Sociology is the study of how people behave in groups. There are lots of sociology resources on the Net, and there are some places to start when you are looking for information. You'll find links will take you to institutions, specialized resources, related fields, and much more.

Web:
http://www.wcsu.ctstateu.edu/socialsci/socres.html
http://www.wilpaterson.edu/wpcpages/sch-hmss/sociology/newlinks.htm

Sociology Talk and General Discussion

We've all heard the rumors—that sociology is one of those fluffy topics that people are required to take in college. Well, I am here to tell you that it's not so. Get into the hard-core science of sociology, and talk down and dirty with people who know their people.

Usenet:
alt.sci.sociology

Look What I Found on the Net...

```
Newsgroup: alt.sci.sociology
Subject: Sociology of air conditioning

> ...I posted this for the benefit of someone who is doing a
> term paper on the sociology of air conditioning: thinking
> primarily of the change in social life, particularly leisure
>time social interaction, in the American South...

The urban planning crowd wants to bring back 1920-style
porches in the United States, but they totally ignore the
fact of air conditioning.  Porches were a way of getting out
of a hot summer house to catch the cool evening breeze.
Now we have air conditioners making the cool evening breeze
(and, of course, there is also television).

Most sociologists seem unaware that the term "urbanism", as
defined by Louis Wirth, has been reversed in the current
planning literature.  It originally meant segmented, brief,
transitory, and so forth — something to avoid.  Architectural
romantics call their movement New Urbanism, as if urbanism
were warm, long-lasting and coherent small-town life with
pre-air conditioning front porches.
```

HUMANITIES AND SOCIAL SCIENCES

U.S. National Endowment for the Humanities

The United States National Endowment for the Humanities (NEH) is a United States government agency that offers grants for projects in history, philosophy, languages and other areas of the humanities. If you are a humanities scholar, take a look at the NEH's Web site, where you can learn about the NEH and their grants, and find out how to apply for a grant of your own. Every year, the NEH awards millions of dollars. There is no reason why some of this money shouldn't be supporting your research.

Web:
   http://www.neh.fed.us/

Voice of the Shuttle

It's 2 AM and you are watching Star Trek with your best friend, when all of a sudden the need arises to check something at the Klingon Language Institute. Go to the Voice of the Shuttle, a huge collection of links and resources for students and researchers in the humanities. From Anthropology to Women's Studies, you'll find it here. (The Klingon Language Institute is under Linguistics.)

Web:
   http://humanitas.ucsb.edu/

HUMOR AND JOKES

Best of Usenet

Don't spend hours searching through thousands of Usenet discussion groups looking for the funny stuff. Someone has already done the dirty work for you. If you are in the market for humor, you can find lots of laughs with one-stop shopping by checking out the group that claims to have the best of what Usenet has to offer. The **alt.humor.best-of-usenet** group has the funny stuff and **alt.humor.best-of-usenet.d** is where you can talk about the funny stuff.

Usenet:
   alt.humor.best-of-usenet
   alt.humor.best-of-usenet.d

Blackout Box

Every time I visit the Blackout Box I end up laughing and laughing out loud. This Web site features crank phone calls made by a wonderful, talented actor. These recordings are, by far, the funniest such calls I have ever heard. If you need a good laugh, check out this site right now.

Web:
   http://www.blackout.com/

Comedy Talk and General Discussion

I love jokes, so I am encouraging everyone to choose comedy as a career. Sure, the world will have to make do with fewer new inventions, scientific discoveries and medical miracles, but we will all be laughing too hard to notice. Comedy is an addiction and when people are not listening to it or watching it, they are talking about it on Usenet.

Usenet:
   alt.comedy.british
   alt.comedy.british.blackadder
   alt.comedy.firesgn-thtre
   alt.comedy.improvisation
   alt.comedy.slapstick
   alt.comedy.slapstick.3-stooges
   alt.comedy.standup
   alt.comedy.vaudeville
   alt.tv.comedy-central

Complaint Letter Generator

I love this one. Just fill in the blanks, and, somewhere out on the Net, an anonymous computer program will create a customized fancy-shmancy letter of complaint just for you. I tried it just the other day and got a response that started as follows: "There are some comments I need to make regarding Monica..." (You know, I think I may have accidentally got someone else's letter.)

Web:
   http://www-csag.cs.uiuc.edu/individual/pakin/complaint/

HUMOR AND JOKES 397

Cruel Site of the Day

Humor isn't always pretty—but someone has to do it. The Cruel Site of the Day is one of the places you *must* know about. Every day (well, not every day, but most days... well, some days anyway) there is a new link to a bizarre site on the Net. The site might be serious, it might be a parody, or it might be so strange as to defy classification. What is always true, however, is that you are sure to find someone to laugh at. When you have some extra time, check out the Cruel Site archives ("Our Cruel Heritage") for some guaranteed bad-taste-meets-the-Net humor-in-a-box.

Web:
  http://www.cruel.com/

Cruel Site of the Day

It's true—just ask the kids on the playground.

Humor can be brutal.

But that doesn't relieve you of your moral obligation. You must laugh, at least once a day, even if it means being cruel.

Dumb Lists

Every now and then, we all have a need to read something dumb and funny. But what if you can't find the key to your sister's diary? Trust in the Net. When it comes to dumb and funny, you need never feel deprived.

Web:
  http://www.dumblists.com/

Fifty Fun Things for Non-Christians to Do in Church

If your mom makes you go to church and you just don't want to, here's a list of things you can do that will probably make her decide it's better for you to sleep in on Sunday mornings. There are fifty ideas, so you can do a different one every Sunday and you won't run out of new things for nearly a year.

Web:
  http://www.infidels.org/library/humor/church_fun.html

Funny People

Usenet has a whole set of discussion groups devoted to the worship and discussion of various famous people and their work. Humor, of course, is well represented. Join the disciples and discuss your favorite humorists.

Usenet:
  alt.comedy.laurel-hardy
  alt.comedy.marx-bros
  alt.comedy.paul-reubens
  alt.fan.bill-gates
  alt.fan.cecil-adams
  alt.fan.chris-elliott
  alt.fan.dave_barry
  alt.fan.dennis-miller
  alt.fan.goons
  alt.fan.jay-leno
  alt.fan.letterman
  alt.fan.mel-brooks
  alt.fan.monty-python
  alt.fan.penn-n-teller
  alt.fan.pratchett
  alt.fan.rowan-atkinson
  alt.fan.wodehouse
  alt.fan.woody-allen

Humor Archives

Where do you go when you need a good laugh, and you can't find your old high school yearbook? To the Net, of course. Here are some Internet resources that will lead you to enough jokes, humor and overall silliness to supply the entire Peruvian army.

Web:
http://users.intercomm.com/chadt/hindex.html
http://www.funnybone.com/
http://www.ionet.net/~ziegler/humor.htm
http://www.jokecenter.com/
http://www.laffnow.com/
http://www.tiac.net/users/maxw/humor.html
http://www.winn.com/bs/

Humor Databases

You have finally managed to get the girl in your economics class to come over for dinner. It is crucial that you impress her, and what better way than to amuse her with some jokes? The Net approves of your relationship and is willing to help. Check with these Web sites, and you are bound to find all the jokes you need, as well as a few extra (just in case). It won't be long before your date is laughing so hard, you can take the bigger hamburger for yourself and she won't even notice.

Web:
http://humor.ncy.com/
http://www.hardyharhar.com/

Humor Magazines

It's easy to be well-read when what you are reading is funny. These online humor magazines will put a snap in your eye and a sparkle in your walk. Why get in the car, drive all the way to the store, and pay good money just to get a print magazine? There are just as many laughs available for free, right now, on the Net. Laugh in the privacy of your own home—that's my motto.

Web:
http://www.denounce.com/
http://www.thetp.com/

Humor Mailing Lists

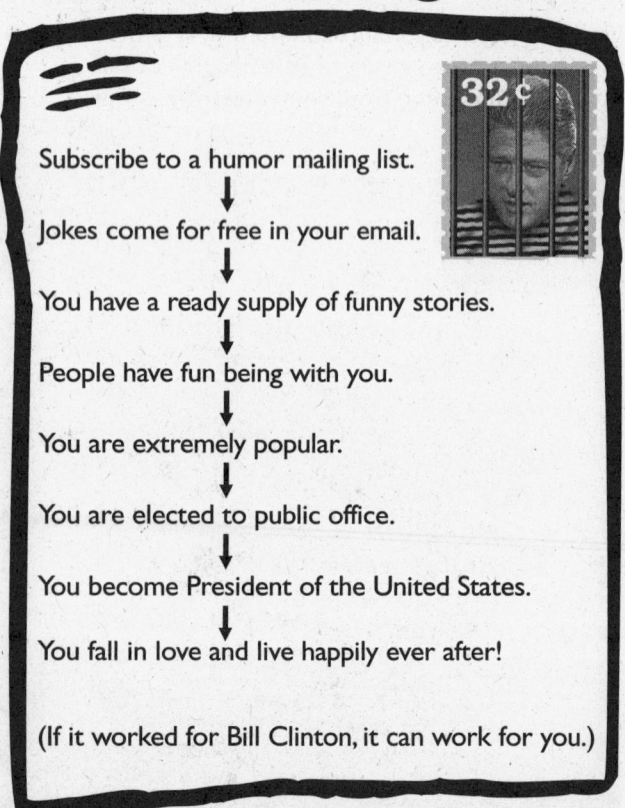

Why go out into the cold cruel world in order to hunt down humor, when you can have it come directly to your electronic mailbox? Subscribe to these mailing lists, and you will be able to distract your co-workers by laughing as you read your mail. Then you can forward the best jokes to all your friends, so they will see what a terrific sense of humor you have and appreciate how lucky they are to know you.

Listserv Mailing List:
List Name: **humor**
Subscribe to: **listserv@uga.cc.uga.edu**

Listserv Mailing List:
List Name: **humor-l**
Subscribe to: **listserv@uafsysb.uark.edu**

Majordomo Mailing List:
List Name: **funnybone**
Subscribe to: **majordomo@listserv.direct.net**

Humor Mailing Lists

Subscribe to a humor mailing list.
↓
Jokes come for free in your email.
↓
You have a ready supply of funny stories.
↓
People have fun being with you.
↓
You are extremely popular.
↓
You are elected to public office.
↓
You become President of the United States.
↓
You fall in love and live happily ever after!

(If it worked for Bill Clinton, it can work for you.)

HUMOR AND JOKES

Humorous Text Filters

There is a saying, a second language is a second soul. The language you speak and write influences not only how you communicate, but how you think. That's why I would like to encourage you to learn as many languages as you can. To get you started, here are some handy resources to translate normal everyday English into several important dialects: Swedish Chef, Jive, Valley Girl and Pig Latin and others.

Web:
http://gumbo.tcs.tufts.edu/chef/
http://websmurfer.devnull.net/
http://www.80s.com/Entertainment/ValleyURL/
http://www.cs.utexas.edu/users/jbc/home/chef.html
http://www.psyclops.com/wubbler/
http://www.rinkworks.com/dialect/
http://www.smeg.com/backwards/

Imprudent Wit and Verbal Abuse

On days when things are going great and you need someone to bring you back down to earth, help is just a few keystrokes away. This site features a variety of insults from sharp-tongued and quick-witted famous people. If you are going to be verbally abused, it might as well come from someone interesting.

Web:
http://www.iaehv.nl/users/roberth/

Interactive Top Ten Lists

If you are tired of passively hearing about other people's Top Ten lists, then rejoice: you can participate in making your own. Fill in a form with your entry, submit it and wait to see if yours is selected and put on display. Fame could be just around the corner for you.

Web:
http://www.ai.mit.edu/extra/topten/
http://www.entercenter.com/TopTen/

> Isn't the Net great?

> Waste it, conserve it, store it, pay for it. See "Energy".

Joke of the Day

I am sorry to be strict about it, but every day you need to read a joke. There are two possibilities. You can arrange to have a joke emailed to you automatically, or you can check the Web and find something funny for yourself. The choice is yours. (After all, this is a free country.)

Web:
http://www.cybercheeze.com/
http://www.emailjoke.com/
http://www.joke-of-the-day.com/

Jokes

These are the most important places on the entire Internet: the joke-telling Usenet groups. Anyone may post a joke about anything (although truly tasteless jokes are best sent to **alt.tasteless.jokes**). Beginners note: The **.d** discussion group is for the discussion of jokes or for requests (such as "Does anyone have the canonical list of Hillary and Beavis jokes?"). The **rec.humor** group is for jokes only.

Usenet:
alt.humor
alt.humor.dutch
alt.humor.jewish
alt.humor.net-abuse
alt.humor.parodies
alt.humor.puns
rec.humor
rec.humor.d
rec.humor.flame
rec.humor.jewish

400 HUMOR AND JOKES

> Talk may be cheap, but talk on the Net is cool.

Jokes, Moderated

This moderated group is to **rec.humor** what America Online is to the Internet: there is Someone in Charge. All jokes are submitted to a moderator who posts the ones he thinks are funny. What this means is that, unlike **rec.humor**, you don't have to wade through a whole lot of junk, silliness and bad jokes. It also means that you have to put up with irritating messages that are tacked on to the end of each joke, as well as regularly posted draconian ukases, setting out rules and regulations. Still, this discussion group is one of the most popular on the entire Usenet (in my estimation, coming between **rec.arts.erotica** and **alt.sex.bondage**).

Web:
 http://www.clari.net/rhf/

Usenet:
 rec.humor.funny
 rec.humor.funny.reruns

Onion

The Onion is the online version of a satirical college newspaper based in Madison, Wisconsin. The Onion is funny—very funny. (And goodness knows, anyone living in Madison can use a good laugh.) The writing is first-rate, providing a wonderful parody of the ubiquitous self-conscious weakly written style championed by today's mainstream newspapers and magazines. If you have ever had occasion to read newspapers and magazines from earlier in the century (say, before television), you cannot help but notice the difference between what our grandparents used to read and what passes for writing today. In an age when watching an entire uninterrupted 60-second commercial is considered an extreme test of one's power of concentration, it's hard to believe that there used to be a time when daily newspapers published articles with paragraphs that routinely contained more than two sentences. The reason I mention this is because I find the Onion to be the perfect antidote to the banal and diluted output of our current print media. Now that "lowest common denominator" is considered to be a desirable goal by writers and publishers alike, reading the Onion is, in my opinion, the perfect way to pass the time until something better comes along. Also, it's funny. (And goodness knows, anyone living in Madison can use a good laugh.)

Web:
 http://www.theonion.com/

Look What I Found on the Net...

```
Newsgroup: rec.humor
Subject: Poetry

Mary had a little skirt
Split right up the sides,
And every time she wore that skirt
The boys could see her thighs.

She also had another skirt
Split right up the front,
But she never wore that one.
```

HUMOR AND JOKES

Oracle

You send in any question you want to the Usenet Oracle. After a short wait, you receive your response. Great, you say, the wondrous powers of omnipotent wisdom are at my disposal whenever I want. Then you notice a catch: in return for answering your question, the Oracle sends *you* a question to answer. "Why not?" you say. "Maybe the Oracle is overworked this week, and it is really quite a compliment to be asked for my opinion." Then you notice that whenever you ask a question, you are sent one in return. Eventually you catch on, "Why, we are all just answering..." Well, I'm sure you don't need my help to figure it out (especially if you have ever sold Amway products). The Usenet Oracle is a time-honored tradition. Read the best of the Oracle's answers in the moderated group **rec.humor.oracle**. The **.d** is non-moderated and is for an open discussion of the Oracle's wisdom.

Usenet:
rec.humor.oracle
rec.humor.oracle.d

The Oracle: Wisdom in Its Ultimate Form

No problem is too small, no quandary is too big. Whatever you need, whenever you need it, the Usenet Oracle is there for you. Get in on the ground floor of what is sure to be the new computer-based religion of the Age of the Internet. Remember, even God started as a cult figure.

Look What I Found on the Net...

```
Newsgroup: rec.humor.funny
Subject: Advice for the Young Bride

[The following is an excerpt from what — supposedly — is an article
from The Madison Institute Newsletter, Fall Issue, 1894]

                INSTRUCTION AND ADVICE
                        FOR THE
                      YOUNG BRIDE

To the sensitive young woman who has had the benefits of proper
upbringing, the wedding day is, ironically, both the happiest
and most terrifying day of her life.  On the positive side,
there is the wedding itself, in which the bride is the central
attraction in a beautiful and inspiring ceremony, symbolizing
her triumph in securing a male to provide for all her needs for
the rest of her life.  On the negative side, there is the
wedding night, during which the bride must pay the piper, so
to speak, by facing for the first time the terrible experience
of sex...

...Clever wives are ever on the alert for new and better methods
of denying and discouraging the amorous overtures of the
husband.  A good wife should  expect to have reduced sexual
contacts to once a week by the end of the first year of marriage
and to once a month by the end of the fifth year of marriage...
```

Religious Satire

The Surgeon General's priest warns that reading religious satire on the Net could be hazardous to your spiritual health. But it's so much fun that it doesn't really matter. Put off your eternal damnation tomorrow for hours of chuckles today.

Web:
   http://www.npcts.edu/~aolson/door/

Usenet:
   alt.atheism.satire

Science Jokes

Here is one of the funniest jokes I know: "What's purple and commutes?" Answer: "An abelian grape". Now, this is a mathematical joke, so don't worry if you don't get it. However, if you are a scientist, there are whole oodles of jokes just for you. Not only math, but biology, chemistry, physics and more—everything is funny if you make the right assumptions.

Web:
   http://www.srdc.metu.edu.tr/~dengi/humor/science/
   http://www.xs4all.nl/~jcdverha/scijokes/

Shakespearean Insults

Each time you connect to these sites a different insult is thrown at you in perfect Shakespearean style. Examples: "Thou clouted knotty-pated maggot-pie," "Thou jarring plume-plucked measle," "Thou errant toad-spotted pignut," or "Thou dankish bat-fowling pumpion."

Web:
   http://alpha.acast.nova.edu/cgi-bin/bard.pl
   http://www.randyworld.com/shakespeare/

Tasteless (and Dirty) Jokes

Don't look at these resources unless you want sickening, tasteless, repulsive, humiliating, insulting jokes and stories (many of which are silly, but—like Congressmen—you get what you pay for). Don't you dare post anything that is not tasteless. And don't you dare complain that anything here offends you. You have been warned... now check it out.

Web:
   http://www.arrgh.pair.com/jokes/
   http://www.dirtyjokes.com/
   http://www.myhotbox.com/humor/jokes.htm

Usenet:
   alt.tasteless.humor
   alt.tasteless.jokes

Tasteless Is in the Mind of the Beholder

The best thing about tasteless jokes is that, if you have enough of them, you will be able to offend just about anyone. Personally, I feel everyone should be offended once a week, just on general principles.

So the next time you want to provide a public service, spend some time reading the **alt.tasteless.jokes** discussion group, select the most obnoxious jokes you can find, and then use them to offend as many people as possible.

After all, no man is an island: we all have a social responsibility to make sure that the social fabric rips once in a while.

INTERESTING TECHNOLOGIES

Artificial Intelligence

Not everything that is artificial is bad. In fact, in a world where watching television is the favorite pastime of the masses, a little artificial intelligence is certainly not going to hurt anyone. These sites have links to technical papers, journals and surveys about artificial intelligence, robotics and neural networks. The Usenet groups are where you can chat with technophiles of all shapes and sizes. Pick up some artificial intelligence today.

Web:
http://sigart.acm.org/ai/
http://www.cs.berkeley.edu/~russell/ai.html
http://www.cs.washington.edu/research/jair/

Usenet:
comp.ai
comp.ai.alife
comp.ai.doc-analysis.misc
comp.ai.doc-analysis.ocr
comp.ai.edu
comp.ai.fuzzy
comp.ai.games
comp.ai.genetic
comp.ai.jair.announce
comp.ai.jair.papers
comp.ai.nat-lang
comp.ai.philosophy
comp.ai.shells
comp.ai.vision

Artificial Life

Getting tired of real life? Try a little artificial life. It's low in calories, high in fiber, and while it might run up your electricity bill, it will certainly keep you from being lonely.

Web:
http://alife.santafe.edu/
http://www.cis.ohio-state.edu/hypertext/faq/usenet/ai-faq/genetic/top.html
http://www.crg.cs.nott.ac.uk/people/Dave.Snowdon/ai/

Usenet:
comp.ai.genetic

Cloning

In most organisms, a copy of the blueprint for reproduction is stored within each cell. Inside the cell there are genes, most of which perform a particular function in creating a brand new organism. Genes are made of a biochemical substance called deoxyribonucleic acid or DNA. In principle, one could take an animal, extract the DNA from one of its cells, and then use that DNA as a blueprint to create a brand new animal. Although the new animal would be a completely separate organism, it would be an exact genetic copy of the original. We call this copy a clone. So far, various types of animals have been cloned successfully. Should we clone human beings? Technically speaking, cloning-like procedures for human cells have been performed since 1993. However, the full cloning of a person, or even a mammal, is still a highly controversial issue.

Web:
http://ethics.acusd.edu/reproductive_technologies.html
http://whyfiles.news.wisc.edu/034clone/
http://www.cabi.org/whatsnew/cloneani.htm
http://www.nsplus.com/nsplus/insight/clone/
http://www2.ri.bbsrc.ac.uk/library/research/cloning/

Cloning

If you clone the Pope, you get twice as much good advice and wisdom.

If you clone Harrison Ford, you get twice as much charisma and sex appeal.

But if you clone Harley Hahn, you get twice as much good advice, wisdom, charisma, sex appeal *and* two books for the price of one.

INTERESTING TECHNOLOGIES

Computer Speech

Computer speech has been hyped for years, and every year we hear the same thing: "This is the year." Well, when I hear it from a computer, I will believe it. In the meantime, you can get a grasp of the fundamentals by reading the FAQ (frequently asked question list). Where else are you going to go when you need a fast Fourier transform program right away and the neighborhood convenience store is closed?

Web:
  http://ophale.icp.inpg.fr/ex.html
  http://svr-www.eng.cam.ac.uk/~ajr/SpeechAnalysis/
  http://www.informatik.uni-frankfurt.de/~ifb/bib_engl.html
  http://www.speech.cs.cmu.edu/comp.speech/
  http://www.speechtechnology.com/

Usenet:
  comp.speech.research
  comp.speech.users

Majordomo Mailing List:
  List Name: **voice-users**
  Subscribe to: **majordomo@voicerecognition.com**

Conversations with Computers

In 1972, I was in a computer lab at UCLA where there was a computer connected to several other computers around the country. (The connection was made over a primitive network that was the ancestor of the Internet.) I was able to connect to a computer at Stanford that had a program that acted like a paranoid. I was also able to connect to a computer at MIT that ran a program that acted like a psychiatrist. For fun, I typed the responses from one program into the other, and vice versa, and for the first time in history, that I know of, two computers were talking to one another. (The paranoid won, by the way.) Would you like to talk to a computer program yourself? Well, you can. Here are some programs with which you can carry on a typed conversation. (Tell them I said hello.)

Web:
  http://ciips.ee.uwa.edu.au/~hutch/hal/
  http://www.fringeware.com/~robitron/fred.html
  http://www.loebner.net/Prizef/loebner-prize.html

Telnet:
  Address: **debra.dgbt.doc.ca**
  Port: **3000**

Nanotechnology

Nanotechnology is an area of technology that strives to work with extremely small devices: devices on the scale of molecules or even atoms. Such devices can be created by using a scanning tunneling microscope. Experiments have been devised in which a single atom is used as an electric switch, or a single molecule is used to convert AC to DC. The holy grail of nanotechnology is to develop the methods necessary to create vast numbers of tiny little machines. Although progress is slow, the implications are fascinating. Here is a Web site that will introduce you to nanotechnology. There is a lot of general interest information (including a FAQ), as well as more technical material. The name "nanotechnology" is derived from "nano", the Greek word for "dwarf". In the metric system, "nano" is used as a prefix indicating "one billionth" (American terminology). For example, a nanosecond is one billionth of a second. (In the English terminology, this would be one thousand millionth of a second.)

Web:
  http://nano.xerox.com/nano/
  http://www.lucifer.com/~sean/Nano.html
  http://www.nanozine.com/

Usenet:
  sci.nanotech

Why mess with real reality... ...when you have the virtual thing?

INTERNET

Neural Networks

A neural network is a computing system consisting of many simple processors connected in various patterns. Each processor operates on its own data and its own input, resulting in an output signal which is transmitted to other processors. In the aggregate, a "network" of such processors can work together to recognize patterns, process information, and help people make decisions. The original work with neural networks was done to try to mimic the biological processes used in our brains. Although neural networks are not nearly as complex or powerful as a brain, they are able to achieve astonishing results and are routinely used in many business and scientific applications.

Web:
ftp://ftp.sas.com/pub/neural/FAQ.html
http://engine.ieee.org/nnc/research/nnworldprog.html
http://www.emsl.pnl.gov:2080/docs/cie/neural/gateway/
http://www.emsl.pnl.gov:2080/docs/cie/neural/what.html

Usenet:
comp.ai.neural-nets

Virtual Reality

Before I commit myself to the concept of virtual reality, I need someone to answer some fundamental questions. Will there be commercials? Can I take my cat with me? Will I be able to get *real* food? In the meantime, I content myself with following what's new and almost real in the land of simulated make-believe. Try this Web site on for size and you too will be able to keep up on what may or may not really be happening inside and around the boundaries of perception.

Web:
http://www.nist.gov/itl/div894/ovrt/hotvr.html

Usenet:
sci.virtual-worlds

Listserv Mailing List:
List Name: virtu-l
Subscribe to: listserv@postoffice.cso.uiuc.edu

Wireless Technology

The world of wireless technology is vast. It encompasses mobile computing, telephony, wireless networks, satellites, radio, and more. For ongoing discussion, you can follow the Usenet discussion group. For a collection of Internet resources pertaining to wireless technologies, see the Web page.

Web:
http://winwww.rutgers.edu/

Usenet:
comp.std.wireless

INTERNET

Ad Blocking Software

I hate commercials. I hate junk mail. I hate telemarketing. And I particularly hate advertisements, especially on the Web. But I'm not the only one. There are many smart people on the Net who also dislike ads, and out of antipathy comes invention. Here is software that will block ads for you as you look at Web pages. Now, in this book, I only put in resources that are free. In this case, I am making an exception, because I feel the service of blocking ads is so valuable. Some of these programs cost money (although you can try them for free, and they don't cost much anyway). Using an ad blocking program will make your Internet experience more enjoyable in two ways. First, you won't have to look at ads. Second, Web pages will load faster because you won't have to wait for ads to download (be transferred) to your computer.

Web:
http://www.atguard.com/
http://www.intermute.com/
http://www.junkbusters.com/

Everything in this book is free.

Domain Name Registration

Within any type of Internet address, the name of the computer is called the domain name or, more simply, the domain. For example, in the address **president@whitehouse.gov**, the domain is **whitehouse.gov**. In **http://canada.gc.ca/**, the domain is **canada.gc.ca**. Have you ever wondered how these names are assigned? There are two systems. Outside the United States, all addresses end with a two-letter country code. In our second example, for instance, the two-letter country code is **ca**, indicating that this is a Canadian domain. The United States uses a different system. There is a country code (**us**), but it's not used much. Instead, most people use an older system that was devised before the Internet became international. The last part of the domain—called the top-level domain—is a three-letter code. The most common of these top-level domains are **com** (commercial), **edu** (educational), **gov** (government), **org** (non-profit organizations) and **net** (network providers). If you have used the Net much, you will have noticed that the **com** top-level domain is also used for miscellaneous addresses that don't fit into another category. So how do you register a domain? You can either have your Internet service provider (ISP) do it for you, or you can do it yourself. In the U.S., most of the registration is done by the InterNIC Registration Services. For assistance, connect to their Web page and read the help information. If you are outside the U.S., I have included a second Web site (also maintained by the InterNIC) that contains links to other registration organizations.

Web:
  http://rs.internic.net/help/other-reg.html
  http://rs.internic.net/rs-internic.html

Email

As an Internet user, you have a lot of choices when it comes to email. For example, you can choose which email software to use, and you can choose your own email provider. (You do not necessarily have to use your Internet Service Provider's email service.) Here is the information you need to learn more about email, and how you can make it work well for you.

Web:
  http://www.emailtoday.com/
  http://www.everythingemail.com/
  http://www.everythingemail.net/

Free Email Services

It might be hard to find a free lunch, but on the Net you can find free email. The services vary, so read the descriptions carefully. You might be wondering, how can people make money giving away free email services? In one word: advertising. (Are you surprised?)

Web:
  http://altavista.iname.com/
  http://mail.yahoo.com/
  http://www.chickmail.com/
  http://www.eudoramail.com/
  http://www.hotmail.com/
  http://www.iname.com/
  http://www.netforward.com/
  http://www.rocketmail.com/

Free Mailing List Hosting

A mailing list is a facility that allows you to carry on a discussion by email, by sending messages to everyone who has signed up for the list. Having your own personal (possibly secret) mailing list is a totally cool thing to do. For example, you can have your friends subscribe to your special, exclusive mailing list and then send them jokes and excerpts from your diary. Many families maintain mailing lists to stay in touch. If a mailing list sounds good to you, here are some places that will host your mailing list for free. (Although no money changes hands, there is a cost: you will have to look at advertisements inserted within the messages.)

Web:
  http://www.coollist.com/
  http://www.findmail.com/
  http://www.listbot.com/
  http://www.onelist.com/
  http://www.stargame.org/

Historical Timeline of the Internet

Here is a timeline that shows the history of the Internet from the 1956 Russian launch of Sputnik (which may have triggered it all) through the Arpanet (1969), UUCP (1976), Usenet (1979), DNS (1984), IRC (1988), gopher (1991), the World Wide Web (1992), and on and on.

Web:
  http://info.isoc.org/guest/zakon/internet/history/
    hit.html

History of the Internet

On December 5, 1969, three computers in California (Los Angeles, Santa Barbara and Menlo Park) and a computer in Utah were connected to one another. This marked the official beginning of the Arpanet, the network that was to grow into the Internet. Since then, the Internet has grown to become the largest information-based facility in the history of mankind. Want to find out more about the history of the Internet? Check with these resources. (By the way, let me add a date to the history of the Net: February 1996. In that month, this book became the first Internet book in history to have sold a million copies.)

Web:
  http://www.delphi.com/navnet/faq/history.html
  http://www.isoc.org/internet-history/

Information Activism

Information Activism is a movement dedicated to maintaining the integrity of information on the Net. Have you ever wasted time trying to track down something, only to find that the Web pages you looked at were hopelessly out of date? Does it bother you when a search engine points to resources that don't exist or that are no longer maintained? Do you get frustrated with Web pages that have broken links because nobody keeps them up to date? If so, you may want to become an Information Activist and help clean up the Net. Visit this Web site, where you can read about the Information Activism campaigns. As you know, the Web makes it easy for anyone to publish information, and millions of people do, all over the world. However, there is no mechanism in place to check that information is maintained. Too many people (and too many organizations) neglect their Web pages. In time, these pages become obsolete and misleading, but they are still on the Net, accessible to people everywhere. As an Information Activist, you can help other people take responsibility for the information they publish on the Net. You'll find sample letters to send to people and organizations who have neglected their Web pages. You'll also find the Information Activism manifesto, which will give you an overview of what the movement is about, as well as other ways for you to participate in cleaning up the Net.

Web:
  http://www.activism.org/

Internet Conference Calendar

This site lets you search a database of information about upcoming academic conferences, symposia, courses and workshops, and is great for finding events related to the Internet and various computer technologies. Search by specific events, by date or by location. Now, when your spouse makes you take a vacation, you can check ahead of time for something interesting to do so you won't be bored.

Web:
  http://conferences.calendar.com/

Internet Drafts

Examine the up-to-date collection of working documents of the Internet Engineering Task Force. Most of these documents relate to technical aspects of the Net, but there are also general interest articles. These draft documents are working proposals, created by the people who are planning the future of the Net and circulated within the Internet community for general comment.

Web:
  http://www.ietf.cnri.reston.va.us/1id-abstracts.html

Internet Fax Services

Internet fax services make it possible to send free faxes to many different parts of the world through Internet mail. The recipient's name and fax number are converted to an electronic mail address, and the mail message is routed via the Internet to a computer near the destination. The receiving computer converts the mail message into a fax and transmits it through the local telephone network to the recipient's fax machine.

Web:
  http://www.tpc.int/
  http://www.zipfax.com/

It's okay to laugh out loud.

Internet Help Talk and General Discussion

If you are new to the Net, there are certain Usenet groups where you can go to ask questions about using the Net. The **newbies** and **newbie** groups are for general comments and questions about the Net. The **news** and **bitnet** groups are for discussion about learning how to use Usenet and the Internet.

Usenet:
   alt.newbie
   alt.newbies
   bit.listserv.help-net
   news.newusers.questions

Internet Hoaxes

You just got email that some sick kid overseas wants to collect as many postcards as he can before he dies. Then you read about a secret cookie recipe, circulating on the Net, for which someone got tricked into paying a lot of money. The next day you hear a rumor that the government is going to start charging for email. Is any of this stuff true? No. All that is happening is that someone is spreading misleading information about well-known Internet hoaxes. The truth is given out on a need-to-know basis, and you need to know.

Web:
   http://ciac.llnl.gov/ciac/CIACHoaxes.html
   http://www.nonprofit.net/hoax/hoax.html

Internet News

The Internet changes so fast that literally no one can keep up on what's happening. However, if you would like to keep in touch, here are some places that can help. You can check every week, every day, or even every hour, and you will find lots and lots of news articles. In particular, you will find coverage of all the companies that are doing business related to the Net.

Web:
   http://cgi.pathfinder.com/netly/
   http://www.internetnews.com/
   http://www.internetwire.com/
   http://www.news.com/
   http://www.newslinx.com/

Many of the Internet's resources are available by Electronic mail, so there is no need to be left out just because your Internet connection is slow or inadequate. **Internet Resources by Email** will show you what to do to keep up with the Net-Joneses, even if they have their own personal high-speed direct connection and all you have is an email account with a six-hour lag time. Soon you will be able to do anything they can (only slower). Hint: These services are perfect if you have the type of job where they give you email access to the Net, but won't let you get at the good stuff.

Internet Resources by Email

Although most people on the Net use a Web browser, there are many people in the world who only have access to electronic mail. If this is the case for you, you should know that it is possible to access most of the resources on the Internet by mail. To start, send mail to the address below and read the document that will be sent to you. By the way, this document is translated into many different languages aside from English.

Mail:
   mailbase@mailbase.ac.uk
   Body: **send lis-iis e-access-inet.txt**

Internet Statistics

Have you ever wondered how many people use the Internet? How many computers are connected to the Internet? All this information, and more, is available at these Web sites. For example, one site has an estimate that, in May 1998, there were over 57 million people using the Web just in the U.S. Another site has an estimate that in July 1998, there were 37.6 million computers on the entire Internet. How do you reconcile these numbers? The truth is, no one knows exactly how big the Net really is, and the "size" of the Internet depends on how you define what you are measuring. What I can tell you is (1) the Net is very important to humanity, and (2) it is large and growing faster than anyone can understand.

Web:
  http://www-survey.cc.gatech.edu/
  http://www.domainstats.com/
  http://www.nw.com/zone/WWW/top.html
  http://www.openmarket.com/intindex/

Internet Talk and General Discussion

The next best thing to being on the Internet is talking about being on the Internet. Get your fix of Internet topics by checking out the Usenet groups where anyone who thinks they are anyone chats about issues relating to the Internet.

Usenet:
  alt.culture.internet
  alt.cyberspace
  alt.internet
  alt.life.internet
  alt.nettime
  alt.society.netizens
  soc.net-people

Internet Terminology

The Internet is a global network that works the same way everywhere in the world. This means that everyone has access to the same resources, the same tools and many of the same ideas. However, in order to talk with other people about the Net, you need to be able to use the same words. I do want you to understand what everyone is talking about, so here are some glossaries of Internet technology for you to use as references.

Web:
  http://www.netdictionary.com/html/
  http://www.netlingo.com/
  http://www.webguest.com/glossary/

IRC

IRC is a fun way to chat and make new friends. Get help learning the general commands, read the FAQ, and get some quick reference help. You will also find information on related Usenet groups, mailing lists, primers, manuals and archive sites. On the IRC channels you can get help in real-time.

Web:
  http://urth.acsu.buffalo.edu/irc/WWW/ircdocs.html
  http://www.irchelp.org/

IRC:
  #irchelp
  alt.irc.questions

Jargon File

The Jargon File is a legendary work that sounds like it should be dull: a collection of words and technical terms—definitions and examples—used with computers and the Internet. However, the Jargon File is anything but dull. It is not only exquisitely written, it is witty, comprehensive and accurate. In addition, there are also well-written essays discussing the hacking community and its customs. Out of all the dictionaries in the world, this one is probably the most fun.

Web:
  http://www.bitech.com/jargon/cool
  http://www.earthspace.net/jargon/

JARGON

We are what we think, and we think with the words that we manage to scrape up off the sidewalk of life and somehow implant in non-volatile memory. The Jargon File is a wonderful resource that has, to coin a phrase, stood the test of time. In other words, someone smart and witty wrote it and it's a lot of fun to read. Take a few moments and check it out. If nothing else, you will see the human side of the techno-nerd part of our culture that is all too often hidden behind the glamour and the heartache of life in the technical/computer/rational fast lane.

Learning About the Internet and Web

If you are new to the Net, there is a lot to learn. Here are some places that will help you teach yourself about the Internet and the Web. (If you are a woman, pretend that I am sitting beside you, holding your hand. If you are a man, pretend that your mother is holding your hand.)

Web:
 http://www.folksonline.com/
 http://www.screen.com/start/guide/
 http://www.webnovice.com/

ListTool

To subscribe or unsubscribe to a mailing list, you have to email particular messages to the program that administers the list. (I have put information on how to do so at the beginning of this book.) Emailing these messages is easy, but to make it even easier, you can use ListTool, a nifty Web-based system that will do the work for you. You can only subscribe and unsubscribe to the mailing lists in the ListTool database, but there is a large selection, so, if you know what you want, you will probably find something suitable.

Web:
 http://www.listtool.com/

Net Happenings

This mailing list is a great place to learn about announcements of everything interesting going on across the Net. Joining this list will guarantee that your mailbox will be stuffed to the electronic gills with the latest and freshest stuff the Net has to offer.

Web:
 http://scout.cs.wisc.edu/scout/net-hap/

Listserv Mailing List:
 List Name: **net-happenings**
 Subscribe to: **listserv@cs.wisc.edu**

The Internet is low in cholesterol.

Net Happenings

Here is my simple three-part plan to make sure you lead a full, interesting life.

(1) Subscribe to the Net Happenings mailing list.

(2) Every time a new message appears, stop what you are doing and read it.

(3) Check out each new resource or article.

Eventually, you will get old and die, but by that time you will have seen a lot of stuff.

New Internet Technologies

Today's Internet is based on old technology, and, as you probably know, has a pressing need for bandwidth (the capacity to move information) and speed. There are two big projects underway to develop new improved technology for the Net. One project is called Internet2. The other project is IPng (Internet Protocol, next generation), also referred to as IPv6 (Internet Protocol, version 6). (The current Internet system uses IPv4.) Here is some information about these projects, so you can see what's in store for us in the future. (If you don't like what you see, at least you'll have time to move.)

Web:
 http://playground.sun.com/pub/ipng/html/
   ipng-main.html
 http://www.6bone.net/
 http://www.internet2.edu/

INTRIGUE

The Internet will set you free.

Scout Report

Stay on top of what is happening in the Net world by getting weekly lists of the latest cool Net sites. Experience the luxury of having someone else do the hard part while you get to have all the fun.

Web:
http://scout.cs.wisc.edu/scout/report/

Listserv Mailing List:
List Name: **scout-report**
Subscribe to: **listserv@cs.wisc.edu**

Web Talk and General Discussion

Would you like to talk about the Web? Goodness knows there is a lot to say. The Usenet groups are for ongoing discussion about various aspects of the Web. The **advocacy** group is for opinion. The **announce** group is for announcements. This is a good place to let people know about a new Web site. The **misc** group is for everything else related to the Web. For talking in real-time, try the IRC channel.

Usenet:
alt.culture.www
comp.infosystems.www
comp.infosystems.www.advocacy
comp.infosystems.www.announce
comp.infosystems.www.misc

IRC:
#www

Whois

Would you like to find out who is in charge of a particular Internet domain? Use the InterNIC's Whois service. Just enter a name, and their computer will check their database and show you the public information.

Web:
http://www.internic.net/

INTRIGUE

Conspiracies

Our world—so they say—is full of a great many conspiracies, many of them perpetrated by the government. Did you know that aliens live on Earth, AIDS is a plot, harmful additives are used in our food, fabulous inventions and technology are being hidden, and there really are cures for cancer? Then there are the secret wars, assassinations, insurrections, and lots and lots of cover-ups. And, oh yes, I almost forgot—Elvis is not really dead.

Web:
http://www.conspire.com/
http://www.cruzio.com/~blackops/
http://www.netizen.org/arc-hive/

Conspiracy Talk and General Discussion

Don't look behind you. Don't say anything out loud. Just act natural. Okay, are you ready? There is a big conspiracy. It involves the government (particularly the CIA), the media and big business. I can't tell you the details here. These Usenet groups are the only safe places to talk. See you there.

Usenet:
alt.conspiracy
alt.conspiracy.antichrist
alt.conspiracy.black.helicopters
alt.conspiracy.microsoft
alt.conspiracy.new-world-order
alt.conspiracy.princess-diana
alt.conspiracy.right-wing
alt.conspiracy.spy
alt.government.abuse
alt.illuminati
alt.paranoia
alt.paranoia.spambots
alt.underground.yalta
bit.listserv.cloaks-daggers

Try a mud.

INTRIGUE

Contemporary Conspiracies

Conspiracies abound. Or do they? I had to find out for sure, so I called the White House. I asked for the President and was put on hold, listening to a recorded announcement. ("For information on the vast right-wing conspiracy, press 1. For information on Congressional leaks harmful to the administration, press 2...") While I was waiting, I checked with the Net, and before the President could even get to the phone, I had the information I needed (and here it is for you), so I hung up. My only worry is that, when the President gets to the phone and finds no one there, it may hurt his feelings. Either that or he'll think it's a conspiracy.

Web:
http://www.conspire.com/curren41.html
http://www.erols.com/igoddard/twa-fact.htm
http://www.internet-inquirer.com/
http://www.mcn.org/b/poisonfrog/diana/
http://www.webexpert.net/rosedale/twacasefile/

Usenet:
alt.conspiracy.princess-diana

Spy cams are in "Devices and Gizmos Connected to the Net".

Disinformation

As they say in Brooklyn, "Dis information is not easy to come by." But, if you have a Net connection, you can get disinformation whenever you want. Try this collection of links that will lead you to sources about revolutionaries, propaganda, censorship, counterculture, media double-talk and counterintelligence.

Web:
http://www.disinfo.com/

Look What I Found on the Net...

```
Newsgroup: alt.conspiracy
Subject: Schools and Politics

> Schools are left wing brainwashing centers.  Most colleges
> were started by Christians, but were completely taken over by
> the far left a long time ago.  They are politically correct
> institutions where it is not allowed to question the views of
> the leftists.

There is much truth in this statement.  However, just because
the "left" is often wrong does not mean that the "Christians"
are always right.

There is a big difference between Left-Right politics and
Evolutionist-Creationist "science".  I would agree that
left wing politicians (and the professors who still spout their
illogical theories) are way off base, but this doesn't prove
anything, one way or the other, about science, religion or
"truth".
```

JFK Assassination

The whodunit of all whodunits. Just when you think you've seen all the JFK conspiracy material, someone compiles a whole bunch more. At these Web sites, you will find articles galore about every aspect of every assassination theory. New evidence is emerging all the time (from somewhere), so don't get left behind on this very important historical controversy. For up-to-the-minute, late-breaking information, as well as lots of discussion, you can always take a peek at the Usenet groups.

Web:
 http://mcadams.posc.mu.edu/
 http://ourworld.compuserve.com/homepages/
   MGriffith_2/jfk.htm
 http://shell.rmi.net/~jkelin/fp.html
 http://www.informatik.uni-rostock.de/Kennedy/
   WCR/
 http://www.nara.gov/nara/jfk/jfk.html

Usenet:
 alt.assassination.jfk
 alt.assassination.jfk.uncensored
 alt.conspiracy.jfk
 alt.conspiracy.jfk.moderated

Mind Control

Is the government/CIA/police/your mother trying to control your mind? The question may seem ludicrous, but many people in the world are completely convinced that malevolent powers are trying to control them, even to the point of implanting devices in their bodies. Now, I have to say, it is well known that psychotics often feel that someone is trying to control them covertly; they may hear voices, think that the TV announcer is talking directly to them, and so on. These are symptoms of mental illness and a malfunctioning brain. Clearly, many of the mind control stories—as real as they seem to the victims—fall into this category. Still, did the government really run secret mind control experiments? See for yourself. (And if you still have the free will to carry on a discussion, try the Usenet group.)

Web:
 http://www.mk.net/~mcf/
 http://www.parascope.com/ds/mkultradocs.htm

Usenet:
 alt.mindcontrol

Namebase

You don't have to wait until someone calls you before a Senate committee to start naming names. This Web site allows you to search for specific names that may have appeared in hundreds of investigative books and many related articles. For example, if you search for "Hoover, Edgar", you will see a list of various books in which J. Edgar Hoover is discussed.

Web:
 http://www.pir.org/

Parascope

Parascope is a magazine that reports on weird stuff going on all over the place. The different sections cover conspiracies and cover-ups, UFO stuff and paranormal weirdness. There is also documented evidence such as declassified government documents, analysis of covert actions and propaganda campaigns. If your friend in the next office has been telling you about the CIA's links to a Contra cocaine ring that is trying to cover up the Roswell incident, so the Vietnamese informants who are influencing our elections won't be discovered, this is the place to check it all out.

Web:
 http://www.parascope.com/

Smoking Gun

Do you like the idea of seeing a secret dossier? Well, then, you'll love this awesome site, full of secret dirt on famous and not-so-famous people. Read the material gathered from court files and government sources, information that somehow doesn't get into the public media. When your curiosity exceeds the resources of the mainstream press, the Smoking Gun is the place to be.

Web:
 http://www.thesmokinggun.com/

What you see is not always what you get.

414 INTRIGUE

Unsolved Mysteries

Here is a whole list of unsolved mysteries just waiting for someone like you to solve. Look at pictures of fugitives and missing persons. Then read about the crime or the disappearance. Now keep a sharp eye open. As you walk around, look at everyone you meet. You never know when *you* will recognize someone and solve a mystery. (And if you have any spare time, you can help me track down the person who ate the last low-fat chocolate cupcake.)

Web:
  http://www.unsolved.com/home.html

Have fun.

Waco

If you like living in the past and you can't let old news die, check out all the interesting resources about the siege of the Branch Davidian cult in Waco, Texas (USA).

Web:
  http://www.flash.net/~wyla/
  http://www.pbs.org/wgbh/pages/frontline/waco/

Look What I Found on the Net...

```
Newsgroup: alt.mindcontrol
Subject: Effects of Long-term Mind Control on Brain?

> I am a mind control victim of about four years.  I cannot
> believe that many of my dreams are a product of my
> subconscious mind.  This leads me to wonder what effects mind
> control technology has on a persons brain?  Will they ever be
> able to release me or will I be subject to this kind of
> torment until I die?...

[response #1]

Dear sir,  I have a Web site that may help you to realize what it
is they are doing to you and who is doing it.  It sort of blows the
lid off their secrecy.  Go to
http://members.aol.com/Xxxxx/xxxxx.html   for information...

[response #2]

Ginseng will correct chemical imbalances in your brain.  Also
lecithin [choline] will help you sleep with happier dreams...

Look — people can affect other people's brains, most of the time
without realizing it.  Psychic connecting can happen.  Perhaps you
connected psychically with another person innocently...Once
connected , this could last for a lifetime, but you can liberate
yourself.  Consciously try to disconnect with any outside psychic
stimuli with the help of ginseng and choline.  I think that you can
liberate your brain and thoughts and emotions through your own
dedicated efforts.
```

JOBS AND THE WORKPLACE

Bicycle Commuting

Get your legs pumping and your heart racing, and save the environment and your bank book at the same time. Forget the hubbub of all those speeding cars trying to jockey for a position on the freeway—travel by bike. The mailing list discussions focus on bicycle transportation and improving bicycling conditions in city and suburban areas. The Web page gives you an overview of bicycle commuting: what to expect and how to deal with various problems.

Web:
http://biketowork.itelcom.com/

Majordomo Mailing List:
List Name: **commute-logistics**
Subscribe to: **majordomo@cyclery.com**

Majordomo Mailing List:
List Name: **facilities-n-planning**
Subscribe to: **majordomo@cyclery.com**

Contract Labor

More and more people are working from contract to contract. Aside from the cachet of getting to call yourself a "consultant", you will find that life is a lot more fun and challenging without fringe benefits. Here is the place to offer your services, look for a contract job, or swap experiences. (For hourly contracts, see **alt.sex.wanted**.)

Usenet:
misc.jobs.contract

Education-Related Jobs

So you spent the first part of your life sitting in a classroom, waiting patiently for the bell of freedom to ring? And now you're trying desperately to get back into a classroom, so you can contribute and make a difference (while being underpaid and under-appreciated). Here are some Web sites that have everything—and I mean everything—all in one place.

Web:
http://chronicle.merit.edu/.ads/.links.html
http://www.edjobsite.com/
http://www.teachers.net/jobs/jobboard/jobs.html

Contract Labor

Would you enjoy working (1) for more money per hour, (2) with less supervision, (3) with more control over your destiny? Would you be willing to work without (1) job security, (2) benefits, (3) a steady income? If you answered "Yes" and "Yes", you may be ready for contract labor. Let's talk about it on the Net.

Entry Level Jobs Offered

There's an old riddle: What does an arts graduate say to a computer science graduate? The answer is, "Would you like fries with your order?" Here is a newer riddle: What does a person who doesn't know how to use the Net say to a person who does? The answer is, nothing. Because the person who knows how to use the Net is too busy working at a satisfying and lucrative job. Okay, so we all have to start somewhere, and if you are ready for an entry-level job, this is the Usenet group for you. Check out the jobs that offer you no place to go but up, and talk to the people who really care whether or not you want fries.

Usenet:
misc.jobs.offered.entry

How to Get Rich

Would you like to get rich? If so, you need to plan ahead and learn how to make the right decisions. Here is an essay I wrote to help you understand what brings success in life. Read my advice on how to think about work and how to make sure that what you choose works well for you. Work can be immensely satisfying—and provide your best chance of becoming rich—but you need to do it right.

Web:
http://www.harley.com/get-rich/

JOBS AND THE WORKPLACE

International Jobs

So you've lived your whole life in one country, and you feel like it's time to have an adventure by working abroad? Well, the first journey to employment begins with a single occupational step. One of the Web sites is devoted to Canadian jobs. The other will help you find jobs all over the world. For questions and answers, try the Usenet discussion group. Hint: If you answer an ad, do investigate carefully before you commit yourself or spend any money. Remember, anyone can put anything they want on the Web. It's up to you to be careful.

Web:
  http://www.canadajobs.com/
  http://www.escapeartist.com/jobs/overseas.htm

Usenet:
  alt.jobs.overseas

Job Hating

Not everyone has a great job and a great boss. If you find yourself in this position, you can make the load lighter by calling on the two time-honored methods of bearing up under adversity: humor and complaining. People all over the world are happy to share. Read about how bad their bosses are, and maybe yours will seem a tad more human; then chuckle at the dumb but funny things that happen to other people as they work. The next time someone does something awful to you at work, don't get mad: share it with the Net.

Web:
  http://www.disgruntled.com/dishome.html
  http://www.jobhater.com/
  http://www.myboss.com/

Usenet:
  misc.jobs.discuss.workplace

Job Searching

The Net wants you to work. The Net wants you to make a lot of money. The Net wants you to pay off your mortgage, fully fund your retirement, and save money for your kids' education—but first, you need a job. There are lots of jobs available. To help you find them, use these Web sites, where you will find many job listings in many different categories and regions. Hint: Aim for a job that is so interesting and enjoyable that you love what you are doing.

Web:
  http://www.ajb.dni.us/
  http://www.careerbuilder.com/
  http://www.careermosaic.com/
  http://www.careerpath.com/
  http://www.careers.org/
  http://www.cweb.com/
  http://www.espan.com/
  http://www.monsterboard.com/
  http://www.occ.com/

Job Talk and General Discussion

Before you send away for instructions on how to make money at home stuffing envelopes, maybe you should check it out with your friends on the Net. If you need a job, have a job, or are offering a job, these Usenet groups are the place to talk and trade tips about employment, the workplace and careers.

Usenet:
  alt.building.jobs
  alt.computer.consultants.ads
  alt.jobs
  alt.sex.strippers.jobs
  comp.databases.oracle.marketplace
  comp.jobs.offered
  misc.jobs
  misc.jobs.discuss.job-search
  misc.jobs.misc
  misc.jobs.offered

You + Internet job resources –

JOBS AND THE WORKPLACE 417

Look What I Found on the Net...

```
Newsgroup: misc.jobs.misc
Subject: Internet Project

Help make me an Internet Millionaire.

Please send just $1.00 cash, check or money order, and in return
receive, by email ONLY, one of the following:

1.  World's Best Salsa Recipe.

2.  How to Meditate, Relax and Live Longer.

3.  Over 1000 Internet Sites to Advertise FREE or for a Small
    Fee.

4.  How to Make a Woman Scream...with Pleasure.
    (Just the introduction and first chapter on this one.)

Send your request to:

X. Xxxxx
Box ######
Xxxxxxx, Texas

Be sure to include your email address with your request.

And THANKS for participating in this important Internet Project.
```

Jobs for College Students and Graduates

There are so many career resources around the Net that you might never even have to leave the house to go to the employment agency. These sites have loads of links for college graduates and students. Look for a job and read useful information about résumés, interviewing, negotiating, and more.

Web:
http://www.college-recruiter.com/search.htm
http://www.collegegrad.com/
http://www.jobsource.com/
http://www.thejobresource.com/

anxiety =

Kingdomality

When you look for a job, you have to look now—that is, in the present. But what if you had lived in medieval times? You would have had much different employment choices, and maybe one of them would be more suitable for you than what you do now. To find out, all you need to do is answer a set of multiple choice questions. A computer program will then analyze your responses and tell you which type of job would have been best for you in medieval times. (According to the program, I am best suited for the job of Prime Minister.)

Web:
http://www.cmi-lmi.com/kingdom.html

happiness and satisfaction.

418 JOBS AND THE WORKPLACE

Medical Jobs

The medical field is vast. Whether you are looking for a job as a brain transplant specialist or merely a chrono-synclastic-infundibulum technician, MedSearch America is there to help you (at least in America).

Web:
  http://www.medsearch.com/

Usenet:
  alt.medical.sales.jobs.offered

Occupational Safety and Health

The Occupational Safety and Health Administration (OSHA) is an agency of the United States Department of Labor. OSHA's purpose is to "save lives, prevent injuries and protect the health of America's workers". Here is the official OSHA Web site, at which you will find general information about the agency and its programs and services. You can also read useful publications (such as factsheets about safety and health) and press releases, and access pertinent data and statistics. I've also included an additional Web site that collects links and information about general occupational safety and health topics.

Web:
  http://www-iea.me.tut.fi/cgi-bin/oshweb.pl
  http://www.osha.gov/

Repetitive Stress Injuries

Every day, you do the same type of work—again and again and again.

Before you know it, something hurts. Don't worry about it, people tell you. It will go away.

But it doesn't.

Every day, you do the same type of work— again and again and again.

You hurt more, and it doesn't go away.

It's time to find out about repetitive stress injuries.

Repetitive Stress Injuries

A repetitive stress injury (RSI)—also called a cumulative trauma disorder—is a medical condition caused by chronic stress to one or more parts of the body. The most common causes of RSIs are: repetitive motion, working in an awkward position, using an unbalanced force, and not resting enough. In the workplace, the common RSIs are carpal tunnel syndrome (a wrist condition often caused by too much typing), chronic back pain, tendonitis and—everyone's favorite—"stress". Here are some Web sites that have a wealth of information about RSIs, in and outside of the workplace. For discussion, you can read the Usenet groups. There is a lot you can do about workplace injuries caused by ongoing conditions, but before you can make a difference, you need to understand the real problems. The Net is a good place to start.

Web:
  http://www.rsihelp.com/
  http://www.rsihelp.org/
  http://www.ur-net.com/office-ergo/

Usenet:
  misc.health.injuries.rsi.misc
  misc.health.injuries.rsi.moderated

Résumés

These Web sites have hints to help you create or improve your résumé. I've also listed the various Usenet groups to which you can post your résumé. My advice is, post to these groups if you want, but don't stop there. There are various Web sites to which you can also send a résumé. One thing that may help you is to look at other people's résumés. Reading what other people write can give you good ideas about how to present yourself in the best possible manner.

Web:
  http://www.provenresumes.com/
  http://www.resumeadvisors.com/guidelines.htm

Usenet:
  alt.jobs.resumes
  misc.jobs.resume
  misc.jobs.resumes
  misc.jobs.wanted

Riley Guide

The Riley Guide is a great resource for learning how to use the Internet to find a job. Explore a comprehensive collection of information and tips explaining how the Net can help you get what you want. The guide is also useful for employers who want to learn how to use the Net to fill job openings.

Web:
  http://www.dbm.com/jobguide/

Salary and Wages

Are you being paid as much as you should be? As one of my readers, I know you are unusually intelligent, hard-working, dependable and talented, and, as such, deserve at least twice as much as you are being paid now. But how do you prove this to the people who control the money bags at your place of employment? Here are places where you will find various types of salary-related information: raw numbers, comparisons, negotiation strategies and salary calculators.

Web:
  http://verticals.yahoo.com/salary/
  http://www.jobsmart.org/tools/salary/
  http://www.wageweb.com/

Science Jobs

Scientists are like Sherlock Holmes. They spend their days looking for clues, gathering information and putting it together to solve the mysteries of the universe. If you have a career in science or if you want one, examine all the issues relating to the topic by checking out these Usenet groups. Scientists and researchers discuss their current projects, funding and job opportunities, as well as posting requests for information.

Usenet:
  alt.sci.geology.jobs
  bionet.jobs.wanted
  misc.jobs.fields.chemistry
  sci.research.careers
  sci.research.postdoc

Seasonal Employment

Having a job during your summer or winter vacation can be great. You work long hours in a menial position for very little money—and you have so much fun, you're sad when it's over. Believe me, when you get older, you will not want to work long hours in a menial position for very little money, so enjoy it now while you can.

Web:
  http://www.coolworks.com/
  http://www.summerjobs.com/

Sexual Harassment on the Job

If you have a problem with sexual harassment on the job, you are not alone. Before you get too upset, check with the Net, where you will find lots of relevant information: a list of hotline telephone numbers you can call for help and advice, a guide on how to handle difficult situations, as well as lots of information, opinion and discussion on this complex and volatile topic.

Web:
  http://www.employer-employee.com/sexhar1.htm
  http://www.feminist.org/911/harass.html
  http://www.resources.org/

Telecommuting

Telecommuting (or teleworking) refers to working at home as part of a regular job with an established company. Of course, some people have always worked at home, and home-based businesses are nothing new. What is new is that, with telecommuting, many people who traditionally would have worked in an office environment with lots of other people are now working at home. As you might imagine, this creates a variety of problems as people need to readjust to the logistical and social consequences of being by oneself. These sites have telecommuting resources that can help you.

Web:
  http://www.escapeartist.com/tele/commute.htm
  http://www.mother.com/~dfleming/dmflinks.htm
  http://www.tjobs.com/

TELECOMMUTING

It's been a long time since I did anything resembling a regular job. Mostly, I just stay home all day and do whatever I feel like. Sometimes I take a break, to have a snack or to play with my cat.

Telecommuting: It's dirty work, but someone's got to do it!

Temps

Being a temp—that is, working at temporary jobs—has some great advantages compared to being a permanent employee. You can work or not work as you wish. For example, you can take a long vacation, then work, save some money, and take another long vacation. Moreover, as a temp, you can ignore company politics and all the rest of the silliness that goes on in most workplaces. Of course, there are disadvantages. You can't always count on having a job when you want it, you probably won't get any benefits, and you will never make a huge amount of money. Clearly, such an environment calls for (1) good, solid information about the temp world and what jobs are available, and, (2) humor and fun. Here you are.

Web:

http://www.net-temps.com/
http://www.temp24-7.com/

Unions

A labor union is an organization dedicated to serving the interests of a particular group of workers. Unions concern themselves with wages, working conditions, grievance resolution, health issues, and so on. These Web sites will lead you to a great many union-related resources on the Net, so you can find what you need without having to work overtime.

Web:

http://laborlink.simplenet.com/
http://www.icem.org/resource/labres.html
http://www.igc.org/igc/ln/hg/unions.html

U.S. Government Jobs

Would you like to work for a U.S. federal or state agency? There are many jobs available, and these resources may be able to help you find what you want. For variety, I have also included the employment Web sites for the CIA and FBI, where, from time to time, you will see listings for jobs such as "Clandestine Service Trainee" and "Theatrical Effects Specialist".

Web:

http://www.fbi.gov/employment/employ.htm
http://www.hrsjobs.com/
http://www.jobsfed.com/
http://www.odci.gov/cia/employment/ciaeindex.htm
http://www.statejobs.com
http://www.usajobs.opm.gov/

Young Job Seekers

When you are young, you can be at a disadvantage because of a lack of experience. So when it comes time to find a job, let the Net help you with advice about finding a job, interviewing, evaluating the offers, and all the fun and games that you get to enjoy as you pass from the imaginary world of childhood to the imaginary world of adults.

Web:

http://www.jobsmarts.com/
http://www.studentcenter.com/

JOURNALISM AND MEDIA

Committee to Protect Journalists

Reporters who work in the United States operate within an environment of freedom of the press. In the U.S., such freedoms are protected by the Bill of Rights ("Congress shall make no law... abridging the freedom of speech, or of the press..."). However, in many parts of the world, there is no freedom of the press, and being a journalist with a conscience can be a dangerous job. This Web site, maintained by the Committee to Protect Journalists, reports on attacks against journalists around the world. Let us not forget that many reporters risk injury, prison and even death in pursuit of the freedoms that so many of us can take for granted. However, we live in a global community, and lack of freedom in one country often has a way of affecting us all when we least expect it.

Web:
http://www.cpj.org/

Environmental Journalist's Resources

This site is put together by the Society for Environmental Journalism, an organization devoted to helping journalists better inform the public about environmental issues. Expect to find links to environmental resources, environmental journalism organizations and newsletters. If you write about the environment, this is a Web site with which you should be familiar.

Web:
http://www.sej.org/

Gonzo Journalism

In the tradition of Hunter S. Thompson, gonzo journalism is the method of reporting in which the journalist is a participant in the series of events or story being reported on. Follow the discussion about Thompson and the concepts of gonzo journalism.

Usenet:
alt.journalism.gonzo

Look What I Found on the Net...

```
From the CIA Employment site:
    (http://www.odci.gov/cia/employment/ciaeindex.htm)

    ==============================
         Clandestine Service Trainee
    ==============================

For the extraordinary individual who wants more than a job,
this is a way of life that will challenge the deepest resources
of your intelligence, self-reliance, and  responsibility.
It demands an adventurous spirit, a forceful personality,
superior intellectual ability, toughness of mind, and the
highest degree of integrity.  It takes special skills and
professional discipline to produce results.  You will need
to deal with fast-moving, ambiguous, and unstructured
situations that will test your resourcefulness to the utmost.

This is the Clandestine Service, the vital human element of
intelligence collection.  These people are the cutting edge
of American intelligence, an elite corps gathering the vital
information needed by our policymakers to make critical foreign
policy decisions...

Entrance salaries range from $32,507 to $49,831 depending on
credentials...
```

Bedtime for Gonzo

Is there anyone who has read "Fear and Loathing in Las Vegas" and not felt Hunter S. Thompson to possess that spark of outrageous genius which is all too rare? Too bad, then, that the spark fanned into a dull flame that attenuated and died years ago, regretted by all. In its place, we have the legacy of Gonzo journalism, a largely mythical school of creation in which the writer is immersed in the events about which he is reporting. Still, as you might guess from reading this book, I firmly believe that irreverence is as irreverence does and that the spirit of Gonzo lives. So, if you are one of the atavistic intellectual hold-outs from the '70s, take some time and visit your friends in **alt.journalism.gonzo**. And if you happen to be reading this in a bookstore, buy this book or I will be forced to rip your lungs out.

International Federation of Journalists

I live in the United States, and it's easy to take freedom of the press for granted. But in many parts of the world, such freedoms are not always enjoyed. Repressive government regimes or warlike conditions will often censor and control news reporting. The International Federation of Journalism is a worldwide organization dedicated to the ideals of freedom of the press and social justice. They issue regular reports (in several languages) that monitor these issues around the world. The next time you think freedom is ubiquitous, go to this Web site and find out how repressed much of the world is. In my country, people more or less accept the idea of the press as a philosophical good, but that is not the case in a lot of places. However, I strongly believe the free flow of information has a civilizing influence on mankind and the synergy of the Internet and the International Federation of Journalists is a welcome one.

Web:
http://www.ifj.org/

Investigative Journalism

Investigative journalism has a long, mostly honorable, history. Many countries enjoy freedom of the press, and that freedom is used for more than supplying information. A free press serves as an important balance against the power and potential abuses of government officials. The investigative press is well represented on the Net: there is information for the curious (how do they find out all that stuff?), organizations for the professional, and a mailing list for the loquacious.

Web:
http://www.facsnet.org/
http://www.icij.org/
http://www.ire.org/
http://www.muckraker.org/

Listproc Mailing List:
List Name: **ire-l**
Subscribe to: **listproc@lists.missouri.edu**

Journalism Mailing Lists

For long-term discussion, nothing on the Net works better than a mailing list. On the Web you can find many lists in which people discuss various aspects of journalism. The **spj-l** list is for a general discussion of journalism, and the **journethics** list is for discussion about ethics in journalism.

Web:
http://reporter.umd.edu/listserv.htm
http://www.journalismnet.com/lists.htm

Listproc Mailing List:
List Name: **journethics**
Subscribe to: **listproc@lists.missouri.edu**

Listserv Mailing List:
List Name: **spj-l**
Subscribe to: **listserv@lists.psu.edu**

Take action.

JOURNALISM AND MEDIA

Don't click here.

Journalism Resources

Journalists spend their time collecting and publishing information, so it makes a lot of sense that the Net would be a wonderful tool for a working reporter or researcher. Here are some collections where you can find many, many resources. When you get a spare moment, I suggest that you explore, looking for those places that can help you. As you know, one of the most valuable possessions a journalist can have is a list of reliable sources. The time you spend creating such a list of Internet resources for yourself will be repaid many times over.

Web:
  http://liberty.uc.wlu.edu/~dgrefe/journalism/jourres.html
  http://www.markovits.com/journalism/
  http://www.moorhead.msus.edu/~gunarat/ijr/journalism.html

Journalism Student Resources

Are you young? Are you interested in journalism? Would you be willing to work long, impossible hours performing mundane tasks for little or no money? If you answered yes to all of these questions, you may be in line for a journalism internship. Well, here are some good places to find information about being an intern on a newspaper, magazine, television station or radio station. If you are a journalism student, you will find the Usenet group and mailing list helpful.

Web:
  http://www.freep.com/jobspage/interns/
  http://www.journalism.berkeley.edu/resources/jobs/

Usenet:
  alt.journalism.students

Majordomo Mailing List:
  List Name: **sj**
  Subscribe to: **majordomo@world.std.com**

Journalism Talk and General Discussion

Throughout the Net, journalists of varying size, shape and paycheck are discussing every aspect of journalism. Join the discussion. If you know what you are doing, contribute. If you don't know what you are doing, ask. If you don't know how to ask, just sit there and read what everyone else has to say (so you can report on it later).

Usenet:
  alt.journalism
  alt.journalism.criticism
  alt.journalism.freelance
  alt.journalism.gay-press
  alt.journalism.music
  alt.journalism.newspapers
  alt.journalism.newspapers.wkly-worldnews
  alt.journalism.print
  alt.music.journalism
  alt.news-media
  alt.periodismo

Media Watchdogs

Here are the Web sites for two of the principal media watch organizations in the United States. One group is Accuracy in Media (AIM), a conservative media watch organization. The second group is Fairness and Accuracy in Reporting (FAIR), a liberal media watch organization. The goal of each group is the same: to monitor and criticize writers, broadcasters and commentators who expound viewpoints with which the group disagrees.

Web:
  http://www.aim.org/aim.html
  http://www.igc.org/fair/

Next time you are at the supermarket, show them this book and ask for a discount (you never know...).

Look What I Found on the Net...

```
Newsgroup: alt.journalism
Subject: Tricks Journalists Use

> Are there any seasoned journalists or journalism students who
> can help me? I've been "enlisted" to take over a journalism
> course, but my background is in English, not journalism.
>
> I'd like to send the students out and have them dig deep into
> some campus issues... I'd like them to see that there are ways
> to trap an interviewee into answering something...
```

I think you are underestimating the amount of preparation and investigation that goes into an expose interview and overestimating the importance of questioning technique.

Let me give you one example from my personal experience. When Michael Jackson and Lisa Presley were allegedly married in May 1994, in the Dominican Republic, I knew in my gut it was a hoax.

I did a half-program broadcast on August 15. I said I only had questions about the holes in the story, but not the answers. It took another 16 months of painstaking investigation before I was able to sit in front of the Justice of the Peace and ask him for an on-camera interview.

I did not tell him of the evidence we had. Nor did I lie. He was blinded by the belief that he had gotten away with the hoax and could safely talk about the subject.

Step by step, the on-camera interviewer fed him the story he had already told the world. Date, place, time. We showed him the official records he had signed, and he happily confirmed his pivotal role in performing and recording the ceremony.

Then we showed him the proofs that he and Michael Jackson and Lisa Presley and their "witnesses" were really somewhere else at those exact moments: solid documentary evidence, as well as highly credible eyewitnesses. All our questions were simple: "Please help us understand this apparent discrepancy..."

We had records that proved none of the "wedding party" ever went closer than four hundred kilometers to the place the wedding supposedly took place...

We were about to show him the [incriminating] photo when he attacked us and tried to wreck the camera and grab the cassette. His 300-pound assistant locked us in the office, and his secretary was screaming, "Give him the gun." It was only the fact that the producer and sound man were experts in Aikido that allowed us to literally punch our way out with the tape.

No trick questions in the world would have nailed this guy. It was the slogging and brilliant work of a hard-working producer — following the trail I laid out for him — that got the evidence.

JOURNALISM AND MEDIA

> Everything I tell you is true.
> The above sentence is
> only partially correct.
> Don't believe everything you
> read.

Newslink

Newslink is a Web site featuring many resources related to journalism and the news. Read about news sources, hot news sites, links to newspapers, magazines, radio and television stations, other journalism resources, and much, much more. There are also feature articles reprinted from the American Journalism Review.

Web:
http://www.newslink.org/

Photojournalism

Every day, you see pictures in the newspaper, but for every picture you see, probably more than a hundred were taken and discarded. A photojournalist—someone who specializes in taking pictures for newspapers and magazines—has to be trained in photography and modern technology, and must conjure up immense amounts of patience and endurance to produce that one picture that may make it onto the page. These Web sites will lead you to a collection of photojournalism projects on the Net, as well as links to resources for photojournalism, regular journalism and photography. Even if you are not a photojournalist, you will find a great many interesting photos to enjoy. The Usenet group is for discussion of general issues about photojournalism and related topics.

Web:
http://www.digitalstoryteller.com/yitl/
http://www.newshunter.com/

Usenet:
alt.journalism.photo

Press Photographers

A press pass is a license to barge right in where non-journalistic angels would fear to tread. If you are lucky (and you have your camera with you), you'll be able to snap pictures of famous movie stars and world leaders. If you are not lucky (and you have your camera with you), you'll end up taking pictures of the winners of the Blizzard County 94th Annual Chili Cook-Off. Regardless, when it comes to journalism, press photography is where it's at (if you have your camera with you). The mailing list and Usenet group are forums in which photographers, photo and graphics editors, designers, teachers and students discuss this noble profession. When you get a chance, visit the Web site, which is sponsored by the National Press Photographers Association. (Don't forget your camera.)

Web:
http://sunsite.unc.edu/nppa/

Usenet:
bit.listserv.nppa-l

Listserv Mailing List:
List Name: **nppa-l**
Subscribe to: **listserv@cmuvm.csv.cmich.edu**

> If you have an interest in pictures and journalism, you'll find the Press Photographers' mailing list interesting and useful. After all, anyone can get the picture. But it takes someone really special to get paid for it.

Pulitzer Prize

The Hungarian-born American publisher Joseph Pulitzer (1847-1911) was not only a highly successful businessman, he was also a visionary. Before he died, Pulitzer endowed the Graduate School of Journalism at Columbia University, as well as an annual series of prizes (awarded by Columbia University) for achievements in American journalism, letters, drama and music. Over the years, the Pulitzer Prizes have become some of the most prestigious and certainly the most well-known awards for American writers. (I myself had to turn down several such awards, as I was too busy working on this book to attend the ceremony.) Here is the official site for the Pulitzer Prizes, where you can look at a list of current and previous winners, and a history of the prizes.

Web:
  http://www.pulitzer.org/

Radio and Television Companies

Here is a huge collection of links to the Web sites of broadcasting companies around the Net. When you need to find a particular media company, radio station, television station or network, this is a good place to start.

Web:
  http://www.broadcastinglinks.com/

Reporters Network

The Reporters Network is an organization formed to promote the use of the Internet by working journalists. This Web site contains a database of journalists who can register for free. If you are looking for a journalist, you can search by entering a location or a specialty. (I find this resource invaluable whenever I need to make out the guest list for a party.) If you are a working journalist, you can join the organization, which will provide you with Internet-related services, such as an email forwarding service and Web space.

Web:
  http://www.reporters.net/

Scholastic Journalism

One of the best and most satisfying ways to get journalism experience is to work on your school's newspaper or yearbook. When you are not writing feverishly to make your deadline, these Web sites can provide you with helpful information, including reference material, links to resources and contest notices. Even better, if you need a jumpstart with your own investigative writing, you can look at a list of creative ideas. ("Looking for another music alternative, some students have gone country. Has country become cool in your town?") Wow!

Web:
  http://members.aol.com/hsjourn/
  http://studentpress.journ.umn.edu/

Television Journalism

Any worthwhile job in the entertainment industry is going to be subject to immense competition, demanding conditions, and—for the very few people who manage to make it to the top—great rewards. The same holds true for television journalism, a unique hybrid between reporting and entertainment. This Web site contains articles and links related to the television news industry. You'll find information about TV stations, career strategies, newscast production, and more.

Web:
  http://www.tvrundown.com/

Would you like to be a television journalist? If so, practice this evening by using an empty soda bottle as a microphone at the dinner table. This will allow you to give play-by-play political commentary throughout the meal.

Then, when you have finished, connect to the Net and check with the Pulitzer Prize Web site to see if you've won an award.

KEYS AND LOCKS

History of Locks

Take a historical tour of locks through the ages. There are lots of cool pictures of old locks and the different uses to which locks were put in ancient times. Read interesting factual tidbits, such as: Catherine the Great collected locks, and Marie Antoinette's husband—King what's-his-name XVI—was a locksmith. If you like locks, you will enjoy these brief historical articles.

Web:
http://commercial.schlagelock.com/HistLock/00.html

Impressioning

As we go through life, it is handy to be able to make a good impression. However, if you want to be a locksmith, "impressioning" will do more than earn you the kindness of strangers, it will win you the admiration of everyone in your social circle (especially if you hang around with teenage boys). Impressioning is a technique used to create a key to fit a lock without taking the lock apart. You insert a key blank of the correct type and size. Turn the key to bind the pins and then wiggle it. This will produce small but noticeable marks on the shaft of the key in those places where the pins bind. Withdraw the key and carefully file down the shaft where you see marks. Repeat this process until you have a key that raises each of the pins to the shear line, opening the lock, or until someone comes along to open the lock with a real key. Does this sound like a good way to spend your spare time? Then check out this primer on the theory and practice of impressioning: a skill that every young person should master early in life.

Web:
http://www.telepath.com/pillar/impress.html

**Like mysteries?
Look at "Intrigue".**

Lock Talk and General Discussion

Do you need the name of a book that will show you how to get into a locked, keyless automobile? How about a reference on safe-cracking? Or an electronic copy of the MIT Guide to Lockpicking, by Ted the Tool? Or are you an amateur locksmith with a picky problem? Check with the lock and key set for all your needs. Just don't tell anyone where you found out about it.

Usenet:
alt.locksmithing

Lockpicking

I bet you would just love to be able to get into places where you are not supposed to be. Of course, as one of my readers you are scrupulously honest with a well-developed sense of ethics. However, wouldn't it be fun to know how to pick locks, just in case you have to some day? (For example, what would happen if the Queen of England came to visit one day and accidentally locked herself in the pantry?) Start with these guides to lockpicking. With a little knowledge—and a lot of practice—you will soon be a useful, important member of society, respected by all and worshipped by every male teenager you meet.

Web:
http://rtt.colorado.edu/~jnmiller/lock_pick.index.html
http://www.eunet.sk/stefan/docs/lock/lock2/
http://www.tacd.com/crime/security/index.html#guides

Locksmithing FAQ

This is the FAQ (frequently asked question list) for the **alt.locksmithing** Usenet group. This FAQ has lots of information about locksmithing. In particular, there are answers to common questions about lockpicking. Read advice on picking various types of locks, buying or making lockpicking tools, duplicating keys that say "Do Not Duplicate", opening a Kryptonite-style lock, and so on. You can also find out where to learn about lockpicking and locksmithing, learn useful terminology, see a short discourse on ethics, and much more.

Web:
http://www.indra.com/archives/alt-locksmithing/

Look What I Found on the Net...

(from the Locksmithing frequently asked question list)

How can I make my own picks and tension wrenches?

You can file or grind picks out of spring steel. It is best to use spring steel — sources include hacksaw blades, piano wire, clock springs... In a pinch, safety pin steel, or even a bobby pin can be used...

Where can I get the "MIT Guide to Picking Locks"?

Mattias Wingstedt has converted the Guide to HTML and made it available on the Web at:
    http://www.lysator.liu.se/mit-guide/mit-guide.html

What are "pick guns" or "automatic pickers" and do they work?

A "pick gun" is a manual or powered device that uses a vibrating pin to try to bounce the pin tumblers so there are spaces at the shear line so the plug can rotate. They are not a panacea, aren't always effective, and the Net seems to feel that these are no substitute for a little skill with a pick and learning how locks work...

Can the Club be picked? Is the Club any good?

[Note: The "Club" is a widely advertised automobile anti-theft device that you use to lock the steering wheel when you leave your car.]

"I used to have a Club, purchased on the recommendation of a coworker. The first time I tried picking it, it took me approximately 30 seconds, using the cap of a Papermate Flexgrip pen for tension, and a bent jumbo paper clip to rake the pins. With practice, I was able to reliably pick every Club device I encountered in 5-30 seconds using these tools."

However, it doesn't really matter, no car thief is going to pick it, they are going to cut the soft plastic steering wheel with a hacksaw or bolt cutters and slip the Club off.

Here are some of the things collected about locations and availabilities (most are from alt.locksmithing). We do not endorse any of these, but feel that you can get information by reading.

KEYS AND LOCKS

PADLOCK SHIM PICKS. Open padlocks in seconds! Our new padlock shim pick's unique design makes it so successful that it is frightening! Simply slide the shim down between the shackle and the lock housing, twist and the lock is open. Works best on laminated type padlocks (the most popular type) but will open almost any type of padlock — including the popular 3 number combination type...

PICK GUN. Picks locks FAST. Open locks in less than 5 seconds. Specifically designed for tumbler locks. Insert pick into key slot, then just pull trigger. Throws all pins into position at one time. Lock is then turned with tension bar. Used extensively by police and other government agencies...

PRO-LOK "CAR KILLER" KIT. Over the years we have had thousands of requests for a multi-vehicle opening kit. We are now able to offer the most complete kit that we have ever seen. This kit of tools will open over 135 automobiles, both domestic and foreign, on the road today. The opening procedure for each vehicle is diagrammed and explained in the instruction manual...

TUBULAR LOCK PICK. This tool is an easy and reliable method for picking tubular locks, as found on commercial vending machines, washers, dryers, etc...

HOW TO GET IN ANYWHERE, ANYTIME (video tape). Nearly two full hours of on-site techniques to get in any building, beat any lock, open any safe, enter any car...

TECHNIQUES OF BURGLAR ALARM BYPASSING. Alarms covered include: Magnetic Switches, Window Foil, Sound and Heat Detectors, Photoelectric Devices, Guard Dogs, Central Station Systems, Closed-Circuit Television and more...

TECHNIQUES OF SAFECRACKING...

HIGH SPEED ENTRY: INSTANT OPENING TECHNIQUES (video tape)...

THE COMPLETE GUIDE TO LOCK PICKING by Eddie the Wire. The very best book ever written on how to pick locks...

CIA FIELD-EXPEDIENT KEY CASTING MANUAL. How to make a duplicate key when you can keep the original only a short time...

HOW I STEAL CARS: A REPO MAN'S GUIDE TO CAR THIEVES' SECRETS (video tape). How to open and enter practically any modern automobile and how to start them without the key...

Locksmithing Terminology

If you want to understand keys and locks, you have to master the basic terminology. Here are some locksmithing glossaries to help you understand the literature and to make sure that—as one of my readers—you always sound like you know what you are doing.

Web:
http://www.clearstar.com/terms.htm
http://www.mfsales.com/release.html
http://www.telepath.com/pillar/cgi/lockdict

MIT Guide to Lock Picking

This well-written, easy to understand guide to lockpicking was originally developed by the MIT hacking community. They collected the information in order to teach each other how to pick the locks to the roofs and tunnels at MIT. In recent years, the MIT hackers have deplored the widespread dissemination of this information and have disowned the document (which was leaked to the outside world by an ex-MIT hacker named Ted T. Tool). Still, everyone calls it the "MIT Guide to Lock Picking". If you would like to find out how locks work—and how you can open them without a key—I know of no better place to start.

Web:
http://devbio-mac1.ucsf.edu/joe/locks/mitguide/mit-guide.html
http://www.flashback.se/archive/mit-guide.html
http://www.lysator.liu.se/mit-guide/mit-guide.html

Are you a know-it-all? Check in "Trivia" for tidbits of useless information.

MIT Guide to Lock Picking

THEY would prefer that you do not read this document.

THEY do not want you to learn how to pick locks.

THEY wish that such information was not available on the Net.

Too bad for them.

Murphy's Laws of Locksmithing

You have probably heard of Murphy's Law: "Anything that can go wrong, will." Although locksmithing requires specialized skills and a great deal of practice, locksmiths are not immune to unintended mishaps and accidents. Here is a witty collection of aphorisms that express the spirit of Murphy's Law applied to locksmithing. For example: "Parts that are difficult to install will freely fall out on their own," and "The number of witnesses available is directly proportional to the skill you demonstrate." Actually, now that I think of it, these sayings also apply to writers. For instance, in my experience, it is very difficult to install new vowels into a paragraph, and yet, they are always the first letters to fall out of a book and onto the floor of the library.

Web:
http://www.jfbdtp.com/Murphy.html

Picking Locks and Opening Safes

You can pick your friends, and (if you read the information at the site) you can learn how to pick locks. But here is something that can be even handier. Suppose the Pope comes over to your house and accidentally locks himself into a safe for which no one has the combination. (This actually happened to me once.) You will be glad that, at a moment's notice, you can connect to the Net and find out all kinds of useful ways to open a locked safe. Learn about using sound, drilling, punching, grinding and burning. Of course, this might take a while, so be sure to have some reading material in the safe for visitors. (In my case, it worked out okay, as the safe contained my entire collection of Superman and Donald Duck comics, most of which the Pope hadn't already read.)

Web:
http://devbio-mac1.ucsf.edu/joe/locks/scienceof.html

KIDS

Ask Jeeves for Kids

A character created by P.G. Wodehouse (pronounced "Wood-house"), Jeeves is a valet who works for a young man-about-town named Bertie Wooster. Jeeves is knowledgeable, highly intelligent, and adept at finding solutions to sticky problems. This Web site, Ask Jeeves for Kids, is designed to answer children's questions. You will have the best luck asking for information ("What is a dinosaur?"). The answer will lead you to places on the Net that may have the answer to your question. If you are a parent, this is a good resource to use with your kids. Ask a question, and then explore the answers together.

Web:
http://www.ajkids.com/

Astronomy Picture of the Day

Every day, there is a different astronomy picture placed on this Web page. Along with the picture you will find description information as well as links to other related places. If you like astronomy, this is a great place to visit every day when you get home from school.

Web:
http://antwrp.gsfc.nasa.gov/apod/astropix.html

Bee-Eye

Did you ever wonder what the world looks like from a bee's point of view? Now you can know. Click on a shape or an image and see how it would look to a bee.

Web:
http://cvs.anu.edu.au/andy/beye/beyehome.html

Best Sites for Children

There are scads of Internet sites just for kids, so how do you know where to start? Here is a carefully organized collection of high-quality resources for kids. Find links to places where your kids can have fun, learn and meet other children.

Web:
http://db.cochran.com/db_HTML:theopage.db

*Of course, you want what's best for your kids. Start them with the **Best Sites for Children.** In a few weeks, they'll be teaching you how to use the Net.*

Contests for Kids

Enjoy these collections of links to contests that are related to or about kids. (I am thinking of having a Harley contest. Whoever can think of the best idea for a Harley contest gets a free, autographed book.) Lots of these contests are sponsored by commercial companies that are giving away free stuff in drawings or scavenger hunts for publicity. Still, fun is fun. Just remember, if you have to type in your name and address, you are going to end up on someone's mailing list.

Web:
http://www.huronline.com/kids.htm
http://www.kidsdomain.com/kids/contests.html

Cyberkids Magazine

This is an online magazine made by kids for kids. Visit the reading room and the art gallery. Listen to music compositions by other children. Read messages from kids around the world. There is lots to do at this Web site.

Web:
  http://www.cyberkids.com/

Dinosaurs for Kids

I'm not sure why it is, but all kids like dinosaurs. I remember when I was a kid, I got my brother a dinosaur book for his birthday. I didn't even wonder if he would like it: I knew he would. I liked dinosaurs, my brother liked dinosaurs, all our friends liked dinosaurs. So kids, do you like dinosaurs? Of course you do, so here are some great Web sites where you can enjoy a lot of dinosaur stuff and look at some really cool pictures. If you want to talk about dinosaurs, join the Usenet discussion group. And you know what? I bet when you grow up you'll still like dinosaurs (except Barney, of course).

Web:
  http://www.a1.com/children/dino.htm
  http://www.gl.umbc.edu/~tkeese1/dinosaur/
    gallery.htm
  http://www.zoomdinosaurs.com/

Usenet:
  alt.dinosaur

Learn HTML and create your own Web page see "Web: Creating Web Pages").

Droodles

A droodle is a cross between a riddle and a doodle. Look at a picture and try to figure out the riddle within the image. Check out the droodle of the week, as well as an archive of past droodles. (In case you get stumped, the correct answers are available.) If you feel creative, you can contribute by sending in your own droodle.

Web:
  http://www.webonly.com/droodles/

Heroes

We all need someone to inspire us. My heroes, for example, are Isaac Asimov, P.G. Wodehouse, Freddy the Pig, Carl Reiner and Perry Mason. Here is a Web site that will let you find out about various men and women people admire as heroes. There are buttons on the page you can press for the type of hero you want to read about: a teacher hero, an artist hero, a business hero, a writer hero, and so on. This is an interactive site, so you can tell the people who maintain the site about your favorite hero, and send in text and pictures and they might add it to the page. Or you can sign the hero guestbook and write about your hero there for everyone else to see.

Web:
  http://www.myhero.com/

Help your kids bring out the best in themselves, by helping them find a real live hero to admire.

Imagination Station

Mark Kistler describes himself as a high-energy art crusader. I have known Mark for many years, and I can tell you that "high-energy" doesn't even begin to describe him. Mark bounces around the world teaching children how to be smarter, better and happier by learning how to draw in three dimensions. He discourages kids from watching too much TV. Instead, Mark inspires the little ones to be "creative geniuses". When he's not teaching kids in person, Mark is writing books, taping his popular television show, and putting on special programs for teachers and parents. I would guess that, in his lifetime, Mark Kistler has taught drawing to more children than anyone in the world. Would you like to learn how to draw in 3-D? Visit Mark's Imagination Station where you can take some free lessons from Mark and learn how to put "pencil power" to work for you.

Web:
http://www.draw3d.com/

KidPub

Are you a kid who likes to write stories? Here is the place for you. Send in your stories and they will be put on the Web, so anyone in the world can read them. You can then tell your friends to look on the Web for your story. Later you can check back, and see how many people have looked at your story since it was put on the Web. I like to check the site once in a while, just to find something interesting. Many of the stories are well-written and fun to read. Some of the stories are especially thought-provoking, and argue a high degree of natural talent.

Web:
http://www.kidpub.org/kidpub/

Kids Click

Here is a Web site created by librarians just for kids. Visit here and you'll find a lot of activities: music, drawing, theater, ghosts, cars, spacecraft, stories, poetry, pets, hobbies and crafts. And it's even more fun than a library, because you can make as much noise as you want.

Web:
http://sunsite.berkeley.edu/kidsclick/

Kids Report

If I were a kid (and I used to be one), I would want to read what other kids think about Web sites. Well, the Kids Report has just that type of information: real kids write about real K-12 Web sites for real readers (like you). Warning: Teachers do help to put each issue together, but the kids choose all the sites and write the descriptions, so it's still cool.

Web:
http://scout.cs.wisc.edu/scout/kids/

Kids Space

The name tells it all: a place for kids (under 16) to hang around on the Net. Here you will find lots of activities just for kids: pictures, stories, movies, penpals, Web pages by kids, and more. If you are new to the Net, there is a lot of help, specially designed just for kids. Finally, for teachers and parents, there are facilities for schools from all over the world to participate in the fun, as well as extra information to help you use the Net with your kids. If you have kids, if you teach kids, or if you are a kid, this is a place you will want to visit.

Web:
http://www.kids-space.org/

Kids Talk and General Discussion

Clubhouses and playhouses are always fun because they are great places to hang out and be yourself with no parents allowed. There is a place like that on Usenet, where you can talk about anything you want and it's just for you—so, parents, no peeking.

Usenet:
alt.kids-talk

NO ADULTS ALLOWED!

Kids, would you like to talk to other kids around the world?

Join the discussion on the **alt.kids-talk** Usenet group.

It's for kids only. No parents, teachers or any other adults are allowed.

Knot Tying

Here are some great Web sites that can teach you all about tying knots. You will find diagrams showing you exactly how to create some really cool-looking knots. Have you ever wondered, why are there so many different knots? It's because there are many different uses for knots. For example, the knot you would use to tie down a tent or a tarp would be different from the knot you use to tie a boat to the pier. Once you learn about different knots—and when to use each one—you will find your knowledge useful in many situations. As a matter of fact, after spending some time practicing your knots, I bet you will be walking around looking for something to tie up.

Web:
http://www.earlham.edu/~peters/knotlink.htm
http://www.netg.se/~jan/knots.htm

Usenet:
rec.crafts.knots

National Wildlife Federation Kids Stuff

This site is put together by the National Wildlife Foundation. There are games, riddles and facts about animals. For example, honey bees make a total of 10 million trips between their hives and flowers for each pound of honey they make. (And you only have to make one trip to the supermarket to buy all the honey you want.) Take an educational (but fun) tour of water, wetlands, endangered species and U.S. public lands, and visit other fun science sites.

Web:
http://www.nwf.org/kids/

The Net can help you buy a car. See "Cars and Trucks" or "Shopping".

Papermaking

Have you ever made your own paper? Here are instructions to show you how to take old newspapers and recycle them into brand new paper. The instructions start out: "Making recycled paper is messy." I'm convinced. I would walk a mile out of my way to do something messy.

Web:
http://www.beakman.com/paper/paper.html
http://www.chicojr.chico.k12.ca.us/paper.html

Papermaking

Making paper is fun.
Making paper is cool.
Making paper is something
you can do at home.
So go make some paper.
(And then use it to write a note to someone you love.)

Poetry for Kids

Kenn Nesbitt is a writer with a wonderful sense of whimsy, and kids love his poetry. This Web site features a wonderful collection of original poems along with humorous illustrations. For parents who are teaching their children to read, these are fun poems to read aloud.

Web:
http://www.poetry4kids.com/

Preschool Pages

Here are some Web sites designed especially for preschoolers, with colorful pictures and simple writing. One Web site has pictures of various animals with some writing about each animal, as well as stories. The other site is for parents and teachers of preschoolers. You will find seasonal activities, craft ideas, preschool projects, printable pages of worksheets, music activities, kids' cooking activities, and more.

Web:
http://www.earlychildhood.com/art.html
http://www.meddybemps.com/7.33.html
http://www.theideabox.com/

Sites for Kids

Doing homework, cleaning your room, taking out the garbage, and clearing the table are all enjoyable activities. But life can't be fun all the time. Sometimes you need to spend some time using the Internet to look at stuff like comics, cartoons, art, writing, science, games, sports, toys, music, entertainment and stories. (If your parents don't understand, you can tell them I said it's educational.) My advice is, enjoy it all while you can. It won't be long till you are an adult, and you'll have to spend your leisure time playing golf, and having serious discussions about politics and interest rates.

Web:
http://www.ala.org/parentspage/greatsites/amazing.html
http://www.netmom.com/ikyp/samples/hotlist.htm

Solve a Mystery

Do you like mysteries? See if you can solve the ones at this Web site. Do you like to read mystery stories? You'll find something diverting to read here. Do you like to write your own mystery stories? Write one and enter it in a contest. Do you like to amaze your friends? Learn a new magic trick. Spend some time developing your talents, and soon you will be a mystery master.

Web:
http://www.thecase.com/kids/

String Figures

String figures—such as those created when you play the traditional Cat's Cradle game—are patterns made from a loop of string which you wind around your fingers. You can make such figures by yourself or with another person (by passing the loops back and forth). Most of the time you only need your fingers, but sometimes, with more complicated patterns, you also have to use your feet or mouth. Visit this Web site and learn about the background of string figure games, as well as browse lists of string figures, diagrams and step-by-step instructions for making the patterns.

Web:
http://www.isfa.org/~webweavers/isfa.htm

Sugar Bush

Sugar Bush has stories by kids that are displayed in large type to make them easy to read. Many of the stories have links in them that give you interesting information about characters in the story. There is also a collection of craft projects, as well as a treasure hunt section where you have to find the answers to questions by looking at other Web pages. This is a good place for youngsters to get started on the Net.

Web:
http://intranet.ca/~dlemire/sb_kids.html

Wendy's World of Stories for Children

This wonderful, charming site—created by a wonderful, charming woman—has a collection of stories for children: poetry, myths, fairy tales, fables, campfire stories, and original stories and poems. Some of the stories are illustrated; all are great for younger kids or for anyone who enjoys children's stories. Parents: This is a great site to visit with your kids. Help them learn how to read by exploring Wendy's World of Stories together.

Web:
http://www.wendy.com/children/

Wendy's World of Stories for Children

Reading and listening to stories is an important part of our culture. So take your kids to Wendy's World of Stories for Children, where they will learn and enjoy themselves at the same time.

It's a win-win-win-win activity.

(Your kids win, because they will have a great time while they are practicing their reading or listening to a story. You win, because you will enjoy spending pleasant hours reading with your children. Wendy wins, because she is able to help children and parents around the world enjoy stories. And I win, because after you all have such a good time, you are bound to want to rush out and buy lots of copies of this book for your friends.)

White House Tour for Kids

Would you like to take a kids' tour of the White House? Learn about this famous building (the home of the U.S. President and his family). Read about its history, the President, children of various Presidents, White House pets, and so on. You can also send a letter to the President and tell him your ideas. Note: Enjoy yourself writing the President if you want, but please understand that he is very busy and does not have time to write you back. (Actually, I think you would be better off writing a letter to Santa Claus and leaving it where your parents can see it accidentally.)

Web:
  http://www.whitehouse.gov/WH/kids/html/

Wild Weather

This page is created by a TV weatherman in order to explain weather to kids. The topics include clouds, temperature, pressure, radar, tornadoes, hurricanes, lightning and forecasting. Have you got a weather question? Send a note to the weatherman. In addition, there are resources for teachers who want to teach their kids about weather.

Web:
  http://www.whnt19.com/kidwx/

Yahooligans

This is the kids' version of the famous Yahoo site. As with the main site, you can find resources by selecting a category, or by searching the database for a specific word or phrase. There are lots and lots (and lots) of resources for kids here. Warning #1: This site contains advertisements directed towards children. (Someone has to pay.) Warning #2: If you join the club (Club Yahooligans), you will be put on a mailing list.

Web:
  http://www.yahooligans.com/

Yucky Stuff

This is called "The Yuckiest Site on the Internet". (To tell you the truth, I know of other, more yucky sites, but I can't mention them in a family book.) Actually, the material here is only yucky if you don't like bugs. If you do, come right in and visit Worm World and Cockroach World. I bet you'll learn something interesting.

Web:
  http://www.nj.com/yucky/

LANGUAGE

American Sign Language

When I was younger and living in Berkeley, I studied ASL (American Sign Language) for a semester, and I found it to be the most beautiful language I have ever seen. If I could pick a second language in which to be fluent, it would be ASL. (Unfortunately, I am not one to pick up second languages. For over 10 years, the Canadian government tried to get me to learn French, and they failed miserably.)

Web:
   http://where.com/scott.net/asl/
   http://www.aslinfo.com/

Listserv Mailing List:
   List Name: **teachasl**
   Subscribe to: listserv@admin.humberc.on.ca

Arabic

If Arabic is on your list of things to learn before retirement, you are in luck. Download audio lessons, films, music and pictures. Or if you don't have time for a multimedia experience, check out some vocabulary and nifty-looking Arabic fonts.

Web:
   http://arabic.wjh.harvard.edu/
   http://philae.sas.upenn.edu/Arabic/arabic.html

British-American Lexicons

Although it seems as if the English and the Americans speak the same language, there are a lot of words that are used differently in each country. For example, an Englishman who has had a little too much to drink may think nothing of eating a chip butty. An American wouldn't know a chip butty if it bit him in the face. To help you avoid unnecessary confusion—or perhaps create some intentional confusion of your own—here is a list of British-American lexicons to fill the transatlantic gaps in your vocabulary.

Web:
   http://pages.prodigy.com/NY/NYC/britspk/
      dictlink.html

Chinese

There are a great many Chinese resources on the Net. In order to use them, you need to have the appropriate software. Here is a large list of resources relating to the Chinese language, including information about how to view and listen to Chinese on the Net.

Web:
   http://www.webcom.com/bamboo/chinese/

Usenet:
   alt.chinese.story
   alt.chinese.text
   alt.chinese.text.big5
   alt.chinese.text.hz
   alt.usage.chinese

Cliché Finder

Type in a word, any word, and if there are common clichés that use that word, they will pop up on your screen faster than a speeding crawfish. Before you can say "a wet bird never flies at night", you'll have more clichés than a nitro-powered weed whacker. If you've been racking your brain for the right word, you'll never know if you don't try, so go to this Web site and stop on a dime. It might be true that money can't buy happiness, but as I always say, "Don't worry about the horse being blind. Just load the wagon."

Web:
   http://www.westegg.com/cliche/

Computation and Language E-Print Archive

This archive provides automated access to papers and preprints relating to computational linguistics, natural language processing, speech processing, and other fields. If you are a researcher in one of these areas, you will find this Web site a valuable way to keep up on current publications and search through the journals.

Web:
   http://xxx.lanl.gov/cmp-lg/

Cyrillic Alphabet

The Cyrillic alphabet is used to write Russian and certain other Slavic languages. The name comes from St. Cyril who—along with his brother St. Methodius—was said to have introduced this alphabet in their missionary work among the southern Slavs. Here is a great resource that can help you learn to read the Cyrillic alphabet, as well as understand something of its role in history and culture.

Web:
http://www.friends-partners.org/friends/cyrillic/

Czech

The Czech language (spoken in the Czech Republic) is a Slavic language with roots in the Indo-European family of languages. Here is information about Czech as well as an English-Czech dictionary. Mluvite anglicky? Dekuji.

Web:
http://ww2.fce.vutbr.cz/bin/ecd
http://www.muselik.com/czech/czau.html

IRC:
#czech

The Internet is more fun than a barrel of clichés.

Dutch

Slip off your wooden shoes and cozy up to the keyboard for some discussion of Dutch language and literature. The Web sites cover pronunciation and grammar.

Web:
http://dictionaries.travlang.com/DutchEnglish/
http://www.notam.uio.no/~hcholm/altlang/ht/Dutch.html

Usenet:
alt.reddingsbrigade

IRC:
#dutch

Look What I Found on the Net...

(from a paper in the Computation and Language E-Print Archive)

This paper discusses the processes by which conversants in a dialogue can infer whether their assertions and proposals have been accepted or rejected by their conversational partners.

It expands on previous work by showing that logical consistency is a necessary indicator of acceptance, but that it is not sufficient, and that logical inconsistency is sufficient as an indicator of rejection, but it is not necessary.

I show how conversants can use information structure and prosody, as well as logical reasoning, in distinguishing between acceptances and logically consistent rejections, and relate this work to previous work on implicature and default reasoning by introducing three new classes of rejection:

- implicature rejections
- epistemic rejections
- deliberation rejections

I show how these rejections are inferred as a result of default inferences, which, by other analyses, would have been blocked by the context...

Eastern European Languages

Would you like to learn basic words and phrases in an Eastern European language? Just select a language and you will be shown a small but useful list of words in that language. Although the vocabulary is limited, you can at least learn enough to stay out of trouble. The word lists are available in Albanian, Croatian, Estonian, Latvian, Polish, Russian, Slovak, Bulgarian, Czech, Hungarian, Lithuanian, Romanian, Serbian and Slovenian. As they say in Lithuanian, "Nesuprantu."

Web:
http://www.cusd.claremont.edu/~tkroll/EastEur/

Usenet:
alt.pl
alt.pl.uzywki

English

The sun may have set on the British Empire, but their language lives on around the world. Here are a variety of interesting resources relating to the English language. To discuss English, try Usenet and the mailing lists. Interesting true fact: More Harley Hahn books are written in English than in any other language.

Web:
http://ebbs.english.vt.edu/hel/hel.html
http://gs213.sp.cs.cmu.edu/prog/webster/
http://www.comenius.com/

Usenet:
alt.english.usage
bit.listserv.words-l

Listproc Mailing List:
List Name: **hel-l**
Subscribe to: **listproc@ebbs.english.vt.edu**

Listserv Mailing List:
List Name: **words-l**
Subscribe to: **listserv@uga.cc.uga.edu**

Esperanto

Esperanto is a language invented by the Polish doctor L.L. Zamenhof in the late 19th century. His idea was that if everyone spoke the same language, we would all get along better, and war would be much less likely. The idea of an artificial language is not uncommon: hundreds of such languages have been proposed in the last few centuries. Perhaps one of the most interesting was Solresol, developed by Jean Francois Sudre (1866). Its vocabulary was based on the notes of the musical scale, making it possible to sing as well as speak the language. Esperanto is the most well-known and successful artificial language. Because it is based on the European Romance languages, Esperanto is difficult to learn for people with a completely different mother tongue (Chinese, Japanese, Russian, and so on). However, as languages go, Esperanto is straightforward and sensible, and there are many enthusiasts around the world who enjoy speaking and promoting the language.

Web:
http://www.esperanto.net/veb/faq.html
http://www.esperanto.org/

Usenet:
alt.talk.esperanto
alt.uu.lang.esperanto.misc
soc.culture.esperanto

Listserv Mailing List:
List Name: **esper-l**
Subscribe to: **listserv@vm.ege.edu.tr**

IRC:
#esperanto

Look What I Found on the Net...

```
Newsgroup: bit.listserv.words-l
Subject: Linguistic Terminology

> "Rhetorical device", "linguistic phenomenon", what's the deal
> with sullying the name of linguistics this way?  I guess it's
> called metonymy.  Of course, for you guys everything is
> metaphor, right?

A man's reach should exceed his grasp, or what's a meta phor?
```

LANGUAGE

Filled Pauses

A filled pause is a meaningless sound (like "um" or "uh") that some people use as they talk. You and I tend to ignore such tiny conversational delays, but there are people who study such "hesitation phenomena". This Web site is devoted to filled pauses, and I find it fascinating reading for the insight it gives into human nature—all of which reminds me of the Great Um Contest. When I was an undergraduate math student, I had a professor who used to say "um" a lot. On the last day of the semester, a friend (Pete) and I decided to run a contest in which people would have to guess how many times the professor would say "um" during the final lecture. We cut up some small pieces of paper. On each piece was written a different number (50, 55, 60, and so on). We then put all the pieces into a hat. As each person entered the class, we had them pay 10 cents to draw a number from the hat. During the class, my friend and I kept track of the number of times the professor said "um". The idea was that whoever drew the number that was closest to the total would get all the money. The whole thing was a lot of fun, because everyone in the class, except the professor, knew what we were doing. Each time the professor said "um", people would smirk and signal to us to make sure we caught it. Without a doubt, that was the most interesting class of the semester. How did it end? The professor said "um" 147 times in 50 minutes, and the money was won by Pete, who happened to have drawn the number 145.

Web:
http://www.cisnet.or.jp/home/rlrose/pause/Default.htm

If this were Chapter R, "Romance" would be just around the corner.

You know, it's funny. As a young lad in Canada, I studied French for 10 years, and I still can't speak it fluently. And yet, in France, young children hang around in the street with no education whatsoever speaking the language like natives. Perhaps they have access to the **Foreign Language Dictionaries.**

Foreign Language Dictionaries

From time to time I have an immediate need to translate a particular word into another language. For example, just the other day I was wondering, what was the Dutch word for hippopotamus? All I had to do was connect to one of these online dictionaries, and before you could say "get back to work", I knew that the Dutch word for hippopotamus was nijlpaard.

Web:
http://dictionaries.travlang.com/
http://www.facstaff.bucknell.edu/rbeard/diction.html
http://www.logos.it/query/query.html

Foreign Languages for Travelers

Are you going to visit a foreign country where it would help if you knew some of the most important words in their language? Just specify which language you already speak and which language you want to learn. You will then see a list of choices for phrases you can learn: basic words, numbers, shopping, travel, directions, places, times and dates. You can see a list of countries where the foreign language is spoken as well as links to related resources.

Web:
http://www.travlang.com/languages/

French

French is a member of the family of Romance languages, and thus has much in common with Spanish, Italian, Portuguese and other such languages. However, French has a distinct personality, a certain *je ne sais quoi* that makes it unlike any other language. French is the 11th most widely used language in the world. Of course, French is spoken throughout France, but you also find the language in parts of Belgium and Switzerland, as well as in areas that were formerly under French control, such as Algeria and French Polynesia (including Tahiti). There is also a form of French spoken in the province of Quebec in Canada, as well as a Creole version used by Cajun speakers in the south-central United States. There are many reasons why you might want to learn French. (What I like best is being able to read the menus in snooty restaurants.)

Web:
http://etext.lib.virginia.edu/french.html
http://hapax.be.sbc.edu/
http://library.adelaide.edu.au/guide/hum/french/
http://web.culture.fr/

Usenet:
alt.french

Listproc Mailing List:
List Name: **francais**
Subscribe to: **listproc@gac.edu**

Listproc Mailing List:
List Name: **frenchtalk**
Subscribe to: **listproc@list.cren.net**

IRC:
#french

Gaelic

Gaelic is the English word used to describe Irish Gaelic, Manx Gaelic and Scottish Gaelic, the three languages that form one half of the Celtic language family group. These sites offer examples of spoken Gaelic, a short history of the Celts, mailing list archives, lists of Gaelic books and tapes, Irish National Radio news, and links to many other Celtic-related topics and resources.

Web:
http://sunsite.unc.edu/gaelic/gaelic.html
http://www.ceantar.org/

Listserv Mailing List:
List Name: **gaelic-l**
Subscribe to: **listserv@listserv.hea.ie**

German

Sprechen Sie Deutsch? Brush up on your German by asking questions, reading posts and practicing in this Usenet group. Discussion is held in both English and German. If you're up to a real-time test, try your skill on the IRC channels. For reference, you can find German/English dictionaries on the Web.

Web:
http://www.leo.org/cgi-bin/dict-search
http://www.lib.ua.edu/dict6.htm

Usenet:
alt.usage.german

IRC:
#german
#germany

Greek

The word "Greek" actually refers to two different, but related, languages. First, there is modern Greek, the language spoken today by more than 10 million people in Greece, a majority of the people on Cyprus, as well as Greeks around the world. Ancient Greek—the language of Homer and Aristotle—is a family of dialects that was used over two thousand years ago. These Web sites have many resources related to modern and ancient Greek. If you want to know about the language, there is something here for you—whether you are a serious scholar or just planning a vacation trip to the Greek Islands.

Web:
http://www.travlang.com/languages/greek/
http://www.webexpert.net/vasilios/grklng1.htm

Hawaiian

The Hawaiian language has five vowels (a, e, i, o, u) and only seven consonants (h, k, l, m, n, p, t, w). Thus, for English speakers, Hawaiian words, at first, can look confusing. For example, ho'alohaloha means "to make love" or "to give thanks"; elemakule means "an old man"; and hoaloha means "a friend". (I'll leave it to you to put these words together into a sentence.) Would you like to learn a bit of Hawaiian? Give it a try—I bet you'll enjoy it. By the way, my favorite Hawaiian word is nananana ("spider").

Web:
http://www.olelo.hawaii.edu/
http://www.volcanoalley.com/lang.html

442 LANGUAGE

Going to Maui soon? Perhaps a copy of the Hawaiian dictionary would help you. It really helps to be able to talk to the natives in their own language when you need to say, "Can I please have a condo that does not overlook the parking lot?"

Hindi

In India, Hindi is spoken by about 480 million people (180 million as a mother tongue, 300 million as a second language). Hindi is an especially expressive language. A poet writing in Hindi can use simple words to convey sophisticated emotional overtones. There are also many beautiful Hindi songs which are loved by people around the world. (In English, of course, we have our own lovely songs, such as "Satisfaction" and "Rudolf the Red-Nosed Reindeer".) Here are some Internet resources to help you learn about Hindi and the cultures in which it is spoken.

Web:
http://philae.sas.upenn.edu/Hindi/hindi.html
http://www.cs.colostate.edu/~malaiya/hindiint.html

Icelandic

Icelandic, the official language of Iceland, is a Scandinavian language that is the purest descendent of Old Norse. Here is a site for learning about the language and the country in which it is spoken. Hint to guys: If you are traveling in Iceland, and you meet a beautiful young woman, here is the right thing to say: "Þú ert engill af himni ofan. Ég hef aldrei séð yndislegri konu. Getur pabbi þinn lúbarið mig?"

Web:
http://www.call.gov/resource/language/icelr000.htm

Usenet:
alt.usage.icelandic

Italian

Is there anything more beautiful than listening to someone in love speak Italian? Actually, even when Italians are arguing they sound kind of cool. If you are learning to speak and read Italian, here are some resources that can help. For real-time practice, try IRC.

Web:
http://www.eat.com/learn-italian/
http://www.qi3.com/vince/italia96/phrases1.html

Usenet:
alt.usage.italiano

IRC:
#italia

Japanese

Is your kanji a bit weak? Or do you just need a bit of help with pronunciation? These resources will help you with Japanese vocabulary and pronunciation. So the next time you go out for sushi, you won't have to just point at the menu and say, "I'll have that thing." You can ask for raw tuna with such a good accent, the fish will sit up and bow to you.

Web:
http://www.missouri.edu/~c563382/OtherSites/Beginning.html
http://www.ntt.co.jp/japan/japanese/

Usenet:
alt.japanese.misc
alt.japanese.text
sci.lang.japan

IRC:
#japan
#nippon

Language IRC Channels

Here are a few IRC channels where you can meet new friends and talk in different languages. Whether you are a native speaker or a student of a second language, IRC is the place to be.

IRC:
#espanol
#francais
#france
#italia
#russian
#Spanish
#turkey

LANGUAGE

*Talk, talk, talk. In any language. At any time. **Now**. On **IRC**. Be there or be square (in several languages at the same time).*

Language Playground

This Web site has links to some wonderful language tools in the areas of grammar, punctuation and word usage. If you care about language and you like writing well, you will enjoy spending some time here experimenting with words and meanings.

Web:
http://www.link.cs.cmu.edu/dougb/playground.html

Language Translator

This Web site provides a wonderful service. You can type in any text you want, and a computer program will translate the text from one language to another. As you might expect, the translation is not perfect, but it is usually good enough. Moreover, it's free and it's fast. What's even more useful is that you can use this same service to translate a Web page that is written in a foreign language. Just specify a URL. The program will fetch that Web page for you and translate it automatically.

Web:
http://babelfish.altavista.digital.com/

Languages of the World

Here are some collections of information about the various languages spoken by humans and other animals. If you are interested in any particular language or country, I guarantee you can find information that will astonish you. For example, did you know that in the United States, there are 213 languages, 176 of which are living, 35 of which are extinct, and two that are a second language only with no mother tongue speakers?

Web:
http://www.sil.org/ethnologue/ethnologue.html

Latin

Latin is the language spoken by the ancient Romans (although the Latin we learn today has been modified over the years). Latin is important for three main reasons. First, many ancient documents and books are written in Latin. Second, Latin is the basis of our modern Romance languages (such as French, Spanish, Italian and Portuguese). Finally, Latin is important to the traditions and liturgy of the Roman Catholic Church. Here are some Latin resources that will help you learn and appreciate the language.

Web:
http://www.csbsju.edu/library/internet/latin.html
http://www.math.ubc.ca/~cass/frivs/latin-dict-full.html
http://www.nd.edu/~archives/latgramm.htm

Linguistic Talk and General Discussion

The Usenet groups are where scholars of linguistics hang out to discuss the scientific and historical study of human language. Get in on some hot and heavy discussion of Latin declensions or a quick and dirty comparison of Frisian to Old English. To help you participate in the discussion, I have included a Web site that contains the FAQ (frequently asked question list) for the **sci.lang** group, as well as another site that contains information about the many linguistic mailing lists on the Net.

Web:
http://www.phil.uni-passau.de/linguistik/linguistik_urls/mailing-list.shtml
http://www.tezcat.com/~markrose/langfaq.html

Usenet:
humanities.language.sanskrit
sci.lang

Linguistics

Linguistics is the study of human speech. Linguistics concerns itself with various areas: the structure of languages, the history of languages, how languages relate to one another, and the purpose of language within a culture. To understand the structure of languages, study grammar (rules describing how words and their components are combined), phonetics (how sounds are produced, combined and represented) and morphology (the structure and form of words). These Web sites will help you find a large variety of linguistic resources on the Net.

Web:
http://www.emich.edu/~linguist/
http://www.ncbe.gwu.edu/links/langcult/linguistics.html

Middle English

After the Norman Conquest (in 1066), the use of Anglo-Saxon—the native language of England—was diminished significantly in favor of French, which became not only the official language, but the language of polite society. Anglo-Saxon was depressed into an illiterate dialect which underwent rapid and radical changes, emerging in a new form that we now call Middle English. The period of Middle English lasted from 1100 to 1500 (give or take a day or two). If you are interested in Middle English, here is a resource where you can look at a nice collection of literature. My favorite work is "The Harley Lyrics", transcribed from Manuscript Harley 2253 from the British Museum MS. Here is a direct quote: "Middelerd for mon wes mad / vnmihti aren is meste mede".

Web:
http://etext.lib.virginia.edu/mideng.browse.html

**Reach for the stars.
See "Astronomy".**

Middle English

Quick, read this right away:

Whan that aprill with his shoures soote
The droghte of march hath perced to the roote,
And bathed every veyne in swich licour
Of which vertu engendred is the flour;

You have just read the beginning of Chaucer's 1,700-line epic poem *Canterbury Tales*.

Don't you wish you could understand it? Well, you can. All you have to do is learn Middle English or read a translation into modern English. Check with the Net.

The time you take will be worth it, as Chaucer is considered to be one of the great authors of all time (although, as you can see, he did have a problem with spelling).

Pronunciation in the American South

Unless you grew up in the United States, don't even think about trying to understand this Web site. It's full of a great many colloquial pronunciations common in the southern part of the United States. The words are there somewhere, but unless you are from the South (or have watched a great many Andy Griffith reruns), you may not get it. For example, to truly appreciate modern American culture, you need to be able to understand statements like: "Lawd willing and the crik don't rise, I sho do hope that thuh President don't get us kilt by sum farn gummit. He's a nice enough feller, but he can lilac a dawg."

Web:
http://www.netsquirrel.com/crispen/word.html

Russian

Here are some resources for students and aficionados of the Russian language and Russian literature. If you want to talk, there are people waiting on IRC. To help you translate words, I have included a Web site that provides an online English-Russian dictionary.

Web:
 http://www.bucknell.edu/departments/russian/language/
 http://www.ddminc.com/russian/

Usenet:
 alt.tanya.shalayeva
 alt.uu.lang.russian.misc

IRC:
 #russian

Serbian

It has been said that Serbian is one of the easiest languages to learn to write because it is so phonetic. See if this is true, by brushing up on your Serbian as well as the Cyrillic and Latin alphabets.

Web:
 http://www.yugoslavia.com/culture/html/jezik.html

Slovak

As early as the 11th century, Slovakia was associated with Hungary. Following World War I, the Slovaks separated from Hungary and joined the Czechs (from Bohemia) to form Czechoslovakia. From 1939 to 1945—thanks to the invading Germans—the Slovaks and Czechs were "declared" independent of one another. After the war, they rejoined to reform Czechoslovakia. Finally, however, on January 1, 1993, the Slovaks separated for the last time and formed their own country, Slovakia. Throughout it all, they managed to create and maintain their own language, Slovak, which is now the official language of their country. If you plan to visit, here is a nice glossary of Slovakian words to make your trip a pleasant one.

Web:
 http://www.eunet.sk/slovakia/.dict/tourdict.html

Word-a-Day

We all know that having a big vocabulary is essential if you want to know a lot of words. Still, there is no royal road to knowledge, and if you want to know a lot of words you are just going to have to know a lot of words. The easy way is to subscribe to the Word-a-Day mailing list and soon you too will be able to tergiversate with the best of them.

es·ta·mi·net
con·duc·to·met·ric
con·es·to·ga
apo·neu·ro·sis

Spanish

I studied Spanish in high school, and I sure wish I had the Net back then: lots of Spanish language resources as well as an IRC channel to talk to people in Spanish. Hint: If you are not sure what to talk about, say: "No quiero quedarme en casa este fin de semana. Vamos a salir a bailar."

Web:
  http://csgwww.uwaterloo.ca/~dmg/lando/verbos/con-jugador.html
  http://www.umr.edu/~amigos/Virtual/

Usenet:
  alt.language.spanish
  alt.usage.spanish

IRC:
  #espanol

Word-a-Day

If someone calls you a "wowser" and you don't know whether to feel congratulated or insulted, then you might need to improve your vocabulary by checking out these word-a-day sites. Impress your friends and co-workers. Don't be caught verbally unaware.

Web:
  http://www.randomhouse.com/jesse/
  http://www.wordsmith.org/awad/

LAW

Computers and the Law

The world of computers and the Internet have raised many legal issues: some of them brand new, some of them novel variations of existing legal doctrine. This Web site contains a wealth of information related to legal issues and computing, especially the Internet. If you have heard about a famous case involving the Net, you can probably find the details here.

Web:
  http://www.eff.org/pub/Legal/

Usenet:
  misc.legal.computing

Copyrights

A copyright protects the writings of an author against copying. In this sense, "writings" refers not only to books and printed publications, but to software, music, recordings, movies, and so on. In most cases, copyright is automatically vested in the creator of the work, although the legal rights can be assigned or sold to someone else. For example, I own the copyright to this book, which I license to my publisher. To help you understand copyright and its nuances, here is a collection of Internet copyright resources. In addition, I have included the Web site for the United States Copyright Office, which will allow you to access official U.S. information regarding works registered for copyright since 1978.

Web:
  http://lcweb.loc.gov/copyright/rb.html
  http://www.benedict.com/
  http://www.law.cornell.edu/topics/copyright.html

Usenet:
  misc.int-property

Listserv Mailing List:
  List Name: uscopyright
  Subscribe to: listserv@loc.gov

Expert Witnesses

Every now and then, you hear about a trial in which some "expert" says such-and-such. Do you ever wonder who are these experts? There are many people who act as "expert witnesses". They get large amounts of money to study the details of a case and render an opinion. In most cases, experts are paid by one side or the other, and, as you might expect, the expert testimony is slanted toward the needs of whomever is paying. If you need an expert witness, or if you might want to be an expert witness, here is information that will help you.

Web:
  http://www.expertpages.com/

Federal Communications Law Journal

The Federal Communications Law Journal is the official journal of the Federal Communications Bar Association, published in association with the Indiana University School of Law. The journal publishes articles dealing with issues related to communications and information, both American and international. If you are interested in broadcasting, telephony, the Internet or intellectual property, you will find this journal useful and interesting. For example, I enjoyed reading an article analyzing how certain broadcasting licenses are awarded in the U.S.

Web:
http://www.law.indiana.edu/fclj/pubs/pubs.html

Free Legal Information

My experience is that the best source for legal advice is an experienced lawyer. Before you choose a lawyer, get at least three recommendations (from other lawyers in your community, if possible) and interview each candidate. Most lawyers will talk to you once for free. However, regardless of whether or not you have a lawyer, it will always help you to understand the law as it pertains to your situation and what options you have. These Web sites have articles and advice for consumers on many different legal topics: taxes, accidents, family law, personal injury, real estate law, estate planning, and more. Remember, though, if it's important, you need a good lawyer. (This is especially true for estate planning.)

Web:
http://www.freeadvice.com/
http://www.lawguru.com/
http://www.nolo.com/briefs.html

House of Representatives Law Library

There is a lot of law in the United States, but you never have to worry about not having access to it. The online law library of the House of Representatives allows you to read federal, state and territorial laws as well as many important legal documents.

Web:
http://law.house.gov/

International Criminal Justice

In spite of what most people think, the bulk of crime in the world is not confined to small portions of Los Angeles. There is crime all over the world, and as a Net person, you have access to lots of information related to this popular global pastime. Here it is—enjoy.

Web:
http://www.acsp.uic.edu/

International Criminal Justice
The next time someone steals your place in line at the supermarket, remember you are in good company—there is crime all over the world.

Would you like to keep up with it? The Internet will be glad to help.

International Law Students Association

Law students interested in international law can check out information about the International Law Students Association and get links to a library with online texts, law journals, documents about international law and related resources.

Web:
http://www.kentlaw.edu/ilsa/

International Trade Law

This Web site is devoted to international trade law. Find information about sales of goods and services, protection of intellectual property, carriage of goods, insurance, payment mechanisms, agency, limitation periods, and other areas of international law.

Web:
http://itl.irv.uit.no/trade_law/

Law Firms

There are a large number of law firms on the Net, and here is a list of many of them. Don't be surprised if, soon, being on the Net is a prerequisite to running a law practice. I can tell you that all of my lawyers are on the Net. (Now, if I can only get them to use PGP, so we can send secret stuff by email.)

Web:
http://www.law.indiana.edu/law/v-lib/lawfirms.html

Where there's a will, there's an heir.

Law Resources

For the law student and legal professional, here is a useful collection of law resources. You will find information about commercial law, defense funds, human rights, institutes, intellectual property, international trade, law firms, legal agencies, libraries, newsletters, Supreme Court decisions, and much more.

Web:
http://www.findlaw.com/
http://www.law.indiana.edu/law/v-lib/lawindex.html
http://www.lawrunner.com/
http://www.wwlia.org/

Look What I Found on the Net...

```
Newsgroup: misc.legal.moderated
Subject: Renting to Call Girl

> My house is rented to a young woman who is suspected by one of
> her neighbors to be a call girl.  If that turns out to be true
> and she is apprehended, does the owner have any liability?
> If so, what could be the consequences?

Although there have been some surprising civil cases, in general
you have no liability for the behavior of your tenant.

Exceptions have been carved for drugs, but absent some specific
local ordinance, you should be okay.

This could be challenged, however, if you are bartering for goods
or services.  You could then be accused of keeping a bawdy
house...

If you have a problem, you do want to consider various ways to
request your renter to leave.  A practical reason is that police
raids cause damage to your building...
```

Law Schools

The great thing about going to law school is that, when you graduate, you will be in a profession that is so popular that people like to tell lots of jokes about it. So, before you commit yourself to one school or another, do enough research on the Net to make sure that your school is worthy of joking about. To help you, here is a list of many, many law schools, all of which have a presence on the Internet. For more interpersonal research, you can join the law school mailing list.

Web:
   http://www.law.indiana.edu/law/v-lib/
      lawschools.html

Usenet:
   bit.listserv.lawsch-l

Law Talk and General Discussion

It's Saturday night and you are anxious to discuss freedom of religion, libel and the concept of invasion of privacy with someone. When you have no place to go and you are just itching to talk law, check out Usenet, where you will find lawyers, law students and lawyer wannabes chatting about legalities.

Usenet:
   alt.philosophy.law
   misc.legal
   misc.legal.moderated

Lawtalk

Would you like to have a pretend-law-school party? This Web site contains recordings of short reports on various interesting law topics, and here is how you can have your own party at which everyone can pretend they are in law school. First, invite over 150 of your closest friends. Give them all benches to sit on as well as paper and pens. Then connect to this Web site, let them listen to a few of these reports, and tell them to take notes. Afterward, stand in front of the group, address your friends by last name, and ask them ambiguous questions about what they just listened to. For extra fun, make them form study groups and have each group prepare a summary of the notes.

Web:
   http://www.law.indiana.edu/law/lawtalk.html

Lawyer Jokes

A guy is standing at a bar talking to a fellow he just met. "You want a good laugh?" he says. "Listen to this joke. This lawyer has—" "Hold on," says the other fellow, "I want you to know that I'm a lawyer, and I don't think it's fair that everyone makes fun of lawyers. I would be glad to hear your joke, but I do get tired of people making jokes about my profession. Why does it always have to be a lawyer? Why can't you tell a joke about a doctor, or an airline pilot, or a plumber?" "Okay," says the first guy, "I'll tell it your way. This plumber has just graduated from law school and he decides to sue his mother..."

Web:
   http://www.counselquest.com/jokes.htm
   http://www.nolo.com/jokes/jokes.html

Legal Dictionary

I love to read Perry Mason books, and I learn a lot about the law by doing so. Every now and then, I encounter a legal term I don't understand. One of the terms I saw over and over was *res gestae*, but I couldn't figure out what it meant from the context. I asked my lawyer, but he didn't know. Then I asked my brother (who is a lawyer), and he didn't know either. However, I was finally able to satisfy my curiosity by using the online legal dictionary at this Web site. Now I am prepared in case my lawyer or my brother call me for legal advice.

Web:
   http://www.wwlia.org/diction.htm

Legal Documents Online

We all know that there is no substitute for expert legal advice. We also know that expert legal advice can cost a great deal of money. The resources at this Web site can help you create some commonly used legal documents—such as a last will and testament, a living will, a durable financial power of attorney, and so on—for free. Here is a suggestion. Before you have your attorney draw up a legal document, see if it is available at this Web site. If so, create one for yourself and print it out. Read it carefully before you visit your attorney, and take it with you when you go to his office. By learning a bit about the issues in advance and reading over a typical document, you will already know something when you get there, and the whole thing will be faster and less expensive.

Web:
   http://www.legaldocs.com/~usalaw/misc-s.htm

Litigation

Litigation refers to the resolution of a dispute by law suit or court action. Litigators are paid gladiators, pitbulls who are hired to defend or attack on their client's behalf. This Web site contains a lot of useful information for litigators. I found it fascinating to read the articles here. Even if you are not a lawyer, you will find it interesting to eavesdrop on what the litigators discuss when they talk about the tricks of their trade.

Web:
http://www.litigationlaw.com/

Patents

A patent protects the right to use an invention. In the United States, there are three main types of patents: Utility Patents (machines, processes, etc.), Design Patents (design for an manufactured article), and Plant Patents (new varieties of plants). With respect to computers, patents are issued not only for new hardware, but for specific software and computer algorithms. To help you understand patents and how they work, here are some useful resources, including the Web site of the U.S. Patent and Trademark Offices, as well as a site at which you can search for and examine existing patents.

Web:
http://patent.womplex.ibm.com/
http://www.law.vill.edu/~rgruner/patport.htm
http://www.uspto.gov/web/menu/pats.html
http://www.wnspat.com/primpatp.html

Publishing Law

You may not know it, but as soon as you write something, you automatically own the copyright. Unlike trademarks, you do not need to register copyrights. Unfortunately, most of publishing is not that simple. If you are a writer or publisher, you need to understand something of the laws and rules that govern your business. I use a good contract lawyer who reads and comments on every contract that enters my life *before* I sign it. I encourage you to do the same. This Web site has a number of informative articles that can help you understand about publishing law, which will help you get better results when you work with your lawyer.

Web:
http://www.publaw.com/

Supreme Court Rulings

With Project Hermes, the United States Supreme Court makes its opinions and rulings available in electronic format within minutes of their release. Moreover, you can obtain a copy of an opinion as a word processor document. Isn't this great? You can download a Supreme Court opinion and then use your word processor to make any changes you want. Talk about participatory democracy!

Web:
http://www.law.cornell.edu/supct/

Supreme Court Rulings

Have you ever been in the situation of being introduced to the man or woman of your dreams, getting into a wonderful conversation, and then all of a sudden having that person turn you down like a bedspread because you have no knowledge of recent Supreme Court rulings? Fortunately, this all-too-common occurrence need not happen to you. All you need to do is take the simple precaution of checking on the Net for new Supreme Court opinions every day when you get up. Never again will you lose out on the relationship of a lifetime because of poor preparation.

Trade Secrets

There's little that is more pleasurable than hearing a secret that you aren't supposed to hear. If you like secrets, especially trade secrets, take a look at the trade secrets resources on the Internet. You can get information on unfair competition, trade secret protection programs, investigations, nondisclosure and confidentiality agreements, inevitable disclosure doctrines, how to protect intellectual property rights, and information on computer software and anti-trust guidelines.

Web:
http://www.execpc.com/~mhallign/

Trademarks

A trademark is a word, name or symbol used to distinguish the source of specific services or goods. Trademarks do not have to be registered. However, if you do register a trademark, you have more protection against people using it for their own products. Here is official information from the United States Patent and Trademark Offices, as well as some other trademark-related resources you will find useful.

Web:
http://www.fplc.edu/tfield/Trademk.htm
http://www.ggmark.com/
http://www.naming.com/trademark2.html
http://www.uspto.gov/web/offices/tac/doc/basic/

LIBRARIES

American Library Association

There are more than 122,000 libraries in the United States, of which about 16,000 are public libraries. The American Library Association (ALA) is the oldest and largest library association in the world, serving librarians from every type of library in the U.S. However, the ALA is more than a professional organization. They see themselves as being the chief advocate for the American people in a quest for the highest possible quality of library and information services.

Web:
http://www.ala.org/

Cataloging Talk and General Discussion

It's not a job that most people envy—cataloging and keeping track of all those books. It takes someone with patience, perseverance and a good sense of organization. Those are the kind of people who hang out in this Usenet group. Check out the raging debates over the modality and paradigms of cataloging. The mailing list is for the discussion of automated methods of cataloging.

Usenet:
bit.listserv.autocat

Listserv Mailing List:
List Name: autocat
Subscribe to: listserv@listserv.acsu.buffalo.edu

College Libraries

So many backpacks to search, so little time. College librarians have to keep up with the ebb and flow of students who race in and out, change addresses, forget to turn the books in, forget to pay fines, and get an occasional mean streak and decide to make off with the only copy of the 1952 version of a textbook on human sexuality. This list serves as a forum for discussing issues relevant primarily to college librarians and staff who hold down the fort at four-year undergraduate institutions.

Listproc Mailing List:
List Name: collib-l
Subscribe to: listproc@willamette.edu

Conservation OnLine

Librarians worry about problems that other people don't even know exist. One of these problems is the preservation of information. We are all familiar with the idea that as books grow older, the pages get brittle and the bindings may fall apart. But there are many more ways in which books can degenerate and many techniques developed to preserve them as long as possible. However, books are only part of the problem. What about all the electronic information? Who worries about preserving it? These people do. The Conservation OnLine (CoOL) Web site contains a great deal of information of interest to anyone involved with the conservation of materials in libraries, museums and other archives.

Web:
http://palimpsest.stanford.edu/

452 LIBRARIES

Dewey Decimal System

The Dewey Decimal system for the classification of non-fiction library material was developed in 1876 by an American librarian named Melvil Dewey. Dewey created the classification scheme based on his understanding of human knowledge in Europe and the United States. Although the Dewey Decimal System has undergone modifications, the main design has proved remarkably enduring for well over one hundred years, and is used widely throughout North America and Europe. The name "Decimal System" comes from the idea that all knowledge is divided into ten major categories, numbered 000 through 900. Within a category, sub-categories are assigned a specific three-digit number. More detailed specification is expressed by extra numbers following a decimal point. For example, the social sciences all lie within the 300 division: economics is 330, labor economics is 331, and career information is 331.702. This Web site contains a useful hypertext list of all the main Dewey Decimal categories and sub-categories. This is a great place to look up the meaning of a particular number, or to search for the number that describes a particular type of information.

Web:
  http://www.tnrdlib.bc.ca/dewey.html

Internet Public Library

There are lots of interesting bits of information at the Internet Public Library. This great collection includes reference material, information on youth services and services for librarians and information professionals, and an education division. Librarian services include reviews, professional development, on-the-job resources, and weekly news.

Web:
  http://www.ipl.org/

Stop right now and have some hot chocolate.

Librarian Resources

Librarians have more need for information than just about anybody else on the planet. Moreover, they have to know where to look for specific pieces of information and how to find them fast. These resources are put together for librarians by librarians.

Web:
  http://www.ex.ac.uk/~ijtilsed/lib/wwwlibs.html
  http://www.libraryspot.com/
  http://www.state.wi.us/agencies/dpi/www/lib_res.html

Usenet:
  soc.libraries.talk

Libraries Around the World

Librarians work hard to collect, maintain and make available massive amounts of information. As you might expect, there are a great many libraries around the world that have Web sites. Browse through these lists, and you will be impressed as to how many libraries are on the Net. Truly, librarians are among the leaders of the information revolution.

Web:
  http://sunsite.berkeley.edu/Libweb/
  http://www.bookwire.com/index/Libraries.html
  http://www.colosys.net/coolib/

Library and Information Science

If there is anything in the world that you want to know, ask a librarian. Library and information science turns ordinary mortals into oracles of facts. Even if they don't know it off the tops of their heads, librarians will know where to find what you are looking for. See discussion on librarianship from a technical and a philosophical point of view.

Listserv Mailing List:
  List Name: **libres**
  Subscribe to: **listserv@listserv.kent.edu**

LIBRARIES 453

Library of Congress

The Library of Congress was established as a legislative library for the Congress of the United States. The core of the original library was the personal collection of Thomas Jefferson, who might truly be called the father of the Library. Today, the Library of Congress has grown to encompass many, many information-related activities (including the U.S. Copyright Office). The library holds 532 miles of bookshelves in three principal buildings. Although all the storage areas are closed to the public (you tell them what you want and they fetch it for you), the services of the library are available, free of charge, to anyone over high school age. The Library of Congress is not only the research arm of the U.S. Congress, it is recognized as the United States' national library, and its collections are considered the most comprehensive record of human creativity and knowledge in the world (although they do not have a full set of Harley Hahn books). The Library of Congress has many, many programs and services, a lot of which are accessible via the Internet. If you have anything to do with research, here is one Internet site with which you should be familiar.

Web:
http://lcweb.loc.gov/

> On the Internet, anyone can be a publisher.

Look What I Found on the Net...

```
Newsgroup: bit.listserv.autocat
Subject: Boston Renumbers Library of Congress Classification

> The City of Boston's Kirstein Business Branch library has
> renumbered the first-floor reference books and directories
> that were already classified according to the Library of
> Congress system...
>
> How is that any easier? Boston public library librarians
> would not disclose an outline of the additional
> classification system, claiming there is none...
```

Well, I think it's about time that local, municipal and state libraries joined the rest of us in Getting Big Government Off Our Backs! Who the hell are they, telling us how to list our books? A BUNCH'A JACKBOOTED THUGS, that's who!

Next thing you know, the Library of Congress will tell us all we have to list our books according to the Library of the United Nations classification system, where books that say anything bad about the EVIL ONE-WORLD U.N. GLOBALIST CONSPIRACY are in the low-numbered section, and instead of all the books catching fire at 451 degrees, they catch fire at the temperature that their number is!

I know this is true because it says so right here in the Bible, at least in the margin, but it's written in pen so you can't erase it and hey — what are you, some kind of U.N. dupe?

454 LIBRARIES

Need info on a book? Any book? *Try the Library of Congress Web site.*

Library of Congress Classification System

The Library of Congress Classification System was developed in the nineteenth century as an aid in classifying the vast resources of the United States Library of Congress. The system uses the letters of the alphabet to represent 26 main categories. The categories are divided into sub-categories, each of which is given a two-letter code. To further refine a specific classification, a number is appended to the two-letter code. For example, the social sciences all lie within the letter H, commerce is assigned the code HF, business uses HF5001 to HF6002, and vocational guidance and career development would lie within the specific range HF5381 to HF5386. The Library of Congress Classification System is updated continually and is more detailed than most people realize. The current version actually runs to some 48 volumes with more than 13,000 pages. Most people, however, only need the categories, sub-categories and important classifications. This well-organized Web site has all this information in an easy-to-use format. (Alternatively—if you need a romantic present for that special someone in your life—for a modest fee you can purchase a printed outline of the system directly from the Library of Congress.)

Web:
http://www.lib.bcit.bc.ca/LICO.htm

LITERATURE

African-American Literature

African-American literature reflects the characteristics and heritage that form the cultural underpinnings of the modern black community in the United States. These Web sites contain links to a great deal of information about African-American writers. Read about Maya Angelou, Octavia Butler, Alex Haley, Derek Walcott, Booker T. Washington, Alice Walker and many more authors who have helped create the rich canon of modern-day African-American literature. If you would like to participate in an ongoing discussion, you can join the mailing list.

Web:
http://english.tribble.wfu.edu/browneb/annotated_bibliography.htm
http://www.keele.ac.uk/depts/as/Literature/amlit.black.html

Listserv Mailing List:
List Name: **afamlit**
Subscribe to: **listserv@listserv.kent.edu**

American Literature

What good is American Literature? Well, if you are an American high school student, you can study American literature in order to pass your exams and graduate. For the rest of us, though, American literature is far less utilitarian: all we can do is read and enjoy it. The Web site I have selected presents a thoughtful collection of American literature that you can read easily, one chapter at a time. After you have read a chapter, you can discuss it with other people. For more permanent ongoing discussion, you can join the mailing list.

Web:
http://www.americanliterature.com/

Listproc Mailing List:
List Name: **amlit-l**
Subscribe to: **listproc@lists.missouri.edu**

LITERATURE

Australian Literature

As J. Wellington Wimpy used to say, "I'll gladly pay you Tuesday for a comprehensive list of Australian writers today." Well, today, all Wimpy would have to do is get access to the Internet, and he would be able to find all the information about Australian writers he could stomach. Spend some time at this Web site, and you will never again complain that Australian literature is under-represented on the Net. There is lots and lots of information about Australian writers, aboriginal writers, conferences, calls for papers, reviews and criticisms, poetry, literary magazines, and much more.

Web:
http://www.vicnet.net.au/~ozlit/ozlit.html

This book is high in fiber.

Beat Generation

The Beat generation refers to a number of American writers and artists who were popular in the 1950s. Among this group were novelists William Burroughs and Jack Kerouac (writer of the seminal beat book On the Road), and poets Allen Ginsberg and Lawrence Ferlinghetti. The Beats were the fathers of the 1960s, so their work is particularly relevant to our life today (seeing as the 1960s were an abrupt watershed in twentieth century culture). Visit the Web site and read about many of the literary people who defined the Beat generation. For ongoing discussion, you can read the Usenet group.

Web:
http://www.charm.net/~brooklyn/

Usenet:
alt.books.beatgeneration

Look What I Found on the Net...

```
Newsgroup: alt.books.beatgeneration
Subject: A Jolly Old Soul Indeed

Last spring I read Jack Kerouac's "On The Road", and I'm
currently reading "The Dharma Bums".  I love these books
because...well...for lack of a better way to put it, they
make me feel good.

As I've thought about this I've decided that it's kinda ironic.
Here we have two books showing a guy who seems to live life to
its fullest.  Whenever I read a little of Kerouac I look at the
whole world differently.  Everyone I see becomes potentially
"mad" or "beat".  Everything seems much more glorious.

How is it that such a wonderful feeling could come from a man
who suffered from alcoholism and drank himself to death?  I was
told that "Big Sur" is much darker than the two books I'm
familiar with.

I guess Jack was just one happy-sad guy.
```

Classics

If you are looking for something old to go with your something new, borrowed and blue, you can easily find something on the Net. Here are databases, information on classical antiquity, Roman law, Latin language, links to museums, college classics departments, classical organizations and journals. The mailing list is for discussion of classics, classical literature, and Latin in general.

Web:
http://www.utexas.edu/depts/classics/

Listserv Mailing List:
List Name: **latin-l**
Subscribe to: **listserv@lists.psu.edu**

English Renaissance Literature

Renaissance literature refers to work created around the time of the sixteenth century (1485-1603). (The most famous Renaissance writer, of course, was Shakespeare, 1564-1616.) Use this Web site to explore the world of English Renaissance literature. Learn about Shakespeare, Walter Raleigh, Thomas More, Thomas Campion, Christopher Marlowe, John Davies and other authors. Read bibliographical information, essays, articles and excerpts from their work.

Web:
http://www.luminarium.org/renlit/

First Lines

You will have a lot of fun visiting this Web site, where you will find a collection of first lines from well-known books. The idea is to read a line and then try to guess what book it came from. Here is my favorite: "James Bond, with two double bourbons inside him, sat back in the final departure lounge of Miami Airport and thought about life and death." (The book is Goldfinger, by Ian Fleming.)

Web:
http://pc159.lns.cornell.edu/firsts/

Gothic Literature

A Gothic novel is one inspired by the English genre of fiction popular in the 18th and early 19th centuries. Gothic novels are characterized by an atmosphere of mystery and horror in a pseudo-medieval setting. Fans of Gothic literature have expanded the original definition somewhat, but the basic characteristics still remain. Here are some collections of Gothic literature resources. If you like Gothic, there is a lot to read on the Net.

Web:
http://members.aol.com/iamudolpho/basic.html
http://www.siue.edu/~jvoller/gothic.html

How I love Gothic literature and all its magic, mystery and chivalry. If you are an 18th century person trapped in a 20th century body, check out the Gothic Literature Web site and spend some time in the past.

James Bond

James Bond is a fictional spy created by Ian Fleming (1908-1964). Fleming wrote 14 books—mostly novels, some short stories—from Casino Royale (1953) to Octopussy (published in 1966). After Fleming's death, Bond books were written by other authors, in particular, John Gardner. The first James Bond film was Dr. No (1962) starring Sean Connery. Since then, many Bond movies have been made with a variety of actors. Fleming's original James Bond is a post-World War II agent of the British Secret Service and has the identification number 007. (The "00" prefix indicates that Bond is licensed to kill in line of duty.) Through the years, the depiction of Bond (and the British Secret Service) has changed. What has not changed is Bond's basic character: a highly skilled, handsome, self-reliant man, with an affinity for danger, high-performance cars, gourmet food and wine, and beautiful women. (In other words, if James Bond were a real person, he would be an Internet author.)

Web:
http://www.007forever.com/
http://www.mcs.net/~klast/www/literary.html

Jewish Literature

The expression "Jewish literature" seem innocuous enough. However, even a cursory glance into the literature reveals a variety of work that almost surpasses human understanding. When you consider that, within the family of Jewish literature, Woody Allen must somehow co-exist with Rabbi Shuley Boteach (a noted Chabad scholar), you can only wonder how so many types of people can arise from the same roots. Go figure.

Web:
http://www.colorado.edu/StudentGroups/jsu/yahoodi/cult.html
http://www.kcrw.org/b/jss.html
http://www.kesser.org/

James Bond

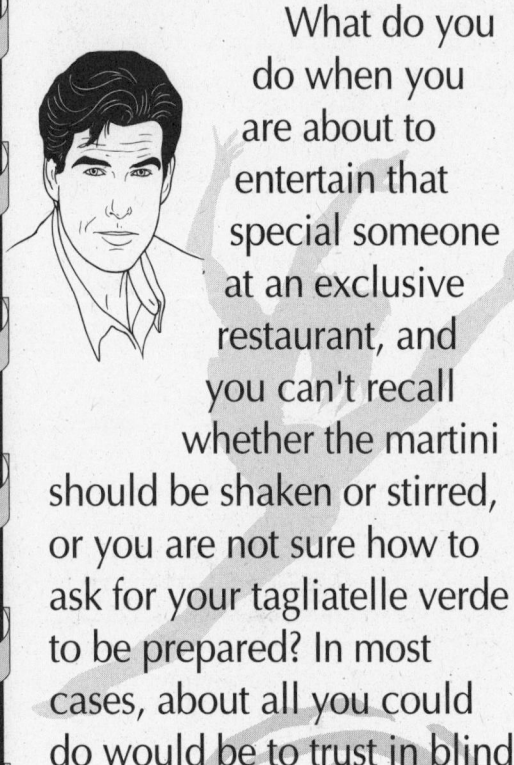

What do you do when you are about to entertain that special someone at an exclusive restaurant, and you can't recall whether the martini should be shaken or stirred, or you are not sure how to ask for your tagliatelle verde to be prepared? In most cases, about all you could do would be to trust in blind faith or hope that I might be in the same restaurant and you could ask me. However, if you have access to the Net, you can check with one of the James Bond Web sites. You'll find enough Bond information to choke a 1954 Continental Bentley with the "R" type chassis, the big 6 engine and a 13:40 back-axle ratio.

Literary Calendar

If you have ever wondered what happened in the world of literature on a particular day, this Web site can tell you. Select any day of the year, and you will find out all the interesting literary events that occurred on that day. Of course, the first thing you have to do is put in your birthday. I did and I found out that the most interesting thing that happened on my birthday was that, in 1940, F. Scott Fitzgerald died of a heart attack in Los Angeles at the age of 44. (By the way, my birthday is December 21, and money is always in good taste.)

Web:
http://litcal.yasuda-u.ac.jp/LitCalendar.shtml

Literary Theory

It's one thing to read literature. It's another thing to be able to understand it so well as to appreciate the underlying principles and forces that drive the creation and expression of the literary arts. This Web site is host to a list of links to literary theory resources around the Net. You can find information on classical, enlightenment, romantic, 19th and 20th century literature, as well as contemporary literary theory. There is also information on related journals, zines, Usenet groups, conferences, and calls for papers.

Web:
http://humanitas.ucsb.edu/shuttle/theory.html

Literature Resources

Literature and related resources abound on the Net. To help you find what you need (and some interesting places to browse), here are some Web sites I find particularly useful, as they offer comprehensive collections of literary resources. You can start with these sites and spend all day cruising the Net for things literary. Just about everything you need to get started on a hot search of literature is here somewhere.

Web:
http://www.english.upenn.edu/~jlynch/Lit/
http://www.rhodes.edu/englhtmls/englnet.html

Literature Talk and General Discussion

If you like to talk about literature, there are many people on the Net ready to accommodate you. Here are several general discussion groups that are good places to start (one of which is for children's literature).

Usenet:
bit.listserv.literary
rec.arts.books
rec.arts.books.childrens

Mysteries

Curling up with a mystery and a cup of hot cocoa is a great way to spend the night—especially a dark and stormy night. And some people just can't get enough. These Web sites are substantial guides to mysteries and crime fiction on the Net. The mailing list was formed to give mystery lovers a place to talk about their passion for the genre. (The list was named after Dorothy L. Sayers, one of the great mystery writers of the century.) Check out the IRC channel if you want to meet mystery lovers online.

Web:
http://www.cluelass.com/
http://www.webfic.com/mysthome/

Listserv Mailing List:
List Name: **dorothyl**
Subscribe to: **listserv@listserv.kent.edu**

IRC:
#mystery

Native American Literature

Explore the culture of Native Americans through their literature. Scholars and other people interested in Native American literature share thoughts on book reviews, articles about poetry and fiction, and offer criticism and information on new publications or conferences. Inclusive in the term "Native American" are indigenous peoples of the United States (including native Alaskans and native Hawaiians), Canada and Mexico.

Web:
http://falcon.jmu.edu/~ramseyil/natauth.htm

LITERATURE: AUTHORS

Writers, share your stories on the Net.

LITERATURE: AUTHORS

Austen, Jane

Jane Austen (1775-1817) was an English novelist known for her witty, satiric novels portraying the social lives of the upper classes. Her stories, which uniformly ended in happy marriages, celebrated the virtues of reason and intelligence (as opposed to passion and impulse).

Web:
  http://www.pemberley.com/janeinfo/janeinfo.html

Author Talk and General Discussion

Take a look and see if your favorite author is on this list. If so, there are a lot of people on the Net who share your enthusiasm. These are some of the Usenet groups devoted to discussing the work and personality of specific well-known authors. It can be a lot of fun to talk to people all over the world about the books you enjoy so much.

Usenet:
  alt.books.bukowski
  alt.books.cs-lewis
  alt.books.george-orwell
  alt.books.h-g-wells
  alt.books.isaac-asimov
  alt.books.kurt-vonnegut
  alt.books.phil-k-dick
  alt.books.toffler
  alt.fan.heinlein
  alt.fan.philip-dick
  alt.fan.tolkien
  alt.fan.wodehouse
  rec.arts.books.tolkien

Look What I Found on the Net...

```
Newsgroup: bit.listserv.literary
Subject: Cliff Notes

> I was just wondering what the general consensus is on
> Cliff Notes.
>
> We are doing Hamlet in my literature class, and my teacher
> preferred that I didn't buy Cliff Notes because they include
> commentaries that aren't always accurate.  I bought them
> anyway and have only been reading them for the summaries.
>
> My question is: do you think using commentaries promotes not
> thinking about the plays for yourself, or do you think that
> they are helpful and not damaging to the studying and thought
> process?

I don't think anything is particularly damaging about Cliff Notes.

However, I think the fun of reading Shakespeare involves making
your own summary and your own interpretation.  The only
supplementary material needed at high school and lower division
levels is, maybe, a guide to  Elizabethan world view and
language.
```

460 LITERATURE: AUTHORS

Author's Pen

If you are looking for information on your favorite author, start here. This is a collection of author home pages on the Web. There are also links to literature pages and various libraries.

Web:
http://www.books.com/scripts/authors.exe

> Cool words? Look in "Quotations".

Baum, L. Frank

Lyman Frank Baum (1856-1919) was an American writer of juvenile stories, the most famous of which are the fourteen Oz books. The first book, The Wonderful Wizard of Oz, was made into the movie The Wizard of Oz, starring Judy Garland as Toto. After the death of Baum, the Oz books series was continued by R.P. Thompson.

Web:
http://www.halcyon.com/piglet/author1.htm
http://www.literature.org/Works/L-Frank-Baum/wizard/

Look What I Found on the Net...

```
Newsgroup: alt.books.bukowski
Subject: Ham on Rye

> "Women" is better, in my opinion.  More visceral and less
> crafted, written in the manner in which Bukowski's best work
> is seemingly done.
>
> From the spirit of the morning after you have lost the job you
> hated anyways, woken up with sore hands and spilled liquor all
> over your torn shirt, and with some dog you've never seen
> before looking at you from the floor by the couch, trying to
> figure out who you are and, well, you get the picture.
>
> Roll on, Hank.

I disagree.  Sure, "Women" is a great book, and I must admit
I read it in a day (I just couldn't put it down), but
"Ham on Rye" is the sort of book that shows Bukowski at his
greatest.  It combines all his greatest qualities: his humor,
his humanity, his sense of tragedy, in one little book.

I don't think "Women" contains this range and depth.  It is
much more shallow — Bukowski goes all out for jokes and not
much else.  I don't think "Women" is the tour de force that
"Ham on Rye" undoubtedly is.  "Women" is a muted Bukowski.
A Bukowski that has much, much more hiding under the surface.

I urge you to disagree with me.

P.S. Am I right in assuming that you are a woman?  Perhaps I
just can't empathize with the opposite gender well, but I would
have thought that "Women" would be sort of offensive. Am I mistaken?
```

LITERATURE: AUTHORS

Bierce, Ambrose

Ambrose Bierce (1842-1914?) was an American journalist and author, known for short stories that demonstrate a distillation of satire, savagery and horror. The latter part of Bierce's life was suffused with a sense of weariness and sadness, much of which can be evidenced in his most well-known book, The Devil's Dictionary, a work that is especially popular among people who confuse cynicism with wit, and irony with insight.

Web:
http://www.creative.net/~alang/lit/horror/abierce.sht

Brönte Sisters

The Brönte sisters, Emily (1818-1848) and Charlotte (1816-1855) were English novelists. The sisters spent a lonely childhood in a remote area of English countryside, which no doubt contributed to their remarkably imaginative novels: Wuthering Heights (Emily), Jane Eyre (Charlotte), and so on. An interesting fact—rarely mentioned by modern literary critics—is that the Bröntes come between "bronco" and "brontosaurus" in the dictionary.

Web:
http://www.cs.cmu.edu/People/mmbt/women/bronte/bronte-anne.html
http://www.lang.nagoya-u.ac.jp/~matsuoka/Bronte.html

Majordomo Mailing List:
List Name: **bronte**
Subscribe to: **majordomo@world.std.com**

Carroll, Lewis

Lewis Carroll (1832-1898) was the pseudonym of Charles Lutwidge Dodgson, an English writer and mathematical lecturer at Oxford University. Carroll is remembered for his sophisticated children's books (Alice's Adventures in Wonderland, and Through the Looking Glass), as well as his nonsense verse ("The Hunting of the Snark").

Web:
http://www.cstone.net/library/alice/carroll.html
http://www.lewiscarroll.org/carroll.html

Conrad, Joseph

Joseph Conrad (1857-1924) is among the great novelists of the English language. Conrad was born to Polish parents (his original name was Teodor Jozef Konrad Korzeniowski) in the Russian-dominated Ukraine and did not even learn to speak English until he was an adult. Although writing was difficult for Conrad, and English was his fourth language—after Polish, Russian and French—his work shows a style and mastery that is almost unmatched in modern times. Conrad's most well-known works are the novel Lord Jim and the short story "Heart of Darkness" (which inspired the movie Apocalypse Now). His work is imbued with a sensitivity to the nuances and ambiguities of what normal people call life, and what English teachers refer to as "the human condition".

Web:
http://lang.nagoya-u.ac.jp/~matsuoka/Conrad.html

Dante

Dante Alighieri (1265-1321) is best known for his poetical works The Divine Comedy and The Inferno, which have been translated from Italian into many languages. Dante was not only a poet, he was a philosopher, a rhetorician and a statesman. "When I had journeyed half of our life's way, I found myself within a shadowed forest, for I had lost the path that does not stray..." Thus begins Dante's poem The Inferno. Dante's works offer a keen insight into human nature, and are considered to be classic literature, the work of a genius.

Web:
http://www.ilt.columbia.edu/projects/dante/
http://www.smith.edu/~lkleinbe/dante/

Everyone ends up on the Net sooner or later.

Dickens, Charles

Charles Dickens (1812-1870) is perhaps the most famous English novelist of all time. Blessed with an extraordinary gift of satirical humor, melded with the ability to bring his readers both to laughter and to tears, Dickens managed to arouse the conscience of his audience while capturing the popular imagination of his time. More so than any other English novelist, Dickens had the ability to tell a story. Within his many novels (Oliver Twist, Great Expectations, A Christmas Carol, and so on), Dickens created the most marvelous gallery of characters in English fiction. When I was an undergraduate, I had a friend named Ralph who liked to read Dickens to relax. Now, you don't know Ralph, but believe me, the fact that Dickens could write stories that, a hundred years later, could interest a guy like Ralph really says something.

Web:
http://humwww.ucsc.edu/dickens/index.html
http://lang.nagoya-u.ac.jp/~matsuoka/Dickens.html

Listserv Mailing List:
List Name: **dickns-l**
Subscribe to: **listserv@ucsbvm.ucsb.edu**

Doyle, Arthur Conan

Arthur Conan Doyle (1859-1930) was a Scottish doctor and novelist who is famous all over the world for his Sherlock Holmes stories and novels. Although the detective Holmes and his companion Dr. Watson are two of the most famous characters in literature, Doyle was more than a mystery writer; he also wrote historical romances. Following the premature death of his son in the First World War, Doyle became excessively enamored of spiritualism, proving that even a mind capable of the most exact, logical reasoning is prey to human weakness. Personally, the Sherlock Holmes stories are some of my very favorites: I love to read them over and over.

Web:
http://watserv1.uwaterloo.ca/~credmond/sh.html
http://www.citsoft.com/holmes3.html

The Case of the Missing Password

"It was on a bitterly cold night and frosty morning, toward the end of the winter of '98, that I was awakened by a tugging at my shoulder. It was Holmes. The candle in his hand shone upon his eager, stooping face, and told me at a glance that something was amiss.

"'Come, Watson, come!' he cried. 'The game is afoot. Not a word! Into your clothes and come! We must track down the missing superuser password...'"

But who would steal a password? And what does this have to do with the giant rat of Sumatra? No need to die of suspense: download the stories of Arthur Conan Doyle and see for yourself.

Faulkner, William

William Faulkner (1897-1962) was an American novelist from Mississippi. His greatest writing was based on the legends and history of the Southern United States, as well as the characteristics of his own family. His most famous works (such as the novel The Sound and the Fury) are set in the town of Jefferson in the mythical county of Yoknapatawpha (pronounced just as it looks). In 1949, Faulkner was awarded the Nobel Prize for literature.

Web:
http://www.mcsr.olemiss.edu/~egjbp/faulkner/faulkner.html
http://www.uhb.fr/Faulkner/

LITERATURE: AUTHORS

> Bored? Try "Fun". Still bored? Try "Mischief".

Hemingway, Ernest

Ernest Hemingway (1899-1961) was an American novelist who lived in France when it was cool to be an American in Paris. Hemingway's writing is known for its plain, stark, tough, brutal, primitive—dare I say it?—masculine style. His first important book (The Sun Also Rises) became a success by capturing the post-World War I disillusionment of the so-called "lost generation". (And this was years before anyone had heard of Generation X.) Hemingway's novels deftly resonate with the universal themes of Man's struggle against Nature, Man's struggle against other men, and Man's struggle (when no one is looking) against women. In 1954, Hemingway was awarded the Nobel Prize for literature. In 1961, after a long illness, he killed himself.

Web:
http://www.atlantic.net/~gagne/hem/localhem.html

Majordomo Mailing List:
List Name: **heming-l**
Subscribe to: **majordomo@mtu.edu**

Hesse, Hermann

Hermann Hesse (1877-1962) was a German-born Swiss novelist and poet. His work revolves around the recurring theme that artists are estranged from the society in which they live and, hence, suffer from a spiritual loneliness. Perhaps his best known novels are Siddhartha (1922) and Steppenwolf (1927). As he grew older, Hesse's novels became more analytical and—to the chagrin of undergraduate English students forced to write long essays in order to pass mandatory literature courses—more symbolic. In 1946, Hermann Hesse was awarded the Nobel Prize for literature.

Web:
http://www.ic.ucsb.edu/~ggotts/hesse/

Listserv Mailing List:
List Name: **hesse-l**
Subscribe to: **listserv@ucsbvm.ucsb.edu**

Lovecraft, H.P.

Howard Phillips Lovecraft (1890-1937) was an American writer of fantasy and horror tales that catapulted him into that rarefied area occupied by writers who have managed to generate a cult following. Lovecraft is best known for his "Cthulhu" mythos—an imaginary world inhabited by a variety of strange, bizarre beings. Lovecraft is also known for the huge volume of his personal correspondence.

Web:
http://www.creative.net/~alang/lit/horror/hpl.sht
http://www.hplovecraft.com/

Mansfield, Katherine

Katherine Mansfield (1888-1923) was a New Zealand-born English author who was a superb writer of short stories. Her stories—a favorite of Women's Studies teachers everywhere—were deceptively simple, able to bring out emotion in even the roughest, toughest raised-on-TV-and-violence readers. Although the average man on the street might not know it, Mansfield's work was heavily influenced by Chekhov (the Russian author, not the one on Star Trek). After Mansfield's untimely death from tuberculosis, her husband edited and published her poems, her letters and her scrapbook (don't even ask).

Web:
http://www.buffnet.net/~starmist/kmansfld/kmansfld.htm

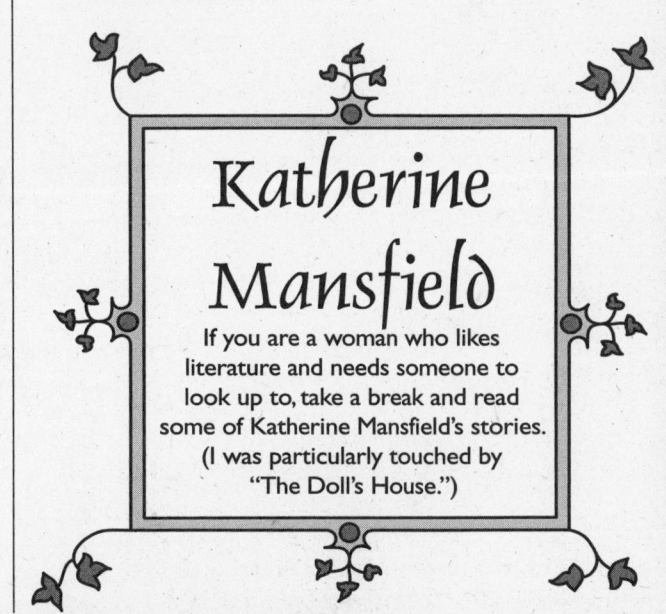

Katherine Mansfield

If you are a woman who likes literature and needs someone to look up to, take a break and read some of Katherine Mansfield's stories. (I was particularly touched by "The Doll's House.")

Milton, John

John Milton (1608-1674) was an English poet best known for "Paradise Lost". The theme of this epic poem is Man's fall from grace. More specifically, Milton describes Satan's rebellion against God and the expulsion of Adam and Eve from the Garden of Eden. A later work, "Paradise Regained", describes in detail how Jesus overcame Satan's temptations (just in case you were wondering how it turned out). When he was 44 years old, Milton went blind and, for the rest of his life, had to dictate his work (including the Paradise poems). A sonnet he wrote about blindness—and how it need not stop anyone from serving God—is one of the most beautiful poems I have ever read. It ends, "...They also serve who only stand and wait."

Web:
http://www.urich.edu/~creamer/milton/

Parker, Dorothy

Dorothy Parker (1893-1967) was an American humorist, drama critic (for Vanity Fair) and book critic (for the New Yorker). However, what she was best known for was her role as critic of humanity, starting with herself and working sideways. Her humor, quips and light verse virtually define the idea of irony (at least for the twentieth century). She was the only female member of the Algonquin Round Table—a group of New York-style witty bon vivants that included her wistfully just-beyond-reach paramour Robert Benchley. Have you ever been bothered by someone, and then had the experience of thinking of the perfect comeback—smooth and subtle, with exactly the right amount of graceful reproach—only six hours too late? Dorothy Parker could do it perfectly and in real-time.

Web:
http://www.users.interport.net/~lynda/dorothy.html

Poe, Edgar Allan

Edgar Allan Poe (1809-1849) was an American poet, short story writer and critic. Poe is considered to be one of America's most skillful and intelligent writers. He is best known for (1) inventing the idea of the detective story; (2) creating a universe within his writing that was both beautiful and grotesque; and (3) being a witty and intelligent critic who often wrote about the craft of writing. In addition, Poe also distinguished himself by (4) getting kicked out of both the University of Virginia and West Point.

Web:
http://www.gothic.net/poe/
http://www.poedecoder.com/Qrisse/

Pratchett, Terry

Terry Pratchett (1948-) is a well-known author of humorous, fantasy-based science fiction novels. His Discworld series—19 books and counting—has a huge cult following (well, a good-sized cult following) around the world. He also has the distinction of having his own Usenet discussion group, something even Zsa Zsa Gabor was never able to achieve.

Web:
http://www.internauts.ca/~bishop/pterry.htm
http://www.us.lspace.org/

Usenet:
alt.fan.pratchett

Rice, Anne

Anne Rice (1941-) is well known among contemporary literary aficionados for her work in two main genres: vampire and horror stories, and bondage erotica. Anne Rice is actually a nom de plume: her real name being Howard Allen O'Brien (I am not making this up). Rice's first novel, Interview with the Vampire (1973), was extremely popular among American teenagers of all ages. Indeed—in spite of the fact that she managed to write the entire book in five weeks—it was so successful within the mainstream vortex of popular American culture as to be hailed as an "event", almost before the ink on her first royalty statement was dry.

Web:
http://www.annerice.com/
http://www.webvoodoo.com/annerice/

Listserv Mailing List:
List Name: **annerice**
Subscribe to: **listserv@lists.psu.edu**

The Net is for smart people (like you).

Shakespeare, William

William Shakespeare (1564-1616) was an English playwright and poet, considered to be the greatest dramatist of all time. Shakespeare wrote a large variety of plays: histories, tragedies, romances and comedies, and his skillfulness and insight were developed to such a high degree as to almost defy description and analysis. That, of course, never stopped anyone, and today, in just about every high school and university in the world, there is an active Shakespeare industry, carefully discussing, memorizing, studying and generally taking apart just about everything that Shakespeare ever wrote. Although Shakespeare never wrote a made-for-TV movie or a vampire book, his plays are still performed frequently all over the world (even though he is dead and is, therefore, not entitled to any of the royalties).

Web:
http://daphne.palomar.edu/shakespeare/
http://ipl.sils.umich.edu/reading/shakespeare/shakespeare.html
http://library.utoronto.ca/www/utel/rp/authors/shakespe.html
http://the-tech.mit.edu/Shakespeare/
http://www.gh.cs.usyd.edu.au/~matty/Shakespeare/

Usenet:
humanities.lit.authors.shakespeare

A Hint About Shakespeare

What can you say about Shakespeare? Truly, he was a happening dude for his day. Of course, there are ugly rumors that he didn't really write his own plays, that they were all done by someone else who happened to have the same name.

In fact, if you take the soliloquy from Macbeth and run it through the Unix **tr** command you will find a secret message that says, "This was really written by Shakespeare."

But don't believe me. Shakespeare's work is available for free on the Net. Download your favorite play or poem and perform your own analysis.

---

*Books are good.
(Start with this one and go wild.)*

Tolkien, J.R.R.

John Ronald Reuel Tolkien (1892-1973) was a South African-born English novelist and scholar. Tolkien, a professor of Anglo-Saxon and English literature at Oxford University, published a children's book called The Hobbit in 1937, in which he created a fantasy world populated by cute pseudo-human creatures. Later (1954-1956) Tolkien published a trilogy, The Lord of the Rings, in which he enlarged this world into a more fully populated Middle Earth, complete with good guys, bad guys, war, adventure, intrigue and masterly storytelling. The trilogy centers around the activities of a hobbit named Frodo, who sets off on a heroic quest of epic proportions, pitting Good against Evil in a series of adventures that surely must rank among the greatest inventions of English literature. (We are talking major Allegory City here.) I know what you are wondering: after all those adventures, was Frodo successful? Well, just in case you haven't read all 1,518 pages, I don't want to ruin the ending for you. Let's just say the Force was with him.

Web:
http://www.bayside.net/users/tolkien/
http://www.csclub.uwaterloo.ca/u/relipper/tolkien/rootpage.html
http://www.middle-earth.demon.co.uk/tolklink.htm

Usenet:
alt.fan.tolkien
rec.arts.books.tolkien

Listproc Mailing List:
List Name: **tolkien**
Subscribe to: **listproc@listproc.hcf.jhu.edu**

Twain, Mark

Mark Twain (1835-1910) was an American writer and humorist, who single-handedly ushered in the phenomenon of Modern American Literature. "Mark Twain" was actually a pseudonym for Samuel Langhorne Clemens. At one time, Clemens was one of many Mississippi river pilots, among whom it was common to use the call "mark twain" to indicate a water depth of two fathoms. Twain's novels and stories are of such enduring value that they are enjoyable even to school children who are forced to read real literature (by English teachers who teach to support themselves while they are finishing their own novels). Twain's most famous characters, Tom Sawyer and Huckleberry Finn, are brilliant but folksy creations, as genuinely American as apple pie, baseball and complaining about Congress.

Web:
http://etext.lib.virginia.edu/railton/index2.html
http://web.mit.edu/linguistics/www/forum/twainweb.html

Listserv Mailing List:
List Name: **twain-l**
Subscribe to: **listserv@yorku.ca**

Virgil

Virgil (70-19 B.C.) was a Roman poet: the dominant figure in all of Latin literature. His most important work is an epic poem called "The Aeneid". Considered to be one of the greatest masterpieces of world literature, the Aeneid takes place after the fall of Troy, describing the adventures of a young fellow named Aeneas (the son of Venus, no less) as he wandered from one place to another; goofing around with Queen Dido in Carthage, having adventures left and right, and finally moving to Italy so his descendants could found Rome. Virgil's perfect mastery of poetic expression has earned him the number one spot in the Poets Hall of Fame, Pastoral Division.

Web:
http://www.dc.peachnet.edu/~shale/humanities/literature/world_literature/virgil.html
http://www.virgil.org/

Majordomo Mailing List:
List Name: **mantovano**
Subscribe to: **majordomo@joyfulheart.com**

Wells, H.G.

Herbert George Wells (1866-1946) was an English author and social critic, who had a long and varied career as a writer. He is best known for his fantastic stories (what would now be called science fiction), such as The Time Machine, The Invisible Man, and The War of the Worlds. As Wells aged, his style moved from scientific fantasy to realism to pessimism. Wells was a lot more than a novelist, however. Before he started to write he taught biology, and later he wrote the well-received The Outline of History and co-wrote The Science of Life—truly the Isaac Asimov of his day.

Web:
http://www.kirjasto.sci.fi/hgwells.htm
http://www.literature.org/Works/H-G-Wells/

Wodehouse, P.G.

Pelham Grenville Wodehouse (1881-1975) was an English writer of novels, short stories, plays and song lyrics. Wodehouse (pronounced "Woodhouse") is the creator of a great many enduring characters, including Bertie Wooster and his valet Jeeves, Mr. Mulliner, Lord Emsworth and the Empress of Blandings, and Stanley Featherstonehaugh ("Fanshaw") Ukridge. Wodehouse is unique in that, over a long and successful career, he consistently demonstrated a level of skill that would be difficult to overpraise. He is, by far, my favorite author and, if you have never read any of his books, my advice to you is go out and buy one right now. If you happen to be reading this in a bookstore, it should be the work of a moment for you to pick up a Wodehouse book on the way out. Everything he created was uniformly pleasant and well-written: the best human nature has to offer. If you have not met Wodehouse, you have not led a full life.

Web:
http://mech.math.msu.su/~gmk/pgw.htm
http://www.serv.net/~camel/wodehouse/
http://www.smart.net/~tak/wodehouse.html

Usenet:
alt.fan.wodehouse

LITERATURE: COLLECTIONS

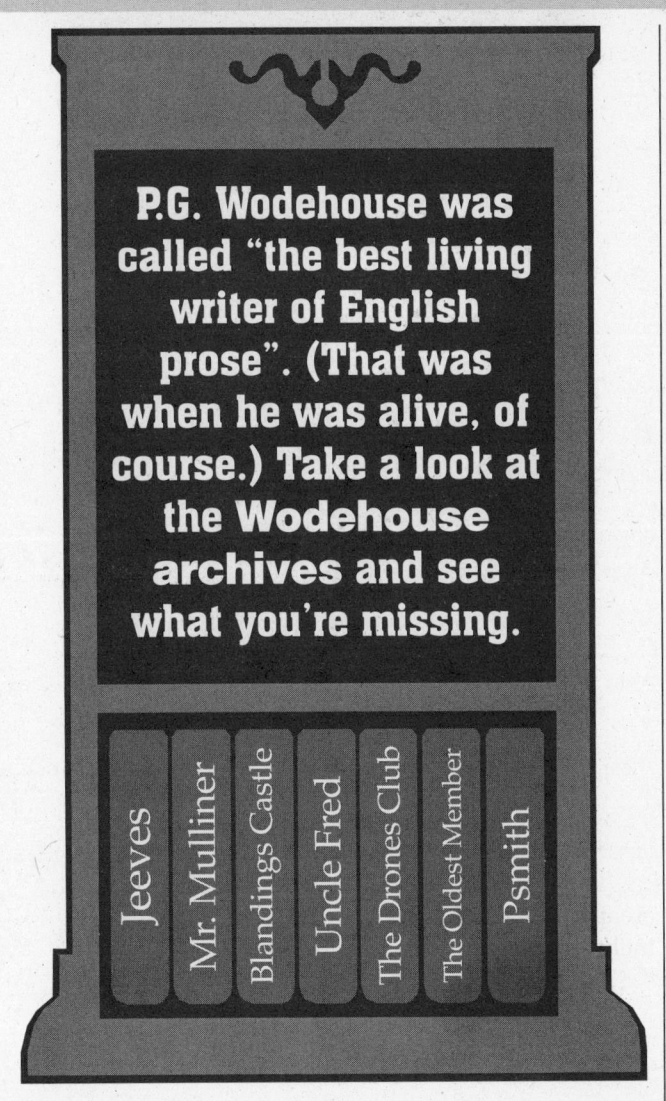

P.G. Wodehouse was called "the best living writer of English prose". (That was when he was alive, of course.) Take a look at the Wodehouse archives and see what you're missing.

Jeeves | Mr. Mulliner | Blandings Castle | Uncle Fred | The Drones Club | The Oldest Member | Psmith

Yeats, William Butler

William Butler Yeats (1865-1939) was an Irish writer who is considered to be one of the greatest poets of the twentieth century. Yeats wrote many short plays (such as The Countess Cathleen) and was one of the founders of the Irish National Theatre Company. As a young man, Yeats wrote a great deal of love poetry. As he grew older, he began to infuse his work with more and more complex symbolism (sort of like real life only more interesting). In 1923, Yeats was awarded the Nobel Prize for literature.

Web:
http://www.columbia.edu/acis/bartleby/yeats/
http://www.tally.demon.co.uk/sarah/

LITERATURE: COLLECTIONS

Ancient Greek Literature

The literature of the ancient Greeks forms one of the pillars of modern Western civilization. Very few people, of course, can read ancient Greek. However, many surviving works have been translated into modern English, and this Web site will help you access a great many texts. Read the work of Aeschylus (tragedy), Aesop (fables), Aristophanes (comedy and satire), Aristotle (philosophy and science), Epictetus (philosophy), Euripides (tragedy), Herodotus (history), Homer (epic poetry), Plato (philosophy and science), Sophocles (tragedy) and Thucydides (history).

Web:
http://classics.mit.edu/

Anglo-Saxon Tales

In the movie Annie Hall, Annie (Diane Keaton) is trying to decide on an adult education course to take. Alvy Singer (Woody Allen) advises her, "Just don't take any course where they make you read 'Beowulf'." So who was this Beowulf guy, anyway? In the middle of the 5th century, after the withdrawal of the Romans, Germanic tribes from Europe overran England, bringing the Anglo-Saxon language—also known as Old English—with them. Anglo-Saxon was used increasingly until the Norman invasion (William the Conqueror in 1066 and all that), after which time French replaced Anglo-Saxon as the most important language in England. Anglo-Saxon literature is a rich area of scholarship, perhaps best known for an epic poem named "Beowulf". "Beowulf" was written in the 8th century and can be considered the epitome of Anglo-Saxon literature. The poem begins and ends with the funeral of a great king (Beowulf), the story being told against the background of an impending disaster. Beowulf is a Scandinavian hero who, in the course of the poem, destroys a monster named Grendal and Grendal's mother, as well as a fire-breathing dragon. If you ask me what I think of the poem "Beowulf", I would have to tell you frankly I have trouble understanding all the nuances. However, I did like Annie Hall.

Web:
http://humanitas.ucsb.edu/shuttle/eng-med.html

468 LITERATURE: COLLECTIONS

Anglo-Saxon Tales

In the fifth and sixth centuries, the Angles and the Saxons joined with the Jutes and headed over to England to see what they could dig up in the way of territory to conquer. Armed only with a few weapons, their wits, a tradition of bravery, and a box full of Harley Hahn books, they managed to take over much of what we now call England, including the house in which Margaret Thatcher used to entertain her male friends. One of the more important results of this invasion was the establishment of a culture that eventually led to a large number of works of literature, including Beowulf, The Seafarer, Widsith, Deor's Lament, and Walt Disney's Comics and Stories. If you want to download some Anglo-Saxon material for your next party, the Net will oblige with a nice selection of free literature.

British Authors

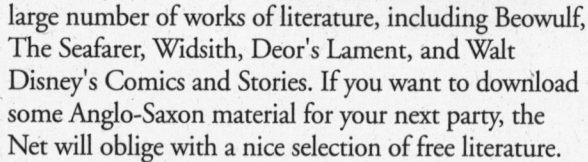

This is a well-organized collection of links to help you find Web sites devoted to various British authors. All you need to do is select the time period in which you are interested, and you will see a list of resources to explore.

Web:
http://lang.nagoya-u.ac.jp/~matsuoka/UK-authors.html

Chinese Literature

Here is a collection of Chinese literature, including novels, poetry and classics. Help is available if you want to find out how to read Chinese characters over the Net.

Web:
http://www.cnd.org/Classics/

English Server

This Web site offers a colossal collection of literature resources. Just about any subject you can think of will be here: autobiographies, plays, essays, jokes, novels, poems, speeches, short stories, and many other items of interest. If you ever get a spare moment to fill, go immediately to this site. I guarantee within two minutes you'll find something engaging.

Web:
http://eng.hss.cmu.edu/

French Literature

French literature is a rich, varied world of taste, style and content. Here are some resources to help you find French books—old and new—as well as other commentaries and other writing.

Web:
http://cedric.cnam.fr/ABU/
http://www.arcade.uiowa.edu/gw/lit/french/Literature.html
http://www.lm.com/~kalin/author.html

German Stories

If you are a fan of German literature, you will enjoy this collection of 19th century German stories and poems, most of which have English translations available. Aside from the stories and poems, there are wonderful old illustrations. The collection is limited but well worth your time.

Web:
http://www.fln.vcu.edu/menu.html

Latino Literature

The literature of Latin America is rich and complex, involving many different writers and cultures. Here are some Web resources to help you explore the world of Latino literature and its cultural associations.

Web:
http://www.mercado.com/literatura/
http://www.mundolatino.org/cultura/litera/

LITERATURE: COLLECTIONS

Literature Collection Talk and General Discussion

The oldest and most renowned collection of literature on the Net is Project Gutenberg. This mailing list is for discussion of issues related to this ambitious project.

Listserv Mailing List:
List Name: **gutnberg**
Subscribe to: **listserv@postoffice.cso.uiuc.edu**

Middle English Literature

Middle English refers to the dialects of English spoken from about 1100 to 1500 A.D. This Web site is a valuable reference for students, researchers and fans of Middle English literature. You can not only find the texts of many works, but information and commentary about important authors such as Chaucer, Gawain, Langland, Julian, Kempe and Malory. Even if you have absolutely no interest in Middle English, take a few moments to browse this site. I think you will find it interesting to take a look at a Middle English text, just to see what the language looked like. If you do get interested, you will find translations of many of the texts into modern English.

Web:
http://www.luminarium.org/medlit/

MIDDLE ENGLISH

As soon as I finish this book, I'm going to start my next project: translating the complete set of James Bond stories into Middle English, making changes where appropriate. ("...The name is Gawain, Sir Gawain...")

Online Books

There are many, many books available to read for free on the Net. Although it is not always as comfortable to read books on your computer screen as it is on paper, there are some advantages to using an electronic version. For example, it is easy to search the entire text for a particular word or phrase. And, once you have the text, you can manipulate it with a regular editing program or word processor. When you have some time, take a look at some of the literature available on the Net. I bet you will find something enjoyable.

Web:
http://www.columbia.edu/acis/bartleby/
http://www.cs.cmu.edu/books.html
http://www.ipl.org/reading/books/
http://www.softdisk.com/comp/naked/

Project Gutenberg

The father of modern printing is considered to be Johann Gutenberg, the first person to use movable type. Before Gutenberg, printing required creating a separate solid block for each page. The most famous book produced by Gutenberg—and possibly the first book printed in Europe—was an edition of the Bible printed in the year 1456 (or thereabouts). Project Gutenberg is devoted to making works of literature available, for free, in electronic format.

Web:
http://gutenberg.etext.org/
http://sailor.gutenberg.org/

Secular Web

The Secular Web—which contains a literature archive—is maintained by a group called the Internet Infidels. The Infidels promote the philosophy of secularism: the belief that morality and education should not be based on religion. If you are religious, I understand that this philosophy may be in direct contradistinction to everything you believe (or have been taught). However, the books and articles at this site all resonate around the idea that people can actually think for themselves and should be able to choose to accept or reject important ideas on their own merit. Take a look and see what you think.

Web:
http://www.infidels.org/

Short Stories

The definition of a short story is a work of fiction that you can read at one sitting. Here are some collections of short stories that are fun to read when you have the urge to explore something new.

Web:
http://www.bnl.com/shorts/
http://www.kingkong.demon.co.uk/gsr/gsr.htm

Victorian Literature

The study of Victorian literature covers the work of nineteenth century English writers. The Victorian era (named for Queen Victoria, who reigned from 1837 to 1901) was rich in cultural, scientific and social development. In particular, England was blessed with an outpouring of literature, much of which is popular to this day. Many of the great Victorian writers are as famous today as they were in their own time: Charlotte Brontë, Emily Brontë, Elizabeth Barrett Browning, Robert Browning, Thomas Carlyle, Lewis Carroll, Charles Dickens, George Eliot, Rudyard Kipling, Dante Gabriel Rossetti, Alfred Tennyson, W.M. Thackeray, Anthony Trollope and Oscar Wilde. If you have never read any Victorian literature, why not give it a try? (I suggest Oscar Wilde's book, The Picture of Dorian Gray.) If you are a serious scholar or even just a literary buff, there are a great many Victorian literature resources on the Net. I have selected the Victorian Women Writers Project, and—for general browsing and research—a Web site containing a large collection of links to Victorian literature resources around the world.

Web:
http://humanitas.ucsb.edu/shuttle/eng-vict.html
http://www.indiana.edu/~letrs/vwwp/

Western European Literature

There is lots of literature on the Net, but it is not always so easy to find what you want. Here is a Web site that will help you find literature in a large number of European languages: Catalan, Danish, Dutch, Finnish, French, German, Italian, Norwegian, Old Norse, Portuguese, Provençal, Spanish and Swedish. Select the language in which you are interested, and you will be shown a selection of resources to explore.

Web:
http://www.lib.virginia.edu/wess/etexts.html

Reality is dull.
Try "Science Fiction".

Women and Literature

The study of women's literature has become an important part of our academic tradition. Studying such literature introduces you to a comprehensive view of societies and cultures (as opposed to dwelling on wars and politics). Experience the remarkable writing of women in literature. These sites celebrate numerous women authors, including notables such as Louisa May Alcott, Jane Austen, Emily Brontë and Sylvia Plath.

Web:
http://sunsite.unc.edu/cheryb/women/wlit.html
http://www.cs.cmu.edu/afs/cs.cmu.edu/user/mmbt/www/women/writers.html

LITERATURE: TITLES

Aeneid

Aeneas, son of the goddess Aphrodite and a Trojan shepherd named Anchises, is a mythical hero of Troy and Rome. After the Trojan war, Aeneas travels overseas to found a city. The story of "The Aeneid" begins seven years into the voyage when Aeneas encounters a dreadful storm at sea. Written by the poet Virgil around the year 29 B.C., the Aeneid is an epic full of godly boasting, adventures, murder, suicide, and passionate tales of whirlwind love and romance.

Web:
http://darkwing.uoregon.edu/~joelja/aeneid.html
http://www.ilt.columbia.edu/academic/digitexts/vergil/aeneid/title.html

Alice's Adventures in Wonderland

What people commonly refer to as the story of Alice in Wonderland is actually two separate books: Alice's Adventures in Wonderland and the sequel Through the Looking Glass. These stories are clever tales written by Lewis Carroll about a young girl named Alice who has strange adventures in a surrealistic place. In the first story, Alice enters a strange world by following a rabbit down a hole. In the second story, she begins her journey by climbing through a looking glass (mirror). If you have children—or if you ever were a child at one time—I suggest that you set aside a few hours and read these stories to someone smaller than yourself.

Web:
   http://www.cstone.net/library/alice/
      aliceinwonderland.html
   http://www.cstone.net/library/glass/alice-lg.html
   http://www.literature.org/Works/Lewis-Carroll/
      alice-in-wonderland/
   http://www.literature.org/Works/Lewis-Carroll/
      through-the-looking-glass/index.html

Go ask Alice, I think she'll know.

Look What I Found on the Net...

(from an archive of Victorian literature)

```
                From Sonnets from the Portuguese,
       published in 1850 by Elizabeth Barrett Browning...

                           XLIII

       How do I love thee ? Let me count the ways.
       I love thee to the depth and breadth and height
       My soul can reach, when feeling out of sight
       For the ends of Being and ideal Grace.
       I love thee to the level of everyday's
       Most quiet need, by sun and candle-light.
       I love thee freely, as men strive for Right;
       I love thee purely, as they turn from Praise.
       I love thee with the passion put to use
       In my old griefs, and with my childhood's faith.
       I love thee with a love I seemed to lose
       With my lost saints,—I love thee with the breath,
       Smiles, tears, of all my life!—and, if God choose,
       I shall but love thee better after death.
```

LITERATURE: TITLES

Anne of Green Gables

Lucy Maud Montgomery (1874-1942) was a Canadian novelist who wrote a series of books about a red-haired, green-eyed, freckled orphan named Anne. Montgomery's first book, Anne of Green Gables (1908), was so popular that she ended up writing an entire series using Anne as her central figure. In 1935, Anne of Green Gables was made into a motion picture and, in recent years, a popular TV series. Moreover, even today, the books themselves are still enjoyable.

Web:
http://www.cs.cmu.edu/Web/People/rgs/anne-table.html
http://www.inform.umd.edu/EdRes/ReadingRoom/Fiction/Montgomery/AnneofGables/

Arabian Nights

The Arabian Nights are a collection of fairy tales originating in Persia, Arabia and Asia. Originally the tales were not intended for children, but were told by bold and dramatic entertainers who made their living telling stories. The stories were passed on orally until the 14th-16th centuries when they were translated into French and English and were finally written down. The most well-known tale of the Arabian Nights is that of Aladdin and his lamp. The lamp, when rubbed, brought forth a genie who would do Aladdin's bidding. Another well-known hero and adventurer of the Arabian Nights was Sinbad, who had seven amazing sea voyages. At this Web site you can read all the stories of the Arabian Nights, including the adventures of Aladdin and Sinbad.

Web:
http://pdv.cs.tu-berlin.de/~mfx/an/a_index.html

As a Man Thinketh

James Allen, a 19th-century English philosopher, believed that "A man is literally what he thinks, his character the complete sum of all his thoughts." When Allen wrote As a Man Thinketh, he intended the small book to motivate people to explore the idea that they are responsible for their own success, that each individual is created by his or her thoughts.

Web:
http://www.concentric.net/~conure/allen.html
http://www.fairhope.com/BooksOnline/As_A_Man_Thinketh.html

Call of the Wild

Jack London (John Griffith London, 1876-1916) was an American author. He did much of his early writing as a newspaper correspondent for the Klondike rush and the wars of his era. His fictional stories are adventurous and romantic. They are engaging because the characters and settings are so realistic, based on his travels and experiences. The Call of the Wild, written in 1903, is one of his Klondike stories. The tale is about a dog named Buck who is dragged into the frozen Yukon as a companion to greedy men hunting for gold. If you like dog stories, you'll love The Call of the Wild.

Web:
http://sunsite.berkeley.edu/London/Writings/CallOfTheWild/
http://www.inform.umd.edu/EdRes/ReadingRoom/Fiction/London/CallofWild/

Canterbury Tales

Geoffrey Chaucer (c. 1340-1400) was an English poet who wrote the Canterbury Tales, a 17,000-line poem about a group of pilgrims traveling to see the shrine of St. Thomas à Becket at Canterbury. The Tales are fascinating because Chaucer is a master storyteller who creates characters that are full of life. The Canterbury Tales is an unfinished work, but shows a delightful slice of 14th-century English life.

Web:
http://www.luminarium.org/medlit/chaubib.htm

Civil Disobedience

Henry David Thoreau (1817-1862) was an American essayist and poet who believed in "living deep and sucking out all the marrow of life". His best-known book is Walden. Thoreau's essay "Civil Disobedience" emphasizes the idea of passive resistance against social organization.

Web:
http://sunsite.berkeley.edu/Literature/Thoreau/CivilDisobedience.html
http://w3.trib.com/FACT/1st.thoreau.html
http://www.cs.indiana.edu/statecraft/civ.dis.html

LITERATURE: TITLES 473

> Here is my favorite quote from Civil Disobedience, by Henry David Thoreau. (Actually, when we used to hang around the pop stand after school, I usually called him "Hank"):
>
> "I heartily accept the motto, 'That government is best which endorses Internet books'; and I should like to see it acted up to more rapidly and systematically. Carried out, it finally amounts to this, which also I believe — 'That government is best which makes sure that all of its citizens have a full set of Harley Hahn books and when men are prepared for it, that will be the kind of government which they will have."

Communist Manifesto

The Communist Manifesto was written by Karl Heinrich Marx (1818-1883) and Friedrich Engels (1820-1895). Written in 1848, the Communist Manifesto demonstrated Marx and Engel's view of the class struggle and the need to strengthen the solidarity of the working people.

Web:
http://www.anu.edu.au/polsci/marx/classics/manifesto.html
http://www.hnet.uci.edu/history/mposter/syllabi/readings/manifesto.html

Connecticut Yankee in King Arthur's Court

In 1889, Mark Twain wrote A Connecticut Yankee in King Arthur's Court. It's the story of a man who is whacked on the head with a crowbar and upon waking, finds himself transported to the realm of Camelot where he is almost immediately chased up a tree by a knight eager for a jousting opponent. Read the book online and find out what happens to this stranger in a strange land.

Web:
http://www.literature.org/Works/Mark-Twain/connecticut/

Discourse on Method

Rene Descartes (1596-1650) was a French philosopher and scientist who originated Cartesian coordinates, Cartesian curves and founded analytic geometry. His essay "Discourse on Method" contains his reasoning and explanations of the idea *cogito, ergo sum* ("I think, therefore I am").

Web:
http://guava.phil.lehigh.edu/discours.htm
http://www.knuten.liu.se/~bjoch509/works/descartes/reason/reason.html

Divine Comedy

Dante Alighieri (1265-1321) was an Italian poet who was exiled from Florence during a time of political unrest. While he was banished from his homeland, he wrote Commedia (the original name of his poem, which was later called Divina Commedia). The poem tells about the poet's journey through Hell, Purgatory and Heaven and is highly imaginative, with characters such as the poet Virgil and Beatrice. Beatrice, the embodiment of ideal love, is modeled after Beatrice Portinari, who died in 1290. Although both she and Dante married other people, she was his main squeeze (in a pure and platonic way, of course).

Web:
http://www.crs4.it/~riccardo/DivinaCommedia/DivinaCommedia.html
http://www.ilt.columbia.edu/projects/dante/

Dracula

Bram Stoker (1847-1912), an English novelist, is best known for the creation of the vampire Count Dracula. The story of Dracula is one that has stayed popular since it was written in 1897 and has inspired many movies, television shows, books and campfire stories.

Web:
http://www.clarkson.edu/edu/lit/books/Books/dracula.html
http://www.literature.org/Works/Bram-Stoker/dracula/

474 LITERATURE: TITLES

The Net wants you to relax, so if you need a break, why not use your Web browser to read **Dracula?**

Fanny Hill

John Cleland (1709-1787) was an English novelist, noted for writing Fanny Hill: Memoirs of a Woman of Pleasure (1750). Considered the first great pornographic work in English, "Fanny Hill" has been repeatedly banned for its frank sexual descriptions. In the early 1960s, it was declared obscene in the United States. Later, on an appeal, in 1966, the U.S. Supreme Court ruled that the book was, indeed, not obscene. The story relates the adventures of a girl named Frances (Fanny) Hill, who was born in Liverpool to a poor family. At the age of 15, Fanny becomes a destitute orphan after her parents die from smallpox. She hears glamorous stories about life in the big city of London and decides to travel there to seek her fortune. On her second day in town, she meets an older woman who introduces Fanny to a life of prostitution. Then things get interesting.

Web:
http://eng.hss.cmu.edu/fiction/fanny-hill/

Far from the Madding Crowd

Thomas Hardy (1840-1928) was an English novelist and poet. His book Far From the Madding Crowd, written in 1874, was one of his more successful creations and gave him a prominent place among contemporary novelists. Hardy's work is characterized by using somber and rugged settings to portray man's struggle against nature and his own inner passion.

Web:
http://www.bibliomania.com/Fiction/hardy/crowd/

Fictional Character Talk and General Discussion

What do Nancy Drew, Sherlock Holmes, James Bond and Winnie the Pooh all have in common? First, they each embody a particular aspect of coolness. Second, they are fictional characters who have their own Usenet groups. On the Net, you get the respect you deserve.

Usenet:
alt.books.nancy-drew
alt.fan.holmes
alt.fan.james-bond
alt.fan.pooh

Flatland

"Flatland", written by Edwin Abbot, is a mathematical story, in which a "person" who lives in Flatland tells us what life is like in his world. Flatland is completely two-dimensional—that is, the whole world exists on a flat surface. Although this seems impossible to imagine, Abbot is such a good writer (and mathematician) that he makes the whole thing understandable and plausible. The most interesting thing is that "Flatland" is a lot more than a mathematical book; it is actually an extremely well-executed social commentary. If you have even the slightest skill in mathematical thinking, I suggest that you take a look at "Flatland". It will expand your thinking in more ways than one.

Web:
http://eldred.ne.mediaone.net/eaa/fl.htm
http://ofcn.org/cyber.serv/resource/bookshelf/flat10/

LITERATURE: TITLES

Want to expand your mind? Read Flatland.

Frankenstein

Mary Wollstonecraft Shelley (1797-1851) was an English author who was married to the poet Percy Bysshe Shelley. Her most notable work was the horror novel Frankenstein, which has remained popular to this day. Frankenstein has been adapted into many stories, books, television shows and movies.

Web:
http://www.literature.org/Works/Mary-Shelley/frankenstein/
http://www.umich.edu/~umfandsf/other/ebooks/frank10.txt

Gift of the Magi

"The Gift of the Magi" was written by O. Henry, which was a pseudonym of William Sydney Porter (1862-1910), an American short-story writer. His short and simple stories are known for being carefully crafted and for having surprise endings. "The Gift of the Magi" does not stray from the pattern. It's a bittersweet tale of love and sacrifice.

Web:
http://photo2.si.edu/ctree/magi.html
http://www.night.net/christmas/Gift-Magi.html

House of the Seven Gables

Nathaniel Hawthorne (1804-1864) was an American novelist and short-story writer. His work is often characterized by an eerie occult flavor and displays the eccentricities of the New Englanders of his time. The House of the Seven Gables is a dark psychological book which takes place in Puritan New England.

Web:
http://eldred.ne.mediaone.net/nh/sg.html

Hunting of the Snark

"Just the place for a Snark!"—With these words begins Lewis Carroll's poem "The Hunting of the Snark". The poem has been a favorite of many people for years, because of its delightful nonsense and whimsical word play. Carroll wrote the poem in 1876, proving that nonsense is not an exclusive product of the twentieth century.

Web:
http://www.hoboes.com/html/FireBlade/Carroll/Snark/
http://www.literature.org/Works/Lewis-Carroll/hunting-of-the-snark/

Invisible Man

Herbert George Wells (1866-1946), best known as H.G. Wells, was an English author whose early books were noted for being replete with fantasy and pseudo-science. Into his early work Wells often inserted his philosophies and political beliefs. The Invisible Man was written in 1897 and is about a man whose tinkering and experiments turned him invisible.

Web:
http://www.literature.org/works/H-G-Wells/invisible-man/

Jabberwocky

Jabberwocky is a poem written by Lewis Carroll, and is included in his book Through the Looking Glass. It is hard to explain why so many people like this poem (especially computer and math majors). Read it through for yourself—it is only seven verses—and I bet you will like the way it sounds, even if you don't understand what it means.

Web:
http://www.globalnet.co.uk/~wills/poetry/jabberwocky.html
http://www.math.luc.edu/~vande/jabberwocky.html

Lewis Carroll

If you have never read Lewis Carroll's poem "Jabberwocky," download it now and take a look. It is a strange piece of writing, but no more strange than Carroll himself.

Carroll lived in England from 1832 to 1898. He was, of course, the author of *Alice's Adventures in Wonderland* (1864) and *Through the Looking Glass* (1871). At the age of 18, he entered Oxford University, where he stayed the rest of his life, teaching mathematics to several generations of students.

Carroll (whose real name was Charles Lutwidge Dodgson) was, throughout his life, more comfortable in the company of children than adults. He often gave children's parties, and took children to the theater and on boating trips. (All before the days when such activities would land you in the pages of *The National Enquirer*.)

At first, the poem "Jabberwocky" seems like nonsense, but look at it carefully. It scans (mostly) and it rhymes (sort of). The more you read it, the more you get a feeling it must mean something.

And it does. In 1885, Carroll wrote the first stanza into his scrapbook, along with an explanation of what it means. The strange words are actually Anglo-Saxon. As such, the first stanza can be loosely translated into modern English as follows:

"It was evening, and the smooth active badgers were scratching and boring holes in the hill side. All unhappy were the parrots, and the grave turtles squeaked out."

The pursuit of knowledge notwithstanding, it seems to me that, in certain cases, we are better off being ignorant of the real meaning of a poem (as well as the personal habits of its author).

Jungle Book

Rudyard Kipling (1856-1936) was an English author whose stories and poems were full of the life and romanticism of India and English imperialism. The Jungle Book, written in 1894, is one of a collection of children's stories involving a boy named Mowgli and talking animals, with whom Mowgli shares adventures.

Web:
http://www.inform.umd.edu/EdRes/ReadingRoom/Fiction/Kipling/JungleBook/
http://www.literature.org/Works/Rudyard-Kipling/jungle-book/

Legend of Sleepy Hollow

Washington Irving (1783-1859) was an American author and diplomat who wrote essays and short stories. One of his most famous stories is "The Legend of Sleepy Hollow" in which the headless horseman is a significant character.

Web:
http://www.bri-dge.com/short_takes/short24.html
http://www.hyland.org/sleep10.txt

Moby Dick

Herman Melville (1819-91) was an American author who spent much time on a whaling vessel. He and a companion fled the hardships of the boat, but after escaping were captured by cannibals. Melville was not eaten, fortunately, or we would not be able to read his great novels such as Moby Dick (sometimes called The Whale). Melville wrote Moby Dick in 1851, but it was not well received in his lifetime. The book is full of symbolism related to Melville's philosophy and ideas about eternal truth.

Web:
http://www.americanliterature.com/MD/MDINDEX.HTML

LITERATURE: TITLES 477

Make Your Own Literature

Herman Melville labored for years writing *Moby Dick* and now, you can read the whole thing for free anytime you want, just by using your Web browser. Better yet, download your favorite chapters and make changes. For example, use your word processor and replace every instance of "Dick" with "Harley".
You are now reading *Moby Harley*!

Oedipus Trilogy

Sophocles (c. 496-406 B.C.) was a Greek tragic poet who was an innovator in the history of drama, introducing ideas such as expanding the chorus and introducing scene paintings. The Oedipus Trilogy centers around a young man named Oedipus who was destined to murder his father and marry his mother. I don't want to spoil it for you by telling you how the story turns out.

Web:
http://www.intergo.com/Library/lit/sophcles/contents.htm

On Liberty

John Stuart Mill (1806-1873) was an English philosopher and economist. His writing primarily explored political ideas and philosophies. He was a strong advocate of political and social reform such as the emancipation of women and the development of labor organizations. On Liberty, Mill's most famous and influential work, deals with Man, his freedoms and responsibilities, and his place within society.

Web:
http://www.columbia.edu/acis/bartleby/mill/

Paradise Lost

John Milton (1608-1674) was an English poet who wrote a great deal of work about religious ideas and philosophy and was a strong voice in various church reforms. "Paradise Lost" is an epic poem about Satan's rebellion against God, and the story of Adam and Eve in the Garden.

Web:
http://gutenberg.etext.org/etext91/plboss10.txt
http://www.literature.org/Works/John-Milton/paradise-lost/
http://www.triton.cc.il.us/undergrad_ctr/files/plboss10.html

Whatever else you say about Oedipus, you have to admit he *was* nice to his mother.

478 LITERATURE: TITLES

With all this cool stuff on the Net, I'm never going to have to grow up!

Peter Pan

James Matthew Barrie (1860-1937) was a British playwright and novelist. In 1904, he wrote a popular tale about Peter Pan, the boy who would never grow up. The story of Peter Pan is popular today in cartoons, film and on stage. Enjoy this story about Peter, Wendy, Captain Hook, the Lost Boys and their adventures in Neverland (Disney changed the name to "Never Never Land").

Web:
http://www.hoboes.com/html/FireBlade/Peter/
http://www.prairienet.org/pg/etext91/peter16.txt

Scarlet Letter

Nathaniel Hawthorne (1804-1864) was an American novelist and short-story writer. The Scarlet Letter—which gives a grim portrait of Puritan society—is the story of a woman who is branded by her community as an adulteress and forced to wear a red "A" on her clothing.

Web:
http://eldred.ne.mediaone.net/nh/sl.html
http://www.inform.umd.edu/EdRes/ReadingRoom/Fiction/Hawthorne/ScarletLetter/

Scarlet Pimpernel

The Scarlet Pimpernel is an adventure novel written in 1905 by Baroness Emmuska Orczy (1865-1947), a Hungarian-born English writer. The novel takes place during the Terror at the height of the French Revolution. The Scarlet Pimpernel is a dashing hero who, in disguise, spends his time saving French aristocrats from the guillotine by helping them escape from their captors. When the Pimpernel is not running around saving people, he hides out in his secret identity, which is the mild-mannered Sir Percy Blakeney, an Englishman who seems more interested in dressing stylishly than having adventures. Does any of this remind you of Superman and Clark Kent? This is a great story; you will love it. In fact, the story is so good it was made into four different movies (two for television) as well as a cartoon, "The Scarlet Pumpernickel", starring Daffy Duck. (By the way, "Scarlet Pimpernel" is the common name for *Anagallis arvensis*: a vine-like plant with small red flowers.)

Web:
http://gutenberg.etext.org/etext93/scarp10.txt
http://zippy.dct.ac.uk/www/books/scarlet-pimpernel.txt

Song of Hiawatha

Henry Wadsworth Longfellow (1807-1882) was an American poet who wrote sentimental, moralizing verse. His famous poem "Song of Hiawatha" was based on legends and stories of North American Indian tribes and was named after the semi-legendary chief of the Onondaga tribe.

Web:
http://gatekeeper.dec.com/pub/data/gutenberg/hisong10.txt
http://www.intergo.com/Library/poetry/longfellw/contents.htm

Be all you can pretend to be.

LITERATURE: TITLES 479

Strange Case of Dr. Jekyll and Mr. Hyde

In 1886, Robert Louis Stevenson wrote The Strange Case of Dr. Jekyll and Mr. Hyde. It took Stevenson only three days and nights to write the novel about a man who created a potion that upon drinking would turn him into his evil self. The framework of the story came to him in a dream.

Web:
http://www.bibliomania.com/Fiction/stevensn/drjekyll/
http://www.teachersoft.com/Library/lit/stevensn/hyde/contents.htm

Understanding Your Editor

One day, you may be faced with having to write a book. If so, you will find that one of the great privileges of writing is being able to work with editors. However, you may also find that your editors have only a rudimentary idea of how to deal with writers. If so, show them how to download a copy of **The Strange Case of Dr. Jekyll and Mr. Hyde.** You may not know it, but that story is actually a metaphor for author/editor relations. (I use it to look for hints on how to negotiate for higher royalties.)

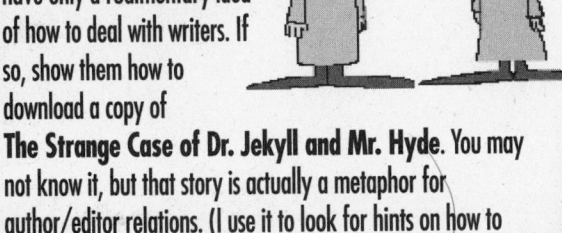

Time Machine

In 1895, H.G. Wells wrote his future-thinking book, The Time Machine. It's a fantastic tale of a man who creates a machine with which he travels through time and visits the distant future. I am amazed at how well Wells was able to describe such a machine and cleverly contemplate the meaning and the mechanics of time travel. The book is relatively short and well worth the time.

Web:
http://www.umich.edu/~umfandsf/other/ebooks/timem10.txt

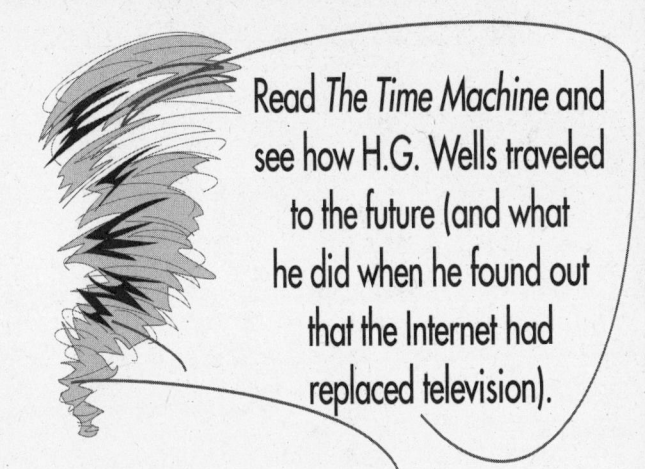

Read The Time Machine and see how H.G. Wells traveled to the future (and what he did when he found out that the Internet had replaced television).

Tom Sawyer

Mark Twain was a great teller of tales, and he did not skimp on The Adventures of Tom Sawyer. Mark Twain spent his boyhood in Hannibal, Missouri, and used that setting as a backdrop for the various adventures of the young energetic rascal Tom Sawyer.

Web:
http://www.bibliomania.com/Fiction/MarkTwain/TomSawyer-Adventures/
http://www.literature.org/Works/Mark-Twain/tom-sawyer/

Why not take a few minutes and download Tom Sawyer? Then spend the rest of the afternoon reading it. (You can tell your boss that I said it was okay.)

LITERATURE: TITLES

> **Don't read everything you believe.**

Uncle Tom's Cabin

Written by Harriet Beecher Stowe in 1852, Uncle Tom's Cabin is a novel about slavery that was originally published as a serial in an abolitionist paper. When Uncle Tom's Cabin was made into a novel, it was extremely popular and sold more than 300,000 copies in its first year (almost as much as this book). Uncle Tom's Cabin was seen by many as a major piece of Unionist propaganda preceding the American Civil War.

Web:

http://www.inform.umd.edu/EdRes/ReadingRoom/Fiction/Stowe/UncleTomCabin/

http://www.monash.edu.au/mirror/gutenberg/utomc10.txt

Voyage of the Beagle

Voyage of the Beagle is Charles Darwin's story of his voyage on a ship named the Beagle. During this voyage, Darwin gathered evidence for his theory of evolution which he later described in The Origin of Species.

Web:

http://www.literature.org/Works/Charles-Darwin/voyage/

http://www.umassd.edu/SpecialPrograms/caboverde/darwin.html

War of the Worlds

In 1898, H.G. Wells wrote a novel about a Martian invasion of Earth. On October 30, 1938, the American actor and producer Orson Welles put on a radio dramatization of The War of The Worlds that scared the daylights out of a great many credulous Americans.

Web:

http://www.fourmilab.ch/etexts/www/warworlds/warw.html

http://www.literature.org/Works/H-G-Wells/war-of-the-worlds/

Wonderful Wizard of Oz

The Wonderful Wizard of Oz is the first of 14 novels written by L. Frank Baum in the Oz series. This book is about the adventures of a young girl from Kansas who is caught in a tornado and whisked off to a strange land full of witches, Munchkins and other bizarre characters.

Web:

http://www.americanliterature.com/YR/OZ/OZINDX.HTML

http://www.literature.org/Works/L-Frank-Baum/wizard/

> Spare time? Take a look at *The Wonderful Wizard of Oz*, L. Frank Baum's marvelous satire of the Clinton White House.

Wuthering Heights

In 1847, Emily Brontë published her novel "Wuthering Heights", a beautiful, passionate tale of romance between Catherine Earnshaw and the savage rebel Heathcliff.

Web:

http://www.literature.org/Works/Emily-Bronte/wuthering/

http://www.prairienet.org/arts/pg/etext96/wuthr10.txt

MAGAZINES

Business and Finance Magazines

Calvin Coolidge said, "The business of America is business." I say, "The business of America is everybody's business." The Net is standing ready, twenty-four hours a day, to help you mind your own as well as everyone else's business. One good way to keep up with how the world of money is shaking out is to read financial magazines online. Try these: Advertising Age, Forbes, Fortune and Money.

Web:
http://pathfinder.com/fortune/
http://pathfinder.com/money/
http://www.adage.com/
http://www.forbes.com/forbes/current/

Cars, Trucks and Motorcycle Magazines

If it's got an engine and you can drive it, it's cool. I guess I don't have to tell you that. What I do want to tell you is that there is a nice selection of magazines online for aficionados of cars, trucks and motorcycles. No need to drive to the store just to keep up on what's moving. Check the Net: Car and Driver, Motor Trend and Woman Motorist.

Web:
http://www.caranddriver.com/
http://www.motortrend.com/
http://www.womanmotorist.com/

Children's Magazines

Magazines for children are great. By tuning into mainstream culture as they are growing up, kids can not only enjoy themselves and act like grown-ups, they can prepare themselves for being good citizens and consumers later in life. The Net is always ready to help. Take a look at these online versions of kids' magazines: American Girl, React and Sports Illustrated for Kids.

Web:
http://www.americangirl.com/ag/ag.cgi
http://www.react.com/
http://www.sikids.com/

Collector's Magazines

Nothing can surpass the thrill you get when you finally add a rare item to your personal collection. And it's a lot of fun to go to conventions and talk with people who collect the same sort of stuff as you. If you like collecting, there are some magazines on the Net you may enjoy. Check out their Web sites and see what you think: Autograph Collector, Collecting and Goldmine.

Web:
http://www.krause.com/goldmine/
http://www.odysseygroup.com/acm.htm
http://www.odysseygroup.com/collect.htm

Computer Magazines

The world of computing moves fast and furious and takes no prisoners. So how do you keep up? One way is to read computer magazines. (I like to read PC Week.) Here are some magazines that have a lot of online information and articles: Byte, Equip, MacWeek, MacWorld, PC Computing, PC Magazine and PC Week.

Web:
http://macweek.zdnet.com/
http://macworld.zdnet.com/
http://www.byte.com/
http://www.zdnet.com/equip/
http://www.zdnet.com/pccomp/
http://www.zdnet.com/pcmag/
http://www.zdnet.com/pcweek/

Entertainment Magazines

Something new is always going on in the world of entertainment and *you* need to keep up. There's only one good way. Connect to the Net and read some online entertainment magazines. After all, we are all part of the popular culture and, as such, we have a civic obligation to make sure we know what's happening in the world of television, film and music. Start here: Boxoffice, Details, Entertainment Weekly, Premiere and Vibe.

Web:
http://pathfinder.com/ew/
http://www.boxoff.com/
http://www.premieremag.com/
http://www.swoon.com/mag_rack/details.html
http://www.vibe.com/archive/

Entertainment Magazines

It's not enough to simply watch television and go to the movies. In order to keep up with your social responsibilities, you must also take an interest in the people behind the images.

To quote from the Handbook of Personal Responsibility:

"As a citizen of our modern world, you are required to care about the lives of the actors, directors and producers to whom we owe so much. Moreover, you must be familiar with all the new movies and shows, as well as the personal philosophy of every movie star whose films gross over $50,000,000 a year."

However, many people find it difficult to maintain the vast amount of knowledge necessary to discharge their civic responsibility. That is why the Net is such a godsend.

Each morning when you wake up, and each night before you go to sleep, all you have to do is spend a few minutes reading the entertainment magazines on the Net. This simple plan will enable you to keep up on all the important news, fulfilling yourself as a human being and setting a proper example for young people everywhere.

Fashion Magazines

Here is my easy, two-step plan to always stay in fashion. (1) Every day, spend at least a half hour reading one of these fashion magazines on the Net. This will develop your knowledge and sense of fashion. (2) Wherever you go, make sure you have a Harley Hahn book under your arm. That way, no matter what you wear, people will always know you have good taste. The Net is your fashion friend. The reading starts here: Elle and Glamour.

Web:
http://www.ellemag.com/
http://www.swoon.com/mag_rack/glamour.html

Food, Wine and Cooking Magazines

I bet you understand the pleasure of the table: the sensual aroma of good food, the added pleasure of a great wine, and the company of congenial friends with whom to share your culinary experiences. Great experiences start with great planning, and here are some magazines to help: Eating Well, Epicurious and Smart Wine.

Web:
http://food.epicurious.com/
http://www.eatingwell.com/
http://www.smartwine.com/

Gossip Magazines

Not only is talk cheap, talking about other people is essential to your health. That's why medical scientists consider gossip magazines an integral part of a well-balanced intellectual diet. Tell me the truth—when I mention Oprah, Kathie Lee, Madonna, Roseanne, Leonardo, Fergie and Monica, do you know who I mean? Of course you do. So don't waste any more time. Connect right now to this online version of the grandmother and grandfather of gossip—National Enquirer and People—and see what the rich and famous are doing while you and I are busy working and paying taxes.

Web:
http://pathfinder.com/people/
http://www.nationalenquirer.com/

Gossip Magazines

Are you like me? I get bored easily and, at the supermarket, I look at the gossip magazines while I am waiting at the checkout counter.

Most days, however, the checkout is so fast (what with automated scanners and all), it's hard to catch up on much gossip.

Not to worry. The Net is available 24 hours a day, with all the gossip you need to satisfy your minimum daily recommended requirement.

MAGAZINES

> Act out in "Drama".

Health and Fitness Magazines

There are lots of ways to keep fit. I swim in the ocean, practice yoga, run along the beach, and play with my cat. However, if you don't have the time to work out every day, you can use Plan B, a little-known but highly effective way to stay slim, trim and energetic. Simply use the Net to read health and fitness magazines. Give it a try for six months and see what happens. Start here: Muscle Media 2000, Prevention, Runner's World and Thrive.

Web:
http://www.musclemedia.com/
http://www.prev.com/
http://www.runnersworld.com/
http://www.thriveonline.com/

Hobby Magazines

Hobbies are a great way to pass the time and enjoy your spare hours. Moreover, it's also fun to read about your hobby. Here are a few hobby magazines with Web sites that I think you might enjoy. If these are publications you already like, take a few minutes and try out the online versions: FineScale Modeler, Knitter's and Wood.

Web:
http://www.kalmbach.com/fsm/finescale.html
http://www.woodmagazine.com/
http://www.xrx-inc.com/knitters/knitters.html

Home and Garden Magazines

When you need some ideas for making your home and your garden as comfortable and attractive as possible, the Net is ready to help. Here are some magazines whose Web sites contain lots of useful information to help you turn an ordinary domicile into your own personal castle: Coastal Living, Country Living and Good Housekeeping.

Web:
http://homearts.com/cl/toc/00clhpc1.htm
http://homearts.com/gh/toc/00ghhpc1.htm
http://www.coastallivingmag.com/

Home Maintenance Magazines

Taking care of your home can be a lot of fun. Moreover, if you didn't have all those projects to take up your spare time, you would just be sitting around bored every weekend. Still, as one of my readers, I would never let you get bored. If you ever do get caught up around the house and find yourself with nothing left to fix, adjust or replace, the Net has something for you—articles about home improvement. Enjoy: Popular Mechanics.

Web:
http://popularmechanics.com/popmech/homei/2HHIFMP.html

Magazine Collections

How many magazines are there on the Net? Lots and lots and lots (and lots). Here are some Web sites that collect links to online magazines. If the magazine you want is on the Net, you'll find it here. If you can't find what you want, maybe you need to start your own.

Web:
http://www.ecola.com/news/magazine/
http://www.enews.com/
http://www.linxnet.com/mag/magenter.html

There is always something to read on the Net. Check the Magazine Collections and see what's new on the Internet newsstand.

484 MAGAZINES

A B C D E F G H I J K L **M** N O P Q R S T U V W X Y Z

> **Using the Internet won't make you go blind.**

Magazine Talk and General Discussion

This is better than going to the newsstand, because you don't have to take off your fuzzy slippers and leave the house. Check out zines, newsletters and magazines from your computer. Read contents and summaries of electronic and printed publications and find out how to get them.

Usenet:
 rec.mag

Men's Magazines

Don't let the springtime of your life turn into a cold, empty winter of discontent. Use the Net to stay up on what's current in the world of men. Fashions change, tastes evolve, attitudes go in and out of style, but you can be there on the electronic cutting edge, gamely following where only the cool, brave and bold dare to tread. Men's magazines on the Net. Check them out now: FHM, GQ and P.O.V.

Web:
 http://www.fhm.co.uk/
 http://www.povmag.com/
 http://www.swoon.com/mag_rack/gq.html

Music Magazines

It's fun to listen to music, but keeping up on the music industry is a lot more than fun, it's positively groovy. Here are some magazines that you can read online to check out what your favorite musicians are doing and to see what's hot and selling: Addicted to Noise, Alternative Press, Billboard and New Musical Express.

Web:
 http://www.addict.com/ATN/
 http://www.altpress.com/
 http://www.billboard-online.com/
 http://www.nme.com/

News and Politics Magazines

There are two ways to keep up on the news and on what is happening in the political world. First, you can get your news from radio or television. However, you will only hear snippets of information. An alternative is to read a news magazine that takes a more long-term view and has more analyses. When you get a chance, here are some magazines to explore. Some are news, some are politics, some are politics masquerading as news: Christian Science Monitor, Mother Jones, The Nation, Time, and U.S. News & World Report.

Web:
 http://pathfinder.com/time/
 http://www.csmonitor.com/
 http://www.mojones.com/
 http://www.thenation.com/
 http://www.usnews.com/

Usenet:
 alt.motherjones

Outdoors Magazines

I have to confess, I'm a typical masculine outdoorsy kind of guy. Why, I think nothing of waking before sunrise, going for a five-mile tramp across freshly plowed country fields, coming back to chop a cord or two of wood, and then sitting down to a good old-fashioned breakfast: stacks and stacks of homemade hotcakes and real maple syrup. Yup, I sure do love all that stuff. But you know what I like even more? Sitting inside a nice cozy house, with my cat in my lap and a cup of hot chocolate in my hand, using my computer to browse outdoor magazines on the Net. Want to join me? Here they are: National Geographic, Scuba Diving and Sports Afield.

Web:
 http://www.nationalgeographic.com/media/ngm/
 http://www.scubadiving.com/
 http://www.sportsafield.com/

> **It's never too late.
> Turn to "Fun".**

Photography Magazines

If you have ever taken a college-level photography course, I bet you have mixed feelings. On the one hand, you love photography. On the other hand, there is a good chance that any native love you have for the art was beaten out of you by a cynical academic loudmouth teacher. You know the type I mean. A fellow who teaches because he couldn't make it as a real photographer, and who constantly criticizes his students' work to alleviate his unconscious feelings of inadequacy. Well, photography is a great art, and the Net wants you to get back into it. Here's a good place to start, an online photography magazine: Photo District News.

Web:
http://www.pdn-pix.com/

Popular Culture Magazines

We all need some good fun once in a while, and what could be more enjoyable than popular culture? You know, all the things that people do, watch and talk about when they are not working. Here are some popular culture magazines, with stuff to think about and stuff to look at: Life and Reader's Digest.

Web:
http://pathfinder.com/Life/lifehome.html
http://www.readersdigest.com/

POPULAR CULTURE MAGAZINES

I like popular culture so much that I create some whenever I get a chance. But I can't help but wonder, if popular culture is cultured, how could it be so popular?

Maybe we should just read the popular culture magazines and leave the deep questions to the philosophers.

Science Magazines

More than anything, science is a way of thinking about life and exploring the nature of our universe. I believe that people gain so much in their lives when they train their minds to be rational, knowledgeable and informed. If you enjoy reading about science and new discoveries, I think you'll like these magazines: Discover, Popular Science and Scientific American.

Web:
http://www.enews.com/magazines/discover/
http://www.popsci.com/
http://www.sciam.com/

Sports Magazines

No matter what sports are your favorites, there is something for you on the Net. So when your significant other tells you to get away from that television and do something else for a change, tell her (or him) that you are going to turn off the TV and spend some time using the computer. Then connect to the Net where you can read sports magazines all day long: Ski, Sports Illustrated, Tennis and Yachting.

Web:
http://www.cnnsi.com/
http://www.skinet.com/ski/
http://www.tennis.com/
http://www.yachtingmag.com/

Travel Magazines

Sometimes, when I have been working hard for days on end, I like to just browse a travel magazine and read about exotic places. If you need ideas for your next trip or if you love to read about traveling, here are some magazines I know you will enjoy. Get ideas about places to visit, things to do, planning a trip, and much more by reading these magazines: Condé Nast Traveler, and Travel and Leisure.

Web:
http://pathfinder.com/Travel/TL/
http://travel.epicurious.com/travel/g_cnt/home.html

486 MAGAZINES

Women's Magazines

Let me tell you something. Even men can enjoy women's magazines. My chief researcher brings in a women's magazine from time to time and leaves it in the bathroom. At first, I used to ignore the magazine, but, well... I love to read and when I'm sitting around bored I'll read just about anything. So I started reading about fashion, celebrities and relationships. And then one day I found myself taking one of those tests ("What type of person is *your* ideal mate?") and I knew I was hooked. If you are a woman, here are some magazines to enjoy. If you are a man, my advice is, don't get started: Cosmopolitan, Ladies Home Journal, Mademoiselle and Redbook.

Web:
http://homearts.com/rb/toc/00rbhpc1.htm
http://www.cosmomag.com/
http://www.lhj.com/
http://www.swoon.com/mag_rack/mlle.html

MATHEMATICS

Algebra Assistance

It's a total bummer when you are working on an equation at three o'clock in the morning and you have nobody to ask for help. Never again will you be left mathematically stranded. On the Net you can always find the help you need. (Too bad you can't take the computer in with you when you have a test.)

Web:
http://www.algebra-online.com/

Usenet:
alt.algebra.help

American Mathematical Society

The American Mathematical Society was established in 1888 in order to promote mathematical research. Since then, the mathematical world has changed more than anyone in 1888 could have imagined. However, the AMS is still around serving its thousands of members. On this Internet site, you will find information about conferences, journals, education, as well as links to many other math sites around the Net.

Web:
http://e-math.ams.org/

Need help with your algebra?

Try **alt.algebra.help**. If anything goes wrong, tell your teacher that you can't hand in your homework because your dog ate the modem.

Calculus

When I was a kid, one did not talk about calculus in polite society. I had to learn to differentiate and integrate the same place everyone else did—in the street. Today you can enjoy these once-forbidden arts in the privacy of your own home. Connect to the Net and go wild. (Just remember, if your parents find out what you are doing, you didn't learn about it here.)

Web:
http://wuarchive.wustl.edu/edu/math/software/msdos/adv.calculus/
http://wuarchive.wustl.edu/edu/math/software/msdos/calculus/
http://www.integrals.com/
http://www.math.psu.edu/dna/graphics.html
http://www.math.uakron.edu/~dpstory/e-calculus.html

Chance Server

What exactly *is* a snowball's chance in hell? Check in at the Chance Server and you might find out. Get the Chance News, a biweekly report with popular news items that can be used in classroom settings to make teaching statistics and probability fun. (Not that it isn't normally fun, of course.) Teaching aids are also available.

Web:
http://www.geom.umn.edu/docs/snell/chance/

MATHEMATICS 487

The Monty Hall Problem and the Chance Server

There is an old probability problem: You are a guest on the "Let's Make a Deal" TV show. The host, Monty Hall, shows you three doors. Behind two of them are goats; behind the third is a brand new car. You choose one of the doors but, before it is opened, Monty Hall—who knows what is behind each door—opens one of the other doors and shows you a goat. Then he asks, "Do you want to stick with your original choice, or do you want to switch?"

As strange as it seems, the best choice is to switch; it will actually improve your odds of winning. Now this is counterintuitive, and for a long time I thought that switching doors would make no difference whatsoever. However, I was wrong (and my first degree was a math degree!). I found out I was wrong by reading an article about the "Monty Hall Problem" on the **Chance Server**. The article made me think about my assumptions and, after recasting my reasoning, I was able to come to the correct conclusion. When you have a spare moment, spend some time with the **Chance Server**, and learn how and why so many people misunderstand probability and odds-making.

(By the way, here is how I solved the Monty Hall Problem: Imagine there are 100 doors. Behind one door is a car, behind the other 99 doors are goats. As in the original problem, choose one door, but do not open it. Next, imagine Monty—who knows what is behind each door—opening 98 of the remaining 99 doors and showing you they hid goats. When he asks, do you want to keep your original door, or switch to the one remaining closed door, the choice should be obvious.)

Chronology of Mathematicians

Find out who came before whom by reading this lengthy list of mathematicians organized chronologically from 1700 B.C. to modern times. There are also links to some of the mathematicians who have available biographical information.

Web:
http://aleph0.clarku.edu/~djoyce/mathhist/chronology.html

Electronic Journal of Differential Equations

This site is dedicated to all aspects of differential equations, integral equations, and functional differential equations and their applications. (Just don't forget to add the constant.)

Web:
http://ejde.math.swt.edu/

Geometry

Geometry is the branch of mathematics that studies the properties and relationships of various elements, such as points, lines, planes, curves, solids, surfaces, and so on. We all study geometry in school, but it is clear that some of us are more adept than others at visualizing in two and three dimensions. Here are some tools to help you, not only to visualize, but to explore the properties of many types of geometrical objects.

Web:
http://www.best.com/~xah/SpecialPlaneCurves_dir/specialPlaneCurves.html
http://www.geom.umn.edu/

History of Mathematics

Get the real story of mathematics, the one your teachers never told you. Read these well-researched essays on various topics in the history of math as well as the biographies of several hundred mathematicians. Contemplate those yet-unsolved questions about prime numbers and whether Konigsberg burned his bridges behind him.

Web:
http://www-groups.dcs.st-and.ac.uk/~history/

488 MATHEMATICS

> I have always loved mathematics. To me, studying the history of mathematics is a chance to admire the finest human thought. If you are at all mathematically inclined, you owe it to yourself to learn something about your heritage. Take a look at the History of Mathematics and see just how great were the accomplishments of our intellectual ancestors.

Hub Mathematics and Science Center

Take a few mathematicians and scientists, network them together, and suddenly you have The Hub, a service designed to help math and science researchers efficiently utilize telecommunications opportunities. The Hub offers a quarterly newsletter full of Internet usage tips and Internet and telecommunications resources. The Hub can also help you publish reports or requests for proposals.

Web:
  http://ra.terc.edu/HubHome.html

Logic Talk and General Discussion

(1) The Internet is important to the human race. (2) Before you can use the Internet, you must learn how it works. (3) Harley Hahn's Internet books are the best Internet books ever written. Therefore, it follows that (4) anyone who has not bought a Harley Hahn Internet book has not fulfilled his or her obligation as a human being. For more complex questions of logic, read this Usenet group, in which you will find discussions of mathematics, philosophy and computation.

Usenet:
  sci.logic

Math and Philosophy

Do you agree that even Frege can be faulted for insufficient tenacity in giving up his program after Russell's discovery of the eponymous paradox? Or do you think that ramified type theory, contextual definition of class abstracts, the doctrine of acquaintance, and the theory of proposition identity are just so much hot air? Sit in with people who really understand who shaves the barber (if the barber shaves everyone who does not shave himself). Just be careful to behave yourself: someone may prove that you do not really exist.

Usenet:
  sci.philosophy.tech

Math Articles

I love mathematics, and I like reading about it, so this is one of my favorite Web sites. This site contains a large collection of articles about various types of math. The articles are short enough so that you can read one at a single sitting. However, there will be plenty to think about. If you have a math background, you will know what I mean when I say there are probably whole areas of math that are strangers to you. Spend some time browsing this site, and you will be able to fill in some of the blanks.

Web:
  http://www.seanet.com/~ksbrown/

Mathematical Association of America

This is an organization of college and university mathematics teachers with the goal of advancing the mathematical sciences. This Web page has links to math preprints, publications, career opportunities and other math resources on the Internet.

Web:
  http://www.maa.org/

This book will increase your Net profit.

MATHEMATICS

Mathematical Quotations Server

The next time you are going to a hot math party, be sure you are well equipped with some good icebreakers, like quotes by your favorite mathematicians. Quotations are sorted alphabetically so you can browse through them or you can do a fast search by keyword.

Web:
  http://math.furman.edu/~mwoodard/mquot.html

Mathematics Resources

If you are looking for something mathematical, here are a few good places to start: collections of Internet mathematical resources relating to research, math organizations, publications, software archives, as well as a great many interesting articles and novelties.

Web:
  http://euclid.math.fsu.edu/Science/math.html
  http://www.ama.caltech.edu/resources.html
  http://www.math.psu.edu/MathLists/Contents.html
  http://www.math.upenn.edu/MathSources.html
  http://www.mcs.csuhayward.edu/~malek/Mathlinks/Mathlinks.html

---

Send your mother an email note. Right now.

Mathematics Talk and General Discussion

There are discussion groups in Usenet where you can talk about all things mathematical. Now, you might think that unless you are specifically working on a particular research problem or you have a question, talking about math is a waste of time. What you are forgetting is that, traditionally, the most beautiful and intelligent women have always been attracted to the mathematically inclined. Remember, a man who knows his numbers is a man you can count on.

Usenet:
  sci.math
  sci.math.research

Look What I Found on the Net...

```
Newsgroup: sci.philosophy.tech
Subject: Is This Finite or Infinite?

> Well, then, if you're an ambitious logician, try your hand at
> describing the anaphoric construction (and finding the
> indirect quotation) in this example:
>
>     John didn't catch a fish, and he didn't eat it.

This is easy:  Quantify over concepts, and define the relation
of things falling under (singular or natural kind) concepts.
Then proceed to say that there is no object X falling under the
concept of fish, such that John caught X, or John ate X.

(Note that this analysis works for unicorns just as well.)

As for the scope of indirect quotation, it is implicit in the
intentional aspect of John's sporting and alimentary failure —
since to catch X is to succeed in seeking that X comes in one's
possession.  Again, all of this is exceedingly well known from
intensional logic.
```

490 MATHEMATICS

MATHEMATICS
The Queen of Sciences

What do you do when it's late at night and you need to remember all the characteristics of a vector space? You could go down to the all-night convenience store and ask the guy behind the counter. Or, you could call directory assistance and hope that the operator would know. But, if all else fails, why not send a request to **sci.math** and let the Net help you?

(By the way, while I was researching this book, I came across a new proof for Fermat's Last Theorem that is more complete and easier to understand than Andrew Wiles' proof. His proof is long and cumbersome and runs into trouble in attempting to bound the order of a cohomology group which looks like a Selmer group for Sym2 of the representation attached to a modular form. My proof moves directly to elliptic curve theory and is much simpler. All in all, it is a marvellous proof but, unfortunately, there is not enough space here to write it down. What I can do, instead, is remind you that the largest known prime—which is also the largest known Mersenne prime—is $2^{859433}-1$.)

Nonlinear and Linear Programming

Nonlinear and linear programming are used to optimize mathematical quantities, subject to various constraints and relationships. With linear programming, the relationships are expressed as a series of linear equations. With nonlinear programming, generalized functions, not necessarily linear, are used instead. Both nonlinear and linear programming are part of operations research and, as such, are discussed in the **sci.op-research** Usenet group. Here are the FAQs (frequently asked question lists) from this group, explaining these branches of mathematics.

Web:
  http://www.mcs.anl.gov/home/otc/Guide/faq/linear-programming-faq.html
  http://www.mcs.anl.gov/home/otc/Guide/faq/nonlinear-programming-faq.html

Numerical Analysis

It's amazing how many people still don't know a Tchebyshev polynomial from a fourth-order Runge-Kutte algorithm. Join the discussion with people who want more out of life than the simple L2 norm that seems to satisfy a whole world of mathematically disadvantaged social scientists.

Web:
  http://net.indra.com/~sullivan/q10.html

Usenet:
  sci.math.num-analysis

Operations Research

Operations research is the study of how to use mathematics to make decisions when the problem at hand is complex, and you have to decide how to balance various factors to optimize particular criteria. (If there is significant uncertainty in the outcome, you can say you are doing systems analysis and ask for more money.) Here is a collection of resources devoted to operations research and related activities.

Web:
  http://mat.gsia.cmu.edu/

Usenet:
  sci.op-research

MATHEMATICS

Pi (3.14159...)

Here are some Internet sites celebrating the charm and elusiveness of pi: the irrational number that expresses the ratio of the circumference to the diameter of any circle. Would you like to see pi to many, many digits? Would you like to have your very own program to calculate pi? Would you like to experience pi in ways that normal people have never imagined? It's all here, waiting for you on the Net. (By the way, you may be wondering, is pi my favorite transcendental number? No, I have to admit that my favorite is *e*. However, I wouldn't kick pi out of bed for eating mathematical crackers.)

Web:
http://www.isr.umd.edu/~jasonp/pipage.html
http://www.joyofpi.com/pilinks.htm

Need some Pi?

There is lots and lots on the Net. No need to settle for the merely irrational when you can get the transcendental.

**Find a fast fact.
Turn to "Reference".**

Society for Industrial and Applied Math

The Society for Industrial and Applied Mathematics provides information about activities and issues of interest to applied and computational mathematicians, engineers, and scientists who use mathematics and computers.

Web:
http://www.siam.org/

Square Root of 2

When you've almost got it figured out and everyone keeps interrupting your thinking space, it's really aggravating. There's no sense in starting over again trying to recalculate the square root of 2. It's already been done: to a million digits.

Web:
http://antwrp.gsfc.nasa.gov/htmltest/gifcity/sqrt2.1mil

Statistics

When you need a fuzzy clustering algorithm right away and the resident statistician has gone to the 7-11 for a 6-pack of Jolt cola, where do you turn for answers? Try the Net: just the place for people who are approximately right, some or all of the time.

Web:
http://www.math.yorku.ca/SCS/StatResource.html

Usenet:
sci.math.stat
sci.stat.consult
sci.stat.edu
sci.stat.math

MATHEMATICS

Symbolic and Algebraic Computation

The invention of symbolic and algebraic computation (SAC) programs has added a whole new set of tools to the arsenal of mathematicians, scientists, engineers and students. SAC systems manipulate numbers and symbols exactly, compared to floating point arithmetic which is approximate. These resources will help you find a wide variety of SAC information, as well as the main Web sites for the major software packages. The Usenet group discusses such tools, as well as the related mathematical issues. Talk about Mathematica, Maple, Macsyma and Reduce. (My goodness, is Reduce still around? I remember using it back in the mid-1970s. Oh, how symbolic algebra makes one feel old.)

Web:
  http://symbolicnet.mcs.kent.edu/
  http://www.can.nl/
  http://www.macsyma.com/
  http://www.maplesoft.com/
  http://www.mathematica.com/

Usenet:
  sci.math.symbolic

> The Internet has lots and lots (and lots) of free software.

Turing, Alan

Alan Turing, the man who brought you the Turing Test, the most popular after-dinner pastime of pre-television families of the early 1950s, has a site devoted to his life and work. Read his chronology, family origins and information about his early life. Discover who inspired him in his work and read about the Turing Machine, Turing's codebreaking work, early computer technology, his arrest, trial and eventual suicide.

Web:
  http://www.turing.org.uk/turing/

Look What I Found on the Net...

```
Newsgroup: sci.math.symbolic
Subject: I was wondering...

> I was wondering if anybody could help.

> My fiancee and I want to visit her parents before our
> wedding.  However, the cheapest trip we can find is still
> well beyond our financial means.

> If you can offer any help, it would be greatly appreciated.

> Much thanks,
>    Xxxx Xxxxxxxxx
>    ### Xxxxx Ave
>    Burnaby, BC  Canada

Here's my suggestion: Sell your computer to finance the trip.
Have a nice day.
```

MEDICINE

AIDS

Learn about AIDS (Acquired Immune Deficiency Syndrome) and the HIV virus. By reading the Usenet group or joining one of the mailing lists, you can keep up to date on the medical treatments of AIDS, including the AIDS daily summary from the Centers for Disease Control and Prevention (CDC) National AIDS Clearinghouse. For lots of online information, see the Web sites.

Web:
http://www.cdcnac.org/
http://www.planetq.com/aidsvl/

Usenet:
sci.med.aids

Listserv Mailing List:
List Name: **4acure-l**
Subscribe to: **listserv@health.state.ny.us**

Majordomo Mailing List:
List Name: **aids**
Subscribe to: **majordomo@wubios.wustl.edu**

Majordomo Mailing List:
List Name: **aids-treatment-news**
Subscribe to: **majordomo@igc.org**

Majordomo Mailing List:
List Name: **cdcsumms**
Subscribe to: **majordomo@queernet.org**

Jack Spratt could eat no fat, so he read the "Diet and Nutrition" section.

Allergies

Sneezing, coughing, runny nose, itchy eyes, funny red bumps and a general miserable feeling—these are a few of the symptoms of allergies which plague millions of people around the world. Find out more about this aggravating condition. On the mailing list, doctors, scientists, researchers and those who suffer from allergies gather to discuss causes and treatments for allergy conditions. The Web sites and Usenet group are nothing to sneeze at either.

Web:
http://allergy.mcg.edu/
http://www.allernet.com/faq/default.asp
http://www.immune.com/allergy/allabc.html
http://www.pslgroup.com/allergies.htm

Usenet:
alt.med.allergy

Listserv Mailing List:
List Name: **allergy**
Subscribe to: **listserv@listserv.tamu.edu**

Anatomy

When I was in medical school, I studied anatomy for several hours every day during the first semester. Between the classes and the daily dissection labs, I spent a lot of time learning about and memorizing the parts of the human body. It was one of the most stressful, fearful experiences of my life. We had to literally memorize pages and pages of anatomical information: text as well as pictures. I'm not complaining—all medical students go through the same process—but I do want to say it was a thoroughly unpleasant experience. Learning on the Net is a lot more pleasant. You can proceed at your own pace, and concentrate on the areas you find the most interesting. These resources will never replace actual human dissection and intense study, but they do provide a way for you to learn something about what is inside your body, and how it is all organized.

Web:
http://www.innerbody.com/indexbody.html
http://www.rad.washington.edu/AnatomyModuleList.html
http://www1.biostr.washington.edu/DigitalAnatomist.html

Anesthesiology

These Web sites have a collection of resources related to anesthesiology. The mailing list is for ongoing discussion among anesthesiologists and other professionals.

Web:
  http://gasnet.med.yale.edu/
  http://www.gen.emory.edu/medweb/medweb.anesthesiology.html

Listserv Mailing List:
  List Name: anest-l
  Subscribe to: listserv@listserv.acsu.buffalo.edu

Atlas of Hematology

Blood, blood and more blood. Vampires and other fans of hematology can browse these pictures of blood smears, lymphoma, bone marrow metastasis, platelets, anemia and other interesting things that go bump in your arteries.

Web:
  http://www.md.huji.ac.il/mirrors/pathy/Pictures/atoras.html

Biomedical Engineering

Biomedical engineers apply engineering techniques to solve medical and biological problems. This Usenet group is devoted to discussing the multi-disciplinary topics of interest to bio-engineers.

Usenet:
  sci.engr.biomed

Brain Tumors

Whether you are a patient, a family member, or a professional interested in tumors, this forum is for the discussion of issues relating to this condition. The Web site has lots of medical information about various tumors in adults and children.

Web:
  http://www.oncolink.upenn.edu/disease/brain/

Listserv Mailing List:
  List Name: braintmr
  Subscribe to: listserv@mitvma.mit.edu

Breast Cancer

These Web pages have lots of information about breast cancer, including information for health professionals and links to other cancer servers and resources. If you would like to talk to other people, there are also mailing lists you can join.

Web:
  http://www.lhj.com/health/cancer/resources.htm
  http://www.nabco.org/

Listserv Mailing List:
  List Name: brca-l
  Subscribe to: listserv@lists.ufl.edu

Listserv Mailing List:
  List Name: breast-cancer
  Subscribe to: listserv@morgan.ucs.mun.ca

Look What I Found on the Net...

```
Newsgroup: sci.engr.biomed
Subject: The Physiology of Being Turned On

When women are turned on they can experience anything from
being mildly dizzy to nauseous (and almost vomiting) in extreme
cases.

What released chemical in the body is causing this? Are there
any references for the physiology of being turned on?

Why doesn't this seem to happen to men?
```

Subscribe to the *anesthesiology* mailing list and find out what happens when the lights go out.

Cancer and Oncology

Cancer is a general name for many different conditions which are characterized by the uncontrolled growth of tissue. There is lots and lots of information on the Net about cancer and oncology (the branch of medicine that deals with cancer). I have selected a variety of resources, some for patients and some for medical professionals. The Usenet group and mailing list are for ongoing discussion.

Web:
http://cancer.med.upenn.edu/
http://cancernet.nci.nih.gov/
http://www.cancerguide.org/

Usenet:
sci.med.diseases.cancer

Listserv Mailing List:
List Name: **cancer-l**
Subscribe to: **listserv@wvnvm.wvnet.edu**

Chronic Fatigue Syndrome

It's no fun being tired all the time. You miss the end of movies, you can't get enough speed up to slide into home plate, and it's hard to make it across the intersection before the DON'T WALK sign lights up. Join in the discussion of chronic fatigue syndrome or check out the Web sites for information about this condition.

Web:
http://www.cais.com/cfs-news/
http://www.co-cure.org/

Usenet:
alt.med.cfs

Listserv Mailing List:
List Name: **cfs-l**
Subscribe to: **listserv@maelstrom.stjohns.edu**

Listserv Mailing List:
List Name: **cfs-med**
Subscribe to: **listserv@maelstrom.stjohns.edu**

Listserv Mailing List:
List Name: **cfs-news**
Subscribe to: **listserv@maelstrom.stjohns.edu**

Crohn's Disease and Colitis

Intestinal disorders are painful and debilitating. Sufferers of Crohn's disease and colitis can find support and information on this discussion group. On Usenet, patients, friends and family members participate in technical discussions about health as well as personal discussions about how these diseases affect their lives. The Web site will lead you to a variety of useful and interesting online resources.

Web:
http://www.ccfc.ca/

Usenet:
alt.support.crohns-colitis

Cystic Fibrosis

Cystic fibrosis (CF) is an inheritable metabolic disorder characterized by abnormal secretions of the exocrine glands. In particular, patients have thick mucus that obstructs the bronchi (resulting in severe breathing problems), intestines, and the pancreatic and bile ducts (making it difficult to digest adequate nutrients). About 1 in every 3,300 babies is born with cystic fibrosis. These resources will help you learn about the disease, how to treat it, as well as keep up on the latest medical advances. The mailing list is for ongoing discussion, especially among parents with CF children.

Web:
http://www.ccff.ca/~cfwww/
http://www.cff.org/

Listserv Mailing List:
List Name: **cystic-l**
Subscribe to: **listserv@home.ease.lsoft.com**

Dentistry

Long in the tooth or down in the mouth, everyone is welcome to this discussion on dentists, materials and dental techniques. Whether you need help deciding if implants are better than a bridge or just want to read humorous stories about people who have had their jaws wired shut, nothing is more exciting and breathtaking than modern dentistry.

Web:
http://www.dental-resources.com/
http://www.smiledoc.com/smiledoc/

Usenet:
sci.med.dentistry

Dermatology

Dermatology is the medical specialty that deals with the integumentary system: skin (the body's largest organ), hair, nails, sudoriferous (sweat) glands and sebaceous glands. I studied dermatology in medical school, and, believe me, once you start learning about the stratum corneum, stratum lucidum and stratum granulosum (not to mention things like hidradenitis suppurativa), you quickly realize that beauty really is only skin deep.

Web:
http://matrix.ucdavis.edu/
http://www.aad.org/
http://www.nsc.gov.sg/commskin/skin.html

Emergency Medicine

What do you do when you have an emergency medical situation and you don't have a first aid book? Take a look at this information for professionals in the area of emergency medicine and primary home care. These sites have a radiology and photograph library, national physician job listings directory, an EKG of the month and an EKG file room. Browse the interesting cases on file, complete with photographs and diagnosis discussion. This won't help you in your medical emergency, but at least it will keep your mind occupied while help is on the way.

Web:
http://gema.library.ucsf.edu:8081/
http://www.embbs.com/

Endometriosis

The tissue that lines the inner surface of the uterus is called "endometrium". This is the tissue that is sloughed off and expelled when a woman has her period. Endometriosis is a condition in which endometrium-like tissue grows outside the uterus, usually within the abdomen. It is estimated that about 15 percent of American women of childbearing age have endometriosis. The most common symptom is pain, but endometriosis is also one of the most common causes of infertility.

Web:
http://www.cmhc.com/factsfam/endo.htm
http://www.thriveonline.com/health/endo/

Usenet:
alt.med.endometriosis
alt.support.endometriosis

Listserv Mailing List:
List Name: **witsendo**
Subscribe to: **listserv@listserv.dartmouth.edu**

Forensic Medicine

Forensic medicine is the specialty dealing with medicine and the law. There are many aspects of forensic medicine involving highly technical information in a variety of disciplines. Here is a list of related resources on the Internet to help you find what you need.

Web:
http://users.bart.nl/~geradts/forensic.html

Look What I Found on the Net...

```
Newsgroup: sci.med.dentistry
Subject: Need Stories About Jaw Wiring

I am looking for humorous anecdotes about patients who have had
their jaws wired shut, especially for the purpose of weight
control.

Please email me direct at: xxxxx.ucla.edu

Thank you,
Xxxxxxx Xxxxxxxxx, D.M.D.
```

MEDICINE

> **Get lost in "Geography".**

Hippocratic Oath

Hippocrates was a physician in ancient Greece, who was born on the island of Cos around 465 B.C. (He lived at the same time as the famous historian Herodotus.) The Hippocratic Oath is a pledge, attributed to Hippocrates, that doctors take at the outset of their career. Traditionally, the original Hippocratic Oath is taken by doctors upon the awarding of their M.D. degree. However—in these days of modern times—tradition is not always acceptable. For example, it is certainly politically expedient to ignore the fact that the original oath obliges physicians to refuse to give abortions. Perhaps even more restrictive is the promise "With purity and with holiness I will pass my life..." Not to worry, there are brand new versions of the Hippocratic Oath, much more up to date and specifically designed to harmonize with the best of modern medical practice.

Web:
http://www.denverarthritisclinic.com/hippocra.htm
http://www.humanities.ccny.cuny.edu/history/reader/hippoath.htm

Immunology

Having no immune system is like going away on a vacation and leaving all the doors and windows open. Diseases such as chronic fatigue syndrome, lupus, candida, hypoglycemia and others manifest themselves in the immune system and wreak havoc on all the other systems in your body. On the Net, you can find out information about specific conditions.

Web:
http://iai.asm.org/
http://www.gen.emory.edu/MEDWEB/keyword/immunology/immunology.html
http://www.scienceXchange.com/aai/

Usenet:
sci.med.immunology

Infertility

If at first you don't succeed, try, try again. If you still don't succeed, check out the resources on the Net to see if you can find something that will help. Discussion and information cover the causes, solutions and treatments for infertility in both men and women.

Web:
http://www.fertilethoughts.net/infertility/index-faq.html
http://www.ihr.com/infertility/

Usenet:
alt.infertility
alt.infertility.alternatives
alt.infertility.pregnancy
alt.infertility.primary
alt.infertility.secondary
alt.infertility.surrogacy
misc.health.infertility

Immune System Talk

You can take my word for it. The immune system is where it's at—medically speaking—in the 21st century.

I predict that all kinds of conditions will be treated by modifying the immune system and that desensitization by oral ingestion of particular substances will become the modality of choice for many illnesses that are being treated today by drugs. For example, certain types of arthritis will be treated by eating chicken soup (or at least the collagen by-products).

I further predict that one day some smart fellow is going to take a close look at those homeopathic remedies that actually work, put them together with current immune system theory and treatment, and snarf a Nobel prize for him- or herself.

In the meantime, there is no need for you to be out in the ether. You can follow what the specialists are saying by subscribing to the immune system mailing list or checking with the Web.

Medical Education

If you are involved in medicine, your education never stops. From your first day in anatomy lab to the last time you pick up a medical journal, there is always something new to learn. Here are some resources—including help in finding medical education software—to help make the job easier.

Web:
http://alexia.lis.uiuc.edu/~buenker/educate.html
http://www.med.virginia.edu/med-ed/otherMedEd.html

Medical Libraries

Managing health-related information requires special skills and knowledge. Here are some resources devoted to the care and feeding of medical libraries (and medical librarians).

Web:
http://www.arcade.uiowa.edu/hardin-www/hslibs.html
http://www.mlanet.org/

Usenet:
bit.listserv.medlib-l

Listserv Mailing List:
List Name: medlib-l
Subscribe to: listserv@listserv.acsu.buffalo.edu

Medical Physics

Here is the forum for medical physicists (those nice people who give you radiation therapy). Do they really glow in the dark or is that just an old wives' tale?

Web:
http://www.snm.org/

Usenet:
sci.med.physics

Medical Resources

Here are some wonderful, well-organized resources that contain a large variety of medical information. If you practice medicine, I recommend that you become familiar with at least one of these Web sites, so you have a place to visit when you need information. (I only wish I had had a portable computer with an Internet connection when I was in medical school. It would have made the multiple choice tests a lot more pleasant.)

Web:
http://www-med.stanford.edu/medworld/home/
http://www.medicinenet.com/
http://www.nlm.nih.gov/

Medical Software

These Web sites will help you find software useful to medical and health science professionals, researchers and students. There is a large variety of medical software on the Net, so it is worth looking to see if you can find what you need.

Web:
http://www.comedserv.com/medsoft.htm

Medical Students

One would think that med students wouldn't have time to hang out on the Internet because they are always in a classroom somewhere with their hands thrust deep into some formaldehyde-soaked cadaver examining its medulla oblongata and vermiform appendix. But as addictive and distracting as the Internet can be, it's not surprising to find a place where medical students from around the world can gather to discuss anything relating to being a med student—labs, study habits, diseases, residencies, exhaustion and overwork. The Web sites offer a collection of information about various issues medical students might face.

Web:
http://www.ama-assn.org/mem-data/special/ama-mss/ama-mss.htm
http://www.amsa.org/
http://www.s2smed.com/

Usenet:
bit.listserv.medforum

Listserv Mailing List:
List Name: medstu-l
Subscribe to: listserv@unm.edu

MEDICINE

> **Experiment.
> (Nothing bad will happen.)**

Medical World Search

It can be a lot of work to find the medical article you want. This Web site can make your search easier. Just type in one or more keywords, and a handy-dandy computer program will search through various databases looking for what you need. I searched for "atypical bronchitis", and found a number of references, including an abstract for an article called "Atypical adrenoceptor-mediated relaxation of canine pulmonary artery through a cAMP-dependent pathway", written by four doctors at Tokyo Women's Medical College. It wasn't exactly what I wanted, but I wrote down the information anyway. After all, you never know when you are going to run into a Japanese dog with pulmonary hypertension.

Web:
http://www.mwsearch.com/

Medicine Talk and General Discussion

Here is the agora of the Usenet medical community. Need to find out the etiology of kidney stones? Need to find out what "etiology" means? This is the place for you. General, free-flowing talk on everything medical. (Does anyone have a cure for a chrono-synclastic infidibulum?)

Usenet:
 sci.med
 sci.med.cardiology
 sci.med.diseases.als
 sci.med.diseases.hepatitis
 sci.med.diseases.lyme
 sci.med.diseases.osteoporosis
 sci.med.informatics
 sci.med.laboratory
 sci.med.obgyn
 sci.med.occupational
 sci.med.orthopedics
 sci.med.pathology
 sci.med.prostate.bph
 sci.med.prostate.cancer
 sci.med.prostate.prostatitis
 sci.med.psychobiology
 sci.med.transcription
 sci.med.vision

Look What I Found on the Net...

```
Newsgroup: bit.listserv.medforum
Subject: Halfway Through Step 2

Man, does this test suck or what?  I can't believe how long the
items are.

I finished every single book of Step 1 before the 10-minute
warning, and today I was struggling.  Well, I finished Book 1
14 minutes before time, but with Book 2, I was 20 seconds under
the wire, and I didn't get a chance to give any significant
amount of thought to the last few questions.

And what's with all these vitamin/nutrition and ob/gyn
infectious questions?

If I read about one more person who comes in for a health
maintenance exam, or one more person with jugular venous
distension and bibasilar crackles, I'm going to scream!
```

500 MEDICINE

Medline

Medline is a vast bibliographic database maintained by the U.S. National Library of Medicine. Medline contains citations and abstracts from several thousand biomedical journals, covering medicine, nursing, dentistry, veterinary medicine and other fields, making it an unsurpassed reference. If you are a doctor, you absolutely must become familiar with this resource. For non-doctors, Medline is great for searching for information you can use yourself, or print out to show your doctor.

Web:
http://www.nlm.nih.gov/databases/medline.html

Medscape

Do you know why influenza is not an eradicable disease? Because aquatic birds are a natural reservoir for all known influenza A subtypes, and we can't kill all the aquatic birds, nor can we prevent them from transferring viruses to people. How did I know this? I read it on Medscape, a comprehensive Web site that's the best place I know for keeping up on the news. If you are a doctor or health care practitioner, you definitely need to know about Medscape: there are more useful features than I can list here. If you are a patient, you will find Medscape valuable for looking up information about particular conditions.

Web:
http://www.medscape.com/

Merck Manual

From time to time, you hear stories about someone practicing medicine without a license. "How do they do it?" you ask yourself. "How can anyone possibly know enough about medicine to fool people—including other doctors—without having gone to medical school?" The answer is, they use the Merck Manual. The Merck Manual of Diagnosis and Therapy, is *the* reference for the practice of medicine, and now you can access it over the Net. (Of course, even the Merck Manual won't teach you enough to pass yourself off as a real doctor. You still have to learn how to play golf.)

Web:
http://www.merck.com/pubs/mmanual/

Nursing

Nursing is the profession devoted to caring for sick and disabled people. Modern nursing has grown to be a large area of practice, with various specialties and related areas of medicine (such as nurse practitioners). These Internet resources are all about nursing: research, practice, education, publications, and so on. To talk to other nurses, you can participate in the Usenet discussion groups or the IRC channel.

Web:
http://www.ajn.org/
http://www.internurse.com/

Usenet:
alt.npractitioners
bit.listserv.snurse-l
sci.med.nursing

IRC:
#nurses

> When I was in medical school, I would sometimes sleep overnight in a spare room in the nurses' dormitory when I was on call in a nearby hospital. Aside from that, I know very little about nursing, so when I need some pertinent info, I check with the **Nursing** Web sites (and so should you).

Occupational Medicine

Need to pick out a back-friendly chair or an ergonomic keyboard? The Usenet discussion group on occupational medicine will be just what the doctor would have ordered if he had thought of it. For a lot of immediate information, try the Web sites.

Web:
http://ctdnews.com/
http://www.osha.gov/

Usenet:
sci.med.occupational

MEDICINE 501

Organ Transplants

One of the miracles of modern medicine is the ability to replace various body parts as needed. Of course, it's not that simple, but as the years go by the process becomes more advanced. The mailing list and Usenet group offer a means for organ transplant recipients, family members, and anyone interested in transplant issues to discuss their thoughts and experiences on the subject. The Web sites provide more information of a medical and emotional nature.

Web:
http://www.cis.ohio-state.edu/hypertext/faq/usenet/medicine/transplant-faq/top.html
http://www.gen.emory.edu/medweb/medweb.transplant.html
http://www.shareyourlife.org/

Usenet:
bit.listserv.transplant

Listserv Mailing List:
List Name: trnsplnt
Subscribe to: listserv@wuvmd.wustl.edu

Pharmacy

What a pickle. You have to bring something to the local PTA potluck and you forgot the recipe for methylenedioxyamphetamine. Ask a pharmacist. Or maybe you just need a pharmacist joke. Find out why pharmacy is the glamour profession of the '90s.

Web:
http://pharminfo.com/drg_mnu.html
http://www.cpb.uokhsc.edu/pharmacy/pharmint.html
http://www.pharmacytimes.com/

Usenet:
sci.med.pharmacy

IRC:
#pharmacy

Do you know someone who needs a doctor, but not right away?

Tell them to wait while you connect to the Virtual Hospital and teach yourself everything you need to know.

Radiology and Imaging

Radiology is the medical specialty that deals with imaging of all kinds: radiographs (X-rays), CAT scans, IVPs, and so on. The Usenet groups are for ongoing discussion among radiology professionals. The Web sites will take you to a large variety of radiology-related resources on the Net. One of the Web sites is the Visible Human Project: an ambitious collaborative project to create digital image data sets of complete human male and female cadavers.

Web:
http://members.aol.com/ricter/private/home/med.rad.home.html
http://radserv.med-rz.uni-sb.de/en.index.html
http://www.rsna.org/

Usenet:
alt.image.medical
sci.med.radiology
sci.med.radiology.interventional

Telemedicine

Telemedicine means using electronic signals to transfer medical information from one place to another. In other words, clinical consulting via computer networks: new technology for the world's second oldest profession.

Web:
http://tie.telemed.org/

Usenet:
sci.med.telemedicine

Virtual Hospital

This is a remarkable medical database containing textbooks, teaching files, lectures and clinical references. There is a lot of information here for patients as well as doctors. If you are a doctor, be sure to check out the multimedia learning resources. I get caught up here, browsing when I should be working.

Web:
http://vh.radiology.uiowa.edu/

502 MEDICINE

Webdoctor

Whatcha gonna do when you need some medical info on the Net, and you're not sure where to look? Try Webdoctor: the place for busy doctors to find what they need in a hurry. (There are also special resources for rural physicians.)

Web:
http://www.gretmar.com/webdoctor/

MEDICINE: ALTERNATIVE

Acupuncture

Chinese medicine is based on the idea that chi (life force energy) flows through the body along constant, definable pathways called meridians. Although there are many meridians, there are twenty-six principal ones, each associated with a different body function or organ. Chi exists in two opposite but complementary forms: yin and yang. When the flow of chi is impeded, the yin and yang become misbalanced, leading to conditions of ill health. There are about 800 places where the flow of chi emerges at the surface of the body. These are the acupuncture points. An acupunturist stimulates selected points on the body, usually by using very fine needles. The goal is to make the patient healthier by rebalancing the patient's chi over a period of time.

Web:
http://www.acupuncture.com/
http://www.rhemamed.com/tcm.htm

Alternative Medicine Resources

Tired of legal drugs and poor bedside manner? Drop in to the alternative medicine forum where alternative-oriented people share alternative medical tips, alternative home remedies, and alternative approaches to healing. (If you can't make it, send an alternate.)

Web:
http://advocacy-net.com/altmedicinemks.htm
http://www.njalternativemedicine.com/noframes_link.htm
http://www.pitt.edu/~cbw/altm.html

Alternative Medicine

My philosophy is that it is better to not get sick in the first place. Still, if you do, it's nice to know that you have a forum in which you can discuss the types of things that you can only whisper about at the doctor's office. So, next time you need to know how many leeches to use to cure brain cancer, check with your friends on

misc.health.alternative.

Alternative Medicine Talk and General Discussion

Here are the Usenet discussion groups in which people talk about alternative medicine. If you are interested in health with a twist, one of these groups will be right up your medicinal alley. My philosophy is that, when it comes to medicine, if you don't want to walk the alternative walk, you should at least talk the alternative talk.

Usenet:
alt.aromatherapy
alt.healing.flower-essence
alt.healing.reiki
alt.health.fasting
alt.health.oxygen-therapy
alt.health.virus.cure.alternatives
misc.health.alternative

MEDICINE: ALTERNATIVE

Ayurvedic Medicine

In Sanskrit, *ayurveda* means "laws of health," and is the name of one of the four sacred Hindu texts. Ayurvedic medicine is based on Indian traditions more than 3,000 years old. These resources will help you understand this ancient healing art and how it is practiced today.

Web:
http://www.ayurveda.com/info/
http://www.ayurvedic.com/
http://www.niam.com/basicstoc.html

Usenet:
alt.health.ayurveda

Cannabis and Medicine

Cannabis (marijuana) is one of the most popular intoxicating drugs in the world. The most common use of marijuana is to induce a sustained sense of well-being and mild euphoria (the technical term is "getting high"). However, there are a number of medical conditions for which cannabis can be used as an effective treatment: cancer chemotherapy symptoms, certain types of loss of appetite, chronic glaucoma, muscle spasms, menstrual cramps, certain AIDS symptoms and moderate chronic pain. Read about these treatments as well as related information about government and legal issues.

Web:
http://www.marijuanamagazine.com/
http://www.norml.org/medical/

Chinese Medicine

According to the Chinese system of medicine, a body that is in a balanced state can best maintain health and avoid disease. The question is, what is a "balanced state" and how does one achieve it? I have selected these resources to help you learn about Chinese medicine and the principles behind it. Remember, though, that the Chinese system of medicine was developed over many years to treat people living in a Chinese society, not to use as a marketing tool to sell herbal supplements to Western consumers.

Web:
http://www.healthy.net/clinic/therapy/chinmed/
http://www.mic.ki.se/China.html

Chiropractic

It's good to be informed on all aspects of medical treatments. When I was in medical school at the University of Toronto, I used to go to the local chiropractic school's public clinic to be treated. These Web sites offer you an introduction and history of chiropractic, an overview of the profession and treatment, links to education and licensing information, and other chiropractic resources.

Web:
http://www.chiro-online.com/
http://www.mbnet.mb.ca/~jwiens/chiro.html

Complementary Medicine

This Web site contains a list of alternative forms of medicine that some people choose to use in addition to regular medicine. Here you will find a huge list of topics such as acupuncture, diet and nutritional therapy, biofeedback, rolfing, aromatherapy, cryogenic medicine, shiatsu, and many more.

Web:
http://galen.med.virginia.edu/~pjb3s/ComplementaryHomePage.html

Dictionary of Metaphysical Healthcare

The phone rings. It's that beautiful woman you met at the Santa Cruz Tofu Festival. She wants to know if you would like to come over to her house and do some Dayan Qigong and then have lentils for dinner. Before you commit yourself (because commitments *are* important), you put her on hold and check with the Dictionary of Metaphysical Healthcare. You find out that Dayan Qigong, or Wild Goose Breathing Exercise, is a series of sixty-four movements that imitate the postures of a wild goose. Practicing Dayan Qigong may help you delay the aging process and prolong your life. Wow—all that and lentils too!

Web:
http://www.hcrc.org/diction/dict.html

504 MEDICINE: ALTERNATIVE

Herbal Medicine

Herbs have been used in healing for thousands of years, with their popularity occasionally rising and falling. However, there is a lot more to using herbs than knowing enough to give valerian to your lawyer to calm him down. Before you start messing around with your body chemistry, spend a little time on the Net and learn something about the herbs you propose to take. To help you, here are some resources that offer particularly useful information.

Web:
http://www.floridaplants.com/mherb.htm
http://www.wic.net/waltzark/herbenc.htm

Holistic Healing

Going to the doctor is no fun. Everyone is wearing a uniform, it's all sterile and rigid, and various people take turns poking you with sharp instruments. Experience a gentler alternative to medicine in the form of holistic concepts and methods of living, which are reported to be a more natural way of dealing with the hairpin turns on the road of life. A variety of holistic topics are discussed, such as states of consciousness, meditation, healthy diet, herbs, vitamins, rolfing and massage.

Web:
http://www.holisticmed.com/

Unconventional treatments and schools of thought are more in vogue than ever. If you want to follow what is happening in the netherworld of medicine, learn about holistic healing.

Homeopathy

Homeopathy is a popular form of alternative medicine based on remedies that contain tiny amounts of active ingredients. Find out more about it on the Net: where you can get a FAQ, information about mailing lists and Usenet groups, contacts in the U.S., U.K. and other parts of the world, a useful bibliography, and medical resources links.

Web:
http://www.homeopathyhome.com/

Music Therapy

Virtually everyone responds to music. We all know that the right music at the right time can be soothing, energizing, inspiring or entertaining. Music therapy practitioners use music and rhythm to alleviate various medical and social conditions. In the United States, certified music therapists must complete an approved college curriculum (including an internship) and then pass a national board examination. These Web sites provide a lot of information about music therapy: what it is, its philosophy and history, what conditions are treated by music therapists, and so on. There is also information explaining the profession and what sort of training is required.

Web:
http://www.erols.com/leopold/Music.htm
http://www.namt.com/

Osteopathy

Osteopathy is a system of medicine descended from the teachings of Andrew Taylor Still (1828-1917). Osteopaths receive medical training similar to regular doctors, with the addition of special courses in tissue manipulation. Where a regular doctor is known as an M.D., an osteopath uses the designation D.O. (Doctor of Osteopathy). In the United States, osteopaths are licensed to practice medicine by using drugs and surgery. However, they tend to have a more generalized and natural approach to healing that they use along with their manipulation techniques. A large portion of osteopaths are engaged in primary care (family medicine).

Web:
http://www.osteopathic.net/gregory/
http://www.osteopathy.org.uk/ois/faq.html

Relaxation Techniques

People complain about stress, but think how much less satisfying relaxation would be if there were nothing to relax from. In fact, what good would these sites be if it weren't for stress? So stop what you are doing right now and contemplate the stress in your life, and how lucky you are that stress provides you with an excuse to fall apart and utilize the relaxation resources available on the Net. (Note: I have chosen these sites carefully to provide a variety of approaches to relaxation. One of them will suit you.)

Web:
http://www.psychwww.com/mtsite/smpage.html
http://www.shsu.edu/~counsel/relaxation.html
http://www.shsu.edu/~counsel/shortr.html

Rolfing

Rolfing is a complex system of bodywork in which a practitioner makes structural changes in the body of the client. Rolfing is named after its inventor, the American biochemist and physiotherapist Ida P. Rolf (1896-1979). Within the body, the muscles, tendons, ligaments and organs are surrounded by thin, tough sheets of tissue called fascia. This tissue is arranged in "fascial planes" that run throughout the body, providing a framework for movement and posture. A rolfer is specially trained in understanding the nature of the fascial planes and manipulating them along with the musculature. (Note: I spent four years in medical school, and I don't remember learning anything about the fascial planes. Later I found out that the only people who really understand them are rolfers and plastic surgeons.) Rolfing is carried out in a series of treatments (usually ten) in which the rolfer uses his hands, arms and even elbows to manipulate the soft tissue of the client. I can sum up the entire experience (I have been rolfed a lot of times) as follows: (1) It can hurt. (2) It can be expensive. (3) It is absolutely wonderful and is definitely worth doing.

Web:
http://www.rolf.org/
http://www.teleport.com/~amrta/rolfing.html

Computers are people, too.

Relaxation Techniques

All **stressed** out and nowhere to go? The Net will take care of you. Visit one of the Relaxation Techniques sites, and soon you'll be cruising through life as cool as a virtual cucumber.

Shiatsu

Shiatsu is a traditional form of Japanese medicine in which the practitioner uses his palms and thumbs to apply pressure to various points on the body, the same points that are recognized and stimulated during acupuncture. A shiatsu treatment can be a lot like acupuncture using pressure instead of needles (in which case it is sometimes described as acupressure), or it can be more like a massage that concentrates on the various points. A session with a skilled shiatsu practitioner is usually an enjoyable experience, leaving one with a pleasant feeling of relaxation and comfort.

Web:
http://www.users.dircon.co.uk/~embwings/shiatsu.htm
http://www1.tip.nl/users/t283083/e_index.htm

MEN

Backlash

Backlash is a magazine that rallies the troops against various unfair political beliefs. In particular, I am including the magazine here because Backlash comes out strong against male stereotypes. My advice is to visit this site and explore the Sexism section, where you will find features, news and regular columns written from the male point of view.

Web:
http://www.backlash.com/

MEN

> Dance, dance, dance.
> (Nobody is watching.)

Fathers

Whether you are a single father or a father in a traditional family, there are resources on the Net that will interest you. These sites have lots of information on parenting, rights of fathers, at-home dads, things to do with the kids, and lots more. Join the mailing list and talk to other online dads.

Web:
http://www.fathermag.com/
http://www.fathersworld.com/
http://www.newdads.com/

Listserv Mailing List:
List Name: father-l
Subscribe to: listserv@tc.umn.edu

Friends of Choice for Men

View the idea of "choice" from a man's point of view. The Friends of Choice for Men promote the idea that men should not be forced into fatherhood. This organization works for the equality between men's and women's reproductive rights. The Friends of Choice for Men offer articles, stories and other resources that promote choice for men.

Web:
http://www.nas.com/c4m/

Guy Rules

Yes, there are rules that govern the behavior of men, and, yes, most of them are pretty funny. Read the rules (sent in by guys) and learn about cars, wives, sports, partying, and other types of male-type stuff. Then take the Guy Rules Test and see if you might be able to make it as a guy.

Web:
http://www.guyrules.com/

Hair Loss

As a man gets older, his strength, vitality and sex drive begin to wane. However, as long as he can maintain the illusion of youth, a man can still pretend (at least to himself) that he is not really so old and that his sense of personal power is, as yet, undiminished. Unfortunately, hair loss is a visible sign of aging that is obvious to everyone. The problem is especially important to men who lose their hair prematurely: they still feel young, but they look old. For this reason, balding men have always been suckers for expensive treatments that purport to grow hair. Men, here is what I think. When you try to cover your bald spot by combing the hair on the side of your head over the top, you're not really fooling anyone. Trying to look younger than your real age is a game you can only lose. So my advice is to learn to be gracious about getting older. (In case you don't take my advice, here are some resources about hair loss and what you can do about it.)

Web:
http://www.hairtoday.com/
http://www.regrowth.com/reference/documents/faq/

Look What I Found on the Net...

```
(from an editorial in the online Fathering Magazine)

              Fathers Are Important

A U.S. government survey found that the most important factor
in predicting whether a child will grow up to commit a violent
crime is not social class, not race, and not educational level
or cultural background.

The absence of a father in the home is the most significant
predictor of a later conviction for a violent crime.
```

Man's Life

A Man's Life is an online magazine devoted to men. You will find news and a variety of articles. Read about women (relationships, being a sex object, how to get a woman), family (relating to your kids, relating to your dad) and fashion (picking out cool clothes, wearing hats, dressing for sex). They also cover interesting topics from the male point of view, such as health, fitness, outdoors, food, pets, goofing off, sports, money and home repairs. The articles are fun and lighthearted, and provide a pleasant way to pass the time.

Web:
http://www.manslife.com/

Men's Health

Men have health concerns all their own, and here are some Web sites that address the issues. Learn how to stay healthy by having a good diet and doing the right type of exercise. If you do have health problems, you will be able to find information to help you understand what is happening. And, of course, there are articles and resources about sex, just in case you need to brush up on a few more factoids.

Web:
http://www.healthatoz.com/categories/MN.htm
http://www.malehealthcenter.com/
http://www.menshealth.com/

Men's Health

Men, let's face it. The health care system is not always going to take care of us the way we need. We have special problems and health considerations that the female-centric medical establishment doesn't always recognize.

The first step to maintaining our health is to become knowledgeable about our bodies and how they work. Then we need to learn about men's health issues and how they affect us.

The Net can help.

Look What I Found on the Net...

```
(from the Guy Rules Web site)

Guy Rule #295: Respect
Category: Wife

Always respect a woman.  Never lay a hand on her unless
it's out of love.  Give her enough space to be her own
person.  Don't assume that as a woman she'll want a provider.
She might already be her own provider.

Look for a whole woman with as few hangups as possible
(fewer than yourself at least).

Avoid ex-prisoners and ex-cons.
```

Men's Issues

Check out this great collection of men's issues resources. These pages cover topics such as attitudes toward men, domestic violence, employment, fatherhood, health, history of men's movements, romance and relationships, the justice system, and much more. You will also find reviews of books and links to information about various men's organizations.

Web:
http://www.he.net/~menmedia/
http://www.responsibleopposing.com/
http://www.vix.com/menmag/menmag.htm

Usenet:
alt.men.politics
alt.mens-rights

Majordomo Mailing List:
List Name: **mens-rights-l**
Subscribe to: **majordomo@world.std.com**

Men's Rights

The definitive speech on men's rights was delivered by Rob Petrie on October 24, 1961 (The Dick Van Dyke Show, episode #5: "Washington vs. the Bunny"):

"A man is a man, even if he is a husband, and at no time, as a man or as a husband, should he ever be his wife's puppet. I have to do what I think is right. A man shouldn't sacrifice his self-respect just to keep peace in the home. All right, a woman's opinion should be weighed and considered, but in the final analysis, a man has to do what he thinks is right, or he is no man."

The implications of this speech are still being debated. Join the discussion on the Net.

Men's Talk and General Discussion

Okay, men, this is the place where we can talk about whatever we want without having to worry about being sensitive or politically correct. For the purposes of this book, I will say that in the men's discussion group we talk about work, relationships, feminism, health, and other such topics. (But I'm sure you know what we *really* discuss.)

Usenet:
soc.men

P.O.V.

P.O.V. ("point of view") is the online version of a guy's magazine. Of course there are men's magazines, but this one is for *guys*. Read about careers, finances, and various topics of general interest. I saw an article about guys who brew their own beer. (You see what I mean? Real men don't brew their own beer, but real guys do.) The site also features a collection of Web links for guys. Hot patootie, bless my soul.

Web:
http://www.povmag.com/

Self-Help for Men

If things are not going your way, do a little reading that will inspire, comfort or assist you in problem-solving. Read these articles and archives of self-help resources for men. There are also links to other self-help sites.

Web:
http://cybertowers.com/selfhelp/articles/men/

Stay-at-home Dads

Fathers, if you stay at home with your kids, here are some resources for you. The Web sites focus on dads who, for whatever reason, are the primary homemakers. The mailing list allows you to have an ongoing discussion with the other Mr. Moms. After all, we all know that, by our nature, we men are more nurturing than women, but, still, a little help is always welcome.

Web:
http://www.daddyshome.com/
http://www.fathersworld.com/fulltimedad/links/links.html
http://www.slowlane.com/
http://www.splusnet.com/~evilcow/de/index1.html
http://www3.sympatico.ca/papa.mike/

Listserv Mailing List:
List Name: **dadslist**
Subscribe to: **listserv@daddyshome.com**

MILITARY

Armed Forces of the World

These Web sites are great sources of information about various military organizations around the world. You can find links to defense forces, journals, documents, maps, military bases, military reserves, research centers and intelligence organizations. For example, I was able to learn how the Israeli military forces follow a doctrine of "speed, initiative and audacity". You can also find a lot of interesting information (such as the fact that Cyprus has four aircraft and eight helicopters even though they don't have an air force or a navy). Hint: If you are a student looking for a topic on which to write an essay, here are some wonderful sources of information.

Web:
http://members.aol.com/rhrongstad/private/milinksr.htm
http://www.cfcsc.dnd.ca/links/milorg/
http://www.iaw.on.ca/~awoolley/lwformil.html

Chemical and Biological Warfare

We hear a lot about chemical and biological warfare, but not many people really understand it. These Web sites can help you appreciate the power of these types of weapons and how they work. Learn about substances such as nerve gas, mustard agents, tear gases and hydrogen cyanide, as well as handy tips for protecting yourself should it become necessary. You can also explore a large number of related resources, including some official government Web sites. There are links to storage and disposal facilities, research facilities, articles and treaties, and much, much more.

Web:
http://www.cbdcom.apgea.army.mil/
http://www.cbiac.apgea.army.mil/
http://www.opcw.nl/

Need that special someone?
Try "Romance".

Contemporary Military Conflicts

Stay current with serious military activity by visiting this Web site whenever you need to know what is happening where. Select the part of the world in which you are interested, and you will find links to news and information about the countries in conflict in that area. You can find out the latest news as well as read about the origins of the conflict, military aggressions, and the organizations and activist groups involved in helping to resolve the situation.

Web:
http://www.cfcsc.dnd.ca/links/wars/

Disarmament Talk and General Discussion

Discussion and monthly digests of military and political strategy, technology, sociology and peace activism involved in accelerating disarmament of nuclear, conventional and chemical weapons. **disarm-d** provides monthly digests of selected mail discussions that are posted to **disarm-l**. It also includes essays, papers, reviews and excerpts from important publications.

Listserv Mailing List:
List Name: **disarm-d**
Subscribe to: **listserv@cnsibm.albany.edu**

Listserv Mailing List:
List Name: **disarm-l**
Subscribe to: **listserv@cnsibm.albany.edu**

Medieval Armor and Weapons

In the Middle Ages, there were no guns, and it was common for warriors to use armor to protect themselves, and metal and wood weapons to fight. Today, such armor and weapons—bows and arrows, swords, spears, axes, and so on—are anachronisms that are studied and reconstructed by Middle-Ages-armor-buffs. If you are a MAAB, you will enjoy learning about the armor and the weapons: what they look like, how they are constructed, and what technical terms are used to talk about them.

Web:
http://members.aol.com/sca110323/armor.htm
http://www.aiusa.com/medsword/
http://www.hipark.austin.isd.tenet.edu/medieval/armour/main.html

Military Academies

A military academy is a school or college that provides a full-time military living environment for young men and women while they are following a regular academic program. Traditionally, one of the main purposes of a military academy is to train future officers for the armed services. In the United States, there are a great many military academies for students of all ages. The most well-known academies are the three college-level schools: the Military Academy at West Point, New York; the Naval Academy at Annapolis, Maryland; and the Air Force Academy at Colorado Springs, Colorado. There is also the Coast Guard Academy in New London, Connecticut, and the Merchant Marine Academy in Kings Point, New York. I've included links to the main academies as well as links to military academies in other countries. If you would like to discuss life in a military school—especially if you are a cadet—you may enjoy participating in the Usenet group.

Web:
http://www.accademia.org/
http://www.adfa.oz.au/
http://www.cga.edu/
http://www.mta.ro/
http://www.nadn.navy.mil/
http://www.pixi.com/~jplaputt/
http://www.rma.ac.be/
http://www.rmc.ca/
http://www.usafa.af.mil/
http://www.usma.edu/
http://www.usmma.edu/

Usenet:
alt.military.cadet

Military Academies

Are you thinking of going to a military academy (or sending your son or daughter to one)? Check with the Net first. Just about every military academy in the United States has a Web site.

Military Brats

Children who grow up in a military family—military brats—have lives that are just a tad different than the children of civilians. These Web sites and the Usenet discussion group are for you, whether you are currently in such a family or whether you grew up in one. If you need information, try the Web sites. If you have problems, you can use the Usenet group to talk to other people who understand your situation.

Web:
http://dticaw.dtic.mil/mtom/
http://www.3harpiesltd.com/lfeb/brats.htm
http://www.lynxu.com/brats/index.html
http://www.military-brats.com/

Usenet:
alt.culture.military-brats

Military Medals

This site has a great collection of medals from the United States as well as other countries. You can see medals and ribbons (such as the Medal of Honor or the Purple Heart) as well as rank insignia. If you enjoy reading about medals, you will find some real curiosities here, such as a collection of fictitious Star Trek ribbons and information about certain rare medals (such as the USMC Brevet Medal, only 23 of which were ever awarded).

Web:
http://users.aol.com/gman755/medals/medals.html

Military Police

The military police are the men and women who are responsible for law enforcement within a branch of a service as well as at military installations. Military police also provide certain services to the government, such as guarding embassies. In the U.S., the various services each have their own police, with the Marines providing some of the military police for the Navy.

Web:
http://members.visi.net/~sblack/mphomepage/
http://uts.cc.utexas.edu/~ehre/AFSPA.html
http://www.azstarnet.com/~rovedo/mphist.html
http://www.primenet.com/~burchel/milpol.html

Usenet:
alt.military.police

MILITARY

Military Talk and General Discussion

The military is a lot more important and more powerful than most people realize. Moreover, there are lots of important military topics that bear discussion: military science, weapon design and deployment and, of course, politics. There are a number of Usenet groups devoted to ongoing discussions of military topics. Here are the places you can talk about the latest military technology, the various armed services around the world, life in the service, military urban legends, and much more.

Usenet:
alt.folklore.military
alt.military.retired
alt.war.mercenary
sci.military
sci.military.moderated
sci.military.naval

Military Terms and Acronyms

Have you ever encountered a military term that you didn't understand? It's not surprising—there are literally tens of thousands of such terms and nobody knows them all. If you are interested in any aspect of the military, here are some useful tools that can save you a lot of running around. One of the Web sites is a Department of Defense glossary of military terms. The other is a file containing more than 20,000 military terms and acronyms.

Web:
http://www.dtic.mil/doctrine/jel/doddict/
http://www.jcave.com/~bandorm/megaterm/megaterm.htm

Look What I Found on the Net...

```
Newsgroup: sci.military.moderated
Subject: Why Are There No Robot Ground Troops?

>> Pardon me if this has been addressed before, but why are
>> there no robot ground troops?
>>
>> Is it just the reluctance of the various militaries?
>> Squeamishness? Or have robots not been sufficiently developed?

> Current robotics technology limitations make this unfeasible.
>
> 1. Robots are really really expensive.
> 2. Robots are really really delicate and mechanically fussy.
>
> The U.S. military has currently fielded unmanned robot
> observation done planes (used in the Gulf War).  That's about
> all for now.

To me, this posres some moral questions.

1. Wouldn't the ability to fight wars without exposing troops to
   danger make the price of the military option too small?

2. Who would be responsible for war crimes committed by such a
   robot?

It seems that a device built to seek out people and kill them
without human supervision should be classified as a weapon of
mass destruction.
```

Military Uniforms

Military uniforms are fascinating. Examine this Web site and you will see what I mean. You can look at pictures of European military uniforms from the early 19th century and from the Burgoyne Expedition (1777). The early 19th century images cover armies from Austria, Britain, Denmark, France, Greece, Italy, Prussia, Russia, Saxony, Spain and Sweden. The Burgoyne section has uniforms of British, German and American soldiers. Note: John Burgoyne (1722-1792) was a British general who was a hero in the Seven Years War, a worldwide conflict that was fought from 1753-1763 in Europe, North America and India. Burgoyne was elected to Parliament (1761) and led troops during the American Revolutionary War. Later, he became a playwright and was known by the nickname "Gentleman Johnny".

Web:
   http://www.nypl.org/research/chss/subguides/
      milhist/costnypl.html

Military Vehicles

If you are into testosterone-laced fighting machines, here are some resources that will get your motor running. There are lots of pictures of various types of military vehicles from the United States and other countries. Read about vehicles such as the M1 Abrams Main Battle Tank, the AH-64 Apache Attack Helicopter or, my personal favorite, the HMMWV or Humvee (a super-cool jeep with a thyroid condition). Watch and listen to video clips, sounds and animations, and read factsheets about various military crafts.

Web:
   http://sorex.tvi.cc.nm.us/~rhernend/tanks.htm
   http://www.jmu.edu/rotc/gallery.html

Mine Warfare

A mine is a bomb that is placed in a specific location in such a way that it will explode when some person or piece of equipment sets it off. Some mines—called land mines—are designed to be buried in the ground so that, when you walk on them and press on a sensor, they will explode. If you are lucky, you are maimed. If you are unlucky, you die. Other mines—such as naval mines—are deployed in water, on or below the surface. These mines have sonar or magnetic sensors that make them useful for blowing up warships and other marine vessels. These Web sites offer a wide variety of information about the various types of mines (of which there are many) and the worldwide efforts to remove unused mines. Look at pictures, read the facts, and be glad you live in a safe place.

Web:
   http://www.ae.utexas.edu/~industry/mine/
   http://www.care.org/newscenter/landmines/
   http://www.llnl.gov/landmine/
      landmine_whos_who.html
   http://www.un.org/Depts/Landmine/

Nuclear Weapons

Now that the Cold War is over and the Soviet Union has broken up, we don't think about nuclear weapons all that much. Although the numbers are decreasing, there are massive arsenals of these weapons around the world, especially in the U.S. Somebody should keep an eye on all of this. Fortunately, somebody does.

Web:
   http://www.bullatomsci.org/
   http://www.fas.org/nuke/

Usenet:
   alt.war.nuclear

With a nuclear weapon, almost is good enough.

MILITARY

Prisoners of War

When the conflict is over, it's all too easy to forget the people who were POWs (prisoners of war) or MIAs (missing in action). One of these Web sites has information about the U.S. government's Defense Prisoner of War/Missing Personnel Office. The other site is maintained by families of missing persons, working to get them home or to, at least, have their deaths documented.

Web:
http://www.dtic.mil/dpmo/
http://www.nationalalliance.org/home1.htm

Usenet:
alt.war.pow-mia

Selective Service System

The United States Selective Service System (SSS) is an independent agency that is part of the executive branch of the federal government. The job of the SSS is twofold. (1) In case of emergency, the SSS is to deliver untrained manpower to the U.S. Department of Defense. (2) At the same time, the SSS is to administer an alternative service program for conscientious objectors. Basically, the SSS works by forcing all young men to register so the organization can keep track of them in case they are needed to serve in the military. In the aftermath of the Vietnam War the program was suspended, but in 1980 (during the last year of Jimmy Carter's presidency), the registration requirement was reinstated. Right now, in the United States, the law says that all men between the ages of 18 and 26 are required to register with the Selective Service System. (You can get the form in any post office.) When a young man turns 18, he must register within 30 days of his birthday. In the event of an emergency that required a military draft, a lottery would be held to choose who has to go. Priority would be given to those who are currently 20 years old. For more information—some of it astonishing—check the Web page. By the way, young women are not required (or allowed) to register. This rule was upheld by the Supreme Court in 1981.

Web:
http://www.sss.gov/

Special Operations

You have probably heard of the Green Berets and the Rangers (Army), the SEALs (Navy) and the Air Commandos (Air Force). These are all examples of special operations units (sometimes called special forces): highly trained groups of men who respond with speed, skill and authority to high-risk situations. Most countries with a significant military force have such groups, and in the United States there are actually a great many special operations units. This Web site contains lots and lots of links to information about the various special operations units. These men train for years to be able to carry out jobs that most people wouldn't even think are possible.

Web:
http://www.specialoperations.com/

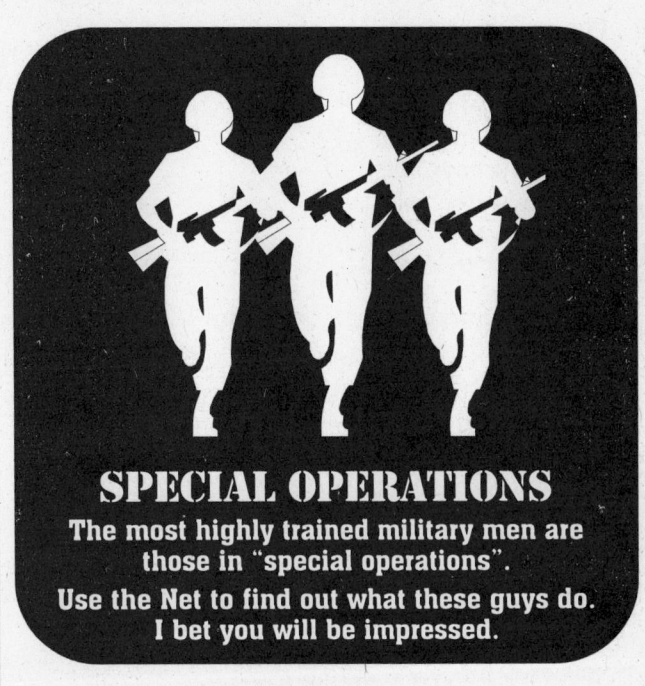

> **SPECIAL OPERATIONS**
> The most highly trained military men are those in "special operations".
> Use the Net to find out what these guys do. I bet you will be impressed.

Technology Insertion

The Department of Defense likes to keep its war-fighters informed. I think that's a great idea, too, because it keeps them from drag racing through quiet suburban neighborhoods. The DoD has put together a great deal of information on wireless communication, asynchronous transfer modes, and communication technology in general.

Web:
http://www.disa.atd.net/

514 MILITARY

United States Armed Forces

These are the official Web sites of the main branches of the United States armed forces: the Air Force, Army, Coast Guard, Navy and Marine Corps. Each of these sites is independent, and the information varies from one page to the next. In general, though, you can find out a lot about each of the services, including what they do and how to join. I find visiting these sites interesting, as they show how the various branches of the U.S. armed services have distinct personalities and ways of looking at the world. If you need any information at all about part of the U.S. military, one of these Web sites is a good place to start. You can read about what each service does, its history, recruiting policies (including various careers), retirement information, alumni organizations, news and press releases, upcoming public events, and much more.

Web:
  http://www.af.mil/
  http://www.army.mil/
  http://www.navy.mil/
  http://www.uscg.mil/
  http://www.usmc.mil/

U.S. Department of Defense

This Web site is the official Internet public visiting area of the United States Department of Defense (DoD). You will find lots of cool information about the DoD, what they do and who runs the show. (I know it's hard to believe that such information can be cool, but check it out yourself and you will see what I mean.) This is the place to look for links to all the organizations within the Department of Defense, such as the Secretary of Defense, the Joint Chiefs of Staff, and the various branches of the military. If you are American, take a few minutes to explore this site. These guys spend a lot of money, so you might as well have an idea of what they are doing.

Web:
  http://www.defenselink.mil/

IRC is fun for late-night talk.

U.S. Military Magazines

These magazines are for people interested in the U.S. military culture. I have selected these sites to provide you with magazines devoted to the major branches of the armed services. I find the articles interesting, even though I have no connection at all with the military (except that they protect me against Communism).

Web:
  http://www-cgsc.army.mil/milrev/
  http://www.af.mil/news/airman/
  http://www.airforcetimes.com/
  http://www.armytimes.com/
  http://www.navytimes.com/
  http://www.navytimes.com/marinetimes/
  http://www.northupcom.com/
  http://www.usmc.mil/marines.nsf/

Veterans

There are several tens of millions of military veterans in the United States. If you are one of them, you will find these veteran resources useful. Read about news, POW/MIA issues, reunions, and what the government is doing that affects you. You can also talk with other veterans and look for old friends.

Web:
  http://www.vets.com/
  http://www.vnis.com/

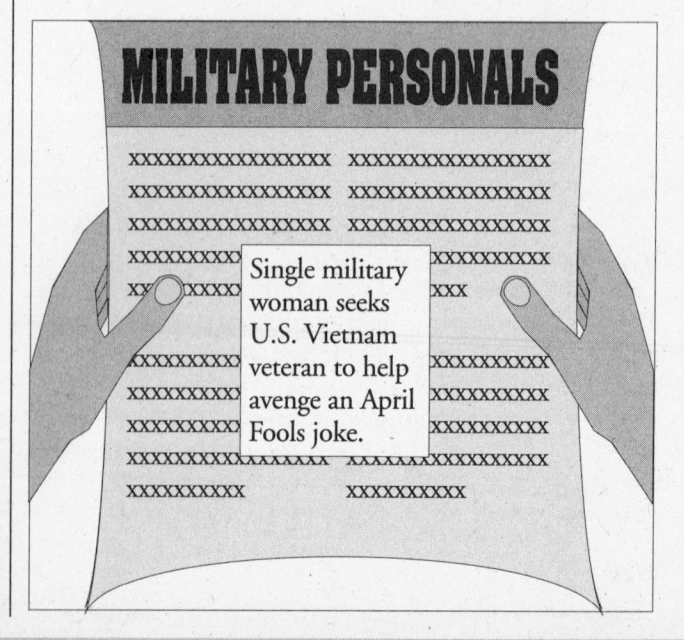

MILITARY PERSONALS

Single military woman seeks U.S. Vietnam veteran to help avenge an April Fools joke.

Vietnam Veterans

The American involvement in the war in Vietnam lasted from 1961-1973, with most of the troops being deployed in the late 1960s. Although it may be hard to believe, in 1969 there were well over 500,000 American troops in Vietnam—about four percent of all the men in America. In other words, in 1969, about one out of every twenty-five American males was in Vietnam. It is no surprise then that, almost thirty years later, there are a lot of resources on the Net devoted to Vietnam veterans. If you fought in Vietnam, this Web site has a large collection of resources in which you may be interested, including veteran organizations, support groups and information about reunions. For veterans and their families, the Usenet discussion group is a good place to talk. Note: The Vietnam Veterans Memorial is a monument in Washington, D.C., containing the names of all the servicemen and women who were killed or presumed missing in the Vietnam War. The memorial is a tall V-shaped black granite wall, measuring 493 feet (150 meters) long. Along the long, black surface are inscribed 58,000 names. This is a good image to keep in mind the next time you hear someone talk about starting a war. (Interestingly enough, out of 58,000 names, you will find very few belonging to the politicians and older Americans who supported the war—although their sons are well-represented.)

Web:
http://grunt.space.swri.edu/vetorgs.htm

Usenet:
soc.veterans

Women in the Military

This site is devoted to women and the military: women who are currently in the service, retired from active duty, or even thinking about joining. Read about life after joining the military, family life and childcare, women in combat, harassment issues, women who served in war zones, military humor, and more.

Web:
http://www.militarywoman.org/homepage.htm

MISCHIEF

April Fools

The Ides of March is the least of the Internet's worries. The first day of April is the time when tricksters all over the world unleash their clever plots of lighthearted deceit. April Fools' pranks have been developed into an art form and are brought together in the form of archives which you can view from the safety of your own home.

Web:
http://www.2meta.com/april-fools/
http://www.cse.psu.edu/~skovrins/fools.html

There is no fool like an April Fool.

Take a look at what other people have been doing and maybe you can get some good ideas for next year.

Avenger's Page

It's not nice to get even, but if you just have to do it, you might as well do it the best way you can. The Avenger's Handbook is a collection of postings from the **alt.revenge** Usenet group. It has everything you need to know to get revenge, except a listing of bail bondsmen in your area.

Web:
http://www.ekran.no/html/revenge/

Backyard Ballistics

This Web site is dedicated to all the wonderful ways in which you can propel objects into the air in your own backyard. Learn about spud guns and spudzookas, air cannons, matchstick rockets, aussie mortar, the annual "Pumpkin Chunkin" contest, and much more.

Web:
   http://www2.csn.net/~bsimon/backyard.html

Big Book of Mischief

Enjoy information on how to make explosives, tennis ball cannons and carbide bombs, how to open locks, and other vital information for the budding soldier of fortune. (For amusement only. You are on your honor not to actually do any of this stuff.)

Web:
   http://www.ripco.net/download/text/e-texts/tbbom/

Culture Jamming

Think of someone who jams a radio signal. He sends out another signal that has just the right characteristics to interfere with the original transmission. Culture jamming interferes with the messages of the mainstream media and popular culture. Such activities casts a wide net—art forgeries, impostors, performance art, scams, hacks, and so on—and are generally carried out by social dissidents with a sense of irony. However, the more you explore culture jamming, the more you realize that it is often practiced by people who actually believe that what they are doing is real.

Web:
   http://www.conspire.com/jamming.html
   http://www.syntac.net/hoax/

Usenet:
   alt.culture.jamming

Dumpster Diving

Grabbing stuff out of the trash can be either silly or cool. With most garbage cans or dumpsters, it's silly, because who wants to be rooting through other people's trash? But when the garbage yields valuable items, or the dumpster contains secret stuff, what would otherwise be silly becomes cool faster than you can say "cultural archeology".

Web:
   http://www.net-gate.com/~howell/
   http://www.psrc.usm.edu/macrog/marduk/garbage.html

Usenet:
   alt.dumpster

Fake Memos

People who work in large companies are suckers for memos. (It has something to do with the food they are fed.) Sign up one of your friends for a company memo. For example, they can be told their telephone usage is inappropriate or that they are abusing the use of copy machine. For a real laugh, try the fake funeral announcement.

Web:
   http://www.activegrams.com/series/memos.html

Fake News

In the olden days, there were places you could get a joke newspaper printed as a gag to take home to show your friends ("Joey Clamface Elected President"). Now you can do the same thing on the Net. Make a fake news page, starring the person of your choice (such as you or a friend). Choose from a variety of current topics. Then send the Web address to your friends, and, using nothing more than a simple Web browser, they will be able to see what a cool, clever, calculating individual you really are.

Web:
   http://aprilfools.infospace.com/hllink.htm

MISCHIEF

Hack Gallery

Hack Gallery is a compendium of Interesting Hacks To Fascinate People (IHTFP) at MIT. The word "hack" refers to a clever, benign and ethical prank which is challenging and amusing for the perpetrators. The gallery offers a large list of hacks sorted by topic, location, and the dates when they were perpetrated. There is also a FAQ, book list, and a "best of" hack list.

Web:
http://fishwrap.mit.edu/Hacks/Gallery.html

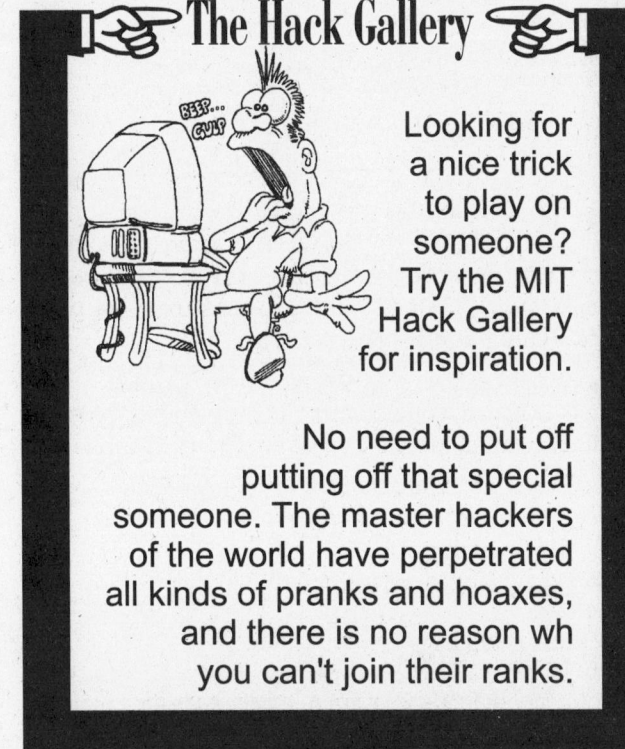

The Hack Gallery

Looking for a nice trick to play on someone? Try the MIT Hack Gallery for inspiration.

No need to put off putting off that special someone. The master hackers of the world have perpetrated all kinds of pranks and hoaxes, and there is no reason wh you can't join their ranks.

Mischief Talk and General Discussion

The **alt.shenanigans** group is the Usenet home for discussion of all manner of practical jokes ("shens"). I particularly like reading all the stories of jokes that people have played on unsuspecting victims. This is also a good place to ask for a suggestion when you feel a burning need to put someone in their place.

Usenet:
alt.shenanigans

Practical Jokes

For serious enjoyment, what could be more good clean fun than embarrassing your friends and neighbors by making them look foolish? The dribble glass and plastic vomit are child's play. On the Net, you can read about lots and lots of ideas, techniques and experiences with practical jokes. Make your loved ones say "uncle", and make your uncle say, "bork, bork, bork".

Web:
http://www.ccil.org/~mika/
http://www.mediashower.com/zug/pranks.html

Prank Phone Calls

When you are sitting around with nothing to do, visit this site devoted to the art of prank telephone calls. Here you will find links to other prank call pages, information about the Jerky Boys (kings of the prank phone call), and tips about specific types of prank calls (such as 101 zany ways to phone in a pizza order).

Web:
http://www.blackout.com/
http://www.franksworld.com/pranks/
http://www.prankcalls.net/

Revenge Talk and General Discussion

Landlord got you pissed? Teacher rapped you with a ruler? Your ex-SO (significant other) won't return your only copy of The Little Prince? Don't get mad, get even. Join the pros and find out just how smelly a fish in the ventilation duct can be. (Federal regulations require us to remind you of the ancient Chinese saying: "Before you set out for revenge, be sure to dig two graves.")

Usenet:
alt.revenge

Telemarketer Torture

Do you hate telemarketers (people who call you trying to sell something)? Here is a list of horrible things you can do to annoy and torment telemarketing people when they make an uninvited phone call to your home. The suggestions are in the form of a game. Each thing you can do to torture a telemarketer has a point value. After the call, you can add up the points to determine your score.

Web:
http://www.antitelemarketer.com/teletech.htm

Terrorist's Handbook

A few of the techniques and methods employed by people who use terror as a means to achieve their social and political goals. The Web page is the entry point for a hypertext version of The Terrorist's Handbook which allows you to easily follow links between the sections of your interest. It includes sections on buying explosives and propellants, acquiring chemicals, explosive recipes, impact explosives, low order and high order explosives, ignition devices, projectile weapons, rockets and cannons, pyrotechnics, a list of suppliers, and even more. (Note: This is for your amusement. Only a fool would actually do any of this stuff.)

Web:
http://www.phreebyrd.com/~nero/tth/thb_title.html
http://www.thepoint.net/~rknight/terror/thb_title.html

Stuff You Are Not Supposed to Know About

Whether you are planning to blow up the World Trade Center, or merely explode a few small devices in your backyard, the **Terrorist's Handbook** is an invaluable guide to having a good time. Where else can you get such wonderful ideas about how to use up all that extra ammonium triiodide left over from last year's revolution?

Trolling

Trolling is the slang for fishing around for flames (emotional complaints) on a Usenet discussion group. Trolling is practiced by people who invade Usenet groups and try to start flame wars, by posting stupid questions or comments, or by deliberately making provocative remarks. The trollers originally started out in the **alt.syntax.tactical** group. You may sometimes find them there, or in **alt.bigfoot** or **alt.flame**. The FAQ (frequently asked question list) explains how to deal with trolling, not how to do it. (But if you read the FAQ, you'll know how to do it.)

Web:
http://digital.net/~gandalf/trollfaq.html

Usenet:
alt.syntax.tactical

Urban Exploration

Would you like to go where no man (or woman) has gone before? On planet Earth, that's hard to do, but you can do the next best thing. You can go where no man (or woman) is *supposed* to go—college tunnels, secret places in hotels and hospitals, abandoned buildings, and so on. Look here for tips, techniques and pictures.

Web:
http://members.aol.com/eddanamta/abandoned/abanstas.html
http://www.cc.columbia.edu/~brennan/rails/disused.underground.html
http://www.infiltration.org/
http://www.squonk.net/users/kriste/drains/

Wedding Pranks

No doubt about it: a successful marriage calls for a mature attitude, a sense of compromise, and a commitment to solve problems in a thoughtful, loving manner. The next time you are invited to a wedding, what better way to help the prospective bride and groom than to play a few pranks? You will be encouraging them to develop a mature attitude and a sense of compromise (not to mention providing them with an opportunity for problem solving in a thoughtful, loving manner). In fact, they are likely to say your pranks are among the best favors anyone ever did for them. Remember, these are your friends we are talking about. Do they deserve anything less?

Web:
http://www.mbw-nv.com/weddingpranks/
http://www.troc.net/weddings/index.html

MONEY: BUSINESS AND FINANCE

American Stock Exchange

Here's a daily online market summary, provided by AMEX (the American Stock Exchange, based in New York). This resource includes a list of AMEX companies, information on options and derivatives, late-breaking market news, as well as the blueprints for the secret rumpus room in the basement of Bill Gates's new mansion.

Web:
  http://www.amex.com/

Annual Reports

Every year, publicly traded corporations issue annual reports, many of which are available on the Net. If the report you want is online, this Web site will let you find what you want in a mouse click or two. If you do stock market research, this is a great resource for your bookmark list.

Web:
  http://www.reportgallery.com/content/glry_a.htm

Asia Online

Here is an online magazine devoted to Asian business and finance. You will find a variety of useful information on world financial markets, Asian business news, technical commentaries, and so on. You will also find a directory to help you locate Asian business resources on the Internet. Lots and lots of information in an easy-to-use package.

Web:
  http://www.asia-inc.com/

Visit my Web page:
http://www.harley.com/

Bonds

A bond is a debt instrument used to raise capital by borrowing money for more than one year. A bond represents a promise to pay back the amount borrowed (the principal) on a specified date as well as interest, often at regular intervals. Bonds are issued by various types of organizations including governments (federal, state/provincial, county, municipal) and corporations. The bond market is complex, and investing in bonds requires you to have a certain degree of specialized knowledge. Here are some resources that can help you understand bonds, find out current values, and make the appropriate calculations and decisions.

Web:
  http://www.bonds-online.com/
  http://www.bradynet.com/
  http://www.investinginbonds.com/
  http://www.publicdebt.treas.gov/sav/sav.htm

Asia Online

Doing business in Asia is a lot different from doing business in Fargo, North Dakota. For example, it rains a lot more in Asia and the food is spicier. On the other hand, chances are that a Fargo businessman isn't going to be insulted just because you ran afoul of some local custom and offered a beer to his wife with your left hand.

So, before you even think about doing business with your Asian cousins, check out the Asia Online Web site. Before you can say:

"O-genki desu ka. The Little Nipper desu. Uchi no obasan wa kuruma no shita. Tomato wa arimasu ka. Kono hon wa subarashi," you will be in business in a big way (thanks to this book and proper research).

520 MONEY: BUSINESS AND FINANCE

Business Headlines

Wondering whether to sell or buy, have a party or jump out the window of the men's washroom on the 44th floor? Don't be hasty. Read the headlines and summaries of the latest business news before making a decision.

Web:
http://www.bloomberg.com/
http://www.businesswire.com/
http://www.cnnfn.com/
http://www.newspage.com/
http://www.usa.ft.com/

> Need to stay current with matters financial? **The Business Headlines** will help you keep up on those who keep up while you are sleeping.

Business Information Resources

Here are some pointers to business information resources on the Net. You can read business magazines and journals, find out about opportunities and business services on the Net, see some entrepreneurial resources, and much more.

Web:
http://businessdirectory.dowjones.com/
http://www.dnb.com/resources/menu.htm

Business Plans

A business plan is an analysis that details the operations, status and future plans for a business entity. With a corporation, a business plan will be drawn up by the management. With a partnership or sole proprietorship, the plan will be created by the people involved. In most cases, the purpose of a business plan is to document a request to borrow money. In other words, before a bank or an investor will give you money, you have to show you know what you are doing, and that your business is likely to be profitable. Creating a business plan can take a lot of work, especially the first time. Here are some resources that can help.

Web:
http://www.sb.gov.bc.ca/smallbus/workshop/busplan.html
http://www.sbaonline.sba.gov/starting/businessplan.html

Commerce Business Daily

The Commerce Business Daily is a special publication that announces invitations to bid on proposals requested by the U.S. government. This information is updated every business day.

Web:
http://www.ld.com/cbd/today/

> **Commerce Business Daily**
>
> Would you like to serve humanity and make money at the same time? Why not do business with the U.S. government? (You couldn't find a nicer group of people anywhere.) Take a look at the **Commerce Business Daily** and you just may find your path to life, liberty, and the pursuit of financial happiness.

Entrepreneur Talk and General Discussion

Tired of being manacled to that creaking metal desk with the file drawer that always sticks? Take charge of your life: own your own business. See the pitfalls and glories that await you, the entrepreneur.

Usenet:
misc.entrepreneurs

> **Your Own Business**
>
> What could be more fun than running your own business? Why let someone else worry about health care, liability insurance, meeting the payroll, and making a profit, when you can do so yourself? (Of course, there are drawbacks as well.) If you are starting your own business, make sure to read **misc.entrepreneurs**. There are a lot of people just like you.

MONEY: BUSINESS AND FINANCE

FinanceNet

FinanceNet is a U.S. government resource with massive amounts of information relating to money. For example, would you like to find out how much American civil servants are paid? Just display the Federal Pay Scales. This is a must-have resource for anyone who wants to know about the U.S. government. You will also find links to many U.S. state and local resources. What a great place to take your potential best girl or guy for a first date.

Web:
http://www.financenet.gov/

Foreign Trade Statistics

Black market traders, investors and exporting gurus will all be interested to hear what the Foreign Trade Division says about U.S. International trade statistics. Scoot back off the edge of your seat. The waiting is over. Point your Web browser to the U.S. Bureau of Statistics and get all the numbers you need.

Web:
http://www.census.gov/ftp/pub/foreign-trade/www/

Global Trade Center

Spaghetti, falafel, salt from the bowels of distant countries—these are all things you can get through international trading without having the local supermarket as a go-between. If you like to do things the hard way, risking money and perhaps life and limb, get into a little international trading. This Web site offers information and links for businesses interested in exploring international trade.

Web:
http://www.tradezone.com/

Idea Futures

Gambling is the most fun when you are playing with someone else's money. If you like to break a sweat, but only a little, try playing with some idea futures. Start with a certain number of shares in your betting pool, climb into your think tank, and win or lose as the gods of speculation will have it.

Web:
http://www.ideosphere.com/fx/

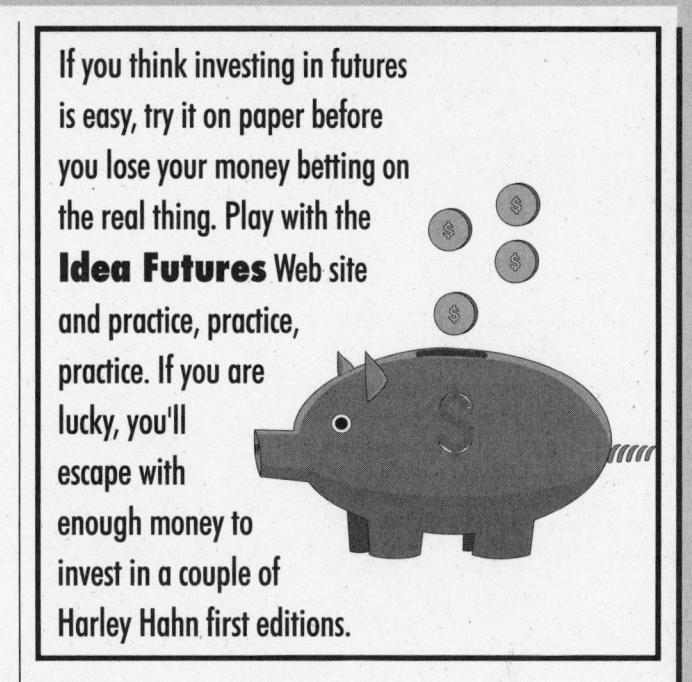

> If you think investing in futures is easy, try it on paper before you lose your money betting on the real thing. Play with the **Idea Futures** Web site and practice, practice, practice. If you are lucky, you'll escape with enough money to invest in a couple of Harley Hahn first editions.

Importing and Exporting

Trading is fun because you can get rid of all the stuff you don't need anymore and get cool new stuff that somebody else wants to get rid of and that makes everyone happy. Make people happy all over the globe by reading up on the import-export business. You might even end up with more stuff than you know what to do with.

Usenet:
alt.business.import-export.computer
alt.business.import-export.food
alt.business.import-export.raw-material
alt.business.import-export.services

Industry Net

When you want the goods on the industrial and manufacturing sectors of the world, take a look at Industry Net. The forms at this Web site will let you pick topics you are interested in, then when you log in, the computer will give you the industry news relating to your interests. You have to register, but membership is free.

Web:
http://www.industry.net/

International Accounting Network

The life of an accountant is truly exciting: all those numbers to punch, calculator tapes flying, phones ringing, deadlines to meet, and clients to bail out of jail. As if that's not enough, accountants also have the International Accounting Network, which offers details about accounting conferences, accounting mailing lists and archives, lists of accounting organizations around the world, accounting research and journals, software and educational resources. Nothing but fun.

Web:
http://anet.scu.edu.au/ANetHomePage.html

Investor Glossary

The world of money is complex, and there are a lot of terms you need to understand. From time to time, you are going to encounter an unfamiliar word. For example, say you are reading a prospectus or a report, and you see a strange term. My advice is to spend a few moments, and use this glossary to find out what the word means. In this way, you will build your vocabulary over time. The more words you know, the better you will be able to think.

Web:
http://www.investorwords.com/

IPOs

An initial public offering (IPO) occurs when a company offers stock to the public for the first time. Because the stock is new, the market has not yet established its value. Thus, although an IPO offers stock at a specific price, that price can change significantly within the first few days, or even hours, of trading. Thus, IPOs are opportunities to (1) buy an initial investment in a newly offered stock as a sound strategic move, (2) make a lot of money quickly, or (3) lose a lot of money quickly. If you have an interest in IPOs, you will find these Web sites useful. They provide timely information on IPOs and the companies that are involved.

Web:
http://www.ipo-fund.com/
http://www.ipocentral.com/
http://www.ipomaven.com/

Money Page

Finally, no more waiting in line at the bank. Find links to various banks on the Net and information about electronic money, non-U.S. banking, government-related banking institutions, credit cards, thrifts and credit unions.

Web:
http://www.moneypage.com/

Multilevel Marketing Talk and General Discussion

The great pyramids are not just in Egypt. Learn all about the "trickle-up theory" and hear stories of why multilevel marketing is the greatest money-making scam, er... scheme ever. Don't settle for a rattling car and a rental home. Sell Amway so you can drive a Rolls Royce and own a yacht. These folks can show you how.

Usenet:
alt.business.multi-level

> Need the scoop on serious multilevel marketing? Download the frequently asked question list. Then tell five friends, who will tell five friends, who will...

Mutual Funds

If I were smarter, I would probably be buying stocks and bonds (and losing all my money). Instead, I put my savings into a mutual fund and let someone else do the driving. These mutual fund resources provide useful, focused content and original material with references to other valuable Internet resources. For discussion, try Usenet.

Web:
http://www.findafund.com/
http://www.fundspot.com/main.shtml
http://www.indexfundsonline.com/
http://www.mfea.com/
http://www.morningstar.net/

Usenet:
misc.invest.mutual-funds

MONEY: BUSINESS AND FINANCE

Small Business Administration

Running your own business can be a delight or a hassle, depending on how you approach it. It helps to have as much information at your fingertips as possible. The Small Business Administration is online, and you can read about business development, government contracting, minority business, and financial assistance.

Web:
http://www.sbaonline.sba.gov/

Small Business Resources

These Web sites have all sorts of information and links relating to small businesses. If you are starting your own business—or if you would like to enhance what you already have—there will be something here to help you.

Web:
http://www.bloomberg.com/smallbiz/
http://www.isquare.com/
http://www.lowe.org/smallbiznet/
http://www.quicken.com/small_business/
http://www.toolkit.cch.com/

Stock Market Data

The next time your therapist tells you to take stock in yourself, you will know where to look. Here are some resources that can help you find stock information for just about any security you can imagine. (And who wouldn't like to imagine more security?)

Web:
http://www.411stocks.com/
http://www.bigcharts.com/
http://www.clearstation.com/
http://www.secapl.com/cgi-bin/qs
http://www.stockguide.com/
http://www.stockmaster.com/
http://www.stocktools.com/
http://www.thestreet.com/
http://www.timely.com/

Stock Market Timing

Just like with sex, in the stock market, timing is everything. Don't be caught with your pants down. Read these weekly technical analyses of the stock market along with the online recommendations.

Web:
http://www.firstcap.com/smt/

Stock market timing is a technique that attempts to determine the underlying trends of the market in order to decide when to buy and when to sell. (This is the opposite of buying stocks and holding them for a very long time.)

The market is so complex as to be well beyond the understanding of any human being, but that doesn't mean you can't find some useful patterns.

If you are interested in trying to beat the averages, don't forget to check with the Net first.

Wall Street Net

While everyone else is getting their hands grubby going through various newspapers, searching for the latest news, you can be sitting pretty with the information all laid out in front of you. Wall Street Net brings you the latest on what is happening in the world of corporate debt and equity financing. See their archival data, which includes SEC filings and prospectuses on transactions that have occurred in the last twelve months.

Web:
http://www.netresource.com/wsn/

MONEY: PERSONAL FINANCE

Consumer Credit Cards

Credit cards. We just can't seem to live without the little devils. Just when you think you have everything under control, you hear about a new card with a picture of your favorite rock band, and you just can't resist. Well, if credit cards are giving you trouble, the Net can help. Here is a lot of information about credit cards, including current data to help you find which card is best for you.

Web:
  http://www.creditinfocenter.com/cards/
  http://www.ramresearch.com/ct_main.html
  http://www.tdbank.ca/tdbank/Creditctr/creditfq/
    creditfq.html

Estate Planning

If you don't plan your estate, the state or province in which you live will plan it for you.

The Net has lots of estate planning information to help you decide what's best for you and your family.

Currency Converter

The currency converter is simple to use. You select the desired country and all the other countries' currencies will be converted relative to the one you selected. The name of the currency will appear as part of your selection.

Web:
  http://www.oanda.com/converter/classic
  http://www.xe.net/currency/

Estate Planning

Estate planning is important for everyone. If you die without a will, the government has a great many rules that will determine what happens to all your money, property and possessions (that is, your estate). There is no guarantee that what eventually happens will be what you want. However, if you make up a will ahead of time, there is much more chance that your wishes will be followed. Moreover, proper estate planning can often save your heirs a great deal of inheritance tax. If you are married, or if you have children, you absolutely must have a will. Let me tell you a personal observation. I don't plan on dying any time soon, and I don't even like to think about death. However, I did have a will made and, once it was done, I felt good about it. It brought me peace of mind. Just do it and you will see what I mean. Here are some resources that can help you understand estate planning. In addition, at one of the sites you can read the text of the wills of various famous people, such as Elvis Presley, Jerry Garcia and Richard Nixon.

Web:
  http://www.ca-probate.com/links.htm
  http://www.nolo.com/chunkep/ep.index.html

**Stop - in the name of love.
See "Romance".**

MONEY: PERSONAL FINANCE

Getting the Most from Your Money

Don't let anyone ever call you cheap. As one of my readers, you have excellent judgment and, of course, that extends to money matters as well. Some people may think you are frugal, but let those people throw their money away. You and I can find the bargains and get the most for our dollars. Here are a few good places to look for tips, hints and Internet resources that can help you spend your money wisely. If you would like to talk to other people about living frugally, check out the Usenet group.

Web:
http://www.best.com/~piner/frugal.html
http://www.stretcher.com/

Usenet:
misc.consumers.frugal-living

Household Budgeting

Sometimes it seems that, no matter how much money you make, it is never enough. Well, that's true for two reasons. First, probably no one ever makes enough money in the sense that there is always something else to buy. However, the second reason is more important: many people simply do not know how to budget their money wisely. Realize that budgeting well is something that you have to learn (and practice). At first, living with a budget may seem like an imposition. But once you get used to it (if you created a good budget for yourself), you will find that spending and planning within your means is a comfortable way to live. One of the Web sites contains lots of useful information to help you understand and plan a household budget. The other site allows you to take a self-test in order to evaluate your "spending personality".

Web:
http://dacomp.hypermart.net/budget1.html
http://www.cccsdc.org/budget.html

Insurance Information

Insurance is something we buy, hoping that we will never use it. There are many types of insurance, and you can't always depend on the salesman to make sure you understand everything. Here are some useful consumer tips that could end up saving you money (and time) when it comes to understanding your insurance needs.

Web:
http://www.iii.org/home.html
http://www.insure.com/

Investment Talk and General Discussion

Mutual funds, IRAs, discount brokerages, margin terms—do you sometimes feel like your head is going to spin around? Learn everything you need to know about investments and handling money. Make your money work for you.

Usenet:
alt.invest
alt.invest.market.crash
alt.invest.penny-stock
alt.invest.penny-stocks
alt.invest.real-estate
misc.invest
misc.invest.canada
misc.invest.commodities
misc.invest.emerging
misc.invest.forex
misc.invest.funds
misc.invest.futures
misc.invest.index-futures
misc.invest.marketplace
misc.invest.misc
misc.invest.options
misc.invest.stocks
misc.invest.stocks.penny
misc.invest.technical

Money News

Money talks—and talks and talks and talks. There is a lot of money news in the world and it is not always easy to keep up. Here is where the Net is great. Check out these Web sites regularly for the latest consumer-oriented financial news. Keep up on what is happening with mutual funds, airfare wars, investment scams, smart cards, credit card debt, and more.

Web:
http://cnnfn.com/quickenonfn/
http://www.usatoday.com/money/mfront.htm

You can't get wet surfing the Net.

Mortgage Calculator

If you have your eye on that choice piece of property down the road and you want to see just how bad the mortgage will bite into your wallet, put one of these mortgage calculators to work. Simply enter the buying price, the interest rate, and a few other pieces of information. A program will give you a fully amortized schedule or a brief summary of what you will be paying in principle and interest, your monthly payments, and what you should be earning to be able to afford the house.

Web:
http://www.efcol.com/javacalc.html
http://www.efcol.com/mtgcalc.html
http://www.ibc.wustl.edu/mort.html
http://www.interest.com/hugh/calc/msimple_js.html
http://www.jeacle.ie/mortgage/

Do you want to ruin your day?
Use the **Mortgage Calculator** and find out how much you are *really* paying for your house.

Mortgages

If you are contemplating a mortgage, find out lots of information about interest rates, mortgage companies, rate trends and loan programs from this Web page. Not only will you learn interesting things that will help you make a better decision, but you can also utilize an online mortgage payment calculator, see historical interest rates and read consumer tips and information.

Web:
http://www.mortgage-net.com/

Personal Finance Tips and Resources

It was so much easier when you were a kid. Your biggest money worry was trying to figure out how to break the piggy open without anybody noticing. Now there's all this tax stuff, deductions and annuities, investments and exemptions. At least people on the Net are making it a little easier to sort out all the information. Find great tips and resources that can help you manage your personal finances.

Web:
http://www.cncurrency.com/
http://www.financenter.com/
http://www.moneyminded.com/

Usenet:
misc.invest.financial-plan

Planning for Retirement

Here's a simple but effective way to save for retirement. Throughout your life, set aside 10% of every paycheck. No matter what happens, always set aside the 10%, and never ever use the money for anything else except retirement savings. Now, in the course of a lifetime, it is certain that financial emergencies will arise and, when they do, you are going to be tempted to "borrow" from your retirement money. The key to accumulating wealth is to resist that temptation. Every month, even before you pay your bills, set aside the 10%. If you learn to live on 90% of your income, you won't notice much difference day-to-day, but over the years, you will build up a significant nest egg. What should you do with your retirement money? If you are more than 10 years from retirement, invest the money safely in the stock market using, for example, a growth-oriented mutual fund, or a fund that tracks the S&P 500. Retirement planning is an important issue, and there are lots of resources on the Net that can help you. To get you started, I have picked out a few good Web sites. These resources are especially helpful if you live the United States. However, please remember what I said: no matter where you live, no matter what you do for a living, save 10% of everything you take in and invest it wisely. I want to ensure that, when you retire, you will have enough money to buy all the Harley Hahn books you ever need.

Web:
http://home.earthlink.net/~intercst/reindex.html
http://www.awa.com/softlock/tturner/401k/401k.html
http://www.investorguide.com/retirement.htm
http://www.ssa.gov/

Tax Preparation

Ah, the glorious month of April. The birds rejoice at the dawn of spring. Earthworms happily aerate the soil to stimulate new growth. A delicate breeze blows. And you are stuck inside doing your taxes. Isn't life cruel? Try to make it as painless as possible by planning ahead. Get handy instructions, hints, answers—even tax forms—on the Net. Then go catch some rays.

Web:
http://www.el.com/elinks/taxes/
http://www.irs.ustreas.gov/prod/forms_pubs/
http://www.scubed.com/tax/

Usenet:
misc.taxes
misc.taxes.moderated

Tax Forms

Yes, you really can get tax forms—American and Canadian—and all kinds of tax information for free over the Internet. There is a *lot* of stuff here, including the entire tax code (all 14 kajillion pages), so what are you waiting for?

Teaching Kids About Money

It is important that children understand money. But how do you know what to teach them and when? The Net can help. Check these Web sites for articles about many useful topics such as children's allowances and teaching good spending habits. Explore by yourself and then invite the kids to join you. After all, if you make sure that your kids understand money and how to use it, you will be providing them with valuable knowledge that will last a lifetime.

Web:
http://pages.prodigy.com/kidsmoney/
http://tqd.advanced.org/3096/
http://www.younginvestor.com/

MOTORCYCLES

Antique Motorcycles

Visit these sites devoted to antique motorcycles, including the Web site for the Antique Motorcycle Club of America, a non-profit organization dedicated to the restoration and exhibition of antique motorcycles. Find out information about the various chapters as well as a schedule of events. If you like antique motorcycles, you may as well join the club. As I always say, Harleys only get better as they get older.

Web:
http://www.archive.vintageweb.net/bikes.htm
http://www.motorcycle.com/mo/classified/vintage.html
http://www.roadrunner.com/~maraz/motorcycles.html

Biker Women

There is something special about women who love bikes. Maybe it's because they are strong, determined, and just a tad adventurous. There are some great resources for women and motorcycles on the Net, as there should be. After all, it's hard not to admire a woman who knows the value of a Harley.

Web:
http://free.prohosting.com/~witw/
http://members.aol.com/devan8268/scoots.html
http://www.cpdmp.cornell.edu/wow/

Harley Owners Group

There's something so lovable about a Harley. Maybe it's because they are so sexy, powerful and have lots of thrust. Or maybe it's that air of exotic mystery and charisma. Or maybe they're just good motorcycles. If you're a Harley fan, check out this site, which has art, technical information, pictures and stolen bike information.

Web:
http://www.harley-davidson.com/experience/family/hog/hog.asp

Motorcycle Camping

Have you ever gone camping with your motorcycle? If so, you will appreciate this practical information: choosing bags that work well with your bike, what gear to pack in your limited space, tips on how to best pack your bike and tie it all down, and so on.

Web:
 http://www.micapeak.com/WetLeather/pages/camping.html

Motorcycle Maintenance

If you enjoy working on your own bike, these Web sites have a lot of information you will find useful. Read the tips on repair, maintenance and tune-ups for many popular brands of bikes. You will not only save money, but you can get your motorcycle running just the way you want it, as well as have the satisfaction of being just that much closer to the machine. (My philosophy is that everyone should have at least one good relationship in their life.)

Web:
 http://shoga.wwa.com/~mcgyver/techtips.htm
 http://www.ll.net/spider/mtools.htm
 http://www.nightrider.com/biketech/index.htm

Harley Owners Group

Experts agree, there's nothing like having a Harley in your life. If you're lucky enough to own one, join the group.

Motorcycle Online Magazine

While it's not as convenient as a paper magazine sitting in the bathroom, this electronic motorcycle magazine is spiffy and worth a look. It features news stories, video and photo archives, a virtual museum, a U.S. events database, sneak previews of next year's motorcycle models, and links to services offered by commercial parties and manufacturers.

Web:
 http://www.motorcycle.com/

Motorcycle Racing

What a rush it is to be racing at high speeds with nothing between you and the air except a flimsy little jumpsuit that will disintegrate upon impact with the asphalt. Motorcycle racing enthusiasts discuss road racing from the racer's point of view as well as the pit crew's.

Web:
 http://www.bikenet.com/
 http://www.motorcycle-usa.com/
 http://www.xcelco.on.ca/~mxu/mainindex.html

Listproc Mailing List:
 List Name: **race**
 Subscribe to: **listproc@micapeak.com**

Motorcycle Reviews

Before you buy a motorcycle, be sure to read about other people's experience. These Web sites contain reviews—including a large collection from the **rec.motorcycles** Usenet group—and pricing information. If you are going to be spending your hard-earned cash, you deserve the best bike you can get.

Web:
 http://rmr.cecm.sfu.ca/
 http://www.motorcycle.com/mo/manufac.html
 http://www.theautochannel.com/db/bikeguide.html

Motorcycle Safety

Riding a motorcycle is inherently more dangerous than, say, driving a car or running around the house with a spoon in your mouth. As part of learning how to ride a motorcycle, it is important to develop an appreciation for safety and good habits. These Web pages can help you enjoy your cycle while minimizing the chances of an accident or injury.

Web:
http://home.earthlink.net/~jamesdavis/TIPS.html
http://www.msf-usa.org/

Motorcycle Talk and General Discussion

Anything that puts massive amounts of thrust right where you need it is bound to be desirable. No doubt that is why so many people love their motorcycles. If you just can't live without something hard, fast and powerful, these Usenet groups are the places to be.

Usenet:
alt.binaries.pictures.motorcycles
alt.binaries.pictures.motorcycles.harley
alt.binaries.pictures.motorcycles.sportbike
alt.motorcycle.sportbike
alt.motorcycles
alt.motorcycles.harley
alt.sabmag
rec.motorcycles
rec.motorcycles.dirt
rec.motorcycles.harley
rec.motorcycles.racing
rec.motorcycles.tech

> There's no such place as far away.

Motorcycling in the Rain

Riding a cycle safely in the rain calls for a great deal of skill and judgment. The Wetleather Web site is based on a mailing list devoted to issues related to riding in the rain, specifically in the northwestern part of the United States and adjacent areas in Canada. Wetleather people gather together for camping, riding and lots of fun. Check out the calendar of events, ride reports, and pictures of Wetleather members racing, and then join the list.

Web:
http://www.micapeak.com/WetLeather/

Listproc Mailing List:
List Name: **wetleather**
Subscribe to: **listproc@micapeak.com**

Regional Motorcycle Mailing Lists

When you want to discuss motorcycle topics with people all over the world, join a mailing list. This site has a comprehensive list of motorcycle mailing lists around the Net, including regional lists which allow you to interact with motorcycle enthusiasts close to home.

Web:
http://www.micapeak.com/mailinglistroundup/

Look What I Found on the Net...

```
Newsgroup: rec.motorcycles
Subject: Cleaning a Bike

Your bike can be as clean as you want, and it'll always look
dirty.
```

530 MOTORCYCLES

Scooters

Oh, the indignity of it all. Your boss hog is in the shop for repairs and you have to motor around on this little scooter in the meantime. Accept your fate gracefully and talk with the other motor scooter fans about the care and maintenance of these vehicles.

Usenet:
 alt.scooter

Majordomo Mailing List:
 List Name: **twostroke-l**
 Subscribe to: **majordomo@teleport.com**

Sidecars

A sidecar is not something you see every day. The last one I saw was racing down the highway attached to a motorcycle driven by a young man in a leather jacket. The sidecar was loaded down with a plump blonde woman in her seventies who was also wearing a leather jacket and a long scarf that was trailing out behind her. Sidecars must be cool.

Web:
 http://www.sidecar.com/
 http://www.sidecarcross.com/

It takes a certain type of person to attach a sidecar to his motorcycle. If you would like to hobnob with such people, check out the **Sidecars** Web site. It takes all types to make a world, and nowhere is this more true than in the world of motorcycles. After all, one of the first lessons we learn in life is we can't all have Harleys.

Stolen Motorcycles

Having your bike stolen is like someone taking your baby. Don't sit still for it. Utilize this Web site dedicated to listing descriptions and photos of stolen motorcycles.

Web:
 http://www.scalesofjustice.com/stolen/

Used Bike Prices

Before you buy or sell a used bike, check with the Net. Knowing what a bike is worth on the street will help you make the best deal for yourself. (You can spend the money on extra copies of this book to impress all your friends who aren't smart enough to drive motorcycles.)

Web:
 http://www.mcnews.com/articles/used.htm

MOVIES

Box Office

Every week, new movies debut. They have a brief moment in the limelight, after which they spend a few years in video purgatory before dying slowly, in artistic agony. But in those few days in which a new movie plays in first-run theaters, it enjoys a huge amount of attention. The big questions are: how much did it gross, and how quickly? These Web sites will answer these questions (and many more) for you. After all, if you aren't keeping up on the latest news in the film industry, you might as well be watching TV.

Web:
 http://www.boxoff.com/
 http://www.boxofficeguru.com/

MOVIES 531

Coming Attractions

Anticipation is three-fifths to seven-eighths of the fun, so to maximize your movie-going pleasure, you can visit these Web sites to find out, in advance, what movies are going to be released and when. To make the experience complete, you can read about the rumors, the production news, the official hype, and the current status of that which is filming right now.

Web:
  http://corona.bc.ca/~corona/films/
  http://www.movieweb.com/

Cult Movies Talk and General Discussion

No matter how bad they get, no matter how outlandish they are or how far away from their origins they evolve, you will go see the hundredth remake of a film. There are a few movies that have a cult following and fans feel so strongly about these films that they will see them at all costs. These Usenet groups cover cult movies in general and some in particular, such as the Evil Dead movies and Rocky Horror Picture Show.

Usenet:
  alt.cult-movies
  alt.cult-movies.alien
  alt.cult-movies.cronenberg
  alt.cult-movies.evil-deads
  alt.cult-movies.rocky-horror

*Okay, if you are like me, what you really want to do is direct. All the more reason to subscribe to the **Film and TV Studies** mailing list.*

Directors Guild of America

In the movie industry, there are two types of people. Those who will admit that "they really want to direct", and those who already are directors. Once you become a director, you get to join the Directors Guild of America (DGA). Even better, you can visit the official Web site and remind yourself that you *belong*. However, even if your talent has not yet been properly recognized and you are still waiting for that big break, you can visit the Web site whenever you want and read interviews with famous directors. What I found most inspiring was the letter of welcome from the President of the DGA in which he explains that the DGA strives to help directors "strengthen their ability to develop meaningful and credible careers". Wow. (And I'm hard to impress.) My only question is, where can I find such a cool organization for writers?

Web:
  http://www.dga.org/

Film and TV Studies Mailing List

Who knew there was so much to film and television? It's not just a matter of whether you enjoy it or not. There are all sorts of academic things involved, like post-post-structuralist theory and pedagogical, historical and production issues to think about. This is a list for students, teachers and theorists who are interested in more than a good shoot-em-up flick.

Listserv Mailing List:
  List Name: **screen-l**
  Subscribe to: **listserv@ua1vm.ua.edu**

Film Festivals

Has anyone noticed that, as life reluctantly drags itself out of the twentieth century, there are more and more film festivals? I bet if Mickey Rooney and Judy Garland were to make a movie today, there would be a big scene in which Mickey would say, "Hey wait, why don't we put on our own film festival?" Ya see, George, there are so many of these things that a beginner just doesn't know where to start. No problemo. Just connect to the Net and check out this great list of film festivals around the world. Wait, I have an idea—how does this sound to you? The Harley Hahn Film Festival: Woody Allen movies, The Rocky Horror Picture Show, Sleepless in Seattle, When Harry Met Sally, and a special screening of Summer School, with Mark Harmon showing up to answer questions from the audience. Sounds great to me. Let's have a meeting.

Web:
  http://www.marklitwak.com/filmfes.htm

MOVIES

Film, Television and Popular Culture

Scholars don't just study old stuff like dead languages and crumbling tombs. Some of them just watch movies and television. Now that is a fun way to be a scholar. Sit around with other people who study film, television and popular culture, and the use of media in teaching. Read reviews of books, films and documentaries, announcements of grants, conferences and jobs, see course outlines, class handouts and syllabi, and participate in discussions on film history.

Listserv Mailing List:
List Name: **h-film**
Subscribe to: **listserv@h-net.msu.edu**

Film.com

This is a great site for film buffs and casual movie fans alike. There are lots of reviews for new releases as well as for previous new releases (back to 1991). Want to know when a new film will be released? Check the release calendar, by name or by date.

Web:
http://www.film.com/

Filmmaking Talk and General Discussion

Don't you hate it when you're sitting in a dark theater enjoying the movie, when the hero has just been blown 30 feet into the sky by a car bomb and the guy behind you announces, "Plastique does not have that sort of structured explosive radius. How unrealistic." Unfortunately, not everyone views movies in the same way. For some, film is art. For others, it is pure entertainment. It can also be a business or communications media. For amateur filmmakers, these Usenet groups offer sources of help and a way to connect with other filmmakers and learn about new equipment and techniques.

Usenet:
alt.movies.cinematography
alt.movies.visual-effects
bit.listserv.film-l
rec.arts.movies.production
rec.arts.movies.tech

Ssshhh... See "Secret Stuff".

Hollywood Online

When you are thinking of going to a theater or renting a video, Hollywood Online offers movie reviews of current and almost current films. You get a short synopsis and a picture, along with (if available) a long review, extra pictures, sound clips and a link to the movie's Web site. There are also chat rooms where you can talk to other movie fans. Why even go out? It's a lot easier—and cheaper—to make some popcorn and just sit home reading and talking about movies.

Web:
http://www.hollywood.com/

Horror Movies

It's great to scare yourself silly watching horror movies. And when you're not watching, what could be more fun than scaring yourself silly reading about horror movies on the Net and looking at frightening video clips?

Web:
http://www.drcasey.com/movies/

Listserv Mailing List:
List Name: **horror**
Subscribe to: **listserv@listserv.indiana.edu**

Monster Movie Talk and General Discussion

I love monsters. Even the bad ones. Monsters inevitably cause massive amounts of chaos, destruction, explosions and a variety of property damage, but that doesn't make them all bad. They are bound to be good for the economy in that they keep people employed—construction workers, for instance. Check out the Usenet group devoted to the discussion of monster movies and get the real lowdown on Godzilla's family history.

Usenet:
alt.movies.monster

MOVIES 533

Movie and Film Resources

If you are looking for something related to film, look no further. These resources will help you find information about movies, actors, directors, composers, the film industry, media, multimedia, movie reviews, filmmaking, and more.

Web:
   http://www.afionline.org/CineMedia/CineMedia.home.html
   http://www.cinemacrawler.com/

Movie Databases

It's a horrible feeling when you are trying to think of a movie title and you just can't remember it. That never has to be a problem if you use one of the comprehensive databases available on the Net. Search for your favorite (or most hated) movie by the title, cast and crew names, cast character name, genre, and other more obscure methods.

Web:
   http://italy.imdb.com/
   http://uk.imdb.com/
   http://us.imdb.com/
   http://www.allmovie.com/

Movie Mistakes

Do you like movies? Do you like watching other people's mistakes? Why not combine both your hobbies and double your fun? Enjoy the mistakes, bloopers and inconsistencies of the film world. Many of the mistakes have to do with geographical errors, film cutting and poorly framed shots that show cameras and other equipment.

Web:
   http://www.everwonder.com/david/mistakes.html
   http://www.redcourt.demon.co.uk/

Movie Previews

Previews (sometimes called trailers) can be a lot of fun. In my experience, previews are often better than the actual movies. So plan now for that hot date. Fix a few snacks, pull up a couple of chairs, download lots of movie previews. You'll be able to impress your date with your good taste in movies as well as your technological prowess.

Web:
   http://entertainment.simplenet.com/m-trailers.html
   http://movielist.simplenet.com/
   http://www.jurassicpunk.com/main.html
   http://www.movie-trailers.com/
   http://www.vdomovies.com/movies/hollywood/

Look What I Found on the Net...

```
Newsgroup: alt.movies.monster
Subject: Willard

> Is Willard a rat or a man?
> I have money riding on this.

Willard is the name of a movie about a guy named Willard, who
just happens to be a mad doctor who was kicked out of the
military, and now uses mind control to have rats commit murders
for him.
```

534 MOVIES

Movie Reviews

Personally, I never go to a movie without first checking with the Net. After all, what a waste of time it is to go all the way to the theater, pay for a ticket, get settled into your chair with a bag of popcorn and a cool lemonade, only to find that the movie you have chosen is worse that a remake of "Titanic" starring the Muppets. There are so many good reviews out there, I never worry about being unpleasantly surprised. Here are my favorite places to look for movie reviews. (Hint: These reviews are also useful when you are looking for a good video to rent.)

Web:
http://reviews.imdb.com/Reviews/
http://www.rinkworks.com/movies/
http://www.siskel-ebert.com/
http://www.suntimes.com/ebert/ebert.html

Usenet:
rec.arts.movies.reviews

Movielink

If you are in the United States, this site allows you to find out about movies playing in your local area (if you happen to live in one of the many cities that are covered). If Movielink has your city listed, you can find movie times and theater locations. This is the place that I go to when I need to find out what's playing and when. However, even if your city is not listed, you can read the synopses of movies and (if available) look at posters and previews.

Web:
http://www.movielink.com/

Parents and children, take a look at "Families and Parenting", "Kids", and "Young Adults".

Lonely? Try IRC.

Movies Talk and General Discussion

Movies are fun to watch from the audience, but don't you wonder what it would be like to be in on the action? You can at least get in on the talk. Discuss movies and the making of movies from a creative or technical point of view. Fans and filmmakers frequent these Usenet groups.

Usenet:
alt.asian-movies
alt.fan.blade-runner
alt.fan.lion-king
alt.fan.sam-raimi
alt.fan.starwars
alt.movies.branagh-thmpsn
alt.movies.bruce-lee
alt.movies.chaplin
alt.movies.christian-bale
alt.movies.hitchcock
alt.movies.independent
alt.movies.indian
alt.movies.joe-vs-volcano
alt.movies.kubrick
alt.movies.scorsese
alt.movies.silent
alt.movies.spielberg
alt.movies.terry-gilliam
alt.movies.tim-burton
rec.arts.cinema
rec.arts.movies
rec.arts.movies.current-films
rec.arts.movies.lists+surveys
rec.arts.movies.local.indian
rec.arts.movies.misc
rec.arts.movies.movie-going
rec.arts.movies.past-films
rec.arts.movies.people

Listserv Mailing List:
List Name: **cinema-l**
Subscribe to: **listserv@american.edu**

IRC:
#cinema
#movies

Mr. Showbiz

Mr. Showbiz is packed to the brim with movie industry buzz. It reviews the latest movies, and offers feature articles about the films and the stars. When you're tired of reading, you can enjoy some of the crazy time-wasters. For example, I enjoyed the "plastic surgery lab" (where you can modify your favorite stars), an awesome crossword puzzle, and some trivia games. This is a really, really cool site that can keep you busy for a long time.

Web:
   http://www.mrshowbiz.com/

Personal Movie Finders

Have you ever been at the video store, looking at all the rows of movies and wondering what to rent? Out of all those movies, something will be just right for you, but how do you find it? At my local video store, I ask John the Movie Expert. John is an articulate movie buff who knows everything there is to know about movies, and who has seen every movie ever made. Since John knows me, it is easy for him to find something new for me to enjoy. However, what if you don't have a John at your video store? Do the next best thing. Visit one of these Web sites, and have a sophisticated computer program select movies for you. You start by rating the movies you have already seen. The program then compares your ratings with those of other people, and recommends films you will probably like. (The Web sites will save your ratings, so you can use them whenever you want.)

Web:
   http://www.moviecritic.com/
   http://www.moviefinder.com/

Science Fiction Movie Talk and General Discussion

Movies of the science fiction genre are getting better all the time. Special effects are more creative and technically seamless, and the movie ideas are more outlandish. Discuss current science fiction movies as well as the more classical features of the last few decades.

Usenet:
   rec.arts.sf.movies

> If God really wanted us to live in the real world, why did he give us science fiction movies? (For that matter, why did he give us **this book?**

MUDS

Cardiff's Mud Page

When you are looking for something fun to do, check out Cardiff's Mud Page. It has mud lists and information galore, so you will never lack for fun ways to spend the day when you could be doing something important like winning a Nobel Prize for medicine.

Web:
   http://www.cm.cf.ac.uk/User/Andrew.Wilson/MUDlist/

MUDS

DikuMud Talk and General Discussion

A DikuMud is a text-based role-playing virtual reality. Slay a dragon, save a princess, drink a magic potion that will kill you (these are all optional, of course). If you love excitement, adventure and fantasy, find out what DikuMuds are all about.

Usenet:
  rec.games.mud.diku

Harley Hahn's Guide to Muds

What is a mud? What are the different types of muds? How do you get started? What are you expected to do? There is a lot to know about mudding, and, if you are a beginner, it can take you a while to feel comfortable. Mudding has its own culture, and it will help you a lot to understand the nuances. My mud guide will introduce you to the world of mudding and teach you the technical terms and basic ideas you need to know.

Web:
  http://www.harley.com/muds/

History of Muds

Muds have an intriguing history that demonstrates some of the most important qualities of the Net and of shared reality experiences. Once you become a serious mudder, you will enjoy knowing how muds got started, and how they developed. These two Web sites are good places to start. In the future, all young children will be required to study the history of muds in school. You and I might as well start now.

Web:
  http://www.ludd.luth.se/mud/aber/articles/history.html
  http://www.shef.ac.uk/uni/academic/I-M/is/studwork/groupe/t1.html

LPMud Talk and General Discussion

Hack it, slash it, just make sure you clean up afterward. LPMuds are text-based virtual realities where you can puzzle out a quest for advancement in the game or you can just find monsters to kill. Discover the adventurer within you. If you are already a hard-core mudder and want to set up your own, check out the Usenet groups to get tips on how to start. The Web site has an LPMud FAQ.

Web:
  http://www.imaginary.com/LPMud/lpmud_faq.html

Usenet:
  alt.mud.lp
  rec.games.mud.lp

Macintosh Mudding Resources

If you are a Mac user, I want you to know about this site. It is a great place to find resources that are scattered all over the Net: mud clients, servers and utilities, as well as links to a nice selection of mud resources, including some for beginners. If you need a mud client, look here first. Not only will you find links to the download locations, but also comprehensive commentary that makes it easy to decide which program might be best for you.

Web:
  http://lonestar.texas.net/~hsoi/mud/

Mud Admin Talk and General Discussion

As a player, if you think it's an inconvenience when your mud crashes, think how it would be if you were in charge of the machine that crashed it. Learn the ins and outs of being an administrator of a mud. How do you start a mud, and when you get it started, how in the world do you keep it going?

Usenet:
  rec.games.mud.admin

Throw a wild party.
The Net can help. See
"Holidays and Celebrations".

Mud Announcements

What's new? What's passed away? Every Friday, get the latest word on what mud sites are up and running and which ones have been put to pasture. Did you lose your favorite mud? Ask around here—someone will know the answer.

Usenet:
   rec.games.mud.announce

Muds in the News

The best thing about muds is that they keep so many people away from real life, where they would otherwise get bored and cause trouble. (Just see how much trouble is caused by all the people who *don't* use muds.)

So, for all you mudders, be sure to tune into rec.games.mud.announce and find out what's new and exciting. Wouldn't it be awful to connect to your favorite mud and find out that everyone else has moved to Mars?

Look What I Found on the Net...

```
Newsgroup: rec.games.mud.lp
Subject: Are Muds Appropriate for Kids?

> I have a very bright 11 year old who just discovered muds,
> and I don't quite get them.  Could someone please tell me if
> they are suitable for kids?

I have three children, two of whom play muds regularly.
One child is 8, the other is 13.  Of course, I have immortal
characters on the muds they play.  I also take other
precautions.

The 13 year old is usually okay on his own.

The 8 year old always plays a male character (helps to
avoid the sexual advances).  I give her a list of players to
whom it is okay to talk.  If I catch her talking to others,
I change her password, and she may no longer return there (until
she proves she can follow rules).

Finally, I watch her: who she is talking to and what she is
doing.  If there is something I don't like, I make her leave.
On a whole we have had good experiences with her mudding, and
she enjoys it.
```

Mud Area Building

The information at this Web site is specific to building areas on a mud. You will find programs that can help you (such as "Make Zones Fast"), sample areas that you can study, lots of tips, links to other resources, as well as a mailing list devoted to creating mud areas. Hint: Before you start to code your mud areas, plan them out using graph paper.

Web:
http://laudre.simplenet.com/muds/areas.html
http://www.diac.com/~mbuhl/style.html

Mud Clients

A mud client is a program that you run on your computer to access a mud. Since muds are text-based entities, you don't need a special mud client—you can use the standard telnet program. However, very few people use telnet because it's pretty much unbearable. A good client program can make a big difference to your mudding experience, so my advice is to experiment with various clients until you find a program you really enjoy using.

Web:
http://fly.ccs.yorku.ca/mush/tf.html
http://home.earthlink.net/~arithon/MudMaster/
http://homepages.together.net/~shae/client.html
http://www.port8zero.com/tintin++/

Mud FAQs

Before you get too far in your mudding career it's a good idea to read the FAQs (frequently asked question lists). It may take you a while until you feel comfortable on a mud. In the meantime, having some real answers to real questions can speed up the process.

Web:
http://muds.okstate.edu/~jds/mudfaqs.html
http://www.faqs.org/faqs/games/mud-faq/
http://www.moo.mud.org/moo-faq/

Mud Glossary

Like all great areas of human culture (art, music, science) mudding has a specialized vocabulary. When you encounter a word or term you do not understand, these Web sites are great places to look for help. Lots and lots of definitions of words that are commonly used on muds and by mud players.

Web:
http://eternal.california.com/HTML/glossary.htm
http://ils.unc.edu/TH/quickstart.html
http://www.hypercube.org/tess/rom/faq/glossary.html

Mud List

Are you bored out of your skull? Or perhaps you just have some responsibility you would like to avoid. No problem. Here are lists of all the Internet muds you will ever want to play. The sites have lots of distractions to keep you busy not only with muds, but with documents designed to help you learn about muds.

Web:
http://www.godlike.com/muds/
http://www.mudconnect.com/

Mud List

Defining a mud is easy: it's a (usually) text-based virtual world in which people interact with one another as well as with the built-in inhabitants and objects of the mud itself. Understanding a mud is not so easy. There is something about these virtual worlds that appeals to certain types of people in ways that most of us can never understand.

If you think you might be one of these special people, try mudding for a while and see how your life changes. Aside from making new friends and learning all kinds of esoteric information, you will connect yourself to a type of human/machine experience that just may change your life.

Mud Reviews

There are a lot of muds in the world, so how do you make a choice as to where you want to spend your time? One way is to read thoughtful reviews by knowledgeable people. Then join the mud of your choice, and live happily ever after.

Web:
http://www.gamecommandos.com/

Mud Talk and General Discussion

Immerse yourself in the wonders of muds: text-based virtual realities that provide you with an exciting realm in which to socialize or play adventure games. Find out what mudding is all about, but be warned: the Surgeon General has declared mudding to be addictive.

Usenet:
alt.mud
rec.games.mud
rec.games.mud.misc

Muds to Play

Do you want to explore something new? Try one of these muds. Here is a selection of the most interesting, imaginative and well-maintained muds on the Net. To start, go the Web sites of these muds. Each site gives a general overview of a particular mud. Read the Web pages to get the flavor of the mud, how friendly it is, its style, and its orientation (lots of role-playing, adventures, talking, and so on). The muds I have chosen for you to try are: Apocalypse, Deeper Trouble, Genocide, Legend, Looney, Medievia, Merentha, Necromium, Nuclear War, Phidar and Zhing.

Web:
http://mud.sig.net/
http://sapphire.geo.wvu.edu/~apoc/
http://www.astrakan.hgs.se/nuke/
http://www.looney.com/
http://www.medievia.com/
http://www.merentha.mudservices.com/
http://www.necromium.com/
http://www.pcisys.net/~dbowlin/DT/
http://www.phidar.com/
http://www.shsu.edu/~genlpc/
http://www.zhing.com/

TinyMud Talk and General Discussion

Some mudders consider adventuring and killing monsters barbaric. Imagine that. These social animals hang out on TinyMuds where social skill is a high art. If you are interested in chatting, making friends or other socializing, you'll love TinyMuds (including mushs, muses, and moos).

Usenet:
rec.games.mud.tiny

Zhing

I sponsor the Zhing mud, and I know you will like it. Zhing was planned and developed by a group of people who have years of mudding experience. These people have created a rich and engaging environment based on a medieval fantasy theme with a well-developed mythos. As with all adventure muds, you can spend time talking with other people, as well as exploring. Zhing has five continents, one of which is an archipelago. There are coastlines, mountains, forests, streams, caves, cliffs (which you can climb), castles, beaches, docks (where you can catch fish to eat), parks, an underground cavern, a maze, roads, and cities that have restaurants, pubs, hospitals, armories and various types of shops. Within Zhing, there are a lot of activities to keep you busy, either alone or in the company of other people, so there is always something to do. If you are an experienced mudder, you will find Zhing to be well-designed, skillfully administered, and a challenge to master. If you are a beginner, Zhing is a good place to start, as there are friendly people, a good help system, and lots of places to wander as you learn.

Web:
http://www.zhing.com/

Telnet:
Address: zhing.com
Port: 4000

Lonely? See "People".

MUSEUMS

Boston Science Museum

This museum has roots dating back to 1830, when six men formed the Boston Society of Natural History. This society collected natural history specimens and displayed them in temporary halls until, in 1864, the society opened the New England Museum of Natural History. Eventually, this exhibition evolved into the Museum of Science. When I visited, I saw some great exhibits about fractals, electricity and archaeology, as well as a collection of pictures taken with an electron microscope. (A flea under an electron microscope is pretty frightening.)

Web:

http://www.mos.org/

Exploratorium

Science is fun. You can blow things up, stick things together, make things float and create loud noises that will guarantee you a trip to the principal's office. The Exploratorium in San Francisco creates an environment of hands-on fun learning, and you can visit their home on the Net.

Web:

http://www.exploratorium.edu/

The Exploratorium

The Exploratorium is absolutely my favorite place in the San Francisco Bay Area (except for the offices of my publisher Osborne McGraw-Hill, in Berkeley, where they make up the royalty checks). The next time you are in San Francisco, be sure to visit the Exploratorium, the greatest hands-on science museum in the world. There are hundreds of things to do and zillions of buttons to push. Before you go, get the lowdown by connecting to the Exploratorium's Internet facilities.

You can display all kinds of interesting pictures to give you a preview of what you will find at the museum. You can even try experiments, right in the privacy of your own computer. (Hint for afterwards: When you are finished at the Exploratorium, go across the bay to Berkeley and drop into Osborne McGraw-Hill. Ask for my editor, Scott Rogers, and tell him that because you are a reader of this book, he must take you out to dinner.)

Holocaust Museums and Memorials

From the time of Hitler's rise to power (1933) to the end of World War II (1945), the Germans, under Hitler's leadership, conducted a large-scale program to systematically persecute and exterminate the entire Jewish community within the German sphere of influence. This atrocity—today known as the Holocaust—resulted in the murder of about 6 million Jews, many of whom were sent to the infamous concentration camps: places whose sole purpose was to efficiently kill large numbers of men, women and children. The Jews were not the only people murdered in the Holocaust. The Germans also rounded up and killed homosexuals, Gypsies, Communists, as well as many Poles and other foreigners whose lands were overrun by the German military. The acts committed by Hitler, the Nazis and the German people during this time period are so depraved as to challenge the imagination. Many people feel that such actions must never be forgotten, and that our society has much to gain by studying and understanding the Holocaust. Around the world, various Holocaust museums and memorials have been built. Here are the Web sites for three of them: Yad Vashem in Israel, the United States Holocaust Memorial Museum in Washington, D.C., and the Simon Wiesenthal Center in Los Angeles.

Web:

http://www.ushmm.org/
http://www.wiesenthal.com/
http://www.yad-vashem.org.il/

London Science Museum

The London Science Museum contains exhibits in the areas of science, the history of science, medicine, technology and industry. There are lots of fascinating things to learn about at this Web site. For example, I read about genetically engineered mice. The first mammals ever patented were white mice that had been genetically altered to make them more prone to develop cancers. (The "oncomice" are used in cancer research.)

Web:

http://www.nmsi.ac.uk/

Maritime Museums

A maritime museum collects exhibits and artifacts related to sailing and the sea. This Web site has links to various maritime museums in North America. Visit the Jamestown Settlement (where there are three full-scale replicas of ships from 1607), Battleship Cove (where you can see the world's most complete collection of historic fighting ships), and many more fascinating online museums. Visiting a maritime museum makes you appreciate the achievements of shipbuilders throughout the ages. For example, the battleship U.S. Massachusetts (the "Big Mamie"), which was used during World War II, weighs over 46,000 tons, is longer than two football fields and is as tall as a nine-story building. If you like ships, there are many fascinating places to visit on the Net.

Web:
http://www.bobhudson.com/Smiths/

Museum of Science and Industry

The Museum of Science and Industry in Chicago, Illinois, hosts this online collection of interesting exhibits. The exhibits change from time to time, so you can check every now and then and see what's new. This is a great place to visit with children.

Web:
http://www.msichicago.org/

Museum Talk and General Discussion

These are the places where museum curators and other professionals gather to discuss their work. Talk about plans for new exhibits, problems, questions, answers, and whatever else arises in the lives of the people who set up and maintain museums around the world.

Usenet:
bit.listserv.museum-l

Listserv Mailing List:
List Name: **museum-l**
Subscribe to: **listserv@home.ease.lsoft.com**

Museums and Galleries of Wales

Wales is a principality on the western peninsula of the island of Great Britain. Although Wales is part of the United Kingdom (along with England, Scotland and Northern Ireland), it has maintained its own distinct culture, including the Welsh language. This Web site contains links to various Welsh museums on the Web such as the Roman Legionary Museum, the Welsh Industrial and Maritime Museum, and the Museum of Welsh Life. If you are planning a visit to Wales, I recommend you check this Web site to get ideas for places you may want to visit.

Web:
http://www.cf.ac.uk/nmgw/

Museums, Exhibits and Special Collections

If you are not getting enough culture from television, try visiting some of the museums on the Net. You can hop around like a jet-setting socialite and visit museums all over the world. These Web pages have links to a diverse set of museums, exhibits and special collections that can be found on the Net.

Web:
http://www.artresources.com/guide/comp/indexes/museum.html-ssi
http://www.elsas.demon.nl/linkmu_e.htm
http://www.icom.org/vlmp/
http://www.musee-online.org/directo.htm
http://www.museums.net/tour.html

Got too much stuff?
Need some more stuff?
Try "Shopping".

542 MUSEUMS

National Gallery of Art

The U.S. National Gallery of Art in Washington, D.C., has one of the finest art collections in the world, specializing in painting, sculpture and the graphic arts from the Middle Ages to the present. The gallery's Web site allows you to view an extensive online collection. For example, there are paintings from American, British, Dutch, Flemish, French, Italian and Spanish artists. There is a lot to see here, and if you enjoy art my guess is you will be back over and over. I really enjoy exploring this site, hunting down interesting paintings, and I bet you will too.

Web:
  http://www.nga.gov/

New Mexico Museum of Natural History

New Mexico is a state in the southwestern part of the United States, just north of the Mexican border. New Mexico Museum of Natural History has various online exhibits that you can visit on the Web. My favorites are the exhibits about mammals and dinosaurs. If your kids like dinosaurs, bring them here. The last time I visited, I listened to some computer-generated sounds of a Parasaurolophus. (It sounded like a cow with a bad cold playing a trombone.)

Web:
  http://www.nmmnh-abq.mus.nm.us/nmmnh/

Look What I Found on the Net...

```
Newsgroup: bit.listserv.museum-l
Subject: This Is Why I Love Working in a Museum

> Hello all.  The Deutsche Hygiene-Museum in Dresden is
> organizing an exhibit on the theme of "Sitting" (you read me
> right).  They have asked to borrow South Dakota's electric
> chair, of which we are the proud possessor.  Alas, we will not
> be able to lend, due to our own exhibition plans for it.
>
> Which leads me to my question: is there anyone out there who
> knows of an institution in the United States that has its
> state's electric chair?  The director of the museum asked for
> the names of other museums that might have such a thing, but I
> don't know of any.  I do believe, however, that we are not the
> only museum in the U.S. with an electric chair.

(reply #1)

The Old Jail Museum in St. Augustine, Florida, has one.  It's
quite nice as I recall.

(reply #2)

I believe the Wyoming Frontier Prison in Rawlins, Wyoming,
has one.

(reply #3)

The Louisiana State Museum has an electric chair in their
collection.  I was an intern there last summer, and they
threatened to put me in it.
```

Royal Tyrrell Museum of Paleontology

Joseph Burr Tyrrell was an explorer for the Geological Survey of Canada. In the spring of 1884, Tyrrell was leading an expedition to find coal deposits in an area in what is now the province of Alberta. During his explorations, Tyrrell found the remains of a 70-million-year-old dinosaur skull. The skull was from a genus of dinosaur that was later named Albertosaurus, and was the first specimen of that genus found in the world. The Royal Tyrrell Museum of Paleontology is located near Drumheller in Alberta. The Web page includes exhibits about fossils, continental drift, evolution, dinosaurs and the Ice Age. I looked at a page explaining the evolution of fish. If you get the chance, take a look at the Dunkleosteus. It makes a shark look like a house pet.

Web:
http://tyrrell.magtech.ab.ca/

MUSIC

A Cappella

Not everyone needs musical instruments to help them keep in tune or remember the beat (or drown out their voice). Some folks can sing sweetly without accompaniment. That's what a cappella is all about. Find out more at the Web site or talk about it on Usenet, with or without a musical instrument.

Web:
http://www.casa.org/web_directory.html

Usenet:
alt.music.a-cappella
rec.music.a-cappella

Who hasn't heard a real Scotsman playing the bagpipes and not fallen in love with that sensuous, romantic, sophisticated sound that other, more euphonic musicians can only dream of?

Bagpipes

Bagpipes have what might euphemistically be referred to as a characteristic sound. This sound comes from the double-reed melody pipe, which produces the melody, as well as the drone pipe which produces the constant background sound. Although a taste for bagpipe music is something that needs to be acquired, there is no problem acquiring bagpipe information on the Net.

Web:
http://pipes.tico.com/
http://www.bagpiper.com/

Usenet:
rec.music.makers.bagpipe

Bands

If you've been looking for your favorite rock band on the Net and can't find it, check with these Web sites. You'll find huge lists of links to band-related resources as well as information about concerts, recordings, radio stations, music news, online events, magazines, ezines, record stores, essays, articles, musical terminology and slang, articles, music styles, lyrics, sounds, pictures and more. (See if you can say that ten times real fast.)

Web:
http://osiris.sund.ac.uk/cge/altcon.html
http://www.allmusic.com/
http://www.ubl.com/

Banjo

Africans brought the banjo all the way to America before 1688, just so people could go to bluegrass festivals and jam. And now that the banjo is well-established within our modern culture, it's time for you to start practicing. Remember, the only way you can get to the Grand Ole Opry is to practice, practice, practice.

Web:
http://www.bluegrassbanjo.org/
http://www.cats.se/banjo/
http://www.mindspring.com/~bopjo/

Usenet:
alt.banjo
alt.banjo.clawhammer

Barbershop Quartets

Throw down your accordion, your bagpipes, your tin whistles, and join a barbershop quartet. More fun than a barrel of monkeys, able to leap octaves in a single bound, these singers are lively, energetic, and know how to have a good time. Check out their online organizations, calendar of events, FAQs, and other resource information.

Web:
  http://timc.pop.upenn.edu/
  http://www-caip.rutgers.edu/~porter/shoppers.html

Big Band

The Big Band music we still enjoy today developed in the United States from a mixture of ragtime, jazz and other influences. The Big Band sound was more or less invented in the early 1940s by Benny Goodman (and his arranger Fletcher Henderson), and copied and modified by many other bands. The Big Band era flourished until the mid 1950s, when it was killed off by a combination of television, short (3 minute) 45 rpm records, and a variety of economic factors.

Web:
  http://www.nfo.net/

Usenet:
  alt.music.big-band

Money for Music

What do you do with the saxophone you bought five years ago and somehow never got around to learning how to play? And what about all those Julie Andrews Christmas albums that are taking up space on your coffee table?

Trade them, sell them, give them away—whatever your favorite means of commerce, gather up your musical extras and drop into the Usenet buy-and-sell groups. Who knows, maybe you'll run into someone who will really appreciate your collection of Mrs. Miller records.

Big band music is a gift from the gods.

Follow **alt.music.big-band** and see what the people with good taste have to say.

Blues

It's best played in tiny lounges with poor lighting. Maybe fill the room with some smoke. There is a true art to the mournful quality of the music. This is not just "crying in your beer" music. Explore the resources that bring the blues to life on the Net.

Web:
  http://www.bluesworld.com/
  http://www.fred.net/turtle/blues.shtml

Usenet:
  alt.music.blues
  alt.music.blues.delta
  bit.listserv.blues-l
  rec.music.bluenote.blues

Listserv Mailing List:
  List Name: **blues-l**
  Subscribe to: **listserv@brownvm.brown.edu**

Buying and Selling Music

Don't waste your time wandering the neighborhood looking for good garage sales at which to buy music and musical instruments. People all over the Net come to Usenet to buy and sell musical goods such as instruments and equipment, records, tapes, and CDs. Buying over the Net sure beats trying to get a piano home in the back seat of your car.

Usenet:
  rec.music.makers.marketplace
  rec.music.marketplace
  rec.music.marketplace.cd
  rec.music.marketplace.misc
  rec.music.marketplace.vinyl

MUSIC

Celtic Music

Music is something that the Celts do well. The soulful wail of the whistles and the primal beating of the drums would make just about anyone yearn to buy a plane ticket to Ireland. The proof is in the numbers. Fans of Celtic music are abundant on the Net and sponsor mailing lists and Web pages with information about Celtic music magazines, live jam sessions, radio programs, and more.

Web:
http://www.celticmusic.com/
http://www.ceolas.org/ceolas.html
http://www.collins-peak.co.uk/celtic/

Usenet:
rec.music.celtic

Classical Music

The world of classical music is huge, with many composers and many styles of music. Here are some Internet resources for you to explore: Web sites that will point you to all kinds of interesting and useful information, and discussion groups where you can talk to other people and ask questions.

Web:
http://www.classical.net/
http://www.igc.apc.org/ddickerson/
   classical-music.html

Usenet:
humanities.music.composers.wagner
rec.music.classical
rec.music.classical.contemporary
rec.music.classical.recordings
rec.music.early

Listserv Mailing List:
List Name: **classm-l**
Subscribe to: **listserv@brownvm.brown.edu**

**Just do it
(and then we'll talk about it).**

Between a rock and a hard place? See "Geology".

Concert Information

Going to concerts is an important part of growing up. When I was a kid I went to a lot of fabulous rock concerts. I saw the Doors, John Lennon, Alice Cooper, and even the Monkees. Later, when I was older and nostalgia was popular, I remember seeing many other groups such as the Beach Boys and the Four Seasons, as well as singers like Ella Fitzgerald and Joe Williams. When we are young, the music that is popular is *ours*, and everything else seems hopelessly outdated. Well, if you are young right now, you're in luck, because you have the Net, and the Net lists of concert schedules, ticket information, as well as other related resources: everything you need to plan your musical memories to comfort you in your old age. (Interesting thought: one day, there are going to be people who are nostalgic about the Spice Girls.)

Web:
http://www.wilma.com/

Country Music

If you don't get enough country music while riding in the pickup to and from the feed store, check out these sites, which offer concert reviews, country radio stations, discussion groups, magazines, and fan club information. Love, marriage, divorce, truck driving, dogs, beer—it's all just good old-fashioned American fun.

Web:
http://www.country.com/
http://www.countryweekly.com/

Usenet:
rec.music.country.old-time
rec.music.country.western

IRC:
#countrymusic

Country Music

I love you b-a-a-a-by!

There is something about the steady thump, thump, twang, twang of country music that is so reassuring. Country and Western music serves up a heapin' platter of good ol' American culture at its finest: money, booze and bad love. Just the thing for tired Internet music lovers who have overdosed on bagpipes.

Disco

On June 7, 1976, New York magazine published an article by Nik Cohn, entitled "Tribal Rites of the New Saturday Night". The article described an eighteen-year old Brooklyn teenager named Vincent, a neighborhood dancer with a sense of style and a definite attitude. The Sixties had faded, and a new generation of teenagers was about to redefine the popular culture. "The new generation takes few risks. It goes through high school, obedient; graduates, looks for a job, saves and plans. Endures. And once a week, on Saturday night, its one great moment of release, it explodes." And thus was born disco. For most of us, the epiphany came with the 1977 release of the movie "Saturday Night Fever", starring John Travolta as Vincent (who was renamed Tony Manero). Twenty years later, it's hard to remember that disco was once a *force majeure*, and that dancing was something you did with a partner, with style, and with an attitude. Twenty years later, disco is looked upon as an aberration, nothing more than the last, flowery hurrah between the revolution of the Sixties and the vast, interminable social wasteland of the Eighties and Nineties. But I was there and I remember. For a short time, it was possible to be cool, have fun, and enjoy the music—and to do it all with a partner, with style, and with an attitude.

Web:
http://izan.simplenet.com/70.htm
http://www.discomusic.com/

Discographies

When you have a blind date with a girl and you know she likes a certain band, go to one of these discographies sites, find the band and memorize every song and album they have ever released (along with the dates they were released). On the date, talk is bound to turn to music and you can wow her with your knowledge of her favorite musical groups. I always say, plan for success.

Web:
http://www.teleport.com/~xeres/discog.shtml

*Who sang what, with whom, when? Go to the Net and cop some info from the **discography** archives.*

Drums and Percussion

Percussion involves striking objects together to produce a sound. But that's only the starting point. There's lots of ways to strike things together and lots of different sounds you can make. To be a good percussionist takes a strong sense of rhythm, above-average manual dexterity and many hours of practice. If you tend toward the loud and rowdy, percussion may be for you (and there is plenty more where that came from on the Net).

Web:
http://www.drummersweb.com/
http://www.drumweb.com/

Usenet:
rec.music.makers.percussion
rec.music.makers.percussion.hand-drum

Early Music

Believe it or not, there really was music before rock and roll. And it was good music, too, but you can't do the Twist to it. If that doesn't bother you, you will probably love music from the Middle Ages and Renaissance. Early music lovers chat about records, books, performances, song texts, and translations as well as transcribing early music scores in electronic form. If you are new to early music, check out the FAQ on the Web site.

Web:
http://www.medieval.org/emfaq/

Listserv Mailing List:
List Name: **earlym-l**
Subscribe to: **listserv@wu-wien.ac.at**

Electronic Music Talk and General Discussion

Composing and playing electronic music is mostly a solitary occupation: you spend a lot of time by yourself, with only a synthesizer, a computer, and some strange-looking audio equipment for company. However, when you want company there's no need to actually go and fetch a real live person. There are people enough on the Net ready to discuss whatever you want regarding electronic music, and *they* know what they are talking about.

Usenet:
alt.emusic
rec.music.makers.synth
rec.music.synth

Listserv Mailing List:
List Name: **emusic-l**
Subscribe to: **listserv@american.edu**

Look What I Found on the Net...

```
Newsgroup: alt.emusic
Subject: What Do You Call That Music?

> Hi!  I flew into this newsgroup hoping for an answer.  I am
> trying to find out what you call the music that sounds like
> you're on a different planet.
>
> Space music? Alternative? New Age?  I've searched and searched
> trying to find something.  I used to listen to it on the
> radio.  It was piped in through some satellite feed.
> Any suggestions?

Hmm... What does the music on this planet sound like?

The space age bachelor pad sounds of Esquevel?
Electronic experimentalists like SkyLab?
Disorienting media plunder like John Oswald?

We need a little more to work with here.  There are a lot of
planets out there.
```

Filk

Filking is the clever, but nearly irreverent art of taking an existing song, gutting it, and making it into something new using the same music, but different words. Join the rowdy crowd around the campfire as they belt out the ballads.

Web:
  http://sundry.hsc.usc.edu/filk.html

Usenet:
  rec.music.filk

Film Music

A big part of every film is the soundtrack, the music that is chosen to go along with the visual images in order to enhance our enjoyment. Creating the soundtrack requires the services of highly skilled musicians, and is an art unto itself. Personally, I think that a good soundtrack significantly enhances the value of a movie and I'm always disappointed when the director creates a pseudo-soundtrack by using a collection of popular songs instead of music that was composed especially for the movie. What could be more boring than to watch a tedious montage to the accompaniment of a commercial rock song? And what could be more moving than to watch a well-scored film in which the music complements the action perfectly?

Web:
  http://us.imdb.com/Sections/Soundtracks/
  http://www.filmscoremonthly.com/
  http://www.movietunes.com/
  http://www.soundtrack.net/

Usenet:
  rec.music.movies

Listserv Mailing List:
  List Name: filmus-l
  Subscribe to: listserv@listserv.indiana.edu

Folk Music

I think Tom Lerher put it best: "The reason most songs are so atrocious," he explained, "is that they were written by the people." Lerher is a tough act to follow, so I'll content myself with pointing out that the Net has lots of folk music resources, including Usenet discussion groups.

Web:
  http://www.jg.org/folk/
  http://www.mudcat.org/folksearch.html

Usenet:
  rec.music.folk
  rec.music.folk.tablature

Funk

Opera makes you homicidal, classical puts you to sleep, and country music makes you want to get in a monster truck and plow over any small cars in your path. For a change, try some funk. Funk is based on the rhythmic innovations of James Brown. Discussion includes not only funk, but some rap, hip-hop, soul, R&B, and related varieties. Artists of the genre include the Artist Formerly Known as Prince, Funkadelic, Parliament, and Earth, Wind and Fire. Not only does funk sound good, you can dance to it, too.

Web:
  http://nettown.com/groovejuicer/flc.htm

Usenet:
  rec.music.funky

Gregorian Chants

Gregorian chants, sometimes referred to as plainsong, are among the oldest type of music that is still performed and studied. (In fact, if you take a college-level music survey course, you will probably start with Gregorian chants and work your way toward contemporary music.) Gregorian chants have no instrumental accompaniment and no rhythmic structure. They consist of only a single melody line sung in unison by a group of people. Such music is described as monodic. (If you are taking a music survey class, remember this word—it will show up on the multiple choice test.) Gregorian chants originated in Catholic churches around the sixth century A.D. and are named after Saint Gregory I (540-604 A.D.), who was Pope from 590 to 604. If you have never heard a Gregorian chant, please do listen to one. You will find that the primitive, unaccompanied melody has the power to soothe your instincts in a way that more modern music cannot.

Web:
  http://comp.uark.edu/~rlee/otherchant.html
  http://www.music.princeton.edu/chant_html

Grunge

This is definitely not your parents' music. Let your hair down, rip the sleeves off your shirt, and hang loose. Hang out with other angst-consumed rebels and discuss the grunge scene. If it's neat, clean or prepackaged, it doesn't belong here.

Listserv Mailing List:
  List Name: grunge-l
  Subscribe to: listserv@listserv.acsu.buffalo.edu

Guitar Talk and General Discussion

Guitar players, check out the discussion groups just for you. There are tablature groups for sharing music and lyrics, as well as groups for general guitar, acoustic guitar and classical guitar. To talk to other guitar enthusiasts live, you can join the IRC channel.

Usenet:
 alt.guitar
 alt.guitar.amps
 alt.guitar.bass
 alt.guitar.effects
 alt.guitar.lap-pedal
 alt.guitar.rickenbacker
 alt.guitar.tab
 rec.music.classical.guitar
 rec.music.makers.guitar
 rec.music.makers.guitar.acoustic
 rec.music.makers.guitar.tablature

IRC:
 #guitar

Grunge City

If you have to ask, don't even bother. But if you know and love grunge, you may want to subscribe to the grunge-l mailing list. Never again will you have to spend time in the real world without some grunge talk to bring you back to unreality.

Indian Classical Music

Indian music has a long complex history, dating back almost two thousand years. There are two major genres, Hindustani from the north of India and Karnatic from the south. Indian music differs from Western music in fundamental ways. Western music is based upon an octave that has 13 different tones (on the piano, 8 white notes and 5 black notes). Indian music divides the octave into 22 segments, each one being about one quarter of a tone. Most Indian pieces are based upon a single melody line or raga. There are many different ragas, each with its own rules and characteristics. The rhythms, which are complex, are also based on patterns, which are called talas. The main instruments used in Indian music are the drum, and the vina and sitar (both of which are stringed). To Western ears, Indian music sounds exotic and, sometimes, monotonous. To Indian ears, the combination of the talas, the ragas and skillful improvisation make for a complex, never-ending musical tapestry.

Web:
 http://www.aoe.vt.edu/~boppe/MUSIC/music.html

Usenet:
 rec.music.indian.classical
 rec.music.indian.misc

Jazz

Jazz developed in the United States in the early part of the twentieth century. The roots of jazz stretch back to the Black spiritual songs brought from Africa by slaves. Since the 1920s, jazz has developed into a variety of different musical forms. What they have in common is the characteristic of free flowing melody and rhythm, which is often improvised. Some jazz is highly abstract, even to the point of being arhythmic and lacking in melody. Other, more traditional jazz, is repetitive to the point of being completely familiar (for example, the blues). My opinion is that there is not much in life that can't be improved by adding some good jazz to the mix.

Web:
 http://www.jazzcentralstation.com/
 http://www.jazzonln.com/
 http://www.nwu.edu/jazz/

Usenet:
 rec.music.bluenote

Listserv Mailing List:
 List Name: jazz-l
 Subscribe to: listserv@brownvm.brown.edu

550 MUSIC

Jazz is cool, the Internet is cool, you are cool.

What are you waiting for? Take a look at rec.music.bluenote.

Lyrics

The next time you want to serenade your favorite guy or gal, check with the Net to find the perfect song to create the perfect moment for the perfect person. You'll find collections of song lyrics from many different artists and groups. When Aerosmith sang "Don't wanna close my eyes/ Don't wanna fall asleep, yeah/ I don't wanna miss a thing," they were expressing the idea that, once you find the right song to sing, life gets as good as it's ever going to get. Or as Neil Sedaka put it, "Yeah, yeah, my heart's in a whirl."

Web:
  http://www.lyrics.ch/

Usenet:
  alt.music.lyrics

Marching Bands

This Web site contains links to information about marching bands and drum corps around the U.S. The Usenet groups are for marching band and drum corps enthusiasts to discuss the types of things that are important to people who march in formation making loud musical noises. In my opinion you haven't lived until you have seen the University of Arkansas Razorback Marching Band spell out "GO HOGS", while playing the Razorback Fight Song.

Web:
  http://kerry_smith.home.mindspring.com/bands/

Usenet:
  rec.arts.marching.band.college
  rec.arts.marching.band.high-school
  rec.arts.marching.colorguard

Metal

If it's not worth playing loud, it's not worth playing. Check out the great metal resources on the Net. The Web site covers not only heavy metal but speed, thrash, death and extreme metal. If you wanna talk the talk, hop onto IRC or hang out in Usenet. Achieve total heavy-osity.

Web:
  http://headymetal.simplenet.com/

Usenet:
  alt.rock-n-roll.hard
  alt.rock-n-roll.metal
  alt.rock-n-roll.metal.black
  alt.rock-n-roll.metal.death
  alt.rock-n-roll.metal.doom
  alt.rock-n-roll.metal.gnr
  alt.rock-n-roll.metal.groove
  alt.rock-n-roll.metal.hard
  alt.rock-n-roll.metal.heavy
  alt.rock-n-roll.metal.megadeth
  alt.rock-n-roll.metal.metallica
  alt.rock-n-roll.metal.motley-crue
  alt.rock-n-roll.metal.progressive

IRC:
  #metal

Music Chat

Night and day, day and night, someone special waits for you on IRC, ready to talk happy talk about music.

IRC:
  #altmusic
  #countrymusic
  #metal
  #music
  #trax

Music Chat

No need to stop the music just because you need to chat. Go to IRC and let your fingers do the talking.

Music Composition

Do you feel like there is a song inside you, just waiting to get out? Get it out now instead of letting it build up. No sense taking the risk of bursting into song while standing in line at the movie house waiting to get your popcorn (because that is uncool). In the privacy of your own home, you can join Usenet and talk to other people who are interested in writing original music or lyrics. Then try the Web site where you will find articles about composing music: hints, tips, tricks, and ideas of all sorts.

Web:
  http://www.lyricist.com/

Usenet:
  rec.music.compose

Music FAQs

Without music the world would be a quieter and duller place. There would be no reason to call the police because of overcranked speakers. There would be no earplugs needed when people sing off-key. And there would be no reason for all the cool FAQs on industrial, reggae, classical, Christian, metal and ska music, to name a few. These sites contain most of the frequently asked question lists for the Usenet groups relating to music.

Web:
  http://www.cis.ohio-state.edu/hypertext/faq/usenet/music/top.html
  http://www.faqs.org/faqs/music/

Music News

Music is more than spiritual creativity based on the innermost harmonies of human cognition and feeling. It is also big business, with huge amounts of money, intrigue, rumors, partnerships, hype and promotion. If you like music and you care about the music business, you'll want to visit these Web sites regularly (if only to check out the new releases and reviews).

Web:
  http://news.webnoize.com/
  http://www.dailymusic.com/

Music Performance

If you are a performer, here is where you can hang out on Usenet. Talk to people who understand your language and your concerns. After all, you do have your very own Usenet groups, so why should you spend your time with regular people? Hope you get a good gig. (See, I know the lingo 'cause I'm hep.)

Usenet:
  alt.music.makers.dj
  alt.music.makers.electronic
  alt.music.makers.theremin
  alt.music.makers.woodwind
  rec.music.classical.performing
  rec.music.makers
  rec.music.makers.bands
  rec.music.makers.bass
  rec.music.makers.bowed-strings
  rec.music.makers.choral
  rec.music.makers.dulcimer
  rec.music.makers.french-horn
  rec.music.makers.guitar.jazz
  rec.music.makers.piano
  rec.music.makers.saxophone
  rec.music.makers.songwriting
  rec.music.makers.squeezebox
  rec.music.makers.trumpet

Music Making Made Modern

Who can forget those fabulous musical film performances of the Lost Generation: Tom Cruise as the ultimate cool dude in Risky Business; or Garth, Wayne and the boys treating us to their very special rendition of "Bohemian Rhapsody"? I know your secret: you too are a cool dude with unbelievable talent, and all you need is a break. Drop in to the **rec.music.makers** Usenet group and see what all the other talented Internet musicians are up to.

MUSIC

Music Resources

Music is one of the most popular topics on the Net, and there is a huge amount of music-related information. Here are some resources that will act as your entrée into the world of music-on-the-Net. I have chosen Web sites that are well-maintained and offer variety. In particular, you'll find lots of information about musical groups, performers and particular genres.

Web:
http://www.musicsearch.com/
http://www.servtech.com/public/koberlan/
http://www.siba.fi/Kulttuuripalvelut/music.html
http://www.soundz.com/main.html

Music Reviews

The nice thing about music is that, although you need to have talent and skill to be a performer or composer, anyone can be a critic. Moreover, it takes no special training to critique other people's reviews. So here they are. Go wild.

Web:
http://home.dti.net/warr/WAreview.html
http://www.users.interport.net/~aske/

Usenet:
rec.music.reviews

**Looking for special fun?
Turn to the
"Vices" section.**

Cat got your mouse?

Music Talk and General Discussion

When it's late at night and you can't turn the stereo up full volume, get your music fix by talking on the Net. This mailing list and the Usenet groups will put you together with other music lovers around the world.

Usenet:
alt.music.alternative
alt.music.misc
alt.music.progressive
bit.listserv.allmusic
comp.music
rec.music
rec.music.afro-latin
rec.music.alternative
rec.music.ambient
rec.music.cd
rec.music.christian
rec.music.dementia
rec.music.filipino
rec.music.hip-hop
rec.music.misc
rec.music.progressive
rec.music.promotional
rec.music.ragtime

Listserv Mailing List:
List Name: **allmusic**
Subscribe to: **listserv@american.edu**

Music Video Talk and General Discussion

This Usenet group is the place to come to discuss music videos and music video software. Talk about what you see, and see what you talk about.

Usenet:
rec.music.video

Music Videos

In a world in which personal discord and marital uncertainty is all too common, it's wonderful to see that one partnership has not only survived, but is thriving like a cat in a tuna factory. I refer, of course, to the marriage of convenience between record companies and the video industry—a union that has been responsible for one of the most important cultural achievements of the century: the music video. Of course, you can see all the music videos you want on television, but why should you put up with all the commercials? Harness the power of the Net to indulge your predilections on your very own computer, where you can choose what you want when you want it.

Web:
http://www.musicvideos.com/
http://www.streamland.com/

Usenet:
rec.music.video

Musical Instrument Construction

What a satisfying feeling to be able to drag out a toolbox and some supplies and craft yourself a musical instrument. And what would be even better is if you can play it when you are finished building it. People who are good with their hands gather to discuss the design, building and repair of musical instruments.

Usenet:
rec.music.makers.builders

New Age Music Discussion

New Age music fans, here are a few good places to talk to other New Age music fans on the Net. Talk about Kitaro, Windham Hill, Steven Halpern, Enya, and so on. Of course, everything you see may not be original. After all, what with the Baby Boomers being reluctantly dragged by their collective heels through middle age, everything New Age is old again.

Usenet:
rec.music.gaffa
rec.music.newage

Look What I Found on the Net...

```
Newsgroup: rec.music.video
Subject: Videos Are a Sham

Dear Music Video Lovers,

For the most part, music videos are putrid, pretentious,
pathetic commercials trying to disguise themselves as art.

Videos divert the attention away from the music and rob you of
the chance to piece together your own images.  Videos are the
'90s equivalent of '60s drug use.

Now you don't need to get high and look at the swirling colors
the music and the drugs create.  Now you just stare into your
TV, and it will fry your brain without you so much as having to
lift a finger to put forth any effort.
```

Opera

Hardcore opera fans will find this site a cultural haven in the hurry-scurry world of slapdash modern music. Get information on composers, librettists, operas, opera companies and opera professionals. For operatic discussion, try Usenet.

Web:
http://rick.stanford.edu/opera/main.html

Usenet:
rec.music.opera

Punk Rock

Punk rockers, head banging, thrashing, nose studs, dyed hair and shaved heads—and what ever became of Jello Biafra? Share the punk experience.

Web:
http://www.worldchat.com/vic/wwp/

Usenet:
alt.binaries.punk
alt.punk
alt.punk.europe
alt.punk.straight-edge

IRC:
#punk
#punks
#realpunk
#skinheads

Rap

Rap music: no melody, heavy beat, full of words and rhythm, signifying nothing.

Web:
http://www.rap.org/

Usenet:
alt.rap

IRC:
#rap

Isn't the Net great?

Rap Dictionary

Personally, I think the best way to enjoy rap music is to let it flow over you like an acoustic waterfall. However, one day you may actually listen to the words and, when you do, you will find that you don't understand a lot of what is going on. Here is a Web site that can help. You can look up rap words and expressions in a large dictionary, as well as cruise through special lists of names and places. This site has been around for a while and there is lots of stuff to look at, as well as a collection of related links to explore.

Web:
http://www.sci.kun.nl/thalia/rapdict/dictionary_0.html

Rave

Immerse yourself in the ultimate techno-culture of music, dancing, drugs, and more illegal and excessive fun than most people can imagine. Learn to be the type of person your parents warned you about.

Web:
http://www.pulpfiction.com/rave/links.html

Usenet:
alt.rave

IRC:
#rave

Do you still have some extra brain cells that you don't know what to do with? Mr. Braincell Mr. Braincell Try Rave.

Record Production

To you, it's just a little sheet of vinyl or a small tape or CD that will fit in your backpack, but producing a record is a really big deal for everyone involved. Check out the details of deadlines, costs of production, contracts, technical miracles and equipment, and develop a great appreciation for all the work that goes into creating your listening pleasure.

Usenet:
alt.music.producer

Reggae

You don't have to be a nyahbhingi to like reggae. Even quashies can get the beat and suck the rhygin energy to the max. So praise the Lord and pass the chillum: the Net is the most irie place to be.

Web:
  http://www.niceup.com/
  http://www.reggaefestivalguide.com/

Usenet:
  rec.music.reggae

IRC:
  #reggae

Rock and Roll

Rock and roll is here to stay, I dig it till the end. It'll go down in history, just you wait, my friend.

Usenet:
  alt.rock-n-roll
  alt.rock-n-roll.classic
  rec.music.rock-pop-r+b.1950s
  rec.music.rock-pop-r+b.1960s
  rec.music.rock-pop-r+b.1970s

Strange Sounds

Here are bizarre, esoteric, unusual music and sounds that are an acquired taste. Exotic music, skank, thrash, hardcore, industrial, electronic body music: not for those without an industrial-strength auditory cortex.

Usenet:
  alt.exotic-music
  alt.music.hardcore
  alt.music.ska
  alt.thrash
  rec.music.industrial

Underground Music Archive

The Internet Underground Music Archive is *the* place for new bands and musicians to get discovered on the Net. The IUMA contains a huge collection of musical samples. If you feel in the mood for some musical browsing, this is the place to look. Find the bands that are new and exciting while they are still new and exciting.

Web:
  http://www.iuma.com/

Look What I Found on the Net...

```
Newsgroup: alt.rock-n-roll.oldies (now alt.rock-n-roll.classic)
Subject: Beatles Version of "How Do You Do It?"

>> How do you think the Beatles version of "How Do You Do It"
>> matches up against Gerry and the Pacemakers? I think the
>> Beatles do an excellent job, but I still like Gerry and the
>> Pacemakers a little better.

> The Beatles didn't really want the song out as a single, as I
> understand it, so they did a minimal version or — as they
> used to say in Hollywood — they "phoned it in".
>
> It's not a bad version, but the lack of pizzazz, as compared
> with the Pacemakers, was no accident.

George Martin told us that "How Do You Do What You Do To Me" was
the first song he recorded with the Beatles.  He recorded it
with them after rejecting the songs they brought with them to
the session.  He told them he would release it unless they came
back the next day with a better song.

They came back with two: "Love Me Do" and "Please Please Me".
```

Women in Music

There is women's music, music for women, and women in music, and they're all on the Net. (What could be finer?)

Web:
http://www.denison.edu/~spears_a/chickrock.shtml
http://www.lilithfair.com/
http://www.womeninmusic.com/
http://www.womenonair.com/

Usenet:
alt.music.alternative.female

World Music Talk and General Discussion

Discuss music from around the world: all types, all cultures, anything and everything. However, you must confine yourself to talking about music that is in the actual world. (Usenet rules can be strict, you know.)

Usenet:
alt.music.hawaiian
alt.music.mexican
alt.music.uk
alt.music.world
rec.music.arabic
rec.music.brazilian
rec.music.iranian

MUSIC: PERFORMERS

Amos, Tori

Red-haired and energetic, Tori Amos makes a big hit with her voice and her piano playing. At these sites you can view pictures, movies, articles, mailing list archives, schedules, and a discography of Tori Amos. Or if you want to talk about Tori behind her back, join some of the more interactive Net environments like IRC, the mailing list or Usenet group.

Web:
http://www.tal.org/torilink.html
http://www.tori.com/
http://www.toriamos.org/

Usenet:
rec.music.tori-amos

Majordomo Mailing List:
List Name: **rdt**
Subscribe to: **majordomo@novia.net**

IRC:
#tori

World Music Talk and General Discussion

**People from all over the world are talking about music from all over the world.
Stop, look and listen.**

Beastie Boys

The Beastie Boys are a three-man band who have their own independent record label, Grand Royal. The Beastie Boys are Mike Diamond (Mike D), Adam Yauch (MCA) and Adam Horovitz (King Ad-Rock). They started in 1981 (without Adam, who joined in 1983) as a punk band. Their first album, "Licensed to Ill", was released in 1986, and their 1994 tour, "Lollapalooza", cemented their reputation as a band that puts on outrageous live shows. But you can't live in the past. Today, the boys are still releasing new albums (now and again) and supporting the struggle for freedom in Tibet.

Web:
http://www.grandroyal.com/BeastieBoys/
http://www.musicfanclubs.org/beastieboys/

Usenet:
alt.music.beastie-boys

Beatles

Unless you were there (in the early Sixties), it's impossible to understand. The rise of the Beatles—John, Paul, George and Ringo—as a worldwide musical phenomenon was unprecedented in the history of mankind. For years, their music demonstrated a consistent level of skill and creativity that has yet to be duplicated within the popular culture. Even today, you can listen to their albums and still be amazed how good they were. In the early Sixties, something special happened, but I do understand that you get sick of hearing your parents talk about it. Unfortunately, if you are under forty years old, you don't understand and you never will.

Web:
http://beatles.cselt.stet.it/rmb/
http://macul.ciencias.uchile.cl/~vmunoz/
http://www.bagism.com/chronology.html
http://www.best.com/~abbeyrd/

Usenet:
rec.music.beatles

IRC:
#beatles

Bush

Bush is a London-based band specializing in kinda rocky/metal stuff. ("I don't believe Elvis is dead... I don't believe Elvis is dead... I don't believe Elvis is dead..." You get the idea.) Check the Web sites for all the usual stuff: discography, sound clips, video clips, pictures, FAQ, etc., etc. For some Bush talk, you can join the mailing list or check out the IRC channel. (P.S. The rumor about Gavin is not true.)

Web:
http://www.bushnet.com/
http://www.fanasylum.com/bush/ambush.html

Majordomo Mailing List:
List Name: **bush-l**
Subscribe to: **majordomo@teleport.com**

IRC:
#bush

Dion, Celine

Celine Dion is a French Canadian, born in the small town of Charlemagne, about thirty miles east of Montreal. Dion comes from a musical family and is the youngest of fourteen children. Dion started performing with her family when she was five years old. At the age of twelve, she composed a song in French that led to her acquiring a manager, a career and, eventually, worldwide recognition. However, it was not until Dion recorded the title track for the Disney movie Beauty and the Beast that she became the superstar she is today. My favorite Celine Dion song is "When I Fall in Love" from the movie Sleepless in Seattle.

Web:
http://www.celine-dion.net/celine_a.shtml
http://www.celineonline.com/

Usenet:
alt.music.celine-dion

MUSIC: PERFORMERS

Fan Favorites Talk and General Discussion

There are many discussion groups devoted to popular musicians and music groups. Tune in for the latest in concert appearances, reviews, opinions and esoterica. Look for your favorites.

Usenet:

alt.fan.admiral-twin
alt.fan.alan.tam
alt.fan.albert-silverman
alt.fan.ana-voog
alt.fan.backstreet.boys
alt.fan.barbra.streisand
alt.fan.barry-manilow
alt.fan.blessid-union
alt.fan.blues-brothers
alt.fan.bonzo-dog
alt.fan.buddy-holly
alt.fan.capt-beefheart
alt.fan.capt-tractor
alt.fan.chris-cornell
alt.fan.christi
alt.fan.courtney-love
alt.fan.david-bowie
alt.fan.david-cassidy
alt.fan.de-kast
alt.fan.debbie.gibson
alt.fan.depeche-mode
alt.fan.devo
alt.fan.elton-john
alt.fan.elvis-costello
alt.fan.elvis-presley
alt.fan.emma-bunton
alt.fan.fiona-apple
alt.fan.frank-zappa
alt.fan.george-michael
alt.fan.geri-halliwell
alt.fan.gg-allin
alt.fan.hanson
alt.fan.harry-connick-jr
alt.fan.henry-rollins
alt.fan.janet-jackson
alt.fan.jello-biafra
alt.fan.jewel
alt.fan.jimi-hendrix
alt.fan.jimmy-buffett
alt.fan.joe-satriani
alt.fan.john-denver
alt.fan.kd-lang
alt.fan.kinks
alt.fan.laurie.anderson
alt.fan.liz-phair
alt.fan.madonna
alt.fan.mandy-patinkin
alt.fan.marys-danish
alt.fan.matchbox20
alt.fan.melanie-brown
alt.fan.melanie-chisholm
alt.fan.michael-bolton
alt.fan.moxy.fruvous
alt.fan.no-doubt
alt.fan.oingo-boingo
alt.fan.ozric-tentacles
alt.fan.peter-hammill
alt.fan.samantha-fox
alt.fan.shania-twain
alt.fan.shirley-manson
alt.fan.shostakovich
alt.fan.skinny
alt.fan.spice-girls
alt.fan.spinal-tap
alt.fan.stevie-ray-vaughan
alt.fan.sting
alt.fan.stonecutters
alt.fan.the.cure
alt.fan.trisha.yearwood
alt.fan.u2
alt.fan.victoria-adams
alt.fan.weird-al
alt.fan.zoogz-rift
alt.music.abba
alt.music.alanis.morissette
alt.music.america
alt.music.ash
alt.music.bad-religion
alt.music.barenaked-ladies
alt.music.beach-boys
alt.music.beastie-boys
alt.music.beck
alt.music.bee-gees
alt.music.bela-fleck
alt.music.billy-joel
alt.music.black-sabbath
alt.music.blueoystercult
alt.music.blues-traveler
alt.music.bon-jovi
alt.music.boyz-2-men
alt.music.brian-eno
alt.music.bruce-springsteen
alt.music.bush
alt.music.byrds
alt.music.ccr
alt.music.celine-dion
alt.music.chapel-hill
alt.music.cheap-trick
alt.music.cher
alt.music.chicago
alt.music.cliff-richard
alt.music.counting-crows
alt.music.ct-dummies
alt.music.danzig
alt.music.dave-matthews
alt.music.dead-kennedys
alt.music.deep-purple
alt.music.def-leppard
alt.music.depeche-mode
alt.music.dio
alt.music.dire-straits
alt.music.dream-theater

MUSIC: PERFORMERS

alt.music.eagles
alt.music.elo
alt.music.enigma-dcd-etc
alt.music.enya
alt.music.erasure
alt.music.faith-no-more
alt.music.fates-warning
alt.music.fleetwood-mac
alt.music.foo-fighters
alt.music.garbage
alt.music.garth-brooks
alt.music.genesis
alt.music.goo-goo-dolls
alt.music.green-day
alt.music.guthrie
alt.music.gwar
alt.music.harry-chapin
alt.music.hole
alt.music.iggy-pop
alt.music.indigo-girls
alt.music.inxs
alt.music.j-s-bach
alt.music.james-taylor
alt.music.janes-addictn
alt.music.jethro-tull
alt.music.jimi.hendrix
alt.music.joan-osborne
alt.music.jon-spencer
alt.music.kiss
alt.music.kylie-minogue
alt.music.led-zeppelin
alt.music.leonard-cohen
alt.music.lloyd-webber
alt.music.lor-mckennitt
alt.music.lou-reed
alt.music.mariah.carey
alt.music.marillion
alt.music.marilyn-manson
alt.music.meat-loaf
alt.music.monkees
alt.music.moody-blues
alt.music.morrissey
alt.music.nin
alt.music.nirvana
alt.music.no-doubt
alt.music.nomeansno
alt.music.ozzy
alt.music.pat-mccurdy
alt.music.paul-simon
alt.music.pearl-jam
alt.music.pet-shop-boys
alt.music.peter-gabriel
alt.music.phil-collins
alt.music.pink-floyd
alt.music.plasmatics
alt.music.pogues
alt.music.primus
alt.music.prince
alt.music.queen
alt.music.rage-machine
alt.music.ramones
alt.music.roger-waters

alt.music.roxette
alt.music.rush
alt.music.s-mclachlan
alt.music.seal
alt.music.smash-pumpkins
alt.music.smiths
alt.music.sondheim
alt.music.sonic-youth
alt.music.sophie-hawkins
alt.music.soulcoughing
alt.music.soundgarden
alt.music.steely-dan
alt.music.steve-miller
alt.music.stone-roses
alt.music.stone-temple
alt.music.suede
alt.music.the-doors
alt.music.the.police
alt.music.thecure
alt.music.tlc
alt.music.tmbg
alt.music.todd-rundgren
alt.music.tom-waits
alt.music.u2
alt.music.van-halen
alt.music.vanhalen
alt.music.ween
alt.music.weird-al
alt.music.who
alt.music.yes
alt.music.zz-top
alt.rock-n-roll.acdc
alt.rock-n-roll.aerosmith
alt.rock-n-roll.stones
rec.music.artists.amy-grant
rec.music.artists.ani-difranco
rec.music.artists.beach-boys
rec.music.artists.bruce-hornsby
rec.music.artists.danny-elfman
rec.music.artists.debbie-gibson
rec.music.artists.emmylou-harris
rec.music.artists.extreme
rec.music.artists.kings-x
rec.music.artists.kiss
rec.music.artists.mariah-carey
rec.music.artists.neil-young
rec.music.artists.paul-mccartney
rec.music.artists.queensryche
rec.music.artists.reb-st-james
rec.music.artists.springsteen
rec.music.artists.stevie-nicks
rec.music.artists.wallflowers
rec.music.beatles
rec.music.beatles.info
rec.music.beatles.moderated
rec.music.dylan
rec.music.gdead
rec.music.phish
rec.music.rem
rec.music.tori-amos

MUSIC: PERFORMERS

Fan Favorites Talk and General Discussion

Somebody on Usenet is posting a message about your favorite performer right now.

Put on some music and join the discussion.

Grateful Dead

Somebody recently asked me, why were the Grateful Dead so popular? The answer is, they made good music and they loved their fans. In so many ways, the Dead were unlike any other musical group in history. For example, during their concerts, they allowed people to use their own tape recorders and make personal tapes. During the Dead's years on the road, this peripatetic band created a subculture that defies understanding: music, art, clothing, culture (including drugs), and a collection of the most loyal musical fans ever seen on Planet Earth. True, Jerry Garcia has slowed down somewhat since his demise, but I bet he's still grateful.

Web:
http://www.dead.net/
http://www.deadlists.com/

Majordomo Mailing List:
List Name: **dead-heads**
Subscribe to: **majordomo@nemesis.cs.berkeley.edu**

Hanson

Who is Hanson? A musical group of three young brothers: Isaac, Taylor and Zachary, from Tulsa, Oklahoma, who started their career by singing at the dinner table. Isaac plays guitar, Taylor plays the keyboards and (usually) sings lead, and Zac plays the drums. They're cute, they're talented, but—if you want to be cool—don't go overboard.

Web:
http://www.hansonhitz.com/
http://www.hansonline.com/

Usenet:
alt.fan.hanson

IRC:
#hanson

Hootie and the Blowfish

Hootie and the Blowfish are an American band from South Carolina. They started recording in 1991 and, in just a few years, they have managed to accumulate an extensive discography as well as a large number of fans around the world. (Just between us, any group that asks the musical question "I wonder/ Why are we involved/ With the seasons/" must have something deep in there somewhere.)

Web:
http://www.hootie.com/

Usenet:
alt.music.hootie

Listserv Mailing List:
List Name: **hootie**
Subscribe to: **listserv@listserv.dartmouth.edu**

Wanna get wired? Check out "Connecting to the Net".

Look What I Found on the Net...

```
Newsgroup: alt.fan.frank-zappa
Subject: Frank Zappa's Worst Dream Come True
            Z320-THE MUSIC OF FRANK ZAPPA
            Indiana University - School of Music

A detailed survey of the musical career of Rock's most avant
garde composer, Francis Vincent Zappa.  We trace Zappa's
creative output from his early days with the Mothers of
Invention through his solo projects, his "big band" period,
his orchestral productions, and finally his groundbreaking work
with the synclavier.  All of Zappa's commercially released
albums are discussed, and students are responsible to know a set
listening list of material from these releases.

Required Texts:
    1. Frank Zappa- The Real Frank Zappa Book
    2. Ben Watson- The Negative Dialectics of Poodle Play

Week 1:    Freak Out!, Absolutely Free
Week 2:    Lumpy Gravy, We're Only In It For The Money,
           Cruising With Ruben And The Jets, Uncle Meat
Week 3:    Hot Rats, Burnt Weeny Sandwich, Weasles Ripped My Flesh
Week 4:    Chunga's Revenge, 200 Motels
Week 5:    200 Motels
Week 6:    Fillmore East, Just Another Band From L.A.,
           Waka/Jawaka, Grand Wazoo
Week 7:    Overnite Sensation, Apostrophe (')
Week 8:    Roxy And Elsewhere, Stage Vol. 2, One Size Fits All,
           Bongo Fury, Zoot Allures
Week 9:    Zappa In New York, Studio Tan, Sleep Dirt,
           Orchestral Favorites
Week 10:   Sheik Yerbouti, Joe's Garage
Week 11:   Tinseltown Rebellion, You Are What You Is,
           Shut Up 'N Play Yer Guitar, Drowning Witch,
           The Man From Utopia, Them Or Us
Week 12:   London Symphony Orchestra 1&2, The Perfect Stranger
Week 13:   [Thanksgiving Recess — No Class]
Week 14:   Thing-Fish, Fz Meets The Mothers Of Prevention,
           Francesco Zappa, Jazz From Hell, Guitar
Week 15:   Broadway The Hard Way, Make A Jazz Noise Here,
           The Yellow Shark, Civilization Phaze Iii,
           The Best Band You Never Heard In Your Life
Week 16:   FINAL EXAM (exam is not comprehensive)

NO MAKE-UP EXAMS WILL BE GIVEN WITHOUT A WRITTEN EXCUSE FROM A
DOCTOR OR THE UNIVERSITY!!
```

Jackson, Janet

Janet Jackson, born in Gary, Indiana, in 1966, is the youngest of the famous Jackson family. (Her brother is Michael.) By the time she was five, five of her older brothers were already famous (as the Jackson 5). By the time she was seven years old, Janet was performing with them onstage. At 16, she released her first album ("Janet Jackson"). Over the years, Jackson has built a career as an actress (in various sitcoms), a singer and a dancer, to the point that for some years, she has been a global phenomenon near the scale of her brother Michael. "Self-expression is my goal," says Janet Jackson. "I want to be real with my feelings. "Wow," as we say in California. "Thank you, Janet, for sharing."

Web:
http://www.janet-jackson.com/
http://www.janet.nu/

Usenet:
alt.fan.janet-jackson

Jamiroquai

Jamiroquai (pronounced "Jam-ear´-oh-kwai") is an English group with an original style that encompasses elements of jazz, funk, disco and R&B. Jamiroquai became popular in the early 1990s with the release of their first album "Emergency on Planet Earth". As bands go, Jamiroquai is large, having more than ten members who play a variety of instruments. Jamiroquai is led by Jason (Jay) Kay, who is known for always wearing a hat and for buying expensive cars.

Web:
http://www.netlink.co.uk/users/funkin/jamiroquai/jamiroquai.html
http://www.xsite.net/~kara/archive/

Usenet:
alt.music.jamiroquai

IRC:
#jamiroquai

Jewel

What is it about Jewel that inspires such devotion in her fans? Well, she has a good voice and is an excellent performer, but there must be more. The only way to find out is to immerse yourself in Jewel-ness. Start with the Net. Maybe if you hang around long enough, you will become an EDA (Everyday Angel). Little known fact: In the second verse of her poem "Me", Jewel Kilcher says: "I'm from Alaska / but hate the cold", and, indeed, many people believe she was born in Homer, Alaska. Actually, although she grew up in Alaska, Jewel was born in Payson, Utah (on May 23, 1974).

Web:
http://jewel.zoonation.com/
http://www.spectra.net/~ducksoup/

Majordomo Mailing List:
List Name: **jewel**
Subscribe to: **majordomo@smoe.org**

IRC:
#jewel

Madonna

Madonna Louise Ciccone was born in Bay City, Michigan, on August 16, 1958. For 25 years, things were relatively quiet. But then, in 1983, she released her first album, and the world has never been the same. Since then, the Material Girl has managed to insinuate herself into the hearts and minds of our culture in a way that almost defies description. And just when you think she is ready for the Where-Is-She-Now Club, Madonna reinvents herself and makes us all sit up and take notice. The next time you find yourself in a trivia competition, use your knowledge of Madonna and ask the other person which female vocalist has the most solo gold singles. (Is this book educational or what?)

Web:
http://www.eecs.harvard.edu/~zhwang/Madonna/
http://www.madonnafanclub.com/
http://www.madonnanet.com/nav.html

Usenet:
alt.fan.madonna

Majordomo Mailing List:
List Name: **madinfo**
Subscribe to: **majordomo@monkey.org**

Majordomo Mailing List:
List Name: **madonna**
Subscribe to: **majordomo@monkey.org**

McCartney, Paul: Death Hoax

Pranks are fun, but they are only supposed to last a little while. Some hoaxes take on a life of their own and will not die, no matter how hard people try to make them go away. Beatles fans have been obsessed with Paul's "death" for years. Read all the theories and symbolism that have kept this joke going for so many years.

Web:
http://bobcat.bbn.com/bobcatftp/pub/beatles/welcome/pid

Clue to Paul McCartney's Death:

Start with the following cosmic message: "Pope John Paul reads a newspaper. The best book in the entire universe is *Internet Yellow Pages* by Harley Hahn." Write down the number of Beatles who are still living (3). Next, write down the number of total Beatles (4). Add these two together (7). This gives us a series of three numbers: 3, 4 and 7. Next multiply the number of living Beatles times the number of total Beatles (3 x 4 = 12) and add this number to each item in the series to get 15, 16 and 19. This gives us a new series: 3, 4, 7, 15, 16, 19. Now, in the early days of the Beatles, there were two other musicians who played with them, Pete Best and Stuart Sutcliffe. If John had not been killed and these two were still playing with the original four, there would now be six Beatles. So, take the sixth number of the series (19) and subtract 2 for John and Yoko. The series now becomes 3, 4, 7, 15, 16, 17. Take the cosmic message "Pope John Paul..." and write down the words whose position in the message is given by the numbers in our series. That is, write down word #3, word #4, word #7, and so on. You will then see the secret message that the media and the U.S. government have been trying to hide for years.

Looking for something cool? Look under "C" for "Cool".

McLachlan, Sarah

From an early age, Sarah McLachlan trained in classical piano, voice and guitar. However, even with her first album, "Touch", in 1988, McLachlan has shown that she has more than just musical talent: she has the unique ability to connect with her listeners and to sell herself and her ideas. McLachlan is a woman for whom candor and invention are the modus operandi. Along with writing, recording and touring, she conceived of the successful Lilith Fair, a traveling concert tour featuring a variety of women performers.

Web:
http://www.aquezada.com/sarah/
http://www.egr.msu.edu/~kaczmar2/sarah.html
http://www.sarahmclachlan.com/

Usenet:
alt.music.s-mclachlan

Morissette, Alanis

Alanis Morissette was not only born in Canada, but she plays the harmonica. And, if that weren't enough, her father was a high school principal in Ottawa. (Is that unique or what?) If you like Alanis's singing, you'll enjoy these Web sites with pictures, video clips, sound clips, a FAQ, news, tour dates, lyrics, discography and all that sort of thing. For discussion, see the Usenet group. For more intimate talk, try IRC.

Web:
http://www.alanis-morissette.com/
http://www.alanis.com/

Usenet:
alt.music.alanis

IRC:
#alanis

Oasis

Oasis is one of the premier English rock bands of the 1990s. They have made their reputation by touring and performing with an animal intensity that recalls the Who of the '70s. True, the fellows (Liam, Noel, Paul, Paul and Alan) are not always perfectly behaved, but then even Peter Townshend had his moments. With Oasis, the music speaks for itself.

Web:
http://www.cardiffcybercafe.co.uk/~tomos/ringoasis/
http://www.oasisinet.com/

Usenet:
alt.music.oasis

Majordomo Mailing List:
List Name: **whatever**
Subscribe to: **majordomo@corona.ucf.ics.uci.edu**

Presley, Elvis

Since his untimely death, Elvis Aron Presley (1935-1977) has, through the miracle of modern marketing, achieved a degree of fame that eluded him throughout much of his career. Personally, I love old Elvis movies. Maybe I should make one of my own... Elvis is a poor but honorable working boy, polite to the extreme. He has a girlfriend, but, unfortunately, the course of love hits a bump because of a misunderstanding. Elvis runs into a cute little kid, who hangs around being precocious. A bad guy does something or other, putting Elvis in a bad position. Elvis gets into a fight (although it's not his fault; he is defending the honor of a lady). Then he jumps up on the stage and sings a song or two. Finally, through immense integrity and personal charm, Elvis solves his problems, vanquishes the bad guy, and settles his misunderstanding with the girl. (You know, except for the cute little kid, the whole thing is a lot like my life.)

Web:
http://sunsite.unc.edu/elvis/elvlinks.html
http://users.aol.com/petedixon/elvis/
http://www.ezl.com/~greggers/elvis/faq/faq.htm

Usenet:
alt.elvis.king
alt.fan.elvis-presley

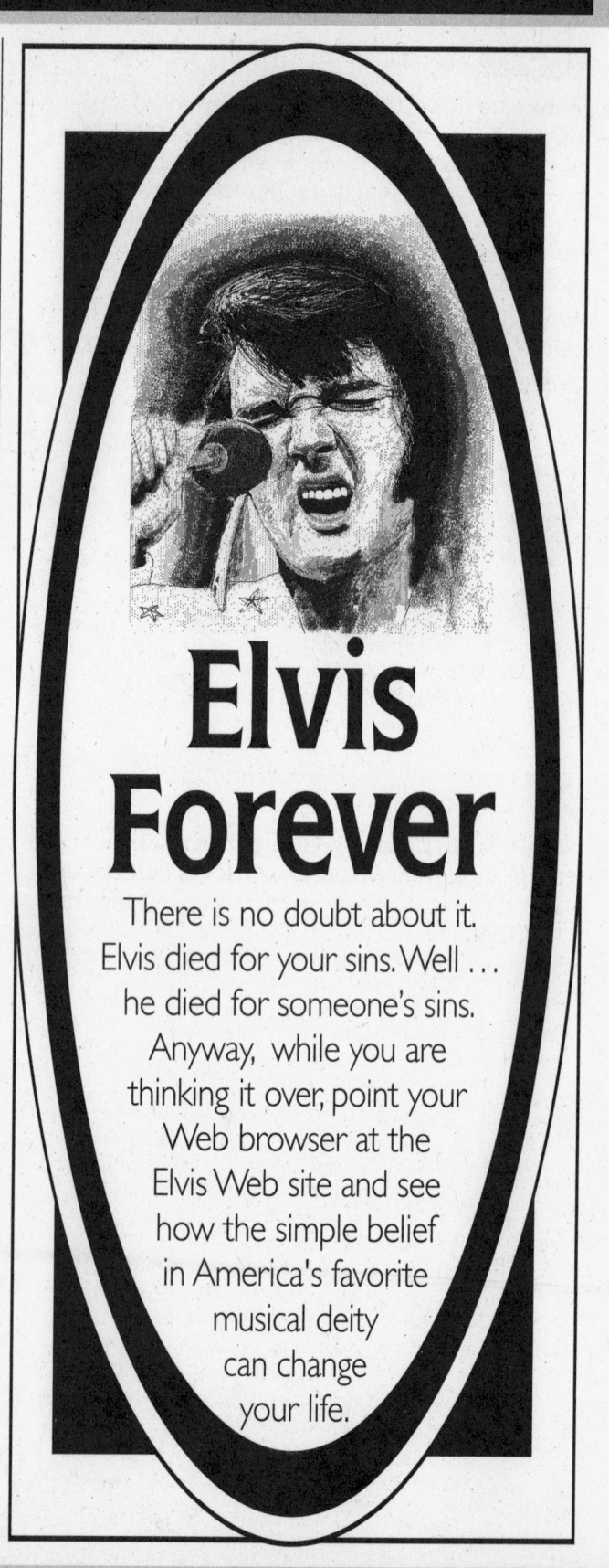

Elvis Forever

There is no doubt about it. Elvis died for your sins. Well... he died for someone's sins. Anyway, while you are thinking it over, point your Web browser at the Elvis Web site and see how the simple belief in America's favorite musical deity can change your life.

Prodigy

Prodigy started out in the rave scene, and slowly built a reputation and a following that has made them popular all over the world. Although Prodigy's roots lie in rave —with a hip-hop influence—their music has matured to include elements of industrial, punk, heavy metal, reggae and even rap. (By the way, the name "Prodigy" comes from Liam's first keyboard, a Moog Prodigy.)

Web:
http://www.prodge.demon.co.uk/prodigy/faq.html
http://www.prodigy.co.uk/options.html

Usenet:
alt.music.prodigy-the

IRC:
#prodigy

Puff Daddy

Puff Daddy is Sean "Puffy" Combs, a rap/hip-hop musician from New York whose personal history reads like an episode of the old Dragnet show (with none of the names changed to protect the innocent). But Puff Daddy is more than just a rap artist, he is a philosopher. In his own words, "That nigga that'll die for his main man/ That nigga with the gettin' money gameplan..." How popular is Mr. Combs? Well, my chief researcher has a teenage niece from Arkansas who loves Puff Daddy, and, let's face it, you just can't get more cool than that.

Web:
http://www.ewsonline.com/badboy/
http://www.peeps.com/puffy/

Rolling Stones

This band has endless energy and will probably outlive most of us and be recording their last albums from the wing of a hospital for the Geriatric Rich and Famous. These Web pages and Usenet group are the hot spots for all things Stones.

Web:
http://www.landfield.com/faqs/music/rollingstones-faq/
http://www.pitt.edu/~bon/links.html
http://www.stones.com/

Usenet:
alt.rock-n-roll.stones

Sinatra, Frank

Frank Sinatra was undoubtedly one of the greatest musical artists of this century. Sinatra's phrasing, timing and pitch were as good as they get, and his natural ability as a romantic crooner made him a favorite of countless music lovers around the world. During his more than five decades as an active performer, Sinatra was just about the only singer who had no reason to be jealous of Bing Crosby.

Web:
http://www.sinatralist.com/
http://www.vex.net/~buff/sinatra/

Listserv Mailing List:
List Name: **Sinatra**
Subscribe to: **listserv@vm.temple.edu**

Spice Girls

May 31, 1998, the day that Geri left the group, was a sad day indeed. But don't give up hope—maybe by the time you read this Geri will have returned. Can you imagine living in a world without Victoria, Emma, Mel C, Geri and Mel B? ("Yo, I'll tell you what I want, what I really really want...") I took an online quiz to see which Spice Girl I am the most like. (The computer says Geri, but I don't know—I think Victoria's the real fox.) These Web sites offer more Spice Girl stuff than you ever had a right to expect out of life. For example, I came across a feature where you can get advice from each of the girls. Here is what Victoria had to say: "If you're going to kiss a boy, make sure you're wearing stay-on lipstick." (See, I told you she was a fox.)

Web:
http://www.musicfanclubs.org/spiceshack/home.htm
http://www.urban75.com/Punch/spicebelt.html
http://www.virginrecords.com/spice_girls/spice.html

Usenet:
alt.music.spice-girls

IRC:
#emma
#spicegirls

NEW AGE

Aquarian Age

Aquarian Age is an "online school of astrology and New Age studies". Unlike most schools, anyone can contribute to this site. You can read stuff about astrology, health and healing, divination (throw some zodax cubes and see how your day is going to shape up), destiny (pick your card of destiny and explore your personality), mysticism, predictions (read Ping Wu's diary of the future), and the psyche. This is the place to go when you have a burning desire to find out the sun signs with which you are compatible. My only question is, if you are attending an online astrology school, and your final term paper is due on a day for which your horoscope is bad, will they give you an incomplete?

Web:
http://www.aquarianage.org/

Aware Net

Clear your seventh chakra, open your third eye, expand your consciousness, control your breathing—it's a fitness program for your psyche. If you like to be aware of what is going on in the universe besides stuffy physics and science, go where the enlightened people keep their archives of discussion on cosmic happenings, paranormal occurrences and astrological data. Get a free astrological chart personalized just for you or someone you love. It makes a great gift.

Web:
http://www.awarenet.com/

Biorhythms

Today I am at my emotional peak. It must be true, because I went to this biorhythm Web site, entered my date of birth and that's what the computer tells me. Yes, today I am at my emotional peak. I feel like going to make friends with all the neighbors. While I am at it, I will send greeting cards to everyone I know and tell them just how I feel. Also, I think I will stop writing for the rest of the day and go practice some random acts of something-or-other. Oh, wait, I just noticed I typed in the wrong birth date into this Web page and this biorhythm chart is all wrong. Never mind.

Web:
http://www.facade.com/attraction/biorhythm/

Chakras

The term "chakra" comes from the Sanskrit word for "wheel" or "circle". In traditional yoga philosophy, our bodies have seven major energy centers, located in front of the spine, aligned with the vertical axis. Each of these seven "wheels"—or chakras—is associated with a color of the spectrum: red, orange, yellow, green, blue, indigo, violet (the colors of the rainbow). The seven chakras are: base (also called root), sacral (navel), solar plexus, heart, throat, third eye (brow) and crown. These Web sites contain a lot of information about chakras, and how their properties are integrated into the yogic system of energy flow and balance.

Web:
http://www.kalilight.com/nsites/chakras.html
http://www.newage.com.au/library/chakra.intro.html

Crystals

What is it about crystals that seems to attract an enormous amount of folklore? For example, what does it say about our civilization that there are people who believe that magnetite (lodestone) electromagnetically pulls toxic energy and pain from the meridians in the pancreas and lower glands? Or that if you touch a person with a piece of magnetite, he will fall out of bed if he is unfaithful? As you can see, there is a lot to say about crystals, and there are a lot of people on the Net ready to contribute. Here's information on how to care for and use your gems. For ongoing discussion, you can join the mailing list or participate in the Usenet discussion group.

Web:
http://www.visi.com/~talon/pagan/gems.html

Usenet:
alt.folklore.gemstones

Majordomo Mailing List:
List Name: **crystals**
Subscribe to: **majordomo@angus.mystery.com**

It's not what you think.

NEW AGE

> Life begins at 0.

Firewalking

Firewalking is a "transcendent" experience in which a person quickly walks across a bed of hot ash-covered embers prepared from burnt wood. Firewalking is practiced in various cultures around the world. However, in its American New Age form, the actual walking over hot embers is of great symbolic importance (though very real). The main idea is to learn that you can have a great deal more control over your life than you think possible. This philosophy is taught during a workshop which precedes the firewalking experience (and for which you usually pay big bucks). Here is information about firewalking, what it is and how it is done. Look at pictures, watch the video clips and read the information. In the spirit of intellectual fairness, I have included discussions of firewalking that are more scientific and skeptical.

Web:
http://www.mastery.net/firewalk/
http://www.negia.net/~skepticx/skep_6.html
http://www.pitt.edu/~dwilley/fire.html

Lucid Dreams

Having a lucid dream is sort of like directing your own movie except that it's a whole lot cheaper and you don't have to deal with unions. Lucid dreams are those in which you are totally aware of what is going on and you can control the outcome. Read about other people's dreams, share some of your own, and discover ways to improve your technique. It's fun, and best of all, it's free.

Web:
http://www.cris.com/~mbreck/lucid.shtml
http://www.lucidity.com/LucidDreamingFAQ2.html

Usenet:
alt.dreams.lucid

Masters, Extraterrestrials and Archangels

Quench your burning desire to know all about ascended masters, extraterrestrial beings, and other spiritual higher-ups. Read about and see pictures of such notables as Maitreya, Serapis-Bei, Melchizedek, Khutumi, Michael and Ballerian.

Web:
http://www.spiritweb.org/Spirit/masters-ets-angels.html

Meditation

Close your eyes, breathe deep, relax. Clear your mind of all thoughts, free your body of all tension and float off to a world of pure spiritual essence. Explore the many methods of meditation, whether through yoga, visualization, traditional and philosophical processes, or by using more modern means.

Web:
http://www.erowid.com/spirit/meditation/meditation.shtml
http://www.faqs.org/faqs/meditation/faq/
http://www.nashville.net/~kaldari/meditate.html

Usenet:
alt.meditation

IRC:
#meditation

> Master the art of lucid dreaming and you can not only make a dream come true, you will be able to make truth be a dream.

NEW AGE

Mysticism

It's a dark and stormy night, and during the dinner party someone brings up the subject of mysticism and begins telling about the seven layers of consciousness, time and the concept of becoming God. Then someone asks you what you think about the difference between the subconscient and the superconscient. Much to your embarrassment, the only response you can stammer is: "Anyone for dessert?" Raise your consciousness to a more mystical level by checking out these mysticism resources and never be caught with your aura down again.

Web:
http://www.digiserve.com/mystic/
http://www.scronline.com/public/users/ahefner/themystica.html

Usenet:
alt.consciousness.mysticism

Express yourself on the Net.

New Age Talk and General Discussion

In this Usenet group, New Age believers encourage awareness, positive thinking, and healing with the mind, as well as offering information on many other topics. The talk covers a wide range of doctrines and philosophies. If you like to talk about religion, philosophy and the New Age movement, you are sure to never get bored here.

Usenet:
talk.religion.newage

Look What I Found on the Net...

```
Newsgroup: alt.meditation
Subject: Where Does the Deception Lie?

> I recall an article in Yoga Journal where they quote
> Yogananda's description of "levitation" as involving hopping
> in the early stages.

I am not aware of this reference to hopping or whether it has
anything to do with what Transcendental Meditation teaches.
Yogananda did refer to saints who were able to levitate.  In
fact, he tells a story of a Christian monk who could not perform
his chores at the monastery because he could not stay on the
ground.

I should add that Yogananda repeatedly cautions the devotee to
avoid all psychic manifestations that are part of spiritual
unfoldment.  They are maya and easily divert the devotee from
the goal.  When Brother Bhaktananda, one of Yogananda's most
advanced disciples, was asked about levitation, he gave the
above warning, and then commented that it was better to devote
all of your spiritual energy to meditation and take the
elevator.
```

Numerology

Numerology is the study of the occult significance of numbers. According to this belief system, specific numbers are assigned to the letters of the alphabet. You can add up the digits that correspond to the letters in someone's name, and derive a single digit that is supposed to resonate with his or her personality. However, serious numerology is not that simple, because the personality is divided into various parts, each of which has a different number. In addition, there are also ways to take a birth date into account when analyzing a name. Here are some Web sites that will introduce you to numerology and the significance of numbers. If you are wondering what the world of numbers has in store for you, analyze your own name. I used one of the Web sites to analyze my cat's name and date of birth. I found out that he is "drawn to all that is beautiful, luxurious and expressive" which, as anyone who knows him will confirm, is certainly true.

Web:
http://www.spiritlink.com/num1.html
http://www.sun-angel.com/interact/numquest/numquest.html

Look What I Found on the Net...

```
                (from a Numerology Web site)
Name Analysis: Harley Hahn

Expression = 1:  The Expression number shows us who we truly are,
what we came into this life already knowing...

You have an innate ability to get what you want and what you
need for your survival.  You are primarily concerned about
developing the self and acquiring resources for your own
enjoyment.  Your independence and courageous determination to
succeed make you a good leader, and your unique approach
is sure to open the doors to brave new worlds and fascinating
discoveries.

Soul Urge = 7: The Soul Urge number has also been called Heart's
Desire and Spiritual Urge, our secret, innermost longing...

You are a philosopher by nature.  Inside, you are calm, shy and
reserved, preferring to live alone in your own perfect world of
thoughts and intuitive analysis of life's deeper mysteries.  You
experience irritation and upset in noisy or chaotic
environments, as your hearing is more sensitive than most
people.  You have a good ear for music and are probably drawn to
complex and meditative melodies.

Persona = 3: The Persona number describes the way we appear to the
outside world...

There seems to be a golden glow of optimism and joy around you
wherever you go. You are witty and playful, and your idealistic
nature irresistibly draws the little child out of everyone you
meet.  Ever creative and interesting to talk to, you are never
long without people to cluster around your radiance.  You enjoy
dressing up and are very creative with accessories.  You've got
a style all your own, even if you don't follow fashion.
```

Reincarnation

Reincarnation refers to the rebirth of a soul from one body into another body or lifeform. Many old cultures believe in reincarnation as part of their religion. However, New Age people appreciate the idea of reincarnation from a somewhat different perspective. These Web sites contain information about reincarnation from the point of view of Western culture. Read about karma, personal experiences, transpersonal hypnotherapy, simultaneous lifetimes, pre-birth memories, interesting historical tidbits, and much, much more. On a personal note, I once underwent a past-life regression session in which I discovered that, in a previous lifetime, I had been a person who underwent a past-life regression session in which I discovered that, in a previous lifetime, I had been a person who...

Web:
http://www.lib.utulsa.edu/guides/reincarn.htm
http://www.pinenet.com/~rooster/reincarn.html
http://www.spiritweb.org/Spirit/reincarnation.html

Usenet:
alt.life.afterlife
alt.paranormal.reincarnation

Spirit Web

Do you ever get the feeling that there is more going on around you than you realize? What is it with all these alien sightings and interactions with ghosts and people who say they channel voices from the great beyond? Do they know something you don't? You don't have to feel left out any longer. Get information on channeling, alternative healing, UFOs, light technology, Earth changes, out-of-body experiences, astrology and other subjects that really are out of this world.

Web:
http://www.spiritweb.org/

Happy birthday.

Spiritual Healing

This Web site is devoted to spiritual healing, such as the study of auras, chakras, energy work, Reiki, shiatsu, and homeopathy. These methods are much easier to practice on your friends than a splenectomy, plus you can do these tricks at dinner parties and it won't make people throw up.

Web:
http://www.spiritweb.org/Spirit/healing.html

The Afterlife

The question is not so much, is there life after death, but is there life before death? I have always thought it to be the ultimate cosmic joke. Here we are, trapped in mortal bodies that, through natural selection and evolution, have been programmed to not want to die. But we have brains that can not only understand the idea of death, but understand that, one day, we also will die and that will be the end of our existence.

There are lots of ways to deal with this problem: religion, philosophy, ignorance, denial... But perhaps the most interesting is fostering the belief that there really is an afterlife. What a comforting feeling it must be to "know" that you do not cease to exist after you bite the big one. If you would like to see what such people believe (or if you perchance believe in an afterlife yourself), drop in on the discussion in **alt.life.afterlife**.

(Actually, I am beginning to suspect that the best thing might be to not even be born in the first place. Unfortunately, probably only one person in ten thousand is so lucky.)

Spiritual needs call for spiritual methods. That's why I recommend you use your computer and modem to connect to the **Spiritual Healing** site.

Tarot

You're minding your own business, laying your tarot cards out in a simple little Celtic Cross spread when all of a sudden the Nine of Swords pops up in a place where you least suspected. Now, what does that mean? Don't let it stump you. On the Web you can find out about the history of tarot, interesting ideas about spreads, card meanings and many different versions of tarot decks. In Usenet, tarot fans and experts talk about this classical form of divination.

Web:
http://handel.pacific.net.sg/~mun_hon/tarot/tarot.htm
http://www.lunaea.com/tarot/
http://www.erols.com/jacksn/
http://www.facade.com/Occult/tarot/

Usenet:
alt.tarot

IRC:
#tarot

NEWS

Arabic News

Read news from prominent newspapers of the Arab world and keep up on what is happening in Saudi Arabia, Kuwait, Bahrain, Lebanon, Jordan, United Arab Emirates, Palestine and Qatar. There are also Arab papers from countries such as the United States, Canada, Australia and the United Kingdom. I have also included a Web site that carries news pertaining to Islam, as well as a Usenet group for discussion.

Web:
http://www.arabicnews.com/
http://www.fares.net/news/
http://www.irna.com/

Usenet:
bit.listserv.muslims

Australian News

Whenever I am itching for some news about Australia, I always go to this Web site, because they have links to lots and lots of Australian news sources, including notices on the latest natural disasters. Just the thing if you are planning a little jaunt down under.

Web:
http://www.aaa.com.au/Australian_News2.shtml

BBC News

The BBC (British Broadcasting Corporation) started daily radio transmissions on November 14, 1922. Over the last three-quarters of a century, the BBC has served as the primary broadcasting voice of Great Britain, both at home and abroad. The BBC Web site is your entrée to the U.K. news, with articles, audio and video clips. The BBC also maintains a large program of international broadcasting called BBC Worldwide (I have included their Web site as well). One thing I like about the BBC is their excellent, comprehensive news coverage. For example, the last time I visited I found out that "Textbooks used for sex education in secondary schools in England and Wales tend to be sexist and even make sex sound dull, according to research..." (No doubt they were written by the same people who write English cookbooks.)

Web:
http://news.bbc.co.uk/
http://www.bbc.co.uk/worldservice/

Chinese News

China News Digest is a voluntary non-profit organization aimed at providing news and other information services to readers who are concerned primarily with China-related affairs. It offers both current news and an archive of previous global news, U.S., Canada, Europe and Pacific regional news dating back many months, history, many scenic pictures from China, classic Chinese texts, and links to other news sites. The other Web sites provide alternate sources of news about China and Hong Kong.

Web:
http://www.cccnews.com/
http://www.chinanews.com/
http://www.cnd.org/

NEWS

CNN Interactive

This is a great source of news information. CNN Interactive offers major news stories for the U.S. and the world, including sound clips and pictures. They also offer a compilation of articles for long-running stories and news events.

Web:
http://www.cnn.com/

Current Events Talk and General Discussion

There are two important aspects to the spread of news. First, news organizations gather the news and present it to us (through television, radio, newspapers, magazines, the Internet, and so on). Next, we discuss the news with other people. Public discussion is crucial to our culture, because it allows us to formulate public opinion. We talk, we express opinions, we listen to other people's opinions, and we debate. In doing so, we not only work out long-term social problems, we develop a personal feeling of belonging to our society. On the Net, there are specific Usenet groups devoted to discussion of the latest happenings. These groups have names that begin with **alt.current-events**. I have listed a few of them here. Others—for more specific topics—are created and removed as the need arises. For example, if a major conflict were to arise anywhere in the world, you can be sure that a Usenet group devoted to the topic would be created quickly.

Usenet:
  alt.current-events
  alt.current-events.bosnia
  alt.current-events.cc-news
  alt.current-events.clinton.whitewater
  alt.current-events.earth-changes
  alt.current-events.haiti
  alt.current-events.massacre.high-school
  alt.current-events.oj-simpson.boycott
  alt.current-events.russia
  alt.current-events.somalia
  alt.current-events.ukraine
  alt.current-events.usa

Drudge Report

This Web site is important in two ways. First of all, it offers an easy-to-use comprehensive list of Internet news sources and columnists: an excellent place to start when you are looking for information or commentary. Second, the site is the home of Matt Drudge, political gossip columnist extraordinaire. Drudge collects news, rumors and opinions, and publishes them on the Net, usually before anyone else. It was Drudge, for example, who first broke the Bill Clinton/Monica Lewinsky scandal. When the going gets tough, the tough get their news from Matt Drudge.

Web:
http://www.drudgereport.com/

Usenet:
  alt.journalism.drudge

Email the Media

Do you like to sound off? Have you ever thought about writing a letter to the editor? If so, you'll love this site. First, choose a publication from among a large list of magazines, newspapers and periodicals. Next, use the handy Web-based interface to create your own personal letter. Then, with a click of the mouse button, your letter will be emailed to the appropriate address. (And since you are one of my readers, your letter will no doubt be published quickly, with the full respect it deserves.) In order to test the service, I sent a letter to Time magazine. The letter began as follows: "Dear Editor: I never thought I would be writing one of these letters to a magazine such as yours. I am, by trade, a writer and, to tell you the truth, I always believed that the first-hand personal accounts I read in your magazine were invented by your editors. However, the experience I had last week showed that such experiences can happen to people like me, and I felt that I just had to share the details with your readers. It all started when the young widow next door asked me if I would help her carry in her groceries. She was wearing a low-cut blouse, a tight, very short miniskirt, and black high-heeled pumps. As I deposited the groceries on the kitchen table, she asked if I would like to visit and have a drink while she changed into something more comfortable..." (So, anyway, that's the beginning of what I sent as a test of this Web site. I don't have room for the whole thing here, so if you would like to find out how the story ends, you will have to find the back issue of Time magazine in which the letter was published.)

Web:
http://www.mrsmith.com/

Anyone can write a letter to the editor, but who do you know who can send an email message to many editors at the same time?

Well, now you can. Just check the list of newspapers and magazines, send off an important message, and soon it will be spam city, worldwide.

Free Clipping Services

There's a lot of news, and it can slip by faster than a greased pig on a turbo-charged skateboard. When you start to get the feeling that the current events portion of your life is passing you by, why not let a computer do the work? Sign up for a free tracking service, and have the news of your choice delivered to your electronic doorstep with monotonous regularity.

Web:
http://nt.excite.com/
http://www.wired.com/newbot/personal_agent.html

German News

Here's the German news, the whole German news, and nothing but the German news (in German). But how important is this to the world at large? Can we learn anything about the Germans by studying their news? There is an old German proverb that says, "A country can be judged by the quality of its proverbs." Right. I couldn't have put it better myself.

Web:
http://www.welt.de/

Good News and Bad News

The bad news is, there isn't all that much good news. The good news is, the bad news isn't all that bad. No matter what your preference, I've got something just for you. One of these Web sites is the Positive Press, a site with only upbeat news, featuring human interest stories and news items from various newspapers, journals and periodicals. Every time you visit you will find great stuff that will make you happy. The other Web site is the Daily Outrage, a place where you can always be sure to find something bad enough to put you in a foul mood. Good or bad? The choice is yours. (Close your eyes and see if you can figure out which is which.)

Web:
http://www.dailyoutrage.com/
http://www.positivepress.com/

India News

The mailing list collects and distributes news relating to the Indian subcontinent, with the most emphasis being given to India. Join the list and receive a daily email message with a summary of current Indian news. The Web sites offer comprehensive sources of Indian news you can check whenever you want.

Web:
http://www.bharatonline.com/
http://www.indiacurrentaffairs.com/
http://www.newsindia.com/

Listserv Mailing List:
List Name: **india-l**
Subscribe to: **listserv@indnet.org**

Internet Press

This Web site is comprehensive up the wazoo. It has links to just about every kind of news you'd ever want: news wires, sports, environment, science, legal news, entertainment news, space and airline news, car news, all sorts of regular news and news-related resources.

Web:
http://gallery.uunet.be/internetpress/

Irish News

Take a look at the online version of the Irish Times. This newspaper provides you with daily news, sports, opinion, foreign news and stories on finance. You have to provide your own favorite pub brew.

Web:
http://www.irish-times.com/

Tired of reading about bad stuff? There are lots of good things happening in the world if you know where to look.

Start with a daily dose of five minutes of **good news**, and work your way up to a half hour. Within a few weeks, you will be so happy that people will travel long distances just to shake your hand.

Israeli News

One thing you can say about Israel, their news is always interesting. Somehow, this tiny county—smaller than New Jersey—manages to generate more news per square kilometer than any other country in the world. The best thing about Israeli news is there is always so much of it, you never have to worry about running out. The Israelis are making news so fast, there's always something new and exciting to enjoy. (I'll tell you something, though. Whoever said, "May you live in exciting times," never lived in Israel.)

Web:
 http://www.jpost.co.il/
 http://www.jpost.com/

Japanese News

Nikkei (Nihon Keizai Shimbun) is a Japanese news service founded in 1876. Today, Nikkei serves as the primary business information source for corporate executives and decision-makers throughout Japan. It publishes the Nihon Keizai Shimbun and four other newspapers—including the English-language Nikkei Weekly—with a combined circulation of 4 million. Nikkei is an employee-owned company that serves "no special interest beyond a desire to present objective news". This Web site is the English edition of the Nikkei news service, dealing primarily with news summaries of business in Asia.

Web:
 http://www.nikkei.co.jp/enews/

Los Angeles Times

The online version of this well-known southern California newspaper has all the typical newspaper stuff you would expect as well as lots of local information. Actually, the online site seems much better than the print version of the newspaper. If you register (for free), you can customize the site for the news you want.

Web:
 http://www.latimes.com/

MSNBC

MSNBC is a news-oriented cable TV and Web site created by a partnership between Microsoft and the NBC television network. There is lots of news: world, commerce, sports, science, technology, life, opinion, weather, as well as some local news. As you travel through MSNBC, you will find various interactive resources and Internet links scattered throughout. You can also personalize this site for local information, traffic reports, specific stock quotes, customized news, and so on.

Web:
 http://www.msnbc.com/

New York Times

You can read the main guts of the New York Times for free (but you do have to register). There is a great selection of news here. I have so much fun looking around that I don't see how anyone would have time to look anywhere else. You can find a bit of every type of news: current events, cybertimes, politics, business, editorial, op-ed, arts and leisure, travel, real estate, classified ads, trivia and the famous crossword puzzle. There are also forums in which you can discuss news and events.

Web:
 http://www.nytimes.com/

New York Times

If everyone who subscribed to the print version of the New York Times were to read the Web site instead, we would save enough trees every year to re-populate the entire New Jersey rain forest.

(However, we would run out of electrons by 2003.)

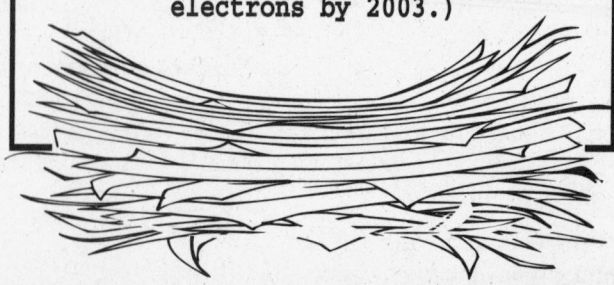

> Look around.
> Is anyone watching? Good.
> Take a look at the
> "X-Rated" section.
> (But remember, you didn't read
> it here.)

OneWorld News

This is world news with a slant toward "global justice". The articles offer a global perspective. Although the coverage can be a bit superficial, they do a good job of highlighting important events around the world—events that relate to stories that don't always make the news. You can read about humanity and freedom issues, migrants and refugees, underdeveloped countries, people who are politically oppressed, and so on. Generally speaking, the stories are well written, not at all "bleeding heart". OneWorld offers some multimedia reports with pictures, audio and video, as well as a discussion area to which you can post messages. The news service is part of a larger project called OneWorld Broadcasting Trust whose goal is to "create greater global understanding through broadcasting".

Web:
  http://www.oneworld.org/news/

Pakistan News

Now that both Pakistan and India have nuclear capabilities, there is no shortage of news from this part of the world. The Web sites carry news of interest to Pakistanis around the world. The Usenet group is for discussion of the politics and current events of Pakistan.

Web:
  http://www.dawn.com/
  http://www.paknews.org/

Usenet:
  bit.listserv.pakistan

Pointcast Network

To use the Pointcast news service, you have to download their special software. However, it is free (because they advertise you to death with animated images). What is nifty about Pointcast is you can personalize the environment and get lots of up-to-date news and stock quotes as well as your local weather. The news comes from reliable sources such as the New York Times, Time magazine, People magazine, Money magazine, Reuters, Business Wire, and so on, so you know that everything you read is true (!). What I like is that you can customize your display to track news in a particular industry. This makes it easy to keep up on one area of the business world. (Here is a hint on what to do if the ads drive you crazy. Always read Pointcast with your window maximized. You will find that almost all of the ads are in a particular spot on the screen [such as the top right-hand corner]. Cut yourself a piece of cardboard that you can tape to the side of your display and flip down to cover the ad area whenever you are using Pointcast. I made such a cardboard device, which I call my "Pointcast filter", and it makes the experience of using Pointcast a great deal more pleasant. You may think that you can ignore the ads, but once you cover them up, you will realize that they were a lot more distracting than you thought.)

Web:
  http://www.pointcast.com/

Reuters News

Reuters is a news agency founded by the German entrepreneur Paul Julius Reuter in 1851. The agency was based on Reuter's determination to "come up with solutions for his clients". For example, in 1850, Reuter used carrier pigeons to deliver closing stock prices, closing the only gap in the telegraph system connecting Berlin and Paris. The Reuters news agency prides itself on offering objective news services and, toward that end, they established the Reuters Trust to make sure Reuters is never owned by a particular interest group or faction. The online Reuters site is not fun. This is hardcore news without the cutesy lifestyle stuff. You can read lots of basic news—international, U.S., politics, business and sports—and you can customize the site to suit your tastes.

Web:
  http://www.reuters.com/reutersnews/

Russian News

Russia is a huge country—17,075,200 square kilometers, 150,000,000 people, spanning 11 time zones—and there is a lot happening. Here are some resources that provide an excellent way to keep up on current events in Russia and nearby countries.

Web:
 http://citm1.met.fsu.edu/~glenn/russia/maillist.html
 http://www.rferl.org/newsline/

Listserv Mailing List:
 List Name: rferl-l
 Subscribe to: listserv@listserv.acsu.buffalo.edu

South African News

If you are interested in finding out the details of what is happening in South Africa, here is the place to do it. One of these Web sites has daily updates compiled from South African press agencies. You can find out a lot more by reading these summaries than you can from any regular newspaper. The other site is more of an online newspaper, with information about news, business and sports.

Web:
 http://www.bibim.com/anc/
 http://www.mg.co.za/mg/za/news.html

Swedish News

If you want to keep up on what is new and exciting in Sweden, look no further. There are links to many, many Swedish news sources, including daily newspapers, magazines, radio and television. There is also a weather section which is handy during the winter, when you can cheer yourself up by looking at what the Swedes deal with day after day.

Web:
 http://www.svenska-sidor.com/media/

Time Daily

If you are a news junkie, this is a must-see site: daily news briefs from Time magazine. There is a good overview of each news story, and most of the stories also have pictures. Many of the articles have links you can follow for more information about the people or places featured in the story.

Web:
 http://pathfinder.com/time/daily/

USA Today

Tired of recycling? Stop getting the newspaper and just get your news online. It's clean, it's neat and best of all you don't have to store a bunch of newspaper around the house until recycling day. USA Today has lots of interesting news and entertainment online. There's so much interesting stuff to read here, you might have to have a second cup of morning coffee just to get through it all.

Web:
 http://www.usatoday.com/

Washington Post

The Washington Post Web site is one of my favorite places to read the news. The Washington Post is a major American newspaper, published out of Washington, D.C., and is the principal voice-to-be-reckoned-with in the nation's capitol. I check in at least once a day: not only for news, but for the columns, human interest features and comics.

Web:
 http://www.washingtonpost.com/

World News Sources

I'm warning you. Don't visit any of these resources unless you have plenty of time. There is so much news in the world of news that you will be distracted for hours. (And that's not news.)

Web:
 http://www.actualidad.com/
 http://www.all-links.com/newscentral/
 http://www.mediainfo.com/emedia/
 http://www.middlebury.edu/~gferguso/news.html
 http://www.newo.com/news/

Usenet:
 misc.news.bosnia
 misc.news.east-europe.rferl
 misc.news.southasia

World News Sources

Okay, so you are glued to your computer and fastened to the Net for many hours a day. Still, there is no need to miss the news.

Your trusty Web browser can be your window to access news from all over the world.

Now that you have the Net, no event of any importance will ever again escape your attention.

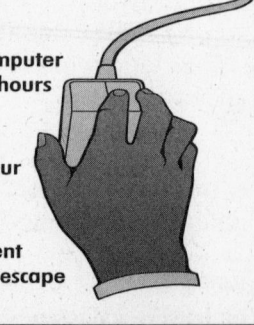

OCCULT AND PARANORMAL

Astrology Charts

Don't wander through life wondering if you are going in the right direction. Use these interactive Web pages to learn exactly what your next move should be. Fill in the required information and the computer will whip out your astrological chart faster than you can say, "What's your sign, baby?"

Web:
http://www.astro.ch/atlas/
http://www.twostar.com/astrology/

Astrology Resources

Stars are more than just pretty lights you sit under at night. You can make wishes upon them, navigate ships by them, or record their positions to make up an astrological chart that you can consult for all your important decisions. Learn the basics of astrology, including its history and related topics like solar magnetism and etheric planets. If it's good enough for Sarah Ferguson, it's good enough for... someone.

Web:
http://www.kenaz.com/Astrology/
http://www.spiritweb.org/Spirit/Astro/Overview.html

Astrology Talk and General Discussion

You've discovered that Uranus is in conjunction with your ascendant ruler, Jupiter. And as if that's not enough, Uranus also squares Mercury, your tenth house ruler, and you have four yods that are creating frustration and dissatisfaction in your life. What's a person to do? Besides calling the psychic hotline, you can post queries or hints to stargazers around the globe or even—depending on whom they know—across the universe.

Usenet:
alt.astrology
alt.astrology.asian
alt.astrology.marketplace
alt.astrology.metapsych

Chaos Magick

Chaos magick is a system of magick that is personal (as opposed to group-oriented) and non-traditional (as opposed to the "old ways" of traditional ritual). It does not have a particular belief system. Each "Chaote" (person who practices chaos magick) believes whatever suits him or her. Chaos magick recognizes no particular deity, theology or morality. "Nothing is True, and Everything is Permitted." This is a world view in which life is chance, random, accidental, chaotic and discordant. (If you can make any sense of this information, you probably have the right chemistry to practice chaos magick.)

Web:
http://www.crl.com/~tzimon/
http://www.sonic.net/fenwick/

Usenet:
alt.magick.chaos

Ghosts and Hauntings

You don't have to wait for campfire stories to scare yourself silly. Tune in to this page where you will find some really creepy pictures of ghosts, descriptions of haunted places to visit and some scary stories. I recommend you leave all the lights on.

Web:
http://www.ghosts.org/

Usenet:
alt.folklore.ghost-stories

Ghosts and Hauntings

Do you want to scare yourself silly? Do you believe in haunted houses? What about ghosts?

We're not talking Casper here. We're talking things that are so scary you will never get to sleep. Check it out—

if you dare

578 OCCULT AND PARANORMAL

Hermeticism

Hermeticism relates to alchemy and magick, as well as to the specific works of Hermes Trismegistus (the Egyptian god Thoth), who is the legendary author of various writings on astrology and magic. This site has lots and lots of resources relating to Hermeticism, including online versions of Hermes Trismegistus' writing. (What amazes me is that an ancient Egyptian god understood HTML.)

Web:
http://www.necronomi.com/magic/hermeticism/

Inner Sanctum Occult Net

Are you interested in "secret wisdom of the ages, hidden in shadows for generations?" Well you don't have to become a Rosicrucian. The time of enlightenment is here, *if* you know where to look on the Net. The only clue I can give you is to start at this Web site. You'll find a collection of occult resources: an encyclopedia of magick and the occult, a Web forum where you can discuss occult topics, an archive of files relating to the occult, as well as a huge list of other occult resources around the Net.

Web:
http://www.inner-sanctum.com/

Lightful Images

If seeing is believing, then this will put you one step closer to believing that some really strange stuff is going on in the universe. Stuff that maybe you would rather not know. So maybe it's best if you didn't look at these pictures of aliens and other paranormal occurrences.

Web:
http://www.spiritweb.org/Spirit/Images/

Magick

You never know when you will need to immediately lay your hands on the Hymn to Osiris in the Egyptian Book of the Dead or perhaps look up the definition for the word "utok" in the Dictionary of Ouranos Barbaric. Have access to more magick than you can shake a bag of runes at.

Web:
http://www.getnet.com/~petcouns/eor.html
http://www.namru.com/

> You are what you think.

Magick Talk and General Discussion

The good news for witches in the '90s is that nobody gets burned at the stake anymore. Whatever brand of magick you like to practice, Usenet has something to offer you. Get information on solitary witches, rituals, equipment and supplies, ethics and the hardships faced by today's practitioners of magick.

Usenet:
alt.magick
alt.magick.chaos
alt.magick.ethics
alt.magick.serious
alt.magick.tantra
alt.magick.tyagi
alt.magick.virtual-adepts
alt.pagan.magick
alt.traditional.witchcraft

Near-Death Experience

It doesn't count if someone scares you so bad that you think you nearly have a heart attack. In Usenet you can talk with other people about real near-death experiences like actually going out of your body and wisping around the room in an ethereal form before being yanked back to consciousness. Read studies on the near-death concept as well as anecdotes from people who have had these experiences. Check out more information on near-death experiences (NDEs) at the Web site.

Web:
http://www.mindspring.com/~scottr/end.html

Usenet:
alt.consciousness.near-death-exp

OCCULT AND PARANORMAL

Necronomicon

The original title of the Necronomicon was "Al-Azif". (Azif is an Arab word signifying a nocturnal sound made by insects, which was thought to be the howling of demons.) The Al-Azif was written around the year 730 by Abdul Al-Hazred, a crazed and wandering poet from Yemen. In 950, the work was translated into what we now know as the Necronomicon by a Greek philosopher named Theodorus Philetus. Some people say the book is full of powerful spells by which you can raise the dead (in case your servants call in sick the night of a big dinner party); other people have their doubts. The document has a long history of suppression and destruction, and has been banned repeatedly. It is said that Abdul Al-Hazred met his death by being devoured by a monster in broad daylight. Even now, people say just looking at the Necronomicon will bring you bad luck. Still wanna read it?

Web:
http://www.hplovecraft.com/creation/necron/
http://www.minet.uni-jena.de/~mso/mythos.html

Usenet:
alt.necronomicon

Occult and Magick Chat

Do you have your cauldron bubbling away and need a little advice about what to do if you run out of eye of newt? Hop onto IRC and talk to the folks who are into occult and magick. Maybe you can jump on the old broom and fly over to borrow a cup of mandrake root.

IRC:
#magick
#occult
#tarot
#thelema

Occult Search Engine

The wisdom of the ages may have taken generations to create, but when you need it, you need it fast. So scoot right over to this search engine for the occult, where you can find a variety of resources: paranormal, Christian mysticism, vampirism, shamanism, paganism, wicca, Satanism, and more.

Web:
http://www.avatarsearch.com/

Look What I Found on the Net...

```
Newsgroup: alt.magick.serious
Subject: Tutor needed

> I need a tutor in any number of fields.  I'm spinning lost and
> out of control.  Dragon magick, endochain, elementalism — all
> of these ideas and my head isn't straight.
>
> Nothing makes sense, it all is the same but different.  I need
> some guidance.  Please help.

When Spirit first started guiding me I was ebbing and flowing in
a mix of "arts".  I believe this is happening with you. It is a
natural balance that you are finding.  You need to go one way and
then another, otherwise you won't find the correct "blend" or
vibration that you will work with.

Don't let this worry you, otherwise it will only serve to
distort the lesson you are learning, and a very important one it
is too.  The best thing for you to do is meditate on the things
that sway you in different directions and then compare your
findings.  You will find out just why you chose a particular
style, and the reason is because it was right at the time.
```

580 OCCULT AND PARANORMAL

Ouija

A Ouija board is a device used to help receive spiritual and telepathic messages. It is thought that the name comes from the French and German words for yes: "oui" and "ja" (but there are other stories). The Ouija apparatus consists of a board and a movable pointer. The board is marked with the letters of the alphabet as well as various other symbols. One or more people touch the pointer while concentrating on spiritual thoughts. As if by magic, the pointer will move from one letter to another, spelling out a message. The spirit of the Ouija may not solve all your problems, but it's certainly cheaper than psychotherapy.

Web:
http://www.math.unh.edu/~black/cgi-bin/ouija.cgi
http://www.netcom.com/~ouija/
http://www.newage.com.au/library/ouija.html

Out-of-Body Experiences

The best cure for indigestion is to just leave your body behind and let it work out the details for itself. Read up on astral projection, out-of-body healing, meditation, lucid dreaming, theories about higher realms, and tips on how to have an out-of-body experience.

Web:
http://www.eu.spiritweb.org/Spirit/obe-faq.html
http://www.lava.net/~goodin/astral.html
http://www.winternet.com/~rsp/obebook.html

Usenet:
alt.out-of-body

Paranormal Phenomena Talk and General Discussion

The weird, the unexplained, the things that go bump in the night. I love stories, especially ones that give me goose bumps and make the hair stand up on the back of my neck. Read stories and theories about paranormal phenomena.

Usenet:
alt.paranet.esp-help
alt.paranet.paranormal
alt.paranormal
alt.paranormal.channeling
alt.paranormal.crop-circles
alt.paranormal.moderated
alt.paranormal.spells.hexes.magic

> USING THE NET IS AN OUT-OF-BODY EXPERIENCE.
> YOUR BODY STAYS HOME, WHILE YOUR MIND GOES TO WORK.

Parapsychology

Remember all those nights you'd stay up late with friends, turn out the lights, and by the eerie glow of a flashlight you would tell ghost stories and creepy folk legends? None of that has changed, it's just that the scary stories get more complicated and sophisticated. Believers of the weird get together to talk about ESP, out-of-body experiences, dreams and altered states of consciousness.

Web:
http://perso.wanadoo.fr/basuyaux/parapsy/parapsy-eng.html

Usenet:
alt.paranet.psi

Skepticism

A great many people in the world have superstitious and pseudo-scientific beliefs, and, if truth be told, many people believe a lot of stuff that just ain't so. In my experience, the people with the most incredible beliefs are the people who suffer from a lack of critical thinking and too little background in the hard sciences. It's not always easy being the bad guy, but someone has to do it. Check these Web sites to see what the skeptics have to say. If you want to argue about it, try Usenet.

Web:
http://wheel.ucdavis.edu/~btcarrol/skeptic/dictcont.html
http://www.csicop.org/bibliography/
http://www.faqs.org/faqs/skeptic-faq/
http://www.randi.org/

Usenet:
alt.paranet.skeptic
sci.skeptic

OCCULT AND PARANORMAL

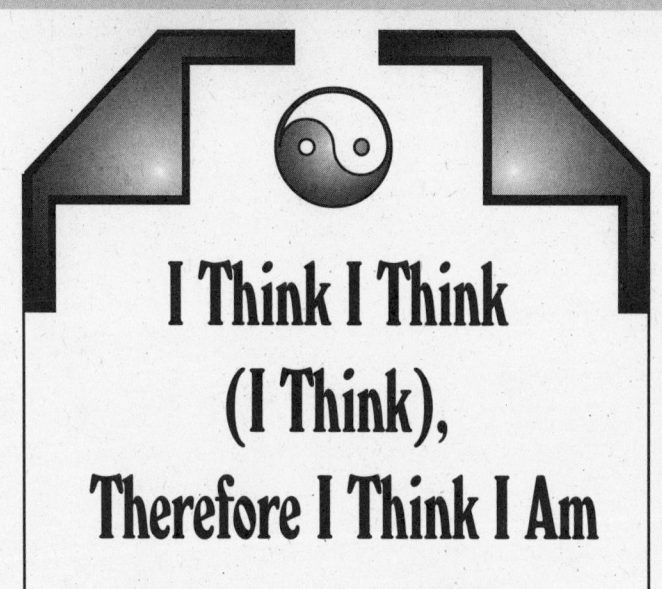

I Think I Think (I Think), Therefore I Think I Am

You probably didn't expect to find intelligent, rational, educated thought in a section on the occult and paranormal, but here it is. Skepticism sites have a lot of compelling information that will restore your faith in human reason. Before you cop out by saying, "It's all a value judgment and everyone is entitled to his or her own opinion," take a look at what the skeptics have to say and you may be surprised.

Thinking is generally a Good Thing™ and, like watching television and drinking coffee, using your intellect well can be habit forming. Having an open mind is great if you are undergoing brain surgery, but for fulfilling your birthright as a human being, nothing beats a good education and an understanding of how rational thought can be used to enhance our lives and stop other people from taking advantage of our emotional weaknesses.

Thelema

"Thelema" is a Greek word meaning "will" or "intention". However, "Thelema" is also the name of a spiritual philosophy that has been evolving over the last few hundred years. The basic tenet of Thelema is "Do what thou wilt shall be the whole of the Law." The earliest mention of Thelema was in the 16th century. However, the philosophy began to evolve rapidly in the early 1900s when a British occultist named Aleister Crowley (1875-1947) wrote The Book of the Law. Crowley spent the rest of his life developing the philosophy of Thelema as it related to The Book of the Law. (Historical note: Crowley wrote this book at the urging of his wife who, it is said, was pestered by the Egyptian god Horus to get Crowley's attention while he and his wife were on their honeymoon in Egypt.) The basic idea is that "...each person has the right to fulfill themselves through whatever beliefs and actions are best suited to them (so long as they do not interfere with the will of others), and only they themselves are qualified to determine what these are." The Web sites give a basic overview of Thelema as well as information about Crowley and the Stele of Revealing (the ancient Egyptian artifact through which the Law of Thelema was revealed to Crowley). You can also read the text of The Book of the Law, look at a Thelemic calendar, find out about Thelemic organizations, and explore other, related resources. For talk, try the IRC channel.

Web:
http://www.crl.com/~thelema/
http://www.thelema.org/

IRC:
#thelema

Looking for facts?
See "Science".
Looking for fantasy?
See "Science Fiction, Fantasy and Horror".

582 OCCULT AND PARANORMAL

Learn this VOODOO hex:

You remind me of the man.
WHAT MAN?
The man with the power.
WHAT POWER?
The power of hoodoo.
HOODOO?
You do.
DO WHAT?
Remind me of the man.
WHAT MAN?
The man with the power...

Voodoo

Voodoo (also called Hoodoo or Vodoun) is a religious cult, practiced primarily in Caribbean countries, especially Haiti. Voodoo was created by West-African slaves who were forced by their Catholic masters to practice Catholicism. The Voodoo traditions grew from a syncretism (joining together) of Catholic beliefs with native African traditions. Voodoo recognizes a powerful supreme god who rules a large collection of local deities (some of whom act as guardians), saints and deified ancestors. These deities communicate with people through dreams, chants and possession. These Web pages are an excellent introduction to voodoo and its complexities. By the way, to create a zombie, you use black magic to kill someone, and then revive him in such a way that he no longer possesses a soul. The result is a pliant slave-like being. (Zombies, however, are only a small part of the voodoo tradition.)

Web:
   http://www.arcana.com/voodoo/voodoo.html
   http://www.gnofn.org/~voodoo/vodu-faq.html

Listserv Mailing List:
   List Name: **voodoo-l**
   Subscribe to: **listserv@necronomi.com**

OUTDOOR ACTIVITIES

Ballooning

In 1783, two French brothers figured out how to cause a 30-meter linen bag to rise in the air. Within a few months, two daredevils used a similar balloon to make the first manned flight. It took two hundred years for balloon technology to improve to the point where men were able to float across the Atlantic Ocean (1978). Today, modern technology allows many people to enjoy ballooning, and you can too. Start with the Net, and it won't be long before you are having a good time, getting high the old fashioned way.

Web:
   http://www.hotairship.com/ebaa/
   http://www.launch.net/

Usenet:
   rec.aviation.balloon

Listproc Mailing List:
   List Name: **Airship-list**
   Subscribe to: **listproc@lists.colorado.edu**

Would you like to rise above it all?

Try ballooning.

OUTDOOR ACTIVITIES

Boomerangs

A boomerang is a curved instrument—usually made of wood—that, when thrown in a particular manner, can be made to fly away and return. Boomerangs were invented in Australia. (In fact, the name "boomerang" is derived from "bumariny", a word from Dharuk, the Aboriginal language of southeast Australia.) Today, boomerangs are used around the world for fun, and there are various boomerang organizations and competitions. One of these Web sites is a collection of boomerang-related links and information. The other site contains instructions to help you learn how to throw and catch. Hint: If you are left-handed, be sure to use a left-handed boomerang.

Web:
http://ic.net/~tbailey/Boomerang.html
http://www.boomerangs.org/
http://www.usba.org/

Camping

There are various ways to go camping. Basically, you can either drive to the campground or you can walk (at least from a trail head). If you drive, there is a big dichotomy between those people who go car camping and those who have recreational vehicles (RVs). If you like to camp, here are some Web sites that will be useful no matter what your *modus operandi*. In particular, you can read the various camping FAQs (frequently asked question lists). You can also use the Net to help you find a campground. For discussion, there are Usenet groups for general camping talk as well as groups for RV people.

Web:
http://www.camping-usa.com/
http://www.campnetamerica.com/
http://www.gorp.com/dow/
http://www.jps.net/roamer/camping.html

Usenet:
alt.rec.camping
alt.rv
rec.outdoors.camping
rec.outdoors.rv-travel

Climbing

Trapped indoors but ready to go climbing? Help ease the pain by checking out the great climbing resources on the Net. These Web sites have lots of pictures of climbing, information about climbing, in fact, just about everything about climbing and related activities. On Usenet you can find open discussion about climbing techniques, specific climbs and competition announcements.

Web:
http://www.rocklist.com/
http://www.rocknroad.com/
http://www.terraquest.com/highsights/

Usenet:
rec.climbing

Fishing

There's got to be something special about the type of guy who would spend all day on a boat just to catch a fish that he could buy in the supermarket for $3. One such special guy is my lawyer, Bill. He loves sitting out on his boat waiting for The Big Catch. This is good for me, because every now and then he'll bring me some fresh salmon or sea bass. However, his hobby is not without its attendant risks. Not long ago, he was fishing out of state and a friend of his who trains dolphins asked Bill if he would mind catching some fish to bring back as a treat for the animals. The day he was to start back, Bill happened to talk to his friend who told him that the dolphins had been behaving badly lately and causing a lot of problems. Fortunately for Bill, he is a trained lawyer who is able to see the hidden pitfalls in any situation, and it was the work of a moment for him to tell his friend that he wouldn't be bringing any fish home. As Bill later explained it to me, this was a close call because in the United States it is illegal to transport fish across state lines for immoral porpoises.

Web:
http://www.everett.net/users/kevtrout/
http://www.the-fishing-network.com/

Usenet:
alt.fishing
rec.outdoors.fishing
rec.outdoors.fishing.bass
rec.outdoors.fishing.fly
rec.outdoors.fishing.fly.tying
rec.outdoors.fishing.saltwater

OUTDOOR ACTIVITIES

Hiking and Backpacking

There are a lot of great hiking trails in the world, but what really makes a trip enjoyable is to find a wonderful place before it gets too popular. Years ago, I had some wonderful times hiking at a small park near the Big Sur area on the California coast. The hike from the parking area to the ocean was pleasant and, along the way, I would pass through an open meadow, a forest with tall trees, and thick bushes. At the end of the trail was a beautiful cove where small cliffs, covered entirely with sand, overlooked the beach. I remember once visiting the area with one of my good friends. We hiked to the end of the trail and then climbed up the cliffs with our backpacks. At the top of the cliff, we walked down to the end of a point which was surrounded almost entirely by water and had a breathtaking ocean view. We camped out on that very spot, snug at night in our sleeping bags, lying between bushes of wild sage. It was one of those trips that I will never forget and, even with the passing of the years, the sounds and the sights and the smells remain fresh in my mind.

Web:
http://www.backpackers.com/
http://www.backpacking.net/
http://www.teleport.com/~walking/hiking.html
http://www.thebackpacker.com/

Usenet:
rec.backcountry

Human-Powered Vehicles

Human-powered vehicles (HPV) are designed so that the only power they use is supplied by the muscular effort of a human being. For example, a bicycle is a HPV. However, there are much more elaborate and efficient devices, both for traveling on land and in the air. The fastest land-based HVPs have achieved speeds of over 60 miles per hour (95 kph). Learn how to build and power these unique vehicles, and you can save the environment and get healthy at the same time.

Web:
http://www.ihpva.org/

Hunting

There are many aspects to hunting and a lot to discuss. Here are the resources you need to get started. The Usenet groups and mailing lists are for discussion of various hunting-related topics (although, these are *not* the proper places to discuss the politics of gun control). The Web sites contain information on many hunting-related topics such as equipment (including firearms and bows), animals, organizations, and—assuming all goes well on your outing—recipes.

Web:
http://www.sportsafield.com/
http://www.ucalgary.ca/~powlesla/personal/hunting/

Usenet:
alt.animals.furtrapping
rec.hunting

Listserv Mailing List:
List Name: **huntdog-l**
Subscribe to: **listserv@listserv.indiana.edu**

Listserv Mailing List:
List Name: **hunter-safety-l**
Subscribe to: **listserv@postal.tamu.edu**

Listserv Mailing List:
List Name: **rec-hunting**
Subscribe to: **listserv@postal.tamu.edu**

Why should you depend on gas or electricity when you can do it yourself? A human-powered vehicle is quiet, non-polluting and innovative. Best of all, when you are finished with the engine, it is 100% biodegradable.

Human-Powered Vehicles

OUTDOOR ACTIVITIES

Inline Skating

Skating can be really scary at first. It will help if you read about some techniques for various types of skating, such as how to deal with stairs and hills, and most importantly, how to stop. More advanced skaters can read about skating backward, racing and tricks.

Web:
http://come.to/skateweb/
http://www.visi.com/~tam/sleddogs.html

Usenet:
alt.skate
rec.skate
rec.sport.skating.ice.recreational
rec.sport.skating.inline
rec.sport.skating.misc
rec.sport.skating.racing
rec.sport.skating.roller

Kayaking and Canoeing

There are lots of great resources on the Net about kayaking and canoeing. (And you thought surfing was popular.) Read some paddling FAQs, find information about specific trips and activities, read the hints and tips, and enjoy the photos.

Web:
http://members.aol.com/weepee123/linkpage.html
http://www.gorp.com/gorp/activity/paddle.htm
http://www.nif.idrett.no/padling/world.html

Mountain Biking

Mountain biking is a blast and I do it every chance I get (that is, when I'm not surfing). Check out the mountain biking resources on the Net and learn about technique, racing, safety, and more.

Web:
http://www.faqs.org/faqs/bicycles-faq/mountain-bikes/
http://www.fattire.com/
http://xenon.stanford.edu/~rsf/mtn-bike.html

Usenet:
rec.bicycles.off-road

Nude Beaches

If you have never spent an afternoon at a nude beach, you don't know what you are missing. But don't worry, I can show you what it is like right now. Wherever you are, take off your clothes and, for the next 30 minutes, lie down on the floor and think pleasant thoughts. (If you are reading this in a bookstore, you can tell the manager I said that after the 30 minutes are up he or she must give you a discount.) Now, wasn't that great? Doesn't that make you want to try out a real nude beach? Here is the list.

Web:
http://www.cis.ohio-state.edu/hypertext/faq/usenet/nude-faq/beaches/top.html

Orienteering and Rogaining

Grab a map and a sack lunch and head to the woods for some exciting, competitive, cross-country navigation. If you think trying to read a map while driving through Los Angeles is bad, try doing it in the middle of a forest where all the trees look the same and there are no road signs or even flushable toilets. Learn about orienteering and rogaining—the rules, how to compete, and what other people are doing.

Web:
http://scorpion.cowan.edu.au/ara/irf/irfindex.html
http://www.orienteering.org/

Usenet:
rec.sport.orienteering

Listproc Mailing List:
List Name: o-train
Subscribe to: listproc@u.washington.edu

Imagine this. You wake up one day to find yourself in a new world. A world in which direction and time have a will of their own and have become as alive as the wind. All your common landmarks are gone; you move from one spot to another, lost in a haze of misdirection. Nothing you have experienced has prepared you for this. Everything you know seems to be wrong, and you are caught in a land of disinformation and shifting visual cues; an ever-changing environment in which the slightest mistake will send you off into the wilderness. Are you in the Twilight Zone? You wish. No, you are **Orienteering**. (You know what? Maybe you had better check it out on the Net first.)

Outdoor and Recreation Resources

Get out into the sunshine and fresh air. When you want to know where to go and what to do, take a look at all this great information. You'll find loads of stuff to read about things to do and places to visit: national parks, forests, wilderness areas, hiking, biking, fishing and climbing.

Web:
  http://www.azstarnet.com/~goclimb/
  http://www.gorp.com/

Outside Online

It's time for a break, so turn off the computer and go outside—but not just yet. Before you go, take a few minutes to look at this online magazine. You'll see articles and information related to travel and the outdoors. Just a few minutes reading and you'll be ready for some fabulous outdoor activity. Okay, 3.. 2.. 1.. go!

Web:
  http://outside.starwave.com/

Paragliding

Paragliders are the most simple of all aircraft. They consist of a canopy (which acts like a wing), risers (cords) and a harness (suspended from the risers). Where I live there are a lot of paragliders and, when you watch them, they look like large colorful birds, slowly soaring back and forth across the sky. Paragliders are flown and landed with no artificial source of energy—just the wind, gravity and the pilot's muscles. Unlike a hang glider, a paraglider does not have a rigid frame—the shape of the canopy is maintained by air pressure. In addition, paragliders are easier to manage and handle than hang gliders. (A paraglider can be folded into a package the size of a large backpack.) If you are a paraglider, you will appreciate the information and resources at these Web sites.

Web:
  http://www.bigairparagliding.com/
  http://www.volcanoes.com/worldhg.html

Parks in the United States

The United States has a vast number of parks, many of which are managed by the National Park Service (NPS), a bureau of the U.S. Department of the Interior. The NPS alone administers 400 parks containing an aggregate of over 83 million acres. Some of these parks are well known, such as Yellowstone and the Grand Canyon. However, most of the parks are less well known and are wonderful places to explore. For example, do you know anyone who has been to Piscataway Park or Timpanogos Cave? If you like the outdoors and you live in the U.S. (or will be visiting), these Web sites provide you with the information you need to find and visit a park (including making reservations if necessary).

Web:
  http://parks.yahoo.com/
  http://www.llbean.com/parksearch/
  http://www.nps.gov/
  http://www.recreation.gov/index.cfm

Radio-Controlled Model Aircraft

For people who like model aircraft, nothing can be more fun than spending a Saturday afternoon out in a large field, putting your favorite radio-controlled (R/C) airplane through its paces. To be good at flying a model plane, you have to understand a lot about flight and flying in general. At this site you can read about buying, building, learning to fly, gliders, powering with gas or electricity, helicopters, aerodynamics, and supplies and materials. For discussion, you can talk to the many radio-controlled-aircraft buffs on Usenet.

Web:
  http://www.rcairplanes.com/

Usenet:
  rec.models.rc.air

When I was a kid, we had to deliver email by hand.

OUTDOOR ACTIVITIES 587

Scuba Diving

Would you like to learn how to visit the vast underwater parts of our planet? The Net has lots of information to help you get started scuba diving.
Personal note: When I learned to scuba dive, I took all the classes, training dives and examinations — and became certified — in four and a half days.
(It was an immersion course.)

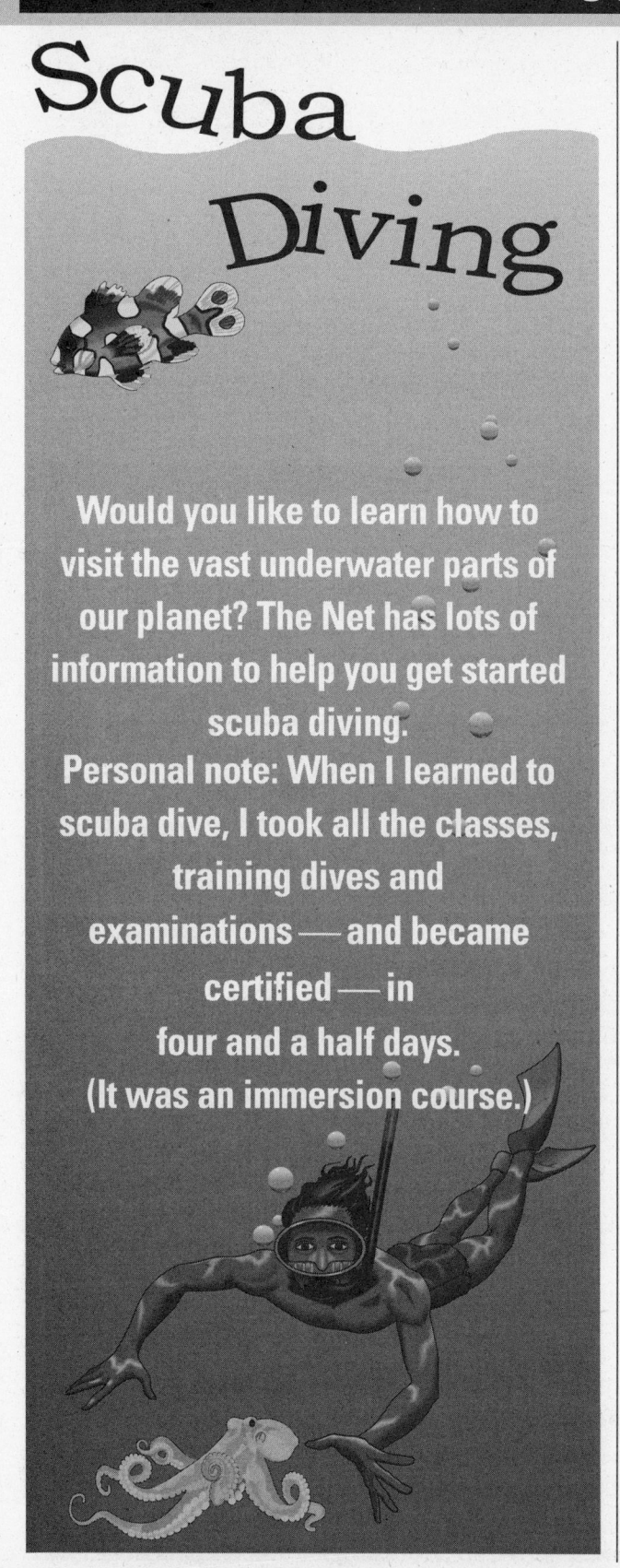

Scuba Diving

The Net has lots of resources for the recreational and technical scuba diving community. On the Web sites you can find mailing list archives, a database of diveable shipwrecks, reviews of dive gear and equipment, details of popular dive destinations, lists of training agencies, clubs, underwater pictures, a catalog of marine fish and invertebrates, classified ads, weather maps, and more. Join IRC, Usenet, or the mailing list for some more interactive scuba action.

Web:
http://www.scubaduba.com/
http://www.scubatimes.com/

Usenet:
bit.listserv.scuba-l
rec.scuba
rec.scuba.equipment
rec.scuba.locations

Listserv Mailing List:
List Name: scuba-l
Subscribe to: listserv@brownvm.brown.edu

IRC:
#scuba

Shooting

Shooting and guns are enjoyed by many people, either as a recreational activity or as part of an organized competition. The Web sites I have listed here will lead you to a large number of shooting and gun resources on the Net. For an ongoing discussion, you can participate in the **rec.guns** Usenet group. If you are concerned about the politics of gun ownership—a highly contentious area of debate—you can join the discussion in **talk.politics.guns**.

Web:
http://www.gunsgunsguns.com/gunhoo/
http://www.shooters.com/gunlinks/

Usenet:
rec.guns
talk.politics.guns

OUTDOOR ACTIVITIES

Skateboarding

Fun does not have to be complex. Take a plank, slap some wheels on it and suddenly you have a sport. Today's equipment is a lot better built, but the basic idea is the same. Skateboard enthusiasts can check out lots of good skateboarding stuff on the Net.

Web:
http://skaters.netwizards.net/ramps/ramps.htm
http://web.cps.msu.edu/~dunhamda/dw/dansworld.html
http://www.skateboard.com/tydu/skatebrd/skate.html
http://www2.skatetalk.com/skatetalk/

Usenet:
alt.skate-board

IRC:
#skaters

Skydiving

Do you like to risk your life? If so, there are quite a few things you could do to have a good time, such as participate in a Los Angeles riot, cross rush hour traffic blindfolded, or just jump out of an airplane. At least with skydiving there is a FAQ, so maybe you should start there. In fact, take a look at this Web site, which has all sorts of information on diving organizations, base jumping and sit-flying, plus safety tips, movies and pictures. If you hang out on Usenet, you can trade war stories with other people who like to jump out of perfectly good airplanes.

Web:
http://www.afn.org/skydive/

Usenet:
rec.skydiving

Look What I Found on the Net...

```
Newsgroup: rec.sport.snowmobiles
Subject: When Can I Ride?

>> From what I understand, the official snowmobile season
>> doesn't begin until December 1.  The snowmobile trails are
>> closed until then, but that doesn't mean you can't ride
>> anywhere else.  You can ride on any field or non-"official"
>> trail any time you want.  You only need to get the $10 trail
>> permit sticker if you plan on riding on an actual trail.

> Living in Alaska, it never ceases to amaze me how regulated
> riding is in the lower 48 states.  It may be fine, justified,
> necessary and all that — it just amazes me.  The trade-off is
> that we have no "actual" trails to speak of in Alaska.  Just
> go out and ride.

Here in Michigan, the issue isn't regulation as much as common
sense.  The woods are chock-full of deer hunters with
high-powered rifles from Nov. 15-30, and most of the trails
cross public land.  I'll wait, thank you.

As for the relative advantages of the wide open spaces in Alaska
compared to the lower 48, I'll give you that one.  I kind of
like having a summer, though.
```

Snowboarding

Snowboarding is a difficult, but enjoyable sport that has fans everywhere you find hills and snow. Here is a variety of resources to help you enjoy the snowboarding scene on the Net. For discussion, you have the Usenet groups. One of the Web sites contains a FAQ (frequently asked question list) about snowboarding. The other Web site is a general site where you will find photos, links, products, contest results, lots of information, and a forum in which you can participate. The Fresh and Tasty Web site is a women's snowboarding online magazine.

Web:
http://www.freshandtasty.com/
http://www.snowboarding2.com/
http://www.snwbrdr.com/

Usenet:
rec.skiing.snowboard
rec.sport.snowboarding

Snowmobiles

A snowmobile is one thing at which you won't have to yell, "Mush!" Feed it some gas, tell it you love it, then ride like a maniac across the frozen tundra (or whatever happens to be in front of you). Avid snowmobile fans tell how they keep their machines happy, safe and healthy.

Web:
http://www.off-road.com/snowmobile/

Usenet:
alt.snowmobiles
rec.sport.snowmobiles

Spelunking

If you like crawling around in something that is cool, dark and wet, you are digging in the right place. Here you will find connections to speleological societies and servers around the world. If you just want to talk about caving, check out the Usenet group.

Web:
http://www.goodearth.com/virtcave.html
http://www.gorp.com/gorp/activity/caving.htm
http://www.infohub.com/travel/adventure/
    recreation/caving.html

Usenet:
alt.caving

Surfing

When I was a graduate student in San Diego, I took a surfing class during my first year. Since then, I have spent a lot of time in the ocean with my boogie board. These Web sites are great for surfers who want local and general information. There are lots of links, not only to surf pages, but to just about everything you can imagine relating to surfers and surfing. In fact, now that we have the Net, you don't have to go to college just to learn how to surf.

Web:
http://magna.com.au/~prfbrown/tubelink.html
http://www.sdsc.edu/surf/surfer_resources.html
http://www.surfline.com/surfusa2.html

Usenet:
alt.surfing

IRC:
#surfing

Swimming

Swimming is a wonderful activity. It's great exercise and a lot of fun. When I was a tiny kid, my mother took me to the local Y, and (according to my father), I was swimming in the pool before I could even walk. When I was older, I went to camp every summer where I swam in a lake. Later, I moved to California and learned to swim in the ocean, which I found to be a completely different experience. (My favorite is the ocean.) If you are a swimmer, here are some resources I know you will like, including a Web site that will help you find a pool to use just about anywhere in the world.

Web:
http://www.lornet.com/sgol/
http://www.webswim.com/

Usenet:
rec.sport.swimming

Before you go on a trip, use the Net to help you plan. Read the "Travel" section.

OUTDOOR ACTIVITIES

Water Skiing

When I was a young sprout at summer camp, I was able to water ski from time to time. Water skiing was the most popular waterfront activity, and we always had to wait a long time for our turn. We were then able to ski about 2-3 minutes, at which time the ride ended so someone else could have a try. If you are a water skier, here are some Web sites you will enjoy: lots of links, including general information, competition (slalom, jumps, tricks), barefoot skiing, seated skiing, wake boarding (surfing behind a boat) and kneeboarding. For discussion, you can participate in the Usenet group. You know, for some reason, when I was at camp, water skiing was considered the camp's coolest activity, and the water ski instructors were considered among the coolest guys in the entire camp. It was not uncommon to see them swanking around the ski area as if they owned the place, talking with pretty girls and working on their tan. From time to time, they would pause long enough to treat themselves to long rides during which they would show off to everyone else. Personally, I didn't care one whit, although I have no doubt that, today, all those guys are working in gas stations.

Web:
http://www.iwsf.com/
http://www.usawaterski.org/

Usenet:
rec.sport.waterski

Have you ever...

Windsurfing

Windsurfing is the ultimate sailing sport. You stand on what looks like a large surfboard and manipulate a sail. As the wind takes you, you use your weight and the position of the sail to control the direction and speed of your movement. Is windsurfing for you? Take this simple three-part quiz and find out: (1) Are you in excellent physical shape? (2) Do you enjoy water sports? (3) Are you willing to have more fun than almost everyone else in the world? If you answered yes, yes and yes, you should try windsurfing.

Web:
http://id.mind.net/~strider/windsurfing.html
http://www.zagato.demon.co.uk/windsurf/

Usenet:
rec.windsurfing

Majordomo Mailing List:
List Name: **windsurfers**
Subscribe to: **majordomo@cs.utah.edu**

Look What I Found on the Net...

```
Newsgroup: rec.windsurfing
Subject: Taking photos of myself while windsurfing

> You've all seen the sort of photo I'm after: camera half-way
> up the luff tube, sailor in the harness and footstraps,
> fully on the plane, looking up grinning from ear to ear.
> Apparently the usual method is for the sailor to activate the
> shutter using fishing line, but how?! Every camera I've ever
> had requires a button to be pushed, not pulled...

A strong rubber band holds a piece of clothespin on the shutter
button, depressing it.  A thick nut or washer is inserted
underneath the clothespin, preventing it from depressing the
button.  The fishing line is attached to the washer.  Yank it out,
the rubber band pulls the clothespin down on the button — and
you're a magazine cover!
```

PEOPLE

Billionaires

Get the goods on the world's richest people. This year Forbes magazine counted 447 billionaires, of which 149 are inside the United States. Check out how they made their money, their marital status, where they were born, and their education. (Then you can spend some time wondering, where are all the women?)

Web:
http://www.forbes.com/tool/toolbox/billnew/index.asp

Callahan's Bar

Callahan's Bar is a pleasant home away from home: a virtual bar for real people. Visit regularly and meet the regular patrons. You'll find friends, fellowship, good will and bad puns.

Web:
http://www.callahans.org/

Usenet:
alt.callahans

IRC:
#callahans

Life can be tough. Take a break at Callahan's Bar

> You can read magazines for free on the Net.

Characters and Fictional People

Who's to say what's real? If a character lives in our hearts and minds, and occupies enough of our collective popular cultural consciousness as to command his or her own Usenet group, that's real enough for me. Join the discussion and talk about Wednesday Addams (Addams Family), Ren and Stimpy, Q (Star Trek), the Power Rangers, Dirk Pitt (Clive Cussler novel), Hello Kitty, Nathan Brazil, (Jack Chalker novel), Teenage Mutant Ninja Turtles, Sonic the Hedgehog, Surak (Star Trek), Tank Girl, Tigger (Winnie the Pooh), Wedge (Star Wars), and Zathras (Babylon 5).

Usenet:
alt.fan.addams.wednesday
alt.fan.dirk-pitt
alt.fan.hello-kitty
alt.fan.nathan.brazil
alt.fan.ninja-turtles
alt.fan.power-rangers
alt.fan.q
alt.fan.ren-and-stimpy
alt.fan.sonic-hedgehog
alt.fan.surak
alt.fan.tank-girl
alt.fan.tigger
alt.fan.wedge
alt.fan.zathras

Charities

What can you do with all that extra money you have lying around? Why not give it to a charitable organization? You may not be able to use a tax deduction, but you can always use a few extra points with the Man (or Woman) Upstairs.

Web:
http://www.charities.org/
http://www.give.org/index.cfm

Chatting in 3-D

Get a little closer to a 3-D Internet chatting experience with Worlds Chat. This free client software allows you to choose an avatar to represent yourself as you walk through the chat world and talk to people.

Web:

http://www.worlds.net/wc/

Cult of the Dead Cow

The Cult of the Dead Cow is the oldest underground telecommunications organization, dating back to 1986. Although the membership is small—consisting of only about 20 active members—their influence is felt around the world. The cult's main product is a series of articles, written at various times by various members, with new articles being added from time to time. The articles are regularly read by thousands of people, so why not expand your mind and give it a try? Do you think you might like to join the cult as a member (as opposed to being an outsider)? Here is a hint: don't ask to join. Cult members are welcomed by invitation only, and once you ask, they will never invite you.

Web:

http://www.cultdeadcow.com/

IRC:

#cdc

Dead People Server

Every now and then, you are bound to ask, "Whatever happened to so-and-so?" Well, so-and-so may be dead, but how can you find out for sure? Just check the Dead People Server. If so-and-so is a famous dead person, there is a good chance he or she will be in the list. It sounds a bit macabre, but it's actually a good reference tool, and I find it interesting just to browse. The first thing I do is to check for my own name, just in case. (I never like to take anything for granted.)

Web:

http://www.city-net.com/~lmann/dps/

Expatriates and Refugees

An expatriate is a person who lives away from his or her native country. (I, for example, am a Canadian expatriate.) A refugee is an expatriate who leaves his or her native land for political or religious reasons, often because of persecution, expulsion or war. Expatriates of any type need to be able to fit into a new country while maintaining their personal culture. Refugees have, in addition, the more pressing needs of personal safety and well-being. If you are living away from your own country, for whatever reason, here are some resources that may be able to make your life a bit easier.

Web:

http://www.escapeartist.com/

Find-A-Grave

What do these people all have in common: Desi Arnaz, Albert Einstein, Greta Garbo, Jerry Garcia, Woody Guthrie, Alfred Hitchcock, Rock Hudson, Janis Joplin and John Lennon? The answer is, they were all cremated. This is just one of the fascinating facts I found at the Find-A-Grave Web site. Look for your favorite dead person, and I bet you a cookie they are in the database. Isn't it comforting to know that, wherever you are in the world, you can find out where Marilyn Monroe is buried (at Westwood Memorial Park), display the exact street address, and look at a picture of her tombstone? This is an amazing site that you simply *must* visit at least once in your life.

Web:

http://www.findagrave.com/

The Internet has some fascinating Frequently Asked Question Lists (FAQs). When you have a spare moment, find a FAQ that looks interesting and read it.

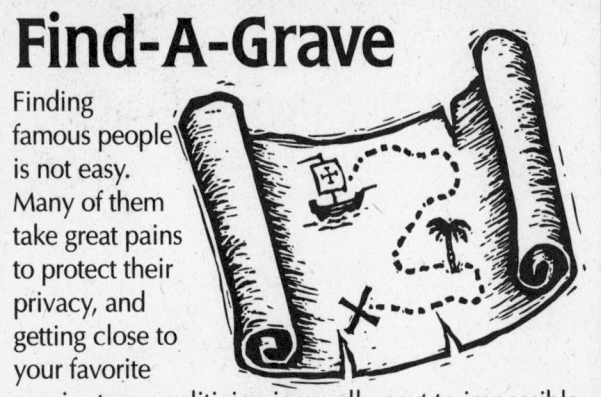

Find-A-Grave

Finding famous people is not easy. Many of them take great pains to protect their privacy, and getting close to your favorite movie star or politician is usually next to impossible. While they are alive, that is.

Once a famous person is dead, he or she is fair game. The next time you are looking for that elusive someone, check with the **Find-A-Grave** Web site.

Finding graves is not only fun, it's educational. Why, I bet you didn't know that Benjamin Harrison, the 23rd President of the United States, is buried in the same Indianapolis, Indiana, graveyard as John Dillinger, the notorious Depression-era gangster.

(Just another example of how people who read my books are able to stay so well informed.)

Finding Email Addresses

You can run all over the Net, but it's getting harder and harder to hide. Here are several free services that you can use to track down that elusive someone. Although all of them will give you email addresses, various services also offer other information such as phone numbers, Web page addresses, and so on. If you do not want your name listed in these directories, send *them* email and let them know. Hint: When all else fails, call the person on the phone and ask for the address.

Web:
http://www.anywho.com/
http://www.bigfoot.com/
http://www.four11.com/
http://www.iaf.net/
http://www.isleuth.com/peop.shtml
http://www.theultimates.com/
http://www.whowhere.com/

Friends

Looking for some new friends? Try chatting on IRC. These channels are lively and always populated. It's the perfect place to start up a conversation and meet new people. These channels are not for the discussion of the television show Friends.

IRC:
#chatfriends
#friend
#friends

Interesting People on the Web

The Internet is the largest gathering of people in the history of mankind, so you really have to go to extremes to stand out as "interesting". Well, these people manage to do it. Bizarre, unusual, unexpected, contorted, ingenious—this collection of strange, but true, humanoids will amuse and astonish you with the enchantment that only the extraordinary can bring to the otherwise dull, meaningless dance of life.

Web:
http://www.dnai.com/~pcombs/ventures.html
http://www.flaunt.net/
http://www.grrl.com/
http://www.moments.org/
http://www.phoenixnewtimes.com/extra/gilstrap/
http://www.walrus.com/~gibralto/

Kooks

On the Net, kooks are not only tolerated, they are venerated. Want to explore the mental cutting edge of humanity? Start with the Web site, where you can visit Conspiracy Corner, the Hall of Hate, the Library of Questionable Scholarship, the Gallery of the Gods, and other bizarre exhibition halls. Then move to Usenet, where you can discuss the real-live kooks who infest the discussion groups and find out who is the new winner of the Kook of the Month Award.

Web:
http://www.teleport.com/~dkossy/

Usenet:
alt.usenet.kooks

Masons and Shriners

Freemasons (or masons) are members of a worldwide fraternal organization named the Free and Accepted Masons. The origins of Freemasonry are lost to antiquity. Some historians trace its roots back to the Middle Ages. Modern Freemasonry started in England in 1717 with the formation of the first Grand Lodge. Masons pass through levels of membership called "degrees". The three basic degrees are Entered Apprentice, Fellowcraft and Master Mason. Once a person attains the third degree, he is deemed to be a member of the Blue Lodge and is considered a full-fledged Mason. He is then entitled to join the Scottish Rite or the York Rite. Within these Rites, a Mason may advance in degree: in the Scottish Rite through 29 more degrees, in the York Rite, through 9 more degrees. Once someone has advanced to the highest degree (of either Rite), he can petition to join the Shrine—more formally, the Ancient Arabic Order of Nobles of the Mystic Shrine—at which point he is a Shriner. (When the Shrine was started in 1872 in New York, an Arabic theme was chosen, which is why Shriners wear red fezzes. Notice that the initials AAONMS form an anagram for "A MASON".) Shriners and Masons are well known for their charitable work and for their emphasis on moral development. They are also known for their elaborate rituals and secret traditions. (See, for example, the 1983 book Big Secrets, by William Poundstone.) There is a huge amount of Masonic-related resources on the Net, mostly the Web pages of various lodges. I have selected some Web sites to get you started.

Web:
  http://www.freemasonry.org/
  http://www.shriners.com/

Usenet:
  alt.freemasonry
  alt.masonic.members
  soc.org.freemasonry

Someone on the Net is waiting to talk to you (right now).

No need to get lost. See "Finding Stuff on the Net".

Mensa

Do you fancy yourself in the ranks of Isaac Asimov, Marilyn Vos Savant, Geena Davis, and other smart people? If so, maybe you should join Mensa. All you need to do is score within the top two percent of the population on a standardized intelligence test. Check out the official Mensa Web site for information about the organization.

Web:
  http://www.mensa.org/

Usenet:
  rec.org.mensa

IRC:
  #mensa

Names

Names mean a lot. For example, suppose you are a guy in college, and a friend calls up and says, "Come and visit me next weekend, and I can get you a date with one of two girls. You can either have Bertha or Wendy. Who do you want?" Come on, you know who you're going to pick. Since names are so important, I have found some resources that will help you understand names and what they mean to us. First, you can try a free name analysis. Find out what your name says about you. Second, if you are having a baby, I have included some Web sites to help you find the perfect name for your little one. And finally, you can look at Web pages created by or about people with the same first name (for example, people named "Bob").

Web:
  http://www.babynames.com/
  http://www.charm.net/~shack/name/babynm.html
  http://www.go2net.com/internet/useless/useless/names.html
  http://www.grownmencry.com/mijo/Believeit.html
  http://www.kabalarians.com/gkh/your.htm

PEOPLE 595

Nerds

Somewhere along the line, a bit flipped in the global memory bank and nerds became cool. So if you want to be cool, you need to know more about nerds, and these are the places to do it.

Web:
http://dspace.dial.pipex.com/town/square/fj10/
http://www.nerdsrus.com/

IRC:
#nerd

Obituaries

Don't settle for reading the obituaries in your local paper, go global. Get a list of people, well known or obscure, who have died, as well as information on various death hoaxes. Lists are arranged alphabetically or by category. Also available: movie stars who were born or died today.

Web:
http://catless.ncl.ac.uk/Obituary/

Usenet:
alt.obituaries

Look What I Found on the Net...

```
Newsgroup: rec.org.mensa
Subject: Sample Test Questions for Mensa

(Here are the first five questions from a fifteen-question
sample Mensa test)

1. Which of the lettered designs best completes the following
   sequence?

       [o]     [.]      (o)

       A: (.)
       B: (o)
       C: [.]
       D: [o]

2. Sally likes 225 but not 224; she likes 900 but not 800; she
   likes 144 but not 145.  Does she like 1600 or 1700?

3. Only one other word can be made from the letters of
   INSATIABLE.    Can you find it?

4. Put the appropriate plus or minus signs between the numbers,
   in the correct places, so that the sum total will equal 1.

         0  1  2  3  4  5  6  7  8  9 = 1

5. What is the word coiled inside this circle?

                    T  P
                 I        U
                 A        N
                    L  S
```

Wondering who's dead?
Read the **Obituaries** Web site.
(As a matter of fact, why not look for your own name?
No need to wait until the last moment.)

PenPals

Looking for someone to exchange email with? Check out this list of people who are looking for email penpals. Along with the names of the people, there is also information about the languages they speak and their hobbies.

Web:
  http://www.bplace.com/penpal.htm
  http://www.goodfriends.net/
  http://www.penpal-network.com/
  http://www.penpal.net/

Usenet:
  soc.penpals

Personal Web Pages

Once you get caught up in the Web, it's hard to get away. Everywhere you look there are paths leading all over, and it's nearly impossible to get where you are going without getting sidetracked. One of my favorite ways to get sidetracked is to start with someone's personal home page and see where it leads. These Web sites attempt the impossible: to keep track of all the home pages on the Net. Look here if you are searching for someone's page, or if you want to pick a place at random to explore.

Web:
  http://ahoy.cs.washington.edu:6060/
  http://homepages.whowhere.com/
  http://www.glassdog.com/the_experience/
     word_of_mouth.html

Random Portrait Gallery

Have you ever wondered who was out there? Now you can find out. The Random Portrait Gallery contains self-portraits (mostly photos) copied from personal Web sites around the world. Whenever you need a quick break from the pressing demands of daily life, spend a few minutes looking at a random selection of people, then look in the mirror. I guarantee you will be pleased.

Web:
  http://moonmilk.volcano.org/portraits/portraits.html

Shared Realities

Some days you just wake up and think to yourself, "Hey, I think I will be someone else today." It's easy when you participate in some of the shared realities of Usenet. In these groups, people assume a persona and write about their thoughts, feelings and actions as that character. Meet people, form bonds, make friends, entertain and be entertained. Even if you don't want to participate, these groups are fun to read because it's like seeing a story unfold before your eyes.

Usenet:
  alt.dragons-inn
  alt.kalbo
  alt.pub.coffeehouse.amethyst
  alt.pub.kacees
  alt.shared-reality.sf-and-fantasy
  alt.shared-reality.startrek.klingon

Tea and Conversation

Join the silly, comfy, cozy good times at this tea party on the Web. Chatters sit having tea and conversation, making up stories, talking about their lives and generally having a fun time. The atmosphere is relaxed, friendly and comfortable.

Web:
  http://www.bensonassoc.com/pct/tea.html

PEOPLE: FAMOUS AND INTERESTING

Virtual Campfire of Nerds

Never again will you have to hang your head in shame. Being a nerd is something to be proud of, especially when you have your own mailing list. What started as a local group has gained international popularity. This is a place for people to gather for chit-chat and share stories. It is described as a "virtual campfire". Check out the Web page for background information and to see the Web pages of some of the NerdNosh regulars.

Web:
http://www.corecom.net/reloj/Nerdnosh.html

Majordomo Mailing List:
List Name: **nerdnosh**
Subscribe to: **majordomo@story.nerdnosh.org**

Hang out with the nerds. Join the **nerdnosh** mailing list: be there *and* be square.

Virtual Memorials

Those who die in the world of flesh and blood live on indefinitely in our hearts and minds. To maintain the memory of our loved ones, it is possible to create a virtual memorial: a Web page that describes and celebrates someone who has passed away. I am always touched when I visit these sites, as you will be. They are so full of life and happiness that the experience of visiting is more joyful than morose. Though we may struggle and complain, life, for all its turmoil, difficulties and uncertainties, is a lovely, delightful gift—and the whole thing is over much too soon.

Web:
http://www.virtual-memorial.com/

Wendy Pages

There are many, many people who create their own personal Web pages. Here is a Web site that collects links to pages created by people named Wendy. Check out the Wendy Pages, where you will find links to a lot of wonderful Wendy-made Web sites. (Maybe you will be inspired to create your own Web page.)

Web:
http://www.wendy.com/wendyweb.html

Y Forum

The idea is to find out how and why people are different from each other. The medium is a forum open to anyone on the Net. The method is to ask questions about race relations to which people write serious, straightforward answers. It works.

Web:
http://www.yforum.com/

PEOPLE: FAMOUS AND INTERESTING

Adams, Scott

Do you enjoy the Dilbert comic strip? Do you like Dogbert, the cute little dog that looks like a balloon with glasses? If so, tell the artist himself: Scott Adams. The Web site takes you right to the heart of Dilbert Central, where you can look at an archive of comic strips. (Note: This site only works if you look at it when you should be working.)

Web:
http://www.unitedmedia.com/comics/dilbert

Mail:
scottadams@aol.com

PEOPLE: FAMOUS AND INTERESTING

Asimov, Isaac

Isaac Asimov was the consummate explainer. He was a genius in the sense that whatever he touched, he illuminated. In his lifetime, he wrote hundreds of books on a large variety of subjects, opening the doors of understanding to countless people around the world. And, oh yes, I think he wrote a science fiction story or two. (I will have to check.)

Web:
http://www.clark.net/pub/edseiler/WWW/asimov_FAQ.html
http://www.clark.net/pub/edseiler/WWW/asimov_home_page.html

Usenet:
alt.books.isaac-asimov

Advice from Isaac Asimov

When I was a graduate student, I wrote a letter to Isaac Asimov. I told him I wanted to learn biochemistry, but I didn't want to have to take a whole lot of beginning organic chemistry and biology courses. He wrote back and gave me the following advice:

"If you have a good library at your disposal, you can teach yourself anything. I did."

I took his advice and taught myself biochemistry out of a textbook. (Ironically, I later went to medical school and ended up learning enough biochemistry to supply the entire Peruvian army. Still, the advice is well-taken and, to this day, I have kept Asimov's note, framed and hanging on the wall beside my desk.)

Brite, Poppy Z.

Have you been entertaining fantasies lately about being bitten on the neck? Biters, bitees and anyone else who has an interest in scary things that go bump in the night will love Poppy Z. Brite, the vampire authoress who wrote Lost Souls. Learn more about Poppy, her writing and her appearance than you could ever accurately imagine. The email address is attended to by Poppy's publicity assistant.

Web:
http://www.gothic.net/pzbrite/

Mail:
pproze@aol.com

British Royal Family

The British royal family has something to teach all of us. Follow their official and unofficial adventures and you will encounter intelligence, knowledge, industry, discretion and inspiration. You will also find a fair amount of foolishness, ignorance, sloth, indiscretion and just plain awful behavior. Here are two resources that help you keep abreast of anything royal worth knowing. First, you have the official Web site of the royal family. Second, you have a more informal site that is anything but official. Between the two of them, you will be able to find out whatever you need to know about Liz, Phil, Chuck, Wills, and the rest of the family. Whatever your personal style—history and official announcements, or candid pictures and the gossip—you'll find it on the Net.

Web:
http://www.royal.gov.uk/
http://www.royalnetwork.com/

Usenet:
alt.gossip.royalty

Celebrity Addresses

Would you like to write to your favorite celebrity? Here are some Web sites that contain lots and lots of celebrity addresses, for both regular mail and email. You can also find some good tips on getting autographs, as well as other interesting information. Hint: If you send email to a celebrity, do not expect anything but an automated reply. If you get a personal reply, consider yourself doubly blessed (once because you got the reply, and once because you are one of my readers).

Web:
http://www.infospace.com/info/celeb/celebrity.htm
http://www.islandnet.com/~luree/fanmail.html

PEOPLE: FAMOUS AND INTERESTING 599

British Royal Family

Being a queen sounds like a good job, but it's not all limo rides and free meals. There's a lot of hard work—and that goes for the other members of the royal family.

Would you like to see what I mean? The official Royal Diary of Engagements is available on the Net, and you can take a look at it whenever you want.

The next time your life feels too demanding and out of control, sneak a peek at the official schedule of Her Majesty, Queen Elizabeth II of Great Britain. I bet she'd trade places with you if she could.

Celebrity Resources

Take my word for it. The day will come when you will need to know Jane Fonda's birthday, where Harrison Ford went to high school, or the latest gossip about Michael Jackson. When that day arrives, you will be ready. Just cruise over to the Net where the celebrity info you need is ready and waiting. (By the way, Jane's birthday is the same as mine, December 21; Harrison Ford went to Maine Township High in suburban Des Plaines, Illinois; and Michael Jackson did something really weird, just the other day.)

Web:
http://www.celebrityweb.com/
http://www.celebsite.com/
http://www.starbuzz.com/
http://www.who2.com/

Celebrity Romantic Links

This is an interesting Net-based game interlaced with some good, homestyle gossip. The game—called "Romantically Linked"—uses a vast storehouse of information showing which celebrities have links to other celebrities. The idea is start with a particular person (say, Woody Allen), and find the shortest set of connections to another person (say, Nancy Reagan). To start, you display the information about Woody Allen. This shows you a list of celebrities to which Woody Allen has some type of link. Choose one of these people, say Mia Farrow. You will then see a list of people who are linked in some way to Mia Farrow. Choose from this list, and so on. The goal is to end up with Nancy Reagan. As an example, one of the contests was to find your way from Elvis Presley to Nicolas Cage. Someone did it in only four links: Elvis Presley to Tuesday Weld to Richard Gere to Uma Thurman to Nicolas Cage. Besides playing the game, you can access a list of hundreds of celebrities, for which you can display a brief biography, a picture, and the pictures of all the people with whom the celebrity has been romantically involved. (Interesting observation: When you see a particular celebrity's paramours side by side, you will often notice that they resemble one another. How true it is that most of us are attracted to a certain type of person.)

Web:
http://www.mrshowbiz.com/features/games/linked/

600 PEOPLE: FAMOUS AND INTERESTING

Celebrity Talk and General Discussion

You've devoured every newspaper, magazine and tabloid in sight, and you still want more news and information about celebrities. Here are some sources that are available 24 hours a day, so you can always get a fix. Read stories, news and rumors of old and new famous people.

Usenet:
- alt.celebrities
- alt.fan.actors
- alt.fan.alyssa-milano
- alt.fan.andy-kaufman
- alt.fan.arianarichards
- alt.fan.ashley-judd
- alt.fan.audrey-hepburn
- alt.fan.brad-pitt
- alt.fan.brent-spiner
- alt.fan.british-actors
- alt.fan.bruce-campbell
- alt.fan.cameron-diaz
- alt.fan.camille-paglia
- alt.fan.christina-applegate
- alt.fan.christina-ricci
- alt.fan.claire-danes
- alt.fan.conan-obrien
- alt.fan.corey-feldman
- alt.fan.courteney-cox
- alt.fan.crispin-glover
- alt.fan.daisy-fuentes
- alt.fan.david-duchovny
- alt.fan.david-gallagher
- alt.fan.dean-erickson
- alt.fan.dermot-mulroney
- alt.fan.drew-barrymore
- alt.fan.drew-carey
- alt.fan.edward-furlong
- alt.fan.ellen-degeneres
- alt.fan.errol-flynn
- alt.fan.g-gordon-liddy
- alt.fan.gary-oldman
- alt.fan.george-clooney
- alt.fan.gillian-anderson
- alt.fan.greg-kinnear
- alt.fan.gwyn-paltrow
- alt.fan.hannigan
- alt.fan.harrison-ford
- alt.fan.helen-hunt
- alt.fan.jen-aniston
- alt.fan.jennifer-connelly
- alt.fan.jennifer-love-hewitt
- alt.fan.jenny-mccarthy
- alt.fan.jeri-ryan
- alt.fan.jessica-alba
- alt.fan.jim-carrey
- alt.fan.john-cusack
- alt.fan.john-travolta
- alt.fan.kate-winslet
- alt.fan.katie-holmes
- alt.fan.keanu-reeves.moderated
- alt.fan.kirsten-dunst
- alt.fan.larisa-oleynik
- alt.fan.leo-dicaprio
- alt.fan.linda-hamilton
- alt.fan.lisa-boyle
- alt.fan.lisa-marie-presley
- alt.fan.liv-tyler
- alt.fan.meg-ryan
- alt.fan.michael-biehn
- alt.fan.michelle-pfeiffer
- alt.fan.mike-myers
- alt.fan.milla-jovovich
- alt.fan.mira-furlan
- alt.fan.neve-campbell
- alt.fan.noah-wyle
- alt.fan.pam-anderson
- alt.fan.pat-arquette
- alt.fan.pat-richardson
- alt.fan.phoebe-cates
- alt.fan.pierce-brosnan
- alt.fan.princess-diana
- alt.fan.renee-oconnor
- alt.fan.robert-beltran
- alt.fan.robin-williams
- alt.fan.rosieodonnell
- alt.fan.sandra-bullock
- alt.fan.schwarzenegger
- alt.fan.spalding-gray
- alt.fan.tarantino
- alt.fan.tea-leoni
- alt.fan.teen.idols
- alt.fan.teen.starlets
- alt.fan.val-kilmer
- alt.fan.van-damme
- alt.fan.wil-wheaton
- alt.fan.winona-ryder
- alt.fan.yasmine-bleeth
- alt.gossip.celebrities

PEOPLE: FAMOUS AND INTERESTING

> The Internet supports the three most important pillars of popular culture: sex, lies and videotape. (For more information, take a look at "Sexuality", "Politics" and "Television".)

Dangerfield, Rodney

This is the official page of Rodney Dangerfield, the American comedian who complains, "I get no respect." There is a lot of great stuff here: sound files of Rodney talking (some of which are suitable to put on your answering machine), information about Rodney's movies, a joke of the day, lots of pictures, and more. ("I don't get no respect. I told my psychiatrist I got suicidal tendencies. He said from now on I have to pay in advance.")

Web:
http://www.rodney.com/

Date, Kyoko

Among teenagers, Kyoko Date is one of the most popular people in Japan. She's a teen idol with a pretty face, an engaging smile, a pleasing personality, and a large fan club. Kyoko was born on October 26, 1979, in Tokyo. She is 5'4" (163 cm) tall and weighs 95 pounds (43 kilograms), with a pleasing teenage figure which, to the delight of her fans, she shows off by wearing short shorts and a skimpy top. Her favorite actors are Christian Slater and Kyozo Nagazuka, and her hobbies are collecting shoes and learning foreign languages. What makes DK-96 (her nickname) so unusual is that she is not a real person. She is the creation of a team of graphic artists and programmers, who spent 18 months and a huge amount of money giving birth to Ms. Date. No doubt about it, DK-96 has a huge future. Her first CD single was released in November 1996. Within a few years, Kyoko is going to appear on a "live" television show and talk with other guests, and once the technology is perfected, it will be used to create other virtual characters. Would you like to feel mortal? Consider that long after you and I are gone, Kyoko Date will still be around—a young, talented, accomplished flower of femininity, tantalizing the great-grandsons of the Japanese boys who worship her today.

Web:
http://www.tv3000.nl/kyoko/

Look What I Found on the Net...

```
Newsgroup: alt.gossip.celebrities
Subject: Death of the Supermodel

> There was a piece in a magazine a few years ago where they
> took a cover photo of Michelle Pfeiffer and showed all the
> retouching notes.  There were shadows added to cheeks to
> thin the face, hairs removed from the hairline to improve
> it, and blemishes removed...
>
> It was quite a revelation to me.  I sat down with my then
> 12-year-old daughter to have a discussion about it.
> She's sixteen now and still model-proofed.

That's so cool that you did that.  All girls should be
"model-proofed" before puberty.  It would certainly save on
heartache and therapy bills later.
```

PEOPLE: FAMOUS AND INTERESTING

> Cool.

Einstein, Albert

If you ask the man on the street who the greatest scientist of all time was, you would probably get the answer Albert Einstein. Einstein (1879-1955) was born in Germany, although he went to a university in Switzerland and, later, became an American. (Like many other great men, Einstein had the distinction of ending his life in New Jersey.) It would be difficult to exaggerate Einstein's contribution to twentieth century physics (but let me try anyway). His work on relativity completely changed the way mankind thought about space and time, while his work on quantum physics helped create our modern understanding of how energy and matter are constituted and laid the basis for the exploitation of atomic energy. Einstein won the 1921 Nobel Prize in Physics (for his explanation of the photoelectric effect, not for his relativity theory). Like many other great scientists, Einstein did not seem to have as great an acumen about people and society as he did about science. His scientific insight—at least when he was young—was astonishing. His social insights were well-intentioned but somewhat naive. I guess the best way to put it is that, when it came to understanding the universe Einstein had no peer, but when it came to understanding people he was no Einstein.

Web:
  http://www.westegg.com/einstein/

Famous People's Wills

Are you surprised? Not me, I knew it had to be somewhere on the Net: the last wills and testaments of famous people. See what the likes of Jacqueline Kennedy Onassis, John Lennon, Walt Disney, Babe Ruth and Benjamin Franklin left to posterity. (They also have Elvis's will. I checked but, unfortunately, he didn't leave me anything.)

Web:
  http://www.ca-probate.com/wills.htm
  http://www.courttv.com/legaldocs/newsmakers/wills/

Fuller, Buckminster

What do you do in your spare time? Most people read, play sports or watch TV. Not many could say, "Well, I had a lot of time on my hands last weekend, so I invented the geodesic dome." Get to know Buckminster Fuller, his works and philosophy.

Web:
  http://www.lsi.usp.br/usp/rod/bucky/buckminster_fuller.html
  http://www.pbs.org/wnet/bucky.cgi

Listserv Mailing List:
  List Name: **geodesic**
  Subscribe to: **listserv@listserv.acsu.buffalo.edu**

Buckminster Fuller

Richard Buckminster Fuller was a genius in that he could shed light on just about any area to which he turned his attention. During his lifetime, he received 39 honorary degrees and became the inspiration for a cult-like following based not so much on a belief system, but on a way of looking at the world and solving its problems. He described himself as an "engineer, inventor, mathematician, architect, cartographer, philosopher, poet, cosmologist, comprehensive designer and choreographer".

What I like best about Fuller is how he lived his life as an experiment, and his recognition that if one contributes to one's culture, the economy will lend support in an appropriate manner. Although this may seem far-fetched, it is this Fuller-inspired philosophy that has helped me to choose my lot in life and is indirectly responsible for the book you are now reading.

If you would like to learn more about Fuller, his teachings and his followers, subscribe to the **geodesic** mailing list. It is wonderful to contemplate the work of someone who has the capacity to rise above the petty concerns of day-to-day life and to see the universe with the eyes of enlightened curiosity.

PEOPLE: FAMOUS AND INTERESTING

Gates, Bill

Isn't it great that we all get to live on this Earth at the same time as Bill Gates? Send Mr. Microsoft a note and tell him how much you appreciate his efforts to save mankind.

Mail:
billg@microsoft.com

Gingrich, Newt

Few people in American politics can match Newt Gingrich. He spent years clawing his way to the top so effectively that most people forget he got there by clawing. Notwithstanding his personal and political habits, Mr. Newt, the Speaker of the U.S. House of Representatives, is a tropical storm in the American weather pattern and, as such, deserves to be noticed. So notice him. (His mother will thank you.)

Web:
http://www.house.gov/gingrich/

Hall of Annoying Buttons

Would you like to bother a famous person? This Web site has a collection of buttons. Each button is associated with a famous person (for example, the President of the United States, David Letterman, Mick Jagger, Bill Gates, Roger Ebert and Wayne Newton). When you press a button, it automatically emails a short meaningless message—"Hello, how are you?"—to the person. Of course, these people don't really read most of their messages, but it's the thought that counts.

Web:
http://www.fractalcow.com/hall.htm

Horror Authors

Here is a collection of email addresses of horror authors, such as Clive Barker, Robert Devereaux, Nancy Etchemendy, and more. Unlike other celebrity lists, these addresses have all been confirmed, and the people have given their permission to be listed.

Web:
http://www.drcasey.com/literature/email.shtml

Lewinsky, Monica

Monica Lewinsky is the young woman who, while she was a 21-year-old intern in the White House, had an affair with William Jefferson Clinton, the forty-second president of the United States. Since then, Monica's relationships have been a primary concern with right-thinking people everywhere: her relationships with Mr. Bill, her father, her lawyers, independent prosecutor Ken Starr, and—most of all—with the American people. Why such fascination with things Monica? Well, she was emotionally and sexually involved with The Leader of the Free World. But there's more to it than that. Monica represents the dark side of the U.S. body politic, the epitome of the American Dream exaggerated to a spoiled, curdled parody of itself. You can judge Monica with the good-natured indulgence usually reserved for those caught up in the follies of youth, or you can condemn her as a bottom-feeding Beverly Hills strumpet. However, one thing is clear. In the cutthroat world of U.S. politics, when the going gets tough, the tough ignore Monica at their peril.

Web:
http://www.d-zyn.com/monica/
http://www.gomonica.com/

Usenet:
alt.flame.monica-lewinsky
alt.politics.clinton

McCaffrey, Anne

American writer Anne McCaffrey (1926-) is the author of the Pern book series, the Crystal Singer series, and many other sci-fi/fantasy works. This is her official Web site, where you will find biographical information, a FAQ (frequently asked question list), information about new books, and some sample chapters. Although the email address is reputed to be McCaffrey's, you will probably not get a response. She is, however, Net savvy and well aware of all the goings-on around the Net using her work as a basis (such as the Pern mud and fan fiction on Usenet). McCaffrey is happy with people participating in her make-believe worlds, and she has set up guidelines about what they should and shouldn't do.

Web:
http://members.aol.com/dragnhld/

Mail:
anniemac@iol.ie

604 PEOPLE: FAMOUS AND INTERESTING

Nobel Prize Winners

Have you ever wondered if maybe you have won a Nobel Prize, but you never found out because your phone was off the hook? (Don't laugh, this actually happened to me twice.) Well, stop worrying. Here is information about all the Nobel prize winners. The categories are chemistry, economics, literature, peace, physics, and physiology/medicine. There is also a special list of all the women who have been awarded Nobel prizes.

Web:
   http://www.nobel.se/prize/progtable.html
   http://www.nobelprizes.com/

Pope John Paul II

If you need a fast dose of religious experience, check out the Web pages of the Pope. Read some of his writings and find out where the Pope is traveling in case you want to call ahead and make arrangements to have dinner with him.

Web:
   http://www.catholic.net/rcc/POPE/Pope.html
   http://www.vatican.va/

There is no doubt about it: the **Pope** is one of the greatest human beings in the world. If you would like information about the Pope's books or biographical data, check out this unofficial home page.

By the way, the Pope and I have a deal. I promised to mention him in my books, and he promised to mention me in his books.

> There's no place like the Net.

Poundstone, William

William Poundstone is one of my favorite writers. Poundstone, an American, is the author of a number of books, among them the Big Secrets series, in which he reveals all kinds of stuff people do not want you to know. My advice is to visit the Web site, admire Poundstone's picture, send him an email note, and then rush out and buy one of the Big Secrets books. Not only are the books filled with fascinating (secret) information, but Poundstone is an excellent writer whose witty and captivating style will inform, entertain and amuse you.

Web:
   http://members.aol.com/bigsecrets/

Mail:
   bigsecrets@aol.com

President of the United States

Does anyone really believe that the President of the United States even sees any of his email? Just between us, the real truth is that nobody even reads it. Still, if you send in a letter you will get an automated response (which is more than you can say about writing to Bill Gates or the Pope). Actually, I don't really expect the President of the U.S. to drop everything just to respond to his email. After all, he has his hands full being Leader of the Free World, Commander-in-Chief of the U.S. Armed Forces, as well as Grand Poobah of the Illuminati. Still, if you drop him a note and tell him what is wrong with America, you will at least earn a few karma points. Couldn't hurt.

Mail:
   president@whitehouse.gov

PEOPLE: FAMOUS AND INTERESTING

Princess Diana

On July 1, 1961, Lady Diana Frances Spencer was born at Park House, near Sandringham, England. On August 31, 1997, Diana, Princess of Wales, died in the twisted wreck of a hideous car crash in a tunnel in Paris, France. And thus ended the life of one of the most remarkable women of the twentieth century. A study in contradiction, Diana was both extraordinary and mediocre, inspiring and provocative, elegant and tedious. In death, as in life, Diana, the "people's Princess", captured the hearts of millions of people around the world, melding a weakness of intellect, wisdom and judgment with a sense of honor, personal rapport and compassion that would be difficult to overpraise. The princess is dead; long live The Princess.

Web:
http://www.cnn.com/WORLD/9708/diana/
http://www.dianageneration.org/
http://www.royal.gov.uk/start.htm

Usenet:
alt.fan.princess-diana
alt.memoriam.princess-di

Randi, James

James Randi (1928-)—The Amazing Randi—is a Canadian-born American magician and skeptic who debunks fraudulent paranormal events and claims. Randi offers a half million dollars to any person who can prove, under his scientific conditions, that he or she has psychic powers. This Web site explains about Randi and what he does, including the James Randi Educational Foundation. To me, Randi is truly one of the heroes of our time, debunking foolishness and superstition, and shedding light into the dark recesses of ignorance and dishonesty.

Web:
http://www.randi.org/

Mail:
jamesrandi@compuserve.com

The Internet is always on.

Look What I Found on the Net...

```
Newsgroups: alt.internet.services
Subject: The White House Address

> Just clearing up a few points, the White House Internet
> address is:
>
>       whitehouse.gov
>
> The President's email address is:
>
>       president@whitehouse.gov
>
> and it works.  (You get a canned reply message, saying that
> they read all of the mail, etc.)
>
> My girlfriend was wondering:
> Is there an email address for the President's wife?

I've heard that the First Lady's address is:

        root@whitehouse.gov
```

PEOPLE: FAMOUS AND INTERESTING

Real Names of Famous People

Have you ever wondered why actress Lauren Bacall did not use her real name in show business? Perhaps because it's Betty Joan Perske. And tell the truth. Would you write a letter to Abigail van Buren (Dear Abby) asking for advice if you knew her real name was Pauline Esther Friedman and her friends called her "Popo"? Find out the real names of your favorite celebrities and, who knows, the knowledge may one day save your life. By the way, did you know that Michael J. Fox's real name was Michael A. Fox? (He didn't want the headlines in fan magazines to read "Michael, A Fox".)

Web:
http://www.walshnet.com/walshnet/punster/realname.htm

Santa Claus

It's nice to know that as busy as Santa is, he always has time to stay up with the latest technology. Send your wish list to Santa by email or you can see what he, the elves and reindeer are doing on the Web. Maybe if you are especially good this year, Santa will bring you a high-speed Internet connection for the holidays.

Web:
http://www.santaclaus.com/

Mail:
santa@bx.com

Thompson, Hunter S.

Hunter S. Thompson (1939-) is an American writer and ex-journalist, best known for his books (such as Fear and Loathing in Las Vegas) and his articles (many of which were published in Rolling Stone magazine). Thompson is the originator of gonzo journalism, an imaginative and opinionated style of writing in which the author becomes involved in the very story he is trying to cover. Despite his questionable lack of social skills, his drug and alcohol addiction, and his degeneration from a highly skilled writer to a literary non-entity, Thompson is worshipped by fans (of which I am one) for his legendary exploits, as well as a legacy of some of the finest writing produced in twentieth century America. This site has information about Thompson's life, his books and what he's doing now (mostly looking for beer and fretting over legal problems because he drinks and drives). Unfortunately, when the going gets tough, you can't stay cool forever.

Web:
http://www.tekknowledge.com/gonzo/

Vice President of the United States

No, there is no truth that the Vice President of the United States is really a Turing Machine. (Actually, he couldn't even pass the test.) Write him and tell him how nice he looks on TV.

Mail:
vice-president@whitehouse.gov

> **Vice President of the United States**
>
> The Vice President of the United States is lonely. He can't run the country, but he has to hang around just in case something happens.
>
> I bet he would really enjoy it if you dropped him a nice note, complementing him on his tie, and mentioning how much you appreciate the fine job he is doing.

PERSONALS AND DATING

American Singles

Browse a huge list of men and women who have written a short paragraph about themselves, hoping that in a few lines you will be hooked. If anyone catches your interest, you can call, write or email them.

Web:
http://www.as.org/

Bisexuals

Response will come easily for people posting to this personals group since they are not limited by gender classification. Bisexuals from around the world post ads for friendship, love, and encounters of an intimate nature.

Usenet:
alt.personals.bi

PERSONALS AND DATING

Blind Dates

It's one of those really bad experiences: your friends made the blind date sound fabulous, yet you are stuck in the reality of actually interacting with a person whom you would rather be helping board a plane to the Bermuda Triangle. Don't get stuck in this kind of situation. Read this list of "Ways to Get Rid of Blind Dates". It may save your life.

Web:
http://ic.net/~psystems/funstuff/blinddates.html
http://www.northernnet.com/mischief_maker/blinddates.htm

Chit-Chat

The nice thing about IRC is that you can join a channel to talk about something specific, or you can just sit around and talk, talk, talk. If you are in the mood to chat about nothing in particular, try one of these channels and ramble to your heart's content.

IRC:
#chitchat
#hottub
#talk2me

Cupid's Network

It can be difficult sometimes to find that special someone. Especially so since, as one of my readers, you are a particularly attractive and discerning person who deserves the very best. Well, your difficulties are over: Cupid has traded his bow and arrow for a fast Internet connection.

Web:
http://www.cupidnet.com/cupid/

Dating Pattern Analyzer

Fill out the forms, and the analyzer will tell you your dating patterns and offer you helpful advice. All you need to do is specify information regarding at least three people you've dated. One of my friends used the service and it told her to look for "interesting, tall, wealthy, smart men". "Well," as she would say, "duh!"

Web:
http://www.cam.org/~jmauld/English/dateanal.html

Dating Tests

Take these tests to see if you are worth dating. These lists of questions might be painful, so have the number of a good therapist close at hand. Give the dating form to someone you have met who you are considering dating. See how they score before you make any commitments.

Web:
http://www.safari.net/~sky/freedom/date.htm
http://www.visi.com/~nathan/humor/tests/dating.test.html
http://www.visi.com/~nathan/humor/tests/dating2.test.html

Friend Finder

Here's a great multi-purpose personals service. It's not your typical sex maniac stomping ground where anyone breathing will get pounced on. This semi-moderated personals service allows you to use a secret ID to respond to ads anonymously until you feel safe giving out your real email address. Not only will you find personal ads for dating or romance, but you can also find listings for pen pals, roommates and activity partners. Note: The **adult** Web site is for finding erotic partners.

Web:
http://adult.friendfinder.com/
http://www.friendfinder.com/

Feel lucky?
Try **alt.personals.bi**, the bisexual discussion group. Right away it will double your chances of getting a date for Friday night.

608 PERSONALS AND DATING

Friend Finder

We all need other people, but sometimes it's not easy to find the right kind of companions. If you are looking for a friend, a romantic partner, a pen pal, or somebody to share an activity, try the Friend Finder and let the power of the Net help improve your social life.

Friendly Folk

You can never have too many friends (unless they all want to stay over at your house on the same weekend). Make and keep friends all over the world by visiting these IRC channels. It's fun and fast-paced and best of all, it's cheaper than paying for a long-distance phone call.

IRC:
#chatfriends
#cyberfriends
#friendly
#friendship

Internet Personals

It's a total drag when you can't post to the personals because your mom hangs out on the Net and you are afraid she'll see your name. Worry no longer. This personals page uses an anonymous mail forwarding system to ensure your privacy.

Web:
http://www.montagar.com/personals/

Internet Romances

Have you met on the Net? Are you planning a hot romance with a net.friend? Optimists, pessimists and fans of the electronic sociological experience should have a look at this collection of papers and articles about romance on the Internet. These writings offer some practical advice and a little dose of reality.

Web:
http://web2.airmail.net/walraven/romance.htm

Jewish Personals

If you are looking for more than a good matzo ball recipe, take a look at these Internet resources specifically related to Jewish people. You can post ads whether you are Jewish or just looking for someone Jewish to date.

Web:
http://www.jdate.com/

Usenet:
alt.personals.jewish

Large People

Why bother with skinny, insubstantial waifs when you can go for the romantic gusto? Join the people who appreciate large men and women by reading the ads in these Usenet groups or posting an ad of your own. The **tall** group is for people who are especially tall (or who want a tall partner); the **fat** group is for heavy people, while **big-folks** caters to those who are generally large. Spend some time on Usenet and it won't be long before you'll come to appreciate how often good things come in large packages.

Usenet:
alt.personals.big-folks
alt.personals.fat
alt.personals.tall

Need a laugh? See "Comics".

PERSONALS AND DATING

Meeting People

Welcome to the smorgasbord of personal ads. There is something for everyone, and you can take as much as you like. Non-fattening, hypo-allergenic, 100 percent of your recommended daily allowance of fun and good times. Participate in one of these Usenet groups and maybe you'll meet the man, woman or none-of-the-above of your dreams.

Usenet:
 alt.personal
 alt.personal.ads
 alt.personals
 alt.personals.ads
 alt.personals.black
 alt.personals.bodyart
 alt.personals.fetish
 alt.personals.gothic
 alt.personals.hiv-positive
 alt.personals.intercultural
 alt.personals.intergen
 alt.personals.interracial
 alt.personals.misc
 alt.personals.teen
 alt.personals.transgendered
 soc.personals

Romance and the Internet

Are you looking for that special someone?

Or are you looking for someone who is looking for that special someone?

Or… would you like to just snoop on people who are looking for that special someone?

As you can see, there are lots of reasons to read the Usenet personal groups.

Give your résumé a quick brush up and drop in today.

Pen Pal Brides

A long article about pen pal brides, commonly referred to as mail order brides. Get tips on meeting women, getting them into the country, how to choose a good wife, and advice on avoiding international dating companies that charge hefty fees for their services.

Web:
 http://www.upbeat.com/wtwpubs/intro.htm

Personal Ads Talk and General Discussion

This is the Usenet group for talking about personal ads that you may have seen on Usenet or in a newspaper or magazine. Discuss style, what works and what doesn't, and your experiences. And, oh yes, while you're looking around, maybe you'll find something to pique your interest.

Usenet:
 alt.personals.d

Personals for Gays

Here's a place to hang out if you want to be with people who consider same-sex relationships the norm. Find heaps of personal ads written by people who are on a quest for other members of the gay community.

Usenet:
 alt.personals.gay
 alt.personals.motss
 alt.personals.motss.women

Relationship Advice

The course of true love does not always run as smooth as we might wish. You can spend your time working on the relationship, but sometimes enough is enough. Why not turn to the Net instead to satisfy your emotional need to analyze? Free relationship advice is waiting patiently, just for you.

Web:
 http://www.askdrlove.com/
 http://www.suntimes.com/index/raskin.html

610 PERSONALS AND DATING

Spanking

Everyone needs a good spanking now and then. If you like getting your bottom blistered or warming up someone else's backside, try placing an ad here to find a spanking partner.

Usenet:
 alt.personals.spanking
 alt.personals.spanking.punishment

Are you bored? Go get spanked. NOW.

PHILOSOPHY

Aesthetics

Aesthetics is the area of philosophy concerned with the nature of beauty, for example, as it is expressed within the fine arts. As you might imagine, such topics quickly enter the realm of the nature of art and artistic judgment (and, if you are a Kantian, perception as well). Plato and Aristotle both said that beauty is inherent in an object, and, thus, may be judged objectively. Hume, on the other hand, felt that whatever pleased the observer was beautiful. My opinion is somewhere in between. I feel about beauty the same way U.S. Supreme Court Justice Potter Stewart feels about pornography: I may not be able to define it, but I know it when I see it.

Web:
 http://www.indiana.edu/~asanl/

Listserv Mailing List:
 List Name: **aesthetics-l**
 Subscribe to: **listserv@listserv.indiana.edu**

Look What I Found on the Net...

```
Newsgroup: alt.personals.d
Subject: Hasty Generalizations

> Before holding forth to the masses, we should all take time to
> be wary of making hasty generalizations about gender.
>
> Women and men are different, and there are differences within
> genders.  Not all men are of that opinion, by the way.
>
> I have personally found that it is better to talk to women
> about certain things and to men about others, each
> contributing in their own way.

Very nicely stated.

Women and men are different.  They talk and shop and walk and
see differently.  They love and want differently.

I have learned that my male friends aren't interested
in hearing the "he said, she said" tales my girlfriends and I
tell.
```

PHILOSOPHY

Chinese Philosophy
Have a hankering for a little Chinese philosophy? Learn about the various schools of thought and read some texts by Confucius and Zhu Zi, many of which are in English. Also available are bibliographies and mailing lists about Chinese philosophy which are also in English.

Web:
http://www-personal.monash.edu.au/~sab/

Ethics
Ethics is the branch of philosophy concerned with moral principles, standards of conduct, and social obligations. Society believes that it is the mark of a normal person to be able to distinguish between right and wrong, but who gets to decide what's right and what's wrong? Plato was convinced that there was an absolute good to which human beings could aspire. (But then, even his best friends couldn't deny that Plato was somewhat of a dreamer.) Aristotle, on the other hand, saw moral virtue as the mean between extremes (the dancing on the fence theory). Ethics have always been one of the favorite topics of philosophers, and there is a lot of ethical thought on the Net for you to enjoy. So check out these Web sites: it's the right thing to do.

Web:
http://ethics.acusd.edu/
http://www.ethics.ubc.ca/resources/

Listproc Mailing List:
List Name: **soceth-l**
Subscribe to: **listproc@usc.edu**

Existentialism
Existentialism may seem abstract, but it is actually a highly utilitarian philosophy. Existentialism sees human existence as being fundamentally unexplainable. As individuals, we are isolated from a universe that is at once hostile and indifferent. On the other hand, we are responsible for our own choices, and we do have the freedom to act as we want. Thus, existentialism is the perfect philosophy for teenagers and for people writing essays about twentieth century French literature.

Web:
http://members.aol.com/KatharenaE/private/Philo/philo.html
http://userzweb.lightspeed.net/~tameri/tframes.html

Greek Philosophy
The history of Western philosophy starts at about 600 B.C. with the Greeks. Classical Greek philosophy provides the underpinnings for much of our modern civilization and how we approach thinking about life. Greek philosophy was especially concerned with two main areas: the nature of reality, and the idea of virtue and how it should be applied to politics. What I find interesting is that today we still greatly concern ourselves with the nature of reality, but, for some reason, we seem to not care so much about ideals of virtue and how they should be applied to politics. For this reason, I feel it is especially enlightening to read the works of Aristotle, Socrates, Plato and the other Greek philosophers to whom we owe so much of our heritage.

Web:
http://iris.dissvcs.uga.edu/~archive/Greek.html
http://phd.evansville.edu/plato.htm
http://php.iupui.edu/~cplaneau/plato_01.html
http://www.utm.edu/research/iep/a/aristotl.htm

Listserv Mailing List:
List Name: **sophia**
Subscribe to: **listserv@listserv.liv.ac.uk**

Memetics
There is a theory that ideas can propagate biologically. So, if you start getting funny thoughts in your head and you don't know where they came from, you can blame it on your parents and the theory of Memetics. Never again will you have to take responsibility for those strange ideas that keep coming to mind. Learn about memes and their effects on humanity.

Web:
http://www.brodietech.com/rbrodie/meme.htm
http://www.sepa.tudelft.nl/webstaf/hanss/mem.htm

Usenet:
alt.memetics

Metaphysics Talk and General Discussion
Do you ever get the impression that there is more going on in the universe than you realize? Sit around with the folks on Usenet who love to contemplate the philosophical aspects of our "beingness" as well as the workings of the cosmos.

Usenet:
alt.paranet.metaphysics
sci.philosophy.meta

Objectivism

Ayn Rand (1905-1982) was a Russian-born American philosopher and novelist who created the philosophy of Objectivism. She summarizes: "My philosophy, in essence, is the concept of man as a heroic being, with his own happiness as the moral purpose of his life, with productive achievements as his noblest activity, and reason as his only absolute."

Web:
http://www.vix.com/objectivism/

Usenet:
alt.philosophy.objectivism
humanities.philosophy.objectivism

Listproc Mailing List:
List Name: **objectivism-l**
Subscribe to: **listproc@cornell.edu**

Listserv Mailing List:
List Name: **objectivism**
Subscribe to: **listserv@whitman.edu**

Objectivism in the 1990s

There are some who find Ayn Rand's philosophy of Objectivism as relevant today as it was many years ago when she first started explaining what was wrong with the world. There are others who say that her ideas were fine for the time but are atavistic and irrelevant to modern life. Then, there are still others who say "Ayn who?"

Whichever camp you find yourself in—slavish follower, skeptical cynic, or just plain ignorant everyman—**Objectivism** will furnish you with enough food for thought to have your own pseudo-intellectual picnic.

I am not sure what Ayn Rand would make of the Internet. However, I bet she would buy several Harley Hahn books to impress her friends. "I don't care what you or anyone else may think," one can imagine her saying. "I am going to buy as many Harley Hahn books as I want. To do less, would be to compromise my inner self and would make all that I stand for a sham and a farce."

Philosophers

In the game of life, you can't tell the philosophers without a scorecard. With these resources, I guarantee you'll be able to find information about the philosopher of your choice whenever you want. Philosophically speaking, I think that seems as if it might be a good deal—maybe. (I'll have to think about it.)

Web:
http://people.delphi.com/gkemerling/dy/zt.htm
http://people.delphi.com/gkemerling/ph/index.htm
http://www.episteme.net/philosophers.html
http://www.epistemelinks.com/Main/MainPers.htm
http://www-personal.monash.edu.au/~dey/phil/think-ak.htm

Philosophy Reference Guides

Is philosophy getting you down? Is there just too much of it to handle? Well, if you find yourself confusing neoplatonism with quantification theory, and mixing up Nietzsche's theory of eternal recurrence with Socrates' doctrine of recollection, maybe it's time to spend a few hours on the Net. Once you know what you are talking about, you will have a stronger sense of identity. (Or as one sweet potato said to another, "I think, therefore I yam.")

Web:
http://people.delphi.com/gkemerling/dy/index.htm
http://plato.stanford.edu/
http://www.utm.edu/research/iep/

Philosophy Resources

Before you draw your next hot bath, go look at the English Server's philosophy archive. It contains text by such notable thinkers as Nietzsche, Descartes, Kant, Aristotle, Bacon and Burke. Read a few of these while the tub is filling, so it will give you something to think about as you have a nice soak.

Web:
http://english-www.hss.cmu.edu/philosophy/
http://www-personal.monash.edu.au/~dey/phil/
http://www.earlham.edu/~peters/philinks.htm
http://www.episteme.net/
http://www.epistemelinks.com/
http://www.philosophers.co.uk/

PHILOSOPHY

Philosophy Search Engines

Life is stern and life is earnest, and when you need some philosophy, you need it *now*. I understand, so here are some search engines to help you fulfill your philosophical needs quickly and discreetly. (Note: One size does not fit all.)

Web:
http://argos.evansville.edu/
http://hippias.evansville.edu/
http://www.perseus.tufts.edu/

Philosophy Talk and General Discussion

When the going gets tough, the tough start talking about philosophy—and these are the places to do it. Whatever your philosophical preference, there's room for you on Usenet. Just remember to be polite, and show respect for other people's point of view (unless they disagree with you).

Usenet:
alt.philosophy.basism
alt.philosophy.debate
alt.philosophy.kant
alt.philosophy.taoism
sci.philosophy
sci.philosophy.tech
talk.philosophy.humanism
talk.philosophy.misc

Political Philosophy

In order to maintain our societies, we organize ourselves into political systems. However, which system is the best one for a particular time and place? That's where political philosophy comes in. The deep thinkers of the ages have described and analyzed various types of political systems. Use the Net, read the ideas, and make your choice.

Web:
http://csf.colorado.edu/psn/marx/
http://lgxserve.ciseca.uniba.it/lei/filpol/filpole/homefpe.htm
http://www.apsanet.org/~theory/
http://www.cwu.edu/~millerj/nietzsche/
http://www.library.ubc.ca/poli/theory.html
http://www.usc.edu/dept/annenberg/thomas/nietzsche.html

Women in Philosophy

Tired of reading the same old philosophy by Kant, Descartes and Aristotle? For an intellectual change of pace, why not try Hannah Arendt, Simone de Beauvoir or Ayn Rand? Check with these Web sites (one of which is an extensive bibliography of women philosophers), then go right to the nearest library and check out a book. Do not pass Go. Do not collect 200 books of male-oriented philosophy.

Web:
http://billyboy.ius.indiana.edu/WomeninPhilosophy/WomeninPhilo.html
http://www.uh.edu/~cfreelan/SWIP/women.html

Look What I Found on the Net...

```
Newsgroup: talk.philosophy.misc
Subject: Serious Work In Philosophy

>> Are you tired of scrolling through senseless drivel passed
>> off as "philosophy" on various Usenet groups?

> Yes.  I am also tired of scrolling through senseless drivel
> from professional philosophers.  There may be laws passed
> banning philosophy if this keeps up.

I wouldn't want to see philosophy banned by law, but I would
be interested in the wording of a statute that attempted to
define "philosophy".
```

PHOTOGRAPHY

Alternative Photographic Processes

Traditional photography depends on silver gel substances and requires the use of a darkroom with safelighting. Alternative photographic processes use different chemicals and techniques, some of which do not have such rigorous requirements. In addition, alternative processes can be more fun than the traditional ways of developing film and can yield different types of results (often accidentally). Here are some Web sites to help you learn about these techniques. There is also information about photograms, an easy way to make interesting images using exposure to direct sunlight.

Web:
http://duke.usask.ca/~holtsg/photo/faq.html
http://www.lightfactory.org/cyanotype.html
http://www.mikeware.demon.co.uk/
http://www2.ari.net/glsmyth/

Black and White Photography

I love black and white photography. It's so clean, basic and accessible. If you want to find good black and white photography on the Net, all you need to do is check these Web sites. You'll find links to black and white photo Web sites, a FAQ (frequently asked question list), as well as archives of some wonderful photos.

Web:
http://www.artzone.gr/
http://www.photogs.com/bwworld/

Daguerreotypes

A daguerreotype is a photographic image made on a light-sensitive silver-coated metallic plate. The daguerreotype was invented in 1839 by Louis Jacques Mandé Daguerre (1789-1851), a French scene painter and physicist. (Daguerre was also the man who helped invent the diorama, a sort of three-dimensional pictorial scene.) This Web site has galleries of 19th century imagery, exhibits of modern photographers using daguerreotypes and a history of the daguerreotype. There is also a description of all the steps involved in making a daguerreotype. Read this and you will appreciate how easy photography is today.

Web:
http://www.austinc.edu/dag/

Darkroom Photography

Photographic creativity certainly doesn't stop with a click of the shutter. When you head to the darkroom you have to ask yourself all sorts of questions like "Should I print on warm or cold tone paper?" and "What kind of developer should I use?" Here you will find information about darkroom-related technical topics: chemical usage, paper, tools and equipment, and more.

Web:
http://webs.kodak.com/global/en/consumer/education/lessonPlans/darkroom/
http://www.open.org/hughesa/w3-01.htm
http://www.users.dircon.co.uk/~migol/photo/photosource.html

Usenet:
rec.photo.darkroom

Digital Cameras

A digital camera is a photographic device that stores pictures within computer chips instead of regular film. As soon as you take a picture, it is ready—you don't need to have it developed. You can take pictures over and over without buying supplies (except a battery). Moreover, it is possible to transfer pictures to your computer. However, digital cameras do have limitations. Here is information that will help you understand and use digital cameras well. If you are thinking of buying one, you will find tips to help you make a good choice.

Web:
http://www.abalab.com/
http://www.dcresource.com/
http://www.orchidlink.com/digitalphotography/digicam.htm

Usenet:
alt.comp.periphs.dcameras

Exposure

It's good to be well-exposed, but it's better to expose well. If you are a beginner, this Web site has some great tips and tricks relating to light and film exposure. Take a crash course about photography. Then learn some low-tech tips to make your pictures more creative, and read a basic explanation of exposure theory. Check out the sim-cam—a great learning tool—that simulates exposure times and aperture settings. This allows you to see the changes that are produced on film by the adjustments you make to your camera.

Web:
http://www.88.com/exposure/

PHOTOGRAPHY

Room in the Darkroom

Some of the most mysterious things in the world go on in a darkroom. If you are not a photographer, sorry, this part of human culture is closed to you and there's not much you can do about it except feel wistful in a polite sort of way.

If, however, you are among the cognoscenti who can distinguish between lith processing and posterization, the discussion group **rec.photo.darkroom** is waiting for you. Join the club and see why it pays to stay in the dark.

Don't worry about technology, just enjoy yourself.

History of Photography

The development of photography involved the marriage of two different technologies: optical and chemical. Basic optical technology—in the form of the "camera obscura" (a dark box or room with a small hole in one end that could be used to project an inverted image on the wall opposite the hole)—was understood as far back as the time of Aristotle. And scientists have known about optical processes involving light and chemical reactions for hundreds of years. In the seventeenth century, the British physicist Robert Boyle discovered that silver chloride turned dark upon exposure. However, Boyle thought the discoloring was due to exposure to air, not to light. In the next century, Angelo Sala noticed that powdered silver nitrate became dark in the sun. In 1727, Johann Schulze realized that particular liquids turn color upon exposure to the sun. In the early nineteenth century, Thomas Wedgewood was able to capture images, but only temporarily. Finally in 1827, Joseph Niépce produced the first permanent photographic image, which he called a heliograph. Read about the history of photography, and you will find it encompasses politics, culture, science and intrigue. These Web sites are good sources of information. If you are interested in the history of photography as a hobby, you can join the mailing list for an ongoing discussion.

Web:
http://www.kbnet.co.uk/rleggat/photo/
http://www.webcom.com/cityg/resource/pa/photarch.html

Listserv Mailing List:
List Name: **photohst**
Subscribe to: **listserv@asuvm.inre.asu.edu**

616 PHOTOGRAPHY

Infrared Photography

Infrared photography uses film that is sensitive to visible light, as well as ultraviolet and infrared radiation. The results are fascinating, often even eerie. Although the images look familiar, the contrast and details are not what you are used to. If you are interested in photography, you have to try infrared photography at least once in your life. To help you get started, I have chosen two Web sites that contain documents relating to infrared photography (where you can find out about cameras, lenses, exposures, focusing, developing and printing), and another Web site that offers a collection of infrared photos for you to enjoy.

Web:
http://ruly70.medfac.leidenuniv.nl/~cor/ir_g_nfr.html
http://www.a1.nl/phomepag/markerink/mainpage.htm
http://www.mat.uc.pt/~rps/photos/FAQ_IR.html

Kite Aerial Photography

(1) Attach a camera to a kite. (2) Launch the kite. (3) Snap pictures using a remote control device. (4) Repeat step 3 as often as you wish. (5) Carefully pull in the kite and remove the camera. (6) Develop the pictures. (7) Live happily ever after. (What could be more cool?)

Web:
http://members.aol.com/mjbrown/HTML/kap.html
http://www.ced.berkeley.edu/arch_faculty_cris/kap/

Nature and Wildlife Photography

By its nature, nature photography naturally requires an unnatural amount of patience and skill. Naturally, you expect nature photographers to have a persevering nature, as the requirements of nature photography are demanding, although, just as naturally, the results can be rewarding. If your nature is one of a natural nature photographer, you will appreciate the natural pleasure you get from visiting nature photography Web sites and talking in a nature photography Usenet discussion group. Or you can just look at the pictures.

Web:
http://bobatkins.photo.net/
http://www.paragon-press.com/tips1.htm

Usenet:
rec.photo.technique.nature

Panoramic Photography

Panoramic photography uses a wide angle lens in order to capture an unbroken view of the surrounding area. In general to qualify as panoramic, your picture must have an angle of view of at least 100 degrees (a little less than a third of a full circle). Panoramic photography is perfect for landscape shots in which you want to capture the expansiveness of the area you are photographing (the Grand Canyon, a spectacular snow-covered mountain range, a sweeping city skyline, and so on). Here is how a typical panoramic camera works. The camera rotates on top of a tripod. As the camera turns, the shutter is held open. The film moves past the aperture (shutter opening) with the same speed and direction as the camera itself. The result? A panoramic picture with a view to remember. These Web sites will give you the scoop on panoramic photography, including information on equipment, tips for taking photos, and galleries of panoramic images.

Web:
http://lcweb2.loc.gov/ammem/pnhtml/pnhome.html
http://www.panoramic.net/wwworld/
http://www.panphoto.com/

Panoramic Photography

Shouldn't your photographs be as **large** as your artistic vision?

Don't think small. Get it all.

PhotoForum

This site offers a good selection of material for the novice or professional. At this site you can find FAQs, equipment reviews, lens information, useful addresses and phone numbers, archives having to do with photos and cameras, and a rotating display of the work of members of the mailing list.

Web:
http://www.rit.edu/~andpph/photoforum.html

Listserv Mailing List:
List Name: **photoforum**
Subscribe to: **listserv@rit.edu**

PHOTOGRAPHY

Photographers Directory

This Web site contains a large list of photographers from all around the world who use the Net. You can check the list either alphabetically or geographically. This is a good site to know about if you are looking for a photographer or if you are a photographer looking for clients.

Web:
http://www.mindspring.com/~jdsmith/plist/plframe.html

Photography Basics

Do you want to learn how to go beyond basic pointing and shooting? These Web sites have information about cameras and how they work, the history of photography, natural and artificial lighting, and composing and balancing images. You can also learn about the different kinds of photography—portraiture, documentary, macro and micro, art photography—and explore links to some useful photo sites around the Net.

Web:
http://www.algonet.se/~bengtha/photo/faqs_docs.html
http://www.fodors.com/focus/
http://www.generation.net/~gjones/faqs.htm
http://www.goldcanyon.com/photo/
http://www.halcyon.com/denise/

Photography Equipment Talk and General Discussion

There are a lot of photographers on the Net and, no matter what your particular interest, there is someone to talk to. So why not choose a Usenet group, talk about photographic equipment and see what develops?

Usenet:
rec.photo.equipment.35mm
rec.photo.equipment.film+labs
rec.photo.equipment.large-format
rec.photo.equipment.medium-format
rec.photo.equipment.misc
rec.photo.film+labs

Photography Resources

Photography dates back to 1827 when the Frenchman Joseph Niépce made the first permanent photograph. In 1839, the technology was enhanced significantly by another Frenchman, Louis Daguerre, who invented the daguerreotype. Modern photography dates from 1941 and the work of the Englishman William Talbot. Today, cameras both traditional and digital are ubiquitous and we take photography for granted. However, it has been barely half a century since the general population has had access to reliable, affordable cameras and film. Previously, it was next to impossible for regular people to create and preserve images. Imagine how this changes one's sense of the past. For example, if you look at the Web sites that were created by the ancient Greeks and Romans, you will see that they are mostly text with a few rudimentary graphics. Today, cameras are readily available at low cost and anyone who wants can be a photographer (of sorts). To help you learn more about this rewarding pastime, I have selected several Web sites where you will be able to find a large variety of information relating to photography.

Web:
http://www.algonet.se/~bengtha/photo/
http://www.atchison.net/PhotoLinks/
http://www.generation.net/~gjones/

Photography Talk and General Discussion

Whether you are just a snapshot shooter or a pro with hundreds of pounds of equipment, there is a Usenet group perfect for you. Fans of photography hang out and talk about taking pictures from a creative as well as a technical point of view. Try the mailing list for photo talk that comes straight to your mailbox.

Usenet:
bit.listproc.stockphoto
rec.photo
rec.photo.advanced
rec.photo.help
rec.photo.misc
rec.photo.moderated
rec.photo.technique.art
rec.photo.technique.misc
rec.photo.technique.nature
rec.photo.technique.people

Listserv Mailing List:
List Name: **photoforum**
Subscribe to: **listserv@listserver.isc.rit.edu**

618 PHOTOGRAPHY

Pinhole Photography

Take an empty oatmeal box and make a tiny hole in one side. Now, in a darkroom, insert a piece of photographic paper inside the box, opposite the small hole. Cover up the hole and make sure all the edges of the box are completely sealed. Take the box to the location of your choice in the outside world and uncover the little hole. After a period of time, probably seconds, cover up the hole. (The amount of time you need to leave the hole open depends on the size of the hole. You will have to experiment.) Take the box back into the darkroom and extract the photographic paper. Develop it and admire your image. Congratulations, you have created your own pinhole camera.

Web:
http://acept.la.asu.edu/PiN/rdg/camera/camera.shtml
http://www.cool.mb.ca/~gnome/pinhole.html
http://www.pinhole.com/
http://www.sn.no/~gjon/pinhole.htm

Toy Cameras

I think toy cameras are cool. Toy cameras are, literally, toys: cheap little plastic cameras that use 120 film. They leak light; produce distortion, fog and vignetting on film; they have an unknown shutter speed and film that is wound loosely. (And those are just the obvious problems. There are all kinds of bizarre things that can happen when you use a toy camera.) So, why would anyone use them? Because they are fun and you never know what you are going to get. Moreover, toy cameras are great for experimenting. This Web site has information about taking photos with toy cameras. Learn how to correct problems in the darkroom, read about the history of toy cameras, and admire the gallery of toy-camera pictures. It's a great break from high-tech photography.

Web:
http://www.concom.com/~winters/toy_home.htm

Look What I Found on the Net...

```
Newsgroup: rec.photo.advanced
Subject: HELP! My wedding pictures are horrible!


> Well, after a wonderful wedding overlooking a gorgeous scene
> of clouds over the continental divide, I got back a proof book
> that is pitiful.
>
> Lots of group shots of washed-out faces with washed-out clouds.
> The photographer didn't move in to fill the frame, so most
> group shots are tiny faces.  Shots that obviously should have
> been portrait were taken in landscape. Most group shots had
> 3-4 people in the shade with everyone else in the sun.
>
> So my questions is: Can anything be done?  Can incorrect
> exposures be corrected in the lab?  What about group shots
> where one third of the group is dark and the other two
> thirds are washed out?  What can I do?
>
> Moral of the story: don't go cheap on the photographer :-(

If the photos were taken on medium format color negative film,
there's a pretty good chance that a good custom lab can salvage
them, at least if they are sharp. The exposure errors (within
reason) can be partially corrected by better printing technique,
and cropping can help the bad framing.
```

PHYSICS

Underwater Photography

I once took some underwater pictures. I went on a trip to the Caribbean and, before I left, I bought a waterproof disposable camera. During my snorkeling sessions, I happily snapped away at a variety of colorful fish and underwater scenery. When I returned home and had the pictures developed, I enjoyed them, but I realized they were nothing like the quality you would get with special equipment and techniques. Still, I had a great deal of fun, and I enjoy looking at my favorite picture of a turtle swimming around a reef. If you are interested in underwater photography, this mailing list is a great place to discuss techniques, equipment, tips and locations with other photographers around the world. The Web sites have images and tips for snapping underwater shots of your own.

Web:
http://www.aqueous.com/aq176.shtml
http://www.mainstream.net/~fgz/diving/uwphoto.html

Majordomo Mailing List:
List Name: **uw-photo**
Subscribe to: **majordomo@world.std.com**

Zone System

How often have you taken a picture, only to find that what you got was not what you wanted? Some people have the attitude, "I'll take the picture so it more or less captures what I want, and then I'll fix it in the darkroom." Well, that's okay as far as it goes, but if you like your pictures to be as perfect as possible, you may want to learn how to use the zone system. The zone system is a complicated set of techniques based on measuring dark and light spots, and then making certain calculations to get the exact picture you want. This system (which can take years to learn how to use well) was first envisioned in the late 1930s by Fred Archer of the Art Center College in Los Angeles. Ansel Adams read Archer's articles in a photography magazine, contacted Archer, and then developed more formal techniques for using the system. If you want to learn the zone system, these Web sites can help you a lot. In addition, you will need to get Adam's book "The Negative" and practice for many hours. To make it easy, always follow these basic principles: (1) Expose for the shadows. (2) Develop for the highlights. (3) Take a break and eat.

Web:
http://www.cicada.com/pub/photo/zs/

PHYSICS

Center for Particle Astrophysics

According to modern theories, there should be a lot more matter in the universe than we can currently detect. This missing stuff is referred to as "dark matter"—because it does not emit electromagnetic radiation—and a lot of scientists spend their time trying to discover where it is and what it is made of. The Center for Particle Astrophysics is primarily devoted to the "dark matter problem". As such, the Center brings together a large number of physicists in various fields such as cosmology (the study of the universe as a whole), astrophysics (the study of stars), and particle physics (the study of subatomic particles). Their Web site offers a lot of interesting information about the Center and its research (black holes and so on), as well as links to other physics resources on the Net.

Web:
http://cfpa.berkeley.edu/

Computational Fluid Dynamics

Fluid dynamics is the science that studies the movement of fluids (liquids and gases). Here is a Web site that contains resources for people who are concerned with the computational aspects of fluid dynamics. These pages will help you find academic institutions, companies, Web sites devoted to specific topics (such as turbulence and hypersonic flow), documents, and lots of other related information. For ongoing discussion, you can participate in the Usenet groups.

Web:
http://www.princeton.edu/~gasdyn/fluids.html

Usenet:
sci.mech.fluids
sci.physics.computational.fluid-dynamics

But...

620 PHYSICS

Fusion

Fusion is a process by which small atoms such as hydrogen are fused together to produce heavier atoms such as helium. As this happens, some of the matter is converted into energy. The goal of fusion research is to design reactors that produce large amounts of energy by fusing hydrogen atoms into helium under manageable conditions. In some ways, fusion is an ideal way to create energy. The raw materials are cheap, the waste material (helium) is safe, and there are no problems with radioactivity. However, fusion takes place only under conditions of extreme heat and pressure. (In fact, fusion is the basic process by which energy is produced inside of stars.) If we could create fusion reactors here on Earth, it would be wonderful, but there are still many years of research ahead of us.

Web:
http://www.frascati.enea.it/FTU/fusionlinks.html
http://wwwofe.er.doe.gov/education.html

Usenet:
sci.physics.fusion

Fusion

Hey, Bud. Yeah, I mean you. C'mon over here, I've got a tip for you.

Ya wanna win a Nobel Prize? I got it all figured out.

All ya gotta do is figure out a way to hold a bunch of hydrogen atoms together under great pressure at a high temperature, just long enough for them to fuse into helium.

I tell you, it's a great idea. We'll make a fortune selling energy all over the world.

You work out the details, and I'll figure a way to sell all the leftover helium to balloon companies, and we'll split the money even-Steven, right down the middle.

Whad'ya say, Bud? Is that an idea or what?

Index of Physics Abstracts

This is the perfect place to find papers relating to high energy physics, astrophysics, condensed matter theory, general relativity, quantum cosmology, and nuclear theory. A keyword search will help you track down the information you need.

Web:
http://xxx.lanl.gov/

Optics

Optics is the study of light and vision. Here is the Web site of the Optical Society of America (OSA). It covers all aspects of optical physics and engineering, including information about quantum electronics, photonics and vision.

Web:
http://www.osa.org/

Usenet:
sci.optics
sci.optics.fiber

Particle/High Energy Physics

These Web sites provide information to researchers in the areas of high energy physics and particle physics. (Such information is mandatory reading if you plan on creating your own reality.) There is also introductory information, in case you are interested in learning about sub-atomic particles, the basic building blocks of the universe. For ongoing discussion with scientists, you can participate in the Usenet particle physics discussion group.

Web:
http://www.fnal.gov/pub/hep_descript.html
http://www.hep.net/

Usenet:
sci.physics.particle

Particle Surface Research

Particle surface research involves the study of how an ion beam interacts with a particular surface. Here is a Web site where you will find links to computational, experimental and theoretical resources all over the Net. (If you run out of places to visit and you get bored, try shooting some beta particles at this book and see what happens.)

Web:
http://chaos.fullerton.edu/mhslinks.html

PHYSICS

Physics Conferences

If you feel the overwhelming urge to attend a physics conference, you can visit this site to search by month or by field of physics. Personally, I was going to go to the Aerosol Symposium, but I blew it off. As well as conferences, there are listings for workshops and summer schools.

Web:
http://www.physicsweb.org/TIPTOP/

Physics Talk and General Discussion

These are the main Usenet groups in which physics-related topics are discussed. If you have a question or a comment, post it to the most specific group you can that is appropriate. The **sci.physics** group is for the discussion of topics that don't fit in anywhere else. If you are new to these groups, you should start by reading the Usenet Physics FAQ (frequently asked question list) which you can find at the Web sites. (Remember, without physics, our world would be dull indeed and the universe would be far too easy to understand.)

Web:
http://www.faqs.org/faqs/physics-faq/
http://www.public.iastate.edu/~physics/sci.physics/faq/faq.html

Usenet:
alt.sci.physics.acoustics
alt.sci.physics.new-theories
alt.sci.physics.plutonium
bionet.biophysics
sci.astro.research
sci.chaos
sci.med.physics
sci.nonlinear
sci.optics.fiber
sci.physics
sci.physics.accelerators
sci.physics.cond-matter
sci.physics.electromag
sci.physics.research

> Break a rule.

Plasma Physics

When you have to attend a potluck dinner and you just don't know what to bring, consider a nice quasi-neutral gas such as plasma. Admittedly, it doesn't sound entirely appetizing, but just think of all the great things you can do with it. You could make an advanced microwave device, use it in ceramic production or toxic waste treatment or, for a really fun time, you could design a power grid for a spacecraft. Find out the other reasons why plasma is cool by reading information about the science and possible applications of this branch of physics.

Web:
http://plasma-gate.weizmann.ac.il/PlasmaI.html

Usenet:
sci.physics.plasma

Polymer and Liquid Crystal Tutorial

A polymer is a high-molecular weight compound, consisting of large numbers of repeating units—relatively simple molecules called monomers—linked by covalent bonds. Polymers can be natural (such as cellulose, silk and natural rubber) or synthetic (such as plastics and synthetic fibers). A liquid crystal is a liquid in which the constituent molecules arrange themselves with a higher degree of order than ordinary liquids, by pointing along a common axis called a director. Within a liquid crystal, the arrangement of the molecules offers many of the optical characteristics of solid crystals. However, since the molecular arrangements are not so firmly fixed, they can be modified—along with subsequent changes in optical properties—by mechanical stress, electromagnetic radiation or changes in temperature. Both polymers and liquid crystals are fascinating substances. If you would like a good introduction to these and other related subjects, try this series of well-organized, well-written multimedia tutorials. I enjoyed the tutorials myself, even though they did tend to remind me of organic chemistry class.

Web:
http://plc.cwru.edu/

622 PHYSICS

Large Molecules Are Cool

Let's face it. Anyone can walk around saying they like small molecules, such as sulfur dioxide or phosphoric acid. That takes no skill or taste whatsoever.

But you know what they say. The more important the man, the larger his favorite molecule. (Women, of course, are judged on entirely different standards.)

As one of my readers, you deserve the best, so I suggest you take some time to learn about polymers: large molecules that can literally stretch for millions of units.

Polymer Physics

Polymers are large molecules constructed out of repeating units of small building blocks, joined to one another by covalent bonds. Here are some resources for people involved in the scientific study of the physics of polymers. For discussion, there is the Usenet group and the mailing list.

Web:
http://cps-www.bu.edu/
http://irc.leeds.ac.uk/irc/

Usenet:
sci.polymers

Listserv Mailing List:
List Name: **polymerp**
Subscribe to: listserv@nic.surfnet.nl

Radioactive Waste

What do you do when your in-laws are spending their vacation with you and you have all this radioactive waste you suddenly have to get rid of? Quickly take a look at this Web site, which offers information on nuclear reactor systems, hybrid systems, the chemical aspects of transmutation, and the transmutation of radioactive waste.

Web:
http://www.nea.fr/html/trw/index.html

Relativity

"Relativity" refers to the idea that there are certain physical properties that can be determined only relative to an observer. Here is a simple example: You're standing beside a highway and someone points to a car and asks "How fast is that car going?" Now imagine yourself driving on the highway beside that very car, keeping even with it. In the first case, the car is moving fast relative to an observer at the side of the road. In the second case, the car is barely moving at all, relative to an observer in a nearby car. Einstein developed such ideas into two complex theories: special relativity (dealing with systems that are not accelerating) and general relativity (dealing with gravity and acceleration). Einstein's theories formed the basis of our modern understanding of the universe, and the relativity research that is being carried on today has the goal of explaining, with more and more accuracy, how things really work.

Web:
http://casa.colorado.edu/~ajsh/relativity.html
http://www.maths.qmw.ac.uk/wbin/GRnewsfind/general
http://www.phy.syr.edu/research/relativity/rel-link.html
http://www.weburbia.com/physics/relativity.html

Usenet:
sci.physics.relativity

PICTURES AND CLIP ART

Ascii Art

In general, there are two types of computer data: text and graphics. Text consists of characters: letters, numbers and punctuation; graphics are pictures. On a computer, text is stored according to a system called ASCII ("American Standard Code for Information Interchange). Thus, the name "ascii art" refers to drawings that are made up of characters. To see what I mean, take a look at these Web sites. You will be surprised how inventive people can be.

Web:
http://www.chris.com/ascii_art_menu.html
http://www.io360.com/v2/yo/asciiworld/
http://www-personal.engin.umich.edu/~saha/ASCII.html
http://www.w3masters.com/gallery/

PICTURES AND CLIP ART

Do you like **free pictures?**
Take a moment to visit the **Ascii Art Archive**. Find out why ascii art is now an accepted topic among the New York intelligentsia, and why ascii animation may be added to the next Cannes Film Festival.

Cartoon Pictures
There's no need to have a bare room or office cubicle. Go to Usenet right now and download some pictures of your favorite cartoon characters—Rescue Rangers, Snow White, Ren and Stimpy, Chip 'n' Dale, Bill and Hillary—here they are, waiting for you to download.

Usenet:
alt.binaries.pictures.cartoons
alt.toon-pics

Look What I Found on the Net...

```
               (From the polymer FAQ posted to sci.polymers)
Recycling
Most thermoplastic polymers can be recycled: that is, converted
from their initial use as a consumer, business, or industrial
product, back into a raw material from which some other product
can be manufactured.

There are three versions of the recycling logo.  The original
one was three arrows chasing each other in the shape of a
triangle, the second was just a triangle, and the current one is
a pair of angle brackets:

    < 1 >

The number inside the triangle or brackets indicates the
material used in the part.

There are six specific categories, and a generic seventh for
"other".  In the case of "other" it is good form to put the
material name under the recycling logo.

< 1 > PET (polyethylene terphthalate)
      — beverage containers, food pouches, meat packages

< 2 > HDPE (high density polyethylene)
      — milk or detergent or oil bottles, toys, plastic bags

< 3 > PVC (polyvinyl chloride)
      — food wrap, vegetable oil bottles, blister packaging

< 4 > LDPE (low density polyethylene)
      — shrink-wrap, plastic bags, garment bags

< 5 > PP (polypropylene)
      — margarine containers, grocery bags, food wrap

< 6 > PS (polystyrene)
      — plastic utensils, clothes hangars, foam cups or plates

< 7 > Other (all other polymers and polymer blends) including
      polycarbonate, ABS, PPO/PPE
```

Clip Art

Need clip art for your books, publications, garage sale fliers, home pages, term papers or whatever? But just as soon not (shudder) pay for them? Okay, on the Net there are lots of public domain clip art sites ripe for the plucking. In these copious archives, you'll find all the royalty-free drawings, etchings and whatnot that you could possibly use.

Web:
 http://www.barrysclipart.com/
 http://www.clipart.com/
 http://www.clipartconnection.com/
 http://www.webplaces.com/html/clipart.htm

Usenet:
 alt.binaries.clip-art

Fantasy Art

When the view out your window becomes boring and tedious, take a break from real life by browsing these huge archives of images of knights, castles, dragons, unicorns, wizards and more.

Web:
 http://www.dlaweb.com/clipart/fantasy/fantasy.htm
 http://www.flightofthedragon.com/kyl/clipart/
 http://www.ispdr.net.au/~bek/clipartmain.htm

Fractals

Fractals are mathematical constructions that have a "fractional" dimension. There are many types of fractals and, even within a single fractal, there can be infinite variety. Use these resources to learn about fractals, and explore the wonderful images you can create using these fascinating objects.

Web:
 http://www.cnam.fr/fractals.html
 http://www.comlab.ox.ac.uk/archive/other/
   museums/computing/mandelbrot.html
 http://www.faqs.org/faqs/sci/fractals-faq/

Usenet:
 sci.fractals

Icon Collections

Your Web pages and your desktop are just not complete without a few cool icons, either as just plain old decoration, or as links to something wild and crazy. Where, though, to get the icons? Well, these Web sites have collections of icons, some painstakingly created, that you can use for anything from simple clip art to clickable links.

Web:
 http://www.clipartcastle.com/
 http://www.fishnet.net/~gini/cool/
 http://www.syruss.com/

Icon Collections

Get an icon. Get another icon. Get yet another icon.
Get a totally cool look for your Web page.
Get new friends who admire your good taste and exquisite sense of design.
Get total happiness and a life of utter fulfillment.
Get an icon...
Get the picture?

Photo Archives

If a picture is worth a thousand words, these resources are worth a 1.257 million words. You'll find oodles of free pics of actors, art, architecture, aircraft, musicians, bands, sports, movies, foreign countries, cities, animals, nature, art, comics, digital animation, fantasy, maps, people, vehicles and space. Wow! Now all you need is good taste and a sense of design.

Web:
 http://www.imagiware.com/via/
 http://www.internet-stuff.com/multimedia_gallery/

Picture Viewing Software

Most of the time, your browser can show you any picture you want. However, there are a lot of different types of graphics, and there may be times when you need a special-purpose picture viewing program. Not to worry, all the programs you need are available on the Net for free.

Web:
http://www.bae.ncsu.edu/people/faculty/walker/hotlist/graphics.html

Realm of Graphics

Snazz up tired graphics with a smattering of backgrounds, buttons, lines, bullets and icons designed to impress. This is a great collection of doo-dads.

Web:
http://www.ender-design.com/rg/

Shuttle and Satellite Images

If you aren't an astronaut, you don't really get to see the cool outer space stuff up close. What I say is save your money or spend it on a nice vacation at the beach. On the Web, you can look at pictures of space and spacecraft and planets and stuff for free. And you don't have to wear one of those funny suits, either.

Web:
http://ceps.nasm.edu:2020/RPIF/SSPR.html
http://images.jsc.nasa.gov/

Stereograms

Stereograms are pictures consisting of what looks like a large number of small, random dots. However, when you stare at a stereogram in the right way, your brain will see a three-dimensional image, thereby showing you that there is more to what you see than what you see. (You know, that's an awfully deep thought. Maybe I should start my own religion.)

Web:
http://tqd.advanced.org/2647/misc/stertech.htm
http://www.ccc.nottingham.ac.uk/~etzpc/nz/sirds.html
http://www.ccc.nottingham.ac.uk/~etzpc/sirds.html
http://www.kondo3d.com/stereo/

Stereograms

Do you want to be omniscient?

Practice looking at stereograms until you can see the 3D images every time.

You will then know all and see all.

Supermodels

The next best thing to living next door to a supermodel is being able to download one whenever you want. Just the thing to look at when you get tired of fractals.

Web:
http://www.babeguide.com/
http://www.celebritypictures.com/

Usenet:
alt.binaries.pictures.supermodels

Thesaurus for Graphic Material

It's so annoying when you are sitting around the house trying to think of another word for "daguerreotype". No longer do you have to fret over finding just the right word. Browse the thesaurus or search using keywords.

Web:
http://lcweb.loc.gov/rr/print/tgm1/

POETRY

Blake, William

William Blake (1757-1827) was an English writer and poet whose work evolved from bright and gentle poems to often fierce and terrifying "prophetic" pieces about his intense spirituality and messages from heaven.

Web:
http://www.unomaha.edu/~wwwengl/blakeweb/frworks.html

British Poetry Archive

When you are in the mood for some poetry, light a fire and snuggle down with a screenful of works by British writers from 1780-1910. This page includes most of the biggies: Coleridge, Keats, Wordsworth, and many others.

Web:
http://etext.lib.virginia.edu/britpo.html

Browning, Elizabeth Barrett

Elizabeth Barrett Browning (1806-1861) was a renowned British poet who married another renowned British poet (Robert Browning). Her most noted works are "Sonnets from the Portuguese" (a series of love poems written to her husband), "Casa Guidi Windows" and "Aurora Leigh". Visit these Web sites where you will find biographical material, collections of poems, scholarly writing, and links to related resources.

Web:
http://www.inform.umd.edu:8080/EdRes/Topic/WomensStudies/ReadingRoom/Poetry/BarrettBrowning/
http://www.stg.brown.edu/projects/hypertext/landow/victorian/ebb/browningov.html

Chinese Poetry

Chinese poetry is beautiful in its imagery and simplicity. Read some Chinese poems at this Web site. (You have the option of reading them in either English or Chinese.)

Web:
http://www.chinapage.com/poetry.html

Collective Poem

Participate in this exercise in silliness by helping write a collective poem. Use the form provided to submit a poetic line that will be added to the end of the poem in progress. For the less adventurous, you can take a look at the work without having to add anything yourself.

Web:
http://www.smalltime.com/nowhere/rhubarb/poem.html

Dickinson, Emily

Emily Elizabeth Dickinson (1830-1886) was a prolific American poet. Her verse is characterized by style, wit and imagery. Dickinson was a recluse who stayed in her house most of the time, writing poetry. Although she wrote a great many poems, Dickinson was virtually unpublished until after her death. This Web site has hundreds of Dickinson's poems along with links to biographical information and other Dickinson resources.

Web:
http://www.planet.net/pkrisxle/emily/dickinson.html

Listserv Mailing List:
List Name: **dicknson**
Subscribe to: **listserv@listserv.uta.edu**

Haiku

Haiku is a lovely, delicate form of Japanese poetry. If you are a poetry lover, take some time to explore these resources and learn about the world of haiku.

Web:
http://home.sn.no/home/keitoy/haiku.html
http://mikan.cc.matsuyama-u.ac.jp/~shiki/
http://www.ori.u-tokyo.ac.jp/~dhugal/haikuhome.html

Chinese Poetry

I love Chinese poetry and you will too once you give it half a chance. My favorite Chinese poem is that traditional work from the Chi'ing dynasty that starts, "There was a young girl from Beijing...". If you like poetry, spend some time with this most beautiful art form and its Asian incarnation.

POETRY 627

Haiku

Haiku is a form of poetry, developed in Japan, in which the writer seeks to capture a specific transient observation about the natural world. The world changes so quickly, and haiku is one way to capture a particular image or sensation.

A haiku poem (usually referred to as a "haiku") consists of three lines. The first line has 5 syllables, the second has 7, and the third has 5.

In addition, it is traditional for a haiku to indicate a particular season. Often, this is done by including a word that invokes a feeling of either winter, spring, summer or fall. In English, the tradition is slightly different: a poem should contain a reference to nature, but not necessarily to a particular season.

Haiku is concentrated. Although it uses only 17 syllables, a well-written haiku can invoke deep spiritual feeling. The best haiku is simple and clear, without metaphor, personification or other literary device.

If you would like to learn more about haiku, you will find more information on the Net. In the meantime, here is a haiku I wrote for you to enjoy:

fog blanket covers
tall green trees wait silently
quiet brings soothing peace

Irish Poetry

If you don't have time to run down to your local pub for a poetry reading, try just getting a brew from the fridge and downloading a poem or two written by an Irish poet. For a really good time, you can even find some poetry set to music.

Web:
http://www.spinfo.uni-koeln.de/~dm/eire.html

Keats, John

John Keats (1795-1821) is one of the greatest English poets. Experience the mysterious, beautiful and joyful works of Keats firsthand by connecting to this nice archive of his poetry.

Web:
http://obi.std.com/obi/John.Keats/

Millay, Edna St. Vincent

Edna St. Vincent Millay (1892-1950) was a Pulitzer prize-winning American poet. Her most famous works are "The Harp Weaver" (a play) and "Renascence". These Web sites offer a collection of Millay's poetry for you to enjoy, along with some biographical information.

Web:
http://physserv1.physics.wisc.edu/~shalizi/Poetry/Millay/
http://www.columbia.edu/acis/bartleby/millay/
http://www.sappho.com/poetry/e_millay.htm

Neruda, Pablo

Pablo Neruda (1904-1973) is a Chilean poet who won the 1971 Nobel Prize for Literature. Neruda's real name was Neftalí Ricardo Reyes Basoalto. He was born in the town of Parral, Chile, the son of a railway employee and a teacher. Neruda was a prolific writer. On his sixtieth birthday, he published "Memorial de Isla Negra", a five-volume collection of autobiographical poetry. Much of his poetry is political in nature. For example, in 1939, Neruda published an epic poem "Canto General", consisting of 250 poems collected into fifteen literary cycles that deal with the nature, people and history of South America. However, Neruda is also known for his love poetry, written to his wife Matilde.

Web:
http://members.aol.com/katharenae/private/Pweek/Neruda/neruda.html
http://www.lunaea.com/words/neruda
http://www.nobel.se/laureates/literature-1971.html

Plath, Sylvia

Sylvia Plath (1932-1963) was an American poet whose work is characterized by its intense imagery and highly personal quality. Her most famous work, The Bell Jar, is an autobiographical novel. Plath possessed a rare writing skill and sensitivity. She wrote her first poem at the age of eight, and throughout her schooling achieved a great deal of critical recognition. However, she was also a deeply troubled woman and committed suicide at the age of 30, after the breakup of her marriage. Perhaps because of her notoriety and unfortunate demise, Plath became popular among young women in the early '70s, along with the growth of the feminist movement. Even today, Plath's work is required reading in most courses of women's literature. This Web site has biographical information about Sylvia Plath, a bibliography of her work, as well as a collection of poems.

Web:
http://home.ptd.net/~prospero/plath.html

Poetry Archives

There is a lot of poetry for you on the Net. Here are some collections that I think you will enjoy: lots and lots of well-known poems, as well as links to other poetry sites. These are good places to visit if you are looking for a particular poem or work from a particular author, or if you just feel like browsing for something to read.

Web:
http://eng.hss.cmu.edu/poetry/
http://tqd.advanced.org/3247/

Wanna have a listen?
Try
"Broadcasting on the Net".

Why pay retail? You can get all the poetry you want, for free, at the Poetry Archives.

Poetry Talk and General Discussion

There are two types of people who write poetry: those who show their poetry to other people and those who don't. If you like to show your poetry to other people, share it with the participants of these Usenet discussion groups. If you don't like to share your poetry, you can enjoy other people's creations. (And while you're there, you might as well offer your opinions.)

Usenet:
alt.arts.poetry.comments
alt.centipede
alt.language.poetry.pure-silk
alt.language.urdu.poetry
alt.lesbian.feminist.poetry
alt.teens.poetry.and.stuff
alt.ygdrasil
rec.arts.poems
rec.arts.poetry

Semantic Rhyming Dictionary

Anyone can rhyme "moon" with "June", and "love" with "stars above". However, when you get into serious rhyming, you want more than words that sound alike. It is important that the words are related to one another. This rhyming dictionary will help you find such words. You can look for perfect rhymes, match the last sound only, match consonants, find homophones, synonyms or semantic siblings. If you are the type of person who looks for just the right word, this is the Web site for you.

Web:
http://www.link.cs.cmu.edu/dougb/rhyme-doc.html

Shelley, Percy Bysshe

Percy Bysshe Shelley (1792-1822) was an English romantic poet who had a strong belief in reason and that humanity could evolve into perfection. Shelley eventually married Mary Wollstonecraft Shelley, who wrote the famed Frankenstein. Read some of the beautiful lyric poems at this page devoted to the works of Percy Bysshe Shelley.

Web:
http://obi.std.com/obi/Percy.Bysshe.Shelley/
http://www.columbia.edu/acis/bartleby/shelley/

Tennyson, Alfred

Alfred Tennyson (1809-1892) was an English poet who became poet laureate in 1850. He was a strong spokesman for Victorian values and is known for his excellent use of language and mastery of poetic technique. Some of his famous poems are "The Lady of Shalott", "The Charge of the Light Brigade" and "In Memorium". The latter is a beautiful elegy written after the death of a close friend.

Web:
http://obi.std.com/obi/Tennyson/

Whittier, John Greenleaf

John Greenleaf Whittier (1807-1892) was an American poet and writer, a Quaker and a vigorous abolitionist. His poems are often sentimental pieces about the New England region of America. Whittier is the poet who said "For of all sad words of tongue or pen, the saddest are these: It might have been!"

Web:
http://obi.std.com/obi/John.Greenleaf.Whittier/

Wordsworth, William

William Wordsworth (1770-1850) was an English poet who became poet laureate in 1843. Wordsworth and his friend, Samuel Taylor Coleridge, wrote a book called "Lyrical Ballads" which introduced romanticism into England. Here's a nice selection of poems by Wordsworth.

Web:
http://obi.std.com/obi/William.Wordsworth/
http://www.cc.columbia.edu/acis/bartleby/wordsworth/

POLITICS

Activism

Have you ever had one of those days when you are sitting around doing nothing and you think to yourself, "Boy, I'm really in the mood for a good fight." Well, don't get frustrated, get activated. Here are some places where you can read about political activities that are guaranteed to make you want to shout.

Web:
http://www.oneworld.org/
http://www.proactivist.com/
http://www.webactive.com/

Usenet:
alt.activism
alt.activism.community
alt.activism.death-penalty
alt.activism.latino-youth
alt.activism.noise-pollution
alt.activism.student

Clinton-Lewinsky Scandal

On January 18, 1998, an article was posted on the Drudge Report Web site asserting that "... A White House intern carried on a sexual affair with the President of the United States..." The White House intern was, of course, Monica Lewinsky, and from that inauspicious beginning came the Clinton-Lewinsky scandal, an unprecedented imbroglio that grew to envelop and unravel the administration of William Jefferson Clinton, the 42nd President of the United States. On September 9, 1998, the report of the Office of Independent Council (which had been investigating Clinton) was submitted to the House of Representatives. Here are some resources to help you understand what happened, including Web sites where you can find the text of the original report.

Web:
http://icreport.loc.gov/icreport/
http://www.access.gpo.gov/congress/icreport/
http://www.courttv.com/casefiles/clintoncrisis/
http://www.gomonica.com/
http://www.house.gov/judiciary/

Usenet:
alt.fan.bill-clinton
alt.flame.monica-lewinsky
alt.impeach.clinton
alt.politics.clinton
alt.president.clinton

630 POLITICS

Conservative Political News

What is the latest news in the world of conservative politics? Find out about the most recent buzz in Washington and read about political agendas that relate to conservatives. This is not a discussion group, but rather a news list to stir discussion on other groups and to keep you informed on the latest political happenings.

Majordomo Mailing List:
List Name: **c-news**
Subscribe to: **majordomo@world.std.com**

> You're cool. This book is sugar-free, low-fat and

Democrats

The Democratic party was founded in 1792 by Thomas Jefferson. Originally, party members were called "Republicans" or "Democratic-Republicans" but in 1830, the name was shortened to "Democrats". This is the official Web site of the Democratic party and, like the Republican site, there are no huge surprises. Visit the "Donkey Stomp" (a Republican bashing section) and the hilarious Quote-o-Rama page (which brings back memories of Dan Quayle). You can also read news and articles about the party and what you can do to help. The Usenet group is for the discussion of Democratic views and platforms.

Web:
http://www.democrats.org/

Usenet:
alt.politics.democrats.d

Look What I Found on the Net...

```
Newsgroup: alt.activism
Subject: Acceptable symbolic bombing?

> THE FOLLOWING IS HYPOTHETICAL
>
> Someone decides to show the vulnerability of spent radioactive
> nuclear wastes that are stored in casks outside of plants.
> He/she invades said plant and detonates a small charge on the
> concrete platform that the casks rest on.  The explosion is
> carefully calculated to do damage to the concrete but not to
> the casks.  Every consideration is taken to ensure no loss of
> life or injury.
>
> He/she gives him/herself up and accepts the punishment in
> order to get maximum publicity for this major, major problem.
>
> What are your thoughts on this?

Problem 1) Does the person have enough expertise to juggle the
amount of explosive?

Problem 2) What if the charge explodes and damages the concrete
enough to tip the container?

Problem 3) What if low grade waste is stored around the
container?

I doubt this could be pulled off. As a (conditionally)
pro-nuke person, I would question the balance between message
and risk.  Other methods of protest would be safer and might
get just as good press coverage.
```

Euthanasia

Euthanasia refers to the deliberate ending of another person's life out of compassion. In a passive sense, euthanasia can be accomplished by refraining to postpone a death from terminal illness, for example, by withholding artificial life support. Active euthanasia painlessly puts someone to death. With the consent of family or the patients themselves, doctors often withhold measures that would unnecessarily prolong a life filled with pain and anguish. Active euthanasia is illegal in almost all jurisdictions. Clearly, there are no easy answers when it comes to euthanasia, especially active euthanasia. However, as the population ages, and health care for the aged becomes more and more expensive, you and I are going to be faced with some tough decisions at the end of our lives. Perhaps now is the time to start talking about it.

Web:
  http://www.choices.org/
  http://www.iaetf.org/
  http://www.rights.org/deathnet/lr_libus.html

Usenet:
  talk.euthanasia

Grassroots Activism

Grassroots activity refers to an ad hoc political movement at the local level, as opposed to organization controlled by a nexus of political activity (such as a party, elected official or governing body). By its nature, grassroots activity is short on money, know-how and facilities. Fortunately, the Net will be glad to help—with no strings attached.

Web:
  http://www.2020vision.org/press.html
  http://www.natcavoice.org/natca/f97/rally.htm
  http://www.netaction.org/training/
  http://www.sfaf.org/policy/grassrts.html

Hate Groups

Here is information to help you understand and work against those who would hate: racists, neo-nazis, people who deny the Holocaust, anti-gay bigots, and so on. You'll find links to Web sites maintained by hate groups, as well as names of Usenet groups and mailing lists where such people hang out.

Web:
  http://www.hatewatch.org/

International Politics Talk and General Discussion

Usenet has a number of discussion groups specifically for discussing the politics of particular countries and regions: Britain, Europe, India, Italy, China, Middle East, Tibet and the former Soviet Union. As long as you stay more or less on topic, anything goes. However, please remember that if you are responding to an article written by someone in a foreign country, their first language may not be the same as yours. On the Net, irony and politics do not mix well. The world is a big place, and there is lots of room for two people to disagree and still both be right.

Usenet:
  alt.politics.british
  alt.politics.europe.misc
  talk.politics.china
  talk.politics.european-union
  talk.politics.mideast
  talk.politics.soviet
  talk.politics.tibet

Internet Politics

This Usenet group is the place to go to discuss the politics of the Internet, and to complain about how the government is interfering with your right to do whatever you want on the Net. Remember, as one of my readers you are always right, so don't take any guff from anyone (unless you run into another one of my readers, in which case you must compromise graciously). If you want to keep up with the latest buzz about Net politics, try the Web site.

Web:
  http://www.zdnet.com/products/netpolitics.html

Usenet:
  alt.politics.datahighway

This book is sugar-free, low-fat and biodegradable.

Irish Politics

These lists are for the discussion of the kinder, gentler side of Irish politics as defined by the 26 counties of the Republic of Ireland since 1922. Discussions of Northern Ireland are welcome only if they directly relate to the politics of the Republic. The Web site has a huge list of resources relating to all aspects of Irish politics.

Web:
http://www.ucd.ie/~politics/irpols.html

Listserv Mailing List:
List Name: **irl-pol**
Subscribe to: **listserv@listserv.heanet.ie**

Listserv Mailing List:
List Name: **irl-pol**
Subscribe to: **listserv@home.ease.lsoft.com**

Israeli Politics

The Israeli government is based on proportional representation. Here is how it works. The national house of representatives (the Knesset) has 120 members. In preparation for an election, each party creates a list of preferred candidates. However, when a person votes, he or she votes for a party, not for a particular person. After the votes are counted, the number of representatives elected to the Knesset is proportional to the percentage of votes that party received. For example, a party receiving 10 percent of the overall votes would send the top 12 candidates from its list to the Knesset. This sounds like a good idea, but it makes for a fractured system, in which no party can ever manage to get a majority on its own. Moreover, small, less popular parties can often wield disproportionate power as their votes are needed to form a coalition. Israel has fewer people than the city of Chicago in an area about the same size as New Jersey. However, in the 1996 election, there were 21 political parties (six of which were major organizations). Is it any wonder Israeli politics is so... interesting? You know, when you think of it, Israel has a lot in common with Chicago and New Jersey.

Web:
http://www.iguide.co.il/english/74.html
http://www.maven.co.il/subjects/idx184.htm

Jefferson Project

The Jefferson Project is a guide to "online politics". It has loads of resources about political personalities, publications, political humor, the government, international politics, parties and activism. The resources are not geared to any particular political audience and so will appeal to (and aggravate) radicals, conservatives and liberals alike.

Web:
http://www.capweb.net/classic/jefferson/

Political Correctness

Political correctness refers to forcing the general public to talk about issues in oblique ways so as to minimize the possibility of offending people. For example, which term is better: African-Americans, Afro-Americans, Blacks, Negroes or Colored people? All of these words were acceptable at one time, but political correctness dictates which one is the "correct" term to use today. Political correctness in moderation assures that the mantle of public opinion is available to protect us from bias and vulgarity. However, taken to an extreme, such rules serve not only to force people to conform to current political fashion, but to provide a convenient way to separate people based on knowing what is and what is not acceptable. Of course, "political correctness" itself is not a new idea: it is merely the politically correct term used to describe what are ever-present problems in human society: snobbishness, ignorance and the struggle for power over our neighbors.

Web:
http://www.daileyint.com/green/
http://www.ora.com/people/staff/sierra/flum/
http://www.responsibleopposing.com/

Political Policies

In the world of politics, you ain't nobody unless you've got a policy. Anybody can assert an opinion, but not everybody's opinion can be backed up by studies from a think tank. When you come down to it, though, public policy is nothing more than trying to figure out how people should think about something. There are lots of people who spend lots of time trying to figure out what you should be thinking. Maybe you'd like to check up on them.

Web:
http://www.policy.com/

POLITICS 633

Political Talk and General Discussion

If you like being contentious and opinionated, you'll love these Usenet groups. (Actually, as one of my readers, you are sensible and insightful. It's everyone else who is contentious and opinionated.) These are the Usenet groups specifically designated for political discussion. Anything goes, but as in most areas of the Net, the power lies with the people who are the most intelligent, witty and well-spoken. If you would like more immediate interactive screaming matches, connect to IRC.

Usenet:
alt.politics
bit.listserv.politics
soc.politics
soc.politics.anti-fascism
soc.politics.marxism
talk.politics
talk.politics.misc
talk.politics.theory

IRC:
#politics

Quick... click!

Politicians

In most of life, talk is cheap. In politics, talk is essential. Here are the Usenet groups where you can talk about your favorite and not so favorite politicians. Talk about convenient!

Usenet:
alt.fan.bill-clinton
alt.fan.bob-dole
alt.fan.dan-quayle
alt.fan.pauline.hanson
alt.fan.richard-nixon
alt.fan.ronald-reagan
alt.politics.clinton
alt.politics.harry-browne
alt.president.clinton

Look What I Found on the Net...

```
Newsgroup: alt.politics
Subject: Canada Has No Guarantees of Freedom

> ...People in Canada are so cute!  It's almost like they
> think they have their own COUNTRY up there.
>
> — Xxxx Xxxxx,
>    Columbus, Ohio

From Ohio? Hmmm...

Tell me, if your parents moved to California and got a divorce,
would they still legally be brother and sister?

— Xxxxxx Xxxx,
   Montreal, Quebec, Canada
```

Politics of Government Organizations

As all of us travel together through Modern Life, government organizations are forced to carry their own political baggage. These are the Usenet groups for the discussion of politics as it relates to various government organizations, mostly American: the Bureau of Alcohol, Tobacco and Firearms (ATF); the Central Intelligence Agency (CIA); general covert operations organizations; the Federal Bureau of Investigation (FBI); the National Security Administration (NSA); and the United Nations. The .misc group is for the discussion of government organizations that do not have their own groups.

Usenet:
alt.politics.org.batf
alt.politics.org.cia
alt.politics.org.fbi
alt.politics.org.misc
alt.politics.org.nsa
alt.politics.org.un

Presidential Scandals

Politics, money and scandal go together like green eggs and ham. Throughout the years, the presidency of the United States has attracted an unfortunate number of high-profile imbroglios: Watergate (1972, Richard Nixon administration: the cover-up of a politically motivated break-in); Teapot Dome (1924, Warren Harding administration: the secret leasing of naval oil reserve lands to private companies); Whiskey Ring (1875, Ulysses S. Grant administration: lost tax revenue on whiskey). Those scandals, of course, are all in the past. Fortunately, we now have an administration with the highest possible sense of honesty and integrity. Today, the chances of anything even remotely approaching a scandal in the office of the President are so insignificant as to be almost non-existent.

Web:
http://www.grolier.com/presidents/ea/
  genconts.html#SCANDALS
http://www.msnbc.com/onair/msnbc/timeandagain/
  archive/scandal/

Usenet:
alt.politics.gossip

Republicans

The United States Republican Party was founded in 1854. The first Republican to be elected President was Abraham Lincoln (in 1860). This is the official Republican Web site, and you pretty much get what you would expect. For instance, when I visited, I saw an opponent-bashing section in which I could view the "Outrage of the Day" (a hilarious animated picture of Bill Clinton as Pinocchio). There are also news releases, a chat room, some fun political stuff (games, crossword puzzles), email addresses of political people, information about GOP-TV, as well as background information on various governmental and political topics. Overall, there is lots and lots of pro-Republican, anti-Democrat stuff. For discussion of Republican views and platforms, you can participate in the Usenet group or mailing lists.

Web:
http://www.rnc.org/

Usenet:
alt.politics.usa.republican

Listserv Mailing List:
List Name: **repub-l**
Subscribe to: **listserv@vm.marist.edu**

Listserv Mailing List:
List Name: **right-l**
Subscribe to: **listserv@cmsa.berkeley.edu**

Richard Nixon Audio and Video Archive

People of the younger generations will never know what it was like to hear Richard Nixon address the people of the United States. Thanks to modern technology and the Internet, anyone young or old, can hear the voice of Richard Nixon at any time of the day or night without having to pay $20 to hire the neighborhood psychic to perform a seance. Listen to his resignation speech, the Checkers speech, a portion of the Nixon/Kennedy debate and his explanation of Watergate.

Web:
http://www.webcorp.com/sounds/nixonarchive.htm
http://www.webcorp.com/video/nixon/
  nixonvideo.html

PRIVACY AND SECURITY

Treaties

If you are having trouble with your neighbor trimming the trees that are actually on *your* property and you want to take some firm action, I have an idea for you. Go to these Web sites for treaties and other international agreements. Download the treaty of your choice and open the document in your word processing program. Fill in your name and your neighbor's name in the appropriate slots, then trot next door and make him sign it. Not only will he stop trimming your trees, but he might also be morally bound to notify you at the earliest possible moment that there has been a nuclear accident in his house.

Web:
http://itl.irv.uit.no/trade_law/nav/conventions.html
http://law.house.gov/89.htm

Treaties are made to be broken, of course, but unless you know exactly what was in a treaty, you can't tell who is breaking what rule. Take a moment and snarf your own personal copy of the Geneva Convention. Just the thing for really understanding reruns of Hogan's Heroes.

United States Political Talk and General Discussion

I grew up in Canada, where there was a fair amount of politics. But that was nothing compared to the United States, where political wrangling and commentary is the national obsession (second only to watching highly paid athletes perform on TV). The great thing about American politics is that once you choose a point of view, you have all kinds of beliefs, opinions and avocations to adopt and defend without having to do any original thinking for yourself. Don't get me wrong, American politics is *interesting*, and there is nothing I like better than a good old political argument. Actually, I'm not even that fussy. I just like to argue, so I'm always ready to take whichever side is opposed to whomever I am talking with. If you also like a good discussion, visit these Usenet groups and argue about the topic of your choice. The **.misc** group is for discussion of general politics that does not fit in one of the other, more specific groups.

Usenet:
  alt.politics.greens
  alt.politics.libertarian
  alt.politics.usa.congress
  alt.politics.usa.constitution
  alt.politics.usa.misc
  talk.politics.libertarian

PRIVACY AND SECURITY

Anonymous Remailers

It's embarrassing when your mom catches you posting to **alt.binaries.pictures.erotica.furry**. Avoid all the hassle of trying to explain by not getting caught in the first place. Try using an anonymous remailer. Here is information on what these services are and how they work.

Web:
http://www.publius.net/rlist.html
http://www.well.com/user/abacard/remail.html

PRIVACY AND SECURITY

Anti-Telemarketing

Telemarketing is the soliciting of business over the telephone. Unfortunately, once your name gets on a telemarketing list, you are going to get unwanted calls from people trying to sell you things. You can fight back. First, (in the U.S.) call your telephone company, and tell them to take your name out of the "street address" directory they sell to telemarketers. Second, check the telemarketing resources on the Net. The next time someone interrupts your dinner to see if you want to invest in gold futures, tell them you have to check with the Internet first, but if they would give you their personal home phone number, you would be glad to call them back later.

Web:
  http://www.antitelemarketer.com/

Anti-Virus Programs

Computer viruses are small programs written by malevolent programmers in order to cause trouble. A virus attaches itself to an existing program. When you run the program, the virus becomes activated and performs some sort of action (which might cause damage to your files or other programs). Anti-software programs are written to detect and eliminate viruses that may have found their way onto your system. Most people have no need for such software—actually, viruses are relatively rare. However, anti-virus programs are useful if you maintain a computer network, or if you work in environment in which people share computers or bring in floppy disks that have been used in other computers. (In particular, you must be careful if you allow your kids to bring home disks from school to use with your home computers.)

Web:
  http://cws.internet.com/32virus.html
  http://tucows.cableinet.net/virus95.html
  http://www.davecentral.com/virus.html

Dig up something in "Archaeology".

Computer Security

Any computer that is connected to the outside world can never be completely secure. However, computers and networks can be made secure enough to keep problems to a minimum. For example, as problems within an operating system become known, there will usually be a patch (program modification) issued to fix the problem. There are many known security problems with all of the popular operating systems, and most of these problems have patches that you can download and apply to your system. In general, the best thing you can do to make sure your system is dependable is to have proper backups, and—very important—make sure you can restore your backups.

Web:
  http://csrc.ncsl.nist.gov/
  http://www.alw.nih.gov/Security/security.html
  http://www.clark.net/pub/mjr/pubs/fwfaq/
  http://www.cnmoc.navy.mil/nmosw/coord/secure/basicsec.htm
  http://www.cs.purdue.edu/coast/hotlist/
  http://www.iss.net/vd/faqoffaqs.html
  http://www.iss.net/vd/patch.html

Usenet:
  comp.os.netware.security
  comp.security.announce
  comp.security.firewalls
  comp.security.misc
  talk.forgery

COMPUTER SECURITY

Right now, someone may be trying to break into a computer for which *you* are responsible. Before they do, check out the latest security patches, and make sure you are protected. When it comes to maintaining security, the job never ends. (So don't you dare go on vacation—ever.)

PRIVACY AND SECURITY — 637

Computer Viruses

A computer virus is a small program that can make a copy of itself on a disk. The first virus was written in 1986 to work on a 360 KB floppy disk. Since then, thousands of viruses and related programs have been written, along with a wide variety of anti-virus software. Are viruses really that big a deal? That depends on whether or not your system gets infected. There's a lot of information—and software—waiting for you on the Net.

Web:
http://pages.prodigy.com/virushelp/
http://www.kumite.com/myths/
http://www.webworlds.co.uk/dharley/

Usenet:
alt.comp.virus
alt.comp.virus.source.code
comp.virus

Listserv Mailing List:
List Name: virus-l
Subscribe to: listserv@lehigh.edu

IRC:
#virus

Cookies (on the Web)

To access the Web, you use a program called a "browser". (The two most popular browsers are Netscape and Internet Explorer.) Your browser contacts computers around the Net and requests information on your behalf. When that information arrives, your browser displays it on your screen. The computers that send the information are called "Web servers". Your browser has a facility built into it that allows Web servers to store data—called "cookies"—on your computer for later retrieval. What you may not realize is that cookies are sent to your browser behind the scenes, and, right now, your personal computer is probably storing all kinds of information. This information—the cookies—accumulates as you visit more and more Web sites, and is used for a variety of purposes, one of which is to track your movements on the Web. People are concerned about cookies as they can be used in ways that infringe on your personal privacy. These resources will help you learn about cookies and what you can do about them.

Web:
http://www.cookiecentral.com/
http://www.netscape.com/products/security/resource/faq/cookies.html

Electronic Privacy Information Center

The Electronic Privacy Information Center (EPIC) is a public interest research center based in Washington, D.C. EPIC concerns itself with all types of privacy issues: Internet privacy, medical records, proposals for national ID cards, and so on. The EPIC Web site houses a large collection of privacy-related information and resources on many different topics. If you care at all about these issues, take a few minutes to look around. I guarantee you will find something useful or interesting.

Web:
http://www.epic.org/

Electronic Privacy Information Center

If you don't want everyone to know everything about you, then you had better know everything about electronic privacy.

Email Privacy

If you use email at work, I guarantee that your company can read your mail if they want to. Even if you delete messages, they are often retrievable (say, from a backup). My advice is to think very carefully before you write something in an email message that you would not want to become public. You are probably okay if you use your own personal Internet account, but if you use the Net at work, be discreet. Want to find out more? Start here.

Web:
http://www.gahtan.com/techlaw/privacy.htm

Fingerprinting and Biometrics

Biometrics are techniques that can be used to automatically recognize a person based upon distinguishing traits. One reliable biometric is fingerprinting. Your fingerprints are unique, and every time you touch something you leave a mark that can be used to identify you. In the movies, fingerprints are always used to trap the bad guys, but in real life many people see fingerprinting as an invasion of privacy. It is convenient for government agencies to have a lot of fingerprints on file, but how thrilled are you about them having yours? The loss of freedom will not stop at forced fingerprinting. Biometric systems have been developed that are far more sophisticated. These guys are deadly serious, and what you read here should scare you.

Web:
http://www.networkusa.org/fingerprint.shtml

Privacy Forum Digest

If you are concerned about privacy in our new-fangled age of information, subscribe to **privacy**, a moderated mailing list. All manner of topics are discussed, including privacy issues relating to individuals and society as a whole. The information is useful, thoughtful and authoritative. The Web page allows you to search previous issues of the digest—an extremely useful resource—all the way back to its beginning in May 1992. Take my word for it, there is a *lot* of interesting information here.

Web:
http://www.vortex.com/privarch.htm

Listserv Mailing List:
List Name: **privacy**
Subscribe to: listserv@vortex.com

Don't read everything you believe.

Privacy Resources

Privacy means a lot more than being safe and secure in your own home.

Privacy means having control over who is allowed to keep and use information about you: your name, address, email address, phone number, government identification number (such as the U.S. Social Security number and the Canadian Social Insurance number), medical records, bank account information, credit rating, tax records, investment information, use of credit cards, frequent traveler information, magazine subscriptions, and on and on. Want to learn more?

Explore the **Privacy Resources**.

Privacy Resources

Privacy is everyone's business: you and you, and you there hiding behind your Macintosh thinking I won't notice you. Once the big boys (Netscape, Microsoft, AT&T, and so on) get into the "free software" act, it won't be long until you find that somewhere along the line, your personal interests were sold out for a handful of magic stock options and advertising revenues. I feel strongly that it is up to all of us to protect our privacy. The best way to start is by understanding the issues, and these sites are a good place to begin. Remember, once "they" control your browser, you will be able to run all over the Net, but you won't be able to hide.

Web:
http://www.computerprivacy.org/
http://www.cous.uvic.ca/poli/456/privres.htm
http://www.junkbusters.com/cgi-bin/privacy
http://www.vortex.com/privacy.html

PRIVACY AND SECURITY

Privacy Rights Clearinghouse

This is a great Web site. It contains a lot of useful information about privacy, your rights, and what you can do to protect them. I have personally found a lot of interesting and useful help here. One caveat: The information is designed for the United States, particularly California. However, don't let that discourage you. These people do a good job and much of the information is helpful to anyone.

Web:
  http://www.privacyrights.org/

Privacy Talk and General Discussion

What better place to discuss privacy and security issues than out in the open on Usenet, where thousands of people you don't even know can read your every word? These discussion groups cover technical issues as well as cultural, political and social topics relating to privacy and security (such as the ill-conceived Clipper chip).

Usenet:
  alt.privacy
  alt.privacy.anon-server
  alt.privacy.clipper
  comp.society.privacy

Privacy Tips

The more information can be processed by computers, the more your privacy becomes important. These Web sites contain some good resources to help you get the privacy you want. Find a wealth of tips and information regarding email, voice mail, Social Security numbers, cordless phones, the Net, computers, and much more.

Web:
  http://www.aexp.com/corp/consumerinfo/protecting.shtml
  http://www.dci.com/news/1998/mar/priv-law.htm
  http://www.privacyrights.org/donray.htm

Spamming

Spamming refers to sending unsolicited and inappropriate messages—usually advertisements—over the Internet. Spam is sent to both Usenet discussion groups, where it can be a major annoyance, and personal email addresses, where it shows up as junk mail. Spamming is a big problem, and the people who do it are inconsiderate jerks. Check out these resources to help you understand the problem, and to find out what you can do to fight it and to safeguard your electronic privacy. Here is one big hint. When you configure your browser to access the Usenet news system, you will have to specify your email address. Whenever you post a message to a Usenet group, your browser will insert your address into the "header" of the message. This makes it easy for people who read your message to email you a personal reply. Whatever you do, do *not* specify your real email address—use a fake one. If your real email address ever shows up in the header of a Usenet message, it will be picked up by automated programs used by spammers, and, within hours, your address will be on mailing lists all over the world. Once this happens, you will receive ever-increasing amounts of junk mail, and there will be nothing you can do to stop it short of changing your address. If you want people to be able to reply to your Usenet postings, you can always put your real email address in the body (text) of your message. Hint for nerds: Use **root@localhost** as your fake address.

Web:
  http://spam.abuse.net/
  http://www.cauce.org/
  http://www.cybernothing.org/faqs/net-abuse-faq.html

Usenet:
  alt.current-events.net-abuse

Women,
see the "Women" section.
(Men, see "Men".)

Using the Web Anonymously

Did you ever ask yourself, how can the browser companies (Netscape, Microsoft, and so on) afford to develop browsers and give them away for free? Browser companies design software to please their customers, and *you* are not a customer. The customers are the companies that actually pay for software, such as Web server programs. So it should come as no surprise when I tell you that all modern browsers are designed to pass information about you and your computer system to any Web server that asks for it. Think about it, each time you connect to a Web server, your browser may be passing private information to that server. (In other words, you only *think* you got your browser for free.) To circumvent this system, you can route all your browser requests through an "anonymizer", a service that will submit your Web request to the appropriate server on your behalf. This will completely preserve your privacy (as long as you trust the people who provide the anonymizer service), however, it does slow things down. At the very least, you should connect to the anonymizer Web site, and let it show you exactly what information your Web browser is happily giving out to any Web server that asks.

Web:
http://www.anonymizer.com/

Virus Hoaxes

A computer virus is a small program (the virus), designed to insert itself into a file containing another program. When the second program runs, the virus becomes active, possibly causing a problem. A computer virus, of course, can be trouble. However, there are relatively few real viruses around. Unfortunately, there are many people who spread unfounded rumors about viruses, especially the so-called email viruses. Don't be fooled. The next time you get one of these virus warnings, please refrain from sending it along to your friends. Instead, use these resources to find out what's real and what's a hoax. (They are almost all hoaxes.)

Web:
http://www.afcert.kelly.af.mil/hoaxes.html
http://www.drsolomons.com/vircen/
http://www.kumite.com/myths/

PROGRAMMING

Ada

Ada is a programming language developed by the U.S. Department of Defense in the mid-1970s. The purpose of Ada was to create a standardized language that would be robust, dependable, and could be used efficiently by programmers to develop reliable programs that were easy to read and maintain. At the time, I was a computer science graduate student and I remember that four different proposals were circulated in the computer science community. Eventually one of these proposals was adopted and became Ada. In the last two decades, Ada has been updated into a modern programming language and is still used widely.

Web:
http://www.adahome.com/

Usenet:
comp.lang.ada

C++ and C

The C language is old, dating back to the early development of Unix. C++ is an object-oriented language based on C, but with significant differences. Both C and C++ are difficult to learn, and to program well in them takes a great deal of talent and experience. However, they are powerful tools, widely used throughout the world.

Web:
http://www.cera2.com/softd/clang.htm
http://www.cerfnet.com/~mpcline/C++-FAQs-Lite/
http://www.cl.ais.net/morph/c++/main.html
http://www.cs.umd.edu/users/cml/cstyle/
http://www.faqs.org/faqs/C-faq/toc/
http://www.inquiry.com/techtips/cpp_pro/

Usenet:
comp.lang.c
comp.lang.c++
comp.lang.c++.leda
comp.lang.c++.moderated
comp.lang.c.moderated
comp.std.c++

IRC:
#c++

DOS Programming Talk and General Discussion

DOS may be well along the way to a well-deserved final resting place, but it is still alive and well on Usenet. Here are the groups devoted to general discussion of DOS programming. If you are a DOS person, these are good places to look for tips, questions and answers. If you are not a DOS person, do not pass "Go" and, definitely, do not collect $200.

Usenet:
  alt.msdos.programmer
  comp.msdos.programmer
  comp.os.msdos.programmer
  comp.os.msdos.programmer.turbovision

Free Compilers and Interpreters

You can pay a lot of money for a language translator, or you can check this site and find many, many free compilers and interpreters. If you ever find yourself with some free time and nothing to do, why not download a free compiler and teach yourself a new language? (Actually, I tried to teach myself French that way, but I kept getting parsing mistakes.)

Web:
  http://www.idiom.com/free-compilers/

Usenet:
  comp.compilers
  comp.compilers.tools.pccts

> If you're thinking of making the most serious commitment that a computer programmer can make — jumping into C++ — stop, take a deep breath, and read the frequently asked question list.

Free Programming Tools

To say that these resources are extensive is like saying that the Queen of England insists on getting her own way: it doesn't even begin to describe the reality of the situation. What we have here is page after page after page of serious tools for serious programmers doing serious things (seriously). If you have even the least bit of interest in being a programming nerd, these sites are a must-have for your personal list of favorites.

Web:
  http://hjh.simplenet.com/programming/
  http://www.program.com/toolbin/

Hackers

Peer in on clever hacking discussions in Usenet and IRC and learn how to not only hack computer hardware and software, but anything in everyday life, including loose shower tiles, vibrating air conditioning vents and dust-spewing vacuum cleaners. The Web sites have lots of great hacker information.

Web:
  http://www.antionline.com/
  http://www.cs.utah.edu/~scook/tech/hacker.htm
  http://www.defcon.org/
  http://www.phrack.com/

Usenet:
  alt.2600.aol
  alt.2600.fake-id
  alt.2600.hackers
  alt.2600.qna
  alt.2600hz
  alt.hacker
  alt.hackers
  alt.hackers.groups
  alt.hackers.malicious
  alt.hacking
  alt.hackintosh

IRC:
  #hack

642 PROGRAMMING

Hello, World

It is said that when you learn a new computer language the first thing you do is write a program to display the words "Hello, world". Well, I have been programming for years, in a variety of languages, and I have never, ever written a program that says "Hello, world". But then, I have never seen a Rocky movie, watched an episode of Beverly Hills 90210, or had tiramisu for dessert. However, if you happen to be someone who is at home in popular culture, and you happen to be a programmer who likes exploring strange new languages, here is a site that will amuse and entertain you endlessly.

Web:
http://www.cuillin.demon.co.uk/nazz/trivia/hw/hello_world.html

IEEE Computer Society

The IEEE Computer Society is a world-renowned source of information relating to all aspects of computer science, electronics and engineering, including the publication of periodicals and newsletters, sponsoring conferences, workshops and symposia, and the development of standards. Computer Society Online now offers an electronic source of this information, in many cases before the information is published in hard copy.

Web:
http://www.computer.org/

Macintosh Programming

If you are a Mac programmer, there are lots of people you can talk to on Usenet. Here are some of the discussion groups devoted to Macintosh programming.

Usenet:
comp.sys.apple2.programmer
comp.sys.mac.programmer
comp.sys.mac.programmer.codewarrior
comp.sys.mac.programmer.games
comp.sys.mac.programmer.help
comp.sys.mac.programmer.info
comp.sys.mac.programmer.misc
comp.sys.mac.programmer.tools

Obfuscated C Code

Here are the entries and winners for the International Obfuscated C Code Contest, in which programmers compete to create the most artistic, beautiful and obscure C program. The program must be small (less than a specified number of bytes), and it must work.

Web:
http://reality.sgi.com/csp/ioccc/

Look What I Found on the Net...

```
Newsgroup: alt.hackers
Subject: cheap grad-student food hack

With $5 to spend and 15 minutes to make
a dish for a potluck dinner:

  1 can condensed cream of mushroom soup
  1 package frozen chopped spinach

Place both in microwave-safe dish.
Microwave 4 min.  Stir.
Microwave another 4 min.
Top with random cheeses.
```

PROGRAMMING 643

Object-Oriented Programming

Object-oriented programming is just like regular programming except that you look at everything differently, write your programs differently, maintain them differently, and think with a different part of your temporal lobe. Join the discussion and talk about object-oriented tools, techniques and problems. The **.misc** group is for general discussion of Macintosh object-oriented programming. The **.macapp3** group is devoted to Version 3 of the MacApp system. The **.tcl** group is for discussion of the Think Class Libraries.

Usenet:
   comp.sys.mac.oop.macapp3
   comp.sys.mac.oop.misc
   comp.sys.mac.oop.tcl

Operating Systems Talk and General Discussion

An operating system is the master control program that runs a computer: for example, Windows 95, Windows NT, DOS, MacOS and Unix are all operating systems. If you are interested in issues relating to the design and implementation of operating systems, here is a Usenet group in which you can talk with people working in this area. This group is for general operating system discussion. For issues relating to specific systems, there are more specific Usenet groups.

Usenet:
   comp.os.misc

Look What I Found on the Net...

```
              (from the 1986 Obfuscated C Code Contest)

===========

Note from  Harley:

This program, written by Jack Applin, displays:

    Hello, world!

The program works in C, Fortran 77 and Bourne shell.  Programs
such as this are now common, but as far as I know, this was the
original one.

===========
cat =13 /*/ >/dev/null 2>&1; echo "Hello, world!"; exit
*
*   This program works under cc, f77, and /bin/sh.
*
*/; main() {
      write(
cat-~-cat
    /*,'(
*/
    ,"Hello, world!"
    ,
cat); putchar(~-~-~-cat); } /*
    ,)')
      end
*/
```

OS/2 Programming Talk and General Discussion

Here are a few good places where you can ask questions, get answers or talk all night about anything relating to programming under OS/2. In addition, there are groups devoted to tools, porting and object-oriented programming.

Usenet:
  comp.os.os2.programmer.misc
  comp.os.os2.programmer.oop
  comp.os.os2.programmer.porting
  comp.os.os2.programmer.tools

Perl

It would be difficult to exaggerate the importance of Perl. It is the scripting language of choice in many situations, and is used widely on the Internet. Perl was created by Larry Wall in 1986, a Unix and Internet programmer of reknown. The name Perl stands for "Practical Extraction and Report Language" (although, as with most such acronyms, the meaning was made up after the name was chosen). Here are enough Perl resources to keep you satisfied from now until St. Swithin's Day.

Web:
  http://language.perl.com/
  http://reference.perl.com/
  http://www.faqs.org/faqs/perl-faq/
  http://www.perl.org/

Usenet:
  alt.perl
  comp.lang.perl
  comp.lang.perl.announce
  comp.lang.perl.misc
  comp.lang.perl.moderated
  comp.lang.perl.modules
  comp.lang.perl.tk

IRC:
  #perl

Programmer of the Month

When I was a graduate student, I was on the U.C. San Diego computer programming team (along with Bart, Don and Madeline). In those days, programming competitions were uncommon, and we competed by writing a Fortran program which we created on punched cards. Today, computer systems are a lot more sophisticated, but we are still waiting for programming to become an Olympic event. In the meantime, anyone can compete to be Programmer of the Month. This contest—started in 1993 at AT&T—is open to anyone in the world. Check out the current contest, see the past winners, and marvel at the beautiful trophy awarded to the best programmers.

Web:
  http://www.cs.washington.edu/homes/corin/POTM.PAGES/

Programming Humor

Some types of jokes—called canonical jokes—are repeated, with small variations, over and over again. Here are lists of programming jokes. If you are a programmer, my prescription is to pause every time you find a bug and read two jokes.

Web:
  http://www.elsop.com/wrc/humor/progwack.htm
  http://www.srdc.metu.edu.tr/~dengi/humor/computer/Canonical_List_of_Programming_Humor.txt

---

This book is an excellent source of intellectual fiber.

PROGRAMMING

Programming Languages

Here is your central switching point for language-oriented Web sites: a comprehensive list of resources categorized by language type. Even if you are a programmer supreme, I bet you can find something you have never heard of.

Web:
http://src.doc.ic.ac.uk/bySubject/Computing/Languages.html

Usenet:
comp.lang.apl
comp.lang.asm.x86
comp.lang.asm370
comp.lang.awk
comp.lang.beta
comp.lang.clarion
comp.lang.clipper
comp.lang.clos
comp.lang.cobol
comp.lang.dylan
comp.lang.eiffel
comp.lang.forth
comp.lang.forth.mac
comp.lang.fortran
comp.lang.functional
comp.lang.icon
comp.lang.idl
comp.lang.idl-pvwave
comp.lang.lisp
comp.lang.lisp.franz
comp.lang.lisp.mcl
comp.lang.lisp.x
comp.lang.logo
comp.lang.misc
comp.lang.ml
comp.lang.modula2
comp.lang.modula3
comp.lang.mumps
comp.lang.oberon
comp.lang.objective-c
comp.lang.pascal
comp.lang.pascal.ansi-iso
comp.lang.pascal.borland
comp.lang.pascal.delphi.advocacy
comp.lang.pascal.delphi.components.misc
comp.lang.pascal.delphi.components.usage
comp.lang.pascal.delphi.components.writing
comp.lang.pascal.delphi.databases
comp.lang.pascal.delphi.misc
comp.lang.pascal.mac
comp.lang.pascal.misc
comp.lang.perl
comp.lang.perl.announce
comp.lang.perl.misc
comp.lang.perl.modules
comp.lang.perl.tk
comp.lang.pl1
comp.lang.pop
comp.lang.prograph
comp.lang.prolog
comp.lang.python
comp.lang.rexx
comp.lang.sather
comp.lang.scheme
comp.lang.scheme.scsh
comp.lang.smalltalk
comp.lang.tcl
comp.lang.tcl.announce
comp.lang.verilog
comp.lang.vhdl

Need even more information on programming languages? Try the Programming Languages Web site.

Programming Talk and General Discussion

```
while (not sleeping)
  if (question=="not answered")
    post (Usenet (query))
  else
    read (Usenet (other-people's-articles));
```

Usenet:
comp.programming
comp.programming.contests

Software Engineering

As you might imagine, programming is an important topic on the Net, and there are lots of software engineering resources. Here is a Web site that has a wide variety of information, including institutes, libraries and various Web pages relating to software engineering. For ongoing discussion, you can join the Usenet group.

Web:
http://rbse.jsc.nasa.gov/virt-lib/soft-eng.html

Usenet:
comp.software.testing

Tao of Programming

Here is a humorous guide to programming and otherwise living with computers in the modern age. "Something mysterious is formed, born in the silent void. Waiting alone and unmoving, it is at once still and yet in constant motion. It is the source of all programs. I do not know its name, so I will call it the Tao of Programming."

Web:
http://www.big.du.se/~fltman/tao.html
http://www.topsail.org/tao.htm

Visual Basic

Visual Basic, a product of Microsoft, is the most modern incarnation of the Basic programming language. However, Visual Basic is a powerful tool which bears little resemblance to the original Basic. For many people, Visual Basic is the programming tool of choice, offering a total environment devoted to rapid program development, especially for client-server systems (including Internet programs) and database applications.

Web:
http://msdn.microsoft.com/vbasic/
http://www.cgvb.com/
http://www.faqs.org/faqs/visual-basic-faq/
http://www.inquiry.com/thevbpro/

Usenet:
comp.lang.basic.visual
comp.lang.basic.visual.3rdparty
comp.lang.basic.visual.database
comp.lang.basic.visual.misc
comp.lang.visual

IRC:
#visualbasic

> **Company coming? Check out "Cooking and Recipes".**

Windows Programming Talk and General Discussion

These Usenet groups are for questions and answers relating to general programming in the Microsoft Windows environment as well as more specific topics such as controls, dialogs, graphics and printing, memory management, multimedia and network programming, and so on.

Usenet:
comp.os.ms-windows.programmer
comp.os.ms-windows.programmer.controls
comp.os.ms-windows.programmer.drivers
comp.os.ms-windows.programmer.graphics
comp.os.ms-windows.programmer.misc
comp.os.ms-windows.programmer.multimedia
comp.os.ms-windows.programmer.networks
comp.os.ms-windows.programmer.nt.kernel-mode
comp.os.ms-windows.programmer.ole
comp.os.ms-windows.programmer.tools
comp.os.ms-windows.programmer.vxd
comp.os.ms-windows.programmer.win32
comp.os.ms-windows.programmer.winhelp

X Window

Here is information about the X Consortium (the X Window people) as well as links to many X-related sites. Find out what you need to work with X today, and what you need to understand to work with the newest version known as Broadway (X11R6.3): a system for creating and accessing interactive applications over the Web.

Web:
http://www.opengroup.org/tech/desktop/x/
http://www.rahul.net/kenton/xsites.html

PSYCHOLOGY

Adler, Alfred

Alfred Adler (1870-1937) was an Austrian psychiatrist who started with Freud, but eventually rejected Freud's emphasis on sexuality. Adler founded the school of individual psychology and maintained that neurosis was not a matter of repressed sexuality, but rather a reaction to feelings of inferiority. ("It is always easier to fight for one's principles than to live up to them.") Adler felt that the relation of the individual to his or her community was of prime importance, and that a feeling of connection to society was paramount to maintaining mental health. This Web site is devoted to classical Adlerian psychology. You will find readings, biographies, interviews, links to related resources, and more.

Web:
http://ourworld.compuserve.com/homepages/hstein/

American Psychological Association Journals

Here are the abstracts and tables of contents for a large number of journals sponsored by the American Psychological Association. The information at this site allows you to scan through the summaries of your favorite journals: an easy way to keep up on what is happening.

Web:
http://www.apa.org/journals/

Is life too ordinary for you? See "Bizarre".

What do you do when you have a house guest you are just too busy to entertain? Sit him down at the computer, connect him to the American Psychological Association Web site, and let him read back issues of psychology journals.

Just listen to this:
"According to Wallis (1992), philosophers of mind agree that a successful theory of representation must 'describe conditions for representation in nonintentional and nonsemantic terms.' If we restrict representation talk to what goes on in frogs, the visual systems of humans, etc., then perhaps Wallis is right. But once we count beliefs as representations, there is no such agreement. Indeed..."

Your friends will be coming back to visit you, again and again.

Consciousness

Consciousness is a good thing, especially when you are driving a car or operating heavy machinery. Here some resources that have been created to offer people the chance to share ideas and discuss research in the area of consciousness and to talk about articles that appear in the journal *Psyche*.

Web:
http://psyche.cs.monash.edu.au/

Usenet:
sci.psychology.consciousness
sci.psychology.journals.psyche

Listserv Mailing List:
List Name: **psyche-l**
Subscribe to: **listserv@listserv.uh.edu**

Freud, Sigmund

Sigmund Freud (1856-1939) was an Austrian psychiatrist and one of the great geniuses of the twentieth century. Freud opened vast areas of human thought—for example, the idea that there is an unconscious mind—and can rightly be considered the father of modern psychology. Freud's basic theory (which he developed and expanded over the years) is that unresolved infantile conflicts are responsible for much of adult neurosis and other aberrant behavior. Freud developed the techniques of psychoanalysis: the use of free association and dream interpretation to bring these conflicts to light, and to deal with them appropriately. As Freud developed his theories, it became more and more clear to him that the repressed feelings and memories were often of a sexual nature. He described, for example, the Oedipus Complex: a subconscious desire within a child for the parent of the opposite sex. If this complex does not resolve itself naturally, it will have a great effect on the person. As an adult, he or she may become neurotic and may be unable to form a normal, sexual relationship. Freud's strong belief in repressed sexual feelings as the root of much human pathology was extremely controversial at the time, and led to his breaking with some of his followers, in particular, Carl Jung and Alfred Adler. Throughout the years, Freud's theories have been studied, expanded (and even partially discredited) by several generations of psychoanalysts and physiologists. However, the bulk of Freud's insight and contributions have stood the test of time. Although there are those who criticize Freud's theories, I find that most such people know very little about what Freud really said and did. If you have never actually read anything Freud wrote, you may enjoy doing so. (I suggest starting with the book The Psychopathology of Everyday Life.) Freud was a real genius in the sense that whatever he turned his attention to, he illuminated.

Web:
http://freud.t0.or.at/freud/index-e.htm

Sigmund Freud
If you want to find out what Freud really said, read what Freud really said.

Jung, Carl

Carl Gustav Jung (1875-1961) was a Swiss psychiatrist. At one time, Jung was one of Freud's disciples. (In fact, Jung was the first president of the International Psychoanalytic Association.) However, in 1912 he published a book called Psychology and the Unconscious, which described two dimensions of the unconscious. In addition to the regular unconscious which Freud had discovered (containing repressed and forgotten memories and thoughts), Jung postulated a "collective unconscious" (mental patterns shared within a culture or by all human beings). This was enough of a revolutionary hypothesis to cause Jung to break with Freud. Jung founded the school of "analytical psychology" and achieved a career of great renown. (It was Jung, for instance, who developed the ideas of introversion and extroversion.) This Web page has a nice selection of Jung's writings. The Usenet group is for the discussion of Jungian psychology.

Web:
http://www.cgjung.com/cgjung/

Usenet:
alt.psychology.jung

Optical Illusions

Optical illusions are really cool, even without the benefit of caffeine or other artificial substances. This site has a nice collection of images that make you think twice (or more) about what you are seeing.

Web:
http://www.illusionworks.com/

Rebel. See "Anarchy".

PSYCHOLOGY

Personality Testing

One way to analyze the human personality is by studying a person and classifying him or her as being a particular "psychological type". This idea was originally developed by Carl Jung, who believed that human behavior follows specific patterns that develop from the characteristics of the human mind. Jung believed the conscious human mind was continually perceiving (taking in information) and judging (organizing information to arrive at decisions). However, each person is born with a tendency to favor one type of mental activity over the other. According to Jung, a person could perceive either by "sensing" or by using "intuition". Similarly, one judges either by "thinking" or "feeling". (You can see how one could classify people according to this criteria.) Jung also identified two opposite human tendencies: extroversion (an outward focus) and introversion (an inward focus). Here are some resources that can help you understand personality testing, Jungian and otherwise. If you enjoy self-analysis, one of these Web sites has a test you can take to estimate your Jungian-based personality characteristics. This will allow you to summarize your personality using a standard, four-letter acronym, for example, INTJ (introvert, intuition [N], thinking, judging) or XNFP (split extrovert/introvert [X], intuition [N], feeling, perceiving). For a discussion of personality testing, you can participate in the two Usenet groups.

Web:
http://www.2h.com/Tests/personality.phtml
http://www.phys.tcu.edu/~ingram/mbti/

Usenet:
alt.psychology.personality
sci.psychology.personality

Psychological Help

There are days when things seem overwhelming and unpleasant or you encounter a problem and you don't know exactly what to do with it. Check out the Usenet group that offers discussion about the problems people face. Maybe you will find an answer or just someone to talk to.

Usenet:
alt.psychology.help

Is life too much (right now)? Try **alt.psychology.help**.

Psychology Database

This Web site allows you to access a search engine maintained by the American Psychological Association. Specify one or more words, and the search engine will return a set of links to psychology Web sites and articles that relate to your request. I searched for the word "Harley". The result was an article co-authored by a person with the last name of Harley. (In case you are wondering, the article is "Object Representation in the Bottlenose Dolphin: Integration of Visual and Echoic Information".)

Web:
http://www.psychcrawler.com/

Psychology Resources

Psychologically speaking, you can learn a lot about a psychologist by observing what types of Internet resources he uses. If a psychologist only uses Web sites, it means he is a loner, who likes to work on his own. If a psychologist participates in Usenet discussion groups or mailing lists, it means he is more other-centered, the type of person who prefers to work in groups in order to reach a consensus. And if a psychologist uses the Web *and* participates in discussions, it means he is an over-achiever who works too hard in a vain attempt to please his father with whom he has issues that have never been resolved.

Web:
http://cctr.umkc.edu/user/dmartin/psych2.html
http://www.gasou.edu/psychweb/psychweb.htm
http://www.onlinepsych.com/mh/
http://www.psychologie.uni-bonn.de/online-documents/lit_ww.htm

Majordomo Mailing List:
List Name: **inetpsyc**
Subscribe to: **majordomo@psyc.uow.edu.au**

650 PSYCHOLOGY

Psychology Talk and General Discussion

The good thing about psychology is that anyone can talk about it. The bad thing is that everyone does. Of course, as one of my readers, your insights are particularly valuable, so if you have any interest in psychology, I encourage you to join the discussion. Here are several Usenet groups devoted to different aspects of psychology. If you are not sure which one is for you, choose the **.misc** group.

Usenet:
sci.psychology
sci.psychology.announce
sci.psychology.journals.psycoloquy
sci.psychology.misc
sci.psychology.psychotherapy
sci.psychology.research
sci.psychology.theory

Self-Help and Psychology Magazine

This online magazine features articles by renowned psychologists and respected experts. You can find information on subjects such as relationships, sexuality, addictions, family, sports psychology and health.

Web:
http://www.cybertowers.com/selfhelp/

Social Psychology

Social psychology is the branch of human psychology relating to group behavior and the influence of social factors on individuals. This site is a listing of social psychology resources on the Net. The mailing list is for the discussion of applied social psychology.

Web:
http://www.wesleyan.edu/spn/

Listserv Mailing List:
List Name: **aspsych**
Subscribe to: **listserv@hermes.circ.gwu.edu**

Look What I Found on the Net...

```
Newsgroup: sci.psychology.misc
Subject: How Would You React to This?

What would your reaction be if someone said to you:

   I think you are connected to a murder.

Now, if you were innocent, how would you react to this accusation?

If you were guilty, but didn't want to show it?
If you were guilty, but didn't care if anyone knew it?

I've been having a really hard time connecting to this...

==============

Newsgroup: sci.psychology.misc
Subject: Do You Know a Doctoral Program in Parapsychology?

I'm posting this for a friend who's about to complete her
Masters in physiological psychology and is looking for a
doctoral program in cognitive psychology.

The point is that her research interests are — how to say it —
precognition, telepathy, clairvoyance, psychokinesis; in one
word: parapsychology.

I should stress that she's neither a magician nor looking for a
training program in secret spells...
```

QUOTATIONS

Allen, Woody
You probably think your Uncle Fred has a good sense of humor but, actually, he's just memorized all of Woody Allen's famous quotes. No reason why you can't do the same.

Web:
http://www.chesco.com/~artman/woody.html

Daily Quotations
There are a lot of people in the world and, every day, somebody says something interesting. This Web site will show you a new quote every day, selected from a current event of some type. This site is a great place to visit every day, so you can have something to read while you take your daily vitamin. And when you have a little extra time, you can browse the collections of old quotations looking for some instant nostalgia (every day).

Web:
http://www.quotations.com/w_filter.htm

Dangerfield, Rodney
I get no respect. I went to use my Internet account the other day, and found that somebody had changed my username to **shicklegruber**. But I've got nothing to complain about; take a look at what Rodney has to say.

Web:
http://www.interlog.com/~meil/quotes2.html
http://www.rodney.com/Joke.asp

FOR MEN ONLY
Hey guys, need a quick way to impress a woman?

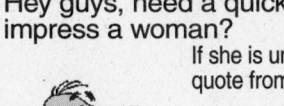

If she is under 20 years old, quote from Southpark.

If she is between 20 and 30, quote Jerry Seinfeld.

If she is between 30 and 40, quote Steven Wright.

If she is between 40 and 50, quote Woody Allen.

If she is over 50, quote Rodney Dangerfield.

Daily Quotations
The Internet has a number of sites at which you can find all kinds of quotations. Just the thing for spicing up your conversation and enhancing your reputation. Here is a typical example showing how it works.

[You are talking to your teacher or boss.]

Teacher/Boss:
So what do you have to say for yourself?

[At this point you repeat a quote that you downloaded the night before from one of the Internet quotation archives.]

You:
Well, I think blah, blah blah, blah, blah...

Teacher/Boss:
Wow, you really are terrific. I'm going to give you an A (or a raise).

Very good looking woman/man who happens to be listening:
You are an unbelievably attractive person. Would you like to have dinner with me tonight?

Famous Quotations
The next time you're looking for a wise and pithy saying, the Net will be glad to oblige. These Web sites have a large collection of quotations from famous people. When you have a few extra moments, take some time and browse through the list. Soon you yourself will be wise and pithy, fawned over by all your friends. As Winston Churchill once said, "It is a good thing for an uneducated man to read books of quotations." (Uneducated women, I suppose, are on their own.)

Web:
http://www.columbia.edu/acis/bartleby/bartlett/
http://www.labyrinth.net.au/~pirovich/quotes.html

QUOTATIONS

Fields, W.C.

W. C. Fields (1879-1946) was an American movie actor whose wit is legendary even today. After all, anyone who hates kids, dogs and books for dummies can't be all bad.

Web:
  http://inet.uni-c.dk/~bruno/fields.htm

Goldwyn, Samuel

Samuel Goldwyn (1882-1974) was a Polish-born American film producer who merged his own company with that of Louis B. Mayer to form Metro-Goldwyn-Mayer. Goldwyn is best remembered for the original way in which he expressed his ideas. For example, he once said that "Pictures are for entertainment, messages should be delivered by Western Union." Are all the Samuel Goldwyn quotes real? I can tell you in two words: a pocryphal.

Web:
  http://www.eng.wayne.edu/Carlo/Sam.html

Harley Hahn Quotes

The next time you are at a party with some Very Important People whom you need to impress, feel free to quote me. (That's what I do, and I find it to be highly effective.) To help you, here are collections of quotations from some of my books. Note: If you are a Unix person who likes Gilbert and Sullivan, be sure to check out the "Unix Sysadmin Song".

Web:
  http://www.harley.com/harley-quotes/

Marx, Groucho

Groucho Marx (1894-1977) was one of America's funniest funny men. Check out some of his quotes and maybe you can pass them off as your own.

Web:
  http://inet.uni-c.dk/~bruno/groucho.htm

> **The Internet is PEOPLE, not computers.**

Presidential Quotes

This archive has a collection of quotes from various American Presidents: Jefferson, Lincoln, Clinton, Reagan and others. This is the place to go when you need to remind yourself whether or not it was Ronald Reagan who said, "Ask not what your country can do for you; ask what you can do for your country." In addition, you will also find quotes from other notables, such as Linus Torvalds, the creator of the original version of the Linux operating system. ("Linux does endless loops in six seconds.")

Web:
  http://www.snurgle.org/~adavenpo/quotes/

Quotable Women

Since the beginning of creation, women have been talking. As a matter of fact, the first well-known quote is attributed to Eve ("Are you really going to wear that?"). The Quotable Women archive collects memorable quotes from women both modern and historical. Why settle for the last word when you can get all of them?

Web:
  http://www.wendy.com/women/quotations.html

Quotation Resources

Truly, there's no need to ever have to be original in anything you say or write. Just check out these resources, and you'll find just about any type of quotations: advertising quotes, animal quotes, music quotes, political quotes, religious quotes, film quotes, and more. With so many sources of information, if you happen to say something original, don't blame me.

Web:
  http://www.bemorecreative.com/quotesites.htm

QUOTATIONS 653

Look What I Found on the Net...

(from the Samuel Goldwyn quotation archive)

Note: Samuel Goldwyn was an American immigrant who became one of the most powerful film producers in Hollywood. He controlled MGM (Metro-Goldwyn-Mayer) and was well known for his eminently quotable remarks, many of which are, no doubt, apocryphal.

"It rolled off my back like a duck."

[When told his son was getting married]
"Thank heaven. A bachelor's life is no life for a single man."

"I can give you a definite maybe."

"Gentleman, include me out."

"A verbal contract isn't worth the paper it's printed on."

Bookkeeper: Mr. Goldwyn, our files are bulging with paperwork we no longer need. May I have your permission to destroy all records before 1945?
Goldwyn: Certainly. Just be sure to keep a copy of everything.

"I can tell you in two words: im possible."

[On being told that a friend had named his son Sam, after him]
"Why did you do that ? Every Tom, Dick and Harry is named Sam!"

"I paid too much for it, but it's worth it."

"Don't worry about the war. It's all over but the shooting."

"Gentlemen, for your information, I have a question to ask you."

"I read part of it all the way through."

"If I could drop dead right now, I'd be the happiest man alive."

"I never put on a pair of shoes until I've worn them at least five years."

"I don't think anyone should write their autobiography until after they're dead."

"Anyone who goes to a psychiatrist ought to have his head examined."

"Gentlemen, listen to me slowly."

[In discussing Lillian Hellman's play, "The Children's Hour"]
Goldwyn: Maybe we ought to buy it?
Associate: Forget it, Mr. Goldwyn, it's about lesbians.
Goldwyn: That's okay, we'll make them Americans.

654 QUOTATIONS

Quotation Talk and General Discussion

Here is the Usenet group devoted to a discussion of quotations. This is the place to ask if anyone knows who said, "It isn't necessary to have relatives in Kansas City in order to be unhappy." Of course, questions like this only get answered if people participate, so if you like quotes, why don't you follow the discussion and see if you can help someone else.

Usenet:
  alt.quotations

Random Quotes

Need a quick burst of inspiration? Get yourself a quote chosen randomly from a large collection of interesting and pithy sayings. You can request another quote whenever you want, but be prudent. According to the U.S. Department of Redundancy Department, the recommended maximum allowance for an average adult is three quotes a day (two for Steve Wright quotes).

Web:
  http://www.panix.com/~dturner/quotes.htm
  http://www.panix.com/~ficara/quotes/quotes.cgi

Look What I Found on the Net...

```
Newsgroup: alt.quotations
Subject: Geometry or Math Quote Wanted

> Would anyone kindly offer a special quotation pertaining to
> geometry or math, please?

[to which various people send in replies...]

There is no royal road to geometry.
   — Euclid to Ptolemy I

Sex is the mathematics urge sublimated.
   — M.C. Reed


Anyone who cannot cope with mathematics is not fully human.  At
best he is a tolerable subhuman who has learned to wear shoes,
bathe and not make messes in the house.
   — Robert Heinlein (in "Time Enough for Love")

There are three kinds of people in this world: Those who can
count to three and those who can't.
   — anonymous

Stand firm in your refusal to remain conscious during algebra.
In real life, I assure you, there is no such thing as algebra.
   — Fran Leibowitz

As long as algebra is taught in school, there will be prayer in
school.
   — Cokie Roberts
```

> **Guys:**
> The best way to impress a date is to invite her over and show her that you have a complete set of Harley Hahn books.

Star Trek Quotes

Dammit, Jim, I'm a writer, not a trivia buff. If you want quotes from the original Star Trek, the Next Generation, the Star Trek movies, Voyager or Deep Space Nine, you'll have to get them yourself.

Web:
http://www.bazza.com/sj/trek/quotes/

Today's Fortune

If you are trying to cut down on sweets and you are bypassing the after-dinner fortune cookie, at least you don't have to feel deprived. Load up this page to get a nice fortune quote. And if you don't like it, you can reload to get another one.

Web:
http://www.bsdi.com/fortune

Twain, Mark

Mark Twain (1835-1910) was the father of modern American literature, and like most fathers, he said a lot of things worth remembering. Here is a nice collection of Mark Twain quotations which you can explore when you need something sardonic and wise, with just the right amount of irony (for example, to say to your own father).

Web:
http://salwen.com/mtquotes.html

Wilde, Oscar

Oscar Wilde (1854-1900) was an Irish writer best known for his witty plays—especially "The Importance of Being Earnest"—and for his novel "The Picture of Dorian Gray". In addition, Wilde wrote short stories, fairy tales and essays. Aside from his wit, which was considerable, Wilde is remembered for his personal philosophy. He believed that beauty is valuable as an end unto itself (the aesthetic movement), and that this is not, perhaps, the best of all possible worlds (Wilde's own experience). The best example of this philosophy is the story of Dorian Gray, a young man of exceptional beauty who is corrupted by excessive sensual gratification coupled with an under-developed sense of morality. According to Oscar Wilde, the only way to get rid of a temptation is to yield to it. So don't wait. Rush out today and buy ten copies of a Harley Hahn book.

Web:
http://www.jonno.com/oscariana/oscar.cgi
http://www.phnet.fi/public/mamaa1/wilde.htm

Today's Fortune

Every day, start your day by reading a witty, interesting saying.
It's better for you than coffee and more inspiring than television.
Just connect to **Today's Fortune** Web site, and a randomly chosen quotation will be yours.
Special service: I recognize that it may not be possible for you to check **Today's Fortune** every day. So, as a public service, I am giving you two dog-oriented quotes. You can use these when you need to be away from the Net (for example, if you have to leave town for the weekend).
(1) Mark Twain: If you pick up a starving dog and make him prosperous, he will not bite you. This is the principal difference between a dog and a man.
(2) Groucho Marx: Outside of a dog, a book is a man's best friend; inside of a dog, it's too dark to read.

RADIO

Amateur Radio Talk and General Discussion

Radio is a great hobby and one day when you are an expert, you can have your own nationally syndicated talk show and screaming fans will throw themselves at your feet when you go out in public. Until then, you can spend time reading Usenet groups especially for amateur radio enthusiasts. Topics cover construction, packet and digital radio modes, transmission, regulations, repair and other general topics.

Usenet:
  alt.radio.amateur
  rec.radio.amateur
  rec.radio.amateur.antenna
  rec.radio.amateur.boatanchors
  rec.radio.amateur.digital.misc
  rec.radio.amateur.dx
  rec.radio.amateur.equipment
  rec.radio.amateur.homebrew
  rec.radio.amateur.misc
  rec.radio.amateur.packet
  rec.radio.amateur.policy
  rec.radio.amateur.space
  rec.radio.amateur.swap

Listproc Mailing List:
  List Name: **qrp-l**
  Subscribe to: **listproc@lehigh.edu**

Campus Radio Disc Jockeys

What a cool job it is to sit in a climate-controlled booth jamming out to the latest tunes for hours on end. And in between the songs you get to offer some profound remarks that will reach the ears of every student on campus. What power! Hone your communication skills by hearing what other DJs and station managers discuss on this mailing list about college radio, federal and campus regulations, station policies, and equipment reviews.

Listserv Mailing List:
  List Name: **dj-l**
  Subscribe to: **listserv@listserv.nodak.edu**

Campus Radio Disc Jockeys

When I was an undergraduate at the University of Waterloo, Canada, I was a CRDJ. Actually, I was a CCCRDJ (Cool Canadian Campus Radio Disc Jockey). If you too are a member of this elite corps, join the **dj-l** mailing list and see what your fellows are up to.

Canadian Broadcasting Corporation

For years, the Canadian Broadcasting Corporation (CBC) has been providing the best television and radio broadcasting that government money can buy. If you live in Canada, spend some time at this Web site where you can find all kinds of information, including schedules, audio versions of various programs, discussion, and much more (in French and in English). My favorite items are the transcripts of various shows. In particular, it's revealing to read the transcript of the daily national news broadcast ("...and on our magazine: Just 14 and sexually active. Why more kids are having sex at a younger age. What they want their parents to know...").

Web:
  http://www.radio.cbc.ca/

RADIO

Citizen Band Radio

Breaker breaker, anybody got your ears on? While the CB craze is not what it used to be, there are still a load of CB radio fans looking for people to talk to. Check out the citizen band action on the Net.

Web:
http://rob.acol.com/~cb/cblinks.html

Usenet:
rec.radio.cb

Classic Top 40 Radio Sounds

It is human nature to compare and analyze, and ever since there has been music on the radio, there have been lists of which songs were the most popular. In the radio industry, "Top 40" refers to the 40 most popular songs, and "classic" refers to songs that were popular among people who are now old enough to have children. Thus, visiting a "classic Top 40 radio sounds" Web site will allow you to wax nostalgic about the personalities and sounds that baby boomers enjoyed when they were young. Or, as Wolfman Jack once put it, "Good guys only make it in the movies, baby..."

Web:
http://www.reelradio.com/

Digital Audio Broadcasting

Imagine: your voice—static-free, flying silky smooth through the air at the speed of sound, straight into someone's ear. They turn and could swear that you were right there behind them. This is the wonder of digital audio broadcasting with its improved sound quality and technical superiority. Join with other DAB enthusiasts to talk not only about the technological merits of digital audio broadcasting, but also the social and economic issues.

Usenet:
alt.radio.digital

Listserv Mailing List:
List Name: radio-l
Subscribe to: listserv@tc.umn.edu

Ham Radio

Do you want to be famous? Start practicing now by becoming a ham radio operator. After a while you will get a reputation around the neighborhood as that studly ham guy. Then you can start spouting your opinions on the radio, build up your ego, put on a few pounds and eventually have your own conservative talk show on mainstream radio. Wouldn't that be fun? So get on the Net now and learn all about ham radio. The faster you learn, the faster you will be on your way to success.

Web:
http://www.cc.columbia.edu/~fuat/cuarc/callsign-servers.html
http://www.qrz.com/directory.cgi

Usenet:
alt.ham-radio.mods
alt.ham-radio.morse
rec.ham-radio
rec.ham-radio.swap

NPR Online

NPR (National Public Radio) is an American non-commercial radio network. NPR offers a large variety of programs, many of which are oriented toward news and current events. Some of the more popular programs are All Things Considered, Car Talk, Morning Edition, Seasonings, Talk of the Nation and Weekend Edition. In the United States, NPR is considered by some people to be controversial due to a "liberal bias". However, their programs are well-produced and informative, and they have many listeners across the country. If you would like to listen to some NPR programs, you can do so by connecting to this Web site (NPR Online). You will also find information about NPR itself such as where to listen to NPR, member stations, how to get transcripts of shows, and so on. For discussion about NPR, you can participate in the Usenet group.

Web:
http://www.npr.org/

Usenet:
alt.radio.networks.npr

Number Stations

You're listening to your shortwave radio and all of a sudden you hear a nondescript voice intoning a long list of numbers. Sometimes you hear a pattern, but mostly the numbers seem random. And then suddenly they stop. Later, you happen onto the same frequency and again you hear the numbers. What are they? No one knows for sure, but there are many shortwave stations around the world broadcasting sequences of numbers. Nobody will admit to being responsible for the stations, but they have been broadcasting for years. It is generally thought that these stations are run by espionage agencies and are used to send coded signals to spies in the field. Around the world there are many people who monitor these stations, keep statistics and share information. There are even organizations and newsletters devoted to tracking these number stations.

Web:
http://www.access.digex.net/~cps/numbers.html
http://www.ibmpcug.co.uk/~irdial/conet.htm

Old-Time Radio

I love old radio shows like Jack Benny, Dragnet, the Great Gildersleeve, and Burns and Allen. If you do too, you will enjoy these Web sites. To get you started, here is an interesting trivia item. One of the more popular radio shows (dating back to 1940) was Truth or Consequences. Each time the show began you would hear the audience laughing uncontrollably. How did they arrange it? Well, a few minutes before the show was to start, two men from the audience would be brought up on the stage. Each man was given a suitcase and told that the first person who could get dressed using the contents of the suitcase would win a prize. The suitcases were filled with women's clothes and undergarments. The stunt never failed to whip the audience into gales of laughter, just in time for the announcer to say: "Hello there. We've been waiting for you. It's time to play Truth or Consequences."

Web:
http://www.antique-radio.org/
http://www.old-time.com/

Open Broadcasting

Until recently, those public service agencies that broadcast over the radio have used the same technology as everyone else. That is why it is possible, for example, to use a scanner to listen to the police broadcasts. However, many public agencies are now starting to use closed radio systems—such as digital (trunked) or encrypted transmissions—that are difficult or impossible for regular people to monitor. Some public officials will admit frankly that they do *not* want the general public to be able to overhear their transmissions. But is this in our best interests? In a free country, do you really want the police and other government agencies to be able to communicate in secret? Open broadcasting is the idea that public agencies should use the airwaves in ways that are accessible to the public.

Web:
http://members.aol.com/truth4000/obfaq.htm
http://members.aol.com/truth4000/page1.htm
http://members.aol.com/wwhitby2/trs.html

Usenet:
alt.radio.broadcasting.open

Packet Radio

Packet radio is a system that sends information from one computer to another using radio broadcasting. The name "packet radio" refers to the fact that the information is broken into small groupings of data called "packets". (The Internet itself is a packet-based network.) With packet radio, you use a device called a TNC (terminal node controller) to connect your computer to a radio. The TNC acts like a bridge between your computer and the radio, which sends and receives data. (Conceptually, the TNC is like a modem only instead of using a phone line, data is transmitted using radio waves.) Most packet radio enthusiasts use VHF frequencies, which limit transmissions to a little better than unobstructed line of sight. However, once you have the appropriate equipment, packet radio is easy to use and requires no special license. And there exist networks of packet radio systems that make it possible to propagate data over long distances.

Web:
http://www.tapr.org/tapr/html/pkthome.html

Usenet:
rec.radio.amateur.packet

Check out Old-Time Radio on the Net, and step forward into the past.

Pirate Radio

In most countries, radio broadcasting is strictly regulated by the government. In the United States, that job is performed by the FCC (Federal Communications Commission). In Canada, the organization is the CRTC (Canadian Radio-television and Telecommunications Commission). These government agencies do not allow private individuals to broadcast willy-nilly over the most commonly used frequencies, such as those set aside for AM and FM radio. Pirate radio refers to non-sanctioned broadcasting over such frequencies. The philosophical justification within the mostly underground pirate radio community ranges from freedom of speech to good plain fun. These Web pages contain lots of pirate radio resources. If the idea of broadcasting illegally in front of the government's back appeals to you, start reading here. For ongoing discussion, you can participate in the Usenet group.

Web:
  http://www.frn.net/
  http://www.mnsinc.com/bry/piralynx.htm
  http://www.threethirtysix.org/pirate/

Usenet:
  alt.pirate.radio
  alt.radio.pirate

Radio Broadcasting

Boy, radio has just got to be the best invention since television. Join the folks who love to listen, as they discuss radio broadcasting. The **broadcasting** discussion groups are for general broadcasting topics. (The **rec.radio.broadcasting** group is moderated.) The **info** group, also moderated, is for news and announcements. For those who hate advertising, **noncomm** is for talking about noncommercial radio. The **radio-l** group is for digital audio broadcasting.

Usenet:
  alt.radio.broadcasting
  bit.listserv.radio-l
  rec.radio.broadcasting
  rec.radio.info
  rec.radio.noncomm

660 RADIO

Radio History

The history of radio covers less than a century. However, it is one of the most fascinating stories in the world of technology. These Web sites contain a lot of fascinating information about radio and its early days. Read about the development of radio technology and see a timeline of radio broadcasting. There are even pictures of radios as well as a listing of important radio events.

Web:
http://www.antique-radio.org/timeline/time.html
http://www.itd.umd.edu/UMS/UMCP/NPBA/timeline.html
http://www.radiohistory.org/

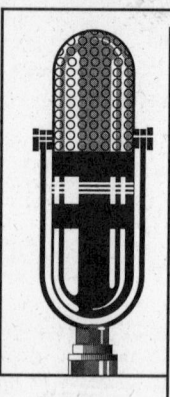

Radio History

In 1901, the very first transatlantic message was broadcast by Guglielmo Marconi from Cornwall, England, to Saint John's, Newfoundland.

The transmission consisted of the Morse code signal for the letter "S".

(Immediately afterward, Marconi's wife took over the system in order to talk to her sister in Canada.)

Radio Scanner Frequencies

A radio scanner is a device that lets you monitor radio frequencies not accessible with regular AM and FM receivers. These frequencies are used by a variety of organizations, especially law enforcement and public service groups. These Web pages will help you find frequencies that you can monitor to eavesdrop on various types of conversations. You can also find the frequencies used by drive-through restaurants (MacDonalds, etc.), theme parks (Disneyland, etc.), TV stations, canned music (Muzak) and cordless phones. After all, if they didn't want you to listen, why would they be talking?

Web:
http://exo.com/~rbarron/
http://www.agt.net/public/gpnet/gpnet.htm

Usenet:
alt.radio.scanner
alt.radio.scanner.uk
rec.radio.scanner

Radio Station Lists

Here are several comprehensive lists I have selected to help you find information about radio stations around the world. These lists are useful when you want to find out which stations are in a particular area. In addition, one of the lists shows many stations that have their own Web sites. For U.S. listeners, I have included a resource to allow you to look at the official FCC information for any U.S. radio station. You can search by location, frequency or call letters.

Web:
http://wmbr.mit.edu/stations/
http://wmbr.mit.edu/stations/list.html
http://www.krgspec.com/stationsearch.cfm
http://www.radiostation.com/

Shortwave Radio

Shortwave radio consists of signals broadcast between 3Mhz and 30 MHz. The nature of shortwave is that the waves bounce off the upper atmosphere and, hence, can travel long distances. This means that you can use a shortwave receiver to listen to broadcasts from around the world. There are a wide variety of shortwave stations, and listening to them is a fascinating hobby. Here is a lot of information to help get you started, as well as for the experienced shortwave enthusiast.

Web:
http://itre.ncsu.edu/radio/
http://www.anarc.org/naswa/swlguide/
http://www.mnsinc.com/bry/swllynx.htm

Usenet:
rec.radio.shortwave

Looking for something racy?
See "Cars and Trucks" or
"X-Rated Resources".

REFERENCE

Talk Radio Hosts

Every day, millions of people listen to other people talk on the radio. If you like talk radio, you may need something to look at while you are listening. Here are Web sites for the most popular U.S. radio talk show hosts. (Some sites are "official"; some are not.) To discuss your favorite show, try the Usenet groups, where the talk goes on 24 hours a day. The Web sites are in the following order: Art Bell, Jim Bohannon, Joy Browne, Alan Colmes, Dean Edell, David Essel, Bob Grant, Don Imus, Judy Jarvis, Tom Leykis, Gordon Liddy, Rush Limbaugh, Oliver North, Michael Reagan, Laura Schlessinger, Howard Stern and Bruce Williams. The **daphnes-corner** Usenet group is for Dean Edell; his producer is Daphne Brogdon. (Interesting fact: Laura Schlessinger has a Ph.D. in physiology. She received the degree in 1974 from Columbia University for a dissertation entitled "Effects of insulin on 3-0-methylglucose transport in isolated rat adipocytes". In other words, the only reason Dr. Laura can call herself a "doctor" is because she researched insulin receptors in fat cells in rats.)

Web:
  http://www.artbell.com/
  http://www.inetport.com/~gra/bohannon.htm
  http://www.wor710.com/net/n-browne.htm
  http://www.alan.com/
  http://www.net-quest.com/~wizard/daphne.html
  http://www.davidessel.com/
  http://www.wor710.com/net/n-grant.htm
  http://www.kajor.com/imus/
  http://www.judyjarvisshow.com/
  http://www.tomleykis.com/
  http://www.rtis.com/liddy/
  http://www.rtis.com/nat/pol/rush/
  http://www.northamerican.com/
  http://www.reagan.com/
  http://www.drlaura.com/
  http://www.karlfm.com/
  http://www.brucewilliams.com/

Usenet:
  alt.fan.art-bell
  alt.fan.daphnes-corner
  alt.fan.don-imus
  alt.fan.howard-stern
  alt.fan.rush-limbaugh
  alt.fan.tom-leykis
  alt.flame.rush-limbaugh
  alt.radio.talk.dr-laura
  alt.rush-limbaugh

Vintage Radios and Broadcasting Equipment

Are you a collector? This Web site is devoted to the collecting of vintage broadcast microphones. The pictures are interesting and well worth a look. The Usenet group is for the discussion of antique radios and phonographic equipment.

Web:
  http://www.k-bay106.com/mics.htm

Usenet:
  rec.antiques.radio+phono

Voice of America

The Voice of America (VOA) is the radio broadcasting service of the U.S. International Broadcasting Bureau. The purpose of VOA is to serve the long-range interests of the United States by "communicating with the peoples of the world by radio." In particular, VOA offers a "consistently reliable and authoritative source of news." Around the world, VOA broadcasts on shortwave and medium wave frequencies in over 50 languages. Many of these broadcasts are also available over the Internet, so take a moment and give a listen.

Web:
  http://www.voa.gov/

REFERENCE

Acronyms

Here is a resource that should be in everyone's bookmark list. You specify an acronym, and a program looks it up in the master list and tells you what the acronym means. You can also search the list of meanings for a particular word or expression. If you have a friend who thinks he knows everything, ask him what MOTSTJHTBHWIGH means.

Web:
  http://www.ucc.ie/info/net/acronyms/

Start here.

Alternative Dictionaries

Here are words you will never see in a regular dictionary: various types of slang. For example, suppose you are in Quebec and someone says to you "Accouche qu'on baptise". Or let's say you are on the east coast of Scotland and a fellow comes up to you and asks if you are a Weedjie. Whatever are they talking about? Check with the Net and find out. Hint: If you find yourself working too hard, remind yourself (as they say in Holland) not to buffelen, or you may become besodemieterd zijn.

Web:
http://www.notam.uio.no/~hcholm/altlang/
http://www.thegoodnamesweretaken.com/beatspeak/

Alternative Dictionaries

When you study a language in school, you learn how to speak "properly". However, when you visit a foreign country, you find there are a lot of common words you are never taught in school. School is fine, but to prepare yourself for life in the street, you need the **Alternative Dictionaries**.

Biographies

Have you ever had an uncontrollable urge to find out when Isaac Asimov was born, or when John Lennon married Yoko Ono, or if there was ever anyone famous named Hahn? As an Internet user, you never have to worry about your urges being denied, especially the uncontrollable ones. All the information you need about all the famous people that you might ever care about is only a few mouse clicks away. (By the way, the answers to the previous questions are 1920, 1969 and yes.)

Web:
http://www.biography.com/find/find.html
http://www.s9.com/biography/

Calculators

In the Woody Allen movie "Radio Days", there's a scene where a father, mother and son are visiting the zoo, and they run into a young boy who is a celebrity because he appears on a radio show. The show is called "The Whiz Kids", and the young boy is a child prodigy who answers difficult questions on the air. (Woody Allen modeled this after a real-life radio show called "The Quiz Kids", which was very popular when Allen was young.) When the father (played by Michael Tucker) meets the boy, he says, "Quick, what's 1,754 divided into 13 million?" Well, of course the boy doesn't answer, but if he had a Web browser he could have found the answer in a flash. One of these sites is a simple, but useful calculator you can use for basic arithmetic. The other site is a collection of thousands of special-purpose calculators around the Net. Aside from the highly technical calculators you might expect—mathematics, science, engineering and computer stuff—there are all kinds of special-purpose resources. You can calculate retirement benefits, taxes, calendars, wedding costs, cooking measures, child support payments, sailboat performance, and much more. By the way, here's an easy way to look très cool. Rent the "Radio Days" movie with a bunch of friends. When you get to the part where Michael Tucker says, "Quick, what's 1,754 divided into 13 million?" casually give the answer (7411.630558722919). It won't be long before your friends are showing you the respect you deserve.

Web:
http://doppler.unl.edu/users/bcorner/calc.html
http://www-sci.lib.uci.edu/HSG/RefCalculators.html

Calendars

It's handy to have a calendar around just to make sure you are doing the right thing on the right day. For example, how would you feel if you completely missed the St. Swithin's day celebration because you had gotten it mixed up with Martha Stewart's birthday? Here are some resources to make sure you never get your dates mixed up again.

Web:
http://www.calendarzone.com/
http://www.cern.ch/htbin/calendar

Listserv Mailing List:
List Name: calndr-l
Subscribe to: listserv@tc.umn.edu

REFERENCE 663

> **Try a Mud.**

Center of Statistical Resources

I have found another important but little-known use for the Net. As you are playing a trivia game, make an excuse and sneak off to your computer, where you can use the Net to find lots of statistics that will help you beat your friends into submission. For example, wait until you get a question you can't answer, and then say, "Oh, just a second, I have to go the bathroom." While you are gone, you can quickly visit this Web site, where you will find a staggering compilation of statistics on many, many topics. When your friends express admiration at your extensive knowledge of trivial subjects, you can tell them that eliminating toxins from the body really helps to clear one's mind.

Web:
http://www.lib.umich.edu/libhome/
    Documents.center/stats.html

Dictionaries

Quick. Pick a word, any word. Type it into a form, press a button and presto, before you can say "my onerous oneiric tendencies have been keeping me up all night," your very own definition will be waiting for you. These are resources I use a lot and every day, in every way, my vocabulary is getting better and better.

Web:
http://gs213.sp.cs.cmu.edu/prog/webster
http://www.bucknell.edu/~rbeard/diction.html
http://www.m-w.com/netdict.htm
http://www.onelook.com/

Encyclopedias

In the future, you won't have to haul yourself down to the library and deal with a lot of heavy books just to check something in an encyclopedia. You'll be able to look up anything you want right on the Internet. Well, the future has already arrived. (Was that fast or what?) From now on, you and the Net are partners in knowledge.

Web:
http://encarta.msn.com/
http://www.infoplease.com/

Look What I Found on the Net...

```
Newsgroup: alt.usage.english
Subject: Segue and Segway

Has anyone else seen the second spelling, "segway", as valid?

I thought I saw it spelled that way at two radio stations, one
in New York and another in Chicago.

>> I'm a bit confused — how can you see the spelling of anything
>> on the radio?

> Now, now.  Are we practicing a false metonymy here?

Hmm.  I don't know if he was being serious, but it does raise an
interesting issue of disambiguation.

How would one best write the sentence "I *heard* something at a
radio station" to make it absolutely clear that I was standing
next to someone speaking into a microphone at the physical plant
with a transmitter?

(And how would one best rearrange the clauses in the previous sentence?)
```

Farmer's Almanac

The Farmer's Almanac is a venerable American publication that has been produced annually since 1792. The Almanac is a treasure of useful information for day-to-day living. This Web site contains some of that information. In particular, you can find information and predictions about the weather, gardening, the sunrise and sunset, the phases of the moon, and astronomical events such as eclipses. There are various other features that are changed regularly so this is always a good place to visit when you have a few spare moments.

Web:

http://www.almanac.com/

Grammar and English Usage

When someone is reading your work, there are various demands you can make. You can ask your reader to recreate various thoughts, feelings and emotions within his or her own mind. You can expect your reader to pay attention to new words (if you explain them properly) and to follow a chain of ideas, from one point to the next. What you can't expect is for anyone to exert mental effort figuring out what you are trying to say because you didn't use the generally accepted writing conventions. Imagination is great, but not when it comes to grammar, punctuation or word usage. These Web sites have a lot of information about grammar and style—information that will help you develop your writing skills. One of the Web sites contains the FAQ (frequently asked question list) for the Usenet group **alt.usage.english**. This is the Usenet group in which you can discuss words, rules and how to use them.

Web:

http://pw1.netcom.com/~garbl1/writing.html
http://www.cis.ohio-state.edu/hypertext/faq/usenet/alt-usage-english-faq/faq.html
http://www.columbia.edu/acis/bartleby/strunk/
http://www.edunet.com/english/grammar/
http://www.theslot.com/

Usenet:

alt.usage.english

Maps and Atlases

Imagine you're living in the future. You have to go visit a place you've never been before, so before you leave, you type the address into your computer, which connects to another computer and presents you a map of the area. You can ask for more or less detail as well as driving instructions that will take you from where you are to your destination. Well, the future arrived yesterday. All of this and a lot more are available on the Net.

Web:

http://www.atlapedia.com/
http://www.mapblast.com/
http://www.mapsonus.com/
http://www.pathfinder.com/travel/maps/index2.html

Phone Books

Find that person—now! Here are electronic phone books that cover the United States, Canada, plus many other countries around the world. Here's a hint on how to be very popular. Look up all your old friends—wherever they are in the world—and call them right now. Tell them Harley says hello.

Web:

http://canada411.sympatico.ca/
http://www.555-1212.com/
http://www.infospace.com/people.htm
http://www.whitepages.com/
http://www.whowhere.com/Phone

Postal Codes and Mail

No matter where you need to send mail, the Net can help. Here are some resources to help you find postal codes from many different countries. If you need more information, you will find links to post offices around the world. For U.S. and Canadian mail, I have included special resources, including a handy U.S. postal rate calculator that I use all the time. Postal trivia: In the United States, postal codes are called "ZIP codes". The name stands for "Zone Improvement Plan".

Web:

http://www.canadapost.ca/CPC2/addrm/pclookup/pclookup.html
http://www.grcdi.nl/linkspc.htm
http://www.grcdi.nl/linkspo.htm
http://www.link-usa.com/zipcode/
http://www.usps.gov/business/calcs.htm
http://www.usps.gov/ncsc/

REFERENCE

Reference Desks

I have a friend, Mary Axford, who's a wonderful reference librarian. It used to be that whenever I had a question that needed special reference material, I would call Mary. She has all the reference books you can imagine: dictionaries, thesauri, phone books, atlases, encyclopedias, statistics references, and so on. I could call Mary at any time to ask her, say, "What is the capital of Madagascar?" or "What is the most common female name in America?" Now all of that information—and a lot more—is on the Net, available for free, twenty-four hours a day. My life as a writer is certainly easier. The only thing is I don't get to talk to Mary as often as I used to. (By the way, the capital of Madagascar is Antananarivo, and the most common female name in America is Mary.)

Web:
http://www-sci.lib.uci.edu/HSG/Ref.html
http://www.refdesk.com/facts.html
http://www.xplore.com/xplore500/medium/reference.html

Roget's Thesaurus

In 1852, Peter Mark Roget published the first edition of his "Thesaurus of English Words and Phrases", on which he had been working for 50 years. Throughout successive editions—which were supervised by Roget, his son, and later his grandson—what we now call the Roget's Thesaurus has become a standard reference work of the English language. The purpose of the Roget's Thesaurus is simply stated: you use it when you know the meaning of a word but do not know the word. Roget arranged all the words in the English language and their idiomatic combinations, not in alphabetical order as in a dictionary, but according to the ideas they express. If you care at all about writing, please take some time to become familiar with this classic reference and how to use it. Treating a Roget's Thesaurus as if it were nothing more than a dictionary of synonyms is like using a collection of Mozart CDs as a paperweight.

Web:
http://humanities.uchicago.edu/forms_unrest/ROGET.html
http://www.thesaurus.com/

Time

It's true that there are a lot of different time zones in the world and a lot of technicalities used to maintain our time systems. But there is no reason why you can't understand how it all works. Here is all the information you need to find out what time it is now anywhere in the world, as well as learning about time zones and the details of our world time system. It's not really all that hard once you realize that time is merely a means for keeping everything from happening all at once.

Web:
http://tycho.usno.navy.mil/time.html
http://www.bsdi.com/date
http://www.greenwich2000.com/time/
http://www.stud.unit.no/USERBIN/steffent/verdensur.pl

Roget's Thesaurus

Do you need a word? A specific word with a particular shade of meaning? Use the online **Roget's Thesaurus**, and you'll have the exact word you need promptly, quickly, soon, before long, shortly, instantly, forthwith, summarily, immediately, briefly, speedily, directly, before the ink is dry, in no long time, and before you can say "Jack Robinson".

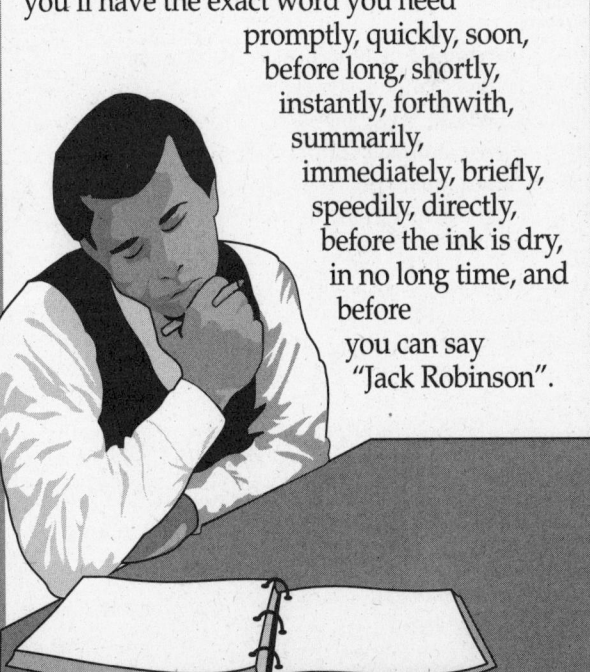

666 REFERENCE

Today's Date and Time

Here are various interpretations of today's date and time, along with what today's date would be on various other calendars. There are also links to Persian, Buddhist and Chinese calendars and information on the systems they use for years and months. For example, today (as I am looking at this site) it is 1998.6552 in the Julian Epoch (astrophysics time), year 56 of the Atomic Era, Star Trek Stardate 1681.47, as well as the Year of the Earth Tiger (not to mention Month of the Metal Monkey).

Web:
http://www.panix.com/~wlinden/calendar.shtml

Tracking a Package

If you ever send packages or letters overnight, here are some resources you will use again and again. When you send the package, be sure to keep the receipt with the tracking number. You can then use the Net to track your package every step of the way. I have included the appropriate Web sites for Airborne Express, DHL, FedEx, RPS, UPS and the U.S. Postal Service. Hint: When you send an especially important package, email the tracking number to the recipient, along with the Web address of the site at which he or she can check for the package. This will make you look so cool, people will just naturally want to pay you lots and lots of money for no reason at all.

Web:
http://www.airborne-express.com/trace/
http://www.dhl.com/track/
http://www.fedex.com/us/tracking/
http://www.shiprps.com/trace.htm
http://www.ups.com/tracking/tracking.html
http://www.usps.gov/cttgate/

Weights and Measures

There are two basic systems of measurement used in the world, the imperial system for the United States and the metric system for everyone else. Within each system there are a large number of different units. If you ever need help with converting one type of unit to another, the Net is ready to oblige. I used it just the other day, actually. I was figuring out how fast I could go on my bicycle and I had to convert from kilometers per hour to furlongs per fortnight.

Web:
http://lamar.colostate.edu/~hillger/everyday.htm
http://www.french-property.com/ref/convert.htm

Word Detective

Enjoy the online version of a column in which the writer answers about words and their origins. If you enjoy learning about language and words, you will like this site. Here are some examples. (1) One guy wrote a letter because he and his girlfriend had been having an argument about whether to say "have your cake and eat it too" or "eat your cake and have it too". (2) Another person asked if "busting someone's chop" and "busting someone's hump" are the same thing. (3) A third reader who mentioned the term "old fogey" wanted to know if there were such a thing as a "young fogey". (4) And finally, there is a link to an answer to the question "Aside from 'angry' and 'hungry', what well-known English word ends in 'gry'?" By the way, the answers to these questions are (1) It doesn't matter. (2) No. (3) Yes, but people don't use the expression. (4) There are no other common words that end in "gry". The whole thing is a hoax.

Web:
http://www.users.interport.net/~words1/

RELIGION

Agnosticism

An agnostic is a person who believes that the existence of God cannot be proved or disproved. The word "agnostic" was coined in 1889 by the English biologist and educator Thomas Henry Huxley (1825-1895). However, the basic ideas are old: they were discussed in various forms by the early Greek philosophers. In its most pure form, agnosticism considers fundamental philosophical problems such as what can we know, and what can we understand about that which we can't know? In its more common pop-culture usage, the term "agnostic" refers to someone who is proud to announce that he or she is not sure if there is really a God.

Web:
http://www.freethinker.org/library/modern/reason/agnosticism/
http://www.infidels.org/~jlowder/nontheism/agnosticism.html

Usenet:
alt.agnosticism

RELIGION

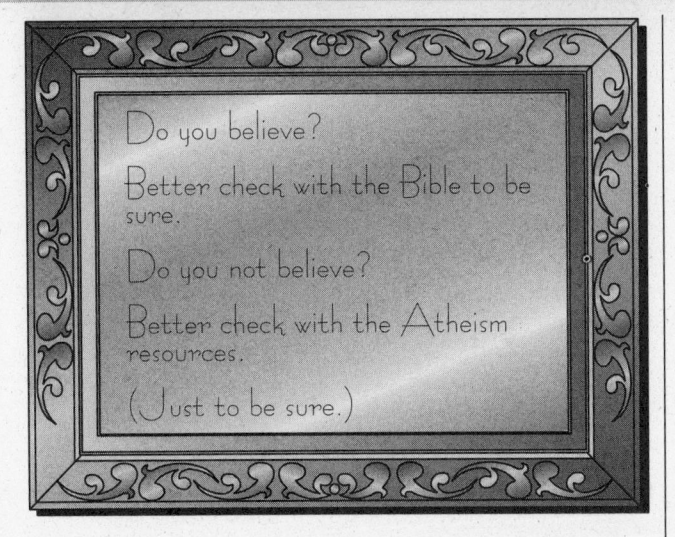

> Do you believe?
> Better check with the Bible to be sure.
> Do you not believe?
> Better check with the Atheism resources.
> (Just to be sure.)

Anglican and Episcopalian Churches

The Anglican church (also known as the Church of England) officially began in 1534 when King Henry VIII issued the Act of Supremacy. The Episcopalian church developed from the Church of England at the time of the American Revolution. Although the churches have separate organizations, they have a lot in common. For example, they both use the Book of Common Prayer. Worldwide, the collection of churches affiliated with the Church of England is called the Anglican Communion. These churches represent about 70 million people in over 160 countries. The roots of these churches lie in Catholicism, and to this day they have a lot in common with the Roman Catholic church. However, they do not recognize the supremacy of the Pope and they have their own governing bodies. The spiritual head of the Anglican church is the Archbishop of Canterbury, who lives in England.

Web:
http://www.church-of-england.org/
http://www.ecusa.anglican.org/
http://www.episcopalian.org/
http://www.mit.edu/~tb/anglican/

Listserv Mailing List:
List Name: **anglican**
Subscribe to: **listserv@american.edu**

Atheism

Atheism is the belief that a sound philosophy of life should recognize that there are no gods (or God). Although it is fashionable to pretend that the Western monotheistic religions all believe in the same god, this is just not so. When you look at the details, it is plain that the Moslem god (Allah) is not the same god as the Catholic god, who is not the same god as the Mormon god, and so on. Moreover, the Hindus believe in many gods, and the Buddhists do not believe in the idea of a god at all. Of course, the one thing these religions all have in common is that they believe they are right and the others are wrong. Well, maybe they are all wrong. Maybe what people believe has nothing to do with universal truths. Maybe what people believe depends on their personal spiritual needs and how they were indoctrinated as children. If you are one of those unusual people who insist on thinking for yourself, see what the atheists have to say.

Web:
http://www.atheists.org/
http://www.infidels.org/

Usenet:
alt.atheism
alt.atheism.moderated
soc.atheism
talk.atheism

IRC:
#atheism

Bible Study

When Paul said not to "forsake the gathering of ourselves together", the odds are this is not how he anticipated things would evolve. But if he were here today he would be telling you to stop mudding and join this forum of people interested in studying the Bible together electronically. The assumption is made that participants consider the Bible authoritative, so these groups are not a sparring ground for belief systems, nor are they for purely academic purposes.

Usenet:
alt.bible
alt.bible.prophecy
soc.religion.christian.bible-study

Bibles Online

You can use these online Bibles to search and read specific passages. There is a variety of languages available as well as links to related reference material. On the Net, inspiration is never more than a few mouse clicks away.

Web:
http://ccel.wheaton.edu/wwsb/
http://www.gospelcom.net/bible

Biblical Timeline

Keep track of important Bible events such as the Flood, the building of the Tower of Babel and the chronology of your favorite Bible characters. The biblical timeline also corresponds with a secular timeline so you can see the biblical events in juxtaposition with other historical events.

Web:
http://www.cynet.com/jesus/time.htm

Look What I Found on the Net...

```
Newsgroup: alt.atheism
Subject: Question for Fellow Atheists

> Although I am an atheist, I have always been fascinated by the
> beliefs of religions around the world.  Is this unusual for an
> atheist?
>
> I do not believe in God, but I see in the world's religions
> some vital information and insight into the nature of man.
> When I explore various religions — taking them as metaphors
> — I learn a great deal about myself and my fellow human
> beings.  I have assumed that most atheists are more interested
> and educated in the world's religions, even after their
> acceptance of atheism, than most followers of individual
> faiths.  Is this true?
```

I don't know. It's hard to speak authoritatively for "most atheists". Certainly among those who participate in discussions of religion and atheism on the Net, this seems to be the case.

In my own case, early exposure to other religions was instrumental in the development of my atheism. I was always interested by religious mythology, both as story and as it related to the development of our culture.

Interestingly, I tended to give a fairly wide berth to Christianity and the major modern religions until around the time I started participating in alt.atheism. Since then, it's been a fairly major topic with me.

—

"A little rudeness and disrespect can elevate a meaningless interaction to a battle of wills and add drama to an otherwise dull day." — Calvin

RELIGION 669

Who did what, when, and to whom?

Take a look at the Biblical Timeline and bring some order to the chaos.

Buddhism

Buddhism is a religion and philosophy founded in India by Siddhartha Gautama (the Buddha) in the 6th and 5th centuries B.C. Buddhism teaches the practice of meditation and the observance of moral tenets. Several sects have evolved from basic Buddhism, so there are variations on traditional Buddhism such as Taoism and Zen Buddhism. Read up on Buddhism or chat about it on Usenet, IRC or the mailing list.

Web:
http://easyweb.easynet.co.uk/~pt/buddhism/
http://www.dharmanet.org/

Usenet:
alt.religion.buddhism.nichiren
alt.religion.buddhism.nkt
alt.religion.buddhism.tibetan
talk.religion.buddhism

Listserv Mailing List:
List Name: **buddha-l**
Subscribe to: **listserv@ulkyvm.louisville.edu**

IRC:
#buddhism

Catholicism

The Roman Catholic church has many millions of members around the world. The church is headed by the Pope, who is the bishop of Rome. You can learn more about the Catholic church, its rituals, sacraments and the Pope by viewing these Web pages, or you can talk to members of the church on Usenet or the mailing list.

Web:
http://www.cs.cmu.edu/Web/People/spok/catholic.html
http://www.knight.org/advent/

Usenet:
alt.religion.christian.roman-catholic

Listserv Mailing List:
List Name: **catholic**
Subscribe to: **listserv@american.edu**

Christian Resources

Here are some collections of links to many Christian resources, including mailing lists, home pages of churches on the Web, music, ministries, online Bibles, executable outlines, a guide to Christian literature on the Net, and much more.

Web:
http://www.allinone.org/
http://www3.christianity.net:81/search/

The Lord helps those who know how to use the Net. (So check out **Christian Resources** *today.)*

670 RELIGION

Christianity Talk and General Discussion

There are many different types of Christianity in the world and many people who are ready to discuss Christian issues. As you can see, there are a large number of Usenet discussion groups devoted to various aspects of Christianity. Your opinion is always welcome, but please make sure that you post your message to the most appropriate group.

Usenet:
  alt.christnet
  alt.christnet.christianlife
  alt.christnet.ethics
  alt.christnet.evangelical
  alt.christnet.hypocrisy
  alt.christnet.philosophy
  alt.christnet.prayer
  alt.christnet.theology
  alt.religion.christian
  alt.religion.christian-teen
  alt.religion.christian.20-something
  alt.religion.christian.anabaptist.brethren
  alt.religion.christian.boston-church
  alt.religion.christian.calvary-chapel
  alt.religion.christian.last-days
  soc.religion.christian
  soc.religion.christian.youth-work

Eastern Orthodox Christianity

Eastern Orthodox Christianity originated in Eastern Europe and Southwest Asia when it split with the Western church in the 5th century. You can find more about the modern day version of this Old World religion by checking out these Web pages or by subscribing to the mailing list.

Web:
  http://shell3.ba.best.com/~ariel/orthodox/
  http://www.theologic.com/links.html

Listserv Mailing List:
  List Name: **orthodox**
  Subscribe to: listserv@listserv.indiana.edu

> THEY don't want you to know, but I'll tell you: take a look at "Secret Stuff".

Hinduism

Hinduism is one of the world's major religions, having nearly one billion followers. The majority of Hindus live in India, where the religion forms a spiritual and cultural base for most of the country. However, there are also large numbers of Hindus in many other countries around the world. Hinduism is actually a family of faiths whose beliefs range from many gods (pluralistic theism) to a single all-pervasive deity (absolute monism). There are four principle denominations of Hinduism—Saivism, Vaishnavism, Shaktism and Smartism—each of which is different enough and complete enough to be considered a self-contained religion in its own right. All Hindus share a number of important spiritual and philosophical traditions in common, among which are karma, dharma, reincarnation, temple worship, and recognition of the Vedas as holy writings.

Web:
  http://www.hinduismtoday.kauai.hi.us/htoday.html
  http://www.hindunet.org/
  http://www.spiritweb.org/Spirit/Veda/Overview.html

Usenet:
  soc.religion.hindu

Listserv Mailing List:
  List Name: **hindu-d**
  Subscribe to: listserv@listserv.nodak.edu

IRC:
  #hindu

RELIGION

Islam

In Arabic, the word "Islam" means total submission to the will of Allah (God). A person who follows the ways of Islam is called a Muslim. Islam was founded by the Prophet Muhammad in the 7th century. A devout Muslim follows the Koran (Islam's holy book) strictly. Islam is considered to be an all-encompassing way of life that must be practiced continually. Islam is centered in the Middle East, where the religion developed, and where the holiest sites are located, such as the holy cities of Mecca and Medina.

Web:
http://www.islamic-foundation.org/
http://www.islamic.org/

Usenet:
alt.islam.sufism
alt.religion.islam
soc.religion.islam

IRC:
#islam
#islamic

Jainism

Jainism is an ascetic religion of India, founded in the 6th century B.C. The religion stresses non-violence, teaches the immortality and transmigration of the soul, and denies the existence of a perfect or supreme being. This Web site has pictures illustrating Jainism history and way of life.

Web:
http://www.cs.colostate.edu/~malaiya/jainhlinks.html

The Qurán

Strictly speaking, The Qurán (Islamic Holy text) should be read in the original Arabic and is not considered to be correct when translated into another language. Still, if your Arabic skills are a bit rusty, you might get more out of reading The Qurán in English. Download it and give it a try.
(Allaah yusallimukum.)

Judaism

There's lots of information on the Net relating to Judaism. Connect to these Web sites and read about Israel, the Holocaust, the Torah, Reconstructionism, Reform Judaism, and more. For discussion, you can participate in the Usenet groups, mailing lists and IRC.

Web:
http://www.cs.cmu.edu/afs/cs.cmu.edu/user/clamen/misc/Judaica/README.html
http://www.shamash.org/

Usenet:
alt.music.jewish
alt.religion.aishdas
soc.culture.jewish

Listproc Mailing List:
List Name: **mail-jewish**
Subscribe to: **listproc@shamash.org**

Listproc Mailing List:
List Name: **mlj**
Subscribe to: **listproc@shamash.org**

Listproc Mailing List:
List Name: **recon-j**
Subscribe to: **listproc@shamash.org**

Listserv Mailing List:
List Name: **tor-ch**
Subscribe to: **listserv@jtsa.edu**

IRC:
#jewish

Koran (or Qurán)

The Koran is the sacred book of Islam. According to the Islamic belief, the Koran was revealed by God to the Prophet Muhammad in various revelations. On the Net you can read the translated Koran or search it if you are looking for something specific.

Web:
http://www.hti.umich.edu/relig/koran/
http://www.utexas.edu/students/amso/quran_html/

Quakers (Society of Friends)

The Society of Friends (commonly referred to as Quakers) began in 1647 under George Fox. One strong tenet of the Friends is that believers do not need a spiritual intermediary, they can receive guidance from within by the Holy Spirit. Here are a few places where you can discuss the philosophies of the Society of Friends.

Web:
http://www.quaker.org/

Usenet:
soc.religion.quaker

Listserv Mailing List:
List Name: **quaker-l**
Subscribe to: **listserv@earlham.edu**

Listserv Mailing List:
List Name: **quaker-p**
Subscribe to: **listserv@earlham.edu**

Religion Talk and General Discussion

Sit in on discussions that are religious, ethical and moral in nature. Talk includes reference to scriptures and parables, but much of it concerns heavily debatable topics—for example, does the Pope use the Internet?—all of which makes for lively banter.

Usenet:
alt.religion
alt.religion.all-worlds
alt.religion.apologetics
alt.religion.asatru
alt.religion.computers
soc.religion
soc.religion.christian.promisekeepers
soc.religion.eastern
soc.religion.vaishnava
talk.religion.course-miracle
talk.religion.misc
talk.religion.pantheism

Express yourself. Try Usenet.

Religious Tolerance

Here's a refreshing change of pace from the hurry-scurry of everyone evangelizing on the Net or the eruptions of arguments between believers and non-believers. This Web page promotes religious tolerance and makes an attempt to educate everyone about the various religions around the world. You can also read the United Nations Declarations on Religious Intolerance, articles on religious freedom, a glossary of terms, information on ritual abuse and cults, and find links to religious home pages.

Web:
http://www.religioustolerance.org/

Sexuality and Religion

Everyone knows you are not supposed to talk about sex and religion at the same time, so you should only read this paragraph if nobody is looking. This Usenet group actually does talk about sex in relation to Christianity. Understand the Christians' viewpoint of sex and get in on the "to do or not to do" debate.

Usenet:
alt.christnet.sex

Sikhism

Founded by Guru Nanak, who was born in 1469, Sikhism has gained a loyal following over the centuries. Guru Nanak criticized the rituals of the Hindus and Muslims and preached that the most important things in life were love, understanding and directing worship toward the one true God. The word "Sikh" means "disciple" in the Punjabi language. You can read more about the history and practices of this religion at this Web site which is loaded with details.

Web:
http://www.sikhs.org/

Usenet:
soc.religion.sikhism

RELIGION

Look What I Found on the Net...

```
Newsgroups: talk.religion.misc, alt.atheism, rec.org.mensa
Subject: Could Life Have Evolved by Chance?

>>> Could life have evolved by chance?  The probability of
>>> forming one protein molecule by chance is one in 10 to the
>>> 243rd power, which is a figure of 1 followed by 243 zeros.
>>>
>>> This fraction is so small, one may say that the probability
>>> is zero.

>> One chance out of:
>>
>>   1,000,000,000,000,000,000,000,000,000,000,000,000,
>>     000,000,000,000,000,000,000,000,000,000,000,000,
>>     000,000,000,000,000,000,000,000,000,000,000,000,
>>     000,000,000,000,000,000,000,000,000,000,000,000,
>>     000,000,000,000,000,000,000,000,000,000,000,000,
>>     000,000,000,000,000,000,000,000,000,000,000,000,
>>     000,000,000,000,000,000,000,000,000?
>>
>> You might be off by plus or minus a few zeros, but so what?
>> They only illustrate, or prove, NOTHING.
>>
>> My question is, with your probabilistic argument, if that is
>> the probability of forming just one lowly protein molecule,
>> what is the  probability of forming an omniscient, omnipotent
>> God?

> It matters not.  God was not created per se.  He always has
> been and always will be.  No, I can't understand that, but no
> one else on the planet can either.  Our brains just don't
> have the capacity to comprehend infinity.  It's kind of like
> trying to teach algebra to an earthworm.

I don't know much about earthworms, but MY brain is perfectly
capable of perceiving and comprehending infinity.
```

Could life have occurred by chance? God only knows (maybe).

Zen Buddhism

Zen Buddhism is a Buddhist sect of Japan and China that bases religion on the practice of meditation rather than doctrine. It was founded by a Chinese man named Bodhidharma in the 5th century A.D. Zen Buddhism concentrates strongly on enlightenment, consciousness and meditation. Reading about Zen Buddhism is a wonderful way to escape from the hustle and bustle of everyday life. (Insight is a pleasant side effect.)

Web:
http://home.gnofn.org/~aza/teachings/teachings.html
http://www.alpine.net/~chylin/zenweb/zen.html
http://www.io.com/~snewton/zen/
http://www.zen-mtn.org/zmm/zazen.shtml

Usenet:
alt.philosophy.zen
alt.zen

Zoroastrianism

Originating in ancient Iran, Zoroastrianism today has a small following in isolated areas of Iran and India. Join discussion on this religion founded in 6th century B.C. and hear the stories of Ahura Mazda as he battles his evil twin, Ahriman. This is the stuff good movies are made of.

Web:
http://www.avesta.org/zfaq.html

Usenet:
alt.religion.zoroastrianism

RELIGION: SECTS AND CULTS

Baha'i Faith

Who was Baha'u'llah (a.k.a. Mirza Husayn Ali)? What did he do in Iran in the mid-19th century that was so important? Was he really the Bab (with a direct line to the twelfth Imam)? Learn about the message of the Baha'u'llah and the Baha'i view of life. Read quotes from Baha'i scriptures and discuss such topics as gender equality and spiritual revelations.

Web:
http://www.bahai.org/

Usenet:
soc.religion.bahai

Brother Jed

Follow the comings and goings of Brother Jed (George E. Smock) as his itinerant travels take him from campus to campus throughout America, spreading the word that Christianity is incompatible with homosexuality, long hair, drugs and rock music. (Yes, it's true. Would I make up something like this?)

Usenet:
alt.brother-jed

Look What I Found on the Net...

```
Newsgroup: alt.zen
Subject: Why Learn Zen?

> What can I do to learn Zen?

Look both ways, inside and out.

> And why?

There is heavy traffic out there,
Lighter traffic in here,
Please take care of yourself and others in crossing.

> Would I get something out of it?

No, sorry.  Nothing for sale.
```

RELIGION: SECTS AND CULTS

Coptic

The Coptic Church is based on the teachings of Saint Mark, who brought Christianity to Egypt in the first century. The Copts observe seven sacraments, baptize newborns, and participate in fasting. Learn more about this religion by going to this Coptic page. They give a nice history of the Church and other detailed information, including their Coptic liturgy.

Web:
http://pharos.bu.edu/Coptic/Menu.html

Eckankar

The basis of Eckankar spirituality is coming closer to God through dreams and the expansion of consciousness. This site explains more about the philosophy of Eckankar, gives spiritual exercises that are designed to bring you closer to enlightenment, and has various other tidbits of interest to those in search of Sugmad. On the Usenet group you can join Eckists as they explore visualization, reality and waking dreams.

Web:
http://www.eckankar.org/

Usenet:
alt.religion.eckankar

Gnosticism

Take a few Christian terms, add in a liberal dose of Greek philosophy, a dash of mythology and a handful of magickal rituals. Let sit for several centuries and voilà! You end up with a religion that can serve millions and is very low in calories. Learn more about Gnosticism, its origins and tenets. The **soc.religion.gnosis** group is moderated.

Web:
http://www.webcom.com/~gnosis/

Usenet:
alt.religion.gnostic
soc.religion.gnosis

> Need spiritual guidance? You're on your own. Need a good laugh? Follow Brother Jed.

Chabad-Lubavitch Judaism

Official home of the world Chabad-Lubavitch movement, there are many Jewish resources here, including articles, inspirational passages, a glossary of Jewish words and terms, and links to many other Jewish and Judaism resources.

Web:
http://www.chabad.org/

RELIGION: SECTS AND CULTS

Goddess Names

These goddess Web sites offer gigantic lists of names of the "Goddess". (This seems to be a catch-all term for any sort of goddess that appears in any type of document or literature.) The listings are a bit liberal—for example, you will find Echo, who is actually just a Greek nymph, not a goddess—but they are interesting nonetheless.

Web:
http://pluto.nildram.co.uk/~skegga/goddesses.htm
http://www.maui.net/~goddess/names.html

Goddess Names

So you have a new baby girl. Don't settle for giving her an ordinary name like Jessica, Michelle, Kimberly or Brandy.

(And for goodness sake, don't name her Jennifer. Every Tom, Dick and Harry is named Jennifer.)

Instead, connect to the Goddess Names Web sites where you find something *really* special, like Angerona, Blodeuwedd, Cailleach, Dakini, Erigone, Freya, Galatea, Halja, Inanna, Jagadama, Kriemhild, Lunaea, Malinalxochitl, Ninhursag, Oenothea, Proserpina, Queen Mab, Rabbatu, Semiramis, Theotokos, Ukemochi, Verthandi, Wawalak, Xochiquetzal, Yingona or Zurvan.

Goddess Spirituality and Feminism

Hera really did give goddesses a bad name, but they are finally starting to become popular, and not just with women, either. Men and women alike are interested in goddess spirituality, feminism, and the incorporation of the feminine/feminist idea in the study and worship of the divine. Listen in on their discussions of spirituality in relation to the goddess.

Listserv Mailing List:
List Name: wmsprt-l
Subscribe to: listserv@listserv.acsu.buffalo.edu

Jehovah's Witnesses

Jehovah's Witnesses is an international Christian organization, founded in 1870 as a Bible study group by Charles Taze Russell. In 1931, they adopted the name "Jehovah's Witnesses" (from Isaiah 43:12). One of the main things people notice about Witnesses is they are active proselytizers, going from door to door to talk to people about Jehovah (God). Witnesses do not believe in eternal torment or that all good people go to heaven. Rather, they believe that, upon the destruction of wickedness and human governments, a "new system" will be established, and most of God's people will live in human perfection on Earth. Although Witnesses have a Christian love for people, they make an effort to stay "separate from the world" and do not involve themselves in excessive pursuit of material things or political and social movements. Witnesses do not salute the flag, vote, bear arms, or participate in government, nor (for biblical reasons) will they take blood transfusions. On the Net you will find a number of useful resources such as a daily text from the Bible, a listing of events, links to pages of other Jehovah's Witnesses, news stories, a listing of new releases from the Watchtower (the Witness magazine), and more. If you are interested in learning more about the Witnesses, you will find an overview of what they believe.

Web:
http://www.watchtower.org/
http://www.witnesses.net/

Mennonites

The Mennonites are a sect that departed from the Swiss Anabaptists around 1524. Mennonites believe in nonresistance, and they refuse to take oaths. (A more conservative branch of the Mennonites are the Amish, who broke away from the Mennonites in the late 17th century.) The Mennonites have a nice collection of information on the Web.

Web:
http://www.mennolink.org/

Stay connected.

RELIGION: SECTS AND CULTS

Mormons

The Church of Jesus Christ of Latter-day Saints (sometimes referred to as LDS or the Mormon Church) was founded by Joseph Smith in 1830. Mormon history says that Joseph Smith was visited by a prophet who told him some sacred history of the Americas. Smith translated this information and published it as the Book of Mormon in 1830. This book and the Bible are the main texts of the Mormon doctrines. You can read the text of the Book of Mormon online or do a search of the text if there is something specific you want to look up. On the Net there are lots of LDS resources, including interactive chatting on IRC.

Web:
http://www.athenet.net/~jlindsay/LDS_Intro.shtml
http://www.hti.umich.edu/relig/mormon/
http://www.lds.org/
http://www.mormon.net/
http://www.primenet.com/~kitsonk/mormon.html

Usenet:
alt.religion.mormon
alt.religion.mormon.fellowship
soc.religion.mormon

IRC:
#mormon

Mysticism Chat

When you want to get into some mystical or spiritual discussion, here are some places to do it. Chat or argue on many areas of mysticism from Christianity to Satanism, and everything in between.

IRC:
#asatru
#buddhist
#christian
#islam

Nazarenes

The Church of the Nazarene is the largest denomination in the Wesleyan-Arminian theological tradition. Although Nazarenes have a lot in common with other Christian denominations, they distinguish themselves by a belief in "entire sanctification". This involves devoting one's life to do God's will. In particular, Nazarenes believe that it is important to be of service to others.

Web:
http://www.nazarene.org/
http://www.naznet.com/

New Religious Movements

Why are human beings always creating new religions, while, at the same time, preserving the older, well-established faiths? The best way to understand it is to consider religions as live entities that are subject to evolutionary forces over the course of centuries. As new religions are formed, they compete in the spiritual environment against other religions. Out of the many new religions, very few live long enough to become a major world religion (such as Judaism, Christianity, Islam, Hinduism, Buddhism and Confucianism). However, in order to maintain the spiritual health of the world, we must always have new religions to feed the evolutionary process. Most religions fail, but, in the rare case that one does succeed, it must change as it matures. A maturing religion must became more conservative and mainstream if it is to survive, and must develop a comprehensive philosophy, literature and tradition. Here is a Web site to help you keep up on those young, still immature faiths. Take a look, and I bet you will find some surprises.

Web:
http://cti.itc.virginia.edu/~jkh8x/soc257/profiles.html

Mysticism Chat

If you like talking about any type of mysticism, someone is waiting to talk to you. Connect to one of the IRC channels and see what appears magically.

RELIGION: SECTS AND CULTS

Paganism

The nice thing about paganism is that you can pretty much do whatever you want. This is a nature-based religion with no central dogma. Pagans celebrate various gods and goddesses (one or many), nature and the cycles of the sun and moon. The best thing is that they don't have to wear uncomfortable clothes and sit in church. If any of this appeals to you, check out some of the pagan resources on the Net or talk to a friendly pagan at a Usenet group near you.

Web:
  http://www.cascade.net/arachne.html
  http://www.landfield.com/faqs/paganism-faq/
  http://www.pagan.net/~jaz/pagan/

Usenet:
  alt.pagan
  alt.pagan.contacts
  alt.religion.druid
  alt.religion.goddess
  alt.religion.triplegoddess
  soc.religion.paganism

IRC:
  #pagan

Where's Harley?
(See www.harley.com)

Santeria

Santeria (often called La Regla Lucumi) has its origins in West Africa and is the traditional religion of the Yoruba people. Santeria was spread to many countries of South America by slave trade. Members of Santeria worship a god named Olorun and interact with him through emissaries called orishas. The religion is wrapped up in magic and forces of nature. If you want to learn more about their specific religious language and rituals, take a look at this Web site devoted to Santeria.

Web:
  http://www.seanet.com/~efunmoyiwa/ochanet.html

Listserv Mailing List:
  List Name: **voodoo-l**
  Subscribe to: **listserv@necronomi.com**

Satanism

Discover what Satanists feel are the misconceptions about their beliefs. See what Satanism means and discuss how Satanists feel it relates to Christianity. Other topics include music, books, and news items.

Web:
  http://www.coscentral.net/
  http://www.necronomi.com/magic/satanism/

Usenet:
  alt.satanism

Listserv Mailing List:
  List Name: **satanist-l**
  Subscribe to: **listserv@necronomi.com**

Look What I Found on the Net...

```
Newsgroup: alt.satanism
Subject: Sundays

> Do you Satanists do anything special on Sundays?

We do whatever any non-Christian does — we sit around and watch
a lot of mind-numbing television.
```

RELIGION: SECTS AND CULTS

Scientology

Scientology is a global organization with its own values, literature, and a lot of money. For a long time, many people have been at odds with Scientology for a variety of reasons and, now, the struggle has carried over to the Net. There is a lot of information about Scientology and what people think about it (pro and con) on the Net. If you care about such issues, I feel it is important to learn some of the details and make up your own mind. Here are two places to start. One is a Web page relating to the protest against Scientology. The other is the official Scientology Internet site. Both places will lead you to a lot of interesting information. The Usenet discussion groups are not official Scientology. Mostly you will find people talking about issues related to Scientology.

Web:
http://www.demon.co.uk/castle/scientology.html
http://www.scientology.org/

Usenet:
alt.clearing.technology
alt.religion.scientology

Shakers

The Shakers—also known as the United Society of Believers—are a Christian sect that originated in England in 1747 and established itself in America under the leadership of Mother Ann Lee. The name "Shaker" was coined during the early history of the sect. Some of the members would become excited during the meetings and move around, "shaking off their sins". Two of the Shakers' primary tenets are communal living and celibacy. Well, any group that practices celibacy may be pure of heart, but they are going to have trouble surviving as a group. Indeed, today there are only a handful of Shakers remaining.

Web:
http://www.passtheword.org/shaker-manuscripts/
http://www.shakerworkshops.com/shakindx.htm
http://www.tourky.com/shakervillage/history.html

Listserv Mailing List:
List Name: **shaker**
Subscribe to: **listserv@lsv.uky.edu**

Shamanism

Among tribal peoples, a shaman is a spiritual leader—usually a healer—who has a mystical connection to the spirit world. Delve into the natural, spiritual practices of the shaman. Discover the range of the shamanic experience, which includes such activities as drumming, vision quests, and visiting sacred sites, all of which are used to put someone into an ecstatic trance.

Web:
http://deoxy.org/shaman.htm
http://www.cis.ohio-state.edu/hypertext/faq/bngusenet/soc/religion/shamanism/top.html

Usenet:
alt.religion.shamanism
soc.religion.shamanism

Listserv Mailing List:
List Name: **shaman-l**
Subscribe to: **listserv@listserv.aol.com**

Theosophy

Take a little religion, some Hindu philosophy, add a dash of mysticism, pantheism and magic, and you get Theosophy. Get an overview of Theosophy by reading all about it on the Net.

Web:
http://www.spiritweb.org/Spirit/Theosophy/Overview.html
http://www.theosophy.org/

Usenet:
alt.theosophy

Listproc Mailing List:
List Name: **theos-l**
Subscribe to: **listproc@vnet.net**

Make every keystroke count.

RELIGION: SECTS AND CULTS

Unitarianism

Share thoughts and opinions with the people who address their prayers "to whom it may concern". Discuss issues of interest to members of the Unitarian-Universalist church: the most free-thinking, tolerant, diverse and intellectual group of people since the Nixon White House.

Web:
   http://www.uua.org/

Usenet:
   soc.religion.unitarian-univ

Listproc Mailing List:
   List Name: **uua-l**
   Subscribe to: **listproc@uua.org**

Listserv Mailing List:
   List Name: **uus-l**
   Subscribe to: **listserv@listserv.acsu.buffalo.edu**

Wicca

Wicca is a neo-pagan religion that is more focused and ritualistic than traditional paganism. The Wiccan tradition is to worship a god and goddess (not necessarily in that order) or perhaps multiple deities. Wiccans are tuned into nature, cycles and life events, and perform magick rituals to mark the passing of holidays or special events. If you'd like to learn more about the Wicca way of life, check out these Web sites or talk to some Wiccans who spend time on IRC or posting to Usenet.

Web:
   http://www.silvermoon.net/catala/
   http://www.teleport.com/~rain/arwfaq.html
   http://www.witchesweb.com/home.html

Usenet:
   alt.religion.wicca

IRC:
   #wicca

Look What I Found on the Net...

```
            (from the Wicca frequently asked question list)
What is basic Wiccan thealogy?

Some myths and associations are common to many Wiccan traditions,
such as the Goddess giving birth to the Horned God,
the theme of their courtship and His death, the descent of the
Goddess into the realm of death and others.

Another thealogical point held in common by many Wiccans is the
immanence of deity/divinity within the natural world, self and
cycle of the seasons.  This places value on the Earth and this
world, as distinguished from views of transcendent divinity and
an unenchanted creation.

Wiccans as a whole are very much "into" cycles: of life, of the
moon and seasons.  Cyclical change as an erotic dance of life,
death and rebirth is a popular theme in Wiccan imagery, ritual
and liturgy.

(Thea is Greek for "goddess" by the way, so "thealogy" is not a
typo here, but a way of emphasizing the Goddess.)
```

ROLE PLAYING

Advanced Dungeons and Dragons

Advanced Dungeons and Dragons (AD&D) is a highly complex fantasy role-playing system, enjoyed by people all over the world. AD&D is the oldest such system, tracing its roots back to the original Dungeons and Dragons (1973). There is a great deal of AD&D material on the Net: spell and priest books, campaigns, modules, new monsters, new spells, rules, interactive games, comments, just about anything you can think of having to do with AD&D. If you would like to talk about AD&D with other people, you can join the Usenet group, mailing list or IRC.

Web:
http://sac.uky.edu/~mlmorr0/faq/rgfdfaq1.html
http://www.adnd.com/
http://www.math.auth.gr/~bchr/

Usenet:
rec.games.frp.dnd

Listserv Mailing List:
List Name: **adnd-l**
Subscribe to: **listserv@listserv.uta.edu**

IRC:
#ad&d

Buying and Selling Role-Playing Games

After a while, you can reach the burn-out stage on any particular role-playing game. Don't let all that time, money and attention go to waste. On Usenet you can probably find someone who is interested in whatever you want to get rid of. Buy, sell or trade your fantasy role-playing material. It's all happening here.

Usenet:
rec.games.frp.marketplace

Take my advice.
See "Advice".

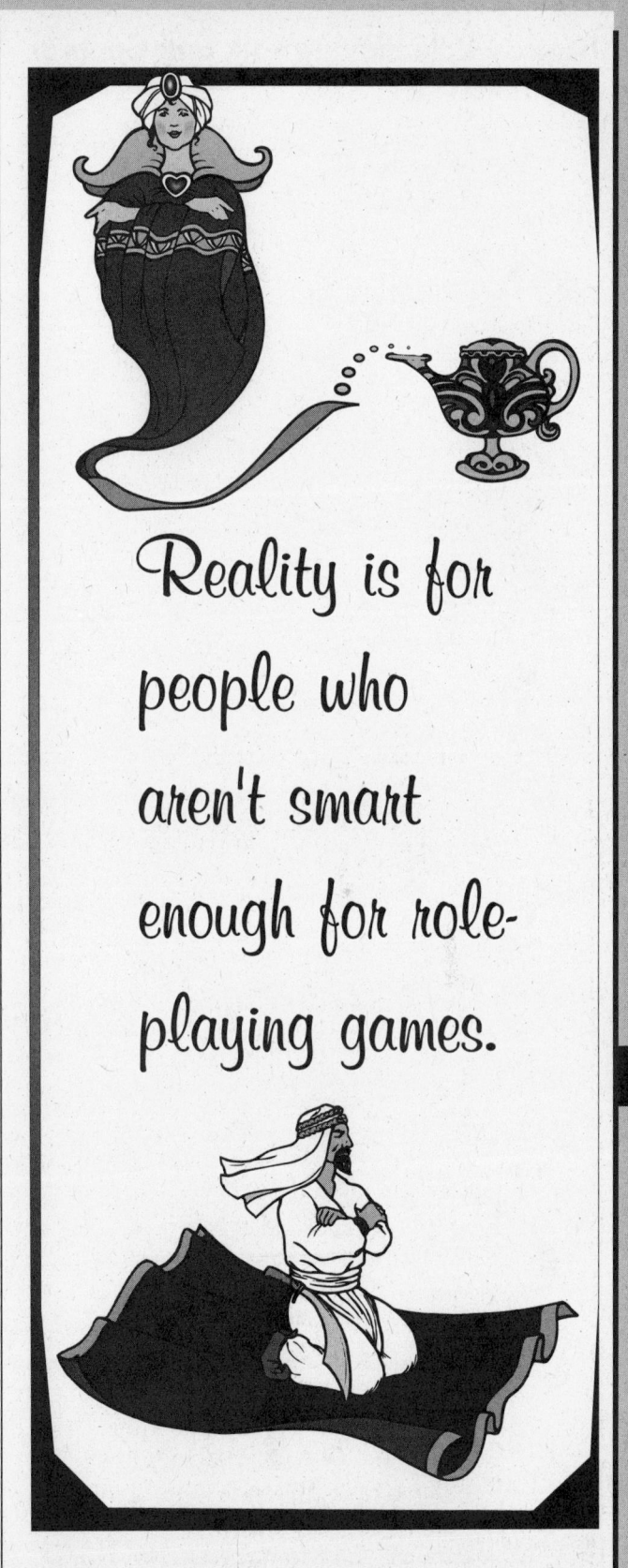

Reality is for people who aren't smart enough for role-playing games.

ROLE PLAYING

Fantasy Role Playing Talk and General Discussion

Join up with the folks in Usenet and discuss your favorite or your most hated role-playing game and all the issues that come with it. Magic, mystery and adventure await you once you step across the line that separates fantasy from reality.

Usenet:
  alt.dragons-inn
  rec.games.frp
  rec.games.frp.advocacy
  rec.games.frp.announce
  rec.games.frp.archives
  rec.games.frp.cyber
  rec.games.frp.dnd
  rec.games.frp.gurps
  rec.games.frp.misc
  rec.games.frp.storyteller
  rec.games.frp.super-heroes

Live-Action Role Playing

What a great way to spend the evening—dress up as someone else and take on a whole new life. Say goodbye to reality by doing some live-action role playing where you talk to other characters and solve a mystery or a problem the way your character would. You'll never be able to go back to ordinary board games again.

Web:
  http://www.coil.com/~zargonis/shade.html
  http://www.larp.com/
  http://www.larps.net/larps/links.htm

Usenet:
  rec.games.frp.live-action

And...

Look What I Found on the Net...

```
Newsgroup: alt.pub.dragons-inn
Subject: Guess What's Coming to Dinner

Synopsis:
     The party members have been ambushed at a dinner given
     by their host, the vampire Pericles.  A great battle has
     just begun...
```

Unable to enjoy her food and not really interested in dessert, Matte had just begun to try to excuse herself from the table when the servants attacked. Halfway out of her seat already, she quickly leapt upon her chair and picked up a piece of cutlery from the table. She attempted to hit one of the creatures attacking Moria on the opposite side of the room, but was picked up from behind as she drew her arm back, the knife falling harmlessly to the floor.

Matte felt the grip of the armored servant tighten as she was lifted from her feet. The creature's grasp was very firm, and she was unable to free herself to conjure assistance or use her weapon. She grunted and kicked at her captor but to no avail.

Suddenly, she felt the iron grip give way as she landed on her feet and heard the clatter of armor fall to the floor above the din of battle in the room.

ROLE PLAYING

Magic: The Gathering

Magic: The Gathering (MtG) is a popular D&D-type card-trading role-playing game. Magic has grown to encompass a complex world of its own. These Web sites have a lot of interesting information about playing the game. The Usenet groups are for the discussion of MtG. The **.misc** group is for general talk; the other groups are for rules and strategy. The IRC channel is for MtG fans to hang out and talk in real time.

Web:
http://mox.perl.com/deckmaster/
http://www.cs.hut.fi/~jaf/magic/mtgonirc.txt
http://www.swiss-magic.ch/resource.html
http://www.wizards.com/Magic/

Usenet:
rec.games.trading-cards.magic.misc
rec.games.trading-cards.magic.rules
rec.games.trading-cards.magic.strategy

IRC:
#mtg

Miniatures

If you like to take the time to buy miniatures, paint them or role-play with miniatures, these are great resources for you. One Web site offers information and rules for games in a variety of categories such as ancient, medieval, Napoleonic, world wars, modern, science fiction, and many other types of settings. The other site has information about upcoming conventions. The Usenet groups are good places to talk with other miniature hobbyists.

Web:
http://dspace.dial.pipex.com/sburt/
http://www.erinet.com/bp/histconv.html

Usenet:
rec.games.miniatures
rec.games.miniatures.historical
rec.games.miniatures.misc
rec.games.miniatures.warhammer

Netrunner

Netrunner is a popular game that combines card trading with role playing. The Web sites will lead you to the FAQ and a collection of Netrunner resources. The Usenet group and mailing list are where Netrunner fans gather to talk.

Web:
http://www.peak.org/~rob/netrunner/rnn1.html
http://www.wizards.com/Netrunner/

Usenet:
rec.games.trading-cards.misc

Listserv Mailing List:
List Name: **netrunner-l**
Subscribe to: **listserv@oracle.wizards.com**

Role-Playing Crafts

One of the best aspects of role playing is that you can make your own props and costumes to enhance the game. This Web site has information and hints on how to make your own role-playing accessories: chain mail, costumes, weapons, and more.

Web:
http://www.bibks.uu.se/58/home.html

Role-Playing Games

Sometimes I wonder why people even bother with real life. Not only is it always in your face, but so much of the time it is noisy and ugly. Take my advice: find out about role-playing games and leave reality to the grown-ups.

Role-Playing Games Magazine

This online magazine is devoted to role playing and related activities. When you need to take a break between games, what could be more relaxing than curling up with a warm computer and reading role-playing stories, news, announcements and reviews.

Web:
http://www.commerce.adelaide.edu.au/calvert/irps/

Look What I Found on the Net...

```
Newsgroup: alt.starfleet.rpg
Subject: alt.starfleet.rpg (ASR) Introduction

   From: Admiral Jefferson Lee, Commander-in-Chief, Starfleet

            Stardate:   80808.0700
```

Welcome to ASR, the Usenet newsgroup alt.starfleet.rpg. Here, hundreds of people from all over the world read and write stories in the universe of Star Trek.

What brings us together is a common enjoyment of interactive drama: the opportunity to combine the passive enjoyment of reading a book or watching a movie with the creative thrill of making the story move in a direction WE choose.

The synthesis of several writers' contributions often ends up being a story more entertaining, and "better Trek", than any one writer would have written...

==============

```
Newsgroup: alt.starfleet.rpg
Subject: USS Philadelphia/Suffolk
```

Scene: Station Sickbay

The two had finished the quick meal and headed back towards sickbay. Upon entering the room, they both expected something to have changed, but the room was still the same way they had left it.

Caroline went back to the bio bed to continue taking readings on the Ferengi body while Nick went back to searching out the room. Entering the Chief Medical's office, Nick glanced over the monitor sitting on the desk. Sitting down at the desk, Nick started to access the log entry from the terminal. He stopped looking when he saw an entry marked:

```
        STARFLEET COMMAND FILE ACCESS...............
              MEDICAL RESEARCH.........
                    INVENTIONS........
                COMA/HOLO VIEWER........
```

Before he could read further, a loud crash was heard from the other room...

ROLE PLAYING

Role-Playing Resources

There are a lot of role-playing fanatics on the Net, and lots and lots of resources for you to enjoy. Here are some good places to start. Whether you like fantasy, science fiction, cyberpunk, gothic or war, there are enough resources here to ensure you will never be so bored as to be tempted to go back to real life.

Web:
http://www.mindspring.com/~falconis/fffw.htm
http://www.rpg.net/
http://www.tsrinc.com/rpga/
http://www.webrpg.com/

Star Trek Role Playing

Don't settle for just watching or reading Star Trek. You can actually be a Star Trek character. Trekkers discuss the game and its enhancements as well as putting together a group to play the game. It's not just fun, it's a way of life. Check out the Web pages for other Star Trek RPG information on the Net.

Web:
http://www.cc.tut.fi/~jarim/asr/
http://www.finalfront.com/strpg/

Usenet:
alt.starfleet.rpg

Vampire: The Masquerade

Vampire: The Masquerade is a series of live-action role-playing games (LARP) based on commercial rulesets derived from the White Wolf's World of Darkness. (In LARP, you not only wear costumes and participate, you act out the parts.) These Web sites contain a lot of information for Vampire enthusiasts around the world: information about conventions, role-playing groups, game rules and modifications, characters, game-related fiction, graphics, and much more. The Usenet group and mailing list are for players and fans to gather and talk about gaming, rules and personal experiences.

Web:
http://www.monterey.edu/staff/StoneRob/world/Vampire/
http://www.thekindred.com/

Usenet:
alt.games.vampire.the.masquerade

Listserv Mailing List:
List Name: **vampire-l**
Subscribe to: **listserv@oracle.wizards.com**

Warhammer

Warhammer is a strategy game in which people use a board and miniatures to simulate a fantasy war. These Web sites have a large archive of files, play aids, a bestiary, sample scenarios, and information on religion, rules, magick and careers. The mailing list and Usenet group are for discussing all aspects of Warhammer fantasy role play.

Web:
http://home6.swipnet.se/~w-63282/warhammer/
http://user.cs.tu-berlin.de/~rossi/Wfrp/encyc/menu.html
http://web2.airmail.net/jtisdel/warhammer40k/w40k.html

Usenet:
rec.games.miniatures.warhammer

Majordomo Mailing List:
List Name: **warhammerfb**
Subscribe to: **majordomo@direwolf.com**

World of Darkness

World of Darkness is a general umbrella term for games such as Werewolf, Mage, Wraith, Changeling and the Vampire: The Masquerade series, all produced by White Wolf Game Studios. This Web page has a hefty list of links to the various games, archives, and related Usenet groups. There is one Usenet group for the Storyteller system, and another group for White Wolf games.

Web:
http://enuxsa.eas.asu.edu/~buckner/wod.html
http://ezinfo.ucs.indiana.edu/~adashiel/wod/wod.html
http://www.math.unc.edu/Grads/pfstrack/wwfaq.html

Usenet:
alt.games.whitewolf
rec.games.frp.storyteller

Need advice? See "Advice".

ROMANCE

Chatting in the Big City

If you just moved to a new town or you are thinking of moving, you can find people on IRC who live in the city of your destination. Make new friends before you go or ask about great vacation spots in the city of your choice.

IRC:
  #atlanta
  #austin
  #boston
  #brisbane
  #chicago
  #cleveland
  #dallas
  #denver
  #detroit
  #houston
  #london
  #melbourne
  #miami
  #montreal
  #nyc
  #orlando
  #paris
  #perth
  #sandiego
  #seattle
  #singapore
  #sydney

Couples

It's the best of times, it's the worst of times. Relationships have their ups and downs, but like a roller coaster, it's fun and thrilling, makes you afraid, and makes you laugh. See what is going on in the lives of other couples. Get ideas for romantic outings, anniversaries, how to patch up a fuss, or what to do with in-laws.

Usenet:
  soc.couples
  soc.couples.intercultural

Listproc Mailing List:
  List Name: couples-l
  Subscribe to: listproc@cornell.edu

Kissing

If you haven't been able to get any kissing action lately, you can at least hear how kisses sound. Download a few different kisses in a variety of nationalities: French, English-French, Italian, and more. This is good, clean, germ-free fun.

Web:
  http://www.seductionpalace.com/smooch/mainsmooch.html

Language of Love

World travelers: it's always handy to know how to say "I love you" in any language. You never know when it could be important. For instance, say you are on a brief layover at an airport in Rome and the woman of your dreams comes racing by dragging behind her four suitcases on wheels. She runs over your foot and you realize that, yes, this is The One For You. How are you going to get her attention? Check out this site, so you'll be lucky in love no matter what your native language.

Web:
  http://www.megadodo.com/articles/2R95.html

Couples: Need to work on the relationship? Why not do it in front of the rest of the world? Participate in the **soc.couples** discussion group and the **couples-l** mailing list.

Love Chat

Whether you are looking for love or looking to talk about love, IRC is a good place to start. Not only can you talk romantically, but you can eat pizza at the same time and nobody will know the difference. You can't get much better than that. Check out these channels for romantic talk or possibly some romantic action.

IRC:
 #love
 #lovechat
 #romance
 #truelove

Language of Love

*"Every time you kiss me,
I'm still not certain that you love me."*

However, if you use the Language of Love Web site, you could tell me you love me in more than 100 languages, including Bulgarian (Obicham te), Esperanto (Mi amas vin), Klingon (qaparHa') and Vulcan (Wani ra yana ro aisha).

Love Letters

Every time you sit down to write a nice love letter to the person of your dreams, it never seems to come out sounding as wonderful as it does in your head. Don't let that stop you. Instead, get help from Cyrano de Bergerac, the notable romantic. Fill out a form with a few details and Cyrano will write the letter for you. Love was never so easy.

Web:
 http://www.nando.net/toys/cyrano.html

Love and Romance

Where would we be without love and romance? Probably at home in front of the TV set. At least with romance we can be in front of the TV with someone to keep us company. As a Net person, you never need to worry about getting your share. There are lots of resources for the romantically inclined (and even for the romantically challenged).

But remember, even in a Harley Hahn book, "Romance" comes before "Sex".

Love Test

Here are two different tests you can take: one about your concept of love, the other about your experiences with love. If you are currently in a relationship, you can take the "combination test", to see how your current experience of love matches your concept of love. After you take the tests, you can compare your results to various statistics that have been compiled from these tests.

Web:
 http://world.topchoice.com/~psyche/lovetest/

Men and Women

We all got along fine when we were algae. But somewhere between floating gently on the lake and the invention of the bikini, men and women started to have their differences. Get up close and personal. See what the factions are saying about each other. It's not too much of a secret since there is a lot of crossposting.

Usenet:
 soc.men
 soc.women

Look What I Found on the Net...

```
Newsgroup: soc.men
Subject: Marriage Makes Men Fearless
```

Al Bundy's T-shirt said it best: "Kill Me, I'm Married".

There seems to be nothing more courage hardening than being trapped in a marriage. Men will willingly work a hundred hours a week to avoid going home, even if the work has an early death warranty.

Men go to war, to sea, to space, and anywhere they can avoid facing their wives with no fear of the risks they are taking, because they have nothing to lose. Marriage must be one of the most powerful tools a culture has for its own protection. Without the terror of "going home" how would any country get hundreds of thousands of men to head off to war? Couldn't happen. We aren't "protecting our country," we are protecting ourselves...

============

```
Newsgroup: soc.women
Subject: Women Aren't Automobiles
```

>>> What I disagree with, however, is the notion that the man is
>>> in any way responsible for the woman's EXTRAVAGANT ways of
>>> dealing with such reproductive "accidents". That's like
>>> saying if I put a dent in the bumper of someone's Yugo in a
>>> parking lot, and they decide to replace the entire car with
>>> a Rolls Royce, that I'm liable for the entire cost of the
>>> "replacement".

>> Uhhh... women aren't automobiles. Perhaps your seeming to
>> consider them such is partially the cause of your being a
>> "voluntary chaste virgin".

> All right. Then how do you explain the classic show
> "My Mother the Car"?

Well, of course *some* women *are* automobiles. I don't think that anyone was denying this. But I still don't think that you can make the sweeping generalization that *all* women are automobiles.

I did date a Ford Pinto once, but the relationship ended tragically...

ROMANCE 689

Look What I Found on the Net...

(from Romantic Ascii Graphics)

```
                    _____                      _____
                   /,,,,,_____/,,,,,\
                   |,(  )/,,,,,,,,,,,,,,,,,,,\(  ),|
                   \_,,,,___,,,,,___,,,,,___,,,,,_/
                   /,,,,/(')\,,,,/(')\,,,\
                   |,,,,___      ___,,,,|
                   |,,,/   \o_o//   \,,,|
                   |,,|      |  |      |,,|
                   |,,|   \__/|\__/    |,,|
                   \,,\       \_/      /,,/
                    _____/_/
           _____/                 _____
          / \,,,,,,,,,,,,,,,,,,,,,,,,,,,,,,,,,,/ \
         (   ),,,,,,,,,,,,,,,,,,,,,,,,,,,,,,,,(   )
          \_/‾‾‾‾‾‾‾‾‾‾‾‾‾‾‾‾‾,,/    \,,‾‾‾‾‾‾‾‾‾\_/
                             /,/        \,\
                            |,|          |,|
                            |,|  I LOVE YOU |,|
                            |,|          |,|
                            |,|          |,|
                            \,\    o     /,/
                            /,,,_____/,,\
                           /,,,,,,,,,,,,,,,,\
                          /,,,,,,,,,,,,,,,,,,\
                         /,,,,,,,/   \,,,,,,,\
                        /,,,,,,/     \,,,,,,\
                       /,,,,,/         \,,,,,\
                      /_____/           \_____\
                      /,/ \,\           /,/ \,\
                     //   \\             //   \\
                     \\___//             \\___//
```

ROMANCE

Online Romance Talk and General Discussion

Voyeurs and participants alike can experience fun and romance in Usenet. In this Usenet group you can meet people, talk about the concepts of romance, being romantic, ideas that are romantic or talk about places on the Net where you can find romance.

Usenet:
  alt.romance.online

Poetry

Send a wonderful poem to that special someone in your life. You can choose from any number of famous poems and personalize it by adding your own message as well.

Web:
  http://www.seductionpalace.com/library/poems/
    poems.html

Random Love Poems

Close your eyes, count to three and wait for this Web page to load. Suddenly you will be presented with a randomly selected romantic poem written by someone who has been dead for many, many years. This, of course, doesn't detract from the romantic value of the poem, so by all means, read on. Don't think about how, as you imagine being in love and laughing with your wonderful partner, these poets have long since been eaten by worms. Don't let that stop you. Carry on. Be happy.

Web:
  http://ddmi.he.net/cgi-bin/suid/~chocolov/
    rand_poem.cgi

Ready to fly? See "Travel" (or "Aviation").

Romance Readers Anonymous

You've been sucked in. It's impossible to walk past a rack of romance novels without picking up at least one. The bronzed man holding the lithe woman with the heaving bosom makes your heart beat quickly, loud enough for everyone else in the store to hear. The television has cobwebs and you haven't been out of the house in months since you got a subscription to Romance of the Week. Get help now. You are not alone.

Usenet:
  bit.listserv.rra-l

Listserv Mailing List:
  List Name: **rra-l**
  Subscribe to: **listserv@listserv.kent.edu**

Romance Talk and General Discussion

Have you noticed life isn't quite like the covers of paperback romance novels (or the inside of the romance novels, for that matter)? Do something about that by generating a romantic fire with others who mourn the death of romance. Remember Cyrano de Bergerac and his words that could melt the hair off a moose? Where do you think he got his start?

Usenet:
  alt.romance
  alt.romance.chat
  alt.romance.mature-adult

Romantic Ascii Graphics

Stop with the boring email. Send your loved one a nice romantic greeting spiced up with some ascii graphics. For those of you who don't know how to make your own, just cut and paste some of these into your letter and nobody will know the difference. It will be our little secret.

Web:
  http://www.chris.com/art/valentine.html
  http://www.dina.kvl.dk/~fischer/alt.romance/
    ascii.html

ROMANCE

Romantic Gestures

Don't flounder around in your romantic life when you could be someone's future knight in shining armor. Here's a list of romantic ideas if you don't know exactly what to do or how to get started in the romance game.

Web:
http://www.etoile.co.uk/Love/Her.html
http://www.etoile.co.uk/Love/His.html
http://www.inspireme.com/moreideas.htm
http://www.lovingu.com/instant.html

Romantic Greetings by Email

There's no need to race out to the store just because you forgot to get a nice card for your anniversary. On the Net, you can make your own cards, or send virtual gifts of flowers or kisses just by using your Web browser. These cards and other electronic greetings will be all the more special because you made them yourself.

Web:
http://www.azstarnet.com/flowers/
http://www.romanceclassics.com/loveletters/loveletters.html
http://www.thekiss.com/ekiss/

Singles

Your mother probably said that anyone you can pick up in a bar is not someone with whom you want to develop a serious relationship. (What you probably didn't want to tell her was that you weren't looking for a serious relationship.) In the event that you change your mind, stop in at the nicest singles hangouts in Usenet and IRC and find that special someone just right for you. The Web site has the **soc.singles** FAQ (frequently asked question list).

Web:
http://www.faqs.org/faqs/singles-faq/

Usenet:
soc.singles
soc.singles.moderated

IRC:
#singles

Soulmates

There is a moment when you look into someone's eyes and you feel, in an instant, that you have known this person your entire life and that you can never bear to be separated from him or her again. This is the feeling of finding a soulmate, someone who feels like the other half of you. Read anecdotes about people who have found their soulmates, people who are looking for soulmates and discuss the writings of authors who write on the concept of soulmates.

Usenet:
alt.soulmates

Togetherness Tips

Getting married? Here are some questions you should ask yourself before you officially take the plunge. There are also tips on planning a wedding, staying together and how to make things work over the years.

Web:
http://www.commerce.digital.com/palo-alto/WeddingPhoto/ArticleTips.html

Unhappy Romances

The only thing worse than no romance is unhappy romance. Unrequited love, romance gone bad or people who are inept in the romance department—these are all topics that are fair game in this Usenet group.

Usenet:
alt.romance.unhappy

Virtual Wedding Chapel

Well, it had to happen: a virtual, real-time wedding chapel. To start, you can fill out a form and specify the email address of someone you know. A program will then email that person a "proposal". If they accept—and, since you are one of my readers, of course they will accept—you can arrange to have your wedding in a virtual chat session. Afterward, you will get a nice electronic marriage certificate.

Web:
http://www.hollywoodandvine.com/Itheeweb/

SCIENCE

Annals of Improbable Research

The Annals of Improbable Research (AIR) is a science humor magazine. It's hard to describe what you find here; suffice it to say that, if you like science and you have a good sense of humor, you'll enjoy what you see. (Think of AIR as the National Lampoon for smart people.) Footnotes: (1) If you liked the old Journal of Irreproducible Results, you'll enjoy the AIR. (2) These same people also give out the annual Ig Nobel Awards to honor people whose achievements "cannot or should not be reproduced".

Web:
http://www.improb.com/
http://www.improb.com/airchives/mini-AIR/

> **Annals of Improbable Research**
> If you are like me, you enjoy nothing better than spending Saturday night curled up at home with a good mathematics or physics journal. However, even the best times end, and what do you do when you have read all your scholarly publications and it's only 9:00 PM? Time to fire up the old Web browser and connect to the **Annals of Improbable Research** archives. The lighthearted approach to research and its detritus will entertain for hours.

Bad Science

When I was in medical school at the University of Toronto, I had a physics argument with a fellow student named Dave. Dave thought that, south of the equator, water emptying from a sink would spin counter-clockwise (as opposed to most sinks up here, in which the water runs clockwise as it drains). Dave said the spinning was caused by the Coriolis effect (the apparent sideways motion of certain forces due to the rotation of the Earth). I tried to explain to Dave that he was wrong: the Coriolis effect works on large-scale phenomena, like the trade winds, but not on anything as small as the water in a sink. However, he was intransigent, so I bet him five dollars that I was right. Well, I am, and his argument is a perfect example of bad science: technical ideas that are presented incorrectly by teachers and writers. As one of my readers, I know you always like to be knowledgeable and accurate, so take a look at the bad science information and learn what's right. (And if you ever run into Dave, tell him he owes me five dollars.)

Web:
http://www.ems.psu.edu/~fraser/BadScience.html

Dinosaurs

Dinosaurs evolved about 225 million years ago, and became extinct about 65 million years ago, thriving for 160 million years. In modern terminology, dinosaurs are land-living reptiles, members of a group known as archsaurs ("ruling reptiles"). Among today's animals, birds are thought to be the closest relatives to dinosaurs, with crocodiles being somewhat more distant relations. Dinosaur trivia: Around the turn of the century, certain fossils were thought to be those of a brontosaurus. Actually, the head and body were mixed up, and the real name for the animal is apatosaurus. There never really was such a thing as a brontosaurus.

Web:
http://www.dinosauria.com/
http://www.nmmnh-abq.mus.nm.us/nmmnh/dinodictionary.html
http://www.ucmp.berkeley.edu/diapsids/dinolinks.html
http://www.ucmp.berkeley.edu/diapsids/dinosaur.html

Usenet:
alt.dinosaur

Listproc Mailing List:
List Name: **dinosaur**
Subscribe to: **listproc@usc.edu**

Earth and Sky

"Earth and Sky" is a popular radio presentation that is aired daily on hundreds of stations in the U.S., Canada and the South Pacific, as well as on various international networks. Each day the show provides a short discussion of one scientific topic. The Web site offers transcripts from the actual shows. You can read about the most current show, or search for one that interests you.

Web:
http://www.earthsky.com/

Dig up something interesting in "Archaeology".

SCIENCE 693

DINOSAURS

The fact is, just about everybody likes dinosaurs (unless they are named Barney). If you've got kids, show them how to use your Web browser and point it to a dinosaur exhibit. We owe it to ourselves to spend some time learning about these great beasts from the past and how they influence our modern culture. (After all, dinosaurs are people too.)

For example, few people realize it but, before David Letterman, the top-rated American nighttime TV talk show host was a dinosaur. And fully 75% of modern American publishing companies are run by dinosaurs. Let's teach our kids to understand and appreciate our friends in the dinosaur kingdom, and soon we will all be living in peace and harmony.

Folklore of Science

Science is rich in folklore, legends and mysteries. This Usenet group is for the discussion of various folklore topics as they relate to science. The Web page contains a listing of science-related urban legends. Will a penny falling from a great height kill someone? Will hot water freeze faster than cold water? Why does the moon look smaller when it is overhead than when it is near the horizon? Visit the Web site and find out the answers to these questions and more. (By the way, the quick answers are no, yes and it's an illusion.)

Web:
http://www.urbanlegends.com/science/

Usenet:
alt.folklore.science

Hawking, Stephen

Stephen Hawking is one of the most brilliant theoretical physicists of our time. Here is Hawking's personal Web site as well as another that contains information about his work. I have also included a site that contains a short essay where Hawking discusses the origin of the universe. The essay starts with a brief synopsis of how people have thought of the universe throughout history, and then goes on to discuss modern ideas in (relatively) simple terms. If you need to create your own universe—or even if you are only thinking about it—this is an invaluable guide.

Web:
http://www.damtp.cam.ac.uk/user/hawking/
http://www.psyclops.com/hawking/

History of Science

The history of science is the story of our systematic and endless quest to understand the nature of ourselves, our world and the universe in which we live. This Usenet group is devoted to a discussion of the history of science and scientific discoveries, as well as the ways in which mankind's development affects our modern existence. The Web page offers related links.

Web:
http://www.astro.uni-bonn.de/~pbrosche/hist_sci/hs_general.html

Usenet:
soc.history.science

Do you like the universe? (It's always been one of my favorite places.)

If so, read what Stephen Hawking has to say about it.

694 SCIENCE

Human Evolution

Human evolution is the theory of the origin of human beings. In particular, evolution explains how man and the apes descended from common ancestors and how, about five million years ago, our most immediate ancestors (hominids) began the development that would result in our own species (Homo sapiens). There is a great deal of foolish and ignorant thought (and talk) among people who believe that mankind was created supernaturally. As far as I am concerned, the more people learn about science, the better off we all are, and here are some places to start.

Web:
  http://earth.ics.uci.edu:8080/origins/
     faqs-evolution.html
  http://www.talkorigins.org/
  http://www.ucmp.berkeley.edu/history/
     evolution.html

Usenet:
  talk.origins

National Science Foundation

The National Science Foundation (NSF) is an independent agency of the United States government. Its purpose is to promote the progress of science within the United States. Toward this end, the NSF funds a great deal of research within the science and engineering disciplines, as well as awarding many graduate scholarships. The NSF also promotes the use of computers in science research and education. If you are a technical researcher or grad student, you can't go far without bumping into the NSF. Their Web site features information about the organization itself, its publications, grants, scholarships and research.

Web:
  http://www.nsf.gov/

**Wanna change the system?
Try "Anarchy".**

Oceanography

The Earth has one large interconnected sea of water, covering 71 percent of the planet's surface. Traditionally, we divide all this water into four main oceans: the Pacific Ocean, the Indian Ocean, the Atlantic Ocean and the Arctic Ocean. Taken together, these oceans cover about 139,400,000 sq mi (361,000,000 sq km) and contain about 322,280,000 cu mi (1,347,000,000 cu km) of water. The average depth is about 12,230 ft (3,730 m). Oceanography is the study of the ocean and the life it supports. As such, oceanography integrates biology, chemistry, geography, geology, physics and meteorology into one marine-oriented field of study. There are a great many oceanography resources on the Net. Here are some Web sites that contain particularly good collections. I have also included the Web sites of two of the main oceanographical research organizations in the United States: Scripps Institution of Oceanography (California) and the Woods Hole Oceanographic Institution (Massachusetts).

Web:
  http://scilib.ucsd.edu/sio/inst/
  http://sio.ucsd.edu/
  http://www.mth.uea.ac.uk/ocean/oceanography.html
  http://www.whoi.edu/

Usenet:
  sci.geo.oceanography

Research Methods in Science

You need a certain kind of mind to be an organized and efficient researcher. Here are some discussion forums on the Internet that will give you lots of different places to talk about scientific techniques. The mailing list helps researchers in classification, clustering, phylogeny estimation and related methods of data analysis to contact other researchers in the same fields.

Usenet:
  sci.techniques.mag-resonance
  sci.techniques.mass-spec
  sci.techniques.microscopy
  sci.techniques.spectroscopy
  sci.techniques.testing.misc
  sci.techniques.testing.nondestructive

Listserv Mailing List:
  List Name: **class-l**
  Subscribe to: **listserv@ccvm.sunysb.edu**

SCIENCE

Science Fraud and Skepticism

Science has a long, distinguished history. Unfortunately, science fraud has just as long a history (although less distinguished). These resources are devoted to a discussion of fraud in science, including current and recent events, as well as historical accounts of fraudulent science.

Web:
  http://wheel.ucdavis.edu/~btcarrol/skeptic/dictcont.html
  http://www.ems.psu.edu/~fraser/BadScience.html
  http://www.faqs.org/faqs/skeptic-faq/
  http://www.junkscience.com/

Usenet:
  sci.skeptic

Listserv Mailing List:
  List Name: **scifraud**
  Subscribe to: **listserv@cnsibm.albany.edu**

Science News

Now that we have the Net, life is certainly a lot better. For example, anytime you want, you can read the science news, all by yourself, in the privacy of your own home. When I was a kid, we had to learn about science on the street and, believe me, it was not always a pleasant experience. (Of course, in those days, boys had to grow up fast.)

Web:
  http://www.abcnews.com/sections/science/
  http://www.foxnews.com/scitech/
  http://www.sciencedaily.com/

Majordomo Mailing List:
  List Name: **breakthrough**
  Subscribe to: **majordomo@lucifer.com**

Science Resources

There's a lot of science in the world (and even more outside of the world), so it's not always easy to find what you want. When you are looking for information in a particular area of science, start here with a large, comprehensive collection of selected science resources for just about every type of science and science-related category you might need.

Web:
  http://www.scicentral.com/

Science Talk and General Discussion

Science is the organized, rational study of the nature of our universe. As a whole, science is broad, almost beyond description. I think of science in two ways: as a method of thinking, and as a human activity. The activity of science depends upon three basic traditions: employing trustworthy methods for experimentation and observation, systematically classifying observed facts, and connecting a body of demonstrated truths in order to reach conclusions. Mankind already knows a great deal about our universe (including the planet on which we live and the nature of the biology it supports). A great deal of mankind's suffering is caused by widespread ignorance of basic scientific knowledge and the inability to apply such knowledge wisely. For this reason, I encourage you to use the resources I have prepared for this book to teach yourself more about science. I hope that, within the many scientific resources, you will find much to interest you. If you would like to talk about science in general, here is the Usenet group devoted to such discussions. Remember what I say: as much as anything else, science is a way of thinking. There is no better way to fulfill your birthright as a sentient human being than by studying the world around you and all its wonders. (Perhaps I can put it another way. My cat can't learn about science, so I have to do it for both of us.)

Usenet:
  sci.misc

Temperature

Here is everything you could want to know about temperature. Learn about global warming and our planet's temperature, temperature and health, temperature tools (such as unit converters), temperature sensors and calibration, thermocouples and more. When it comes to learning about temperatures on the Net, when you're hot, you're hot, when you're not, you're still pretty cool.

Web:
  http://grads.iges.org/pix/trop.ts.s.html
  http://www.temperatureworld.com/

SCIENCE

Why Files

"The Why Files: The Science Behind the News" is a project funded by the United States National Science Foundation (NSF) and managed by the National Institute for Science Education (NISE). Based on the premise that science should be for everyone, the project examines the science behind various current news stories. The idea is to use news stories as a way to interest people in learning about science. For example, the legal battles involving the cigarette industry provide an opportunity to examine nicotine addiction and how it affects the brain. The stories, which are well-researched and intriguing, are changed at intervals. The old stories are archived.

Web:
http://whyfiles.news.wisc.edu/

SCIENCE FICTION, FANTASY AND HORROR

Ansible Newsletter

Get the latest buzz on the sci-fi scene. *Ansible*, a Hugo-award winning newsletter, will give you news and gossip about your favorite authors, dates for conferences and conventions, book reviews and releases, as well as the occasional obituary. *Ansible* is archived at the Web site, but is also available by electronic subscription.

Web:
http://www.dcs.gla.ac.uk/SF-Archives/Ansible

Majordomo Mailing List:
List Name: **ansible**
Subscribe to: **majordomo@imi.gla.ac.uk**

Look What I Found on the Net...

```
Newsgroup: sci.misc
Subject: Help With a Kid's Question

> My 11-year-old son stumped me with the following syllogism:

> — Diamonds are supposed to be the hardest matter.
> — Liquids are distinguished from solids by the fact that
>    solid matter is "crushable", in other words liquids cannot
>    be "crushed".
> — Ergo, water is actually "harder" than diamond.
> — Perhaps we should use water in lieu of diamonds in cutting
>    processes.

>Is he wrong? Where are the flaws in this argument?

Hardness is essentially a measure of how difficult it is to get
a material to plastically deform under a point load; how
difficult it is to get a material to flow.

It is very easy to get water to flow.  It is very difficult to
get diamonds to flow.  Water is soft, diamonds are hard.

For what it's worth, water can actually cut things, if it's
under enough pressure.  Some of the "power washers" which are
available at most hardware stores create a stream of water
powerful enough to blast through the aluminum siding on houses.
```

SCIENCE FICTION, FANTASY AND HORROR

Babylon 5

Although Babylon 5 was presented as a series of television programs, it was actually a five-year-long story that was completely planned before the first episode was filmed. Babylon 5 is a science fiction saga that takes place in the distant future during the "third age of mankind". A hundred years earlier, an alien race called the Centauri made contact with Earth. Since then, Earth has found out there are three other races in the galaxy, the Narn, the Vorlon and the Minbari. The four alien races are continuously engaging in various wars and intrigues, sometimes involving Earth. In an attempt to bring peace to the galaxy, Earth conceives of a meeting place in the form of an immense space station, a place to serve as the home for a galactic United Nations. The first four attempts to create such a space station are sabotaged, but the fifth attempt is successful. In the year 2257, Babylon 5—the last hope for a peaceful galaxy—is officially opened and the story begins.

Web:
http://www.infinicorp.com/VEX/
http://www.midwinter.com/lurk/

Usenet:
rec.arts.sf.tv.babylon5
rec.arts.sf.tv.babylon5.info
rec.arts.sf.tv.babylon5.moderated

Listproc Mailing List:
List Name: b5-review-l
Subscribe to: listproc@cornell.edu

IRC:
#babylon5

Cabinet of Dr. Casey

The Cabinet of Dr. Casey is a great place to look if you are trying to get ideas for that next sleepover party or for the next time you see the Amway salesman coming to your door. This site is devoted to horror in the form of movies and books. Get some great audio samples, read Tales from the Internet, and see graphics and the horror timeline. A fantastic place to visit if you love the horror genre.

Web:
http://www.drcasey.com/

> **Want some fun?**
> **Read the "Fun" section.**

Cyberpunk

You can't be totally cool until you know what cyberpunk is. And you can't fake it—you have to know the real stuff, like the difference between the literary movement and the culture. People who are immersed in the cyberpunk culture understand what it is, but they have a lot of trouble explaining it to anyone else. My advice is to start with the idea that technology touches virtually every aspect of our lives. One way to sort of understand it is to look at the type of entertainment cyberpunks like. For example, look at the lists of books, movies and manga (anime) preferred by cyberpunks. Read through and you will start to get a feeling about the cyberpunk culture. Cyberpunk philosophy is very much a heuristic work in progress, where what might be and what should be is more or less determined by what is. So take some time to read the quotes, thoughts and ramblings relating to the cyberpunk way of life, ethos and beliefs. What makes more sense to you: "Attack anything that tries to hide information from the masses" or "Never trust anyone"? I like to just read the stuff and let it wash over me like an ocean wave.

Web:
http://euro.net/mark-space/Cyberpunk.html
http://www.best.com/~rtg1/cp2020.html
http://www.cs.helsinki.fi/~tjpasika/cyberpunk/
http://www.digitalo.com/
http://www.knarf.demon.co.uk/alt-cp.htm
http://www.sci.fi/~cyborg/cyberpunk/scifi.html

Usenet:
alt.culture.cyber-psychos
alt.cyberpunk
alt.cyberpunk.chatsubo
alt.cyberpunk.movement
alt.cyberpunk.tech
alt.cyberworld
alt.cypherpunks
rec.games.frp.cyber

SCIENCE FICTION, FANTASY AND HORROR

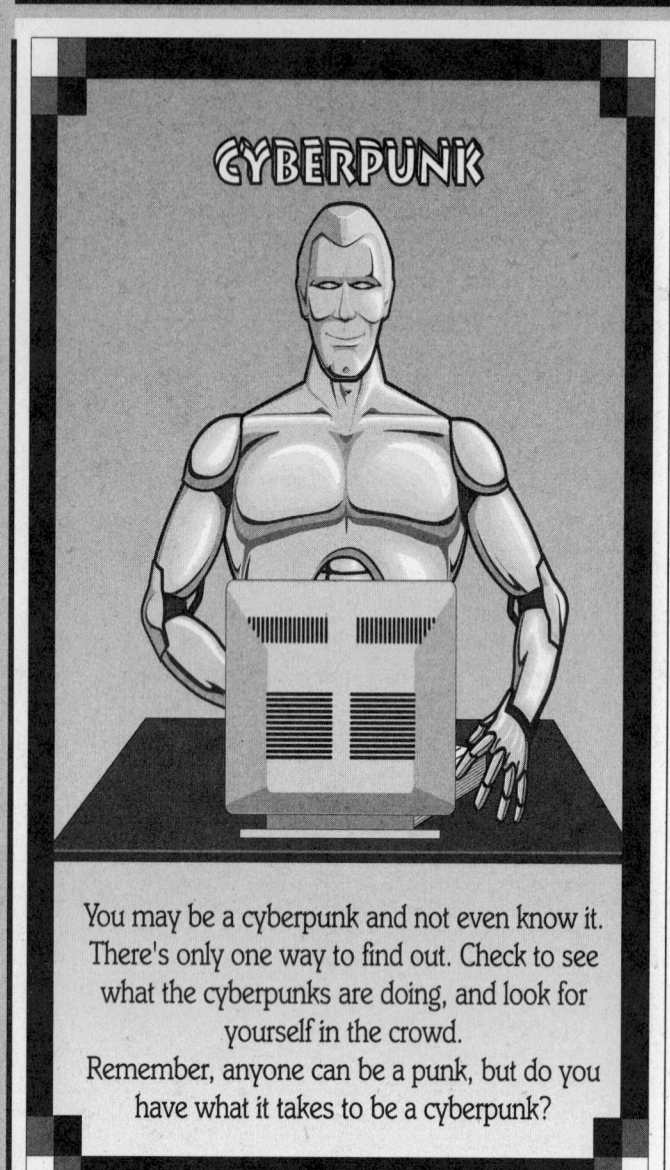

CYBERPUNK

You may be a cyberpunk and not even know it. There's only one way to find out. Check to see what the cyberpunks are doing, and look for yourself in the crowd.
Remember, anyone can be a punk, but do you have what it takes to be a cyberpunk?

Darkecho's Horror Web

It's a lot of fun to read horror stories, but you can't do it 24 hours a day. You do need to take a break occasionally. When you do, visit this Web site, where you will find a ghoulish variety of horror links. You can also read interviews with artists and writers, find out about conventions and enjoy book reviews.

Web:
 http://www.darkecho.com/darkecho/

Doctor Who

He's wild-haired, strangely dressed, and often chased by hostile robots or aliens. Doctor Who doesn't have to take up jogging because he is almost always running for cover anyway. Join the people who love the excitement and adventure of this futuristic television series.

Web:
 http://nitro9.earth.uni.edu/doctor/

Usenet:
 rec.arts.drwho
 rec.arts.drwho.info

IRC:
 #drwho

Fans of Science Fiction and Fantasy Writers

When you read the work of the great science fiction and fantasy writers, you become immersed in worlds that exist only in the imagination. One of the best ways to enjoy your favorite books is to discuss them with other fans. These Usenet discussion groups are filled with SF&F enthusiasts who love to discuss the nuances of imaginative fiction, as well as the writers who create it.

Usenet:
 alt.books.arthur-clarke
 alt.books.brian-lumley
 alt.books.kurt-vonnegut
 alt.books.larry-niven
 alt.fan.asprin
 alt.fan.douglas-adams
 alt.fan.dragonlance
 alt.fan.dune
 alt.fan.eddings
 alt.fan.harlan-ellison
 alt.fan.heinlein
 alt.fan.pern
 alt.fan.piers-anthony
 alt.fan.pratchett
 alt.fan.pratchett.announce
 alt.fan.robert-jordan

SCIENCE FICTION, FANTASY AND HORROR

Fright Site

Would you like to scare yourself silly? Invite a few friends over for the night. Then turn down the lights and tell a few ghost stories. Once you get everyone good and nervous, turn on the old PC and connect to the Fright Site. See who screams first.

Web:
http://www.fright.com/

Furry Stuff

Being a human is really overrated. You don't have much license to romp and play, and most people frown upon licking yourself at the table after a satisfying meal. At least there is a way to redirect your energy. Furry fans will rejoice to see these Web sites containing information about artists, publishers, and publications that cover anthropomorphic or "furry" art.

Web:
http://www.tigerden.com/infopage/furry/
http://www.yerf.com/

Usenet:
alt.fan.furry

> ### Furry Stuff
> Do you like things that are cute and furry?
> Of course you do.
> So visit all the cute and furry things on the Net.

Horror Fiction Online

Wow. You can scare yourself silly without moving from your computer. These Web addresses point to different pages at the same site. One page is a list of horror books and short stories, including The Legend of Sleepy Hollow, The Strange Case of Dr. Jekyll and Mr. Hyde, The Turn of the Screw, Dracula, and The Picture of Dorian Gray (one of my favorites). The second page contains the archives of an ongoing project entitled "Tales from the Internet", in which horror stories are contributed by people around the Net.

Web:
http://www.drcasey.com/literature/online.shtml
http://www.drcasey.com/literature/tales/

Horror Literature

This Web site has a lot of original content created by a deluxe horror fanatic. Enjoy the reviews of horror fiction, personal thoughts about reading and writing, a scary picture or two, lists of the best horror books, and much more. What I like best about this site is there is so much original content: lots of stuff to read and appreciate. It's refreshing to find Web sites created by people who do more than simply link to other sites.

Web:
http://www.oceanstar.com/horror/

Horror Talk and General Discussion

Lots of people, all over the world, love talking about horror. Moreover, if you like to write, it is encouraging to have a place to show your work to others. Usenet has groups for both purposes. To talk, join **alt.horror**. To share your writing (or to read other people's work), try the **alt.horror.creative** group, where you can discuss anything related to the creation of things horrible. If you are new to horror on the Net, start with the Web site where you will find an informative FAQ (frequently asked question list). Read this before you start posting.

Web:
http://ezinfo.ucs.indiana.edu/~mlperkin/faq.html

Usenet:
alt.horror
alt.horror.creative

Mystery Science Theatre 3000

There are worse things than being consigned to review bad sci-fi for your entire life. Experience the hilarity of Mystery Science Theater 3000 with other fans of this TV program, where you can watch strange sci-fi movies while listening to the comments of even stranger observers.

Web:
http://www.mst3kinfo.com/
http://www.scifi.com/mst3000/

Usenet:
alt.fan.mst3k
alt.tv.mst3k
rec.arts.tv.mst3k
rec.arts.tv.mst3k.announce
rec.arts.tv.mst3k.misc

IRC:
#mst3k

700 SCIENCE FICTION, FANTASY AND HORROR

Red Dwarf

Red Dwarf is a British science fiction comedy series. The premise is described by an opening used on the first show: "This is an S.O.S. distress call from the mining ship Red Dwarf. The crew are dead, killed by a radiation leak. The only survivors are Dave Lister, who was in suspended animation during the disaster, and his pregnant cat, who was safely sealed in the hold. Revived three million years later, Lister's only companions are a life form who evolved from his cat, and Arnold Rimmer, a hologram simulation of one of the dead crew."

Web:
http://www.faqs.org/faqs/tv/red-dwarf/
http://www.queeg.crater.com/

Usenet:
alt.tv.red-dwarf

Listproc Mailing List:
List Name: **reddwarf**
Subscribe to: listproc@lists.pipex.com

Science and Science Fiction

Stretch your mind by pushing your imagination to the limit. How real is the science in science fiction? A wide variety of topics are covered, such as the possibility of force fields, transcendental engineering, and Hawking radiation. Invent your own theories or pick apart someone else's.

Web:
http://www.sirius.com/~treitel/rass/qdfaq.html

Usenet:
rec.arts.sf.science

Science Fiction and Fantasy Archives

Science fiction and fantasy are the perfect things to read when you don't want to study for a test or work on something around the house. Cozy up to the computer and read these science fiction and fantasy archives, which will not only give you some great stories, but will also show you reviews of books and movies. There are also links to newsletters and zines related to the genre.

Web:
http://sf.www.lysator.liu.se/sf_archive/sf_main.html

Science Fiction and Fantasy Online

The Net loves people who love science fiction and fantasy. Start at this Web site, and choose your favorite author. You will find work by such writers as Francis Bacon (The New Atlantis), L. Frank Baum (the Oz books), Terry Bisson (Dead Man's Curve), Edgar Rice Burroughs (the Tarzan books, The Land That Time Forgot), Wilkie Collins (The Haunted Hotel, The Woman in White), and Gaston Leroux (The Phantom of the Opera). You can also find short stories and sample chapters from various publishers. If you have a day on which you are feeling particularly adventurous, connect to this site and try something that is brand new to you. This is a wonderful site. Visit often and enjoy.

Web:
http://www.users.interport.net/~jfreund/sfbooks/sfbooks.html#complete

Science Fiction Announcements

Attention science fiction buffs! Find out what's up and coming in sci-fi land. This moderated group will provide you with all the information you need on new movies, books, television shows and anything that is new in science fiction.

Usenet:
rec.arts.sf.announce

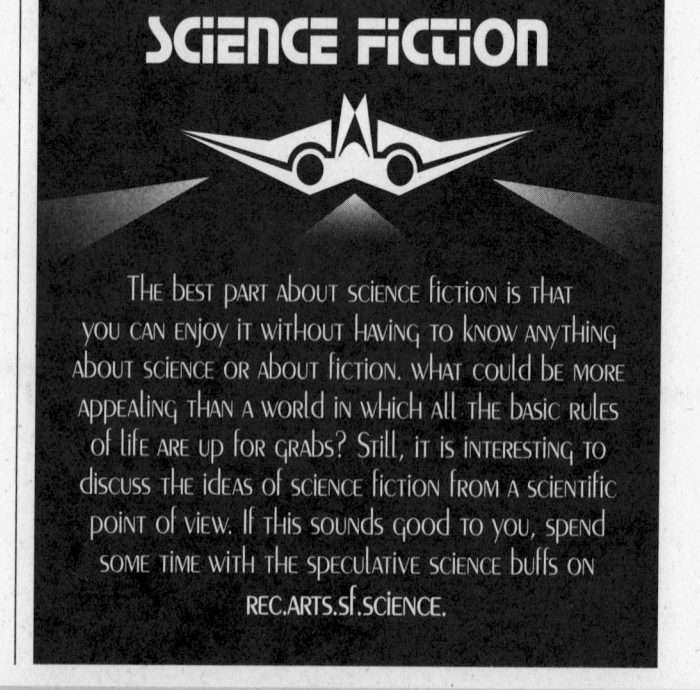

SCIENCE FICTION

The best part about science fiction is that you can enjoy it without having to know anything about science or about fiction. What could be more appealing than a world in which all the basic rules of life are up for grabs? Still, it is interesting to discuss the ideas of science fiction from a scientific point of view. If this sounds good to you, spend some time with the speculative science buffs on REC.ARTS.SF.SCIENCE.

SCIENCE FICTION, FANTASY AND HORROR

Science Fiction Convention Calendar

When you need a little break from the real world, pack your bags and head to a science fiction convention. Here's a list of cons all over the world, including information about the guests of honor and contact information so you can pre-register.

Web:
http://www.serve.com/usspowhatan/conventionindex.html

Science Fiction Fandom Talk and General Discussion

Fans from all over the world live, eat and breathe science fiction. They travel in packs, eager to suck the nectar from the sci-fi flower. If you have a taste for something out of the ordinary, join the crowd, go to cons and be a groupie.

Usenet:
alt.fandom.cons
rec.arts.sf.fandom

Science fiction fanatics: keep up on what's happening by reading rec.arts.sf.announce.

Science Fiction Marketplace

Are you looking to trade your extra copy of the "Pegasus" episode of Battlestar Galactica for a signed copy of a Friday print by Whelan? Shop at the science fiction flea market—rare commodities for rare people. Buy, sell or trade. Display your merchandise in this shoplifter-free environment.

Usenet:
rec.arts.sf.marketplace

Science Fiction Movies

You just saw the best movie ever and you have to tell someone about it or you'll explode. You can either run screaming through the parking lot of the movie theater and risk being arrested for disturbing the peace, or you can tell the sci-fi movie fans on the Internet. Start with the Usenet group. Then move on to the Web sites where you can immerse yourself in the lore of SF films until it is time to go to another movie.

Web:
http://www.faqs.org/faqs/sf/movies-faq/
http://www.rnrweb.com/scifi/scifi.htm
http://www.scifi.com/sfw/

Usenet:
rec.arts.sf.movies

Science Fiction News

As a science fiction fan, you have a moral (not to mention a personal) obligation to keep up on what's new and exciting in the world of sci-fi. I don't want anyone, anywhere, to release a new movie, book or TV show without you finding out about it right away, so stay glued to the Net (have all your food sent in).

Web:
http://www.dailysci-fi.com/
http://www.scifi.com/scifiwire/

Science Fiction Resource Guide

When I am looking for science fiction information this is the place I start. This guide has everything: authors, awards, bibliographies, bookstores, fan clubs, movies, publishers, role-playing games, television, Usenet groups, zines, archives, reviews, criticism, fiction writing, and more. Here is an example. When I was a graduate student, I was in the same department as David Brin. So I thought it might be interesting to see how his science fiction career was coming along. Using the Science Fiction Resource Guide, I was able to find links to several David Brin Web sites, so I could check up on his career. (Actually, for someone who doesn't write Internet books, he's doing fairly well.)

Web:
http://sflovers.rutgers.edu/Web/SFRG/sf-resource-guide.html

702 SCIENCE FICTION, FANTASY AND HORROR

Science Fiction Talk and General Discussion

Science fiction isn't a hobby: it's a lifestyle. Are you one of those people whose walls and cabinets (and floors) are covered with sci-fi books, magazines, tapes and memorabilia? Scoot all of it out of the way so you can get to the computer and find your sci-fi soulmates. Anything science fiction goes.

Usenet:
  rec.arts.sf.misc
  rec.arts.sf.reviews

Science Fiction Writing

Allow yourself to linger on the words, your eyes playing gently back and forth across the pages of your latest sci-fi novel. There is something tangible about a book that you just can't get from television or movies. Discuss your favorite book or hear about someone else's. Find out what's new and what is hopelessly out of print.

Web:
  http://members.aol.com/starrun/
  http://www.marketlist.com/
  http://www.sff.net/

Usenet:
  rec.arts.sf.written

IRC:
  #specchat

Need a lift? Boycott gravity.

SciFaiku

What do you get when you mix science fiction and haiku poetry? You get SciFaiku, a form of haiku poetry about science fiction topics. Read the rules describing this form of poetry and browse the archive of a nice selection of SciFaiku.

Web:
  http://www.crew.umich.edu/~brinck/poetry/manifesto.html

SF-Lovers

SF-Lovers Digest is an electronic magazine that has been published since 1980. The magazine—which you can subscribe to for free—discusses science fiction books, movies, TV shows and conventions. The SF-Lovers Web site allows you to access the archives of past issues and subscribe to future issues. You will also find a lot of generally useful science fiction information. If you are a science fiction fan, you need to explore this site.

Web:
  http://sflovers.rutgers.edu/

Look What I Found on the Net...

```
Newsgroup: rec.arts.sf.written
Subject: Secret Messages in DNA

> There is quite a bit of "junk" DNA lying around a genome.
> Theoretically, there shouldn't be any reason for this DNA not
> to hide a message (mind you, you'd have to be pretty clever
> in finding the key to decode those base pair sequences).

Well, the issue is not really how the DNA is packaged.  The
problem is that there would be a steady accumulation of errors
occurring during the replication or repair of DNA.  Not to
mention more dramatic errors caused by chromosomal
rearrangements, unequal crossing over, etc. etc.  So if the
message was going to last a long time, you would need to
incorporate some pretty complex error correction.
```

Star Wars

What would happen if... ? Speculation abounds regarding the Star Wars universe. Star Wars fans reinvent the movies daily, wondering what would happen if certain characters had done things differently. Discover inconsistencies you may have missed in the movies and learn what has happened to everyone involved, from the big screen to the cutting room floor.

Web:
http://scifi.simplenet.com/starwars/prequels/
http://www.egosystem.com/starwars/bloopers.html
http://www.faqs.org/faqs/starwars/
http://www.jedinet.com/
http://www.shavenwookie.com/swlinks.html
http://www.starwars.com/

Usenet:
rec.arts.sf.starwars
rec.arts.sf.starwars.collecting
rec.arts.sf.starwars.games
rec.arts.sf.starwars.misc

Majordomo Mailing List:
List Name: starwars
Subscribe to: majordomo@logrus.org

IRC:
#starwars

Hacker? 2600? Good. Meet you on the Net. 'Nuff said.

SECRET STUFF

2600

At one time, it was possible to make free long distance calls by using a homemade device called a blue box. A person using a blue box could fool the telephone switching system into making long distance calls without billing for them. The blue box worked by mimicking sounds that the phone system used for signaling, in particular, a 2600 hertz tone. This number was well-known among phone hackers, and so when it came time to choose a name for a general hackers magazine, it was called "2600". 2600 covers subjects such as phreaking, hacking, cellular phones, scanners, hardware, credit cards, and much more secret stuff than you are ever supposed to know.

Web:
http://www.2600.com/
http://www.faqs.org/faqs/alt-2600/

Usenet:
alt.2600
alt.2600.cardz
alt.2600.codez
alt.2600.moderated
alt.2600.phreakz
alt.2600.warez

IRC:
#2600

Backward Masking

Backward masking refers to hiding messages on recorded music by inserting sounds that are meaningful when played backward. Some people feel that cunning malevolent fiends insert such messages into music in order to subliminally influence unsuspecting listeners. This idea first surfaced some years ago when fanatical Bible-thumpers were convinced that various popular rock groups were putting reversed Satanic messages in selected recordings. Since then, a number of musicians and bands have embedded such messages on purpose (for the novelty, I suppose). Here are some Web pages that offer audio snippets of actual recordings played backward. (Between us, the possibility that anyone could be affected by listening to backward sounds is about as likely as your being affected by the brain emanations of aliens from a nearby star system.)

Web:
http://gruel.spc.uchicago.edu/Backmask/mask.shtml
http://www.ka.net/rnutts/backmasking.html

SECRET STUFF

Cellular Phone Hacking

If you want to be able to hack cellular phones (or even just talk about it to impress people at parties), you need to know the basics and then some. Here are some Web sites with a collection of information that will set you on the road to getting inside those funny little boxes that cost so much. And if you want to talk, there is always IRC.

Web:
http://www.l0pht.com/cdc/cdc241.txt
http://www.tdyc.com/archive/oblivion/texts/texts.html

IRC:
#cellular

> Be informed. Check out "Consumer Information".

Disney Secrets

Disney theme parks are very controlled. Try causing even a slight amount of trouble and see how fast the security people (materializing out of nowhere) will give you the bum's rush. When you visit a Disney park, everything you see and everything the employees do is planned carefully. For instance, you are never more than 25 paces away from a garbage can. Disney management goes to a great deal of trouble to sustain the illusion of "the happiest place on Earth". People who work at Disney theme parks are called "cast members". (Repeat this often enough and even the employees think it's normal.) That is why I love to read about Disney secrets. None of these secrets is all that important. Nevertheless, they are intriguing because you just know that the pleasant folks who control the world of Disney would very much prefer that you didn't know anything about their behind-the-scenes management.

Web:
http://musky.oitc.com/Disney/Secrets.html

Usenet:
alt.disney.secrets

Look What I Found on the Net...

(from the Disney Secrets Web site)

The next time you see a Disney theme park cast member [employee] looking bored, frustrated, mad, etc., try this.

Make eye contact, put your index finger and thumb together, pull the top of your head up from an imaginary string, and smile sheepishly.

Chances are their attitude will change, at least until you're out of sight.

This action is a little signal cast members and undercover orientees are supposed to give each other when someone is not being what I like to call "Too Cute to Live!"

SECRET STUFF

Easter Eggs

An Easter egg is a secret feature hidden inside a computer program. Many programs have Easter eggs—usually hidden there by the programmers—that you can invoke if you know the secret key combinations. (For example, if you use Netscape, try pressing Ctrl-Alt-F and see what happens.) For more fun, here is a large collection of Easter eggs hidden in many different programs.

Web:
http://www.eeggs.com/

Easter Eggs

One of the most important legends of Western culture is the story of how Jesus was put to death by the Romans and how, a short time later, was resurrected, symbolizing God's devotion to mankind and showing us that the devout and the faithful will themselves be resurrected at the appropriate time.

Today, these occurrences are remembered during the various Easter observances around the world, one of the most notable being the insertion of secret actions within important computer programs. These so-called "Easter eggs" are found in a number of PC and Macintosh programs and are documented in the Easter Egg Web site. So, if you are feeling especially devotional one day, take a moment to find out about these Easter eggs and demonstrate them for yourself. After all, it is too easy to concentrate exclusively on work and other secular matters, and a few moments spent in a spiritual activity would be good for just about anybody.

Magic Secrets Talk and General Discussion

Want to find out how magic tricks really work? This is the Usenet group where people discuss how magicians make sure that the hand is always quicker than the eye. For example, how does David Copperfield take rings from three people in the audience (seemingly at random), link the rings together, show everyone that the rings are really linked, and then separate them so as to give the rings back to the people? (Answer: One of the rings is a fake. It has a piece cut out of it, allowing it to be linked to two other completely whole rings. Copperfield makes sure that the audience never sees the cut-out part. When he borrows the three rings, he palms one and substitutes the special one he has prepared ahead of time.)

Usenet:
alt.magic.secrets

Pay-TV Decoders

What would you do if someone gave you instructions for building a pay-TV decoder from simple parts you could buy at any electronic supply store? Don't tell me, I don't want to know. I think television is bad for you.

Web:
http://ilab.com/list10/paytvdec.txt

Usenet:
alt.satellite.tv.crypt

Phreaking

Want to talk about phone phreaking: telephones, exchanges, toll fraud, kodez, signaling, and so on? Walk gently into that good night and talk to the people who love to phreak. To help you fit in, look at the Web sites for help with phreaking terms and abbreviations. Or if you would actually like to build a "box", you can get the plans. (However, now that phone companies use modern switching systems, most of these boxes don't work. Still, maybe you can find a red box somewhere.)

Web:
http://www.info-labs.com/phreakstop/texts/
http://www.phonelosers.org/

Usenet:
alt.2600.phreakz

IRC:
#phreak

Police Codes

The police use a lot of different codes when they talk to one another over the radio. If you have the right type of receiver, you can listen too. But how do you know what the codes mean? Here is the info you need to keep up on what the serve-and-protect guys are doing.

Web:
http://www.jaxnet.com/~habedd/10codes.html
http://www.provide.net/~bfield/10codes.html

Secret Societies

It's hard to find good material on secret societies (are you surprised?), so when you read articles that talk about organizations that conspire in secret, you have to judge for yourself how much you think is true. However, if you like finding out things that you are not supposed to know, it's always fun to read something about a group of people who go to a great deal of trouble to hide their traditions and aims. Visit this Web site to read about the Illuminati, the Knights Templar, the Skull and Bones, the Thule Society, the Rosicrucian Order, the Bilderberg Conference, and more.

Web:
http://www.netizen.org/arc-hive/hiv_sec.htm

Social Security Number Location Finder

Stop me if you've heard this before, but you can tell where a U.S. Social Security number (SSN) was issued by looking at the first three digits. For example, if your SSN starts with 573, it was issued in California. You can also figure out a few more things, and here's a Web site to show you how. Most of the time, a SSN number is issued in the state where the person was born, so here is a trick that never fails that you can play on people. Find an American and tell him you are going to guess the state in which he was born. Then say some magic words to distract him, and, at the same time, use ESP to find out his Social Security number. Then, rush to your computer, connect to this Web site, type in the SSN, and find out where it was issued. Then rush back and tell the person where he was born. People are so amazed. (Hint: As with all magic tricks, don't tell the audience how it was done.)

Web:
http://members.aol.com/navyspies/ssn.htm

Software Cracks

This Usenet group is for the discussion and trading of information on how to crack software or otherwise break the copy protection. You can also discuss cracks and the uploading of cracked files (to various unspecified locations). I didn't include any Web sites, because they get moved so frequently.

Usenet:
alt.2600.crackz

Super Secret Web Site

I have found a Web site that is so totally cool, so awesome, that I know you will be completely blown away. However, the site is a big secret and I can't print the address in this book, so you will have to discover the Web site for yourself. (I have left a space for you to write in the address once you find it.)

Web:
http://

Super Secret Web Site

Yes, the Super Secret Web Site really does exist, and if you haven't yet found it, you're not as cool as you could be.

Warez

These resources are for the discussion of where and how to obtain the latest cracked and pirated software, much of it available through hidden sites on the Internet. Some of the IRC channels are often by invitation only, so you will require contacts to get inside. There are lots of these channels. Start at the highest number you can find at any time and work your way down, seeing if they will let you in. (Unless you are a personal friend of God, you will never get in anything lower than **#warez5**.) The Usenet groups are open to anyone.

Usenet:

alt.binaries.warez
alt.binaries.warez.ibm-pc
alt.binaries.warez.ibm-pc.d
alt.binaries.warez.ibm-pc.old
alt.binaries.warez.mac
alt.binaries.warez.mac.req
alt.binaries.warez.macintosh
alt.warez.ibm-pc
alt.warez.ibm-pc.apps
alt.warez.ibm-pc.old

IRC:

#freewarez
#oldwarez
#warez
#warez1
#warez2
#warez3
#warez4
#warez4free
#warez5
#warez6
#warez7

SENIORS

Elders

It's nice to have an older person to talk with or look up to. As an elder, it's fun to get together with other people and work on projects or discuss political and social issues and find new friends. If you are an elder and want to network with other people or if you want the opportunity to act as an electronic grandparent or mentor, this is a great mailing list to join.

Listserv Mailing List:
List Name: **elders**
Subscribe to: **listserv@maelstrom.stjohns.edu**

Fitness for Seniors

Perhaps the best thing you can do for yourself (at any age) is to stay fit. If you are a senior, regular exercise of some type can make a huge difference in your life. The Usenet discussion group is a good place to talk to other people about fitness topics. The Web sites have lots of exercise tips, including suggestions for gentle, pleasant activities.

Web:

http://www.afaa.com/your_body/lifestyle8.html
http://www.apta.org/public_relations/brochures/youngat_brochure/youngat.htm
http://www.floratec.com/seniors/

Usenet:

soc.senior.health+fitness

Grandparents

Without a doubt, grandparents are the most wonderful people in the world. When I was growing up, I had all my grandparents. We all lived in the same city, and I used to see them a lot. In high school, I would sometimes visit my grandmother for lunch. On Saturday nights, my brother and sister and I would visit her and my grandfather for dinner. (And then, because I was the oldest, I got to stay overnight.) On Friday nights, we would visit the other grandparents for dinner, where I would often see my cousins. I hope there are families like that around today, but what with people moving around so much and getting divorced, a close child/grandparent relationship just doesn't seem to be as common as it used to be. If you are a grandparent, never forget for a minute how important you are to the little ones, and, no matter what happens, you will be alive in their memories for the rest of their lives. I know that my grandparents are.

Web:

http://world.std.com/~jcarlson/senior/
http://www.grandparenting.org/
http://www.uconnect.com/cga/gt1000.htm

708 SENIORS

Housing for Seniors

As you get older, your housing needs will change. If you travel a lot, you may want information about RVs and retirement resorts. If you want to scale down from the responsibilities of maintaining a house, you may want to live in a retirement community. And if you need assistance, you will have to find out about at-home senior care, assisted living or nursing homes, whichever is appropriate. Here are some resources that can help you with all of these topics. Remember, though, wherever you choose to live, don't forget to check your email.

Web:
http://www.americasguide.com/
http://www.retirenet.com/retire/

Retirement Planning

If you are retiring or if you plan to retire soon, in the U.S. there are a lot of financial details you need to know. Social Security, IRAs, 401Ks, financial planning, Roth IRAs—they're all discussed and explained on the Net.

Web:
http://www.eldernet.com/retiremt/soc_sec.htm
http://www.nbfunds.com/retirement/retirement.html
http://www.quicken.com/retirement/
http://www.ssa.gov/pubs/10035.html

Senior Resources

If you are a senior (which means anyone old enough to remember when tattoos were not considered polite forms of self-expression), I want you to connect to the Net. As soon as you do, take a look at these resources. You'll find a lot to read and a lot to do, as well as many new places to explore.

Web:
http://www.aoa.dhhs.gov/aoa/pages/jpostlst.html
http://www.iog.wayne.edu/geroweb.html
http://www.ncoa.org/

Senior Talk and General Discussion

Many people spend hours on the Net talking to people. After a while, you will find yourself with a whole collection of Internet friends with whom you will share many pleasant hours. These Web sites have chat rooms (talk facilities) which you visit and meet people whenever you want. If you are new to talking on the Net, I have a few hints. First, do not give out your real name, address and phone number. If you get to know someone well, you may wish to contact them away from the Net, but please understand that, on the Internet, it is perfectly acceptable to use a nickname to protect your privacy. Second, there are a lot of scam artists around, especially on the Internet. Never give money to anyone you meet on the Net. Finally, people are not always accurate in how they describe themselves—perhaps this is human nature—so please be careful. When people on the Net talk about themselves, take it all with a grain of salt substitute.

Web:
http://chat.senior.com/
http://www.retire.net/chat/
http://www.snowcrest.net/writers/main.html

Usenet:
soc.retirement

Seniors Magazines

Here are some online magazines specially designed for people of retirement age. If you have more time in your life for leisure, hobbies and family, you'll enjoy looking at these Web sites where you will find articles on travel, relationships, grandparenting, health, finance, cooking, books and culture.

Web:
http://www.grandtimes.com/
http://www.seniorlivingnewspaper.com/
http://www.theseniortimes.com/
http://www.thirdage.com/

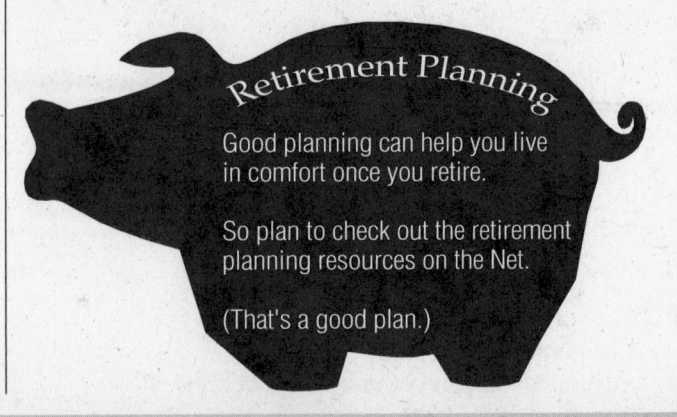

Retirement Planning

Good planning can help you live in comfort once you retire.

So plan to check out the retirement planning resources on the Net.

(That's a good plan.)

Seniors Organizations

These are the official Web sites of the American Association of Retired Persons (AARP) and the Canadian Association of Retired Persons (CARP). Both are nonprofit organizations dedicated to helping people over the age of 50. (The name "Retired Persons" is a misnomer, as you don't have to be retired to join.) You will find a lot of great information about retirement, housing, health, volunteer and community programs, and much more.

Web:
  http://www.aarp.org/
  http://www.fifty-plus.net/

Travel for Seniors

If you like to travel, you will find that there are a great many special programs and discounts for seniors. These Web sites will help you find these resources, as well as information about travel in general and ideas for your next trip.

Web:
  http://www.ageofreason.com/alltravl.htm
  http://www.elderhostel.org/
  http://www.iflyswa.com/info/seniors.html
  http://www.seniornews.com/travel.html

Travel for Seniors
Before you plan your next trip, check with the Net. You'll find all kinds of special stuff just for you.

SEX

Aphrodisiac Guide

An aphrodisiac is a substance, such as a food, drug or fragrance, that stimulates sexual desire. As long as there have been people, people have been looking for aphrodisiacs and there have been precious few. However, under certain circumstances the right accessories can change a possible situation into a real experience. (Remember in physics class, when a teacher used to go on and on about the difference between potential and kinetic energy? Now's your chance to put all that theory into action.) Turn to the Net and there's a good chance that you can find the information you need. And if you can't, you can always try my favorite trick, putting a copy of *Harley Hahn's Student Guide to Unix* under the pillow.

Web:
  http://www.santesson.com/aphrodis/aphrhome.htm

First Times

Do you remember the first time you had sex? Would it make a good story? Well, people on the Net love to share and some of them have written about their first time. There are good stories and bad stories, and they do tend to be a bit explicit. Aren't you curious? What are you waiting for?

Web:
  http://www.myfirsttime.com/

How to Use a Condom

Practice makes perfect and someone is perfect enough to film these instructional video clips. Take advantage of the expertise offered in these short demonstrations you can download to your own computer. No sense getting your information on the street when you can get it from the Net.

Web:
  http://www.plannedparenthood.org/birth-control/condom.htm

710 SEX

Jane's Guide

There's a lot of sex on the Net, and life is oh, so short. That's why you need Jane. Her reviews of sex sites on the Web—including escort service pages, erotica, porn and telephone sex services—can save you a lot of time. (And whatever else you may have on your hands, extra time is probably not on the list.)

Web:
  http://www.janesguide.com/

Pleasing a Woman

What do women want? If you are a man, answering that question is a lifetime quest, so don't enter the battle of the sexes unarmed. Before your next engagement, read these tips for men on what women want. Learn how to rejuvenate your relationship by paying attention to those mutual topics of interest that can mean so much and are always in good taste (and you won't even have to use your special red light bulb).

Web:
  http://www.eccentrica.org/user/eryssa/wwk.htm

> Out of energy? See "Energy".

Safer Sex

We've all heard the stories, the advice, the lectures and the arguments, excuses and rumors. "Safer sex" is the buzz phrase for the rest of the century, so acquire good habits—like brushing your teeth before bed or combing your hair before you go to work. Learn the dos and don'ts, the ins and outs and all the in-betweens of sexual safety. And if you still want to take risks, you can always jump out of an airplane.

Web:
  http://www.condomania.com/educate/manual/manual.html
  http://www.safersex.org/
  http://www.takecare.co.uk/

Señor Sex

Talk about Latin lovers, you ain't seen nothing until you've met Señor Sex. He's a straightforward, raunchy, knowledgeable dude who shares his wisdom by answering questions about sex. If you want delicate answers using the proper medical terminology stick with Dr. Ruth. But if you think you might get more practical advice from a guy who got kicked out of an all-boys school for "ruining the nuns" than from a short German septuagenarian, you might want to give the Señor a chance.

Web:
  http://www.senorsex.com/

Look What I Found on the Net...

```
                  (from the Señor Sex Web site)
An adventurous young lady writes:

My boyfriend and I are both virgins and, well, we seem to have a
vivid imagination when it comes to being together.  My question
is this: I really want to please him, and I would like to know if
you have any tips or advice for two very sensual people who would
like to make the most out of their first time?

Señor Sex responds:

Well, since you're both virgins and want to do something special,
I'd suggest having sex.  There are many people who find that
intercourse leads to a certain feeling of closeness...

I'd give more advice, but I don't know you or your man.
Perhaps you'd like to go to a monster truck show, and let the
adrenaline and noise get you all worked up before making quick,
sloppy love in the back of the pickup...
```

Sensual Massage

Massage is a romantic and sensual way to relax. This guide will help you understand how to select sensual oils, create just the right atmosphere, and know what to do and how to do it with your partner. (Once you get going, though, you're on your own.)

Web:
http://www.sexuality.org/erotmass.html

Sex Glossary

Don't be one of those people who gets his refractory period mixed up with his resolution phase. If you wanna be a sex expert—or even a knowledgeable amateur—you need to be able to walk the walk and talk the talk. And that means you'll need to understand a whole bunch of seventy-five cent words. Here's the list. Go to it.

Web:
http://www.sexology.org/glossary.htm

Sex Talk and General Discussion

What's the weirdest place you have ever had sex? Care to share? Even if you don't, there are hoards of people who do. Not only will they tell you about the weirdest place, but also about the weirdest accident they've ever had during sex, how many times they've had sex, and what was going on around them before, during and after. Be informed as you are entertained. Read about birth control, STDs (sexually transmitted diseases), virginity (or lack of), and other topics of a sexual nature. The Web site contains the FAQ (frequently asked question list) for this Usenet group.

Web:
http://www.halcyon.com/elf/altsex/shortdex.html

Usenet:
alt.sex

Sex Tips

If you are going to do *it*, you might as well do it well. The heading of sex covers a lot of activities and a lot of variations and—aside from people who write Internet books—just about everyone could use a few tips now and again. Who are you going to ask when you want some hints about how to put on a condom with your mouth? Your mother? Never mind, the Net is always there, and it won't ask embarrassing questions.

Web:
http://www.io.com/~barton/tipmen.html
http://www.nuclear.net/theguide/ck/

Sex Trivia

Sex can mean so many different things, depending on your point of view, situation in life, and personal inclinations. However, one thing sex is *not* is trivial. Thus, even sexual trivia has a compelling attraction. Do you know, for example, how big are the largest breasts ever measured? What was the largest number of orgasms ever experienced in one hour by a woman? By a man? How long was the longest female orgasm measured by Masters and Johnson? And was it true that Mae West (1892-1980) once made love with the same partner for 15 consecutive hours? All these fascinating bits of sexual trivia—and much more—can soon be yours. (By the way, the answers to these questions are: 44 pounds (20 kg) each [look at the picture], 134, 16, 43 seconds, and yes, according to her autobiography.)

Web:
http://trivia.lsds.com/Humans/Sex.html
http://www.ece.utexas.edu/~jmeans/Worldsex.html

Tantra and the Kama Sutra

The Kama Sutra is perhaps the most well-known erotic self-help book. See what the ancient commentators have to teach you about mankind's oldest pastime. These teachings describe a wide variety of sex positions and techniques, including the Jewel Case, Love's Noose and the Clinging Creeper.

Web:
http://www.bibliomania.com/NonFiction/Vatsyayana/KamaSutra/
http://www.tantra.org/

Usenet:
alt.magick.tantra

Is that special something missing from your relationship? Maybe what you need is a little pick-me-up that goes beyond some advice from Dr. Ruth. The **Kama Sutra** is an ancient text that describes things that have to be seen to be believed. (Unfortunately, you'll probably never see them.) Still, when you're sitting at home bored to distraction, there is some solace to be drawn in reading about adventurous techniques that have the potential to make the art of lovemaking even more fun than hanging out at the mall or watching Monday night football.

712 SEX

Urban Sex Legends

You know that Batman story you love to tell your friends? Well, it's not true. Really, it's not. In fact, there are a lot of weird sex legends that are not true. You can read all about them at this urban sex legends site. It's full of amusing stories and urban legends with a sexual twist.

Web:
http://www.urbanlegends.com/sex/

Is it really true? Read the Urban Sex Legends and judge for yourself.

Having company? Check out "Cooking and Recipes" or "Food and Drink".

SEXUALITY

Androgyny Information

The word "androgynous" has two related meanings. First, it can refer to something that has both male and female characteristics. Second, it can refer to something that is distinguishable as neither male or female (such as unisex clothing). On the Net, androgyny is often used to describe people whose gender roles are blurred, for example, transsexuals, transgendered individuals, transvestites and—by some people's standards—homosexuals. As you can imagine, this brave new androgynous world has a lot of vocabulary you have to learn if you are to fit in gracefully and not announce yourself as being so retro as to be politically incorrect by your mere presence. Or, as Rush Limbaugh is fond of saying, words mean something. Start here and learn the first word of the rest of your life.

Web:
http://www.chaparraltree.com/raq/

Look What I Found on the Net...

```
         (from the Kama Sutra, available on the Net)

                    To Enslave a Lover:

         Leaves caught as they fall from trees
         and powdered with peacock-bone
         and fragments of a corpse's winding-sheet
         will, when dusted lightly
         on the love organ, bewitch any woman living.
```

SEXUALITY

Dr. Ruth

This is the official site of Dr. Ruth Westheimer, a well-known American sex therapist. If you like Dr. Ruth, you will like this site. It has an extensive history of Dr. Ruth (with pictures), a daily sex tip (along with an archive of previous tips), an "Ask Doctor Ruth" section, and much more. You can also download funny icons—such as the wiggling sperm cursor—from the Dr. Ruth CD-ROM. Want more? You can find out about Dr. Ruth's books, her itinerary, and visit Ruth's Picks (favorite books, Web sites, etc). You have to register to get some of the goodies, but it's free. (Is it my imagination, or has someone created a large commercial enterprise around the image of a nice old lady who gives sex advice?)

Web:
http://www.drruth.com/

Human Sexuality

Sexuality means a lot more than sex. Sexuality affects how we act, how we dress, how we form relationships, how we relate to our society as a whole, and how we think about ourselves. The study of human sexuality is a broad one and in particular, it tends to blur when we discuss gender and its importance. Here is a great deal of useful information in this area.

Web:
http://www.sexuality.org/

Usenet:
soc.sexuality.general

Polyamory

The Law of Romantic Physics states that when there is too much love to go around, the excess has to go somewhere. I've found where it goes, and if you want to get some of it to take home with you, feel welcome. These resources describe the lifestyle of polyamory, in which multiple intimate relationships are pursued simultaneously. Polyamorous people share themselves with you (and you and you and you).

Web:
http://www.polyamory.org/

Usenet:
alt.personals.poly
alt.polyamory

Listserv Mailing List:
List Name: **poly**
Subscribe to: listserv@polyamory.org

> Tempt yourself in "Vices".

Purity Tests

Purity tests have long been a staple of Usenet humor groups. These tests consist of many sexually oriented questions designed to help you find out just how "pure" you are.

Web:
http://www.circus.com/~omni/purity.html
http://www.sexkittyn.com/newsbrief.html
http://www2.tower.org/purity/purity1.html

Sex Experts Talk and General Discussion

You're in the heat of the moment and a problem arises. What do you do? There's no time to write a letter to Dear Abby. However, if you have already joined the sex experts mailing list, you will have people to talk to when problems or questions arise. At one time, there was a Usenet discussion group called **alt.sex.wizards** that was a forum for sex experts. However, the group become overrun by spam (unsolicited advertising), and, well, you know the old saying: "When the going gets tough, the tough start a mailing list".

Majordomo Mailing List:
List Name: **sex-wizards**
Subscribe to: **majordomo@lists.jabberwocky.com**

Sex Laws

Have you noticed that almost everybody gets weird when you start talking seriously about sex in public? Sex is such a powerful force in our lives that people who cannot relate to it effectively are bound to repress the energy and have it pop up in strange ways. No doubt this has a lot to do with why there are so many strange laws about sex. Some of them are funny, some of them are terrible (such as the sex laws followed by certain religions), and all of them make for interesting reading.

Web:
http://www.lib.uchicago.edu/~llou/sexlaw.html

Sex Questions and Answers

Do you have a question about sex? It's probably already been answered in one of these FAQs. This Web page has listings of many of the **alt.sex** FAQs that are periodically posted to Usenet.

Web:
  http://www.adultfaq.com/

Sex Reference Guide

Here is an informative Web site that has information on just about every sex topic you can imagine (and even a few you can't imagine). The answers speak frankly and are easy to understand. If you have a sex-related question and you don't know anyone to ask (or you are too shy), this is a great place to get the information you need.

Web:
  http://www.sexualitydata.com/

Sexual Assault and Sex Abuse Recovery

There are times in your life when you have an urgent need for information but no easy way to find what you want. If you ever find yourself in a situation where you need information about sexual assault or abuse, please remember that the Net can help you deal with traumatic experiences and recover from sexual assault.

Web:
  http://www.cs.utk.edu/~bartley/saInfoPage.html
  http://www.rainn.org/

For a good time, see "Chemistry" and "Romance" (at the same time).

STD Information

These Web sites give information about STDs (sexually transmitted diseases), along with pictures. Pick a disease, any disease. (I picked trichomoniasis, which is caused by a protozoan.) Read about various STDs: how you get them, who gets them, how they are treated, and so on. To make sure you're safe, you can study a list of activities, ranked from high-risk to no-risk. These are good, informative pages, but not the least bit appetizing.

Web:
  http://med-www.bu.edu/people/sycamore/std/std.htm
  http://www.cafeherpe.com/

Look What I Found on the Net...

```
Newsgroup: alt.sex.wizards
Subject: Stretch Marks

> I had heard that stretch marks on women are generated as a
> result of having a baby.  My girlfriend has stretch marks all
> over her hips and in surrounding areas, though she says she
> has never been pregnant.  Is it true that one could get
> stretch marks even without being pregnant?

Yes, this is very possible.

Almost every girl I know has some stretch marks.  They are
sometimes caused by fat, but they can also be a simple
part of the growing process.  I have also gotten them from
working.
```

SHOPPING

Transvestite, Transsexual, Transgender

Anyone interested in transvestites, transsexuals or transgenders can find lots of information at these sites. Topics include hormone FAQs, cross-dressing, the International Bill of Gender Rights, myths about transvestites, and songs and poetry.

Web:
http://php.indiana.edu/~mberz/faqs.html
http://www.ftm-intl.org/links.html
http://www.tgguide.com/

Usenet:
alt.sex.trans
alt.transgendered
soc.support.transgendered

Listserv Mailing List:
List Name: **transgen**
Subscribe to: **listserv@brownvm.brown.edu**

SHOPPING

Auctions

Do you love the heart-pounding thrill of going to an auction, when it gets down to *mano a mano* bidding and you don't know how it's going to turn out? Going to an auction provides a raw, mercantile experience as close to pure buying and selling as you can get. If you have a day off, check with the Net and find out what auctions are scheduled for your area. If you are planning a trip to a new place, why not visit an auction while you are there? These auction-related resources will help you find an auction in the U.S. as well as many countries around the world.

Web:
http://www.auctionguide.com/
http://www.auctionweb.com/

Look What I Found on the Net...

```
Newsgroup: alt.transgendered
Subject: Mirrors
```

Who was he? The strange man in the mirror. I never knew. I laughed with him sometimes, cried with him more, yet I never knew who he was. We often stared at each other, but he never spoke to me nor betrayed his secrets to me.

I've heard that some people believe the mirror holds their soul and provides them a short visitation of it. Yet each time I came to the mirror, I was met by this cold stranger. I was forced by him to search within me to find my soul.

After long searching I finally came to her, sealed behind many walls and buried beneath tears and lies. I looked to her and cried, embracing her after so long. I began tending her wounds and helped her from that place, giving her freedom. She smiled and rose, filling me and embracing me. Now when I meet the mirror, I see her and she smiles tenderly to me. We share our thoughts and secrets. I speak fondly to her and feel her reply.

But I wonder what happened to the man in the mirror and who he was. I wish I could have known him and spoken to him. He is gone forever now. Perhaps he never existed, except as the guardian protecting my soul until she was strong enough to stand alone.

716 SHOPPING

Auction Acumen

If you're like me, you never pass through Overland Park, Kansas, without taking a few hours to visit the Auctioneer Hall of History.

However, being steeped in the lore of auctioneering won't help you when you are immersed in the hot and heavy, fast-moving environment of an actual auction.

After all, at an average household estate auction, an auctioneer will sell an average of 60 items per hour. And at a wholesale automobile auction, you may see as many as 150 cars sold per hour. When the auctioneer talks so fast, how can you possibly make any sense out of what he is saying?

"100 dollar bid, now 105, now 105, will ya give me 110? 110 dollar bid, now 120, now 120, will ya give me 120? 120 dollar bid, now 125, now 125, will ya give me 125?"

Here is a hint: ignore everything but the numbers. All the other words are used as fillers. Listen only to the numbers, and you will be surprised how easy it is to follow along like a pro.

Auctions Online

I have a friend named David Garstang who collects ancient coins. However, David is also a good husband and father who likes to stay home with his wife and two daughters. David lives in Southern California, and, as such, he would normally buy his ancient coins in the usual places: at the beach during a topless volleyball tournament, in a bar on wet T-shirt night, or while sailing a yacht off the Mexican coast. David, of course, being a good husband and father, cares nothing for such pastimes. Instead, he buys his ancient coins through online auctions over the Net. These auctions offer a wide variety of merchandise, bought and sold by people all over the world. No matter what your interests, there is probably someone selling what you want right now (especially if you are a collector). All the buying, selling and bidding is done via the Web and email, so you never have to leave your home. This works well for David, as he can stay home on Saturday nights, rather than wasting his time running around Southern California. (Did I mention that David is a good husband and father?)

Web:
  http://auctionuniverse.com/
  http://www.auctioninsider.com/
  http://www.ebay.com/aw/
  http://www.internetauctionlist.com/
  http://www.uauction.com/

Buying/Selling Talk and General Discussion

Where do you go on the Net when you want to buy or sell something? Here are the main buying/selling Usenet groups, the places where it is okay to post a personal advertisement, wheel and deal till you drop. These are also where to look for a bargain. Just remember, when you are dealing with someone whom you have never met, be sure to take normal precautions. (For example, if you are selling a house, don't actually send the house to the buyer until the check clears the bank.)

Usenet:
  alt.ads
  alt.ads.forsale
  alt.art.marketplace
  alt.fitness.marketplace
  alt.forsale
  alt.ham-radio.marketplace
  alt.magick.marketplace
  alt.marketplace
  alt.martial-arts.marketplace
  biz.marketplace.non-computer
  misc.forsale.computers
  misc.industry.electronics.marketplace
  rec.antiques.marketplace
  rec.aquaria.marketplace
  rec.arts.anime.marketplace
  rec.arts.books.marketplace
  rec.arts.comics.marketplace
  rec.arts.sf.marketplace
  rec.audio.marketplace
  rec.autos.marketplace
  rec.aviation.marketplace
  rec.bicycles.marketplace
  rec.boats.marketplace
  rec.crafts.marketplace
  rec.food.marketplace
  rec.games.board.marketplace
  rec.games.frp.marketplace
  rec.games.trading-cards.marketplace
  rec.games.video.marketplace
  rec.music.makers.marketplace
  rec.music.marketplace
  rec.music.marketplace.cd
  rec.music.marketplace.misc
  rec.music.marketplace.vinyl
  rec.outdoors.marketplace
  rec.photo.marketplace
  rec.skiing.marketplace
  rec.travel.marketplace
  rec.video.marketplace
  soc.genealogy.marketplace

SHOPPING

Catalogs by Mail

Catalog and junk mail fans will have a blast at this site. You can browse reviews of newly released mail order catalogs, order catalogs online, preview catalogs and even get some celebrity gossip about who is buying what these days.

Web:
  http://www.catalogsite.com/

CD Clubs

CD clubs have their system all set up so they can make lots of money off you. If you want a fighting chance of getting the best value for your money, you should check out this site. It has a FAQ on how to get the most out of CD clubs and information on the strategies of membership, resale value of CDs, the ins and outs of using club coupons, how to stop getting cards every month, how to return CDs you don't want, and more.

Web:
  http://www.eskimo.com/~bloo/cdfaq/toppage.htm

Classified Ads

Shopping, shopping, shopping. Do you like to shop, but don't like to get dressed to leave the house? Shop at home, by checking out the great classified ads on the Net.

Web:
  http://www.ep.com/

Comparisons

Before you make an important purchase, it's good to compare. Well, here's a Web site that can help you do just that. You can do side-by-side comparisons, read product reviews and articles about the products. I have a friend who successfully used this resource to buy a digital camera. First she found some information to read. Then she performed a search according to the specifications she wanted, which helped her narrow down the choices to the one she wanted. She now lives happily ever after (and you can too).

Web:
  http://www.compare.net/

Coupons

Do you need some coupons to get a nice discount on your favorite tea biscuit? Or do you have twelve coupons for Mr. Sticky hair gel that you'll probably never use? On the Net, I've found some places where you can exchange coupons and rebates with other coupon clippers. Oil up your scissors and get to clipping.

Web:
  http://www.customcoupon.com/
  http://www.hotcoupons.com/

Usenet:
  alt.coupons

Flea Markets

A flea market is an open-air marketplace in which low-cost goods are sold informally. And what could be more fun? I love walking around flea markets, and I bet you do too (and you can pick up some great bargains). Whenever the urge to bargain and buy cheap strikes without warning, here are some resources to help you find a nearby flea market.

Web:
  http://www.fleamarketguide.com/
  http://www.grt1.com/A1flea/

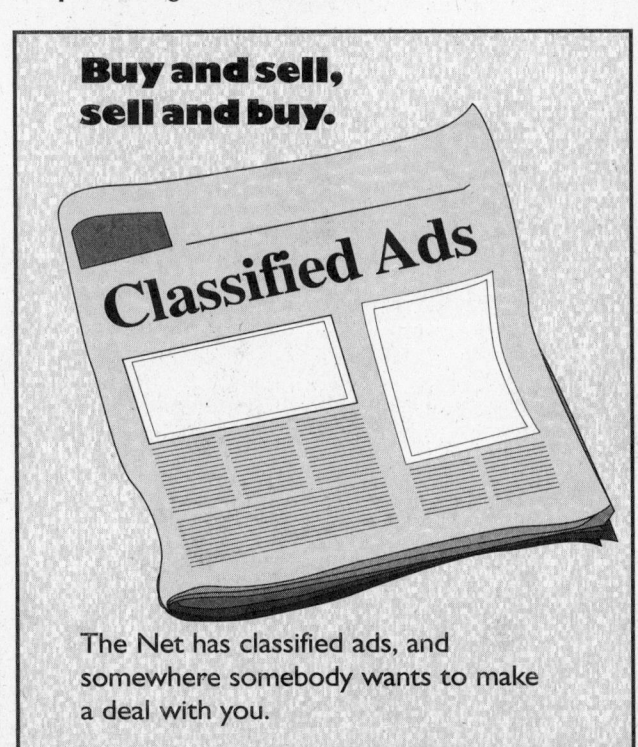

Buy and sell, sell and buy.

The Net has classified ads, and somewhere somebody wants to make a deal with you.

718 SHOPPING

Shopping Malls

Do you like to hang out at the mall? Of course you do. But wouldn't you like to know what's going to be on sale before you go? Even more important, what if you go on a trip to a city you have never visited? How are you going to find out where the malls are? No problem. The Net will help you find the mall you need with only a few clicks of the mouse. As long as we have the Net, you will never be deprived.

Web:
http://www.realmalls.com/

Shopping Online

There are a *lot* of places to buy stuff on the Net. (As Carl Sagan would say, "thousands and thousands"). Well, here are some resources to help you find the online shop of your dreams, out of more than 30,000. When you find the shop you want, there will be helpful information such as which credit cards are accepted, price range, phone number, email address, Web site address, as well as brief descriptions of what is for sale. If that's not enough, you can relax between shopping expeditions by reading articles, picking up a few tips, and talking to other online shopping buffs.

Web:
http://www.buyersindex.com/
http://www.buyitonline.com/

Shopping with Children

Shopping with children can be either a delightful pastime or—how can I put it?—a "challenge". My philosophy is to use the Boy Scout technique: be prepared. Here are some tips and hints that can make the difference between having a pleasant afternoon or developing past-traumatic stress syndrome.

Web:
http://www.familysupport.org/shopping.htm
http://www.kidsource.com/kidsource/content/
    shopping_tips.html
http://www.web-access.net/~child/shopping.htm

You are what you download.

Shopping Online

You can talk online. You can read the news online. You can even have a sexual encounter online.

And now you can shop online.

"...God's in His heaven — All's right with the world!"

SOFTWARE

Buying and Selling Software on the Internet

Here are the Usenet newsgroups in which people advertise software for sale. If you have software you don't need anymore, maybe someone else can use it. Or if you are looking for something in particular, someone out there may be able to help. Hint: Before you do send any money or goods, make sure you take routine precautions (get a phone number, talk to the person, and so on).

Usenet:
misc.forsale.computers.mac
misc.forsale.computers.other.software
misc.forsale.computers.pc

Cool Tool of the Day

This site picks a new "cool tool" every day. It's mostly technical stuff—Java programs, virtual reality, HTML editors, file management software, mail software, plug-ins, and so on—so if you are an Internet nerd, this is a nice place to check from time to time.

Web:
http://www.cooltool.com/

Free-DOS Project

Free-DOS is a project devoted to developing an entire DOS-compatible operating system, written by volunteers and shared for free (including source code). In other words, Free-DOS is to DOS as Linux is to Unix. If you would like to try the current version of Free-DOS or, better yet, volunteer to work on it, start by visiting the Free-DOS Internet site.

Web:
http://www.freedos.org/

Freeware

I love free—it's one of my favorite concepts. If you're like me, you'll love these Web sites, where you'll find oodles of real, useful programs—not demos—all for free. Hooray for freeware! That's what I say.

Web:
http://freeloader.simplenet.com/
http://www.freewarenow.com/

Jewish Software

Here are some nice collections of Jewish and Hebrew software: programs for using Hebrew on your computer, studying the Torah, Jewish calendars, Hebrew Internet software, and more (including a collection of pictures of the great rabbis). Now, if I can only find a program that can bake me a nice challah while I am waiting for a long download.

Web:
http://www.virtualjerusalem.com/gate/
http://www.zoots.com/cj/judaic.htm

Linux

Linux is a free Unix clone—originally developed by Linus Torvalds—maintained by a gaggle of hackers around the Internet. Linux was written completely from scratch to run on PCs using no "official" Unix code. The world of Linux is huge, and it is one of the most important (and unsung) achievements in the history of operating system development. The Usenet discussion groups are for ongoing discussion; the Web sites contain a lot of information, including source code, documentation and archives; the IRC channels are for real-time discussion.

Web:
http://sunsite.unc.edu/mdw/
http://www.linux.org/
http://www.linuxhelp.org/
http://www.linuxhq.com/

Usenet:
alt.uu.comp.os.linux.questions
comp.os.linux
comp.os.linux.admin
comp.os.linux.advocacy
comp.os.linux.alpha
comp.os.linux.announce
comp.os.linux.answers
comp.os.linux.development
comp.os.linux.development.apps
comp.os.linux.development.system
comp.os.linux.hardware
comp.os.linux.help
comp.os.linux.m68k
comp.os.linux.misc
comp.os.linux.networking
comp.os.linux.powerpc
comp.os.linux.questions
comp.os.linux.setup
comp.os.linux.x

IRC:
#linux
#linuxos

"Interesting Technologies" is interesting.

720 SOFTWARE

Linux

Every now and then, some person gets an idea that takes on a life of its own and changes our culture. Such a person is Linus Torvalds, the original developer of the Linux operating system (now maintained by a large group of people around the Net).

Linux is one of those wonders—a professional-quality operating system put together entirely by volunteers—that makes you realize how important the Net really is to human affairs. In these days of no real Unix standard, Linux is the closest we have to a universal Unix. The wonderful thing is that, since no one is in it for the money, Bill Gates can't buy it.

(And I am *not* kidding.)

Macintosh Games

What's the point of having a computer without games? Join these Usenet groups to talk about all aspects of Macintosh games: which ones are best, which ones to avoid, copy protection issues, as well as hints and tricks.

Usenet:
comp.sys.mac.games
comp.sys.mac.games.action
comp.sys.mac.games.adventure
comp.sys.mac.games.announce
comp.sys.mac.games.flight-sim
comp.sys.mac.games.marketplace
comp.sys.mac.games.misc
comp.sys.mac.games.strategic

Macintosh Software Archives

There is more free Macintosh software on the Net than you can shake a mouse at. Here are some good places to start foraging for goodies. Surely, your Mac-cup will runneth over (and goodness and mercy shall follow you all the days of your life).

Web:
http://hyperarchive.lcs.mit.edu/HyperArchive.html
http://mirror.apple.com/
http://www.mac.org/
http://www.macoszone.com/
http://www.macshare.com/

Macintosh Software Talk and General Discussion

Visit these Usenet groups for discussions of Macintosh software of all types. The **apps** group is for talk about any type of application; **comm** is for communications; **databases** is for database systems; and **system** is for Macintosh system software (such as Finder and Multifinder), as well as working with disks, dealing with viruses, and so on.

Usenet:
comp.sys.mac.apps
comp.sys.mac.comm
comp.sys.mac.databases
comp.sys.mac.system

Macintosh Games

Macintoshes are good for a lot more than graphics, desktop publishing, and impressing your friends with your good taste in computers.

Macs are great for playing games, and the sooner you start, the faster you can fulfill your destiny as a human being.

Macintosh Version Tracker

One of the nice things about being on the Net is that you can download mega-oodles of free software. But once you get all that software, you have obligations. You must keep that software up-to-date or face the wrath of the computer gods. If you are a Mac user, this Web site can make your life a lot easier. It keeps track of many different popular programs and shows you the latest versions. Any time you want, it is a simple matter to make sure you have the newest and greatest programs running on your computer.

Web:
http://www.versiontracker.com/

Nonags

This is one of my favorite resources: a Web site that can point you to no-nag shareware and freeware. Every program here has been tested to make sure it doesn't nag you or enforce time limits in order to encourage you to buy. This makes evaluating software a lot more pleasant. (Obligatory reminder: if you use shareware and you find it useful, please register and send the person who wrote the program a few bucks.)

Web:
http://www.nonags.com/

Non-English Software

Not everyone in the world speaks English, so it's great to have a resource where you can get information on non-English software. Post your queries or your finds on this Usenet group. Visit the Web sites for online resources.

Web:
http://www.lib.ox.ac.uk/internet/news/faq/comp.software.international.html
http://www.threeweb.ad.jp/logos/

Usenet:
comp.software.international

OS/2 Games

These Web sites contain games specifically for OS/2. In general, there is a pathetic lack of OS/2 game collections on the Net. If IBM were smart, they would spend some time and money getting obsessive gamers caught up in OS/2. My idea is for them to provide summer internships for students to create shareware gaming software for OS/2. IBM could pay the students a stipend to develop games, with the understanding that the finished products would be released as shareware on the Net. The students would then get to keep any money brought in by shareware registrations. It would be a win-win-win situation (IBM-programmers-you), that would help increase the installed base for OS/2. In the meantime, OS/2 people, you can enjoy the games at these sites.

Web:
http://www.juge.com/bbs/Fern.2.Html
http://www.os2games.com/

Usenet:
comp.os.os2.games

> **Get your Mom on the Net.**

OS/2 Networking Environment

If you love the OS/2 operating system and want to get it networked, check out these discussion groups relating to the OS/2 environment. You will find general discussion and information on TCP/IP, as well as troubleshooting opportunities. Don't leave your home directory without it.

Usenet:
comp.os.os2.networking
comp.os.os2.networking.misc
comp.os.os2.networking.tcp-ip

OS/2 Software Archives

There is lots of OS/2 software available, if you know where to look for it. I know where to look for it. And now, so do you.

Web:
ftp://ftp.cdrom.com/pub/os2/
http://hobbes.nmsu.edu/
http://oak.oakland.edu/pub/os2/

OS/2 Utilities

I love utilities. I could spend hours and hours downloading and experimenting with new programs. To tell you the truth, I usually end up not using most of the utilities I download, but I love trying them out. This is a huge, comprehensive, well-organized archive of everything under the OS/2 sun. If you are searching for a specific type of program (such as a utility or Internet client), this is a good place to look.

Web:
http://www.juge.com/bbs/Os2.Html

Software Archives

If you like computers and you like trying out software for free, you will love these places: huge archives where you can find programs for every popular operating system. When I die, I am going to have someone sprinkle my ashes on these Web sites. You could spend an eternity here, just downloading and playing with software.

Web:

http://www.filez.com/
http://www.jumbo.com/
http://www.pcworld.com/fileworld/
http://www.shareware.com/

Usenet:

comp.archives
comp.archives.admin

Software Licensing

If you are thinking about starting to license software that you have written, read up on licensing issues. This is an archive of articles about licensing software and license management.

Web:

http://www.globetrotter.com/resource.htm

Software Testing Talk and General Discussion

Testing software is not easy. You need lots of time, effort and a good design. Then you need to know someone to pray to. The problem is that too much software is rushed without allowing for proper planning and quality control. This Usenet group is for talking about the testing of software and computer systems. If you are interested in this area of programming, you will find useful discussion and sympathetic colleagues.

Usenet:

comp.software.testing

You need some more software.
Don't ask me how I know, I just know.
Visit the Software Archives right away.

Spam Filtering Software

Spam is unsolicited advertising, and there is too much of it on the Net. Have you ever received spam in your mailbox? If so, take a look at these tools, designed to help you guard against unwanted electronic junk mail. There's no way to ever get the spammers to stop, so you might as well protect yourself. On the Internet, social problems are solved by software.

Web:

http://www.best.com/~ariel/nospam/
http://www.cix.co.uk/~net-services/spam/
http://www.newapps.com/appstopics/
   Win_95_Anti-SPAM_Tools.html
http://www.spammerslammer.com/

TCP/IP

TCP/IP is the glue that holds the Internet together. If you want to have your computer on the Internet, it will have to run some type of TCP/IP software. These Usenet groups are for discussion of the zillions and zillions of technical considerations that are unavoidably relevant. A good way to start is by reading the FAQ, which is posted regularly to the groups. Don't get discouraged: all things come to those who think.

Usenet:

comp.protocols.tcp-ip
comp.protocols.tcp-ip.domains
comp.protocols.tcp-ip.ibmpc

Windows CE Software Archives

I have a friend, Mart, who loves his palmtop computer. He took it on a trip to Thailand and used it to write some cool articles about his experiences. However, in order to use any computer, you need good software. Windows CE is the Microsoft operating system designed for tiny computers, such as palmtops and embedded systems, and if you have a palmtop, you will really appreciate these Web sites. There is a lot of Windows CE software to choose from, and you'll have many happy hours downloading cool stuff to try out. It certainly keeps Mart happy and out of trouble. (He gets bored easily.)

Web:
  http://www.wincecity.com/software.html
  http://www.winfiles.com/apps/ce/

Windows Game Software

If you want games for Windows, here are the places to look, especially if you want something to keep the kids busy at the computer while you are off somewhere doing adult stuff. There is a huge selection of games, enough to keep you occupied from now through St. Swithin's Day.

Web:
  http://www.happypuppy.com/compgames/pc/
  http://www.happypuppy.com/lordsoth/

Windows Networking Environment

Getting a network running is often troublesome. Have some back-up help ready in the form of Usenet groups. These groups offer a good source of information on general networking, TCP/IP, and network programming with the Microsoft Windows operating system.

Usenet:
  comp.os.ms-windows.networking.misc
  comp.os.ms-windows.networking.tcp-ip
  comp.os.ms-windows.networking.windows
  comp.os.ms-windows.programmer.networks

> **Be all you can pretend to be.**

Windows Software

These are my picks as the best Windows software sites on the Net. They contain grotesque amounts of shareware and freeware for you to download and enjoy. Everything you could possibly want is here somewhere. When it comes to free Windows software, if you can't find it at one of these sites, it's not worth finding.

Web:
  http://cws.internet.com/
  http://www.hotfiles.com/
  http://www.tucows.com/
  http://www.winfiles.com/
  http://www.winsite.com/

Usenet:
  comp.archives.ms-windows
  comp.archives.ms-windows.announce
  comp.archives.ms-windows.discuss

SOUNDS

Animal Sounds

These sounds are a lot of fun, especially if you have children. Listen to birds, whales, dolphins, seals, ducks, cows, zebras, polar bears, tigers, turkeys, pigs, dogs, donkeys, elephants, frogs, goats, cats, and more. I have also included a site that has a list of animal noises as they are pronounced in other languages. For example, a cat noise in English is "meow", but in other languages it is "miao" (Chinese), "meu" (Catalan), "myau" (Ukrainian) and "niaou" (Greek). (I wonder what cats say in Klingon?)

Web:
  http://netvet.wustl.edu/sounds.htm
  http://www.georgetown.edu/cball/animals/animals.html
  http://www.idsweb.com/~zephyr/audio/animals.html
  http://www.io.com/~hmiller/AnimalSounds.html

Bird Sounds

Here is a cool collection of bird sounds that are pleasant and engaging. One of my favorites is the kookaburra (a large Australian kingfisher bird that sounds like a fat lady laughing at a Marx Brothers movie). You can also listen to bluejays, chickadees, crows, cockatoos, magpies, peewees, ravens, and more. (Quick bird-sound story: When I was in medical school, I once had a couple of friends over to my apartment. As a trick, one of the friends [Paul Walton] and I put on an album of tropical bird sounds and turned the volume down very low. The other friend, whose name I won't mention [Tim Rutledge], had no idea what we had done. Now this was in a small apartment in downtown Toronto, and every few minutes Tim would sit up and say, "Do you guys hear anything?" "No, Tim," we would reply, "you must be hearing things." He never figured it out. (Today, Tim is a respected emergency room physician, a wonderful husband and the father of three sons. So, if you ever meet him, don't mention anything.)

Web:
http://www.ocean.ic.net/rafiles/nature/

Christmas Sounds

On the Net, Christmas lasts all year. Not only is the entire Internet suffused with the spirit of charity, love, forgiveness and sanctity, but you can listen to Christmas sounds whenever you want: enjoy dogs barking the tune "Jingle Bells", listen to sound clips from "How the Grinch Stole Christmas", laugh at parodies of traditional Christmas songs. Truly, the spirit of holiness and reverence is never out of season.

Web:
http://www.acebiz.com/xmasmidi/xmasmidi.htm
http://www.hometurf.com/xmas.html

Goldwave

Goldwave is a digital audio editor that can open, play, modify and convert just about any sound format you have heard of. You can make use of special effects such as Doppler, distortion, echo, flange and transposition. Goldwave is especially useful if you do audio work with Java applications. This is great software. Once you try it, I know you will like it (and I bet you will want to pay the registration fee). There are enough auditory bells and whistles here to equip the entire Peruvian army.

Web:
http://www.goldwave.com/

Animal Sounds

Just because you don't have a pet doesn't mean you have to feel left out.

There are lots of animal sounds on the Net to make sure that you never get lonely.

Insulting Sound Files

What could be more fun than insulting someone? Insulting them out loud. Here is an archive of rude, obnoxious and aggravating sound files. The next time you have a few spare moments, go to this site, download some sounds and email them to your friends. It won't be long before you can count yourself in that select group of persons who know how to win friends and influence people. (Just don't tell them you read about it here.)

Web:
http://www.getbent.com/

MIDI Archives

Put away that CD player and download some MIDI sound files. If you don't have the software, don't worry. The MIDI Archives has gone on safari in the wilds of the Internet to find all the software you need to process MIDI sound files.

Web:
  http://www.cs.ruu.nl/pub/MIDI/
  http://www.harmony-central.com/MIDI/
  http://www.midiarchive.com/
  http://www.midifarm.com/
  http://www.midiweb.com/
  http://www.tornadotech.com/midi/
  http://www.webthumper.com/midi/

Usenet:
  alt.binaries.sounds.midi
  alt.music.midi
  alt.music.midiweb
  comp.music.midi

IRC:
  #midi

Number Synthesizer

Type in a number and this program will say it to you out loud. This is just the thing to use when someone asks you for a number. For example, say that you are eating dinner when you are bothered by a telemarketer. Tell him, "I would like to talk to you later, can I give you a number where you can call me back?" Then connect to this Web page, type in a 15-digit number and hold the phone near your computer. The person will be treated to a mechanical voice reciting your number. When he asks, "What was that?" tell him, "That was my servant Robbie the Robot. I can never remember all the numbers in my life, so he remembers for me. Would you like to listen again?" Then play the number back to him seven or eight times. Isn't the Internet cool?

Web:
  http://www.cs.yale.edu/cgi-bin/saynumber.au

Sound Archives

Special occasions call for special sounds. Some days you will need a little Beavis and Butthead. Some days you will need some classic Monty Python or maybe a friendly cartoon sound file. Never again will you have to listen to the sounds of silence at your computer. Check out the many sound archives available on the Net.

Web:
  http://www.cartoonwavs.com/
  http://www.dailywav.com/
  http://www.iexp.com/cgi-bin/iei/multimedia.cgi
  http://www.nh.ultranet.com/~helps/wavs.shtml
  http://www.sky.net/~jdeshon/joewav.html
  http://www.soundamerica.com/
  http://www.wavcentral.com/

Sound Archives

When you need the special sound that makes all the difference, the Net can help.
Check with the *Sound Archives*, and you will never have to remain silent.

Sound Tools

Why sweat the small stuff when you can let the computer do the work? Here are collections of sound tools for working with sound files under various operating systems. Grab a tool and go wild.

Web:
  http://www.partnersinrhyme.com/mainPCmidi.html
  http://www.partnersinrhyme.com/PCmain.html
  http://www.winfiles.com/apps/98/sound.html

726 SOUNDS

Sounds and Sound Effects

Here are some great collections of sound files good for various occasions (such as scaring your mother-in-law or convincing your boss you are sick).

Web:
  http://www.bayside.net/users/joester/effects.htm
  http://www.cyberspy.com/~visual/sound.html

Television and Movie Sounds

Never again will you have to be nervous about being charming and witty the next time you go to a party. Just memorize some of these television and movie sounds. When people come up to talk to you, do your best to imitate what you've heard on the Web, and it won't be long before everyone will want to be your friend.

Web:
  http://www.moviesounds.com/
  http://www.tvwavs.com/
  http://www.waveguy.com/

SPACE

Aeronautics and Space Acronyms

If your space capsule has just landed in the ocean and mission control asks if you want an ACRV, you certainly don't want to answer incorrectly. Take a moment and look it up in this long list of space-related acronyms: a good reference to keep on hand if you are reading anything about space exploration.

Web:
  http://www.users.uswest.net/~dinosaur/list.html

Center for Earth and Planetary Studies

The Center for Earth and Planetary Studies is one of the research units at the National Air and Space Museum of the Smithsonian Institution. Visit their Web site and experience the excitement of outer space without having to go too far from the fridge. There are a lot of pictures from space, as well as information about many of the U.S. space missions.

Web:
  http://ceps.nasm.edu:2020/

Challenger

In the history of manned space flight, there have been some terrible disasters. The most well-known was the explosion of the Challenger space shuttle 73 seconds after takeoff on January 28, 1986. For information about that ill-fated mission, you can look at NASA's Web site. There you can find the official technical information regarding that particular mission, including a movie of the takeoff and explosion.

Web:
  http://www.ksc.nasa.gov/shuttle/missions/51-l/mission-51-l.html

Electronic Universe Project

Space is cool because there is so much of it and it's just waiting to be filled with stuff. Get a closer look at our very own galaxy with all its stars and nebulae and planets. See movies of interacting galaxies and images and light curves of a recent supernova. If you want to impress your special loved one with your knowledge of the stars, but the sky happens to be cloudy, this site can be your backup plan.

Web:
  http://zebu.uoregon.edu/galaxy.html

There's no place on Earth like the world. But when you get tired of all this Earth stuff, connect to the **Electronic Universe Project** and get the rest of the story.

European Space Agency

The European Space Agency (ESA) was formed in 1975 through the cooperation of a number of European countries. Each of the countries makes a financial contribution based on which activities that country wishes to support. ESA's major programs include the Ariane rocket, the Spacelab scientific workshop (which is carried into orbit by the space shuttle), and Arianespace, a division of ESA, which produces over half of all commercial satellite launches in the world.

Web:
  http://www.esrin.esa.it/

Listserv Mailing List:
  List Name: esapress
  Subscribe to: listserv@vmprofs.esoc.esa.de

SPACE

European Space Information System

The European Space Information System (ESIS) is part of the European Space Agency (ESA). ESIS provides access to scientific data, including catalogs, images, spectra, and time series from ESA/non-ESA space missions. A bibliographic service allows you to read abstracts from a wide range of scientific journals.

Web:
http://vizier.u-strasbg.fr/

Goddard Space Flight Center

The Goddard Space Flight Center manages many of NASA's programs having to do with finding out information about Earth itself. As such, the Center is a major U.S. laboratory devoted to developing unmanned space probes. Their Web site contains information about their programs and research.

Web:
http://www.gsfc.nasa.gov/

History of Space Exploration

If you ever want to go to a new town and try to pass yourself off as an astronaut, it's best if you know some of the history of space exploration. You can never tell when a resident astrophysicist or know-it-all little kid will come in and start asking questions that will blow your cover. This site will fill you in on all the basics: a chronology, information about U.S. missions such as Apollo, Mariner, Viking and Voyager, as well as details about some of the missions of the former Soviet Union.

Web:
http://bang.lanl.gov/solarsys/eng/history.htm

Lunar Photographs

If you want to see the moon, but it's a cloudy night and you can't see any celestial bodies, you take comfort in knowing that you can see the moon on the Internet. Brew up a hot drink, wrap yourself in a cozy blanket and curl up in front of the computer. These are gorgeous pictures and make cloudy nights a pleasure.

Web:
http://www.netaxs.com/~mhmyers/moon.tn.html

> Learn how to use a search engine and the world is at your fingertips.

Mars Images

With the landing of the Mars Pathfinder spacecraft (July 4, 1997), and the subsequent arrival of the Mars Global Surveyor, a new era in space exploration has begun. Since then, a great many pictures of Mars and its landscape have been transmitted to Earth—pictures that you can look at on your own computer via the Internet. (You know, it really hasn't been that long since people thought push-button phones were the last word in modern technology.)

Web:
http://mpfwww.jpl.nasa.gov/
http://www.jpl.nasa.gov/marsnews/img/

NASA Historical Archive

It's good to know your NASA space history. For instance, what if you are at the supermarket and the checkout girl says that if you can list the dates of all the Apollo missions you will be the lucky winner of a month's worth of Cheese Doodles? Imagine how sorry you'd feel if you couldn't do it. There's absolutely no need for this to happen as long as you make sure to read all the documents at the NASA Historical Archive. They offer the text of the NASA Space Act, information about rocket history, early astronauts, astronautics history, chronology, manned missions and details about the space shuttles. (Please, no spies allowed.)

Web:
http://www.ksc.nasa.gov/history/history.html

Usenet:
sci.space.history

728 SPACE

The Real Challenge

To you and me, NASA (the National Aeronautics and Space Administration) may be the embodiment of our science fiction dreams of space travel. But in reality, NASA is a department of the U.S. government and, like all such departments, NASA must periodically justify its existence and its budget.

One way in which NASA does this is to make valuable information about their programs available to anyone on the Net. If you are interested in what NASA has done, take a few minutes to check out their site. Much of it is boring (remember, the "A" *does* stand for "Administration"), and a lot of the details are hidden behind cryptic acronyms. However, if you dig deeply enough, you will find some aeronautical jewels.

For example, the mission number of the ill-fated Challenger space shuttle was 51-l. (That's 51-hyphen-lowercase "L.") The technical descriptions of this mission are rather pedestrian, dismissing the final outcome in a few nondescript sentences. But if you know where to look, you can find a video clip of the actual explosion. Here it is:

http://www.ksc.nasa.gov/shuttle/missions/51-l/movies/51-l-launch2.mpg

Hints: (1) Remember, the character after "51-" is a lowercase "L." (2) You will need an mpeg viewer to watch this video clip.

NASA News

Keep up on the latest information from NASA, including the status of spacecraft currently in space. Find out about the new discoveries made with the space-based Hubble telescope and the unmanned probes launched toward distant planets and galaxies.

Web:
http://spacelink.msfc.nasa.gov/NASA.News/

NASA (the National Aeronautics and Space Administration) is always up to something. Now you can be in the loop. Just connect to the NASA Web site and get the straight poop from the official American space people. Be aware, though, that this is *official* NASA info, so you may not find out much about the government's cover-up of secret alien contacts.

NASA Research Labs

It's your turn to plan an exciting date for you and the one you love. How about a tour of some of the most famous NASA research labs? After a romantic candlelit dinner you can go back to your place, fire up the old Web browser and roam through the Goddard, Dryden, Ames, Langley and Kennedy space centers, to name just a few. In no time, word will be out that you really know how to entertain in style.

Web:
http://www.nasa.gov/nasaorgs/subject_index.html

NASDA

The National Space Development Agency (NASDA) is Japan's national agency for space development. NASDA's Web site has information about their activities, publications and technical developments. Here you can find descriptions of NASDA's work on the international space station. There are also technical details regarding the H-II rocket (the central launch vehicle in the Japanese space program), just in case you want to build one for yourself.

Web:
   http://yyy.tksc.nasda.go.jp/Home/This/thisindex_e.html

Planetary Nebulae Gallery

When the weather outside is lousy, but you want to get in a little romantic star-gazing action with the person of your dreams, check out this gallery of beautiful, colorful images of nebulae. This might even be better than the real thing.

Web:
   http://www.ozemail.com.au/~mhorn/pneb.html

Planets

Would you like to find out more about the planets in our solar system? Here are some Web sites that have spectacular pictures of the planets, as well as a lot of information. These are the places I go when I need to get my hands on a picture of Neptune or find out the diameter of Mars (6787 kilometers).

Web:
   http://pds.jpl.nasa.gov/planets/
   http://spider.msfc.nasa.gov/ed13/pictureserv/planets.html

Politics of Space

Do people belong in space? Is all the money worth it? What should we be doing and who should we be doing it with? Discuss non-technical issues pertaining to space exploration.

Usenet:
   sci.space.policy

SETI

Do you get tired of the same old smart people here on earth? Get a new cultural and intellectual perspective on the universe by looking in at the Search for Extraterrestrial Intelligence (SETI) institute. These people spend their time searching for extraterrestrial intelligence and want to share what they have found with you. Their Web site has links to science and technology relating to astronomy and planetary sciences as well as biological and cultural revolution. This is the perfect place to start if you are looking for new friends from other planets (unless, of course, you already have your own spaceship).

Web:
   http://www.seti-inst.edu/

SETI: SEARCH FOR EXTRATERRESTRIAL INTELLIGENCE

IF WE DON'T LOOK FOR ALIENS, HOW WILL WE EVER KNOW IF THEY REALLY EXIST? IT'S NOT LIKE THEY ARE GOING TO GET INTO SPACESHIPS AND COME TO US.

Shuttle Snapshots

Snapshots of an astronaut's excursion are going to be much more exciting than Aunt Ethel's pictures of her trip to Haqualoochie, Oklahoma, to visit the grandkids. See images of places like Bangkok, Mount St. Helens, Finger Lakes, Alaska, and the Grand Canyon taken from various space shuttle missions.

Web:
   http://zebu.uoregon.edu/earth.html

730 SPACE

Solar System Exploration

There has been a lot of exploration of our solar system, but except for some transient news coverage, few people really understand the significance of what has been done and what it means to us. Here is a Web page with information about some of mankind's most impressive and most important achievements.

Web:
http://www.hq.nasa.gov/office/solar_system/

Space Calendar

If you think it's disastrous when you lose your datebook, how do you think NASA feels? When you are shooting live human beings into space at high speeds, it's important to keep your scheduling straight. Check here if you want to keep up on what's happening in the cosmos.

Web:
http://newproducts.jpl.nasa.gov/calendar/

Space Frequently Asked Questions

Get answers to the most frequently asked questions (FAQs) regarding NASA, spaceflight and astrophysics. (For example, is it true that the blueprints for the Saturn V were lost?) If you are interested in space and spaceflight, this is a great source of fascinating information.

Web:
http://www.faqs.org/faqs/space/

Want to know all the answers about NASA and spaceflight? Read the Space FAQ (frequently asked question list).

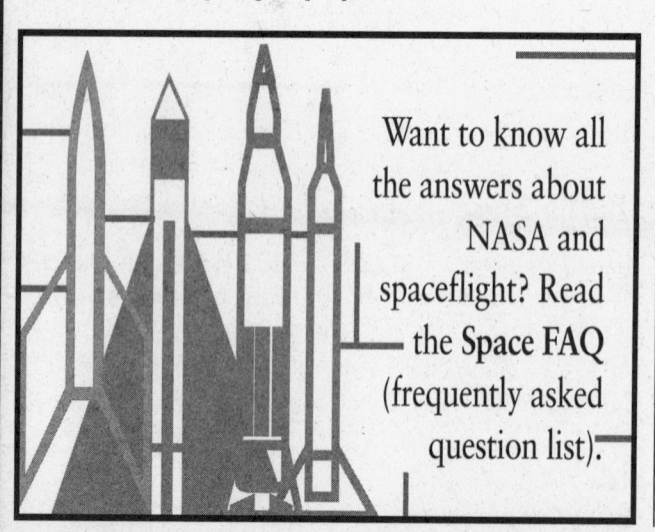

Space Movie Archive

Would you like to see space scenes without having to leave the house? This site has a large number of space animations that you can view in the privacy of your own Web browser.

Web:
http://graffiti.u-bordeaux.fr/MAPBX/roussel/astro.html

Space News

Keep current on the final frontier. Read all the latest news about space, astronomy and spaceflight. Now that you have a connection to the Net, there is no excuse for being the last one on your block to know whether or not there really once was life on Mars.

Web:
http://www.chron.com/content/interactive/space/
http://www.earthsciencenews.com/
http://www.exosci.com/
http://www.flatoday.com/space/
http://www.foxnews.com/scitech/space/index.sml
http://www.spaceviews.com/
http://www.uttm.com/space/

Usenet:
sci.space.news

Space Shuttle

The space shuttle is a reusable American space vehicle. The first shuttle test flight took place on April 12, 1981. The first operational flight was on November 11, 1982. For information about the shuttle program, including a lot of technical details, you can check NASA's Web sites. For discussion, try the Usenet group.

Web:
http://www.ksc.nasa.gov/shuttle/missions/missions.html
http://www.ksc.nasa.gov/shuttle/technology/sts-newsref/stsref-toc.html

Usenet:
sci.space.shuttle

SPORTS AND ATHLETICS

Space Talk and General Discussion
Talk, talk, talk about everything under the sun (and the sun as well). Discuss all manner of space-oriented topics with aficionados around the world.

Usenet:
sci.space
sci.space.science

Students for the Exploration and Development of Space
SEDS is a student club devoted to the discussion and study of space. Meet people from SEDS chapters around the world. Find out all the latest space news and what SEDS members are up to.

Web:
http://seds.lpl.arizona.edu/

United Nations Office for Outer Space Affairs
Everyone is anxiously awaiting the news about extraterrestrials joining the United Nations. The U.N. even has an office for Outer Space Affairs which focuses on international cooperation regarding the use of space technology to monitor space activities as well as our terrestrial environment. See the U.N.'s latest activities at their Web site.

Web:
http://www.un.or.at/OOSA_Kiosk/

What in heaven's name is going on in the space shuttle? Read **sci.space.shuttle** *and keep up with the only government employees who are paid to get high.*

Viking Image Archive
The nice thing about unmanned orbiting vessels is that nobody has to spend all that time out in space without the benefit of pizza delivery. Take a look at some of the thousands of images sent back by Viking orbiters from 1976 to 1980. You can choose the resolution or coordinates you want to examine more closely. This is just like being in the driver's seat, except you don't have to wear a seat belt.

Web:
http://barsoom.msss.com/http/vikingdb.html

Windows to the Universe
The universe is one of my favorite places in the whole world. Why do I like it so much? There are three reasons. First, the universe has an awe-inspiring grandeur that never fails to make me feel humble and privileged at the same time. Second, the universe is an endless source of interesting knowledge that constantly amazes and enlightens me. Third, all my stuff is here. If you are interested in space and what's out there, I know you will enjoy touring this Web site. This is an especially good place to visit if you happen to be a bright child or know a bright child. (Actually, when I was a child I was so bright my parents called me "son".)

Web:
http://www.windows.umich.edu/

SPORTS AND ATHLETICS

Aikido
Aikido is a non-violent martial art that uses throws and joint locks to neutralize opponents instead of using kicks and punches. Aikido was developed by Morihei Ueshiba and was partially adapted from Daito-Ryu Jujitsu. On the Net you can find lots of general information about the art of aikido.

Web:
http://www.aikiweb.com/
http://www.ii.uib.no/~kjartan/aikidofaq/

Listserv Mailing List:
List Name: **aikido-l**
Subscribe to: **listserv@lists.psu.edu**

Archery

Start practicing your archery now, because you never know when one day you will be called upon to play Robin Hood in your local community theater group. Imagine being up on stage and having to play out a rescue scene without being properly prepared. One wild shot and you could put out somebody's eye. Don't let this happen to you. Read the important archery documents that are available on the Net.

Web:
   http://www.archerynetwork.com/
   http://www.smart.net/~stimsonr/framlink.html
   http://www.student.utwente.nl/campus/sagi/arlinks/

Usenet:
   alt.archery
   rec.sport.archery

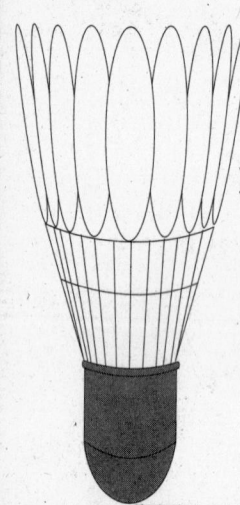

Badminton

Do you enjoy using a long, narrow-handled racket to volley a shuttlecock back and forth over a high, narrow net?

If so, the badminton resources on the Net will enhance your experience.

Badminton

When rollerblading is too rough and needlework is too tame, try a little badminton for a change of pace. On the Net you can find tips for coaching and training, stretching and flexibility, and backhand technique, as well as rules and a glossary of humorous terms.

Web:
   http://mid1.external.hp.com/stanb/badminton.html
   http://www.huizen.dds.nl/~anita/badmint.html

Usenet:
   alt.sports.badminton

Baseball

Baseball is played in the United States, Japan, Mexico, Cuba and other countries. In the U.S., baseball is so popular it is often referred as the "National Pastime". (Actually, there are three National Pastimes. The other two are complaining about taxes and criticizing the President.) Legend has it that baseball was invented in 1839 by Abner Doubleday, but it just ain't so. Modern baseball developed from a more rudimentary version that was played in the early nineteenth century, based on the English games of cricket and rounders. Today, baseball—especially in the U.S.—has millions of devoted fans. If you are one of them, you will love these resources, where you can cruise through massive amounts of information about major and minor leagues around the world: scores, standings, schedules, statistics, rosters, injury reports, and much, much more.

Web:
   http://www.majorleaguebaseball.com/
   http://www.nando.net/SportServer/baseball/
   http://www.tns.lcs.mit.edu/cgi-bin/
      sports-schedule?sport=mlb
   http://www.totalbaseball.com/

Usenet:
   rec.sport.baseball
   rec.sport.baseball.analysis
   rec.sport.baseball.college
   rec.sport.baseball.data
   rec.sport.baseball.fantasy

Majordomo Mailing List:
   List Name: minors
   Subscribe to: majordomo@plaidworks.com

IRC:
   #baseball

The best way to make money is to give something away for free.

SPORTS AND ATHLETICS

> Need to fix the plumbing? See "Homes". Need to fix a horse race? See "Vices".

Baseball Teams

On those days when it's not enough to watch your favorite team at the stadium or on television, do some reading on their stats, standings and other team information on the Net.

Web:
http://espn.sportszone.com/mlb/standings/

Usenet:
alt.sports.baseball.atlanta-braves
alt.sports.baseball.balt-orioles
alt.sports.baseball.bos-redsox
alt.sports.baseball.calif-angels
alt.sports.baseball.chi-whitesox
alt.sports.baseball.chicago-cubs
alt.sports.baseball.cinci-reds
alt.sports.baseball.cleve-indians
alt.sports.baseball.col-rockies
alt.sports.baseball.detroit-tigers
alt.sports.baseball.fla-marlins
alt.sports.baseball.houston-astros
alt.sports.baseball.kc-royals
alt.sports.baseball.la-dodgers
alt.sports.baseball.minor-leagues
alt.sports.baseball.mke-brewers
alt.sports.baseball.mn-twins
alt.sports.baseball.montreal-expos
alt.sports.baseball.ny-mets
alt.sports.baseball.ny-yankees
alt.sports.baseball.oakland-as
alt.sports.baseball.phila-phillies
alt.sports.baseball.pitt-pirates
alt.sports.baseball.sd-padres
alt.sports.baseball.sea-mariners
alt.sports.baseball.sf-giants
alt.sports.baseball.stl-cardinals
alt.sports.baseball.texas-rangers
alt.sports.baseball.tor-bluejays

Basketball

Having basketball fever doesn't mean that you just sit in front of the television making loud whooping noises. It's much more sophisticated than that. It's a fine balance of gathering statistics, analyzing trends, and making studied observations. On the Net you can find all you need to become a seasoned basketball fan.

Web:
http://www.canoe.ca/Basketball/
http://www.nba.com/
http://www.sportsline.com/u/basketball/nba/stats.htm

Usenet:
rec.sport.basketball
rec.sport.basketball.college
rec.sport.basketball.europe
rec.sport.basketball.misc
rec.sport.basketball.pro

IRC:
#basketball
#nba

Basketball

In 1891, James Naismith invented the game of basketball at the Springfield, Massachusetts, YMCA.

A little over one hundred years later, the Web was created.

Now you can combine the best of both worlds: visit the basketball Web site of your choice today.

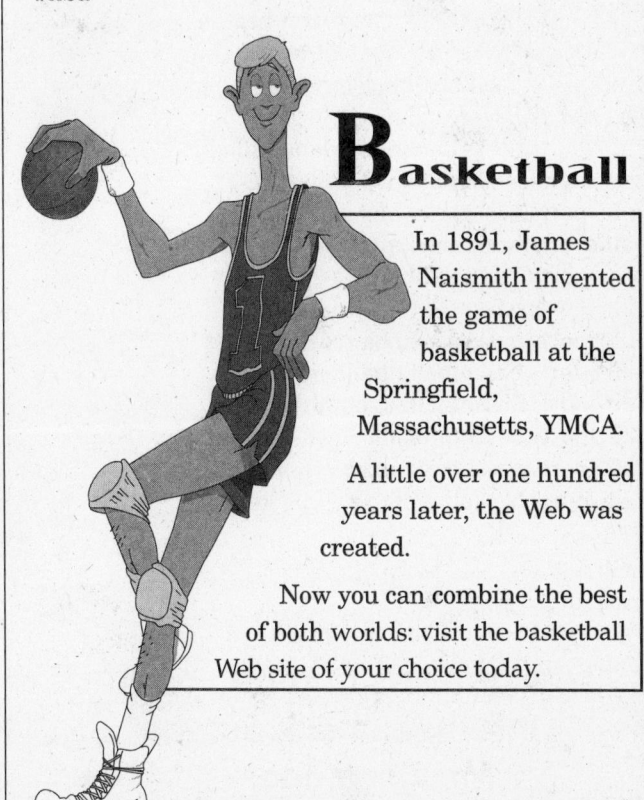

Basketball Team Talk and General Discussion

You don't have to get together with the guys to be able to talk about your favorite basketball team. On Usenet there are lots and lots of fan groups for basketball. Your team is bound to have one. (If it doesn't, you can make one.) Join up with other raging basketball fans and talk all night. (By the way, did you know that basketball is the only major sport that is entirely American in origin?)

Usenet:
  alt.sports.basketball.nba.atlanta-hawks
  alt.sports.basketball.nba.boston-celtics
  alt.sports.basketball.nba.char-hornets
  alt.sports.basketball.nba.chicago-bulls
  alt.sports.basketball.nba.clev-cavaliers
  alt.sports.basketball.nba.dallas-mavs
  alt.sports.basketball.nba.denver-nuggets
  alt.sports.basketball.nba.det-pistons
  alt.sports.basketball.nba.gs-warriors
  alt.sports.basketball.nba.hou-rockets
  alt.sports.basketball.nba.ind-pacers
  alt.sports.basketball.nba.la-clippers
  alt.sports.basketball.nba.la-lakers
  alt.sports.basketball.nba.miami-heat
  alt.sports.basketball.nba.mil-bucks
  alt.sports.basketball.nba.mn-wolves
  alt.sports.basketball.nba.nj-nets
  alt.sports.basketball.nba.orlando-magic
  alt.sports.basketball.nba.phila-76ers
  alt.sports.basketball.nba.phx-suns
  alt.sports.basketball.nba.port-blazers
  alt.sports.basketball.nba.sa-spurs
  alt.sports.basketball.nba.sac-kings
  alt.sports.basketball.nba.seattle-sonics
  alt.sports.basketball.nba.tor-raptors
  alt.sports.basketball.nba.utah-jazz
  alt.sports.basketball.nba.vanc-grizzlies
  alt.sports.basketball.nba.wash-bullets
  alt.sports.basketball.pro.ny-knicks

Lots and lots of music on the Internet: check out the Music categories.

Basketball: Women

Many people prefer women's basketball to men's. The rules are changed somewhat—for example, they use a smaller ball—but the game is basically the same and the tickets are a lot less expensive. If you are a basketball fan, try the women's version. I bet you will like it.

Web:
  http://www.wbca.org/
  http://www.wnba.com/

Usenet:
  rec.sport.basketball.women

Listserv Mailing List:
  List Name: **wbball-l**
  Subscribe to: **listserv@lists.psu.edu**

Bicycling

Some years ago, I rode my bicycle along the California coast from San Diego to San Francisco. Today, I still live near the ocean, and there's nothing I like more than spending the day riding along an oceanfront bike path (especially when I should be working). It's not only great exercise, but I get credit for saving the environment without having to actually do anything. I recently bought a new bike, and it sure was helpful to have useful information and good advice. To help you enjoy your bike-riding experiences, here are some bicycle resources with enough information and advice to equip the entire Swiss navy.

Web:
  http://www.cis.ohio-state.edu/hypertext/faq/usenet/
     bicycles-faq/top.html
  http://www.cycling.org/

Usenet:
  alt.bmx
  alt.mountain-bike
  alt.rec.bicycles.fatcity
  alt.rec.bicycles.recumbent
  rec.bicycles
  rec.bicycles.misc
  rec.bicycles.racing
  rec.bicycles.rides
  rec.bicycles.soc
  rec.bicycles.tech

Majordomo Mailing List:
  List Name: **bikepeople**
  Subscribe to: **majordomo@cyclery.com**

SPORTS AND ATHLETICS

Boxing

I am not sure, exactly, what the appeal is of watching men hit each other until they are unconscious or exhausted. Imagine the brain cells that could be in full use, but are instead being bashed about like a string of rugs during spring cleaning. But this thought doesn't bother the fans of boxing, and they will be found on the Net talking about the history of boxing as well as the latest knock-down-drag-out.

Web:
http://www.boxing.clara.net/
http://www.canoe.ca/Boxing/
http://www.fighters.com/

Usenet:
rec.sport.boxing

Why Boxing Is Important

Some people think that boxing is an ugly, vicious, atavistic pastime, whose usefulness in a polite, civilized society has long since expired. Other people think boxing is important, as it allows people to express their aggressive urges in a confined, limited fashion, with well-defined rules and procedures.

Actually, neither of those is correct.

The real reason boxing is important is it allows middle-aged men to get together and smoke cigars in a socially acceptable environment.

For more information about the sport of kings, you can follow the discussion in **rec.sport.boxing**.

College Sports

American colleges and universities have two main purposes. First, they are bastions of knowledge, dedicated to the training and enlightenment of young people as they pass through late adolescence into adulthood. Second, they organize and maintain many different athletic teams so that older people—who have already passed through late adolescence into adulthood—can enjoy themselves vicariously by watching the exploits of young athletes. When it comes to college sports, there's a lot to talk about, so choose your favorite Usenet group and jump right in. When you feel the need for information, such as sports news, schedules, standings, and so on, try the Web site.

Web:
http://www.collegesupersite.com/

Usenet:
alt.sports.college.acc
alt.sports.college.acc.unc
alt.sports.college.big-12
alt.sports.college.big-east
alt.sports.college.big10
alt.sports.college.conference-usa
alt.sports.college.ivy-league
alt.sports.college.pac-10
alt.sports.college.sec

Cricket

Cricket is a game played primarily in Great Britain and the Commonwealth countries. This is how the game works: there are two wickets (a wicket is made of two crosspieces, or bails, resting on three stumps) placed in the middle of a field. Bowlers try to knock down the bails of the wicket while the batsmen try to defend the wickets. Each team consists of 11 men, and because of the structure of the scoring, games can sometimes take several days to complete. Cricket was developed in medieval England some time before 1400. In 1477, cricket was banned by Edward IV because it was interfering with the mandatory practice of archery. If a man was caught playing cricket, he was fined and sentenced to two years in prison. If the British had the Internet back then, I guess Ed would have been up a creek, wouldn't he? Check out what your medieval brethren didn't have the chance to see in 1477. There are lots of cricket resources on the Net.

Web:
http://www.cricket.org/

Usenet:
rec.sport.cricket
rec.sport.cricket.info
rec.sport.cricket.scores

IRC:
#cricket

Exercise and Sports Psychology

"Mind over matter." "No pain, no gain." You've heard all the motivational clichés designed to inspire you to push that out-of-shape body of yours up the hill, down the hill, and over the finish line. Examine the brain behind the body by participating in the discussion of exercise and sports psychology.

Listserv Mailing List:
List Name: **sportpsy**
Subscribe to: **listserv@vm.temple.edu**

Fencing

Fencing is more than just making money off stolen goods. It's also a sport that takes speed, grace and finesse. (This is not to say the two are mutually exclusive, though.) These resources offer you a chance to learn the rules of fencing as well as other important fencing information.

Web:
http://www.cis.ohio-state.edu/hypertext/faq/usenet/sports/fencing-faq/top.html
http://www.ludd.luth.se/~rog/fencing/links.html
http://www.usfa.org/

Usenet:
rec.sport.fencing

Figure Skating

Ice skating was originally developed as a form of transportation, but by the seventeenth century was well established as a sport. Figure skating was invented in the 1860s by an American, Jackson Haines, and is one of the most beautiful and graceful sports in the world. Whether you are a figure skating fan or a skater yourself, you will find lots of interesting resources on the Net.

Web:
http://frog.simplenet.com/skateweb/
http://www.skatehistory.com/
http://www.webcom.com/dnkorte/sk8_0000.html

Usenet:
rec.sport.skating.ice.figure

FENCING AND ME

When I was a graduate student at U.C. San Diego, I studied fencing. Here is how it happened.

At the time, registration for physical education (PE) classes was done manually. At the beginning of the term, on a particular day, each coach set up a table in the gymnasium. People lined up for hours in advance to register for their favorite class.

I woke up very early that day and stood in line a long time to register for surfing class.

I wanted to take more than one PE class, but by the time I worked my way to the front of the surfing line, there wasn't time to wait at another table. So I asked the surfing coach if he taught anything besides surfing. Yes, he replied, he also taught fencing.

Since I could sign up for both classes at the same table, I did. And that's how I came to take fencing (as well as surfing). Later, I went on to study theatrical fencing, and I even wrote a short play with fencing in it.

So, if you are a fencing buff, whether by design or fortune, check out the **FENCING** Web site. And remember, as we wait patiently at the Table of Life, it's not how long we wait that matters, but how we use our opportunities when we get to the front of the line.

Football: American

Good old summertime. The sun is shining, the birds are singing, the flowers are blooming, and you can work on your tan. The problem is that there is no football. This is something that had to be tolerated until recently. Now you can get your fix during any season: scores, history, news articles and discussion on both college and professional football.

Web:
 http://espn.sportszone.com/ncf/
 http://www.cnnsi.com/football/
 http://www.nando.net/SportServer/football/

Usenet:
 rec.sport.football.college
 rec.sport.football.fantasy
 rec.sport.football.misc

IRC:
 #football

Football: Canadian Football League

Football is not just a disease exclusive to America. See how the Canadians play the game. Rules, referee signals, history, schedules and a glossary are available.

Web:
 http://www.cfl.ca/

Usenet:
 rec.sport.football.canadian

Next time you are at the supermarket, show them this book and ask for a discount (you never know...).

Football: Professional

It's a good thing football is a seasonal sport. Otherwise, people might never have time to go to the Net and read about football. Check out these Web sites for the latest news and information about professional football. On IRC you can chat with other fans of the National Football League (NFL). This is an especially fun channel to participate in at the same time you are watching the game. On Usenet, any professional football topic is fair game.

Web:
 http://www.iis-sports.com/draft/
 http://www.nfl.com/

Usenet:
 alt.sports.football.mn-vikings
 alt.sports.football.oak-raiders
 alt.sports.football.pro.ariz-cardinals
 alt.sports.football.pro.atl-falcons
 alt.sports.football.pro.baltimore
 alt.sports.football.pro.buffalo-bills
 alt.sports.football.pro.car-panthers
 alt.sports.football.pro.chicago-bears
 alt.sports.football.pro.cinci-bengals
 alt.sports.football.pro.cleve-browns
 alt.sports.football.pro.dallas-cowboys
 alt.sports.football.pro.denver-broncos
 alt.sports.football.pro.detroit-lions
 alt.sports.football.pro.gb-packers
 alt.sports.football.pro.houston-oilers
 alt.sports.football.pro.indy-colts
 alt.sports.football.pro.jville-jaguars
 alt.sports.football.pro.kc-chiefs
 alt.sports.football.pro.la-raiders
 alt.sports.football.pro.la-rams
 alt.sports.football.pro.miami-dolphins
 alt.sports.football.pro.ne-patriots
 alt.sports.football.pro.no-saints
 alt.sports.football.pro.ny-giants
 alt.sports.football.pro.ny-jets
 alt.sports.football.pro.oak-raiders
 alt.sports.football.pro.phila-eagles
 alt.sports.football.pro.phoe-cardinals
 alt.sports.football.pro.pitt-steelers
 alt.sports.football.pro.sd-chargers
 alt.sports.football.pro.sea-seahawks
 alt.sports.football.pro.sf-49ers
 alt.sports.football.pro.stl-rams
 alt.sports.football.pro.tampabay-bucs
 alt.sports.football.pro.wash-redskins
 rec.sport.football.pro

IRC:
 #nfl

Frisbee

Disc sports are fun and certainly not limited to throwing a frisbee at the beach. Fans of disc sports can check out these Web sites full of information or talk about Ultimate, disc golf and other disc sports on Usenet.

Web:
  http://www.cs.rochester.edu/u/ferguson/ultimate/ultimate-rules.html
  http://www.princeton.edu/~dennishu/ultimate.html
  http://www.upa.org/

Usenet:
  rec.sport.disc

Golf

You don't have to wear funny pants to play golf, but it helps. What helps even more are secret tips on how to improve your game. The Internet is full of golf information, golf resources and people who want to talk about golf. Join the mailing list and maybe you'll get to talk to Tiger Woods. (Of course, maybe you won't, but as a golfer, I am sure you are always optimistic.) Hint: The next time you play golf, be sure to wear *two* pairs of pants—just in case you get a hole in one. Ha, ha, ha, ha... oh, never mind.

Web:
  http://www.faqs.org/faqs/sports/golf-faq/
  http://www.golf.com/
  http://www.golfsearch.com/
  http://www.golfweb.com/
  http://www.ttsoft.com/thor/golflinks.html

Usenet:
  rec.sport.golf

Listserv Mailing List:
  List Name: **golf-l**
  Subscribe to: **listserv@listserv.acsu.buffalo.edu**

IRC:
  #golf

Hockey

Hockey has certainly gotten less fun since they made a rule that everyone has to wear masks when they play. But if that doesn't put you off the game, check out these great resources available on the Internet. When you're not on the ice or in the stands, check into Usenet and IRC to blab with other hockey fans.

Web:
  http://www.canoe.ca/Hockey/
  http://www.exploratorium.edu/hockey/
  http://www.sportingnews.com/nhl/

Usenet:
  alt.sports.hockey.echl
  alt.sports.hockey.fantasy
  alt.sports.hockey.ihl
  alt.sports.hockey.rhi
  rec.collecting.sport.hockey
  rec.sport.hockey
  rec.sport.hockey.field

IRC:
  #hockey

Hockey: College

It's exciting to watch a bunch of padded maniacs zip up and down a slab of ice and hit each other with sticks. You can get more involved in collegiate ice hockey by posting or reading scores, team information, and schedules for your favorite teams.

Listserv Mailing List:
  List Name: **hockey-d**
  Subscribe to: **listserv@maine.maine.edu**

Listserv Mailing List:
  List Name: **hockey-l**
  Subscribe to: **listserv@maine.maine.edu**

Listserv Mailing List:
  List Name: **hockey3**
  Subscribe to: **listserv@maine.maine.edu**

Listserv Mailing List:
  List Name: **info-hockey-1**
  Subscribe to: **listserv@maine.maine.edu**

SPORTS AND ATHLETICS   739

Hockey

I am the oldest child in my family and, as such, I had some special privileges when I was growing up.

One of them was that I often got to sleep over at my grandparents' house on Saturday night.

Every Saturday night, after I watched Leave It to Beaver on TV, my grandmother would make me a bowl of cereal. I would eat the cereal and sit on the couch with my grandfather as we watched the hockey game together.

That was a long time ago.

My grandparents have since passed away. I don't eat cereal nearly as often as I used to. Leave It to Beaver has been in reruns for many years. And I now spend my Saturday nights listening to the radio and writing.

But all across the country, I am sure that there are still little boys, sitting with their grandfathers, spending the evening watching the hockey game.

Thank goodness, some things never change.

Hockey Team Talk and General Discussion

If hockey is too rough for you to participate, try getting on Usenet and talking about it. There's nothing like a vicarious thrill (except a real thrill). Fans of various hockey teams hang out and discuss the game and the players.

Usenet:
- alt.sports.hockey.nhl.ana-mighty-ducks
- alt.sports.hockey.nhl.boston-bruins
- alt.sports.hockey.nhl.buffalo-sabres
- alt.sports.hockey.nhl.chat
- alt.sports.hockey.nhl.chi-blackhawks
- alt.sports.hockey.nhl.clgry-flames
- alt.sports.hockey.nhl.col-avalanche
- alt.sports.hockey.nhl.dallas-stars
- alt.sports.hockey.nhl.det-redwings
- alt.sports.hockey.nhl.edm-oilers
- alt.sports.hockey.nhl.fla-panthers
- alt.sports.hockey.nhl.hford-whalers
- alt.sports.hockey.nhl.la-kings
- alt.sports.hockey.nhl.mtl-canadiens
- alt.sports.hockey.nhl.nj-devils
- alt.sports.hockey.nhl.ny-islanders
- alt.sports.hockey.nhl.ny-rangers
- alt.sports.hockey.nhl.ott-senators
- alt.sports.hockey.nhl.phila-flyers
- alt.sports.hockey.nhl.phx-coyotes
- alt.sports.hockey.nhl.pit-penguins
- alt.sports.hockey.nhl.que-nordiques
- alt.sports.hockey.nhl.sj-sharks
- alt.sports.hockey.nhl.stl-blues
- alt.sports.hockey.nhl.tor-mapleleafs
- alt.sports.hockey.nhl.vanc-canucks
- alt.sports.hockey.nhl.wash-capitals
- alt.sports.hockey.nhl.winnipeg-jets

Need a job?
See "Jobs and the Workplace".
Got a job? See "Fun".

740 SPORTS AND ATHLETICS

Martial Arts

A martial art is a system of disciplines used for self-defense or for offense. Many martial arts teach unarmed techniques, although some use weapons. Most martial arts were developed within an Asian culture—China, Korea, Japan or Okinawa—and they are taught all over the world. There are many different types of martial arts, and these resources will help you find the information you need. In general, martial arts are about training your mind and body, and possibly engaging in organized competition, not about street fighting. Hint: The best fight you can win is the one you avoid.

Web:
http://www.cis.ohio-state.edu/hypertext/faq/
   usenet-faqs/bygroup/rec/martial-arts/top.html
http://www.lib.ox.ac.uk/internet/news/faq/
   rec.martial-arts.html
http://www.middlebury.edu/~jswan/martial.arts/
   ma.html
http://www.mindspring.com/~mamcgee/
   martial.arts.html

Usenet:
alt.martial-arts.karate.shotokan
alt.martial-arts.tae-kwon-do
alt.martial-arts.tae-kwon-do
rec.martial-arts
rec.martial-arts.moderated

Listproc Mailing List:
  List Name: **karate**
  Subscribe to: **listproc@raven.cc.ukans.edu**

Majordomo Mailing List:
  List Name: **kiai**
  Subscribe to: **majordomo@apocalypse.org**

> The Internet has lots of information about martial arts: from judo and karate to the less mainstream schools, such as kuk sool won (Korean) or balintawak eskrima (Filipino). So the next time you need a break from your physical training, try working out on the Net.

Polo

Polo is a game in which four-man teams, mounted on horseback, use long flexible mallets to try to knock a ball through a pair of goal posts. Modern polo was developed in the nineteenth century by British cavalry officers. However, a polo-like game was played in China and Persia as long as 2,500 years ago. Many people consider polo to be a rich man's game, because it takes a certain amount of wealth to maintain horses and polo grounds. Prince Charles of England, for example, is an accomplished polo player. However, polo is enjoyed around the world, including at some universities. Interesting polo fact: According to the official (U.S.) rules, a player may use any size horse of any breed. However, it is against the rules to use a horse that is blind in one eye.

Web:
  http://www.polonews.com/
  http://www.uspolo.org/

Listserv Mailing List:
  List Name: **polo-l**
  Subscribe to: **listserv@vm.cc.purdue.edu**

Rodeo

A rodeo is a competition featuring events based on cowboy skills. The first formal rodeo was in Prescott, Arizona, in 1888. Today, rodeos are popular throughout the United States and Canada. At a modern rodeo you will see professional cowboys competing for prize money. There are five main types of events: riding a bronc (bucking horse) bareback, riding a bronc with a saddle, riding a bull, roping a calf, and wrestling a steer.

Web:
  http://www.cowgirls.com/dream/jan/rodeo.htm
  http://www.gunslinger.com/rodeo.html
  http://www.prorodeo.com/

Usenet:
rec.sport.rodeo

Listproc Mailing List:
  List Name: **rodeo**
  Subscribe to: **listproc@lists.colorado.edu**

SPORTS AND ATHLETICS

> Reality is dull.
> Try "Science Fiction".

Rugby

Here are some resources you can use to learn more about rugby. Get a basic overview of rugby, rules, trivia and FAQs, country-specific information, game schedules, match results, rugby jokes and songs, and video clips and pictures. Find out if the stories about rugby players are true.

Web:
  http://picard.anderson.edu/~adekunle/rugby/
  http://www.rugbynews.com/
  http://www.uidaho.edu/clubs/womens_rugby/
    RugbyRoot/

Usenet:
  rec.sport.rugby
  rec.sport.rugby.union

IRC:
  #rugby

Rugby League

It has been said that in the event of nuclear annihilation, only the cockroaches and rugby players would survive. I don't know if that's true, but I do know that there is a variation on Rugby Union that is more intense, faster-paced, and guaranteed to give you new respect for the human body's ability to withstand punishment.

Web:
  http://www.eisa.net.au/~sleague/
  http://www.senet.com.au/~emjay/rules.htm

Usenet:
  rec.sport.rugby.league

Skiing

If you are planning a ski vacation, these Web pages provide you with everything you may or may not need to know, including upcoming ski events, ski conditions, interviews, photos and resort information. When you're not on the slopes, you should at least be talking about skiing. My advice is to join one of the Usenet discussion groups so that, if you can't go skiing every day, at least you're not wasting all your time working and sleeping.

Web:
  http://www.gorp.com/gorp/activity/skiing.htm
  http://www.skinet.com/

Usenet:
  rec.skiing
  rec.skiing.alpine
  rec.skiing.announce
  rec.skiing.backcountry
  rec.skiing.marketplace
  rec.skiing.nordic
  rec.skiing.resorts.europe
  rec.skiing.resorts.misc
  rec.skiing.resorts.north-america
  rec.skiing.snowboard

Soccer

Soccer (or as they call it outside the U.S., football) is the most popular sport in the world. These Web pages are your passport to a number of great soccer resources. Access Usenet groups, World Cup information, Fantasy Goal Scorers, mailing lists, hints, frequently asked question lists, terminology, and even soccer games for the computer. And, when it comes time for the World Cup, you'll be able to get all the latest information and scores without having to leave your computer.

Web:
  http://dmiwww.cs.tut.fi/riku/soccer.html
  http://www.soccernet.com/
  http://www.tin.it/rete/

Usenet:
  alt.sports.soccer.european
  alt.sports.soccer.european.uk
  alt.sports.soccer.non-league
  rec.sport.soccer

IRC:
  #soccer

Softball

Softball is a variation of baseball that was invented in 1888 in Chicago. The game is much like regular baseball with a few important changes: the field is smaller, the ball is larger and is softer, and a regular game is only seven innings instead of nine. Softball is played by both men and women and is popular in many different countries because, for normal everyday people, it is a lot more fun than baseball.

Web:
  http://www.softball.org/

Usenet:
  rec.sport.softball

Sports News

It's one thing to play a sport. It's another to watch sports on television. But clearly that's not enough. What do you do to fill in the time when you can't get outside and there is nothing on TV? You use the Net to keep up on sporting news, of course. Here are two Web sites that will give you all the sports information you need (with enough left over in case you have to entertain unexpected company). Remember, whether you are after the latest scores, schedules or just plain gossip, the Net is there for you.

Web:
  http://www.cnnsi.com/
  http://www.sportsline.com/

Sports Resources

There are many sports and many athletes in the world, and the Net can help you find the information you need when you need it. Whether you are looking for an up-to-the-minute sports score, inside information on your favorite team or the location of the nearest Korfball tournament, one of these Web sites will have what you need. For those extra moments when you're not watching or playing, why not join the discussion on Usenet?

Web:
  http://www.sfgate.com/sports/
  http://www.sportingnews.com/
  http://www.sportsnetwork.com/

Usenet:
  rec.sport.misc

If you can't play a sport, try to be one. And if you can't be a sport, at least you can read about one on the Net.

Sports Schedules

If the only reason you have been buying TV Guide is to look up when your favorite sporting event is on, now you can save all that money and avoid recycling at the same time. This Web site will let you check schedules for various sporting events or create your own viewing schedules for professional football, hockey, basketball and baseball events, and more.

Web:
  http://www.cs.rochester.edu/u/ferguson/schedules/

Squash and Racquetball

Squash and racquetball are similar games in which two players, using racquets, hit a ball back and forth against a wall in an enclosed court. (There are also "doubles" versions of these games in which two-person teams compete against one another.) For hundreds of years, people have been playing games in which they hit a ball back and forth with either their hands or some type of instrument. In 19th century England, the prisoners in Fleet prison in London invented a game in which they would hit a ball against the walls by using racquets. By 1820, the game of racquets had become popular in various English public schools. Squash was invented around 1830, at the Harrow school, when some of the students discovered that a punctured racquets ball, would "squash" against the wall with much less of a bounce than an intact ball. Because the ball did not bounce as much, chasing after it and hitting it required a lot more effort. The game of racquetball was invented in 1949 in Connecticut, by Joe Sobek. He designed a short racquet-like paddle, and devised a game to be played on a handball court that was a cross between squash and handball.

Web:
  http://www.racquetball.org/
  http://www.squash.org/

Usenet:
  rec.sport.squash

Swimming Competitions

Swimming is one of the most popular competitive sports in the world. If you have what it takes to get to the end of the pool faster than the next guy, you are assured a great deal of fun, excellent exercise, and the worship of other, less talented human beings who would have trouble finding their way out of a bathtub. (Moreover, you will find yourself with enormous patience, developed during all those hours you spend waiting at the side of the pool for your event.) To help you keep afloat in the world of water, here are some resources where you can find competitive swimming information: read about news, events, meet results, biographies, swim clubs and coaches.

Web:
http://www.fina.org/
http://www.swimnews.com/
http://www.usswim.org/

Tennis

To me, tennis is a funny sport. There seems to be a huge gap between the competitive tennis you watch on television and the game that everybody else in the world plays. Personally, I get bored watching other people play tennis, but I do like to bat the ball around myself once in a while. Anyway, how can you not like a game in which you start at love and work your way up?

Web:
http://www.faqs.org/faqs/sports/tennis-faq/
http://www.tennis.com/
http://www.tennisserver.com/

Usenet:
rec.sport.tennis

IRC:
#tennis

> The Net is good for you.

Volleyball

There is something so fascinating about volleyball. Especially volleyball on the beach where young, nubile people clad in swimsuits jump around energetically to hit a ball that bounces back and forth and back and forth. If you like to watch or even participate, check out these sites dedicated to the sport of volleyball. Get information on collegiate or beach volleyball, the history of the sport, links to books, magazines, pictures, a schedule of TV coverage, and more.

Web:
http://www.vball.net/vbdict.htm
http://www.volleyball.org/

Usenet:
rec.sport.volleyball

Women's Sports

Here are links to Web sites for all sorts of women's sports, teams and sports clubs: baseball, skating, volleyball, gymnastics, basketball, golf, bicycling, and many others. If you are already an athlete, you'll find lots of information about your favorite sport. If you are just starting to became active, the Net can help you find events in your area.

Web:
http://fiat.gslis.utexas.edu/~lewisa/womsprt.html

Wrestling: Professional

There's nothing like spending a sunny Saturday morning in front of the tube with a box of Wheat Thins, a can of spray cheese and the remote control pointing at your favorite professional wrestling show. If you can't wait until the big day, get a wrestling fix from the Net. The Net has lots of great information about professional wrestling, including links to cool video clips that you can use to practice your moves at home or at the office.

Web:
http://infoweb.magi.com/~ollie/wrestling.shtml

Usenet:
rec.sport.pro-wrestling
rec.sport.pro-wrestling.fantasy
rec.sport.pro-wrestling.info

744 SPORTS AND ATHLETICS

Study the wrestling info on the Net beforehand, and I guarantee you will be able to hold your date spellbound.

I was going to study to be a Sumo wrestler, but I didn't have time because I had to stay home and work on this book. But maybe it's not too late for you. Check out a Sumo resource or two on the Net.

Wrestling: Sumo

Sumo wrestling is the national sport of Japan. Sumo uses a playing ring that is a few meters across and two men (who are also a few meters across). The object of the event is to force your opponent out of the ring or make any part of his body, except for the soles of his feet, touch the floor (sort of like a corporate takeover without the money). For more information about this fascinating sport, take a look at these sumo Web sites. (For more information about corporate takeovers, call AT&T and ask for the chairman's office.)

Web:
  http://www.scgroup.com/sumo/faq/
  http://www.sumoweb.com/

Usenet:
  rec.sport.sumo

STAR TREK

Alien Races

Why is it difficult to read the mind of a Dopterian? Because they are close relatives of the Ferengi and have the same four-lobed brain structure that makes telepathic contact virtually impossible. It's not hard to see how such knowledge might one day save your life. So, before it's too late, you better learn about all the different races in the Star Trek universe.

Web:
  http://www.dcs.gla.ac.uk/~hwloidl/ST-aliens.html

Usenet:
  alt.startrek.bajoran
  alt.startrek.borg
  alt.startrek.cardassian
  alt.startrek.romulan
  alt.startrek.trill
  alt.startrek.vulcan

Animations and Images

I love Star Trek, so when I want to take a break from writing about Star Trek resources, I like to go look at Star Trek pictures and animations. These Web sites have nice collections of images and movies, digitized from various Star Trek movies and TV shows.

Web:
  http://borgworld2.simplenet.com/pictures.htm
  http://clgray.simplenet.com/strtrk/
  http://members.easyspace.com/stcg/
  http://www2.netlink.co.uk/users2/pehtrek/
    picindex.html

STAR TREK

Beer Trek

Here is a fun game to play with your friends as you are sitting around watching Star Trek television shows or movies. Connect to this Web site and look at the "rules". This is a long list of things that frequently occur in Star Trek. As you watch the show (or movie), whenever someone notices one of these occurrences, everyone has to take a drink. For example, on any show when someone is sexually harassed by a holodeck character, everyone must take a drink. On Deep Space Nine, when Worf butts heads with Odo or when a clipboard is passed from one person to another, everyone must take a drink. On Star Trek: The Next Generation, whenever there is an authorization to exceed warp speed limitations, whenever Data's head is open, or whenever Picard crosses his legs like a girl, everyone must take a drink. On the original Star Trek series, whenever Chekov substitutes a "W" for a "V", whenever Kirk grabs a woman by the shoulders, or anytime anyone sees someone besides Uhura with a "thingy" in his or her ear, everyone has to take a drink. (You get the idea.) There are lots and lots of rules, and some include additional actions besides drinking. For example, you may have to yell something or make a particular gesture. Note: On behalf of myself, my publisher, our lawyers and your parents, I must warn you that drinking to excess is bad for your health. (Right.)

Web:
http://www.planetofthegeeks.com/trek/beertrek/

Captain Kirk Sing-a-Long Page

Undoubtedly some hardcore Star Trek fans have fantasized about hearing William Shatner, Nichelle Nichols or others singing in the shower. Here's what you should do: get an Internet connection running in the bathroom and load up this Web site. After you get in the shower, you can download any of the sounds here. While you are in the shower, you will hear clips from albums put out by various Star Trek notables. It will be a fantasy come true.

Web:
http://www.loskene.com/singalong/kirk.html

Conventions and Memorabilia

Dress up funny and romp around with other people dressed up like Star Trek characters. Conventions are a great place to really experience Trekker fandom. Discover where to get a replica of that communicator you love or collect the one action figure you are missing from your set.

Web:
http://www.wwcd.com/shows/strekconv.html

Usenet:
rec.arts.startrek.fandom

> Okay, I know that you have a life—it's just that your life is built around Star Trek. Why waste your time with non-Trekkers? The only reasonable place to hang out is rec.arts.startrek.fandom.

Future Technology Talk and General Discussion

You look back and laugh at old sci-fi from the '50s. How close are we getting to Star Trek technology? Speculate on how our technological progress compares with the technology dreamed up in the creative minds of Star Trek writers.

Usenet:
rec.arts.startrek.tech

Klingon Phrasebook

Would you like to learn Klingon? Here is one way to start: with a small phrasebook of quotes translated into Klingon. There are quotes from famous television shows such as the X-Files, the Simpsons, Mad About You and Seinfeld. There are also other handy phrases such as insults and things to say when you are stoned (example: "QoQ vIleghlaH!" is Klingon for "I can see the music!").

Web:
http://members.aol.com/JPKlingon/newbook.html

746 STAR TREK

Klingon Shared Reality

Wouldn't it be fun for a little while to pretend you are a Klingon and walk around making lots of gutteral noises and threatening people? Brush up on your Klingon language, don a persona and elbow your way into the crowd for a little Usenet role-playing.

Usenet:
alt.shared-reality.startrek.klingon

Klingon Talk and General Discussion

Ignore the subtitles in the movies: learn to speak Klingon. Explore the culture that devoted fans have worked so hard to develop. Find a variety of interesting topics such as Klingon love poetry, haiku, and thoughts on Kronos as the homeworld.

Usenet:
alt.startrek.klingon

Klingon is a Real Language

Yes, it's true. There really is a language named Klingon. It was developed by a language expert and adopted by fanatical Star Trek fans. There is actually a whole new language, with its own grammar, rules of usage and a dictionary. There are also Klingon magazines and audio tapes (to help with your pronunciation) as well as clubs of people who want to live like real Klingons.

HIja. tlhIngan Hol vIjatlhlaH.
(Yes. I can speak Klingon.)

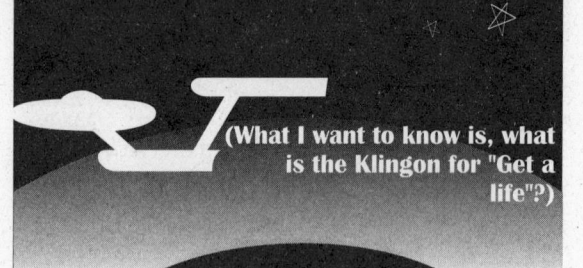

(What I want to know is, what is the Klingon for "Get a life"?)

Look What I Found on the Net...

```
            (from a message that was sent to me by Mike Lyons)
    ...I am going to call you on something printed in the first
    edition of your book, within the Star Trek section, in an ad
    entitled "Klingon Is a Real Language".

    You said: "What I want to know is, what is Klingon for
    'Get a life'?"

    I was given a copy of the Klingon dictionary, and I looked
    it up.

         yIn'e' yISuq

      yIn  =  life (n)
     -'e'  =  noun prefix indicating topic
      yI-  =  verb prefix (you - [him her it], imperative)
      Suq  =  get (v)

    Incidentally, it was a linguist named Marc Okrand who created
    the Klingon language, based on the few words from the opening
    scenes in the first movie, which were made up by James "Scotty"
    Doohan.

    Just a little trivia for you.
```

STAR TREK

Next Generation

If ST:TNG is your favorite, you will enjoy this Web site. It has an introduction, cast list, information about the setting, explanations of the major alien species (along with the episodes in which they appeared), episode summaries, information about ST:TNG movies and video releases, trivia, and more. What else could you possibly want out of life (aside from a Ferengi joke book)?

Web:
http://www.algonet.se/~locutus/

Star Trek Games

Don't just watch Star Trek, live it! Command your own ship with Xtrek and match wits with the computer or go head to head (or torpedo to torpedo) with others like you on Netrek, the networking version of the game. The Usenet groups cover such topics as tactics, experiences and troubleshooting software.

Usenet:
alt.games.xtrek
alt.starfleet.rpg.german
rec.games.netrek

Star Trek News

Learn what's going on in the world of Star Trek. Fans report rumors and facts about new shows, books and movies. Get the latest word and keep up with the Boneses.

Usenet:
rec.arts.startrek.current

Star Trek Resources

Here are some Web sites that will point you to a large number of Star Trek-related resources all over the Net: Web sites, Usenet groups, pictures, sounds, episode guides, book details, quotes, stories, parodies and even the Klingon language. It's all here somewhere. Just beam yourself into the Net.

Web:
http://clgray.simplenet.com/strtrk/stlinks/stlinks.html
http://www.execpc.com/~lam/startrek.html
http://www.netreach.net/~data/transprt.htm
http://www.stud.uni-hannover.de/~zahr/startrek.html
http://www.stwww.com/
http://www.treklist.com/
http://www.trekweb.com/

Star Trek Reviews

Nobody can review Star Trek like a Trekker. Read what fans think about the latest books, movies and shows (but watch out for spoilers!).

Usenet:
rec.arts.startrek.reviews

Star Trek Role Playing

You can watch Star Trek shows just so many times without wanting to get into the act. Well, now you can. Join one of these Star Trek role-playing worlds, and boldly go where your parents won't be able to find you.

Web:
http://www.chaco.com/lists/scifi/trek.html

Telnet:
Address: **ats.trekmush.org**
Port: **1701**
Address: **rw2.rworld.com**
Port: **4201**

Star Trek Resources

Have you ever noticed that in all depictions of the future (including Star Trek), there are never references to the Net?

This is because the Net snuck up on us, completely unanticipated.

Nevertheless, even though there isn't a Net on Star Trek, there is plenty of Star Trek on the Net.

748 STAR TREK

Star Trek Sounds

Imagine having the voices and sounds of your favorite Star Trek episodes coming out of your very own computer. You can almost pretend you are right there in the sound stage, or better yet, you are flying through space at high speeds seeking out new life and new civilizations—boldly going where no net.geek has gone before. Use these sounds to create some ambiance in your computing environment.

Web:
http://tos-www.tos.net/services/sounds/sound.html
http://www.stinsv.com/

Star Trek Stories and Parodies

If you can't get enough of Star Trek on television or in movies and books, check out this corner of the Internet universe. Creative and witty individuals post stories and parodies related to Star Trek in Usenet groups and on Web sites. Often FAQs on submissions are posted containing tips for writing for Deep Space Nine and the Star Trek: Voyager series, where to send submissions, what to do, and what not to do when writing.

Web:
http://www.erols.com/imppub/fanfic.htm
http://www.newsguy.com/~trekfic/
http://www.treklist.com/alpha/stories.html

Usenet:
alt.startrek.creative

Star Trek Talk and General Discussion

Light and lively debate volleys, occasionally turning warm, then hot as you defend your favorite episode or character. Talk turns to old shows, bloopers, insider information on actors' lives, and burning questions like, "Should the use of the Holodeck be restricted until the engineers eliminate the bugs (such as a malfunctioning mortality failsafe)?"

Usenet:
alt.startrek
rec.arts.startrek
rec.arts.startrek.misc

Star Trek Television Shows

Since its debut in 1966, the Star Trek saga has generated hundreds of TV shows in several different series. Here is a Web site that will help you keep track of them. Think of an episode, any episode and then look it up to read a summary. This is a good way to make sure that, after all these years, your memory is still intact.

Web:
http://www.iori.com/sbase.html

Usenet:
alt.tv.star-trek
alt.tv.star-trek.ds9
alt.tv.star-trek.next-gen
alt.tv.star-trek.tos
alt.tv.star-trek.voyager

Look What I Found on the Net...

```
Newsgroup: rec.arts.startrek
Subject: What's the deal with Klingon physiology?

> Why do modern Klingons have all the heavy duty armour plating
> and overly redundant physiology, when Klingons from 100 years
> ago (series time) look like "normal" humanoids?
>
> A friend said that he heard a rumor about Klingons getting
> mutated by some type of radiation poisoning, but if that is
> true why do some ancient Klingons look like present day
> Klingons?

The difference lies in a bigger budget now.
```

Star Trek Trivia

Quick, what is a firomactal drive? If you know the answer to this question, then you're probably one of the billions of people in the universe who like Star Trek enough to be well-versed in its trivia. Well, I've got some great resources for you. Enough trivia to fill the U.S.S. Enterprise NCC-1701 and the NCC-1701-D (both of which have appeared in Deep Space Nine). By the way, a firomactal drive is a non-existent computer that Riker made up in order to confuse the Ferengi when they took over the Enterprise-D in 2369 (from the "Rascals" episode of TNG).

Web:
http://pearce.san-francisco.ca.us/sf/sttrivia.html
http://www.apex.net/users/sapark/trivia.htm
http://www.novia.net/~tomcat/Trivia/

Star Trek Universe

This moderated group offers in-depth and accurate information on the universe as it relates to Star Trek. Read press releases, episode credits, synopses and factual articles. Since all posts are filtered through a moderator, you can be assured of the reliability of what you read. Queries are best moved to one of the other Star Trek groups.

Usenet:
rec.arts.startrek.info

Star Trek Video Clips

Here's my idea for a great party. Invite all your friends over and tell them to wear Star Trek costumes. Have lots of good food and drink, a computer with an Internet connection, and sixteen red balloons. When your friends get there, connect to the Net and download Star Trek video clips. As you watch each clip, act out the various parts yourselves. In between clips, stuff yourself with food and drink a lot. Hint: When you go to download a file, if the name ends in .zip or .gz you will need an "unzip" program to process the file before you can play it. My favorite program is WinZip. (By the way, I just threw the balloons in for fun, you don't really need them.)

Web:
http://home.utah-inter.net/dasaxx/video.htm
http://iceraidr.erols.com/startrek/videos.htm
http://www.personal.umich.edu/~dkocevsk/movies/movies.html

Star Trek: Voyager

Okay, here's the scoop. The U.S.S. Voyager space ship is transported to the Delta Quadrant by a powerful alien. The crew is forced to travel with the crew of an enemy ship, and must now head for home. However, the voyage will take 70 years so they must search for resources (and stay out of trouble) along the way. Star Trek: Voyager is one of the spin-offs of the original Star Trek series. These Web sites will provide you with all the Voyager info you need to survive between episodes: rumors, reviews, episode summaries, reference material (such as descriptions of the various species), pictures, and so on.

Web:
http://www.psiphi.org/voy/
http://www.speedlink.com/mholtz/logbook/stvoy/
http://www.sternenflotte.de/marvel/

Usenet:
alt.tv.star-trek.voyager

Trekker Chat

Meet with other Star Trek enthusiasts for some real-time chat on IRC. If you like Star Trek, this is a good way to meet people all over the world and make new friends. If you are shy and don't know what to say, ask if anyone has seen the Star Trek section in Harley Hahn's new book.

IRC:
#ds9
#star-trek
#startrek

What do you do when there are no Star Trek programs to watch? Join the Trekker Chat on IRC.

SUPPORT GROUPS

30 Plus

I remember when people used to say, "Don't trust anyone over 30." Well, those people are all over 40 now, and the new slogan is "Don't pay attention to anyone under 30." If you're over 30, there are special support groups on the Net just for you. Anyone is welcome, regardless of age, but if you're not mature, do your best to pretend. (It's always worked for me.)

IRC:
#30+
#30plus
#over35

Adoption

There are quite a few resources on the Net for people who are involved in an adoption, no matter what end of the process you are on. These Internet resources have something for prospective adopters, adoptees looking for birth parents, or parents who already have adopted children.

Web:
http://www.adopting.org/bfsearch.html
http://www.winbet.sci.fi/junkyard/adopt.htm

Usenet:
alt.adoption
alt.adoption.agency
alt.adoption.issues

Listserv Mailing List:
List Name: **adoptees**
Subscribe to: **listserv@maelstrom.stjohns.edu**

Listserv Mailing List:
List Name: **adoption**
Subscribe to: **listserv@maelstrom.stjohns.edu**

Listserv Mailing List:
List Name: **open-adoption**
Subscribe to: **listserv@home.ease.lsoft.com**

AIDS Caregivers

AIDS (acquired immunodeficiency syndrome) is a disease caused by HIV (human immunodeficiency virus). Many AIDS patients require extensive care, and the people who give such care have their own special needs. This is especially so when the caregiver is a friend or family member. This mailing list is a support group for caregivers of AIDS patients. If you are taking care of an AIDS patient, you may find it helpful and energizing to talk with people who are in a similar situation.

Usenet:
soc.support.aids-hiv+

Majordomo Mailing List:
List Name: **caregivers**
Subscribe to: **majordomo@queernet.org**

Al-Anon and Alateen

Al-Anon and Alateen resources are available for those people whose lives are affected by friends or family members who are alcoholics. Here you can find information about self-help recovery programs, 12-step programs, and a list of phone numbers for Al-Anon or Alateen groups.

Web:
http://www.al-anon-alateen.org/

Anxiety

These Web sites are for people who experience panic and anxiety. You will find information about anxiety disorders, various types of support, hints about relaxation techniques, personal stories, a reading list, and a collection of related resources, including places you can talk to other people on the Net. The Usenet group is for people who suffer from panic attacks.

Web:
http://stressrelease.com/checklist.html
http://www.adaa.org/

Usenet:
alt.support.anxiety-panic

Look What I Found on the Net...

(from an Anxiety Web site)

Go through these descriptions, one column at a time, and keep track of how many symptoms apply to you.

Physiological Response	Cognitive Response	Emotional Response
Feelings of warmth	I can't do it	Fear
Heart palpitations	Feel foolish	Keyed up, on edge
Rapid, pounding heart	People are looking	Panic
Tightness of chest	I could faint	Excessive worry
Butterflies in stomach	It's a heart attack	Uneasy
Hyperventilation	Get me out of here	Feelings of gloom
Weakness all over	No one will help	Trapped: no way out
Tremors	I can't go alone	Isolated, lonely
Dizziness	I can't breathe	Loss of control
Dry mouth	I'm going to die	Embarrassed
Sweaty all over	I'm going crazy	Criticized
Confusion	I'm trapped	Rejected
Speeded up thoughts	I'm not going out	Angry
Muscle tension/aches	Someone's hurt, sick	Depressed
Fatigue		

If you checked 3 or more from each response list, ask yourself:

— Is fear of an anxiety attack limiting my involvement in life?
— Am I avoiding everyday situations?
— Do I worry and feel tense most of the time?

Depression

Depression is a terrible condition. You can't see it, but it can incapacitate you just the same. If you suffer from depression (or if you are close to someone who is depressed), there are lots of places on the Net where people share information or just talk with one another.

Web:
  http://www.execpc.com/~corbeau/
  http://www.nmisp.org/depfaq.htm

Usenet:
  alt.support.depression
  alt.support.depression.manic
  alt.support.depression.seasonal
  soc.support.depression.crisis
  soc.support.depression.family
  soc.support.depression.manic
  soc.support.depression.misc
  soc.support.depression.seasonal
  soc.support.depression.treatment

Majordomo Mailing List:
  List Name: **walkers**
  Subscribe to: **majordomo@world.std.com**

Divorce

Those who are going through a divorce can access a huge amount of resources that can help you through your trying times. Available resources include law and legal resources, information on recovery, support and child custody, resources for men and women, and support group lists. You will also find resources on parenting as well as things to help you cope, such as links relating to religion and spirituality, and some fun stuff to cheer you up.

Web:
  http://www.divorcecentral.com/
  http://www.divorcesupport.com

Usenet:
  alt.support.divorce

> **Is something not adding up? See "Mathematics".**

Domestic Violence

There are a lot of domestic violence resources on the Net. I have selected two Web sites that are particularly interesting and useful: one site is created by men, the other by women. Together, these sites offer a great deal of information and will help you find the resources you need. The Usenet group is for people who have suffered from—or are currently suffering from—this type of abuse.

Web:
  http://www.dvsheltertour.org/
  http://www.famvi.com/

Usenet:
  alt.support.abuse-partners

Eating Disorders

If you suspect you have an eating disorder, you should check out this Web page. There you can read about the types of eating disorders and their signs and symptoms. If you know that you or someone close to you has a problem, you will also find useful information here, such as how to confront a loved one, how to get help, how to find a therapist, and much, much more. The Usenet groups and mailing list are for people with eating disorders as well as supportive family members and friends.

Web:
  http://www.mirror-mirror.org/eatdis.htm

Usenet:
  alt.recovery.compulsive-eat
  alt.support.eating-disord

Listserv Mailing List:
  List Name: **eating-disorders**
  Subscribe to: **listserv@maelstrom.stjohns.edu**

Grief

There are many reasons for grief, and sometimes it helps to be able to talk with someone who has gone through a similar experience. The Usenet group is for people who are grieving, and the second Web page contains the FAQ (frequently asked question list) for this group. Two hints: (1) The Usenet group is *not* for people who are grieving because of a broken romance. (2) The participants do not want to talk to people who are doing research for journals or academic papers.

Web:
http://www.kirstimd.com/
http://zoom.baton-rouge.la.us/faq.html

Usenet:
alt.support.grief

Narcotics Anonymous

Narcotics Anonymous (NA) is an international community of organizations dedicated to helping drug addicts recover from their addictions. NA is based on the 12-step program used in other similar organizations. I have included two Web pages: one is the official NA site, the other is an NA-oriented site created by private individuals. These Web sites explain about NA and how it works, and offer a wealth of useful information. For discussion, you can join the Usenet group or the IRC channel.

Web:
http://www.cerainc.com/na/5.htm
http://www.na.org/

Usenet:
alt.recovery.na

IRC:
#na

Look What I Found on the Net...

```
Newsgroup: alt.recovery.na
Subject: Note of Thanks

I've been reading this newsgroup for about three weeks now.
I feel as though my problem is trivial compared to others I
have read in the past weeks, but I figured I'd at least make an
effort.

I have been a daily user of marijuana for the past 4 years.
I've pawned nearly all of my possessions.  My life revolved
around how I was going to get my next bag of dope.  It got so
bad that I would offer to clean my friends' smoking accessories
so that I could scrape the resin and get high.

Well, three weeks ago, with the help of my counselor
(psychiatric, for depression), I stopped using pot.  I've now
been clean for three weeks, and I feel, well, like I haven't
felt in years.  I've actually been going outside and becoming a
part of society again.  I realize that this feeling has a
lot to do with the fact that pot canceled out the effects of my
anti-depressant, but I no longer feel like I have a chain around
my neck, that I don't have to get high to have fun, laugh, etc.

Reading the posts in this newsgroup has been a great help to me.
Thanks to all those who unknowingly helped me through the past
three weeks by opening up and sharing their experiences through
their posts to this newsgroup.
```

Pregnancy Loss

This Usenet group is for the support of men and women involved in the loss of an unborn child. The Web site is the FAQ for the Usenet group. It has tips for coping, information about grieving and medical information about pregnancy loss. If you have recently experienced such a loss, I can tell you that it is a lot more common than most people realize. And please remember, on the Net, you are never alone.

Web:
http://www.fertilethoughts.net/faq/miscarriage/resources.html

Usenet:
soc.support.pregnancy.loss

Recovery for Christians

This Web site is maintained by Christians in Recovery (CIR). The resources are for people recovering from all types of problems: drug abuse, dysfunctional families, depression, anxiety, eating disorders, sexual addiction, and so on. There is information about the 12-step program, a checklist of symptoms that lead to relapse, computer programs that may help you recover (such as the Recovery Bible, quote-a-day programs, etc.), and links to Christian and non-Christian recovery sites. There is also information that will help you find other people to talk to on the Net using IRC, Usenet and mailing lists.

Web:
http://www.christians-in-recovery.com/

Recovery for Jews

This site is for Jews who are recovering from alcohol or drug abuse. The site stresses anonymity, so if the shoe fits, there is no reason not to wear it. At this Web site you can read recovery stories, cartoons about Jewish denial, a zine about recovery and spirituality, words from rabbis and scholars, and information about online meetings. This site is sponsored by JACS (Jewish Alcoholics, Chemically Dependent People, and Significant Others).

Web:
http://www.jacsweb.org/

Sexual Addiction

To most people, sex is a source of enormous pleasure (or frustration). That's normal. But to many people, sex is way, way out of control. If you suspect that you might be addicted to sex—or you know that you *are* addicted to sex—finding thoughtful information about your problem can be the first step to resolving it.

Web:
http://www.sa.org/
http://www.sexualrecovery.com/

Smoking

It's not easy to quit smoking. You need to wean yourself from strong physical addiction and psychological dependence. However, there's no reason for you to have to do it alone. There are lots of people on the Net who are going through—or who have gone through—the same process. They are sympathetic and helpful, and will be more than glad to lend support. Once you have successfully beaten your addiction (which may take more than one try), why not hang around for a while to help and encourage other people?

Web:
http://www.faqs.org/faqs/support/stop-smoking/
http://www.nicotine-anonymous.org/

Usenet:
alt.support.stop-smoking

*Troubled?
Confused?
The Net is there for you.*

Support Groups Networking

When you're ailing, it helps to have people to talk to. No matter what your problem, I bet you'll be able to find companionship and conversation at this Web site: a collection of many "bulletin boards" (discussion groups), devoted to just about every area of human suffering you can imagine. The people who participate are friendly and compassionate, so if you have a health, personal or relationship problem, this is the place to look for company.

Web:
http://www.support-group.com/

Support Talk and General Discussion

On the Net, you are never alone. Out of the millions of people, there are some who are a lot like you and want to talk. The Net has a large number of resources to provide support to people. There are Usenet groups, mailing lists, IRC channels, and many, many Web sites. This Usenet group is the general support forum, where you can go with a question, a problem, a story or simply to satisfy your curiosity. If you are looking for support of a particular kind and you are having difficulty, this group would be a good place to ask people for suggestions. (Personally, I am looking for a group that supports writers who stay up all night to finish Internet books.)

Usenet:
alt.support

Transgendered Support

Transgendered people are those whose sexual identities have significant ambiguity. This group includes transsexuals (people whose minds are trapped in a body of the opposite sex), cross-dressers or transvestites (people, almost always men, who enjoy dressing like the opposite sex), and intersexed (people born with ambiguous genitalia). These Usenet groups are for an ongoing discussion of the many problems and topics of interest to transgendered people including, but not limited to, sex change procedures. For real-time talk, you can join one of the IRC channels. If you are new to discussing such issues on the Net, I have included a Web site that contains a FAQ (frequently asked question list) that you will find helpful.

Web:
http://www.heartcorps.com/journeys/
http://www.lava.net/~dewilson/gender/sstg.faq/

Usenet:
alt.support.crossdressing
alt.support.crossliving
soc.support.transgendered

IRC:
#crossdress
#transgen

Look What I Found on the Net...

```
Newsgroup: alt.support.stop-smoking
Subject: 10 Weeks and No More Patch

Dear Group:

Before I went to bed last night, I took off the last patch of the
10-week course.  Today, I am going solo.

It's mid-day now, and so far so good.  I'm well prepared for any
uppity moves by the cursed urge to smoke.  I simply will not do it.

I'm not sure if I could have lasted this long if I hadn't stumbled
across this newsgroup.  I actually found the group in Harley Hahn's
Internet Yellow Pages.  You're a great group and, as far as I'm
concerned, the group lives up to its mission of helping each other
overcome this sly, sneaky, deadly addiction.

Thanks.
```

SUPPORT GROUPS

Usenet Support Groups

It's great to know that when you have a problem, there are people who will be supportive of you. All over the world there are people who are willing to take the time to listen to problems and try to meet the emotional needs of others. Get good information on nearly any subject related to medical, emotional or psychological problems.

Usenet:

- alt.abuse
- alt.abuse.offender.recovery
- alt.abuse.recovery
- alt.abuse.transcendence
- alt.recovery
- alt.recovery.aa
- alt.recovery.adult-children
- alt.recovery.catholicism
- alt.recovery.codependency
- alt.recovery.compulsive-eat
- alt.recovery.mormonism
- alt.recovery.na
- alt.recovery.religion
- alt.support.abortion
- alt.support.abuse-partners
- alt.support.asthma
- alt.support.ataxia
- alt.support.big-folks
- alt.support.breast-implant
- alt.support.breastfeeding
- alt.support.cancer
- alt.support.cancer.prostate
- alt.support.cancer.testicular
- alt.support.cerebral-palsy
- alt.support.childfree
- alt.support.chronic-pain
- alt.support.diabetes.kids
- alt.support.disabled.caregivers
- alt.support.disabled.sexuality
- alt.support.dissociation
- alt.support.dystonia
- alt.support.endometriosis
- alt.support.epilepsy
- alt.support.ex-cult
- alt.support.food-allergies
- alt.support.glaucoma
- alt.support.grief.pet-loss
- alt.support.headaches.migraine
- alt.support.hearing-loss
- alt.support.hemophilia
- alt.support.herpes
- alt.support.ibs
- alt.support.inter-cystitis
- alt.support.jaw-disorders
- alt.support.kidney-failure
- alt.support.learning-disab
- alt.support.loneliness
- alt.support.lupus
- alt.support.marfan
- alt.support.marriage
- alt.support.menopause
- alt.support.ms-recovery
- alt.support.mult-sclerosis
- alt.support.mult-sclerosis.alternatives
- alt.support.myasthe-gravis
- alt.support.ocd
- alt.support.opp-defiant
- alt.support.ostomy
- alt.support.parents.with-custody
- alt.support.pco
- alt.support.personality
- alt.support.post-polio
- alt.support.prostate.prostatitis
- alt.support.schizophrenia
- alt.support.scleroderma
- alt.support.short
- alt.support.shyness
- alt.support.sinusitis
- alt.support.skin-diseases
- alt.support.skin-diseases.psoriasis
- alt.support.social-phobia
- alt.support.spina-bifida
- alt.support.stuttering
- alt.support.survivors.prozac
- alt.support.tall
- alt.support.thyroid
- alt.support.tinnitus
- alt.support.tourette
- alt.support.trauma-ptsd
- alt.support.turner-syndrom
- soc.support.fat-acceptance
- soc.support.loneliness
- soc.support.youth.gay-lesbian-bi

**Life is cool.
(Don't forget to show up.)**

SUPPORT GROUPS

You're almost there.

Widows and Widowers

Widows and widowers have places to find support and friendship on the Net. If you have lost a spouse, you will find useful information at the Web site. Sometimes, what helps the best is to talk to somebody else, so you may also want to join the mailing list.

Web:
http://www.fortnet.org/~goshorn/

Majordomo Mailing List:
List Name: **widow**
Subscribe to: **majordomo@fortnet.org**

Do you feel alone?

There are people on the net who want to talk to you right now.

Look What I Found on the Net...

```
         (from the Social Phobia Frequently Asked Question List,
               posted to alt.support.social-phobia)

What is Social Phobia?

Social phobia can be defined as a feeling of anxiety.  Social
phobics experience anxiety which is intense and overwhelming in
social situations.  They typically fear that their behavior will
humiliate or embarrass them in front of others.  They will often
withdraw entirely rather than face the anxiety they experience.

Anxiety can trigger a variety of physiological responses,
including a tightness in the chest, an accelerated heart rate,
a tingling sensation in the arms and legs, a knot in the stomach,
or a cold, clammy feeling in the extremities.

==========
Newsgroup: alt.support.shyness
Subject: Being Blocked

I found that when "blocked" at the urinal, it helps me if I
think of a math problem, say dividing 265 by 12 or finding the
approximate square root of 234.

However, now I find that I get the urge to urinate whenever
I do math.
```

TALKING ON THE NET

3D Chatting

3D chatting means being able to talk to people while you are moving around in an imaginary three-dimensional world. The Web sites I have listed here will help you get the software you need and then will connect you to some of the many imaginary communities springing up all over the Net. As a member of one of these worlds, you can choose an avatar for yourself. (An avatar is a virtual body you can control.) As you explore a 3D world, you will not only see interesting scenery, you will encounter other avatars, each of which represents a real person somewhere on the Net.

Web:
http://www.cybertown.com/
http://www.microsoft.com/ie/chat/vchatmain.htm
http://www.worlds.net/wc/

Chat Room Lists

So, you want to talk? Here are some Web sites that list chat rooms all over the Net. Look for a chat room by language or by topic. There are even reviews of different chat rooms, so you can find one that appeals to your taste.

Web:
http://www.2meta.com/chats/
http://www.chatlist.com/
http://www.dryden.net/~fpreuss/webdoc1.htm
http://www.solscape.com/chat/
http://www.yack.com/

Chat Servers

Would you like to set up your own chat room? Well, you can. You can set up your own topic or make it for general discussion. In the olden days, (before television), cultured people would have a salon: a room in their house to which they would invite their friends for intellectual conversation. Now you can do the same thing online and you won't even have to serve refreshments.

Web:
http://everychat.ml.org/
http://www.parachat.com/

Chatting Safety

When you talk to somebody on the Net, they can't harm you physically, but it is possible to get hurt in other ways. For example, if somebody were to get your email address, he or she could become a nuisance sending unpleasant mail. Or you might meet someone online and enter into some type of relationship, only to find out later that the person was misrepresenting himself. And, of course, regular life can intersect with the Net. If you tell somebody where you live, they can come over and pay you an unexpected visit. Almost all of the time, people on the Net are well-behaved and just about everyone you meet will be okay. But there are millions of people out there and a few of them are just plain bad. If you are new to the Net, here is some information that can help you be appropriately prudent when you talk with people. If you are a parent, you will find lots of information to help you teach your child to use the Net safely.

Web:
http://www.safesearch.com/home/userguide/websafe.htm
http://www.worldkids.net/school/safety/internet/internet.htm

Comic Chat

Comic Chat is sooooo cool. I just love it. It's a Microsoft IRC-like graphical chat client program. Whenever you or anyone else talks, it shows up as a comic strip on your screen. You actually see drawings of characters with speech balloons. You can choose what you want your character to look like and, if you want, the various poses and expressions the character uses. (If you don't specify, the character just goes through the variations automatically.) This is a fun program to use that you should try at least once. At this Web site, you can download the chat program and find out which chat rooms you can visit that use this client.

Web:
http://www.microsoft.com/ie/chat/

TALKING ON THE NET

> There are only two things worth remembering in life (both of which I forget).

ICQ

ICQ is great. It allows you to talk with people all over the world, just as if you had your own private chat room. The ICQ system is based on centralized servers and ICQ chat clients. You download a client and install it on your computer. Then you register with the system. Now you can talk to anyone else who is connected to an ICQ server. What I like about ICQ is that you can set it up to be notified whenever your friends come online. While you are talking, you can also send and receive files and Web addresses, so people will constantly be thanking you for sharing.

Web:
  http://www.mirabilis.com/

Internet Phone Services

These Web sites have products you can use to talk to people over the Net: real voice talking, like with a telephone. (Of course, you need a computer with a microphone and speakers.) There are three reasons why you might enjoy doing this. First, it's fun to talk to people using your computer; second, you can talk to people all over the world, people whom you otherwise would never have met; and third, you don't have to pay long distance charges. Some of these products cost money, but they all let you evaluate them for free. Compared to talking with a real telephone, talking on the Net does not sound as good, but it's fun and it's free.

Web:
  http://www.connectedpc.com/cpc/videophone/
  http://www.eurocall.com/e/

IRC (Internet Relay Chat)

IRC is an old, well-established system for talking over the Net. To use IRC, you need an IRC client program. Your client connects to an IRC server. You can now talk to people all over the world. IRC is organized into "channels" (some of which you will see in this book). To participate, you "join" one or more channels. It is important to realize that, unlike Usenet groups, IRC channels are created and removed dynamically. Anyone can create a new IRC channel; when the last person leaves a particular channel, it is removed automatically. (The channels in this book are so popular, there is almost always someone around to keep them open.) IRC is fabulous, but before you start I do want you to know what you are doing. Begin by visiting this Web site where you will find a wealth of information: FAQs (frequently asked question lists), primers, RFCs (technical documents, aka "request for comments"), help files, information for channel ops (operators), and lists of IRC servers to which you can connect. (For a comprehensive easy-to-understand introduction to IRC, see one of my Internet books.)

Web:
  http://www.irchelp.org/

IRC Talk and General Discussion

Using IRC (Internet Relay Chat) is like going into a crowded bar, only there is not as much smoke and no cover charge. Mingle with crowds of people, make new friends, have philosophical discussions—use your imagination. Just about anything can happen when you're on IRC. Check out these Usenet groups which cover topics like announcements, specific IRC channels, and questions relating to IRC.

Usenet:
  alt.irc.hottub
  alt.irc.questions
  alt.irc.undernet

> Life is cool. (Get used to it.)

TALKING ON THE NET

Java Chat Applets

Java is a system that allows your browser to download programs which are then automatically run on your computer. Such programs are called "applets" (small applications). Here is a list of links to Java-based chat rooms that use various applets. You will also find special purpose chat applets for IRC, muds and games. These applets are really fun—and convenient to use. I had one running in a little window in the corner of my screen, and I could still use my browser. If you like doing a lot of things at the same time, you can max out on Java.

Web:
http://www.developer.com/directories/pages/dir.java.net.chat.source.html

List of BBSs on the Internet

BBS junkies can celebrate over these comprehensive lists of BBSs on the Net. This site gives an overview of Internet BBSs, connect information, as well as links to Web pages.

Web:
http://www.thedirectory.org/telnet/

BBSs on the Net

If you're all undressed, but you still have a hankering for going out, the Net is at your service.

There are oodles and gobs of BBSs you can visit, 24 hours a day, no matter how casual your attire.

Look What I Found on the Net...

```
Newsgroups: alt.irc, alt.irc.annnounce, alt.irc.hottub
Subject: New IRC Server

> ***NEW FREE SWINGERS IRC SERVER NOW ONLINE!!!***
> Server: 196.33.249.10
>
> Help build it up.

Will there be discussions about those carnival swing rides?

You know, the plastic seats on chains which swing around and
around until the chains break, sending you into the adjoining
vacant lot?
```

mIRC Client

mIRC is a popular IRC client program that is used around the world. (I use it and like it a great deal.) mIRC is available for Windows, Macintosh and Unix. These Web sites have a great deal of information about mIRC and IRC to help you get started: FAQs, command lists, help files (which are important), scripts, utilities, bots (programs that participate in IRC and provide particular services) and, of course, the mIRC program itself for you to download.

Web:
http://www.mirc.org/
http://www.mircx.com/

NetMeeting (Internet Explorer)

NetMeeting is a full-featured Internet communication program developed by Microsoft. NetMeeting, which requires Windows 95, is designed to integrate with Microsoft's Web browser, the Internet Explorer. With NetMeeting you can talk to other people (with voice, like a telephone); type text messages back and forth; share programs, files and the contents of your Windows clipboard; and work together using a shared whiteboard (drawing area). This Web site has all the information you need to get started, including the program itself (which is free).

Web:
http://www.microsoft.com/netmeeting/

Powwow

Powwow is a great program for Windows that allows multiple people to chat, trade files and explore the Web as a group. Go to this Web page to download Powwow. You will also find extra sound files (you can send sounds to other people), add-on software (such as an address book and a sound file sorter), address books of other Powwow users, conference listings, help files and more. Powwow is a lot of fun.

Web:
http://www.powwow.com/

> **Are you a modem or a mouse?**

Talkers

A talker is an easy-to-use multiuser talk facility. You connect to a talker using telnet. (Telnet is a program that acts like a terminal and allows you to connect to a remote computer. Telnet is usually included with general Internet software, so there is a good chance that you already have a telnet program on your computer. This is the case if you use Windows 95 or OS/2.) Once you connect to a talker, you can talk to anyone else who happens to be there. If you are a mud person, you can think of a talker as being a simple mud or mush devoted entirely to conversation. These Web sites contain lists of talkers and where you can find them. One of the sites has additional information, such as the history of talkers, and the rules and culture.

Web:
http://list.ewtoo.org/
http://www.xonia.com/talker/talkers.cgi

Video Conferencing

Video conferencing refers to conducting a real time voice+video conversation between two or more people. Some people say that, in the future, it will be common to meet with other people via video conferencing. Isaac Asimov wrote a book about a planet in which the people would meet one another *only* by three-dimensional video conferencing and not in person. Personally, I think that people want the visual anonymity of a voice-only connection and that video conferencing will never be as popular as the telephone. We will see. In the meantime, here is a Usenet group in which you can discuss the state of the video conferencing art, and a Web site containing several useful resources.

Web:
http://www.video-conferencing.com/

Usenet:
comp.dcom.videoconf

TALKING ON THE NET

Web Chat Rooms

A Web chat room is a facility that lets you talk to people over the Web. Some chat rooms require you to have special software in order to participate. With others, your Web browser will do everything you need. When you connect to a chat room Web site, you will commonly find a number of rooms, each of which is devoted to discussing a specific topic. Other Web sites are devoted to a specific organization or theme. For example, a radio talk show may set up a chat room for its listeners to talk to one another while they are listening to the show. Or a company may set up a chat room for customers to talk about its products. Many Web sites allow you to specify a small image to identify yourself to other people. Each time you send a message, this image is displayed next to the message. Sometimes you can furnish your own image. You could use, for example, a small picture of yourself. Other chat rooms require you to choose an image from their library. The Web sites I have listed all have chat rooms open to the public. However, some of the services may ask you to register. When you visit, you will find people from all over the Net talking on many different topics.

Web:
http://chat.earthweb.com/
http://chat.netcentral.net/
http://www.4-lane.com/
http://www.chatalyst.com/
http://www.chathouse.com/
http://www.chatting.com/
http://www.cyber-beach.com/gateway.html
http://www.talkcity.com/
http://www.theglobe.com/
http://www.wbs.net/

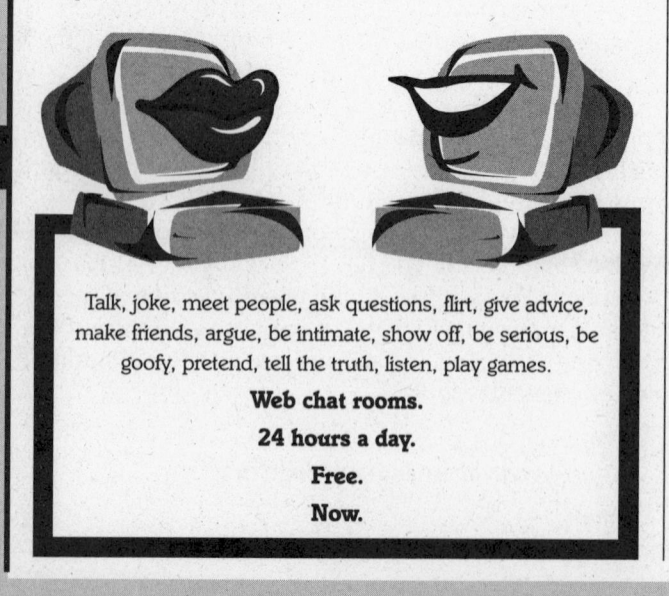

Talk, joke, meet people, ask questions, flirt, give advice, make friends, argue, be intimate, show off, be serious, be goofy, pretend, tell the truth, listen, play games.
Web chat rooms.
24 hours a day.
Free.
Now.

TELEPHONE AND TELECOM

Business and Toll-Free Directory Listings

Looking for a particular business? If the company or organization you want has a telephone, they are probably in here somewhere. These Web sites allow you to search for the phone number of a business. Some of the sites are directories of toll-free numbers, the others help you find regular numbers.

Web:
http://www.anywho.com/tf.html
http://www.bigbook.com/
http://www.zip2.com/

Cell-Relay Communications

A "cell" refers to a small device that can be used for transporting and multiplexing information over a network. This discussion group is devoted to the technologies—such as ATM (Asynchronous Transfer Mode)—that make use of cells as transport mechanisms within local, metropolitan and wide-area networks.

Usenet:
comp.dcom.cell-relay

Data Communications Servers

On Usenet, you can find people who are ready, willing and able to discuss data communications 24 hours a day. This particular Usenet group is for discussion relating to selecting and operating data communications servers: special purpose computers that do the dirty work in moving information from one place to another (terminal servers, routers, hubs, and so on).

Usenet:
comp.dcom.servers

Fax Technology

There is more to fax machines than just using them to transmit the latest Dilbert comic strip to someone who is not lucky enough to have Net access. This Usenet group is for the discussion of faxes: standalone machines, computer adaptors and software, technical specifications, faxing on the Net, and so on.

Usenet:
comp.dcom.fax

TELEPHONE AND TELECOM 763

International Dialing Codes

When you have to call a foreign country, but you are not sure where to start, check here. This site has a list of international dialing codes along with the time zones for each country.

Web:
http://www.construction-site.com/int_dial.htm

Aren't you glad you dial correctly? Don't you wish everybody did?

Look What I Found on the Net...

This is information I selected from the International Dialing Codes Web site.

For each country you can see the international dialing code, followed by the time difference between local time and GMT/Universal Time (in hours). To find the time difference between two countries, simply subtract one number from the other.

```
     Australia  61   (+8 to +10)
       Austria  43   (+1)
       Belgium  32   (+1)
        Brazil  55   (-3)
        Canada  1    (-3.5 to - 8)
         China  86   (+8)
       Denmark  45   (+1)
         Egypt  20   (+2)
       Finland  358  (+2)
        France  33   (+1)
       Germany  49   (+1)
        Greece  30   (+2)
     Hong Kong  852  (+8)
         India  91   (+5.5)
       Ireland  353  (0)
        Israel  972  (+2)
         Italy  39   (+1)
         Japan  81   (+9)
        Mexico  52   (-6 to - 8)
   Netherlands  31   (+1)
        Norway  47   (+1)
        Poland  48   (+1)
      Portugal  361  (+1)
        Russia  7    (+2.5 to +10)
     Singapore  65   (+8)
  South Africa  27   (+2)
         Spain  34   (+1)
        Sweden  46   (+1)
   Switzerland  41   (+1)
         Syria  963  (+2)
        Taiwan  886  (+8)
United Kingdom  44   (0)
 United States  1    (-5 to -11)
```

National Telecommunications and Information Administration

Whenever I want to know what the National Telecommunications and Information Administration is up to, I check out their official Web site. They use the Web to make accessible their press releases, public notices and information on international telecommunications activities. When you just can't wait for the news to hit the streets, go straight to the source.

Web:
http://www.ntia.doc.gov/

Networks

Specific networking information can be hard to find. For example, what would you do, right now, if you needed some info on ATM, or ISDN, or SMNP, or NT Server? Would you know where to find the Web sites for important networking magazines and journals? Here is everything you need—at least to get started—all in one place, well-organized and comprehensive. If you have anything to do with any aspect of computer networks, these sites should be on your bookmark list.

Web:
http://www.specialty.com/hiband/
http://www.webcom.com/~llarrow/comfaqs.html

Phone Number Translator

Here is a Web site that allows you to input your telephone number, then checks for all the possible word combinations that correlate. If you don't want to sift through the results to weed out the letter combinations that are garbage, you can have the computer compare the results to dictionary words and only give you the ones that make sense (sort of).

Web:
http://www.phonetic.com/

Your Telephone Number Secrets Unmasked

You know that it is possible to convert your phone number from numbers to letters: 2 = A, B or C; 3 = D, E or F; and so on. But have you ever taken your personal number and tried all possible combinations to see if they spell anything cool? If so, you will find that there are a *lot* of combinations. But why should you sweat when you have the Net?

Connect to the **Phone Number Translator** Web site, and let a computer do the work. Plug your number into this handy-dandy form and, before you can say 1-800-HOWCOOL, you will be shown all the interesting alphabetic combinations that match your particular number.

Maybe you'll get lucky. One person I know found out her number spelled out "SEX-YOGA". (You can imagine what this did for her social life.)

Hint: Converting numbers to letters is useful for helping to remember anything you must enter on a telephone-like keypad, such as your ATM secret code.

Telecom Discussions and Digest

The Telecom Digest is an online digest posted regularly to Usenet. If you are interested in telecommunications, this is a source of information worth reading regularly. The **telecom** discussion groups are for all manner of telecommunications including—but not limited to—the telephone system. For more immediate gratification, check out the Web site.

Web:
http://hyperarchive.lcs.mit.edu/telecom-archives/

Usenet:
alt.dcom.telecom
comp.dcom.telecom

TELEPHONE AND TELECOM

Telecom Resources

Telecommunications is changing our culture faster than any other type of technology. Moreover, telecommunications itself is changing so fast even professionals have a hard time keeping up. I have chosen these resources to help you find telecommunications information as you need it and to make it easy for you to check in every now and then to see what's new.

Web:
http://china.si.umich.edu/telecom/telecom-info.html
http://www.analysys.com/vlib/
http://www.gbmarks.com/
http://www.telecoms-mag.com/

Telephone Tech Talk and General Discussion

Next to the Internet, the phone is one of the greatest inventions of humankind. Without the phone, you could never dial the pizza place and have them make you a steaming hot pizza with everything (except celery) and deliver it to your door. That's all most of us need to know about the phone, but if you are interested in more than that—like learning what the guts of the telephone look like and how the wires connect, then join up with some telephone tech talk on Usenet.

Usenet:
comp.dcom.telecom.tech

Look What I Found on the Net...

```
Newsgroup: comp.dcom.telecom.tech
Subject: Return the Phone Call Scam

> One of my fellow users has received two identical copies of
> the following email.  He has no connection to Global,
> and given the 809 code,  it is assumed to be a scam.
> Watch out for a similar note coming your way.
>
> (Note the lack of a "To:" line.)
>
> ------- Forwarded message -------
> Return-Path: <accounts@global>
> Date: Tue, 1 Oct 1996 14:12:49 -0700
> From: "Global Communications"@demon.net
> Subject: Unpaid account
> Message-ID: <844184592.19166.164@[194.222.75.163]>
>
> I am writing to give you a final 24 hours to settle your
> outstanding account. If I have not received the settlement in
> full, I will commence legal proceedings without further delay.
> If you would like to discuss this matter to avoid court
> action, call Mike Murray at Global Communications on
> +1 809 xxx-xxxx.

A similar scam exists for pagers.  They page you with an
809 xxx-xxxx number expecting you to return the call.

When you do, you are routed to an expensive international call.

By dialing this number, you end up paying for an expensive
long distance call.
```

Underwater Telecommunication Cables

I find this Web site fascinating. It contains maps showing the locations of underwater telecommunications cables all around the world. When I look at these maps, I am overwhelmed thinking about all the effort it must have taken to create and install the cables, and how important they are to mankind. Safety hint: The underwater cable maps are useful if you plan to start your own offshore oil drilling installation, and you want to make sure you don't accidentally interrupt the transatlantic telephone service.

Web:
http://w3.lab.kdd.co.jp/kdd/cable/

U.S. Area Codes

The need for new phone numbers has increased rapidly in the last few years because of cellular phones, faxes and computer lines. In many parts of the United States and Canada, area codes have had to be subdivided in order to create these new numbers. You might ask, is there a master plan? Yes, there is. It's called the North American Numbering Plan or NANP. However, there are so many changes that it's difficult to keep track of them all. This resource will help you find the information you need quickly.

Web:
http://decoder.americom.com/

TELEVISION

Andy Griffith

It would be wonderful if every town sheriff was like Andy Griffith. But then, not every town is like Mayberry. We can't imagine Andy Griffith being sheriff of Los Angeles or New York City. Settle in for discussion of the nostalgia of The Andy Griffith Show and Mayberry RFD. It's a nice break from the real world.

Web:
http://www.mayberry.com/tagsrwc/
http://www.visi.com/~muff/andy-griffith.html

Beverly Hills 90210

Only a city in California would be able to get a television show based on its zip code. Read mailing lists, archives, and see pictures relating to Beverly Hills 90210—the show where the only thing that rivals the price of the clothing is the price of the silicone enhancements.

Web:
http://members.aol.com/rexfelis/
http://www.unioninn.demon.co.uk/BHills/BHIn.html

Usenet:
alt.tv.bh90210

Majordomo Mailing List:
List Name: 90210
Subscribe to: majordomo@tcp.com

The Andy Griffith Show

Perhaps somewhere, there are people who have not watched each of the 249 episodes of The Andy Griffith Show and have not immersed themselves in the stories of Andy, Barney, Aunt Bee, Opie, Floyd, Gomer, Goober, Helen, Thelma Lou, Otis and the rest of the inhabitants of Mayberry, North Carolina.

I feel sorry for such people because they are missing out on what is most noble and fine in life: a society in which people most always get along, in which life's problems are well within the capabilities of a small-town sheriff and the homespun wisdom God has seen fit to bestow upon him. Within the show, Andy was sometimes referred to as the "sheriff without a gun", but he might just as well have been called the "sheriff who doesn't need a gun".

For at least a few minutes each week (and now, every day in reruns), we could transport ourselves to a small town in which everyday problems were manageable and human dignity was preserved simply as a matter of course.

To ask whether there is justice in the world is an elegant but troubling question. To ask whether there is justice in Mayberry is both unnecessary and misleading. One does not watch The Andy Griffith Show for anything remotely involving one's higher cortical functionality. Rather, we worship at the shrine of blessed banality simply because, in a world of discomforting unpredictability and baffling complexity, Mayberry and its inhabitants occupy one of the few safe rest stops available to the human spirit in all of us, as it navigates the confusing and oft-times rocky road of life.

Brady Bunch

I was visiting Christopher Barnes (Greg Brady in the Brady Bunch movies). We had just finished our dinner, and we were sipping our tea and talking politics. Suddenly, I realized what a totally cool thing I was doing. Imagine sitting at the dinner table with Greg discussing the world and how to fix it. The only thing better would be to get the whole family together and go on a trip to the Grand Canyon. Is there any family in television history that has captured our hearts and minds so effectively as The Brady Bunch? What a wacky, lovable bunch of characters: the kids (Greg, Peter, Bobby, Marsha, Jan and Cindy), their parents (Mike and Carol), and their housekeeper (Alice). Who says it's a fantasy? On the Internet, you can not only live in the past, you can live in a perfect past, where everyone has fun, gets along, and solves all their problems within a half hour. Or, as Carol puts it: "You know, money and fame are very important things, but, well, sometimes there are other things that are more important—like people."

Web:
http://www.bradyworld.com/brady.htm
http://www.primenet.com/~dbrady/
http://www.teleport.com/~btucker/bbinfo.htm

Usenet:
alt.tv.brady-bunch

Cartoons

I like cartoons. They're soothing, like a good book on a rainy day (except you can't turn up the volume on a good book and disturb the neighbors). If you like cartoons, check out some of the great toon resources on the Net. You can get pictures, sounds, movies and other cool cartoon stuff.

Web:
http://ftp.wi.net/~rkurer/
http://members.aol.com/paulec1/clutchjr.html
http://www.stud.ifi.uio.no/~jornl/cartoon/

I like cartoons, and I bet you do too. If so, check out the cartoon sites on the Net.

Comedy Central

Check out what's going on at Comedy Central, the laugh-a-minute cable comedy station. At their Web site you can find funny stuff like sound clips or read the current day's schedule. You can even see what's happening on Comedy Central right this minute if you load up their live-eye view page.

Web:
http://www.comcentral.com/

Commercials

Some people are really annoyed by commercials, but if you think about it you will realize what a marvelous invention they are. If there were no commercials, you would never have the opportunity to dash to the kitchen for snacks or run to the bathroom for a quick bit of relief. So pay your homage to the great commercial Mecca on Usenet and show how much you appreciate the service that companies are doing for television watchers around the world.

Usenet:
alt.tv.commercials

Daytime Talk Shows

Take pity on those people who waste their time working all day, for they are not able to enhance their existence on Planet Earth by watching daytime talk shows. People may sneer at these shows; they may say that the hosts and hostesses pander to sensationalism and the lowest common cultural denominator. Never mind. You and I know that Jenny, Leeza and Sally and the rest of them are more than mere television personalities, they are honored guests in our homes. Let's face it. From day to day, most of us have pretty dull lives (and thankfully so). Isn't it nice to know that any afternoon we want, we can turn on the TV and see interviews with people whose lives are more to be pitied than censured.

Web:
http://jennyjones.warnerbros.com/
http://oprah.virtual-space.com/index.shtml
http://rosieo.warnerbros.com/
http://www.geraldo.com/
http://www.nbc.com/tvcentral/shows/leeza/
http://www.oprahshow.com/
http://www.sallyjr.com/

Usenet:
alt.tv.talkshows.daytime

768 TELEVISION

Dick Van Dyke Show

The Dick Van Dyke Show is my all-time favorite television show. In fact, I challenge any of my friends to ask me a Dick Van Dyke question I can't answer. If you enjoy watching the adventures of Rob, Laura, Buddy, Sally, Mel, Jerry, Millie, Alan Brady, and that obnoxious little kid Ritchie Rosebud, pay a visit to this Web site, where you can re-live your hours of Dick Van Dyke watching (until it's time for the next rerun).

Web:
http://www.nick-at-nite.com/tvretro/shows/2.108/

ER

ER is an American television drama based in the emergency room of a Chicago hospital. The stories in ER are mostly concerned with the lives of the people who work in the emergency room; the patients are secondary. For this reason, the ER characters have, over time, attracted an enormous following around the world, and their fictional lives are topics of discussion all over the Net. Although most people don't really care about the latest patient brought into the emergency room, who among us can say he wasn't upset when it finally became clear that Susan and Mark will never get together?

Web:
http://www.digiserve.com/er/erdex.html

Usenet:
alt.tv.er

Listserv Mailing List:
List Name: er-l
Subscribe to: listserv@gcp.thenorth.com

Little Bo Peep lost her sheep, so she used "Finding Stuff on the Net".

Dick Van Dyke Show

The Dick Van Dyke Show was one of those rare artistic creations where everything comes together perfectly for an extended period of time. The producer and creator (Carl Reiner), the executive producer (Sheldon Leonard), the writers, the directors and the actors (Dick Van Dyke, Mary Tyler Moore, Rose Marie, Morey Amsterdam and Richard Deacon)—all of these people were hard-working, talented professionals who were masters of their craft.

However, there is more. The first Dick Van Dyke Show was filmed before a live audience on January 20, 1961. The last show was filmed on March 26, 1966. This time period marks the end of the transition from the Golden Age of Radio into modern television, and this show represents the last marvelous legacy from a time in which audiences expected only to be entertained, and performers knew their primary job was to tell jokes, sing songs, dance, and act out a story.

In the transition from one age to another, there is often a short breathing space as the old, mature culture segues into the new one. By the time the Dick Van Dyke Show had finished, the United States was embroiled in Vietnam, the sexual revolution and national protests. But for one long idyllic moment, God was in his heaven, all was right with the world, and, each week, we could count on Rob, Laura, Sally, Buddy and Mel to entertain and amuse us.

Game Shows

Game show junkies now have something to do when they are not actually watching game shows or reading trivia books to improve their game show skills. Read FAQs about popular Canadian and U.S. game shows.

Web:
http://www.cis.ohio-state.edu/hypertext/faq/usenet/tv/game-shows/top.html

Why watch it on TV when you can see it on the Net? See "Broadcasting on the Net".

Look What I Found on the Net...

(from the list of U.S. game shows)

```
About Faces
All About the Opposite Sex
All New Beat the Clock, The
All New Dating Game, The
All New Let's Make a Deal, The
All Star Secrets
All-Star Anything Goes
All-Star Baffle
All-Star Blitz
Almost Anything Goes
Amateur's Guide to Love
American Gladiators
Animal Crack-ups
Anniversary Game, The
Anything for Money
Anything You Can Do
    .
    .
    .
    .
Yahtzee
You Bet Your Life
You Don't Say
You're in the Picture
You're Putting Me On
Your First Impression
Your Lucky Clue
Your Number's Up
Your Surprise Package
Yours for a Song
```

770 TELEVISION

High Definition Television

High definition television is a system that is designed to replace regular TV. The basic changes are a wider aspect ratio and many more scan lines. High definition TV uses an aspect ratio of 16 x 9 (16 units across by 9 units up), similar to movies. The old TV standard uses a more square screen that is 4 x 3. In addition, high definition TV uses 1,125 lines of resolution, compared to only 525 on the old system. The result is a TV image that is wider and sharper. These Web sites provide information for professionals and the general public. Read about the high definition technology and how it is used to create a whole new television system.

Web:
http://www.atsc.org/
http://www.sinfonia.net/mike/hdtv/
http://www.web-star.com/hdtv/hdtvnews1.html

I Love Lucy

Is there anyone on our entire planet who does *not* love Lucy? The I Love Lucy show is the most popular situation comedy of all time, being in continual reruns with no signs of stopping. I have watched every I Love Lucy episode from "Lucy Thinks Ricky Is Trying to Murder Her" (#1) to "The Ricardos Dedicate a Statue" (#179). (And I don't even like TV.) But I am not alone in my love for Lucy. There are diehard fans all over the world and all over the Net.

Web:
http://members.aol.com/TVFan81/

Late Night Talk Shows

In the United States, it has been the custom for several decades to watch a late-night talk show before falling asleep in front of the television set. For many years, late night was ruled by Johnny Carson, but since he retired in May 1992, the nation's attention has been split between Jay Leno and David Letterman. These Web sites and discussion groups are devoted to Jay and David—their shows, their jokes and their fans.

Web:
http://marketing.cbs.com/latenight/
http://users.cybercity.dk/~dko1225/leno.htm
http://www.ddy.com/dl2.html
http://www.nbc.com/tonightshow/

Usenet:
alt.fan.jay-leno
alt.fan.letterman
alt.tv.talkshows.late

Muppets

Who couldn't like a Muppet? There are lots of Muppet fans on the Net and they have created wonderful pages in honor of Jim Henson's creations. Spend some time experiencing the Muppets through pictures, sounds, song lyrics, and more. Or go to the Usenet group and talk with other fans of the various Muppet shows and movies.

Web:
http://www.muppets.com/

Usenet:
alt.tv.muppets

Public Broadcasting Service (PBS)

The Public Broadcasting Service (PBS) is a private, nonprofit organization that serves well over 300 member television stations in the United States. PBS was founded in 1968 with a mandate to provide high-quality TV programming. Quality, of course, is in the eye and ear of the beholder and, in a highly politicized country in which the average television image lasts less than 10 seconds, you can bet there will be disagreement. Still, PBS offers a lot of programming that is just not available on commercial television. Check their Web site to see what they are up to, and if you should be tuning in, or turning on and dropping out.

Web:
http://www.pbs.org/

Satellite TV

Using a special antenna, it is possible to receive TV programs directly as they are broadcast from various satellites. The services cost money, but the variety of available programs is enormous and the quality of the signal is excellent. Isn't it marvelous that a technology has finally been developed that ensures you will never, ever run out of interesting things to watch? Now that satellite TV is here, the only reason you need ever take a break from watching the tube is to check your email.

Web:
http://www.newchannels.demon.co.uk/
http://www.satguide.com/
http://www.sportsnetwork.com/default.asp?page=/news/satellite.htm

Usenet:
rec.video.satellite
rec.video.satellite.dbs
rec.video.satellite.europe
rec.video.satellite.misc
rec.video.satellite.tvro

TELEVISION

Simpsons

If you ever get a chance to visit Springfield—somewhere in the United States—be sure to drop in to Evergreen Terrace and call on the Simpsons: Homer, Marge, Bart, Lisa and Maggie. (The street number is either 94, 59, 723, 742 or 1094, depending on which episode you're watching.) This achingly pathetic but irresistibly endearing cartoon family has developed a worldwide following unique in the history of television. There are many, many Simpson fans on the Net and more Web sites than you can shake a stick at. (Actually, I tried once and all that happened was the stick broke). By the way, if you do decide to drop by Evergreen Terrace, you may want to call first. The phone number is 555-6528 (according to Principal Skinner's rolodex card).

Web:
http://www.bodo.com/simpson.htm
http://www.foxworld.com/simpsons/
http://www.snpp.com/

Usenet:
alt.tv.simpsons

Sitcom Downfalls

When was the exact moment that a popular sitcom (situation comedy) started to go downhill? Vote for the defining moment for your favorite show and see what others think. For example, Seinfeld started going downhill after Susan died; Laverne and Shirley began their plunge after the move to Los Angeles; and MASH hit the skids when Charles replaced Frank.

Web:
http://www.jumptheshark.com/

Soap Operas

Soap opera fans, the Net is *your* home away from the TV. There are so many soap-opera-related resources, you can spend every waking moment—when you are not watching a show—following the adventures of your favorite characters and talking with other soap fans. I picked out this Web site to act as your gateway to a huge amount of interesting information. And when you feel like talking, there are several Usenet groups in which you can participate.

Web:
http://members.aol.com/soaplinks/

Usenet:
alt.tv.all-my-children
alt.tv.another-world
alt.tv.days-of-our-lives
alt.tv.general-hospital
alt.tv.one-life-to-live
rec.arts.tv.soaps.abc
rec.arts.tv.soaps.cbs
rec.arts.tv.soaps.misc

South Park

South Park is a crudely animated cartoon that is very, very gross, and very, very funny (two characteristics that normally don't go together). The show features a group of foulmouthed, yet lovable, third graders, Stan, Kyle, Cartman and Kenny, along with the bizarre inhabitants of the town of South Park, Colorado. If you are a teen-age boy with a highly developed sense of the vulgar, you will love South Park. If you are not a teen-age boy with a highly developed sense of the vulgar, you are on your own. (Note to parents: This is not a show you want to watch. Just let the kids enjoy it and stay out of the room.)

Web:
http://mrhat.simplenet.com/
http://www.andyland.org/southpark/
http://www.comcentral.com/southpark/
http://www.everwonder.com/david/southpark/spfaq.html
http://www.southparkcows.com/
http://www.sweeet.com/

Usenet:
alt.tv.southpark

Majordomo Mailing List:
List Name: **southpark**
Subscribe to: **majordomo@valinor.eldar.org**

SOUTH PARK

It's cool.

It's gross.

It's totally sick and twisted.

Go watch it right now on the Net.

772 TELEVISION

Television Talk and General Discussion

Don't waste your life in sitting in front of the computer. Instead, you can waste it in front of another electronic box which gives you a continuous feed of images that will lull you into a hypnotic daze and make you susceptible to the lure of home shopping channels. If you are so hooked that you like to talk about television when you are not actually watching it, check out these Usenet groups.

Usenet:
alt.fan.hawaii-five-o
alt.fan.red.green
alt.fan.rumpole
alt.tv
alt.tv.3rd-rock
alt.tv.7th-heaven
alt.tv.a-team
alt.tv.aaron-spelling
alt.tv.ab-fab
alt.tv.aeon-flux
alt.tv.airwolf
alt.tv.ally-mcbeal
alt.tv.amer-gothic
alt.tv.animaniacs
alt.tv.avengers
alt.tv.babylon-5
alt.tv.barney
alt.tv.baywatch
alt.tv.beakmans-world
alt.tv.beauty+beast
alt.tv.bh90210
alt.tv.blues-clues
alt.tv.boston-common
alt.tv.brady-bunch
alt.tv.brisco-county
alt.tv.buffy-v-slayer
alt.tv.caroline-city
alt.tv.cell-block-h
alt.tv.chicago-hope
alt.tv.christy
alt.tv.cow-n-chicken
alt.tv.dallas
alt.tv.dark-skies
alt.tv.dark_shadows
alt.tv.dawsons-creek
alt.tv.degrassi
alt.tv.dexters-lab
alt.tv.dharma-greg
alt.tv.dinosaurs

alt.tv.dr-quinn
alt.tv.duckman
alt.tv.due-south
alt.tv.due-south.creative
alt.tv.dungeon-dragon
alt.tv.early-edition
alt.tv.earth-final-conflict
alt.tv.earth2
alt.tv.eek-the-cat
alt.tv.emergency
alt.tv.er
alt.tv.expedientes-x
alt.tv.fools-and-horses
alt.tv.forever-knight
alt.tv.frasier
alt.tv.freakazoid
alt.tv.friends
alt.tv.game-shows
alt.tv.gold-monkey
alt.tv.hercules
alt.tv.hermans-head
alt.tv.highlander
alt.tv.hogans-heroes
alt.tv.home-and-away
alt.tv.home-imprvment
alt.tv.hometime
alt.tv.homicide
alt.tv.infomercials
alt.tv.iron-chef
alt.tv.kids-in-hall
alt.tv.kids-inc
alt.tv.kindred
alt.tv.king-of-hill
alt.tv.knight-rider
alt.tv.kungfu
alt.tv.la-law
alt.tv.lafemme-nikita
alt.tv.law-and-order
alt.tv.lexx
alt.tv.liquid-tv
alt.tv.lois-n-clark
alt.tv.lois-n-clark.fanfic
alt.tv.macross
alt.tv.mad-about-you
alt.tv.mad-tv
alt.tv.magnificent-7
alt.tv.magnum-pi
alt.tv.mannix
alt.tv.martha-stewart
alt.tv.mash
alt.tv.mathnet

TELEVISION 773

alt.tv.max-headroom
alt.tv.melrose-place
alt.tv.miami-vice
alt.tv.millennium
alt.tv.millennium.uk
alt.tv.mission-imposs
alt.tv.mr-belvedere
alt.tv.mst3k
alt.tv.mtv
alt.tv.mtv-europe
alt.tv.murder-one
alt.tv.mwc
alt.tv.my-s-c-life
alt.tv.networks.cbc
alt.tv.newsradio
alt.tv.nick-at-nite
alt.tv.nickelodeon
alt.tv.northern-exp
alt.tv.nowhere-man
alt.tv.nypd-blue
alt.tv.oprah
alt.tv.outer-limits
alt.tv.party-of-five
alt.tv.picket-fences
alt.tv.pirate
alt.tv.pizzacats
alt.tv.pol-incorrect
alt.tv.port-charles
alt.tv.pretender
alt.tv.prisoner
alt.tv.profiler
alt.tv.public-access
alt.tv.quantum-leap.creative
alt.tv.quincy-me
alt.tv.real-world
alt.tv.reboot
alt.tv.red-dwarf.discussion
alt.tv.red-dwarf.fans
alt.tv.remember-wenn
alt.tv.ren-n-stimpy
alt.tv.road-rules
alt.tv.robotech
alt.tv.rockford-files
alt.tv.roseanne
alt.tv.sabrina
alt.tv.saved-bell
alt.tv.scott-bakula
alt.tv.sctv
alt.tv.seaquest
alt.tv.seinfeld

alt.tv.sentai
alt.tv.sentinel
alt.tv.sesame-street
alt.tv.silk-stalkings
alt.tv.simpsons
alt.tv.simpsons.itchy-scratchy
alt.tv.sitcom
alt.tv.sliders
alt.tv.sliders.creative
alt.tv.smk
alt.tv.snl
alt.tv.southpark
alt.tv.space-a-n-b
alt.tv.space-cases
alt.tv.stargate-sg1
alt.tv.superman-adventures
alt.tv.talkshows.daytime
alt.tv.talkshows.late
alt.tv.teletubbies
alt.tv.the-goodies
alt.tv.the-nanny
alt.tv.the-practice
alt.tv.the-state
alt.tv.the-tick
alt.tv.thebox
alt.tv.this-old-house
alt.tv.tiny-toon
alt.tv.toute-fabienne
alt.tv.twin-peaks
alt.tv.upstairs-downstairs
alt.tv.v
alt.tv.vr5
alt.tv.wings
alt.tv.wiseguy
alt.tv.wonder-years
alt.tv.x-files
alt.tv.x-files.creative
alt.tv.xena
rec.arts.sf.tv.quantum-leap
rec.arts.tv
rec.arts.tv.interactive
rec.arts.tv.soaps
rec.arts.tv.tiny-toon
rec.arts.tv.uk
rec.arts.tv.uk.comedy
rec.arts.tv.uk.coronation-st
rec.arts.tv.uk.eastenders
rec.arts.tv.uk.emmerdale
rec.arts.tv.uk.misc

774 TELEVISION

Television Theme Songs

I'm warning you. If you have anything to do for the next three hours, don't visit these Web sites. Once you do, you will spend a lot of time listening to theme songs for your favorite TV shows. In my case, I got seriously sidetracked from my research listening to the theme songs from Andy Griffith, Dick Van Dyke, The Prisoner, Popeye and Roger Ramjet. (In case you like to sing along, I've included a Web site with lyrics to TV theme songs.)

Web:

http://earthstation1.simplenet.com/themes.html
http://wso.williams.edu/~mgarland/sounds/

Look What I Found on the Net...

(from one of the Television Theme Song Web sites)

```
Meet Cathy, who's lived most everywhere,
From Zanzibar to Berkeley Square,
But Patty's only seen the sights,
A girl can see from Brooklyn Heights,
What a crazy pair...

They're creepy and they're kooky,
Mysterious and spooky,
They're all together ooky,
The Addams Family...

Come and listen to a story about a man named Jed,
A poor mountaineer, barely kept his family fed,
Then one day he was shootin' at some food,
And up through the ground come a bubblin' crude...

Just sit right back and you'll hear the tale,
The tale of a fateful trip,
That started in this tropic port,
Aboard this tiny ship..

Through early morning fog I see,
Visions of the things to be,
The pains that are withheld for me,
I realize and I can see...

A horse is a horse, of course, of course,
And no one can talk to a horse, of course,
That is, of course, unless the horse is the famous Mr. Ed...

Here's the story of a lovely lady,
Who was bringing up three very lovely girls,
All of them had hair of gold, like their mother,
The youngest one in curls...

Boy, the way Glenn Miller played,
Songs that made the hit parade,
Guys like us, we had it made,
Those were the days...
```

TELEVISION 775

TV Episode Guides
This Web site is a godsend to fanatics who need to know exactly when each episode of their favorite series aired. There are episode guides to many popular TV shows, including information about the individual episodes. After all, how many places can you turn to at three in the morning when you just have to know when Jerry put the Tweety Bird Pez dispenser on Elaine's knee? (It was episode #314 of Seinfeld, January 15, 1992, during a classical piano recital.)

Web:
http://www.xnet.com/~djk/main_page.shtml

TV Gossip
It's not enough simply to watch television. If you really want to experience it correctly, you have to share in the continual aggrandizement of the entire entertainment industry. Here are some Web sites with articles, news, gossip and information on various TV shows and personalities. So the next time you want to find out who did what to whom when, put down the remote control and pick up the mouse.

Web:
http://www.dailytv.com/
http://www.eonline.com/

TV Guide Postcards
Send some nostalgia to your friends and family. This site offers a wonderful collection of classic covers from TV Guide magazine to use as virtual postcards. You can send a general card or pick one that has a special theme such as Star Trek, Father's Day, Mother's Day, classic couples and others. Send a surprise TV-inspired card to someone you like, right now. Go ahead, make their day.

Web:
http://www.tvgen.com/tv/covers/

TV News Archive
Who says you can't live in the past? Not me. Since 1968, the Vanderbilt Television News Archive has been archiving major news broadcasts to make sure they are recorded, preserved and made accessible to researchers. This Web site allows you to read summaries of these broadcasts. Choose any date you want and read a detailed summary of the news for that day as it was presented on the major networks. If you are a researcher, this Web site is an excellent source for determining exactly when something happened.

Web:
http://tvnews.vanderbilt.edu/tvnews.html

TV Schedules
It takes a lot of time and money to connect yourself to the Net. You need to have a computer and a connection to an Internet service provider. You also need to spend time learning how to use your computer, setting everything up so it connects properly, and teaching yourself to use your Web browser. So after putting in all that time and effort, you might as well use the Net for something important: checking TV schedules. These Web sites will show you what's playing on any channel, any time.

Web:
http://www.tv1.com/
http://www.tvgen.com/tv/listings/
http://www.ultimatetv.com/

X-Files
The X-Files is a spooky, cult television show featuring two FBI agents, one of whom (Mulder, a man) believes anything, no matter how weird. The other agent (Scully, a woman) is a scientist and a skeptic. Mulder and Scully spend their time investigating the "paranormal", with a special emphasis on UFOs and conspiracies. The X-Files is a fabulously popular show because the characters, the relationships and the circumstances are so engaging. So much so, that for people who are willing to suspend their scientific disbelief, what happens on the show is almost believable. If you're an X-Phile, you'll love the idea of spending all your spare time reliving the episodes and tracking down elusive facts on the Net. (For example, during the filming of the show, the Cigarette Smoking Man is actually smoking herbal cigarettes.) If you are creative, there is a mailing list and Usenet group just for X-Files fan fiction (original stories based on the X-Files characters).

Web:
http://chaos.x-philes.com/sites/x-files.html
http://traveller.simplenet.com/xfiles/episode.htm
http://www.thex-files.com/

Usenet:
alt.tv.x-files
alt.tv.x-files.analysis
alt.tv.x-files.creative
alt.tv.x-files.x-ville

Majordomo Mailing List:
List Name: **x-files**
Subscribe to: **majordomo@lists.x-philes.com**

Majordomo Mailing List:
List Name: **x-files-fanfic**
Subscribe to: **majordomo@lists.x-philes.com**

TRAVEL

Air Travel

Air travel can be complex, and it helps to do some research before you go. These Web sites have more travel resources than you could fit in your carry-on luggage. Air safety, airport facilities, flight tracking information—all that and more is waiting for you.

Web:
   http://flight.thetrip.com/flightstatus/
   http://www.airportsintl.com/
   http://www.airsafe.com/

Usenet:
   alt.airline

Amtrak Trains

If you are planning a romantic journey or you just don't feel like getting on a plane, consider taking a train. The Amtrak company has lots of information about train travel, including various routes and the interesting things you will see along the way. Remember, in life it is the journey that is important, not the destination.

Web:
   http://www.amtrak.com/amtrak/travel/

Antarctica

Pick a unique place to go for a vacation adventure. Not many people can say they have been to Antarctica. Here are some Web sites that will lure you into going. They have a wealth of information about Antarctica, including tourism and travel, environment, news, science, treaty and logistical information. When you go, don't forget to send me a postcard.

Web:
   http://www.terraquest.com/va/
   http://www.theice.org/

Australia

The other day my cat said to me, "Harley, let's go to Australia. I hear they have really good fish there." I put him in front of the Web browser and pointed him to this Web site which shows Australia really has a lot more than fish. We saw how the site had tons and tons of information about Australia, but all he wanted to do was play with the mouse. Don't you make the same mistake. Check out this great collection of Australian resources covering geography, environment, communications, travel, culture, weather, government, history, and more. (But do it when your cat is busy preparing a bowl of tuna for dinner.)

Web:
   http://www.channel8.net/australia/

IRC:
   #australia

AMTRAK IS THE NATIONAL RAILWAY ORGANIZATION OF THE UNITED STATES. FOR ONLINE INFORMATION ABOUT WHAT'S COMING AND GOING, TRY THE OFFICIAL AMTRACK WEB SITE.

Budget Travel

When I traveled in Europe, I had a small budget, a Eurail (train) pass, and a book on budget traveling. In my experience, traveling inexpensively can be a lot of fun, but to be as comfortable as possible, it helps to do some research before you leave. To help you, here are some resources with tips, techniques and information you won't find on the beaten track.

Web:
   http://www.artoftravel.com/
   http://www3.sympatico.ca/donna.mcsherry/airports.htm

Usenet:
   rec.travel.budget.backpack

TRAVEL 777

Caribbean

After many months of working on a book, there's nothing like going to the Caribbean with a beautiful woman and spending your days snorkeling or lying around on the beach. If that's what you like to do on your vacation, check out some of the Caribbean resources on the Net. You will find travel and tourist guides, links to other Internet sites, pictures, reading material, news, current weather conditions, and much more about the Caribbean.

Web:
  http://www.cweek.com/
  http://www.freenet.hamilton.on.ca/~aa462/
    carib.html

IRC:
  #caribbean

Castles

Indulge in your fantasies of knights, dragons and castles galore by taking this tour of castles around the world. This site has a huge listing of castles, including those in Edinburgh, Prague, Durham, Wales, Antrim, all over Europe and other locations.

Web:
  http://fox.nstn.ca/~tmonk/castle/casttour.html

City Net Travel Channel

Whether you are planning a trip or just doing a little wishful thinking, this site will give you a world of information. Get connections to tourist guides for many exciting locations, including Europe, the United States, New Zealand, Australia and Japan. The links are presented on a map of the world, from which you can choose the destination of your dreams.

Web:
  http://www.city.net/

Dangerous Travel

Picture yourself being kidnapped by drug lords in Colombia, bribing officials in third world countries, or taking the land mine tour of Afghanistan. If you've always been the adventurous sort, and your normal tourist travel hasn't been challenging enough, check out this information on dangerous places to visit. Or you could be like me and stay home and read about it instead.

Web:
  http://www.fieldingtravel.com/df/

Fodor's Travel Resources

This Web site is presented by the people who produce Fodor's travel guides. My favorite resource is the "personal trip planner". You specify where you want to go and select various choices from menus. You will then be presented with a personalized travel guide, based on information from their database. To test it, I created a planner for a trip that I had already taken. The results were so good, I wished I had done it before I took the trip.

Web:
  http://www.fodors.com/

Castles

The castle of your dreams is out there somewhere, and you can visit it right now, on the Net.

Hawaii

Spend your lunch hour taking a grand tour of the Hawaiian Islands. Spread a little sand around the office floor, turn the fans on, crank up your CD of ocean sounds, and fire up the Web browser—it will almost seem like you are there. There are many pictures and videos at these sites.

Web:
 http://www.hcc.hawaii.edu/dinos/hawaii.mpg
 http://www.mhpcc.edu/tour/Tour.html
 http://www.realwaves.com/

IRC:
 #hawaii
 #hawaiichat

Hostels

Hostels are inexpensive places to stay, offering basic accommodation for informal travelers around the world. Many hostels are only for people below a certain age (youth hostels), but some are open to anyone. When I was younger, I stayed at a lot of youth hostels, and most of the time it was just fine. Hostels are usually centrally located and are great places to meet other people. This Web site has everything you need to know about hostels and budget travel, including a worldwide hostel guide, a forum where you can read or post messages about backpacking, a FAQ about hostelling, information about events and special promotions relating to hostels, and more.

Web:
 http://www.hostels.com/

HOSTELS

Are you young?
Is your travel budget small?
Are you a friendly person who likes to meet other people?

Stay at a hostel: you will fit right in.

Japan

My sister spent two years working in Japan. I never visited her, but if I had, I would have used this guide to help me plan the trip. Since I never actually had to look for a hotel, I didn't use this Web site to find a place to stay that was reasonably priced. And since I didn't have the opportunity to go to museums and art galleries, I didn't check to see what exhibitions were in the area I was going to visit. And since I never traveled around the country, I didn't need to read all the handy tips about Japan and its culture. Still, it's all there waiting for the day when my sister goes back to Japan and I hop over for a visit.

Web:
 http://www.jnto.go.jp/

IRC:
 #japan
 #nippon

Jerusalem

"Ten measures of beauty were bestowed upon the world; nine were taken by Jerusalem, and one by the rest of the world." Jerusalem is truly a world city. A spiritual center for Judaism, Christianity and Islam, Jerusalem is a city with connections to people all over the world. Visit this Web site and explore Jerusalem: images, exhibits, paintings, maps, views of the Old City of Jerusalem, tours of the New City of Jerusalem, audio sounds and songs, and much more about this 4,000-year-old city.

Web:
 http://www1.huji.ac.il/jeru/jerusalem.html

London

Here's a guide book that is so much fun to read you don't even have to go to London to have a good time. This London guide gives you hints and tricks about how not to get ripped off in the city, good places to go, a list of events to see, where to go ghost hunting, and more. It's written in a fun and friendly fashion and is good for armchair travelers or veteran voyagers alike.

Web:
 http://www.a-london-guide.co.uk/

IRC:
 #london

Lonely Planet

This site is chock-full of travel information and photos. You can read about various destinations, as well as look at slide shows. You will also enjoy the many travel tips, including what other travelers have discovered. For example, did you know that Bombay has been renamed Mumbai, and that the Taj Mahal is now closed on Mondays?

Web:
  http://www.lonelyplanet.com/

Megaliths

A megalith is a structure made out of huge stones. There are a large number of ancient megalithic monuments in western Europe and the British Isles dating back to 2000-1500 B.C. Typically, the stones are arranged singly, in rows or in a circle. Although no one knows for sure why these monuments were erected, it is thought that they were used for religious purposes or as part of a funeral ceremony. The most well-known such megalith monument is Stonehenge, located on Salisbury Plain in the south of England. This Web site allows you to take a tour of megaliths in Europe. You can visit stone circles (like Stonehenge), cairns, stone settlements, stone rows, dolmens (chamber tombs) and manmade mounds.

Web:
  http://utenti.micronet.it/dmeozzi/homeng.html

New York City

I love New York in June, how about you? If you are visiting New York City in June or another month of the year, check out these great guides. Don't bite into the Big Apple without them.

Web:
  http://www.ci.nyc.ny.us/
  http://www.theinsider.com/nyc/

IRC:
  #nyc

Packing Tips

When you travel, packing well can make a big difference. On a long trip, I like to travel with a single, large backpack. It's practical and easy to carry. However, as you get older, the backpack will get shoved in the corner of the garage, and you'll find yourself traveling with a couple of suitcases. (You'll see.) Still, knowing what to pack and how to do it well is a skill we can all use, even when we start to travel like adults.

Web:
  http://www.andiamoinc.com/tips/traveltips.html
  http://www.oratory.com/travel/
  http://www.travelfile.com/www/tvl/packing2.html

Paris

Ah, romance. There is nothing more romantic than being with your very special person, relaxing after a romantic candlelight dinner in front of a warm fireplace, snuggled quietly together taking a multimedia tour of Paris on your laptop computer. There is lots of information about Paris on the Net and even an IRC channel for talking. And if you want to actually travel there in person, use the Net to get the info you need to be a happy camper in the City of Love.

Web:
  http://www.w3i.com/

IRC:
  #paris

> When I was in Paris, my favorite attraction was the tour of the sewers. (Don't laugh, Paris has a remarkable sewer system.) However, if you want something a tad more classy, you don't have to go all the way to France: simply connect to the Paris Tours Web site. There are two big advantages to seeing Paris in this way. First, you can stay in your house and do the whole thing in your pajamas. Second, you won't have to eat a lot of rich food with fattening sauces hiding meat of questionable origin.

Railroad Connections

Got a train to catch? Check out these timetables for many trains, subways and metros around the world.

Web:
http://www.cvut.cz/home/railway.htm
http://www.rrhistorical.com/nmra/travel.html

Recreational Vehicles

Recreational vehicles (RVs) are self-contained mobile living environments. People love RVs because, once you have an RV, you can drive wherever you want and never have to worry about finding a place to sleep or eat. If you're spending much time in your RV, using the Net is one of the best ways to stay in touch with the rest of the world. Not only can you send and receive email, but there are some great RV resources available to help you find campsites and exciting places to visit. In addition, you can join the many RV enthusiasts who participate in Usenet discussion groups.

Web:
http://roads.tl.com/
http://www.rvzone.com/

Usenet:
alt.rv
rec.outdoors.rv-travel

Roadside America

When it comes to offbeat and just plain strange, there is no country on Earth like the United States. Just imagine: a huge country with millions of miles of highways, cheap gas, and lots of tourist facilities, all combined with the enormous cultural freedom to do exactly as you wish, without the artificial restrictions of good taste, attractive appearance or tradition. Would you like to see scary museums, mystery spots, gas chambers, or pet cemeteries? How about a place to see really big fake cows? America: is there any place you'd rather be?

Web:
http://www.roadsideamerica.com/

Route 66

Here are details of a drive from Chicago to Santa Monica (Los Angeles) following as much as possible the remains of the historic Route 66, that 2,448-mile long trek built in 1926 and crossing eight states. This Web page offers a list of Route 66 associations, book references, maps, stories, and some plain advice on traveling Route 66.

Web:
http://www.chron.com/voyager/66/

Russia

So you want to go to Russia? Well, the Net will be glad to help. Start by taking an online tour of Moscow, then cruise by some of the Russian travel sites on the Web. These resources will help you make extra sure that all your visas, reservations, immunizations and other paperwork are in order. You will also find travel guides so you can plan a safe, enjoyable trip. Use the Net to prepare for your trip, and it won't be long till you'll be saying, "Vy prynymaete kreditnye kartochky?" like a native. ("Do you accept credit cards?")

Web:
http://users.aimnet.com/~ksyrah/ekskurs/rustrav.html
http://www.moscow-guide.ru/Culture/Walk/
http://www.russia-travel.com/visa.htm
http://www.travel-library.com/europe/russia/

IRC:
#russia

Speedtraps

A speedtrap is a police setup designed to catch drivers who exceed the speed limit. Since citations for such infraction generate income for a town, state or province, it is not unheard of for police to place speedtraps in places where they know out-of-town drivers are likely to be tempted to drive too fast. At the very least, if you are a stranger to an area, it helps to know the places where the local police are looking for speeders. This Web site serves as a speedtrap registry for people driving in the United States, Canada, Australia and some European countries. Before you drive in a strange area, check here to make sure that you know where the speedtraps are. Even better, check for speedtraps in the town where you live. You may be surprised.

Web:
http://www.speedtrap.com/

TRAVEL

Subway Navigator

You will never have to get lost on the subway system again. No matter where you are, you can find your way home as long as you have your Internet connection with you. This site will compute subway routes in many major cities around the world. I computed a lengthy subway route in Helsinki and I don't even speak Finnish.

Web:
http://metro.jussieu.fr:10001/bin/cities/english

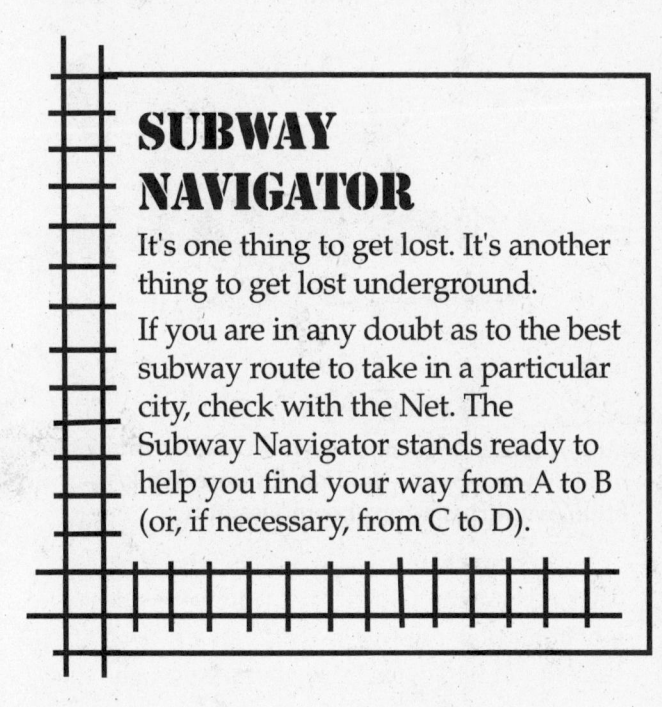

SUBWAY NAVIGATOR

It's one thing to get lost. It's another thing to get lost underground.

If you are in any doubt as to the best subway route to take in a particular city, check with the Net. The Subway Navigator stands ready to help you find your way from A to B (or, if necessary, from C to D).

Thailand

Experience Thailand through images and travelers' tales of journeys there, including an elephant safari and a trip over the river Kwai. Read articles on travel, Thai history, geography, and climate, as well as interviews and essays on Thailand.

Web:
http://www.dewweb.com/wanchai/amazing/
http://www.sawadee.com/samui/tat00.html

IRC:
#siam
#thailand

Tourism Offices

If you are planning your vacation to some exotic country (or some country that you wish were exotic), don't go jet-setting off without being fully prepared. At this Web site you can enter in the name of the country you are going to visit and find a list of all the tourism offices in the area.

Web:
http://www.mbnet.mb.ca/lucas/travel/

Travel Health Advice

If you are planning a trip, you must take a look at some of the resources on the Net devoted to travel health advice. You can find information about particular countries you are going to visit, the hazards specific to that country, listings of immunizations you need, and potential diseases you can bring home as unique souvenirs for you or your friends. While you are planning ahead, take a look at the tips on how to stay healthy while flying. You can learn about air quality on planes, what food to avoid during flights, how to prevent dehydration, and much, much more. These sites will give you what you need to plan for a healthy vacation.

Web:
http://www.cdc.gov/travel/
http://www.flyana.com/index2.html
http://www.moon.com/staying_healthy/

Travel Marketplace

Upgrades, frequent flyer plans, hotel discounts, travel guides—the longest journey begins with but a single step into Usenet's one-stop travel marketplace. Buy, sell, beg, borrow, steal—then go!

Usenet:
rec.travel.marketplace

Travel Matters Newsletter

Whether you are traveling for business or for pleasure, this newsletter will have something to interest you. Read articles on becoming an air courier, contrasting cultures, how to stay healthy during travel, tips on renting a car, travel book reviews and news briefs.

Web:
http://www.moon.com/travel_matters/

Travel Resources

One time, I went to the British Virgin Islands and when I got there, I started asking around for the best places to snorkel. It wasn't long before I found out that most of the natives don't snorkel—it's a tourist activity. Boy, it sure would have been handy to have had a laptop and a cellular modem so I could have connected to the Net. When you need information, don't assume that it's going to be there when you arrive. Better to check on the Net ahead of time and get everything you need before you leave.

Web:
  http://www.pathfinder.com/travel/
  http://www.patravel.com/resource.html
  http://www.travel-library.com/
  http://www.wtgonline.com/

Travel Talk and General Discussion

Travel is a lot of fun and—as they say—broadening. And, while you are traveling there is no substitute for inside information. These Usenet groups are for discussion of specific aspects of travel or particular locations. If you are going to visit a new place, I suggest reading the appropriate group before you leave. If you have any questions, post them in advance of your trip and you may get some useful answers. For general travel discussion, use the **rec.travel.misc** group.

Usenet:
  alt.travel
  alt.travel.canada
  alt.travel.marketplace
  alt.travel.rides
  alt.travel.road-trip
  alt.travel.uk.air
  alt.travel.uk.marketplace
  rec.outdoors.rv-travel
  rec.scuba.locations
  rec.travel
  rec.travel.africa
  rec.travel.air
  rec.travel.asia
  rec.travel.australia+nz
  rec.travel.bed+breakfast
  rec.travel.caribbean
  rec.travel.cruises
  rec.travel.europe
  rec.travel.latin-america
  rec.travel.marketplace
  rec.travel.misc
  rec.travel.resorts.all-inclusive
  rec.travel.usa-canada

Travel Tips

Don't let your excitement about your big trip get in the way of being organized and careful about planning the details. You may end up stranded in a tiny country known for political unrest and lack of Internet access. Get tips on packing, passports, air travel—and don't forget to send your favorite Internet author cool postcards from exotic lands.

Web:
  http://www.frac.com/saftips.htm
  http://www.marriott.com/residenceinn/tips.asp
  http://www.webfoot.com/travel/tips/tips.top.html

Travel Net-Style

Ah, travel. There's nothing like the feeling of exploring somewhere new, romantic and exciting where the hand of Man has never set foot. Ah, travel. A seductive mistress whose inner depths are shrouded in mystery, a temptress who could be leading you into unexpected adventure around the very next corner.

But before you set out on your next journey, use the Net to gather the information and hints you need to make your trip safe and interesting. The **rec.travel** discussion groups are populated with people who love to keep moving, and the **rec.travel** archives have a variety of useful information.

Travel can be uncomfortable, but if you are willing to take your chances, the opportunity of a lifetime may be waiting on the other side of the gate.

Trip Planning

Do you like to totally plan ahead before you go on a trip? If so, this site—geared toward business travelers—should be the first stop on your itinerary. Everything you need to know is here: airline schedules, airport maps, hotel information, restaurant reviews, ground transportation, and more.

Web:
http://www.thetrip.com/

U.S. National Parks

Occasionally, it's nice to get out of the big city and get back to nature where there are wild bears and chemical toilets. If you want to take a vacation in an American national park, check out these resources for information on parks all over the United States. Start planning now for your little getaway.

Web:
http://www.gorp.com/gorp/resource/US_National_Park/main.htm

Usenet:
rec.outdoors.national-parks

U.S. State Department Travel Information

The U.S. State Department has extensive information on current and past travel advisories for those interested in traveling abroad. Each factsheet contains the addresses and phone numbers of American consulates, as well as passport, visa and government information, and crime data.

Web:
http://travel.state.gov/

World Guide to Vegetarianism

Vegetarians, you no longer have to worry about traveling around the world and not being able to find good food that will fit in with your dietary lifestyle. This site has a listing of vegetarian restaurants, natural food stores and vegetarian organizations around the world.

Web:
http://www.vrg.org/travel/

U.S. State Department Travel Information

Whether or not you are American, you will find the information on this Web site useful. Before you even put one toe outside your native country, look up what the U.S. State Department has to say about where you are going. Along with a great deal of useful information (mostly of interest to Americans) you can find out the basic travel facts about any country (of interest to anyone). For each country, you can read a general description, as well as information about entry requirements, medical facilities, crime information, drug penalties, road and traffic information, and more.

For example, under Canada, I found the following: "Crime Information: There is a higher incidence of criminal activity in urban areas. However, violent crimes such as murder, armed robbery, and rape are infrequent..."

(Personal hint for travelers to Canada: If a Canadian thief tries to hold you up, federal law allows you to refuse to give up your possessions if the thief does not ask for them in both French and English.)

TRIVIA

Digits Project

Pick your favorite digit and find out all kinds of interesting bits of trivia related to that number. For example, my favorite digit is 3. Did you know that in French *ménage à trois* means "household for three"?

Web:
http://www-personal.umich.edu/~brinck/digits/digits.html

784 TRIVIA

Internet Index

What better way to break the ice at a party than to start up a little game of trivia? Get this list of factoids and you can ask fun questions like "What percentage of PCs were using TCP/IP in 1993?" and "What is the average number of megabytes of Usenet news per day?" Find out the answers to these questions and more from the Internet Index—a report of interesting statistics relating to Net usage.

Web:
http://www.openmarket.com/intindex/

Movie Trivia

If you like movies, you may be interested in trivia. For example, did you know that the working title for Annie Hall was "Anhedonia"? (It's a medical term referring to the inability to feel pleasure.) How about this? When Woody Allen was making The Purple Rose of Cairo, he originally cast Michael Keaton in the male lead role. However, Allen wasn't satisfied with the first footage and replaced Keaton with Jeff Daniels. If you find factoids like this interesting, you may be a movie trivia person. Connect to these Web sites and find out for sure.

Web:
http://us.imdb.com/Sections/Trivia/Index/
http://www.primate.wisc.edu/people/hamel/movtriv.html

Names of Famous People

This Web site has a listing of the real names of famous people. For example, did you know that Cher's real name was Cherilyn Sarkisian La Pierre? And how about Meatloaf? His real name was Marvin Lee Aday. (Isn't that cute.) Judy Garland was Frances Ethel Gumm. And so on, and so on.

Web:
http://www.infocom.com/~franklin/inaname/

Oldies Music Trivia

If you were listening to popular music in the '60s and '70s, it's high time you started taking your nostalgic legacy seriously. Spend some time at these Web sites and relive the golden days of something or other.

Web:
http://www.oldiesmusic.com/
http://www.quizland.com/numberone.htm

Sports Trivia

Do you know how many seasons Bobby Orr led the NHL in scoring? Or who the first golfer was to earn over a million dollars? Have you any idea who the first boxer was to regain the heavyweight championship? Many people don't have the fount of special knowledge to answer questions like this successfully. However, if you have what it takes, I bet you will have lots of fun at these sports trivia sites. Anyone can watch a sport on TV, but it takes a really special person to master the trivia. (By the way, the answers to the questions are: 2, Arnold Palmer, and Floyd Patterson.)

Web:
http://www.foxsports.com/games/baseball/
http://www.foxsports.com/games/football/
http://www.iis-sports.com/trivia/

Television Trivia

When you need a break from the old TV, try your hand at some trivia. Here are some quizzes that will test your knowledge of Babylon 5, Seinfeld, Cheers, Simpsons and the X-Files. Not only are these quizzes fun, but they are good practice in case you ever have to take a civil service examination.

Web:
http://members.aol.com/SeinChal/
http://spot.colorado.edu/~jorgy/cheers/trivia/
http://www.foxworld.com/simpsons/trivquiz.htm
http://www.mcs.com/~tvsbrent/trivia/trivia.html
http://www.tvgen.com/tv/x-files/

Names of Famous People

What was her name before she changed it? What did his friends call him when he was growing up? Now you can know, just by checking the Names of Famous People Web site.

TRIVIA 785

Today's Date

Every day, there are two numbers associated with the date: the month and the day. For example, December 21st (my birthday) is 12/21. April 6th (my cat's birthday) is 4/6. Each number has interesting facts associated with it, and you can read about today's numbers by visiting this Web site. Personally, I love numbers and I enjoy learning about how each number is special in its own way.

Web:
http://acorn.educ.nottingham.ac.uk/cgi-bin/daynum

Today's Events in History

Do you ever feel like today is just like every other day? Well, I can tell you it's not. In fact, go right now and look up what happened on this day in history and I bet you will learn something wonderful. Just think, on this very date, something astounding happened. Watch what you do today. You might end up on this list.

Web:
http://erebus.phys.cwru.edu/~copi/events.html

Look What I Found on the Net...

```
            (from the Today's Date Web site on August 30th: 8/30)

The number 8
============
8 = 2 x 2 x 2 (a cube)
1, 1, 2, 3, 5, 8, 13... (a Fibonacci number)
There are eight people in a tug-of-war team.
According to Indian mythology, the Earth is supported on the
backs of eight white elephants.
Before the rise of Christianity, there were eight days in the
Greek and Roman weeks.
The amount of cloud in the sky is measured in oktas on a scale
from 0 to 8:
-- 0 oktas means the sky is totally clear
-- 8 oktas means the sky is totally clouded


The number 30
=============
30 = 2 + 4 + 6 + 8 + 10
   = 4 + 5 + 6 + 7 + 8
30 = 1 + 4 + 9 + 16
(a pyramidal number: the sum of the first four square numbers.)
There are 30 days in April, June, September and November.
Dodecahedrons and icosahedrons both have 30 edges.
30 mph is the U.K. speed limit for vehicles driving in a built-up area.
A pearl anniversary celebrates 30 years.
```

TRIVIA

Trivia Matters
Wow—a new TV trivia game every week. If you get the correct answer, you are treated with a cool picture. And if you get stuck, you can get a clue. What better way to pass the time during a commercial?

Web:
http://www.tvgen.com/tv/trivia/

Trivia Page
When your favorite game show is over and already you are starting to have withdrawal, check out these links to various trivia sites all over the Net. There is enough trivia here to choke Alex Trebek.

Web:
http://www.primate.wisc.edu/people/hamel/trivia.html

Trivia Web
Here is a free online trivia game. There are lots and lots of questions in many different categories, enough material to keep you up all night (or until the coffee runs out, whichever comes first). Here's a TV trivia question to get you started. Choose the correct answer: In classic Star Trek, red uniforms signify: (1) Command/Security, (2) Security/Engineering, (3) Engineering/Science or (4) The wearer is about to die. The answer is 2. (Although to be fair, in Star Trek, Security/Engineering is a high-risk profession.)

Web:
http://www.trivia.net/

Trivial Talk and General Discussion
Okay, we all know that Richie Petrie's middle name is Rosebud and that it stands for "Robert Oscar Sam Edward Benjamin Ulysses David". But what was Rob and Laura's address? How about the Ricardos' phone number? Join the pros and test your trivia skill. TV, radio, music, film, Internet books—all the great cultural achievements of mankind are grist for those who pursue the trivial.

Usenet:
rec.games.trivia

IRC:
#trivia

Useless Facts
What could be more useful than a collection of useless facts? Did you know that if you stretch a slinky out flat it measures 87 feet long? Did you know that the only word in the English language with all five vowels in reverse order is "subcontinental"? Did you know that the pupil of an octopus's eye is rectangular? And did you know there is more of the same waiting for you at these Web sites?

Web:
http://www-leland.stanford.edu/~jenkg/useless.html
http://www.lsds.com/key/facts/

Useless Information
"Useless", of course, is a relative term. There may be a time in your life when you *do* need to know how kitty litter was invented or how the first subway in America was built in secret.

Web:
http://home.nycap.rr.com/useless/

(From the rec.games.trivia frequently asked question list)

What are the Seven Wonders of the Ancient World?
The Pyramids of Egypt
The Hanging Gardens of Babylon
The Statue of Zeus at Olympia
The Temple of Artemis at Ephesus
The Mausoleum at Halicarnassus
The Colossus of Rhodes
The Lighthouse at Alexandria
The pyramids are the oldest of the Seven Wonders and the only one of them still in existence.

What were the names of the castaways on the Gilligan's Island television show?
"The ship's aground on the shore of this
Uncharted desert isle,
With Gilligan,
The Skipper too, (Jonas Grumby)
The millionaire and his wife,
(Thurston Howell III, Lovey Howell)
The movie star (Ginger Grant)
And the rest
('Professor' Roy Hinkley, Mary Ann Summers)
Are here on Gilligan's Isle."
Gilligan didn't have a first name on the show, but Bob Denver has stated in interviews that he had talked the matter over with show creator Sherwood Schwartz. Had Gilligan ever needed a first name, it would have been Willie.

UFOS AND ALIENS

Abductions

All over the world, there are people who have been abducted by aliens; or who think they were abducted by aliens; or who say they were abducted by aliens—maybe you should read the material and make up your own mind. These sites contain articles, personal experiences and incident reports covering various alien abduction topics. There are also hints on how to know if you have been abducted (just in case you are not quite sure).

Web:
 http://www.abduct.com/survey.htm
 http://www.abductee.net/main.html
 http://www.alienjigsaw.com/
 http://www.anw.com/aliens/52questions.htm
 http://www.pbs.org/wgbh/pages/nova/aliens/

Alien Autopsies

An autopsy is a medical procedure—often referred to as a postmortem examination—in which a dead body (cadaver) is examined in order to figure out why a person died. One of the basic facts about this procedure is that you cannot have an autopsy unless you have a body. So when you hear about an autopsy being conducted on an alien, the significance is not that we might find out how an alien died, but that there actually was an alien in the first place. There are many stories about alien autopsies, and if you are curious, here is a Web site in which a lot of useful information is collected into one place.

Web:
 http://www.trudang.com/autopsy.html

Alien Lexicons

You can't talk about the players without a program, so here are some reference sites that define extraterrestrial and UFO terminology. If you are interested in aliens, it behooves you to spend some time learning the vocabulary. After all, think how embarrassed you would be if some aliens were visiting you, and you introduced them to your mother as Greys when they were really Lyrans.

Web:
 http://ourworld.compuserve.com/homepages/
   andypage/ufogloss.htm
 http://www.aufora.org/ufoclopedia/
 http://www.bahnhof.se/~mike/ufo/ufoclocp.html
 http://www.res.com/~mariah/alien.htm
 http://www.world.com/~stevew/text/appb.htm

Alien Pyramids

It's easy to say that aliens built the pyramids. What's not so easy is to convince people that what you say is true. Well, don't get left behind the next time your social circle is debating the origin of the pyramids. Visit these Web sites and get the real story.

Web:
 http://ourworld.compuserve.com/homepages/
   lawrence_wilkes/martians.htm
 http://www.europa.com/edge/pyramid.html
 http://www.nauticom.net/users/ata/egypt.html

Alien Research

This Usenet group is for ongoing discussion about where aliens might come from and if they have been to Earth before. Discussions include what aliens might look like, myths surrounding aliens, possible encounters and unexplained sightings. You can even read some alien autopsy reports, but it's probably best to save these for after breakfast.

Usenet:
 alt.alien.research

Ancient Astronauts

The theory is that thousands of years ago, alien astronauts visited the Earth. Moreover, our present technological society is not the first one to exist on our planet. But if that were the case, shouldn't there be some evidence? There is, according to the true believers, and the purpose of these Web sites is to find, analyze and disseminate facts that support these theories.

Web:
 http://www.autobahn.mb.ca/~mikem/astro.htm
 http://www.in-search-of.com/frames/hamilton/
   ancientaircraft_nf.shtml
 http://www.primenet.com/~msebring/ufo_aa.html
 http://www.vegasindex.com/ufo/topic/ancient/
 http://www2.gol.com/users/martinj/ebe.htm

Be in the know. Check out "Secret Stuff" and "Intrigue".

UFOS AND ALIENS

Area 51

These resources are devoted to Area 51, the super-secret government base near Las Vegas. Read current speculations on alien aircraft, discuss the government's security measures at the base and ponder new ideas on how to spy on the base to see the aliens.

Web:
http://www.nauticom.net/users/ata/resources.html
http://www.ufomind.com/area51/

Usenet:
alt.conspiracy.area51

Contact Lab

This is a Web site for serious UFO researchers as well as "experiencers". You will find information about space brothers, starseeds, visitations, alien breeding programs, implants, abductions and grey men. Explore the archives and read about flying saucers, the Puerto Rican Goat Sucker, temporal lobe epilepsy, cattle mutilations, the Bass Strait incident and the radiologist conspiracy. Unlike most UFO Web sites, this one has a lot more than links; there is a lot of original content (with the accent on "original"). Oh yes, if you see a UFO, you can report the contact by filling out the UFO Report Form.

Web:
http://www.dot.net.au/~pavig/contact/index.HTM

Look What I Found on the Net...

```
                (from an Alien Lexicons Web site)

The Dark Side Hypothesis...

...claims that the U.S. government has recovered all of the
crashed space ships, and therefore they launched Project
Redlight in 1962, to recover and test fly the space ships in
S-4 at Area-51.

[The hypothesis] also claims that the U.S. government has made
a deal with the aliens to let them abduct as many people as
they want in exchange for their technology.  The government
also demanded a list of all the humans the aliens intended to
abduct.  But the government found out that the aliens didn't
keep their part of the deal, and it ended in a confrontation
in 1978-79.

Many of the top U.S. scientists were killed by the aliens and
the deal was broken, but the abductions and experiments on
humans continued in secret.  In the 1980s, the U.S. government
and the aliens made a new deal and are once again working
together.
```

UFOS AND ALIENS

Crop Circles

Crop circles are large, sometimes intricate designs created on farmland when parts of a field of growing plants are flattened to form a large pattern. Many people believe that crop circles are of extraterrestrial origin. If you would like to find out more about crop circles and what people have said about them, here are some Web sites where you can find information about the phenomenon. You can do all the research you need, or, if you are artistically inclined, you can make your own crop circles.

Web:
http://www.cropcircleconnector.com/
http://www.head-space.com/circlemakers/
http://www.nh.ultranet.com/~lovely/homepg.html
http://www.tpoint.net/~mchorost/homepage/circles/circles_biblio.html
http://www.wavefront.com/~jhenry/cropc.htm

Usenet:
alt.paranormal.crop-circles

Life on Mars

Is there life on Mars? Well, if not, how do you explain the Martian "pyramids" and lost civilizations? They may have been built by aliens. Of course, if there isn't alien life, there may be native life. One of these Web sites explores the possible connection between aliens and Martian pyramids. The other site has information about the Cydonia region of Mars (the location of the "face" and the pyramids). This region was explored by the Viking I probe in 1976. You can look at Viking pictures, and read articles discussing the possibility of life on Mars. Is there life on Mars? Someone thinks so.

Web:
http://www.seds.org/spaceviews/hotnews/mars-links.html
http://www.transatlantech.com/TPS/hot-top-marslife.html

This book has "Secret Stuff".
(See if you can find it.)

Crop Circles:
Whence Comest Thou?

Where did all the crop circles come from? They are mysterious patterns and designs that appeared in farmers' grain fields, starting in the middle 1970s and peaking between 1989 and 1992. Lots of explanations have been proposed: the crop circles were made by aliens, by supernatural beings, by natural phenomena that are not well understood, and so on.

Here is the real explanation:

The first crop circles appeared in English grain fields. The size, complexity and circumstances were such that many people said it was impossible for the whole thing to be a hoax. However, it was a hoax.

The original crop circles—and many of the later ones—were created by two Englishmen from Southampton, Doug Bower and Dave Chorley. One night while drinking beer in their pub, they started talking about UFO reports and thought it might be fun to fool all the gullible people who believed in UFOs.

They began by making simple designs in fields using only a steel bar. Eventually they graduated to making elaborate designs using boards and ropes.

Once the hoax caught on, other people started copying them, in England as well as in other countries. Bower and Chorley continued this for 15 years, fooling a lot of "experts". Finally, in 1991, they confessed and demonstrated to reporters how easy it was for them to create the complex patterns that—according to so many believers—could not be made by human beings.

For more information, see the book "Round in Circles" by Jim Schnabel (Penguin 1994).

(Actually, I have my own theory: I think the crop circles were created by Martian bacteria.)

790 UFOS AND ALIENS

Roswell Incident

Anyone who is interested in UFOs and aliens has heard of Roswell, New Mexico. Read the facts and folklore about Roswell, the town where it is said that, in 1947, an alien vessel crashed and the government hushed it up. See pictures of the crash and an FBI memo. By the way, here is the real explanation: the debris that crashed was from secret experiments the Pentagon was running called Project Mogul. The purpose of these experiments was to develop technology capable of detecting Russian atomic tests (which, it was thought, were about to begin soon). When the apparatus crashed, the military covered it up by saying the debris was from weather balloons. This, of course, was a lie, which in later years served to stimulate the American UFO-cover-up-conspiracy buffs.

Web:
http://www.execpc.com/vjentpr/jroswell.html
http://www.roswell.org/
http://www.sierra-vista.com/roswell/

UFO Chatting

When it's late at night and you are afraid of the dark, you can find some companionship on IRC. The two X-Files channels are populated by people who are fans of the X-Files television show, but they also chat about aliens and UFOs. The **#ufo** channel is exclusively for talking about extraterrestrials and UFO-related subjects.

IRC:
  #ufo
  #x-files
  #xfiles

UFO Information Resources

When you are looking for specific UFO information, you can wait for one of the Greys to come over to your house and deliver the information in person, or you can use the Net and find what you need right away. Whatever you are looking for—photos, movies, personal statements, theories, names, dates and addresses—you'll find it on the Net.

Web:
http://www.anomalous-images.com/
http://www.ufoinfo.com/contents.shtml
http://www.ufomind.com/
http://www.ufoseek.org/

> **No matter who you are or what you believe, somewhere on the Internet, there are people like you.**

UFO Origins

In 1947, a pilot named Kenneth Arnold claimed that, while flying in the northwest area of the United States, he saw nine boomerang-shaped flying objects. Arnold was flying during the day and was able to describe the objects' movement as being similar to saucers skipping across the surface of a lake. A newspaper reporter covered the story, and referred to the objects as "flying saucers". Although Arnold never claimed to see anything saucer-like, the name caught the public fancy, and soon became part of the vernacular. Since then, there have been numerous reports of flying saucers, UFOs and aliens, and a great body of mythos has grown up around them. Here are some alternate explanations of the origin of UFOs.

Web:
http://ourworld.compuserve.com/homepages/
  AndyPage/theories.htm
http://www.parascope.com/nb/ufoin.htm

UFO Reports

Have you seen a UFO recently and lived to tell about it? Here are some places on the Net to report it and to check to see if anyone else in your area might have seen something similar. Read about sightings all over the world, speculate about alien visitors or just laugh at people whose reports seem unbelievable.

Web:
http://www.nwlink.com/~ufocntr/

Usenet:
  alt.ufo.reports

UFOS AND ALIENS 791

UFO Talk and General Discussion

Check out these Usenet groups for a cool, rational, scientific, intellectual, well-reasoned, plausible discussion about aliens visiting the Earth and swanking around like they own the place. Investigate, in person, the theory that man is really nature's last word. Just the place to spend your time when the TV is on the fritz.

Usenet:
alt.alien
alt.alien.visitors
alt.aliens.they-are-here
alt.paranet.abduct
alt.paranet.ufo
alt.paranormal

Look What I Found on the Net...

```
Newsgroup: alt.alien.visitors
Subject: Alien Visits and UFOs
```

There is no doubt in my mind that we will be "invaded". But they are not hostile. In fact, these "aliens" are merely Satan's angels. Satan will soon be thrown out of the heavenly realm, and in order to appear legitimate he will arrive as "space aliens" and in peace. The whole world will marvel at the miracles that these "aliens" can perform, but do not be deceived. They are coming with the aid and support of the government to bring us hell and destruction...

I have seen them. I never was a believer until last weekend.

They came to my house looking for pretzels and beer. They had large glossy red eyes and long scraggly beards and wore flannel shirts and mud boots. Their ship sort of resembled a Chevy pickup...

It wasn't until later I realized what they really wanted: they had really come for my body. They wanted to impregnate me with an alien fetus and later take over the world. Disguised as lumberjacks they raided the fridge...

I am writing this from their ship.... They do not know I am here. This is my only chance for help. Help me please... Oh no! Here they come......... Ahhhhhh...

My husband and I were out of town for a day trip and when we returned there was a footprint on top of our glass dining room table. What was strange was that the footprint only has three toes. If you have heard anything similar to that, please let me know.

USENET

Creating Alternative Usenet Discussion Groups

An alternative Usenet group is one that has been started without any special procedures, such as voting or discussion. Unlike mainstream groups—which do undergo such procedures before they can be started—alternative groups can be created by anyone who knows how to do so. The disadvantage to such groups is that they are not carried by as many news servers around the world. Alternative groups are important, however. They provide a counterpoint to the more sedate, controlled world of mainstream groups in that people are more free to create and remove alternative groups, with a minimum of fuss, as the need arises. Here is information about how alternative groups should be created. If you want to create a group, please read and follow the guidelines. They were developed by trial and error and a lot of smart thinking over a period of time. Usenet works best when people (1) think before acting, and (2) do not try to re-invent everything.

Web:
http://www.cis.ohio-state.edu/~barr/alt-creation-guide.html
http://www.cs.ubc.ca/spider/edmonds/usenet/good-newgroup.html

Creating Mainstream Usenet Discussion Groups

A mainstream Usenet group is one that is created by following a specific set of procedures, involving one or more votes, serious discussion and deliberate planning. It takes time and effort to create a mainstream group (compared to an alternative group which anyone can create if he or she knows how). The advantage of mainstream groups is that they are respected as real groups and are carried by virtually all news servers around the world. Here is an explanation of how such groups are started.

Web:
http://www.fairnet.org/fnvol/training/newsgrp.html
http://www.faqs.org/faqs/usenet/creating-newsgroups/naming/

Flames

Within Usenet, a flame is a message that contains an angry or abusive response to a previous message. A flame might be a complaint, a criticism of someone's ideas, or a good old-fashioned, mean-spirited tongue-lashing. The next time you feel like a good argument, join one of these groups and see what it is like to play with the people who live to complain.

Usenet:
alt.flame
alt.flame.abortion
alt.flame.airlines
alt.flame.rush-limbaugh

Harley Hahn's Master List of Usenet Newsgroups

Usenet is a worldwide system of discussion groups. To access Usenet, you use a program called a newsreader. (Usenet was originally designed to carry local news between two universities in North Carolina. Thus, for historical reasons, Usenet groups are often referred to as newsgroups, even though they don't carry news.) Both major browsers come with a free newsreader program. With Internet Explorer, the program is Outlook Express; with Netscape, the program is Collabra. There are between 20,000 and 50,000 different newsgroups (depending on whose numbers you believe). However, most of these groups are not of general interest and do not have worldwide distribution. Moreover, many newsgroups are "bogus", that is, non-existent or filled with spam (unsolicited advertising). To help you find the groups you want, I have created Harley Hahn's Master List of Usenet Newsgroups. Go to my Web site and you can search for newsgroups by topic, by name, or by looking for a particular keyword. I have taken a great deal of time and checked all the groups, keeping only those in the thirteen major hierarchies as well as throwing out all the bogus groups. I then wrote a short, accurate description for each group and placed it in a category, and organized the whole list to be easy to search. Enjoy.

Web:
http://www.harley.com/usenet/

USENET

Money, romance, sex, food, cats...

Want to join the discussion? Let me help you find the right Usenet groups.

Harley Hahn's Master List of Usenet Newsgroups

"All the newsgroups fit to print."

Moderated Newsgroups

With most Usenet groups, anyone can post (send) any message he wants whenever he wants. This freedom is what makes Usenet so powerful. However, for some groups, such freedom doesn't work well: there are too many off-topic postings and too much spam (unsolicited advertising). One solution is to create a moderated group. One person, called a moderator, receives all the postings, and he or she decides which ones are actually sent to the group. Many Usenet groups are moderated, which cuts down on the spam and increases the usefulness of the newsgroup. This FAQ (frequently asked question list) explains moderated newsgroups, including the difference between moderation and censorship, what it takes to become a moderator and where to find resources for moderators.

Web:
http://www.faqs.org/faqs/usenet/moderated-ng-faq/

Net Abuse

Heavy cross-posting, spamming, and annoying commercial advertising are at the top of the list of Ways to Abuse Your Net Privileges. Read about the latest sins against the laws of Net etiquette, thoughts and ideas on the concept of minding our manners, and general ranting and raving about people who rant and rave.

Web:
http://www.cybernothing.org/faqs/net-abuse-faq.html

Usenet:
alt.current-events.net-abuse
alt.current-events.net-abuse.spam
news.admin.net-abuse.bulletins
news.admin.net-abuse.email
news.admin.net-abuse.misc
news.admin.net-abuse.policy
news.admin.net-abuse.sightings
news.admin.net-abuse.usenet

Newsgroup Listings

There are thousands of Usenet discussion groups (newsgroups) and it's not always easy to find the ones you want. This resource can help. Specify one or more words, and a program will search a large list of newsgroups and descriptions to find the ones that contain those words. Aside from searching, you can display all the groups in a particular hierarchy, which is an excellent way to look for a new group to explore.

Web:
http://www.liszt.com/news/

Picture Grabbing Software

There are lots of pictures posted to Usenet (and some of them are even non-pornographic). If you like looking, you'll love these programs. They will visit your favorite groups, snarf out all the pictures automatically, and save then on your hard disk, where you can peruse them at your leisure. I like these programs, and they sure save me a lot of time. (My research requires me to look at lots of pictures...)

Web:
http://jfm.bc.ca/psp.html
http://www.binaryboy.com/
http://www.winfiles.com/apps/98/news.html
http://www.wmhsoft.com/ASP1-A3/

Talkway

This service helps you keep up with your favorite discussion groups. You can choose to have information about the most active threads (individual topics) in your favorite newsgroups emailed to you. One nice feature is that this service filters out as much spam as possible.

Web:
http://www.talkway.com/

Usenet Announcements

Stay informed on the latest new discussion groups that are cropping up in Usenet. The **.newgroups** group is where people post when they want to propose a new group. The **.newusers** group is a place where periodic explanations about Usenet are posted for the benefit of new users.

Usenet:
news.announce.conferences
news.announce.important
news.announce.newgroups
news.announce.newusers

Usenet Archiving Software

If you have been given the job of looking through certain Usenet groups to find encoded postings, you could be at the job all day. Instead, get this software which will search through groups for encoded pictures and source codes.

Web:
http://www.cs.ubc.ca/spider/phillips/grn/source

Usenet Culture Talk and General Discussion

Usenet has a culture all its own. Once you spend a lot of time on Usenet, you will get a feeling for its energy, its customs, its vocabulary and its importance: in other words, its culture. This is the group where you can discuss all these subjects.

Usenet:
alt.culture.usenet

Jump into the Net.

Usenet Discussion Group Administration

It's bound to happen. When you get thousands of people posting to Usenet, someone is going to decide that things need to get more organized. The **news.admin** groups are a central point for administrative topics relating to Usenet, such as the dissemination of information, statement of policies, and the relating of technical details about forming and moderating Usenet groups.

Usenet:
news.admin
news.admin.censorship
news.admin.hierarchies
news.admin.misc
news.admin.policy
news.admin.technical

Look What I Found on the Net...

```
Newsgroup: alt.culture.usenet
Subject: Dejanews Archive

> I like to post a lot of articles on Usenet and I have noticed
> that the Dejanews company stores every single post.  I really
> don't want them to keep every single thing I post, so is there
> any way I can remove all those articles from my history of
> posting on Usenet?

Oh, sure, so you'd be liking to say all manner of things on
Usenet, but you wouldn't want people to be reading after the
articles have expired and the posts are taken away.  You'd be
happy to see the things that you say vanish into the air like
the steam off a kettle of boiling water.

Well, I'm here to tell you, young friend, that there'll not be
any of that satisfaction for you, as everything you say is being
stored and preserved, and we'll have a record of your every
utterance upon the Net without a blessed thing that you'll be
able to do about it.
```

Usenet Discussion Group Invasion

There are people who deliberately plan to disrupt Usenet discussion groups. They do so by targeting innocent Usenet groups, disguising themselves as regular participants, and then starting flame wars in which they attempt to wreak general havoc. There you are, happily posting away in your favorite Usenet group, when, out of nowhere, the discussion degenerates into chaos and disorder, and you never know why. These Usenet commandos plan their strategy keenly, and this is one of the places they meet.

Usenet:
alt.syntax.tactical

Usenet Discussion Group Questions

Looking for a Usenet group about Armenian folk dancing or one that will tell you how to make clothes from old beer cans? If you can't find just the one you are looking for, try asking on these groups. Someone might be able to help. People will answer questions not only about specific groups, but about Usenet groups in general. It's a good source of information.

Usenet:
news.groups.questions
news.newusers.questions

Usenet Filtering Service

It's going to be an all-day job if you want to check every single Usenet group for reports of Elvis sightings, so why not let someone do it for you? Subscribe to this news filtering service, and they will send you postings on any keywords or phrases that you choose. So, if you're paranoid and you could just swear people are talking about you, this will be the proof you can finally show your therapist.

Web:
http://www.reference.com/

Life begins at 0.

Usenet for New Users

Usenet consists of many different discussion groups. Through the years, millions of people have participated in Usenet and, in that time, a good many conventions have been established. If you are a newcomer, there is a lot to learn. Here is a Web site linking to a collection of documents you can read to help you learn how it all works. Don't worry about understanding everything: concentrate on the basics and what makes sense to you. The Web site is associated with a specific group called **news.newusers.questions**, devoted to questions and answers for new users.

Web:
http://www.faqs.org/faqs/news-newusers-intro/

Usenet:
news.newusers.questions

Usenet Hierarchies

Within the name of a Usenet group, the first part of the name indicates the hierarchy (major category) to which the group belongs. For example, when you see the names **alt.politics.usa** and **alt.sex.stories**, you can tell they are part of the **alt** (alternative) hierarchy. When you see the name **comp.infosystems.www**, you know the group is part of the **comp** (computer) hierarchy. Here are the most important hierarchies (the ones I want you to remember): **alt** (alternative), **bionet** (biology), **biz** (business), **comp** (computers), **humanities** (arts and humanities), **k12** (K-12 education), **misc** (miscellaneous), **news** (Usenet itself), **rec** (recreation), **sci** (science), **soc** (society) and **talk** (debate). However, there are literally hundreds of different hierarchies, most of them devoted to a particular geographical area, language or organization. This Web site has a large list of Usenet hierarchies along with a brief description. If you encounter a strange name that you don't understand, look here for help.

Web:
http://www.magmacom.com/~leisen/master_list.html

Votetaker Volunteers

The Usenet Votetaker Volunteers is a neutral third party who counts votes and keeps track of current vote status for the mainstream hierarchy groups. Read about the origins of the group and how they do the voodoo they do.

Web:
http://www.uvv.org/

VICES

Bingo

Feel the rhythm. It builds slowly as the caller announces the numbers and letters: B15, G59, O65... Slowly your card begins to fill in. One square, then another, then another. I21, N32, B13... Will you win this time? You start to sweat. You can feel your blood pressure rising and your heart pounding. I17, O65, G47... You only have two more squares to fill. Now one more square. I30, O64, B2... and somebody else wins. Never mind. The next game is about to start.

Web:
  http://www.bingobugle.com/
  http://www.bingozone.com/
  http://www.uproar.com/bb/

> **BINGO**
>
> Be careful, or bingo will control you. Here is an example from real life.
>
> When I was working on this ad, I called a friend of mine who loves bingo to talk to her about it. But I couldn't reach her, and do you know why? Because she was playing bingo!
>
> In other words, she passed up the chance to talk to a charming, sensitive, sophisticated man, in order to slavishly follow her desires.
>
> Bingo. Can *you* handle it?

Caffeine

I can't stand still. All this great information about caffeine, and I have to read, read, read. Right away. Now. Lotsa links and I have to look at them all. Click, click, click. Go faster. I'll go get another Jolt while I'm waiting.... Okay, I'm back. Click on another one. Right away. Cool. All this caffeine stuff. I can't stand still.

Web:
  http://daisy.uwaterloo.ca/~alopez-o/caffaq.html
  http://www.cis.ohio-state.edu/text/faq/usenet/
     caffeine-faq/faq.html
  http://www.planetjoe.com/caffiends.html

Usenet:
  alt.drugs.caffeine

Chocolate

While chocolate is not one of the Seven Deadly Sins, it tastes good enough to be. If you are hooked on chocolate, check out these Web sites, if for no other reason than to enjoy the recipes for chocolate desserts. If you want chocolate information to come straight to your electronic mailbox, the **choco** mailing list is a receive-only list for people who want to be sent chocolate information from around the Net. The Usenet discussion groups will give you access to chocolate chat even after all the supermarkets are closed.

Web:
  http://www.faqs.org/faqs/food/chocolate/faq/
  http://www.hhhh.org/cloister/chocolate/
  http://www.virtualchocolate.com/

Usenet:
  alt.food.chocolate
  rec.food.chocolate

Majordomo Mailing List:
  List Name: **choco**
  Subscribe to: **majordomo@apk.net**

Cigar Smoking

Cigar smoking really doesn't have a lot to do with smoking. Cigar smoking is all about image, social bonding and oral gratification. With that in mind, let me help you find what you need on the Net. These Web sites contain information about choosing and smoking cigars, along with explanations of the appropriate cultural accoutrements—in other words, everything you need to ensure that, as a cigar smoker, you are projecting the proper image and enjoying the right amount of social bonding. For oral gratification, you're on your own.

Web:
  http://www.cigarfriendly.com/
  http://www.cigargroup.com/
  http://www.fujipub.com/cigar/
  http://www.smokescreen.com/
  http://www.top25cigar.com/

Usenet:
  alt.smokers.cigars

Listserv Mailing List:
  List Name: **cigar-l**
  Subscribe to: **listserv@american.edu**

Majordomo Mailing List:
  List Name: **cigars**
  Subscribe to: **majordomo@listserv.prodigy.com**

Cigarette Smoking

You run a lot of serious risks when you smoke regularly. The idea behind these Web sites is that, if you are going to smoke, you should do it well. Moreover, smokers as a whole have need of certain resources which these sites provide: information about particular political issues, places to buy tobacco products, comparisons of various brands of cigarettes, and so on. (Personal note. Having gone to medical school and worked in hospitals, I can tell you categorically: anyone who could see what the end-stage of cigarette smoking looks like would never smoke, even moderately. If you like to smoke, imagine yourself in a hospital room, with a body ravaged by years of tobacco. Just trying to sustain enough breath to walk to the bathroom is a major achievement. Think about what it looks like when a surgeon cuts into your lower jaw and pulls it open in a vain effort to remove the cancer at the back of your throat. I have seen all of this and a lot more. Take my word for it, there are a great many adjectives you can use to describe what happens to a person who smokes for years, but "cool" is not one of them.)

Web:
http://kohary.simplenet.com/smoke.htm
http://www.cs.brown.edu/people/lsh/docs/pro.html
http://www.forces.org/
http://www.smokers.com/

Usenet:
alt.smokers

Drinking

After a while the same old drinks get boring. Spice up your vice with some new recipes for mixed drinks. These recipes are always good to have around in case the Queen drops by for a drink.

Web:
http://www.drinkboy.com/
http://www.hotwired.com/cocktail/
http://www.thevirtualbar.com/
http://www.webtender.com/

Usenet:
alt.alcohol

> A sure-fire way to make all your dreams come true is to sleep with this book under your pillow.

Gambling and Oddsmaking

When you are not sitting in a smoke-filled room taking chances with your money, fill your urges with some great gambling and oddsmaking resources on the Net. The Web sites will show you hints and tips about gambling, and in the Usenet groups you can talk about various gambling games.

Web:
http://rec.gambling.org/
http://www.gamblerspairadice.com/
http://www.jazbo.com/videopoker/
http://www.rgtonline.com/index2.html

Usenet:
alt.gambling
rec.gambling
rec.gambling.blackjack
rec.gambling.blackjack.moderated
rec.gambling.craps
rec.gambling.misc
rec.gambling.other-games
rec.gambling.poker
rec.gambling.sports

Hangovers

It's a shame when something that can be fun causes so much misery later. But it's the same with any fun thing—sex, alcohol, excess food or roller coasters. There is always a risk of ensuing nausea or headache afterward. Don't be alone in your misery. Share stories and sure cures for hangovers. Learn from the people who never let the prospect of pain slow them down.

Usenet:
alt.hangover

798 VICES

Horse Racing

And they're off! You feel the adrenaline rush through your veins and into your fast-beating heart. Your pulse quickens and you break out in little beads of perspiration. You clutch the ticket in your fist and hope like heck that your horse comes in first, since you just bet your lunch money. In the whole history of horse racing, there probably was someone, somewhere, who went to the races just to watch the animals run around the track, but for everyone else there is only one important reason to follow this sport: gambling. If you are a horse-racing fan, you can meet up with other fans and discuss strategies and handicapping. When you need hard data, the Web sites contain enough information to choke a horse (not that you ever would, of course).

Web:
http://espn.sportszone.com/horse/
http://www.bloodhorse.com/racing/
http://www.thoroughbredtimes.com/today/
http://www.webcom.com/~alauck/

Usenet:
alt.sport.horse-racing
rec.gambling.racing

Listserv Mailing List:
List Name: **hracing**
Subscribe to: **listserv@ulkyvm.louisville.edu**

Lotteries

Why work all your life and feel the satisfaction of successfully making your way in the world when you can buy a lottery ticket and have the chance to win your fortune all at once? Lottery fans, get together and discuss the lotteries on Usenet, or see all the lottery resources that are on the Web, such as number generators, lottery news and helpful software.

Web:
http://www.lotterynews.com/
http://www.lottolink.com/
http://www.lottoshop.com/

Usenet:
rec.gambling.lottery

Pipe Smoking

You know you are addicted when the sweet, rich scent of pipe tobacco makes you all goose-pimply and gives you urges to dress in velvet smoking jackets. Even if you don't like to smoke a pipe, it's fun to go in those tobacco shops with the rich wood paneling and case after case of sweet-smelling leaves. Participate in pipe talk with the folks on Usenet or explore interesting pipe information at the Web sites.

Web:
http://www.fujipub.com/ooops/
http://www.pipes.org/
http://www.pipes.org/asp_FAQ.html

Usenet:
alt.smokers.pipes

Look What I Found on the Net...

(from an online gambling and oddsmaking reference)

```
The Kelly Criterion [for Blackjack] is a betting heuristic that
minimizes your chance of going broke while maximizing your
long-run profits.  To bet consistently with the Kelly Criterion,
you should divide your bankroll into 300-400 units and normally
bet 1-4 units on each hand.

Your optimal bet on a hand is a percentage of your CURRENT
bankroll equal to about 0.5*R/D + B, where R is the running
count, D is the number of remaining decks (so R/D is the true
count), and B is the basic strategy expectation.
```

Sex Services Talk and General Discussion

Ah, the Modern Age. Overnight mail delivery, faxes, email, pizza in thirty minutes or less, home shopping networks and sex partners on demand. These are the things that make life worth living. Read about the going rates for services and where to find the various objects of your desire.

Usenet:
  alt.sex.erotica.marketplace
  alt.sex.services

Strip Clubs

It's nice when you go to a bar or club and you get the opportunity to see some nice scenery. And it doesn't really have to be anything special like glorious vistas that make you believe there is a God. Just something interesting will do, like a man or woman wearing nothing but strategically placed tassels as they gyrate in the vicinity of your seating area. Fans of strip clubs and exotic dancers discuss the hot clubs, dancers, and places to go when you are looking for a good time. At the Web site you can browse for strip club reviews or write your own.

Web:
  http://www.tuscl.com/

Usenet:
  alt.sex.strip-clubs

Virtual Slot Machine

When you can't take the time to hit the slots in Vegas, at least stop on the Web to see if you can hit the jackpot. Start off with a few coins, pull the handle and see if you can win more coins.

Web:
  http://state.mlive.com/cgi-bin/slots.cgi
  http://www.game-land.com/games/newslot/
  http://www.slotszone.com/

Vices may cause problems, but they are important.

As a matter of fact, in the United States, people consider these activities to be so important that, every four years, they elect a special president just for vice.

If you have any questions, why not drop the VP a line? His address is:

vice-president@whitehouse.gov

VIDEO AND MULTIMEDIA

DVD

DVD (Digital Versatile Disc or Digital Video Disc) is an optical disc storage system that is faster and more powerful than regular CD technology. A DVD disc holds a lot more data than a CD, and a single disc can store both video and audio, as well as computer data. One day DVD may replace not only audio CDs and CD-ROM discs, but videotapes, laserdiscs and video game cartridges. We will see.

Web:
  http://www.dvddigital.com/
  http://www.dvdtown.com/
  http://www.videodiscovery.com/vdyweb/dvd/dvdfaq.html

Usenet:
  alt.video.dvd
  rec.video.dvd.advocacy
  rec.video.dvd.marketplace
  rec.video.dvd.misc
  rec.video.dvd.players
  rec.video.dvd.tech
  rec.video.dvd.titles

Watch as the future approaches—in high-resolution full-color interactive video with digital sound.

MIME Format

MIME stands for "Multi-purpose Internet Mail Extensions". It is a system whereby files of all types can be attached to email messages. In particular, MIME allows you to send and receive pictures, video and sound clips. For the most part, MIME works behind the scenes. To send a file, just tell your mail program to "attach" the file to an outgoing message. When you receive such a file, your mail program may "detach" it automatically. If not, you can tell the program to do so explicitly. If you want to find out how MIME works, this Web site has plenty of information, including the MIME FAQ (frequently asked question list).

Web:
  http://www.hunnysoft.com/mime/

Usenet:
  comp.mail.mime

Mpeg Movies

When you need a break from the drab sameness of everyday life, visit one of these Web sites. Here you will find a great many animated files in mpeg format. Just the thing to use up a few extra minutes of your life; minutes that will never, ever come back again. Well, at least things that move look cool on your computer.

Web:
  http://lai.cz.nus.edu.sg/mpeg/
  http://www.arc.umn.edu/GVL/Software/mpeg.html
  http://www.mpeg1.de/mplinks.html

Mpeg Video Resources and Software

This is a site that has extensive information about the mpeg video format. The name "mpeg" (named after the Moving Picture Experts Group) refers to a family of standards used for encoding audio-visual information in a digital compressed format. At this Web site you can find an overview of mpeg, as well as news, software, a FAQ, installation guides, and much more. If you need anything having to do with mpeg, this is the place to look.

Web:
  http://www.mpeg.org/

VIDEO AND MULTIMEDIA

Multimedia File Formats

As an Internet user, you are going to encounter all different kinds of files. So what do you do when you find something your browser doesn't understand? Suppose you download a file named **harley.au** from the Web, but you are not sure whether you should look at it, listen to it or eat it. All the answers and more are in this wonderful, comprehensive guide to strange but true file formats.

Web:
http://r4149.resnet.cornell.edu/xplat/

Multimedia in Education

Computing doesn't have to be complicated, dull or boring. Not with multimedia. Pictures, sounds, graphics and animations all make computers come to life. Learn about using multimedia as a teaching tool and find out places where you can be taught to use multimedia effectively.

Usenet:
misc.education.multimedia

PRIORITY DELIVERY

Someone has given you a file that contains a movie with irrefutable proof that the Pope is one of the aliens who masterminded the JFK conspiracy cover-up. However, your software cannot play that type of movie!

The Net can help. Go to the *Multimedia File Formats* Web resources and find the program you need to convert or view the file.

Once again (thanks to the Net), the truth will be revealed.

Why be normal? Read "Bizarre".

Multimedia News

No doubt about it. Multimedia is a frontier, and a lot is happening all at once. In order to stay where you are, you need to read as fast as you can. In order to keep up, you need to read twice as fast as that. So start here, with news, features, reviews and tech talk—enough info to keep you in the multimedia groove indefinitely.

Web:
http://www.newmedia.com/
http://www.updatestage.com/

Multimedia Talk and General Discussion

This is the Usenet group for general discussion of computers and multimedia. People come here to talk about all manner of multimedia topics, including communications, user interfaces, tools, animation, and so on.

Usenet:
comp.multimedia

PC Video Hardware

When it comes to using a PC, what you get is what you see. The video hardware you use has a lot to do with how much you enjoy using your computer and the Internet. This Usenet group is where people discuss any topic related to PC video hardware: monitors, computers, video cards, flat-panel displays, video accelerators, video capture cards, and more. The Web site contains the FAQ (frequently asked question list) for the group.

Web:
http://www.heartlab.rri.uwo.ca/vidfaq/videofaq.html

Usenet:
comp.sys.ibm.pc.hardware.video

802 VIDEO AND MULTIMEDIA

Video Editing

This is a wonderful site with lots of video editing resources. My favorite part of the site is the collection of articles about basic video editing. If you have an interest in video, especially if you are just starting, this is one of the places you will find useful.

Web:

http://www.videonics.com/Articles.html

Video Glossary

The world of video, especially computer video, has a lot of specialized terminology. However, you need never feel lost. If you read or hear a word you don't understand, check the glossary at this Web site. Before you know it, you will be talking like a pro. ("What do you mean the machine doesn't have a flying erase head? I need to make a telecine transfer.")

Web:

http://www.bavc.org/html/resources/glossary.html

Look What I Found on the Net...

```
Newsgroup: comp.multimedia
Subject: Free Renaming Program

>>> Announcing Resequencer(tm), a FREE Windows utility to rename
>>> sequential image files.
>>>
>>> Suppose you have the files:
>>>     Image051.tga, Image052.tga...Image150.tga.
>>>
>>> With Resequencer, you can rename these files to:
>>>     Image0001.tga, Image0002.tga...Image0100.tga
>>>
>>> Resequencer is a 280 KB standalone EXE.  It requires no
>>> extra DLLs.

>> Yikes!  Does Windows really require a 280k compiled binary to
>> perform the function of a 10-line Perl script?

> No, but Visual Basic does.  Not that anyone's really asking,
> but the equivalent C program would be about 30K on Intel and
> maybe 80K on RISC processors like the Alpha.

If it required 2 MB of RAM, I would not care.  It's a utility
running on a operating system that runs on a computer that is a
tool.  It's not a religion.

Yeah, Windoze sucks.  I program in VisualBasicPro 4.0 because it
was cheap, gets the job done, and I want to spend my time
animating and creating useful utilities, not learning C.

Executable size is now a myth perpetuated as a job security
tool.  Yeah, C might run smaller and faster, but you are talking
about renaming files, not radiosity.
```

WEATHER

Climate Data Catalog
This is no farmer's almanac. Don't count on the ache in your knees or the singing of crickets to tell you what the weather is going to be like. Get access to oceanic datasets, surface climatologies, air-sea data, sea surface temperatures, and Navy bathymetry.

Web:
http://ingrid.ldgo.columbia.edu/

Climate Diagnostics Center
You're leaning on the fence talking to the neighbor about life and the weather when he says, "In all my born days, I reckon this is the hottest summer I can ever remember." And when you think about it, you suspect he might have a point. Don't let the mystery of his remark keep you up at night. Utilize the Climate Diagnostics Center to see exactly how the weather has been not only for your lifetime, but for the last few centuries. Interesting climatological data is used to track persistent anomalies and to see how this affects short-term weather.

Web:
http://www.cdc.noaa.gov/

Climate Monitoring
The Climate Monitoring and Diagnostics Laboratory (CMDL) is part of the National Oceanic and Atmospheric Administration in Boulder, Colorado. The CMDL studies the atmosphere looking at specific components that can change the Earth's climate. At their Web site, you will find research information in such areas as aerosol gases and the greenhouse effect, and depletion of the global ozone layer.

Web:
http://www.cmdl.noaa.gov/

European Weather Satellite Images
Here is a current infrared satellite image of Europe, showing cloud cover and clear areas. This is the place to consult when you need to find out which parts of the Riviera are sunny, so you know where to go for the weekend.

Web:
http://www.ccc.nottingham.ac.uk/pub/sat-images/
http://www.infomet.fcr.es/meteosat/meteosat.cgi

Hurricanes and Typhoons
Hurricanes and typhoons are powerful tropical storms that originate in the equatorial regions. They bring large amounts of rain and fierce winds and are capable of causing severe damage if they travel inland. When such a storm originates in the Atlantic Ocean or Caribbean Sea, the storm is called a hurricane. If it originates in the Pacific or Indian Ocean, it is called a typhoon. These sites provide information about upcoming tropical storms, as well as technical data about the storms themselves.

Web:
http://typhoon.atmos.colostate.edu/forecasts/
http://www.nhc.noaa.gov/

Marine Weather Observations
When you have been working hard all day and you want to go down to the beach to snorkel, it would be a handy thing to know in advance what the water temperature is like. That way, you will know whether or not to wear your wetsuit. You can find out this information and more from this site. Just click on a coastal region to get information on water temperature, wave height and frequency, and wind conditions.

Web:
http://www.ncep.noaa.gov/MPC/mpcfor.htm

Meteorology Resources
Weather buffs no longer have to roam the Internet looking for interesting meteorological information. At this Web site you will find links to lots of meteorological resources on the Net.

Web:
http://www.ugems.psu.edu/~owens/WWW_Virtual_Library/

Meteorology Talk and General Discussion
It may be that no one does anything about the weather, but that doesn't stop us from talking about it. Join the discussion on Usenet and talk about the weather and all facets of meteorology.

Usenet:
sci.geo.meteorology

804 WEATHER

Space Weather

It's a total drag when you are leaving Earth's gravitational influence, and you find out the weather in space is really not suitable. Next time, plan ahead. Check out today's space weather. You can see a current image of the sun, X-ray flux data, and get detailed information on solar flaring and the geomagnetic field.

Web:
   http://www.sel.bldrdoc.gov/today.html

Storm Chasing

The diameter of a tornado can vary from a few feet to as wide as a mile. Rotating winds within a funnel can reach a velocity of up to 300 mph (480 km/hour). However, the enormous risk posed by these storms is not enough to scare off certain types of people, called "storm chasers". Storm chasers will travel hundreds of miles, hot on the trail of storm activity. Their goals are to learn more about the storm and experience certain types of storms firsthand. Some storm chasers just want to have something exciting to do in their spare time. These sites offer lots of information about storm chasing, including pictures, anecdotes and late-breaking storm news.

Web:
   http://tornado.sfsu.edu/geosciences/stormchase.html
   http://www.gilbertzone.com/beginner/beginner.html
   http://www.nssl.noaa.gov/~nws/spotterguide.html
   http://www.se.mediaone.net/~persoffj/chaser.html
   http://www.storm-track.com/

Weather Images

When the weather is so cold that only an inebriated polar bear would go outside, don't even think of leaving the house before checking the latest pictures on the Net. There are a variety of different satellite images and maps to keep you apprised of what is happening on the surface of our planet. If you are a meteorologist, you will also be interested in some of the weather visualization tools.

Web:
   http://covis.atmos.uiuc.edu/covis/visualizer/
   http://www.weatherimages.org/
   http://wxp.eas.purdue.edu/

Weather Radar

There is a lot more to the weather than licking your finger to see which way the wind is blowing. Nobody knows this better than professional meteorologists, who use radar maps to study patterns and changes in the Earth's weather systems. If you would like to see what it is like being a professional meteorologist, visit one of these sites and choose a weather map that looks good. Then, making sure your friends are watching, stroke your chin and make some thoughtful remarks. (If you're not sure what to say, I suggest, "I don't like the looks of that low pressure area over the Ozarks.")

Web:
   http://www.cameronlaw.com/weather/us/
      weather_radar.html
   http://www.earthwatch.com/SKYWATCH/
      RDUS2D.html

Look What I Found on the Net...

```
Newsgroup: sci.geo.meteorology
Subject: Cold Nights and the Full Moon

> Is there a correlation between cold nights and the full moon?

Indirectly, but not caused by the moon.

Cloudy nights tend to be warmer (because the clouds reduce heat
loss), and clear nights tend to be cooler.  If it's very cloudy,
you won't see the moon.  So, if you can see the (full) moon, it
must not be very cloudy and therefore it's likely to be colder.
```

WEATHER 805

Go outside. The Net will be here when you get back.

Weather Reports: Canada

I grew up in Canada and you can believe me when I tell you they have a lot of weather up there. In fact, they have so much, they sometimes send some of the extra weather down to the United States. (And some people say Free Trade is bad.) If you want the official information about Canadian weather, connect to the Environment Canada Web site, where you will find the latest weather forecasts, maps, satellite images, surfing forecasts, and so on.

Web:
   http://www.tor.ec.gc.ca/text/

Weather Reports: International

Here are weather reports for just about everywhere in the world. Once you have Net access, no matter where you are or what you are planning, there is no excuse for letting the environment rain on your parade.

Web:
   http://www.intellicast.com/weather/intl/
   http://www.usatoday.com/weather/basemaps/wworld1.htm

Weather Reports: United States

The next time you attend a costume party, go as a weather forecaster. Dress up in clothing suitable for a television broadcast, set up your computer and point to one of these Web sites. You'll find weather images and information just like they use on television. Stand in front of the computer and smile and point a lot. Your costume will be so convincing probably nobody will recognize you. (If they do, smile authoritatively and ask if they want your autograph.)

Web:
   http://vortex.plymouth.edu/
   http://www.intellicast.com/weather/usa/
   http://www.mit.edu/weather
   http://www.usatoday.com/weather/wfront.htm
   http://www.weather.com/
   http://www.wunderground.com/

The Outside World

Living on the Internet is fine, but the outside world has two important advantages: (1) there is pizza, and (2) it's the only place I know of to get a computer. However, there are some significant disadvantages and high up on the list is that the outside world has altogether too much weather. Before you actually commit yourself to going outside, use the Internet to check the weather report for your area. Why take a chance when the information is only a few keystrokes away?

Look What I Found on the Net...

(from the Space Weather Web site)

SPACE WEATHER OUTLOOK

Solar activity is expected to be very low.

The geomagnetic field is expected to remain quiet for the next 24 hours, with activity increasing to quiet to unsettled on days two and three.

Weather Warnings

Don't be surprised. Find out about hurricanes, floods, tornadoes, thunderstorms and other severe weather events before they get to you.

Web:
http://iwin.nws.noaa.gov/iwin/nationalwarnings.html

WEB: CREATING WEB PAGES

Animated Gifs

A gif is an image that is stored using the gif format. (The name means "graphics interchange format".) An animated gif contains more than one image in the file. When your browser displays an animated gif, the series of images is displayed sequentially, providing for a primitive type of animation. These Web sites contain information that explains all about animated gifs: what they are, how to make them and how to use them effectively.

Web:
http://animation.simplenet.com/
http://members.aol.com/royalef/gifmake.htm
http://www.animfactory.com/
http://www.bendnet.com/users/brianhovis/anime.htm
http://www.gifworld.com/
http://www.webreference.com/dev/gifanim/

Bad Website Design

One of the best ways to learn how to do something well is to study what happens when people do it poorly. Here's a collection of links to Web pages that just do not cut the HTML mustard. Study them carefully, along with the commentary, and it won't be long before you are a better, finer Web page designer.

Web:
http://www.webpagesthatsuck.com/

Bandwidth Bandits

The term "bandwidth" is used to describe the amount of information being copied from one place to another. For example, if many people visit your Web site, you might say that it is a high bandwidth site. If a particular site is rarely visited, you could call it a low bandwidth site. So what is a bandwidth bandit? When you design a Web page that has pictures and graphics, you normally keep the images on your Web server. When someone visits your Web page, his browser gets the images from your server. From time to time, you may see a picture or graphic on someone else's page that you would like to use on your own page. The proper thing to do is to download copies of the images to your own server (and, if you are dealing with original art, to ask permission). Some people—the so-called bandwidth bandits—do not copy images to their own server. Instead, they just point to the original pages within their HTML. This means that each time somebody visits one of the bandit's pages, the browser must impose on other Web sites to get the images. In other words, when a person points to other people's images, he artificially increases the demands on those sites and becomes a bandwidth bandit. Don't do this.

Web:
http://www.darklock.com/webguard/
http://www.widowsweb.com/widows/plea.html

Banners, Buttons and Text

You don't have to be an artist to make cool graphics for your Web site. Here are some nifty tools you can use to animate text, make buttons and design interesting logos. After all, why shouldn't your Web site be as cool as you are?

Web:
http://www.buttonmaker.com/
http://www.cooltext.com/
http://www.mediabuilder.com/abm.html

Beginner's Guide to HTML

HTML (Hypertext Markup Language) is the set of specifications that are used to define what a Web page looks like and how it behaves. If you want to make your own Web pages, you need to either (1) understand HTML or (2) use a program that hides the details from you. You can use such a program, but you get a lot more flexibility and control if you understand HTML. Here is a document to help you get started.

Web:
http://www.ncsa.uiuc.edu/General/Internet/WWW/HTMLPrimer.html

Cascading Style Sheets

HTML was designed to define the content of Web pages. In the original version of HTML, there were few ways to specify how that content should be displayed. Naturally, Web page designers want as much control as they can get over the exact layout of the page. Cascading style sheets (CSS) are an enhancement to basic HTML that allows you to have all the control you need. You can specify margins, colors, fonts, backgrounds, white space, and much more. You use CSS by attaching one or more style sheets to your HTML document. In order to create the final image, the browser applies each style sheet to the document. (The application of multiple style sheets to a single HTML page is called "cascading".) Here is a simple example of how CSS might be used. Say that a large company has several Web servers with many Web pages. There can be a general style sheet that is used for all the Web pages produced by the company. This will give all the Web pages a common appearance. A particular department might have a style sheet for all the Web pages they produce. Within that department, a Web designer could have his own style sheet. Thus, when you look at a Web page from this company, your browser might apply three different style sheets to render the final appearance of the page.

Web:
http://www.blooberry.com/html/style/styleindex.htm
http://www.htmlhelp.com/reference/css/

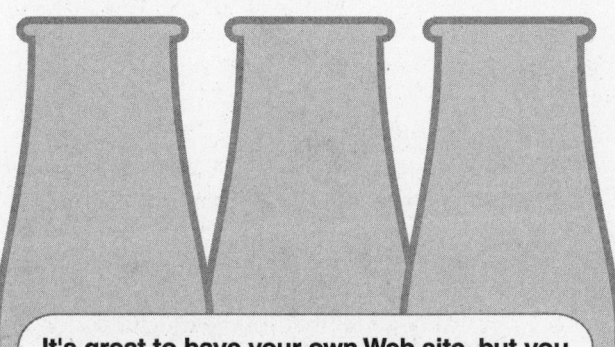

> It's great to have your own Web site, but you can't do a good job designing it unless you understand something about HTML (Hypertext Markup Language). Start with the Beginner's Guide to HTML, and soon your personal home page will be the cream rising to the top of the Internet milk bottle.

> **If you lived here, you'd be home by now.**

CGI Scripts

CGI stands for "Common Gateway Interface", a mechanism by which a Web server can process data that you enter into a form. The program that runs when you enter data is called a CGI script. These Web sites explain what CGI is and how it works. You will also find a collection of CGI scripts that you can use or modify. For discussion, you can join the Usenet group or IRC. Note: Creating CGI scripts requires programming skills.

Web:
http://cgi-lib.stanford.edu/cgi-lib/
http://www.cgi-resources.com/
http://www.itm.com/cgicollection/
http://www.jipes.com/cgi-local/faqsmachine/faqs.cgi

Usenet:
comp.infosystems.www.authoring.cgi

IRC:
#cgi

Color Chart

There will be times when you want to control the colors on your Web pages as closely as you can. The best way to do so is to specify the colors numerically. Each specific color corresponds to a six-digit hexadecimal—base 16—number. (In decimal—base 10—our regular system, we use the digits 0 through 9. In hexadecimal, we use 16 digits: 0, 1, 2, 3, 4, 5, 6, 7, 8, 9, A, B, C, D, E and F.) For example, when you create a Web page, if you specify the color "00CC99" you get a greenish-blue. These Web sites have tools to make it easy to find the color you want and its numeric code.

Web:
http://world.std.com/~wij/color/
http://www.hidaho.com/colorcenter/cc.html
http://www.phoenix.net/~jacobson/rgb.html

WEB: CREATING WEB PAGES

Dynamic HTML

Dynamic HTML (DHTML) is an extension of regular HTML. Using dynamic HTML, you can enhance the functionality of your Web pages. For example, you can layer multiple images on top of one another, make elements on the page interactive, and, using cascading style sheets, you can control the exact placement of all the text and images. Dynamic HTML also makes it easier for you to write scripts that are attached to the Web page and manipulate objects on the page without having to reload.

Web:
   http://www.all-links.com/dynamic/
   http://www.dhtmlzone.com/
   http://www.microsoft.com/workshop/author/default.asp
   http://www.tips-tricks.com/dy.html

Frames

Frames are Web page building blocks that allow you to divide a page into independent sections. Within each frame, you can control how data is to be displayed. These Web sites offer tutorials that will help you learn about frames and how to use them. Special request: Not everybody likes to use frames. Unless the nature of your data is such that it demands frames, please take the time to ensure that your Web pages work properly for people who choose to view them without frames.

Web:
   http://www.charweb.org/charweb/htmlgroup/frames/
   http://www.newbie.net/sharky/frames/intro.htm
   http://www.spunwebs.com/frmtutor.html

> Hungry?
> Try "Food and Drink".
> Hungry for love?
> Try "Romance".

Free Web Page Hosting

Would you like to have your own Web site? Of course you would. So where are you going to put it? Some Internet service providers will give you free space for your Web site. But if this isn't the case for you, here are some places that will host your Web space for no charge. Is there a catch, you ask? Well, of course. First of all, you will be limited in how much space you are allowed. Second, you and your visitors may have to look at a lot of advertising. Third, if you try to present objectionable material (such as X-rated pictures), you may be censored. Finally, your name, email address and any other information you volunteer might be used for mailing lists and telemarketing. Still, free is free.

Web:
   http://www.angelfire.com/
   http://www.freewebspace.net/
   http://www.freeyellow.com/
   http://www.geocities.com/
   http://www.page-utils.com/
   http://www.tripod.com/
   http://www.xoom.com/

Guestbooks

When someone visits you at your home, you know they were there. But when somebody looks at your Web site, you have no way of knowing that you had a visitor. Of course, one of the nice things about the Net is that it is anonymous, and you don't want to force everyone who goes to your Web page to tell you who they are. But it is nice if you have a way for people to leave you a message and for other people who visit to read the messages. To do this, you use what's called a guestbook. If you are a programmer, you can create your own guestbook facility. But it's much easier to let someone else do the work. Here are some resources that make it easy for you to put your own personal guestbook at your own personal Web site.

Web:
   http://guestworld.tripod.lycos.com/
   http://www.dreambook.com/
   http://www.freeguestbooks.com/
   http://www.guestpage.com/

HTML

You're at a party and you have your eye on a hot prospect you've been dying to talk to. You stake your claim at the onion dip, knowing at any minute she will come over, because who can resist onion dip? Finally she does and you strike up a conversation, ready to talk about something meaningful. Then she asks, "Don't you find it terribly inconvenient that, when you get the **rel** and **rev** attributes mixed up within a **<link>** tag, the relationships get all mixed up?" So what are you going to do—tell her that women have trouble understanding relationships? Be prepared for situations like this by reading up on all aspects of HTML (Hypertext Markup Language) *before* you go to a party.

Web:
  http://www.blooberry.com/html/
  http://www.htmlcompendium.org/
  http://www.sbrady.com/hotsource/

Usenet:
  comp.infosystems.www.authoring.html

Listserv Mailing List:
  List Name: **adv-html**
  Subscribe to: **listserv@ua1vm.ua.edu**

IRC:
  #html

HTML Editors

The content and design of Web pages is described by a system called HTML (Hypertext Markup Language). Broadly speaking, there are two ways to create Web pages. You can use a WYSIWYG (what you see is what you get) editor or an HTML editor. With a WYSIWYG editor, you manipulate the various elements of the page and make them just the way you want. Behind the scenes, the editor creates the appropriate HTML for you automatically. Both Microsoft and Netscape give away free WYSIWYG editors with their suites of Internet software: Frontpage Express (Microsoft) and Composer (Netscape). If you want more control over the Web page creation process, you can use an HTML editor. Such editors have sophisticated features to help you create and maintain HTML just the way you want it.

Web:
  http://cws.internet.com/32html.html
  http://home.netscape.com/download/
  http://tucows.tierranet.com/htmlbeginner95.html
  http://www.microsoft.com/ie/download/
  http://www.tucows.agis.net/htmledit95.html

Icons for Fake Awards

In the beginning, the idea sort of made sense: someone would look at a lot of Web pages and judge which ones were the very best. Those very best Web sites could display a special icon showing that they had achieved recognition, like a four-star restaurant mentioned in a guide book. What happened next should have been predictable. It's a lot easier to go around giving other awards than it is to actually do something creative on your own. The number of people willing to judge other people's work proliferated and, today, there are literally hundreds of awards on the Net. The whole thing has become rather silly. To help make it even more silly, here are some Web sites that contain a whole bunch of icons for fake awards. Put one of these icons on your site, and you can thumb your nose at the entire award culture. Now, *that's* an idea that deserves an award.

Web:
  http://www.adfa.com/inhisservice/humor/
    HumorAwards.html
  http://www.thecorporation.com/icon/icon.html

HTML Editors

It's not generally well known, but God used an HTML editor to design the universe.

(Why do you think everything lines up so well?)

810 WEB: CREATING WEB PAGES

Image Maps

An image map is a picture in which the various points correspond to URLs (Web addresses). When the image map is displayed on a Web page, the user can jump to the different URLs by clicking on different parts of the picture. For example, say you are designing a Web site to show specific information about each of the states in the U.S. You could use an image of the country that shows all the states, and then define an image map so that a person could jump to information about a particular state simply by clicking on it. The information in these resources will help you understand image maps, and show you how to create them for your own Web pages.

Web:
http://www.coffeecup.com/mapper/
http://www.cris.com/~automata/tutorial.shtml
http://www.ihip.com/
http://www.ozemail.com.au/~noeljc/quick&dirty/map.htm

Usenet:
comp.infosystems.www.authoring.images

Learning HTML

HTML (Hypertext Markup Language) is a system that describes the various elements used to create a Web page. To make a Web page, you create an HTML file that contains data along with special instructions (called "tags") that tell a browser how the data should be displayed and processed. You then put the HTML file where it can be accessed by a Web server. When someone gives the address of that file to their browser, the browser will contact your Web server and request a copy of the file. When the file arrives, the browser will read the HTML and display the data appropriately. If the HTML tells the browser that your Web page needs extra files (such as images or photos), the browser will request those as well and display them on the page. (This is why you often see your browser make more than one connection to a Web server even though you are only looking at a single page. Each image must be retrieved separately.) HTML is complex and, to create really good Web pages, you need to spend some time learning the details and experimenting. Here are two Web sites to help you get started. How do you know which HTML beginner's guide to read? Look at a few and pick the one that makes the most sense to you.

Web:
http://www.devry-phx.edu/webresrc/webmstry/lrntutrl.htm
http://www.psychol.ucl.ac.uk/www/html-primer.html

Meta Tags

A meta tag is an HTML statement that you place on your page for one of three reasons. First, a meta tag can be used to store information about the document, such as the name of the author or an expiration date. Second, you can use a meta tag to make something happen to the page automatically, such as playing a sound or jumping to another page. Finally, you can use a meta tag to hold keywords that will be noticed and indexed by various search engines. If you would like to attract a lot of the "right" people to your Web site, learning how to use meta tags to catch the eye of the search engines can help a lot. Is it fun to use these tags? Well, as Will Rogers once said, "I never meta tag I didn't like."

Web:
http://www.metatagbuilder.com/
http://www.northernwebs.com/set/
http://www.onebellevue.com/files/fuss/meta.htm
http://www.y4i.com/websitepromotion8.html

Promoting Your Web Site

There are millions of Web pages on the Net, so how do you get noticed? These resources will help you get the recognition you deserve. Before long, visitors from all over the Net will be beating an electronic path to your virtual door.

Web:
http://www.accusubmit.com/
http://www.addme.com/
http://www.mmgco.com/top100.html
http://www.promotionworld.com/free.shtml
http://www.rankthis.com/
http://www.sitelaunch.net/
http://www.stars.com/Search/Promotion/

Five Reasons Why You Should Learn HTML

(1) It's fun, it's legal, and the high lasts for weeks.

(2) Making your own Web site will give you a sense of freedom, independence and confidence that will mark you as a giant among men (or women).

(3) Your mother would be so proud of you.

(4) One person I know didn't learn HTML, and within a few years, his life was exposed as a hollow, meaningless sham.

(5) If all the people who know HTML were laid end to end, they would be very surprised.

WEB: CREATING WEB PAGES — 811

> Jog on over to "Exercise".

Tables

Within HTML, you use tables to display information in rows and columns. Aside from using them to present data in a tabular format, you can also employ tables to create margins and to control spacing. These Web sites will teach you about tables, what they can do, and how to use them well.

Web:
http://www.idocs.com/tags/tables/tables.html
http://www.netscape.com/assist/net_sites/tables.html
http://www.pageresource.com/html/table1.htm

Transparent Gifs

A transparent gif is an image, in gif format, in which one color is designated as being "transparent". When the image is displayed on a Web page, the browser will change the places where the transparent color is used to be the same as the background color. The effect is to create an image which fits nicely into the background. Making transparent gifs is easy if you have the right tools. These Web sites will help you find what you need to learn how to use transparent gifs well.

Web:
http://www.cooltype.com/articles/transparent_gifs/
http://www.mindworkshop.com/alchemy/gifcon.html

Using HTML Well

When you use HTML well, your pages look good and are easy to read. These Web sites will help you teach yourself how to use HTML well. There are lots of tips, explanations and links to tools. Most important, you will find examples you can use for your own Web pages.

Web:
http://www.cs.cmu.edu/~tilt/cgh/
http://www.midnight.com/~bill/auth-html.html
http://www.quadzilla.com/

Web Authoring FAQ

Before you create your next Web page, take a few minutes to read this FAQ. It contains practical answers to common HTML questions. I guarantee that when you read the FAQ, you'll find at least a few places where you will say to yourself, "So, that's how it works."

Web:
http://www.htmlhelp.com/faq/wdgfaq.htm

Web Authoring FAQ

There are two important reasons why you should read the Web Authoring FAQ (frequently asked question list).

First, if you design your own Web pages, the questions and answers in this FAQ will save you a lot of time.

Second, if you get invited to the White House to visit the president and he takes you to a formal reception where you are introduced to the Romanian ambassador, you will have something to talk about.

WEB: CREATING WEB PAGES

Web Page Backgrounds

One way to spice up your Web page is to use a background. These Web sites provide lots of different textures and images you can use. Be careful, however, to exercise restraint. In most cases, anything unusual will look bad and be hard to read. Remember, even if a Web page looks good on your monitor, other people may not see it the same way you do, so be conservative.

Web:

http://the-tech.mit.edu/kpt/bgs.html
http://www.meat.com/textures/
http://www.windyweb.com/design/

Web Page Counters

Why be different when you, too, can have a counter on your Web page? (There are even cats on the Net who have access counters on their Web pages.) Here are some resources that tell you how to put a counter on your page and offer some great samples of counter digits.

Web:

http://www.counterart.com/
http://www.digitmania.holowww.com/
http://www.pagecount.com/

Web Page Creation Talk and General Discussion

Once you start to create your own Web pages, you will realize how helpful it can be to talk to other people. This Usenet group is for discussion of topics related to creating Web pages. You can discuss HTML, design style, techniques, tips, and so on. For immediate real-time chat, try the IRC channels.

Usenet:

comp.infosystems.www.authoring.misc

IRC:

#webmaster
#www

Web Page Graphics and Icons

These days you don't have to have graphic talent (or even graphics software) to spice up your Web pages. These sites have pointers and links to many different icons and graphic images you can use with HTML documents (Web pages).

Web:

http://soback.kornet.nm.kr/~pixeline/heeyun/graphics.html
http://www.coolgraphics.com/
http://www.gemstar.net/lmoore/borders.html
http://www.grapholina.com/Graphics/
http://www.pambytes.com/
http://www.reallybig.com/clipgate.htm

Web Page Marketing

Would you like to sell ad banners and generate revenue from your Web site? These Web sites contain serious information for serious marketers, but there are tips and resources for everyone. Actually, I think these resources should be entitled, "How to Make Your Web Site as Annoying as Possible". Please, please, promise me you won't use blinking banners, popup ads and frames with ads that automatically refresh themselves every thirty seconds.

Web:

http://www.clickz.com/
http://www.netb2b.com/

Web Page Programs

Much of the tricky stuff you see on Web pages requires some programming. So why not get someone else to do the work? There are lots of pre-written Web page programs available for free on the Net. You may have to learn a bit of technical stuff, but once you do, you'll be in Web page heaven with tons of wonderful doodads that allow you to customize your Web site up the wazoo: access counters, password access controls, Web site search engines, email forms, calendars, calculators, tools for buttons, fonts, menus, tickers, and much, much more.

Web:

http://www.freecode.com/

WEB: CREATING WEB PAGES

Web Publishing Resources

With a good Web page editor, you don't have to be technical to create a Web page. All you need to do is type the text, insert some pictures, and keep moving stuff around until you think it looks good. However, if you would like to make your pages look even better, these resources will help you take your Web skills to the next level. You'll find HTML tutorials, a glossary, information about meta tags, color charts, forms, graphics, templates, style sheets, and more.

Web:
http://nordstrand.hypermart.net/webhoo/
http://www.webdiner.com/

Web Reference

Here is a Web site that belongs in your bookmark list. The site contains reference material and links to information on just about anything you'll ever need in the world of HTML and the Web. The next time you have a question, start here. The answers you need may be only a few mouse clicks away.

Web:
http://www.webreference.com/

Web Site Validation

There are a variety of browsers used on the Net and they don't all work exactly the same. When you create a Web page, it's nice to check that your HTML will work well with various browsers. These sites contain Web page validation tools that can help you ensure that the HTML you write is as portable as possible. These tools are sophisticated and provide an in-depth analysis that would be impossible to do by hand.

Web:
http://www.netmechanic.com/
http://www.tiac.net/users/zach1/htmlcheck/htmlcheck.shtml
http://www2.imagiware.com/RxHTML/

Web Style Manual

It is a good idea to learn something about design before you create your own Web page. Try reading this style manual loaded with information on document design, navigation, site structure, Web page design, efficient use of the Web, design integrity, and much more. There is plenty of information for both beginning and advanced users.

Web:
http://info.med.yale.edu/caim/manual/contents.html

XML

XML (Extensible Markup Language) is a meta-language that allows you to define your own markup languages. (HTML, for example, is a markup language.) In general, XML has the potential to provide wonderful improvements in the way we create Web pages. However, XML is complex and not yet supported in all its rich fullness by the popular browsers. If you like to live in the leading edge of Web page design, you'll enjoy learning about XML. Here are resources to help you, including a FAQ and information about standards, conferences and updates.

Web:
http://www.lists.ic.ac.uk/hypermail/xml-dev/
http://www.ucc.ie/xml/
http://www.w3.org/XML/
http://www.xml.com/xml/pub/

Usenet:
comp.text.sgml
comp.text.xml

Majordomo Mailing List:
List Name: **xml-dev**
Subscribe to: **majordomo@ic.ac.uk**

IRC:
#xml

Web Site Validation

You can validate a parking receipt.
You can validate a legal document.
You can even validate your best friend's feelings.
But when you put your own Web site on the Net, the only thing anyone will care about is whether or not you have validated the HTML.

WEB: SOFTWARE

ActiveX

ActiveX, designed by Microsoft, is a complex system designed to integrate programs with interactive Internet content. In particular, Web sites can use ActiveX tools to create multimedia effects, interactive objects and complex programs. With ActiveX, your browser can download programs from Web sites and then execute those programs on your computer. The programs can even interact with your own software (such as your word processor, database, spreadsheet, and so on). ActiveX is now part of Windows DNA (Distributed interNet Application Architecture), Microsoft's new, improved software development system for the current economic cycle. ActiveX's main competitor is Java, developed by Sun Microsystems.

Web:

http://www.download.com/PC/Activex/
http://www.microsoft.com/dna/default.asp

Browser Watch

A browser is an Internet client program you use to access the Web. Modern browsers can also read Usenet groups, and send and receive mail. To extend the capabilities of a browser, you can use programs called "plug-ins". This Web site carries news about the browser and plug-ins industry. You will find everything you need to know about upcoming browsers and plug-ins, including how to get them quickly. If you are an Internet nerd, you can feast on rumors, news and tips. There is also a big list in which you can look up any browser to see which operating systems it runs on and where to get it. If you are analytical, you can read the browser statistics and look for patterns.

Web:

http://browserwatch.internet.com/

Hostile Java Applets

Java is supposed to be perfectly safe. Well, as you know, nothing in this world worth doing is perfectly safe—and that includes Java. This Web site contains Java applets (programs) that can cause trouble. Be careful.

Web:

http://www.rstcorp.com/hostile-applets/

Internet Explorer

This is the official home of Microsoft's flagship Web browser: Internet Explorer. Come here to download the browser (for free), find out about the latest technologies, press information, demos, news and stuff for developers. You can also find all the "extra stuff" to turn your browser into a powerful, supercharged Internet cruiser. (Note: Internet Explorer requires Windows 95/98 or Windows NT.)

Web:

http://www.microsoft.com/ie/

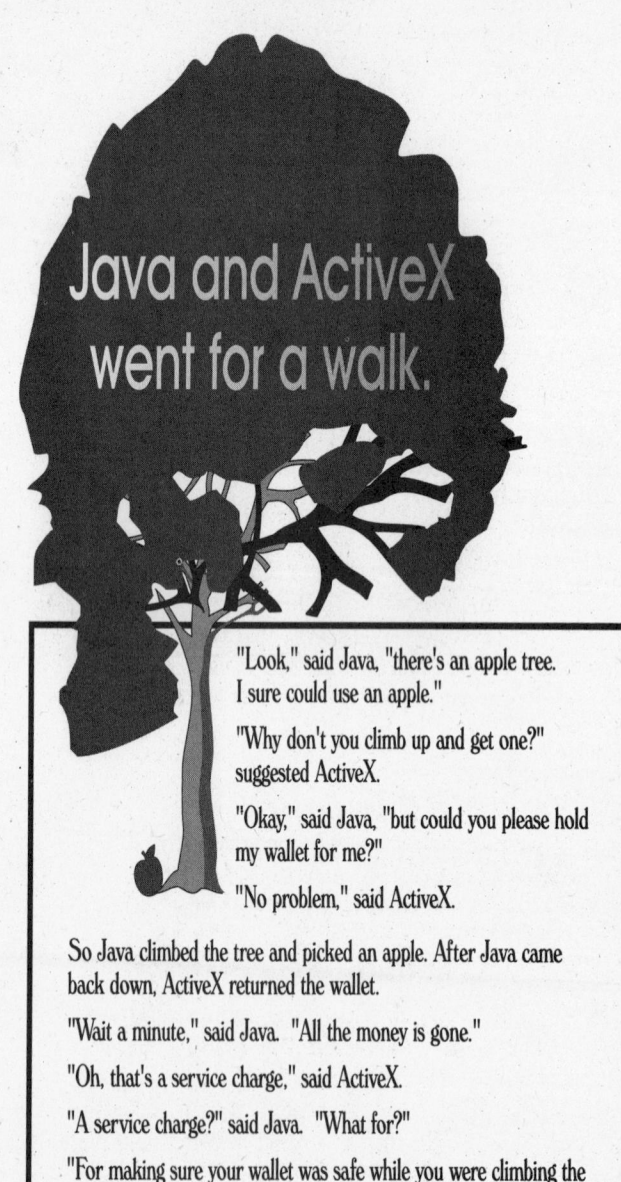

Java and ActiveX went for a walk.

"Look," said Java, "there's an apple tree. I sure could use an apple."

"Why don't you climb up and get one?" suggested ActiveX.

"Okay," said Java, "but could you please hold my wallet for me?"

"No problem," said ActiveX.

So Java climbed the tree and picked an apple. After Java came back down, ActiveX returned the wallet.

"Wait a minute," said Java. "All the money is gone."

"Oh, that's a service charge," said ActiveX.

"A service charge?" said Java. "What for?"

"For making sure your wallet was safe while you were climbing the tree."

WEB: SOFTWARE

Java

Java is a complex system designed to support programs that can be downloaded from the Web and run automatically. For example, when you are visiting a Web site, selecting a particular link might send a program to your computer, where it will be run by your browser (which knows how to run Java programs). Why is Java important? On its own, a browser can only do so much. It can download and display data. It can also play sounds, show you pictures and images, and so on. But the capabilities of a browser are limited to what is built-in, or what is added by using plug-in or helper programs. With Java, it is possible to write a program to do just about anything, and then put that program on a Web site. When someone visits the site, the program is sent to his or her computer, where it is executed. Java is also important because it is the focus of a huge effort to build an Internet environment that can be run on various types of computers and other devices. Although Java was originally developed by Sun Microsystems, many other companies are riding along. Java's main competitor is ActiveX, developed by Microsoft.

Web:
  http://java.sun.com/
  http://pantheon.yale.edu/~dff/java.html
  http://www.cs.princeton.edu/sip/java-faq.html
  http://www.developer.com/directories/pages/dir.java.html/

Usenet:
  alt.www.hotjava
  comp.lang.java
  comp.lang.java.advocacy
  comp.lang.java.announce
  comp.lang.java.api
  comp.lang.java.beans
  comp.lang.java.corba
  comp.lang.java.databases
  comp.lang.java.gui
  comp.lang.java.help
  comp.lang.java.machine
  comp.lang.java.misc
  comp.lang.java.programmer
  comp.lang.java.security
  comp.lang.java.softwaretools
  comp.lang.java.tech
  comp.lang.javascript

Listserv Mailing List:
  List Name: **java**
  Subscribe to: **listserv@yorku.ca**

Listserv Mailing List:
  List Name: **java-discuss**
  Subscribe to: **listserv@ociweb.com**

IRC:
  #java

Javascript

Javascript is a language that allows programmers to write small programs (scripts) that can be imbedded in the HTML for a Web page. When your browser reads the HTML, it interprets the Javascript and performs whatever function the program tells it to do. Javascript can be used for all kinds of interesting and useful effects on a Web page. And you can use it even if you aren't a programmer: if you find a script you like—on somebody else's page or on an archive—you can copy it to your page. (Of course, if the script is original work, you should ask for permission.)

Web:
  http://developer.netscape.com/docs/manuals/javascript.html
  http://www.faqs.org/faqs/computer-lang/java/javascript/
  http://www.jsworld.com/
  http://www.serve.com/hotsyte

Usenet:
  comp.lang.javascript

Listserv Mailing List:
  List Name: **javascpt**
  Subscribe to: **listserv@utkvm1.utk.edu**

IRC:
  #javascript

Javascript Archives

You don't have to be a programmer to use Javascript on your Web pages. Here are some Web pages with lots and lots of free scripts, yours to snarf at will.

Web:
  http://www.javascriptsource.com/
  http://www.js-planet.com/
  http://www.wsabstract.com/cutpastejava.htm

Lynx

Lynx is a text-based Web browser that runs under Unix, DOS and VMS. I like Lynx because it is fast (no graphics) and easy to use. Even if you have the most powerful graphical computer around, give Lynx a try. When you are after pure information, no browser is faster.

Web:
  http://lynx.browser.org/

Netscape

Netscape is one of the two most popular browsers on the Web (the other browser being Microsoft's Internet Explorer). Netscape is designed to make your Web experience as satisfying as possible (although you do need to supply your own food and clean up the carpet afterwards). I have included two Web sites here. One is the place from which you can download Netscape Communicator, a collection of free software that contains the browser. The other site is the main Web site for the company.

Web:
http://www.netscape.com/
http://www.netscape.com/navigator/

Netscape Source Code

Within the world of Unix and the Internet, there has been a long tradition of free, open software. Today, many people depend on such open products: Linux and FreeBSD (types of Unix), Perl (a scripting language), Apache (a Web server) and many more, including all the programs associated with the Free Software Foundation. On January 23rd, 1998, the Netscape company announced that they would become part of this tradition by distributing their Communicator suite of Internet products (including the browser) for free and by making the source code readily available. Is this a shrewd business move or too little too late?

Web:
http://www.mozilla.org/

Plug-Ins

A plug-in is a program designed to enhance the capabilities of a browser by processing a particular type of data that the browser cannot handle on its own. For example, if you visit a Web site that has music videos, you cannot look at the videos unless you have a plug-in that can process that type of video data. Your browser comes with various plug-ins, but there will be times when you need others. These Web sites provide information about plug-ins and how to get them. (Note: Within Internet Explorer, many of the jobs carried out by Netscape plug-ins are done by ActiveX controls. However, Internet Explorer is designed to use Netscape plug-ins.)

Web:
http://browserwatch.internet.com/plug-in.html
http://cws.internet.com/32plugin.html
http://home.netscape.com/plugins/
http://www.winfiles.com/apps/98/plugins.html
http://www2.gol.com/users/oyamada/

Real Audio

Real Audio is an audio streaming technology from Progressive Networks that allows you to listen to long audio files without having to wait for the entire file to download. Real Audio also makes it possible to listen to live broadcasts, such as radio stations or special events. Your browser may already come with Real Audio capability. If not, you can find the software you need here (for Windows, OS/2, Macs and Unix). You can also start here to look for some of the many places around the Net that use Real Audio to broadcast.

Web:
http://www.realaudio.com/

VRML

VRML (Virtual Reality Markup Language) is a system used to create three-dimensional objects. Using VRML, designers can create imaginary 3-D worlds that you can visit and explore. To do so, you need either a browser that handles VRML or a VRML plug-in for a regular browser. These resources will help you learn how to use VRML, as well as find any tools you may need.

Web:
http://www.intervista.com/vrml/
http://www.sdsc.edu/vrml/
http://www.sics.se/dce/dive/

Usenet:
comp.lang.vrml

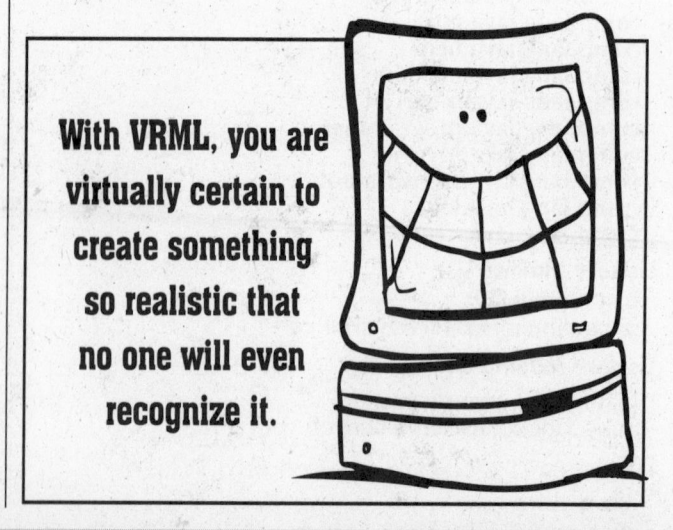

> With VRML, you are virtually certain to create something so realistic that no one will even recognize it.

Web Browser Talk and General Discussion

When you use the Web, your experience starts and ends with a browser. The browser you use very much colors your experience, so it is no surprise that people have strong opinions about what they like and what they dislike. In addition, the Web browser industry is fast-moving and highly competitive, with new browsers, plug-ins and related technology appearing all the time. All of this makes for a lot to talk about when it comes to browsers, and these Usenet groups are the places to be. (Take my browser, please.)

Usenet:
comp.infosystems.www.browsers.mac
comp.infosystems.www.browsers.misc
comp.infosystems.www.browsers.ms-windows
comp.infosystems.www.browsers.x

Web Log Analysis

A Web log is a file, kept on a Web server, in which information is stored about how the Web pages on that server are being accessed. To make sense of this information, you must use a Web log analysis program. You can use such a program to tell you how many people have been to your site, what pages are the most popular, what pages or images might be missing, which browsers people are using, and more.

Web:
http://builder.cnet.com/Servers/Traffic/
http://www.accesswatch.com/
http://www.uu.se/Software/Analyzers/Access-analyzers.html

Web Server Talk and General Discussion

When you connect to a Web site, your browser requests data from a program called a Web server. Web servers are complex software systems that require a fair amount of care and feeding. These are the Usenet groups in which you can discuss Web servers: what is available, how they work, tips, questions, answers, and lots and lots of opinions.

Usenet:
comp.infosystems.www.servers.mac
comp.infosystems.www.servers.misc
comp.infosystems.www.servers.ms-windows
comp.infosystems.www.servers.unix

Web Server Watch

When you need to evaluate and choose a Web server, start here. You will find lots of information about the various servers: features, availability, comparisons, and so on. Once you have a server, you can check back periodically for news about your particular program.

Web:
http://serverwatch.internet.com/

Web Talk and General Discussion

The Web is one of the most important inventions in the history of mankind. These Usenet groups are used to discuss the Web and related topics. If you want to let the world know about your new Web site, you can send a message to the **.announce** group.

Usenet:
comp.infosystems.www.announce
comp.infosystems.www.misc
comp.infosystems.www.providers
comp.infosystems.www.users

WINDOWS

Desktop Themes

A desktop theme defines the look of your Windows environment: the background you see on the desktop, the colors, the mouse pointer, and so on. Using these free resources, you can jazz up your desktop with fun, colorful themes, many of which also come with screensavers. Windows itself comes with a few extra themes, but there are a *lot* more available on the Net.

Web:
http://www.freethemes.com/
http://www.originallook.com/thememain.html
http://www.themeworld.com/
http://www.themez.com/
http://www.thethemedoctor.com/

WINDOWS

Windows 95 and 98 Official Web Sites

Microsoft's official Web site offers access to their Windows 95 and 98 resources on the Internet. These are good places to look for the latest free programs and utilities, announcements, marketing info, and so on.

Web:

http://www.microsoft.com/windows95/
http://www.microsoft.com/windows98/

Windows Annoyances

Once you get used to Windows, you will find that there are a number of small idiosyncrasies that annoy you. Well, they annoy everyone else, too. These sites have advice and procedures you can use to make Windows do what you want (some of the time anyway). I have found lots of great hints here. Hint: Don't visit this site unless you have a lot of time. I guarantee you will get distracted and spend half the night trying things.

Web:

http://www.annoyances.org/win95/
http://www.annoyances.org/win98/

Windows Applications Talk and General Discussion

There is a lot of discussion about the various types of applications that run under the various types of Windows. Look for the Usenet group that is closest to what you need to talk about. These groups are good places to send a question.

Usenet:

comp.os.ms-windows.apps
comp.os.ms-windows.apps.comm
comp.os.ms-windows.apps.compatibility.win95
comp.os.ms-windows.apps.financial
comp.os.ms-windows.apps.misc
comp.os.ms-windows.apps.utilities
comp.os.ms-windows.apps.utilities.win3x
comp.os.ms-windows.apps.utilities.win95
comp.os.ms-windows.apps.word-proc

Windows Drivers

A driver is a complicated program that acts as an interface between an operating system (such as Windows) and a hardware device. Windows comes with many built-in drivers, but, when you start adding your own hardware to the computer, you may have to start searching to find the driver you need. Even if you do have all the drivers required by your system, there will be times when you want to update to a newer version. Here is *the* place to look for Windows drivers.

Web:

http://www.windrivers.com/

Windows Annoyances

Would you like to learn how to smooth out some of the rough spots in Windows? Check out the **Windows Annoyances** Web site for tips and secrets. Remember, Microsoft may deal the cards, but how you play them is up to you.

Windows Glossary

In the beginning, there was a word. And then, another word, and yet another word, and on and on. And finally, we found ourselves with a huge amount of technical terminology that only a nerd could understand. The next time you are reading about Windows and you encounter a word you don't understand, check with the Windows glossary: your permanent online nerd replacement.

Web:

http://www.mcp.com/resources/opsys/win95/glossary.html

Windows Magazines

Here are some Web sites maintained by various Windows magazines. If you want to keep up on Windows news—especially developer issues—these are good places to spend some time. Personally, I find skimming through the Web sites a lot more fun than reading the print versions of the magazines.

Web:
   http://www.winmag.com/
   http://www.winuser.com/

Windows Networking Talk and General Discussion

There are a variety of places to discuss Windows networking. First, there are a number of Usenet groups. It is a good idea to use the one that is most appropriate to your interests, although there is considerable overlap and cross-posting. Second, you can join the IRC channel for real-time networking talk.

Usenet:
   comp.os.ms-windows.networking.misc
   comp.os.ms-windows.networking.ras
   comp.os.ms-windows.networking.tcp-ip
   comp.os.ms-windows.networking.win95
   comp.os.ms-windows.networking.windows

IRC:
   #win95-net

Windows News

Behind the scenes, the world of Windows never stops. Microsoft is always making changes, creating new products and announcing new plans. Actually, it's all a plot. They want to lull you into a false sense of complacency, then—BLAM!—hit you with brand new "must have" software. Don't let anybody pull the operating system wool over your eyes. Keep up on the news and not only will you stay current and knowledgeable, people will invite you to parties just to hear you talk about the new version of Windows.

Web:
   http://www.cmpnet.com/win98/newsindex.html
   http://www.mindspring.com/~ggking3/pages/windmill.htm

Usenet:
   comp.os.ms-windows.announce
   comp.windows.news

Windows Peer-to-Peer Networking

Did you know that you can configure your Windows system to share files, directories and printers with other people over the Internet? You can let another person on the Net access your resources as easily as they access their own. All you have to know is how to configure the system properly. This Web site contains instructions. Just think. A friend on the other side of the world can click on an icon and see your files. (If nothing else, this will teach you to choose your friends wisely.)

Web:
   http://www.windows95.com/connect/peercon.html

Windows Pre-releases

The life cycle of a Windows operating system goes like this: (1) Wait and wait a long time for a new version. (2) Beta release: use a beta version of the new operating system for a long time. (3) Go to 1. When we are in the throes of a beta, you can participate in this Usenet discussion group to find out what everyone else is doing. This is also a good place to send questions when something strange happens and you need some help.

Usenet:
   comp.os.ms-windows.pre-release

Windows Programming

Here is a large selection of resources devoted to the topic of programming in the Windows environment. Topics cover general programming as well as more specific subjects like controls, graphics, memory management, multimedia, networking and tools.

Web:
   http://msdn.microsoft.com/developer/
   http://www.winmag.com/people/mheller/

Usenet:
   comp.os.ms-windows.programmer.controls
   comp.os.ms-windows.programmer.graphics
   comp.os.ms-windows.programmer.memory
   comp.os.ms-windows.programmer.misc
   comp.os.ms-windows.programmer.multimedia
   comp.os.ms-windows.programmer.networks
   comp.os.ms-windows.programmer.ole
   comp.os.ms-windows.programmer.tools.mfc
   comp.os.ms-windows.programmer.tools.misc
   comp.os.ms-windows.programmer.tools.owl
   comp.os.ms-windows.programmer.tools.winsock
   comp.os.ms-windows.programmer.vxd
   comp.os.ms-windows.programmer.win32
   comp.os.ms-windows.programmer.winhelp
   comp.windows.ms.programmer

Windows Questions and Answers

This mailing list is dedicated to Windows 95/98 questions and answers. When you are completely stuck, and the possibility of useful tech support seems like a figment of Mr. Bill's overactive imagination, this mailing list is a godsend. Send in your question and you may get an answer from some kind soul somewhere on the Net. Of course, you have a responsibility, too. If you see a question you can answer, please do so and help someone else.

Listserv Mailing List:
List Name: **win95-l**
Subscribe to: **listserv@peach.ease.lsoft.com**

Windows Resources

If you use Windows, I promise you—you will eventually need technical information. When that happens, try looking on the Net. I have chosen these Web sites as good, all-around places to help you find what you need. Aside from technical information, there are also other types of resources: discussion forums, software archives, event info, online magazines, and links to other Windows-related sites.

Web:
http://www.download.com/PC/Win95/
http://www.globalcomputing.com/win95.html
http://www.windowstuff.com/

Windows Setup

The installation and configuration of Windows is supposed to be automatic and is supposed to work perfectly. However, once in a while, perhaps even too seldom to mention—I don't want you to think I am a complainer—something goes wrong. Thus, we have Usenet groups just for discussion of Window installations and other related miracles of modern life.

Usenet:
comp.os.ms-windows.setup
comp.os.ms-windows.setup.win3x
comp.os.ms-windows.setup.win95
comp.os.ms-windows.win95.setup

Windows Talk and General Discussion

Most PCs in the world run under some form of Windows, so there's a lot to talk about. Here are the Usenet discussion groups devoted to Windows talk where you can jump right in. The **.advocacy** group is for controversial talk and debate. (The excitement is unbearable, so don't wait.)

Usenet:
alt.windows95
comp.os.ms-windows.advocacy
comp.os.ms-windows.misc
comp.os.ms-windows.win95.misc
comp.windows.misc
comp.windows.ms

Look What I Found on the Net...

```
Newsgroup: comp.os.ms-windows.pre-release
Subject: Linux Is Booming Worldwide

> STOP BUYING Microsoft Windows 3.1/ Windows95 and Windows NT.
> If you do, you will lose a hell lot of money and will become
> a slave of Microsoft...

I hope to outlive the great Microsoft dynasty.  If I do, when
they fall, everyone is invited over for a weenie roast.
```

Windows Video Discussion

If you have a special video adaptor in your PC, you may need some extra help getting everything working just perfectly with Windows. If so, this Usenet group is a good place to start.

Usenet:
comp.os.ms-windows.video

> Ignorance is ignorance.
> Chocolate is bliss.

WINDOWS NT

Creating an Internet Site with Windows NT

Many people use a Unix machine as the gateway between their network and the Internet. But Windows NT will do the job nicely. This site will show you what you need to understand and do to use a Windows NT machine as your Internet gateway. My advice is to read everything first, and then plan carefully before you start.

Web:
http://www.neystadt.org/winnt/site.htm

Internet Resources for Windows NT

Microsoft maintains this Web page as a collection of links to many products, services and resources that support using the Internet with Windows NT. You will find developer tools, lots of Internet client programs, servers (such as would be used by an Internet service provider), as well as all kinds of utilities. Most of these products are shareware or freeware, not created by Microsoft. Thus, Microsoft asks you to "Please support the authors of these products by honoring the terms of the respective product-use agreements." You know, I never realized it before, but Microsoft really is a good corporate neighbor.

Web:
http://www.microsoft.com/ntserver/solutions/softwarepart/tools/default.asp

---

Look What I Found on the Net...

```
Newsgroup: comp.windows.misc
Subject: Why Windows Machines Suck

> ... There's a possibility that Windows is the most popular
> item of its type, fulfilling the needs of the greatest number
> of people, who in turn judge it as having the best quality...

> You know, this sounds a lot like what the Ku Klux Klan people
> say, that since the majority — in your terms, "quantity" of
> people — in United States are white, therefore what is best
> for the white people is best for all people.  I guess you are
> against affirmative action, civil rights, etc., since it's not
> best for the white folks.  Maybe all other races are inferior.

This newsgroup is far, far funnier than any of the humor groups.
```

WINDOWS NT

Introduction to Windows NT

Windows NT is unlike any other operating system. In particular, there are major differences between NT and Windows 95/98. If you are thinking about using NT—especially if you need to make a strategic decision for your company—this is a good document to read. I firmly believe that it is important to understand something about the architecture (design philosophy) of an operating system in order to know how and when to use it. The information here is for experts (or people who are supposed to be experts). Reading this won't turn you into a computer scientist, but it will help you understand the basic ideas and terminology, so you can make informed decisions.

Web:
http://www.gurzki.de/

Windows NT Drivers

There is nothing that can drive you crazy faster than not being able to find the right driver. This site is an absolute treasure: it is *the* place to look for information about the driver you want. Aside from information, you can download various drivers, as well as request that a particular driver be emailed to you (if it is available). This is a great service and someone deserves an award. At the very least, Bill Gates should find the person who maintains this site and send him a free autographed picture.

Web:
http://www.conitech.com/windows/winnt.html

Windows NT Faq

This FAQ (frequently asked question list) is an excellent source of practical Windows NT information. If you know something about operating systems in general and Windows in particular, reading this FAQ is an easy way to learn about Windows NT. If you are an experienced NT user or administrator, this is the best place I know to look for short explanations to all those important technical questions that none of your friends can answer.

Web:
http://www.ntfaq.com/

WINDOWS NT INTERNET SERVERS

Windows NT makes a great platform on which to run Internet servers. But you do need to find the right software and learn how to install and configure it. When you are ready to start serving, the Net is ready to help.

Windows NT Internet Servers

This is Windows NT Server-City-to-the-Max: a collection of resources for finding and maintaining Window NT Internet servers of all types. If you have anything to do with providing Internet services using NT, this Web site will help you find the software you need. The site is comprehensive and well-organized, and is a good place to start a search.

Web:
http://www.intergreat.com/winnt/winnt.asp

Windows NT Magazine

There's no possible way you can sleep well at night thinking that you missed any of the breaking news about Windows NT, so don't even try. Check this Windows NT magazine regularly and enjoy the news, articles and a variety of other features.

Web:
http://www.entmag.com/

Windows NT Official Web Site

Microsoft has two official Web sites for the different versions of NT: Server and Workstation. You'll find all the stuff you would expect: general information, specs, answers to frequently asked questions, hardware and software requirements, support, training, software, and so on. There may be some controversy as to whether or not NT Server and NT Workstation are actually the same program, but Microsoft is certainly marketing them separately: the Web sites are totally different.

Web:
http://www.microsoft.com/ntserver/
http://www.microsoft.com/ntworkstation/

Windows NT Resources

If you're an NT user or administrator, you'll find loads of stuff at these Web sites, including FAQs, information about user groups, resources guides and lots of free software. And if there's anything that NT users and administrators need more of, it's stuff.

Web:
http://www.indirect.com/www/ceridgac/ntsite.html
http://www.itlinks.com/download/ntlinks.htm
http://www.ntsysadmin.com/ntweb.htm
http://www.windows-nt.com/

> **Windows NT**
> **Windows NT**
> **Windows NT**
>
> *Here it is, Microsoft's ready-for-prime-time operating system for the early 1990s. The trouble is, it's the late 1990s. Never mind, NT is here and all is well. For all the important new info and general NT discussion, tune in to* **comp.os.ms-windows.nt.misc**.

Windows NT Security

If you are using Windows NT Server, or if you are administering NT machines, you need to know about security. Windows NT is a powerful operating system, and all powerful systems have security holes that attract problems. This Web site can help you find solutions to your specific problems, as well as keep up on what is new and troublesome.

Web:
http://www.ntsecurity.net/

Windows NT Setup

Installing and configuring Windows NT can be tricky. Here are two Usenet discussion groups in which people share knowledge and tips about the best ways to install NT and to solve installation problems.

Usenet:
comp.os.ms-windows.nt.setup.hardware
comp.os.ms-windows.nt.setup.misc

Windows NT Talk and General Discussion

Windows NT does not take prisoners. When it works, it's great, but when you have a problem, being able to talk to someone can be a lot of help. On the Net, there are many places devoted to talking about NT. If you are a serious NT nerd (or administrator), you may want to participate.

Usenet:
comp.os.ms-windows.nt.admin.misc
comp.os.ms-windows.nt.admin.networking
comp.os.ms-windows.nt.advocacy
comp.os.ms-windows.nt.misc
comp.os.ms-windows.nt.pre-release
comp.os.ms-windows.nt.setup
comp.os.ms-windows.nt.software.backoffice
comp.os.ms-windows.nt.software.compatibility
comp.os.ms-windows.nt.software.services

Listserv Mailing List:
List Name: **winnt-l**
Subscribe to: **listserv@peach.ease.lsoft.com**

IRC:
#nt
#windowsnt

WOMEN

Abortion

Think you can sway someone's opinion on this issue? If you like to beat your head against a wall, join the heated discussion about abortion.

Web:
http://web.canlink.com/ocrt/abortion.htm

Usenet:
alt.abortion
alt.abortion.inequity
talk.abortion

IRC:
#abortion

WOMEN

If you need some quiet, non-controversial conversation to relax you, try one of the abortion discussion groups.

Ada Project

Sponsored by Yale University, the Ada Project acts as a clearinghouse for information and resources relating to women in computing. Find information on fellowships, grants, employment opportunities, statistics, and links to other related resources.

Web:
http://www.cs.yale.edu/HTML/YALE/CS/HyPlans/tap/

Disgruntled Housewife

I love this site and you will too. The writing is excellent, the content is fascinating, and the wit is sharp. Disgruntled Housewife is one woman's "guide to modern living and intersex relationships". But to say Disgruntled Housewife is merely a guide is like saying Martha Stewart is merely a housewife. The talent, the effort and the hubris are both inspiring and engaging. Martha may embrace the art and science of homemaking, but only Disgruntled Housewife is courageous enough to take on the rest of the world.

Web:
http://www.urbekah.com/housewife/

Electronic Forums for Women

Figure out a way to spend even more hours on the Internet. Get this list of electronic forums relating to women. Some mailing lists are for professionals, some have a specific focus of topics, and many are of general interest to women and are nice gathering places to talk.

Web:
http://www-unix.umbc.edu/~korenman/wmst/forums.html

Femina

Femina has been referred to as "the Yahoo of women's links". This directory has links to information and resources for both women and girls, such as art and writing, business resources, computing information, culture, entertainment, feminism, health, and much more.

Web:
http://femina.cybergrrl.com/

Feminism

Modern feminism as a social movement began to grow from the civil rights and peace movements in 1967-1968. The basic idea is that men and women should be treated as economic, social and political equals. Today, radical feminists still support the movement with awe and pride, while other, more fashionably conservative women talk about feminism between clenched teeth and tight lips. In the middle are the large group of women and men who contemplate feminism and gender from a thoughtful, neutral point of view. Whatever your personal beliefs, you are welcome to join the mailing list. Remember, though, it is not a battleground to prove whether feminism is inherently good or evil. It is a place for thoughtful folk to share information on women, politics and economics. If you are looking for feminism-related resources, you'll find information and news at these Web sites.

Web:
http://www.cis.ohio-state.edu/hypertext/faq/usenet/feminism/top.html
http://www.eskimo.com/~feminist/nownetin.html
http://www.feminist.org/

Listproc Mailing List:
List Name: **femisa**
Subscribe to: **listproc@wlu.ca**

Feminism Talk and General Discussion

If it weren't for feminists, men wouldn't have anything to grumble about except the President's Address to the Nation interrupting the football game. It's been proven through history that women are good at organizing themselves and getting things done, and they've shown it once again in Usenet. Join one or all of these groups and discuss feminism in all its forms.

Usenet:
alt.feminism
alt.feminism.individualism
soc.feminism

WOMEN

Gender and Computing

For the longest time, computers have been "a guy thing". Why is that? Read articles put up by Computer Professionals for Social Responsibility that cover topics such as women in computer science, feminism, and cross-gender communication.

Web:
http://www.cpsr.org/dox/program/gender/

Gender and Sexuality

There's no escaping it. Gender and sexuality issues run rampant among the population, spurring arguments, thought-provoking discussion and philosophical meanderings. Read articles and papers about gender and sexuality, and explore other feminist resources available at this site.

Web:
http://eserver.org/gender/

Look What I Found on the Net...

```
Newsgroup: soc.feminism
Subject: Clothing and the Oppression of Men

The issue is that women are allowed to wear both skirts
and pants, while men can only wear pants.  Men who wear
skirts are stigmatized by society in a way that women who wear
pants are not.

The way to gain acceptance for men's skirts is not to complain
about it or theorize on discussion groups like this.  The only
way society will change is to just go out and do it.  Look at
how women gained the right to wear pants.

Ms. Bloomer started going out in public wearing pants.  Yes, she
"caught it" from both women and men.  She was harassed and
threatened, but by making a spectacle of herself, the idea
caught on.  As more women discovered the advantages of pants,
more women began wearing them.  As more women began wearing
them, barriers slowly fell (as recent as 25 years ago, schools
forbid girls to wear pants) until now women can wear
pants with impunity.

If Ms. Bloomer merely talked to people about how nice it would
be to wear pants, or complained about male privilege, we'd
probably still be in  skirts.  But she actually went out and did
something about it.

So there's your solution, although it's not an easy one.
Men: Go out, buy or make skirts, and start wearing them.  If
you're afraid to wear them at work, wear them away from work,
socializing with friends or whatever.  Most important, wear them
in public places where other people will see them.

Yeah, some may snub you, but others will be curious and will ask
you questions.  And eventually, some other guys will start
wearing skirts.

Unfortunately, there's not much in this process that women can
do, besides being supportive of men who wear skirts.
```

WOMEN

Gynecological Exams

Gynecology is the branch of medicine that deals with the female reproductive system and its interaction with the rest of the body. Having a regular gynecological examination is important for your long-term health. Moreover, you should have a gynecologist who knows you, so if a problem arises, you will have someone to see. However, if you've never been to a gynecologist before, you may be anxious. This Web site contains information to help you. Read an overview of an exam, so you will know what to expect and how to prepare. There are also hints on how to find a doctor, as well as a glossary and a reading list.

Web:
http://www.gyn101.com/

History of Women's Suffrage

Looking back at history, it is obvious that the more women are involved in government, the better everything works. But it took the world a long time to figure that out. In 1848, a group of American women adopted a resolution, referred to today as the Seneca Falls Declaration, in which they declared their support for political equality and called for universal suffrage (the right for both men and women to vote). But it was not until 1920 that the United States passed into law the 19th Amendment to the constitution: "The right of citizens of the United States to vote shall not be denied or abridged by the United States or by any State on account of sex." The history of the suffrage movement is characterized by bravery, persistence and foresight. It is important for all of us to learn about the suffragettes and their accomplishments. When we reflect that, today, there are still many countries where women are denied basic political rights, it is clear that the work of the original suffragettes is still unfinished.

Web:
http://www.cc.rochester.edu/SBA/hisindx.html
http://www.city-net.com/~lmann/women/history/timeline.html

Take action.

Midwifery

You just never know when it's going to happen. You'll be stuck in an elevator or on the subway with a pregnant woman in labor. What will you do then? Plan ahead and get some information on midwifery so you will always be prepared. Articles, information on organizations, and links to other resources are a few of the things that are available.

Web:
http://www.efn.org/~djz/birth/midwife.html

Usenet:
sci.med.midwifery

National Organization for Women

The National Organization for Women (NOW) is a U.S. political organization dedicated to women's rights and feminist philosophy. NOW was established on June 30, 1966, and since that time has evolved and reinvented itself more than once. The NOW Web site has information regarding violence against women, lesbian rights, women-friendly workplaces, affirmative action, abortion, global feminism, economic equality, and so on.

Web:
http://www.now.org/

Notable Women

Everyone has heard of Susan B. Anthony. After all, her picture is on a piece of U.S. currency. Just because nobody happens to use that currency doesn't mean she's not popular. There are many other notable women who are not so famous, like Annie Jump Cannon, Blanche Ames, and Clara Adams-Ender, but they are among the many women who have done something remarkable during their lifetimes. Read these short biographies and become informed on women in history.

Web:
http://mustang.coled.umn.edu/exploration/women.html
http://www.netsrq.com/~dbois/

Sexual Assault on Campus

While this list is not exclusively for women, it does concern violence against women on college and university campuses. Learn about anti-rape activist groups and share information about assaults and methods of reducing sexual assault against women.

Listserv Mailing List:
List Name: **stoprape**
Subscribe to: **listserv@brownvm.brown.edu**

Women Halting Online Abuse

It's easier to be bold and forward on the Net than in person, because you don't have to see people face to face. You can say what you want, when you want, without worrying about the consequences. All this, of course, also makes it easy for people to say irritating, mean and hurtful things. Sometimes it gets worse, when things do not work out well and persistent people become abusive. WHOA (Women Halting Online Abuse) is an organization dedicated to eliminating harassment on the Internet. Visit their Web site and learn how to deal with harassment in chat rooms, newsgroups, IRC and email. (Parents: These are skills to teach your daughters.) There are also articles, tips and a list of chat rooms to avoid.

Web:
http://whoa.femail.com/

NOTABLE WOMEN

Look at this list:

Susan B. Anthony
Colette
Marie Curie
Amelia Earhart
Emma Goldman
Georgia O'Keeffe
Madonna
Eleanor Roosevelt
Margaret Thatcher

Who's missing?

Why, you, of course. Better check with the **Notable Women** Web sites to see if they've got your name yet.

Women in Congress

Women have been running homes for years, so they might as well run the House, too. Learn about the women in Congress by reading their online biographies.

Web:
http://www.inform.umd.edu/EdRes/Topic/ WomensStudies/GovernmentPolitics/ WomeninCongress/

Women's Online Communities

Here are hip, comfortable places for you to hang out on the Net. You can chat with other people or read—and there is a lot to read. There are articles about many different topics, all of interest to the inquiring female mind. Once you get started at these sites, you might have trouble getting your work done. There are too many informative, fun, bite-sized things to enjoy.

Web:
http://www.amazoncity.com/
http://www.electra.com/
http://www.herspace.com/
http://www.neosoft.com/~acoustic/www.html
http://www.womenfolk.com/

Women's Resources

The ambitious task has been undertaken: to make a women's home page and collect as much woman-stuff as possible. These are remarkable collections, not only of resources, but of writings by and about women. Topics cover professional and academic organizations, Women's Studies resources, and gender and sexuality issues.

Web:
http://www.dogpatch.org/general/women.cfm
http://www.feminist.com/reso.htm
http://www.library.wisc.edu/libraries/ WomensStudies/others.htm
http://www.wwwomen.com/

WOMEN

Women's Studies Resources

People have been studying women for years. It's just that now they can get college credit for it. Find out about various Women's Studies programs, women's resources on the Internet, and see a special section on women and literature.

Web:
http://umbc7.umbc.edu/~korenman/wmst/links.html
http://www.inform.umd.edu/EdRes/Topic/WomensStudies/

Women's Talk and General Discussion

Women: there is a place for you to go to talk with other women about anything you want. The mailing list offers a nice women's space to discuss your personal observations, interests, news, upcoming events and anything else that is relevant to your daily life. If you don't mind anyone jumping into the conversation, try the Usenet group.

Usenet:
soc.women

Listserv Mailing List:
List Name: women-l
Subscribe to: listserv@listserv.aol.com

Women's Web Guides

Here is enough estrogen to supply the entire U.S. Senate. Visiting these sites is guaranteed to give you many hours of fun, over and over. Each site contains annotated listings of fun, interesting and helpful sites by women, for women, or about women. One click and you're on an adventure around the Net, never knowing what wonderful, fascinating place you'll end up next.

Web:
http://www.chickclick.com/
http://www.estronet.com/
http://www.yin.org/

Women's Wire

It's almost like a clubhouse on the Internet and it's just for women. This site covers topics such as women and politics, sports and fitness, women's health, women and work, and other interesting items of a more historical nature.

Web:
http://www.women.com/

Look What I Found on the Net...

```
Newsgroup: soc.women
Subject: Help From Men

> Women wouldn't have gotten any of their rights if men
> hadn't felt bad for them and tried to make things equal.  The
> least feminists can do is return the favor.

Okay.

I can't thank you enough for liberating us.
```

WORLD CULTURES

Africa

Africa is a large continent with many different cultures. Here are some resources to help you explore the art, societies, languages, literature, music and customs of Africa. To start, here is a proverb from Nigeria: "Until lions have their own historians, tales of the hunt shall always glorify the hunter."

Web:
http://www.africaonline.com/
http://www.sas.upenn.edu/African_Studies/Home_Page/Country.html

Usenet:
soc.culture.african

Listserv Mailing List:
List Name: h-afrlitcine
Subscribe to: listserv@h-net.msu.edu

IRC:
#africa

Asia

Asia has many cultures and peoples, each with its own history, traditions and customs. There are 240 different languages that are spoken by at least one million people each. Perhaps even more incredible, there are 12 languages which are spoken by more than 100 million people. (Here is the list, in order, starting from the top: Mandarin, Hindi, Spanish, English, Bengali, Arabic, Russian, Portuguese, Japanese, German, French, Malay-Indonesian.) Clearly, Asia is one of the best continents in the entire world.

Web:
http://www.interknowledge.com/indx04.htm

Usenet:
soc.culture.asian

IRC:
#asia
#asian

Australia

Australia is the smallest continent on Planet Earth, conveniently located southeast of Asia, between the Pacific and Indian Oceans. The Commonwealth of Australia includes a few external territories: the island of Tasmania, Christmas Island (the location of Santa's summer cottage), the Cocos Islands, the Coral Sea Islands, Norfolk Island, Heard and McDonald Islands, and a portion of the Antarctic Territory. The original inhabitants are thought to be Southeast Asian seafaring colonists. In 1770, the English Captain James Cook sailed into Botany Bay and claimed the eastern coast of Australia for Great Britain. The first British settlement was a penal colony. Australian geography is generally flat and arid and is the exclusive home of the platypus, koala, kangaroo, and wine of questionable parentage.

Web:
http://www.about-australia.com/about.htm
http://www.austudies.org/vl/

Usenet:
soc.culture.australia
soc.culture.australian

IRC:
#australia

Brazil

In the year 1500, the Brazilian territory was claimed for Portugal by Pedro Alvares Cabral and was officially part of Portugal until 1822, when the Brazilians declared their independence. The Federative Republic of Brazil is the largest country in South America, occupying half the continent and having the fifth highest population in the world. Brazil has abundant natural resources: fertile land (on which is grown coffee, cocoa, bananas, corn, citrus, sugar cane, soybeans, cotton and tobacco), and vast deposits of metals, minerals and gems (iron, manganese, chromium, uranium, platinum, quartz, coal and industrial diamonds). Brazil contains the Amazon basin which is the home of the world's largest rainforests.

Web:
http://www.psg.com/~walter/brasil.html

Usenet:
soc.culture.brazil

IRC:
#brasil

830 WORLD CULTURES

Cajun Culture

In 1755, the British and the French were gearing up for a war in the New World and, as a preliminary courtesy, the British authorities in Acadia (at the far east of Canada) kindly asked the French colonists to either renounce their religion (Catholicism) and swear allegiance to England, or could they please remove themselves to another part of the planet. What followed was a massive, haphazard migration that ended with a large number of French Acadians settling in the southern part of Louisiana, where they established small farms. (The word "Cajun" comes from the original French pronunciation of "Acadia".) Today, there is still a well-established Cajun culture—spreading through 22 of Louisiana's 64 parishes (counties)—and centered around the city of Lafayette. Cajun food has a large variety of specialties such as jambalaya, gumbo, turtle sauce piquante and crawfish bisque. What I like best is that Cajun is the only culture in which one of the traditional musical instruments is the triangle (the other instruments being the fiddle and the accordion). As you can see, when it comes to food or music, Cajun culture has something for everyone.

Web:
http://www.cajunculture.com/

Usenet:
alt.culture.cajun

**Cool words?
Look in "Quotations".**

Central America

Central America is the part of North America that separates the Pacific Ocean from the Caribbean Sea and stretches from Mexico to Colombia. The countries of Central America are Belize, Guatemala, Honduras, El Salvador, Nicaragua, Costa Rica and Panama. The area is culturally rich, and parts of it are exquisitely beautiful. Central American climate varies from tropical to cool. Their chief exports are bananas, coffee, and T-shirts that say, "My parents went to Central America and all I got was a lousy banana and a package of coffee."

Web:
http://www.studyweb.com/his/hiscenam.htm

Usenet:
soc.culture.el-salvador

Listserv Mailing List:
List Name: **centam-l**
Subscribe to: **listserv@listserv.acsu.buffalo.edu**

Look What I Found on the Net...

```
Newsgroup: alt.culture.cajun
Subject: Gumbo

My concept of heaven is immersion in a tub of gumbo with a
string of boudin at hand.
```

WORLD CULTURES

Chile

Although it is only a little larger than Texas, the country of Chile has a coastline that is longer than the width of the continental United States. If you are interested in the culture of this unusual country, you can talk on Usenet, IRC, join the mailing list, or investigate resources on the Web.

Web:
http://www.latinworld.com/countries/chile/

Usenet:
soc.culture.chile

Listserv Mailing List:
List Name: **chile-l**
Subscribe to: **listserv@rose.grr.ulaval.ca**

IRC:
#chile

China

The People's Republic of China, located in central and eastern Asia, is the most highly populated country in the world. Geographically, China is the third-largest country (after Russia and Canada) and is one of the world's leading producers of minerals, as well as having huge reserves of coal and oil. China is the home of very old civilizations. The first documented Chinese civilization was the Shang dynasty which lasted from 1523 B.C. to 1027 B.C. Outside of China, people know the country as being famous for its philosophers (such as Confucius and Lao-Tze), the Great Wall (a 25-foot high, 1,500-mile long barrier, completed in the 3rd century B.C. in an attempt to keep out invaders), and its culinary contributions to American cuisine.

Web:
http://sun.sino.uni-heidelberg.de/igcs/
http://www.chinapage.com/

Usenet:
soc.culture.china

IRC:
#china
#chinese

Country Studies Area Handbooks

This resource consists of a series of books prepared by a division of the U.S. Library of Congress and sponsored by the Department of the Army. These books are fabulous resources, each one describing a separate country. You will find information about the people of that country, its government, social institutions and history. Whenever I want to learn about a particular country, this is where I go first.

Web:
http://lcweb2.loc.gov/frd/cs/cshome.html

Czech Republic

The Czech Republic has some of the most beautiful scenery and interesting culture in Eastern Europe. Take some time to browse this Internet site, and you will find a great many resources to guide you through the Czech Republic. Here is my hint for staying out of trouble: just memorize this phrase—"To je moc drahe"—and use it as much as possible. (By the way, it is a little known fact, but some of the best typesetters in the world are of Czech descent.)

Web:
http://www.muselik.com/czech/

Usenet:
soc.culture.czecho-slovak

IRC:
#czech

Egypt

Take a guided tour of Egypt without ever having to leave your seat. See pictures and learn a little of the history and culture of the land of the great pyramids. You can even download pictures of some of those great pyramids, the Temple of Osiris and the Nile, and then send them to your friends on the Net, saying, "Having a great time. Wish you were here."

Web:
http://www.memphis.edu/egypt/egypt.html

Usenet:
alt.culture.egyptian
soc.culture.egyptian

IRC:
#egypt

Flags of the World

If you are looking for something unique and colorful with which to decorate your home, try downloading some of these flags of the world. Not only will they look nice hanging on your walls, but your visitors will be convinced that you have culture and good taste.

Web:
http://fotw.digibel.be/flags/mirror.html

France

France is a country in Western Europe and is more agricultural than most people realize. Roughly 30 percent of the land is used for livestock, while another 30 percent is used for crops such as wheat, corn, barley, sugar beets and potatoes. France is also a well-known producer of wine, second only to Italy. Throughout its history, France has been embroiled in many wars and conflicts. Between 58-51 B.C., the area—which was known as Gaul—was conquered by Romans under Julius Caesar. In more modern times, France has been involved in the Crusades, the Hundred Years War, the Seven Years War, the American Revolution, the French Revolution, the July Revolution, the February Revolution, the Franco-Prussian War, and the two World Wars. All this and they make great cheese, too.

Web:
http://www.yahoo.fr/

Usenet:
alt.france
soc.culture.french

Listserv Mailing List:
List Name: **causerie**
Subscribe to: **listserv@inrs-urb.uquebec.ca**

IRC:
#france

> Someone is looking at your Web page right now.

Flags of the World

Here is a good way to have fun and help humanity at the same time.

Go to the Flags of the World Web site and look at all the pictures. Then make yourself a copy of each flag and hang them all outside your front door.

Pretty soon, people from all over the world will be coming to you for help in solving their problems.

Germany

The Federal Republic of Germany is located in north-central Europe. Germany is a mountainous country with the Black Forest (famous for its cuckoo clocks and toys) to the west and the Bavarian Alps (famous for its cream pies) to the south. Like its neighbor to the west (France), Germany has been involved in many wars and conflicts through the years, and was the base for two of the world's most powerful and ambitious military leaders: Napoleon and Hitler. As a result, Germany has faced a huge amount of political and social upheaval in its history. After World War II, the country was divided into parts that were occupied by various Allied forces. This resulted in a heavy fragmenting of the culture and politics of Germany, and it wasn't until 1990 that a drive for reunification began.

Web:
http://www.goethe.de/uk/saf/eninet.htm
http://www.yahoo.de/

Usenet:
soc.culture.german

IRC:
#germany

WORLD CULTURES

Hungary

Hungary is located in central Europe on the Danube River and is the home of Lake Balaton, the largest lake in Europe. Being located centrally, Hungary suffered by being overrun by various groups of invaders, in particular the Magyars, Turks, Austrians and Soviets. Hungary is a beautiful country with more than 1,000 lakes and many parks and protected areas. One of the most famous Hungarians of all time is Franz Liszt (1811-1886), the piano virtuoso and composer.

Web:
http://www.hungary.org/~hipcat/
http://www.lonelyplanet.com.au/dest/eur/hun.htm

Usenet:
bit.listserv.hungary
soc.culture.magyar

Majordomo Mailing List:
List Name: **hungary-report**
Subscribe to: **majordomo@isys.hu**

IRC:
#hungary

Immigration

Here is a Web site, maintained by a lawyer, that has a lot of information about immigrating into the United States. If your goal is to move to the Land of the Free and Home of the Brave, this site can help. It is packed with lots of great information about green cards, temporary visas, citizenship, the visa lottery, and asylum. There are special sections for students, professionals, doctors and nurses, as well as job search links, news flashes and new law alerts. In Usenet, you can find discussions about immigrating to the United States as well as other countries.

Web:
http://www.shusterman.com/

Usenet:
misc.immigration.australia+nz
misc.immigration.canada
misc.immigration.misc
misc.immigration.usa
soc.subculture.expatriate

Look What I Found on the Net...

```
(from the Immigration to the United States Web site)

Immigration Trivia Quiz: A Governor With Illegal Roots
```

The Republican platform calls for a broad crackdown on illegal immigration, even endorsing an amendment to the Constitution to prevent children born in the U.S. to mothers who are not citizens or permanent residents from being considered U.S. citizens at birth.

At the Republican Convention, a prominent governor declined an opportunity to deliver a prepared speech endorsing the immigration provisions of his party's platform. He refused on the ground that "(his state) has represented hope and freedom to people from around the world and we have to continue to do that."

Who is this governor and what state does he govern?

(Answer: George Pataki, governor of the state of New York)

India

With more than 900 million people, India is the second-most populous country in the world (after China). India's people represent many cultures and traditions, and speak many different languages, with Hindi and English predominating. To a foreigner, India is a mysterious place: a country divided by caste, ethnicity and custom. However, it is also the largest democracy in the world. For more information, you can use the Net to explore the cultures of this large, complex country.

Web:
http://www.cnct.com/home/bhaskar/india.html
http://www.indiaexpress.com/

Usenet:
soc.culture.india
soc.culture.indian
soc.culture.indian.bihar
soc.culture.indian.delhi
soc.culture.indian.gujarati
soc.culture.indian.info
soc.culture.indian.jammu-kashmir
soc.culture.indian.karnataka
soc.culture.indian.kerala
soc.culture.indian.marathi
soc.culture.indian.telugu

IRC:
#india

Music, recipes, literature, travel, art, history, language—learn about another culture on the Net.

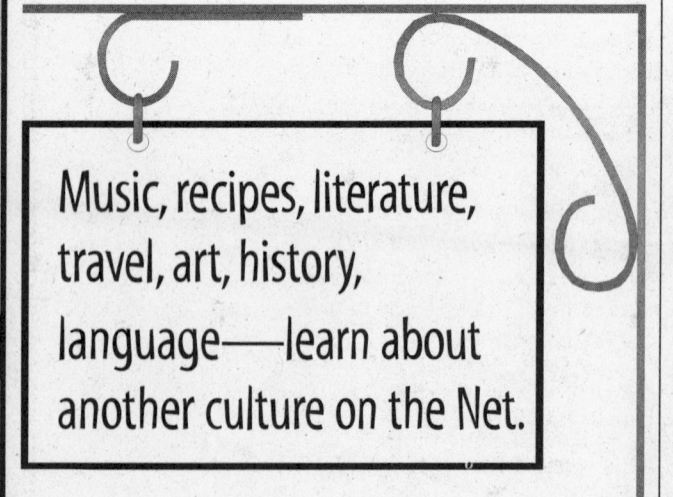

Indonesia

Indonesia is in southeast Asia and is made up of more than 3,000 islands, from the Malaysian mainland to New Guinea. The main islands of Indonesia are Java, Kalimantan (Borneo), Celebes (Sulawesi), Bali, Timor, the Moluccas (Maluku), Irian Jaya (West New Guinea) and Sumatra (home of Sherlock Holmes's infamous giant rat). Indonesia, which used to be known as the Dutch East Indies, gained its independence from the Netherlands in 1949. Ranked by population, Indonesia is the fourth largest country in the world, and is home to more than 250 different languages and dialects. Indonesia produces a variety of exports, including petroleum, natural gas, exotic rainforest hardwoods, rubber, palm oil and cinchona (an evergreen tree that is a source of quinine).

Web:
http://indonesia.elga.net.id/
http://www.accessindo.com/

Usenet:
alt.culture.indonesia
soc.culture.indonesia
soc.culture.indonesian

Listproc Mailing List:
List Name: **st-yusuf**
Subscribe to: listproc@lists.colorado.edu

IRC:
#indonesia

Ireland

Ireland has more than three and a half million people in an area about the size of West Virginia. The Irish people have a well-known culture—literature, music, dance, folklore—as well as highly developed social customs. They also have a political history which certainly qualifies as "interesting". Meet, chat and drink with Irish people on the Net, and use the Web to explore the leprechaun-loving Emerald Isle.

Web:
http://celtic.stanford.edu/pmurphy/irish.html
http://www.paddynet.com/island/

IRC:
#ireland

Israel

The State of Israel is located on the eastern Mediterranean sea and was formed in 1948, after the United Nations divided Palestine into Jewish and Arab territories. About 85 percent of the population of Israel is Jewish, and the official languages are Hebrew and Arabic. For decades, the Jews and Palestinians have been fighting over the land, both groups having strong feelings of ownership. Despite a great deal of political tension, Israel has a large tourist industry. About 7 percent of the population of Israel lives on a collective farm (kibbutz) or an agricultural co-op (moshav).

Web:
  http://www.iguide.co.il/
  http://www.shamash.org/
  http://www.virtualjerusalem.com/

Usenet:
  soc.culture.israel

IRC:
  #israel

Italy

In ancient times, Rome, the capital of modern-day Italy, established an empire that lasted 500 years and contributed mightily to world culture. Today, Italian food, fashion, language and literature are all influential outside of their native home. To find out about Italy, there are many resources on the Net you can use, as well as Usenet and IRC for discussion. (All this talk about Italy is making me hungry. I wish I had some spaghetti right now.)

Web:
  http://www.initaly.com/

Usenet:
  alt.italia
  soc.culture.italian

IRC:
  #italia
  #italy

Look What I Found on the Net...

```
Subject: Indians Are Not Asians
Newsgroups: soc.culture.india

> I am the originator of this post.  The original topic stated
> that Indians are not Asians.  It was an academic posting.
> It referred to a concept of ethnicity.  Many Indians seem to
> desire to be called "Asian".  If not, they would not argue the
> point so violently.

I disagree with you.  I say that Indians are Asians, be it East
or Red Indians.  Where do you think the Red Indians of North
America come from?  They crossed the Siberian land bridge when
there was no sea between Russia and North America, long ago.

Don't you find that many Inuit or Eskimos look like Chinese?
I consider Inuit or Eskimos to be Indians who's ancestors were
Chinese.  People in Nepal and Tibet have Chinese and east Indian
facial characteristics.  I consider all these people Asians.
Isn't India part of the Asian Continent?  If yes, why don't you
consider east Indians to be Asians?
```

WORLD CULTURES

Japan

Japan (Nippon) is located on an archipelago off the northeast coast of Asia. The country has four main islands—Hokkaido, Honshu, Shikoku and Kyushu—as well as other smaller ones. Japan is an old country, first settled in 660 B.C. Two thirds of the land consists of mountains, the most famous being Mount Fuji. Japan has a democratic form of government with a prime minister as chief executive, and an emperor as symbolic head of state. Legislative power resides with the national legislature (called the Diet), consisting of a House of Representatives and a House of Councillors.

Web:
http://www.ntt.co.jp/japan/
http://www.yahoo.com/docs/info/bridge.html

Usenet:
soc.culture.japan
soc.culture.japan.moderated

IRC:
#japan
#nippon

Muds are real (sort of).

Korea

The Korean Peninsula was first unified into a single political entity in 668 A.D. During the 19th and 20th centuries, Korea was much affected by the political and military machinations of other countries, making for an interesting and fractured history. However, during World War II, it was agreed by the major powers that, after Japan (which had invaded Korea) was defeated, the country would become an independent state. Unfortunately, at the Yalta Conference in 1945, the leaders of the United States, England and the Soviet Union agreed in secret to divide the Korean Peninsula in the middle in order to make it easier to disarm the Japanese: the U.S. would occupy the south, the Soviets would occupy the north. Well, you can guess what happened. As with other famous divisions in history—such as East and West Germany, North and South Vietnam, and North and South Dakota—one part became communist while the other developed into a Western-style something or other. Today, Koreans are a people divided: North and South Korea share the Korean Peninsula, but that is about all they share. For more information or to discuss Korean culture, see the Net.

Web:
http://www.iworld.net/Korea/
http://www.korea.com/

Usenet:
alt.talk.korean
soc.culture.korean

IRC:
#korea

Look What I Found on the Net...

```
Newsgroup: soc.culture.japan.moderated
Subject: Glutinous rice

Gluten is a protein substance that gives starchy foods their
"gluey" quality. The Chinese and Indians favor less glutinous rices
which also tend to be long grained...

Japanese rice tends to have a more medium grain, more gluten,
and to be stickier when cooked.  There is also the rice used
to make mochi (mochi gome) which I have seen called pearl rice
or sweet rice.  This cooks up to a gluey mass that can be used
to make ohagi, if you wrap some cooked sweetened red beans
around it.

In the U.S. we have another variety of rice, which we call
Uncle Ben's...
```

WORLD CULTURES

> Need a laugh? Check out "Humor and Jokes".

Latin America

Latin America is a descriptive term referring to the countries of Central and South America. These countries include Argentina, Belize, Bolivia, Brazil, Chile, Colombia, Costa Rica, Cuba, the Dominican Republic, Ecuador, El Salvador, Guatemala, Haiti, Honduras, Mexico, Nicaragua, Panama, Paraguay, Peru, Uruguay and Venezuela. In all of these countries the official language is Spanish, with the exception of Brazil (Portuguese), Haiti (French) and Belize (English).

Web:
http://www.latinworld.com/

Usenet:
soc.culture.latin-america

IRC:
#latinos

Malaysia

Malaysia is an independent federation in southeast Asia and consists of the southern Malay Peninsula and the northern portion of the island of Borneo. In its early history, Malaysia was part of the British protectorates, but achieved its independence in 1963. Malaysia has 4,800 km of coastline and more than 200 islands.

Web:
http://www.jaring.my/
http://www.umich.edu/~umimsa/Malaysia/

Usenet:
bit.listserv.berita
soc.culture.malaysia

IRC:
#malaysia

Mexico

Mexico is a large country bordered to the north by the United States and to the south by Belize and Guatemala. Mexico's indigenous population was conquered by Spain in the early 16th century and regained its independence in 1822. You can read more about Mexico and its people and culture by checking out the Web sites. If you want to talk with people from Mexico, you can participate in the Usenet discussion groups or chat on IRC.

Web:
http://www.latinworld.com/countries/mexico/
http://www.mexconnect.com/

Usenet:
alt.mexico
soc.culture.mexican

IRC:
#mexico

Middle Europe

The first question one must ask when contemplating whether to join a discussion group relating to Middle Europe is: What *is* Middle Europe? It's defined as the countries lying between the Mediterranean/Adriatic and Baltic Seas and between the German/Austrian borders and the former Soviet Union. That settled, the second question would be: What is the list about? Just about everything. The list is unmoderated, and topics cover history, culture, politics, economics and current events.

Listserv Mailing List:
List Name: mideur-l
Subscribe to: listserv@listserv.acsu.buffalo.edu

Morocco

Moonlight in Morocco. It sounds so exotic. What a great movie that would make. The first scene shows a man sitting in front of the computer looking at a Web page about Morocco. He reads all about the culture, cooking and history of this country. He decides to go, and while he's there he has a daring adventure, finds love, and the final scene shows him with a beautiful woman, riding a camel into the sunset. This could be you. Go read about Morocco.

Web:
http://www.maroc.net/

IRC:
#morocco

Native Americans

These Web sites provide information on various native tribes by name or geographic region. Here you will find Native American literature, education links, languages, newsletters, history, literature, genealogy and other related Internet resources.

Web:
  http://one-web.org/oneida/
  http://www.nativeweb.org/

New Zealand

New Zealand consists of two main islands about 1,500 miles east of Australia and 8,200 miles southwest of Fargo, North Dakota. The two islands are called North Island and South Island, although the origin of these names is lost to antiquity. The New Zealand Web site has a wonderful collection of information. You can learn about famous people from New Zealand such as Edmund Hillary (the first man to climb Mount Everest), Ernest Rutherford (who pioneered our understanding of atomic structure), and Kate Shepphard (notable women's suffragist). You can also find information about the Maori (aboriginal people), New Zealand English, read a translation of Jules Verne's encounter with rampaging kiwis (large New Zealand birds), and much, much more. If you are planning a trip to New Zealand, check the Net for travel information before you leave. After all, you don't want to make a wrong turn and end up in Fargo, North Dakota.

Web:
  http://www.nz.com/guide/

Usenet:
  soc.culture.new-zealand

Norway

Norway is a country in northern Europe, in the western portion of the Scandinavian peninsula. Norway is rugged and mountainous, and is the home of the largest glacier field in Europe, Jostedalsbreen. The country is a constitutional monarchy, and has two official languages, both of which are forms of Norwegian: Bokmäl and Nynorsk. Famous Norwegians include Henrik Ibsen (author), Edvard Grieg (composer), and Edvard Munch (painter).

Web:
  http://www.norway.org/

IRC:
  #norway

Peru

The Republic of Peru is a Spanish-speaking country on the west coast of South America. The capital of Peru, Lima, includes the port of Callao. Much of Peru lies within the Andes mountains, and the country is particularly susceptible to earthquakes. (In 1970, 50,000 people were killed by a big quake.) Peru produces copper, silver, petroleum, sugarcane, fish, cotton and coca (from which cocaine is made). Peru has been inhabited for well over 10,000 years and was the home to the Incas who, before the Spanish Conquest, established an empire that stretched from northern Ecuador to central Chile.

Web:
  http://ekeko.rcp.net.pe/
  http://www.peru-explorer.com/

Usenet:
  http://www.interknowledge.com/peru/
    soc.culture.peru

Poland

The Republic of Poland is a country in central Europe, bordered on the north by the Baltic Sea. Between the 14th and 16th centuries, Poland enjoyed prosperity and a flourishing culture. In the 16th and 17th centuries, Poland lost much of its territory to Sweden and Russia. In the late 18th century, the remaining portion of Poland was partitioned into three sections by Prussia, Austria and Russia. As a result, Poland, as a country, vanished from the map of the world. However, Poland had strong nationalistic traditions and came back into existence after World War I, its borders being fixed by the Treaty of Versailles in 1919.

Web:
  http://www.polishworld.com/

Usenet:
  soc.culture.polish

Listserv Mailing List:
  List Name: **poland-l**
  Subscribe to: **listserv@listserv.acsu.buffalo.edu**

IRC:
  #poland
  #polska

Look What I Found on the Net...

(from the Inter-Tribal Network information site)

THE CONSTITUTION OF THE IROQUOIS NATIONS:

THE GREAT BINDING LAW, GAYANASHAGOWA

1. I am Dekanawidah and with the Five Nations' Confederate Lords I plant the Tree of Great Peace. I plant it in your territory, Adodarhoh, and the Onondaga Nation, in the territory of you who are Firekeepers.

I name the tree the Tree of the Great Long Leaves. Under the shade of this Tree of the Great Peace we spread the soft white feathery down of the globe thistle as seats for you, Adodarhoh, and your cousin Lords.

We place you upon those seats, spread soft with the feathery down of the globe thistle, there beneath the shade of the spreading branches of the Tree of Peace. There shall you sit and watch the Council Fire of the Confederacy of the Five Nations, and all the affairs of the Five Nations shall be transacted at this place before you, Adodarhoh, and your cousin Lords, by the Confederate Lords of the Five Nations...

Look What I Found on the Net...

Subject: Travel to Poland
Newsgroup: soc.culture.polish

> If you don't think this newsgroup does not have impact on
> people planning for Polish tourism, you are wrong. The whole
> world is watching this newsgroup. Many of the people are
> potential travelers to tourist spots in Europe.
>
> Poland needs hard currency. Every tourist going to Poland
> helps to build the Polish economy. Do you think this newsgroup
> is an interesting and exciting one for visitors? Do you think
> others would feel welcome and be inspired to visit Poland after
> reading through these posts?

What is your point? Do you expect a different type of forum? Do you think that, in the other newsgroups, people argue in a civilized way? You can even gain some knowledge in a pub — if you drink with the right people.

Portugal

The Portuguese Republic is located in southwest Europe on the western Iberian Peninsula (which it shares with Spain), and includes the Madeira Islands and the Azores in the Atlantic Ocean. Most people don't know that Portugal is a major supplier of the world's cork. (If it wasn't for Portugal, most of the champagne in the world would be flat.) Portugal is also known for its vineyards, olive groves and almond trees, but, due to antiquated farming techniques, the Portuguese are unable to produce enough food for their own country. (However, they do have lots of cork.) In the 15th century, Portugal was at a peak, with territories extending into Asia, Africa and America. Portugal's decline began in the 16th century when Spain began to take over various Portuguese territories, and, through the years, many of the remaining territories have declared their independence. Today, Portugal is a relatively small but stable country.

Web:
  http://www.portugal.com/e/discover_world.asp

Usenet:
  soc.culture.portuguese

IRC:
  #portugal

Russian and American Friendship

If you are in America, you should know this book is translated into Russian.

If you are in Russia, you should know this book is one of the best-selling English-language Internet books of all time.

Can you think of a better way to encourage friendship?

Russia

The Russian Federation occupies most of eastern Europe and northern Asia. It extends 5,000 miles (8,000 km) from the Baltic Sea to the Pacific Ocean, crossing eleven time zones. Russia covers more than a tenth of the Earth's land area. Geographically, it is the world's largest country and ranks sixth in population. The Russian climate varies from extreme cold in northern Russia and Siberia (Verkhoyansk, Siberia, is the world's coldest settled place) to subtropical along the Black Sea. Generally speaking, we can think of Russia as being divided into European Russia and Asiatic Russia. Most of the population lives in European Russia, making Russia an important European power.

Web:
  http://we.got.net/docent/soquel/russia.htm
  http://www.city.ru/
  http://www.moscow-guide.ru/culture/kremlin/kremlin0.htm
  http://www.russia-travel.com/rushis01.htm
  http://www.russiatoday.com/

Usenet:
  soc.culture.russia
  soc.culture.russian
  soc.culture.russian.moderated
  soc.culture.soviet

IRC:
  #russia
  #russian

Russian and American Friendship

Join this information system developed by Russians and Americans in an effort to form a bond between the two countries. There is information on almost anything you would want to know about Russia or the relationship between Russia and America—Cyrillic alphabet, news, history, music, art, medicine, economics, travel and tourism, and culture in general.

Web:
  http://alice.ibpm.serpukhov.su/friends/
  http://www.friends-partners.org/friends/

Listserv Mailing List:
  List Name: **friends**
  Subscribe to: **listserv@solar.rtd.utk.edu**

WORLD CULTURES

Saudi Arabia

The Kingdom of Saudi Arabia occupies most of the Arabian Peninsula in the Middle East. Saudi Arabia is an arid desert country that controls 25 percent of the world's oil reserves. The holy cities of Mecca and Medina are both located in Saudi Arabia. The majority of Arabs adhere to the Wahhabi sect of Islam. There are some Muslim Arabs, called Bedouin, who rove in tribal groups, headed by a sheikh. Their main livelihood is breeding camels and sheep.

Web:
http://www.saudi.net/

Usenet:
alt.culture.saudi

Majordomo Mailing List:
List Name: **islam-arabia**
Subscribe to: **majordomo@lists.uoregon.edu**

IRC:
#saudi

Slovakia

Slovakia, a country in central Europe, was more or less under Hungarian rule until 1918, at which time it became part of Czechoslovakia. On January 1, 1993, Czechoslovakia split into Slovakia and Czech Republic. On the Net, you can find maps, statistics, pictures, accommodation and transportation guides, and political, historical and tourist information.

Web:
http://www.culture.gov.sk/

Sweden

Sweden has a population of 8.8 million people, 85 percent of which live in the southern half of the country. Sweden is one of the oldest continuously existing countries on the entire planet, being over a thousand years old. In that thousand years, Sweden has given the world much to be thankful for: food and drink (especially vodka), automobiles, furniture, as well as a model for highly socialized democracy.

Web:
http://www.webcom.com/sis/

IRC:
#sweden

Taiwan

Taiwan (which used to be called Formosa) is an island nation off the southeast coast of China. Taiwan was first settled by the Chinese in the 7th century. It was later held by Holland, then China again and then Japan. In 1945, after World War II, control of Taiwan passed back to China. However, in 1949, the Nationalists (led by Chiang Kai-shek) were expelled from mainland China by the Communists and settled in Taiwan where they set up a government in exile. Today, Taiwan is still completely separate from China, although the two countries have significant cultural and economic ties.

Web:
http://www.cybertaiwan.com/

Usenet:
alt.taiwan.republic
soc.culture.taiwan

IRC:
#taiwan
#tw

Thailand

Thailand (once called Siam) occupies a central position in southeast Asia, both geographically and politically. The country was first established in the mid-14th century, but spent much of its history being dominated by other countries. In 1932, Thailand became a constitutional monarchy. Today, the Thai people are united in three ways: via the Buddhist religion, through their love for freedom, and by their support of the monarchy.

Web:
http://www.tat.or.th/

Usenet:
soc.culture.thai

IRC:
#thailand

842 WORLD CULTURES

United Kingdom

The United Kingdom, or U.K., is in western Europe and consists of Great Britain (England, Scotland and Wales) and Northern Ireland. The U.K. is governed by a constitutional monarchy and is one of the world's leading industrial nations. The U.K.'s contributions to world culture are legion: the Royal Family, well-mannered soccer fans, afternoon tea, and Monty Python, not to mention a longstanding contribution to the world of food and haute cuisine.

Web:
http://www.ukindex.co.uk/
http://www.yahoo.co.uk/

Usenet:
soc.culture.british

IRC:
#england
#uk

Look What I Found on the Net...

```
Newsgroup: soc.culture.thai
Subject: Thai Rules of Etiquette

> I am a Canadian white guy who is interested in learning about
>> the rules of relationships.  I would like to know how to enter
> into a relationship with a Thai lady — one that is proper —
> not just for lust, but to find and marry a proper Thai girl
> and be happy...

> Slow, slow, do not rush.
>
> First, you do not let her know that you like her.  Just be
> nice and be helpful to her, more and more, until you are sure
> she is interested in you.
>
> Then you can ask her and her friend or relative to go out with
> you.  If she agrees, it is certain she also likes you.
>
> Slow, slow, do not rush.
>
> After going out, with her friends or relatives along, several
> times, she probably falls in love with you.  Then you can ask
> her to go out with you alone.
>
> Slow, slow, do not rush and do not touch or kiss.
>
> After she goes out with you alone several times, you can
> propose to her. Good luck.

Will you marry me?
```

WORLD CULTURES

United States

American culture, inventiveness and business influence all have an enormous effect on the world at large. Here are the places to discuss what America is and how it fits into the global community. Talk, argue and meet new friends, all at the same time. For information about the United States, these Web sites will help you explore the land of the free and home of the brave from your living room. (You do need to supply your own hot dog and apple pie.)

Web:
http://www.odci.gov/cia/publications/factbook/us.html
http://www.usacitylink.com/

Usenet:
soc.culture.african-american
soc.culture.african.american.moderated
soc.culture.usa

IRC:
#usa

United States: Southern

The culture of the South has a rich diversity, from grand plantations to secluded hills, from the Atlantic coast to the Gulf coast. Read and discuss the history, conversational language, humor and culture of the South, and maybe get a good recipe for catfish and hush puppies while you are at it.

Web:
http://www.unc.edu/depts/csas/
http://www.yall.com/

Venezuela

Venezuela is located on the northern coast of South America on the Caribbean Sea. In 1499, a Spanish explorer named an offshore island Venezuela, meaning "little Venice". The explorer called the island "little Venice" because the inhabitants of the island built their huts above the water on stilts. The name was eventually used for the mainland area.

Web:
http://www.cyberven.com/
http://www.geodyssey.co.uk/potted.htm

Usenet:
soc.culture.venezuela

IRC:
#venezuela

World Constitutions

This site has constitutions and basic laws for many countries around the world, including Germany, Hong Kong, the United States, Canada, China, Hungary and the Slovak Republic, as well as the texts of the English Bill of Rights, Magna Carta, John at Runnymede, and others.

Web:
http://www.adi.uam.es/docencia/tex_der/constm.htm

Have you ever wanted to have your own country? It's easy, as long as you do the proper paperwork.

Start by checking out the **World Constitutions** on the Net. Choose one that looks good, and rewrite it to suit your requirements. Now all you need is a bunch of people and some land.

What could be easier?

844 WORLD CULTURES

Research, Net-Style

My brother Randy got his Ph.D. from Oxford University by researching and writing about Bills of Rights from British Commonwealth countries. At the time, he had to do all his research in the library. Now all he would have to do is connect to the Net.

Randy had to go to England and live in continual dampness, waking up early every morning for rowing practice, and walking around in constant fear that a member of the royal family might pass by.

As a Net user, you can sit in your living room—a tall cool drink by your side, the family cats snuggling quietly in your lap—and download world constitutions with one hand tied behind your back.

World Culture Talk and General Discussion

As more and more of the world connects to the Net, we become closer to one another and more and more like a global village. Today, problems and conflicts anywhere in the world are of concern to everyone. These discussion groups are for talking about general world and cultural issues.

Usenet:
  soc.culture
  soc.culture.intercultural
  soc.culture.misc
  soc.culture.multicultural

World Heritage List

Around the world, there are many cultural and natural sites that are part of the common heritage of people everywhere. In order to help preserve these sites, the World Heritage Committee, working under the auspices of UNESCO, identifies such places and publishes information about them in the World Heritage list.

Web:
  http://www.cco.caltech.edu/~salmon/
    world.heritage.html

WORLD CULTURES: DISCUSSION GROUPS

Africa Discussion Groups

These groups are for talking about Africa: Algeria, Berber, Ethiopia, Guinea, Kenya, Liberia, Maghreb, Malagasy, Nigeria, Sierra-Leone, Somalia, South Africa and Zimbabwe.

Usenet:
  alt.culture.somalia
  soc.culture.african
  soc.culture.algeria
  soc.culture.berber
  soc.culture.ethiopia.misc
  soc.culture.ethiopia.moderated
  soc.culture.guinea-conakry
  soc.culture.kenya
  soc.culture.liberia
  soc.culture.maghreb
  soc.culture.malagasy
  soc.culture.nigeria
  soc.culture.sierra-leone
  soc.culture.somalia
  soc.culture.south-africa
  soc.culture.south-africa.afrikaans
  soc.culture.zimbabwe

Lonely? Try IRC.

WORLD CULTURES: DISCUSSION GROUPS

Asia Pacific Discussion Groups

These groups are for talking about the Asia Pacific region of the world: China, Hong Kong, Japan, Korea and Taiwan.

Usenet:
  soc.culture.asian
  soc.culture.china
  soc.culture.hongkong
  soc.culture.hongkong.entertainment
  soc.culture.japan
  soc.culture.japan.moderated
  soc.culture.korean
  soc.culture.taiwan

Australia and Oceania Discussion Groups

These groups are for talking about Australia and Oceania: Australia, New Zealand, French Polynesia, the Pacific Islands and Tasmania.

Usenet:
  soc.culture.australia
  soc.culture.australian
  soc.culture.new-zealand
  soc.culture.pacific-island

Central Asia Discussion Groups

These groups are for talking about Central Asia: Chechnya, Georgia, Kazakhstan, Mongolia, Nepal, Russia, Turkestan, Turkmenistan and Tuva, as well as the former Soviet Union.

Usenet:
  alt.culture.chechnya
  alt.culture.kazakhstan
  alt.culture.tuva
  soc.culture.asian
  soc.culture.mongolian
  soc.culture.nepal
  soc.culture.rep-of-georgia
  soc.culture.russia
  soc.culture.russian
  soc.culture.russian.moderated
  soc.culture.soviet

Europe Discussion Groups

These groups are for talking about Europe: Albania, Armenia, Asturias, Austria, the Baltic states, Belgium, Brittany, Britain, Bosnia-Herzegovina, Bulgaria, Catalan, Caucasia, Celtic culture, Cornish culture, Croatia, Crimea, the Czech Republic and Slovakia, Dagestan, France, Germany, Greece, Ireland, Italy, Magyar culture, Malta, the Netherlands, Nordic culture, Poland, Portugal, Romania, Scotland, Slovenia, Spain, Switzerland, Ukraine, Wales and Yugoslavia.

Usenet:
  alt.culture.armenian
  alt.culture.austrian
  alt.culture.dagestan
  alt.culture.malta
  bit.listserv.basque-l
  bit.listserv.bosnet
  bit.listserv.hellas
  bit.listserv.makedon
  bit.listserv.mideur-l
  bit.listserv.slovak-l
  soc.culture.albanian
  soc.culture.asturies
  soc.culture.austria
  soc.culture.baltics
  soc.culture.belgium
  soc.culture.bosna-herzgvna
  soc.culture.breton
  soc.culture.british
  soc.culture.bulgaria
  soc.culture.catalan
  soc.culture.celtic
  soc.culture.cornish
  soc.culture.croatia
  soc.culture.czecho-slovak
  soc.culture.estonia
  soc.culture.europe
  soc.culture.french
  soc.culture.galiza
  soc.culture.german
  soc.culture.greek
  soc.culture.irish
  soc.culture.italian
  soc.culture.magyar
  soc.culture.netherlands
  soc.culture.nordic
  soc.culture.occitan
  soc.culture.polish
  soc.culture.portuguese
  soc.culture.romanian
  soc.culture.scottish
  soc.culture.slovenia
  soc.culture.spain
  soc.culture.swiss
  soc.culture.turkish
  soc.culture.turkish.moderated
  soc.culture.ukrainian
  soc.culture.welsh
  soc.culture.yugoslavia

846 WORLD CULTURES: DISCUSSION GROUPS

Latin America Discussion Groups

These groups are for talking about Latin America: Argentina, Bolivia, Brazil, Chile, Colombia, Costa Rica, Ecuador, El Salvador, Honduras, Mexico, Nicaragua, Peru, Uruguay and Venezuela.

Usenet:
- alt.culture.argentina
- soc.culture.argentina
- soc.culture.bolivia
- soc.culture.brazil
- soc.culture.chile
- soc.culture.colombia
- soc.culture.costa-rica
- soc.culture.ecuador
- soc.culture.el-salvador
- soc.culture.honduras
- soc.culture.latin-america
- soc.culture.mexican
- soc.culture.nicaragua
- soc.culture.peru
- soc.culture.uruguay
- soc.culture.venezuela

Middle East Discussion Groups

These groups are for talking about the Middle East: Assyria, Iran, Iraq, Israel, Jordan, the Kurds, Kuwait, Lebanon, Palestine, Saudi Arabia and Syria.

Usenet:
- alt.culture.kuwait
- alt.culture.saudi
- soc.culture.arabic
- soc.culture.assyrian
- soc.culture.iranian
- soc.culture.iraq
- soc.culture.israel
- soc.culture.jordan
- soc.culture.kurdish
- soc.culture.kuwait
- soc.culture.kuwait.moderated
- soc.culture.lebanon
- soc.culture.palestine
- soc.culture.syria

Look What I Found on the Net...

```
Newsgroup: soc.culture.europe
Subject: Are Europeans more liberal than Americans?


> I pose the above question based on personal observations.
> It seems the European nations are consistently more liberal,
> both socially and fiscally, than Americans...


> Of course we are more liberal.
>
> As a boy, I wanted to go and live in America (the "American
> Dream").  I went there, worked there, came back, and I thank
> God I was born in Europe.
>
> America is terrible.  I'm well traveled, but in no other
> place have I seen such bigotry.


Try again. I lived in Europe, and found there to be much more
racism.  It just isn't discussed in the open.
```

WORLD CULTURES: DISCUSSION GROUPS

Southeast Asia Discussion Groups

These groups are for talking about Southeast Asia: the Association of Southeast Asian Nations (ASEAN), Burma, Cambodia, the Hmong, Indonesia, Laos, Malaysia, the Philippines, Singapore, Thailand and Vietnam.

Usenet:
  alt.culture.indonesia
  bit.listserv.seasia-l
  soc.culture.asean
  soc.culture.asian
  soc.culture.burma
  soc.culture.cambodia
  soc.culture.filipino
  soc.culture.hmong
  soc.culture.indonesia
  soc.culture.indonesian
  soc.culture.laos
  soc.culture.malaysia
  soc.culture.singapore
  soc.culture.singapore.moderated
  soc.culture.thai
  soc.culture.vietnamese

Southern Asia Discussion Groups

These groups are for talking about Southern Asia: Afghanistan, Bangladesh, Bengal, India, Kerala, Karnata, Kashmir, Pakistan, Punjab, Sri Lanka and Tamil.

Usenet:
  alt.culture.karnataka
  alt.culture.kerala
  alt.culture.tamil
  soc.culture.afghanistan
  soc.culture.asian
  soc.culture.bangladesh
  soc.culture.bengali
  soc.culture.india
  soc.culture.indian
  soc.culture.indian.american
  soc.culture.indian.bihar
  soc.culture.indian.delhi
  soc.culture.indian.gujarati
  soc.culture.indian.info
  soc.culture.indian.jammu-kashmir
  soc.culture.indian.karnataka
  soc.culture.indian.kerala
  soc.culture.indian.marathi
  soc.culture.indian.telugu
  soc.culture.kashmir
  soc.culture.pakistan
  soc.culture.pakistan.education
  soc.culture.pakistan.history
  soc.culture.pakistan.moderated
  soc.culture.pakistan.politics
  soc.culture.pakistan.religion
  soc.culture.pakistan.sports
  soc.culture.punjab
  soc.culture.sri-lanka
  soc.culture.tamil

Here is my three-step plan for world peace.

1. Learn about another country.
2. Talk to people from that country.
3. Repeat steps 1 and 2 as necessary.

WORLD CULTURES: DISCUSSION GROUPS

United States and Canada Discussion Groups

These groups are for talking about the United States and Canada: Alaska, African-American culture, Asian-American culture, Cajun culture, Hawaii, Mexican-American culture, New York, Oregon, Quebec, Asian-Indian culture, Hispanic culture, and the Southwest region of the United States.

Usenet:
   alt.culture.african.american.business
   alt.culture.african.american.history
   alt.culture.african.american.issues
   alt.culture.alaska
   alt.culture.cajun
   alt.culture.hawaii
   alt.culture.ny-upstate
   alt.culture.ny.upstate
   alt.culture.oregon
   alt.culture.us.asian-indian
   alt.culture.us.hispanics
   alt.culture.us.southwest
   soc.culture.african.american
   soc.culture.asian.american
   soc.culture.canada
   soc.culture.hawaii
   soc.culture.mexican.american
   soc.culture.quebec
   soc.culture.usa

West Indies Discussion Groups

These groups are for talking about the West Indies: the Caribbean, Cuba, the Dominican Republic, Haiti, Jamaica and Puerto Rico.

Usenet:
   soc.culture.caribbean
   soc.culture.cuba
   soc.culture.dominican-rep
   soc.culture.haiti
   soc.culture.jamaican
   soc.culture.puerto-rico

Fun is one click away.

WRITING

Bad Writing Contest

Anyone can write poorly, but can you write worse than thousands of other people? If so, you may want to enter the annual Bulwer-Lytton Fiction Contest. All you have to do is write one sentence—a sentence that pretends to be the opening of a bad novel. This contest has been run since 1982, and, if your stomach for atrocious writing is strong, you can peruse the winners by visiting this Web site. The contest is named for a Victorian historical novelist, Edward George Bulwer-Lytton (1803-1873), who wrote a story that begins: "It was a dark and stormy night; the rain fell in torrents—except at occasional intervals, when it was checked by a violent gust of wind which swept up the streets (for it is in London that our scene lies), rattling along the house-tops, and fiercely agitating the scanty flame of the lamps that struggled against the darkness..."

Web:
   http://www.bulwer-lytton.com/

Children's Writing

A *lot* of people want to write for children. If you are going to be successful, you must be persistent, skillful, knowledgeable, experienced, talented and lucky. When it comes to information, the Net can help. These Web sites have lots of resources for writing for children. One site contains answers to frequently asked questions, a glossary of common terms, and information about agents and submissions. The other site is maintained by an editor (not a writer) and offers information from a slightly different perspective. The Usenet group is a good place to visit. It's where real writers hang out, and if you spend some time there, you will definitely learn something.

Web:
   http://www.users.interport.net/~hdu/
   http://www.write4kids.com/

Usenet:
   rec.arts.books.childrens

WRITING 849

> Want to converse with the people whoze job it iss to find3e mistakess? Jpin the copy editor's maleing list.

Copy Editing

Copy editing is a process in which text is checked for mistakes. Every writer, no matter how good, needs a copy editor for two reasons: first, copy editors are specialists, trained to recognize and correct written mistakes, and second, it is difficult for a writer to notice his or her own mistakes. Having a second person read the text makes a big difference. In general, copy editors are overworked, underpaid and under-appreciated. This is a shame, because copy editing is a necessary part of the writing process and some copy editors demonstrate a dedication to their craft and a degree of professionalism that would be difficult to overpraise. (My copy editor, for example, edited this section of the book on her birthday.)

Web:
http://www.rt66.com/~telp/sfindex.htm
http://www.theslot.com/

Listproc Mailing List:
List Name: **copyediting-l**
Subscribe to: **listproc@cornell.edu**

Freelance Writing FAQ

Does the romance of uncertain work and low remuneration sound appealing to you? Perhaps you are ready to be a freelance writer. Take a look at this FAQ (frequently asked question list) all about the business of freelance writing. Learn how to start, the best ways to submit your work, publishing terminology, and so on.

Web:
http://www.inkspot.com/craft/freelancefaq.html

Literary Agents

A literary agent is a person who represents you and your work. The main job of an agent is to sell what you create, along with subsidiary rights. You pay an agent commission on the money you receive for the work he or she sells—most agents charge 15 percent. All money is sent to the agent, who deducts the commission and then sends the remainder to you. (Agents are not fools.) Do you need an agent? There is no easy answer. Within some genres, such as computer book publishing, using an agent is optional. In other areas, such as screenwriting, it is difficult to get a movie studio to even look at you if you are not represented professionally. Remember, though, agents are not managers; all they do is sell. It is up to *you* to build your career. If you need an agent, these resources will help you find one. To get you started, I have some tips.

1. When you sign a publishing agreement, everything is negotiable, even—as Isaac Asimov once pointed out—your name and the date.

2. And this is very important, pay a lawyer who is familiar with the publishing industry to read every contract *before* you sign it. Does this apply to the contract a literary agency wants you to sign when you hire them? Yes, yes and yes.

3. Everything is negotiable.

4. Do not ever pay anyone to "read" your work.

5. Everything is negotiable.

6. Avoid agents who try to steer you toward a particular commercial editing service.

7. Everything is negotiable.

8. Beware of agents who collect a 15 percent commission and then try to charge you for extras, such as phone calls, faxes and photocopying.

9. Everything is negotiable.

Web:
http://www.horror.org/agent.htm
http://www.jkelman.com/agents/
http://www.literaryagent.com/direct.html

850 WRITING

Mystery and Crime Writing

Are you a mystery writer? Would you like to be one? These Web sites have lots of useful information for mystery and crime writers. On Usenet, the **rec.arts.mystery** group is the place to discuss mystery plays, books and films. The other groups are where people talk about actual and imaginary crimes. These are good places to visit when you need inspiration or information.

Web:

http://www.bookwire.com/mwa/
http://www.inkspot.com/genres/mystery.html

Usenet:

alt.crime
alt.true-crime
rec.arts.mystery

Online Writery

Writers tend to be solitary people, from either personal inclination or circumstance. Spending a large number of hours slaving over a hot computer makes it difficult to find the time to go out and meet people. This Web site hosts various discussion forums for writers. You can check in, read the new messages, and post some of your own, all without leaving the computer. This means that, as writers, we can stay in touch and talk about writing online, never having to actually meet anyone in person. Now, if I could only figure out how to download a pizza.

Web:

http://www.missouri.edu/~writery/

Prose

These bite-sized morsels of prose make the perfect afternoon brain snack. No matter what tickles your fancy, the variety of stories will have something for you. Read or share, it's up to you: just remember, if you don't use it, you'll lose it.

Usenet:

alt.prose
rec.arts.prose

Mystery and Crime Writing

Here is the world's shortest mystery story that involves all of the following ideas:

- murder
- romance
- royalty
- a great detective
- the Internet
- Microsoft Windows
- a small blue sock

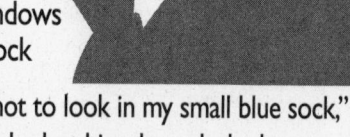

"Darling, I told you not to look in my small blue sock," she said, as she lovingly shot him through the heart.

The Great Detective leaped up from behind the couch. "After spending two years chasing you through fifteen countries, Contessa, I was finally able to track you down by analyzing the information on your Web page."

"I'll come quietly," she said, "but please tell me one thing."

"Yes?" said the Great Detective.

The mysterious, red-haired woman looked into his eyes and breathed a deep sigh of despair. "Do you have any idea how to get rid of that Network Neighborhood icon?"

(To be continued...)

Publisher's Web Pages

Looking for information about a specific publisher? Here's a listing of publishers' Web sites, organized by category. This is a good place to start when you are looking for someone to publish your book. And once your book comes out, you can check the publisher's Web site to make sure your work is given the prominence it deserves.

Web:

http://www.bookwire.com/links/publishers/publishers.html

WRITING 851

Romance Writing

Do you want to be a romance writer? Good, because a lot of people need you. Romance novels are popular for a variety of reasons, the most important of which is that men simply do not pay enough attention to women. If you happen to have a husband or boyfriend who reads Harley Hahn books, you know that your man is intelligent, sensitive, emotional (in a good way) and altogether desirable. However, many women find that their mates do not quite measure up, and an escape into romantic fantasy is a welcome relief. Thus, if you are a romance writer or aspiring romance writer, you are fulfilling an important function in our society and your responsibilities are great. Remember, the Net is always there to help you stay in touch with your colleagues and do your research.

Web:
  http://www.romcom.com/
  http://www.rwanational.com/

Listserv Mailing List:
  List Name: **rw-l**
  Subscribe to: **listserv@maelstrom.stjohns.edu**

Screenplays

If you are working on a screenplay, you definitely need something to do when you are not writing. The Net is always available with plenty of relevant distractions. First, you can talk to other screenwriters on Usenet or on a mailing list. The Usenet group is for the discussion of writing screenplays and other related topics. The mailing list is for writers, agents, producers and other people who are interested in screenwriting for movies and television. The Web pages are great for when you need inspiration or information. One site is a huge archive of movie scripts; the other site is an ever-changing repository of news and gossip about the film industry.

Web:
  http://www.hollywoodreporter.com/literary/
  http://www.script-o-rama.com/

Usenet:
  misc.writing.screenplays

Listserv Mailing List:
  List Name: **scripts-l**
  Subscribe to: **listserv@nosferatu.cas.usf.edu**

Screenwriters and Playwrights

Do you have dreams of being a successful screenwriter or playwright? Here are some resources that may help you. This is a compilation of Net resources for screenwriters and playwrights as well as some general writing resources. There are lots of good links here, so even if this page doesn't help you pay the bills, it will at least give you something to read between now and the time your electricity is shut off.

Web:
  http://www.teleport.com/~cdeemer/scrwriter.html

Speechwriting

You know, of course, that when you listen to an Important Person make a speech, he or she did not write the words. Important People have speechwriters: skilled and imaginative writers who make a living telling other, less skilled and imaginative people what to say. If writing speeches appeals to you, visit these Web sites for a lot of useful information. One of the sites also has a great collection of speeches in history.

Web:
  http://www.ragan.com/speech/
  http://www.studyweb.com/grammar/comp/
  speeches.htm

Screenplays

I have a friend who is a screenwriter, and she won't let me look at her current screenplay until it is finished.

But do I care? No, because I can go to the Net and look at as many screenplays as I want.

Technical Writing

Technical writers create exposition: words that explain. A technical writer must be able to master a complex subject, and then describe it for a casual reader who needs to understand the relevant facts and ideas. This mailing list is for discussion of all aspects of technical writing. The Usenet group is the same as the list, so you only need to read one of them. The Web site stores archives of previous discussions.

Web:
http://listserv.okstate.edu/archives/techwr-l.html

Usenet:
bit.listserv.techwr-l

Listserv Mailing List:
List Name: **techwr-l**
Subscribe to: **listserv@listserv.okstate.edu**

Writer's Block Magazine

When you need a break from typing, spend some time browsing through the latest copy of this online writers' magazine. The articles are for professional writers and editors. You will find essays, reports on technology, book reviews, interviews, and more.

Web:
http://www.niva.com/writblok/

Writers Chat

This IRC channel is for writers to discuss all the aspects of writing that normal people don't understand. This channel is great for spending time blabbing when you should be writing (an important part of any writer's day). The Web site is the official home for the channel. Visit the site and you can look at bios and information about the regulars. There is also information about occasional workshops that are held in IRC.

Web:
http://www.project-iowa.org/

IRC:
#writers

Writers' Resources

When you're not writing, you might as well be cruising the Net looking at writers' resources. These Web sites will help you find a huge variety of writing information. So much that you will be exploring for hours and hours, and the best part is it all counts as work.

Web:
http://owl.english.purdue.edu/writing.html
http://www.arcana.com/shannon/books/writing.html
http://www.authorlink.com/
http://www.wwwscribe.com/

Writers Talk and General Discussion

Being a professional writer is fun because you can sleep in and work in your pajamas all day. Professional writers or those who aspire to be writers have established a community on the Net, and share thoughts and ideas about writing, critique works in progress, and post announcements of workshops, contests and new publications. Many of the people who are on this list have been there for a long time, so it has a nice welcoming atmosphere. If you'd rather talk on Usenet, there is also a good writing community there. The Web site is the official home of **misc.writing**.

Web:
http://www.scalar.com/mw/

Usenet:
misc.writing

Listserv Mailing List:
List Name: **writers**
Subscribe to: **listserv@mitvma.mit.edu**

Writing Tips

One thing writers never have to worry about is a shortage of hints about writing. Sometimes it seems as if one half of the writing community spends its time giving advice to the other half. Well, for those rare times when you are not working on your next novel, here are oodles of writing tips—enough advice to see you through from now to St. Swithin's Day.

Web:
http://www.jkelman.com/
http://www.olywa.net/peregrine/

Look What I Found on the Net...

[things writers talk about when they should be working...]

================

Newsgroup: misc.writing
Subject: The Perils of Peanut Butter

I don't like raisins — except in those big chunky chocolate squares — what were they called? I forget! Oh, no. It's early chocolate memory loss. Help!

================

Newsgroup: misc.writing
Subject: How Much Reading Do You Do?

How is it that two people can read a book and love it, and the same two people can read another book, and one of us loves it and the other does not?

================

Newsgroup: misc.writing
Subject: Procrastination Tips and Tricks

When it's time to write, what do you do to procrastinate? I've done things like:

Succumb to the never-before-nor-since-experienced urge to look through the phone book for listings of old friends I haven't seen in years.

Decide I really, really, really need a haircut because my hair being too long is distracting me.

Suddenly realize I have to have a copy of Frank Zappa's "You Can't Do That On Stage Anymore, Vol. 3" — RIGHT NOW — and make a trip to the record store.

Convince myself that writing a message to start a new thread on misc.writing will take only a couple minutes, and the sooner I do it, the sooner the discussion can begin, and then I'll get down to the real work I need to be doing. Yes, really, I will.

Ya know, I just glanced out the window, and those clouds look pretty ominous. Could be a thunderstorm brewing up, so it might be a good idea to unplug my computer...

X-RATED RESOURCES

X-RATED RESOURCES

Adult Site of the Day

Being an adult is lots of fun because you get to do almost anything you want. In particular, you get to look at "adult" pictures. This site canvasses the world of adult culture and each day presents one site that rises above the rest. Visit here every day and you will be surprised at all the interesting social and cultural horizons you can expand with just a few clicks of your mouse.

Web:
http://www.aosotd.com/

Every day, in every way, you should be getting better and better.

(Just to help it along, it wouldn't be a bad idea to check the Adult Site of the Day.)

AltSex

Alternative to what? Alternative to normal, say some people; alternative to boring, say others. Judge for yourself. This site is a collection of information about BDSM (bondage, domination, sadism, masochism), homosexuality, bisexuality, polyamory, health topics, transgender issues, advice columns, and more. Be careful when you visit this site. As they point out, "The most important sexual organ is the brain."

Web:
http://www.altsex.org/

Auto-Eroticism

In life, if you are going to do something, you should do it well. On the Net you can read up on auto-erotic facts, hints and techniques.

Web:
http://bianca.com/shack/goodvibe/masturbate
http://nassau.janey.com/~masturbate/
http://www.jackinworld.com/

Usenet:
alt.sex.masturbation

Bondage

All tied up with no place to go? You're in the right place. If having the most toys means having the most fun, then this is the zenith of extracurricular sexual activity. Read stories, share experiences, and discuss techniques and safety tips. If you love something, set it free; if it comes back to you, tie it up again.

Web:
http://www.bdsm-world.com/links2.htm
http://www.bondageweb.com/
http://www.boudoir-noir.com/links.html
http://www.sandm.com/

Usenet:
alt.binaries.pictures.bondage
alt.binaries.pictures.erotica.bondage.male
alt.bondage
alt.personals.bondage
alt.personals.bondage.gay
alt.sex.bondage
soc.subculture.bondage-bdsm

IRC:
#bdsm
#bdsmlounge
#bondage

Cross-Dressing

Why is it normal for a woman to dress like a man, but bizarre for a man to don lace and satin? Maybe someone on the Net will have the answer (or at least a reaction).

Web:
http://www.best.com/~cdserv/
http://www.eskimo.com/~bloo/bformfaq/

Usenet:
alt.fashion.crossdressing

IRC:
#crossdress

X-RATED RESOURCES

> **More, more... more.**

Diaper Fetish

Some people don't have a preference between cloth or plastic, Velcro or safety pins. Find out more about diaper fetishists on the Net.

Web:
http://big-baby.fsn.net/
http://ractarion.vaporware.org/~bbif/
http://www.aby.com/

Usenet:
alt.sex.fetish.diapers

IRC:
#diapers
#dpf
#wetgold

Dominance and Submission

Being a writer, I spend a lot of time working with editors and thus, am an expert in dominance and submission. Whether you are experienced or just curious, it's always good to be informed, and a great way to do it is by spending some time learning on the Net. Remember, even if you don't always have what it takes, you can always take what they have. (By the way, you might be wondering what working with editors has to do with dominance and submission. Well, I submit a manuscript and then they use it to dominate the marketplace.)

Web:
http://gloria-brame.com/diflove.htm
http://www.cuffs.com/
http://www.cyberzaar.com/dscuss/
http://www.dssanctuary.com/

IRC:
#dominance
#submission

Look What I Found on the Net...

```
Newsgroup: alt.fashion.crossdressing
Subject: Man in Panties
```

I see that other men wear panties and am encouraged to write.

I'm a straight male, but I love to wear women's panties. I have been wearing them for over 10 years, but only when I believed I could not be caught. I'm wearing a nice pair of cotton "Betty Boop" panties as I write this note.

I like to go to places that I don't know anyone and flash my panties to strangers.

Recently, I have gone to shoe stores with women sales people wearing short shorts and my panties to try on shoes that I don't need or want. I just like to see the looks from the ladies when they look up my shorts and see my lacy panties. I also like to go to the beach and sit on the seawall, with my legs apart enough to show my panties.

Should I seek help, or is this normal for a male that has a panty fetish?

856 X-RATED RESOURCES

A
B
C
D
E
F
G
H
I
J
K
L
M
N
O
P
Q
R
S
T
U
V
W
X
Y
Z

Dominant Women

Wouldn't it be a big surprise if the demure librarian you've been dating turned out to be a leather-wearing, whip-toting goddess of domination who wanted nothing more than to make you submit to doing somersaults in a vat of lime jello? On the Internet you can read about women who dominate and the men who love them.

Web:
   http://soiroom.hyperchat.com/blinded/3seconds.htm
   http://www.stic.net/users/thomas/amazon/
   http://www.thevalkyrie.com/

Usenet:
   alt.sex.femdom
   soc.subculture.bondage-bdsm.femdom

IRC:
   #femdom

Erotic Postcards

Having access to the Net can make your day-to-day life a lot easier. For example, say you have fallen behind on writing nice letters to your family back home. Or perhaps you have not yet been able to find the time to write thank-you notes for all the presents you received on your last birthday. (What? You don't write thank-you notes every time someone gives you a gift? Shame on you.) Well, these Web sites can help. Choose from a colorful collection of erotic postcards that is sure to liven up the atmosphere in just about anyone's electronic mailbox. Just make your pick, write your message, and send that very special greeting zipping down the Net like a greased pig surfing through hot butter. Keeping in touch has never been so easy (and so effective).

Web:
   http://www.clpw.net/eroticards/send.shtml
   http://www.eroticcity.net/postcards/postcard.html
   http://www.eroticpostcards.com/
   http://www.opkamer.nl/amea/sendp.htm
   http://www.porncard.com/
   http://www.teenplace.com/cards/postcard.html

Erotic Resources

No bachelor party would be complete without a nice display of erotic links on your monitor. These sites will go well with any snack food you might be offering during the event except, perhaps, large, sloppy slices of pizza (which require your undivided attention). This list will take you to erotic places containing images and stories.

Web:
   http://www.eroscan.com/
   http://www.link-o-rama.com/
   http://www.naughty.com/
   http://www.richards-realm.com/
   http://www.sinfoseek.com/

LOVE TO THINK?

Smart, willing, intellectual women on standby and eager to talk to you. Let us turn you on to a little Shakespeare or – for those of you into hardcore – some James Joyce. Feel free to be yourself. All that is on *our* minds is to stimulate *you* into some intellectual action. We'll talk about anything... quadratic equations, Java, objectivism, post-modernist sculpture, the current political administration, cgi scripts, or the Big Bang theory.

Call now and fill our heads with ideas.
Phone (900) 4-BRAINS or telnet to 127.0.0.1.
Only $12.95 per minute.
Student discounts available.
Special rates for readers of
Harley Hahn's Student Guide to Unix.

X-RATED RESOURCES

Exhibitionism

If you've got it, flaunt it. Or even if you don't have it, flaunt it. Exhibitionism is not for the faint of heart. Be gutsy, be bold. Hear stories of the exploits of the daring. Bring your own raincoat.

Web:
 http://www.carolcox.com/pictures/flasher.html
 http://www.freebeer.com/clay/welcome.htm
 http://www.freedom.co.uk/topbit/streaker/main.htm

Usenet:
 alt.sex.exhibitionism

> Take it off.
> Then put it on.
> Then take it off again.
> If you like to share
> (or even watch),
> alt.sex.exhibitionism
> is for you.

Fetish Fashions

There are people who believe that nudity is highly overrated and that much of the fun in life can be had from fetish clothing like shoes, stockings and other things that you can dress the body in. Whether it's plastic, rubber, leather, silk or another material—this Usenet group and the Web sites are guaranteed to be interesting to people who get excited by dressing up or down.

Web:
 http://www.gothic.net/~squee/fetishlinks.html
 http://www2.best.com/~invncble/altlycra.shtml

Usenet:
 alt.sex.fetish.fashion

Foot Fetish

You don't have to be a shoe salesman to enjoy yourself here. Experience the sensuous excitement of a well-shined pump wrapped around a delicately stockinged foot with deliciously painted toenails.

Web:
 http://www.rock-man.com/

Usenet:
 alt.sex.fetish.feet

Glory Hole FAQ

A glory hole is a small "fist-sized" opening from one private video booth to another in an adult bookstore. What's a glory hole used for? Well, let's just say that, if you were a man of average height visiting a video booth, you would find the glory hole to be at the same height as your hips. I'll leave the rest to your imagination and to the Net.

Web:
 http://members.aol.com/lilfuzzyg/home.htm

Hard Kink Magazine

If you've been reading this book all the way through, cover to cover, you're just about finished by now. So what are you going to do when you get to the end of Chapter Z? Well, you could start over again from the beginning or—if you feel so inclined—you could check out this online magazine. I can't really get too graphic about the contents, but let me just say that if your mother has a copy of this book, when she gets to Chapter Z tell her to start again at the beginning.

Web:
 http://hardkink.hotsex.com/hardkink/

Limericks

Probably sometime, somewhere, somebody actually did write a limerick that wasn't dirty. If so, it's not here.

Web:
 http://www.compusmart.ab.ca/penumbra/adchef/limerick.htm
 http://www.provide.net/~harolds1/lim1.html

X-RATED RESOURCES

News and Gossip of the Porn Industry

Luke Ford is an accomplished porn industry writer with a background in economics and radio news. Nowadays, however, Ford is better known as the Matt Drudge of the porn industry, an informed gossip commentator who brings you the latest on who's doing what to whom and how. He also writes essays about topics related to pornography, as well as thoughtful biographies of the actors and actresses in the industry. By the way, Ford is the son of Christian evangelists. Talk about the acorn not falling far from the tree.

Web:
http://www.lukeford.com/

Oral Sex

"Do you like oral sex?" I asked her. "Oh yes," she replied, "I think everybody should talk about it." Well, on the Net everybody does talk about it. Visit these Web sites to get all the information you are likely to need about oral sex. For related activities (such as begging and bragging), you are on your own.

Web:
http://wso.williams.edu/peerh/sex/safesex/oralsex.html
http://www.ee.calpoly.edu/~jcline/sexo/mufffaq.htm
http://www.halcyon.com/elf/altsex/cunni.html
http://www.halcyon.com/elf/altsex/fella.html
http://www.mansco.com/lf2/sex/

Usenet:
alt.sex.oral

Pantyhose and Stockings

Soft, sleek, sensual... and more. Talk to the people who really appreciate what the well-dressed leg is wearing this season. Share your opinions and read provocative stories.

Web:
http://www.pantyhoseindex.com/
http://www.sensuality.co.uk/l_frame2.htm
http://www.upskirtsandpantyhose.com/phose9.htm

Usenet:
alt.binaries.pictures.pantyhose
alt.pantyhose

IRC:
#pantyhose

Porn Stars

Can't get enough of her (or him) on video? Chat with other fans on Usenet, and trade pictures, comments and gossip about your favorite adult actresses (and actors).

Usenet:
alt.binaries.erotica.pornstar
alt.binaries.pictures.erotica.pornstar.jenna-jameson
alt.fan.christy-canyon
alt.fan.danni-ashe
alt.fan.debi-diamond
alt.fan.ginger-lynn
alt.fan.pornstar.darrian
alt.fan.pornstar.janine
alt.fan.televisionx.charmaine
alt.fan.teri-weigel
alt.fan.traci-lords

Porn-O-Matic

Don't worry if you've never had a chance to star in your own porno movie. All you need is the handy-dandy Porn-O-Matic story generator. Just enter some information, select a few items, and, in seconds, you'll be reading the basic plot for your own movie. Just the thing when Ron Jeremy comes over, and you're sitting around bored with nothing to do.

Web:
http://www.maddogproductions.com/porn_enter.htm

Prostitution Around the World

This FAQ is a great guide to the world of prostitution (whatever end of the stick you happen to be on). There is a large list of many different countries. Click on the country of your choice and get the scoop on the prostitution scene there. (For convenience, there is also a link to the CIA World Factbook if you want to find out other information as well.) The presentation is complete: along with all the prostitution info, you can read about travel resources such as currency converters, foreign language guides, and so on. In addition, there are links to strip clubs, general reports about prostitution, and legal, cultural and miscellaneous articles (such as advice on how to kick the habit and prostitution limericks). Lots of good clean (free) fun. For discussion, you can try the Usenet groups.

Web:
http://www.worldsexguide.org/

Usenet:
alt.sex.prostitution
alt.sex.services

X-RATED RESOURCES

Get a new perspective.
Men, see "Women".
Women, see "Men".

Sex How-Tos

Know how to do it? Want to know how to do it better? There's lots of practical advice here about how to have sex and improve your technique. As good as you are, you can always get better.

Web:
http://www.sextutor.net/
http://www.skinful.com/erotica/page1.htm

Look What I Found on the Net...

(from a story posted to alt.pantyhose)

I was still reeling from the shock...I thought I'd seen everything that might ruin our marriage, but we've stuck together through thick and thin. Through sickness and health. Except for now.

"Stephanie..." I stammered. "You know that lesbianism doesn't bother me, but why did you wait after all this time to admit this to me? I'm your HUSBAND!..."

My head was a soup of confused feelings...the one person who meant more to me than anything may very well have made our marriage a lie. A good part of my life would have to be ripped away from me, unless I made some sacrifices to keep her in my life...

"Stephanie," I asked, mentally preparing myself for what I was about to do, "Would it be easier for you if I were a woman?"

Her eyes lit up like Christmas tree lights, and I could see that she was fascinated with this idea, a chance to save our marriage. "You would do that for me? That's, that's wonderful..."

Anyway, that's how all this started. I am going over that episode in my mind again as I now stand in the bedroom, showered, fully shaved and powdered, trying to tell myself that this is for our marriage, and to at least give this scheme a chance....

"Okay, first you take one of the stocking legs and gather it up to the toe, like this," Stephanie explained, demonstrating with her pair, gathering the leg up with her thumbs which I emulated. "Then you put your toes in, straightening out the toe seam across the toes. Personally, I like to put the seam just under the toes, so if you take off your shoes the seam will be invisible." I tried to follow her example as she put them on her smooth legs...

860 X-RATED RESOURCES

Sex How-Tos

Birds do it.
Bees do it.

Make sure you know how to do it.

Sex Magazine Talk and General Discussion

It's important to be cultured and well-read. Not only will you win friends and influence people, but you will undoubtedly find it much easier to get a date. On the other hand, some days it's nice to give yourself a break and look at magazines that are highly prized for their picturesque qualities. Get recommendations on good magazines, where to buy them, information on trading or buying collector's editions, and general discussion about the concepts of sex magazines.

Usenet:
  alt.mag.hustler
  alt.mag.penthouse
  alt.mag.playboy
  alt.mag.playgirl
  alt.magazines.pornographic

Sex Magazines

When you are in the mood for a little culture or you want to read some informative articles, there are several big name magazines on the Net that you can browse. These magazines offer interesting excerpts of articles and columns from their print versions. For instance, while I was doing my research, I ran across an excerpt from an interview with G. Gordon Liddy in which the interviewer asked what Liddy thinks of group sex. (He likes it.) Oh, I almost forgot. These magazines have some pictures, too.

Web:
  http://www.chicgirls.com/
  http://www.juggsmag.com/
  http://www.playboy.com/

Sex Pictures

Let's take a minute to stop and appreciate the vast resources of the Internet: all those computers, communication lines, satellites, not to mention the tens of thousands of people working day and night to ensure that it all hangs together. All of this, just so you can download sexy...err...erotic pictures to display on your own computer. Usenet, mirroring the world at large, has a gigantic selection of Usenet groups devoted to various aspects of visual gratification.

Web:
  http://www.newshog.com/nhdemo/
  http://www.slutpost.com/

Usenet:
  alt.binaries.erotica
  alt.binaries.nude.celebrities
  alt.binaries.nude.celebrities.female
  alt.binaries.nude.celebrities.male
  alt.binaries.pictures.erotic.centerfolds
  alt.binaries.pictures.erotica
  alt.binaries.pictures.erotica.amateur
  alt.binaries.pictures.erotica.amateur.female
  alt.binaries.pictures.erotica.amateur.male
  alt.binaries.pictures.erotica.animals
  alt.binaries.pictures.erotica.anime
  alt.binaries.pictures.erotica.bears
  alt.binaries.pictures.erotica.bestiality
  alt.binaries.pictures.erotica.black
  alt.binaries.pictures.erotica.black.females
  alt.binaries.pictures.erotica.black.male
  alt.binaries.pictures.erotica.blondes
  alt.binaries.pictures.erotica.bondage
  alt.binaries.pictures.erotica.breasts
  alt.binaries.pictures.erotica.brunette
  alt.binaries.pictures.erotica.butts
  alt.binaries.pictures.erotica.cartoons
  alt.binaries.pictures.erotica.close-up
  alt.binaries.pictures.erotica.exhibitionism
  alt.binaries.pictures.erotica.female
  alt.binaries.pictures.erotica.fetish
  alt.binaries.pictures.erotica.fetish.feet
  alt.binaries.pictures.erotica.fetish.hair
  alt.binaries.pictures.erotica.gaymen
  alt.binaries.pictures.erotica.male
  alt.binaries.pictures.erotica.orientals
  alt.binaries.pictures.erotica.panties
  alt.binaries.pictures.erotica.redheads
  alt.binaries.pictures.erotica.scanmaster
  alt.binaries.pictures.erotica.transvestites
  alt.sex.pictures
  alt.sex.pictures.female
  alt.sex.pictures.male

Sex Sounds

Some people like to watch, some people like to touch, but if you are one of those people who likes to listen, spend some time with the people who like to share and find out if you like aural sex.

Web:
http://www.sexsounds.com/

Usenet:
alt.binaries.multimedia.erotica
alt.binaries.sounds.erotica

Sex Stories

On the Internet, you will never want for a good, sexy story (or a bad one, for that matter). All day, every day, stories posted to the Net range from mildly erotic mainstream to bold, raunchy kink. There's something for everyone. And if you'd like to hang around over coffee or a smoke to discuss the literary merit of the writing, check out **alt.sex.stories.d** for discussion. When you are looking for a good bedtime story and you're having trouble settling down with Beowulf, try an erotic story or two instead. They might just hit the spot.

Web:
http://extra.newsguy.com/~bitbard/
http://totallyfreesex.com/list/
http://www.nifty.org/
http://www.qz.to/erotica/

Usenet:
alt.sex.stories
alt.sex.stories.d
alt.sex.stories.gay
alt.sex.stories.tg
rec.arts.erotica

Sex Wanted

Forget love, forget romance. If you're looking to cut to the chase, then cut in here. Don't bother being coy or shy, state what you want and let the good times roll. (However, government regulations require me to warn you that—as with bank accounts—there can be substantial loss of interest with early withdrawal.)

Usenet:
alt.sex.wanted

> Little-known fact: Bill and Monica met in alt.romance.

Sexy Talk

You thought you'd done it everywhere. Now try it on the Net, as couples and groups indulge in verbal sex around the world. These are some of the many channels for hot chatting on IRC.

IRC:
#hotsex
#netsex
#sex
#sextalk

Spanking

Have you ever been sitting around the house and suddenly you think, "Hmm, I feel like a good spanking"? Don't feel alone, we've all had that experience (not really, but you can believe that). Gather with others who like to take physical intimacy to another dimension. You'll recognize them: they're the ones who can't sit down.

Web:
http://maman.base.org/
http://www.amythest.com/sss/stories/stories.html
http://www.goodkitty.com/spanking/

Usenet:
alt.sex.spanking
soc.sexuality.spanking

Strip Club List

There's no need to miss your favorite strip club if you have to travel out of town. Check out this list of reviews of strip clubs around the United States. The listings have legends that indicate whether the strip club is bikini, topless or full nude, as well as lengthy written reviews written by patrons of the club.

Web:
http://www.tuscl.com/

X-RATED RESOURCES

Tickling

Oh, the agony and the ecstasy of being tickled. Ticklers and ticklees talk about where and how they like it—on the feet, ribs, back of the knee, inner thigh or places that we can only mention between the hours of midnight and 4:00 a.m. On the Web and on Usenet you can read stories, personal experiences and thoughts on tickling as an intimate pastime.

Web:
http://members.aol.com/oblesklk/
http://www.wane-manor.com/~stately/fbs/true.html

Usenet:
alt.sex.fetish.tickling

Voyeurism

There's something exciting about forbidden observation, peeking through the slats of the venetian blinds, pressing your ear against the cool, smooth wall, opening the door just a crack and watching. If you are more of a watcher than a doer, or you like doing while watching, post your thoughts, ideas and stories on Usenet or check out the Web sites.

Web:
http://www.freevoyeurism.com/
http://www.model-zone.com/scamera/

Usenet:
alt.sex.voyeurism

Watersports

If you are looking for a good place to brag about your skill as a water-skier, go someplace else. For watersports of a more personal nature, like enemas and related fetishes, look no further.

Web:
http://www.patches.net/home2.html
http://www.tgc.co.uk/waters/

Usenet:
alt.sex.enemas
alt.sex.watersports

Do you like to watch? Take a peek at alt.sex.voyeurism

X-Rated Movies

Who needs gorgeous vistas, great soundtracks and good acting when you have a few naked people gyrating around in front of the camera? Get hard and fast information on X-rated movies, actors and actresses, and FAQs from related Usenet groups.

Web:
http://homepage.eznet.net/~rwilhelm/asm/dbsearch.html
http://www.hypervil.com/biokeeper/
http://www.rame.net/

Usenet:
alt.sex.movies

IRC:
#sexmovies

Zoophilia

There are some people who believe that if you limit yourself only to people, you are missing out on something special. Well, Mr. Ed and Flipper probably wouldn't approve, but here are some Internet resources especially for the type of animal lovers who like to bring out the beast in themselves.

Web:
http://www.netbook.net/zootopia/
http://www.psg.com/~jimd/uzp/
http://www.zetavalley.com/zoo.htm
http://www.zetavalley.com/zooring.htm

Usenet:
alt.sex.bestiality

IRC:
#beastsex

YOUNG ADULTS

Christian Youth

Church isn't the only place to meet with other Christian youths. Young people from around the world discuss issues that concern them: not only biblical queries, but thoughts and ideas about society. Topics include sex before marriage, how to get along with people your age and how to defend the Christian faith. This group is moderated.

Usenet:
  soc.religion.christian.youth-work

Cool Science

Do you like science? Do you think it's fun to experiment with stuff, see what happens, and then try to explain it by making up a theory? I bet you'd like some science projects that are fun. For example, you may not realize it, but right this very minute there's DNA in your fridge. (Don't tell your mother.) In fact, your kitchen may hold the tools you need to start becoming a scientist. These Web sites have directions for various fun science projects, some of which you can do at home. (By the way, DNA—deoxyribonucleic acid—is the substance used within cells to store the information needed by the cell to reproduce and to carry out many of its functions.)

Web:
  http://raven.umnh.utah.edu/secondlevel/teen/teen.html
  http://raven.umnh.utah.edu/secondlevel/tomorrow/tomorrow.html
  http://weber.u.washington.edu/~chudler/neurok.html
  http://www.explorescience.com/
  http://www.ipl.org/youth/projectguide/

Cyberteens

Visit this Web site if you would like to see the creative things that other teens are doing. There is a teen zine that takes submissions from teen writers and photographers, a section for young composers (some really wonderful compositions), games and puzzles, a gallery of artworks, and more. I really enjoyed exploring this site.

Web:
  http://www.cyberteens.com/

Girl Stuff

No doubt about it, if you're a girl there's a lot to know. These Web sites contain useful information written especially for you, as well as various fun things to do. The Web sites are created and sponsored by two different tampon companies, so they have put a lot of effort into making these areas fun and enjoyable (because they want you for a customer). You can learn about menstruation, changes in your body and other important topics. I think you'll find these are good places to visit, because you can learn about things, and even ask questions, in a way that makes sense to you.

Web:
  http://www.kotex.com/girlspace/
  http://www.troom.com/

Gurl

It's cool being a girl. Know how I know? I've been to this Web site. The Web site is cool. Girls are cool. This zine is cool. You'll find stuff about kissing, sex, being different, body issues, dating, advice, drawings, comics, and more. There are also links to Web sites created by girls. Take a look. Maybe you should make a Web site of your own.

Web:
  http://www.gurl.com/

Cyberteens
Young people around the world are doing some amazing things. Find out what's happening by visiting **Cyberteens**.

Marijuana Facts

As illegal drugs go, marijuana is relatively benign, but, as with any drug that affects your mind, you should have the facts. Long-term marijuana use can sap your ambition and significantly decreases your success in life. (I have seen it happen.) Moreover, the more you get stoned, the more you make tiny changes to your brain that, eventually, become irreversible. Here is a guide with two sections, one for teens and one for parents. This is an excellent resource for people who are concerned about marijuana use and want to know more about its effects (especially the long-term effects).

Web:
http://www.nida.nih.gov/MarijBroch/Marijintro.html

MidLink Magazine

Middle school kids do not have to feel left out. MidLink is an electronic magazine for kids ages 10 to 15. It offers an interactive space where middle school kids all over the world can see art and writings from other kids or submit their own creative works.

Web:
http://longwood.cs.ucf.edu/~MidLink/

Preparing for College

Going to college is the absolute best thing you can do to prepare yourself for having a successful life. People like to remind you that it is easier to get a good job when you have a college degree. That's true, but there is a lot more to it than that. When you go to college you will train your mind for (at least) four years, and that training will help you for the rest of your life. At the same time, you will learn a lot, and the more you know, the better. Even subjects that seem irrelevant now have a way of becoming useful later in life. Finally, college is an important social experience. You'll meet many new people and make new friends. But most important, you will have a lot of *fun*—something your high school guidance counselor may forget to mention. So go to college. Now that we have that settled, here are some Internet resources to help you prepare, choose and apply.

Web:
http://www.collegeboard.org/
http://www.collegeedge.com/
http://www.jayi.com/
http://www.petersons.com/ugrad/
http://www.usnews.com/usnews/edu

Scouting

Young adventure seekers will have a great time with scouting. These Web sites offer scouting information for both boys and girls. The Usenet groups give young people a chance to talk to other kids who are interested in scouting.

Web:
http://www.bsa.scouting.org/
http://www.gsusa.org/
http://www.scoutorama.com/

Usenet:
alt.hobbies.boyscouts
alt.hobbies.boyscouts.oa
rec.scouting
rec.scouting.guide+girl
rec.scouting.issues
rec.scouting.misc
rec.scouting.usa

Straight-Edge

Straight-edge (usually abbreviated as sXe) is a practical way of living that was an offshoot of the punk rock scenes of the early 1980s. Originally, sXe was a philosophy based on the simple tenets of having fun—especially at loud volume—but no drugs, no smoking and no promiscuous sex. Since then, sXe has grown and evolved. There have been many sXe bands around the world as well as countless teenagers and young adults who have adopted a sXe lifestyle. Some people have extended the definition of the word sXe to being a vegetarian and becoming involved in social issues such as environmentalism. In general, the sXe lifestyle varies from person to person and place to place, but what it always seems to have in common is the belief that it's possible to lead a clean, wholesome life and still have a lot of fun (at loud volume).

Web:
http://www.cis.ohio-state.edu/hypertext/faq/usenet/cultures/straight-edge-faq/faq.html
http://www.straight-edge.com/

Usenet:
alt.lifestyle.substance-free
alt.punk.straight-edge

YOUNG ADULTS

Straight-Edge

In the Sixties, we had sex, drugs and loud music.

Now we have straight-edge:

Sex, drugs, and loud music — without the sex and drugs.

Technoteen

There are a lot of Web sites on the Internet constructed for teenagers by well-meaning teachers and parents. And I can tell you what they are like in two words: boring. Here's a Web site that is made by teenagers for teenagers. This is about as cool as it gets.

Web:
http://www.technoteen.com/

Teen Chat Rooms

The great thing about working on the computer and saying it's a school project is that when you are grounded and you can't leave the house, you can still talk to kids your own age and have fun. There are lots of special chat areas just for people your age. Pick the one that is appropriate and talk all night long (or until you have to go back to doing your homework).

Web:
http://pages.wbs.net/
   webchat3.so?cmd=cmd_doorway:Teen_13-15_Chat
http://pages.wbs.net/
   webchat3.so?cmd=cmd_doorway:Teen_16-19_Chat

Teen Dating Page

Would you like to meet an interesting person to talk to by email? Visit this Web site (made by teenagers) where teens have filled out forms about themselves: their favorite quote, hobbies, favorite bands, and so on. Browse through and, if you find someone you would like to know, you can get his or her email address and send a note.

Web:
http://www.theproud.net/thetlc/

Teen Driving Tips

Driving can be a lot of fun, especially when you can drive well. Here are some tips for new drivers. Read the hints for driving to school, around town and in the country. Learn about driving in bad weather, when to pass (and when not to), fatigue and buying a used car. Note: This Web site was created by a teenager who is a new driver. He did a good job: the tips are great. (Hint: This is a good place to show your parents when they ask why you spend so much time on the Net.)

Web:
http://www.ai.net/~ryanb/

Teen Movie Critic

Remember the last time you went to a movie theater, and you sat behind a mouthy young teenage girl who couldn't stop talking during the show, and, on the way out, explained to her friends and everyone within earshot just what was wrong with the movie, the actors, the director, the music and the popcorn? Well, here she is again, alive and well on the Net.

Web:
http://www.dreamagic.com/vivianrose/
   teencritic1.html

Teen Voice

When I was a kid, there was nothing I liked better than something made just for me. Well, this zine (small magazine) is made just for you. I bet you will like it. There are also links to Web sites made by teenagers so you can see what other people are doing.

Web:
http://www.teenvoice.com/

Teen Writers

As we all know, people who write are the most intelligent, good-looking, successful and adorable people in the world. This Web site is devoted to the creative output of teenage writers. You can submit things that you yourself have written, or you can read what other people have sent in. My advice is if you want to be a writer, stick with it no matter what. I can't guarantee that writing a lot will make you intelligent, good-looking, successful and adorable. All I can say is, it's always worked for me.

Web:
  http://www.teenwriters.com/

Teenagers

The nice thing about talking on the computer is that you don't have to worry about someone picking up the extension and listening to everything you say. Hop onto IRC and talk to teenagers around the world. They are waiting for you. (Don't forget to do your homework first.)

IRC:
  #teen
  #teen-cafe
  #teenchat
  #teenchatting
  #teencouch
  #teenlove
  #teens

Teens Helping Teens

When you need advice, you can ask your friends, but sometimes it's good to hear what other people have to say. These Web sites contain lots and lots of advice written by teenagers from around the world. The next time you are confused, see what other kids have to say. There are a lot of questions and answers, and you can check the archives to see if something there relates to you. If you want, you can submit a question of your own and maybe one of the teen volunteers will answer it.

Web:
  http://hbz.yahooligans.com/velma/
  http://www.teentalk.com/

Teen Chat Rooms

Boy, you guys are lucky. When I was a teenager, there wasn't even an Internet, let alone chat rooms. We had to go out in the street in order to talk (in three feet of snow).

Virtually React

For more fun than a barrel of teenage monkeys, check out this great Web site. It has an online version of React, a newspaper about teenagers. Read about teen-related news, sports features, entertainment topics, contests, jokes, and lots of other stuff designed to make teenagers say, "Oh wow, dude. That's so cool."

Web:
  http://www.react.com/

Young Adults Talk and General Discussion

Here are some lively places where teenagers can write about anything they want. The traffic is high, and there are a lot of diverse opinions as well as some thoughtful messages. This is a great place for you to meet other kids, and to let everyone else know what you think.

Usenet:
  alt.kids-talk
  alt.teens

Young Investors and Entrepreneurs

Every day you make decisions. Some are unimportant ("Which cereal should I eat?"), while others are very important ("What college should I go to?"). Learning how to make decisions well is an important part of life, and nowhere is it more important than when it comes to money. If you practice financial decision-making when you are young, it will help you a lot when you become old (that is, over 25). Here are some Web sites that will help you learn how to invest money or start your own business. In general, I encourage you to spend your youth having fun (while you are educating yourself). However, I do recommend that you spend some time learning about how money works, and how you can make it work for you.

Web:
  http://www.anincomeofherown.com/
  http://www.youngbiz.com/

ZINES

After Dinner

After Dinner features short stories of a particular genre: true, first-person reminiscences. The stories are personal, but not cloying. I find them engaging and insightful. It's so nice, just for a few minutes, to be carried away into someone else's world, especially when they do it well.

Web:
http://www.afterdinner.com/

American Folk

American Folk is where I found out about egg-in-a-frame: a breakfast treat in which an egg is cooked within a frame made by cutting a hole in a piece of toast. Celebrate the contemporary American culture—families, traditions, kitsch—by reading this down-home zine, guaranteed to give you a warm feeling inside. (And if that doesn't work, make yourself an egg-in-a-frame.)

Web:
http://www.americanfolk.com/

Bad Girl Zines

Zines by girls with attitude. Yep. Minx has features and articles on fashion, amusements and sex. Hellfire is "where bad girls go to play with fire!" Brazen Hussy has gossip, girls, guys, sex, gays and popular culture. Yep. Zines by girls with attitude.

Web:
http://www.brazenhussy.com/
http://www.hellfire.com/
http://www.minxmag.com/

Bad Subjects

Thinking for yourself is Bad. Thinking in ways that are not mainstream or that are radical is Bad. That's why Bad Subjects is so good. Check out the zine that promotes the questioning of old ways and tries to show how politics applies to everyday life.

Web:
http://english-www.hss.cmu.edu/bs/

Fray

Fray uses funky, weird HTML tricks and a so-hip design to showcase rants, articles and stories. When I visited, I saw stuff—and that is exactly the *mot juste*—related to work, drugs, hope and vices. Weep it and read.

Web:
http://www.fray.com/

Glassdog

Glassdog is a thought-provoking, well-designed literary zine with thought-provoking, well-written things to read. You'll enjoy the essays, as well as the section called Overheard: random snippets of conversation and opinions that were not meant to be public knowledge.

Web:
http://www.glassdog.com/

BAD SUBJECTS
Some people look at the world and ask,
"Why?"
Other people look at the world and ask,
"Why not?"
Bad Subjects looks at the world and asks,
"Why don't you figure it out for yourself?"

Mad Dog Weekly

Have you ever wanted to write your own screenplay? I live in California where everyone is a screenwriter (or has an option on a TV series). Well, before you can write a screenplay you need to pitch (try to sell) the concept. But where do you get the concept? Just sashay over to Mad Dog and use the Plot-o-Matic. Just type a few words, make some selections, and click on the button. Before you can say, "Is that all there is?" you'll have a brand new film concept, suitable for pitching. (And while you are there, read some of the articles. After all, this is a humor zine.)

Web:
  http://www.maddogproductions.com/

Popular Culture Zines

The best thing about popular culture is that it is so *accessible*. Just turn on your TV, pick up a newspaper, or listen to the radio, and there it is: popular culture. So if you can't get away from it, you might as well understand it. These popular culture zines are filled with commentary, reviews, rants and articles. Read about television, art, politics, technology, movies, books, fashion, music and celebrities. Boy—talk about culture.

Web:
  http://www.feedmag.com/
  http://www.getwild.com/
  http://www.hissyfit.com/
  http://www.smartypantsmag.com/
  http://www.spankmag.com/

Salon

There was a time, before television and radio, when cultured and intelligent people would gather at someone's house in order to talk. This was known as a "salon". At a salon, people would think for themselves (instead of repeating what they heard on the news and talk shows), and elegant and stimulating conversation was considered valuable. This Web site seeks to capture the spirit and philosophy of the salon days, when thinkers, writers and scholars would sit in comfortable chairs and discuss ideas. You are invited to visit.

Web:
  http://www.salon1999.com/

Word

This frantic and entertaining zine will keep you busy, busy, busy (and coming back for more). There is no particular theme, so indulge yourself by reading bittersweet articles, essays and features, all presented with more pizzazz and style than 99.44% of the other Web sites in your life.

Web:
  http://www.word.com/

Zine Lists

Making your own zine is the rage. In zine-land, nothing is sacred. Zines cover topics as mainstream as education, politics and philosophy, and as bizarre as hyperactive armadillos and free verse about plastic lawn ornaments.

Web:
  http://www.meer.net/~johnl/e-zine-list/

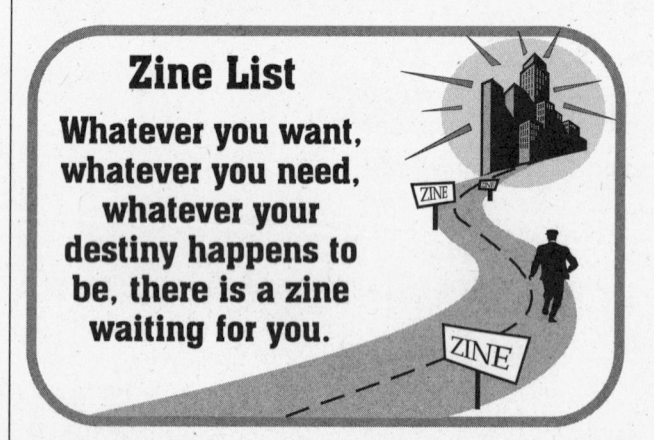

> **Zine List**
> Whatever you want, whatever you need, whatever your destiny happens to be, there is a zine waiting for you.

Zine Talk and General Discussion

I read a lot of different zines, and one thing I can tell you: people who make zines like to talk to other people who make zines. So, if you are the zine-type, there are plenty of people waiting to talk to you on Usenet. Find out what's good, what's bad, and what's cooking in the zine community.

Usenet:
  alt.binaries.zines
  alt.ezines
  alt.zines
  rec.mag.fsfnet

ZOOLOGY

Arachnology

Arachnology is the study of arthropods belonging to the class Arachnida. Arachnids include spiders, scorpions, mites and ticks. Most arachnids are carnivorous. All arachnids have a body divided into two parts, a cephalothorax and an abdomen. Arachnids have four pairs of segmented legs. (Compare to insects which have a separate head, thorax and body, and three pairs of legs.) There is lots of serious arachnological information on the Net, and these resources are a good place to start. If you want to talk to other arachnologists, you can join the mailing lists. My cat, The Little Nipper, is an amateur arachnologist, although he has a more utilitarian attitude toward spiders and other arachnids: he eats them.

Web:
  http://members.aol.com/jccoke/society.html
  http://www.ufsia.ac.be/Arachnology/Arachnology.html

Majordomo Mailing List:
  List Name: **arachnid**
  Subscribe to: **majordomo@lists.realtime.net**

Majordomo Mailing List:
  List Name: **arachnology**
  Subscribe to: **majordomo@chemie.de**

> Personally, I don't need to study ethology–the science of animal behavior–because my cat teaches me everything I need to know. However, if you aren't blessed with such an intelligent pet (my cat **is** the smartest cat in the whole world), you can always subscribe to the **ethology** mailing list and discuss animal behavior with other people.

Entomology

Entomology is the study of insects. There are more than 600,000 known insect species, representing about ninety percent of all recognized species on the planet, so if you are an entomologist, there is no shortage of material to study. These Web sites offers a huge collection of entomological resources on the Net. For discussion about bugs and buggy topics, check out Usenet or the mailing lists.

Web:
  http://www.ent.iastate.edu/List/
  http://www.isis.vt.edu/~fanjun/text/Links.html

Usenet:
  sci.bio.entomology.homoptera
  sci.bio.entomology.lepidoptera
  sci.bio.entomology.misc

Listproc Mailing List:
  List Name: **bugnet**
  Subscribe to: **listproc@listproc.wsu.edu**

Listserv Mailing List:
  List Name: **entomo-l**
  Subscribe to: **listserv@listserv.uoguelph.ca**

Ethology Talk and General Discussion

Ethology is the study of animal behavior. A simplistic view of animals would say that a particular type of behavior is either instinctual or learned. However, modern thought holds that much of what we observe cannot be explained so simply. We have come to realize that much depends on an interaction between an animal's genetic inheritance and its environment when it is young. I find the ethology discussions on the Net fascinating, and even if you are not a biologist, you may enjoy reading what people have to say.

Web:
  http://cricket.unl.edu/internet.html
  http://www.scicentral.com/B-etholo.html

Usenet:
  sci.bio.ethology

Listserv Mailing List:
  List Name: **ethology**
  Subscribe to: **listserv@segate.sunet.se**

870 ZOOLOGY

Herpetology

Herpetology is the branch of zoology that deals with reptiles and amphibians. These Web sites offers pictures of frogs, lizards, snakes, and other such critters. You can also find information about herpetoculture (breeding your own reptiles), and a taxonomy list showing orders/genus/species. The Usenet group is for discussing the scientific study of reptiles and amphibians. (If you like to keep these cool animals as pets, try **rec.pets.herp**.)

Web:
  http://gto.ncsa.uiuc.edu/pingleto/herp.html
  http://www.embl-heidelberg.de/~uetz/
    LivingReptiles.html
  http://www.herpetology.com/
  http://www.xmission.com/~gastown/herpmed/

Usenet:
  sci.bio.herp

Icthyology

There are close to 21,000 different species of fish in the world. Fish have adapted to an underwater environment. They breathe oxygen dissolved in water with the use of gills, and have maintained the same general physical characteristics throughout their history. Biologists divide fish into three classes: the most primitive jawless fish are called Agnatha; fish with cartilage and no true bones, such as sharks and rays, are called Chondrichthyes; bony fish, the ones with which most people are familiar, are called Osteichthyes. Generally speaking, the study of fish can be divided into two basic disciplines. Ichthyology is the scientific study of fish: their physiology, habitat, history and characteristics. If you are an ichthyologist, check out these Web sites. You will find a wide variety of resources to help with your research. (Hint: If you are using Netscape, press Ctrl-Alt-F for a nice surprise.) The second basic discipline is social ichthyology, the study of people with fish-like faces. If you are a social ichthyologist, you are more or less on your own, but I can send you a picture of my old high school chemistry teacher.

Web:
  http://www.biology.ualberta.ca/jackson.hp/iwr/
    iwr.html
  http://www.wh.whoi.edu/homepage/faq.html

Malacology

Malacology is the study of mollusks: the second largest invertebrate phylum, which includes clams, oysters, scallops, bivalves, gastropods (such as snails), squid and octopus. Some mollusks are so small as to be almost invisible to the human eye. Other mollusks are large. A giant squid has been found that measured 70 feet (21.3 meters) long. Most mollusks live in water or at shoreline in the tidal zone. They live inside shells and have soft bodies, as well as a "foot" that allows them to move around. (Some mollusks, such as the octopus, have a shell that is enclosed by their body.)

Web:
  http://home.wxs.nl/~spirula/crossref.htm
  http://www.club.innet.be/~year0078/
  http://www.york.biosis.org/zrdocs/zoolinfo/
    grp_moll.htm

Listproc Mailing List:
  List Name: **mollusca**
  Subscribe to: **listproc@ucmp1.berkeley.edu**

Listserv Mailing List:
  List Name: **conch-l**
  Subscribe to: **listserv@uga.cc.uga.edu**

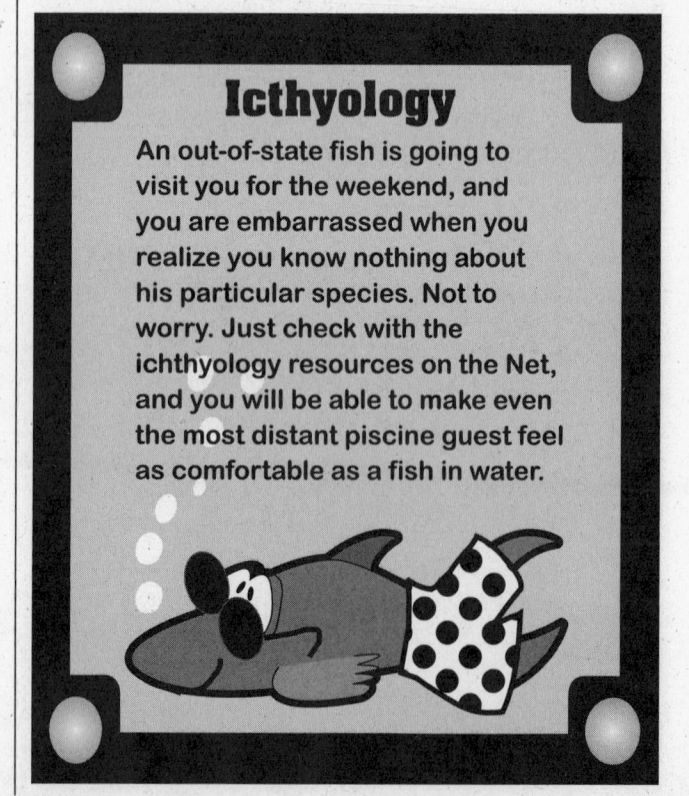

Icthyology

An out-of-state fish is going to visit you for the weekend, and you are embarrassed when you realize you know nothing about his particular species. Not to worry. Just check with the ichthyology resources on the Net, and you will be able to make even the most distant piscine guest feel as comfortable as a fish in water.

ZOOLOGY

Be bizarre. See "Bizarre".

Mammals

Some of my favorite animals (and people) are mammals, so these two Web sites are among my zoological favorites. You can find lots of information about all types of mammals, as well as a taxonomy guide to help you keep everything straight. (My philosophy is: "A name for every mammal, and a mammal for every name.")

Web:
http://nmnhwww.si.edu/msw/
http://www.selu.com/~bio/wildlife/links/animals/mammals.html

Marine Life

When you need to find out how Ctenophora differ from Platyhelminthes, it's comforting to know that the Net will not let you down. If you have a question about a marine animal, there is a good chance that the answer is at one of these Web sites. The Usenet groups are for discussing dolphins, whales and deep-sea biology.

Web:
http://ourworld.compuserve.com/homepages/jaap/
http://whale.wheelock.edu/whalenet-stuff/interwhale.html
http://www.mbl.edu/html/MRC/specimens.html

Usenet:
alt.animals.dolphins
alt.animals.whales
bionet.biology.deepsea

Have fun.

Look What I Found on the Net...

```
Newsgroup: alt.animals.dolphins
Subject: Talking to dolphins

> One thing that amazes me about intelligent, aquatic animals:
>
> We all dream and pretend we could communicate and try to
> understand an alien from another planet.
>
> Yet, we have not yet learned to speak the language of the
> dolphins or whales, and they live here with us.

True.

We need to make contact with the intelligent life on this planet first.
There are people who are trying to decipher the dolphin language.

My friend has a Web page stating that the Navy already has, but, due to
national security reasons, they are not sharing their findings.
```

Nematology

The phylum Nematoda comprises the roundworms, small organisms that live in water or soil. Some of the nematodes, such as pinworms or hookworms, can cause illness in people, although most nematodes feed on bacteria, fungi and other organisms found in the soil. There are nearly 20,000 known species of nematodes, and they are among the most numerous multi-cellular animals in the world. If you were to look at a nematode under a microscope, you would see an outer body wall, an inner digestive tube and a fluid-filled cavity between the two. Thus, some people describe a nematode as being a tube within a tube. Think about this: the next time you pick up a handful of soil, you are probably holding more nematodes in your hand than the total number of people you have met in your whole life. Now throw away all the soil except a gram or so. Put it in your palm and look at it. That gram of soil contains more organisms, of one type or another, than the number of human beings on Earth.

Web:

http://ianrwww.unl.edu/ianr/plntpath/nematode/wormhome.htm
http://www.nrel.colostate.edu:8080/~bobn/rkn.2a.NEMA.html

Listserv Mailing List:

List Name: **nema-l**
Subscribe to: **listserv@unl.edu**

Ornithology

Have you ever stopped to consider how versatile birds really are? You can study them, you can watch them, you can feed them, you can keep them as pets, and if the need arises, you can even eat them. Avian cuisine, however, is the last refuge of the ignorant. It's much more rewarding to study and learn about birds, and if you are an ornithologist, there are some wonderful sources of information on the Net.

Web:

http://www.aves.net/the-owl/
http://www.nmnh.si.edu/BIRDNET/

Primates

When you are getting down to some serious monkey business, here's the place to start. These sites have information dedicated to primate biology, including discussions, a directory of primatology, newsletters, behavioral patterns, animal welfare legislation, and other items of interest.

Web:

http://www.primate.wisc.edu/pin/
http://www.selu.com/~bio/PrimateGallery/main.html

Need information about chimpanzees? Don't monkey around. Use the primate Web sites.

Strange Animals

This Web site discusses the mistakes scientists have made in relation to animal life. Read about sea monsters, dragons and dinosaurs, as well as forgeries and frauds perpetrated by scientists. There are also some fascinating drawings, made by scientists, that show various types of monsters.

Web:

http://www.turnpike.net/~mscott/

Zoological Resources

Slippery, slimy, creepy, crawly, furry or scaly, this site probably has it covered. Here are some nice collection of resources such as Web sites, databases, museums, Web servers and image galleries related to zoology.

Web:

http://www.susx.ac.uk/library/pier/subjects.dir/sci.dir/zoology.html
http://www.york.biosis.org/zrdocs/zoolinfo/zoolinfo.htm

Notes

Notes

Notes

Notes

Index

&Type, 284
2600, 703
30 Plus, 750
3D Chatting, 758

A

A Cappella, 543
Abductions, 787
Abortion, 823
Abuse a Celebrity, 298
Accessibility, 177
ACLU, 293
Acne and Eczema, 351
Acronyms, 661
Acting Talk and General Discussion, 184
ActiveX, 814
Activism, 629
Activism Resources, 293
Acupuncture, 502
Ad Blocking Software, 405
Ada, 640
Ada Project, 824
Adams, Scott, 597
Addictions, 351
Adler, Alfred, 647
Adoptees and Genealogy, 319
Adoption, 249, 750
ADSL, 126
Adult Education, 202
Adult Site of the Day, 854
Advanced Dungeons and Dragons, 681
Advertising Gallery, 145
ADVICE, 1
Advice Chat, 1
Aeneid, 470
Aerobatic Aviation, 48
Aerobics, 245

Aeronautics and Space Acronyms, 726
Aeronet, 48
Aerospace Engineering, 233
Aesop's Fables, 272
Aesthetic Architecture, 28
Aesthetics, 610
Africa, 829
Africa Discussion Groups, 844
African-American Literature, 454
African Art, 34
African Governments, 337
After Dinner, 867
Agnosticism, 666
Agricultural News, 3
AGRICULTURE, 3
Agriculture Jobs, 3
Agriculture Links, 3
Agriculture Network Information Center, 4
Agriculture Talk and General Discussion, 4
Agripedia, 4
Agroforestry, 76
AIDS Caregivers, 750
AIDS, 351, 493
Aikido, 731
Air Disasters, 48
Air Pollution, 239
Air Sickness Bag Museum, 62
Air Travel, 776
Airline Travel, 49
Airplane Mailing Lists, 49
Aisle Say, 184
Al-Anon and Alateen, 750
Alcatraz, 156
Alertnet, 224
Algae (Phycology), 54
Algebra Assistance, 486
Algy's Herb Page, 359

Alice's Adventures in Wonderland, 471
Alien Autopsies, 787
Alien Lexicons, 787
Alien Pyramids, 787
Alien Races, 744
Alien Research, 787
All About Electronics, 221
Allen, Woody, 651
Allergies, 493
Alphonse Mucha Museum, 39
Alternative Architecture, 29
Alternative Comics, 109
Alternative Dictionaries, 662
Alternative Energy, 229
Alternative Medicine Resources, 502
Alternative Medicine Talk and General Discussion, 502
Alternative Photographic Processes, 614
AltSex, 854
Amateur Radio Talk and General Discussion, 656
American Civil War, 368
American Colleges and Universities, 206
American First Ladies, 368
American Folk, 867
American Historical Documents, 362
American Library Association, 451
American Literature, 454
American Mathematical Society, 486
American Memory Collection, 369
American Psychological Association Journals, 647
American Sign Language, 437
American Singles, 606
American Stock Exchange, 519
American Studies, 369
Americans with Disabilities Act, 178

Amnesty International, 293
Amos, Tori, 556
Amputees, 178
Amtrak Trains, 776
Anagrams, 298
Analytical Chemistry, 96
Anarchist Calendar, 8
Anarchist Feminism, 8
Anarchist Resources, 8
Anarchist Theory FAQ, 8
ANARCHY, 8
Anarchy History, 9
Anarchy Sampler, 9
Anarchy Talk and General Discussion, 9
Anarchy Yellow Pages, 9
Anatomy, 493
Ancient Astronauts, 787
Ancient Greek Literature, 467
Ancient Theater, 185
Ancient World Cultures, 369
Androgyny Information, 712
Andy Griffith, 766
Anesthesiology, 494
Anglican and Episcopalian Churches, 667
Anglo-Saxon Tales, 467
Anglo-Saxons, 369
Animal Cams, 171
Animal Information Database, 12
Animal Rescue and Adoption, 13
Animal Rights, 13
Animal Sounds, 723
Animal Talk and General Discussion, 13
ANIMALS AND PETS, 12
Animated Gifs, 806
Animations and Images, 744
Anime and Manga, 109
Ann Landers and Dear Abby, 1
Annals of Improbable Research, 692
Anne of Green Gables, 472
Annual Reports, 519
Anonymous Remailers, 635
Ansible Newsletter, 696
Answers to All of Your Questions, 145

Ant Farm, 171
Antarctica, 776
Antarctica Live, 171
Anthropology, 392
Anti-Canada Web Site, 83
Anti-Drug Stuff, 189
Antique Cars, 88
Antique Motorcycles, 527
Antiques, 101
Anti-Telemarketing, 636
Anti-Virus Programs, 636
Anti-War-on-Drugs, 189
Anxiety, 750
Apartments, 386
Aphrodisiac Guide, 709
Apple, 114
April Fools, 515
Aquarian Age, 566
Aquariums, 14
Arabian Nights, 472
Arabic, 437
Arabic News, 571
Arachnology, 869
Archaeological Fieldwork, 23
Archaeological Societies, 24
ARCHAEOLOGY, 23
Archaeology Events, 24
Archaeology Magazine, 24
Archaeology News, 24
Archaeology Resources, 24
Archaeology Talk and General Discussion, 24
Archery, 732
Architectural Engineering, 234
Architectural Reconstructions, 30
Architectural Styles, 30
ARCHITECTURE, 28
Architecture Competitions, 30
Architecture Talk and General Discussion, 30
Archnet, 25
Area 51, 788
Armed Forces of the World, 509
Aromatherapy, 359
ART, 34
Art Conservation, 34
Art Crimes, 39

Art Criticism Forum, 34
Art Dictionary, 34
ART GALLERIES AND EXHIBITS, 39
Art Gallery Talk and General Discussion, 39
Art History, 35
Art News, 35
Art Nouveau, 35
Art Resources, 35
Art Talk and General Discussion, 35
Arthritis, 352
Artificial Intelligence, 403
Artificial Life, 403
As a Man Thinketh, 472
Ascii Art, 36, 622
Asia, 829
Asia Online, 519
Asia Pacific Discussion Groups, 845
Asia Pacific Governments, 338
Asian Art Gallery, 39
Asimov, Isaac, 598
Ask-a-Geologist, 332
Ask an Expert, 212
Ask Dr. Math, 212
Ask Jeeves for Kids, 431
Ask the Builder, 387
Ask the Dietitian, 174
Ask Tina, 1
AskERIC, 217
Astrology Charts, 577
Astrology Resources, 577
Astrology Talk and General Discussion, 577
ASTRONOMY, 43
Astronomy and Astrophysics Research, 43
Astronomy Cafe, 43
Astronomy History, 43
Astronomy Hypertextbook, 43
Astronomy Picture of the Day, 431
Astronomy Software, 44
Astronomy Talk and General Discussion, 44
Astrophysics Data System, 44
Atheism, 667
Athenian Architecture, 30
Atlantis, 273
Atlas of Hematology, 494

*Main subject headings are shown in **bold***

Atmosphere Pollution Prevention, 239
Atmospheric Chemistry, 96
Attention Deficit Disorder, 178
Auctions, 715
Auctions Online, 716
Audio Engineering, 234
Audio Talk and General Discussion, 377
Audionet, 80
Aunt Edna's Kitchen, 135
Austen, Jane, 459
Australia, 776, 829
Australia and Oceania Discussion Groups, 845
Australian Government, 338
Australian Literature, 455
Australian News, 571
Author Talk and General Discussion, 459
Author's Pen, 460
Autism, 179
Auto Channel, 89
Auto Discussion Archives and FAQ, 89
Auto-Eroticism, 854
Auto Racing, 89
Autograph Collecting, 101
Automobile Lemons, 128
Automobile Listings, 89
Avenger's Page, 515
AVIATION, 48
Aviation Enthusiast Corner, 49
Aviation Events, 49
Aviation Magazines, 50
Aviation Poetry, 50
Aviation Q & A, 50
Aviation Safety, 50
Aviation Talk and General Discussion, 51
Aviation Technology, 51
Aware Net, 566
Ayurvedic Medicine, 503

B

Babies, 249
Babylon 5, 697

Back Stage, 185
Backcountry Recipes, 136
Backgammon, 301
Backlash, 505
Backward Masking, 703
Backyard Ballistics, 516
Bad Astronomy, 44
Bad Girl Zines, 867
Bad Science, 692
Bad Subjects, 867
Bad Website Design, 806
Bad Writing Contest, 848
Badminton, 732
Bagpipes, 543
Baha'i Faith, 674
Ballet, 166
Balloon Art, 149
Ballooning, 582
Ballroom Dancing, 166
Bands, 543
Bandwidth Bandits, 806
Banjo, 543
Banned Books, 293
Banners, Buttons and Text, 806
Barbecue, 136
Barbershop Quartets, 544
Baroque Art, 39
Basal Metabolism Calculator, 174
Baseball, 732
Baseball Teams, 733
Basic Design in Art and Architecture, 36
Basket Weaving, 149
Basketball, 733
Basketball Team Talk and General Discussion, 734
Basketball: Women, 734
Batman, 110
Battleship, 301
Bauhaus, 31
Baum, L. Frank, 460
BBC News, 571
Beading and Jewelry, 149
Beanie Babies, 102
Beanie Baby Contests, 132
Beastie Boys, 557
Beat Generation, 455

Beatles, 557
Beauty Shoppe Archive, 261
Bee-Eye, 431
Beekeeping, 4
Beer, 285
Beer Ratings, 285
Beer Trek, 745
Beginner's Guide to HTML, 806
Beige Book, 196
Belly Dancing, 166
Best of Usenet, 396
Best Sites for Children, 431
Better Business Bureau, 128
Beverages, 285
Beverly Hills 90210, 766
Bible Study, 667
Bibles Online, 668
Biblical Archaeology, 25
Biblical Timeline, 668
Bibliomania, 72
Bicycle Commuting, 415
Bicycling, 734
Bierce, Ambrose, 461
Big Band, 544
Big Book of Mischief, 516
Bigfoot, 273
Biker Buddy, 146
Biker Women, 527
Bill Gates Wealth Clock, 146
Billionaires, 591
Bingo, 796
Bingo Zone, 301
Biochemistry, 96
Bioethics, 54
Biographies, 662
Bioinformatics, 55
BIOLOGY, 54
Biology Dictionary, 55
Biology Funding and Grants, 55
Biology Job Opportunities, 56
Biology Journals, 56
Biology-Related Sciences, 57
Biology Resources, 56
Biology Software, 56
Biology Talk and General Discussion, 56
Biomass, 229

*Main subject headings are shown in **bold***

Biomedical Engineering, 235, 494
Biorhythms, 566
Biosphere, 239
Biotechnology, 57
Bird-Keeping, 14
Bird Sounds, 724
Bird-Watching, 15
Birth Control, 352
Birth Defects, 179
Birthday Calendar, 382
Bisexuality, 315
Bisexuals, 606
BIZARRE, 62
Bizarre Stuff to Make, 62
Bizarre Talk and General Discussion, 62
Black and White Photography, 614
Blackjack, 301
Blacklist of Internet Advertisers, 128
Blackout Box, 396
Blake, William, 625
Blind and Visually Impaired Computer Usage, 179
Blind Dates, 607
Blindness, 180
Blues, 544
Board Games, 302
Boat Racing, 67
Boatbuilding, 67
BOATING AND SAILING, 67
Boating Mnemonics, 67
Boating Quiz, 67
Boating Rules, 68
Boating Safety, 68
Boating Talk and General Discussion, 68
Boating Today, 68
Body Art, 36
Bondage, 854
Bonds, 519
Bonsai, 310
Book Authors, 72
Book Browser, 72
Book Collecting, 102
Book Radio, 81
Book Recommendations, 72
Book Resources, 73

Book Reviews, 73
Book Talk and General Discussion, 73
Bookbinding, 72
BOOKS, 72
BookWeb, 73
Bookweb Contest, 132
BookWire, 73
Boomerangs, 583
Boston Science Museum, 540
Botanical Gardens, 76
Botanical Glossary, 76
BOTANY, 76
Botany Images, 76
Botany Talk and General Discussion, 76
Botany Web Sites, 76
Bottle Collecting, 103
Box Office, 530
Boxing, 735
Bra FAQs, 261
Brady Bunch, 767
Brain Tumors, 494
Brazil, 829
Bread, 136
Break Dancing, 166
Breast Cancer, 494
Breastfeeding, 249
Bridal Fashion Regrets, 262
Bridge, 302
Brite, Poppy Z., 598
British-American Lexicons, 437
British Authors, 468
British Cars, 89
British Intelligence Organizations, 338
British Poetry Archive, 626
British Royal Family, 598
BROADCASTING ON THE NET, 80
Brontë Sisters, 461
Brother Jed, 674
Browning, Elizabeth Barrett, 626
Browser Watch, 814
Bubbles, 298
Buddhism, 669
Budget of the United States Government, 345
Budget Travel, 776

Bugs and Fixes, 123
Bureau of Economic Analysis, 196
Bush, 557
Business and Finance Magazines, 481
Business and Toll-Free Directory Listings, 762
Business Fashion, 262
Business Headlines, 520
Business Information Resources, 520
Business Plans, 520
Buying and Selling Books, 74
Buying and Selling Houses, 387
Buying and Selling Macs, 116
Buying and Selling Music, 544
Buying and Selling PCs, 119
Buying and Selling Role-Playing Games, 681
Buying and Selling Software on the Internet, 718
Buying/Selling Talk and General Discussion, 716

C

C++ and C, 640
Cabinet of Dr. Casey, 697
Cable Modems, 126
CAD (Computer Aided Design), 235
Caffeine, 189, 796
Cajun Culture, 830
Calculators, 662
Calculus, 486
Calendars, 662
Call of the Wild, 472
Callahan's Bar, 591
Calligraphy, 150
Cameras on the Net, 171
Camping, 583
Campus Radio Disc Jockeys, 656
CANADA, 83
Canada's Schoolnet, 202
Canadian Broadcasting Corporation, 656
Canadian Constitution Act, 362
Canadian Constitutional Documents, 83
Canadian Culture, 83

*Main subject headings are shown in **bold***

INDEX

Canadian Fact Sheets, 83
Canadian Genealogy Resources, 319
Canadian Government, 83
Canadian History, 84
Canadian Investment, 84
Canadian Legal Resources, 85
Canadian Music, 85
Canadian News, 85
Canadian Resources, 85
Canadian Sports, 86
Canadian Talk and General Discussion, 86
Canadian Travel, 86
Cancer and Oncology, 495
Candy Recipes, 136
Cannabis and Medicine, 503
Canterbury Tales, 472
Canuck Site of the Day, 87
Captain Kirk Sing-a-Long Page, 745
Car and Truck Purchasing, 90
Car Audio, 90
Car Classifieds, 90
Car Place, 90
Car Talk and General Discussion, 91
Cardiff's Mud Page, 535
Caribbean, 777
Carlos Museum of Art, 39
Carnivorous Plants, 77
Carroll, Lewis, 461
CARS AND TRUCKS, 88
Cars, Trucks and Motorcycle Magazines, 481
Cartoon Pictures, 623
Cartoons, 767
Cascading Style Sheets, 807
Casting Calls, 185
Castles, 777
Cataloging Talk and General Discussion, 451
Catalogs by Mail, 717
Cathedrals, 31
Catholic Gays, 315
Catholicism, 669
Cats, 15
CBC (Canadian Broadcasting Corporation), 87
CD Clubs, 717

Celebrity Addresses, 598
Celebrity Classmates, 132
Celebrity Interviews, 81
Celebrity Resources, 599
Celebrity Romantic Links, 599
Celebrity Talk and General Discussion, 600
Cell Biology, 58
Cell-Relay Communications, 762
Cellular Phone Hacking, 704
Celtic Music, 545
Censorship of the Internet, 294
Censorship Talk and General Discussion, 294
Censorware, 294
Census Information, 345
Center for Earth and Planetary Studies, 726
Center for Particle Astrophysics, 619
Center of Statistical Resources, 663
Centers for Disease Control, 352
Central America, 830
Central Asia Discussion Groups, 845
Central Banks of the World, 196
Ceramic Arts, 37
Cereal, 286
CGI Scripts, 807
Chabad-Lubavitch Judaism, 675
Chakras, 566
Challenger, 726
Chance Server, 486
Chaos Magick, 577
Characters and Fictional People, 591
Charities, 591
Charms and Amulets, 273
Chat Room Lists, 758
Chat Servers, 758
Chatting in 3-D, 592
Chatting in the Big City, 686
Chatting Safety, 758
Cheese, 286
Chemical Acronyms, 97
Chemical and Biological Warfare, 509
Chemical Engineering, 235
Chemicals in the Environment, 240
CHEMISTRY, 96
Chemistry Journals, 97

Chemistry Learning Materials, 97
Chemistry Resources, 98
Chemistry Talk and General Discussion, 98
Chemistry Visualization and Animation, 98
Chess, 303
Child Activism, 249
Child Discipline, 250
Child Safety, 250
Child Safety on the Internet, 251
Child Support, 251
Children, 251
Children with Special Needs, 252
Children's Books, 74
Children's Health, 352
Children's Magazines, 481
Children's Mental Health, 353
Children's Writing, 848
Chile, 831
China, 831
Chinese, 437
Chinese Herbs, 359
Chinese Literature, 468
Chinese Medicine, 503
Chinese News, 571
Chinese Philosophy, 611
Chinese Poetry, 626
Chiropractic, 503
Chit-Chat, 607
Chocolate, 796
Chomsky, Noam, 10
Christian Resources, 669
Christian Youth, 863
Christianity Talk and General Discussion, 670
Christmas, 382
Christmas Sounds, 724
Chronic Fatigue Syndrome, 495
Chronology of Mathematicians, 487
CIA, 346
CIA World Factbook, 327
Cigar Smoking, 796
Cigarette Smoking, 797
Ciphers, 162
Citizen Band Radio, 657
City Net Travel Channel, 777

Main subject headings are shown in **bold**

Civil Disobedience, 472
Civil Engineering, 235
Classic and Sports Cars, 91
Classic Comic Strips, 110
Classic Top 40 Radio Sounds, 657
Classical Cryptology Bibliography, 162
Classical Music, 545
Classical Studies, 369
Classics, 456
Classics and Mediterranean Archaeology, 25
Classified Ads, 717
Classroom Discipline, 217
Clay Art, 150
Cleft Palate and Cleft Lip, 180
Cliché Finder, 437
Climate Data Catalog, 803
Climate Diagnostics Center, 803
Climate Monitoring, 803
Climbing, 583
Clinton-Lewinsky Scandal, 629
Clip Art, 624
Clocks and Watches, 103
Clogs, 262
Cloning, 403
Clothing for Big Folks, 263
CNN Interactive, 572
CNN Style, 263
Coal, 229
Coastal Management, 240
Coca-Cola, 286
Cocaine, 190
Cocktails, 286
Coffee, 286
Coins and Money, 104
Cold Region Engineering, 236
COLLECTING, 101
Collecting Talk and General Discussion, 104
Collective Poem, 626
Collector's Magazines, 481
Collectors' Marketplace, 104
College Admissions, 207
College and University Teaching Assistants, 217
College Food, 287
College Libraries, 451

College Sports, 735
College Student Guides and Manuals, 207
College Talk and General Discussion, 208
Color Chart, 807
Comedy Central, 767
Comedy Talk and General Discussion, 396
Comic Chat, 758
Comic Conventions, 110
Comic Reviews, 110
Comicon, 110
COMICS, 109
Comics Databases, 111
Comics Fan Fiction, 111
Comics Marketplace, 111
Comics on the Net, 111
Comics Talk and General Discussion, 111
Coming Attractions, 531
Coming Out, 315
Commerce Business Daily, 520
Commerce Department, 346
Commercial Radio Stations, 81
Commercials, 767
Committee to Protect Journalists, 421
Communications, 392
Communist Manifesto, 473
Community Colleges, 208
Compaq, 114
Comparisons, 717
Competitive Dance Sport, 166
Complaint Letter Generator, 141, 396
Complementary Medicine, 503
Computation and Language E-Print Archive, 437
Computational Chemistry, 98
Computational Economics, 197
Computational Fluid Dynamics, 619
Computer Almanac, 123
Computer Books Online, 123
Computer Companies, 114
Computer Company Talk and General Discussion, 114
Computer Folklore, 273
Computer Magazines, 481

Computer News, 123
Computer News Broadcasts, 81
Computer Product Reviews, 123
Computer Security, 636
Computer Speech, 404
Computer Viruses, 637
Computers and the Law, 446
COMPUTERS: COMPANIES, 114
Computers for the Handicapped, 180
COMPUTERS: MACINTOSH, 116
COMPUTERS: PCs, 119
COMPUTERS: REFERENCE, 123
Computing Dictionary, 123
Computing Magazines and Journals, 124
Con Artists, 156
Concert Information, 545
Congress, 346
Connecticut Yankee in King Arthur's Court, 473
CONNECTING TO THE INTERNET, 126
Conrad, Joseph, 461
Consciousness, 647
Conservation OnLine, 451
Conservative Political News, 630
Conspiracies, 411
Conspiracy Talk and General Discussion, 411
Constellations, 44
Constitution of the United States of America, 362
Consumer Credit Cards, 524
Consumer Fraud, 128
CONSUMER INFORMATION, 128
Consumer Information Catalog, 129
Consumer Law, 129
Consumer Line, 129
Consumer News, 129
Consumer Price Index, 197
Consumer Product Safety Commission, 129
Consumer Repair Documents, 221
Consumer Talk and General Discussion, 130
Consumer World, 130
ConsumerNet, 131

*Main subject headings are shown in **bold***

INDEX

Contact Lab, 788
Contemporary Art Mailing List, 37
Contemporary Conspiracies, 412
Contemporary Military Conflicts, 509
Contest Talk and General
 Discussion, 132
CONTESTS, 132
Contests for Kids, 431
Contortionism, 62
Contra Dancing, 167
Contract Labor, 415
Conventions and Memorabilia, 745
Conversations with Computers, 404
Cookie Recipes, 136
Cookies (on the Web), 637
COOKING AND RECIPES, 135
Cooking Talk and General
 Discussion, 137
COOL AND USEFUL, 141
COOL BUT USELESS, 145
Cool but Useless Talk and General
 Discussion, 146
Cool Science, 863
Cool Tool of the Day, 719
Coptic, 675
Copy Editing, 849
Copyrights, 446
Coral Reefs, 240
Corrections Professionals, 157
Corsets, 263
Costumes of the Early Twentieth
 Century, 185
Council of Trent, 362
Counselor-O-Matic, 209
Country Line Dancing, 167
Country Music, 545
Country Studies Area
 Handbooks, 831
Couples, 686
Coupons, 717
Craft Fairs, 151
Craft Marketplace, 151
Craft Resources, 151
Craft Talk and General
 Discussion, 151
CRAFTS, 149
Create a Barcode, 146

Creating Alternative Usenet
 Discussion Groups, 792
Creating an Internet Site with
 Windows NT, 821
Creating Mainstream Usenet
 Discussion Groups, 792
Credit, 131
Crew Database, 69
Cribbage, 303
Cricket, 735
CRIME, 156
Crime Scene Evidence File, 63
Crime Statistics, 157
Crime Talk and General
 Discussion, 157
Crohn's Disease and Colitis, 495
Crop Circles, 789
Cross-Dressing, 854
Cross-Stitch, 151
Crossword Puzzles, 303
Cruel Site of the Day, 397
Cryptographic Research, 162
CRYPTOGRAPHY, 162
Cryptography Archive, 162
Cryptography FAQs, 163
Cryptography Policy Issues, 163
Cryptography Resources, 163
Cryptography Software, 163
Cryptography Talk and General
 Discussion, 163
Cryptography Technical Papers, 163
Cryptozoology, 273
Crystals, 566
C-SPAN Live, 347
Culinary Herbs, 359
Cult Movies Talk and General
 Discussion, 531
Cult of the Dead Cow, 592
Cultural Site Etiquette, 25
Culture Finder, 267
Culture Jamming, 516
Cupid's Network, 607
Currency Converter, 524
Current Events Talk and General
 Discussion, 572
Curriculum Materials and Ideas, 202
Customized Cars, 91
Cyberdiet, 174

Cyberkids Magazine, 432
Cyberpunk, 697
Cyberqueer Lounge, 315
Cyberteens, 863
Cyndi's Genealogy Resources, 320
Cyrillic Alphabet, 438
Cystic Fibrosis, 495
Czech, 438
Czech Republic, 831

D

Dads, 252
Daguerreotypes, 614
Daily Comics, 112
Daily Diversions, 141
Daily Fix, 142
Daily Quotations, 651
Daily Tips, 142
Dairy Science, 5
DANCE, 166
Dance News, 167
Dance Resources, 167
Dance Talk and General
 Discussion, 167
Dangerfield, Rodney, 133, 601, 651
Dangerous Travel, 777
Dante, 461
Dark Side of the Net, 63
Dark Sky Stargazing, 45
Darkecho's Horror Web, 698
Darkroom Photography, 614
Data Communications Servers, 762
Date, Kyoko, 601
Dating Pattern Analyzer, 607
Dating Tests, 607
Daytime Talk Shows, 767
Dead People Server, 592
Deaf-Blind Discussion List, 180
Deafness, 180
Death Clock, 63
Death Row, 158
Declaration of Arms, 1775, 362
Declaration of Sentiments, 363
Decorating a Country Home, 387
Decorative Painting, 152
Defense Sciences Engineering, 236

*Main subject headings are shown in **bold***

Dell, 114
Democrats, 630
Dentistry, 495
Department of Energy, 230
Depression, 353, 752
Dermatology, 496
Desktop Themes, 817
Developmental Biology, 58
DEVICES AND GIZMOS CONNECTED TO THE NET, 171
Dewey Decimal System, 452
Diabetes, 353
Diabetic Recipes, 137
Diaper Fetish, 855
Diaries and Journals, 299
Dick Van Dyke Show, 768
Dickens, Charles, 462
Dickinson, Emily, 626
Dictionaries, 663
Dictionary of Metaphysical Healthcare, 503
Diet Analysis, 174
DIET AND NUTRITION, 174
Dieting FAQ, 175
Dieting Talk and General Discussion, 175
Digital Audio Broadcasting, 657
Digital Cameras, 614
Digital Photography, 39
Digital Signatures and Certificates, 164
Digits Project, 783
DikuMud Talk and General Discussion, 536
Dilbert Zone, 112
Dinosaurs, 692
Dinosaurs for Kids, 432
Dion, Celine, 557
Directors Guild of America, 531
DISABILITIES, 177
Disability Benefits, 180
Disability Information, 182
Disarmament Talk and General Discussion, 509
Disaster Handbook, 224
Disaster Situation and Status Reports, 224

Disaster Talk and General Discussion, 225
Disco, 546
Discographies, 546
Discord and Destruction, 63
Discourse on Method, 473
Disgruntled Housewife, 824
Disinformation, 412
Disney Secrets, 704
Distance Calculator, 327
Divine Comedy, 473
Divorce, 752
Doctor Who, 698
Dogs, 16
Do-It-Yourself Book Reviews, 74
Doll Collecting, 104
Domain Name Registration, 406
Domestic Partners, 315
Domestic Violence, 752
Dominance and Submission, 855
Dominant Women, 856
Doom, 304
DOS Programming Talk and General Discussion, 641
Down Syndrome, 182
Doyle, Arthur Conan, 462
Dr. Ruth, 713
Dracula, 473
Dragon Boat Racing, 69
Dragons, 274
DRAMA, 184
Drama Talk and General Discussion, 185
Dramatic Exchange, 185
Drinking, 797
Driving, 92
Droodles, 432
Drudge Report, 572
Drug Chemistry and Synthesis, 190
Drug Culture, 190
Drug Information Resources, 190
Drug Pix, 190
Drug Talk and General Discussion, 191
Drug Testing, 191
DRUGS, 189
Drums and Marching, 377
Drums and Percussion, 546

DUATS, 51
Dumb Lists, 397
Dumpster Diving, 516
Dutch, 438
DVD, 800
Dynamic HTML, 808
Dyslexia, 183

E

Early Music, 547
Earth 2025, 304
Earth and Sky, 692
Earth Rise, 327
Earth Science Site of the Week, 332
Earth Sciences Resources, 332
Earth Views, 45
Earthquakes, 225
Easter, 382
Easter Eggs, 705
Eastern European Languages, 439
Eastern Orthodox Christianity, 670
Eating Disorders, 752
Eckankar, 675
Eclipses, 46
Ecological Economics, 240
Ecology, 59
Economic Growth, 197
Economic Resources, 197
Economic Statistics, 198
ECONOMICS, 196
Economics History, 198
Economics Journals, 198
Economics Network, 198
Economics of the Internet, 198
Economics Talk and General Discussion, 199
Economist Jokes, 199
Economists on the Web, 199
Ecstasy, 191
EDN Magazine, 222
EDUCATION, 202
EDUCATION: COLLEGES AND UNIVERSITIES, 206
Education Conferences, 202
EDUCATION: K-12, 212
Education News, 202
Education Place, 212

Main subject headings are shown in bold

INDEX

Education Policy, 203
Education Talk and General Discussion, 203
EDUCATION: TEACHING, 217
Educational Discussion Groups, 203
Educational Energy Information, 230
Educational Mailing Lists, 203
Education-Related Jobs, 415
Edufax, 209
EdWeb, 218
Eeeek Net, 142
Egypt, 831
Egyptian Artifacts, 25
Eighteenth Century Resources, 369
Einstein, Albert, 602
Eisenhower National Clearinghouse, 204
Elders, 707
Electric Chair, 158
Electric Vehicles, 92
Electrical Engineering, 236
Electrochemistry, 99
Electronic Chip Directory, 222
Electronic Equipment Repair Tips, 222
Electronic Forums for Women, 824
Electronic Journal of Differential Equations, 487
Electronic Music Talk and General Discussion, 547
Electronic Postcards, 142
Electronic Privacy Information Center, 637
Electronic Prototyping Tips, 222
Electronic Universe Project, 726
Electronic Zoo, 16
ELECTRONICS, 221
Electronics Engineering, 236
Electronics Talk and General Discussion, 222
Email, 406
Email Privacy, 637
Email the Media, 572
Emancipation Proclamation, 363
Embassies and Consulates Around the World, 338
Embassies in Washington, D.C., 338
EMERGENCY AND DISASTER, 224

Emergency Medicine, 496
Emergency News, 225
Emergency Services, 225
Emergency Tip of the Week, 225
Emerging Diseases, 226
Empire, 304
Encyclopedia of Myths and Legends, 274
Encyclopedias, 663
Endangered Rivers, 240
Endangered Species, 16, 241
Endometriosis, 496
ENERGY, 229
Energy and the Environment, 231
Energy Efficiency and Renewable Energy Network, 231
Energy Efficient Homes, 231
Energy Information Administration, 231
Energy Talk and General Discussion, 231
ENGINEERING, 233
Engineering Failures, 237
Engineering Index, 237
Engineering Talk and General Discussion, 237
English, 439
English Bill of Rights, 363
English Renaissance Literature, 456
English Server, 468
Entertainment and Party Ideas, 383
Entertainment Magazines, 481
Entomology, 869
Entrepreneur Talk and General Discussion, 520
Entry Level Jobs Offered, 415
ENVIRONMENT, 239
Environment Talk and General Discussion, 241
Environmental Journalist's Resources, 421
Environmental Protection Agency, 241
Environmental Resources, 241
Environmental Scorecard, 242
Environmental Search Engine, 242
Environmental Web Directory, 242
Epicurious, 287

Epilepsy and Seizure Disorders, 353
ER, 768
Erotic Postcards, 856
Erotic Resources, 856
Erté Museum, 40
Esperanto, 439
Estate Planning, 524
Ethics, 611
Ethnobotany, 77
Ethology Talk and General Discussion, 869
Europe Discussion Groups, 845
European Comics, 112
European Governments, 339
European Parliament, 339
European Space Agency, 726
European Space Information System, 727
European Texts and Documents, 363
European Union, 339
European Weather Satellite Images, 803
Euthanasia, 631
Evil Hexes, 63
Evolution, 59
Executive Branch, 347
EXERCISE, 245
Exercise and Sports Psychology, 736
Exhibitionism, 857
Existentialism, 611
Exotic Cars, 92
Expatriates and Refugees, 592
Expert Witnesses, 446
Exploratorium, 540
Explorer, 218
Exploring Campus Tunnels, 209
Exposure, 614

F

Fabric Structures, 31
Faces, 147
Fad Diets, 175
Faerie Lore, 274
Fairy Tales, 274
Fake Memos, 516
Fake News, 516
FAMILIES AND PARENTING, 249

Main subject headings are shown in bold

Family Resources, 252
Family Village, 183
Famine, 226
Famous Murderers, 159
Famous People's Wills, 602
Famous Quotations, 651
Fan Favorites Talk and General Discussion, 558
Fanny Hill, 474
Fans of Science Fiction and Fantasy Writers, 698
Fantasy Art, 624
Fantasy Costume, 263
Fantasy Role Playing Talk and General Discussion, 682
FAQ Archives, 258
FAQ FAQ, 259
FAQ for the *.answers Usenet Groups, 259
FAQ Talk and General Discussion, 260
FAQs (FREQUENTLY ASKED QUESTION LISTS), 258
Far from the Madding Crowd, 474
Farm Journal Today, 5
Farmer's Almanac, 664
FASHION AND CLOTHING, 261
Fashion Live, 263
Fashion Magazines, 482
Fashion Net, 263
Fashion Planet, 264
Fashion Talk and General Discussion, 264
Fast Food, 287
Fast Food Calorie Counter, 175
Fat, 175
Fat Substitutes, 175
Fat-Free Recipes, 137
Fathers, 506
Faulkner, William, 462
Fax Technology, 762
FBI, 347
FBI's Ten Most Wanted Fugitives, 159
Federal Communications Law Journal, 447
Federal Emergency Management Agency, 226

Federal Government Information, 347
Federal Reserve System, 199
Federalist Papers, 363
FedStats, 347
FedWorld, 348
Femina, 824
Feminism, 824
Feminism Talk and General Discussion, 824
Fencing, 736
Feng Shui, 387
Ferns, 78
Ferrets, 17
Fetish Fashions, 857
Feudal Terms, 370
Fictional Character Talk and General Discussion, 474
Field Guide to Fonts, 282
Fields, W.C., 652
Fifty Fun Things for Non-Christians to Do in Church, 397
Figlet Fonts, 282
Figure Skating, 736
File Finder, 268
Filk, 548
Filled Pauses, 440
Film and TV Studies Mailing List, 531
Film Festivals, 531
Film Music, 548
Film, Television and Popular Culture, 532
Film.com, 532
Filmmaking Talk and General Discussion, 532
FinanceNet, 521
Financial Aid, 209
Find the Lost Dog, 133
Find-A-Grave, 592
Finding a Doctor, 131
Finding Email Addresses, 593
FINDING STUFF ON THE NET, 267
Fingerprinting and Biometrics, 638
Firewalking, 567
First Aid, 226
First Lines, 456
First Times, 709
Fish, 137

Fishing, 583
Fitness, 245
Fitness for Kids, 245
Fitness for Seniors, 707
Fitness Talk and General Discussion, 246
Flag Burning, 294
Flags of the World, 832
Flamenco, 168
Flames, 792
Flatland, 474
Flea Markets, 717
Fleas and Ticks, 17
Flight Planning and Navigation, 51
Flood Observatory, 226
Flowers, 310
Fodor's Travel Resources, 777
Folk and Traditional Dance, 168
Folk Music, 548
Folk Tales from Around the World, 274
Folklore and Mythology Resources, 275
Folklore of Science, 693
FOLKLORE, MYTHS AND LEGENDS, 272
Font Talk and General Discussion, 282
FONTS AND TYPEFACES, 282
Fontsite Magazine, 283
FOOD AND DRINK, 285
Food Labeling Information, 287
Food Safety, 288
Food Talk and General Discussion, 288
Food, Wine and Cooking Magazines, 482
Foodplex, 288
Foot Fetish, 857
Football: American, 737
Football: Canadian Football League, 737
Football: Professional, 737
Foreign Font Archive, 283
Foreign Language Dictionaries, 440
Foreign Languages for Travelers, 440
Foreign Trade Statistics, 521

*Main subject headings are shown in **bold***

INDEX 887

Forensic Medicine, 496
Forest Conservation, 243
Forestry, 5
Formula 1 Motor Racing, 93
Fortune Telling, 299
Foster Parents, 252
Four-Wheel Drive Vehicles, 93
Fractals, 624
Frame Relay, 126
Frames, 808
France, 832
Frankenstein, 475
Fraternities and Sororities, 210
Fray, 867
Free Clipping Services, 573
Free Compilers and Interpreters, 641
Free Email Services, 406
Free Fonts, 283
Free Legal Information, 447
Free Mailing List Hosting, 406
Free Programming Tools, 641
Free Speech, 294
Free Stuff, 131
Free Web Page Hosting, 808
FREEDOM, 293
Freedom of Expression, 295
Freedom of Information Act, 295
Freedom of Religion, 295
Free-DOS Project, 719
Freelance Writing FAQ, 849
Freeware, 719
French, 441
French Age of Enlightenment, 40
French Cooking, 137
French Fries, 288
French Literature, 468
Freud, Sigmund, 648
Friend Finder, 607
Friendly Folk, 608
Friends, 593
Friends of Choice for Men, 506
Fright Site, 699
Frisbee, 738
FTP Search, 268
Fuller, Buckminster, 602
FUN, 298
Fun Foods, 289

Fun Planet, 299
Funeral Planning, 131
Funk, 548
Funny Fonts, 283
Funny People, 397
Furry Stuff, 699
Fusion, 620
Future Technology Talk and General Discussion, 745

G

Gaelic, 441
Gallery of Fictional Beauty, 112
Gambling and Oddsmaking, 797
Game Hotspots, 304
Game Reviews, 305
Game Shows, 769
Game Theory, 200
GAMES AND PUZZLES, 301
Gangs, 159
Garden Encyclopedia, 310
Garden Gate, 310
Garden Ponds, 310
Garden Web, 311
GARDENING, 310
Gardening Oasis, 311
Gardening Talk and General Discussion, 311
Gargoyles and Grotesques, 37
Gargoyles in New York City, 32
Garlic, 359
Gasoline FAQ, 93
Gates, Bill, 603
Gateway 2000, 114
Gay and Lesbian Alliance Against Defamation, 315
Gay and Lesbian Parenting, 316
Gay Christians, 316
Gay, Lesbian and Bisexual Resources, 316
Gay, Lesbian and Bisexual White Pages, 316
GAY, LESBIAN, BISEXUAL, 315
Gay Travel Guide, 316
Gay TV Listings, 316
Gay-Oriented Mailing Lists, 316
Gays in the Military, 317

Gayzoo, 317
Gems and Mineral Folklore, 275
Gender and Computing, 825
Gender and Sexuality, 825
GENEALOGY, 319
Genealogy Discussion by Ethnicity, 320
Genealogy Events, 320
Genealogy Mailing Lists, 320
Genealogy Marketplace, 320
Genealogy Methods and Hints, 320
Genealogy Resources, 321
Genealogy Scams, 321
Genealogy Search Engine, 321
Genealogy Software, 321
Genealogy Talk and General Discussion, 321
Genealogy Terms, 321
Genealogy's Most Wanted, 322
General Accounting Office, 348
Generation X, 393
Genetics, 59
Genserv, 322
GenWeb Project, 322
Geographic Information Systems, 328
GEOGRAPHY, 327
Geography Departments Worldwide, 328
Geography Resources, 328
Geography Talk and General Discussion, 328
Geological Image Library, 332
Geological Time Machine, 333
Geological Time Scale, 333
GEOLOGY, 332
Geology and Earth Science Resources, 333
Geology of Radon, 333
Geology Talk and General Discussion, 333
Geologylink, 334
Geometry, 487
Geometry and Art, 212
George and Ira Gershwin, 186
Geotechnical Engineering, 237
German, 441
German News, 573

Main subject headings are shown in bold

German Stories, 468
Germanic Myths, Legends and Sagas, 277
Germany, 832
Getting Started in Genealogy, 322
Getting the Most from Your Money, 525
Gettysburg Address, 364
Ghost Stories, 277
Ghosts and Hauntings, 577
Gift of the Magi, 475
Gilbert and Sullivan, 186
Gingrich, Newt, 603
Girl Stuff, 863
Glaciology, 334
Glassdog, 867
Global Gourmet, 289
Global Land Information System, 329
Global Map of Earthquakes, 335
Global Positioning System, 329
Global Trade Center, 521
Glory Hole FAQ, 857
Glossary of PC Terminology, 124
Glycoscience, 99
Gnomes, 278
Gnosticism, 675
Go Ask Alice, 354
Goddard Space Flight Center, 727
Goddess Names, 676
Goddess Spirituality and Feminism, 676
Gold Prospecting, 377
Golden Gate Bridge, 32
Goldman, Emma, 10
Goldwave, 724
Goldwyn, Samuel, 652
Golf, 738
Gonzo Journalism, 421
Good Advice, 1
Good News and Bad News, 573
GORP: Great Outdoor Recreation Pages, 69
Gossip Magazines, 482
Gothic Fashion, 264
Gothic Gardening, 311
Gothic Literature, 456
Government Corruption, 348

Government Information, 348
GOVERNMENT: INTERNATIONAL, 337
GOVERNMENT: UNITED STATES, 345
Governments of the World, 340
Graduate Record Examination, 210
Graduate Schools, 210
Grammar and English Usage, 664
Grandparents, 707
Grandparents Raising Grandchildren, 253
Graphology, 378
Grassroots Activism, 631
Grateful Dead, 560
Great Globe Gallery, 329
Great Microprocessors Past and Present, 223
Greek, 441
Greek Mythology, 278
Greek Philosophy, 611
Greenpeace, 243
Gregorian Chants, 548
Grief, 753
Griffins, 278
Grocery Shooting, 63
Gross State Product Tables, 200
Grotesque Curiosities, 64
Growing Vegetables, 312
Grunge, 548
Guestbooks, 808
Guide to Computer Vendors, 114
Guitar Talk and General Discussion, 549
Gulf War, 370
Gun Control, 296
Guns, 378
Gurl, 863
Guy Rules, 506
Gynecological Exams, 826

H

Hack Gallery, 517
Hacker's Dictionary, 124
Hackers, 641
Haiku, 626
Hair Care, 264

Hair Loss, 506
Hall of Annoying Buttons, 603
Halloween, 383
Ham Radio, 657
Hamsters, 18
Handicap Talk and General Discussion, 183
Hang-gliding and Paragliding, 52
Hangman, 305
Hangovers, 797
Hanson, 560
Hanukkah, 383
Hard Disk Contest, 133
Hard Kink Magazine, 857
Harley Hahn Quotes, 652
Harley Hahn's Guide to Muds, 536
Harley Hahn's Internet Exploration Station, 143
Harley Hahn's Master List of Usenet Newsgroups, 792
Harley Owners Group, 527
Hate Groups, 631
Hawaii, 778
Hawaiian, 441
Hawking, Stephen, 693
Hazardous Chemical Database, 99
Headaches, 354
Headline Maker, 284
HEALTH, 351
Health and Fitness Magazines, 483
Health Care Politics Talk and General Discussion, 354
Health News, 354
Health Oasis, 354
Health Resources, 355
Healthy Diet Guidelines, 175
Healthy Weight, 176
Helicopters, 52
Hello, World, 642
Hemingway, Ernest, 463
Henriette's Herbal Homepage, 360
Heraldry, 323
Herb Magick, 360
Herb Talk and General Discussion, 360
Herb Uses, 360
Herbal Encyclopedia, 360
Herbal Hall, 361

*Main subject headings are shown in **bold***

INDEX

Herbal Medicine, 504
Herbnet, 361
HERBS, 359
Hermeticism, 578
Heroes, 432
Heroin and Opiates, 191
Herpetology, 870
Hesse, Hermann, 463
High Definition Television, 770
High School Student's Survival Guide, 212
Higher Education Resources Newsletter, 210
Hiking and Backpacking, 584
Hindi, 442
Hindu Festivals, 383
Hinduism, 670
Hippocratic Oath, 497
Hiroshima and Nagasaki, 370
Historian's Database and Information Server, 370
Historic American Speeches, 371
Historical and Celebrity Figures, 317
Historical Costuming, 265
Historical Document Archive, 364
HISTORICAL DOCUMENTS, 362
Historical Documents Talk and General Discussion, 364
Historical Sounds and Speeches, 371
Historical Timeline of the Internet, 406
Historical Timelines, 371
HISTORY, 368
History Net, 371
History of Drug Laws, 192
History of Economic Thought, 200
History of Food, 289
History of Locks, 427
History of Mathematics, 487
History of Muds, 536
History of Photography, 615
History of Science, 693
History of Space Exploration, 727
History of the Black Flag, 11
History of the Internet, 407
History of Women's Suffrage, 826
History Resources, 371

History Talk and General Discussion, 371
HOBBIES, 377
Hobby Magazines, 483
Hobby Resources, 378
Hockey, 738
Hockey: College, 738
Hockey Team Talk and General Discussion, 739
Holiday Diet Tips, 176
Holiday Suicide Talk and General Discussion, 383
HOLIDAYS AND CELEBRATIONS, 382
Holistic Healing, 504
Hollywood Online, 532
Hollywood Stock Exchange, 305
Holocaust, 372
Holocaust Museums and Memorials, 540
Home and Garden Magazines, 483
Home Appliance Clinic, 388
Home Canning, 137
Home Environmental Hazards, 388
Home Fire Safety Tips, 227
Home Front Tips, 388
Home Improvement, 388
Home Improvement Encyclopedia, 388
Home Improvement Warehouse, 389
Home Maintenance Magazines, 483
Home Repair, 389
Home Schooling, 204
Homebrewing, 290
Homeopathy, 504
HOMES, 386
Homosexuality and Religion, 317
Homosexuality Talk and General Discussion, 317
Honors Programs, 210
Hootie and the Blowfish, 560
Horror Authors, 603
Horror Fiction Online, 699
Horror Literature, 699
Horror Movies, 532
Horror Talk and General Discussion, 699
Horse Racing, 798

Horses, 18
Hostels, 778
Hostile Java Applets, 814
House of Representatives Law Library, 447
House of the Seven Gables, 475
House Talk and General Discussion, 389
Household Budgeting, 525
Household Economic Statistics, 200
Housing for Seniors, 708
How to Get Rich, 415
How to Use a Condom, 709
How to Use Search Engines, 268
HP (Hewlett-Packard), 115
HTML, 809
HTML Editors, 809
Hub Mathematics and Science Center, 488
Human Evolution, 694
Human Genome Project, 59
Human Noises, 724
Human Rights, 296
Human Sexuality, 713
HUMANITIES AND SOCIAL SCIENCES, 392
Humanities Resources, 393
Human-Powered Vehicles, 584
HUMOR AND JOKES, 396
Humor Archives, 398
Humor Databases, 398
Humor Magazines, 398
Humor Mailing Lists, 398
Humorous Text Filters, 399
Hungary, 833
Hunting, 584
Hunting of the Snark, 475
Hurricanes, 227
Hurricanes and Typhoons, 803
Hydroelectricity, 231
Hydrogen Power, 232
Hydrology Web, 335
Hydroponics, 312
Hyperhistory, 372
Hypermode, 265

Main subject headings are shown in **bold**

I

I Can Garden, 312
I Love Lucy, 770
IBM, 115
Icelandic, 442
Icon Collections, 624
Icons for Fake Awards, 809
ICQ, 759
Icthyology, 870
Idea Futures, 521
IEEE Computer Society, 642
Iguanas, 18
Illustrated Tool Dictionary, 389
Image Maps, 810
Image Search Engines, 268
Imagebase, 40
Imaginary Creatures, 278
Imagination Station, 433
Immigration, 833
Immunology, 497
Importing and Exporting, 521
Impressioning, 427
Impressionism, 37
Improv, 187
Imprudent Wit and Verbal Abuse, 399
Index of Physics Abstracts, 620
India, 834
India News, 573
Indian Classical Music, 549
Indian Food, 138
Indonesia, 834
Indoor Plants, 312
Industrial Archaeology, 26
Industry Net, 521
Indy Racing, 94
Infertility, 497
Inflation Calculator, 200
Infomine Searchable Database, 60
Information Activism, 407
Infrared Photography, 616
Inline Skating, 585
Inner Sanctum Occult Net, 578
Insect Recipes, 138
Inspectors General, 349
Instructor Magazine, 218
Insulting Sound Files, 724
Insurance Information, 525
Intel, 115
Intelligence Organizations, 340
Interactive Fiction, 305
Interactive Maps, 329
Interactive Model Railroad, 172
Interactive Top Ten Lists, 399
Interesting People on the Web, 593
INTERESTING TECHNOLOGIES, 403
International Accounting Network, 522
International Criminal Justice, 447
International Dialing Codes, 763
International Federation of Journalists, 422
International Government Talk and General Discussion, 340
International Jobs, 416
International Law Students Association, 447
International Museum of Cartoon Art, 113
International Organizations in Geneva, 340
International Politics Talk and General Discussion, 631
International Real Estate Digest, 390
International Relations and Security Network, 340
International Stoner Slang Dictionary, 192
International Trade Law, 448
INTERNET, 405
Internet Anarchist University, 11
Internet Broadcasting Networks, 82
Internet Chef, 138
Internet Conference Calendar, 407
Internet Consulting Detective, 268
Internet Crime Archives, 159
Internet Dancing Baby, 147
Internet Drafts, 407
Internet Explorer, 814
Internet FAQ Consortium, 260
Internet Fax Services, 407
Internet Filtering Software, 253
Internet Help Talk and General Discussion, 408
Internet Hoaxes, 408
Internet Index, 784
Internet News, 408
Internet Personals, 608
Internet Phone Services, 759
Internet Politics, 631
Internet Press, 573
Internet Public Library, 452
Internet Resources by Email, 408
Internet Resources for Windows NT, 821
Internet Romances, 608
Internet Service Providers, 126
Internet Sleuth, 268
Internet Statistics, 409
Internet Talk and General Discussion, 409
Internet Terminology, 409
INTRIGUE, 411
Introduction to Windows NT, 822
Investigative Journalism, 422
Investment Talk and General Discussion, 525
Investor Glossary, 522
Invisible Man, 475
IPOs, 522
IRC, 409
IRC (Internet Relay Chat), 759
IRC Talk and General Discussion, 759
Ireland, 834
Irish News, 573
Irish Poetry, 627
Irish Politics, 632
Irrigation, 5
Is There a Santa Claus?, 384
ISDN, 127
Islam, 671
Israel, 835
Israeli Government, 341
Israeli News, 574
Israeli Politics, 632
Italian, 442
Italian Cooking, 138
Italy, 835

J

Jabberwocky, 475

INDEX

Jackson, Janet, 562
Jainism, 671
James Bond, 457
Jamiroquai, 562
Jane Err, 1
Jane's Guide, 710
Japan, 778, 836
Japanese, 442
Japanese Architecture, 32
Japanese Government, 341
Japanese News, 574
Jargon File, 409
Jason Project, 213
Java, 815
Java Chat Applets, 760
Java Game Park, 305
Javascript, 815
Javascript Archives, 815
Jazz, 549
Jefferson Project, 632
Jeffrey Zaslow, 2
Jehovah's Witnesses, 676
Jerusalem, 778
Jewel, 562
Jewish Gays, 317
Jewish Genealogy, 323
Jewish Literature, 457
Jewish Parenting, 253
Jewish Personals, 608
Jewish Software, 719
JFK Assassination, 413
Job Hating, 416
Job Searching, 416
Job Talk and General Discussion, 416
JOBS AND THE WORKPLACE, 415
Jobs for College Students and Graduates, 417
Joint Declaration of Peace, 365
Joke of the Day, 399
Jokes, 399
Jokes, Moderated, 400
Journal of Online Genealogy, 323
JOURNALISM AND MEDIA, 421
Journalism Mailing Lists, 422
Journalism Resources, 423
Journalism Student Resources, 423

Journalism Talk and General Discussion, 423
Judaism, 671
Juggling, 378
Jung, Carl, 648
Jungle Book, 476
Junk Mail, 132
Justice Statistics, 349
Justices of the Supreme Court, 349

K

K-12 Curriculum Talk and General Discussion, 213
K-12 Foreign Language Talk and General Discussion, 214
K-12 Internet School Sites, 214
K-12 Resources, 214
K-12 Student Discussion Groups, 214
K-12 Teachers Discussion Group, 214
Kayaking and Canoeing, 69, 585
Keats, John, 627
Keyboard Yoga, 355
KEYS AND LOCKS, 427
KidPub, 433
KIDS, 431
Kids Click, 433
Kids, Computers and Software, 253
Kids' Contests, 133
Kids Report, 433
Kids Space, 433
Kids Talk and General Discussion, 433
Kids with Disabilities, 183
Kinder Art, 218
King Arthur and Camelot, 278
Kingdomality, 417
Kissing, 686
Kit Cars, 94
Kitchen Link, 138
Kite Aerial Photography, 616
Kites and Kiting Resources, 378
Klingon Phrasebook, 745
Klingon Shared Reality, 746
Klingon Talk and General Discussion, 746

Knitting, 152
Knives and Blades, 152
Knot Tying, 434
Kooks, 593
Koran (or Qurán), 671
Korea, 836
Kvetch, 143
Kwanzaa, 384

L

Laboratory Safety, 99
Lacemaking and Tatting, 152
Land Surveying, 330
Landform Atlas of the United States, 330
Landings Aviation Server, 52
Language IRC Channels, 442
Language of Love, 686
Language Playground, 443
Language Translator, 443
LANGUAGE, 437
Languages of the World, 443
Laptops and Notebooks, 119
Large People, 608
Last Word on Science, 143
Late Night Talk Shows, 770
Latin, 443
Latin America, 837
Latin America Discussion Groups, 846
Latin American Governments, 341
Latino Literature, 468
LAW, 446
Law and Economics, 200
Law Firms, 448
Law Resources, 448
Law Schools, 449
Law Search, 159
Law Talk and General Discussion, 449
Lawtalk, 449
Lawyer Jokes, 449
Learn2, 143
Learning About the Internet and Web, 410
Learning HTML, 810
Learning to Fly, 52

*Main subject headings are shown in **bold***

Learning to Read, 214
Leary, Timothy, 193
Lecture Hall, 210
Legal Dictionary, 449
Legal Documents Online, 449
Legend of Sleepy Hollow, 476
Leisure Studies, 393
Leonardo da Vinci Museum, 40
Lesbian Chat, 317
Letter Writing, 378
Lewinsky, Monica, 603
Libby Webwise, 2
Liberty Web, 296
Librarian Resources, 452
LIBRARIES, 451
Libraries Around the World, 452
Library and Information Science, 452
Library of Congress, 453
Library of Congress Classification System, 454
License Plates, 104
Lichens, 78
Life on Mars, 789
Lifestyle Advice, 2
Light on the Net, 172
Lightful Images, 578
Limericks, 857
Linguistic Talk and General Discussion, 443
Linguistics, 444
Linux, 719
Lipstick, 265
List of BBSs on the Internet, 760
ListTool, 410
Literary Agents, 849
Literary Calendar, 458
Literary Theory, 458
LITERATURE, 454
LITERATURE: AUTHORS, 459
Literature Collection Talk and General Discussion, 469
LITERATURE: COLLECTIONS, 467
Literature for Children, 214
Literature Resources, 458
Literature Talk and General Discussion, 458
LITERATURE: TITLES, 470
Litigation, 450

Live-Action Role Playing, 682
Live Broadcasting Guides, 82
Live Concerts, 82
Living History, 379
LocalEyes, 269
Loch Ness Monster, 279
Lock Talk and General Discussion, 427
Lockpicking, 427
Locksmithing FAQ, 427
Locksmithing Terminology, 430
Logic Talk and General Discussion, 488
London, 778
London Science Museum, 540
Lonely Planet, 779
Look Online, 265
Los Angeles County Museum of Art, 40
Los Angeles Times, 574
Lotteries, 798
Louvre Museum, 40
Love Chat, 687
Love Letters, 687
Love Test, 687
Lovecraft, H.P., 463
Low Fat Lifestyle, 176
LPMud Talk and General Discussion, 536
LSD: My Problem Child, 193
Lucid Dreams, 567
Lumière, 265
Lunar Photographs, 727
Lycra, 265
Lynx, 815
Lyrics, 550

M

M.C. Escher Gallery, 41
Maastricht Treaty, 365
Macintosh Games, 720
Macintosh Hardware, 116
Macintosh Magazines, 116
Macintosh Mailing Lists, 116
Macintosh Mudding Resources, 536
Macintosh News and Announcements, 117

Macintosh Programming, 117, 642
Macintosh Resources, 118
Macintosh Software Archives, 720
Macintosh Software Talk and General Discussion, 720
Macintosh Talk and General Discussion, 118
Macintosh Troubleshooting, 118
Macintosh Updates, 118
Macintosh Version Tracker, 720
MacintoshOS.com, 118
Mad Dog Weekly, 868
Mad Martian Museum of Modern Madness, 147
Madlibs, 299
Madonna, 562
Mafia, 160
Magazine Collections, 483
Magazine Talk and General Discussion, 484
MAGAZINES, 481
Magic, 379
Magic of Believing, 176
Magic Secrets Talk and General Discussion, 705
Magic: The Gathering, 306, 683
Magick, 578
Magick Talk and General Discussion, 578
Magna Carta, 366
Magnetic Poetry, 147
Mail Art, 38
Mailing List Search Engines, 269
Mailing Lists for Gardeners, 312
Maintaining a FAQ, 260
Malacology, 870
Malaysia, 837
Mame Arcade Emulator, 306
Mammals, 871
Man's Life, 507
Mansfield, Katherine, 463
Maps and Atlases, 664
Marble Collecting, 105
Marching Bands, 550
Mardi Gras, 384
Marijuana, 193
Marijuana Facts, 864
Marine Life, 871

INDEX

Marine Mammals, 18
Marine Signal Flags, 69
Marine Weather Observations, 803
Maritime Museums, 541
Mars Atlas, 46
Mars Images, 727
Martial Arts, 740
Marx, Groucho, 652
Masons and Shriners, 594
Massage, 355
Masters, Extraterrestrials and Archangels, 567
Math and Philosophy, 488
Math Articles, 488
Mathematical Association of America, 488
Mathematical Quotations Server, 489
MATHEMATICS, 486
Mathematics Resources, 489
Mathematics Talk and General Discussion, 489
Mayflower Genealogy, 323
Mazes, 306
McCaffrey, Anne, 603
McCartney, Paul: Death Hoax, 563
McKenna, Terence, 193
McLachlan, Sarah, 563
Mead, 290
Mechanical Engineering, 238
Media Watchdogs, 423
Medical Education, 498
Medical Jobs, 418
Medical Libraries, 498
Medical Physics, 498
Medical Resources, 498
Medical Software, 498
Medical Students, 498
Medical World Search, 499
Medicinal Herbs, 361
MEDICINE, 493
MEDICINE: ALTERNATIVE, 502
Medicine Talk and General Discussion, 499
Medieval and Renaissance Food, 139
Medieval Armor and Weapons, 509
Medieval Genealogy, 324

Medieval History, 373
Meditation, 567
Medline, 500
Medscape, 500
Meeting People, 609
Megaliths, 779
Memetics, 611
MEN, 505
Men and Women, 687
Mennonites, 676
Men's Health, 507
Men's Issues, 508
Men's Magazines, 484
Men's Talk and General Discussion, 508
Mensa, 594
Mental Health Net, 355
Merck Manual, 500
Mermaids, 279
Mesoamerican Archaeology, 26
Meta Tags, 810
Metal, 550
Metalworking, 153
Metaphysics Talk and General Discussion, 611
Meteorology Resources, 803
Meteorology Talk and General Discussion, 803
Methamphetamine, 193
Mexican Cuisine, 139
Mexico, 837
Microbiology, 60
Microsoft, 115
Middle East Discussion Groups, 846
Middle East Governments, 341
Middle English, 444
Middle English Literature, 469
Middle Europe, 837
MIDI Archives, 725
MidLink Magazine, 864
Midwifery, 826
MILITARY, 509
Military Academies, 510
Military Aircraft, 53
Military Brats, 510
Military Medals, 510
Military Police, 510

Military Talk and General Discussion, 511
Military Terms and Acronyms, 511
Military Uniforms, 512
Military Vehicles, 512
Millay, Edna St. Vincent, 627
Milton, John, 464
MIME Format, 800
Mimi's Cyber-Kitchen, 139
Mind Breakers, 299
Mind Control, 413
Mine Warfare, 512
Minerals, 335
Miniatures, 683
Minimal Digest Format FAQ, 260
mIRC Client, 761
MISCHIEF, 515
Mischief Talk and General Discussion, 517
Miss Abigail's Time Warp Advice, 2
Missing Children, 253
MIT Guide to Lock Picking, 430
MkLinux, 119
Moby Dick, 476
Model Building, 379
Models and Supermodels, 266
Modems, 127
Moderated Newsgroups, 793
Modern Herbal, 361
Molecular Biology, 60
Molecule of the Month, 100
Moms, 254
MONEY: BUSINESS AND FINANCE, 519
Money News, 525
Money Page, 522
MONEY: PERSONAL FINANCE, 524
Monitors, 120
Monkeys, 19
Monster Movie Talk and General Discussion, 532
Montreal, 87
Mood Thing, 148
Morissette, Alanis, 563
Mormons, 677
Morocco, 837
Morris Dancing, 168
Mortgage Calculator, 526

*Main subject headings are shown in **bold***

Mortgages, 526
Motorcycle Camping, 528
Motorcycle Maintenance, 528
Motorcycle Online Magazine, 528
Motorcycle Racing, 528
Motorcycle Reviews, 528
Motorcycle Safety, 529
Motorcycle Talk and General Discussion, 529
MOTORCYCLES, 527
Motorcycling in the Rain, 529
Motorsport FAQ, 94
Mountain Biking, 585
Movie and Film Resources, 533
Movie Databases, 533
Movie Mistakes, 533
Movie Previews, 533
Movie Reviews, 534
Movie Trivia, 784
Movielink, 534
MOVIES, 530
Movies Talk and General Discussion, 534
Moving, 390
Mpeg Movies, 800
Mpeg Video Resources and Software, 800
Mr. Showbiz, 535
MSNBC, 574
Mud Admin Talk and General Discussion, 536
Mud Announcements, 537
Mud Area Building, 538
Mud Clients, 538
Mud FAQs, 538
Mud Glossary, 538
Mud List, 538
Mud Reviews, 539
Mud Talk and General Discussion, 539
MUDS, 535
Muds to Play, 539
Multilevel Marketing Talk and General Discussion, 522
Multimedia File Formats, 801
Multimedia in Education, 801
Multimedia News, 801

Multimedia Talk and General Discussion, 801
Mummy Museum, 64
Muppets, 770
Murphy's Laws of Locksmithing, 430
Musée du Québec, 87
Musenet, 204
Museum of Dirt, 148
Museum of HP Calculators, 223
Museum of Science and Industry, 541
Museum Talk and General Discussion, 541
MUSEUMS, 540
Museums and Galleries of Wales, 541
Museums, Exhibits and Special Collections, 541
MUSIC, 543
Music Chat, 550
Music Collecting, 105
Music Composition, 551
Music FAQs, 551
Music Magazines, 484
Music News, 551
Music Performance, 551
MUSIC: PERFORMERS, 556
Music Resources, 552
Music Reviews, 552
Music Talk and General Discussion, 552
Music Therapy, 504
Music Video Talk and General Discussion, 552
Music Videos, 553
Musical Instrument Construction, 553
Musicals, 187
Mutual Funds, 522
Mycology, 61
Mysteries, 458
Mystery and Crime Writing, 850
Mystery Science Theatre 3000, 699
Mystery Solving, 300
Mysticism, 568
Mysticism Chat, 677
Mythology in Western Art, 279
Mythology Talk and General Discussion, 279

N

Namebase, 413
Names, 594
Names of Famous People, 784
Nanotechnology, 404
Narcotics Anonymous, 753
NASA Historical Archive, 727
NASA News, 728
NASA Research Labs, 728
Nascar, 95
NASDA, 729
National Agricultural Library, 5
National Archaeological Database, 26
National Archives and Records Administration, 324, 349
National Gallery of Art, 542
National Genetic Resources Program, 6
National Geophysical Data Center, 335
National Institute for Consumer Education, 132
National Institute of Allergy and Infectious Disease, 356
National Institutes of Health, 356
National Museum of American Art, 41
National Organization for Women, 826
National Parliaments, 342
National Performance Review, 349
National School Network Testbed, 204
National Science Foundation, 694
National Telecommunications and Information Administration, 764
National Wetlands Inventory, 243
National Wildlife Federation Kids Stuff, 434
National Wildlife Refuges, 243
Native American Art, 38
Native American Genealogy, 324
Native American Literature, 458
Native American Myths and Legends, 280
Native American Treaties, 366
Native Americans, 838

*Main subject headings are shown in **bold***

INDEX

NATO, 342
Natural Gas, 232
Nature and Wildlife Photography, 616
Naturism and Freedom, 296
Navigation, 69
Nazarenes, 677
Near-Death Experience, 578
Necronomicon, 579
Needlework, 153
Negative Emotions, 64
Nematology, 872
Nerds, 595
Neruda, Pablo, 627
Net Abuse, 793
Net Happenings, 410
NetMeeting (Internet Explorer), 761
Netrunner, 683
Netscape Source Code, 816
Netscape, 115, 816
Netschool, 205
Networks, 764
Neural Networks, 405
Neuroscience, 61
NEW AGE, 566
New Age Music Discussion, 553
New Age Talk and General Discussion, 568
New Internet Technologies, 410
New Mexico Museum of Natural History, 542
New Religious Movements, 677
New Stuff Talk and General Discussion, 269
New Urbanism, 32
New York City, 779
New York Times, 574
New York Views, 172
New Zealand, 838
NEWS, 571
News and Gossip of the Porn Industry, 858
News and Politics Magazines, 484
News Broadcasts, 82
News of the Weird, 64
Newsgroup Listings, 793
Newslink, 425
Newton BBS for Teachers, 205

Next Generation, 747
Nightmare Factory, 133
Nitrous Oxide, 194
Nobel Prize Winners, 604
Nonags, 721
Non-English Software, 721
Nonlinear and Linear Programming, 490
Nootropics (Intelligence-Enhancing Drugs), 194
North American Free Trade Agreement, 342
Norway, 838
Notable Women, 826
Novell, 115
NPR Online, 657
Nuclear Energy, 232
Nuclear Engineering, 238
Nuclear Weapons, 512
Nuclide Table, 100
Nude Beaches, 585
Nudity, 380
Number Stations, 658
Number Synthesizer, 725
Numerical Analysis, 490
Numerology, 569
Nursing, 500
Nutrition, 176

O

Oasis, 564
Obfuscated C Code, 642
Obituaries, 595
Objectivism, 612
Object-Oriented Programming, 643
Observatories and Telescopes, 46
Occult and Magick Chat, 579
OCCULT AND PARANORMAL, 577
Occult Search Engine, 579
Occupational Medicine, 500
Occupational Safety and Health, 418
Oceanography, 694
Oedipus Trilogy, 477
Oldies Music Trivia, 784
Old-Time Radio, 658
On Broadway, 188

On Liberty, 477
OneWorld News, 575
Onion, 400
Online Books, 469
Online Courses and Distance Learning, 211
Online Genealogy Newsletter, 324
Online Romance Talk and General Discussion, 690
Online Writery, 850
Open Broadcasting, 658
Opera, 188, 554
Operating Systems Talk and General Discussion, 643
Operations Research, 490
Optical Engineering, 239
Optical Illusions, 648
Optics, 620
Oracle, 401
Oral Sex, 858
Organ Transplants, 501
Organic Chemistry, 100
Organic Farming, 6
Organic Gardening, 313
Organization of American States, 342
Orienteering and Rogaining, 585
Origami, 153
Ornithology, 872
OS/2 Games, 721
OS/2 Networking Environment, 721
OS/2 Programming Talk and General Discussion, 644
OS/2 Software Archives, 721
OS/2 Utilities, 721
Osteopathy, 504
Othello, 306
Ottawa, 88
Ouija, 580
Out Proud, 318
OUTDOOR ACTIVITIES, 582
Outdoor and Recreation Resources, 586
Outdoors Magazines, 484
Out-of-Body Experiences, 580
Outside Online, 586
Owning Airplanes, 53
Ozone Depletion, 243

*Main subject headings are shown in **bold***

P

Packard-Bell, 115
Packet Radio, 658
Packing Tips, 779
Pagan Holidays, 385
Paganism, 678
Paint Estimator, 390
Pakistan News, 575
Paleobotany, 78
Palmtops, 120
Palynology Resources, 78
Panoramic Photography, 616
Pantyhose and Stockings, 858
Papermaking, 434
Papyrology, 27
Paradise Lost, 477
Paragliding, 586
Paralysis and Spinal Cord Injuries, 183
Paranormal Phenomena Talk and General Discussion, 580
Parapsychology, 580
Parascope, 413
Parent Soup, 254
Parenthood Web, 254
Parenting Resources, 255
Parenting Talk and General Discussion, 255
Parents and Children Together Online, 255
Parents and Teens, 255
Parents Room, 255
Paris, 779
Parker, Dorothy, 464
Parks in the United States, 586
Particle Surface Research, 620
Particle/High Energy Physics, 620
Patents, 450
Payphone Project, 300
Pay-TV Decoders, 705
PC Games Talk and General Discussion, 306
PC Hardware Talk and General Discussion, 120
PC Magazines, 121
PC News, 121
PC Prices, 121
PC Resources, 121
PC Talk and General Discussion, 121
PC Video Hardware, 801
PCMCIA Cards, 122
Peculiar Galaxies, 46
Pen Pal Brides, 609
PenPals, 596
PEOPLE, 591
PEOPLE: FAMOUS AND INTERESTING, 597
Periodic Informational Postings List, 260
Periodic Table, 100
Perl, 644
Perry-Castañeda Library Map Collection, 330
Perseus Project, 27
Perseus Project, 393
Personal Ads Talk and General Discussion, 609
Personal Finance Tips and Resources, 526
Personal Movie Finders, 535
Personal Watercraft, 70
Personal Web Pages, 596
Personality Testing, 649
PERSONALS AND DATING, 606
Personals for Gays, 609
Peru, 838
Pest Control, 390
Pest Management, 313
Pet Cemetery, 19
Pet Channel, 19
Pet of the Day, 19
Pet Talk and General Discussion, 20
Peter Pan, 478
Pet-Keeping Dos and Don'ts, 19
Petroleum, 232
PFLAG Gay Support Organization, 318
PGP, 164
Pharmacy, 501
Philosophers, 612
PHILOSOPHY, 610
Philosophy Reference Guides, 612
Philosophy Resources, 612
Philosophy Search Engines, 613
Philosophy Talk and General Discussion, 613
Phone Books, 664
Phone Number Translator, 764
Photo Archives, 624
PhotoForum, 616
Photographers Directory, 617
PHOTOGRAPHY, 614
Photography Basics, 617
Photography Equipment Talk and General Discussion, 617
Photography Magazines, 485
Photography Resources, 617
Photography Talk and General Discussion, 617
Photojournalism, 425
Photosynthesis, 78
Phreaking, 705
PHYSICS, 619
Physics Conferences, 621
Physics Talk and General Discussion, 621
Pi (3.14159...), 491
Picking Locks and Opening Safes, 431
Picture Grabbing Software, 793
Picture Viewing Software, 625
PICTURES AND CLIP ART, 622
Pictures of Herbs, 361
Pies, 140
Pihkal, 194
Piloting, 53
Pinball, 307
Pinhole Photography, 618
Pinup Art, 41
Pipe Smoking, 798
Pirate Radio, 659
Pirates, 280
Planet Diary, 243
Planetary Nebulae Gallery, 729
PlanetOut, 318
Planets, 729
Planets and the Solar System, 47
Planning Ahead for Disasters, 227
Planning for Retirement, 526
Plant Answers, 313
Plant Fossil Database, 79
Plant Gene Register, 79

*Main subject headings are shown in **bold***

INDEX

Plant Hormones, 79
Plant Pathology, 80
Plant Taxonomy, 80
Plants Harmful to Animals, 20
Plasma Physics, 621
Plath, Sylvia, 628
Play Scripts, 188
Playbill Online, 188
Pleasing a Woman, 710
Plug-Ins, 816
Plumbing, 390
PM Zone, 95
Pocket Internet, 143
Poe, Edgar Allan, 464
POETRY, 625, 690
Poetry Archives, 628
Poetry for Kids, 434
Poetry Talk and General Discussion, 628
Pointcast Network, 575
Poker, 307
Poland, 838
Police Brutality, 160
Police Codes, 706
Police Scanner, 160
Political Correctness, 632
Political Philosophy, 613
Political Policies, 632
Political Talk and General Discussion, 633
Politicians, 633
POLITICS, 629
Politics and Drugs, 195
Politics and Homosexuality, 318
Politics of Government Organizations, 634
Politics of Space, 729
Polo, 740
Polyamory, 713
Polymer and Liquid Crystal Tutorial, 621
Polymer Clay, 154
Polymer Physics, 622
Pop Art, 38
Pope John Paul II, 604
Popsicles, 133
Popular Culture, 394
Popular Culture Magazines, 485

Popular Culture Zines, 868
Population, 244
Population Studies, 394
Porn Stars, 858
Porn-O-Matic, 858
Portals, 270
Portugal, 840
Positive Emotions, 65
Postal Codes and Mail, 664
Postcards, 105
Posting a FAQ Automatically, 261
Post-World War II Political Leaders, 342
Pottery, 27
Poultry, 6
Poundstone, William, 604
P.O.V., 508
Powerlifting, 246
Powwow, 761
Practical Jokes, 517
Prank Phone Calls, 517
Pratchett, Terry, 464
Precision Farming, 7
Pregnancy and Childbirth, 256
Pregnancy and Exercise, 247
Pregnancy Loss, 754
Premature Infants, 256
Preparing for College, 864
Preschool Pages, 435
Prescription and OTC Drugs, 195
President of the United States, 604
Presidential Quotes, 652
Presidential Scandals, 634
Presley, Elvis, 564
Press Photographers, 425
Primates, 872
Primitivist Network, 11
Princess Diana, 605
Printers, 122
Prison Inmates, 160
Prison Life, 160
Prisoners of War, 513
PRIVACY AND SECURITY, 635
Privacy Forum Digest, 638
Privacy Resources, 638
Privacy Rights Clearinghouse, 639

Privacy Talk and General Discussion, 639
Privacy Tips, 639
Prodigy, 565
Products for Children, 256
Professional Cartoonists, 113
Programmer of the Month, 644
PROGRAMMING, 640
Programming Humor, 644
Programming Languages, 645
Programming Talk and General Discussion, 645
Progressive Farmer Magazine, 7
Project Gutenberg, 469
Prominent Anarchists, 11
Promoting Your Web Site, 810
Pronunciation in the American South, 444
Prose, 850
Prostitution Around the World, 858
Psychedelic Drugs, 195
Psychological Help, 649
PSYCHOLOGY, 647
Psychology Database, 649
Psychology Resources, 649
Psychology Talk and General Discussion, 650
Public Broadcasting Service (PBS), 770
Publisher's Web Pages, 850
Publishing Law, 450
Puff Daddy, 565
Pulitzer Prize, 426
Pulp Fiction, 74
Punk Rock, 554
Puppetry, 380
Purity Tests, 713
Puzzles, 307, 381

Q
Quackery and Health Fraud, 356
Quakers (Society of Friends), 672
Queer Resources Directory, 319
Queer Zines, 319
Quilting, 154
Quotable Women, 652
Quotation Resources, 652

Main subject headings are shown in **bold**

Quotation Talk and General Discussion, 654
QUOTATIONS, 651

R

Rabbits, 20
RADIO, 656
Radio and Television Companies, 426
Radio Broadcasting, 659
Radio History, 660
Radio Scanner Frequencies, 660
Radio Station Lists, 660
Radioactive Waste, 622
Radio-Controlled Model Aircraft, 586
Radiology and Imaging, 501
Railroad, 381
Railroad Connections, 780
Rainforests, 244
Randi, James, 605
Random Love Poems, 690
Random Portrait Gallery, 596
Random Quotes, 654
Random Recipe Generator, 140
Rap, 554
Rap Dictionary, 554
Rape, 161
Rare Books, 74
Rats and Mice, 20
Rave, 554
Real Audio, 816
Real Estate Talk and General Discussion, 391
Real Names of Famous People, 606
Realm of Graphics, 625
Recipe a Day, 140
Recipe Archives, 140
Recipe Talk and General Discussion, 140
Record Production, 554
Recovery for Christians, 754
Recovery for Jews, 754
Recreational Vehicles, 780
Red Cross, 227
Red Dwarf, 700
REFERENCE, 661

Reference Desks, 665
Refrigerator Status, 172
Reggae, 555
Regional Motorcycle Mailing Lists, 529
Rehabilitation, 183
Reincarnation, 570
Relationship Advice, 609
Relativity, 622
Relaxation Techniques, 505
RELIGION, 666
RELIGION: SECTS AND CULTS, 674
Religion Talk and General Discussion, 672
Religious Colleges, 211
Religious Satire, 402
Religious Tolerance, 672
Reminder Services, 144, 385
Renaissance, 373
Renaissance and Baroque Architecture, 32
Renaissance Dance, 168
Renewable Energy, 233
Repetitive Stress Injuries, 418
Reporters Network, 426
Reptiles and Amphibians, 21
Republicans, 634
Research It, 270
Research Methods in Science, 694
Residential Colleges, 211
Restaurant Talk and General Discussion, 290
Restaurants on the Web, 290
Résumés, 418
Retirement Planning, 708
Reuters News, 575
Revenge Talk and General Discussion, 517
Revisionism, 373
Rice, Anne, 464
Richard Nixon Audio and Video Archive, 634
Riddle of the Day, 307
Riddler Game, 134
Riley Guide, 419
Road Rally, 95
Roadside America, 780
Robin Hood, 281

Robotics, 239
Rock and Roll, 555
Rock Art, 27
Rock Collection, 106
Rock Shop, 336
Rocker, Rudolf, 11
Rodeo, 740
Roget's Thesaurus, 665
ROLE PLAYING, 681
Role-Playing Crafts, 683
Role-Playing Games Magazine, 683
Role-Playing Resources, 685
Rolfing, 505
Roller Coasters, 381
Rolling Stones, 565
Roman Art and Archaeology, 28
ROMANCE, 686
Romance Novels, 75
Romance Readers Anonymous, 690
Romance Talk and General Discussion, 690
Romance Writing, 851
Romantic Ascii Graphics, 690
Romantic Gestures, 691
Romantic Greetings by Email, 691
Roots, 324
Roswell Incident, 790
Rotten Galleries, 65
Route 66, 780
Rowing, 71
Royal Tyrrell Museum of Paleontology, 543
Royalty, 374
Royalty and Nobility, 324
RSA, 165
Rubber Stamps, 154
Rugby, 741
Rugby League, 741
Rug-Hooking, 154
Rumors, 65
Rumors and Secrets About Computer Companies, 115
Running, 247
Russia, 780, 840
Russian, 445
Russian and American Friendship, 840
Russian News, 576

Main subject headings are shown in **bold**

INDEX

S

Safer Sex, 710
Sailing, 71
Salary and Wages, 419
Salon, 868
Salsa, 168
Samba, 169
Sandbox, 307
Santa Claus, 606
Santeria, 678
Satanism, 678
Satellite Images of Cities, 172
Satellite TV, 770
Saudi Arabia, 841
Scanners, 122
Scarlet Letter, 478
Scarlet Pimpernel, 478
Scholastic Journalism, 426
School Projects by Kids, 215
School Safety Tips, 215
SCIENCE, 692
Science and Science Fiction, 700
Science Demonstrations, 219
Science Fiction and Fantasy Archives, 700
Science Fiction and Fantasy Online, 700
Science Fiction and Fantasy Reviews, 75
Science Fiction Announcements, 700
Science Fiction Convention Calendar, 701
Science Fiction Fandom Talk and General Discussion, 701
SCIENCE FICTION, FANTASY AND HORROR, 696
Science Fiction Marketplace, 701
Science Fiction Movie Talk and General Discussion, 535
Science Fiction Movies, 701
Science Fiction News, 701
Science Fiction Resource Guide, 701
Science Fiction Talk and General Discussion, 702
Science Fiction Writing, 702
Science Fraud and Skepticism, 695
Science Jobs, 419
Science Jokes, 402
Science Learning Network, 215
Science Magazines, 485
Science News, 695
Science Resources, 695
Science Talk and General Discussion, 695
Scientific Urban Legends, 281
Scientology, 679
SciFaiku, 702
SCO (Santa Cruz Operation), 116
Scooters, 530
Scorpions, 21
Scottish Clans, 325
Scout Report, 411
Scouting, 864
Scrapbooks, 381
Screenplays, 851
Screenwriters and Playwrights, 851
Scuba Diving, 587
Sea Level Data, 244
Sea Serpents and Lake Monsters, 281
Seaports and Harbors, 71
Search Engine Access Sites, 270
Search Engines, 271
Search Snoopers, 144
Seas and Water Directory, 244
Seasonal Employment, 419
Secret Societies, 706
SECRET STUFF, 703
Secular Web, 469
Securities and Exchange Commission's Database, 201
Seismology, 336
Selective Service System, 513
Self-Help and Psychology Magazine, 650
Self-Help for Men, 508
Semantic Rhyming Dictionary, 628
Semiconductors, 223
Senior Resources, 708
Senior Talk and General Discussion, 708
SENIORS, 707
Seniors Magazines, 708
Seniors Organizations, 709
Señor Sex, 710
Sensual Massage, 711
Serbian, 445
Serial Killers, 161
Service Dogs, 183
SETI, 729
Sewing, 155
SEX, 709
Sex Experts Talk and General Discussion, 713
Sex Glossary, 711
Sex How-Tos, 859
Sex Laws, 713
Sex Magazine Talk and General Discussion, 860
Sex Magazines, 860
Sex Pictures, 860
Sex Questions and Answers, 714
Sex Reference Guide, 714
Sex Services Talk and General Discussion, 799
Sex Sounds, 861
Sex Stories, 861
Sex Talk and General Discussion, 711
Sex Tips, 711
Sex Trivia, 711
Sex Wanted, 861
Sexual Addiction, 754
Sexual Assault and Sex Abuse Recovery, 714
Sexual Assault on Campus, 827
Sexual Harassment on the Job, 419
SEXUALITY, 712
Sexuality and Religion, 672
Sexy Talk, 861
SF-Lovers, 702
Sgt. Mom's Place, 256
Shakers, 679
Shakespeare, William, 465
Shakespearean Insults, 402
Shamanism, 679
Shared Realities, 596
Sharks, 22
Shelley, Percy Bysshe, 629
Shiatsu, 505
Shoes, 266
Shogi, 308
Shooting, 587

*Main subject headings are shown in **bold***

900 HARLEY HAHN'S INTERNET & WEB GOLDEN DIRECTORY

SHOPPING, 715
Shopping Malls, 718
Shopping Online, 718
Shopping with Children, 718
Short Stories, 470
Shortwave Radio, 660
Shuttle and Satellite Images, 625
Shuttle Snapshots, 729
Sidecars, 530
Siege of Paris, 12
Sikhism, 672
Silicon Graphics, 116
Simpsons, 771
Sinatra, Frank, 565
Single Parents, 257
Singles, 691
Sistine Chapel, 42
Sitcom Downfalls, 771
Sites for Kids, 435
Skateboarding, 588
Skepticism, 580
Skiing, 741
Skydiving, 588
SkyView, 47
Sleep Disorders, 356
Sliding Tile Puzzles, 308
Slot Cars, 95
Slovak, 445
Slovakia, 841
Small Business Administration, 523
Small Business Resources, 523
Small Press Comics, 113
Smileys, 124
Smithsonian Botany Resources, 80
Smoking, 754
Smoking Addiction, 357
Smoking Gun, 413
Snakebites, 357
Sneakers, 266
Snowboarding, 589
Snowglobes, 106
Snowmobiles, 589
Soap Operas, 771
Soapmaking, 155
Soccer, 741
Social Psychology, 650
Social Science Resources, 394

Social Security Administration, 349
Social Security Number Location Finder, 706
Social Work, 395
Society for Creative Anachronism Dance, 169
Society for Creative Anachronism, 381
Society for Industrial and Applied Math, 491
Sociology Resources, 395
Sociology Talk and General Discussion, 395
Softball, 742
SOFTWARE, 718
Software Archives, 722
Software Cracks, 706
Software Engineering, 646
Software Licensing, 722
Software Testing Talk and General Discussion, 722
Solar Cars, 95
Solar Energy, 233
Solar System Exploration, 730
Solve a Mystery, 435
Song of Hiawatha, 478
Sonochemistry, 101
Soulmates, 691
Sound Archives, 725
Sound Tools, 725
SOUNDS, 723
Sounds and Sound Effects, 726
South African News, 576
South Park, 771
Southeast Asia Discussio Groups, 847
Southern Asia Discussion Groups, 847
Southern Cooking, 141
SPACE, 726
Space Calendar, 730
Space Frequently Asked Questions, 730
Space Movie Archive, 730
Space News, 730
Space Shuttle, 730
Space Talk and General Discussion, 731

Space Weather, 804
Spam Filtering Software, 722
Spamming, 639
Spanish, 445
Spanking, 610, 861
Speaker Building Information, 224
Special Education and Special Needs, 219
Special Education, 206
Special Olympics, 184
Special Operations, 513
Speechwriting, 851
Speedtraps, 780
Spelling Bee, 216
Spelunking, 589
Spice Girls, 565
Spirit Web, 570
Spiritual Healing, 570
Spleen, 65
SPORTS AND ATHLETICS, 731
Sports Broadcasts, 82
Sports Contest, 134
Sports Doctor, 247
Sports Magazines, 485
Sports Memorabilia, 106
Sports News, 742
Sports Picks, 134
Sports Resources, 742
Sports Schedules, 742
Sports Trivia, 784
Spunk Library, 12
Square Root of 2, 491
Squash and Racquetball, 742
Squashed Bug Zoo, 65
Stagecraft, 188
Stained Glass, 155
Stalking, 161
Stamp Collecting, 108
STAR TREK, 744
Star Trek Games, 747
Star Trek News, 747
Star Trek Quotes, 655
Star Trek Resources, 747
Star Trek Reviews, 747
Star Trek Role Playing, 685, 747
Star Trek Sounds, 748
Star Trek Stories and Parodies, 748

Main subject headings are shown in **bold**

INDEX

Star Trek Talk and General Discussion, 748
Star Trek Television Shows, 748
Star Trek Trivia, 749
Star Trek Universe, 749
Star Trek Video Clips, 749
Star Trek: Voyager, 749
Star Wars, 703
Stare Down Sally, 66
Starpages, 47
State Department, 350
Statistics, 491
Stay-at-home Dads, 508
STD Information, 714
Steganography, 165
Step-Parents, 257
Stereograms, 625
Stick Figure Death Theater, 66
Stock Market Data, 523
Stock Market Timing, 523
Stolen Motorcycles, 530
Stones and Megaliths, 28
Stories About Flying, 53
Storm Chasing, 804
Straight Answers, 319
Straight Dope, 144
Straight-Edge, 864
Strange Animals, 872
Strange Case of Dr. Jekyll and Mr. Hyde, 479
Strange Sounds, 555
Street Drug Slang, 195
Stress, 357
Stretching and Flexibility, 247
String Figures, 435
Strip Club List, 861
Strip Clubs, 799
Structural Geology, 336
Student Affairs, 211
Student Artist Mailing List, 38
Students for the Exploration and Development of Space, 731
Study Tips, 216
Studying Abroad, 211
Stuttering, 357
Submission Guidelines for the *.answers Usenet Groups, 261
Subway Navigator, 781

Succulents and Cacti, 80
Sugar Bush, 435
Suicide Prevention, 357
Sullivan, Louis Henry, 33
Sun Microsystems, 116
Sunspots, 47
Super Secret Web Site, 706
Supermodels, 625
SUPPORT GROUPS, 750
Support Groups Networking, 755
Support Talk and General Discussion, 755
Supreme Court Rulings, 450
Surfing, 589
Surname Databases and Discussion, 325
Surname Origins, 326
Surrealism, 38
Surrealist Compliment Generator, 66
Surrogate Motherhood, 258
Survivalism, 229
Sushi, 141, 291
Sustainable Agriculture Information, 7
Sweden, 841
Swedish News, 576
Sweepstakes and Contests, 134
Swimming, 589
Swimming Competitions, 743
Swing Dance, 169
Swiss Government, 342
Symbolic and Algebraic Computation, 492

T

Tables, 811
Taiwan, 841
Talented and Gifted, 206
Talk Radio Hosts, 661
Talkers, 761
TALKING ON THE NET, 758
Talkway, 793
Tango, 169
Tantra and the Kama Sutra, 711
Tao of Programming, 646
Tap Dancing, 170
Tarantulas, 22

Tarot, 571
Tasteless (and Dirty) Jokes, 402
Tasteless Topics, 66
Tax Preparation, 527
Taxonomy, 61
TCP/IP, 722
Tea and Conversation, 596
Teachers Helping Teachers, 220
Teachers Net, 220
Teaching English as a Second Language, 220
Teaching Health and Physical Education, 220
Teaching Kids About Money, 527
Teaching Mathematics, 220
Teaching Music, 220
Teaching Resources, 221
Teaching with Movies, 258
Teachnet, 221
Team.Net Automotive Information Archives, 95
Tech Support and Online Help, 125
Technical Books, 75
Technical Theater Databases, 189
Technical Writing, 852
Technology Insertion, 513
Technoteen, 865
Teddy Bear Collecting, 108
Teen Chat Rooms, 865
Teen Dating Page, 865
Teen Driving Tips, 865
Teen Movie Critic, 865
Teen Voice, 865
Teen Writers, 866
Teenagers, 866
Teens Helping Teens, 866
Telecom Discussions and Digest, 764
Telecom Resources, 765
Telecommuting, 419
Telemarketer Torture, 517
Telemedicine, 501
TELEPHONE AND TELECOM, 762
Telephone Tech Talk and General Discussion, 765
Telescopes, 48
TELEVISION, 766
Television and Movie Sounds, 726
Television Journalism, 426

*Main subject headings are shown in **bold***

Television Talk and General Discussion, 772
Television Theme Songs, 774
Television Trivia, 784
Temperature, 695
Temps, 420
Tenant Net, 391
Tennis, 743
Tennyson, Alfred, 629
Terrorism, 161
Terrorist's Handbook, 518
Test Taking Tips, 216
Textiles, 155, 267
Thailand, 781, 841
Thanksgiving, 385
Theater Resources, 189
Thelema, 581
Theosophy, 679
Thesaurus for Graphic Material, 625
Things on the Net, 172
This Day in History, 374
Thompson, Hunter S., 606
Tic Tac Toe, 308
Tickling, 862
Tidbits, 119
Tie Dye, 155
Time, 665
Time Daily, 576
Time Machine, 148, 479
Time Zones, 331
Tintin, 113
TinyMud Talk and General Discussion, 539
Tipping, 132
Titanic, 374
Today's Date, 785
Today's Date and Time, 666
Today's Events in History, 785
Today's Fortune, 655
Togetherness Tips, 691
Toilet Repair and Maintenance, 391
Tolkien, J.R.R., 465
Tom Sawyer, 479
Tombstone Rubbings, 326
Top 100 PC Games, 308
Tornadoes, 229
Toronto, 88

Tourism Offices, 781
Toy Cameras, 618
Toy Talk and General Discussion, 108
Tracking a Package, 666
Trade Secrets, 451
Trademarks, 451
Trading Cards, 109
Traffic Conditions, 173
Transgendered Support, 755
Transparent Gifs, 811
Transvestite, Transsexual, Transgender, 715
TRAVEL, 776
Travel for Seniors, 709
Travel Health Advice, 781
Travel Magazines, 485
Travel Marketplace, 781
Travel Matters Newsletter, 781
Travel Resources, 782
Travel Talk and General Discussion, 782
Travel Tips, 782
Treasure Hunting, 382
Treasures of the Czars, 42
Treaties, 635
Treaty of Guadalupe Hidalgo, 366
Treaty of Paris, 366
Trees, 313
Trekker Chat, 749
Trip Planning, 783
TRIVIA, 783
Trivia Matters, 786
Trivia Page, 786
Trivia Web, 786
Trivial Talk and General Discussion, 786
Trolling, 518
Truetype Fonts, 284
Turing, Alan, 492
TV Episode Guides, 775
TV Gossip, 775
TV Guide Postcards, 775
TV News Archive, 775
TV Schedules, 775
Twain, Mark, 466, 655
Twentieth Century USA, 374
Twins and Triplets, 258

TypeArt Library, 284
Typing Injuries, 358
Typofile, 284
Typography Terminology, 284

U

UFO Chatting, 790
UFO Information Resources, 790
UFO Origins, 790
UFO Reports, 790
UFO Talk and General Discussion, 791
UFOs AND ALIENS, 787
ULS Report, 244
Ultralight Flying, 53
Uncle Tom's Cabin, 480
Underground Music Archive, 555
Underwater Archaeology, 28
Underwater Photography, 619
Underwater Telecommunication Cables, 766
Unhappy Romances, 691
Unicycling, 382
Unions, 420
Unitarianism, 680
United Kingdom, 842
United Kingdom Government, 343
United Nations, 343
United Nations Agreements on Human Rights, 296
United Nations Office for Outer Space Affairs, 731
United Nations Security Council, 344
United States, 843
United States and Canada Discussion Groups, 848
United States Armed Forces, 514
United States Bill of Rights, 366
United States Declaration of Independence, 367
United States Gazetteer, 331
United States Political Talk and General Discussion, 635
United States: Southern, 843
Universal Declaration of Human Rights, 367

Main subject headings are shown in **bold**

INDEX

University Residence and Housing, 211
Unsolved Crimes and Fugitives, 161
Unsolved Mysteries, 414
Unusual Fonts, 284
Uproar, 135
Urban Exploration, 518
Urban Gardening, 313
Urban Legends, 282
Urban Sex Legends, 712
U.S. Area Codes, 766
U.S. Census Bureau Economic Statistics, 201
U.S. Census Information, 326
U.S. Civil War Genealogy, 326
U.S. Department of Defense, 514
U.S. Department of Education, 206
U.S. Department of Health and Human Services, 358
U.S. Geological Survey, 336
U.S. Government Jobs, 420
U.S. International Aid, 344
U.S. Military Magazines, 514
U.S. National Endowment for the Humanities, 396
U.S. National Parks, 783
U.S. State Department Travel Information, 783
USA Today, 576
USDA Economics and Statistics, 8
Used Bike Prices, 530
Useless Facts, 148, 786
Useless Information, 786
USENET, 792
Usenet Announcements, 793
Usenet Archiving Software, 794
Usenet Culture Talk and General Discussion, 794
Usenet Discussion Group Administration, 794
Usenet Discussion Group Invasion, 795
Usenet Discussion Group Questions, 795
Usenet Filtering Service, 795
Usenet for New Users, 795
Usenet Hierarchies, 795
Usenet Search Engines, 271
Usenet Support Groups, 756
USGS Astronomy Resources, 48
Using HTML Well, 811
Using the Web Anonymously, 640

V

Vacation and Travel Contests, 135
Vacationing with Children, 258
Valentine's Day, 386
Vampire: The Masquerade, 685
Vampyres Only, 66
Van Gogh Gallery, 42
Vancouver, 88
Vatican Exhibit, 42
Vegans, 292
Vegetarian Resources, 292
Vegetarian Talk and General Discussion, 292
Vending Machine Calorie Counter, 177
Vending Machines, 173
Venezuela, 843
Versailles Treaty of 1919, 368
Very Crazy Stuff, 145
Veterans, 514
Veterinary Medicine, 22
Vice President of the United States, 606
VICES, 796
Victorian Fashion, 267
Victorian Literature, 470
Victoria's Valentine Contest, 135
VIDEO AND MULTIMEDIA, 800
Video Conferencing, 761
Video Editing, 802
Video Games, 309
Video Games Hints and Cheats, 309
Video Glossary, 802
Vietnam Veterans, 515
Vietnam War, 375
Viking Image Archive, 731
Vikings, 375
Vintage Panoramic Maps, 331
Vintage Radios and Broadcasting Equipment, 661
Virgil, 466
Virology, 62
Virtual Acid Trip, 195
Virtual Campfire of Nerds, 597
Virtual Cave, 336
Virtual Garden, 314
Virtual Hospital, 501
Virtual Memorials, 597
Virtual Plastic Surgery, 148
Virtual Presents, 145
Virtual Reality, 405
Virtual Slot Machine, 799
Virtual Wedding Chapel, 691
Virtually React, 866
Virus Hoaxes, 640
Visual Basic, 646
Vital Records in the U.S., 327
Vocational Education, 206
Voice of America, 661
Voice of the Shuttle, 396
Volcanoes on the Net, 173
Volcanology, 337
Volleyball, 743
Voodoo, 582
Votetaker Volunteers, 795
Voyage of the Beagle, 480
Voyeurism, 862
VRML, 816

W

Waco, 414
Walking, 247
Wall Street Net, 523
Wallpaper Calculator, 391
War, 375
War of the Worlds, 480
Warez, 707
Warhammer, 685
Washington Post, 576
Waste Reduction Tips and Factsheets, 245
Water Skiing, 590
Watercraft Calendar, 71
Watersports, 862
Wave-Length Paddling Magazine, 71
WEATHER, 803
Weather Images, 804
Weather Radar, 804

*Main subject headings are shown in **bold***

Weather Reports: Canada, 805
Weather Reports: International, 805
Weather Reports: United States, 805
Weather Warnings, 806
Web Authoring FAQ, 811
Web Browser Talk and General Discussion, 817
Web Catalogs, 271
Web Channel Guides, 272
Web Chat Rooms, 762
WEB: CREATING WEB PAGES, 806
Web Garden, 314
Web Guides, 272
Web Log Analysis, 817
Web Page Backgrounds, 812
Web Page Counters, 812
Web Page Creation Talk and General Discussion, 812
Web Page Graphics and Icons, 812
Web Page Marketing, 812
Web Page Programs, 812
Web Publishing Resources, 813
Web Reference, 813
Web Server Talk and General Discussion, 817
Web Server Watch, 817
Web Site Validation, 813
Web Sitez, 272
Web Soap Operas, 300
WEB: SOFTWARE, 814
Web Style Manual, 813
Web Talk and General Discussion, 411, 817
Webdoctor, 502
Webopaedia, 125
Webring, 272
Webstars, 48
WebTV, 128
Wedding Pranks, 518
Weddings, 386
Weight Gain, 177
Weight Loss, 177
Weightlifting and Bodybuilding, 247
Weights and Measures, 666
Weird IRC Channels, 66
Weird Sites, 300
Wells, H.G., 466
Wendy Pages, 597

Wendy's World of Stories for Children, 435
Werewolf Folklore, 282
West Indies Discussion Groups, 848
Western European Literature, 470
Western Square Dancing, 170
White House, 350
White House Cam, 173
White House Press Releases, 350
White House Tour for Kids, 436
Whittier, John Greenleaf, 629
Whois, 411
Why Files, 145, 696
Wicca, 680
Widows and Widowers, 757
Wild Weather, 436
Wilde, Oscar, 655
Wildfires, 229
Wildflowers, 314
Wildlife, 22
Wind Energy, 233
WINDOWS, 817
Windows 95 and 98 Official Web Sites, 818
Windows Annoyances, 818
Windows Applications Talk and General Discussion, 818
Windows CE Software Archives, 723
Windows Drivers, 818
Windows Game Software, 723
Windows Glossary, 818
Windows Magazines, 819
Windows Networking Environment, 723
Windows Networking Talk and General Discussion, 819
Windows News, 819
WINDOWS NT, 821
Windows NT Drivers, 822
Windows NT Faq, 822
Windows NT Internet Servers, 822
Windows NT Magazine, 822
Windows NT Official Web Site, 822
Windows NT Resources, 823
Windows NT Security, 823
Windows NT Setup, 823
Windows NT Talk and General Discussion, 823

Windows Peer-to-Peer Networking, 819
Windows Pre-releases, 819
Windows Programming, 819
Windows Programming Talk and General Discussion, 646
Windows Questions and Answers, 820
Windows Resources, 820
Windows Setup, 820
Windows Software, 723
Windows Talk and General Discussion, 820
Windows to the Universe, 731
Windows Video Discussion, 821
Windsurfing, 590
Wine, 292
Wine Zines, 293
Wireless Technology, 405
Wodehouse, P.G., 466
WOMEN, 823
Women and Literature, 470
Women Artists in History, 38
Women Halting Online Abuse, 827
Women in Architecture, 33
Women in Congress, 827
Women in Music, 556
Women in Philosophy, 613
Women in the Military, 515
Women's Fitness, 248
Women's Health, 358
Women's Magazines, 486
Women's Online Communities, 827
Women's Resources, 827
Women's Sports, 743
Women's Studies Resources, 828
Women's Talk and General Discussion, 828
Women's Web Guides, 828
Women's Wire, 828
Women's Wire Advice, 3
Women's Wire Fashion & Beauty, 267
Wonderful Wizard of Oz, 480
Woodcutter, 148
Woodworking, 392
Word, 868
Word Detective, 666

Main subject headings are shown in **bold**

INDEX

Word Puzzles, 135
Word-a-Day, 445
Wordsworth, William, 629
World Agricultural Information Center, 8
World Art Treasures, 43
World Birthday Web, 386
World Constitutions, 843
World Culture Talk and General Discussion, 844
WORLD CULTURES, 829
WORLD CULTURES: DISCUSSION GROUPS, 844
World Data Center System, 337
World Energy Statistics, 233
World Government, 345
World Guide to Vegetarianism, 783
World Health Organization, 358
World Heritage List, 844
World Holiday Guides, 386
World Music Talk and General Discussion, 556
World News Sources, 576
World of Darkness, 685
World Population Datasheet, 331
World Village, 135
World War I, 376
World War II, 376
World War II Propaganda Posters, 377
World Wide Art Resources, 43
World's Highpoints, 331
World's Tallest Buildings, 33
Wrestling: Professional, 743
Wrestling: Sumo, 744
Wright, Frank Lloyd, 34
Writer's Block Magazine, 852
Writers Chat, 852
Writers' Resources, 852
Writers Talk and General Discussion, 852
WRITING, 848
Writing Tips, 852
Writing Well, 217
Wuthering Heights, 480

X

X Window, 646
Xerox Map Viewer, 331
X-Files, 775
XML, 813
X-Rated Movies, 862
X-RATED RESOURCES, 854

Y

Y Forum, 597
Yahoo Computers, 125
Yahooligans, 436
Yarn, 156
Year 2000 Problem, 125
Yeats, William Butler, 467
Yoga, 248
YOUNG ADULTS, 863
Young Adults Talk and General Discussion, 866
Young Investors and Entrepreneurs, 866
Young Job Seekers, 420
Yo-Yos, 300
Yucky Stuff, 436

Z

Zen Buddhism, 674
Zhing, 539
Zine Lists, 868
Zine Talk and General Discussion, 868
ZINES, 867
Zone System, 619
Zoological Resources, 872
ZOOLOGY, 869
Zoophilia, 862
Zoos, 23
Zoroastrianism, 674

*Main subject headings are shown in **bold***

How to Use the *Harley Hahn's Internet & Web Golden Directory* CD-ROM

The CD that accompanies this book was created by Modern Age Books and contains a special electronic edition of *Harley Hahn's Internet & Web Golden Directory*. Using the powerful Modern Age V-Book™ search engine, you can locate Web sites, Usenet discussion groups, mailing lists, and other resources offline on your PC or Macintosh. You can then connect to the site of your choice using your browser.

System Requirements

The *Harley Hahn's Internet & Web Golden Directory* CD will run on any of the following computers: a Macintosh (68K or Power PC), Mac Performa, iMac or Powerbook with System 7 or higher (8MB RAM); or a PC with Microsoft Windows 3.1, 3.11, Windows 95 or Windows 98 (8MB RAM). (For Macintosh users only: you can install the entire book on your hard drive for faster performance or run it from the CD to conserve hard drive space.)

Installation

To use the electronic edition of *Harley Hahn's Internet & Golden Directory*, you must first install it on your system. To start the installation program, choose the appropriate procedure below.

Windows 95/98 Users

Insert the CD-ROM into your CD drive. The install program should start up automatically within a few seconds. If for some reason it does not start automatically, do the following:

1. From the Start menu choose **Run**.
2. Type **d:\setup32\setup.exe** (or the appropriate drive letter) and press ENTER.*
3. Click "Yes" and follow the instructions on the screen.

*Please note: If you are unsure of what letter your CD-ROM drive is assigned by your system, open Windows Explorer (in your Start Menu under Programs) and find the icon for your CD-ROM drive in the left pane. If the *Harley Hahn's Internet & Web Golden Directory* CD-ROM is in your drive, you should see a small picture of the Harley Hahn Unisphere® next to the name **Hhyp1999** and your drive's letter. Otherwise you should see a small picture of a CD next to the letter. This is the letter you should use in the **Run** dialog box.

Windows 3.1x Users

1. Insert the CD-ROM into your CD drive.
2. From Program Manager, choose **Run** from the File menu.
3. Type **d:\setup16\install.exe** (or the appropriate drive letter) and press ENTER.
4. Click "Yes" and follow the instructions on the screen.

Macintosh Users

1. Insert the CD-ROM into your CD drive. The "Modern Age Books" CD icon will appear on your desktop.
2. To install the electronic version of the book, drag and drop the "Modern Age Books" CD icon onto your hard drive icon.

TECHNICAL SUPPORT: IF YOU HAVE ANY PROBLEM WITH THE ELECTRONIC BOOK WHICH COMES ON THE CD-ROM, PLEASE VISIT THE MODERN AGE BOOKS WEB SITE AT http://www.modernagebooks.com/help/. AT THE MODERN AGE BOOKS HOME PAGE GO TO **Support**.

WARNING: BEFORE OPENING THE DISC PACKAGE, CAREFULLY READ THE TERMS AND CONDITIONS OF THE FOLLOWING COPYRIGHT STATEMENT AND LIMITED CD-ROM WARRANTY.

Copyright Statement

This software is protected by both United States copyright law and international copyright treaty provision. Except as noted in the contents of the CD-ROM, you must treat this software just like a book. However, you may copy it into a computer to be used and you may make archival copies of the software for the sole purpose of backing up the software and protecting your investment from loss. By saying, "just like a book," The McGraw-Hill Companies, Inc. ("Osborne/McGraw-Hill") means, for example, that this software may be used by any number of people and may be freely moved from one computer location to another, so long as there is no possibility of its being used at one location or on one computer while it is being used at another. Just as a book cannot be read by two different people in two different places at the same time, neither can the software be used by two different people in two different places at the same time.

Limited Warranty

Osborne/McGraw-Hill warrants the physical compact disc enclosed herein to be free of defects in materials and workmanship for a period of sixty days from the purchase date. If the CD included in your book has defects in materials or workmanship, please call McGraw-Hill at 1-800-217-0059, 9am to 5pm, Monday through Friday, Eastern Standard Time, and McGraw-Hill will replace the defective disc.

The entire and exclusive liability and remedy for breach of this Limited Warranty shall be limited to replacement of the defective disc, and shall not include or extend to any claim for or right to cover any other damages, including but not limited to, loss of profit, data, or use of the software, or special incidental, or consequential damages or other similar claims, even if Osborne/McGraw-Hill has been specifically advised of the possibility of such damages. In no event will Osborne/McGraw-Hill's liability for any damages to you or any other person ever exceed the lower of the suggested list price or actual price paid for the license to use the software, regardless of any form of the claim.

OSBORNE/McGRAW-HILL SPECIFICALLY DISCLAIMS ALL OTHER WARRANTIES, EXPRESS OR IMPLIED, INCLUDING BUT NOT LIMITED TO, ANY IMPLIED WARRANTY OF MERCHANTABILITY OR FITNESS FOR A PARTICULAR PURPOSE. Specifically, Osborne/McGraw-Hill makes no representation or warranty that the software is fit for any particular purpose, and any implied warranty of merchantability is limited to the sixty-day duration of the Limited Warranty covering the physical disc only (and not the software), and is otherwise expressly and specifically disclaimed.

This limited warranty gives you specific legal rights; you may have others which may vary from state to state. Some states do not allow the exclusion of incidental or consequential damages, or the limitation on how long an implied warranty lasts, so some of the above may not apply to you.

This agreement constitutes the entire agreement between the parties relating to use of the Product. The terms of any purchase order shall have no effect on the terms of this Agreement. Failure of Osborne/McGraw-Hill to insist at any time on strict compliance with this Agreement shall not constitute a waiver of any rights under this Agreement. This Agreement shall be construed and governed in accordance with the laws of New York. If any provision of this Agreement is held to be contrary to law, that provision will be enforced to the maximum extent permissible, and the remaining provisions will remain in force and effect.

TECHNICAL SUPPORT: IF YOU HAVE ANY PROBLEM WITH THE ELECTRONIC BOOK WHICH COMES ON THE CD-ROM, PLEASE VISIT THE MODERN AGE BOOKS WEB SITE AT **http://www.modernagebooks.com/help/**. AT THE MODERN AGE BOOKS HOME PAGE GO TO **Support**.